Health Care Needs Assessment

The epidemiologically based needs assessment reviews

Second Edition

Volume 1

Edited by

Andrew Stevens
Professor of Public Health
Department of Public Health and Epidemiology
University of Birmingham

James Raftery
Professor of Health Economics
Health Services Management Centre
University of Birmingham

Jonathan Mant
Senior Clinical Lecturer
Department of Primary Care and General Practice
University of Birmingham

and

Sue Simpson
Research Fellow
Department of Public Health and Epidemiology
University of Birmingham

RADCLIFFE PUBLISHING
OXFORD • SAN FRANCISCO

Radcliffe Publishing Ltd
18 Marcham Road
Abingdon
Oxon OX14 1AA
United Kingdom

www.radcliffe-oxford.com
Electronic catalogue and worldwide online ordering facility.

© 2004 Andrew Stevens, James Raftery, Jonathan Mant and Sue Simpson

British Library Cataloguing in Publication Data

A catalogue record for this book is available from the British Library.

ISBN 1 85775 891 9 (volume 1)

ISBN 1 85775 892 7 (volume 2)

ISBN 1 85775 890 0 (set)

Typeset by Advance Typesetting Ltd, Oxford
Printed and bound by TJ International Ltd, Padstow, Cornwall

Contents: VOLUME 1

Preface   v

List of contributors   vi

An Introduction to HCNA: the epidemiological approach to health care needs assessment
Andrew Stevens, James Raftery and Jonathan Mant   1

1 Diabetes Mellitus
Rhys Williams and Heather Farrar   17

2 Renal Disease
Roger Beech, Martin C Gulliford and Paul Roderick   75

3 Stroke
Jonathan Mant, Derick Wade and Simon Winner   141

4 Lower Respiratory Disease
Sarah Walters and Derek J Ward   245

5 Coronary Heart Disease
David A Wood, Kornelia P Kotseva, Kevin Fox, Ameet Bakhai and Tim J Bowker   373

6 Colorectal Cancer
Hugh Sanderson, Andrew R Walker and Denise Young   449

7 Cancer of the Lung
Hugh Sanderson and Stephen Spiro   503

8 Osteoarthritis Affecting the Hip and Knee
Jill Dawson, Ray Fitzpatrick, John Fletcher and Richard Wilson   549

9 Cataract Surgery
John R Thompson   635

10 Groin Hernia
Wendy Phillips and Mark Goldman   671

Index   721

Contents: VOLUME 2

11 Varicose Veins and Venous Ulcers
Sue Simpson and Paul Roderick   1

12 Benign Prostatic Hyperplasia
David E Neal, Rebecca R Neal and Jenny Donovan   91

13 Severe Mental Illness
John K Wing   159

14 Alzheimer's Disease and Other Dementias
David Melzer, Katherine Pearce, Brian Cooper and Carol Brayne   239

15 Alcohol Misuse
Christopher CH Cook   305

16 Drug Misuse
John Marsden and John Strang with Don Lavoie, Dima Abdulrahim, Matthew Hickman
and Simon Scott   367

17 Learning Disabilities
Siân Rees, Chris Cullen, Shane Kavanagh and Paul Lelliott   451

18 Community Child Health Services
David Hall, Sarah Stewart-Brown, Alison Salt and Peter Hill   543

19 Contraception, Induced Abortion and Fertility Services
Mary W Lyons and John R Ashton   631

Index   677

Preface

This book is the second edition of the *Health Care Needs Assessment Reviews*, first published in 1994. The objective of the first edition was to produce definitive assessments of the 'need' for health services of a typical health authority's population by individual disease or health problem. This was undertaken for 20 key topics. Each topic was dealt with under a standard protocol designed by the editors. Authors were asked to include: (i) a statement of the problem (disease); (ii) sub-categories of the problem meaningful to commissioners of health care; (iii) information on incidence and prevalence of the problem; (iv) a description of current services available to address the problem and their costs; (v) a summary of what is known about the effectiveness and cost-effectiveness of the main services; and (vi) recommendations and quantified models of care. The authors were also invited to give their opinion on suitable outcome measures and audit methods which might be used to monitor services and to indicate any research requirements arising from the review of needs assessment.

The same protocol has been used in this second edition, but the content has been updated. The evidence base of health care has moved on, new technologies and practices for tackling health problems have been introduced and the structure of the UK's health services has changed. In April 2002, 302 primary care trusts replaced 99 health authorities and 481 primary care groups in England, with similar changes in Scotland and Wales. The responsibilities of primary care trusts, however, specifically those to do with planning and commissioning services to meet the needs of their population, remain very similar to those of health authorities.

This second edition updates the 20 topics included in the original version. It is accompanied by a second series, published in 1997, covering a further eight topics (accident and emergency departments; child and adolescent mental health; low back pain; palliative and terminal care; dermatology; breast cancer; genitourinary medicine services; and gynaecology). A third series is in preparation. This will include adult critical care; black and minority ethnic groups; continence; dyspepsia; hypertension; obesity; peripheral vascular disease; pregnancy and childbirth; and prison health.

Each chapter has been reviewed by the editors and by external anonymous peers. The chapters are the work of individuals or groups of authors chosen for their expertise in the topic area. Authors work to the standard protocol but with freedom of emphasis according to the topic. As such, chapters do not necessarily reflect the professional consensus or the views of the sponsors of this project and should not be regarded as setting an obligatory norm. Rather the chapters present the evidence and arguments on which commissioners of health care might base their decisions.

The editors wish to acknowledge the contributions of Anne Kauder, Mike Dunning and Graham Winyard, who all helped devise the original project and steer it into its present form, of Graham Bickler and of other steering group members for their advice over the years. We would also like to thank the many external experts who have reviewed the individual chapters and whose comments have helped to contribute to the value of the needs series.

Andrew Stevens
James Raftery
Jonathan Mant
Sue Simpson
May 2004

List of contributors

Dima Abdulrahim
Advisor
National Treatment Agency
Email: Dima.Abdulrahim@nta-nhs.org.uk

John R Ashton
Regional Director of Public Health
Government Office for the North West
Email: John.R.Ashton@doh.gsi.gov.uk

Ameet Bakhai
Senior Fellow and Cardiology Specialist Registrar
Clinical Trials and Evaluation Unit
Royal Brompton Hospital
Email: a.bakhai@cteu.org

Roger Beech
Senior Lecturer
Director of Research
Centre for Health Planning and Management
Keele University
Email: r.beech@keele.ac.uk

Tim J Bowker
Associate Medical Director
British Heart Foundation, and
Consultant Cardiologist
St Mary's Hospital, Paddington, and
Honorary Senior Lecturer
National Heart and Lung Institute
Imperial College London
Email: bowkert@bhf.org.uk

Carol Brayne
Professor of Public Health Medicine
Department of Public Health and Primary Care
University of Cambridge
Email: cb105@medschl.cam.ac.uk

Christopher CH Cook
Professorial Fellow
St Chad's College
University of Durham
Email: c.c.h.cook@durham.ac.uk

Brian Cooper
Honorary Research Fellow
Section of Old Age Psychiatry
Institute of Psychiatry
Email: spjubco@iop.kcl.ac.uk

Chris Cullen
Professor of Clinical Psychology
Department of Psychology
Keele University
Email: c.cullen@keele.ac.uk

Jill Dawson
Reader in Health Services Research
School of Health and Social Care (OCHRAD)
Oxford Brookes University
Email: jdawson@brookes.ac.uk

Jenny Donovan
Professor of Social Medicine
Head of Health Services Research
Department of Social Medicine
University of Bristol
Email: jenny.donovan@bristol.ac.uk

Heather Farrar
Consultant in Public Health
Bournemouth Teaching Primary Care Trust

Ray Fitzpatrick
Professor of Public Health and Primary Care
Division of Public Health and Primary Health Care
Institute of Health Sciences
University of Oxford
Email: raymond.fitzpatrick@nuf.ox.ac.uk

John Fletcher
Consultant Public Health Physician
Oxford City Primary Care Trust
Email: john.fletcher@post.harvard.edu

Kevin Fox
Consultant Cardiologist and Honorary Senior Lecturer
National Heart and Lung Institute
Imperial College London
Email: k.fox@imperial.ac.uk

Mark Goldman
Chief Executive
Birmingham Heartlands and Solihull NHS Trust
Email: mark.goldman@heartofwmids.nhs.uk

Martin C Gulliford
Senior Lecturer
Department of Public Health Sciences
King's College London
Email: martin.gulliford@kcl.ac.uk

David Hall
Professor of Community Paediatrics
Institute of General Practice
University of Sheffield
Email: d.hall@sheffield.ac.uk

Matthew Hickman
Senior Lecturer
Centre for Research in Drugs and Health Behaviour
Division of Primary Care and Population Health Sciences
Imperial College London
Email: m.hickman@imperial.ac.uk

Peter Hill
Honorary Consultant in Child and Adolescent Psychiatry
Department of Psychological Medicine
Great Ormond Street Hospital for Children
Email: strandend@dial.pipex.com

Shane Kavanagh
Director of Health Economics
Johnson & Johnson Pharmaceutical Services
Beerse
Belgium
Email: skavanag@psmbe.jnj.com

Kornelia P Kotseva
Senior Clinical Research Fellow
National Heart and Lung Institute
Imperial College London
Email: k.kotseva@imperial.ac.uk

Don Lavoie
Deputy Regional Manager, London
National Treatment Agency
Email: don.lavoie@nta-nhs.org.uk

Paul Lelliott
Director
The Royal College of Psychiatrists Research Unit
London
Email: plelliott@cru.rcpsych.ac.uk

Mary W Lyons
Senior Lecturer
Centre for Public Health
Faculty of Health and Social Sciences
Liverpool John Moores University
Email: M.Lyons@livjm.ac.uk

Jonathan Mant
Senior Clinical Lecturer
Department of Primary Care and General Practice
University of Birmingham
Email: j.w.mant@bham.ac.uk

John Marsden
Senior Lecturer in Addictive Behaviour
Division of Psychological Medicine
Institute of Psychiatry
King's College London
Email: J.Marsden@iop.kcl.ac.uk

David Melzer
Clinical Senior Research Associate
Department of Public Health and Primary Care
University of Cambridge
Email: dm214@medschl.cam.ac.uk

David E Neal
Professor
Oncology Department
Addenbrooke's Hospital
Cambridge
Email: den22@cam.ac.uk

Rebecca R Neal
Clerk
House of Lords
London

Katherine Pearce
Consultant in Public Health Medicine
Cambridge and Huntingdon Health Authority

Wendy Phillips
Consultant in Communicable Disease Control
South Yorkshire Health Protection Service
Email: wendy.phillips@doncastereastpct.nhs.uk

James Raftery
Professor of Health Economics
Health Services Management Centre
University of Birmingham
Email: j.p.raftery@bham.ac.uk

Siân Rees
Senior Policy Advisor
Mental Health Services Branch
Department of Health
London
Email: sian.rees@doh.gsi.gov.uk

Paul Roderick
Senior Lecturer in Public Health Medicine
Health Care Research Unit
University of Southampton
Southampton General Hospital
Email: pjr@soton.ac.uk

Alison Salt
Consultant Paediatrician
Wolfson Centre
Institute of Child Health
London

Hugh Sanderson
Consultant in Public Health
Central South Coast Cancer Network
Hampshire and Isle of Wight Strategic Health Authority
Email: hugh.sanderson@hiowha.nhs.uk

Simon Scott
Lead Commissioner, Substance Misuse
Brighton and Hove City PCT
Email: simon.scott@bhcpct.nhs.uk

Sue Simpson
Research Fellow
Department of Public Health and Epidemiology
University of Birmingham
Email: s.l.simpson.20@bham.ac.uk

Stephen Spiro
Professor of Thoracic Medicine
The Middlesex Hospital, London

Sarah Stewart-Brown
Professor of Public Health
Division of Health in the Community
Warwick Medical School (LWMS)
University of Warwick
Email: sarah.stewart-brown@warwick.ac.uk

Andrew Stevens
Professor of Public Health
Department of Public Health and Epidemiology
University of Birmingham
Email: a.j.stevens@bham.ac.uk

John Strang
Director and Professor of the Addictions
National Addiction Centre
Institute of Psychiatry
King's College London
Email: j.strang@iop.bpmf.ac.uk

John R Thompson
Professor of Ophthalmic Epidemiology
Department of Ophthalmology
University of Leicester
Email: john.thompson@le.ac.uk

Derick Wade
Professor and Consultant in Neurological Rehabilitation
Oxford Centre for Enablement
Email: derick.wade@dial.pipex.com

Andrew R Walker
Robertson Centre for Biostatistics
University of Glasgow
Email: A.Walker@stats.gla.ac.uk

Sarah Walters
Senior Clinical Lecturer
Department of Public Health and Epidemiology
University of Birmingham
Email: S.Walters@bham.ac.uk

Derek J Ward
Specialist Registrar in Public Health
Public Health Directorate
South Worcestershire Primary Care Trust
Email: djward@btinternet.com

Richard Wilson
Senior Public Health Information Specialist
South Birmingham Primary Care Trust
Moseley Hall Hospital
Email: Richard.Wilson@SouthBirminghamPCT.nhs.uk

John K Wing
Retired

Rhys Williams
Professor of Clinical Epidemiology
The Clinical School
University of Wales Swansea
Email: D.R.R.Williams@swansea.ac.uk

Simon Winner
Consultant Physician
Department of Clinical Geratology
Radcliffe Infirmary, Oxford
Email: simon.winner@geratology.ox.ac.uk

David A Wood
Garfield Weston Chair of Cardiovascular Medicine
National Heart and Lung Institute
Imperial College London
Email: d.wood@imperial.ac.uk

Denise Young
Greater Glasgow Health Board

Date of acceptance for publication

Chapter	Date accepted for publication
Diabetes Mellitus	April 2000
Renal Disease	January 2000
Stroke	December 2001
Lower Respiratory Disease	March 2003
Coronary Heart Disease	April 2002
Colorectal Cancer	May 2000
Cancer of the Lung	May 2000
Osteoarthritis Affecting the Hip and Knee	April 2000
Cataract Surgery	October 2000
Groin Hernia	October 2000
Varicose Veins and Venous Ulcers	September 2002
Benign Prostatic Hyperplasia	July 1999
Severe Mental Illness	May 2000
Alzheimer's Disease and Other Dementias	July 1999
Alcohol Misuse	November 1999
Drug Misuse	September 2000
Learning Disabilities	August 2002
Community Child Health Services	November 2001
Contraception, Induced Abortion and Fertility Services	September 2002

An Introduction to HCNA

The epidemiological approach to health care needs assessment

Andrew Stevens, James Raftery and Jonathan Mant

The need for needs assessment

Some form of health care needs assessment has always been necessary in health service planning. In the early 1990s, as a consequence of health service reforms in the UK and elsewhere, including The Netherlands, New Zealand, Australia and the USA,[1-7] it took on a more central role. In the UK, the late 1990s saw a second round of reforms, which stressed the importance of collaboration and partnership, while continuing to emphasise the role of health care needs assessment.[8]

Four overlapping periods of changing perspective on need can be identified.[9] The first may be characterised as a period of 'social concern' in the 1960s – identifying gaps in health service provision relating to deprivation and patchy facilities. There followed a period of 'rational planning' in the 1970s – attempting to plan services systematically, but with no formal needs focus. The Resource Allocation Working Party (RAWP) review then placed a focus on spatial inequity, i.e. the relative under-provision of services in different regions.[10,11] Need was recognised and measured by surrogate means, notably demographic. The NHS and Community Care Act of 1991 by contrast required that need be identified so that service requirements could be specified fairly closely.[1] We might now add a fifth period of 'collaborative action' – in the 2000s – in which the need for health care and the need for other interventions to improve health are to be collectively identified by a range of players, but principally strategic health authorities, primary care trusts (PCTs) and local government.[12]

The most important change, and indeed the period when needs assessment became established as a critical process in health care, was the transition from the 1980s to the 1990s, although this period has its roots in the policy context stemming from the 1970s.

The policy context

From the 1970s the expansion of public services and public expenditure that had characterised the post war era came under critical review. Prompted by the oil price shocks of the 1970s and the recourse of the UK to the International Monetary Fund (IMF), public expenditure became tightly controlled as Keynesianism was challenged by monetarism in the UK and in the USA. Tax resistance in both countries also contributed to a fundamental reappraisal of the public–private relationships.

The 'new public management' offered an agenda for taking these issues forward.[13] In the UK its early manifestations included:

- increased attention to financial control
- stronger, more hierarchical management with target setting
- an extension of audit, transparency, benchmarking and protocols
- increased consumer responsiveness
- deregulation of the labour market
- a reduction in the self-regulating power of the professions
- some empowerment of less bureaucratic and more entrepreneurial management
- new forms of corporate governance, with a shift to a board of directors model.[14]

This went beyond rhetoric, with two-thirds of formerly state-owned businesses transferred to the private sector, requiring in turn that either competition or regulation be established to stimulate efficiency.[15]

Given that the UK health sector was predominantly public in both finance and provision, it was a strong candidate for the kinds of reforms outlined above. Although the bulk of attention has been devoted to the structural reforms introduced in 1991, each of the above themes was picked up and continues to be played out in the NHS today.

The structural reforms of 1991 resulted from *Working for Patients*,[16] which was the product of a ministerial review established by Margaret Thatcher in 1988, when hospital bed closures and cancellations of elective surgery were being blamed on a perceived under-funding of the NHS. The review explored and rejected many options before focusing mainly on the delivery of services. It drew heavily on the ideas of Alain Enthoven and a key slogan was that 'money should follow patients'.[17] This encapsulated the idea that hospitals should receive funding in proportion to the number of patients treated, not as hitherto on the basis largely of historical patterns of allocation.

Competition was to be introduced between hospitals and with other providers, including the small private sector. Core elements included:

- separation of purchaser and provider roles in health care
- creation of self-governing NHS Trusts
- transformation of health authorities (now PCTs) to become purchasers
- introduction of 'fundholding' by groups of general practitioners
- the use of contracts to link purchasers and providers.

The only significant modification to these has been the abandonment of (individual practice) general practitioner fundholding.

Central role of needs assessment in the NHS health care reforms

The creation of purchasers of health care in the 1991 National Health Service (NHS) and Community Care Act put the formal purchasing of health care centre stage in the new NHS. Although the reforms initially emphasised the increased freedom around the independent provider role through the creation of NHS Hospital Trusts, it later became obvious that cost-effective targeting of health care could not happen without a significant role for purchasers.[18–20] These were to be capitation funded, a move that had been started by the report of the 1976 Resource Allocation Working Party and its precursors.[10,11] These new cost-constrained purchasers required a mechanism for determining what services they should purchase and at what volume that was not simply a product of what was currently provided. This mechanism was to be 'needs assessment'.

An initial analysis of the role of district health authorities (now PCTs) set needs assessment as the first of a series of tasks as follows:[18]

1 assessment of the health needs of the local population, including a more positive emphasis on the views of that population
2 appraisal of service options for meeting those needs, including close co-operation with (the then) family practitioner committees and general practitioners, both in the short term and strategically
3 specification of the chosen pattern of service provision
4 choosing between providers and placing contracts compatible with the districts' cash limits
5 monitoring the provision of contracted services and the health of the population
6 controlling expenditure on contracts within the districts' cash limits.

For needs assessment to anchor the process in this way, it was necessary to develop a protocol for the assessment of health care needs, and to drastically improve the information available to health authorities on baseline aspects of their service, and nationally available data relevant to their needs assessment activities. This series tackles those challenges by developing a protocol for health care needs assessment, and then using that protocol to provide data around the protocol headings for disease and client groups.

While the role of health authorities has changed again as a result of the latest reforms, with commissioning of services now being the responsibility of primary care trusts,[8] there is continuity with the previous reforms. In particular, the responsibility for planning health services is kept separate from provision, and funding of health services will continue to be for a defined population, rather than for a service. Therefore a protocol for health care needs assessment remains as relevant now as it did when the first edition of this series was published. Indeed, the audience for this material is now wider, as a greater proportion of primary health care professionals will assume a commissioning role.

Characteristics of health care needs assessment

The requirements of the role of purchasing authorities (primary care trusts) has the following effects.

First, *need for health care* must be distinguished from the *need for health*. The need for health care is much more specific than the need for health. The latter concerns who is needy in general terms, and can be measured by morbidity, deprivation and sociodemographic measures. Health problems with no realistic treatments are included here. But these measures alone have little to say that helps the specification of health care services, except perhaps in distinguishing relative levels of need between large areas. The need for health care is much more specific and is now widely accepted as meaning the *population's ability to benefit from health care*.[21-23] It depends on the potential of preventive or treatment services to remedy health problems.

Second, needs assessment for practical purchasing requires a *usable level of detail* for those who will subsequently specify services. The definition, the population's ability to benefit from health care, leaves open the level of detail at which health care is defined. However, it is important not to specify needs so generally that different populations and interventions cannot be distinguished, nor to specify needs in so much detail that the activity of health care needs assessment becomes overwhelming. A reasonable compromise should be sought.

Third, *need* is quite different from *supply* and *demand*. Put simply, need is what people might benefit from, demand is what people would be willing to pay for in a market or might wish to use in a system of free health care, and supply is what is actually provided. Although this distinction is uncontroversial, the difficulty of measuring need makes it tempting to measure supply and demand as surrogates for need. This is complicated by the price being zero for services free at the point of use. Supply and demand are not tempered by each other as they might be in a market with a price mechanism. Furthermore, supply is the consequence of historical patterns mixed with the consequences of political pressure for change. It is clearly misleading to measure the existing service provision as though it were an indicator for need. Similarly, the measurement of waiting lists, reflecting as they do demand mediated by doctor as agent, is also misleading. Figure 1 illustrates how need, demand and supply might overlap or differ.[9] It shows eight fields of services divided into (1) those for which there is a need but no demand and supply, (2) those for which there is a demand but no need or supply, (3) those for which there is a supply but no need or demand, and then (4–7) the various degrees of overlap.

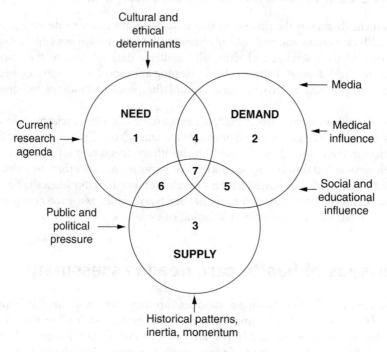

Figure 1: Need, demand and supply: influences and overlaps.

The diagram indicates where work is required not just in assessing health care needs, but also in attempting to make the three circles of need, demand and supply more congruent. This includes demand management and changing supply as well as better definition of need. Demand management may involve curtailing it where it is inappropriate (areas 2 and 5 in Figure 1), stimulating it (areas 1 and 6), or coping better with it (area 4).[24] Varied mechanisms with which demand can be influenced include the accessibility and organisation of services, the provision of health information, education, and financial incentives.[25–27] Supply changes may require subtle mechanisms not easily captured in service agreements. Where the cause of the mismatch between supply and need is clinical practice, effective strategies to promote behaviour change among professionals are required. These can include educational outreach visits, reminders, interactive educational meetings, audit and feedback, use of local opinion leaders, local consensus processes and patient-mediated interventions.[28] Even need can be shifted somewhat, given that research programmes can be altered, with new findings on pathology and degrees of benefit which matter to patients, and the identification of forms of health care that are effective.

Fourth, needs are probably best explored basing the assessment on *disease groups*. The logic is that a need arises when there is a lesion rather than when a person has reached a certain age, belongs to an ethnic sub-group, or because a particular service is provided. However, this is not an absolute rule. The ability to benefit from health care can be assessed at the level of the subpopulation who may benefit from a particular intervention (provided competing interventions are considered). Such units can be reassembled around particular services, or population subgroups such as demographic minorities. Some chapters in this series are therefore oriented around services such as family planning, and around mixed groups such as people with learning disabilities. In primary health care needs assessment it is often argued that a good starting point is around a particular intervention.[29]

Fifth, often the key element of health care needs assessment is the measurement of the *effectiveness of interventions*. The evidence-based medicine and evidence-based health care movements are relatively recent and it remains the case that clear information on effectiveness is often absent in service planning. But it cannot be argued that ineffective services are needed. Therefore, where effectiveness is in doubt, a first step is the gathering of effectiveness information.

Sixth, health care needs assessment is only ever artificially divorced from *setting priorities* in health care. Some 'needs assessors' would prefer not to acknowledge resource shortages, and argue that all needs should be met. The untenability of this view as the proliferation of new potentially effective health care technologies continues apace becomes ever clearer. Needs assessment can be integral to prioritisation, because it is only a short step from need as the ability to benefit from health care to a utilitarian view of relative need as the *relative ability to benefit per unit cost*. This is not to deny an exploratory phase of needs assessment, a sort of scanning exercise, before such hard calculations are made, nor to deny that precision in quantifying priorities is very elusive.

Seventh, it is worth noting the distinctions between *individual need* and *population need*. Population need can be viewed as the sum of individuals' need. But the viability of this assumption is dependent on how the individual needs assessment is undertaken. If it strays into an assessment of demand, or it is unconcerned with proven ability to benefit, it is likely to distort assessed population needs. Clearly there are differences between the view of a carer dealing with (assessing the needs of) an individual, and a planner looking at a population. The former is likely to be a strong advocate for the patient, to take no account of people who are in need but do not come to the clinic, and (as regards relative need) to take little account of costs. The circumstances in which individual needs assessment is a practical means of assessing health care needs at a population level are those in which individual patients are few, highly costly, very heterogeneous and countable (i.e. not hidden from the view of routine data).

Eighth, one can also distinguish between needs for (public sector) *services other than health care* and *services for health care*. 'Benefit' in the former tends to be more open-ended. In health care, increasing inputs of care can be associated with zero benefit or negative benefit (harm). The limits of benefit are not so clear with education, housing or transport (although even here diminishing returns and even negative benefit are evident sometimes). However, other public sector services have an impact on health, and with a collaborative approach to health care needs assessment across different sectors, the relative contribution of different investment (relative needs assessment) will be important.

Ninth, needs assessment itself incurs costs. This means that short-cuts can be necessary, and indeed it is argued below that surrogate measures (making comparisons and taking a corporate view) have a valid place in health care needs assessment.

Aim of health care needs assessment

The overall *aim* of health care needs assessment is to provide information to plan, negotiate and change services for the better and to improve health in other ways. In other words the assessment can be done with an eye to any activities which have an impact on health, whether directly in the hands of health services or not. The working definition of health care need as the population's ability to benefit from health care reflects this (and can be expanded to cover 'services' more widely).

It is worth noting that each element of the definition is important.

Table 1: The need for health care – the population's ability to benefit from health care.

- The **population's** ability to benefit from health care equals the aggregate of individuals' ability to benefit. For most health problems this will be deducible from epidemiological data, rather than from clinical records.
- The **ability** to benefit does not mean that every outcome is guaranteed to be favourable, but rather that need implies potential benefit which on average is effective.
- The **benefit** is not just a question of clinical status, but can include reassurance, supportive care and the relief of carers.* Many individual health problems, especially infectious diseases and long-term disabilities, have a social impact via multiple knock-on effects or via a burden to families and carers. Consequently, the list of beneficiaries of care can extend beyond the patient.
- Health **care** includes not just treatment, but also prevention, diagnosis, continuing care, rehabilitation and palliative care.

* Diagnosis and reassurance constitute an all-important component of primary and ambulatory care, including accident and emergency services where a high proportion of people may require no more than a negative diagnosis.

Objectives of health care needs assessment

1 The principal objective of health care needs assessment is *to specify services* and other activities which impinge on health care. The principal activities involved in health care needs assessment are therefore:

- the assessment of incidence and prevalence (how many people need the service/intervention)
- the effectiveness and cost-effectiveness of their services (do they confer any benefit, and if so at what cost, i.e. what is the relative benefit?)
- the baseline services (changing provision for the better necessitates knowledge of the existing services, both to know which services ought to change and to identify opportunities for the release of resources to enable the change to happen).

These three components – incidence and prevalence, health service effectiveness and baseline services – form the basis of 'triangulation' (*see* Figure 2), whereby health care purchasers and planners can determine

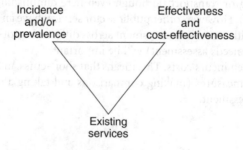

Figure 2: The triangulation of health care needs assessment.

the policy directions they wish to pursue. They form the three main elements of the protocol used to structure the needs assessment in subsequent chapters of this series.

There are, however, also other objectives in health care needs assessment which flow from the aim of planning, negotiating and changing services for the better.

2   Improving the *spatial allocation of resources*. This was the principal objective of national needs assessment in the UK at the time of the Resource Allocation Working Party and before, right up to the 1990 NHS reforms. It seems a reasonable supposition that if broadly equal populations are to receive services, the most efficient deployment of services will be to give them broadly equal resources. This supposition works well at a macro-level, but weakens as the scale gets smaller – because the chances of small areas having equal needs, other things being equal, reduces. And given that resources will continue to be allocated between sub-national units, spatial allocation continues to be important.

3   Third, *target efficiency* (the accurate targeting of resources to those in need) is often a central activity of needs assessors. Strictly, the measurement of target efficiency is the measurement of whether or not, having assessed needs, resources have been appropriately directed. In this sense, target efficiency is related to audit. But it is always important to know whether, having defined the need, those who get a service need it, and those who need it get it.

A number of new objectives for health care needs assessment have been suggested following the expansion of needs assessment into general practice. They include (in various guises) the three listed above, but to these can be added the following.

4   The *gathering of general intelligence* to get a perspective on population health and population health needs. This objective is, of course, important not just for new primary care needs assessors, and in many respects can be considered the first stage of needs assessment, rather than a separate objective.

5   Fifth, the objective of health care needs assessment *to stimulate the involvement and ownership of different players* in the process has been noted. The more members of the primary care team and others are involved in the assessment, the more likely attention will be paid to the findings of the activity. Again, this argument could be extended to needs assessment undertaken outside primary care.

Scales of needs assessment

Although the aim of needs assessment remains the same at all scales, the principal objectives and the process are likely to vary according to the scale of assessment. These scales can be summarised as follows:

* national (circa 50 million)
* regional (circa 5 million)
* local authority/health authority/primary care trust (circa 50 000 to 500 000)
* individual general practice (circa 5000 to 10 000).

National needs assessment

There are many national health care concerns. National needs assessment is necessary for areas of legislative change. These include modifications of health services – particularly including elements of the public health agenda such as seat-belt and tobacco control legislation. It also applies to elements of planning affecting the national economy – including, for example, very large capital investments – and to politically and media-sensitive areas such as those issues raised by 'postcode prescribing'. Indeed, part of the rationale for the establishment of the UK's National Institute for Clinical Excellence was to end 'unacceptable geographical variations in care'.[30] National needs assessment is also the level for the assessment of spatial equity between large sub-national regions.

Regional health care needs assessment

Despite both a policy of centralisation and a wish to delegate planning to a unitary level of health authority below that of the region, regional planning has been remarkably durable. There are certain services for which the region is an obvious scale of activity. These concern not just large spatial issues such as fluoridation, but also medical specialties where provision needs to be at the scale of a population of several million.

Spatial equity, specific service planning (sum of) and target efficiency are all relevant at the regional level.

Health authority/primary care trust/local authority needs assessment

This is the traditional level of health care needs assessment with PCTs now the UK's principal purchaser of care. There is, however, a big difference between the traditional agenda of health authorities/PCTs and of local authorities, the former with a tradition of technical planning – increasingly for effective and efficient services – and the latter with a tradition of working with the politics of local democracy. The scope of the services provided by both differs as well, and the combined agenda addressing principally service specification, but also target efficiency, is very large and will need to be highly selective.

In the UK planning at the level of the small primary care trusts is likely to have elements both of health authority scale planning and of individual practitioner planning. This has opportunities both for service specification, and for individual clinical insights, and can make use of the potentially fertile practice register data available at individual practitioner level.

Individual practitioner needs assessment

The individual practitioner has long had much promise as a needs assessor, given his or her access to case registers, his or her role as a consumer of secondary care, and therefore at arm's length from it, and his or her feel for a patient perspective on service. However, these advantages are tempered by the difficulties of needs assessment at this level, including the conflict of needs assessment with general practitioners' business interests, and the ease with which practitioners can ignore unseen patients.

Needs assessment activities at this scale can only include service specification for the most prevalent of diseases, and of primary care services, but target efficiency (audit) can be reviewed intensely.

Different types of health care needs assessor/assessments

It should also be recognised that technical needs assessors do not have a monopoly of the words 'needs assessment'. Those who might consider themselves needs assessors could include:

- politicians – both national and local
- clinicians – both generalist and specialist
- patients
- technocrats.

The different perspectives of these assessors will obviously influence the characteristics of the assessment. In theory all can undertake valid assessments, but it is worth examining any product against understood criteria.

The following questions have been identified in judging assessments.[31]

1   *Is there a clear context of allocating scarce resources?* Needs assessments that fail to acknowledge resource limitations are common, but are of restricted value to health care commissioners. This can be a problem with individual clinical needs assessment, which can put great pressure on health budgets and squeeze the care available to patients with weak advocates. Some population approaches also fail to acknowledge resources used. This is a difficulty, for example, with specialty-specific documents recommending levels of service within a single specialty.

2   *Is the needs assessment about priority setting within the context of a variety of competing needs or is it about advocacy for a single group or individual?* This is closely related to the resource context question. Specialty-specific documents, client group surveys and even policy directives which focus on single groups often represent advocacy rather than balanced contributions to priority setting. Surveys about, for example, the needs of a particular ethnic minority are of limited help in guiding health care planners unless seen in the context of equivalent surveys of other groups. Policy recommendations based on lobbying would be much more prone to distorting resource use than policy directives based on research.

3   *Is the needs assessment exploratory or definitive?* Some approaches to needs assessment are exploratory in that they highlight undefined or under-enumerated problems. This is particularly true of lifestyle surveys that estimate the size of risk groups such as alcohol abusers or teenage smokers. Exploratory surveys are best thought of as just a first stage in a more specific needs assessment process.

4   *Is the determination of the most important needs expert or participatory?* Technocratic needs assessment tends preferentially to be expert, although the Oregon experience demonstrates that participatory approaches and expert ones can be merged. Expert approaches seek to be as objective as possible, although objectivity soon reaches its limits.

Approaches to needs assessment

The approach to needs assessment based on the triangulation of incidence and prevalence, effectiveness and cost-effectiveness, and existing services (*see* Figure 2) we have labelled 'the epidemiological approach to needs assessment'. This method is described more fully below.

Needs assessment will usually aim to make incremental changes to existing services. The epidemiological approach to needs assessment can usefully be supplemented by other tools. Indeed, in view of the shortage of information both on effectiveness and on prevalence, and because of the size of the task of reviewing and applying such information even when it is available, health care purchasers have tended to use two other simple methods, namely the 'comparative' and the 'corporate' approach.[22]

Comparative approach to needs assessment

The comparative approach to needs assessment contrasts the services received by the population in one area with those received elsewhere. Comparisons can be powerful tools for investigating health services, especially in the context of capitation-based funding. Variations in costs and service use may be appropriate depending on local circumstances, but with capitation funding of health care, gross departures from the mean require justification. The literature on differential rates of surgery, for example, shows that the more loosely defined the clinical indications are for a particular problem, the more likely considerations other than need and benefit are to influence levels of activity undertaken.[32,33]

Comparative service provision should take account of local population characteristics, including demographic and morbidity data, such as those provided by the English Public Health Common Data Set.[34] To the extent that such sources are beginning to provide detailed mortality and morbidity information, they may start to act as population outcomes data. The use of such data in this way, however, relies on the assumption that health care is a major determinant of mortality and morbidity, which may not be justified.[35]

Corporate approach to needs assessment

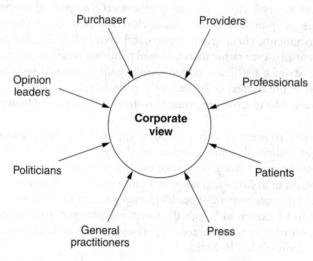

Figure 3: Contributors to the corporate view of local service needs.

The corporate approach to needs assessment is based on the demands, wishes and alternative perspectives of interested parties, including professional, political and public views (*see* Figure 3). While such an approach blurs the difference between need and demand, and between science and vested interest, it also allows scope for managing supply and demand at the same time as assessing need as affected by local circumstances. It would be surprising if important information were not available from those who have been involved in local services over many years. In the National Health Service context, this corporate approach has been widely used, and was encouraged in both the 1989 reforms with its 'local voices',[36] and the emphasis on partnership and collaboration in the 1997 White Paper.

A protocol for (the 'epidemiological approach' to) needs assessment

Each of the chapters in this series has been written following a standard protocol that utilises the headings shown in Table 2. The approach is based on the belief that non-local epidemiological data are valuable to local needs assessment, and that both costs and cost-effectiveness have to be considered. While need is a

Table 2: Components of the epidemiological approach to needs assessment.

1	Statement of the problem
2	Sub-categories
3	Prevalence and incidence
4	Services available and their costs
5	Effectiveness and cost-effectiveness of services
6	Quantified models of care and recommendations
7	Outcome measures, audit methods and targets
8	Information and research requirements

function of benefit, not of cost, the purpose of population needs assessment is to help decide between competing priorities. Such decision making requires information on both.

Statement of the problem

A necessary first step is a precise statement of the problem and its context, including major issues and controversies relevant to health care commissioners. It is not possible (or desirable) to divorce the process of health care needs assessment from contemporary controversies, though a broad population-based needs assessment should also provide an appropriate context and perspective from which such controversies can be viewed. Thus the emergence of new drugs is a relevant contextual issue in a health care needs assessment of dementia, but a comprehensive needs assessment will not consider these drugs in isolation from other aspects of dementia services, such as provision of basic nursing care and carer support (*see* Chapter 14 on dementia).

Sub-categories

There are many different ways of subdividing a disease, such as by aetiology, pathology, anatomy, severity or prognosis. In the context of health care needs assessment, what is most useful to a planner or commissioner of health care is a sub-categorisation that is predictive of requirements for services. The most appropriate sub-categorisation will depend upon the disease in question. Thus aetiological sub-categories are chosen for diabetes (type 1, type 2 and gestational diabetes), severity sub-categories for dementia, and presence or absence of health problems and dependence for alcohol misuse.

Prevalence and incidence

Prevalence and incidence form the first corner of the needs assessment triangle (*see* Figure 3). It is a truism to state that identification of the frequency of occurrence of disease is a core part of the epidemiological approach to needs assessment. However, in isolation of information about treatments available and their effectiveness, prevalence and incidence are not synonymous with need.

Prevalence and incidence are most useful in health care needs assessment when they can be directly related to sub-categories that predict service requirements. Thus the prevalence of radiological osteo-arthritis is a poor predictor of need, whereas prevalence based on symptoms and clinical features is a better estimate of the number of people who might benefit from hip replacement surgery (*see* Chapter 8 on osteoarthritis of hip and knee).[37] This approach, which involves identifying the number of people in a population with a condition that would benefit from treatment as opposed to simply identifying the number of people with the condition, has been termed the 'epidemiology of indications'.[38] However, epidemiologists have in general been more interested in the aetiology of diseases than in the scope for benefit, so prevalence and incidence data on sub-categories relevant to service planning are often not available.

The source material for this section comes either from the epidemiological literature or from official statistics, such as *Cancer Statistics: Registrations*[39] and the *Health Survey for England*.[40] One caveat on using national data or data from epidemiological surveys carried out in other parts of the country is that incidence and prevalence vary with such factors as age, sex, region, socio-economic status and ethnicity. Therefore, appropriate adjustments need to be made to estimate the frequency of disease in one locality from these data.

Services available and their costs

Services available form a corner of the needs assessment triangle (*see* Figure 2). Although current services are only weakly related to need, it is important to understand them, since local levels are required for comparative analysis, and they are the starting point for change. Data about both structure (how many specialists per unit of population) and process (how many people treated per unit of population) are relevant to this section. Health resource groups offer a possible 'currency' for measuring health care activity,[41] and combining such data with finance data in a programme-budgeting approach can assist the sensible analysis of existing services.[42] Data sources include audits and surveys, and official statistics, in particular the hospital episode statistics (HES) for secondary care and GP morbidity surveys[43] for primary care. Costing studies of health care remain relatively sparse, but the availability of official data such as the National Health Service Reference Costs (a product of the 1997 White Paper) and Trust Financial Returns allow some cost estimates to be made.

Effectiveness and cost-effectiveness of services

The availability of data concerning the third element of the health care needs assessment triangle, namely effectiveness and cost-effectiveness of services, has improved dramatically in recent years. Initiatives such as those of the Cochrane Collaboration and the evidence-based medicine movement have led to a growing recognition of the importance of randomised controlled trials and systematic reviews in the evaluation of health care. It is beyond the scope of this series to present new systematic reviews of the evidence, but each chapter draws from systematic reviews that have been carried out, and the key studies in the topic area. Authors have been asked to grade the evidence for an intervention in terms of the size of the effect and the quality of the supporting evidence as shown in Table 3.

The population benefit achieved by health care depends not just on the efficacy of the service under study conditions, but also on its effectiveness in real life and its acceptability to patients. It can be argued that it is difficult to generalise the results of some randomised controlled trials, since all the types of patients to whom the results would be of potential relevance may not be included.[44] In these circumstances, the findings of non-randomised studies may be of use since they are generally less selective in terms of recruitment. However, a non-randomised study is an inherently weaker design in terms of internal validity, since it is prone to selection bias in that treatment allocation is likely to be influenced by

Table 3: Grading of evidence of effectiveness.

SIZE OF EFFECT

A	The procedure/service has a strong beneficial effect
B	The procedure/service has a moderate beneficial effect
C	The procedure/service has a measurable beneficial effect
D	The procedure/service has no measurable beneficial effect
E	The harms of the procedure/service outweigh its benefits

QUALITY OF EVIDENCE

I-1	Evidence from several consistent or one large randomised controlled trial
I-2	Evidence obtained from at least one properly designed randomised controlled trial
II-1	Evidence obtained from well-designed controlled trials without randomisation, or from well-designed cohort or case–control analytical studies
II-2	Evidence obtained from multiple time series with or without the intervention. Dramatic results in uncontrolled experiments (such as the results of the introduction of penicillin treatment in the 1940s) could also be regarded as this type of evidence
III	Opinions of respected authorities, based on clinical experience, descriptive studies, or reports of expert committees
IV	Evidence inadequate and conflicting

factors that might affect outcome. While some of these differences can be adjusted for, it is not possible to adjust for factors that are unknown, unmeasured or unmeasurable.

Quantified models of care and recommendations

Since need is derived from incidence and prevalence on the one hand and effectiveness on the other, it is tempting to seek a simple formula combining both in order to generate estimates of the need for services. Recommendations would logically emerge from any disparities between the estimates of need and current service provision. For most diseases and treatments, however, no such logic exists for the following reasons:

- inadequate data on incidence and prevalence
- inadequate data on effectiveness and cost-effectiveness
- lack of agreement on thresholds for intervention
- severity levels may be ill-defined
- treatment pathways are complex, with numerous filters.

Given these uncertainties and the need to quantify services when planning, a more flexible approach to models of care based on needs has been developed in some of the chapters in this series. Most include recommendations drawn from incidence and prevalence and effectiveness findings. These are often, quite reasonably, at the margin, rather than as gross service transformations.

Outcome measures, audit methods and targets

The principal objective of health care needs assessment is the specification of services and other activities that impinge upon health care. Under *The New NHS*,[8] health care commissioners will negotiate long-term agreements with NHS Trusts. It is intended that these are based on specific services, and include health and quality objectives. Authors have the opportunity to suggest what measures and targets might be used to monitor such long-term agreements. The National Performance Framework puts forward six areas of performance:[8]

- health improvement
- fair access
- effective delivery of appropriate health care
- efficiency
- patient/carer experience
- health outcomes of NHS care.

Information and research requirements

A health care needs assessment can help to clarify what information and research priorities should be in a given area, in terms of both epidemiology and effectiveness research. With the development of the National Research & Development Strategy and the National Health Technology Assessment programme, a greater proportion of clinical research in the UK is now carried out in response to specific calls for research to answer questions that have been identified as NHS priorities. Epidemiological health care needs assessment is one process by which such questions can be identified.

Conclusion

While the organisational context of health care needs assessment has changed in recent years, the process remains a core component of health service planning. In this chapter, a protocol for the epidemiological approach to needs assessment has been outlined. Each of the following chapters adheres to this protocol, though more information is available for some topic areas than others. The key target audience is people involved in the planning and monitoring of health services. In England, this includes both primary care trusts and strategic health authorities as bodies charged with the commissioning of local health services, development of health strategy and monitoring. Health care systems in the twenty-first century will need to address the challenges posed by demographic change, technological development and changing public expectations within a context of limited resources. An epidemiological approach to health care needs assessment provides a rational framework within which these issues can be tackled.

References

1 House of Commons. *National Health Service and Community Care Act*. London: HMSO, 1990.
2 Organisation for European Corporation and Development. *The Reform of Health Care: a comparative analysis of seven OECD countries*. Health Policy Studies No. 2. Paris: OECD, 1992.
3 Borren P, Maynard A. *Searching for the Holy Grail in the Antipodes: the market reform of the New Zealand health care system*. Discussion Paper. York: University of York Centre for Health Economics, 1993.
4 Matthews L. Health reforms in New Zealand. *BMJ* 1991; **303**: 327.
5 Leeder SR, Alexander J. Australia's national health strategy. *BMJ* 1992; **305**: 1042–3.

6 Pepper Commission. *A Call for Action.* US Bipartisan Commission on Comprehensive Health Care. Washington, DC: US Government Printing Office, 1990.

7 Roberts J. Clinton outlines plan to fix American health care system. *BMJ* 1993; **307**: 819–20.

8 Secretary of State for Health. *The New NHS.* Cm 3807. London: The Stationery Office, 1997.

9 Stevens A, Gabbay J. Needs assessment, needs assessment. *Health Trends* 1991; **23**: 20–3.

10 Department of Health and Social Security. *Sharing Resources for Health in England.* Report of the Resource Allocation Working Party. London: DHSS, 1976.

11 Buxton MJ, Klein R. *Allocating Health Care Resources: a commentary on the Report of the Resources Allocation Working Party.* London: HMSO, 1978.

12 Stevens AJ, Bickler G. Health care needs assessment and health improvement programmes. In: Rawaf S, Orton P (eds). *Health Improvement Programmes.* London: RSM Press, 2000.

13 Hood CA. Public management for all seasons. *Public Administration* 1991; **69** (Spring): 3–19.

14 Ferlie E, Ashburner L, Fitzgerald A, Petttigrew A. *The New Public Management in Action.* Oxford: Oxford University Press, 1996.

15 Foster CD, Plowden FJ. *The State Under Stress.* Buckingham: Open University Press, 1996.

16 Department of Health. *Working for Patients.* London: HMSO, 1989.

17 Enthoven A. *Reflections on the Management of the NHS.* London: Nuffield Provincial Hospitals Trust, 1985.

18 National Health Service Management Executive. *Role of District Health Authorities: analysis of issues.* London: Department of Health, 1989.

19 Audit Commission. *Their Health, Your Business: the new role of the District Health Authority.* London: HMSO, 1993.

20 Mawhinney B, Nichol D. *Purchasing for Health: a framework for action.* London: NHS Management Executive, 1993.

21 Culyer AJ. *Need and the National Health Service.* London: Martin Robertson, 1976.

22 National Health Service Management Executive. *Assessing Health Care Needs.* London: Department of Health, 1991.

23 Matthew GK. Measuring need and evaluating services. In: McLachlan G (ed.). *Portfolio for Health.* London: Oxford University Press, 1971 (*Problems and Progress in Medical Care: essays on current research*, 6th series.)

24 Pencheon D. Matching demand and supply fairly and efficiently. *BMJ* 1998; **316**: 1665–7.

25 Coulter A. Managing demand at the interface between primary and secondary care. *BMJ* 1998; **316**: 1974–6.

26 Gillam S. Managing demand in general practice. *BMJ* 1998; **316**: 1895–8.

27 Rogers A, Entwistle V, Pencheon D. A patient-led NHS: managing demand at the interface between lay and primary care. *BMJ* 1998; **316**: 1816–19.

28 Bero LA, Grilli R, Grimshaw JM, Harvey E, Oxman AD, Thomson MA. Closing the gap between research and practice: an overview of systematic reviews of interventions to promote the implementation of research findings. *BMJ* 1998; **317**: 465–8.

29 Scottish Needs Assessment Programme. *Needs Assessment in Primary Care.* Glasgow: SNAP, 1998.

30 Dobson F. *About NICE.* Foreword on NICE website: www.nice.org.uk (accessed on 9/10/2000).

31 Stevens AJ, Raftery J (eds). *Health Care Needs Assessment*, 2nd series. Oxford: Radcliffe Medical Press, 1997.

32 Saunders D, Coulter A, McPherson K. *Varieties in Hospital Admission Rates: a review of the literature.* London: King's Fund Centre, 1989.

33 Wennberg JE, Malley AG, Hanley D *et al.* An assessment of prostatectomy for benign urinary tract obstruction: geographic variations and the evaluation of medical care outcomes. *JAMA* 1988; **259**: 3027–30.

34 Department of Health. *Public Health Common Data Set 1996: incorporating Health of the Nation indicators and population health outcome indicators* (four volumes). Guildford: University of Surrey, National Institute of Epidemiology, 1997.

35 McKeown T. *The Role of Medicine.* Oxford: Blackwell, 1979.

36 National Health Service Management Executive. *Local Voices.* London: Department of Health, 1992.

37 Frankel S, Eachus J, Pearson N *et al.* Population requirement for primary hip replacement surgery: a cross-sectional study. *Lancet* 1999; **353**: 1304–9.

38 Frankel S. The epidemiology of indications. *J Epidemiol Community Health* 1991; **45**: 257–9.

39 Office for National Statistics. *Cancer Statistics: registrations, 1992.* Series MB1, No. 25. London: The Stationery Office, 1998.

40 Prescott-Clarke P, Primatesta P (eds). *Health Survey for England 1996.* London: The Stationery Office, 1998.

41 Buckland RW. Health care resource groups: a more sensitive and less costly approach to contracting [editorial]. *BMJ* 1994; **308**: 1056.

42 Lockett T, Raftery J, Richards J. In: Honigsbaum F, Richards J, Lockett T (eds). *Priority Setting in Action: purchasing dilemmas.* Oxford: Radcliffe Medical Press, 1995.

43 Office for National Statistics. *Morbidity Statistics from General Practice. Fourth National Study, 1991– 1992.* Series MB5, No. 3. London: ONS, 1995.

44 McKee M, Britton A, Black N, McPherson K, Sanderson C, Bain C. Interpreting the evidence: choosing between randomised and non-randomised studies. *BMJ* 1999; **319**: 312–15.

1 Diabetes Mellitus

Rhys Williams and Heather Farrar

1 Summary

This chapter provides:

- information to assess the need for services for people with diabetes and its complications
- criteria to assess the success of programmes for the care and early detection of this group of disorders.

The chapter does not aim to provide a systematic review of the literature on diabetes epidemiology and health care. There are a number of systematic reviews available in the Cochrane Library and other sources. Instead, the chapter highlights the most recent important studies in these areas and suggests issues, particularly in the domain of health services research, where more information is needed. Considerable documentation and a large measure of agreement exist on the aims of diabetes care and how these might be achieved. The most important consensus documents on the subject are listed in Appendix II, and some feature as specific references in the text.* (Further explanation and relevant references for the statements made below are included in subsequent sections.)

Statement of the problem/introduction

Definition and diagnostic criteria

Diabetes mellitus is a group of disorders with common features, of which a raised blood glucose level is the most evident. It is a chronic disease which can cause substantial premature morbidity and mortality.

The diagnosis of diabetes is based on clinical symptoms and/or measurements of plasma glucose. Existing World Health Organization (WHO) diagnostic criteria for diabetes have been revised following recommendations by a WHO Consultation Group. The American Diabetes Association (ADA) has also suggested a revision. Impaired glucose tolerance (IGT) and impaired fasting glucose (IFG) are indicators of increased risk of diabetes. The definition of gestational diabetes mellitus (GDM) is controversial, although guidelines for its detection and diagnosis are available for the UK.

The problem

- Diabetes mellitus and its complications can cause severe problems for affected individuals and their families. They impose a heavy burden on health services.
- The primary prevention of some cases of type 2 diabetes is potentially feasible, but has yet to be implemented as a public health measure.

---

*This chapter was written before the publication of the various National Service Frameworks (NSFs) for diabetes. They are not referred to in detail in the text, but are listed in Appendix II.

- The organisation of services for the care of people with diabetes is complex, involving hospital-based diabetes teams, community services, those working in primary care, patients and their families.

The solution

- There is now proof that, in both type 1 and type 2 diabetes (*see* below for explanation), effective control of hyperglycaemia prevents the development and progression of the microvascular complications of diabetes (retinopathy, neuropathy and nephropathy). Attainment of near-normal glycaemic control, while minimising the risk of hypoglycaemia, is a priority.
- The impact of diabetes and its complications can be reduced by providing well-organised, integrated care including, in particular, the education and empowerment of patients and their families and the early identification of complications.
- Primary care trusts (PCTs) and their equivalents elsewhere in the UK, together with providers of hospital-based diabetes services and community services, must work together, with the patient and the family at the centre of the process.

The challenges

- Some of the greatest current challenges to those involved in planning and delivering diabetes services are (1) the involvement of all people with diabetes in a continuing, planned programme of care, (2) resolving local issues of where and by whom that care should be given, and (3) ensuring that, wherever that care is provided, its quality is set and maintained at the highest possible level.
- Assessing the impact of diabetes services also presents considerable challenges. However, the relevant process and outcome measures necessary for this are largely agreed and, with some exceptions, are measurable with the careful use and interpretation of routine sources of information and ad hoc studies.
- Keeping pace with new developments in diabetes care will also be a challenge. Some of the main areas relevant to future prevention and care are summarised below.

Sub-categories of diabetes

There are four sub-categories of diabetes:

1   type 1
2   type 2
3   other specific types (e.g. drug induced)
4   gestational.

It has been suggested that the terms 'insulin-dependent diabetes mellitus' (IDDM) and 'non-insulin-dependent diabetes mellitus' (NIDDM) be replaced by the aetiologically based categories type 1 and type 2 diabetes. Any form of diabetes may require insulin therapy. In type 1 diabetes this therapy is essential to maintain life. In type 2 diabetes it is a treatment option used to improve control of blood glucose.

Complications of diabetes may be classified into macrovascular (coronary heart disease, cerebrovascular disease and peripheral vascular disease) and microvascular (retinopathy, nephropathy and neuropathy).

Prevalence and incidence

The prevalence of type 2 diabetes is increasing because of the ageing population and an increase in the prevalence of risk factors (e.g. obesity). An increasing incidence of childhood diabetes is also contributing to this.

There are many published studies on the incidence and prevalence of diabetes in various parts of the UK. Most studies involve Caucasian populations and the results are not applicable to non-Caucasian populations. It is known that the prevalence of diabetes is higher in people of South Asian and Afro-Caribbean origin. When estimating local incidence or prevalence it is preferable, rather than extrapolating findings from elsewhere, to use data from local studies if these are available. The incidence of type 2 diabetes in adults is difficult to determine given the latency of the condition. The incidence in children is easier to estimate, and has been shown to be around 14 per 100 000 children aged 14 and under per year. The overall prevalence of clinically diagnosed diabetes in people of all ages in the UK is between 2 and 3%. The prevalence of diabetes in children and young people (aged under 20) is around 0.14%. The prevalence of self-reported diabetes in adults is around 3%.

Macrovascular and microvascular complications contribute to premature mortality and morbidity. For example, mortality due to coronary heart disease is 2–3 times higher in people with diabetes than in those without. Also, the complications of diabetes have been shown to be more prevalent in areas of socio-economic deprivation, with increased mortality rates.

Services available

People with diabetes are cared for by a wide range of health care staff in primary and secondary care. Staffing levels and facilities vary between localities. People with diabetes have been shown to utilise health services in general more than people without. It is also likely that those who do not attend for regular review of their diabetes are likely to be the most frequent users of secondary care services for ensuing complications.

The direct health care costs of diabetes include those associated with prevention, diagnosis and treatment. It has been estimated that 8.7% of acute-sector costs are spent on the care of people with diabetes. It has been predicted that the overall cost of hospital care for people with diabetes will increase by 15% by 2011.

Effectiveness and cost-effectiveness of services

Screening

Currently, population screening is an issue only in relation to type 2 diabetes. Screening for diabetes for all people aged 40 or over has been recommended by the ADA. In the UK the National Screening Committee (NSC) is reviewing the issue of screening for diabetes. Screening for retinopathy has been shown to be an effective and cost-effective intervention. Current recommendations are that eye examinations should be performed annually as part of regular surveillance. Further research is required to determine whether this is the optimum frequency for all people with diabetes.

As a method of screening for diabetes itself, urine testing is known to have a low specificity, with between 140 and 170 people identified for each true positive detected. It is also uncertain whether early diagnosis affects outcome, although several studies have clearly shown that complications are present in many people at diagnosis. This is an important area for further research. Opportunistic screening (also known as case finding) is recommended good practice when adults present in primary or secondary care for other reasons. In 2003, the WHO published a WHO/International Diabetes Federation (IDF) report summarising expert views on screening for type 2 diabetes (*see* Appendix II).

Optimal glycaemic control

Robust evidence has now shown that, in type 1 diabetes, intensive insulin therapy (IIT) delays the onset and slows the progression of retinopathy, nephropathy and neuropathy. Any improvement in glycaemic control in type 1 diabetes is likely to reduce the risk of these complications. However, IIT carries with it an increased risk of hypoglycaemia.

Similarly, robust evidence has also shown that intensive treatment with oral hypoglycaemics and/or insulin in type 2 diabetes reduces the risk of microvascular complications. Tight control of high blood pressure is also important for the reduction of diabetes microvascular complications. These measures may also be effective in preventing or delaying macrovascular complications.

Delivery of care

Patients with diabetes are cared for in primary care, secondary-based care or a combination of both. It is still unclear which is the most effective setting, although it is clear that primary care with a recall system ('prompted care') can be as effective as secondary care in terms of glycaemic control and adherence to follow-up. It is the quality of care, rather than its location, which is likely to be the main determinant of patient satisfaction and outcome.

Models of care

The appropriate model of care for a locality will depend on the current service arrangements and the enthusiasm and motivation of staff to make improvements in the quality of care. Planning these improvements should involve a multidisciplinary approach across primary and secondary care with representation of user and carer views. Primary care trusts (PCTs), and their equivalents elsewhere in the UK, should assess the health care need of the local population, and develop and monitor in collaboration with their local diabetes services advisory groups (LDSAGs), or their equivalent, a local strategy for diabetes care.

There is a plethora of nationally and internationally agreed standards for care, protocols for treatment and measures for monitoring improvements. There are also several established and innovative planning tools. These include population databases (also known as 'registers'), case-mix systems (e.g. Health Care Resource Groups [HRGs]) and commissioning matrices.

Outcome measures

There are established process and outcome measures for diabetes services which are useful for clinical audit or for monitoring purposes. Process measures include clinic waiting times and quality of communication with health care workers, the proportion of people receiving planned care, in particular an annual review, and the frequency with which key examinations and investigations are carried out and recorded.

Outcomes of diabetes care depend on whose perspective is being considered (patient, clinician or commissioner of services). They include quality of life and well-being, the achievement of optimal blood glucose, blood lipid and blood pressure levels and reduced incidence of short- and long-term complications.

Information and research requirements

The main requirements are:

- more evidence on the effectiveness and cost-effectiveness of population screening for diabetes
- more research into the primary prevention of diabetes
- further use and development of population databases to ensure that those with diagnosed diabetes are able to maintain contact with appropriate services.

2 Introduction

Diabetes: the problems and challenges

Diabetes mellitus and its complications can cause severe problems for affected individuals and their families. In turn, these impose a heavy burden on health services. There is no cure for diabetes. However, the primary prevention of some cases of type 2 diabetes is potentially feasible but has yet to be implemented as a public health measure. A further problem is the organisation of services for the care of people with diabetes. This is complex, involving hospital-based diabetes teams, community services, those working in primary care, patients and their families.

Some of the greatest current challenges to those involved in planning and delivering diabetes services are:

- the involvement of all people with diabetes in a continuing, planned programme of care
- resolving the local issues of where and by whom that care should be given
- ensuring that, wherever that care is provided, its quality is set and maintained at the highest possible level.

Assessing the impact of diabetes services also presents considerable challenges. However, the relevant process and outcome measures necessary for this are largely agreed and, with some exceptions, measurable with the careful use and interpretation of routine sources of information and ad hoc studies.

Definition and diagnostic criteria

Diabetes is a group of disorders with common features, of which a raised blood glucose level is the most evident. Existing WHO diagnostic criteria for diabetes have been revised following recommendations by a WHO Consultation Group.[1] The ADA has also suggested a revision.[2] Future WHO recommendations will also include criteria for the definition of diabetes complications and for the clinical staging of these complications.

The ADA and WHO recommendations are similar (although not, unfortunately, identical) but both differ from the 1985 WHO recommendations which were the previous worldwide standard.[3] The essential features of the ADA recommendations (for non-pregnant adults) are listed in Table 1 together with the main differences between these new recommendations and the previous WHO recommendations.[3]

If the ADA or new WHO recommendations are adopted in the UK,* there will be little impact on clinical management. The main consequences are likely to be:

- an *increase* in the estimated prevalence of diabetes as a result of the *lowering* of the minimum fasting plasma glucose (FPG) concentration necessary for diagnosis
- a reduced emphasis on the oral glucose tolerance test (OGTT) in the diagnosis of diabetes, although this is still likely to be regarded as the investigation of choice for epidemiological research.

The magnitude of the effect on prevalence is likely to differ between groups of different ethnic origin. For example, Unwin et al.[4] reported results from men and women aged 25–74 years living in Newcastle and participating in an epidemiological study of diabetes (i.e. including previously known and unknown cases). They calculated that the effect of changing from a definition of diabetes based on previous WHO criteria to the new ADA criteria was an increase in the prevalence of diabetes from 4.8% to 7.1% in Caucasians, from 4.7% to 6.2% in people of Chinese origin and from 20.1% to 21.4% in people of South

---

* Since this chapter was written Diabetes UK have recommended that all health care professionals adopt the WHO diagnostic criteria.

Table 1: Essential features of the American Diabetes Association (ADA) recommendations for diabetes (in non-pregnant adults)[2] and the main differences between these and the *previous* WHO recommendations.[3]

Provisional ADA recommendations	Previous WHO recommendations
General: Based on clinical *stages*	Based on clinical *states*
Diabetes: Symptoms of diabetes plus 'casual' PG ≥ 11.1 mmol/l *or* FPG ≥ 7.0 mmol/l *or* 2 h PG ≥ 11.1 mmol/l during an OGTT Any of the above need to be confirmed on a subsequent day for the diagnosis to be made	Same FPG ≥ 7.8 mmol/l or 2 h PG ≥ 11.1 mmol/l during an OGTT
Impaired glucose tolerance (IGT): 2 h PG ≥ 7.8 mmol/l but < 11.1 mmol/l	Same
Impaired fasting glucose (IFG): FPG ≥ 6.1 mmol/l and < 7.0 mmol/l	Not previously recognised
Normal glucose tolerance: FPG < 6.1 mmol/l *or* 2 h PG < 7.8 mmol/l	Not specified

'Casual' is defined as any time of day without regard to time since last meal. FPG, fasting plasma glucose; PG, plasma glucose; OGTT, oral glucose tolerance test.

Asian origin. Note that these findings differ from those already published for the US population aged 40–74 years in which the prevalence of diabetes was *reduced* (from 6.34% to 4.35%) by the use of the new criteria.[2]

Impaired glucose tolerance and impaired fasting glucose

The 1985 WHO recommendations introduced the term 'impaired glucose tolerance' (IGT) (*see* Table 1 for diagnostic criteria).[3] IGT has long been recognised as a risk factor for ischaemic heart disease, and in some people it is a precursor of type 2 diabetes.[5] The recent ADA recommendations proposed the adoption of an additional category – impaired fasting glucose (IFG).[2] The diagnostic criteria for this are also included in Table 1.

IGT and IFG are not yet regarded as clinical entities in their own right, but as indicators of increased risk for the future development of diabetes and for cardiovascular disease. Abnormal glucose tolerance is a component of the 'insulin resistance syndrome', also known as 'Reaven–Modan syndrome' or 'syndrome X'. In addition, this syndrome has one or more of the following features: obesity, dyslipidaemia (usually high triglyceride and/or low HDL cholesterol) and hypertension.[6,7]

Gestational diabetes

The ADA criteria summarised in Table 1 refer to non-pregnant adults. The definition of gestational diabetes mellitus (GDM), the magnitude of its effects on the outcome of pregnancy and the best method of screening for this condition are controversial. Opinions and practices in the UK vary considerably from place to place and differ from those of the USA.[2,8] The most recent summary of UK practice is that published by the Pregnancy and Neonatal Care Group of the joint (British Diabetic Association [BDA] and Department of Health [DH]) Saint Vincent Task Force, which proposed that new diagnostic criteria for gestational diabetes should be formulated based on prospective studies of pregnant women.[8] In the mean time, it recommended the screening procedures and definitions summarised in Box 1.

Box 1: Screening procedures and definition of gestational diabetes.[8]

Urine should be tested for glycosuria at every antenatal visit.
Timed random laboratory blood glucose measurements should be made:

- whenever glycosuria (1+ or more) is detected
- at the booking visit and at 28 weeks' gestation.

A 75 g OGTT with laboratory blood glucose measurements should be carried out if the timed random blood glucose concentrations are:

- > 6 mmol/l in the fasting state or 2 h after food
- > 7 mmol/l within 2 h of food.

The interpretation of the OGTT during pregnancy is as follows:

Category	Fasting plasma glucose	2 h after glucose load
Diabetes	> 8 mmol/l	> 11 mmol/l
IGT	6–8 mmol/l	9–11 mmol/l
Normal	< 6 mmol/l	< 9 mmol/l

The management of established diabetes in women who become pregnant is a separate issue from GDM and gestational IGT. There is no controversy about the fact that stringent control of blood glucose during pregnancy is beneficial in terms of perinatal mortality and that the prevention of congenital malformation requires careful pre-pregnancy care.[8]

The diagnosis of type 1 diabetes, especially when it occurs in children, does not usually pose problems of definition because there are usually one or more of the classical symptoms of diabetes – thirst, polyuria, malaise and weight loss. The clinical picture, taken with the result of a urine glucose or 'casual' blood glucose estimation (Table 1), is usually sufficient to make the diagnosis. On the rare occasions when an OGTT is required in a child, the dose is calculated on a dose per body weight basis.

3 Sub-categories of diabetes

The ADA and WHO recommend that the sub-classification of diabetes based on insulin dependency, IDDM and NIDDM should now be abandoned in favour of the aetiologically based classification shown in Box 2. This is partly because patients with *any* form of diabetes may require insulin treatment at some stage of their disease. The most important sub-categories in public health terms are type 1 and type 2 diabetes. The most important long-term vascular complications of diabetes are also outlined in Box 2. Diabetes may also predispose to non-vascular conditions, such as cataract. Table 2 lists the relevant categories in the *International Classification of Diseases (ICD)*.

Box 2: Aetiological classification of diabetes mellitus.[2]

> **Type 1 diabetes:** β-cell destruction, usually leading to absolute insulin deficiency.
>
> **Type 2 diabetes:** may range from predominantly insulin resistance with relative insulin deficiency to a predominantly secretory defect with insulin resistance.
>
> **Other specific types:**
>
> - genetic defects of β-cell function, e.g. chromosome 7, glucokinase (formerly MODY2)
> - genetic defects in insulin action, e.g. leprechaunism
> - diseases of the exocrine pancreas, e.g. pancreatitis
> - endocrinopathies, e.g. acromegaly
> - drug- or chemical-induced diabetes, e.g. caused by thiazides
> - infections, e.g. congenital rubella
> - uncommon forms of immune-mediated diabetes, e.g. due to anti-insulin antibodies
> - other genetic syndromes sometimes associated with diabetes, e.g. Down's syndrome.
>
> **Gestational diabetes mellitus.**
>
> **Long-term vascular complications of diabetes.**
>
> **Macrovascular complications:**
>
> - coronary heart disease
> - cerebrovascular disease
> - peripheral vascular disease.
>
> **Microvascular complications:**
>
> - retinopathy
> - nephropathy
> - neuropathy.

Table 2: Diabetes categories in the *International Classification of Diseases (ICD)*, 10th revision.

Number	Title	Includes
E10	Insulin-dependent diabetes mellitus	Diabetes (mellitus): • brittle • juvenile-onset • ketosis-prone • type I
E11	Non-insulin-dependent diabetes mellitus	Diabetes (mellitus) (non-obese) (obese): • adult-onset • maturity-onset • non-ketotic • stable • type 2 Non-insulin-dependent diabetes of the young
E12	Malnutrition-related diabetes mellitus	Malnutrition-related diabetes mellitus: • insulin-dependent • non-insulin-dependent
E13	Other specified diabetes mellitus	
E14	Unspecified diabetes mellitus	Diabetes NOS
E15	Non-diabetic hypoglycaemic coma	

4 Prevalence and incidence

The epidemiological information needed for health care needs assessments of diabetes

One of the first steps in assessing need in a locality involves assembling information on the frequency of occurrence of diabetes:

- the number of individuals with clinically diagnosed diabetes in a given population (prevalence)
- the number of new patients needing diagnosis, stabilisation and programmes of education and long-term care (incidence)
- the number of individuals with, or likely to develop, specific complications.

There are a number of ways to estimate the above. In practice, a trade-off between precision and feasibility will need to be made. The following list is roughly in descending order of precision:

- examining a validated, up-to-date population database of those with diabetes living in the locality. (We prefer to use the term 'population database' rather than 'register', in keeping with advances in information technology. The term 'register' has, at least to us, the connotation of a list of affected people which is held at one location. The term 'population database' might also encompass systems in which data may be distributed over a number of different sites.)
- using a recently conducted epidemiological study of diabetes in the locality, or part of it, calculating 'indicative prevalences' (and/or incidence and mortality rates) by extrapolation from data collected elsewhere[9]
- estimating the number of people with diabetes from prescribing data and knowledge of 'average daily dose'.

The text below gives brief descriptions of prevalence, incidence and mortality. Appendix III is intended to be used in the practical tasks of calculating local numbers of people affected by diabetes and its complications. A computer-based model using the data from Appendix III is now available to assist local planning of diabetes services (Appendix III gives details of how to obtain a copy of this model). The Trent and Humberside Public Health Observatory is the lead observatory for diabetes and has co-ordinated more detailed modelling work for PCT use. Further information is available on its website.

Published data on diabetes incidence and prevalence

Since 1980, diabetes incidence[10–26] and prevalence[27–46] estimates for the UK have been published from a number of local and national studies. Clearly, when estimating local incidence or prevalence it is preferable, rather than extrapolating findings from elsewhere, to use data from local studies if these are available. For that reason, the references to these published studies are given in full. Some of these are now quite dated and most, although not all, were of populations that were largely Caucasian in origin. For localities in which no suitable data are available, age- and sex-specific incidence and prevalence estimates, derived from published studies, are given in Appendix III to allow locally relevant calculations to be made.

Incidence is well documented in children because of the relatively clear-cut nature of the condition in this age group and the presence of well-validated population databases.[11–25] An estimate from one of these databases[24] gives an annual incidence, in children aged 0–14 years, of 13.91 per 100 000 (95% confidence interval: 13.51–14.66), when age- and sex-standardised to an external reference population.[47] The prevalence of diabetes in children and young people (aged under 20) is reported as 14.0 per 1000.[48]

For diabetes in adults, 'incidence' is not a useful concept because the diagnosis of diabetes may be made a considerable time after the disease process has begun. Information on the frequency of diagnosis of new cases is sparse and some of this is now outdated (e.g. Barker *et al.*[10]), although some more recently published data are available.[26]

The prevalence of diabetes in adults is well documented, for specific localities, by means of ad hoc epidemiological studies. Poole, in the south of England, estimated the crude prevalence of diabetes in 1996 to be 2.13% in males, 1.60% in females and 1.86% overall.[46] The equivalent age-adjusted (to the 1991 UK Census population) prevalences were 1.74, 1.37 and 1.55%, respectively.

Routine data are available from general practice.[49] The General Practice Morbidity Survey provides data on prevalence, 'incidence' (more correctly, frequency of presentation of new cases) and consultation rates from a number of general practices with a total patient population base of around 2.5 million.[49] Cases are defined as those permanently registered with a general practitioner (GP) who have a clinical diagnosis of diabetes recorded at any time and/or treatment with diabetic drugs from defined sections of the *British National Formulary*. The overall prevalence of diabetes (all ages, types 1 and 2 combined) estimated from this source is 1.19% for males and 1.02% for females.

The National Health Survey for England[45] has also published prevalence data, in this case self-reported diabetes recorded by interview questionnaire in a sample of just under 12 000 adults. The survey has also estimated the prevalence of undiagnosed diabetes, as defined by a glycosylated haemoglobin concentration of 5.2% or more. In men, the prevalence of self-reported diabetes was 3%, whereas the corresponding figure in women was 1.8% (overall, men and women combined, 2.4%). The prevalence of previously undiagnosed diabetes was 1% in men and 1% in women. Thus the prevalence of all diabetes, diagnosed and undiagnosed, estimated from this source was 4% in men, 2.8% in women and 3.4% in all adults.

The main advantages of using data from ad hoc epidemiological studies are that diabetes is usually defined in a consistent manner (most commonly following the 1985 WHO definition[3]) and that information on IGT and the prevalence of previously undiagnosed diabetes has often been estimated by means of the OGTT. The main disadvantages of using national GP morbidity statistics are that no consistent definition of diabetes has been used and that the burden on local services may be underestimated due to the failure to ascertain some cases, particularly those treated by dietary therapy alone. The problem of definition also applies to self-reported diabetes, although this method is more likely to identify people treated with dietary therapy alone.

Some of the listed epidemiological studies make specific reference to populations of non-Caucasian origin.[28,31,36,38,41] In general, the prevalence of diabetes in these groups is higher, sometimes much higher, than in Caucasian populations of the same age. For diabetes in children, there is little difference in incidence between the various ethnic groups.[20] However, for adults, diabetes (mainly type 2 diabetes) is 2–4 times as common (depending on gender and age) in people of South Asian origin as in those of Caucasian origin.[36,48] People of South Asian origin are heterogeneous and prevalence may vary among them, although detailed analysis of prevalence in relation to area of origin and religion suggests that there is much less difference between South Asian groups than there is between them and their Caucasian neighbours.[50] In people of Afro-Caribbean origin, prevalence is also high and the majority of diabetes is again type 2.[31,48]

Prevalence and incidence of diabetic complications

The most important consequence of diabetes is premature death from coronary heart disease (CHD). It has long been known, and is still the case, that mortality rates from CHD are 2–3 times higher in people with diabetes than in their non-diabetic peers, and that the additional risk of CHD in people with diabetes cannot be explained in terms of the 'classic' risk factors for CHD, i.e. smoking, hypertension and serum lipid concentrations.[51–53]

There is now a large number of studies of mortality rates in people with diabetes.[54–66] Again, these are listed in full to enable specific local rates to be calculated if the relevant studies exist.

Other macrovascular complications of diabetes are cerebrovascular disease (CVD) and peripheral vascular disease (PVD). The consequences of these are premature mortality and morbidity as a result of stroke or circulatory problems of the lower limb resulting in ischaemic pain, ulceration, gangrene and amputation.

The pathognomonic sequelae of diabetes are the microvascular complications, i.e. retinopathy, nephropathy and neuropathy. Alone or, more frequently, in combination these contribute greatly to morbidity from diabetes and, particularly in the case of nephropathy, to premature mortality from renal failure.

Diabetes and socio-economic deprivation

The complications of diabetes, e.g. retinopathy or cardiovascular disease, have been shown to be more prevalent in areas of high socio-economic deprivation.[67,68] Also, the use of insulin in these areas has been shown to be less than elsewhere.[67,69] Mortality due to diabetes is higher in people from lower socio-economic groups, the unemployed and those with a 'low attained level of education'.[65,70,71]

Future epidemiological trends

The prevalence of diabetes will increase in the next decade, if only because of the ageing of the population. In addition to this influence, however, a number of other temporal trends, particularly the increase in childhood and adult obesity, will contribute to the increase in the number of people with type 2 diabetes in the population of the UK.[72] It is already occurring at increasingly younger ages – in teenagers, and in children as young as 8 years. The incidence of type 1 diabetes in children has also been found, in some population studies, to be increasing. The rate of this increase has been put as high as a doubling of incidence every 20–30 years.[73] A general increase in incidence in children has not been confirmed by all studies.[74] However, the best evidence for such an increase relates to the youngest age group (birth to 4 years) – children who will have the longest time to develop complications.

Estimates of the future prevalence of diabetes have been made on a global basis and for the UK.[75,76] The latter highlights the inadequacy of current data, particularly for mortality, for the prediction of future prevalence in the UK. Their 'best guess' is that the total prevalence of diabetes will increase by 25% for males and 14% for females between 1992 and 2010.

5 Services available

Structure and process

As with all chronic diseases, services for people with diabetes must be organised around the evolving, individual needs of the affected person. With this in mind, the WHO and the International Diabetes Federation (IDF) have consistently stressed self-care and the role of patients and patients' organisations in determining how care should be provided. Thus the strategic recommendations of the Saint Vincent Declaration[77] (see Appendix IV) and the related Acropolis Affirmation[78] were formulated by joint discussion between professional carers, affected individuals and patients' organisations. Similarly, the best of national and local policies and protocols have been drawn up in consultation with patients and their relatives (e.g. a 'Patients' Charter'[79] [Appendix V]), often under the guidance of LDSAGs[80] or similar bodies.

The main components of diabetes services are the hospital-based diabetes team or teams (usually one or more consultant diabetologists, or paediatricians, other consultant staff, specialist nurse, dietitian and podiatrist, with suitable junior medical, laboratory and administrative support), the primary care team (GP, practice nurse and administrative support) and other community support (podiatrist, dietitian and community nurse). Seventy-five per cent of districts or their equivalent have a 'diabetes centre'.[81] More detailed information on the facilities offered by diabetes centres is given in Appendix VI. The range of components is outlined in Table 3.

Table 3: Staff necessary for a comprehensive diabetes service.

Service	Staff	Service	Staff
Services provided in primary care	General practitioners Practice nurses Supported by: • dietitians • podiatrists • optometrists • district nurses • laboratory services • administrative staff and, in some localities: • diabetes facilitators • and/or specialist nurses	Services provided in hospitals, for children	Paediatrician with a special interest in diabetes† Specialist nurses/liaison health visitors Supported by: • dietitians • podiatrists • optometrists • clinical psychologists • laboratory services • administrative support
Services provided in hospitals, for adults	Diabetologists* Specialist nurses Supported by: • dietitians • podiatrists • optometrists • clinical psychologists • laboratory services • administrative support	Services provided in hospitals, for pregnant women with pre-existing diabetes and women who develop diabetes during pregnancy	As for adults, with the addition of obstetricians and midwives
Services for the management of patients with complications	As for adults, with the addition of ophthalmologists, vascular surgeons, cardiologists, renal physicians and psychosexual counsellors	Preventive and support services in the community	Health promotion staff Local authority staff Social services Residential/nursing home staff Voluntary services

* Older people may be cared for by a geriatrician with a particular interest in diabetes, or in jointly run clinics.
† Increasingly, young people with diabetes are managed in clinics run jointly by paediatricians and diabetologists. Staffing levels and facilities vary from place to place. More detailed information on staff and facilities has been collected by the BDA.[31,32]

Service utilisation

The frequency of diabetes 'episodes' in general practice (i.e. 'an instance of diabetes-related sickness in which there were one or more general practitioner consultations') is 11.1 per 1000 persons at risk per year.[49] This is more than twice the rate of the general population. Age- and sex-standardised admission rates are available for use as primary care effectiveness indicators, a part of the National Framework for Assessing Performance.[83]

A study in South Glamorgan has shown that patients with diabetes accounted for 5.5% of hospital admissions and 6.4% of outpatient attendances, and that patients with diabetes occupy 9.4% of acute-sector bed days.[84] Inpatient and outpatient activity was studied for patients with and without diabetes for all diagnoses and procedures, even if not related to diabetes.[84] Some results are summarised in Table 4.

Table 4: Hospital utilisation by patients with and without diabetes.

Patients with diabetes	Patients without diabetes
Mean length of stay of 11.4 bed days	Mean length of stay of 7.1 bed days
Mean of 5 outpatient attendances per patient per year (for patients aged 25–34 years)	Mean of 0.5 outpatient attendances per patient per year (for patients aged 25–34 years)
Mean of 4 outpatient attendances per patient per year (for patients aged over 75 years)	Mean of 1.5 outpatient attendances per patient per year (for patients aged over 75 years)
Occupy 5–6 acute hospital bed days per person per year[85,86]	Occupy one acute hospital bed day per person per year

The use of hospital resources by people with diabetes is heavily influenced by the presence or absence of complications. The CODE-2 (Cost of Diabetes in Europe – Type 2, a registered trademark of SmithKline Beecham plc) study demonstrated that, compared with patients with no recorded complications, those with only microvascular complications use just over twice the amount of hospital resources.[87] For patients with macrovascular complications this figure is around three, and those with both microvascular and macrovascular complications require around five and a half times the hospital resources of those without complications.

These crude estimates of service usage mask a substantial unmet need, the two most important aspects of which are:

- the numbers of individuals whose diabetes is currently undiagnosed
- the proportion of patients with clinically diagnosed diabetes who have no planned programme of care.

The proportion of patients with no established programme of care will vary from district to district. There are data on the proportion who have a programme of follow-up care at a hospital (estimates range from 29 to 46%), but these studies are now rather dated because they were carried out before the establishment of diabetes centres, which are likely to have increased access to hospital-based care.[81,88–90]

Although there is little published evidence on the subject, it is likely that patients not attending for regular clinical review (either in primary or secondary care) will be the most frequent users of hospital inpatient facilities, particularly for problems such as diabetic ketoacidosis and for complications such as diabetic foot disease.

Screening

One of the issues which urgently requires clarification is whether population screening for undiagnosed diabetes (almost exclusively type 2 diabetes) is effective and cost-effective. This issue is dealt with in detail below but it is mentioned briefly here, before a summary of current information on costs, beacuse policies on screening for diabetes are closely linked to the economics of diabetes care.

Any population-based screening programme for diabetes clearly has cost implications for the health service, those of publicising and administering the programme, taking and testing blood or urine samples, communicating the results to those screened and dealing with the resulting newly identified cases. There are also costs to the individual, not only the direct costs of attending screening sessions, which apply to all those screened, but the cost, to those found likely to have diabetes, of a diagnosis brought forward in time, with its implications for lifestyle, life assurance and, in some cases, employment.

These costs may be severe for both false positives and true positives, and there are also potential costs for false negatives, unwarranted reassurance and time lost for therapeutic intervention. The latter statement implies that earlier therapeutic intervention has its benefits. This is currently not proven although accumulating indirect evidence suggests that it may be the case. Relevant observations are (1) evidence proving the role of near-normal blood glucose control in preventing or delaying complications in both type 1 and type 2 diabetes (*see* below) and (2) evidence that a substantial proportion of patients with type 2 diabetes already have microvascular complications at diagnosis (20%, according to the United Kingdom Prospective Diabetes Study (UKPDS); again, *see* below).

Costs of diabetes in the UK

Information on the costs of diabetes, in particular its health care costs, is available for many countries, including the UK.[84,91–97] The economic aspects of diabetes are currently of considerable interest internationally.[87,98]

- In 1989 at least 4–5% of total health care expenditure, including primary, secondary and community care, was estimated to be devoted to the care of people with diabetes.[92] This amounted to around £1 billion in the UK in that year. Of this, an estimated 3.2% (£32 million in 1986–87) was estimated to have been spent in primary care.
- More recently, Currie *et al.*[94] estimated that 8.7% of acute-sector costs is spent on care for patients with diabetes. This was calculated to be an average of £2101 per year per resident with diabetes compared with £308 per year per resident without diabetes.
- In one district, people with diabetes accounted for 5.5% of hospital admissions and 6.4% of outpatient attendances.[84] The relative risk of hospital admission for diabetes-related complications in this district was around 12 for coronary heart disease and cerebrovascular disease, 16 for neuropathy and peripheral vascular disease, 10 for eye complications and 15 for renal disease.[84]
- Patients with diabetes have around a fourfold increased probability of undergoing a cardiac procedure, and the total cost of the hospital treatment for coronary heart disease in people with diabetes was estimated (at 1994–95 prices) to be £1.1 billion.[95]
- The overall cost of hospital care for people with diabetes in one district was predicted to increase by 15% by the year 2011. This is greater than the predicted overall increase of 9.4% for all inpatient care.[94]

Although the health care costs of secondary and tertiary care for people with diabetes are reasonably well quantified, the costs of primary and community care have received little attention. Costs per episode are considerably higher for secondary and tertiary care than for primary care, but the number of episodes is greater in the latter. The costs per patient are likely to be lower in the short term in primary care. However, unless this care is of sufficient quality to prevent or delay complications, or at least identify them early, the long-term costs are likely to be higher.

Most of the economic impact of diabetes results from its complications. Foot problems (caused by diabetic neuropathy and peripheral vascular disease) and cardiovascular disease in particular account for a high proportion of hospital admissions, considerable disability and, in the case of cardiovascular disease, considerable premature mortality.[57,99] Of the currently preventable complications of diabetes, diabetic foot disease and diabetic eye problems incur the greatest levels of service use and hence costs. Renal replacement therapy is expensive but needed less often than other services. Estimated costs, for patients with type 1 diabetes, are available for each of these complications.[93]

The economic impact of diabetes can be categorised into direct and indirect costs. Direct costs, such as those quoted above, include the costs of preventing, diagnosing, managing and treating diabetes, including hospital costs and social services. Indirect costs result from the consequences of morbidity, disability and premature mortality and the loss of productive output for society.[98,100] Owing to a number of methodological problems, indirect costs are difficult to estimate. When they have been estimated (e.g. Gray *et al.*[93]) they have been found to be at least as great as the direct costs.

6 Effectiveness and cost-effectiveness of services

In this section, where appropriate, evidence is assessed according to a scoring system outlined in Appendix VII.

Screening

Screening for diabetes

Screening ('the systematic application of a test or inquiry, to identify individuals at sufficient risk of a specific disorder to warrant further investigation or direct preventive action, among persons who have not sought medical attention on account of symptoms of that disorder'[101]) may be proactive or opportunistic. In proactive screening, members of a specific population are targeted, whereas opportunistic screening, sometimes referred to as 'case finding', is the 'invitation for testing of apparently asymptomatic individuals not otherwise seeking medical care'.[102]

Although the ADA advocates 3-yearly testing for diabetes in all adults aged 45 or over, screening for diabetes in the general population is not currently advocated in the UK.[2] The professional advisory committee of the BDA is undecided about the benefits of screening for diabetes in the general population, describing the role and value of screening as 'unclear'.[103] The report advocates opportunistic screening 'alongside screening for other problems such as hypertension and obesity'. It also suggests that screening may take the form of 'a single-point initiative of a practice (or Health District) across a larger population'.[103] If screening is to be carried out, it recommends restricting this to adults between the ages of 40 and 75, using a rescreening frequency of 5 years and adopting the criteria listed in Box 3. In 2003, a WHO/IDF document, *Screening for Type 2 Diabetes*, was published (*see* Appendix II).

Box 3: Procedures, criteria and practice for testing asymptomatic individuals for diabetes as advocated by the professional advisory committee of the BDA.[103]

If blood glucose testing is used then a 'positive' result is a FPG of > 6.6 mmol/l or a venous PG 2 h after a 75 g oral glucose load of > 8.0 mmol/l.

If urine testing is used then any glucose in a sample passed 2 h after a main meal is a 'positive' result. An FPG in the range 5.5–6.6 mmol/l is an equivocal result which should be repeated in 6–12 months if there is any risk factor for diabetes (obesity, a family history of diabetes or 'Asian/African' racial origin).

If blood glucose or urine tests are 'negative' then they should be repeated in 5 years, or 3 years if any of the above risk factors are present.

The BDA report also summarises the elements of a diabetes screening test.[103] The sensitivity, specificity and predictive value of, for example, varying thresholds of FPG as a screening test for diabetes (as defined by the previous WHO criteria[1]) are provided and are also shown in Table 5.[103]

Table 5: Sensitivity, specificity and predictive value of various fasting plasma glucose (FPG) thresholds compared with 1985 WHO criteria[1] for diabetes.

FPG (mmol/l)	Sensitivity (%)	Specificity (%)	Predictive value of a positive test (%)*
> 7.8	32	100	100
> 6.7	30–60	> 90	45–55
> 5.5	70–90	c. 90	20–45
> 4.5	100	< 90	
			< 10

* Prevalence unspecified.

Screening the general population, using a self-testing method for the detection of postprandial glycosuria, has been reported in a study based in Ipswich.[104] In this study, 13 795 subjects aged between 45 and 70 years and not known to have diabetes were posted a urine testing strip with instructions and a result card. Of the 10 348 (75%) who responded, 343 (3.3%) were found to have glycosuria and diabetes was confirmed in 99 (30%) of the 330 who attended for OGTT. A further 65 had an OGTT result in the IGT range. Thus large-scale screening is possible and is relatively cheap in terms of the cost of materials, postage, etc. However, at least in this study, around 140 people had to be contacted for each true positive case detected, and the short- and long-term consequences of these early diagnoses were not evaluated.

The issues surrounding population screening for diabetes are complex and important, and are currently being addressed in the UK by the National Screening Committee. For this reason, screening for diabetes, particularly type 2 diabetes, has been highlighted as an issue which PCTs and their equivalents need to keep in mind as a potential future development. Terminology is often used loosely. In particular, the terms screening, case finding and opportunistic screening are often used in different senses, and the screening test is sometimes endowed with a degree of certainty (either positive or negative) which even the 'gold standard' does not merit.

Greenhalgh[105] emphasised the last of these points in her anecdote about a patient who described symptoms of diabetes and was tested, once, for glycosuria. On being found to be negative, he was reassured that he did not have the disease. Casual (or random) testing for glycosuria is grossly insensitive (Greenhalgh quotes a sensitivity of 22%). This is improved by postprandial testing but, as shown by Davies et al.,[104] can still remain below 30%.

Greenhalgh, quoting data from Andersson et al.,[106] provides a similar estimate of yield of true positives to Davies et al.[104] – around 170 people need to be contacted for each true positive detected.

Screening for diabetic retinopathy

The effectiveness and cost-effectiveness of screening for diabetic retinopathy have been reviewed.[107–110] Bachman and Nelson's comprehensive review indicates that an organised programme of early detection and treatment would be likely to reduce blindness among people with diabetes.[110] The results of this review are summarised in Box 4.

Box 4: Screening for diabetic retinopathy.

- 'Gold standard' screening tests are stereoscopic multi-field photography and direct plus indirect ophthalmoscopy performed by an ophthalmologist.
- The most widely used screening tests are direct ophthalmoscopy, performed by a variety of health professionals, and non-stereoscopic retinal photography. Individually, these tests may achieve high sensitivity and specificity under optimal conditions, with increased sensitivity when combined.
- Screening programmes reported in the UK have resulted in an overall yield of 1.2% of screening episodes leading to laser photocoagulation.
- Cost-effectiveness analyses suggest that screening by retinal photography or by an optician may be at least as efficient as retinal examination by GPs or ophthalmologists.
- Studies in the USA have shown that annual screening would lead to net cost savings for people with type 1 diabetes.
- Treatment of proliferative retinopathy or maculopathy by laser coagulation has been shown to be effective. Treatment at earlier stages of retinopathy is less effective.
- For every 100 patients with treatable disease, 55 would be expected to become blind or severely visually impaired within 10 years if none were treated. This is compared with 13 if all were treated in the same period. The pick-up rate diminishes after the first round of screening.

Source: Bachman and Nelson.[110]

The National Screening Committee has considered in some detail the question of population screening for diabetic retinopathy. Their recommendation is that this should be introduced and a commitment has been made for this to be a national policy. The recommended methods are likely to be digital retinal photography with or without direct ophthalmoscopy.

Effectiveness of optimal glycaemic control

Type 1 diabetes

The Diabetes Control and Complications Trial (DCCT) research group reported its findings for type 1 diabetes in 1993.[111] By providing robust evidence (I-1), the DCCT confirmed the consensus opinion that improving glycaemic control in type 1 diabetes is effective in the primary and secondary prevention of retinal, renal and neurological complications. A Swedish study[112] (I-2), among others, came to similar conclusions and a meta-analysis (I-1), which preceded the reporting of the DCCT, found that intensive blood glucose control was effective in the secondary prevention of microvascular complications.[113] The DCCT and its results are summarised in Box 5.

Box 5: Summary of the DCCT.

- A randomised controlled trial based in the USA commenced in 1986.
- 1441 patients with type 1 diabetes were randomly allocated to 'intensive insulin therapy' (IIT) or conventional therapy.
- The patients were highly motivated, with 99% completing the study.
- The trial had primary and secondary prevention arms.
- The results showed that IIT delays the onset and slows the progression of diabetic retinopathy, nephropathy and neuropathy.
- Analysis of the results showed that any improvement in diabetes control will prevent complications: the better the control, the fewer the complications.
- The trial was terminated prematurely at a mean of 6.5 years due to convincing results.
- IIT increased the risk of severe hypoglycaemia by threefold.

Some questions remained unanswered, such as the applicability of the results of the DCCT to patients with type 2 diabetes, patients with advanced complications and young children.[114]

Some of the implications of the DCCT for the UK are listed below.

1   DCCT was a trial of efficacy (outcomes under ideal circumstances) rather than effectiveness (outcomes in 'the real world'). Therefore replication of its approach may not be applicable to everyday UK clinical practice.[115,116]
2   The costs of implementing the recommendations were not addressed, although subsequent economic 'modelling' has been carried out.[117]
3   The role of patients and patient empowerment was not addressed in the DCCT, and this is seen as increasingly important in the UK.[116]
4   Full implementation or a pragmatic partial implementation of the DCCT results in the UK would:

- require increased resources in the short term, unless reorganisation of diabetes care or other activities releases existing resources
- improve the quality of care for people with type 1 diabetes
- be likely to result in increased efficiency of the NHS care of diabetes in the long term through the prevention or delay of microvascular complications.

Type 2 diabetes

The DCCT led to debate and speculation about the implications of its results for people with type 2 diabetes.[118] However, two studies now provide direct evidence of the beneficial effect of improved blood glucose control on the development of complications in type 2 diabetes. These studies were already underway when the DCCT was published.

The first of these is the Kumamoto study, published in 1995.[119] Using a study design similar to the DCCT, Ohkubo *et al.* examined the effect of 'multiple insulin injection therapy' in patients with type 2 diabetes on the progression of microvascular complications (I-2). The study was small, involving 110 Japanese patients who did not have the characteristics typical of patients with type 2 diabetes in the UK. For example, none of the Japanese patients were obese and, as a group, they had significantly lower body mass indices than most UK patients. The results were similar to those of the DCCT in that they showed that improved glycaemic control delayed the onset and progression of retinopathy, nephropathy and neuropathy. The extent to which these results could be applied to people with type 2 diabetes in the UK was uncertain, however.

Since the publication of the Kumamoto study, the results of the UKPDS have become available.[120–124] The main aims of the UKPDS (I-1) were (1) to determine whether intensive control of blood glucose would prevent complications in type 2 diabetes, (2) to answer the same question for the tight control of high blood pressure, and (3) to determine whether any specific treatment (specific oral hypoglycaemic agent and/or insulin) confers particular benefit. The UKPDS is summarised in Box 6.

Editorial commentaries on the final results of the UKPDS highlighted the fact that 'intensive therapy of type 2 diabetes is beneficial, despite the associated weight gain' but that the study 'did not unequivocally show whether an intensive [blood glucose] strategy influences cardiovascular disease'.[125–128] With regard to the latter, however, its results are reassuring in terms of the 'absence of an obvious pernicious effect [on death from cardiovascular disease] of either insulin or sulphonylureas'.[125] Orchard[126] draws attention to the benefit, in relation to survival with cardiovascular disease, of simvastatin-mediated cholesterol lowering in type 2 diabetes (the 4S study[129]).

Morgensen[127] emphasised that the UKPDS demonstrated the advantages of effective control of high blood pressure in people 'even more convincingly' than the effect of tight blood glucose control. This was influential in reducing deaths from diabetes-related causes (*see* Box 6), whereas the 'difference between the treatment regimens in their effect on haemoglobin A_{1c} concentrations (7.0% v. 7.9%) was probably not large enough to result in great differences in cardiovascular outcome'. Combination therapy was often needed to produce this effective decrease in blood pressure. The proportion of UKPDS subjects requiring three or more antihypertensive treatments to achieve effective blood pressure control was 27% and 31%, respectively. This editorial also re-emphasises the 'double jeopardy' of type 2 diabetes combined with high blood pressure and the third 'bad companion' of type 2 diabetes, namely dyslipidaemia.

Box 6: Summary of the United Kingdom Prospective Diabetes Study.

- The UKPDS was a multi-centre randomised controlled trial that commenced in 1977 and was carried out in the UK.
- Initially, 4209 patients (aged 25–65 years) with newly diagnosed type 2 diabetes were randomly allocated to different therapies: 'conventional' diet and exercise therapy, or 'intensive' diet and exercise *and* oral hypoglycaemic or insulin therapy.
- Over the 10 years of the study, the mean HbA_{1c} in the intensively treated group was 11% lower than in the conventionally treated group (7.0% [SD 6.2–8.2] vs. 7.9% [SD 6.9–8.8]).[120]
- Compared with the conventional group, the risk for any diabetes-related endpoint in the intensive group was 12% lower (95% CI: 1–21%, $p = 0.029$). This represented a reduction, in the absolute risk of death, from 46.0 events per 1000 patient years to 40.9 events per 1000 patient years.[120] The reduction in risk of diabetes-related death, in relation to this difference in glycaemic control, was not statistically significant.[120]
- There was a statistically significant 25% (95% CI: 7–40%, $p = 0.0099$) reduction in risk for the microvascular endpoints considered. This represented a reduction in absolute risk from 11.4 events per 1000 patient years to 8.6 events per 1000 patient years.[120]
- There was no significant difference in any diabetes-related endpoints between the three intensive agents (chlorpropamide, glibenclamide and insulin).[120]
- A statistically significant improvement in blood pressure control was achieved during the course of the study. Mean blood pressure in the tightly controlled blood pressure group was 144/82 mmHg compared with 154/87 mmHg ($p < 0.0001$).
- This difference was clinically significant in that the risk of death from diabetes-related causes, in relation to this difference in blood pressure, was reduced by 32%, that of stroke was reduced by 44% and that of microvascular endpoints by 37%.[122]
- There was no perceptible difference in the effectiveness of captopril and atenolol, and the majority of subjects randomised to the blood pressure control groups required more than one anti-hypertensive treatment to achieve effective control.

Watkins[128] observed that the 'use of insulin *per se* confers neither additional advantages nor disadvantages, while the use of sulphonylureas does not lead to additional risks'. He also emphasised the importance of the findings concerning blood pressure control and 'that ACE [angiotensin-converting enzyme] inhibitors or β-blockers are equally effective in achieving the benefits of lowering blood pressure'. Despite the emphasis in the trial's results of the advantages of adding oral hypoglycaemic or insulin treatment to the basic dietary therapy, Watkins considered that the 'role of diet, exercise and weight reduction remains, of course, paramount in treatment of Type 2 diabetes'.

Effectiveness of risk factor modification

Although the achievement of as normal a blood glucose as possible is a contributory factor in the prevention of long-term complications (and is clearly fundamental to the avoidance of hypoglycaemia and hyperglycaemia), other factors are also known to be important. Some of these are amenable to therapy or behavioural modification, e.g. the control of hypertension for nephropathy, cardiovascular disease and cerebrovascular disease.

The importance of smoking cessation in people with diabetes has received some attention. This suggests that smoking is associated with poor glycaemic control and increased prevalence and progression of microvascular complications.[130–132] A study in Atlanta, USA, showed that people with diabetes are as likely to smoke as those without, and that 40% of smokers with diabetes reported that their doctor had not advised or helped with cessation.[133] Programmes designed to encourage smoking cessation specifically in people with diabetes are rare and, where evaluated, have proved unsuccessful.[134]

Effective delivery of care

The most effective setting for delivery of care for people with diabetes is open to debate. Randomised controlled trials of hospital vs. primary care have been reviewed by the Cochrane Diabetes Group (I).[135] Only five trials were sufficiently robust to be included in their meta-analysis. The results suggest that 'prompted' primary care, i.e. a programme including a system of recall and regular review of diabetes, can be as good as hospital care in terms of glycaemic control. Such prompted care is better than hospital care in terms of maintaining contact with patients.

The results of this meta-analysis should be interpreted with caution, however, because of inter-study variation and statistical heterogeneity. The results are, though, consistent with an earlier review.[136] The effective element appears to be the computerised recall with prompting for patients and their family doctors. The extent to which care should be 'shared' (between the hospital team and primary care) is likely to vary from practice to practice, from patient to patient and from time to time during the natural progression of diabetes in any given patient. There will be times (e.g. during childhood, during and immediately prior to pregnancy and when complications are developing) when care by a hospital team is necessary.

Cost-effectiveness of care

Cost-effectiveness studies of diabetes care in the UK and in countries with similar health care systems are relatively rare. However, components of this care, such as screening for diabetic retinopathy, preventive foot care and intensive control of hypertension in people with diabetes, have received some attention. In general, it is reasonable to follow the widely held consensus that prompt diagnosis, patient education and regular, high-quality clinical review are likely to contribute to the cost-effectiveness of local diabetes programmes.

Preventive foot care, incorporating an educational component and organised on an outpatient basis, is an option which has been shown in Australia to reduce the need for hospital admission for lower limb complications, in the UK to reduce amputation rates and in The Netherlands to reduce the cost of diabetic foot disease.[137–139] Given the large contribution of diabetic foot disease to acute-sector costs, preventive foot care would have to be either very ineffective, very costly or both not to be cost-effective.[140–142]

Recently, the effective control of blood pressure, with ACE inhibitors or β-blockers, in people with diabetes has been shown to be cost-effective.[124] The additional resources required to achieve this control were recouped within the 10 years of the UKPDS trial by the cost savings associated with the reduced frequency of complications and the life years gained. This conclusion from direct observation in a trial of type 2 diabetes in the UK supports the general conclusion of a US modelling study of type 1 diabetes (based on the results of the DCCT) and the US study of type 2 diabetes (based on extrapolation of DCCT results to type 2 diabetes).[117,143,144] Intensive therapy, directed at improved control of blood pressure or control of hyperglycaemia, although more costly than routine care, achieves significant reductions in health care costs in the long run. This 'long run' is measured in years, but ultimately this intensive therapy is cost-effective in terms of direct health care costs and benefits.

7 Models of care

Introduction

The organisation of services for the care of people with diabetes is complex, involving hospital-based diabetes teams, community services, those working in primary care, patients and their families. The most appropriate model of care for people with diabetes is not readily apparent given the lack of effectiveness data on the relative importance of primary or secondary care.[135,136] One thing is certain, however, as stated by Greenhalgh:[145] 'inadequacies in the provision of diabetes care in the UK will not be redressed simply by sounding the trumpet for a primary-care-led system, nor by the formation of political factions to protect the traditional territory of the [hospital] diabetologist'. Instead, services need to be designed from the point of view of the user, 'tailored to the individual patient' and not rigid in their adherence to district or hospital protocols.[145]

The provision of care for people with chronic diseases, including diabetes, is shifting from secondary to primary care with the benefits of increased access to care and increased patient satisfaction because of this increased access.[146,147] In England, PCTs have taken over from health authorities (HAs) as commissioners of health care.[148] This policy shift has led to PCTs (and their equivalents elsewhere in the UK) emerging as the commissioners and providers of care for people with diabetes. Specialist expertise, 'hi-tech' facilities and, in most localities, leadership are likely to remain in secondary care. Part of the role of PCTs or their equivalent is to ensure health and health care needs are met appropriately and that the quality of care is monitored and maintained, for example by taking the lead in the development of local Health Improvement Programmes (HImPs) and similar plans.[148]

National guidance on the key features of a good diabetes service has been issued [NHS Executive HSG(97)45], and this emphasises the need for a process of continual improvement of diabetes services at a district level. The balance between primary and secondary care for people with diabetes can and will vary between districts and this is justifiable with one proviso – that nobody with diabetes should receive inexpert, unstructured care at any location. The BDA has also issued guidance on the ways in which diabetes can feature in local HImPs (*Health Improvement Programmes: an opportunity to improve the health of people with diabetes* – available from the BDA). This document emphasises the multi-agency nature of HImP implementation, with 4 of 11 designated areas for action citing the local authority as the lead organisation.

Planning district services for people with diabetes

Integrated district diabetes services have frequently been developed with support and leadership from the local hospital-based diabetes team. This team should consist of at least one consultant trained in diabetes care, although the exact number will depend on the size of the district, and the prevalence of diabetes, and the appropriate number of diabetes specialist nurses, dietitians and podiatrists. Recommendations for the structure of specialist diabetes care services have been published by the BDA.[149]

The main clinical roles of the team will be in education and specialist patient care, particularly of those with newly diagnosed type 1 diabetes, active complications, pregnant women with diabetes and diabetes of any kind which is difficult to control. Children with diabetes should be looked after by a team which includes a paediatrician with a special interest in diabetes. The hospital team will also give advice on the management of acute problems and ensure that proper clinical links are made with other hospital services such as ophthalmology, cardiology, renal medicine, medicine for the elderly, obstetrics, and general, vascular and orthopaedic surgery.

The key elements to be followed when planning service or health improvements for district residents with diabetes mellitus are shown in Box 7.

Box 7: Key elements for planning diabetes service or health improvements.

- Setting up a multi-disciplinary group to exchange ideas, develop partnerships and plan and implement change. In the late 1990s, at least 60% of HAs had set up an LSDAG or their equivalent.[150]
- Assessing the health care needs of the local population using this health care needs assessment with additional corporate or comparative elements as appropriate.[151] This should identify problems specific to individual districts, such as a large ethnic population, or specific local service issues, such as problems of recruiting medical staff.
- Using nationally and internationally available standards to develop and agree aims and objectives of the local diabetes service and local standards (in terms of structure, process and outcome) of care.[80,150,152]
- Developing local protocols of care including local policies on screening for diabetes, the use of population databases, health promotion, foot care and retinal screening.
- Developing protocols on management of patients at the primary/secondary care interface.
- Ensuring the training and professional development of those caring for people with diabetes.[152]
- Planning service reconfiguration where appropriate, e.g. the development of outreach clinics.
- Planning evaluation and clinical audit, including economic evaluation.

The greatest current economic and organisational challenges to those involved in commissioning diabetes services are related to the four key areas (A, B, C and D) illustrated in Figure 1. Within these areas are the boundary between not having diabetes and having diabetes (A, primary prevention), between diagnosed

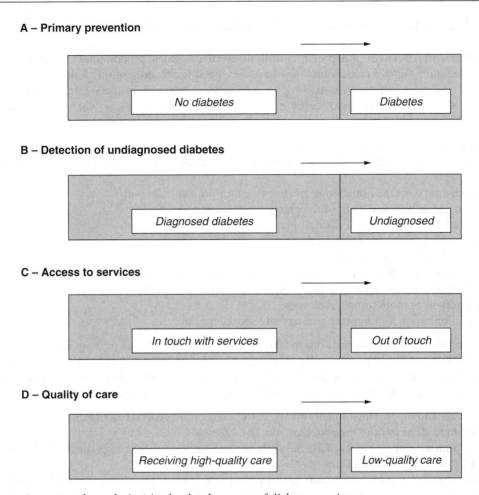

A – Primary prevention

| No diabetes | Diabetes |

B – Detection of undiagnosed diabetes

| Diagnosed diabetes | Undiagnosed |

C – Access to services

| In touch with services | Out of touch |

D – Quality of care

| Receiving high-quality care | Low-quality care |

Figure 1: Important boundaries* in the development of diabetes services.

and undiagnosed diabetes (B, screening and early diagnosis), between being in contact and out of contact with health services (C, access to services) and between receiving effective care and receiving ineffective care (D, quality of care).

Considerable documentation and a large measure of agreement exist on the aims of diabetes care and how these might be achieved. These should include:

- opportunistic screening in those at high risk of diabetes
- involvement of all those identified in planned programmes of care
- ensuring that all those with diabetes and their carers have access to appropriate education
- maintaining optimal metabolic control to prevent or delay the development of complications
- eliminating the acute problems of hypoglycaemia and hyperglycaemia
- ensuring the early identification and treatment of complications
- improvement of glycaemic control in pregnancy, thereby reducing fetal wastage and the incidence of congenital malformations.

---

* Service developments should move all these boundaries to the right.

Planning diabetes services in the primary care setting

Many general practices have taken part in 'chronic disease management programmes' (*see The Red Book*[153]) for diabetes and asthma. Practices may also have developed health promotion clinics for their diabetic patients.[154] As more patients with diabetes are seen predominantly in primary care, the care provided must be of the highest quality. Quality care is most likely to take place when the following are available:[155]

- trained and motivated practice personnel
- a practice-based database of patients with diabetes (linking to a district population database where possible)
- protected time for the initiation of treatment, education and follow-up
- clinical and educational audit of the practice's activities
- recognition of a practice (or district) protocol for diabetes care
- regular recall of patients for clinical review
- a curriculum for patient education
- well-defined liaison with the hospital-based team and easy access to those facilities not normally available in primary care, e.g. group education programmes, specialist nurse and dietetic advice and management of more complicated cases
- good information flow between primary and secondary care.

Revised and updated recommendations for the management of diabetes in primary care are included in a BDA publication with that title, as listed in Appendix II. The improvement of diabetes services in a primary care setting should occur as part of a PCT strategy. This is explored above. As a minimum, PCTs or their equivalents can encourage high-quality diabetes care at primary care level if they:

- encourage and support high-quality diabetes care in all or most general practices, but particularly those which fulfil all or most of the above criteria
- assist primary care teams that lack the skills or facilities to carry out high-quality diabetes care to acquire those skills and facilities
- ensure that the essential community services of dietetics and chiropody are provided to support the primary care team in their work with people with diabetes.

Tools for planning

Population databases

Developments in information technology have enabled more and more comprehensive databases of diabetes care to be established and used. These have progressed from simple card indices of individuals known to have the disorder through to sophisticated distributed databases which allow information on health care episodes occurring in many different locations to be accessed from a number of sites. Access to such data, carefully controlled and monitored to ensure confidentiality, can enhance both the care of the individual patient and the planning and monitoring of services for populations.

The work involved in establishing such population databases must not be underestimated. Particularly in inner cities, any one ascertainment source may grossly underestimate the number of people that need to be included. Burnett *et al.*,[35] working in inner London, found that only 40% of 4674 patients identified from multiple sources had Prescription Pricing Authority (PPA) returns. Only 43% appeared on general practice diabetes registers and only 57% could have been identified from attendances at the district hospital. The message from this research is clear – multiple, frequently overlapping sources must be used in the compilation (and updating) of population databases on diabetes. The resource consequences of this must be identified from the outset.

Another later study came to the opposite conclusion to Burnett et al. Howitt and Cheales,[39] based in south-east England, felt that ascertainment through general practices alone was adequate. They based this on their findings that most (41 of 43) practices approached contributed to their register and that the estimates of prevalence obtained were close to those expected from epidemiological studies carried out in other places. This is relatively weak evidence because they had no independent validation of completeness of ascertainment in their locality.

Patchet and Roberts[156] sounded a cautionary note about over-ascertainment (or over-diagnosis) of people included on practice-based registers. Of 112 patients listed by their practice as having diabetes, 26 had had normal HbA_{1c} concentrations in the preceding 6 months. Their conclusion was that nine of these people had been investigated by OGTT but had been found not to have diabetes. Such inflation of databases does no doubt occur, but the net effect of over- and under-ascertainment is most likely to give an underestimation of the numbers of people with diabetes, especially those treated with dietary therapy alone.

Recent years have seen the standardisation, both in the UK and elsewhere, of data items for inclusion on practice- and population-based diabetes data sets. The Diabetes Audit Working Group of the Research Unit of the Royal College of Physicians and the BDA,[157] for example, has listed and defined 101 data items which it considers should be included in a diabetes data set. This suggestion may be regarded as unnecessarily complex, especially in the context of primary care. It is more sensible, however, to advocate the use of subsets of such databases, applying the standard definitions of the items selected, rather than compiling, de novo, local databases that lack comparability with others elsewhere.

There is little published evidence on the effectiveness or cost-effectiveness of registers or population databases. Jones and Hedley,[158] in 1984, estimated that their diabetes register, when considering only the advantages it provided for retinal screening, had a benefit-to-cost ratio of 15:1. The costs of establishing such a resource are greater than the costs of maintaining it so, once established, the cost-effectiveness of such databases should increase as benefits accrue.

More recently, Elwyn et al.[159] questioned the usefulness of population databases, suggesting that they may be 'more trouble than they're worth'. However, they do admit to the potential of these databases to improve the quality of individual care by prompting call and recall for regular review. Also, they acknowledge that they can facilitate local needs assessment and the monitoring of quality of care from aggregated district or regional data. Despite the fact that diabetes databases have been in use in the UK for almost three decades, they consider that, in relation to their cost-effectiveness, it may be 'too early to tell and perhaps too late to ask'. Further information about the benefits of using population databases will emerge when localities such as Salford publish longitudinal data on process and outcome. Thus far, such data are only available in abstract form.[160]

Elwyn et al.[159] also highlight important ethical issues surrounding the compilation of these databases. They are probably correct in believing that, in most places where such databases exist, individuals with diabetes are largely ignorant of the fact that their demographic and clinical details are held in this form, in addition to the clinical record. These authors cite several items of guidance (including an NHS Executive Letter [EL (96) 72])[161] which emphasise that patients should 'opt in' rather than 'opt out' to such databases. The EL itself states that 'patients should be made aware of the existence and the purpose of a register'.[161] In practice, it is likely that the majority of people with diabetes, given reasonable safeguards in relation to confidentiality, would not object to their personal data being held in this way. However, although some information exists on this question in relation to population databases for cervical screening, no information exists for diabetes databases.[162]

Future developments in this area will need to take account of the current NHS Information Strategy[163] and the move, as part of that strategy, towards electronic patient records. In addition, software systems, such as MIQUEST, are used for example in the extraction of data used in the DiabCare project.[164]

Health care Resource Groups

Health care Resource Groups (HRGs) are one way of developing a system based on case-mix. 'Case-mix is a system which classifies types of patients treated, and costs each category to enable consistent pricing for each patient'.[165] HRGs are 'groupings of acute inpatient care episodes which are likely to consume the same amount of resource'[166] and are based on the patient record and inpatient events.[167] They are adapted from diagnosis-related groups (DRGs) which were developed in the USA in the early 1980s.

HRGs have been used for contracting and are being used in commissioning, internal resource management (e.g. within a trust) and 'benchmarking'. The NHS Information Authority co-ordinates progress in the development of HRGs. Costing of surgical hospital episodes by HRGs is well developed, with the extension of the use of HRGs in the acute medical specialties complete by 2000.[168,169]

The allocation of a particular episode of care to a group is dependent on a number of characteristics of the episode, including:

- the age of the patient
- the primary diagnosis
- the secondary diagnosis/diagnoses
- the surgical procedure, if any
- whether the patient was alive or dead at discharge.

Although admissions and episodes for medical reasons, e.g. diabetes, are more difficult to classify into HRGs than surgical procedures, the NHS Information Authority has developed HRGs for diabetes. Costs of diabetes HRGs are being developed, and preliminary figures are included in Appendix VIII.

Commissioning matrices

Health service planners and commissioners, based in PCTs, should ensure that the full spectrum of health care for people with chronic diseases meets local needs and is of a high quality. Health care frameworks have been developed to assist in assessing needs, commissioning services and improving quality of care. These are, in essence, highly developed 'checklists' to ensure that the task of planning and commissioning care is approached in a logical manner and does not neglect any important area.

The 'Health Benefit Group Development Project' by the NHS Information Authority has led to the development of health care frameworks for different diseases and conditions, matching HRGs with 'Health Benefit Groups' (HBGs) and associated performance indicators.[170-172] These health care frameworks are intended to be used in drawing up local HImPs (or their equivalent) and service agreements. A diabetes health care framework is being developed with emphasis on assessing need and its resource implications. A draft version of this framework is shown in Appendix IX. This health care framework is not suitable for use as a decision-making tool for individual patient care.

A condition-specific health care matrix which can be applied to different health care programmes, including care for people with diabetes, has been developed and is included in Appendix X.[173-176] This can be used as a tool for commissioning and planning services.

Although not necessarily a commissioning matrix, the National Service Framework (NSF) for diabetes is available to guide the development of local services. There is considerable evidence surrounding 'best practice' in diabetes care, and there are a number of improvements that can and should be made in many localities to put this evidence into practice.

Note: HBGs and HRGs are being developed by Clinical Working Groups to NHS Information Authority (Case-mix Programme) specification.

8 Outcome measures

The monitoring of diabetes care using measures of process and outcome occurs at two levels:[177]

- the individual patient level, by clinicians as part of the continuing care and treatment of the patient
- the aggregated group/population level, by health care commissioners (PCTs) and/or trust managers to ensure that desired outcomes are being delivered.

A Department of Health (DoH) working group report[178] lists 32 'candidate indicators' ranging from the prevalence of clinically diagnosed diabetes to summary measures of satisfaction with diabetes services. Among the working group's recommendations are that six of these candidate indicators should be used on a routine basis. These are listed below.

Measures of process

In its recommendations for the audit of diabetes services, the Diabetes Audit Working Group of the Research Unit of the Royal College of Physicians and the BDA[157] suggested a number of process measures, of which the following are likely to be the most useful for evaluating diabetes services:

1 average waiting times in hospital clinics
2 average time spent with doctor, nurse or other health worker
3 quality of communication with primary care team
4 the frequency with which the following are recorded in the clinical notes:

- body weight
- state of optic fundi (observed through dilated pupils), visual acuity
- blood pressure
- concentration of urinary albumin
- percentage of glycosylated haemoglobin
- serum cholesterol, total and high-density lipoprotein (HDL) cholesterol
- state of injection sites (in insulin-treated patients)
- state of the feet
- presence of peripheral pulses.

Measures of outcome

The outcomes of diabetes care to be measured at PCT level can be formulated from the aims and objectives agreed as part of the local HImP. Health care commissioners, clinicians and patients have different perspectives on the desired outcomes for a diabetes service (*see* Box 8).[177] Chosen outcomes must achieve a balance between the different perspectives.

Box 8: Different perspectives on outcomes of diabetes care.

Health care commissioners
- Provision of high-quality, cost-effective care.
- Reduced incidence and prevalence of diabetes.
- Reduced incidence and prevalence of complications.

Clinicians
- Achievement of optimal glucose levels.
- Prevention of long-term complications.
- Tailoring regimen to meet the needs of the individual.

Patients
- Avoidance of short-term complications, e.g. hypoglycaemia.
- Psychosocial needs, e.g. to achieve a balance between health and well-being.
- Involvement in treatment decisions.

Examples of outcomes

Population health outcome indicators have been available for districts since 1993 and are shown in Table 6.[179] These have been developed further, and a wide range of outcome measures for implementation is included in Appendix XI.

Table 6: Population health outcome indicators for diabetes.

Outcome	Indicator
Ketoacidosis and coma	Age-standardised rates for hospital episodes and coma among residents of area per 1,000,000 residents by sex
Lower limb amputation	Age-standardised rates for operations for lower limb amputations among patients with diabetes resident in the area per 1,000,000 residents by sex
Standardised mortality ratio (SMR)	SMR for diabetes mellitus for ages 1–44 years by sex

General and diabetes-specific patient-centred outcomes have been developed in recent years.[177,180] These measure the knowledge, attitudes and beliefs of patients and the psychosocial impact of living with diabetes, e.g. the quality of life measure used in the DCCT.[181] Choice of measure depends on the research question, instrument validity and practicality, e.g. length of the questionnaire.

The collection and assessment of outcomes are limited by the difficulties of dealing with data derived from routine information systems.[86,177,182,183] Although many data items are collected as part of the clinical review of patients, they are not always available in a standardised form which is easily collated for analysis.

Recent initiatives aim to improve the quality of diabetes care by standardising the collection and aggregation of outcome information:[177]

- DiabCare[164] – monitors the achievement of the Saint Vincent targets throughout Europe
- UK Audit Feasibility study[157,184] – development of a UK diabetes data set compatible with DiabCare
- Dialog[185,186] – a system designed to create diabetes population databases and record information for monitoring care.

Recommendations of the Department of Health working group

The six indicators recommended for use on a routine basis are:

1 the prevalence of clinically diagnosed diabetes
2 the number of patients who have had at least one hypoglycaemic emergency within the last year that required therapeutic intervention by a health professional expressed as a proportion of a population known to have diabetes
3 the number of patients who have had at least one hyperglycaemic emergency within the last year that required hospital admission expressed as a proportion of a population of patients known to have diabetes
4 SMR for death due to diabetes mellitus
5 years of life lost per 10 000 resident population by death due to diabetes mellitus
6 years of life lost by death due to diabetes mellitus.

It can be seen that knowledge of the population denominator of people with diabetes is crucial for the calculation of these indicators. This knowledge is available locally in the few districts with comprehensive diabetes population databases. For the remainder, extrapolation from published prevalence estimates must be made.

9 Information and research requirements

Some likely future developments in diabetes were mentioned at the beginning of this chapter. The following list of information and research requirements re-emphasises some of these and includes some other issues.

- There is a need for more evidence on the costs and benefits of population screening, as distinct from opportunistic screening, for type 2 diabetes. Costs and benefits need to be assessed in as wide a sense as possible – to include both financial and intangible costs and benefits affecting both the health care system and those being screened. Allied to this are issues surrounding the acceptability of screening to various groups, such as people of Asian origin, for example, in whom diabetes is already common and becoming more so.
- Primary prevention of type 1 and type 2 diabetes is a goal that may be achievable within a few years. The results of the Diabetes Prevention Program (in the USA), the Finnish Diabetes Prevention Study and STOP-NIDDM have clearly shown the prevention, or at least delay, of the transition from IGT to type 2 diabetes (in people who were also obese) by lifestyle changes or therapy with metformin or acerbose. This chapter, which was written before these results were published, has not been able to deal with them in detail. However, it does emphasise the vital importance of translating this RCT evidence into everyday clinical and public health practice.

- A substantial proportion of type 2 diabetes has long been potentially preventable – that associated with obesity. Unfortunately, viable strategies for the prevention of obesity continue to elude us. A more feasible approach may be the identification of people with IGT or other risk markers for type 2 diabetes and the encouragement of lifestyle changes in them, or their treatment with oral hypoglycaemic agents as attempts to reduce the likelihood of progression to diabetes. Many therapies for obesity are notoriously ineffective in the long term. As new drugs appear (e.g. orlistat) they need to be evaluated thoroughly. Research is already available on these questions and further results are awaited.
- The further development of population databases, with relevant outcome measures for the assessment of the quality of care, needs to be encouraged. Although the goal should be the complete ascertainment of all with diabetes in a defined population, the quality of care can be improved considerably by using currently available data to monitor the health and follow-up of those already identified. Proposed changes to the NHS, such as the NHS Information Strategy[163] nationally, and HImPs locally, may well contribute to this, as will the prospective analysis of outcome data already being recorded on population databases. The development of psychosocial outcome measures suitable for routine clinical use will contribute to this area.

In addition, a number of other less wide-ranging but nonetheless important questions need to be tackled, including:

- the introduction of new forms of insulin, e.g. fast-acting insulin analogues and the administration of insulin intranasally
- the introduction of digital systems for the recording and interpretation of retinal photographs
- evidence relating to new methods for the treatment of leg ulcers, e.g. ketanserin and growth hormone
- demand for new, more effective treatments of erectile dysfunction, such as sildenafil (Viagra)
- further development of combination therapy (oral hypoglycaemic agents and insulin) for the treatment of type 2 diabetes.

Despite the fact that insulin has been available for more than 75 years and oral hypoglycaemic agents for almost as long, diabetes is still responsible for considerable morbidity and premature mortality in the UK. Most of these effects are the results of the complications of diabetes, many of which are potentially preventable. The delivery of continuous, effective, comprehensive care to people with diabetes is an important component in realising this potential for prevention.

Appendix I: Abbreviations

ACE	angiotensin-converting enzyme
ADA	American Diabetes Association
BDA	British Diabetic Association
CVD	cerebrovascular disease
DCCT	Diabetes Control and Complications Trial
DoH	Department of Health
FPG	fasting plasma glucose
GDM	gestational diabetes mellitus
HBG	Health Benefit Group
HDL	high-density lipoprotein (cholesterol)
HImP	Health Improvement Programme
HRG	Health care Resource Group
ICD	*International Classification of Diseases*
IDDM	insulin-dependent diabetes mellitus
IDF	International Diabetes Federation
IFG	impaired fasting glucose
IGT	impaired glucose tolerance
IIT	intensive insulin therapy
LDSAG	Local Diabetes Services Advisory Group
NHS	National Health Service
NIDDM	non-insulin-dependent diabetes mellitus
NSC	National Screening Committee
NSF	National Service Framework
OGTT	oral glucose tolerance test
PCT	primary care trust
PG	plasma glucose
PPA	Prescription Pricing Authority
PVD	peripheral vascular disease
UKPDS	United Kingdom Prospective Diabetes Study
WHO	World Health Organization

Appendix II: Consensus documents on diabetes care

Some of the following feature as specific text references.

Alberti KGMM, Gries FA, Jervell J, Krans HMJ for the European NIDDM Policy Group. A desktop guide for the management of non-insulin-dependent diabetes. *Diabet Med* 1994; **11**: 899–909.

American Diabetes Association. Clinical practice recommendations 1998. *Diabetes Care* 1998; **21** (Suppl. 2): 1–81.

British Diabetic Association. *Care of Diabetics with Renal Failure.* London: British Diabetic Association, 1988.

British Diabetic Association. *Diabetes and Chiropodial Care.* London: British Diabetic Association, 1990.

British Diabetic Association. Saint Vincent and improving diabetes care. Specialist UK workgroup reports. *Diabet Med* 1996; **13** (Suppl. 4).

British Diabetic Association. *The Principles of Good Practice for the Care of Young People with Diabetes.* London: British Diabetic Association, 1996.

British Diabetic Association. *Training and Professional Development in Diabetes Care.* London: British Diabetic Association, 1996.

British Diabetic Association. *Recommendations for the Management of Diabetes in Primary Care.* London: British Diabetic Association, 1997.

British Diabetic Association. *Diabetes Centres in the United Kingdom. Results of a survey of UK diabetes centres.* London: British Diabetic Association, 1998.

British Diabetic Association. *Guidelines for Residents with Diabetes in Care Homes.* London: British Diabetic Association, 1998.

British Diabetic Association. *Health Improvement Programmes: an opportunity to improve the health of people with diabetes.* London: British Diabetic Association, 1998.

British Diabetic Association. *Recommendations for the Structure of Specialist Diabetes Care Services.* London: British Diabetic Association, 1999.

British Diabetic Association. *Local Diabetes Services Advisory Groups. Update report including the results of 1996 survey of LDSAGs.* London: British Diabetic Association, 1999.

British Diabetic Association. *Diabetes Care: what you should expect.* London: British Diabetic Association, 1999.

British Diabetic Association. *What Care to Expect When Your Child has Diabetes.* London: British Diabetic Association, 1999.

British Diabetic Association. *What Care to Expect in Hospital.* London: British Diabetic Association, 1999.

British Diabetic Association. *Catalogue for Health Care Professionals 1999.* London: British Diabetic Association, 1999.

British Diabetic Association. *Catalogue: information and promotional items for people living with diabetes.* London: British Diabetic Association, 1999.

Clinical Standards Advisory Group. *Standards of Clinical Care for People with Diabetes.* London: HMSO, 1994.

Department of Health, British Diabetic Association. *St Vincent Joint Task Force for Diabetes. The report.* London: British Diabetic Association, 1995.

Department of Health. *National Service Framework for Diabetes: standards.* London: Department of Health, 2001.

Department of Health. *National Service Framework for Diabetes: delivery strategy.* London: Department of Health, 2002.

Guy M. *Model Specification for Diabetes Services.* Cambridge: East Anglian Regional Health Authority, 1991.

Guy M. *The Development of a Specification for Diabetes Services.* Cambridge: Cambridge Health Authority, 1991.

International Diabetes Federation (Europe) and World Health Organization (Europe). The European Patients' Charter. *Diabet Med* 1991; **8**: 782–3.

International Diabetes Federation. *International Consensus Standards of Practice for Diabetes Education.* London: International Diabetes Foundation, 1997.

NHS Executive. Key features of a good diabetes service. *Health Service Guidelines* 1997; **45**.

Nutrition Subcommittee of the British Diabetic Association's Professional Advisory Committee. Dietary recommendations for people with diabetes: an update for the 1990s. *Diabet Med* 1992; **9**: 189–202.

Royal College of Physicians (Research Unit) and British Diabetic Association Audit Working Group. Proposal for the continuing audit of diabetes services. *Diabet Med* 1992; **9**: 759–64.

Scottish Intercollegiate Guidelines Network (SIGN). *The Care of Diabetic Patients in Scotland: National Clinical Guidelines numbers 4, 9, 10, 11, 12 and 19.* Edinburgh: Royal College of Physicians, 1996–97.

World Health Organization (Europe) and International Diabetes Federation (Europe). Diabetes care and research in Europe: the Saint Vincent Declaration. *Diabet Med* 1990; **7**: 360.

World Health Organization. *Screening for Type 2 Diabetes: Report of a World Health Organization and International Diabetes Federation meeting.* Geneva: World Health Organization Department of Noncommunicable Disease Management, 2003.

Appendix III: Data for the calculation of local estimates

Note: data similar to those below form the basis of a computer model 'Health Care Needs Assessment – Diabetes' produced by SmithKline Beecham and Abacus International, as a planning tool for PCTs and their equivalents elsewhere in the UK.

Data in the computer model may, in some details, differ from those listed below if more recently published studies have been incorporated into the more recent versions of the model. The model also includes additional information over and above that included here.

In the following tables, age- and sex-specific prevalences and incidence rates (as appropriate) for clinically diagnosed diabetes and its complications have been taken from various studies referenced in the above text. Using local population figures, the expected numbers of cases, and the likely maximum and minimum estimates, based on 95% CI can be calculated.

Table A1: The incidence of diabetes in childhood.[24]

Age group (years)	Incidence
0–4	9.74 (7.93–11.55)
5–9	13.60 (12.33–14.87)
10–14	17.80 (16.94–18.66)
0–14	13.91 (13.51–14.66)

Incidence rates are per 100,000 persons per year (95% CI). *Note*: updated incidence rates from this source, with separate values for boys and girls, may be available in the near future.

Table A2: The frequency of diagnosis of new cases of diabetes in adults.[26]

Age group (years)	Frequency of diagnosis of new cases (95% CI not available)
15–24	2.5
25–34	4.5
35–44	8.0
45–54	18.0
55–64	35.0
65–74	46.0
75–84	37.0
85 years and over	37.0

Rates are per 10,000 persons per year.

Table A3: The prevalence of clinically diagnosed diabetes in a predominantly Caucasian population (Poole, Dorset) showing the increase in prevalence between 1983[27] and 1996.[46]

Age group (years)	Males		Females	
	1983	1996	1983	1996
0–29	2.5	2.4	2.3	2.3
30–39	4.3	8.2	3.9	4.7
40–49	8.0	13.3	7.3	7.1
50–59	16.1	22.3	9.9	18.1
60–69	24.2	54.2	16.6	37.1
70–79	41.0	66.6	31.2	35.3
80 and over	48.5	79.6	24.8	52.3
All ages	11.0	21.3	9.3	16.0

Prevalences are per 1000 persons. Age/sex-adjusted prevalences (with 95% CI). Crude prevalences have been adjusted to 1991 age and sex distribution of the UK.
All males: 10.4×10^3 (9.5–11.4) (1983); 17.4×10^3 (16.3–18.6) (1996)
All females: 8.9×10^3 (8.1–9.7) (1983); 13.7×10^3 (12.7–14.7) (1996)
Both sexes: 9.7×10^3 (9.0–10.3) (1983); 15.5×10^3 (14.8–16.3) (1996).

Table A4: The 'incidence' (I) and prevalence (P) of clinically diagnosed diabetes as assessed from the General Practice Morbidity Survey[49] together with consultation rates (C) for diabetes.[49]

Age group (years)	Males			Females		
	I	P	C	I	P	C
0–4	–	0.1	0.1	0.1	0.1	0.3
5–15	0.2	0.8	1.2	0.3	0.7	1.0
16–24	0.7	2.4	5.5	0.4	1.5	3.5
25–44	1.5	4.9	11.3	0.8	3.4	8.6
45–64	5.8	21.7	54.4	4.3	15.4	39.4
65–74	10.9	42.8	105.3	9.5	33.7	85.8
75–84	12.0	47.5	116.4	10.3	37.4	93.2
85 and over	6.5	32.7	77.8	7.1	23.8	49.6

All ages prevalence = 11.9×10^3 (males) and 10.2×10^3 (females). 'Incidence' rates are per 1000 persons per year. Prevalences are per 1000 persons. (*Note:* the source document gives prevalence 'per 10,000 person years at risk' which is incorrect.) Consultation rates are per 1000 persons per year.

Table A5: The prevalence, in adults, of self-reported, clinically diagnosed diabetes and previously undiagnosed diabetes assessed by glycosylated haemoglobin concentration > 5.2%.[45]

	Diagnosed diabetes	Previously undiagnosed diabetes
Men	29.8	10.0
Women	17.6	10.0
Both sexes	23.6	10.0

Prevalences are per 1000 persons.

Table A6: The prevalence of clinically diagnosed diabetes in adults of South Asian origin.[36]

Age group (years)	Men		Women	
	Diagnosed	Previously undiagnosed	Diagnosed	Previously undiagnosed
20–29	2.0	8.0	–	6.0
30–39	12.5	24.1	23.7	11.3
40–49	56.3	45.7	24.5	47.5
50–59	110.3	62.5	120.3	60.0
60–69	140.0	81.2	193.7	98.7
70 and over	170.5	145.0	125.8	102.5

Prevalences are per 1000 persons. Overall, age-adjusted prevalences are 124.0×10^3 (men) and 112.0×10^3 (women).

Table A7: The prevalence of clinically diagnosed and previously undiagnosed diabetes in adults (people aged 40 and over) of Afro-Caribbean origin.[48]

Men	Women	Both sexes
167.0	177.0	172.0

Prevalences are per 1000 persons. *Note*: the 'both sexes' prevalence has been calculated on the assumption that the male/female ratio in this age group in the Afro-Caribbean population is 1:1. *Comment*: peer-reviewed, published age- and sex-specific data for clinically diagnosed and previously undiagnosed diabetes (separately) in people of Afro-Caribbean origin are urgently needed.

Table A8: The prevalence of diabetic retinopathy, maculopathy and levels of Snellen visual acuity.[187]

Age group	Prevalence (95% CI)
People with diabetes aged 28–91 years (mean age 67.7 ± 11.9 years) Mean duration of diabetes 7.2 ± 5.8 years	Retinopathy • None: 48.0 (40.0–56.0) • BGR: 48.0 (39.0–56.0) • PLR: 4.0 (2.0–9.0) Maculopathy • None: 90.0 (85.0–95.0) • Some: 10.0 (5.0–15.0) Snellen visual acuity • 6/6: 33.0 (26.0–41.0) • 6/9: 22.0 (15.0–28.0) • 6/12: 21.0 (14.0–27.0) • 6/18: 12.0 (7.0–17.0) • 6/24: 3.0 (1.0–8.0) • 6/36: 3.0 (1.0–7.0) • 6/60: 1.0 (0.4–6.0) • < 6/60: 5.0 (2.0–10.0)

Prevalences are per 100 persons with clinically diagnosed diabetes. *Note*: (1) BGR is background retinopathy (Wisconsin grades 1.5–5); PLR is proliferative retinopathy (Wisconsin grades 6–8). (2) 'Some' maculopathy is Early Treatment of Diabetic Retinopathy Study (ETDRS) clinically significant maculopathy. (3) Retinopathy and maculopathy data above are based on combined photographic, clinical and hospital record observations ($n = 145$ for retinopathy; $n = 144$ for maculopathy). (4) Snellen visual acuity data are for people with diabetes not treated with insulin ($n = 144$).

Table A9: The prevalence of diabetic neuropathy.[188]

Age group (years)	Prevalence (95% CI)
20–29	5.0 (2.5–6.0)
30–39	9.5 (6.0–12.5)
40–49	16.0 (13.0–18.0)
50–59	25.5 (23.5–28.0)
60–69	36.0 (34.0–38.0)
70–79	43.0 (39.5–46.0)
80–89	60.5 (54.0–67.0)

Prevalences are per 100 persons with clinically diagnosed diabetes.

Table A10: The prevalence of microalbuminuria, incidence of proteinuria and prevalence of proteinuria in people with diabetes. This table is adapted from Chattington.[189] The original data are from Hasslacher[190] and Borch-Johnsen.[191]

Complication	Type 1 diabetes	Type 2 diabetes
Prevalence of microalbuminuria	10–25	15.0–25.0
Incidence of proteinuria	0.5–3.0	1.0–2.0
Prevalence of proteinuria	15.0–20.0	10.0–25.0

Prevalences are per 100 persons with clinically diagnosed diabetes. Incidence rates are per 100 persons with clinically diagnosed diabetes per year.

Table A11: The prevalence of hypertension in adults with diabetes.[192]

Age group (years)	Prevalence (95% CI)
Men	
25–34	13.5 (7.4–22.0)
35–44	28.0 (22.9–33.1)
45–54	33.8 (30.7–36.9)
55–64	40.2 (37.0–43.4)
25–64	34.7* (32.7–36.7)
Women	
25–34	16.6 (8.3–28.5)
35–44	36.5 (29.7–43.3)
45–54	43.9 (39.6–48.1)
55–64	53.4 (49.8–57.0)
25–64	46.5† (43.9–49.0)

Prevalences are per 100 persons with clinically diagnosed diabetes. *20.7% were on antihypertensive therapy, 14.0% had blood pressure > 160/90 and were untreated. †22.2% were on antihypertensive therapy, 24.3% had blood pressure > 160/90 and were untreated.

Table A12: The prevalence of peripheral vascular disease in adults with diabetes.[193]

Age (years) [diagnostic group]	Prevalence (95% CI)	Age (years) [diagnostic group]	Prevalence (95% CI)
Type 1 diabetes		*Type 2 diabetes*	
Men		Men	
0–29	–	0–29	–
30–39	11.0	30–39	–
40–49	–	40–49	6.0
50–59	11.0	50–59	3.0
60–69	14.0	60–69	9.0
70–79	65.0	70–79	32.0
80 and over	–	80 and over	46.0
All ages	12.0 (6.0–19.0)	All ages	22.0 (18.0–27.0)
Women		Women	
0–29	–	0–29	–
30–39	–	30–39	–
40–49	–	40–49	–
50–59	18.0	50–59	4.0
60–69	7.0	60–69	19.0
70–79	25.0	70–79	28.0
80 and over	24.0	80 and over	45.0
All ages	5.0 (2.0–12.0)	All ages	25.0 (20.0–30.0)

Prevalences are per 100 persons with clinically diagnosed diabetes. *Note:* (1) Peripheral vascular disease was identified by a combination of palpation of pulses, blood pressure and Doppler measurements (for exact definitions see original paper). (2) Prevalences were based on 213 subjects with type 1 diabetes and 864 subjects with type 2 diabetes.

Table A13: The incidence of heart disease in adults with diabetes.[194]

Age group (years)		
35–64	Myocardial infarct	1.8
	ECG abnormality	2.2
	All IHD	4.1

Rates are per 1000 per year.

Appendix IV: Saint Vincent Declaration[77]

Representatives of government health departments and patients' organisations from all European countries met with diabetes experts under the aegis of the Regional Offices of the WHO and the IDF in St Vincent, Italy, on 10–12 October 1989. They agreed unanimously upon the following recommendations and urged that they should be presented in all countries throughout Europe for implementation.

General goals for people (children and adults) with diabetes

- Sustained improvement in health experience and a life approaching normal expectation in quality and quantity.
- Prevention and cure of diabetes and of its complications by intensifying research effort.

Five-year targets

- Elaborate, initiate and evaluate comprehensive programmes for the detection and control of diabetes and of its complications with self-care and community support as major components.
- Raise awareness in the population and among health care professionals of the present opportunities and the future needs for prevention of the complications of diabetes and of diabetes itself.
- Organise training and teaching in diabetes management and care for people of all ages with diabetes, for their families, friends and working associates and for the health care team.
- Ensure that care for children with diabetes is provided by individuals and teams specialised both in the management of diabetes and of children, and that families with a diabetic child get the necessary social, economic and emotional support.
- Reinforce existing centres of excellence in diabetes care, education and research. Create new centres where the need and potential exist.
- Promote independence, equity and self-sufficiency for all people with diabetes – children, adolescents, those in working years of life and the elderly.
- Remove hindrances to the fullest possible integration of the diabetic citizen into society.
- Implement effective measures for the prevention of costly complications.
- Reduce new blindness due to diabetes care by one-third or more.
- Reduce the numbers of people entering end-stage diabetic renal failure by at least one-third.
- Reduce by one-half the rate of limb amputations for diabetic gangrene.
- Cut morbidity and mortality from coronary heart disease in the diabetic by vigorous programmes of risk factor reduction.
- Achieve pregnancy outcome in diabetic women that approximates that in non-diabetic women.
- Establish monitoring and control systems using state-of-the-art information technology for quality assurance of diabetes health care provision and for laboratory and technical procedures in diabetes diagnosis, treatment and self-management.
- Promote European and international collaboration in programmes of diabetes research and development through national, regional and WHO agencies, and in active partnership with diabetes patients' organisations.
- Take urgent action in the spirit of the WHO programme 'Health for All' to establish joint machinery between WHO and IDF, European Region, to initiate, accelerate and facilitate the implementation of these recommendations.

Appendix V: What diabetic care to expect

The British Diabetic Association Patients' Charter[79]

When you have been diagnosed, you should have:

- a full medical examination
- a talk with a registered nurse who has a special interest in diabetes. She will explain what diabetes is and talk to you about your individual treatment
- a talk with a state-registered dietitian, who will want to know what you are used to eating, and will give you basic advice on what to eat in the future. A follow-up meeting should be arranged for more detailed advice
- a discussion on the implications of diabetes for your job, driving, insurance, prescription charges, etc., and whether you need to inform the DVLA and your insurance company, if you are a driver
- information about the BDA's services and details of your local BDA group
- ongoing education about your diabetes and the beneficial effects of exercise, and assessments of your control.

    PLUS
    If you are treated by insulin:

- frequent sessions for basic instruction in injection technique, looking after insulin and syringes, blood glucose and ketone testing and what the results mean
- supplies of relevant equipment
- discussion about hypoglycaemia (hypos); when and why it may happen and how to deal with it.

    If you are treated by tablets:

- a discussion about the possibility of hypoglycaemia (hypos) and how to deal with it
- instruction on blood or urine testing and what the results mean, and supplies of relevant equipment.

    If you are treated by diet alone:

- instruction on blood or urine testing and what the results mean, and supplies of relevant equipment.

    Once your diabetes is reasonably controlled, you should:

- have access to the diabetes team at regular intervals – annually if necessary. These meetings should give time for discussion as well as assessing diabetes control
- be able to contact any member of the health care team for specialist advice when you need it
- have more education sessions as you are ready for them
- have a formal medical review once a year by a doctor experienced in diabetes.

    At this review:

- your weight should be recorded
- your urine should be tested for protein
- your blood should be tested to measure long-term control
- you should discuss control, including your home-monitoring results
- your blood pressure should be checked

- your vision should be checked and the back of your eyes examined. A photo may be taken of the back of your eyes. If necessary you should be referred to an ophthalmologist
- your legs and feet should be examined to check your circulation and nerve supply. If necessary you should be referred to a state-registered chiropodist
- if you are on insulin, your injection sites should be examined
- you should have the opportunity to discuss how you are coping at home and at work.

Your role:

- you are an important member of the care team so it is essential that you understand your own diabetes to enable you to be in control of your condition
- you should ensure that you receive the described care from your local diabetes clinic, practice or hospital. If these services are not available to you, you should:

  - contact your GP to discuss the diabetes care available in your area
  - contact your local community health council
  - contact the BDA or your local branch.

Appendix VI: Diabetes centres

Purpose

Diabetes centres ideally should (and some do) provide the hub of the local diabetes services, and a place where patients and their carers, and staff from the hospital and community can meet. They offer clinical advice and education on diabetes to all on a single site where most of the professional and social services required are accessible. In many cases their operational philosophy and organisation take account of the special bridging role between specialist and primary care diabetes services.

Diabetes centres should offer some or all of the following facilities:

- education services for patients and their carers, staff working in the centre and professionals from primary and secondary care
- each group requires an agreed educational curriculum
- facilities for clinical advice and regular review, including the annual review
- drop-in access for people with diabetic problems
- referrals for further diagnosis and the treatment of diabetes
- joint clinics with ophthalmologists, nephrologists and other specialists
- dietary advice – information, teaching and review by specialist dietitians
- chiropodial (podiatric) advice, education and treatment
- psychological and social advice and treatment
- a flexible outreach service
- a 24-hour telephone helpline
- a secure and effective computerised information system
- a venue for the audit of local diabetes services
- a place to house and update the diabetes register
- a meeting place for primary and secondary care staff to hold joint clinical meetings
- a focus for integrated care, providing the opportunity for creating individualised programmes of care for people, sufficiently flexible to meet their changing needs through a lifetime with diabetes
- the opportunity for people with diabetes to obtain all or a large part of the services relevant to diabetes care in one place
- children's play area
- a place where people with diabetes and their families can meet and share their problems, experiences and solutions, e.g. local BDA branch meetings
- a place where other meetings relevant to diabetes can be held, e.g. LDSAG meetings
- a place for advising groups of people with diabetes special needs, e.g. children, young adults, pre-pregnancy counselling.

Source: British Diabetic Association.[81]

Appendix VII: Size of effect and quality of evidence

Size of effect

A: The procedure/service has a strong beneficial effect.
B: The procedure/service has a moderate beneficial effect.
C: The procedure/service has a measurable beneficial effect.
D: The procedure/service has no measurable beneficial effect.
E: The harm of the procedure/service outweighs its benefits.

Quality of evidence

I-1: Evidence from several consistent or one large randomised controlled trial.
I-2: Evidence obtained from at least one properly designed randomised controlled trial.
II-1: Evidence obtained from well-designed controlled trials without randomisation, or from well-designed cohort or case–control analytic studies.
II-2: Evidence obtained from multiple time series with or without the intervention. Also, dramatic results in uncontrolled experiments.
III: Opinions of respected authorities, based on clinical experience, descriptive studies, or reports of expert committees.
IV: Inadequate and conflicting evidence.

Appendix VIII: HRG costs for diabetes (based on 1999 Schedule of Reference Costs)

	HRG code	HRG label FCEs	n	Mean average £	Range for 50% of NHS trusts		Range for all NHS trusts	
					Minimum £	Maximum £	Minimum £	Maximum £
ELIP	K11	Diabetes with hypoglycaemic emergency >69 or with complications and comorbidities	35	1,093	524	1,395	1,115	3,300
ELIP	K12	Diabetes with hypoglycaemic emergency <70 without complications and comorbidities	182	618	328	779	43	1,884
ELIP	K13	Diabetes with hyperglycaemic emergency >69 or with complications and comorbidities	15	1,458	637	1,988	117	3,242
ELIP	K14	Diabetes with hyperglycaemic emergency <70 without complications and comorbidities	19	724	367	943	251	1,609
ELIP	K15	Diabetes and other hyperglycaemic disorders >69 or with complications and comorbidities	438	1,154	569	1,518	143	6,599
ELIP	K16	Diabetes and other hyperglycaemic disorders <70 without complications and comorbidities	407	768	490	1,058	124	8,167
ELIP	K17	Diabetes with lower limb complications	459	1,743	806	2,285	99	8,140
ELIP	Q16	Foot procedures for diabetes or arterial disease, and procedures to amputate stumps	1,011	1,453	777	1,714	112	8,002
NELIP	K11	Diabetes with hypoglycaemic emergency >69 or with complications and comorbidities	2,120	872	561	1,220	25	8,952
NELIP	K12	Diabetes with hypoglycaemic emergency <70 without complications and comorbidities	1,900	557	330	790	84	2,785
NELIP	K13	Diabetes with hyperglycaemic emergency >69 or with complications and comorbidities	2,760	1,002	700	1,454	50	4,885
NELIP	K14	Diabetes with hyperglycaemic emergency <70 without complications and comorbidities	5,304	638	453	884	55	2,239

NELIP	K15	Diabetes and other hyperglycaemic disorders >69 or with complications and comorbidities	6,319	1,185	830	1,638	129	9,221
NELIP	K16	Diabetes and other hyperglycaemic disorders <70 without complications and comorbidities	5,664	662	479	1,000	92	12,096
NELIP	K17	Diabetes with lower limb complications	4,422	1,553	912	2,024	113	9,542
NELIP	Q16	Foot procedures for diabetes or arterial disease, and procedures to amputate stumps	1,279	2,079	943	2,813	124	10,337
DC	K14	Diabetes with hyperglycaemic emergency <70 without complications and comorbidities	17	231	183	273	151	416
DC	K15	Diabetes and other hyperglycaemic disorders >69 or with complications and comorbidities	715	197	145	329	26	1,478
DC	K16	Diabetes and other hyperglycaemic disorders <70 without complications and comorbidities	2,938	249	156	323	33	1,480
DC	K17	Diabetes with lower limb complications	62	268	183	428	109	1,162
DC	Q16	Foot procedures for diabetes or arterial disease, and procedures to amputate stumps	305	312	265	490	103	918

ELIP, elective inpatients; NELIP, non-elective inpatients; DC, day case.

Appendix IX: HBGs/HRGs for diabetes – summary matrix

HBGs	HRGs Prevention and health promotion	Investigation and diagnosis	Clinical management	Continuing care
At risk	Health promotion:			
Whole population	Health education			
At specific risk	Primary prevention			
Type 1 diabetes	Surveillance			
Type 2 diabetes	Screening			
Secondary diabetes	Clinical management of at-risk groups			
		Clinical assessment		
		Diagnostic investigations:		
Presentation		Pathology		
Hyperglycaemia		Imaging		
Hyperglycaemic emergencies		Specialised tests and procedures		
			Acute inpatient admission	
Confirmed disease			Medical management	
Diabetes without complications			Surgical management	
Diabetes with complications			Nursing voluntary sector	
Continued consequences of disease				To be decided

Source: NHS Information Authority (Version control no. B13 CW 31.01.00). Crown Copyright 1999.
The material herein remains the property of the Crown. It is made available in this publication via delegated authority of the NHS Information Authority and may not be reproduced, adapted, or used for any other purpose without the permission of the Secretary of State for Health.

Appendix X: Health care programme matrix

Service level	Needs	Effective action	Location	Input	Activity targets	Output	Service outcome	Health objective
Primary prevention	Fill in this box first							Reduced incidence and prevalence of the condition
Screening and early treatment								Reduced incidence and prevalence of illness
Acute care								Reduced premature mortality
Rehabilitation and continuing care							Fill in this box last	Reduced mortality, incidence and prevalence of disability and handicap

Source: O'Brien and Singleton.[176]

Appendix XI: Recommendations of the Working Group on Outcomes[178]

Recommendations for implementation were made for each indicator using the following categories

A: To be implemented generally on a routine basis.

B: To be implemented generally by periodic survey.

C: To be implemented where local circumstances allow on a routine basis.

D: To be implemented where local circumstances allow by periodic study.

E: To be implemented following IT developments on a routine basis.

F: To be further developed because either the link with effectiveness is not clear or the indicator specification is incomplete.

Indicators related to reducing or avoiding risk of diabetes and appropriate detection of diabetes

1   Prevalence of clinically diagnosed diabetes (Category A).

2   Percentage prevalence of retinopathy and maculopathy at the time of diagnosis of diabetes (Category E).

3A Prevalence of obesity in persons aged 16–64 (defined as BMI $= 30.0 \, kg/m^2$) (Category B).

3B Proportion of people undertaking rigorous physical activity in the previous 28 days (Category F).

3C Proportion of people who on average consume fruit or vegetables or salad each day, within the general population (Category F).

Indicators related to reducing risk of complications

4   Percentage of patients, aged 16 and over and known to have diabetes, who smoke (Category C).

5   Percentage of patients, aged 16–64 and known to have diabetes, who have a BMI $> 30 \, kg/m^2$ (Category C).

6   Percentage of patients known to have diabetes with elevated blood pressure: type 1 $> 140/90 \, mmHg$, type 2 $> 160/90 \, mmHg$ (Category C).

7   Percentage of patients known to have diabetes with HbA_{1c} that was $> 7.5\%$ on a DCCT standardised assay, at time of last recording within the previous year (Category C).

8   Percentage prevalence of retinopathy and maculopathy within a population known to have diabetes (Category C).

9   Percentage prevalence of microalbuminuria within a population known to have type 1 diabetes (Category C).

10 Percentage prevalence of protective sensation loss within a population known to have diabetes (Category C).

11 Percentage prevalence of absence of both pulses in at least one foot within a population known to have diabetes (Category C).

12 Percentage of patients known to have diabetes where there is no record of blood pressure. The retina or the feet have been assessed within the previous year (Category C).

13 Percentage prevalence of symptomatic angina within a population known to have diabetes.

14 Percentage prevalence of claudication within a population known to have diabetes.

Indicators related to reducing impact of diabetes

15 Number of patients who have had at least one hypoglycaemic emergency, within the last year, that required therapeutic intervention by a health professional, expressed as a proportion of a population of patients known to have diabetes (Category A).

16   Number of patients who have had at least one hyperglycaemic emergency, within the last year, that required hospital admission expressed as a proportion of a population of patients known to have diabetes (Category A).

17   Case fatality rate associated with acute diabetic episodes treated in hospital (Category C).

18A   SMR for death due to diabetes mellitus (Category C).

18B   Years of life lost per 10 000 resident population by death due to diabetes mellitus (Category C).

18C   Years of life lost by death due to diabetes mellitus (Category C).

19   Annual incidence of severe visual impairment (visual acuity < 6/60 in the better eye) within a population of patients known to have diabetes (Category C).

20   Annual incidence of amputation above the ankle within a population of patients known to have diabetes (Category C).

21   Annual incidence of amputation below the ankle within a population of patients known to have diabetes (Category C).

22   Annual incidence of myocardial infarction within a population of patients known to have diabetes (Category C).

23   Annual incidence of stroke within a population of patients known to have diabetes (Category D).

24   Number of patients who have started renal replacement therapy or have had a creatinine level > 500 μmol/l recorded for the first time within the last year, expressed as a proportion of a population of patients known to have diabetes (Category C).

25   Rates of late stillbirth and perinatal mortality in deliveries from a population of patients known to have diabetes and who become pregnant (Category C).

26   The rate of delivery by Caesarean section, in deliveries from a population of patients known to have diabetes and who become pregnant (Category C).

27   The incidence of delivered babies with birth weight greater than the 90th centile (allowing for gestational age) from within a population of patients known to have diabetes and who become pregnant (Category C).

28   The incidence of occurrence of specific congenital malformations (i.e. neural tube defects, cardiac and renal malformations) in deliveries from a population of patients known to have diabetes and who become pregnant (Category C).

29   The rate of admission to special care baby units (and nurseries) of babies delivered from a population of patients known to have diabetes and who become pregnant (Category F).

30   Summary of a measure of psychological well-being within a population of patients known to have diabetes and who become pregnant (Category F).

31   Summary of a measure of health status/health-related quality of life within a population of patients known to have diabetes (Category F).

32   Summary of a measure of satisfaction with service within a population of patients known to have diabetes.

Source: Working Group on Outcome Indicators for Diabetes, Report to the Department of Health, 1997.[178]

References

1 WHO Consultation Group. The definition, diagnosis and classification of diabetes mellitus and its complications. Part 1: the definition, diagnosis and classification of diabetes. *Diabet Med* 1998; **15**: 539–53.

2 The Expert Committee on the Diagnosis and Classification of Diabetes Mellitus. Report of the Expert Committee on the Diagnosis and Classification of Diabetes Mellitus. *Diabetes Care* 1997; **20**: 1183–97.

3 World Health Organization. *Diabetes Mellitus: report of a WHO study group.* Geneva: World Health Organization, 1985.

4 Unwin N, Alberti KGMM, Bhopal RS, Harland J, Watson W, White M. Comparison of the current WHO and new ADA criteria for the diagnosis of diabetes mellitus in three ethnic groups in the UK. *Diabet Med* 1998; **15**: 554–7.

5 Kannel WB, McGee DL. Diabetes and glucose tolerance as risk factors for cardiovascular disease: the Framingham study. *Diabetes Care* 1979; **2**: 120–6.

6 Modan M, Halkin H, Almog S *et al.* Hyperinsulinemia. A link between hypertension, obesity and glucose intolerance. *J Clin Invest* 1985; **75**: 809–17.

7 Reaven GM. Role of insulin resistance in human disease. *Diabetes* 1988; **37**: 1595–607.

8 Jardine Brown C, Dawson A, Dodds R *et al.* Report of the pregnancy and neonatal care group. *Diabet Med* 1996; **13**: S43–53.

9 Charlton BG, Calvert N, White M, Rye GP, Conrad W, van Zwanenberg T. Health promotion priorities for general practice: constructing and using 'indicative prevalences'. *BMJ* 1994; **308**: 1019–22.

10 Barker DJP, Gardner MJ, Power C. Incidence of diabetes amongst people aged 18–50 years in nine British towns: a collaborative study. *Diabetologia* 1982; **22**: 421–5.

11 Waugh NR. Insulin-dependent diabetes in a Scottish region: incidence and urban/rural differences. *J Epidemiol Community Health* 1986; **40**: 240–3.

12 Patterson CC, Smith PG, Webb J, Heasman MA, Mann JI. Geographical variation in the incidence of diabetes mellitus in Scottish children during the period 1977–1983. *Diabet Med* 1988; **5**: 160–5.

13 Barclay RPC, Craig JO, Galloway CAS, Richardson JE, Shepherd RC, Smail PJ. The incidence of childhood diabetes in certain parts of Scotland. *Scott Med J* 1988; **33**: 237–9.

14 Burden AC, Hearnshaw JR, Swift PG. Childhood diabetes mellitus: an increasing incidence. *Diabet Med* 1989; **6**: 334–6.

15 Bingley PJ, Gale EAM. Incidence of insulin-dependent diabetes in England: a study in the Oxford region 1985–6. *BMJ* 1989; **298**: 558–60.

16 Crow YJ, Alberti KG, Parkin JM. Insulin-dependent diabetes in childhood and material deprivation in northern England 1977–86. *BMJ* 1991; **303**: 158–60.

17 Metcalfe MA, Baum JD. Incidence of insulin-dependent diabetes in children aged under 15 years in the British Isles during 1988. *BMJ* 1991; **302**: 443–7.

18 Green A, Gale EAM, Patterson CC. Incidence of childhood-onset insulin-dependent diabetes mellitus: the EURODIAB ACE study. *Lancet* 1992; **339**: 905–9.

19 Patterson CC, Waugh NR. Urban/rural and deprivational differences in incidence and clustering of childhood diabetes in Scotland. *Int J Epidemiol* 1992; **21**: 108–17.

20 Staines A, Bodansky HJ, Lilley HEB, Stephenson C, McNally RJQ, Cartwright RA. The epidemiology of diabetes mellitus in the United Kingdom. The Yorkshire Regional Childhood Diabetes Register. *Diabetologia* 1993; **36**: 1282–7.

21 Wadsworth E, Shield J, Hunt L, Baum D. Insulin-dependent diabetes in children under 5: incidence and ascertainment validation for 1992. *BMJ* 1995; **310**: 700–3.

22 Gardner SG, Bingley PJ, Satwell PA, Weeks S, Gale EAM. Rising incidence of insulin-dependent diabetes in children aged under 5 years in the Oxford region: time trend analysis. *BMJ* 1997; **315**: 713–17.

23 Patterson CC, Carson DJ, Hadden DR. Epidemiology of childhood IDDM in Northern Ireland 1989–1994: low incidence in areas with highest population density and most household crowding. *Diabetologia* 1996; **39**: 1063–9.

24 McKinney PA, Law GR, Bodansky HJ, Staines A, Williams DRR. Geographical mapping of childhood diabetes in the northern English county of Yorkshire. *Diabet Med* 1996; **13**: 734–40.

25 Rangasami JJ, Greenwood DC, McSporran B, Smail PJ, Patterson CC, Waugh NR. Rising incidence of type 1 diabetes in Scottish children, 1984–93. *Arch Dis Child* 1997; **77**: 210–13.

26 Vanderpump MPJ, Tunbridge WMG, French JM *et al.* The incidence of diabetes mellitus in an English community: 20-year follow-up of the Whickham Survey. *Diabet Med* 1996; **13**: 741–7.

27 Gatling W, Houston AC, Hill RD. The prevalence of diabetes mellitus in a typical English community. *J R Coll Physicians Lond* 1985; **19**: 248–50.

28 Mather HM, Keen H. The Southall diabetes survey: prevalence of known diabetes in Asians and Europeans. *BMJ* 1985; **291**: 1081–4.

29 Forrest RD, Jackson CA, Yudkin JS. Glucose intolerance and hypertension in North London: the Islington Diabetes Survey. *Diabet Med* 1986; **3**: 338–42.

30 Neil HA, Gatling W, Mather HM *et al.* The Oxford community diabetes study: evidence for an increase in the prevalence of known diabetes in Great Britain. *Diabet Med* 1987; **4**: 539–43.

31 Odugbesan O, Rowe B, Fletcher J, Walford S, Barnett AH. Diabetes in the UK West Indian community: the Wolverhampton survey. *Diabet Med* 1989; **6**: 48–52.

32 Gibbins RL, Saunders J. Characteristics and pattern of care of a diabetic population in mid-Wales. *J R Coll Gen Pract* 1989; **39**: 206–8.

33 Waugh NR, Jung RT, Newton RW. The Dundee prevalence study of insulin-treated diabetes: intervals between diagnosis and start of insulin therapy. *Diabet Med* 1989; **6**: 346–50.

34 Croxson SC, Burden AC, Bodington M, Botha JL. The prevalence of diabetes in elderly people. *Diabet Med* 1991; **8**: 28–31.

35 Burnett SD, Woolf CM, Yudkin JS. Developing a district diabetic register. *BMJ* 1992; **305**: 627–30.

36 Simmons D, Williams DRR, Powell MJ. The Coventry diabetes study: prevalence of diabetes and impaired glucose tolerance in Europids and Asians. *Q J Med* 1991; **81**: 1021–30.

37 Yudkin J, Forrest R, Jackson C, Burnett S, Gould M. The prevalence of diabetes and impaired glucose tolerance in a British population. *Diabetes Care* 1993; **16**: 1530.

38 Gujral JS, McNally PG, Botha JL, Burden AC. Childhood-onset diabetes in the white and South Asian population in Leicestershire, UK. *Diabet Med* 1994; **11**: 570–2.

39 Howitt AJ, Cheales NA. Diabetes registers: a grassroots approach. *BMJ* 1993; **307**: 1046–8.

40 Meadows P. Variation of diabetes mellitus prevalence in general practice and its relation to deprivation. *Diabet Med* 1995; **12**: 696–700.

41 Davies MJ, Gujral JS, Burden AC. The prevalence of diabetes in the adult Caucasian and Asian population in Leicester. *Diabet Med* 1996; **13**: S37.

42 Morris AD, Boyle DIR, Chalmers J, Macdonald TM, Newton RW, Jung RT. Using record linkage of drug consumption to facilitate complete diabetes registration: the Diabetes Audit and Research in Tayside Study (DARTS). *Diabet Med* 1996; **13**: S57.

43 Colhoun HM, Dong W, Lampe FC. Diabetes and diabetic care in England: the Health Survey for England. *Diabet Med* 1996; **13**: S57.

44 Connolly V, Unwin N, Sayer E, Bilous R, Kelly F. Increased prevalence of NIDDM but not IDDM in areas of social deprivation. *Diabet Med* 1996; **13**: S56.

45 Bennett N, Dodd T, Flatley J, Freeth S, Boiling K. *Health Survey for England 1993*. London: HMSO.

46 Gatling W, Budd S, Walters D, Mullee MA, Goddard JR, Hill RD. Evidence of an increasing prevalence of diagnosed diabetes mellitus in the Poole area from 1983 to 1996. *Diabet Med* 1998; **15**: 1015–21.

47 Esteve J, Benhamou E, Raymond L. *Descriptive Epidemiology*. Lyon: International Agency for Research on Cancer, 1994.

48 British Diabetic Association. *Diabetes in the United Kingdom – 1996*. London: British Diabetic Association, 1996.

49 OPCS. *Morbidity Statistics from General Practice. Fourth national study, 1991–1992*. London: HMSO, 1995.

50 Simmons D, Williams DR, Powell MJ. Prevalence of diabetes in different regional and religious South Asian communities in Coventry. *Diabet Med* 1992; **9**: 428–31.

51 Garcia MJ, McNamara PM, Gordon T, Kannell WB. Morbidity and mortality in diabetics in the Framingham population. *Diabetes* 1974; **23**: 105–11.

52 Panzram G. Mortality and survival in type 2 (non-insulin-dependent) diabetes mellitus. *Diabetologia* 1987; **30**: 123–31.

53 Turner RC, Millns H, Neil HAW *et al.* Risk factors for coronary artery disease in non-insulin-dependent diabetes mellitus: United Kingdom prospective diabetes study (UKPDS: 23). *BMJ* 1998; **316**: 823–8.

54 Robinson N, Edmeades SP, Fuller JH. Recent changes in diabetic mortality and morbidity in England and Wales. *Health Trends* 1984; **16**: 33–7.

55 Waugh NR, Dallas JH, Jung RT, Newton RW. Mortality in a cohort of diabetic patients. *Diabetologia* 1989; **32**: 103–4.

56 Morrish NJ, Stevens LK, Head J, Fuller JH, Jarrett RJ, Keen H. A prospective study of mortality among middle-aged diabetic patients (the London cohort of the WHO Multinational Study of Vascular Disease in Diabetics). II. Associated risk factors. *Diabetologia* 1990; **33**: 542–8.

57 Wong JSK, Pearson DWM, Murchison LE, Williams MJ, Narayan V. Mortality in diabetes mellitus: experience of a geographically defined population. *Diabet Med* 1991; **8**: 135–9.

58 Botha JL, Parker H, Raymond NT, Swift PGF. Diabetes diagnosed before the age of 2 years: mortality in a British cohort 8–17 years after onset. *Int J Epidemiol* 1992; **21**: 1132–7.

59 Neil A, Hawkins M, Potok M, Thorogood M, Cohen D, Mann J. A prospective population-based study of microalbuminuria as a predictor of mortality in NIDDM. *Diabetes Care* 1993; **16**: 996–1003.

60 Walters DP, Gatling W, Houston AC, Mullee MA, Julious SA, Hill RD. Mortality in diabetic subjects: an eleven-year follow-up of a community-based population. *Diabet Med* 1994; **11**: 968–73.

61 Croxson SC, Price DE, Burden M, Jagger C, Burden AC. The mortality of elderly people with diabetes. *Diabet Med* 1994; **11**: 250–2.

62 Raymond NT, Langley JD, Goyder E, Botha JL, Burden AC, Hearnshaw JR. Insulin-treated diabetes mellitus: causes of death determined from record linkage of population-based registers in Leicestershire UK. *J Epidemiol Community Health* 1995; **49**: 570–4.

63 Mcnally PG, Raymond NT, Burden ML *et al.* Trends in mortality of childhood-onset insulin-dependent diabetes mellitus in Leicestershire: 1940–1991. *Diabet Med* 1995; **12**: 961–6.

64 Mather HM, Fuller JH, Chaturvedi N. Mortality and morbidity from diabetes in South Asians and Europeans: 11-year follow-up of the Southall Diabetes Survey. *Diabet Med* 1996; **13**: S37.

65 Robinson N, Lloyd CE, Stevens LK. The relationship between social deprivation and mortality in people with diabetes. *Diabet Med* 1996; **13**: S37.

66 McKinney PA, Law G, Ghali N *et al.* Mortality and causes of death in a cohort of 1800 people diagnosed with NIDDM in childhood. *Diabet Med* 1996; **13**: S50.

67 Kelly WF, Mahmood R, Kelly MJ, Turner S, Elliott K. Influence of social deprivation on illness in diabetic patients. *BMJ* 1993; **307**: 1115–16.

68 Eachus J, Williams M, Chan P *et al*. Deprivation and cause-specific morbidity: evidence from the Somerset and Avon survey of health. *BMJ* 1996; **312**: 287–92.

69 Kelly WF, Mahmood R, Turner S, Elliott K. Geographical mapping of diabetic patients from the deprived inner city shows less insulin therapy and more hyperglycaemia. *Diabet Med* 1994; **11**: 344–8.

70 Robinson N, Lloyd CE, Stevens LK. Social deprivation and mortality in adults with diabetes mellitus. *Diabet Med* 1998; **15**: 205–12.

71 Nilsson PM, Johansson S-E, Sundquist J. Low educational status is a risk factor for mortality among diabetic people. *Diabet Med* 1998; **15**: 213–19.

72 Department of Health. *Health of the Nation One Year On*. London: HMSO, 1996.

73 Bingley PJ, Gale EAM. The rising incidence of insulin-dependent diabetes in Europe. *Diabetes Care* 1989; **308**: 1019–22.

74 Rangasami JJ, Greenwood DC, McSporran B, Smail PJ, Patterson CC, Waugh NR. Childhood insulin-dependent diabetes: Oxford may not be representative. *BMJ* 1998; **316**: 391–2.

75 Amos A, McCarty DL, Zimmet P. The rising global burden of diabetes and its complications: estimates and projections to the year 2010. *Diabet Med* 1997; **14**: S1–85.

76 Clowes J, Williams R, Vail A. *Diabetes in the UK: now and in the future*. Unpublished, 1998.

77 World Health Organization (Europe), International Diabetes Federation (Europe). Diabetes care and research in Europe: the Saint Vincent Declaration. *Diabet Med* 1990; **7**: 360.

78 World Health Organization (Europe), International Diabetes Federation (Europe). The Acropolis affirmation. *Diabet Med* 1995; **12**: 636.

79 British Diabetic Association. *Diabetes Care. What you should expect*. London: British Diabetic Association, 1992.

80 British Diabetic Association. *Guidance on Local Diabetes Services Advisory Groups*. London: British Diabetic Association, 1995.

81 British Diabetic Association. *Diabetes Centres in the United Kingdom. Results of a survey of UK diabetes centres*. London: British Diabetic Association, 1998.

82 Williams DR, Spathis GS. Facilities in diabetic clinics in the UK: how much have they changed? *Diabet Med* 1992; **9**: 592–6.

83 NHS Executive. *The New NHS: modern, dependable. A national framework for assessing performance*. Wetherby: NHS Executive, 1998.

84 Currie CJ, Williams DR, Peters JR. Patterns of in- and outpatient activity for diabetes: a district survey. *Diabet Med* 1996; **13**: 273–80.

85 Williams DR. Hospital admissions of diabetic patients: information from hospital activity analysis. *Diabet Med* 1985; **2**: 27–32.

86 Macleod CA, Murchison LE, Russell EM, Dingwall-Fordyce I. Measuring outcome of diabetes: a retrospective survey. *Diabet Med* 1989; **6**: 59–63.

87 CODE-2 Advisory Group. *CODE-2: revealing the costs of type 2 diabetes in Europe*. London: SmithKline Beecham, 1999.

88 Williams DRR. Health services for patients with diabetes. In: Jarrett RJ (ed.). *Diabetes Mellitus*. London: Croom Helm, 1986, pp. 57–75.

89 Yudkin JS, Boucher BJ, Schopflin KE *et al*. The quality of diabetic care in a London health district. *J Epidemiol Community Health* 1980; **34**: 277–80.

90 Busch Sorensen M, Elphick AJ, Home PD, Thorsteinsson B. Diabetes care: a guideline to the facilities needed to support internationally endorsed standards. *Diabet Med* 1995; **12**: 833–8.

91 Alexander WD. Diabetes care in a UK health region: activity, facilities and costs. *Diabet Med* 1988; **5**: 577–81.

92 Laing W, Williams R. *Diabetes: a model for health care management*. London: Office of Health Economics, 1989.

93 Gray A, Fenn P, McGuire A. The cost of insulin-dependent diabetes mellitus (IDDM) in England and Wales. *Diabet Med* 1995; **12**: 1068–76.

94 Currie CJ, Kraus D, Morgan CL, Gill L, Stott NCH, Peters JR. NHS acute sector expenditure for diabetes: the present, future, and excess inpatient cost of care. *Diabet Med* 1997; **14**: 686–92.

95 Currie CJ, Morgan CL, Peters JR. Patterns and costs of diabetes and non-diabetes related coronary heart disease hospital care. *Heart* 1997; **78**: 544–9.

96 Currie CJ, Peters JR. The demand and financial cost of hospital care for diabetes mellitus and its related complications. *Diabet Med* 1998; **15**: 449–51.

97 Currie CJ, Morgan CL, Peters JR. The epidemiology and cost of inpatient care for peripheral vascular disease, infection, neuropathy, and ulceration in diabetes. *Diabetes Care* 1998; **21**: 42–8.

98 International Diabetes Federation. *The Economics of Diabetes and Diabetes Care*. Brussels: International Diabetes Foundation, 1996.

99 Morrish NJ, Stevens LK, Fuller JH, Jarrett RJ, Keen H. Risk factors for macrovascular disease in diabetes mellitus: the London follow-up to the WHO Multinational Study of Vascular Disease in Diabetics. *Diabetologia* 1991; **34**: 590–4.

100 Marks L. *Counting the Cost: the real impact of non-insulin-dependent diabetes*. London: King's Fund/ British Diabetic Association, 1996.

101 National Screening Committee. *First Report of the National Screening Committee*. London: Department of Health, 1998.

102 Sackett DL, Holland WW. Controversy in the detection of disease. *Lancet* 1975; **2**: 357–9.

103 Paterson KR. Population screening for diabetes mellitus. *Diabet Med* 1993; **10**: 777–81.

104 Davies MJ, Williams DRR, Metcalfe J, Day JL. Community screening for non-insulin-dependent diabetes mellitus: self-testing for post-prandial glycosuria. *Q J Med* 1993; **86**: 677–84.

105 Greenhalgh T. How to read a paper – papers that report diagnostic or screening tests. *BMJ* 1997; **315**: 540–3.

106 Andersson DKG, Lundblad E, Svardsudd K. A model for early diagnosis of type 2 diabetes mellitus in primary health care. *Diabet Med* 1993; **10**: 167–73.

107 Singer DE, Nathan DM, Fogel HA, Schachat AP. Screening for diabetic retinopathy. *Ann Intern Med* 1992; **116**: 660–71.

108 Mason J, Drummond M. *Centre for Health Economics Discussion Paper 137. Screening for diabetic retinopathy by optometrists: effectiveness and cost-effectiveness*. York: University of York, 1995.

109 Rohan TE, Frost CD, Wald NJ. Prevention of blindness by screening for diabetic retinopathy: a quantitative assessment. *BMJ* 1989; **299**: 1198–201.

110 Bachman M, Nelson S. *Screening for Diabetic Retinopathy: a quantitative overview of the evidence, applied to the populations of health authorities and boards*. Bristol: Health Care Evaluation Unit, University of Bristol, 1996.

111 The Diabetes Control and Complication Trial Research Group. The effect of intensive treatment of diabetes on the development and progression of long-term complications in insulin-dependent diabetes mellitus. *NEJM* 1993; **329**: 977–86.

112 Reichard P, Nilsson BY, Rosenqvist U. The effect of long-term intensified insulin treatment on the development of microvascular complications of diabetes mellitus. *NEJM* 1993; **329**: 304–9.

113 Wang PH, Lau J, Chalmers TC. Meta-analysis of effects of intensive blood-glucose control on late complications of type 1 diabetes. *Lancet* 1993; **341**: 1306–9.

114 Crofford OB. Diabetes control and complications. *Annu Rev Med* 1995; **46**: 267–79.

115 Pugh JA. Intensive insulin therapy for insulin-dependent diabetes mellitus. *ACP J Club* 1994; **120**: 31.

116 Anonymous. Implementing the lessons of DCCT. Report of a national workshop under the auspices of the British Diabetic Association. *Diabet Med* 1994; **11**: 220–8.

117 Diabetes Control of Complications Trial Research Group (DCCT). Lifetime benefits and costs of tight control therapy as practised in the diabetes control and complications trial. *JAMA* 1996; **276**: 1409–15.

118 Nathan DM. Inferences and implications – do the results from the Diabetes Control of Complications Trial apply in NIDDM? *Diabetes Care* 1995; **18**: 251–7.

119 Ohkubo Y, Kishikawa H, Araki E *et al.* Intensive insulin therapy prevents the progession of diabetic microvascular complications in Japanese patients with non-insulin-dependent diabetes mellitus: a randomised prospective 6-year study. *Diabet Med Clin Pract* 1995; **28**: 103–17.

120 UK Prospective Diabetes Study Group. Intensive blood-glucose control with sulphonylureas or insulin compared with conventional treatment and risk of complications in patients with Type 2 diabetes (UKPDS 33). *Lancet* 1998; **352**: 837–53.

121 UK Prospective Diabetes Study Group. Effect of intensive blood-glucose control with metformin on complications in overweight patients with Type 2 diabetes (UKPDS 34). *Lancet* 1998; **352**: 854–65.

122 UK Prospective Diabetes Study Group. Tight blood pressure control and risk of macrovascular and microvascular complications in type 2 diabetes: UKPDS 38. *BMJ* 1998; **317**: 703–12.

123 UK Prospective Diabetes Study Group. Efficacy of atenolol and captopril in reducing risk of macrovascular and microvascular complications in type 2 diabetes. *BMJ* 1998; **317**: 713–19.

124 UK Prospective Diabetes Study Group. Cost-effectiveness analysis of improved blood pressure control in hypertensive patients with type 2 diabetes: UKPDS 40. *BMJ* 1998; **317**: 720–6.

125 Nathan DM. Some answers, more controversy, from UKPDS. *Lancet* 1998; **352**: 832–3.

126 Orchard T. Diabetes: a time for excitement – and concern. *BMJ* 1998; **317**: 691–2.

127 Mogenson CE. Combined high blood pressure and glucose in type 2 diabetes: double jeopardy. *BMJ* 1998; **317**: 693–4.

128 Watkins P. UKPDS: a message of hope and need for change. *Diabet Med* 1998; **15**: 895–6.

129 Pyorala K, Pedersen TR, Kjekshus J *et al.* Cholesterol lowering with simvastatin improves prognosis of diabetic patients with coronary heart disease. *Diabetes Care* 1997; **20**: 614–20.

130 Chaturvedi N, Stevens L, Fuller JH. Which features of smoking determine mortality risk in former cigarette smokers with diabetes? The World Health Organization Multinational Study Group. *Diabetes Care* 1997; **20**: 1266–72.

131 Chaturvedi N, Stephenson JM, Fuller JH. The relationship between smoking and microvascular complications in the EURODIAB IDDM Complications Study. *Diabetes Care* 1995; **18**: 785–92.

132 Sawicki PT, Didjurgeit U, Muhlhauser I, Bender R, Heinemann L, Berger M. Smoking is associated with progression of diabetic nephropathy. *Diabetes Care* 1994; **17**: 126–31.

133 Malarcher AM, Ford ES, Nelson DE *et al.* Trends in cigarette smoking and physicians' advice to quit smoking among people with diabetes in the US. *Diabetes Care* 1995; **18**: 694–7.

134 Muhlhauser I. Smoking and diabetes. *Diabet Med* 1990; **7**: 10–15.

135 Griffen S, Kinmonth AL. Diabetes care: the effectiveness of systems for routine surveillance for people with diabetes. In: Williams R, Bennett P, Nicolucci A, Krans HMJ, Ramirez G (eds). *Diabetes Module of the Cochrane Database of Systematic Reviews.* Oxford: The Cochrane Collaboration, 1998.

136 Greenhalgh PM. *Shared Care for Diabetes. A systematic review.* Occasional paper. London: Royal College of General Practitioners, 1994.

137 Flack JR, Strumfin G, Bauman A, Jan S. *An Assessment of Diabetes in South Western Sydney: does ambulatory stabilisation improve health outcomes?* Sydney: NSW Department of Health, 1995.

138 Edmonds ME, Blundell MP, Morris ME, Thomas EM, Cotton LT, Watkins PJ. Improved survival of the diabetic foot: the role of a specialist foot clinic. *Q J Med* 1986; **60**: 763–71.

139 Bakker K, Dooren J. A specialised outpatient foot clinic for diabetic patients decreases the number of amputations and is cost saving. *Ned Tijdschr Geneeskd* 1994; **138**: 565–9.

140 Ward JD. The costs of diabetic neuropathy. *Pharmacoeconomics* 1995; **8** (Suppl. 1): 52–4.

141 Reiber GE. Diabetic foot care: financial implications and practical guidelines. *Diabetes Care* 1992; **15** (Suppl. I): 29–31.

142 Brown JB, Pedula KL, Bakst AW. The progressive cost of complications in type 2 diabetes mellitus. *Arch Intern Med* 1999; **159**: 1873–80.

143 Eastman RC, Javitt JC, Herman WH *et al.* Model of complications of NIDDM(I): model construction and assumptions. *Diabetes Care* 1997; **20**: 725–34.

144 Eastman RC, Javitt JC, Herman WH *et al.* Model of complications of NIDDM(II): analysis of the health benefits and cost-effectiveness of treating NIDDM with the goal of normoglycaemia. *Diabetes Care* 1997; **20**: 735–44.

145 Greenhalgh T. A primary-care-led diabetes service: strengths, weaknesses, opportunities and threats. *Diabet Med* 1998; **15**: S7–9.

146 Murphy E, Kinmonth AL, Marteau T. General practice-based diabetes surveillance: the views of patients. *Br J Gen Pract* 1992; **42**: 279–83.

147 Kinmonth AL, Murphy E, Marteau T. Diabetes and its care – what do patients expect? *J R Coll Gen Pract* 1989; **39**: 324–7.

148 Department of Health. *The New NHS*. London: Department of Health, 1997.

149 Alexander W. *Recommendations for the Structure of Specialist Diabetes Care Services*. London: British Diabetic Association, 1999, pp. 1–13.

150 NHS Executive. *Key Features of a Good Diabetes Service. HSG(97)45*. Leeds: NHS Executive, 1997.

151 Stevens A, Raftery J. Introduction. In: Stevens A, Raftery J (eds). *Health Care Needs Assessment. The epidemiologically based needs assessment reviews* (second series). Oxford: Radcliffe Medical Press, 1997.

152 British Diabetic Association. *The Principles of Good Practice for the Care of Young People with Diabetes*. London: British Diabetic Association, 1996.

153 NHS Executive. *Statement of Fees and Allowances Payable to General Medical Practitioners in England and Wales*. Leeds: Department of Health, 1998.

154 British Diabetic Association. *Recommendations for Diabetes Health Promotion Clinics*. London: Patient Services Advisory Committee, 1991.

155 Day J. *Report of a Shared Care and District Diabetes Services Working Party*. London: British Diabetic Association, 1990.

156 Patchett P, Roberts D. Diabetic patients who do not have diabetes: investigation of register of diabetic patients in general practice. *BMJ* 1994; **308**: 1225–6.

157 Williams DRR, Home PD, Members of a Working Group of the Research Unit of the Royal College of Physicians and the British Diabetic Association. A proposal for continuing audit of diabetes services. *Diabet Med* 1992; **9**: 759–64.

158 Jones R, Hedley A. Evaluation of a diabetes register and information system. In: Bryant J, Roberts J, Windsor P (eds). *Current Perspectives in Health Computing*. Weighbridge: BJHC, 1986, pp. 80–7.

159 Elwyn GJ, Vaughan P, Stott NCH. District diabetes registers: more trouble than they're worth? *Diabet Med* 1998; **15**: S44–8.

160 New J, Campbell F, Hollis S, McDowell D, Young R. *A Robust Method for Analysing Changes in Diabetes Care Provision*. Chicago: American Diabetes Association Scientific Meeting, 1998.

161 NHS Executive. *Chronic Disease Management Registers: Executive Letter (1996) 72*. Leeds: NHS Executive, 1996.

162 Williams R. Breaking the barriers for improved glycaemic control: primary care and secondary care interface. *Diabet Med* 1998; **15** (Suppl. 4): S37–40.

163 Department of Health, NHS Executive. *Information for Health. An information strategy for the modern NHS 1998–2005: a national strategy for local implementation.* Leeds: Department of Health, 1998.

164 World Health Organization. *Diabetes Care and Research in Europe: the St Vincent Declaration action programme. Implementation document.* Copenhagen: WHO, 1995.

165 Palmer G. Case-mix funding of hospitals: objectives and objections. *Health Care Analysis* 1996; **4**: 185–93.

166 Sanderson HF. The use of Health care Resource Groups in managing clinical resources. *Br J Health Care Manage* 1996; **2**: 174–6.

167 Douglas G. Data for all. *Health Service J* 1990; **22**: 299–300.

168 NHS Executive. *Comparative Cost Data: the use of HRGs to inform the contracting process.* Leeds: NHS Executive, 1994.

169 NHS Executive. *Priorities and Planning Guidelines for the NHS: 1998/99.* Leeds: NHS Executive, 1997.

170 NHS Information Authority. *The Health Benefit Group Development Project.* Winchester: NHS Executive, 1999.

171 National Case-mix Office. *Health Benefit Group/Health care Resource Group Matrices: findings of pilot sites.* Winchester: NHS Executive, 1998.

172 NHS Information Authority. *The Health Care Framework.* Winchester: NHS Executive, 1999.

173 O'Brien M, Halpin J, Hicks N, Pearson S, Warren V, Holland WW. Health-care commissioning development project. *J Epidemiol* 1996; **6**: S89–92.

174 Chappel D, Halpin J, O'Brien JM, Rodgers H, Thomson R. *Health Care Programme Based Purchasing of Services for Patients with Stroke in Gateshead and South Tyneside: a pilot study.* Northumberland: Northumberland Health Authority, 1998.

175 Academy of Medical Royal Colleges. *Health Care Programmes in the NHS, Vols 1–3.* London: Academy of Medical Royal Colleges, 1997.

176 O'Brien M, Singleton S. Health care programmes rule – OK! *J R Coll Physicians Lond* 1998; **32**: 208–10.

177 Greenhalgh J, Georgiou A, Long AF, Williams R, Dyas J. *Measuring the Health Outcomes of Diabetes Care.* Leeds: Nuffield Institute for Health, University of Leeds, 1997.

178 Home P, Coles J, Goldacre M, Mason A, Wilkinson E. *Outcome Indicators for Diabetes.* National Centre for Health Outcomes Development, 1999.

179 Department of Health. *Population Health Outcome Indicators for the NHS, England: a consultation document.* London: Department of Health, 1993.

180 Bradley C. *Handbook of Psychology and Diabetes. A guide to psychological measurement in diabetes research and practice.* Harwood Academic Publishers, 1994.

181 The DCCT Research Group. Reliability and validity of a diabetes quality-of-life measure for the Diabetes Control and Complications Trial (DCCT). *Diabetes Care* 1988; **11**: 725–32.

182 Williams DRR, Fuller JH, Stevens LK. Validity of routinely collected hospital admissions data on diabetes. *Diabet Med* 1988; **6**: 320–4.

183 Leslie PJ, Patrick AW, Hepburn DA, Scougal IJ, Frier BM. Hospital inpatient statistics underestimate the morbidity associated with diabetes mellitus. *Diabet Med* 1992; **9**: 379–85.

184 Wilson AE, Home PD. A data set to allow exchange of information for monitoring continuing diabetes care. *Diabet Med* 1993; **10**: 378–90.

185 Vaughan NJ, Hopkinson N, Chishty VA. DIALOG: co-ordination of the annual review process through a district diabetes register linked to the FHSA database. *Diabet Med* 1996; **13**: 182–8.

186 Vaughan NJ, Shaw M, Boer F, Billett D, Martin C. Creation of a district diabetes register using the DIALOG system. *Diabet Med* 1996; **13**: 175–81.

187 Sparrow JM, McLeod BK, Smith TDW, Birch MK, Rosenthal AR. The prevalence of diabetic retinopathy and maculopathy and their risk factors in the non-insulin-treated diabetic patients of an English town. *Eye* 1993; **7**: 158–63.

188 Young MJ, Boulton AJ, Macleod AF, Williams DR, Sonksen PH. A multicentre study of the prevalence of diabetic peripheral neuropathy in the United Kingdom hospital clinic population. *Diabetologia* 1993; **36**: 150–4.

189 Chattington PCM. New targets for the prevention and treatment of diabetic nephropathy. In: Betteridge DJ (ed.). *Diabetes: current perspectives*, 2000. London: Taylor & Francis.

190 Hasslacher C, Ritz E, Wahl P, Michael C. Similar risks of nephropathy in patients with type 1 or type 2 diabetes mellitus. *Nephrol Dial Transplant* 1989; **4**: 859–63.

191 Borch-Johnsen K. The cost of nephropathy in type II diabetes. *Pharmacoeconomics* 1995; **8**: 40–5.

192 The Hypertension in Diabetes Study Group. Hypertension in Diabetes Study (HDS). 1. Prevalence of hypertension in newly presenting type 2 diabetic patients and the association with risk factors for cardiovascular and diabetic complications. *J Hypertens* 1993; **11**: 309–17.

193 Walters D, Gatling W, Mullee M, Hill R. The prevalence, detection, and epidemiological correlates of peripheral vascular disease: a comparison of diabetic and non-diabetic subjects in an English community. *Diabet Med* 1992; **9**: 710–15.

194 Morrish N, Stevens L, Fuller J, Keen H, Jarrett R. Incidence of macrovascular disease in diabetes mellitus: the London cohort of the WHO Multinational Study of Vascular Disease in Diabetics. *Diabetologia* 1991; **34**: 584–9.

Acknowledgements

The authors gratefully acknowledge the help of Edwina Gerry, Steven Keen, Catherine Oxley and Pam Lillie in preparing this chapter. The studies of incidence, prevalence and mortality were identified in collaboration with Jonathan Clowes. We are also grateful to the managers, clinicians and patients who gave their time to comment on the previous edition and to make valuable suggestions for improvements, most of which we have attempted to incorporate in this edition.

2 Renal Disease*

Roger Beech, Martin C Gulliford and Paul Roderick

1 Summary

Background

This chapter addresses critical questions on the organisation and planning of services for adult patients with renal disease. The chapter summarises:

- information concerning the epidemiology of renal diseases
- needs for services
- current service delivery
- cost-effectiveness data
- the implications for future service development.

The chapter should be read in conjunction with purchasing guidance produced by the Department of Health, and the Renal Association/Royal College of Physicians report, *Treatment of Adult Patients with Renal Failure: Recommended Standards and Audit Measures* (the 'standards' document).[1,2]

Types of renal disease (sections 3 and 4)

Renal disease can be divided into disease without failure of kidney function and kidney failure itself, which divides into chronic and acute forms. These sections of the chapter review the main classification systems and causes of renal disease.

The management of patients with the advanced stage of chronic renal failure (CRF) called end-stage renal failure (ESRF) is the most costly item of care. These patients require chronic renal replacement therapy (RRT), by either dialysis or transplantation. Such treatment is highly effective in providing a good quality of life in an otherwise inevitably fatal condition. This chapter therefore largely focuses on chronic and end-stage renal failure.

Nevertheless there are larger numbers of patients with symptoms/signs of renal disease who will require assessment and/or medical supervision at district hospitals or tertiary centres. A number of patients develop acute renal failure (ARF), and some require dialysis for short periods of time, a few ending up with chronic failure. Prognosis is poor if there is multi-organ damage, but recovery is greater when disease is limited to the kidneys.

---

* Since this chapter was prepared there have been a number of significant developments and several important documents have been published. The reader is referred to the addendum and list of references on p. 140.

Population need (section 5)

Renal replacement therapy

The main sociodemographic characteristics that will influence population need for RRT are those driving the incidence and progression of CRF to ESRF:

- age
- gender
- ethnic origin (specifically Indo-Asian and African-Caribbean).

Indicators of social deprivation will also influence need as CRF is greater in deprived groups.

Age, deprivation and ethnic origin are all associated with relatively common conditions like diabetes mellitus, which can lead to progressive CRF.

Population-based studies show:

- the incidence of ESRF to be 130–150 per million population (pmp) in predominantly white European populations
- approximately 75–80 pmp under age 80 would be suitable for RRT each year in such populations.

However, as the risk of ESRF is higher among the elderly, and among African-Caribbean and Indo-Asian populations, the overall level of need is likely to be significantly higher. Moreover, numbers requiring RRT will increase sharply as these ethnic minority populations age. Several European countries, including Wales and Scotland, which are predominantly Caucasian and do not have large ethnic minority populations, already have annual acceptance rates over 100 pmp.

While it is hard to be precise it is likely therefore that population need in England is likely to be at least 100 pmp and probably 120–130 pmp (new patients accepted on to RRT programmes per year).

This figure will vary substantially between primary care trusts (PCTs) depending on their population characteristics.

The incidence of CRF is less readily available. One study of diagnosed disease with creatinine over 150 μmol/l shows a rate of over 1600 pmp. This will also vary between populations.

Acute renal failure/general nephrology

Current estimates are limited:

- 600 patients pmp per year need assessment for renal disease
- 100–140 individuals pmp per year develop ARF, of whom 70 pmp require nephrological assessment.

Renal services in the UK (section 6)

RRT services only consume around 1% of the NHS budget, but these funds are spent on a disproportionately small number of patients. When the predicted rise in RRT stock levels has levelled, it has been estimated that RRT services will consume between 2 and 4% of the NHS budget, but patients receiving RRT will only account for 0.08% of NHS patients.

The main methods of treatment for ESRF are:

- haemodialysis (HD)
- continuous ambulatory peritoneal dialysis (CAPD)
- transplantation.

These are used in combination in an RRT programme (for further details of these treatments *see* Appendix I). Each method is effective in prolonging survival, but if quality and duration of survival are considered, successful transplantation is the most cost-effective method of treatment. However, this mode is only applied to selected patients. Transplantation is therefore the preferred option for patients but it is limited by the availability of donor organs.

In the past, renal services have been provided through multi-district tertiary centres. Centralisation may allow specialists to achieve better results through greater experience and efficient use of scarce manpower, but populations in districts remote from specialist centres under-utilise renal services. This has resulted in geographical inequity of provision and use, particularly for RRT. In recent years, there has been a recognition of this problem. The national 'purchaser guidance' document encouraged the development of a 'hub-and-spoke' model, geographical factors permitting.[1]

Comparisons of service provision in 1993 and 1995 in England and in Wales demonstrated evidence of expansion and decentralisation. Key findings were:

- an increase in the number of satellite renal units linked to main renal units (most of which provide a full range of services, including transplantation); satellites were heterogeneous in size, location, medical input, NHS/private and other, and patient case-mix
- an increased use of hospital HD in both main and satellite units
- a much slower expansion of CAPD
- a decline in home HD
- an overall improvement in standards of care but still unacceptable variation in the quantity and quality of dialysis delivery
- persisting regional variation in the supply of services and acceptance rates
- the number of main units pmp was low compared to European countries and relatively static, although there was some growth in autonomous district general hospital (DGH)-based renal units
- evidence that some units were operating under considerable pressure which may have limited the quality of dialysis care provided.

In terms of current demand:

- the acceptance rate for RRT in the UK was rising and was 82 pmp by 1995 in England and there was evidence of regional variation
- the prevalent ('stock') rate was 476 pmp
- the characteristics of patients being treated had changed, with an increasing proportion being elderly with associated comorbidity.

There is still evidence of unmet need as this acceptance rate is below the rate in many western European countries and less than the above estimate of population need. Unmet need is higher in older ages and it varies by area.

Further data up to the end of 1998 were published in 2000.

Effectiveness and cost-effectiveness (section 7)

The evidence base for renal services is growing. There is now a Cochrane Collaboration Renal Review Group, which is co-ordinating systematic reviews of the evidence. New trials are being commenced under the auspices of the Renal Association's Clinical Trials Group. The Renal Association's standards document is an important summary of the current evidence, and it has recently been updated.

There is a need for more randomised controlled trials (RCTs) in renal disease although this is complicated by the requirement in most instances for multi-centre studies to achieve adequate numbers.

Prevention

This can be considered as:

- primary – preventing renal disease
- secondary – preventing progression/recurrence
- tertiary – reducing complications and handicap associated with renal failure.

Primary and non-specialist secondary care providers can contribute to the primary and secondary prevention of renal disease through the detection and management of diabetes, hypertension, urinary tract infection, obstructive uropathy and mild CRF. Health improvement strategies for reducing cardiovascular disease (CVD) may contribute to a reduction in renal disease because risk factors such as diabetes and hypertension are important in both conditions. The progression of CRF may be slowed through use of appropriate interventions, particularly the control of hypertension. However, the reduction in the incidence of ESRF, although valuable, is likely to be small in the short term even if greater preventive efforts are made. Their cost-effectiveness remains to be established, although they have been shown to be as effective as and more acceptable and accessible than main renal unit HD for a wide range of HD patients.

Greater efforts are needed to educate GPs and physicians about the management of renal disease. Further research is needed to determine the effectiveness of preventive measures.

Nearly 40% of patients starting RRT are referred to the renal unit less than four months before dialysis is needed. This predicates against appropriate management of CRF and planning for dialysis (secondary/tertiary prevention). Such patients fare badly and use greater resources in establishing dialysis. In some cases this is inevitable (e.g. because of rapid progression), but there is scope for more timely referral of patients with CRF. However, even some patients under longer-term nephrological care start dialysis in emergency. Greater attention is needed to ensure that facilities are available for establishing timely vascular access to reduce this as far as possible.

For ARF, avoidable factors may contribute to some cases, although more research is needed to define the scope for prevention.

Renal replacement therapy

For all modalities there have been marked improvements in survival in the last decade, particularly after transplantation, despite the increasing proportions of elderly and 'high-risk' patients. In general:

- 50% of patients in Europe on RRT are alive after 10 years and 40% after 15 years
- patients under 55 years without diabetes or other coincidental diseases can expect a 94% survival to year one and an average life expectancy of 14.3 years thereafter
- the best patient survival rates are reported following transplantation, but these are a selected patient group (younger, with less comorbidity)
- graft survival is influenced mainly by tissue-type match, the type of donor (live vs. cadaveric), the type of immunosuppression and the underlying cause of the renal disease
- it is difficult to compare CAPD and hospital HD directly because case-mix varies, but there does not appear to be any difference in overall survival when selection factors are taken into account.

Treatment (or modality) survival is better on HD, because of the risk of recurrent peritonitis with CAPD, although this problem has declined with the introduction of disconnect catheters. Dialysis by CAPD can become inadequate over time as any remaining patient renal function declines. Continuous ambulatory peritoneal dialysis has, in the past, been used preferentially in the UK for patients with diabetes, patients with CVD and elderly patients. Some argue that many older patients who are being increasingly accepted on to RRT require accessible, medically supervised hospital HD as an alternative option to CAPD.

Furthermore, the modalities are best considered as interdependent and patients should have a choice between them when first established on RRT. There are concerns that choice is limited due to inadequate HD facilities. There will be increasing need for hospital HD as the older age group expands and as patients first established on CAPD fail on this modality. Although the UK has a much higher proportion of patients on CAPD than other European countries, recent growth in provision has largely been of hospital HD, with CAPD showing much slower growth and home HD declining. There has also been a growth of automated peritoneal dialysis (APD) as an alternative to home HD and CAPD. Further evidence of its cost-effectiveness needs to be established.

Cost-effectiveness studies indicate that the main methods of treatment can be ranked in diminishing order of cost-effectiveness as follows:

- successful transplantation
- CAPD
- home HD
- hospital HD.

However, these comparisons cannot be used directly; in the local context there may be significant variations in case-mix and the costs of expanding different components of the service may depend on local circumstances. Moreover, there are significant problems in separating interdependent modalities. For example, CAPD requires back-up hospital HD for both temporary and permanent technique failures. In addition, cost shifts and the introduction of technology (Y connectors and bicarbonate dialysis fluid) can affect the analyses: many of the studies pre-date these technological changes.

The evidence on relative cost-effectiveness of modalities and the characteristics of the existing stock of patients on RRT, together with the likely sorts of patients who would enter the RRT programme if acceptance rates were to increase, indicate the purchase of a combination of transplantation (within the constraints of organ supply) and a balanced programme of CAPD and HD, though with greater emphasis on HD. HD is increasingly being delivered in satellite units. Their cost-effectiveness in coping with elderly comorbid patients remains to be established.

It has to be accepted that the proportion of patients who are elderly and/or with comorbidity will increase, a development that may reduce the marginal cost-effectiveness of RRT services. The scope for improvement in organ harvesting for transplantation appears modest at present, unless it can be given greater priority (and funding) by provider units, and additional strategies for organ procurement are developed.

Better evidence of the relative cost-effectiveness of hospital HD, CAPD and APD is needed, ideally by randomised methods, as observational studies are problematic because of selection factors in the use of these modalities.

Modelling future demand and its implications (section 8)

Various researchers have used modelling techniques to predict the future prevalence ('stock') of patients who will be receiving RRT when a steady state is reached. Key findings are as follows:

- for an estimated need of 80 new patients pmp under age 80 there will be a rise in the stock levels of between 50 and 90% over the next 15 years depending on the assumed rates of patient survival (this is probably a conservative estimate, with a more realistic figure being a doubling of stock levels to a rate of 800 pmp)
- stock rates will rise even if acceptance rates remain constant

- to meet projected demand, year-on-year growth in provision will be required
- elderly patients with associated comorbidity will increase both in absolute terms and as a proportion of total patient stock
- the main growth in demand by modality will be in dialysis, particularly hospital HD, as transplantation and CAPD may not be appropriate for elderly patients with comorbidity
- the increase in demand will be influenced by the rates of patient acceptance and patient survival
- changes in transplantation rates will only have a small effect on stock levels, though they would alter the dialysis-to-transplantation ratio.

Further modelling is needed to investigate the effects of a higher target acceptance rate (including the impact of demographic change in ethnic minorities), and the balance of dialysis modalities under different assumptions about future case-mix and availability of dialysis facilities.

Transplantation (section 8)

Transplantation is the preferred modality for RRT, but demand outstrips supply of organs. Policies to increase the supply of kidneys for transplantation are required. PCTs and Strategic Health Authorities (SHAs) need to consider how cadaver donation from intensive-care units (ICUs) and neurosurgical units can be maximised. ICUs, neurosurgical facilities and transplant teams must be well resourced. Brainstem death testing and organ harvesting should be audited. Procurement co-ordinators should be adequately funded and supported to fulfil their roles of professional and public education, co-ordination of organ harvesting and bereavement counselling. 'Elective ventilation' of non-ICU patients purely for the purpose of providing organs for transplantation has been declared illegal. The use of asystolic donors needs further pilot studies to demonstrate its feasibility and effectiveness. National policies to enhance the profile and coverage of the donor card scheme and the development of the NHS organ register are important. The opt-out policy of 'presumed consent' needs wider debate. Providers should be encouraged to use the national kidney sharing scheme and to participate in larger local (e.g. regional) lists with clear criteria for allocation. This would enhance the effectiveness and equity of transplantation. Of concern is the difficulty of ensuring equitable access to transplants for ethnic minority groups.

The use of living donors has been less well established in the UK than in some other countries. The programme is expanding and now includes unrelated donors. It has helped to maintain kidney supply in the face of declining cadaver kidneys, though it is not applicable to all recipients.

Organisation of services (section 8)

Renal replacement therapy

The key dilemma is how to enhance the quantity of RRT, invest in quality improvements and ensure geographical access to reduce current inequities. The new infrastructure of regional and sub-regional groups for commissioning specialist services will need to review population needs, trends in demand and current service disposition in order to plan with their constituent PCTs how and where supply could be increased over a 5–10-year time frame.

This would entail, for example, supporting the development of autonomous DGH renal units outside major cities, and satellite units. The former will provide a more complete service which improves the care for all types of renal disease and particularly ARF.

Conversely, there are grounds for rationalising transplant services into fewer large centres to ensure a critical mass of medical, nursing and pathological expertise.

In Scotland, there is a recommendation to develop 'managed clinical networks', which would facilitate seamless care between renal units, transplant centres and primary and community-based services. This concept requires further exploration in England and Wales.

In terms of the delivery of services:

- RRT expansion has knock-on implications for other hospital services (e.g. vascular and cardiac) as well as for primary and community care
- access surgery is key to a timely start to dialysis – surgical manpower must be adequate to cope
- expansion of hospital HD has considerable resource implications in terms of need for buildings, infrastructure, technology, and skilled nursing and technical staff
- a major constraint on service development is a shortage of skilled nurses
- further work is required to identify different skill mixes and to develop policies for recruitment, training and retention of staff
- research is needed to establish good models of satellite units in providing more accessible care for elderly RRT patients
- with the increasing numbers of elderly on RRT, the role of community support linked in with primary care is crucial
- in parallel with RRT expansion, pre-ESRF care needs to develop in order to improve the delivery of secondary/tertiary prevention measures
- primary care also has an important role in the primary prevention of renal disease and in early diagnosis and prompt referral
- explicit rationing of RRT is very difficult to implement; the cost-effectiveness of RRT can be improved by enhancing efficiency of delivery of RRT and earlier referral of patients
- the need to develop policies on withdrawal and terminal support is growing with the increasingly elderly population on dialysis.

There is a need for more information on the organisation of and patterns of care for ARF. Access to nephrologists would be improved by the development of more autonomous renal units/DGH nephrology posts.

Monitoring and evaluation, research needs (sections 9 and 10)

Evaluation is essential for RRT, a highly complex and costly area of health care. Clinical standards for all areas of renal disease, though predominantly for dialysis and transplantation, have been developed by the Renal Association and widely disseminated. Some are evidence based, others are consensus statements.

Comparative audit will be facilitated by the development of the UK and Scottish Renal Registries. The geographical and person-specific equity of RRT delivery can then be evaluated, and comparative audit of units' performance undertaken. PCTs and SHAs should encourage and support the involvement of their units in the Registry, including its funding.

Key evidence-based measures of the quality of care could be introduced into service agreements.

Conclusion

Renal replacement therapy is effective in prolonging life of good quality in patients with ESRF. Provision will have to continue to expand to meet population need and to cope with inbuilt growth in the prevalent pool. To achieve an accessible, high-quality service, specialist service commissioning groups will have to consider how to decentralise nephrological expertise and dialysis facilities and to develop a quality assurance framework. Service delivery will need to be increasingly responsive to the needs of the elderly population on RRT.

Improvements in the quality of RRT will need to be funded alongside growth in quantity. Transplantation services should be restricted to large tertiary centres and measures to increase the organ supply given high priority.

Commissioning groups will need to work together with providers and constituent PCTs to co-ordinate and evaluate these developments with the ultimate goal of achieving more equitable, accessible and cost-effective renal services.

2 Introduction

This section discusses the needs of primary care trust (PCT) populations for specialist services for the treatment of adults with renal disease. The main emphasis is on organising services for patients with ESRF, the end-point of progressive CRF. End-stage renal failure is inevitably fatal unless treated by RRT, including dialysis or transplantation. Renal replacement therapy is a complex treatment that has to be given regularly for the rest of the patient's life. It is a costly form of intervention. Large amounts of NHS resources are therefore spent keeping a relatively small number of patients alive who would otherwise die. It is estimated that 1% of the NHS budget is currently spent on 0.08% of the population, rising to 2% at steady state.[3]

Services required for diagnosis and treatment of ARF and for other renal diseases are also discussed briefly. Conditions that are mainly treated by urologists are not included.

The level of RRT provision has expanded considerably in the UK in the past decade from a position of significant underprovision. Acceptance rates increased from 20 pmp in 1982 to 82 pmp in England and 109 pmp in Wales in 1995.[4] The UK acceptance rate is still below the estimate of population need and lower than several comparable European countries. Older individuals, and patients with associated comorbidity, such as diabetes, formerly had low rates of acceptance on to RRT but are now being treated in greater numbers. The percentage of new acceptances in England who were aged over 65 was 41% in 1995.[4] Such expansion was possible within the resource constraints of the NHS by the widespread use of CAPD and the expansion of the kidney transplantation programme. More recently the main increase in relative and absolute terms has been in hospital HD. This mode predominates in most European countries.

Rationing of RRT has been largely covert; providers (GPs and hospital physicians/surgeons) have not always referred patients to nephrologists for assessment when they might have benefited, but there has been a liberalisation of attitudes to referral of patients with ESRF in the past decade.[5]

Services for patients with renal disease are still largely provided through multi-district renal units, following the regional model first instituted in the 1960s when dialysis first became available. Most units support a full range of specialist services except transplantation, this being largely restricted to academic centres. There has been a considerable increase in renal satellite units, i.e. units without full-time, on-site consultant nephrology staff that are linked to main renal units. There are also some autonomous DGH renal units. Within districts the number of patients receiving services is small, but there is evidence of under-referral of patients at present. This is a greater problem in districts that are remote from renal units,[6] particularly in older individuals.[7]

Commissioning policy has changed from the internal market to the establishment of regional and sub-regional specialist commissioning groups. An important consideration in any PCT/SHA/specialist commissioning group strategy will be to determine the priority to be given to the RRT programme, given its proven effectiveness but significant resource use, and whether the provision of services locally would be advantageous within a regional strategic framework.

There have been significant developments in defining the evidence base for the management of renal disease and for monitoring and evaluating the care provided. These include the Cochrane Collaboration Renal Review Group, the production of regularly updated standards of care by the Renal Association and the development of the UK Renal Registry of patients on RRT which will, among other things, facilitate comparative audit of the quality and equity of care.

This chapter describes what is currently known about the epidemiology of renal disease, the need for renal services, and the effectiveness and cost-effectiveness of these services. It identifies gaps in the knowledge which commissioning groups would find useful in assessing their needs for renal services, and makes recommendations for relevant research.

3 Statement of the problem

The essential functions of the kidney are the excretion of waste products of metabolism, the control of salt and water balance and blood pressure (BP), and the regulation of bone metabolism and haemoglobin production. If kidney function is impaired, all these body systems are affected. The standard measure of renal function is creatinine clearance, which reflects the ability of the kidneys to excrete most waste products of protein metabolism. The normal range is about 100 ml/min; rates less than 30 ml/min imply severe renal impairment. When clearance falls below 10 ml/min patients become severely symptomatic and usually need RRT. For long-term monitoring of renal function, measurement of simple serum creatinine is used.

Categories of renal disease

The following terms are used in this chapter.

- **Renal diseases without renal failure** – acute and chronic diseases of the kidney not resulting in a significant or progressive reduction in renal function. This workload is often termed 'general nephrology', e.g. investigation of proteinuria, haematuria (microscopic and macroscopic), recurrent urinary tract infection.
- **Renal failure** – a reduction in renal function sufficient to cause substantial increases in blood urea and creatinine concentrations.
- **Acute renal failure (ARF)** – this is of sudden onset and is potentially reversible. It develops over days or weeks, and dialysis may be required. Some patients die, usually from the precipitating condition, but full recovery of renal function usually occurs if the patient survives. It is now recognised that some cases of ARF never recover renal function.[8]
- **Chronic renal failure (CRF)** – develops over months or years and is not usually reversible, although intervention may modify the rate of progression. It may present as ARF if there is a precipitating event.
- **End-stage renal failure (ESRF)** – the irreversible reduction of renal function to levels incompatible with the maintenance of life without dialysis or transplantation.

Coding systems

The relevant ICD9 and 10 codes[9,10] are given in Table 1, ONS operation codes[11] in Table 2, and Health Care Resource Groups (HRGs) in Table 3. The HRG classification includes much that is urological rather than nephrological.

Table 1a: Diagnostic codes (ICD ninth revision).

016.0	TB kidney
250.3	Diabetes with renal manifestations
274.1	Gouty nephropathy
403	Hypertensive renal disease
404	Hypertensive heart and renal disease
580	Acute glomerulonephritis
581	Nephrotic syndrome
582	Chronic glomerulonephritis
583	Nephritis and nephropathy, not specified as acute or chronic
584	Acute renal failure (excludes post-operative renal failure and complications of pregnancy)
585	Chronic renal failure (excludes hypertensive renal disease)
586	Renal failure, unspecified
587	Renal sclerosis, unspecified
588	Disorders resulting from impaired renal function
589	Small kidney of unknown cause
590	Infections of kidney
591	Hydronephrosis
592	Calculus of kidney and ureter
593	Other disorders of kidney and ureter
599.7	Haematuria
634-8	Acute renal failure complicating abortion
669.3	Acute renal failure complicating labour and delivery
788.9	Extrarenal uraemia
997.5	Post-operative acute renal failure

Source: ref. 9.

Table 1b: Diagnostic codes (ICD tenth revision).

I12.0	Renal failure with hypertension
I13.0	Hypertensive heart and renal disease
NO1	Rapidly progressive nephritic syndrome
NO2	Recurrent and persistent haematuria
NO3	Chronic nephritic syndrome
NO4	Nephrotic syndrome
NO5	Unspecified nephritic syndrome
NO6	Isolated proteinuria with specified morphological lesion
NO7	Hereditary nephropathy
N10	Acute tubulo-interstitial nephritis
N11	Chronic tubulo-interstitial nephritis
N12	Tubulo-interstitial nephritis, not acute or chronic
N13	Obstructive and reflux uropathy
N14	Drug and heavy metal induced tubulo-interstitial and tubular conditions
N15	Other renal tubulo-interstitial disease
N16	Renal tubulo-interstitial disorders in diseases classified elsewhere
N17	Acute renal failure
N18	Chronic renal failure
N19	Unspecified renal failure
N27	Small kidney of unknown cause
N28.0	Ischaemia and infarction of kidney
N29.1	TB kidney
N99.0	Post-procedural renal failure
0 00-07	Renal failure complicating abortion/ectopic or molar pregnancy
0 90.4	Renal failure following labour
R31	Unspecified haematuria
R39.2	Extra-renal uraemia
	Pre-renal uraemia
R80	Isolated proteinuria
R94.4	Abnormal kidney function test
T79.0	Traumatic anuria
T82.4	Complication of vascular disease
T85.6	Peritoneal dialysis (PD) catheter
T86.1-9	Kidney transplant failure or rejection

Source: ref. 10.

Table 2: OPCS 4 operation codes.

Operation	OPCS code
Transplantation of kidney	M01
Total excision of kidney	M02
Partial excision of kidney	M03
Other open operations on kidney (including open biopsy)	M08
Percutaneous puncture of kidney (including percutaneous biopsy)	M13
Compensation for renal failure	X40
Renal dialysis	X40.1
Peritoneal dialysis (PD)	X40.2
Haemodialysis necessary	X40.3
Other specified	X40.8
Unspecified	X40.9
Placement of ambulatory apparatus for compensation of renal failure	X41
Insertion of ambulatory PD catheter	X41.1
Removal of ambulatory PD catheter	X41.2
Other specified	X41.8
Unspecified	X41.9
Placement of other apparatus for compensation of renal failure	X42
Insertion of temporary PD catheter	X42.1
Other specified	X42.8
Unspecified	X42.9
Donation of organ	X45
Donation of kidney	X45.1
Reconstruction of renal artery	L41
Other open operations on renal artery	L42
Transluminal operation on renal artery	L43

Source: ref. 11.

Table 3: Health Care Resource Groups.

L01	Kidney transplant
L02/3	Kidney major open procedure
L04	Kidney major endoscopic procedure
L05/6	Kidney intermediate endoscopic procedure
L07/8	Non-operating-room admission for kidney or urinary tract neoplasms
L09/10	Kidney or urinary tract infections
L45	Extracorp lithotripsy
L46	Renal replacement-associated procedures
L47/48	Renal replacement therapy
L49/50	Acute renal failure
L51	Chronic renal failure
L52/53	Renal general disorders
L54/55	Renal findings
L99	Complex elderly with urinary tract or male reproductive system primary diagnosis

Source: National Case Mix Office (www.casemix.org.uk).

4 Sub-categories

Renal diseases without renal failure

The clinical and pathological features of renal diseases have been described in standard texts.[12,13] This category includes a wide range of conditions, many of which are rare. The importance of these conditions is their common potential to cause renal damage, which may subsequently progress over a variable time period to renal failure. Thus the aim of diagnosis and treatment should be to prevent or minimise the extent of renal damage.

Acute renal failure

Acute renal failure is characterised by the rapid deterioration in renal function to levels at which dialysis may be required to support life. After an interval, recovery of renal function may occur but there may be residual impairment of renal function. Acute renal failure may result from a number of conditions. Most common are pre-renal causes (e.g. hypovolaemic, cardiogenic and septic shock), but intrinsic renal disease or the effects of toxins or drugs and post-renal causes such as acute obstruction also contribute. In most cases of ARF there are several contributory causes. The Renal Association Standards document[2] recognised the following groups:

- *medical* – glomerulonephritis (GN), infections, adverse drug reactions, renovascular disease (RVD)
- *multiple injuries* – road traffic accidents, industrial injuries, burns, etc.
- *surgical* – following major procedures, e.g. aortic or cardiac surgery, especially when complicated by hypotension or infection
- *obstetric* – obstetric causes of ARF are now rare in the UK
- *urinary tract obstruction* – most often caused by prostatic hyperplasia.

Chronic renal failure

Chronic renal failure results from a number of conditions which cause slow deterioration in renal function. A minority of cases arise after ARF (*see* Figure 1 overleaf). Once significant chronic renal damage is established it tends to be steadily progressive, with the eventual development of ESRF. Most diseases affecting the kidney fall into the following categories.

Auto-immune disease

Glomerulonephritis describes a group of diseases in which the glomeruli (the filters in which starts the process of urine formation) are damaged by the body's immunological response to tissue changes or infection. The more severe forms are treated with immunosuppressive drugs, but treatment makes only a small impact on the progress of this group of diseases to ESRF.

Systemic disease

The most important cause is diabetes, both insulin-dependent (type 1) diabetes and non-insulin-dependent (type 2) diabetes. Progressive renal disease develops in a significant proportion, especially if

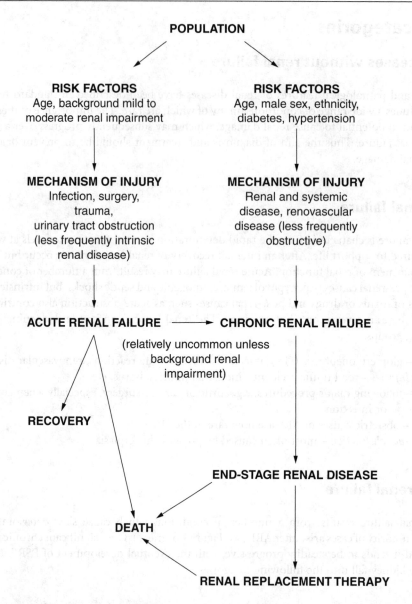

Figure 1: Causes and outcome of renal failure.

BP and blood glucose control have been poor. Diabetes is particularly prevalent in Indo-Asian and African Caribbean populations.

Atherosclerotic vascular disease may also affect the renal arteries, causing progressive impairment of renal function. Renovascular disease is increasingly recognised in the elderly, and carries a poor prognosis as it is associated with generalised vascular disease. Other systemic diseases that affect the kidneys include systemic lupus, vasculitis and multiple myeloma.

High blood pressure

Severe hypertension damages the kidney. Establishing it as a cause is difficult because renal impairment is complicated by hypertension. It is a particular problem in African-Caribbean populations.

Obstruction/infection

Obstruction to urine flow causes back-pressure on the kidneys. The most common form is benign prostatic hypertrophy. When combined with infection it is especially damaging. Two other important conditions are reflux nephropathy in young children and urinary tract stones.

Genetic disease

One important inherited disease, polycystic kidney disease, affects the kidney. It causes no symptoms until middle age or later but is a common cause of ESRF.

Toxic damage

This can be produced by several drugs and environmental toxins (e.g. lead).

End-stage renal failure

The distribution of renal diseases among patients accepted for RRT in the UK in 1985–86 and 1990–91 is shown in Table 4. It is important to note the difficulties in ascribing a cause to ESRF. In a substantial minority no cause is identified ('unknown' group), as patients present with small, shrunken kidneys and invasive investigations are not justified. As mentioned above, ascribing hypertension as the primary cause can be difficult. Moreover, data on RRT acceptances will under-represent certain causes (e.g. diabetes) because of selective referral patterns.

Table 4: Causes of ESRF in patients accepted on to renal replacement therapy in the UK, 1985–86 and 1990–91.

	Percentage of new patients	
	1985–86	**1990–91**
Unknown	20	24
Glomerulonephritis	20	15
Pyelonephritis and interstitial nephritis	15	13
Polycystic kidney	9	8
Renovascular disease[a]	12	14
Diabetes	11	14
Multi-system	6	6
Other	7	6

[a] Includes hypertension.
Source: EDTA 1985–86, 1990–91.

Table 5: Causes of ESRF in patients accepted on to RRT in England and Wales in 1995.

	Percentage of new patients		
	Under 65 ($n = 2058$)	Over 65 ($n = 1429$)	All ages ($n = 3487$)
Glomerulonephritis	14.9	8.9	12.4
Pyelonephritis	9.0	9.3	9.1
Diabetes	15.7	11.1	13.8
Renal vascular disease	4.1	8.2	5.5
Hypertension	7.5	8.3	7.8
Polycystic kidney	7.5	3.5	5.9
Uncertain	14.3	20.9	17.0
Other	13.8	10.7	12.6
Missing	13.2	19.2	15.7

Source: ref. 4.

More recent data for England and Wales from a special survey conducted in 1995–96 show a slight rise in the proportion with diabetes to 14% (*see* Table 5).[4]

A distinction can be made between primary renal diseases and systemic diseases with renal involvement. The prognosis is generally better for patients with primary renal diseases than for patients with systemic disease. Chronic GN and chronic pyelonephritis are the most important primary renal diseases, while hypertension and diabetes mellitus are the most important systemic causes of ESRF.

Patients on RRT have sometimes been grouped according to level or risk according to the following criteria:

Level of risk	Age (years) and diabetes
Standard	< 55 non-diabetic
Medium	< 55 diabetic or 55–64 non-diabetic
High	> 65 diabetic, 55–64 diabetic

However, newer prognostic indices are being developed which take better account of the presence and severity of comorbidity (*see* below).

5 Incidence and prevalence

Data sources

Mortality data are an unreliable source for investigating the epidemiology of renal disease as there is considerable under-ascertainment. The cause of death in renal failure, for example, is often ascribed to an end complication, e.g. heart failure, rather than to the underlying renal disease. Moreover, ICD coding does not reliably distinguish between acute and chronic forms of renal failure. There is, however, evidence of a substantial fall in the mortality from renal diseases over the past century, pre-dating the introduction of RRT.[14] The exact reasons for this decline are not clear, but it may partly reflect reductions in ARF, in turn arising from the decline in infectious causes, and from improvements in the management of shock and of pregnancy.

Hospital episode statistics (HES) data are likewise an unreliable measure of incidence or prevalence. First, they only relate to known cases; second, most RRT is delivered to outpatients or to patients at home; third, although there is a correlation between hospital episodes and numbers of patients on RRT, this is not direct. ICD coding lacks specificity (*see* above).

Renal registries have been set up to describe patterns of RRT, so they reflect access and availability of care as well as incidence of disease.

Renal diseases without renal failure

The epidemiology of renal diseases has been reviewed,[14,15] but further work is needed in this field.[16] There is a wide range of conditions for which specialist facilities for diagnosis and treatment might be required. The Renal Association estimates that there are at least 250 referrals pmp requiring a nephrological opinion per year and 400–800 pmp attending for follow-up (excluding chronic dialysis and transplant patients).[17] Further population-based studies of the epidemiology of renal diseases are required.

Acute renal failure

There is no accepted epidemiological definition of ARF. Two population-based studies have been carried out in the UK. Feest *et al.*[18] considered patients to have ARF if the serum creatinine rose above 500 μmol/l for the first time and either (i) returned below that level and remained there or (ii) the patient died in the acute illness and the history or postmortem findings confirmed a diagnosis of ARF. Khan *et al.*[19] included patients in whom the serum creatinine rose above 300 μmol/l for the first time and either (i) the serum creatinine returned to below that level and remained there or (ii) the patient died and the clinical features were suggestive of an acute deterioration.

Patients in both of these studies who remained dialysis dependent for more than 90 days were considered to have CRF. For patients presenting in renal failure for the first time the distinction between acute and chronic renal failure may be difficult, but it is now recognised that about 17% of patients with ARF may not recover renal function[8] and these may be described as having acute irreversible renal failure.[20]

Incidence of ARF

Results from the studies by Feest *et al.*[18] and Khan *et al.*[19] are shown in Table 6 overleaf. The overall annual incidence of ARF in the study of Feest *et al.* was 140 per million total population. Khan *et al.* found that the overall incidence of ARF with creatinine > 500 μmol/l, after excluding patients with cancer and those over 80 years of age, was 102 per million. Both studies showed a substantial increase in the incidence of ARF with age, but for comparable age groups the more recent study by Khan *et al.* showed incidence rates that were four to five times higher than those documented by Feest *et al.* While these two estimates are in reasonable agreement, detailed comparison of the two studies serves to emphasise the magnitude of

Table 6: Incidence of acute renal failure according to age.

Feest et al.[18]			Khan et al.[19]		
Age group (years)	No. of cases (pmp)	Annual incidence	Age group (years)	No. of cases (pmp)	Annual incidence
16–49	7	17	0–19	4	30
50–59	8	83	20–49	46	157
60–69	20	186	50–69	86	834
70–79	53	660	70–79	76	2,694
80–89	35	949	≥ 80	98	5,188
> 89	2	–			

variations which may arise as a result of different case definitions, different populations and differing patterns of clinical activity. There are several obvious differences between the studies.

- Khan et al. used a lower threshold value for serum creatinine (300 rather than 500 µmol/l).
- Feest et al. excluded patients with obvious terminal illnesses such as cancer, but Khan et al. found that differences between the studies were substantial even after excluding cases with cancer.
- Feest et al. did not attempt to include resident subjects who developed ARF outside the district. For example, they noted that patients were referred out of the district for cardiothoracic surgery.
- Khan et al. studied a population in the north of Scotland, while Feest et al. studied a population in south-west England.

Chronic and end-stage renal failure

As with ARF, the incidence of CRF in the population has been investigated by using a raised serum creatinine as a marker, as creatinine is measured as part of a routine urea and electrolytes test. This is a specific marker of renal failure, which is sensitive to moderate to severe renal failure, creatinine rising above the normal range when 60–70% of renal function is lost.

A population-based study in the Grampian Region showed that the incidence of CRF (creatinine > 300 µmol/l) was 450 pmp.[21] There was a steep age gradient; the gender difference was not reported. A study using Southampton and South West Hampshire Health Authority as the population base has shown that in 1992–94, the incidence of new diagnoses of CRF (creatinine > 150 µmol/l) was 1625 pmp (CI: 1540–1716), and there was a steep age gradient.

The incidence of ESRF in a district population determines the number of new cases that could be accepted for RRT. The prevalence of ESRF is almost the same as the prevalence of patients receiving RRT ('stock') because untreated survival is poor.

The incidence of ESRF (based on routine creatinine results over 500 µmol/l) has been defined by studies undertaken in Devon and the North West by Feest et al.,[18] and in Grampian by Khan et al.[21,22] These two studies gave results which showed that:

- the incidence of ESRF was 148 pmp per annum in the Feest study and 130 pmp in the Khan study
- the incidence of ESRF will vary by district depending on the population age distribution and ethnic composition, and according to indicators of social deprivation.

ESRF and age

The incidence of ESRF increases with age (*see* Table 7), but because of the small numbers of cases in these studies the confidence limits of the age-specific incidence rates are wide.

Table 7: Age-specific incidence rates for end-stage renal disease.

Age group (years)	Annual incidence rate per million population (95% CI)
0–20	6 (−2–14)
20–49	58 (38–78)
50–59	160 (96–224)
60–69	282 (197–367)
70–79	503 (370–636)
≥ 80	588 (422–754)

Source: ref. 22.

ESRF and ethnicity

Ethnicity is an important influence on the incidence of ESRF. Two ethnic groups require separate consideration: people of African or African-Caribbean (AAC) origin and people of Indian subcontinent descent (Indo-Asians). In the USA, the acceptance rate of African-Americans (AA) on to RRT is four to five times higher than for whites.[23–25] Rates of all renal diseases except polycystic disease are higher in AA than in white populations. Although the prevalence and severity of hypertension is greater in AA populations than in whites in the USA, this does not explain the increased acceptance rates, nor does correction for educational level or access to medical care.[26] Similar findings apply to ESRF from diabetes in AA populations in the USA.[27]

Although direct extrapolation to AAC communities in the UK is not appropriate, there is evidence that there is higher mortality from cerebrovascular and hypertensive disease[28] and a higher prevalence of hypertension[29,30] among AAC populations than among white populations in the UK.

Recent work for the 1993 National Renal Review in England found that population-based ethnic-specific acceptance and stock rates in England were almost three times higher in AAC populations than in white populations (*see* Table 8)[31] and the rate ratio increased with age.

Table 8: Ethnic rates of renal replacement therapy acceptance (1991–92) in England.

	White		Indo-Asian		African-Caribbean	
	Male	Female	Male	Female	Male	Female
Number of cases per annum	3,063	1,871	262	178	161	111
Rate per million population	90	50	281	196	272	172
Relative rate	1.0	1.0	3.1	3.9	3.0	3.4

Source: ref. 31.

The National Renal Review found that acceptance and stock rates were likewise higher for Indo-Asians, which in part may be due to higher rates of diabetic ESRF. People of Indian subcontinent descent are known to have a higher prevalence and mortality from diabetes.[32] A study in Leicester found that the rate of acceptance from diabetic ESRF was ten times higher in Indo-Asians compared with whites.[33] The relative rate was even higher when diabetic populations were compared, suggesting that Indo-Asian people with diabetes are more susceptible to renal damage.[34] In the National Renal Review, there was a five- to sixfold higher acceptance rate for diabetic ESRF in both African-Caribbean and Indo-Asian populations compared with whites, and for uncertain cause among Indo-Asians.[31]

The National Renal Review findings were confounded by access to renal units. Multi-level modelling of the data on the characteristics and location of all patients accepted on to RRT in England in 1991–92 demonstrated the independent effects of ethnicity (population levels of Indo-Asians and African-Caribbeans) on acceptance rates, after controlling for access to renal units – indirect evidence of increased population need for RRT in these ethnic groups.[6]

The increased acceptance rates among ethnic minority populations does not rule out inequality in access to services. Population-based data are needed on the epidemiology of CRF in ethnic minorities.

Ethnic minority populations are much younger than white populations. The implication is that as these populations age there will be an increased need; this will be disproportionate because of the age-related increases in relative rates. Age-standardised acceptance rate ratios using the 1991–92 acceptance data were 90 for whites, 422 for Asians and 374 for African-Caribbeans.[31] It has been estimated that the need for RRT in Greater London will grow at 25–33% between 1991 and 2011 due to ageing of ethnic minorities, despite a net loss of the white population.[35]

In summary:

- extrapolating from RRT data, a higher incidence of ESRF is probably found among African-Caribbeans and Indo-Asians than among whites in the UK
- further work is needed to evaluate the incidence, aetiology and treatment of ESRF among the ethnic minorities in the UK.

ESRF and socio-economic status

Another potentially important determinant of the incidence of ESRF is socio-economic status. The evidence for this is indirect.

- There is a strong inverse social class gradient in mortality from renal failure.[36]
- The population-based rates of creatinine over 150 μmol/l in Southampton and SW Hampshire increased in those areas with the highest Townsend deprivation index (personal communication, N Drey).
- There is evidence for socio-economic gradients in underlying causes of ESRF, such as non-insulin-dependent diabetes, hypertension and RVD.[37]
- The modelling study above showed that area deprivation was positively associated with RRT acceptance.[6]

ESRF and diabetes mellitus

ESRF is an important complication of both type 1 (insulin-dependent) and type 2 (non-insulin-dependent) diabetes mellitus (DM). As type 1 DM is the less common form, ESRF secondary to type 2 DM now predominates. Patients with type 1 DM usually present aged 40–50 years and may have other diabetic microvascular complications, such as blindness. Patients with type 2 DM are usually older and often have clinical macrovascular disease. The proportion of diabetic patients accepted for RRT in England and Wales is approximately 14%. In the USA, the figure is much higher at 37%.[25] It has been suggested that the prevalence of diabetic nephropathy is lower in the UK than in North America, although there is little direct evidence to support this contention. There has been concern that the needs of people with diabetes and renal disease have not been met in the UK. This was confirmed in the 1980s by the findings of the Joint Working Party of the British Diabetic Association, the Renal Association and the Royal College of Physicians, which showed that one-third of diabetic patients with renal disease died without receiving RRT.[38,39] Some of the deaths were considered unavoidable, but half of the patients who died were considered to have died from untreated ESRF. However, people with diabetes have been more readily accepted on to RRT in the UK in recent years. Diabetic ESRF will be greater in districts with a high prevalence of ethnic minorities. A recent report estimated that because of increasing numbers of older people in ethnic minority groups, between 1991 and 2011 the number of patients with diabetes will increase by 33.5% in African-Caribbean men, 79.4% in African-Caribbean women, 83% in Indo-Asian men and 137% in Indo-Asian women.[40]

What is the level of population need for RRT?

Feest *et al.*[18] estimated that the overall incidence of ESRF suitable for RRT in those aged less than 80 was 78 pmp per year (95% CI: 63–93).[22] This 'suitability' criterion excludes patients who would have a severely restricted or hospital-based existence if accepted on to RRT (e.g. those with severe vascular disease or advanced malignancy). In the Feest study, 54% of incident cases of ESRF were referred for nephrological opinion and 35% were accepted.

This is probably a minimum estimate of need for the following reasons.

- It does not take into account the needs of ethnic minorities.
- The over-80s should be included, as chronological age is not a bar to treatment.
- Clinical thresholds vary. For example, in Wales in 1995 the acceptance rate was 109 pmp and in several European countries with complete data acceptance rates were well over 100 pmp.[41]
- The population is ageing; population estimates predict increases between 1994 and 2011 of 15% in the 60–74 age group and 14% in over-75s.[42]

It is difficult to be precise about the level of national need for RRT, but a more realistic figure is probably an acceptance rate in the range 120–130 pmp.

At the PCT level it will depend on the sociodemographic factors determining the incidence of ESRF, the most important being age and ethnic structure. Some PCTs with large ethnic minorities may have rates approaching 200 pmp as these populations age.

A final point is that these rates are based on total populations, i.e. they include childhood ESRF cases and the population aged 0–15 in the denominator. The latter may have a disproportionate effect, as ESRF is rarer in children. Ideally all population rates should be age- (and sex-) standardised.

6 Services available

Services for the prevention, diagnosis and treatment of renal disease are provided in the primary care setting, in district hospitals, in renal satellite units (which may be on hospital sites) and in tertiary referral centres. Treatment for ESRF represents by far the most costly item of care.

Renal disease without renal failure (general nephrology)

Diagnosis and initial management of patients with renal disease is the responsibility of GPs and physicians in district hospitals. It can be argued that most cases should be referred for nephrological opinion so that appropriate investigations and treatment can be undertaken. Such work is primarily outpatient based and relatively high volume. Protocols are required to facilitate appropriate referral from GPs and hospital doctors (e.g. for haematuria; *see* below). In addition to routine hospital services, histopathology, specialist radiology and radioisotope imaging services may be required.

A report from the Renal Association of the UK suggests that around 250 new patients pmp annually will require assessment for renal disease.[17] More work is needed to establish this and the overlap with other specialties managing renal problems (e.g. urology).

Acute renal failure

Patients with significant ARF will usually need to be referred to a specialist for diagnosis and temporary RRT, if required. Renal support is usually required for days or weeks. Patients may develop ARF in hospitals with or without nephrological expertise. Many patients with ARF are seriously ill, often with multi-organ failure, and may need high-dependency or intensive care for respiratory and/or other organ failure, and expert medical and nursing care. Ideally, nephrological opinion should be sought, but in some cases ICU staff may have the necessary expertise to manage ARF.

Little is known on a population basis of patterns or outcomes of care. It is not clear whether there is inequitable access to renal advice and dialysis support for ARF. Expansion of nephrology services in DGHs to allow expansion of RRT programmes should also improve the management of ARF. Nephrological input is also particularly important for centres with cardiothoracic surgery units because ARF is a complication of surgery for vascular disease, congenital heart disease and cardiac transplantation.

Feest *et al.* found that only 36% of patients with ARF were referred for specialist advice.[18] They suggested that a further 14% of patients might have benefited from referral to a renal specialist; this would have resulted in a referral rate of 70 pmp per year. The incidence of patients receiving dialysis was 18 pmp per year. Khan *et al.* found that only 23% of patients in their series were referred for a specialist opinion and that younger or lower-risk patients were more likely to be referred.[19] In this study, 50 patients pmp per year received dialysis for ARF.

These observational studies point to the need to develop guidelines for referral of patients with ARF and to disseminate them to doctors responsible for providing acute care in other specialities and in district hospitals. More evaluation of ARF care is needed.

Chronic renal failure

Chronic renal failure can present insidiously with non-specific symptoms, or be detected in patients with hypertension, diabetes or urinary abnormalities. It can be diagnosed by GPs and hospital doctors by measurement of blood urea and creatinine concentrations, although repeated measurement may be required to establish chronicity in some cases. Early referral to nephrologists is desirable, since treatment of hypertension, diabetes, urinary tract infections and obstruction and dietary modification can reduce the rate of progression of CRF, and measures can be taken to reduce the associated morbidity (e.g. renal bone disease, CVD, malnutrition).[43] The Renal Association recommends referral of all patients with a persistently raised creatinine above 150 μmol/l.[2]

Specific interventions may be of benefit in certain types of GN. A programme of management can also be planned before the patient develops ESRF requiring dialysis. Currently 30–40% of patients present late in ESRF,[44] and a similar percentage require emergency access despite prior nephrological follow-up. Patients referred late have more associated comorbidity and poorer survival. Moreover, initial hospitalisation is prolonged and they are more likely to end up on long-term HD (*see* Section 7).

Further research is needed to define the extent to which late-referred cases could have been referred earlier, and the difference in outcome this would achieve.

Most care of CRF patients can take place in outpatients. There has been a growth in the establishment of joint diabetic–nephrology clinics. This is to be welcomed as a strategy to reduce the incidence of diabetic nephropathy. There are effective evidence-based interventions to reduce the risk of nephropathy, such as the use of angiotensin-converting enzyme (ACE) inhibitors in people with diabetes with hypertension and proteinuria.[45–48] Microalbuminuria testing has been recommended, as it appears to be cost-effective on modelling, but there is no formal testing programme in place.[49] Further research is needed on the cost-effectiveness of such screening.

There are also guidelines for the investigation of haematuria and proteinuria produced by the Scottish SIGN group,[50,51] though the recommendations have not necessarily been widely accepted. This is a complex area with limited long-term prognostic information. Local policies are needed to co-ordinate the respective roles of primary care, urologists and nephrologists in diagnosis and follow-up, especially in cases with microscopic haematuria.

End-stage renal failure

End-stage renal failure is incompatible with life and RRT is required. This can be either by transplant (from live or cadaver donor) or by dialysis using an artificial membrane (HD) or the peritoneum (mainly CAPD, though APD is being increasingly used).

A renal service for patients with ESRF includes main renal unit HD, a CAPD training and support programme, home dialysis (though the numbers are falling as few new cases are started on this), a transplant programme and, increasingly, subsidiary satellite units for HD. These modalities are discussed in more detail in Appendix I. Hospital HD requires considerable infrastructure in terms of space, technology and trained staff. Care is provided by a multi-disciplinary team including social workers, dietitians, pharmacists and dialysis technicians (the staffing is more fully described in the Renal Association report).[17] Renal and transplant wards are needed for undertaking transplantation, for treating related complications and unrelated comorbid illnesses, and for establishing vascular or peritoneal access. Inpatient stays can be protracted in complicated cases. Sufficient expertise in vascular and transplant surgery is crucial, as well as theatre time.

Renal facilities in England and Wales, 1993–95

Data on service provision are available from national reviews undertaken in 1993 and 1995.[4] Further data to 1998 was made available in 2000 – *see* Recommended reading, p. 140.

Key findings are presented in Table 9 overleaf (note that station = space for an HD machine).

The number of renal units in England fell by one between 1993 and 1995, three new units opened and there were mergers in London. The size of existing units grew (*see* Table 9). In England, there were 52% more HD stations, and 8% of stations were designated 'temporary', meaning that due to lack of facilities regular outpatients were attending for HD in wards or other areas not designated for the purpose. This indicates the pressure felt by some units in coping with demand for HD. There were also more HD

Table 9: Renal unit facilities in England in 1993–95 and in Wales in 1995.

	England 1993	England 1995	Wales 1995
Main units			
Main renal units	52	51*	5
total beds	990	1,105	59
unit beds median (range)	19 (0–43)	20 (0–64)	11 (0–38)
total HD stations	932	1,423	97
unit HD stations median (range)	15 (3–55)	23 (7–86)	13 (10–35)
fixed stations	743	832	65
satellite stations	189	472	28
Temporary stations	N/A	119	4
HD shifts/week	694	856	62
unit shifts median (range)	12 (0–31)	18 (8–35)	16 (12–18)
Satellite units			
Current satellites	36	60	3
no. of main units with current satellites (range/unit)	17 (1–6)	30 (1–5)	2 (1–2)
Planned satellites	14	37	5
no. of units with planned satellites	9	28	5
no. of planned satellites where unit has no existing satellites	5	8	1
total patients in satellite units	476	1,476	64
median patients per satellite (range)	15 (1–41)	24 (1–68)	32 (25–39)
total HD stations in satellite unit	189	472	28
median HD stations per satellite (range)	6 (2–10)	7 (2–31)	8 (6–14)

* Facilities data from 50/51 units.

shifts per day. The dialysis service in most main units (51/56) remained under NHS management. Continuous ambulatory peritoneal dialysis training and care were provided in 54 units.

The number of satellite units rose by 60%, with many more planned (*see* Table 9). Thirty-three per cent of all HD stations were in satellites, compared with 20% in 1993. Half of the satellite units were located on DGH sites and 19% were privately managed. Medical support varied, only four had permanent medical staff, and nine had 24-hour emergency medical cover on site. The majority (49/60), including these 13, had regular visits from consultant, staff-grade or clinical assistant nephrologists.

Consultant nephrology staffing in England increased by 22 additional posts between 1993 and 1995 and there was an increase in all grades of non-consultant medical staff. Consultant nephrologist whole-time equivalents (WTE) varied by region from 1.5 to 2.6 pmp, the average being 2.0 pmp for England and 1.9 pmp in Wales.

There was geographical variation in service provision. In 1995, regional rates of HD station varied from 21 to 36 pmp, the English rate being 29 pmp, and in Wales 33 pmp. These compare with 1993, when the variation in the old regional rates was from 5 to 29 stations pmp, with a national rate of 20 pmp.

There was one transplant centre in Wales and 24 in England compared with 29 in 1993. The reduction was largely due to reorganisation in London. There were 0.5 WTE transplant surgeons pmp.

The number of renal units per capita in England (1995 rate of about 2.2 pmp including satellites) is low compared with other Western European countries (*see* Table 10 overleaf).

Table 10: Renal centres known to EDTA-ERA Registry in 1994.

Country	Known centres	Known centres (pmp)
Austria	47	5.9
Belgium	61	6.0
Denmark	14	2.7
Finland	26	5.1
France	271	4.7
Germany	566	7.0
Greece	82	7.9
Ireland	5	1.4
Italy	649	11.3
Luxembourg	5	12.5
Netherlands	52	3.4
Norway	20	4.6
Portugal	67	6.8
Spain	227	5.8
Sweden	64	7.3
Switzerland	46	6.6
UK	84	1.4*

* There is a difference between the estimates of renal centres pmp given in Table 10 and in the main text. The estimate in Table 10 covers the UK, as opposed to England, and the data were provided by the EDTA register, as opposed to national reviews in 1993 and 1995. The latter data source is probably the most reliable.
Source: ref. 41.

Processes of care

The use of better-quality process measures, many recommended by the Renal Association's Standards document,[2] increased during this period, particularly use of bicarbonate HD, thrice-weekly HD and disconnect CAPD systems, although there was wide variation between units (*see* Figure 2 overleaf). Twenty-five per cent of units used synthetic HD membranes. There was lower usage in Wales for each of these measures. The proportion of dialysis patients on HD increased from 43 to 50%, with considerable inter-unit variation (27–100% in 1995).

Characteristics of patients

The age distribution for patients accepted in 1995 is shown in Figure 3 overleaf. The median age of new acceptances in England was 61, compared with 59 in 1991–92, and 41% were over 65 compared with 37% in 1991–92. In Wales the median age was 60, with 40% over 65. In both countries, 13% were over age 75. The male:female ratio was 1.58 in England and 1.55 in Wales, compared with 1.71 in England in 1991–92. The main single cause of ESRF was diabetes (14%), but in 17% the cause was defined as 'unknown' (*see* Table 5). Patterns differed by age, with a greater proportion being unknown in the old; the contribution of RVD in the older individuals should be noted. Renal units varied considerably in their case-mix, as indicated by the age distribution and proportion with diabetic nephropathy.

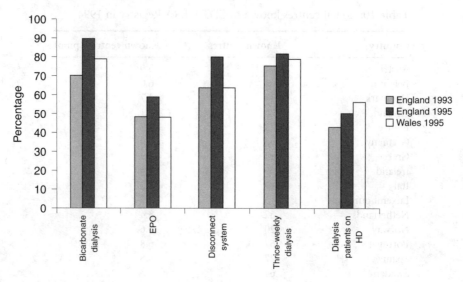

Figure 2: Percentage of patients on selected treatments in England (1993 and 1995) and Wales (1995).

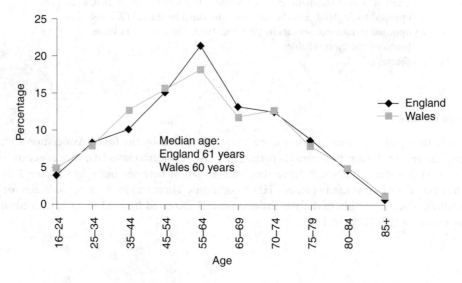

Figure 3: Age distribution for patients accepted on to RRT in England and Wales in 1995.

Constraining factors

Renal unit directors were asked about potential constraints on the development of their dialysis programme. The most common responses were the level of funding, physical space and shortage of trained nurses (76%, 80% and 70% of units, respectively). Only 22% of units found medical staff availability to be a constraint.

What are the current patterns of acceptance rate? Is need being met?

During the 1980s acceptance rates rose from 20 pmp in 1982 to reach 60 pmp by 1990. Unfortunately the completeness of the EDTA resister has fallen in the past decade and it is no longer a reliable source of data on RRT rates in the UK.

This highlights the need for national surveys until the developing UK Renal Register approaches complete coverage.

The annual acceptance rate in England rose from 67 (65–70) pmp ($n = 3247$) in 1991/2 to 82 (80–85) pmp ($n = 4024$) in 1995. Annual increases were 9, 5 and 10%, respectively (*see* Figure 4). The Welsh rate was significantly higher at 109 (98–122) pmp in 1995. Regional acceptance rates in 1995, uncorrected for cross-boundary flows, varied from 64 to 105 pmp. It is clear then that there has been a continued rise in acceptances, largely due to liberalisation of referral to nephrologists rather than changing acceptance policies or rising incidence of ESRF. Nevertheless, this rate in England is below estimates of need. The types of patients being accepted have changed dramatically. In 1982–84 only 11% were over 65 and 8% were diabetic; by 1995 these figures were 41% and 14%, respectively. There is still unmet need which is greater in the old, age- and sex-specific acceptance rates are still lower than the gradients of incidence found by Feest *et al.*[18] Khan *et al.*[19] showed that age and comorbidity were significant determinants not only of survival but also of referral to nephrologists.[52] Significant regional variation in supply and in acceptance rates persists, which is a key issue for the specialist services commissioning groups.

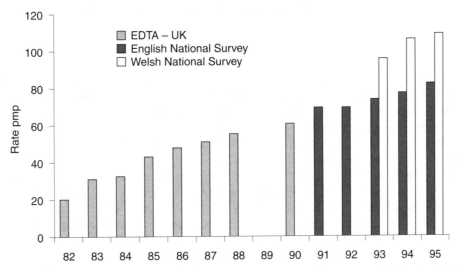

Figure 4: Acceptance rates pmp in the UK in 1982–90, England in 1991–95 and Wales in 1993–95.

Prevalent patients on RRT – 'the stock'

The prevalence of patients in England increased from 396 pmp ($n = 19\,212$) in 1993 to 476 pmp ($n = 23\,115$) in 1995, and it was 487 pmp ($n = 1560$) in Wales. In England, this was largely facilitated by expansion of hospital HD patients and an increase in patients with functioning grafts; PD numbers rose less and home HD declined by 11% (*see* Figure 5 overleaf).

Acceptance for treatment levels of 80 new patients pmp population will lead to much higher levels of patient stock. Eventual 'steady-state' stock levels of 800 patients pmp population have been predicted (*see* Section 8). Even if current acceptance rates remain unchanged, further rises in patient stock are likely

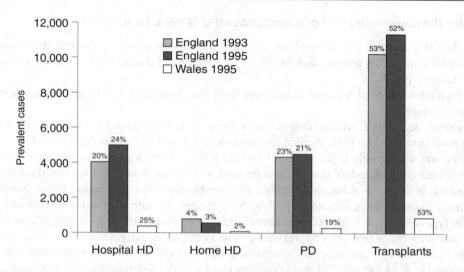

Figure 5: Modalities of treatment for prevalent cases in England (1993, 1995) and Wales (1995).

because the 'steady state' (when the numbers of patients entering and leaving the RRT process balance) has not yet been reached. The UK stock rate is low by European standards and there is considerable inter-regional variation.

Modalities of RRT

UK prevalence rates are increasing. The pattern has been to shift from PD to HD. There are considerable international differences in the use of different modalities of RRT. The UK differs from most European countries in its high proportion of patients on CAPD and transplantation (*see* Table 11). Hospital HD accounted for only 24% of patients treated in 1995 in the UK but for over two-thirds in, for example, Italy and West Germany.[41] The CAPD proportion in the UK is the highest in Europe and the transplant proportion is only exceeded by a few countries, e.g. Norway.

The method of funding health care may be a major reason why there are differences between countries in their use of treatments. In the UK, centres have had to function within a fixed financial budget growth, meaning that expansion in case load could often only be achieved by making more intensive use of existing funds. This has led to its greater use of lower-cost domiciliary treatments such as CAPD, and to transplantation. Renal units were also encouraged to transfer the costs of CAPD fluid to GPs, although this option is not available now. The method of funding services has also contributed to the UK's low geographic dispersion of hospital and specialist services. Availability of skilled staff has also limited the spread of renal units.[4]

It has also been argued that the geographic dispersion of renal units limits the choices regarding the types of treatment offered to individual patients, and means that some have to be assigned to suboptimal treatments. It has been claimed that some patients who should ideally be treated by hospital HD are assigned to CAPD. Distance may make it impossible for patients to travel to centres for hospital HD on a regular basis, hence constraining them to have PD unless there is a satellite unit nearby.

In addition to international differences, there are also differences in the methods of treatment used among the UK units, only part of which can be explained by differences in case-mix between centres. Other factors include past investment decisions, available facilities and resources, and clinical preferences. For example, in England and Wales the proportion of dialysis patients on HD within units varied from 27 to 100%, with a mean of 50%.[4]

Table 11: New patients accepted for RRT in 1994 in a sample of European countries (EDTA-ERA registry).

Country	Haemodialysis		Peritoneal dialysis		Graft		Total*	
	n	pmp	*n*	pmp	*n*	pmp	*n*	pmp
Austria	743	92.8	60	7.5	6	0.7	848	106.0
Belgium	1,128	111.7	100	9.9	106	10.5	1,334	132.1
Denmark	264	50.8	152	29.2	29	5.6	445	85.6
Finland	0	0	11	2.2	0	0	306	60.0
France	3,238	55.8	560	9.6	256	4.4	4,054	69.9
Germany	6,247	76.9	539	6.6	514	6.3	10,170	125.2
Greece	854	82.1	185	17.8	32	3.1	1,071	103.0
Ireland	140	38.9	67	18.6	1	0.3	208	57.8
Italy	3,205	56.0	709	12.4	176	3.0	4,090	71.5
Luxembourg	29	72.5	1	2.5	0	0	30	75.0
Netherlands	895	58.1	369	24.0	23	1.5	1,287	83.6
Norway	218	50.7	40	9.3	44	10.2	302	70.2
Portugal	622	62.8	12	1.2	98	9.9	971	98.1
Spain	2,249	57.4	349	8.9	124	3.2	3,137	80.0
Sweden	618	70.2	341	27.4	35	4.0	894	101.6
Switzerland	456	65.1	117	16.7	12	1.7	585	83.6
UK	1,885	32.3	1,356	23.2	54	0.9	3,295	56.4*

* There are differences between the figures given in Table 11 and those given in the main text. The estimates in Table 11 cover the UK, as opposed to England, and the data were provided by the EDTA Register, as opposed to national reviews. The latter data source is probably the most reliable.
Source: ref. 41.

Survival trends

For all modalities there have been marked improvements in survival in the past decade, particularly after transplantation, despite the increasing proportions of older individuals and 'high-risk' patients.[4] In general, 50% of patients in Europe on RRT are alive after 10 years and 40% after 15 years. 'Standard-risk' patients (i.e. those under 55 years without diabetes or other coincidental diseases) can expect a 94% survival to year 1 and an average life expectancy of 14.3 years thereafter (*see* Table 12).

Table 12: Average life expectancy on RRT by risk group.*

	Standard risk	Medium risk	High risk
All modalities			
1-year survival (%)	94	83	77
Life expectancy at 1 year (years)	14.3	8.6	3.5
Successful transplant	12.7	11.1	Not applicable

* Standard = < 55 years, non-diabetic; medium = < 55 years diabetic, 55–64 years non-diabetic; high = > 65 years diabetic, 55–64 years diabetic.
Source: National Renal Review.

Newer indices have taken into account the presence and severity of comorbidity.[52,53] New survival data will be available from the UK Registry as numbers and follow-up increase,[54] and from an ongoing survey of trends in survival.

The US RDS 1997 report gives life expectancy for patients commencing RRT (actually at day 90) at different ages by age, sex and ethnicity, compared with the general population. Presented below are the figures for US whites, using 1990 national data and 1996 USRDS data.[25]

Years of life expected:

Age group	RRT males	RRT females	General population males	General population females
35–39	12.4	11.9	40.0	45.6
50–54	6.8	6.6	26.5	31.5
65–69	3.4	3.4	15.2	18.9
80–84	2.0	2.0	7.0	8.8

Key findings are that adult RRT patients have only 20–35% of the life expectancy of the general population. The gender difference in the general population is all but lost. Not shown is the improved survival of transplanted patients. In the 1998 UK Registry report, survival databased in four units (458 patients) showed a mortality rate of 21/100 person years; this was considerably greater in those over 65 (39/100 vs. 9.7/100).[54] Current research is under way to determine time trends in mortality on RRT in the UK.

The best patient survival rates are reported following transplantation, but these patients are highly selected. Graft survival is influenced by the type of donor (live vs. cadaveric), the tissue-typing match, the type of immunosuppression and the underlying cause of the renal disease (e.g. patients with diabetes have poorer survival).

The UK Transplant Services Support Authority (UKTSSA) audit evaluated transplantation from 1981 to 1991 in the UK. The following survivals were found (graft survival was taken as survival to death or to loss of the graft).[55]

	Graft	Patient
1 year	78	91
5 year	64	73
10 year	50	50

For regrafts the 1-year graft survival was slightly lower at 71%.

The factors affecting 1-year rates were studied using multivariate analysis. The main factor affecting graft survival was HLA mismatch; donor age > 55, and 'imported' kidneys (i.e. from another unit) (after adjusting for other factors) were also significant. There was evidence of improving graft and patient survival over this period.

Costs of RRT

Renal replacement therapy is expensive relative to other health interventions. Although RRT services consume only around 1% of the NHS budget,[3] these funds are spent on a disproportionately small number of patients. When the predicted rise in RRT stock levels has levelled it has been estimated that RRT services will consume between 2 and 4% of the NHS budget, but patients receiving RRT will only account for 0.08% of the population.[3]

Table 13 includes data from publications that have estimated the annual costs of maintaining a patient on RRT. Where appropriate, the costs in the original papers have been converted to a common price base of 1998 using data on annual pay and price inflation in hospital and community health services. In general, the costs include items directly associated with the treatment modality, such as erythropoietin (EPO) and cyclosporin, and an allowance for the 'knock-on' costs of complications and comorbidities linked to treatment with the various modalities.

Table 13: Annual costs of care by treatment modality.

Source	Annual costs (£) (at 1998 prices)			
	Hospital HD (£)	Home HD (£)	CAPD (£)	Transplant (£): (a) Operation (b) Maintenance
West[56]	25,230	16,790	19,850	(a) 15,270 (b) 4,580
Bolger and Davies[57]	27,550	13,780 (year 1) 11,350 (after)	10,330 (year 1) 9,820 (after)	(a) 17,090 (b) 3,950
Mallick[3]	NA	NA	NA	(a) 14,800 (b) 5,100
Krupa et al.[58]	28,450	18,390	19,250	NA
NHS Executive[1]	31,520	25,530	18,930	(a) 12,550 (b) 5,840
North Thames[59] (patients aged 70 and over)	20,700	NA	15,100	NA
MacLeod et al.[60]	NA	NA	13,900	NA

NA = not available.

The costs derived by Bolger and Davies[57] and by Krupa et al.[58] were based on studies of individual renal units, those derived by the NHS Executive[1] on a study of two units based in large teaching hospitals, and those derived by North Thames on a study of four renal units.[59] The costs of Mallick[3] were based on a survey of all renal units in England. Finally, those quoted by MacLeod et al.[60] were based on a systematic review of the literature.

In addition to the costs given in Table 13, the North Thames study[59] estimated that the annual costs of maintaining an older patient on APD were £24 100.

Mallick[3] argued that in practice it is difficult to separate the costs of the different methods of dialysis. Instead he gave a cost of £26 800 at 1998 prices, this being the average across all dialysis modalities. He also argued that because patients can switch between therapies it is more meaningful to link costs to patients rather than modalities. In his publication, the costs of maintaining a patient on RRT for three years were estimated as ranging from £31 900 to £95 700 (at 1998 prices), for five years from £38 300 to £153 100, and for ten years from £76 500 to £267 900. The wide ranges in costs were linked to the assumed rate at which patients changed modalities and to the assumed rates of occurrence of patient morbidity and complications.

PCTs should only use the above costs as a guide when estimating the costs of care in their local unit. For the estimates in Table 13, there is variation both in the annual costs of modalities and in their relative costliness, although hospital HD is always the most expensive.

Variations in the costs of care in different renal units can be due to variations in the methods that they use to derive costs by modality and in the elements that they cover. In the North Thames study,[59] annual cost estimates covered care provided by GPs, district nurses and social services. These items were only found to account for 2.9% of annual costs.

Assumptions about the use of expensive medications, such as EPO, also affect cost estimates by modality. In the North Thames study, use of EPO accounted for 91% of the costs of medications (mean annual costs per patient, £3100), and 53% of dialysis patients received EPO. Unpublished source material for the Renal Purchasing Guidelines[1] suggests that 70% is a more appropriate value for the percentage of dialysis patients who should receive EPO.

In addition, cost estimates by modality are affected by assumptions relating to the rates of occurrence of treatment complications and comorbidities, with peritonitis being an example of one of the most expensive. The review by MacLeod et al.[60] estimated that an episode of peritonitis costs £2000.

Satellite unit costs are not available in the literature. These will vary as their structure, process and patient case-mix is heterogeneous (see above).

In practice, PCTs and trusts should derive their own estimates of the costs of local renal services. To support them in this task they should refer to the costing templates detailed in the paper by Mallick[3] and in the Renal Purchasing Guidelines.[1] These templates will help them to identify the important elements that should be covered when deriving the costs of local care.

7 Effectiveness of services

The evidence base for renal services should improve as there is now a Cochrane Renal Review Group which is undertaking systematic reviews of the evidence using the Cochrane Collaboration methods. The Group was established in March 1997 and has its base in Lyons, France. A list of ongoing work in 1998 is shown in Appendix II. However, more RCTs are needed in nephrology, and small numbers of patients mean that multi-centre studies are usually required.

Within the UK, the Renal Association has a standing group responsible for the development and implementation of standards of care. The standards recommended are based on existing evidence where possible.[2]

The NHS R&D programme has funded completed reviews in dialysis – namely bicarbonate vs. acetate fluid in HD, disconnect catheters, CAPD vs. HD, frequency of dialysis, type of dialysis membrane and reuse of dialyser.[60]

The Renal Association Clinical Trials Group is co-ordinating multi-centre trials on many aspects of renal disease. Initial trials include CVD prevention using aspirin and simvastatin in CRF and RRT patients, and immunosuppressive treatment of membranous GN. Not all areas of care are amenable to RCT, and evaluating dialysis patients is particularly difficult as dialysis care is a multifaceted intervention with multiple often interdependent effects, especially on pathophysiological measures.

Effectiveness of services for preventing renal disease

A major problem with understanding the aetiology and hence potential for primary and secondary prevention of chronic renal disease is the lack of early markers of renal impairment which can be used in large studies.

The incidence of renal failure could be reduced by the primary and secondary prevention of diabetes and hypertension and their complications, and possibly by better management of reflux nephrology in children and urinary obstruction in older men.

While hypertension and diabetes each contribute to the risk of developing ESRF, they are also important risk factors for the much more common coronary heart disease and stroke. For this reason, national health strategy targets for reducing deaths from coronary heart disease and stroke are also relevant to the prevention of end-stage renal disease (ESRD). This has been recognised in guidelines for the control of hypertension.[61]

More effective diagnosis and treatment of diabetes and hypertension will have some impact in the long term but this is unlikely to be substantial in the short term.

Hypertension (quality of evidence: I)

Hypertension is mainly primary ('essential') but it can also be secondary to both renal and non-renal diseases. There is no doubt that the control of severe and malignant hypertension can prevent the development of end-organ damage, including renal failure. The relationship of mild and moderate hypertension to ESRF is less clear. Observational data from the MRFIT study in the USA suggest that control of hypertension would reduce ESRF.[62] The US National High Blood Pressure Education Working Group concluded that the aim should be for a BP below 140/90 mmHg and this target should be lower for high-risk groups, namely people with diabetes, blacks and those with CRF.[63]

Primary prevention population strategies to reduce hypertension include lower consumption of salt, and reduction in body weight and alcohol intake. Detection and management of hypertension are primarily undertaken by GPs, who require guidelines on the investigation and management of hypertension with input from nephrologists, particularly about the investigation of renal disease in patients with hypertension.

Diabetes mellitus

Type 1 diabetes mellitus (quality of evidence: I)

The Diabetes Control and Complications Trial (DCCT) studied the effect of intensive control of blood glucose in type 1 diabetes on the development of microalbuminuria as a surrogate marker of renal involvement. This study showed that intensive insulin therapy reduced the occurrence of micro-albuminuria (urinary albumin excretion of 40 mg per 24 hours) by 39% (95% CI: 21–52%) and albuminuria (300 mg per 24 hours) by 54% (95% CI: 19–74%). The study provided evidence that intensive insulin treatment can reduce the onset and progression of nephropathy in insulin-dependent diabetes (IDDM).[64]

There is evidence that the rate of progression of diabetic nephropathy in IDDM can be reduced by control of hypertension and that this may lead to reduced mortality.[46] Moreover in short-term studies antihypertensives reduce the progression of microalbuminuria (the precursor stage before actual nephropathy). Reduction of other cardiovascular risk factors is important in improving the survival of people with diabetes.

ACE inhibitors have been shown to be particularly efficacious in the management of hypertension in diabetic patients, and in diabetic patients with proteinuria without hypertension. They appear to reduce proteinuria independently of their effect on BP.[47,48]

It has been argued that screening for microalbuminuria and intensive BP treatment may be used to prevent ESRD in type 1 diabetes.[49]

Type 2 diabetes mellitus (quality of evidence: I)

Prevention of diabetes presents potentially the most productive strategy for the prevention of ESRD from diabetes. Observational studies suggest type 2 diabetes may be preventable by measures to reduce obesity and enhance exercise participation.[65] A large cluster randomised study in China showed that intervention by means of diet and exercise could reduce the progression of impaired glucose tolerance to DM.[66] Another prevention study is currently under way in the USA.[67]

Recently reported results from the United Kingdom Prospective Diabetes Study (UKPDS) analysed the effects of intensive blood glucose control and tight BP control on the occurrence of complications in type 2 diabetes. Over ten years the haemoglobin A1c was 0.9% lower in the intensively treated group and this was associated with a 12% (1–21%) lower risk of diabetes-related events. The study did not have sufficient statistical power to detect a change in the occurrence of renal failure, but at 9 and 12 years the occurrence of microalbuminuria was reduced by approximately one third in the intensively treated group.[68] The effect of tight BP control was to reduce diabetes-related end-points by 24% (8–38%) and deaths related to diabetes by 32% (6–51%). Subjects in the tight BP control group had a 29% (1–49%) reduction in risk of microalbuminuria at 6 years.[69]

Overall, the results of the UKPDS suggest that intensive blood glucose control may reduce diabetic microvascular disease, while hypertension control reduces both microvascular and macrovascular disease.

Treatment of urinary tract infection/reflux nephropathy (quality of evidence: II-2)

Urinary tract infections in childhood secondary to urinary reflux are associated with a risk of permanent renal damage.[70] Although it is not possible, even with optimal management, to prevent renal scars after urinary tract infection in all children, failure to investigate urinary tract infections and arrange appropriate follow-up and prophylactic antibiotics does appear to contribute to avoidable renal damage in some cases.[71] These deficiencies are not confined to general practice but also occur in hospital. There is no evidence on the cost-effectiveness of screening for reflux; this would have to be undertaken in the neonatal period.

Treatment of urinary tract obstruction (quality of evidence: III)

Three to five per cent of ESRF in patients over the age of 65 is due to acquired urinary tract obstruction. End-stage renal failure secondary to urinary tract obstruction is preventable if cases are treated early and the obstruction relieved.[72] A retrospective audit of older male patients presenting with ESRF due to prostatic outflow obstruction identified delays in referral for assessment of renal function in patients with untreated prostatism.[72] The symptoms and clinical size of the prostate did not correlate with the degree of obstruction. Earlier detection of impaired renal function in men with untreated prostatism and closer follow-up of patients with impaired renal function at the time of prostatectomy could avert, in part, progressive nephropathy requiring eventual long-term dialysis.

Other causes of CRF (quality of evidence: variable IV to I)

The scope for the prevention of renal failure secondary to other causes (e.g. GN) requires further study. Some forms, such as rapidly progressive GN, benefit from aggressive immunosuppression; in other forms the balance of risk and benefit is less clear. There is not space to review the evidence for each type of GN, but suffice to say more RCTs are needed.

There are consensus guidelines from the Scottish SIGN group on management of proteinuria and haematuria.[50,51] Neither recommend screening for these abnormalities.

Prevention of ARF (quality of evidence: III)

In cases of ARF acquired in hospital, there is some evidence of avoidable factors in the management of cases that contribute to the incidence of the condition,[73] such as the use of nephrotoxic drugs and the development of post-operative shock. The scope for prevention requires further research.

Effectiveness of services for diagnosing and treating renal disease

Acute renal failure (quality of evidence: III)

Mortality from ARF reflects the severity of the condition and overall is between 50 and 60% at one year.[74,75] It is greater if there is multi-organ failure, especially hepatic failure. The study by Feest *et al.* found that age *per se* was not a prognostic factor, and survival was better for cases secondary to prostatic obstruction.[18] Survival was 34% at two years, similar to Khan's study (30%).[19] In the absence of hospital dialysis, mortality in severe cases would be virtually certain.[74] There has been a progressive though not especially marked improvement in survival after ARF in the past 35 years, despite an increase in the proportion of older patients with complicated medical and surgical conditions.[75]

The prognosis of uncomplicated ARF in young adults has been good ever since the advent of adequate dialysis. Subsequent changes in dialysis technology appear to have made little difference to survival in this group. Improvements in prognosis have occurred in the management of complicated ARF, predominantly in older patients. Recent studies have suggested that dialysis using biocompatible membranes may result in a better outcome. In the main, improvements in prognosis have been brought about not by dialysis alone, which nonetheless remains a prerequisite for recovery, but by attending to the precipitating causes of the episode of ARF and to the related complications. In some cases recovery is not complete, and long-term follow-up may be required; this is especially true in older individuals.[8]

Many patients with ARF will be managed in ICUs and in this clinical setting the APACHE score is of value for prognostic stratification.[76]

Secondary prevention of CRF progression (quality of evidence: I–III)

The main approaches have been control of hypertension and the use of low-protein diets. Systematic review of low-protein diets has demonstrated the beneficial effect in terms of progression of renal disease to ESRF in non-diabetics, and in reducing decline in creatinine clearance in people with diabetes.[77,78] There is debate over the appropriate level and how to ensure patient compliance. The evidence for control of hypertension is less robust, but the Renal Association recommends a target BP of < 140/90 for age < 60 and < 160/90 for those over 60.[2] ACE inhibitors may have a particular role if proteinuria is present.[47]

Renovascular disease (predominantly due to atherosclerotic narrowing of the renal arteries) is an increasingly common cause of ESRF, but the appropriate management of those with CRF and underlying

RVD is uncertain – trials are needed to compare conservative medical treatment with angioplasty and stenting. Guidelines are needed on the appropriate diagnostic and interventional pathways.

Early referral to renal units is recommended by the Renal Association. Despite this, up to 40% of patients requiring dialysis are referred within 4 months of starting RRT.[44] In some cases this is inevitable because of the insidious nature, so that symptoms do not occur until late, and some patients have rapidly progressive forms of renal failure. However, there are patients whose referral is clearly delayed.

The benefits of early referral include establishing an underlying diagnosis (some of which respond to specific treatments), better control of hypertension, judicious use of low-protein diet, reduction in the complications of CRF such as renal bone disease, and elective planning for commencement of dialysis. Detection of obstruction and management of urinary tract infections and attention to fluid balance may also contribute. However, a quantitative estimate of the extent to which the onset of dialysis can be delayed cannot be given, and hence there are few cost-effectiveness data on a more proactive approach to pre-ESRF care.

There is evidence of under-referral by GPs and general physicians to specialist renal services in relation to the population incidence of ESRF, which is associated with insensitivity to a renal diagnosis, or a belief that specialist help would not be appropriate or that resources would not be available to treat the patient.

There is no research focusing specifically on how the diagnosis of renal disease by GPs and general physicians can be improved. It must be recognised that advanced CRF is rare in general practice – the average GP would see only one patient suitable for RRT every six years. The numbers with raised creatinine are more significant. The Southampton incidence study found a rate of 17 new cases in a practice of 10 000 patients. Renal physicians should aim to ensure that GPs and other doctors identify and refer suitable cases in a timely manner.

End-stage renal failure (quality of evidence: II-2)

The aim of RRT is not only to prolong life but also to restore quality by permitting a sufficiently independent existence with minimal support. All modalities of RRT are effective in prolonging life of reasonable quality, even in patient subgroups regarded as 'high risk' (i.e. older patients or patients with diabetes). The quality of life often improves with time after the initial dislocation of starting dialysis and once there is acceptance of the restrictions, e.g. on diet and mobility. Expectations are in general lower in older individuals, and several studies show that they can have a good quality of life on RRT; mental health (SF-36) compares well with the general population of a similar age and gender.[59]

The different modalities do not represent straightforward alternatives in all cases of ESRF since each modality may not be suitable for some individuals, even though the range of indications for each modality has widened. For example, PD may be contraindicated in patients with previous major abdominal surgery or in those unable for physical and mental reasons to cope with undertaking CAPD fluid exchanges themselves. Patient choice is important. For example, PD is more suitable for those patients who desire autonomy (e.g. to carry on working), while HD provides an infrastructure of medical and social support which may be valued in particular by the frail elderly. The 'choice' of modality is then determined by a combination of clinician and patient preference, in turn dependent on patients' social and clinical characteristics and by the availability of the different modes of RRT. Most argue that availability should not limit choice.

Patients may move between modalities, especially between CAPD and transplantation, but also between CAPD and hospital HD, either on a temporary or a permanent basis.

The presence and severity of comorbidity, especially CVD, is the most important predictor of survival.[52,53,59] It is important to adjust for such case-mix differences when comparing unit outcomes.

Cardiovascular disease in CRF and ESRF (quality of evidence: extrapolation of grade I evidence in non-renal patients)

There is substantial evidence that patients with CRF and ESRF are at very high risk of CVD, and it is the major cause of death in both groups. This problem has been highlighted by the National Kidney Foundation Task Force.[79] This is due to enhanced atherosclerotic disease as a consequence of classical risk factors such as hypertension, dyslipidaemia, diabetes, other risk factors for arterial disease (e.g. homocysteinaemia) and other factors leading to cardiac muscle damage (e.g. fluid overload, anaemia, hyperparathyroidism). The Task Force recommended that such patients be considered at very high risk of CVD and that preventive measures be taken accordingly. Most of the evidence for effectiveness has to be extrapolated from studies of CVD in the general population.

Dialysis (quality of evidence: II-2)

Home HD patients are a selected and dwindling group and few patients are now started in this modality. Continuous ambulatory peritoneal dialysis has taken over as the main form of home treatment, though its role is also declining in relative importance. There is still considerable debate about the relative merits and appropriateness of the two main forms of dialysis (hospital HD and CAPD). There have been no RCTs comparing them, and so evidence has been derived from observational studies of large data sets with adjustment for important confounders.[80,81]

Such inter-modality comparisons of survival have to be interpreted with caution because of possible selection effects. Survival rates between modes of dialysis appear very similar, after adjustment for case-mix differences. This suggests that transfer between modalities can be made without undue concern for survival.

Morbidity and quality of life (quality of evidence: II-2)

Successful transplantation is generally regarded as offering the best quality of life of all methods of RRT, although it is not suitable for all types of patient. It reverses the metabolic and haematological effects of renal failure. Quality of life post-transplant has been improved by the use of cyclosporin for immuno-suppression. Newer agents such as mycophenolate have been shown to reduce the acute rejection rate but there is no evidence as yet that they prevent long-term rejection.[82]

The differences between the types of dialysis in morbidity and quality of life are far less clear-cut. In part, the interpretation of inter-modality comparisons depends on whether morbidity, health status, quality of life or social functioning are regarded as most important for judging more or less successful treatment. For example, transplant patients tend to have higher perceived health status than hospital HD patients, despite experiencing more frequent inpatient episodes.

Technique survival (i.e. whether the patient has to change the type of dialysis) is better in most but not all studies with HD,[81] largely because of the problem of recurrent peritonitis with CAPD. This can lead to treatment failure (temporary and permanent) and malnutrition (due to protein loss and appetite suppression). Peritonitis rates have declined with the use of Y-connector systems[60] and newer sterilisation methods. Another problem with CAPD is inadequate dialysis (especially when residual renal function is lost) and evaluating the dialysis dose is more difficult than for HD.[2]

Continuous ambulatory peritoneal dialysis allows more independence than HD and may be beneficial to young people awaiting transplantation. It may also have advantages for people with CVD because of the continuous nature and because there is no need for a fistula. It is unclear whether people with diabetes do better on CAPD. There is no evidence that complication rates of CAPD are greater in the elderly, though some may have difficulty performing it.

There have been innovations in the delivery of hospital HD which enhance its effectiveness, such as monitoring of adequacy and use of bicarbonate dialysate rather than acetate.[60] There is no space here to review the evidence for setting standards for dialysis.[2]

Continued expansion of CAPD is unlikely to be a cost-effective way of increasing acceptance rates. Newer patients are predominantly elderly and more dependent and may do better in the supervised environment of unit HD, not least because of social contact. The main factors affecting the appropriateness of modalities for the elderly are well documented by Nissenson.[83]

Newer methods of APD have been introduced for those with particular clinical (e.g. lower filtration) or psychosocial needs. These are more expensive and their place needs to be evaluated more rigorously. A new development which has not been widely introduced in the UK is the concept of daily home HD. The technology is now available, and patients are reported to have much higher quality of life and less requirement for supportive therapies such as EPO. Its cost-effectiveness and feasibility need to be established.

There is no right solution to the balance of modalities as evidenced by the considerable variation in CAPD:hospital HD ratio worldwide. Most would agree that patients should have a choice of modalities (i.e. they should not be forced to choose CAPD because of a shortage of facilities for HD). The modalities are best viewed as being interchangeable with decisions made on the basis of clinical and social grounds. Whatever the balance of modalities, treatment must be made more accessible to patients to reduce travel times (and costs) and to contribute to improving the equity of service provision.

Erythropoietin

The potential to improve the quality of life of patients on maintenance HD has recently been increased by the availability of recombinant human EPO to combat the anaemia associated with long-term HD.

Erythropoietin increases blood haemoglobin concentration and enhances quality of life for patients on dialysis, in particular reducing fatigue and physical symptoms and improving exercise tolerance. It also removes the risks associated with transfusions. Side-effects include a higher incidence of hypertension and clotting of the vascular access, though these occur less than was first thought. It is generally believed that the patient benefits outweigh the impact of the side-effects on patients, at least in the short term.

According to a European collaborative study of the benefits of EPO in 'transfusion-dependent' (anaemic) ESRF patients, it can improve the quality of patients' lives, according to their own assessments, by between 2 and 5% of a quality-adjusted life year (QALY).[8] There is no evidence to date that EPO increases length of survival.

There is an ongoing systematic review of the use of EPO in ESRF, including route of administration and dosage.

Despite good evidence of effectiveness, the problem is the high cost in an already costly patient group. A fall in EPO prices from one of two drug firms making it would help to ease financial pressures.

Summary

Table 14 overleaf summarises key findings concerning existing evidence about the effectiveness of measures to prevent and treat renal disease.

Cost-effectiveness of preventing CRF/ESRF

There are limited data available. The high costs of RRT services (*see* Table 13) emphasise the importance of measures to prevent the onset of renal disease. A study by Rodby *et al.*[85] indicates that for patients with

Table 14: Summary of levels of evidence of effectiveness.

Intervention	Quality of evidence	Reference
Prevention		
Chronic renal disease		
Hypertension	I	61
Diabetes mellitus, type 1	I	64, 48
Diabetes mellitus, type 2	I	66, 67
Urinary tract infection	II-2	70
Urinary tract obstruction	III	72
Acute renal failure	III	73
Treatment		
Acute renal failure	III	75
Chronic renal failure	I–III	77, 78
End-stage renal failure	II-2	52, 53, 59

diabetic nephropathy, the use of captopril is effective in reducing future spending on RRT services. Studies by Borch-Johnsen et al.[49] and by Kibberd and Jindal[86] also indicate that in type 1 diabetes, screening for microalbuminuria and antihypertensive treatment are cost-effective in reducing future spending on ESRD.

Comparative cost-effectiveness of methods of RRT

Tables 15 (see overleaf) and 16 (see p. 115) summarise the principal studies of the cost-effectiveness of RRT (for further information see MacLeod et al.[60]). The results of the studies presented are not comparable with one another because of different methodologies, base years, currencies, etc. They are presented to give an indication of the general direction of the cost-effectiveness comparisons.

Successful transplantation, especially from a live, related donor, preceded by a period of CAPD, is the most cost-effective means of RRT even when the full range of health service and patient/family and social costs are taken into account.

Economic studies to date show that CAPD is more cost-effective than hospital HD, and since peritonitis rates associated with CAPD have decreased, CAPD is more cost-effective than home HD in most situations. In perhaps the most detailed, recent economic appraisal of dialysis methods in the UK, CAPD emerged as unequivocally the most cost-effective modality, particularly when expansion of RRT was concerned.[87] The investment decision will depend on predictions of the likely patient mix to be treated.

Factors affecting results and interpretation of comparisons

None of the cost-effectiveness comparisons is based on data from RCTs, a fact confirmed by the systematic review conducted by MacLeod et al.[60] This means that selection (case-mix) factors will affect patient outcomes, including factors such as patient rehabilitation and treatment costs, and thereby the results of comparisons.

The magnitude and, on occasion, the direction of cost-effectiveness comparisons are affected by the outcome variable used (life years gained, QALY, etc.), the use of discounting (or not) and the specification of costs (direct treatment costs, social costs, etc.) included in the analysis. All costs should ideally be included regardless of which agency meets the bill.

Table 15: Summary of studies of cost-effectiveness of different methods of RRT.

Study	Currency/year of costs†	Discount rate	Years	LRD Tx*	CAD Tx*	CAPD	Home HD	Hospital HD
Buxton and West‡ (UK)[88]	£/1972	10%	20	–	–	–	2,600	4,720
US General Accounting Office (USA)[89]	$/1981	–	Second	–	–	–	17,767	35,535
Stange and Sumner (USA)[90]	$/1981	5–7%	10	24,900	28,815	–	28,456	44,142
Roberts et al. (USA)[91]	$/1981		Life	12,319	23,839	–	21,212	39,630
Ludbrook (UK)[92]	£			–	–	–	5,150	7,100
Bulgin (Canada)[93]	$			–	–	12,630	–	18,048
Maxwell and Grass, US DHSS (USA)[94]	$/1981		pa	–	–	–	16,706	18,600–23,250
Mancini and Davis§ (UK)[95]	£		First	–	–	9,500–11,400	9,800–9,950	11,200–13,650
	£		Subsequent	–	–	7,550–9,800	7,100–8,700	11,200–13,650
Lameire (Belgium)[96]	£/1984		pa	–	–	11,850	17,260	25,850
Garner and Dardis (USA)[97]								
Low	$/1981	10%	20	22,400	31,148	–	25,177	31,582
High	$/1981	10%	20	16,974	22,578	–	25,381	31,989
Haggar (UK)[98]								
First	£		First	–	–	22,790	30,724	30,403
Subsequent	£		Subsequent	–	–	21,574	18,971	29,029
Smith et al.‡ (UK)[87]	£/1988		pa	–	–	8,196	10,221	14,476–16,291
Sesso et al.‡ (Brazil)[99]								
First	$/1985		First	3,851	7,283	12,578	–	10,981
Second	$/1985		Second	3,022	6,978	12,134	–	10,065
Karlberg and Nyberg (Sweden)[100]	$/1991			–	10,000	30,000	40,000	60,000

* Gross social costs, i.e. excluding output gains due to treatment. LRD Tx = live-related donor transplant; CAD Tx = cadaveric transplant.
† Where different from year of publication.
‡ Net social costs, i.e. including output gains due to treatment.
§ Health service costs only.

Table 16: Cost per QALY: estimates for RRT methods.

Study	Cost per QALY					
	Currency/ year of costs	Discount rate	Transplant	CAPD	Home HD	Hospital HD
Smith *et al.* (1989)* (UK)[87]	£/1988	5%	–	6,731	9,292	15,594–17,549
Hutton *et al.* (1990)† (UK)[101]	£/1988	5%	1,724	–	–	11,071
Maynard (in West, 1991) (UK)[56]	£/1990	5%	4,710	–	17,260	21,970

* Average costs per QALY over 5 years assuming 100% survival.
† Adapted from Gudex.[102] Average annual costs per QALY for a transplant lasting 10 years; hospital HD over 8 years.

The results are also affected by technological change (e.g. the effects of cyclosporin and EPO), which influences survival, complication rates, health service costs, family costs, social costs, quality of life, etc.

- In practice, comparisons between modalities are affected by the efficiency with which each modality of RRT can be used under the specific conditions prevailing locally.
- The practical policy choice concerns the best mix of modalities, since not all patients are suitable for all modes of treatment and optimal therapy for the individual may change over time. Also transplantation is constrained by an absolute shortage of organs.
- More research is required to establish the relative cost-effectiveness of the main methods of RRT in a range of patient subgroups, such as the elderly and people with diabetes. The average cost-effectiveness of RRT methods in the past may not be entirely relevant to the patient mix coming forward for RRT in the future if programmes expand and as populations age. Studies should be on an intention-to-treat basis.

Relative cost-effectiveness of differences in the methods of delivering individual treatment modalities

A recent systematic review of the literature considered the effectiveness and cost-effectiveness of variations in methods of service delivery within treatment modalities.[60] Its conclusions are summarised below.

- *Synthetic vs. cellulose membranes in HD*: synthetic membranes were associated with reduced patient morbidity but higher costs. The authors recommended that cellulose membranes be the preferred option.
- *Bicarbonate- vs. acetate-buffered dialysis*: bicarbonate-buffered dialysis was recommended as it achieved improved patient comorbidity at the same cost as acetate-buffered dialysis.
- *Short-duration (< 3.5 hours) vs. standard-duration (> 3.5 hours) dialysis*: the authors warned against the use of short-duration dialysis based on an assumption that it reduces costs because it may also lead to increases in patient morbidity.

- *Y-set vs. standard spike delivery systems in CAPD*: Y-set systems were found to lead to significant reductions in the incidence of peritonitis. Although they are more expensive than standard systems their use is likely to be cost-effective.
- *CCPD vs. CAPD*: CCPD leads to significant reductions in the incidence of peritonitis but it is more expensive.

Conclusion

RRT is effective in prolonging life and in providing an acceptable quality of life for most patients, including the old. Modality-specific cost-effectiveness analyses are difficult to undertake because patients may undergo two or more modalities in their lifetime on RRT. It is clear that greater resources need to be invested in measures to increase the supply of kidneys for transplantation (*see* Section 9). The appropriate balance between CAPD and hospital HD is a matter for debate, as shown by the variations worldwide and between English Regions. Certainly there will have to be an overall expansion of facilities to cope with the increasing stock.

8 Models of care

This section focuses on the organisation of services for RRT.

The planning of specialist services, of which renal care is one, is changing. Prior to the 1990 NHS reforms, RRT was organised as a regional speciality. Each region decided on the priority accorded to specialist renal services through its budget for regional specialities. Each district's consumption of renal services, particularly RRT, depended on the referral thresholds of GPs and consultants, in turn influenced indirectly by local availability, including the distance to the nearest renal unit. Renal units nominally provided services to a number of districts, but district managers had no say in how this role was performed.

The 1990 NHS reforms placed responsibility on local health authority (HA) purchasers, albeit working together with (in many areas) a 'lead' purchaser taking responsibility for negotiating the contract. The consultation document *The New NHS Commissioning Specialist Services* proposed the establishment of a regional group and area subgroups with representation from each HA.[103] This group had overall responsibility for ensuring an appropriate level and distribution of services in the region.

PCTs are responsible for developing service agreements with providers within the overall regional strategy. They need to know what is their population's need, based on age and ethnic structure, how such need is being met, likely trends in demand and what is the projected growth in the numbers of patients on RRT. They need to know how many of their residents are currently on RRT or have been taken on (i.e. current stock and acceptance rates), by which units, what is the balance of modalities and what is the quality of care (this will be facilitated in future by the UK Renal Registry).

The remainder of this section discusses in greater detail the key tasks and decisions that will be faced by PCT/specialist services commissioning groups.

Estimating future demands for, and costs of, services for RRT

The aim here is to illustrate the ways in which the types of data presented in earlier sections might be synthesised into meaningful information for planning local renal services. The approach focuses on services for RRT.

The issues addressed are:

- the key information that is needed to support local decision making
- the data that will be required to provide this information
- the analytical approaches that can be used to transform these data into useful information.

The discussion draws on previous publications which have either addressed planning issues relating to renal services or developed approaches for projecting future requirements (Davies and Roderick,[104] Krupa et al.,[58] Wight et al.,[105] Davies and Roderick,[106] Bolger and Davies,[57] Forte,[107] Mallick[3]). Some results from these papers are also presented in order to highlight the trends in activity levels and the key variables that affect future demand for RRT services.

Readers are also referred to the *Renal Purchasing Guidelines* produced by the NHS Executive.[1] This document provides further guidance about how to generate information about future activity levels and costs. Since this chapter was written the National Service Framework for Renal Services has also been published (January 2004).

Key information needed to plan and model services for RRT

The main questions surrounding the future provision of RRT services might be summarised as follows.

- How many patients will require RRT services?
- What amount of resources will they require in terms of facilities and both the mix and quantities of modalities?
- What will it cost to provide these resources?
- How will patient numbers and the need for resources and costs evolve over time?

Data needed to generate this information

Staff within PCTs and trusts will need to obtain the following data relating to local services (a regional perspective will also be required to plan the appropriate location of services):

- opening patient stock levels by treatment modality and risk group (at least age)
- the demographic composition of the population to be served and hence an assessment of potential need
- annual patient acceptance rates, preferably by risk category (e.g. age, presence of comorbidities)
- proportionate assignment of new patients to treatment modalities, again preferably linked to risk categories
- annual supply of transplants
- patient survival rates
- mode of dialysis and transplant graft survival rates
- the incidence of key complications and comorbidities
- the unit costs of key elements of the service (e.g. modality costs and the costs of complications such as peritonitis)
- disposition of services in relation to population need – main and satellite, available manpower (medical, nursing, associated specialties).

In practice there may be uncertainty surrounding the values of some of the variables, e.g. future acceptance rates. Here planning assumptions will need to be made and the effects of varying these assumptions tested as part of the analysis. In addition, although average cost data will provide an initial indication of the cost consequences of change, in practice costs do not vary in a linear manner. For example, existing staffing levels may initially be able to meet increases in activity levels. Eventually, extra staff may be needed and there will be a step-change in costs. For more sophisticated analysis, commissioners and providers may want to collect data which allow an analysis of such step-changes.

Methods of analysing the data

Some form of computer modelling package will be needed to analyse the data that are collected. In addition, use of computer modelling will allow 'what if' analysis to be undertaken whereby the impacts of different planning scenarios, assumptions and variables are tested.

Two modelling approaches have been used in the literature: computer simulation (Bolger and Davies[57]) and spreadsheet modelling (Krupa et al.,[58] Wight et al.[105]). A further example of spreadsheet modelling is found in a project undertaken on behalf of the Welsh Office by Paul Forte and Peter Rutherford. They took an existing model, the *balance of care* approach,[107] and adapted it for the planning of renal services.

The two techniques are probably complementary. Supporters of simulation modelling argue that it provides a more realistic and sophisticated technique for estimating long-term trends in activity and costs over time.[104] It is a dynamic technique, which models individuals with specific characteristics, and the effects of resource constraints, such as the supply of transplants, can easily be allowed for. Spreadsheet modelling provides snapshots at points in time and is more relevant to the analysis of short-term needs for resources. The software is probably easier to develop and therefore it may be a more accessible approach for staff in PCTs and trusts.

Whichever approach to modelling is selected, the analysis that will be undertaken can be subdivided into the following components:

- a prediction of patient stock levels year on year, taking account of opening stock levels, acceptance rates and patient survival
- the assignment of patients to treatment packages, taking account of the initial assignment of new patients to treatment modalities and subsequent changes in modality linked to technique survival and complication rates
- a prediction of year-on-year resources required (e.g. stock levels by modality) and the costs of these resources.

Key findings from published research

The following recent publications have projected the future demands for and costs of RRT services: Davies and Roderick[106] and the NHS Executive.[1] These papers provide consistent messages, so their key conclusions are summarised here.

- At current estimated levels of need (80 new patients pmp per annum) there will be a rise in patient stock levels of between 50 and 90% over the next 15 years depending on assumed rates of survival.
- Stock levels will rise by around half this amount even at the average annual acceptance rate in 1991–92 of 65 pmp.
- Predicted steady-state stock levels resulting from differing rates of acceptance are as follows: 65 new patients pmp per annum, steady-state stock around 588 patients pmp; 80 new patients pmp per annum, steady-state stock around 663 patients pmp; 100 new patients pmp per annum, steady-state stock around 769 patients pmp.
- The assumed rates of patient acceptance and survival are the key determinants of future stock levels. A change in the assumed transplant rate has only a small effect on projected stock levels.
- There will be a disproportionate rise in the number of patients using dialysis modalities, reflecting an increase in the proportion of older high-risk patients being accepted on to treatment programmes.

- At steady state around 0.08% of the population will require RRT and they will consume 2% of the NHS budget.
- Future stock and cost levels will vary considerably between districts depending on their socio-demographic characteristics and opening stock.

The above only indicate trends in activity and cost levels and the key variables which affect projections. Specialist services groups/PCTs and providers must generate their own information for planning the development of local renal services. The importance of them addressing this task is emphasised by the projected growth in activity and cost levels.

Planning the supply of services for transplantation

There are two sources of kidneys for transplantation.

- Most kidneys are cadaveric, derived from donors certified as dead while on life support in ICU and who are free of major diseases that would compromise kidney function. Such patients usually have severe head injuries or intracerebral bleeding due to stroke. Death is certified following the application on two separate occasions, normally several hours apart, of standard tests for brainstem functions by clinicians independent of the transplant team.
- A minority come from live donors, traditionally related, but increasingly unrelated (e.g. spouses).

The major problem facing the transplant programme is the shortage of kidneys.

The shortfall of kidneys for transplantation

Figures from the UKTSSA indicated that in 1997 and 1998 there were 2817 cadaver kidneys and 418 live kidneys (13% of total) transplanted in the UK, and there were also 45 kidney and pancreas transplants.[108] Compared to 1995–96 there was an absolute fall of 325 cadaver kidneys, partly offset by an increase of 91 live kidneys. The donor rate was 13.5 pmp in the UK and Eire; this was similar to that in other European countries except Spain (31.5 pmp).

Cadaver kidney donor rates are slowly falling in the UK, consequent on welcome declines in road traffic accidents and cerebral haemorrhage from strokes. Also the wider use of computerised tomography (CT) scanning may have reduced the number of poor-prognosis head injuries that were ventilated on ICU. The gap between the need and supply of kidneys has meant that the transplant waiting list continues to rise, reaching 5702 patients by December 1998.[108]

UKTSSA estimated that the current annual need for kidneys is approximately 2500 in the UK, a rate of 48 kidneys pmp population per year.[109] The Hoffenberg Report argued that the requirement could rise as high as 4000 in the foreseeable future.[110]

As waiting lists for transplantation lengthen, there has been investigation into ways of improving the level of organ procurement. Two main approaches have been suggested.

- Increase cadaveric donation in cases of confirmed brainstem death on ICUs.[111,112] Strategies include reducing relatives' refusal, improving procurement and increasing the pool of donors.
- Make greater use of living donors, particularly by encouraging donations from living, related HLA identical donors and living, unrelated donors.

Barriers to cadaver organ donation from ICUs and elsewhere

It was believed that the demand for organs could be satisfied if an increased proportion of the organs assumed to be available were donated for transplantation. A detailed audit of all deaths in 278 (98%) of the ICUs in England throughout 1989 by Gore identified several principal barriers to organ donation, which affect different stages in the process of obtaining transplantable organs.[112]

1　Brainstem death may not be a possible diagnosis – it was a possible diagnosis in 14% of cases (*c.* 1700 per year).
2　Brainstem death tests may not be performed even though brainstem death is a possible diagnosis – it was not tested in 24% of these cases. In many there were good reasons, but in some, negative attitudes and resource restraints may have contributed. Brainstem death criteria were confirmed in 10% of the total audited cases (*c.* 1200 per year), of which 95% had suitable kidneys for donation.
3　There may be general medical contraindications to organ donation – general medical contra-indications to donation were found in 17% of the cases of criteria-confirmed brainstem deaths in (2) above. Brainstem death, criteria-confirmed, actual donors were achieved in only half the cases in (2) above (i.e. in 5% of the total audited cases, equivalent to *c.* 600 donors per year, a rate of 13.7 heart-beating cadaver solid organ donors pmp). This amounts to a rate of 24 kidneys pmp per year as against an estimated demand of 48 pmp per annum.
4　Brainstem death was confirmed and there were no contraindications in 8% of the audited cases (*c.* 1000 per annum).
5　Ninety-three per cent of families of potential donors were asked about the possibility of donation. Nonetheless, lack of discussion was responsible for the non-retrieval of organs in a number of cases, equivalent to 10% of the actual brainstem donors.
6　Relatives may refuse consent to organ removal – consent for donation was given in 70% of the cases when organ donation had been suggested to relatives.
7　Specific organs may be found to be unsuitable upon investigation, and suitable, offered organs may not be able to be harvested.

With the exception of the level of non-performance of confirmatory tests of brainstem death, there was noticeable regional variation in the frequency with which these obstacles occurred, suggesting that there might be scope for improvements in practice in some ICUs and hospitals. It is important to note that Gore's study did not look at cases taken off ventilation before brainstem death tests.

Possible ways of improving the level of cadaveric organ donation

As a result of the audit described above[112] and other studies,[113] a number of steps which could increase the availability of cadaveric donors have been recently proposed.

- An increase in the number of ICU places which would help to increase the incidence of brainstem death, since the incidence depends in part on the availability of mechanical ventilators and the willingness of staff to refer patients who might become brainstem dead. ICU beds are always scarce in the NHS and are also expensive to support.
- Ensuring that there is adequate funding and staffing of neurosurgical facilities (as these are a major source of donors) and adequately resourced transplant teams.
- Performance of brainstem function tests in all possible patients and if necessary more aggressive cardiovascular support that could contribute to an increase in organ supply.
- Early consultation with the local transplant co-ordinator and/or transplant team which would establish the suitability of organs for transplantation in good time for their eventual use, which

could ensure that irrelevant contraindications are not arrived at in ICUs or on the wards. There is some evidence that transplant teams tend to operate broader criteria of eligibility than ICU staff and others imagine. It has been suggested that clinicians should be obliged to discuss all potential brainstem death patients with the local transplant co-ordinator whether in ICU or elsewhere. A transplant co-ordinator should be available in every region. Such 'required referral' could be audited. Moreover co-ordinators can ensure that the patient is adequately maintained to preserve renal function prior to transplantation.

- Publicity and education programmes which could contribute to increasing the consent level among relatives (70%) still further and thereby increase the proportion of potential donors. Since 1994 there has been a national organ register held at UKTSSA with nearly 5.5 million people registered and indicating their consent.[108] Applications can be made when driving licences, passports or new GP registrations are made. This list is not of sufficient size and there is no evidence that it has maintained donor rates.

- Publicity campaign to increase the acceptability of organ transplantation and hence the donation rate in the South Asian community. These groups have a significant excess of renal disease but there is a particular shortage of kidney donors, compounded by the need for blood group and HLA matching.[114] Strategies to remedy this shortfall include not only increasing the acceptance of organ donation but also ensuring equitable access to ICU and encouraging living donation.

A key component of these approaches is a well-resourced team of transplant co-ordinators. They are responsible for education programmes, co-ordinating the process of transplantation and also providing bereavement support. There are crucial issues to ensure sufficient numbers of staff in each area to fulfil these roles and that they are appropriately trained. The country with the highest donor rate, Spain, is the one which has invested most heavily in procurement co-ordination (with one in each general hospital, often a doctor). While this model may not be suitable for the UK, better links between ICUs and co-ordinators, e.g. by link nurses, represent one positive approach.

Other strategies

- Although the use of previously unventilated patients dying outside ICUs with primary and progressive cerebral disease might contribute substantially to increasing the pool of donors,[115] this process of 'elective ventilation' has been deemed illegal.

- Increased use of asystolic kidney donation (i.e. patients who suffer cardiac arrest). This is limited by the need to remove kidneys within 30 minutes for best results, but this policy has only been successfully implemented in a few centres, e.g. Leicester. Schemes like this are difficult to organise and may not offer a generalisable solution.

- Increase in live donation. UK rates have been low compared with some Scandinavian countries, e.g. Norway, which has a rate of 17 pmp. There is significant variation between units. However, more units are promoting the approach, partly by employing recipient co-ordinators within each renal unit. The results of unrelated transplants (e.g. spouses) are comparable to related. An increase in live donors has meant that kidney supply has been maintained in the face of declining cadaver kidneys.

- Increasing the amount by which the Department of Health reimburses hospitals for each donor to cover the costs of organ retrieval.

'Opt-out policy'

Currently people 'opt in' to organ donation by voluntarily carrying a donor card. Evidence shows that although most people approve of the scheme, only about a quarter carry a card and at the time of consideration the card (and therefore the intentions of the patient) may not be available.

Some countries have introduced 'opt-out' schemes where it is assumed that consent is given unless people actively register to opt out. The impact of this development is unclear and there are obstacles to its introduction in the UK. There is evidence from abroad that because all relatives have to be approached to obtain a medical history for the donor, the system is no longer of particular relevance. It is important that public confidence in the transplant programme is maintained. Any move to a system of presumed consent would have to be carefully debated at national level.

Organisation of transplantation services

Currently, many UK transplant units are small, performing under 50 operations a year.

No. of operations per year	No. of units
> 100*	3
75–99	4
50–74	4
20–49	9
< 20	2

* North and South Thames listed as one centre.
Source: UKTSSA Annual Report 1998.

The London Implementation Group's Review and Purchaser Guidance recommended that all units should undertake about 100 transplants in order to produce economies of scale, concentrate expertise and improve research into transplantation.[116] The Renal Standards document (in conjunction with the British Transplant Society) recommends that units should serve at least a 2 million catchment population, depending on geography, communications and population density, and that they should perform at least 50 transplants per year.[2]

This requires considerable rationalisation of existing small units. The UKTSSA audit found no evidence that transplant survival is associated with unit size, though in other fields of specialist care hospital and physician volume has been shown to influence outcome.

Xenotransplantation

The most appropriate donor is the pig, but this technique is still at an early stage. Although promising in the long term, the current focus is on overcoming early rejection and acute rejection. There are unresolved issues about the safety of such cross-species transplants with regard to transmission of infectious disease.

Equity and effectiveness of transplantation

Kidneys are a scarce resource. It is imperative that they are allocated in a manner that balances effectiveness and equity considerations. Clear policies for putting patients on transplant waiting lists are required. The national allocation system and several regional ones take account of both equity and effectiveness considerations. The proportion of kidneys that are exchanged (i.e. put into the national pool and used outside the donating unit) rather than used locally has been falling with the introduction of some regional waiting lists, as use by these lists counts as local. About a third of cadaver transplants were beneficially HLA matched in 1991–96, hence maximising outcome. This proportion is higher with exchanged kidneys.

The main problem with cadaveric transplantation is chronic rejection. Newer immunosuppressive drugs have shown benefits in reducing acute rejection episodes and graft loss in the first year. Further research is needed to identify successful methods of reducing long-term failure.

Further issues surrounding the organisation and planning of renal services

Funding

With the availability of finite resources, how can one reconcile the need for increased quantity of care, improvements in its quality and greater emphasis on reducing inequity of access? What investment should be made over what time period? Modelling does not predict a steady state for over 15 years so a medium to long-term planning cycle is needed. Moreover there is inbuilt growth in the resources needed even if the acceptance rate were to remain the same, which is very unlikely. If there is an increase in acceptance to meet population need this would add to the resources required. Improvements in quality outlined below also require financial investment. The regional specialist services group and its constituent PCTs will have to grapple with maintaining growth within resource constraints.

Geographical equity of RRT

Existing specialist renal services and personnel are still concentrated, by European standards, in a relatively small number of centres in each region. This leads to continual disparities in accessibility and utilisation. Are there population groups who are distant from existing services? What are their acceptance rates? What practical scope is there for altering the volume, location or balance of services used?

To some extent this pattern is being superseded by the provision of more local renal services – for example, by investing in additional autonomous consultant-led DGH renal units or satellite units. This has reduced the travel costs of patients on hospital HD and in training for other modalities. This could be an important consideration for PCTs if they have to fund the full costs of RRT for their residents, including travel to the main renal unit. Savings on NHS-funded patient travel could be invested in the new renal unit under this option.

Evidence from other countries in Europe and from areas of England and Wales where satellite renal units have been built indicates that the more renal units there are, whatever their precise role, the higher the referral and acceptance rates and the prevalence of patients on RRT in the areas concerned. If units have full- or part-time nephrologists, the effect of decentralisation is likely to be magnified as the local specialists diagnose increasing numbers of cases suitable for RRT. Specialists generally have broader inclusion criteria than GPs or general physicians for RRT. The nephrologists will also act as a focus for local charitable effort and will lobby for a continuing expansion of RRT. PCTs will therefore have to be prepared to face the consequences of encouraging strategies of decentralisation.

Reducing need

What preventive activity is ongoing which might reduce the need for RRT by reducing the incidence of ESRF or delaying progression of CRF? Foremost would be integration of renal services with diabetes care (e.g. joint diabetologist–nephrologist clinics), and policies as part of CVD prevention to identify and manage hypertension. The scope for earlier referral to nephrologists locally needs to be explored.

Appropriateness of care

Stanton describes and analyses policy development in RRT provision in the UK over the last four decades,[117] showing how explicit rationing was replaced by covert rationing by under-referral and how little impact the emerging health economic evidence had on policy.

Given the considerable expansion predicted and high cost of RRT, can explicit criteria be set to ensure the appropriateness of RRT? This is a contentious issue.

There are a few severe comorbidities for which there would be general agreement among nephrologists and physicians that RRT could be withheld (e.g. severe dementia, terminal malignancy).[4] Wiltshire HA prioritised RRT to those most likely to benefit from treatment based on the following criteria: potential life years gained should be over one year; there should be an absence of severe co-morbidity; and the patient should be capable of independent living. All of these criteria are open to debate (e.g. What is independent living? Should we exclude RRT from those who are partially dependent? Can we always predict who will survive one year?).[118] It may be difficult therefore to be explicit, and the decision to treat an individual patient should be left to the clinician, in conjunction with the patient and their family.

A recent study has shown that although it is possible to identify a high-risk group of patients with poor survival on RRT (under 20% at one year), excluding them would only save about 3% of RRT costs and it would deny dialysis to several long-term survivors, i.e. any prognostic index will have false positives and negatives.[53] Many would also argue that the modality of treatment in relation to patient characteristics should not be specified either, but should depend on clinical and social needs. The Renal Association Standards document recommends that decisions on dialysis commencement or withdrawal should be made jointly by the patient and the consultant nephrologist, in consultation with relatives, other members of the renal team and the patient's GP.[2]

A consequence of relatively unrestricted access to dialysis is dealing with the consequences. Withdrawal from RRT is likely to be an increasing feature of RRT programmes, with associated terminal care needs for patients and carers and for staff. Better prospective information on this issue is required.

Further work is required to determine if there are explicit criteria that are acceptable to the public, professionals and PCTs, and to identify prognostic factors that severely limit survival and quality of life on RRT.

Cost-effectiveness

The evidence on relative cost-effectiveness of modalities and the characteristics of the existing stock of patients on RRT, together with the likely sorts of patients who would enter the RRT programme if acceptance rates were to increase, indicate the purchase of a combination of transplantation (within the constraints of organ supply) and a balanced programme of CAPD and HD. As argued above, hospital HD may be the most appropriate option for many of the older individuals who are being accepted, and the predominance of CAPD as the main form of dialysis may have to be reduced, although CAPD is particularly attractive if the objective is to expand the RRT programme over a relatively short space of time, as no major capital investment is required. The scope for improvement in organ harvesting for transplantation appears modest at present, unless it can be given greater priority (and funding) by provider units, and additional strategies for organ procurement are developed. Policies to improve live donation should be encouraged.

Better evidence of the relative cost-effectiveness of hospital HD, CAPD and APD is needed, ideally by randomised methods, as observational studies are problematic because of selection factors in the use of the these modalities. The feasibility of such a trial needs to be established, including overcoming patient and clinician preferences.

It has to be accepted that the proportion of patients who are elderly and/or with comorbidity will increase, reducing the marginal cost-effectiveness. The manpower constraints on RRT expansion need to be considered, e.g. in skilled nurses, transplant surgeons, specialist dietitians. There will be additional knock-on effects on other services, such as vascular surgery, cardiology and community services.

Service changes that inflate costs need to be justified by their impact on the quality of care. Here evidence about the relative cost-effectiveness of different treatment modalities and alternative ways of providing care within individual modalities needs to be consulted.

Where possible, measures which reduce cost per case while maintaining standards of care should be pursued. Possibilities include changes in the skill mix of staff, though further research is needed to identify an appropriate balance in relation to different types of patient case-mix.

Transplantation

The Department of Health's *Renal Purchasing Guidance* recommended rationalisation of transplantation to fewer centres, which would have an academic role, and with the surgical, immunological and medical expertise undertaking sufficient volume of transplantation (though there is no direct evidence for a volume–outcome relationship).[1] Regional specialist services groups will need to review the disposition of renal transplantation.

What contribution can or should the local acute services commissioned by PCTs be expected to make to increasing the number of transplantable kidneys available to district residents and to the UK Transplant Service? Key issues are the role of transplant co-ordinators in co-ordinating a programme of education (public and professional), and liaison with ICUs to facilitate organ donation and harvesting. An increased investment in recipient co-ordinators to promote live donation must be considered.

Service agreements

What form should these take? Given that ESRF is a relatively rare condition with an annual need of only 120–130 pmp or so on average, there are only likely to be about 60 new occurrences of ESRF requiring RRT in a district of 500 000 in any year. The eventual steady-state pool of patients on RRT, although hard to predict exactly, is likely to be well over ten times this.

The majority of the renal budget in any one year will be spent on the opening stock of patients, with fluctuations around this value being due to deaths and the take-on of incident cases. Given this, an appropriate agreement might be a mixture of a basic block budget for the majority of expenditure with appropriate adjustments being made on a cost-per-case basis.

PCT organisation

In order to plan the appropriate disposition of services there is a clear role for regional specialist services groups and their subgroups to co-ordinate activity at PCT and provider level.

In Scotland, the concept of 'managed clinical networks' has been proposed as a way of integrating service provision at primary, secondary and tertiary levels.[119] This requires further consideration.

What is the role of the private sector?

Private operators have demonstrated in England and Wales that they can provide supplementary in-centre HD capacity for the NHS in small subsidiary units flexibly and quickly, as long as specialist clinical support is available from a main NHS renal unit, although there is no evidence that the private HD units are cheaper or more cost-effective than their nearest NHS counterparts. PCTs will have to decide whether to invite private operators to compete for service contracts with NHS main renal units. Private operators are keen to offer centre HD and CAPD support services to NHS purchasers. They offer a possible means of either rapidly expanding RRT or, within the existing resources, altering the balance and location of RRT. Two potential drawbacks are pressures to reduce costs which compromise quality and the necessity in some cases of using a fixed range of products supplied by the private organisation. It is essential therefore that a quality assurance framework is in place to maintain and enhance standards in both public and private sector units.

9 Monitoring and evaluation of renal services

It is imperative that there is good information on the cost-effectiveness and equity of care for these complex and costly services.[120] For RRT this will now be greatly facilitated by the UK Renal Registry. UKTSSA provides valid transplant data. There is a dearth of information on ARF.

Two national initiatives are relevant here. The establishment of the National Institute for Clinical Excellence (NICE) should ensure that there is readily available information on cost-effectiveness of treatments and should disseminate evidence-based guidelines. Standards of care may be performance managed by the Commission for Health Improvement (CHI).

Prevention of renal failure

A reduction in the number of patients developing ESRF with diabetes has been suggested as an outcome measure for diabetic services.[67] The necessary data are currently not routinely available, but should become available in the future. Similar measures could be applied to essential hypertension. Any strategy to reduce CVD should incorporate this.

Acute renal failure

The case fatality from ARF could be monitored and rates interpreted in the light of patient age, disease aetiology and other severity measures, and treatment provided. Further work is needed to develop guidelines on definitions, preventable causes and appropriate management and methods of information collection. More information is required on patterns of care and outcomes.

End-stage renal failure

The effectiveness of RRT in ESRF can be assessed in terms of survival, complications (e.g. renal bone disease (rare), peritonitis, hospitalisations, symptoms, and biochemical/haematological measures such as haemoglobin and calcium level), subjective health status, quality of life, patient satisfaction and the impact on family and carers. Ad hoc studies can be added, e.g. on quality of life.

Traditionally data on patients accepted on to RRT were collected by the European Dialysis and Transplant Association (EDTA) and annual reports produced. In recent years, the completeness of the EDTA Register has fallen in the UK for a variety of reasons, including use of paper data and the lack of feedback to participating centres. To address this, a national UK Renal Registry has been established under the auspices of the Renal Association with support from the British Transplant Society, the Association of Paediatric Nephrologists and the Department of Health. The main aim is to provide UK data on the quantity and quality of RRT services by collating and analysing data on the structure of services, patient characteristics and processes and outcomes of RRT. The Register provides important information for renal units to allow comparative clinical audit, national data to feed into EDTA, and information to PCTs and DH on the development of RRT services, including the equity and effectiveness of care. Its functions are listed below. It is computer based and has extensive validity checks built in. Eventually it is hoped that there will be complete coverage of England, Wales and Northern Ireland. There is already a Scottish Register; data will be pooled to give a UK-wide perspective.

The functions of the UK Renal Registry are:

- to collect demographic and descriptive data for comparison of the equity of care and for planning of service development
- to facilitate comparative audit by means of a carefully defined data set to audit effectiveness of care against recommended national standards and to identify good practice
- to produce national and local data on outcomes with regard to case-mix
- to be a resource for research studies.

In time the Registry will expand to monitor pre-ESRF care.

The first substantive report of the Registry was produced in September 1998, which included data from nine units.[54]

The following are important measures that can be considered. An important caveat is that RRT is rare at district level, relatively small numbers of patients are treated, and random variation in incidence and variations in case-mix have to be taken into account in interpreting local measures.

Population-based rates

PCT, regional and national acceptance and stock rates are required. These must be age- and sex-standardised for comparative purposes. These rates must be compared to estimates of local need taking account of the age, sex, ethnic and deprivation profile of the population. Such data will provide information on the equity of care by 'place' and by 'person' and time trends.

Districts with low acceptance rates should examine the effectiveness of services used for detection and referral of cases and the accessibility of RRT to their residents.

The stock of patients and its breakdown by modality and risk group should be monitored. The balance between CAPD and HD could be a marker of the degree of choice for patients. The growth of care in renal satellite units should be monitored.

The national and regional retrieval and transplant rates are collected by UKTSSA. It is important that targets are not set by PCTs for a specified number of transplants on their patients, as this would be inequitable and ineffective.

Survival

The survival of patients on RRT will be analysed by the Registry, and for transplant patients it is already being monitored by UKTSSA. It is debatable whether this should be analysed at PCT level as there are problems of small numbers, multiple providers and need for case-mix adjustment for valid comparison. Comparisons of renal units have the same problems, but participation of units in national audit would be beneficial. Case-mix adjustment for key prognostic factors such as comorbidity is crucial (*see* above). This must be collected in a complete and standardised format.

Survival analyses are important in providing prognostic data and for monitoring improvements in care. They include survival curves, one-, three- and five-year outcomes, annual mortality rates and life expectancy. More complex analyses can be undertaken to determine the factors influencing survival, particularly treatment input and processes (e.g. adequacy of dialysis).

Quality of dialysis and transplantation

Evaluation of renal services should be expanded to evaluate the quality of dialysis. The morbidity and quality of life of dialysis patients are dependent on the safety and effectiveness of the procedure. Dialysis is in general a safe procedure, long-term survival is improving and a reasonable standard of life is available for most patients. As the proportion of patients being started who are elderly with comorbidity rises, it is incumbent on renal services to evaluate the balance between quality of care and survival.

Chronic problems have been revealed, e.g. dialysis arthropathy, which arises because of the accumulation of a substance that is poorly removed by conventional dialysers. More expensive, high-permeability dialysis postpones the complication. Moreover, the US experience in the 1980s of rising mortality of dialysis patients has been salutary. This has been attributed to the inadequacy of dialysis, in turn brought on by pressure to reduce the time on dialysis and hence costs.

The essential parameters which determine morbidity must be determined and standards set where possible.

The Renal Association, in conjunction with the Intensive Care Society and the British Transplant Society, produced its second report on standards in renal disease in 1998.[2] Standards are evidence based wherever possible and include not only RRT care but also smaller sections on ARF and CRF and general nephrology.

The report will be continually updated to take account of new evidence, particularly that arising from systematic reviews (e.g. those being undertaken by the Cochrane Renal Group) and large trials.

The key areas for evaluation are listed below. For more detail on the rationale, readers should consult the report.

Renal units will be striving to monitor their own performance against these benchmark standards and clearly the Registry will provide an invaluable method for assembling and disseminating relevant data. Improvements in quality will require additional investment and, although they may be cost-effective, few are likely to be cost saving.

Items for comparative audit in RRT include the following:

- demographic data on dialysis patients
- techniques used (e.g. bicarbonate vs. acetate)
- correction of anaemia
- dialysis adequacy and nutrition
- BP control
- phosphate control
- CVD risk factors
- biochemical profiles
- transmissible disease
- hospitalisation
- water quality
- access for dialysis
- outcomes, including peritonitis rates for PD.

Items for transplantation include the following:

- pre-transplant, e.g. number of transplants, donors, waiting list, matching
- first year post-transplant, e.g. post-operative problems, hospitalisation, acute rejection, patient survival, graft survival
- long-term, e.g. survival and cause of death, graft failure, neoplasia, cardiovascular events, BP and creatinine.

Items for ARF include the following:

- demographics
- causes
- techniques used
- severity
- outcomes.

10 Research priorities

Ideally, PCTs require considerably more information than is generally available for most health services. This section sets out the main areas where better data and improved understanding could ensure an optimal pattern of renal services. In general, the research evidence is far better developed for ESRF than any other aspect of renal disease.

The National Health Technology Assessment Programme is an obvious way of identifying and funding renal research priorities. Systematic reviews have already been completed on several aspects of dialysis, and evaluation of renal satellite units is ongoing. An appropriate method of identifying priorities is to take the research recommendations from the systematic reviews that are likely to be forthcoming in the next few years (*see* Appendix II). The Cochrane Renal Group has mapped out the available evidence to identify areas where there are sufficient trials to warrant a review (*see* www.cochrane-renal.org).

The following is a selection of areas where further research could be undertaken.

Epidemiology

In general, there is considerable scope to improve knowledge of the epidemiology of renal diseases. Limited data are available on the incidence of CRF, but further work is needed, particularly to assess the incidence, aetiology and access to treatment of CRF and ESRF among ethnic minorities in the UK. Estimates of the age-specific incidence of ESRF are derived from studies with relatively small numbers of cases and should be improved by performing larger studies. Epidemiological studies to determine the risk factors for renal disease are needed. This requires development of early markers of renal disease that can be used in population studies. Similarly, there is a lack of information on the incidence and determinants of ARF.

Prevention

There is very little literature on the primary prevention of renal disease. Research should be undertaken to determine the scope for primary prevention of acute and chronic renal failure and the steps required to bring this about – for example, the identification of hypertension, the treatment of diabetes and urinary tract problems, and the effective management of ARF. This should include research on screening for urinary abnormalities (e.g. microalbuminuria in diabetes, haematuria, proteinuria) and could involve modelling techniques. The results of the DCC trial and the UKPDS clearly have relevance to the prevention of renal disease in people with diabetes. The Diabetes Prevention Program due to report after 2002 should provide clearer evidence on the feasibility of preventing diabetes, especially in minority groups.[67]

Future research is needed on the determinants of progression and mortality, and secondary prevention of renal disease. Given the high prevalence of CVD in renal disease, studies are needed of the risk factors for CVD in renal patients and secondary CVD prevention trials in such patients. Further trials are needed to identify best treatments of various forms of GN. The most effective management of RVD is uncertain – trials are needed that compare interventional and conservative approaches.

The development of ARF can be considered potentially avoidable in certain cases. All cases should be subject to retrospective evaluation through a system of clinical audit. Evaluation of the scope for reducing late referral in ESRF should be undertaken. Research is also needed to assess the impact of late referral on outcome. Finally, greater efforts are needed to educate GPs and physicians about the management of renal disease.

Diagnosis of CRF/access to care

Research is required to obtain a better understanding of the reasons for variations in diagnosis and referral rates for specialist services, particularly for CRF. Research specifically focusing on how the diagnosis of renal disease by GPs and general physicians can be improved is also required. Finally, renal physicians should aim to ensure that GPs and other doctors identify and refer suitable cases in a timely manner.

Treatment

The workload and costs of treating ARF are not currently known in the NHS. Data should be collected to allow districts to estimate these.

Research is needed to provide better evidence of the relative effectiveness and cost-effectiveness of hospital HD, CAPD and APD. Ideally, this evidence should be generated by RCTs, although this is complicated by the requirement in most instances for multi-centre studies to achieve adequate numbers. Observational studies are problematic because of selection factors in the use of these modalities.

Published comparisons of the relative effectiveness and cost-effectiveness of the different modalities of RRT are all influenced to some degree by the selective recruitment of patients on to the different modalities. Comparisons should control for characteristics such as age, cause of renal disease, co-morbidities, social circumstances, length of time on RRT, etc.

This programme of research should also establish the relative effectiveness and cost-effectiveness of the available modalities (a) in all the principal patient subgroups presenting for RRT (e.g. older individuals, people with diabetes, etc.) and (b) in a range of configurations of services. It is particularly pertinent to assess the relative cost-effectiveness of methods of RRT for those types of patient most likely to be coming forward for RRT in the near future if RRT programmes expand and as populations age. Such research must incorporate the inter-dependence of different modalities.

Research is also required into the determinants of morbidity and mortality and quality of life of patients on RRT, and the relationship with the adequacy of dialysis and other dialysis processes. The impact of early initiation of dialysis also needs to be assessed.

The main problem with cadaveric transplantation is chronic rejection. Newer immunosuppressive drugs have shown benefits in reducing acute rejection episodes and graft loss in the first year. Further research is needed to identify successful methods of reducing long-term failure.

Further comparative research should be encouraged to assess the consequences (e.g. in terms of improved accessibility) and cost-effectiveness of alternative policies and organisational solutions to the provision of RRT (e.g. decentralised patterns of service, including the use of satellite renal units fulfilling a variety of possible functions). The role of satellite units in providing more accessible care for elderly RRT patients needs to be established.

Where possible, measures which reduce cost per case while maintaining standards of care should be pursued. Possibilities include changes in the skill mix of staff, though further research is needed to identify an appropriate balance in relation to different types of patient case-mix.

Cessation of treatment

A consequence of relatively unrestricted access to dialysis is dealing with the consequences. Withdrawal from RRT is likely to be an increasing feature of RRT programmes, with associated terminal care needs for patients and carers and for staff. Better prospective information on this issue is required. Further work is required to determine if there are explicit criteria for the cessation of treatment that are acceptable to the public, professionals and PCTs, and to identify prognostic factors that severely limit survival and quality of life on RRT.

Models of care

Further modelling is needed to investigate the effects of a higher target acceptance rate (including the impact of demographic change in ethnic minorities), and the balance of dialysis modalities under different assumptions about future case-mix and availability of dialysis facilities.

Appendix I: Types of renal replacement treatment

Dialysis

Haemodialysis

Haemodialysis is effective in a wide range of settings. It can be based in hospitals (as an inpatient for acute problems and for establishing dialysis), as an outpatient, in a free-standing unit or at home (HD) for maintenance dialysis.

Hospital outpatient dialysis is the main form. One machine can support up to nine patients. Patients have to travel. The frail elderly and patients with CVD can tolerate it if the quality of dialysis is high. It provides social support and medical supervision.

Home dialysis is for patients who can adapt their home and can manage self-treatment (with carers) and who will be on dialysis long term. It allows independence. Back-up nursing and technical support are needed and training is essential. One machine is needed per person. It has been largely replaced by CAPD.

Continuous ambulatory peritoneal dialysis

As it is continuous there are fewer fluctuations in fluids and electrolytes compared with HD, and it may be more suitable for patients with cardiovascular problems.

The main drawback is the risk of peritoneal infection; if this is recurrent despite changes in catheters, a switch to HD is needed. There is a high demand for consumables and nurse support, and it is time-consuming. It allows greater independence than outpatient HD and is suitable for patients who live some distance from a renal unit.

Automated peritoneal dialysis

This is being increasingly used in subgroups of patients with specific clinical/psychosocial indications. PD is driven by a machine; one approach allows intermittent PD at night.

The technique is more expensive than standard methods of PD.

Transplantation

Cadaver

Success depends largely on the degree of HLA tissue-type matching. There is a shortage of donors and hence a waiting list. If successful, it is the most effective option as it reverses all side-effects of ESRF, although patients need to take powerful immunosuppressants to prevent graft rejection.

Live, related donor

If well matched there is a high success rate. It is not as widely performed.

Indications for assigning patients to appropriate RRT modalities

The modalities have tended to be used in the following individual circumstances in the UK, although the inter-dependence of the modalities must be recognised and the evidence base for some is not clear.

Transplantation:

- age under 55–60 years
- availability of a suitable donor organ.

CAPD:

- disciplined, motivated and alert patients
- remoteness from a hospital centre
- patients with cardiovascular problems.

Hospital HD:

- multi-system disease
- previous persistent peritonitis with CAPD
- patient poorly motivated or lacking alertness
- old, infirm
- repeated transplant failure.

Home HD:

- likelihood of long wait for a transplant
- reasonable home conditions
- co-operation of another household member
- a good level of patient training
- remoteness from a hospital centre.

Appendix II: Systematic review programme of the Cochrane Renal Collaboration 1998

Completed reviews

- Cytomegalovirus prophylaxis with antiviral agents in solid organ transplantation
- Comparison of cellulose, modified cellulose and synthetic membranes in the haemodialysis of patients with end-stage renal disease
- Systematic review comparing continuous cyclic peritoneal dialysis (CCPD) with continuous ambulatory peritoneal dialysis (CAPD) as treatment for patients with end-stage renal disease (ESRD)
- A systematic review comparing short-duration with standard-duration dialysis treatments in haemodialysis as treatment for patients with end-stage renal disease (ESRD)
- A systematic review comparing bicarbonate-buffered dialysate with acetate-buffered dialysate in haemodialysis of patients with end-stage renal disease (ESRD)
- Comparison of CAPD delivery systems: Y-set/modified Y-set vs. standard spike

Protocols

- Prophylactic treatments for recurrent urinary infections in women
- Effects of levocarnitine supplement in chronic renal failure patients
- Corticosteroid, cyclophosphamide and cyclosporin treatment of adult-onset minimal change nephropathy
- Effects of low-protein diet in delaying the onset of end-stage renal disease in non-diabetic adults with chronic renal failure

Titles

- Comparison of haemodialysis with continuous ambulatory peritoneal dialysis
- The use of human recombinant erythropoietin in pre-dialysis chronic renal failure patients
- A comparison of subcutaneous with intravenous erythropoietin in the treatment of anaemia in patients with end-stage renal disease maintained on dialysis
- The effects of corticosteroids in acute drug-induced interstitial nephritis
- Long-term antibiotics vs. surgery for vesico-ureteric reflux in children
- Double or triple immunosuppressive therapy in renal transplantation: patient and graft survival
- Long-term antibiotic administration to prevent recurrent urinary tract infection in children
- Treatment of idiopathic membranous nephropathy
- Early steroid therapy in the prevention of anaphylactoid purpura nephropathy in children
- A comparison of different corticosteroid regimens for children with nephrotic syndrome
- Multiple risk factor interventions and primary prevention of renal disease
- Is stent insertion more effective than angioplasty or conservative medical management in renal artery stenosis?
- Renal function in clinical trials of antihypertensive drug treatment
- Calcium-channel blockers for prevention of cyclosporin A nephrotoxicity
- Correction of metabolic acidosis in pre-end-stage renal failure
- Efficacy and safety of cyclosporin in inducing remission of childhood idiopathic nephrotic syndrome
- Comparison of the renal effects of angiotensin-II antagonists and ACE inhibitors
- The effectiveness of cranberry juice in the prevention and treatment of urinary tract infections in adults
- Short vs. conventional duration of therapy for acute urinary tract infection in childhood

References

1 Department of Health. *Renal Purchasing Guidelines*. London: NHS Executive, 1996.

2 Renal Association. *Treatment of Adults and Children with Renal Failure. Standards and audit measures* (3e). London: Royal College of Physicians, 2002.

3 Mallick NP. The costs of renal services in Britain. *Nephrol Dial Transplant* 1997; **12** (Suppl. 1): 25–8.

4 Roderick PJ, Ferris G, Feest TG. The provision of renal replacement therapy for adults in England and Wales: recent trends and future directions. *Q J Med* 1998; **7**: 90–7.

5 Parry RG, Crowe A, Stevens JM, Mason JC, Roderick PJ. Referral of elderly patients with severe renal failure: questionnaire survey of physicians. *BMJ* 1996; **313**: 466.

6 Roderick P, Clements S, Stone N, Martin D, Diamond I. What determines geographical variation in rates of acceptances on to renal replacement therapy in England? *J Health Serv Res Policy* 1999: **4**: 139–46.

7 Boyle OJ, Kudlac H, Williams AJ. Geographical variation in the referral of patients with chronic end-stage renal failure for renal replacement therapy. *Q J Med* 1996; **89**: 151–7.

8 Bhandari S, Turney JH. Survivors of acute renal failure who do not recover renal function. *Q J Med* 1996; **89**: 415–21.

9 World Health Organization. *International Classification of Diseases*, 9th revision. Vol 1. London: HMSO, 1977.

10 World Health Organization. *International Classification of Diseases*, 10th revision. London: The Stationery Office, 1997.

11 Office of Population Censuses and Surveys. *Tabular List of the Classification of Surgical Operations and Procedures*, 4th revision: consolidated version. London: HMSO, 1990.

12 Weatherall DJ, Ledingham JGG, Warrell DA. *Oxford Textbook of Medicine* (3e). Oxford: Oxford University Press, 1996.

13 Cameron JS *et al*. *Oxford Textbook of Clinical Nephrology*. Oxford: Oxford University Press, 1992.

14 Roderick P, Webster P. Renal disease. In: Charlton J, Murphy M (eds). *The Health in Adult Britain: 1841–1994*. London: The Stationery Office, 1997.

15 Challah S, Wing AJ. The epidemiology of genito-urinary disease. In: Holland WW, Detels R, Knox G (eds). *Oxford Textbook of Public Health. Vol 4*. Oxford: Oxford University Press, 1985.

16 Hoy W, Watkins M. Renal disease epidemiology: an underdeveloped discipline. *Am J Kidney Dis* 1988; **12**: 454–7.

17 Working Group of the Renal Association Subcommittee on Provision of Treatment for Chronic Renal Failure. *Provision of Services for Adult Patients with Renal Disease in the United Kingdom*. London: Royal College of Physicians of London and the Renal Association, 1992.

18 Feest TG, Round A, Hamad S. Incidence of severe acute renal failure in adults: results of a community-based study. *BMJ* 1993; **306**: 431–83.

19 Khan IH, Catto GRD, Edward N, Macleod AM. Acute renal failure: factors influencing nephrology referral and outcome. *Q J Med* 1997; **90**: 781–5.

20 Firth JD. Acute irreversible renal failure. *Q J Med* 1996; **89**: 397–9.

21 Khan IH, Catto GRD, Edward N, Macleod AM. Chronic renal failure: factors influencing nephrology referral. *Q J Med* 1994; **87**: 559–64.

22 Feest TG, Mistry CD, Grimes DS, NP Mallick. Incidence of advanced chronic renal failure and the need for end-stage renal replacement therapy. *BMJ* 1990; **301**: 987–90.

23 Rostand SG, Kirk KA, Rutsky EA, Pate BA. Racial differences in the incidence of treatment for end-stage renal disease. *NEJM* 1982; **306**: 1276–9.

24 Sugimoto T, Rosansky S. The incidence of treated end-stage renal disease in the Eastern United States, 1973–79. *Am J Public Health* 1984; **74**: 14–17.

25 United States Renal Data System. *1997 Annual Data Report. US Department of Health and Human Services, Public Health Service, National Institutes of Health*. Bethesda, MD: National Institute of Diabetes and Digestive and Kidney Disease, 1997.

26 McClellan W, Tuttle E, Issa A. Racial differences in the incidence of hypertensive end-stage renal disease (ESRD) are not entirely explained by differences in the prevalence of hypertension. *Am J Kidney Dis* 1988; **4**: 258–90.

27 Cowie CC, Port FK, Wolfe RA, Savage PJ, Moll PP, Hawthorne VM. Disparities in incidence of diabetic end-stage renal disease according to race and type of diabetes. *NEJM* 1989; **321**: 1074–9.

28 Balarajan R, Bulusu L. Mortality among migrants in England and Wales, 1978–83. In: Britten M (ed.). *Mortality and Geography: a review in the mid-1980s, England and Wales.* OPCS, Series DS no. 9. London: HMSO, 1990, pp. 103–21.

29 McKeigue PM, Shah B, Marmot MG. Relation of central obesity and insulin resistance with high diabetes prevalence and cardiovascular risk in south Asians. *Lancet* 1991; **337**: 382–6.

30 Cruikshank J, Cooper J, Burnett M, Macduff J, Dubra U. Ethnic differences in fasting C-peptide and insulin in relation to glucose tolerance and blood pressure. *Lancet* 1991; **338**: 842–7.

31 Roderick PJ, Raleigh VS, Hallam L, Mallick NP. The need and demand for renal replacement therapy in ethnic minorities in England. *J Epidemiol Community Health* 1996; **50**: 334–9.

32 Soni Raleigh V. Diabetes and hypertension in Britain's ethnic minorities: implications for the future of renal services. *BMJ* 1997; **314**: 209–15.

33 Burden AC, NcNally P, Feehally J, Walls J. Increased incidence of end-stage renal failure secondary to diabetes mellitus in Asian ethnic groups in the United Kingdom. *Diabet Med* 1992; **9**: 641–5.

34 Allawi J, Rao PV, Gilbert R *et al*. Microalbuminuria in non-insulin-dependent diabetics: its prevalence in Indian as compared with Europid patients. *BMJ* 1988; **296**: 462–4.

35 Roderick P, Clements S, Diamond, Storkey M, Raleigh VS. Estimating demand for renal replacement therapy in Greater London: the impact of demographic trends in ethnic minority populations. *Health Trends* 1998; **30**(2): 46–50.

36 Office of National Statistics. *Occupational Health Decennial Supplement No. 10.* London: Office of National Statistics, 1995.

37 Marmot MG, Davey Smith G, Stansfield S *et al*. Health inequalities among British civil servants: the Whitehall II study. *Lancet* 1991; **337**: 1387–93.

38 Joint Working Party on Diabetic Renal Failure. Renal failure in diabetics in the United Kingdom: deficient provision of care in 1985. *Diabet Med* 1988; **5**: 79–84.

39 Joint Working Party on Diabetic Renal Failure. Treatment and mortality from diabetic renal failure in the 1985 United Kingdom survey. *BMJ* 1989; **299**: 1135–6.

40 Gulliford MC, Mejia A. Trends in diabetes mellitus in Greater London 1991–2011: associations with ethnicity. *Diabet Med* 1999; **16**: 174–5.

41 Berthoux FC, Mehls O, Mendel S *et al*. Report on Management of Renal Failure in Europe XXV 1994. *Nephrol Dial Transplant* 1996; **11**(Suppl. 1): 1–47.

42 Government Actuary's Office. *National Population Projections 1994-Based.* Series PP2 No 20. London: Office of National Statistics, 1996.

43 Curtis JR. Interventions in chronic renal failure. *BMJ* 1990; **301**: 622–3.

44 Eadington DW. Delayed referral for dialysis. *Nephrol Dial Transplant* 1996; **11**: 2124–6.

45 Scottish Intercollegiate Guidelines Network (SIGN). *The Care of Diabetic Patients in Scotland. Management of diabetic renal disease. A National Clinical Guideline recommended for use in Scotland* (pilot edition). Edinburgh: SIGN, 1997.

46 Kasiske BL, Kalil RSN, Ma JZ, Liao M, Keane WF. Effect of antihypertensive therapy on the kidney in patients with diabetes: a meta regression analysis. *Ann Intern Med* 1993; **118**: 129–38.

47 Gansevoort RT, Sluiter WJ, Hemmelder MH, de Zeeuw D, de Jong PE. Antiproteinuric effect of blood pressure lowering agents: a meta-analysis of comparative trials. *Nephrol Dial Transplant* 1995; **10**(11): 1963–74.

48 Lovell HG. Are angiotensin-converting-enzyme inhibitors useful for normotensive diabetic patients with microalbinuria? (Cochrane Review). In: *The Cochrane Library. Issue 2.* Oxford: Update Software, 1998.

49 Borch-Johnsen K, Wenzel H, Viberti GC, Morgensen CE. Is screening and intervention for microalbuminuria worthwhile in patients with insulin-dependent diabetes? *BMJ* 1993; **306**: 1772–3.

50 Scottish Intercollegiate Guidelines Network (SIGN). *Investigation of Asymptomatic Microscopic Haematuria in Adults. A National Clinical Guideline recommended for use in Scotland* (pilot edition). Edinburgh: SIGN, 1997.

51 Scottish Intercollegiate Guidelines Network (SIGN). *Investigation of Asymptomatic Proteinuria in Adults. A National Clinical Guideline recommended for use in Scotland* (pilot edition). Edinburgh: SIGN, 1997.

52 Khan IH, Catto G, Edward N, Fleming L, Henderson I, MacLeod A. Influence of coexisting disease on survival on renal replacement therapy. *Lancet* 1993; **341**: 415–16.

53 Chandra SM, Schulz J, Lawrence C, Greenwood R, Farringdon K. Is there a rationale for rationing chronic dialysis? A hospital-based cohort study of factors affecting survival and morbidity. *BMJ* 1999; **318**: 217–23.

54 Ansell D, Feest T. *The UK Renal Registry. The First Annual Report 1998.* Bristol: Renal Registry, 1998.

55 United Kingdom Transplant Support Service Authority (UKTSSA). *Renal Transplant Audit 1981–91.* Bristol: UKTSSA, 1993.

56 West R. *Organ Transplantation.* London: Office of Health Economics, 1991.

57 Bolger PG, Davies R. Simulation model for planning renal services in a district health authority. *BMJ* 1992; **305**: 605–8.

58 Krupa BS, Duggan AK, Haycox A. Costing renal service provision – the Shrewsbury renal revenue model. *Br J Med Econ* 1996; **10**: 15–26.

59 Lamping DL, Constantinovici N, Roderick P *et al.* Why age should not be a barrier to dialysis: evidence of clinical outcomes, quality of life and costs from the North Thames Dialysis Study (NTDS). *Lancet* 2000; **356**: 1543–50.

60 MacLeod A, Grant A, Donaldson C *et al.* Effectiveness and efficiency of methods of dialysis therapy for end-stage renal disease: systematic reviews 1998. *Health Technol Assess* 1998; **2** (5).

61 Ramsay LE, Williams B, Dennis Johnston G *et al.* British Hypertension Society guidelines for hypertension management in 1999: summary. *BMJ* 1999; **319**: 630–5.

62 Klag MJ, Whelton PK, Randall BI *et al.* Blood pressure and end-stage renal disease in men. *NEJM* 1996; **331**(1): 13–18.

63 National High Blood Pressure Program Education Working Group. Report on hypertension and chronic renal failure. *Arch Intern Med* 1991; **151**: 1280–7.

64 Diabetes Control and Complications Trial Research Group. The effect of intensive treatment of diabetes on the development and progression of long-term complications of insulin-dependent diabetes mellitus. *NEJM* 1993; **329**: 977–86.

65 Skarfors ET, Selinus KI, Lithell HO. Risk factors for developing non-insulin-dependent diabetes mellitus. *BMJ* 1991; **303**: 755–60.

66 Pan XR, Li GW, Hu YH *et al.* Effect of diet and exercise in preventing NIDDM in people with impaired glucose tolerance. The Da Qing IGT and Diabetes Study. *Diabetes Care* 1997; **20**: 537–44.

67 The Diabetes Prevention Program Research Group. The Diabetes Prevention Program. *Diabetes Care* 1999; **22**: 623–34.

68 UK Prospective Diabetes Study (UKPDS) Group. Intensive blood glucose control with sulphonylureas or insulin compared with conventional treatment and risk of complications in patients with type 2 diabetes (UKPDS 33). *Lancet* 1998; **352**: 837–53.

69 UK Prospective Diabetes Study (UKPDS) Group. Tight blood pressure control and risk of macrovascular and microvascular complications in type 2 diabetes: UKPDS 38. *BMJ* 1998; **317**: 703–13.

70 Smellie J, Normand I. Urinary infections in children. *Postgrad Med J* 1985; **61**: 895–905.

71 South Bedfordshire Practitioners' Group. Development of renal scars in children: missed opportunities in management. *BMJ* 1990; **301**: 1082–4.

72 Sacks SH, Aparicio SAJR, Bevan A, Oliver DO, Will EJ, Davison AM. Late renal failure due to prostatic outflow obstruction: a preventable disease. *BMJ* 1989; **298**: 156–9.

73 Cameron JS. Acute renal failure 30 years on. *Q J Med* 1990; **74**: 1–2.

74 Eliahou HE, Boichis H, Bott-Kanner G, Barell V, Bar-Noach N, Modan B. An epidemiologic study of renal failure. II. Acute renal failure. *Am J Epidemiol* 1975; **101**: 281–6.

75 Turney JH, Marshall DH, Brownjohn AM, Ellis CM, Parsons FM. The evolution of acute renal failure, 1956–88. *Q J Med* 1990; **273**: 83–104.

76 Rowan KM, Kerr JH, Major E, McPherson K, Short A, Vessey MP. Intensive Care Society's APACHE ll study in Britain and Ireland. 1. Variations in case mix of adult admissions to general intensive care units and impact on outcome. *BMJ* 1993; **307**: 972–7.

77 Pedrini M, Levey A, Lau J, Chalmers T, Wang P. The effect of dietary protein restriction on the progression of diabetic and non-diabetic renal diseases: a meta-analysis. In: *The Cochrane Library. Issue 2.* Oxford: Update Software, 1998.

78 Waugh NR, Robertson AM. Protein restriction in diabetic renal disease. In: *The Cochrane Library. Issue 2.* Oxford: Update Software, 1998.

79 National Kidney Foundation. *Controlling the Epidemic of Cardiovascular Disease in Chronic Renal Disease.* Washington, DC: Executive Summary, National Kidney Foundation, 1998.

80 Burton P, Walls J. Selection-adjusted comparison of life expectancy of patients on continuous ambulatory peritoneal dialysis, haemodialysis and renal transplantation. *Lancet* 1987; **i**:1115–18.

81 Gokal RM, Jakubowski C, King J. Outcome in patients on CAPD and haemodialysis: 4-year analysis of a prospective multicentre study. *Lancet* 1987; **2**: 1105–9.

82 The Tricontinental Mycophenolate Mofetil Renal Transplantation Study Group. A blinded, randomized clinical trial of mycophenolate mofetil for the prevention of acute rejection in cadaveric renal transplantation. *Transplantation* 1996; **61**: 1029–37.

83 Nissenson A. Dialysis treatment in the elderly patient. *Kidney Int* 1993; **43**(Suppl. 40): 51–7.

84 Leese B, Hutton J, Maynard A (eds). *The Costs and Benefits of the Use of Erythropoietin in the Treatment of Anaemia Arising from Chronic Renal Failure: a European study.* York: Centre for Health Economics, University of York, 1990.

85 Rodby RA, Firth LM, Lewis EJ. An economic analysis of captopril in the treatment of diabetic nephropathy. *Diabetes Care* 1996; **19**(10): 1051–61.

86 Kibberd BA, Jindal KK. Screening to prevent renal failure in insulin-dependent diabetic patients: an economic evaluation. *BMJ* 1995; **311**: 1595–9.

87 Smith WGC, Cohen DR, Ascher AW. *Evaluation of Renal Services in Wales with Particular Reference to the Role of Subsidiary Renal Units.* Cardiff: Department of Renal Medicine, KRUF Institute of Renal Disease, Royal Infirmary, 1989.

88 Buxton MJ, West RR. Cost–benefit analysis of long-term haemodialysis for chronic renal failure. *BMJ* 1975; **2**: 376–9.

89 Comptroller General, US General Accounting Office. *Treatment of Chronic Kidney Failure: dialysis, transplant, costs and the need for more vigorous efforts.* Washington, DC: Government Printing Office, 1977.

90 Stange PV, Sumner AT. Predicting treatment costs and life expectancy for end-stage renal disease. *NEJM* 1978; **298**: 372–8.

91 Roberts SD, Maxwell DR, Gross TL. Cost-effective care of end-stage renal disease: a billion dollar question. *Ann Intern Med* 1980; **92**: 243–8.

92 Ludbrook A. A cost-effectiveness analysis of the treatment of chronic renal failure. *Appl Econ* 1981; **13**: 337–56.

93 Bulgin RH. Comparative costs of various dialysis treatments. *Perit Dial Bull* 1981; **1**: 89–91.

94 US Department of Health and Human Services, Health Care Financing Administration. 42 CFR Part 405, proposed rules. *Fed Register* 1982; **47**(30): 6556.

95 Mancini PV, Davis MJS. *The Costs of Renal Replacement Therapy.* London: Department of Health and Social Security, 1982.

96 Lameire NH. Reflections on the status of treatment of end-stage renal disease in Belgium. *Renal Fail* 1983; **5**: 18–22.

97 Garner TI, Dardis R. Cost-effectiveness analysis of end-stage renal disease treatments. *Med Care* 1987; **25**: 25–34.

98 Haggar T. Assessing the cost of a kidney transplant surgeon. *Pub Fin Acc* 1988; **11**: 11–13.

99 Sesso R, Eisenberg JM, Stabile C *et al.* Cost-effectiveness analysis of the treatment of end-stage renal disease in Brazil. *Int J Technol Assess Health Care* 1990; **6**: 107–14.

100 Karlberg I, Nyberg G. Cost-effectiveness studies of renal transplantation. *Int J Technol Assess Health Care* 1995; **11**: 611–22.

101 Hutton J, Leese B, Maynard A. The UK case study. In: Leese B, Hutton J, Maynard A (eds). *The Costs and Benefits of the Use of Erythropoietin in the Treatment of Anaemia Arising from Chronic Renal Failure: a European study.* York: Centre for Health Economics, 1990, pp. 103–18.

102 Gudex C. *QALYs and their Use by the Health Service.* Discussion Paper 20. York: Centre for Health Economics, 1986.

103 NHS Executive. *The New NHS Commissioning Specialised Services.* Consultation Document. London: NHS Executive, 1997.

104 Davies R, Roderick P. Planning services for renal failure throughout UK using simulation. *Eur J Operat Res* 1998; **105**(2): 285–95.

105 Wight J, Olliver A, Payne N. A computer model for predicting the demand for end-stage renal failure (ESRF) treatment, contract setting and monitoring. *Nephrol Dial Transplant* 1996; **11**: 1286–91.

106 Davies R, Roderick P. Predicting the future demand for renal replacement therapy in England using simulation modelling. *Nephrol Dial Transplant* 1997; **12**: 2512–16.

107 Forte P, Bowen T. Improving the balance of elderly care services. In: Cropper S, Forte P (eds). *Enhancing Decision Making in the NHS: the role of decision support systems.* Buckingham: Open University Press, 1997.

108 United Kingdom Transplant Support Service Authority (UKTSSA). *Transplant Activity 1998.* Bristol: UKTSSA, 1999.

109 UK Transplant Service (UKTS). *1989 Annual Report.* Bristol: UKTS, Southmead Hospital, 1989.

110 Working Party on the Supply of Donor Organs for Transplantation (Chairman: Sir Raymond Hoffenberg). *Report.* London: HMSO, 1987.

111 Gore MS, Hinds CJ, Rutherford AJ. Organ donation from intensive-care units in England. *BMJ* 1989; **299**: 1193–7.

112 Gore SM, Taylor RMR, Wallwork J. Availability of transplantable organs from brain-stem death donors in intensive-care units. *BMJ* 1991; **302**: 149–53.

113 British Transplantation Society. *Report of the British Transplantation Society Working Party on Organ Donation.* London: British Transplantation Society, 1995.

114 Higgins RM, West RN, Edmunds ME *et al.* Effect of a strict HLA matching policy on distribution of cadaveric kidneys to Indo-Asian and white European recipients: regional study. *BMJ* 1997; **315**: 1354–5.

115 Salih MAM, Harvey I, Frankel S, Coupe DJ, Webb M, Cripps HA. Potential availability of cadaver organs for transplantation. *BMJ* 1991; **302**: 1053–5.

116 London Renal Services Review Group. *Report of an Independent Review of Specialist Services in London.* London: HMSO, 1993.

117 Stanton J. The cost of living: kidney dialysis, rationing and health economics in Britain, 1965–96. *Soc Sci Med* 1999; **49**: 1169–82.

118 Wiltshire Health Authority. *Renal Replacement Therapy. Purchasing review and recommendations.* Devizes: Wiltshire Health Authority, 1997.

119 The Scottish Office. *Acute Services Review Report 1998.* Edinburgh: The Scottish Office, 1998.

120 Beech R, Mandalia S, Melia J, Mays N, Swan A. Purchasing services for end-stage renal failure: the potential and limitations of existing information sources. *Health Trends* 1993; **15**: 60–4.

Acknowledgements

This is an updated version of the chapter that appeared in the first Health Care Needs Assessment series co-authored by J Melia and N Mays.

We are grateful for the permission of the authors and of the editor of the *British Medical Journal* and the *Quarterly Journal of Medicine* for their permission to reproduce the following tables in this report: Table 7 from Feest TG, Mistry CD, Grimes DS, Mallick NP. Incidence of advanced chronic renal failure and the need for end-stage renal replacement treatment. *BMJ* 1990; **301**: 897–900; Tables 5 and 9 and Figures 2–5 from Roderick PJ, Ferris G, Feest TG. The provision of renal replacement therapy for adults in England and Wales: recent trends and future directions. *Q J Med* 1998; **91**: 518–87.

Addendum

Since this chapter was prepared there have been a number of significant developments with regard to renal disease:

- A new classification for renal disease has been proposed by the US Kidney Disease Quality Initiative (KDOQI) based on estimated glomerular filtration rate (GFR):
  - National Kidney Foundation. KDOQI clinical practice guidelines for chronic kidney disease: evaluation, classification and stratification. *Am J Kidney Dis* 2002; **39**: S1–100.
- International guidelines have been published. The US National Kidney Foundation has initiated the Kidney Disease Outcome Quality Initiative (KDOQI); (www.kidney.org/professionals/kdoqi.guidelines-ckd). CARI guidelines have been produced in Australia (www.kidney.org.au.cari).
- UK Transplant is the new organisation that has replaced UKTSSA. Their business plan outlines the latest initiatives to improve availability of kidneys and other organs for transplantation; www.uktransplant.org.uk/
- The National Renal Workforce Planning Group has produced *British Renal Society. The Renal Team. A multi-professional renal workforce plan for adults and children with renal disease.* London: British Renal Society, 2002; www.britishrenal.org

Several important documents have also been published:

- UK Renal Registry Annual Reports. The 2000 report includes data from the 1998 National Renal Survey (chapter 3), and the 2002 report includes new modelling of future demand (chapter 6).
- Renal Association. *Treatment of Adults and Children with Renal Failure. Standards and audit measures* (3e). London: Royal College of Physicians, 2002.
- National Institute for Clinical Excellence (NICE) appraisal of home dialysis; www.nice.org.uk
- National Service Framework for Renal Services (January 2004); www.doh.gov.uk
- National Service Framework for Diabetes (December 2001).

3 Stroke

Jonathan Mant, Derick Wade and Simon Winner

1 Summary

Introduction

Stroke accounts for 11% of all deaths in England and Wales, and is also an important cause of morbidity, since the majority of patients survive their first stroke, often with significant disability. The significance of stroke as a major health care problem has been recognised in recent Government White Papers, which have set targets for reductions in stroke mortality. Standard Five of the National Service Framework (NSF) for Older People states that: 'The NHS will take action to prevent strokes, working in partnership with other agencies where appropriate. People who are thought to have had a stroke have access to diagnostic services, are treated appropriately by a specialist stroke service, and subsequently, with their carers, participate in a multi-disciplinary programme of secondary prevention and rehabilitation.'

There have been important advances in the evidence base for the prevention, treatment and rehabilitation of stroke in the last decade. Commissioners of health care face important decisions about how to implement this evidence and comply with the NSF and how to allocate priorities to different aspects of stroke care. This chapter aims to provide the background information to support such decision making.

Sub-categories

There are several different ways of categorising the problems related to stroke. From a perspective of health care needs assessment, no single classification is ideal. A pragmatic solution is to use the following sub-categories.

- *People at high risk of stroke*: This category has been included because stroke prevention should have a key role in health strategies, exemplified by local Health Improvement Plans. Mortality targets set by the Government ensure that stroke prevention will remain a priority for primary care trusts.
- *Transient ischaemic attack (TIA)*: Defined as an acute loss of focal cerebral or ocular function with symptoms lasting less than 24 hours, which is presumed after adequate investigation to be due to embolic or thrombotic vascular disease.
- *Stroke (acute phase)*: The World Health Organization (WHO) defines stroke as a syndrome of rapidly developing symptoms and signs of focal, and at times global, loss of cerebral function lasting more than 24 hours or leading to death, with no apparent cause other than that of vascular origin. Although sub-arachnoid haemorrhage is included within this WHO definition, it is appropriately dealt with separately (*see* below).

- *People with sequelae of stroke*: Needs for rehabilitation and continuing care services relate to the medium- and long-term consequences of stroke. Such patients also benefit from therapy aimed at the reduction of risk of further stroke or other vascular events.
- *Sub-arachnoid haemorrhage*: This clinical syndrome is caused by blood in the sub-arachnoid space, typically due to leakage of blood from an aneurysm near the circle of Willis. While sub-arachnoid haemorrhage may lead to cerebral infarction, the acute management is different from that for focal stroke, and therefore it is useful to consider it as a separate sub-category.

Prevalence and incidence

Using data from a number of different sources, including the Health Survey for England, and UK-based prevalence surveys and incidence studies, the following estimates of numbers of cases per 100 000 population in a year were made.

Table 1: Summary of epidemiology of stroke and risk factors for stroke in a population of 100 000.

Sub-category	Expected number of new cases per year (incidence)	Expected number of existing cases (prevalence)
Risk factors for stroke		
Atrial fibrillation	330	1,100
Hypertension (BP > 140/90 mmHg)		34,000
Current smokers		28,000
Diabetes mellitus		2,000
Ischaemic heart disease		5,500
Transient ischaemic attack	35	
Stroke		1,500
First stroke (excluding sub-arachnoid haemorrhage)	164	
Recurrent stroke	57	
People with moderate disability from stroke	N/A	1,000
Sub-arachnoid haemorrhage	10	

These estimates are based upon the population structure of England and Wales as a whole. The prevalence and incidence of stroke rise with age, so these figures need to be adjusted for areas that have different age distributions, such as retirement areas or new towns. The prevalence and incidence of stroke also depend upon other population factors such as ethnic mix and socio-economic status.

Services available and their costs

Prevention of stroke

Both population-based strategies and approaches to reduce the risk in individuals at high risk of stroke are used. Services available to treat people at high risk of stroke include blood pressure reduction, anticoagulation for people in atrial fibrillation, investigation of transient ischaemic attack, and treatment with carotid endarterectomy in appropriate cases. Aspirin is also indicated for many people at high risk of stroke. Other relevant services include those related to smoking cessation, weight reduction and exercise promotion.

Acute management and rehabilitation of stroke

The majority of patients with acute stroke are cared for initially in hospital, though a proportion remain at home. Community services available to facilitate home care in different parts of the country include rapid response teams, hospital at home, day hospital, and outpatient and domiciliary services. In hospital, patients may be cared for in specialist facilities or on general wards. Types of specialist facility that are available under the broad umbrella term of 'stroke unit care' include stroke teams, dedicated stroke units (which may be for acute care and/or rehabilitation) and mixed rehabilitation units. Recent audits suggest that the majority of patients are cared for on general wards. In some areas, intermediate care facilities such as community hospitals and social rehabilitation units are available to facilitate transfer from hospital back into the community. Approximately 19% of stroke survivors are transferred to long-term institutional care.

Services for sub-arachnoid haemorrhage

Acute sub-arachnoid haemorrhage is usually managed in hospital. Both acute medical therapy, in the form of nimodipine, and surgery (to repair underlying vascular defects) are available.

Costs of stroke care

Stroke has been estimated to account for 4–6% of total NHS costs. It has been estimated that approximately two-thirds of these costs arise from the treatment and care of people with 'old' strokes.

Effectiveness and cost-effectiveness

Population strategies to prevent stroke

Evidence from observational studies supports a number of population strategies to lower the incidence of stroke, directed at reducing smoking, reducing socio-economic deprivation, lowering blood pressure and encouraging healthy lifestyles.

Prevention in people at high risk of stroke

Treating hypertension, anticoagulating people in atrial fibrillation, treating people at high cardiovascular risk with antiplatelet agents, treating people with vascular disease with statins, tight control of blood glucose and blood pressure in diabetics, and performing carotid endarterectomy in people with significant carotid artery stenosis are all approaches that have been demonstrated to be effective in randomised controlled trials (RCTs). Evidence from observational studies supports the encouragement of changes in lifestyle, such as stopping smoking, healthy diet, exercise and avoidance of excessive alcohol consumption.

Acute treatment of stroke

There is good evidence that patients receiving organised inpatient or stroke unit care have lower mortality than those cared for in other settings. While many pharmacological interventions in acute stroke have been studied, aspirin and thrombolysis (in certain specific circumstances) are the only ones shown by RCTs to be effective.

Stroke rehabilitation

There is good evidence that organised stroke care given by a co-ordinated specialist team reduces disability and rates of institutionalisation. Within the overall package of stroke unit care, there is a growing evidence base for individual components. There is now evidence from RCTs supporting the use of physiotherapy, occupational therapy and family support for carers.

Treatment of sub-arachnoid haemorrhage

Nimodipine is effective in the treatment of acute sub-arachnoid haemorrhage.

Models of care and recommendations

Guidelines for stroke care

National guidelines and statements on stroke care have been produced by the Intercollegiate Working Party on Stroke, the Edinburgh Consensus Meetings and the Scottish Intercollegiate Guidelines Network (SIGN). These provide an excellent basis for considering the optimum pattern of stroke services for a defined population.

The key components of a strategy for primary stroke prevention include identification and treatment of hypertension, identification and treatment of atrial fibrillation, careful control of hypertension in diabetes, lifestyle advice with regard to smoking, diet, weight, and exercise, and treatment with a statin of patients with known vascular disease and elevated cholesterol.

The same issues apply to treatment of people who have had a stroke or transient ischaemic attack (TIA), but because the risks of subsequent strokes are high, each is of relatively greater importance. In addition, following ischaemic stroke, patients should be on aspirin, or another antiplatelet agent if aspirin-intolerant. Patients with a TIA or minor stroke should be assessed rapidly for eligibility for carotid endarterectomy, which should be performed in a centre with a low complication rate. This might necessitate referral to regional or sub-regional units.

There is consensus that the vast majority of patients with acute stroke should initially be assessed in hospital. Aspirin is an effective acute treatment for ischaemic stroke, and is preferably administered after brain imaging has been performed to rule out intracranial haemorrhage. Thrombolytic therapy is a reasonable treatment to give in selected patients, but only in specialist centres in a carefully monitored environment. Further research is required before such a model of care can be 'rolled out' to a wider population.

There is strong evidence that acute care and rehabilitation of stroke patients is highly effective when carried out in inpatient stroke units that offer an organised, multi-disciplinary approach to care. All stroke patients should have access to such care. The extent to which these results can be reproduced in other settings, such as community hospitals, day hospitals and at home, have not yet been demonstrated. While some studies have been carried out looking at early discharge schemes, the precise contribution that these should make has still to be defined. Nevertheless, it is impractical to expect stroke units (with an average unit size of 6–15 beds) to cater for the needs of a typical district general hospital catchment area serving a population of 300 000, which can anticipate having on average 30 patients with stroke in hospital at a time. Therefore different models of DGH care that conform to the broader definition of 'stroke unit care' need to be employed, and locality-based models of intermediate care need to be developed and evaluated.

Towards a quantified model for stroke care

With regard to services specifically aimed at stroke prevention, in a typical population of 100 000 it is estimated that in a year:

- 539 of the estimated 1100 patients in atrial fibrillation will need anticoagulation
- 99 patients will need rapid neurological assessment and/or assessment for eligibility for carotid endarterectomy
- 14 patients will need carotid endarterectomy.

With regard to acute stroke treatment and rehabilitation, in a typical population of 100 000 which suffers 221 first or recurrent strokes in a year it is estimated that:

- 12 hospital beds will be required (within a setting that conforms to stroke unit care)
- access to neurosurgical services is required for patients with sub-arachnoid haemorrhage and patients with stroke who develop hydrocephalus
- access to community-based specialist rehabilitation services is required – the size of these will depend upon the extent to which hospital-based or community-based rehabilitation is the preferred model within a given area.

Priorities for stroke care

Within the optimum model for stroke care promoted by national guidelines, priority should be given to establishment of stroke units and developing models of care that permit care of equivalent quality to stroke unit care to be applied to a larger proportion of stroke patients. In hospital, this will mean ensuring co-ordinated, multi-disciplinary specialist care in settings other than stroke units, such as neurological and geriatric rehabilitation wards. With regard to stroke prevention, simple interventions such as aspirin in appropriate patients are highly cost-effective. Anticoagulation for atrial fibrillation and carotid endarterectomy in selected patients are also cost-effective treatments, though the former has greater potential, in terms of both numbers of strokes that might be prevented and relative cost (approximately £4000 vs. £28 000 per stroke prevented). More effective treatment of hypertension is the strategy that has the most potential for reducing stroke incidence, but the relative cost-effectiveness is critically dependent upon whether older or newer antihypertensive agents are used.

2 Introduction

Stroke as a major health issue

Stroke is a major health problem in the UK. It accounted for over 56 000 deaths in England and Wales in 1999, which represents 11% of all deaths.[1] The majority of patients survive a first stroke, often with significant morbidity. Overall it has been estimated that caring for people with stroke accounts for 4–6% of the total NHS budget.[2,3] While there is evidence that age-specific mortality from stroke has been declining in recent years,[1] this is unlikely to result in any decline in need for services, since this in part reflects better survival following stroke. Furthermore, ageing of the population will offset any age-specific decline in incidence.

International comparisons of stroke mortality

The burden of stroke in terms of mortality in the UK can be set in a worldwide context. An analysis of World Health Organization (WHO) data shows that mortality is lowest in affluent industrialised countries, and that UK mortality is broadly similar to that in other Western European countries.[4] For example, the mortality rate for men aged 35–74 in 16 Western European countries ranges from 34 per 100 000 (Switzerland) to 162 per 100 000 (Portugal). The UK is ranked ninth in this set of countries, with a mortality of 65 per 100 000. International comparisons of case fatality (i.e. whether or not strokes that occur are fatal) give a slightly different picture, with the UK tending to have higher case fatality than other areas of Western Europe.[5,6] It is difficult to disentangle whether the differences in case fatality are due to differences in methods of data collection, case-mix, or care provided. High case fatality but average mortality from stroke (as experienced in the UK) taken at face value would imply lower incidence, but this is not borne out by comparative incidence studies.[6,7] This would suggest that the likeliest explanation for the discrepancy is methodological artefact (which may affect either or both case fatality and mortality).

Stroke and Government policy

The importance of stroke has been stressed in Government policy over the last decade. Two White Papers, *The Health of the Nation*[3] and *Saving Lives: Our Healthier Nation*,[8] set targets for reductions in stroke mortality. There is a chapter on stroke in the National Service Framework (NSF) for Older People in which Standard Five aims 'to reduce the incidence of stroke in the population and ensure that those who have had a stroke have prompt access to integrated stroke care services'.[9] The standard given is that: 'The NHS will take action to prevent strokes, working in partnership with other agencies where appropriate. People who are thought to have had a stroke have access to diagnostic services, are treated appropriately by a specialist stroke service, and subsequently, with their carers, participate in a multi-disciplinary programme of secondary prevention and rehabilitation.'

The implementation of the NSF standard sets a challenge. The information in this chapter illustrates the dimensions of the task ahead to implement the NSF standard. The chapter summarises the epidemiology of stroke (Section 4), the current pattern of stroke services (Section 5), the evidence of effectiveness of services and interventions (Section 6), and models of care to achieve the aim of the NSF (Section 7).

Key issues

Within a publicly financed health care system with limited resources, a key issue is how best to distribute the health care resources that are available for stroke care. As in other areas of health care, there is controversy over which part of the system is in most need of extra resources. Should the emphasis be on hospital-based or community-based services? On services for prevention or treatment? On acute treatments or longer-term rehabilitation? These questions have no simple answers, and the solutions lie in getting the balance right between these different facets of stroke services. One aim of this chapter is to provide the background information that will help commissioners of health care services to make rational choices in these difficult areas.

There have been significant improvements in the evidence base for stroke in the last decade. Effective strategies are available to prevent stroke, and to treat and rehabilitate stroke patients. However, audits suggest that many people with stroke are not receiving optimal care.[10] This raises important issues of implementation. The Intercollegiate Working Party (IWP) for Stroke has prepared multi-disciplinary guidelines for stroke care which reflect this evidence base,[11] and a key question for commissioners of health care is how best to support implementation of these guidelines, which have been explicitly incorporated into the National Service Framework.

The data that are available from epidemiological studies are only of limited value for a health care needs assessment. While there are now reasonable data on the incidence and prevalence of stroke, data on the incidence and prevalence of disability and impairment, which are a stronger predictor of the need for rehabilitation and continuing care services, are limited. Therefore, there is a danger that needs assessment (and hence service provision) can become too focused on the needs of people with acute stroke, and less on their rehabilitation and longer-term care needs.

3 Sub-categories

Stroke is a neurological impairment of sudden onset which is caused by a disruption of the blood supply to the brain. Stroke is an umbrella term that includes different pathologies and clinical syndromes. This can lead to some confusion in the literature. In this chapter, for pragmatic reasons that are explained below, stroke is distinguished from sub-arachnoid haemorrhage and from transient ischaemic attack (*see* 'Sub-categories used in this chapter' below for definitions of these conditions that are used in this chapter). In fact, the standard definition of stroke[12] includes sub-arachnoid haemorrhage, but because the clinical syndrome of sub-arachnoid haemorrhage is quite distinct from stroke and is managed in a different way, in this chapter sub-arachnoid haemorrhage is considered separately. The standard definition of stroke excludes transient ischaemic attack on the basis of duration of symptoms: to be labelled 'a stroke', symptoms have to last for more than 24 hours, otherwise the label 'transient ischaemic attack' applies. However, the underlying pathology is the same, and the management in terms of secondary prevention is identical. The following section reviews the different ways in which stroke can be sub-classified and explains why the sub-categories used in this chapter have been selected.

Possible sub-categorisations

Stroke can be sub-categorised in different ways: by pathological type; by pathological cause; by associated risk factors; by prognosis; by anatomical site; or by impact on disability and handicap. From the perspective of a health care needs assessment, none of these sub-categorisations is entirely satisfactory on its own.

Pathological type

There are two major pathological types of stroke: cerebral infarction and intracerebral haemorrhage. A third important acute cerebrovascular disease is sub-arachnoid haemorrhage, which may or may not result in a clinical stroke. The vast majority of stroke is cerebral infarction. For example, in the Oxford Community Stroke Project, 81% of first strokes were cerebral infarction, 10% primary intracerebral haemorrhage, 5% sub-arachnoid haemorrhage and 5% of uncertain type.[13] The pathological type of stroke is of prognostic significance (*see* Table 2 overleaf) and of clinical significance in that there are some differences in the acute management of patients with intracerebral haemorrhage and cerebral infarction (*see* Sections 5 and 6). Sub-arachnoid haemorrhage presents and is managed differently from the other acute cerebrovascular diseases.

While it is useful to distinguish the pathological types of stroke, the exercise is of only limited utility in health care needs assessment. The pathological type is only a very crude predictor of disability and handicap, and these are important determinants of medium- and long-term health care needs. Routine data sets do not discriminate well between types,[14] so practical ability to sub-categorise to this level of detail is limited.

Table 2: Case fatality rates by pathological type of stroke: adapted from Bamford *et al.*[13]

Stroke type	Mortality at 1 month (95% CI)	Mortality at 1 year (95% CI)
Cerebral infarction	10% (7–13)	23% (19–27)
Primary intracerebral haemorrhage	50% (38–62)	62% (43–81)
Sub-arachnoid haemorrhage	46% (29–63)	48% (24–72)
Uncertain type	77% (46–100)	84% (52–100)
All	19% (16–22)	31% (27–35)

Pathological cause

The sequence of events leading to permanent brain damage varies considerably, and the underlying mechanisms are interrelated and can lead from one to another (*see* Figure 1). The principal pathological types of stroke are associated with different underlying causes. Cerebral infarction is usually due to thrombosis or embolism, though it can also be a consequence of intracerebral haemorrhage or sub-arachnoid haemorrhage. Embolism may arise either from the heart or from atheromatous arteries. The distinction between thrombosis and embolism and identifying the source of the embolus is of potential relevance in targeting secondary prevention, and for clinical trials of acute treatments. However, accurate classification is usually arbitrary – presence of a source of embolus, for example, does not prove that a stroke had an embolic cause. A classification of sub-type of ischaemic stroke based on presumed underlying pathological cause was proposed by the TOAST (Trial of ORG10172 in Acute Stroke Treatment) investigators: large artery atherosclerosis; cardio-embolism; small-vessel occlusion; stroke of other determined aetiology; stroke of undetermined aetiology.[15] This classification is difficult to apply. The TOAST investigators found that the initial clinical impression of stroke sub-type only agreed with final determination of sub-type (incorporating all investigation results and performed three months after stroke) in 62% of patients, and 15% of patients did not have a clear aetiological sub-type even at three months.[16] Use of modern magnetic resonance imaging techniques can substantially improve the early classification of stroke sub-type.[17] US data from the Stroke Data Bank of the National Institute of

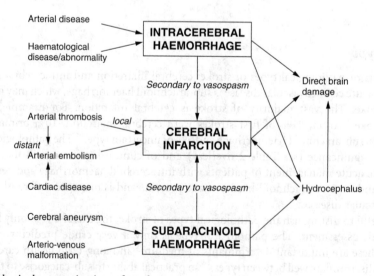

Figure 1: Pathological categorisation of stroke.

Neurological and Communicative Disorders and Stroke and the Framingham study suggest that, using the TOAST classification,[18] 60% of ischaemic stroke is attributed to an embolic cause, 25% of ischaemic stroke to small-vessel occlusion (lacunar stroke), and 15% of ischaemic stroke to large vessel athero-thrombosis.

Simple classification of the pathological cause of the stroke is also of prognostic relevance. Follow-up of patients with ischaemic stroke in Rochester, Minnesota found that this classification predicted risk of stroke recurrence at one month (but not in the long term), and long-term (five-year) survival.[19]

Intracerebral haemorrhage may occur as part of sub-arachnoid haemorrhage, but more commonly occurs on its own. The usual causes are vasculopathy secondary to hypertension or vascular disease, intracranial aneurysm (usually associated with sub-arachnoid haemorrhage), and arterio-venous mal-formations.

Sub-arachnoid haemorrhage is often due to leakage from an intracranial aneurysm, but may also occur as a result of arterio-venous malformations or other vascular abnormalities such as angiomas. Approximately 20% of sub-arachnoid haemorrhage has no demonstrable underlying cause.[20,21]

Associated risk factors

Several medical conditions increase risk of stroke, such as hypertension, atrial fibrillation, diabetes, ischaemic heart disease and carotid artery stenosis. Aspects of lifestyle modify stroke risk, such as diet, smoking, alcohol and exercise (*see* Section 4). Knowledge of the prevalence of such factors and the strength of their association with stroke is relevant for a disease prevention needs assessment. Estimates can be made of the relative contribution of each risk factor to the overall burden of stroke, which in turn can inform prioritisation of stroke prevention initiatives (*see* Section 7).

Prognosis

Prognosis following stroke can be described in terms of survival, risk of a further stroke (recurrence) or extent of long-term disability. Prognostic factors are different for each of these. A number of studies have derived models for predicting outcome of stroke in terms of survival and/or disability.[22-25] These models tend to use a combination of some or all of past medical history (e.g. previous stroke, diabetes), demographic variables (age, sex) and early clinical features (e.g. impaired consciousness, urinary incontinence). Prognosis influences need for health services, so a prognosis-based sub-categorisation could be of value. However, predicting outcome for individuals is very difficult and for groups remains crude. It is questionable whether complex multivariate models are significantly more useful than simple univariate predictors such as level of consciousness or incontinence.[22,25]

Prognostic models have been applied to the process of adjusting data sets for differences in case-mix, which is important for interpreting variations in outcome.[26,27] As such, the models are of possible value in monitoring the quality of stroke services (*see* Section 8).

Anatomical site

Bamford *et al.*, using data from the Oxford Community Stroke Project, defined four sub-categories of cerebral infarction on the basis of presenting symptoms and signs: lacunar infarcts (LACI), total anterior circulation infarcts (TACI), partial anterior circulation infarcts (PACI) and posterior circulation infarcts (POCI) (*see* Table 3 overleaf).[28]

While the classification is based upon bedside clinical features, the labels attached to each sub-category are anatomical, which reflects the close correlation between symptoms and signs and site of cerebral

Table 3: The Oxford Community Stroke Project classification of sub-types of cerebral infarction.[28]

Lacunar infarcts (LACI)	A pure motor stroke, a pure sensory stroke, a sensori-motor stroke or an ataxic hemiparesis.
Total anterior circulation infarcts (TACI)	A combination of new higher cerebral dysfunction (e.g. dysphasia), homonymous visual field defect and ipsilateral motor and/or sensory deficit of at least two areas (out of face, arm and leg).
Partial anterior circulation infarcts (PACI)	Only two of the three components of a TACI, or with higher cerebral dysfunction alone, or with a motor/sensory deficit more restricted than those classified as LACI (e.g. confined to one limb).
Posterior circulation infarcts (POCI)	Any of ipsilateral cranial nerve palsy with contralateral motor and/or sensory deficit, bilateral motor and/or sensory deficit, disorder of conjugate eye movement, cerebellar dysfunction, isolated homonymous visual field defect.

infarction. As shown in Table 4, this classification is of prognostic significance. A TACI is associated with high mortality, and significant disability in most survivors. A PACI is associated with the highest risk of early (i.e. within 3 months) recurrence of stroke. A patient with a POCI has the best chance of a good recovery, and patients with a LACI the best chance of survival. The advantage of this classification is that it uses relatively simple clinical criteria. The disadvantages are that it does not extend to sub-arachnoid haemorrhage or intracerebral haemorrhage, and that for lacunar strokes, the relationship between clinical classification and anatomical site may not be very close. For example, Toni *et al.* found that only 56% (123/219) of patients with clinically defined lacunar strokes had anatomically defined lacunar strokes, while 27% (47/170) of patients with anatomical lacunar strokes did not have clinical lacunar strokes.[29] Nevertheless, as a clinical classification, the system remains of value.

Table 4: Prognostic significance of the Oxford Community Stroke Project stroke sub-types (Bamford *et al.*).[28]

	Case fatality (%)			Functionally dependent (Rankin 3–5) (%)			Dead or dependent		
	1 month	6 months	1 year	1 month	6 months	1 year	1 month	6 months	1 year
LACI	2	7	11	36	26	28	38	34	40
TACI	39	56	60	56	39	36	96	96	96
PACI	4	10	16	39	34	29	44	45	45
POCI	7	14	19	31	18	19	38	32	38
All	10	18	23	39	29	28	50	48	51

Impact in terms of disability and handicap

Disability and handicap are important determinants of rehabilitation and care needs. A fuller discussion of the concepts of disability and handicap, and their relationship to impairments, is given in Appendix 1. Several measures are available and used either in routine clinical practice or for audit and research purposes.[30,31] The Barthel Activities of Daily Living Index is perhaps the most commonly used measure of disability (*see* Table 5).[32] This gives a disability score from 0 (severe disability) to 20 (independent), and can be subdivided into groups. It has limitations, in that it has floor and ceiling effects and is insensitive to small differences.[30] It describes disability at a given point in time, and while this is of relevance to current health care needs, it is only a weak predictor of future disability.

Table 5: Examples of disability measures: the Barthel Index[32] and the Modified Rankin Scale.[13]

Modified Rankin Scale

0 No symptoms
1 Minor symptoms which do not interfere with lifestyle
2 Minor handicap: symptoms which lead to some restriction in lifestyle but do not interfere with the patient's capacity to look after themselves
3 Moderate handicap: symptoms which significantly restrict lifestyle and prevent totally independent existence
4 Moderately severe handicap: symptoms which clearly prevent independent existence, though not needing constant attention
5 Severe handicap: totally dependent, requiring constant attention night and day

Barthel Activities of Daily Living (ADL) Index

Score from 0–20, on the basis of assessment of ten different items:

Bowel control (score 0–2); Bladder control (score 0–2); Grooming (score 0 or 1); Toilet use (score 0–2); Feeding (score 0–2); Ability to transfer from bed to chair and vice versa (score 0–3); Mobility (score 0–3); Dressing (score 0–2); Ability to climb stairs (score 0–2); Bathing (score 0 or 1).

Reliability depends upon accurate application of standardised definitions.

Several scales include elements of both disability and handicap. One of the simplest of these is the Rankin scale, usually used in modified form with six grades,[13] from no symptoms to severe disability (*see* Table 5). This scale has the virtue of simplicity and is therefore suitable for large-scale epidemiological studies and clinical trials. It is often collapsed down to two levels. For example, in the Oxford Community Stroke Project it was reduced to 'functionally independent' (grades 0–2) and 'functionally dependent' (grades 3–5) (*see* Table 4). Measures of handicap may focus on single dimensions such as social activities (e.g. the Frenchay Activities Index)[33] or address handicap more broadly. An example of the latter is the London Handicap Scale,[34] which measures handicap using the six dimensions of the WHO classification.[35] Measures of this type are of value in clinical trials and audits and could have a role in local health care needs assessments where primary data are being collected, but because they are not in routine use, they cannot usefully form the basis of sub-categorisation for the purposes of this chapter.

Sub-categories used in this chapter

Need for health care is defined in terms of both the incidence and prevalence of a condition, and the effectiveness of services to treat that condition (*see* An introduction to HCNA). It follows that the most useful sub-categorisation of stroke would be into categories for which there were data available for both epidemiology and effectiveness. The sub-categories used in this chapter reflect this pragmatic reasoning, rather than being underpinned by a firm theoretical basis. They do not follow any single one of the categorisations described above. Nevertheless, the preceding discussion is important to underline the limitations of the classification that will be used, to raise issues that are of importance in considering local health care needs assessments, and to highlight alternative sub-classifications that would be of value if data were available.

The sub-categories that are used in this chapter are:

- people at high risk of stroke
- transient ischaemic attack
- stroke (acute phase)
- people with sequelae of stroke
- sub-arachnoid haemorrhage.

People at high risk of stroke

This category has been included since stroke prevention should have a key role in health strategy, such as local Health Improvement Plans or their equivalent. Indeed, the mortality targets set by the Government ensure that stroke prevention will remain a priority for primary care trusts.[8] For discussion of who is at high risk of stroke, and therefore included in this sub-category, *see* Section 4.

Transient ischaemic attack

This is a particular subgroup within the high-risk group. A transient ischaemic attack (TIA) may be defined as an acute loss of focal cerebral or ocular function with symptoms lasting less than 24 hours which, after adequate investigation, is presumed to be due to embolic or thrombotic vascular disease.[36] The distinction between TIA and stroke is one of duration of symptoms, with 24 hours representing a watershed between the two. In a significant minority of patients (14% in one series), patients with a clinical TIA have suffered a cerebral infarct in the appropriate area as demonstrated by CT scan.[37] The relevance of including TIA as a sub-category is that patients with a recent TIA are at high risk of suffering a completed stroke (*see* Section 4). Some patients with a carotid territory TIA (as opposed to vertebro-basilar territory TIA) will benefit from carotid endarterectomy to reduce this risk (*see* Section 6). Therefore the incidence of TIA predicts need for health services aimed at assessing whether such patients would be suitable candidates for endarterectomy, and indeed need for the operation itself. The distinction between TIA and minor stroke is arbitrary, and in practical terms for a health care needs assessment TIA should be considered with minor stroke. However, since most of the available epidemiological data separate TIA from minor stroke, the sub-category of TIA on its own is used for pragmatic reasons.

Stroke (acute phase)

Stroke may be defined as a 'syndrome of rapidly developing symptoms and signs of focal, and at times global, loss of cerebral function lasting more than 24 hours or leading to death, with no apparent cause other than that of vascular origin'.[12] This definition includes sub-arachnoid haemorrhage, which is a cause of global loss of cerebral function. However, sub-arachnoid haemorrhage will be considered as a separate category for the purposes of this chapter (*see* below). Patients who suffer a stroke need four types of service: acute treatment, secondary prevention, rehabilitation and continuing care. Unfortunately, none of the sub-categorisations of stroke discussed above adequately predicts need for all these categories of service. Acute treatment and secondary prevention needs are largely determined by stroke incidence, whereas rehabilitation and continuing care needs relate to severity of stroke and persistence of symptoms, whether defined in terms of impairment, disability or handicap.

People with sequelae of stroke

Given that needs for rehabilitation and continuing care services relate to the sequelae of stroke, it is important to have a sub-category that reflects this. The American Heart Association has classified the consequences of stroke in terms of six categories of impairment: motor, sensory, visual, language, cognition and affect.[38] There are some data on the prevalence of these impairments following stroke, so this categorisation has some utility for the purposes of health care needs assessment.

Sub-arachnoid haemorrhage

Sub-arachnoid haemorrhage is characterised clinically by a history of acute onset of headache, meningism and photophobia, often associated with loss of consciousness with no history of trauma.[13] This clinical syndrome is caused by blood in the sub-arachnoid space, typically due to leakage of blood from an intracranial aneurysm near the circle of Willis. While sub-arachnoid haemorrhage may lead to cerebral infarction due to an intracerebral component of haemorrhage or associated spasm of blood vessels, the acute management is different from that for focal stroke, and therefore it is useful to consider it as a separate sub-category.

The chapter will also make use of the available routine classification systems for stroke. These include the International Classification of Disease (ICD) codes and the Health Care Resource Group Codes (HRGs). Therefore, it is useful to outline how these systems classify stroke.

International Classification of Disease (ICD) codes

Routine NHS data such as mortality and hospital episode statistics utilise the International Classification of Disease (ICD) codes. Until recently, data have been coded using the ICD-9 system,[39] but a newer system has been developed, ICD-10.[40] The ICD codes use a classification based on a mixture of pathological type, cause and anatomical site (*see* Table 6 overleaf). The principal ICD-9 codes encompassing stroke are 430–438, but if information is imprecise, then strokes are occasionally placed under less specific codes.[41] Commonly, codes 430–438 are combined to give an overall code group for cerebrovascular disease incidence or mortality. It should be noted that these codes include diagnoses that are not strictly included in clinical definitions of stroke, such as transient cerebral ischaemia, subdural haemorrhage and cerebral arteritis.

Table 6 also illustrates the extent of use of these codes, by showing the number of deaths coded to each three-digit classification in England and Wales in 1998. Approximately two-thirds of stroke deaths were coded as 'acute but ill-defined cerebrovascular disease'. In a study of coding of acute stroke in Oxford hospitals, it was found that 89% of patients who died or were discharged with a diagnosis of stroke confirmed through a prospective stroke register were coded using ICD-9 code 436.[41] Thus however desirable sub-classification of stroke might be using systems such as those outlined in 'Possible sub-categorisations' above, in practice routine data sets do not provide sufficiently detailed diagnostic information to enable their use.

The equivalent alpha-numeric ICD-10 codes are shown in Table 7 overleaf. In ICD-10, cerebrovascular diseases are covered by the codes I 60–I 69. The principal changes compared with ICD-9 are as follows:

- transient cerebral ischaemia is now classified elsewhere
- the four-digit codes (not shown) allow more precise specification of anatomical site and of pathology
- occlusion and stenosis of pre-cerebral arteries now specifies '*not resulting in cerebral infarction*'
- there is a new code allowing for occlusion and stenosis of cerebral arteries that does not result in cerebral infarction.

Table 6: ICD-9 classification of stroke[39] and coding of deaths from stroke in England and Wales 1998.[14]

			Number of deaths in 1998 (% of total 'stroke')
430	Sub-arachnoid haemorrhage		2,686 (4.7)
431	Intracerebral haemorrhage		4,532 (7.9)
432	Other and unspecified intracranial haemorrhage	432.0 Non-traumatic extradural haemorrhage	415 (0.7)
		432.1 Subdural haemorrhage	
		432.9 Unspecified intracranial haemorrhage	
433	Occlusion and stenosis of pre-cerebral arteries	433.0 Basilar artery	222 (0.4)
		433.1 Carotid artery	
		433.2 Vertebral artery	
		433.3 Multiple and bilateral	
		433.8 Other	
		433.9 Unspecified	
434	Occlusion of cerebral arteries	434.0 Cerebral thrombosis	4,644 (8.1)
		434.1 Cerebral embolism	
		434.9 Unspecified	
435	Transient cerebral ischaemia		141 (0.2)
436	Acute but ill-defined cerebrovascular disease		36,919 (64.2)
437	Other and ill-defined cerebrovascular disease	437.0 Cerebral atherosclerosis	7,453 (13.0)
		437.1 Other generalised ischaemic cerebrovascular disease	
		437.2 Hypertensive encephalopathy	
		437.3 Cerebral aneurysm, non-ruptured	
		437.4 Cerebral arteritis	
		437.5 Moyamoya disease	
		437.6 Non-pyogenic thrombosis of intracranial venous sinus	
		437.8 Other	
		437.9 Unspecified	
438	Late effects of cerebrovascular disease		504 (0.9)

Table 7: ICD-10 classification of stroke.

I 60	Sub-arachnoid haemorrhage
I 61	Intracerebral haemorrhage
I 62	Other non-traumatic intracranial haemorrhage
I 63	Cerebral infarction
I 64	Stroke, not specified as haemorrhage or infarction
I 65	Occlusion and stenosis of pre-cerebral arteries, not resulting in cerebral infarction
I 66	Occlusion and stenosis of cerebral arteries, not resulting in cerebral infarction
I 67	Other cerebrovascular diseases
I 68	Cerebrovascular disorders in diseases classified elsewhere
I 69	Sequelae of cerebrovascular disease

These modifications make it easier to differentiate between those conditions that result in cerebral infarction (i.e. stroke) and those that do not.

Health care resource group codes (HRGs)

The NHS Executive has developed health care resource groups as a resource management tool. They group together patients who are expected to consume similar amounts of health care resource. The groups are defined on the basis of diagnoses (using the ICD codes described above) or procedures (using the Office of Population Censuses and Surveys classification [OPCS-4]). NHS reference costs provide data on the average costs for each HRG (*see* Section 5). Table 8 lists the HRG codes and labels for procedures and conditions of particular relevance to stroke. The categories are broad. For example, one would anticipate a very large range of costs within the category of A22, depending upon factors such as the degree of disability and whether or not a patient survived. Such wide variation in costs is indeed seen (*see* 'Costs of stroke care' in Section 5).

Table 8: Health Resource Group codes relevant to stroke.

HRG code	HRG label	Procedures/conditions included
A01	Intracranial procedures except trauma – 1	Drainage of extradural space
A02	Intracranial procedures except trauma – 2	Drainage of subdural space
A03	Intracranial procedures except trauma – 3	Operations on aneurysm of cerebral artery (excision or ligation); ligation of carotid artery; drainage of sub-arachnoid space; evacuation of haematoma (intracerebral, cerebellar)
A04	Intracranial procedures except trauma – 4	Operations on aneurysm of cerebral artery (clipping, obliteration)
A19	Haemorrhagic cerebrovascular disorders	Sub-arachnoid haemorrhage; intracerebral haemorrhage
A20	Transient ischaemic attack, aged > 69 or with complications	TIA
A21	Transient ischaemic attack, aged < 70 with no complications	TIA
A22	Non-transient stroke or cerebrovascular accident, aged > 69 or with complications	Cerebral infarction; stroke not specified as haemorrhage or infarct
A23	Non-transient stroke or cerebrovascular accident, aged < 70 with no complications	Cerebral infarction; stroke not specified as haemorrhage or infarct
Q05	Extracranial or upper limb arterial surgery	Carotid artery surgery, including endarterectomy

World Health Organization classifications of impairment, disability and handicap (ICFDH, ICF)

The classifications of stroke considered so far in this section have mostly focused on the underlying pathology. This is appropriate when considering health care needs for prevention and acute treatment, but less so when considering rehabilitation and continuing care needs. Rehabilitation can be defined as *an active problem-solving and educational process which focuses on the patient's disability (activities affected) and which aims to maximise the patient's social participation while minimising both the patient's somatic and psychological pain and distress and the distress of and stress on family members.* This definition of rehabilitation is based upon the WHO model of impairment, disability and handicap. The original WHO model was published in 1980, but has now been updated as the International Classification of Functioning, Disability and Health.[42] For discussion of the WHO models, *see* Appendix 1. The key ways in which the updated model (ICF) has changed from the original model are that:

- the terms impairment, disability and handicap are replaced by new terms (functions, activities and participation) which extend their meanings to include positive experiences
- environmental factors are explicitly incorporated in the model.

4 Prevalence and incidence

People at high risk of stroke

People may be at higher risk of stroke owing to inherent factors that cannot be altered, such as age, sex, family history and ethnicity. The effect of these will be considered under the epidemiology of stroke in 'Stroke' below. It is possible to produce long lists of potentially modifiable risk factors for stroke. However, these lists are based largely on associations observed in epidemiological studies, and the relationship between the risk factor and stroke is not necessarily causal, and may simply be due to confounding.[43–45] Table 9 (*see* opposite) shows the more important modifiable risk factors. It has been divided into those factors where there is reasonable evidence that treatment or removal of the risk factor does lead to a reduction in stroke risk, and those where the evidence is less certain. A summary of the evidence that treatment/avoidance of these factors is effective in reducing stroke risk is provided in Section 6.

While some of these risk factors (e.g. atrial fibrillation) are either present or absent ('dichotomous variables'), others, such as hypertension and obesity, are continuous variables. Table 9 presents the data using well-accepted (but arbitrary) cut-offs between what is 'normal' and 'abnormal' which can be used to define a 'higher-risk' individual. However, the lower the level of blood pressure, the lower the risk of stroke.[46] This is part of the rationale behind strategies to achieve whole-population risk reduction (*see* 'Prevention of stroke' in Section 5).

The importance of each of the risk factors in population terms depends upon three factors: how strong the association with stroke is (i.e. the relative risk), how common the risk factor is (i.e. the prevalence) and how common the disease is in the population group (i.e. the absolute risk). Thus, among the risk factors in the top half of Table 9, hypertension and smoking are the most important factors, given their high prevalence. Similarly, in the second half of the table, the potential importance of physical inactivity and obesity is underlined by high prevalence. Conversely, transient ischaemic attack is less important because it is relatively uncommon, though the high relative risk emphasises its importance for the individuals in whom it occurs. Oral contraception is of relatively minor importance in population terms as a risk factor for stroke, since it is used in a population in whom the absolute risk of stroke is very low.

Several of the risk factors shown in Table 9 (hypertension, diabetes, ischaemic heart disease, obesity) are dealt with in other chapters in the health care needs assessment series, so will not be considered further here. An important risk factor that does need some further consideration is atrial fibrillation.

Table 9: Prevalence of modifiable risk factors for stroke.

Risk factor	Relative risk of stroke in patient with risk factor	Prevalence of risk factor in England
Good evidence that treatment/avoidance can lower stroke risk		
Hypertension	1.5 for every 5 mmHg increase in diastolic blood pressure[46]	38% of men and 30% of women have either a systolic blood pressure greater than 140 mmHg or a diastolic blood pressure greater than 90 mmHg[47]
Atrial fibrillation	4–5[48,49]	5% of people aged 65 years and older[50,51]
Smoking	1.5[52]	28% of men and 27% of women[47]
Diabetes mellitus	2–3[44]	Diagnosed diabetes: 2–3% of men and 1.5–2.5% of women,[47,53] with an additional 1% of men and women with undiagnosed diabetes (glycosylated haemoglobin > 5.2%)[54]
Ischaemic heart disease	2.5[44]	7% of men and 4.5% of women (self-reported angina or heart attack that has been confirmed by a doctor)[47]
Previous stroke	15 in first year after stroke, dropping to 2 after 5 years[55]	1.5–1.75% of population[56,57]
Transient ischaemic attack	80 within first month; 13 within first year; 7 overall[58]	About 1.5% of people aged 55 or over report symptoms of typical TIA in preceding 3 years (not UK data)[59]
Weaker evidence that treatment/avoidance can lower stroke risk		
Obesity	1–2[44]	17% of men and 21% of women are obese (BMI > 30 kg/m^2), and an additional 45% of men and 32% of women are overweight (BMI 25–30 kg/m^2)[47]
Physical inactivity	2.5[60]	35% of men and 41% of women engage in less than 30 min of moderate exercise per week[47]
Excessive alcohol consumption	1.5–2 for 5 units/day[61,62]	15% of men and 3% of women drink more than 35 units per week[47]
Oral contraception	3, or 2 if low-oestrogen preparation[63]	27% of women aged 16–54 are current users of oral contraception (including injections or implants)[47]

Atrial fibrillation

There have been four UK prevalence surveys of atrial fibrillation (AF), which are summarised in Table 10 (*see* overleaf). It can be seen that given the different age groups and methods used to identify atrial fibrillation, there is a reasonable consistency in the findings. Approximately a quarter of atrial fibrillation is paroxysmal (i.e. episodic) and the rest is chronic.[64–66] Atrial fibrillation is more common in men than women. Longitudinal studies have shown that risk of atrial fibrillation is also independently associated with increasing age, heart failure, valve disease, coronary heart disease, diabetes and hypertension.[67,68] In a prevalence survey of people aged ≥65 (baseline data collection for the Cardiovascular Health Study), 57% of people with atrial fibrillation had clinical cardiovascular disease, and a further 35% had subclinical

Table 10: English prevalence surveys of atrial fibrillation.

Study	Population	Method of identifying AF	Results
Sudlow et al.[50]	Random sample of 4,843 people aged ≥ 65 drawn from HA register of 26 practices in Northumberland	ECG	Overall prevalence: 4.7% 65–74: 3.5% men, 2.4% women 75+: 10% men, 5.6% women
Connell and Gray[64]	Single practice in Gateshead (n = 9,162)	From GP case notes, some verified by ECG	Overall prevalence: 91/9,162 (1%); 76% chronic, 24% paroxsymal
Wheeldon et al.[51]	Single practice in Sheffield: all patients aged ≥ 65 (n = 1,422)	ECG	Overall prevalence: 5.4%; 75+: 6.6%
Lip et al.[65]	Two Birmingham practices (n = 16,519)	From GP case notes	Prevalence: 50+: 2.4%; 73% chronic, 27% paroxysmal

cardiovascular disease (abnormal findings on echocardiography or carotid ultrasound).[69] In other words, atrial fibrillation may be regarded in most cases as a manifestation of underlying cardiovascular disease. Data from the Framingham study suggest that the prevalence of atrial fibrillation has risen over time, from 3.2% in men aged 65–84 in 1968 to 9.1% in 1989.[67]

The best estimate of the prevalence of atrial fibrillation comes from a synthesis of four large population-based surveys carried out in the USA and Australia.[70] The results of this synthesis are consistent with the UK estimates shown in Table 10. Therefore, in Table 11, the age-specific prevalence rates derived from these four population surveys are applied to the population structure of England and Wales[14] in order to obtain best estimates of UK age-specific numbers of cases of atrial fibrillation. It can be seen from Table 11

Table 11: Estimate of age-specific numbers of cases of atrial fibrillation in England and Wales.

Age group (years)	Age-specific prevalence rate	Population of England and Wales (1000s)	Number of cases of AF (1000s)	% of all AF
40–44	0.1%	3,479.8	3.5	0.6%
45–49	0.3%	3,403.8	10.2	1.7%
50–54	0.5%	3,500.1	17.5	2.9%
55–59	0.8%	2,709.4	21.7	3.6%
60–64	1.5%	2,489.9	37.3	6.2%
65–69	3.0%	2,314.7	69.4	11.6%
70–74	5.0%	2,085.7	104.3	17.4%
75–79	7.0%	1,781.2	124.7	20.8%
80–84	10%	1,089.6	109.0	18.2%
85–89	10%	669	66.9	11.2%
90+	10%	347.7	34.8	5.8%
All ages	1.1%	52,427.9		
> 40	2.5%	23,870.9	599.3	
> 65	6.1%			85%
> 75	8.6%			56%

that the prevalence of atrial fibrillation rises with age, and over half (56%) of people with atrial fibrillation are aged 75 or over. A recent (1996–97) prevalence survey of *diagnosed* atrial fibrillation based upon data from a large health maintenance organisation in Canada found similar rates to those shown in Table 11.[71] Given that this survey would have omitted people with undiagnosed atrial fibrillation (in England this is about a quarter of all people with AF[72]) this provides a hint that perhaps the age-specific prevalence of atrial fibrillation is rising.

There have been two incidence studies of atrial fibrillation, Framingham and the Cardiovascular Health Study, neither of which are UK based.[68,73] In the Cardiovascular Health Study, the incidences for men aged 65–74 and 75–84 were 17.6 and 42.7 per 1000 person years, and for women 10.1 and 21.6. The Framingham results were similar, but with smaller differences between men and women. In the Framingham study, during 40 years of follow-up, 621 out of 5209 people developed atrial fibrillation. Atrial fibrillation in this cohort was associated with a 1.5- (men) to 1.9-fold (women) increased risk of mortality after adjustment for pre-existing cardiovascular disease.[74] The median survival of people aged 55–64 in atrial fibrillation was 12.6 years for men and 12.1 years for women, as compared with 18.1 years and 21.3 years, respectively, for people not in atrial fibrillation. Similar excess in adjusted mortality for people in atrial fibrillation has been reported from a smaller cohort (87 patients in AF) in Western Australia.[75]

There is a strong independent association between atrial fibrillation and stroke. Two cohort studies have reported relative risks of stroke in 'lone' atrial fibrillation (i.e. with no other evidence of cardiovascular disease) of between 4 and 5.[48,49] Furthermore, data from Framingham suggest that strokes occurring with atrial fibrillation are more severe and more likely to be fatal.[76] The Oxford Community Stroke Project reported a higher 30-day case fatality rate for cerebral infarction associated with atrial fibrillation (23%) as compared with sinus rhythm (8%).[77] The proportion of strokes in the population that are attributable to atrial fibrillation rises with age. The arrhythmia is associated with 30.7% and accounts for 23.5% of strokes in people aged 80–89, as compared with 8.5% and 2.8%, respectively, in 60–69 year olds.[73] Analysis of the Stroke Data Bank of the US National Institute of Neurological and Communicative Disorders and Stroke suggested that 9% of all ischaemic stroke is due to atrial fibrillation.[18]

Risk of stroke in patients with atrial fibrillation has consistently been found in several studies to be independently associated with increasing age, previous stroke or TIA, and hypertension.[78–80] Recent heart failure has been found to increase risk in some studies[79] but not others.[78,80] Being female[78,80,81] or diabetic[78] has also been identified as independent risk factors in some studies. Echocardiographic features such as global left ventricular dysfunction and left atrial size also predict stroke risk in atrial fibrillation, after clinical factors have been taken into account.[82]

Other risk factors for stroke

In addition to the risk factors for stroke considered in Table 9, there are several other factors that have been found to be associated with stroke risk, listed in Table 12 (*see* overleaf).[44,83]

Two factors in this table that have received some attention in terms of stroke prevention strategies in recent years, and are therefore worth considering in slightly more detail, are hypercholesterolaemia and asymptomatic carotid artery stenosis.

Cholesterol and risk of stroke

There is no strong evidence of any independent association between serum cholesterol and risk of stroke.[84] Despite this, an overview of cholesterol lowering with statin drugs found that treatment with statins reduces risk of stroke.[85] There are possible explanations for this apparent contradiction. Firstly, there is some evidence that low cholesterol is associated with increased risk of haemorrhagic stroke,[86] so it may be

Table 12: Other risk factors for stroke.

Other specific cardiac factors	Infective endocarditis; mitral stenosis; recent large myocardial infarction; left ventricular hypertrophy; cardiomyopathy
Haematological factors	Sickle-cell disease; raised packed cell volume; hypercoagulability, including raised fibrinogen
Biochemical factors	Hyperhomocysteinaemia; hypercholesterolaemia
Clinical factors	Migraine; snoring
Dietary factors	Low potassium; low fruit and vegetable intake
Other factors	Asymptomatic carotid artery stenosis; major life events

that this masks a positive association between serum cholesterol and risk of ischaemic stroke. Secondly, it may be that statins lower stroke risk indirectly by lowering risk of myocardial infarction, which is an established risk factor for stroke. Thirdly, it may be that statins do not reduce stroke risk by lowering cholesterol, but by some other mechanism. As will be discussed in Section 6, the evidence for cholesterol lowering to prevent stroke is strongest for patients with existing coronary heart disease, so in the context of the epidemiology of risk factors for stroke, serum cholesterol is of most relevance in this subgroup of patients.

Asymptomatic carotid artery stenosis

Atherosclerosis of the internal carotid artery is an important cause of stroke. Epidemiological data suggest that it is responsible for 9% of all ischaemic stroke.[18] When associated with symptoms of transient ischaemic attack, severe carotid artery stenosis (i.e. 70–99% stenosis) is associated with a 20% risk of major stroke in three years.[87,88] However, asymptomatic stenosis carries a lower risk of stroke. The risk of ipsilateral stroke or death in the medical control group of the Asymptomatic Carotid Artery Stenosis trial was 11% after 5 years.[89] Patients with an asymptomatic stenosis of 60–99% are at twice the risk of a first stroke compared with patients with stenosis of less than 60%.[90] However, approximately 45% of strokes in this population are attributable to other pathology, such as small-vessel occlusion and emboli from a cardiac source.[90,91] Furthermore, this population is at high risk of ischaemic heart disease. Indeed, Ogren *et al.* found no association between asymptomatic carotid stenosis and risk of stroke in a cohort of men born in 1914, which was perhaps due to the high mortality from ischaemic heart disease in those men with severe carotid stenosis.[92] Therefore, the relevance of the prevalence of asymptomatic carotid artery stenosis is perhaps more in relation to cardiovascular disease prevention strategies in general than it is to stroke prevention. The evidence for carotid endarterectomy to prevent stroke in asymptomatic carotid artery stenosis will be considered in Section 6.

Transient ischaemic attack

While there have been a number of studies worldwide of the epidemiology of transient ischaemic attack, the most robust study in the UK is the Oxfordshire Community Stroke Project, carried out between 1981 and 1986. The age-specific annual incidence rates derived from this study are shown in Table 13.[93] The overall incidence is similar in males and females, though the incidence in 55–84 year olds is higher in men than in women. Oxfordshire has one of the lowest death rates from stroke in the UK, and so it is likely that

Table 13: Age/sex-specific annual incidence rates with 95% confidence intervals (per 1000 population) for transient ischaemic attack in the Oxfordshire Community Stroke Project, 1981–86.

Age band (years)	Males	Females	Persons
< 15	0.00	0.00	0.00
15–44	0.02 (0.00–0.04)	0.02 (0.00–0.04)	0.02 (0.01–0.03)
45–54	0.25 (0.06–0.44)	0.26 (0.07–0.45)	0.25 (0.12–0.39)
55–64	1.22 (0.77–1.66)	0.63 (0.31–0.94)	0.92 (0.65–1.19)
65–74	2.43 (1.68–3.17)	0.90 (0.47–1.33)	1.61 (1.20–2.03)
75–84	3.01 (1.79–4.23)	2.29 (1.45–3.13)	2.57 (1.87–3.27)
85+	0.70 (0.00–2.07)	2.87 (1.26–4.49)	2.32 (1.09–3.67)
All ages	0.39 (0.31–0.46)	0.31 (0.24–0.38)	0.35 (0.30–0.40)

TIA incidence is higher elsewhere in the country. Approximately 80% of the TIAs were in the carotid distribution, and 20% in the vertebro-basilar distribution, which is similar to findings elsewhere.[94,95]

A much higher incidence of transient ischaemic attack (1.9 per 1000 per year) was recently reported from the General Practice Research Database (GPRD).[96] This probably reflects considerable misclassification error. For example, the prevalence of stroke recorded in this data set is only a sixth of what has been recorded in population surveys (see 'Prevalence of stroke' below), and many people with a label of transient ischaemic attack turn out to have other diagnoses.[97]

As shown in Table 9, a transient ischaemic attack is associated with a very high risk of stroke (relative risk of 80, 95% confidence interval: 34–158) in the first month following the event.[58] This falls to a relative risk of 13 in the first year, and to 7 in the first seven years. In absolute terms, this equates to a 4.4% (95% CI: 1.5–7.3%) risk of stroke in the first month, an 11.6% (95% CI: 6.9–16.3%) risk in the first year, and a 29.3% (95% CI: 21.3–37.3%) risk in the first five years, with an average annual risk of 6%.[58] People with TIA are also at significant risk of myocardial infarction, with an approximate annual risk of 2.4%.[58]

For a health care needs assessment, it is the incidence of transient ischaemic attacks rather than prevalence that is of most interest, because this will dictate the need for carotid endarterectomy (see Sections 6 and 7). The prevalence (i.e. the number of people who have had a history of a TIA) is relevant in that it highlights a group of people who are at high risk of future stroke, and therefore targets for secondary prevention. Unfortunately, there are no good UK-based estimates of the prevalence of transient ischaemic attack. In a Dutch study carried out between 1990 and 1993, the prevalence of a history of symptoms suggestive of a transient ischaemic attack within the last three years (assessed by a trained study physician) was 3.7% of men and 2.9% of women aged 55 or over. However, the prevalence was 50% lower if only people with classical features of a transient ischaemic attack were included.[59] In the Atherosclerosis Risk In Communities (ARIC) Study set in the USA between 1987 and 1989, 3% of people aged 45–64 reported the occurrence of symptoms during their life which were classified by diagnostic algorithm as being due to a transient ischaemic attack.[98] Both these prevalence estimates are higher than would be anticipated from the Oxford Community Stroke Project, or from other incidence studies,[94,95] which suggests some over-ascertainment, possibly due to difficulty in accurate assessment of past symptoms.

Stroke

Incidence of first stroke

There have been several studies worldwide of stroke incidence.[7] This report will focus on three incidence studies of first-ever stroke in England: the Oxford Community Stroke Project (OCSP),[99] the South London Stroke Register (SLSR)[100] and the East Lancashire Study (ELS).[101] The methodology of these studies is summarised in Table 14 and the resulting age-specific incidence rates are shown in Table 15. In these studies, cases of sub-arachnoid haemorrhage were included under the broad umbrella of 'stroke'.

Table 14: English studies of first stroke incidence.

	Number of strokes	Period of study	Population	Method of case ascertainment
OCSP	675	1981–86	All patients registered with 50 GPs (10 practices) in Oxfordshire (total population: 105,476)	1 GPs notified all possible strokes. 2 Admission and casualty registers of Oxford hospitals reviewed. 3 Oxford Record Linkage study enabled identification of those who died or were discharged from Oxford hospitals with stroke. 4 Death certificates and post-mortem reports reviewed. Possible cases reviewed by a study neurologist as soon as possible either at home, in hospital, or in a special outpatient clinic. CT scan or post-mortem was sought in every case.
ELS	642	1994–95	All patients registered with 93 practices in East Lancashire (total population: 405,272)	1 GPs notified all possible strokes. 2 Ward log books of local hospitals checked monthly. 3 Discharge diagnoses from routine hospital coding. 4 Death certificates reviewed. 5 Rehabilitation and support service staff were asked to report possible strokes. GP case notes or FHSA records reviewed for possible cases.
SLSR[103]	1,254	1995–98	Residents of 22 wards of Lambeth, Southwark and Lewisham Health Commission (total population: 234,533)	12 notification sources: A&E records; hospital wards; brain-imaging requests; death certificates; Coroner's records; GPs; hospital medical staff; community therapists; bereavement officers; hospital-based stroke registers; GP computer records; others: notification by patients or relatives. Possible cases reviewed by a study physician within 48 hours where possible. Outpatient and domiciliary visits offered.

The all-age (standardised) rates at the bottom of Table 15 reflect the overall incidence rate that would have occurred if the age-specific incidence rates are experienced in England and Wales as a whole. Thus,

Table 15: Age-specific annual incidence of first stroke (per 1000 population) in three English populations, with 95% confidence intervals.

Age group (years)	Oxfordshire	East Lancashire	South London
< 15	0.03		0.01 (0.00–0.04)
15–24	0.06		0.03 (0.00–0.07)
25–34	0.08		0.12 (0.08–0.18)
35–44	0.23		0.30 (0.21–0.42)
< 45	0.09 (0.06–0.13)		
< 50		0.09 (0.06–0.13)	
50–54		0.88 (0.49–1.26)	
45–54	0.57 (0.35–0.79)		0.87 (0.68–1.10)
55–64	2.91 (2.37–3.45)	1.69	2.19 (1.88–2.53)
65–74	6.90 (5.93–7.87)	4.67	4.96 (4.44–5.51)
75–84	14.34 (12.49–16.19)	10.64	9.34 (8.41–10.34)
85+	19.87 (15.78–23.95)	20.86	19.72 (17.08–22.65)
All age (crude)	1.60 (1.48–1.72)	1.58 (1.46–1.71)	1.33 (1.26–1.41)
All age (standardised)	**2.17***	**1.65***	**1.74†**

*Age- and sex-standardised to England and Wales, 1998.[14]
†Age-standardised to England and Wales, 1998.

depending upon which incidence study is used, the incidence of first stroke in England seems to lie between 1.65 and 2.17 per 1000 population. The standardised rates are all higher than the crude rates because these three studies were carried out in populations that overall are younger than England and Wales as a whole. They differ from the previously published standardised rates because a different standard population was used. For example, the OCSP standardised its rates using the 1981 England and Wales population, and quoted an all-age (standardised) rate of 2.0.[99] The higher rate shown in Table 15 reflects changes to the age structure of England and Wales that have occurred between 1981 and 1998. In other words, assuming stable age-specific incidence, there would have been an 8.05% rise in the overall incidence of stroke between 1981 and 1998 due to ageing of the population. It is notable that the Oxfordshire rates are higher than those observed in East Lancashire and South London. Oxfordshire has a lower standardised mortality ratio (SMR) for stroke than the other districts: the SMR for Oxfordshire over the period 1993–95 was 90, compared with 98 in Lambeth, Southwark and Lewisham and 104 in East Lancashire.[102] Therefore, unless case fatality is significantly lower in Oxfordshire than in the other districts, Oxfordshire is unlikely to have a higher incidence than the other areas. Two possible explanations for the variation in observed rates are differences in case ascertainment, and secular changes in stroke incidence.

The methods of case ascertainment in the three studies are summarised in Table 14. It is conceivable that case ascertainment was more complete in Oxfordshire than in the other areas, given that the Oxfordshire study population was smaller, and the GPs involved all had to be 'enthusiastic' to collaborate.[99] There was also a significant 'carrot' for GPs to notify patients, namely rapid review by a study neurologist and access to CT scanning. Research nurses visited practices at least once a week. The South London and East Lancashire studies both aimed to recruit from defined geographical areas, and therefore will have included GPs of varying degrees of enthusiasm. South London compensated for this by having many different methods of identifying possible cases, and also offered early assessment by a specialist. Minor strokes are most likely to be missed by community registers, since such cases may not be admitted to hospital,[104] and the duration of symptoms/residual disability will be shorter. Some evidence that the Oxford Community Stroke Project did indeed detect a higher proportion of minor strokes is provided by the case fatality in the three studies. Thirty-day case fatality in the OCSP was 19%,[13] compared with 26% in South London[103] and 34% in East Lancashire (*see* 'Survival following stroke' below).[101]

The Oxfordshire study was performed a decade before the other studies, so the observed difference may reflect a decline in age-specific incidence of stroke in the intervening decade. There have been significant reductions in age-specific stroke mortality over this period,[1] and it is likely that this in part reflects decline in incidence (*see* 'Trends in stroke incidence and mortality' below).

While the overall rate of stroke was different in the three studies, the general pattern of an increasing incidence with age is similar. The expected number of new first strokes in a population of 100 000 with the age- and sex-specific structure of England and Wales is shown in Table 16, based on the age- and sex-specific incidence rates of the OCSP. Two estimates are made. In the first (A), it is assumed that there has been no reduction in age-specific incidence between 1981–86 and the present day and in the second (B), it is assumed that there has been a 20% reduction in age-specific incidence. These show that although the age-specific rates are generally higher in men than women, more women than men would be expected to have a stroke, owing to the longer life expectancy of women. Eighty-one per cent of strokes (175/216) would be anticipated to occur in people aged 65 or over. The anticipated stroke rate is between 174 and 216 per 100 000 population, depending upon what assumption is made about change in age-specific incidence rates. If a 20% reduction in incidence is assumed between the time when the OCSP was carried out and the present day, then the overall incidence rate matches the rate for the South London Stroke Register (1.74 per 1000) (*see* Table 15). Capture–recapture analysis of the South London register results suggests that it is extremely unlikely that it could be under-counting by as much as 20% (which would be the implication if assumption [A] was adopted).[105] Therefore, the range 1.74–2.16 per 100 000 seems a plausible range of likely stroke incidence, taking all the UK-specific epidemiological data that are available into account. In estimating stroke incidence in a local population, once age structure has been taken into account, it is also important to take into account factors such as ethnic mix (*see* 'Ethnicity and stroke' below) and other sociodemographic factors (*see* 'Other factors affecting stroke incidence' below).

Table 16: Estimated numbers of new first strokes in a typical population of 100,000 in England and Wales.

Age	Males				Females				Total number of strokes	
	OCSP rate (/1000)	Population	Number of strokes		OCSP rate (/1000)	Population	Number of strokes			
			A	B			A	B	A	B
< 45	0.08	31,235	2	2	0.11	29,872	3	3	5	5
45–54	0.67	6,579	4	4	0.46	6,589	3	2	7	6
55–64	3.47	4,900	17	14	2.35	5,017	12	9	29	23
65–74	8.11	3,890	32	25	5.84	4,503	26	21	58	46
75–84	15.87	2,123	34	27	13.39	3,352	45	36	79	63
85+	18.42	514	9	8	20.36	1,425	29	23	38	31
Total		49,241	98	80		50,758	118	94	**216**	**174**

Note: Number of strokes in A assumes stable incidence between 1981–86 (i.e. when OCSP was performed) and present day; B assumes 20% decline in age-specific incidence over this time period.

Incidence of recurrent stroke

While the key incidence studies of stroke have focused on incidence of first stroke, in terms of a health care needs assessment recurrent stroke is of equal importance. The OCSP showed that the risk of suffering a recurrence within five years of a first stroke was 30% (95% CI: 20–39%).[55] The East Lancashire Study identified 642 first strokes and 290 recurrent strokes.[101] In other words, using the East Lancashire data, it would be necessary to inflate the estimated numbers of stroke in a population by as much as 45%. Recent estimates in the USA of the 'inflation factor' for recurrent strokes vary from 30%[106] to 43%.[107] In the WHO MONICA project, the 'inflation factor' was 20%.[108] This is lower than the other studies, probably because it was set in younger populations – the study population was aged 35–64 years. The proportion of recurrent strokes that might be anticipated depends upon factors such as the age of the population (older age means more recurrent stroke) and ethnic mix.[107]

Prevalence of stroke

Surveys carried out in Newcastle and North Yorkshire found the prevalence of stroke to be between 1.5 and 1.75%.[56,57] Prevalence of stroke in adults (aged 16 or over) in the Health Survey from England in 1998 was found to be 2.1 per 1000 in women and 2.3 per 1000 in men.[47] Prevalence rises with age; 9–10% of people aged 75 or over have had a stroke. The prevalence of stroke recorded in general practice is much lower than this. Data from the General Practice Research Database (GPRD) suggests that the prevalence is only 2.3 per 1000.[109] The discrepancy probably reflects both under-recording in GP records and that the stroke had to be recorded between 1994 and 1998 to be included. Interestingly, the recording of TIA in this database is much higher than one would anticipate from epidemiological studies (*see* 'Transient ischaemic attack' above).

Survival following stroke

Survival following first stroke in the three UK-based epidemiological studies is shown in Table 17. The almost twofold variation between Oxfordshire and East Lancashire reflects either differences in case ascertainment or differences in survival. The likeliest explanation is that the OCSP had better ascertainment of minor stroke due to differences in study design (*see* 'Incidence of first stroke' above). After the first year, non-stroke cardiovascular disease is the commonest cause of death in stroke survivors.[110]

Table 17: Case fatality following first stroke.

Time after stroke	OCSP	ELS	SLSR
28 days	19%	34%	26%
90 days		40%	33%
180 days			37%
1 year	31%		

OCSP, Oxfordshire Community Stroke Project; ELS, East Lancashire Study; SLSR, South London Stroke Register.

The prognosis is worse for recurrent stroke – in the USA, the two-year case fatality of first stroke is 43%, compared with 52% for recurrent stroke.[111]

Ethnicity and stroke

Risk of death from stroke in the UK is higher in minority ethnic groups. An analysis of death by country of birth for the period 1989–92 found that mortality was highest among those born in West Africa and

Table 18: Standardised mortality ratios (and 95% confidence intervals) for stroke in England and Wales by country of birth, 1989–92.[112]

Country of birth	Men	Women
Total population	100	100
Scotland	125 (115–136)	125 (113–137)
Ireland	138 (128–148)	123 (113–133)
East Africa	114 (86–147)	122 (88–164)
West Africa	271 (210–344)	181 (118–265)
Caribbean	168 (151–186)	157 (136–179)
South Asia	155 (143–168)	141 (127–157)

the Caribbean, but was also significantly raised in those from South Asia, Ireland and Scotland (*see* Table 18).[112]

In the South London Stroke Register, the age- and sex-adjusted incidence of stroke was 2.2 times higher in people of African or Caribbean origin compared with the white population, but case fatality was similar in the different populations.[103] Similar differences in stroke incidence by ethnicity have been observed in the USA.[107]

Other factors affecting stroke incidence

There are wide variations in stroke mortality throughout England and Wales. Standardised mortality ratios (SMRs) for stroke in health authorities in England and Wales in 1993–95 varied from 74 (95% CI: 67–81) in Redbridge and Waltham Forest to 130 (95% CI: 121–139) in Wigan and Bolton.[102] Socio-economic deprivation appears to be an important factor underlying this variation.[113,114] Regional differences in lifestyle (*see* Table 9 for other factors associated with risk of stroke) may also account for some of the observed variation. There is also some evidence that adverse socio-economic circumstances in childhood may influence subsequent risk of mortality from stroke.[115]

Trends in stroke incidence and mortality

Age-specific mortality from stroke in England and Wales has been declining throughout the twentieth century.[116] For example, in 65–74 year old men, there was an average annual reduction in stroke mortality of 1.5% per year from 1901 to 1939, 0.1% per year from 1940 to 1967, and 2.2% per year from 1968 to 1991. Between 1986 (the last year of the OCSP) and 1999, age-adjusted mortality from stroke fell by 42% in men and by 32% in women.[1] The changes in age-specific mortality rates over this period are shown in Figures 2 and 3 (*see* overleaf).

Between 1986 and 1999, there have continued to be falls in mortality in all ages, but these have been more pronounced in the older age groups, and there is a hint that the decline in mortality has slowed in the younger age groups since 1993 (*see* Figure 2). There are three major categories of explanation for this observed fall in mortality: artefact, decline in incidence or decline in case fatality. While there are important errors in the death certification of stroke,[118] artefactual change in how doctors have been recording death is unlikely to explain the fall, since there have been similar declines in mortality from coronary heart disease, which is the likeliest alternative cause to appear on the death certificate.[1] Data on trends in incidence are not available for England and Wales, so empirical evidence for a fall in incidence needs to be sought from other countries. The evidence is mixed. For example, in Denmark there has been a

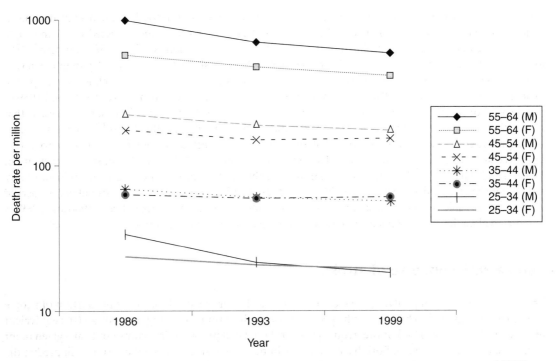

Figure 2: Trends in age-specific stroke mortality in England and Wales, ages 25–64, 1986–99.[1,14,117]

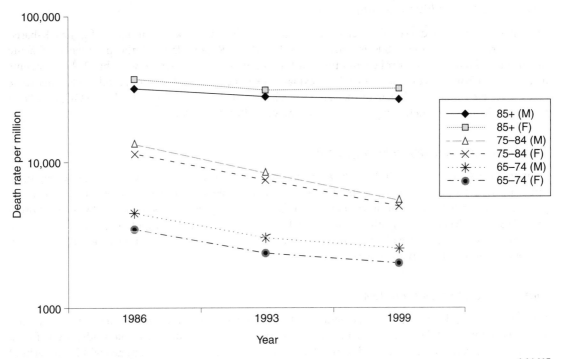

Figure 3: Trends in age-specific stroke mortality in England and Wales, ages 65 and over, 1986–99.[1,14,117]

3% per annum decline in age-adjusted incidence between 1982 and 1991, but no overall decline in incidence due to demographic change.[119] In the WHO MONICA project (which covered stroke in people under the age of 65), incidence declined in the majority of the populations studied (13/17 for men, 15/17 for women) between 1985 and 1990.[120] In the Swedish MONICA site, while incidence fell in under-65s, it rose in 65–74 year olds.[121] In New Zealand, there was no consistent pattern of decline in age-specific incidence between 1981 and 1991,[122] and in the USA rates appear to have fallen between 1985 and 1989 in people aged over 70, and then started to rise again.[123] Data from Rochester, Minnesota, suggested that stroke rates rose between the 1970s and 1980s, but were stable during the 1980s.[124] There are more consistent international data to suggest that there has been a decline in case fatality from stroke (i.e. improved survival after stroke), but not of sufficient magnitude to explain the fall in stroke mortality in England and Wales.[121,125–127] Therefore, the most plausible explanation for the decline in stroke mortality is that there has been a decline in both incidence and case fatality. To reflect this, the estimated numbers of new strokes in Table 16 include an assumption (B) of a 20% decline in incidence between 1986 and 1989, as a partial explanation of the 42% decline in mortality over the same time period.

People with sequelae of stroke

There are two ways of quantifying the sequelae of stroke. Either one can look at the proportion of people who might be expected to have a specific problem after a given time following their stroke (the equivalent of incidence), or one can look at the frequency of stroke-related problems in a community at a given point in time (a prevalence survey). Both have their uses in needs assessment, since the former will predict the need for acute rehabilitation services, and the latter the need for long-term support.

Incidence of disability following stroke

There has been a lack of data on the incidence of disability following stroke. A summary of some UK-based studies carried out in the 1980s is shown in Table 19.[128] Recent data on the prevalence of acute impairments following first stroke from the South London Stroke Register showed that 21% of patients had a normal Barthel score (*see* Table 5 for explanation) and 51% had severe disability (Barthel score < 10).[129] These results are similar to the acute prevalence data shown in Table 19. In the OCSP, 65% of stroke survivors were functionally independent one year after their stroke.[13]

Prevalence of disability following stroke

A prevalence survey in North Yorkshire found that 33% of stroke survivors had some cognitive impairment, 27% had a problem with their speech, and 12.5% had difficulty swallowing.[56] Fifty-five per cent required help in one or more activities of daily living. A prevalence survey in Newcastle reported that 70% were dependent on others (modified Rankin score 3–5).[57] Extrapolating these results to a population with a prevalence of stroke of 1.5–1.75%, one would anticipate the prevalence of stroke with moderate residual disability to be between 0.8% and 1.2%.

Time course of recovery following stroke

It is also useful to know the recovery pattern following stroke, since this will influence need for (and appropriate timing of decisions about) institutional care. In the Copenhagen stroke study, it was found that functional recovery (as measured by the Barthel Index; *see* Table 5) was completed within 13 weeks of the stroke in 95% of patients. However, the more severe the stroke, the longer it took for recovery to take

Table 19: Acute (0–7 days), 3-week and 6-month impairment/disability rates.[131–134]

Phenomenon		Acute	3 weeks	6 months
Impairments	Initial loss/depression of consciousness	5%	–	–
	Not oriented (or unable to talk)	55%	36%	27%
	Marked communication problems (aphasia)	52%	29%	15%
	Motor loss (partial or complete)	80%	70%	53%
Disabilities	Incontinent of faeces	31%	13%	7%
	Incontinent of urine	44%	24%	11%
	Needs help grooming (teeth, hair, face)	56%	27%	13%
	Needs help with toilet/commode	68%	39%	20%
	Needs help with feeding	68%	38%	33%
	Needs help moving from bed to chair	70%	42%	19%
	Unable to walk independently indoors	73%	40%	15%
	Needs help dressing	79%	51%	31%
	Needs help bathing	86%	65%	49%
	Very severely dependent	38%	13%	4%
	Severely dependent	20%	13%	5%
	Moderately dependent	15%	15%	12%
	Mildly dependent	12%	28%	32%
	Physically independent	12%	31%	47%

Note: The acute figures are of limited accuracy as many patients were not assessed within the first week. Many of these were very ill and probably very dependent. Consequently the figures relating to acute disability are minimum estimates.

place. Thus it took up to 20 weeks before maximal recovery was achieved in patients with very severe strokes.[130]

Mood disorders following stroke

Depression and anxiety are important sequelae of stroke.[135] For example, in a follow-up at six months of patients admitted to hospital in Edinburgh who were entered into a trial to assess the effect of a stroke family care worker, 22% were anxious (i.e. scored > 8 on the HAD anxiety scale) and 20% were depressed (> 8 on the HAD depression scale).[136] Estimates of incidence differ between studies due to variations in design, including in particular how depression is defined.[135] For example, 60% of patients in the Edinburgh study scored over 4 on the GHQ-30,[136] and 54% of patients in the control group of a study in Finland were classed as depressed (10 or more on the Beck Depression Inventory).[137]

Effect of stroke on informal carers

Stroke has important effects on the well-being of carers as well as patients. Care giving is associated with significant strain, anxiety and stress.[138–141] A literature review reported the prevalence of depression in carers of stroke patients to vary from 34% to 52%.[142] A more recent study found a 17% prevalence of depression, a 37% prevalence of anxiety and a 55% prevalence of an abnormal score (> 4) on the General Health Questionnaire (GHQ-30) six months after stroke.[143] These problems persist. In the Perth Community Stroke Study, over half of carers of stroke survivors with residual moderate or severe disability at one year had evidence of emotional distress, and the majority reported disruption of social activities (79%) and leisure time (55%).[144] In a matched case–control study, spouses of patients with stroke were significantly more likely to be depressed than controls 1–3 years after stroke.[145]

Sub-arachnoid haemorrhage

The overall incidence of sub-arachnoid haemorrhage in the Oxford Community Stroke Project was 10 per 100 000 per year.[13] This is consistent with international studies, though these show a wide variation in incidence from 2 to 22 per 100 000.[146] In a study in New Zealand, at least 68% of cases were associated with an underlying intracranial aneurysm or arterio-venous malformation.[20] Mortality from sub-arachnoid haemorrhage is high. In the New Zealand study, 36% had died within 48 hours of presentation, and 57% within one year. In the OCSP, 46% were dead within one month, and 48% within one year.

Summary of epidemiology of stroke at level of primary care trust

Table 20 shows that from a primary care perspective, the vast bulk of the workload is concerned with prevention and long-term care. A GP with a list size of 2000 would only expect to see one case of sub-arachnoid haemorrhage every five years, fewer than one transient ischaemic attack per year, and three patients with a first stroke and one patient with a recurrent stroke per year. On the other hand, each GP would expect to have 22 patients with atrial fibrillation under their care, and 20 patients who have moderate disability from a stroke.

Table 20: Summary of epidemiology of stroke and risk factors for stroke in a population of 100,000 and for a GP with a list size of 2,000.

Sub-category	Expected number of new cases per year (incidence)		Expected number of existing cases (prevalence)	
	For a GP	For a PCT	For a GP	For a PCT
Risk factors for stroke				
Atrial fibrillation	7	330	22	1,100
Hypertension (BP > 140/90 mmHg)			680	34,000
Current smokers			560	28,000
Diabetes mellitus			40	2,000
Ischaemic heart disease			110	5,500
Transient ischaemic attack	0.7	35		
Stroke			30	1,500
First stroke (excluding sub-arachnoid haemorrhage)	3	164		
Recurrent stroke	1	57		
People with moderate disability from stroke			20	1,000
Sub-arachnoid haemorrhage	0.2	10		

Note: PCT = primary care trust, with a population of 100,000; numbers of first strokes derived from assumption B in Table 16.

5 Services available and their costs

This section describes the types of service and intervention that are available for stroke care and gives data as to how widely they are used. It does not comment on whether they are effective (this is covered in Section 6), whether they should or should not be available (covered in Section 7), or whether the utilisation rate is appropriate. To interpret whether or not the utilisation rate is appropriate, it is important to consider both the effectiveness and the cost-effectiveness of the intervention.

Prevention of stroke

Rose identified two complementary strategies for disease prevention: the population approach, whereby the aim is to reduce the level of risk in the whole population, and the 'high-risk' approach, which aims to focus attention on reducing risk in individuals known to be at higher risk of the disease.[147] 'High-risk' individuals in this context include people at high risk of stroke, people with transient ischaemic attack and people with previous stroke.

Population strategies

These include both strategies to make environmental and socio-economic conditions more favourable to health, and strategies to influence behaviour in such a way that 'healthy' choices are more likely to be made. Such approaches overlap. For example, provision of no-smoking areas both makes the environment healthier and may discourage people from smoking. The population strategies relevant to stroke highlighted in the White Paper *Saving Lives: Our Healthier Nation* are summarised in Table 21.[8]

Table 21: Population strategies highlighted in *Saving Lives: Our Healthier Nation*.

	Local players and communities	Government and national players
Social and economic	Tackle social exclusion Provide incentives to employees to cycle or walk to work	Raise cost of smoking through taxation Tackle joblessness, social exclusion and poor education
Environmental	Provide smoke-free environments Reduce stress at work Provide safe cycling and walking routes	
Personal behaviour	Enforce ban on illegal sale of cigarettes to children Improve access to affordable food in deprived areas Provide facilities for physical activity	Encourage development of healthy schools and workplaces Control advertising and promotion of cigarettes Develop healthy living centres Ensure access to and availability of foods for a healthy diet Provide information about health risks of smoking, poor diet and lack of exercise
Health services		Encourage health care professionals to give advice on healthier living

Prevention in people at high risk of stroke

Hypertension, diabetes and ischaemic heart disease are dealt with in other chapters in this series of health care needs assessments. Workers in primary care are well placed to offer appropriate lifestyle advice (diet, smoking, alcohol, weight, exercise).

For people in atrial fibrillation, the principal treatments to reduce stroke risk are anticoagulation with warfarin, usually with a target INR (International Normalised Ratio) of 2.5, or use of an antiplatelet agent, commonly aspirin, with newer alternatives available such as clopidogrel. Treatment with warfarin requires regular blood tests in order to ensure that the INR is near the target. Traditionally, INR has been monitored in hospital-based anticoagulation clinics, but newer models are emerging, including monitoring in primary care,[148] use of computerised decision support software to regulate dosing,[149] and patient self-management of INR.[150]

UK-based audits have shown that the majority of patients in atrial fibrillation are treated with aspirin rather than warfarin. Estimates of the proportion of people in atrial fibrillation on warfarin vary between 21% and 36%.[50,51,64,65] Warfarin is used less often in elderly people. For example, Sudlow *et al.* found that only 17% of patients in atrial fibrillation over the age of 74 were on warfarin.[50] This reluctance by clinicians to use warfarin in elderly patients is also reflected in US data.[151–153] Analysis of the National Ambulatory Care Surveys suggests that while warfarin use increased in the USA between 1989 and 1993 (from 13% to 40% of patients in atrial fibrillation), there has been no further rise in warfarin use between 1993 and 1996 (33% of patients in 1996 were on warfarin).[154] As in the other studies, the National Ambulatory Care Surveys showed that warfarin was less likely to be used in the very elderly.

Echocardiography is sometimes used to increase the precision of estimating risk of stroke in atrial fibrillation. In a study in West Birmingham, Lip *et al.* found that about a fifth of patients in atrial fibrillation had had an echocardiograph performed.[65]

Prevention in people who have had a transient ischaemic attack or stroke

Interventions commonly used are summarised in Table 22.

Table 22: Secondary prevention in people who have had a transient ischaemic attack or stroke.

Lifestyle advice	Diet; smoking; alcohol; weight; exercise, where appropriate
Blood pressure reduction	
Antiplatelet agents	Most commonly aspirin; other agents such as dipyridamole and clopidogrel are also used
Anticoagulation	For patients in atrial fibrillation and those with certain types of valvular heart disease, and for those where the stroke was considered to be cardio-embolic in origin
Statins	For patients with known coronary heart disease
Carotid endarterectomy	For patients with significant (> 70%) carotid artery stenosis on the same side

Note: The effectiveness of these interventions is discussed in Section 6.

A survey conducted by the Stroke Association (1378 respondents) found that after a stroke 63% were taking aspirin, 23% were not taking aspirin because of a contraindication, and 14% were not taking aspirin but had no contraindication.[155] While this survey is difficult to interpret owing to a low response rate (less than 34%), it does echo other audits of aspirin use. For example, out of 198 men in the British Regional Heart Study with a history of stroke or transient ischaemic attack, only 80 (40%) were taking aspirin when surveyed in 1992.[156] Analysis of the General Practice Research Database (GPRD) found that between 1992 and 1996 around 37% of patients with a diagnosis of TIA were on aspirin, and 17% of patients with a diagnosis of stroke.[96] A survey of aspirin use in patients identified from GP registers as having coronary heart disease found that 63% were taking aspirin.[157]

Given the high relative risk of stroke early after a transient ischaemic attack (*see* Table 9), systems have been developed for 'fast-track assessment' of patients with a transient ischaemic attack. These include urgent neurology outpatient assessment, and express carotid duplex services.[158] A substantial proportion of people referred with a transient ischaemic attack either do not have this diagnosis confirmed, or do not proceed to surgery. In a review of 332 patients referred to a regional neurovascular clinic, in only 60% of cases did the neurologist agree with the diagnosis.[97] In the first year of an express carotid duplex service in Gloucester, 90 scans were performed, and 14% of these patients went on to have a carotid endarterectomy.[158] The median gap between onset of symptoms and surgery for these patients was 51 days.

An audit of 709 carotid endarterectomies performed in 1994 by 59 participating surgeons in the UK and Ireland found that the mean ipsilateral stenosis was 82% (range: 30–99%).[159] A study in Wessex reported that in 1995–96, the crude rate of carotid endarterectomy was 8.9 per 100 000 population, but estimated that need for the operation was at a level of 15.3 per 100 000.[160] A study of national carotid endarterectomy rates based on Hospital Episode Statistics (HES) found that, between 1990 and 1995, rates increased from 1.2 per 100 000 to 4.8 per 100 000.[161]

Acute management and rehabilitation of stroke

Patients with acute stroke are treated and rehabilitated in a variety of different settings, as illustrated in Figure 4.

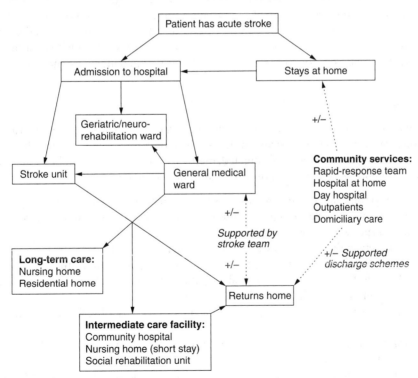

Figure 4: Patient pathways for stroke.

There is wide variation between localities in the proportion of patients with acute stroke who are admitted to hospital. Fifty-five per cent of people with first stroke were admitted to hospital in the OCSP,[162] 70% in the East Lancashire Study,[101] 71–78% of patients under the age of 75 across three districts in Southern England,[163,164] and 84% of patients on the South London Stroke Register.[100] The proportion in the OCSP admitted to hospital is lower than the others probably both because in this study there was more complete ascertainment of minor strokes and because neurologists would visit patients at home or see them in an outpatient clinic. Also it was carried out earlier than the other studies, and there may have been changes in admission patterns over time. Schemes such as 'rapid-response teams', 'hospital at home'[165] and day hospital services have been developed to facilitate keeping people at home. In Oxfordshire, whether or not someone was admitted depended on both the severity of the stroke and whether or not the patient lived alone.[162] The principal reason given by GPs for requesting admission to hospital was for nursing or social care (a factor in 87% of admissions).

Diagnosis of stroke

The diagnosis of stroke can be made on clinical grounds based on history and bedside signs, and this clinical diagnosis is reasonably accurate in that investigations such as cranial imaging seldom show unexpected alternative pathological diagnoses (*see* discussion in 'Diagnosis' in Section 6).[166] The majority of patients admitted to hospital with stroke will have a CT scan or other type of brain imaging primarily to exclude or demonstrate cerebral haemorrhage.[167,168]

Acute treatments

Treatments available for acute stroke are reviewed in Section 6. With the exception of aspirin, acute drug treatments such as heparin and thrombolytic therapies (only recently given a restricted licence in the UK for acute stroke) are used only rarely. A Stroke Association survey of consultants caring for stroke patients carried out during 1998 found that 94.1% 'rarely or never used thrombolysis'.[167] In patients who cannot swallow, 60% of consultants start feeding within the first week, usually (90%) with a nasogastric tube. If unsafe swallowing persists, 75% of consultants favour the use of percutaneous endoscopic gastrostomy (PEG).

Stroke-unit care

Among patients admitted to hospital, a major distinction is whether patients are treated on a stroke unit or in a general medical ward. The term 'stroke-unit' care has come to be synonymous with 'organised in-patient' care.[169] This implies care by a co-ordinated, multi-disciplinary team including nurses and doctors. Under this broad umbrella, several types of 'stroke unit' have been defined:[170]

- *stroke ward*: geographically defined area where stroke patients receive stroke-unit care
- *stroke team*: a mobile team delivering stroke-unit care to patients in a variety of wards; this does not always include a specialist nurse
- *dedicated stroke unit*: a disease-specific stroke unit managing only stroke patients
- *mixed assessment/rehabilitation unit*: a generic disability unit (which fulfils the definition of a stroke unit) specialising in the management of disabling illnesses including stroke; for example, this would include geriatric and neurological rehabilitation wards
- *acute stroke unit*: a stroke unit accepting patients acutely and continuing for several days (usually < 1 week)
- *combined acute/rehabilitation stroke unit*: a stroke unit accepting patients acutely but continuing care for several weeks if necessary
- *rehabilitation stroke unit*: a stroke unit accepting patients after a delay of 1–2 weeks and continuing care for several weeks if necessary

From responses to the Stroke Association survey of consultant physicians in the UK it was estimated that in 1998 approximately half of stroke patients were cared for in an organised stroke service.[167] In the National Sentinel Audit for stroke, which carried out a case-note review of 6894 consecutive stroke patients admitted to 197 trusts in England, Wales and Northern Ireland during 1998, the proportion of patients receiving stroke-unit care was lower.[10] Eighteen per cent of patients were shown to spend more than half of their inpatient stay on a stroke unit, 15% on a rehabilitation unit, and 67% on general wards. This general pattern of results is consistent with the Clinical Standards Advisory Group (CSAG) review of stroke services in a small random sample of 13 districts and boards in the UK that was carried out during 1996–97. Out of 20 trusts that provided rehabilitation services for people with stroke, 13 had a designated stroke service, of which nine could be classified as stroke units.[168] CSAG noted that there 'was rarely a full multi-disciplinary team capable of working in a patient's home'.

The Stroke Association survey (1998) found that the majority of consultants admit stroke patients to an acute admission ward – only 12% admit directly to a stroke unit.[167] Seventy-five per cent of consultants had access to specialised stroke services – either a defined unit, or a multi-disciplinary stroke team. The majority of the stroke units were rehabilitation units, but a minority of consultants (17%) had access to acute stroke units or to combined acute/rehabilitation units (16%). Access to acute stroke-unit care was much higher in Scotland (41%) and Northern Ireland (52%) than in England (29%) and Wales (21%).

In terms of what is different about the medical components of stroke-unit care compared with general ward care supported by a specialist stroke team, Evans *et al.* reported that stroke-unit care was associated with more intensive monitoring, greater use of oxygen and antipyretics, measures to reduce aspiration, and early nutrition.[171]

Components of the multi-disciplinary team

A key feature of stroke-unit or 'organised' care is access to a multi-disciplinary team. The component parts of this team for a ten-bedded unit are summarised in Table 23 (*see* overleaf).[170] The National Sentinel Audit for stroke found that while the majority of trusts had access to core professional staff, other professionals were not necessarily available – for example, only 29% had support from a clinical psychologist.[10] The Stroke Association consultant survey found that a third of consultants did not have access to a multi-disciplinary team for their stroke patients.[167]

Surgical intervention in acute stroke

Neurosurgeons offer two relevant interventions (excluding treatment of sub-arachnoid haemorrhage): evacuation of intracerebral haemorrhage, and the treatment of acute hydrocephalus arising from cerebellar haemorrhage or infarction. Both these operations are uncommon in the UK. There is uncertainty over the value of the former, though it is quite widely used in some countries, such as Japan. The latter is accepted practice, but acute hydrocephalus is a relatively uncommon complication.

Length of stay

In the National Sentinel Audit, the mean age of patients admitted to hospital with stroke was 75 years, with a 28% mortality at 30 days.[10] For those discharged alive, the median length of stay was 21 days. The mean length of stay (including deaths) in a study in Dublin was 31 days,[172] which is similar to the average in Oxfordshire (unpublished data held on file from the Oxford Stroke Register, 1995).

Table 23: Multi-disciplinary involvement with typical WTE staff for a ten-bedded stroke unit (after Langhorne and Dennis[170]).

	Professional	WTE*
Core team	Physicians	Consultant: 0.5–1
	Nurses	Junior medical: 0.4–0.8
	Physiotherapists	7–12
	Occupational therapists	1–2
	Speech and language therapists	0.9–1.3
	Social workers	0.2–0.6
		< 0.4–0.7
Other professionals	Audiologist	
	Chaplain	
	Chiropodist	
	Clinical psychologist	
	Dentist	
	Dietitian	
	Orthoptist	
	Pharmacist	
Other medical/surgical consultants	Neurosurgeon	
	Psychiatrist	
	Ophthalmologist	
	Radiologist	
	Rheumatologist	
	Vascular surgeon	

* WTE, whole-time equivalent.

Community services

These services may be used either to help people with stroke avoid hospital admission, or to support people with stroke after transfer out of hospital. A review of community-based rehabilitation services carried out by the Audit Commission in 12 different areas of England and Wales reported that 80% of localities had access to day hospitals and 50% to a multi-disciplinary team.[173] While most such teams include physiotherapy and occupational therapy, the other professional groups (including nursing and medical) were only represented in a minority.[174]

Intermediate care facilities

There are several definitions of 'intermediate care'.[175] Perhaps the most useful definition for the purposes of this chapter is 'a service that meets the needs of those who because of their age or psychosocial circumstances would benefit from an extended period of rehabilitation from a multi-disciplinary team following acute illness or treatment which could not be reasonably provided in their own homes, in an acute hospital or in a specialist unit'.[176] The National Service Framework for Older People describes intermediate care as a bridge between acute hospital and primary and community care, and gives its aim as 'to provide integrated services to promote faster recovery from illness, prevent unnecessary acute hospital admissions, support timely discharge and maximise independent living'.[9] In the context of stroke care, they have a potential role for patients who 'would otherwise face unnecessarily prolonged hospital stays ... [or] long-term residential care'.[9]

The Audit Commission identified social services residential rehabilitation schemes as an important form of intermediate care. Half of the areas included in the Audit Commission review had social rehabilitation schemes. Typically, such care is based in units that were previously local authority residential homes. Costs tend to be shared between health and social services.[173] Amounts of medical input vary. Because these are 'social' rehabilitation schemes, users also have to pay a contribution.

Another form of intermediate care is the community hospital (CH).[177,178] In 1993, there were around 350 community hospitals in the UK, with about 10 000 beds.[176] Stroke is the commonest medical diagnosis associated with CH admission.[179]

Long-term care

In the National Sentinel Audit, 74% of patients were discharged to independent or warden-controlled housing, 7% were transferred to another hospital, and 19% were transferred into institutional care. There were wide variations between different regions of the UK as to the proportion of patients discharged to institutional care who had been admitted from home with a stroke (6–19%).[180] These results are consistent with an unpublished study (data held on file) of 532 consecutive stroke admissions in patients aged 65 or over to acute hospitals in Oxfordshire. After six months, 228 (43%) were at home, 233 (44%) had died, 56 (10%) were in residential care, and 15 (3%) were still in hospital (mostly a community hospital). This is the equivalent of 19% of survivors being in institutional care. Surveys of nursing homes estimate that between 14%[181] and 23%[182] of beds in nursing homes are occupied by people who have had a stroke.

Carer support

Recognising the wider impact of stroke, services have been developed which target carers as well as patients. These include specific single-faceted interventions such as information giving, educational programmes and counselling,[183] and more generic services where the aim is to provide information and advice, emotional and social support, and liaison with health and social services. These generic services have been variously called 'social work',[184] 'specialist nurse support',[185] 'family support organisation'[186] and 'family care work'.[187]

Services for sub-arachnoid haemorrhage

Someone with a diagnosis of sub-arachnoid haemorrhage, which carries a high mortality (*see* Section 4), would be admitted to hospital. Investigations and treatments used are shown in Table 24 (*see* overleaf). Evidence of the effectiveness of these interventions is summarised in 'Sub-arachnoid haemorrhage' in Section 6.

Costs of stroke care

The overall costs of stroke care to the NHS are variously put at between 4%[2] and 6%[3] of the total expenditure on the NHS. Bosanquet and Franks estimated that people who have had strokes accounted for

Table 24: Management of sub-arachnoid haemorrhage: possible investigations and treatments.

1 To make diagnosis	Brain imaging	CT scan
		MRI scan
	Lumbar puncture	
2 To search for cause of haemorrhage	Vascular imaging	Angiography
		MR angiography
		CT angiography
		Transcranial colour-coded duplex sonography
3 Treatment of acute haemorrhage	Evacuation of intracerebral haematoma	
4 Prevention of re-bleeding	Medical therapy	Antifibrinolytic drugs
	Surgical therapy	Clipping of aneurysm
	Interventional radiology	Coil embolisation
5 Prevention of secondary cerebral ischaemia	Medical therapy	Nimodipine

£2318 million in 1995–96, which is the equivalent of 5.8% of total NHS and social services expenditure.[188] They estimated that £758 million of this was attributable to the cost of treating new patients, and £1560 million to the cost of treatment of 'old patients' (i.e. costs attributable to long-term care, community support and acute admissions for recurrent strokes). If the costs of informal care are also taken into account (estimated at £672 million), then the total cost would rise to £2990 million.[188]

Publication of the NHS reference costs allows simple estimates to be made of some of the hospital-related components of care. The relevant health resource group (HRG) codes (*see* 'Health care resource group codes [HRGs]' in Section 3) and their costs for 1999 are shown in Table 25. This shows the average cost of a Finished Consultant Episode (FCE) in NHS trusts in England. FCEs can be difficult to interpret, because a patient may have several FCEs over the course of a single admission. For example, over a six-month period in one study, 470 FCEs relating to stroke were identified, which corresponded to 318 separate admissions – an average of 1.5 FCEs per admission.[41] There is very wide variation in costs of an FCE between different trusts. Thus, for example, while the average cost of an FCE for an admission with stroke in someone aged 70 or over was £2099, the range for the middle 50% of trusts was from £1179 to £2729, and the total range was from £45 to £16 415![189] The wide range illustrates some of the current limitations of use of HRGs in this context. It is not clear to what extent the wide range reflects erroneous data or differences in case-mix between different trusts. Use of the range for the middle 50% of trusts (as shown in Table 25) gives a more conservative estimate of the spread of cost. However, estimates from research studies suggest that the total cost of an individual stroke case admitted to hospital in the UK is between £5800 and £8500 (1996–7 prices),[170,190] which falls outside this range.

6 Effectiveness and cost-effectiveness

Important sources of data on evidence of effectiveness of stroke services include the Cochrane Library (*see* Appendix 2), the Royal College of Physicians' National Clinical Guidelines for Stroke,[11] *Clinical Evidence*;[191] and the review by the NHS Centre for Reviews and Dissemination of systematic reviews of

Table 25: NHS reference costs relevant to stroke (1999).[189]

HRG code	Mean cost of FCE (range for middle 50% of trusts)	
	Non-elective inpatient	Elective inpatient
Carotid artery stenosis		
Q05 (carotid artery surgery including endarterectomy)	£1,767 (895–2,132)	**£1,940 (833–2,075)**
Transient ischaemic attack		
A20 (age > 69 or with complications)	**£918 (686–1,395)**	£1,384 (556–1,739)
A21 (age < 70 with no complications)	**£624 (459–1,068)**	£1,461 (502–1,413)
Stroke		
A22 (age > 69 or with complications)	**£2,099 (1,179–2,729)**	£2,635 (911–3,365)
A23 (age < 70 with no complications)	**£1,623 (1,004–2,240)**	£2,096 (677–2,142)
A19 (includes intracerebral haemorrhage)	**£1,413 (928–2,004)**	£1,918 (652–2,415)
A03 (includes evacuation of intracerebral/cerebellar haematoma)	**£3,870 (1,141–4,223)**	£3,502 (1,013–3,717)
Sub-arachnoid haemorrhage		
A19 (includes sub-arachnoid haemorrhage)	**£1,413 (928–2,004)**	£1,918 (652–2,415)
A03 (includes drainage of sub-arachnoid space; excision/ligation of cerebral artery aneurysm)	**£3,870 (1,141–4,223)**	£3,502 (1,013–3,717)
A04 (includes clipping/obliteration of cerebral artery aneurysm)	**£5,365 (1,347–6,089)**	£4,715 (1,070–5,370)

Note: **Bold costs** indicate more usual type of admission.

research relevant to the 'wider public health' agenda.[192] This section draws heavily on these sources, with reference to more recent specific studies where relevant.

Population strategies to prevent stroke

Rees *et al.* recently reviewed the evidence relevant to Government policy on heart disease and stroke.[193] Their conclusions are summarised below.

Prevention of smoking

Raising the cost of cigarettes through taxation reduces consumption.[194] The effect is greater on women and younger people, but it creates financial hardship for poorer sections of society.[195] Provision of smoke-free workplaces[196] and control of advertising[197] both reduce overall tobacco consumption. School-based programmes which employ social reinforcement techniques[198] and mass media campaigns[199] may both be effective at reducing uptake in young people. Health education campaigns that simply provide information tend to be effective only in higher socio-economic groups.[200]

Socio-economic deprivation

Evidence on the direct health effects of income supplementation is lacking, since the trials that were performed did not use suitable health outcome measures.[201] Structural and legislative measures are most effective at reducing health inequalities.[200]

Healthy lifestyle

A systematic review of exercise health promotion strategies concluded that public health strategies aimed at changing the environment to encourage walking and cycling would reach a greater proportion of the inactive population than strategies aimed at increasing use of exercise facilities.[202]

While eating more fresh fruit and vegetables has been shown to be associated with a lower risk of stroke,[203] health effects of changes in consumption have not been demonstrated through trials. Public health strategies to reduce salt consumption, such as reducing salt content in processed foods, may have an impact on blood pressure.[204]

Prevention in people at high risk of stroke

The evidence for treatments to reduce risk of stroke in different categories of people is summarised in Table 26. Treatment of hypertension, diabetes and ischaemic heart disease is covered in more detail in other chapters. The grading of the quality of evidence takes into account both the nature of the evidence

Table 26: Effectiveness of treatments to reduce risk in high-risk individuals.

Risk group	Intervention	Reduction in stroke risk	Quality of evidence*
Hypertension	Lowering blood pressure	35–40% with a mean reduction of 5–6 mmHg in diastolic blood pressure[209]	A1
Atrial fibrillation	Adjusted-dose warfarin	59%, with mean achieved INR from 2.0–2.6[210]	A1
	Aspirin	20–22%, with doses in trials varying between 50 mg and 1,300 mg/day[210,211]	B1
	Warfarin vs. aspirin	32–36% reduction if treated with warfarin in preference to aspirin[210,212]	B1
Carotid artery stenosis (asymptomatic)	Carotid endarterectomy	27–38% reduction in risk of ipsilateral stroke or peri-operative stroke or death after mean of 3 years follow-up[213,214]	C1
People at high vascular risk†	Aspirin	27% reduction in risk of MI, stroke or vascular death; 31% reduction in risk of non-fatal stroke[215] There is no evidence that higher doses (e.g. 300 mg/day) are any more effective than lower doses (e.g. 75 mg/day)[216]	A1
	Thienopyridine derivatives (ticlopidine and clopidogrel) in preference to aspirin	12% reduction if treated with a thienopyridine in preference to aspirin[217,218]	C1
	Statin therapy	*See* text for discussion of MRC/BHF heart protection study	
Ischaemic heart disease	Lowering cholesterol with statins	29% reduction if treated with a statin[219]	A1

* *See* introductory chapter to HCNA series for grading used.
† Including peripheral vascular disease, ischaemic heart disease and cerebrovascular disease.

(grade 1–4) and the size of the effect (A–E). The definitions are given in the introductory chapter to this series. The size of the effect incorporates both relative effect (reduction in stroke risk – as shown in Table 26) and absolute effect. Thus, carotid endarterectomy in asymptomatic individuals has been graded C since asymptomatic carotid artery stenosis does not confer significant stroke risk, so the benefits of the operation in absolute terms are small.[90] The published evidence that statins reduce stroke risk is derived largely from two cardiovascular secondary prevention studies – the Cholesterol and Recurrent Events (CARE) Study[205] and the Scandinavian Simvastatin Survival Study (4S).[206] Therefore, cholesterol lowering has been included as a treatment in people with ischaemic heart disease. However, the indications for statins will widen as a result of the recently reported but unpublished MRC/BHF Heart Protection study. This trial involved 20 000 volunteers who were at increased risk of coronary heart disease, regardless of baseline cholesterol level. The results presented at the 2001 American Heart Association Scientific Meeting showed that treatment with statins reduces the risk of heart attacks and strokes 'by at least one-third, not just in people who already have coronary disease, but also in those who have diabetes, narrowing of arteries in their legs or a previous history of stroke'.[207]

With regard to lifestyle interventions to reduce risk of stroke (e.g. smoking cessation, weight loss, healthy diet, exercise, control of alcohol consumption), there is little direct evidence from trials that such interventions are effective. Justification for their use is through extrapolation from observational studies that demonstrate associations between the risk factor and stroke, and that changes in risk factor status are associated with better outcome (quality of evidence: B2). Observational evidence suggests that moderate alcohol consumption may actually protect against ischaemic stroke.[208]

Prevention in people who have had a stroke or transient ischaemic attack

Lowering blood pressure

A meta-analysis of individual patient data on the effects of lowering blood pressure of patients with hypertension and a history of stroke, who had been included in randomised controlled trials of the effects of antihypertensive therapy, found risk of subsequent stroke was reduced by 28% (95% CI: 61–85%) (quality of evidence: A1).[220] The benefits of lowering blood pressure in people with stroke have been confirmed by the PROGRESS trial, which showed similar effects (28% reduction in stroke risk) in both hypertensive and non-hypertensive stroke patients.[221,222] The trial also showed that the more intensive the treatment, the larger was the effect. Thus giving combination therapy (an ACE inhibitor plus a thiazide diuretic) achieved greater reductions in blood pressure (mean reduction: 12/5 mmHg) and stroke risk (43%) compared with a single agent (ACE inhibitor) (5/3 mmHg reduction in blood pressure, and 5% reduction in stroke risk). These findings are consistent with observational data showing that the lower the diastolic blood pressure, the lower the risk of a second stroke.[223]

Treatment of atrial fibrillation

For secondary prevention in atrial fibrillation, warfarin reduces risk of stroke by 68%, a similar order of magnitude to that achieved in primary prevention.[210] Due to the higher risks of stroke in people who have already had a stroke, the benefits of warfarin over aspirin in absolute terms are higher than for primary prevention.

Carotid endarterectomy for symptomatic carotid artery stenosis

In patients with severe carotid artery stenosis (> 80% in the European Carotid Surgery Trial [ECST], which is the equivalent of > 70% in the North American Symptomatic Carotid Endarterectomy Trial [NASCET]) surgery reduces the risk of disabling stroke or death by 48% (95% CI: 27–73%) (quality of evidence: A1).[224] In patients with moderate stenosis (ECST 70–79%; NASCET 50–69%) surgery reduces risk of stroke or death by 27% (95% CI: 15–44%) (quality of evidence: B1). In patients with lesser stenoses, surgery increases the risk of stroke or death by 20% (95% CI: 0–44%) (quality of evidence: E1).[224] The benefits of carotid endarterectomy are outweighed by the harm if the surgical complication rate exceeds 6%.[224] A variety of surgical techniques are used for carotid endarterectomy, but there is insufficient evidence to favour one approach over another.[225–31] The recently reported CAVATAS trial found that endovascular treatment (i.e. percutaneous transluminal balloon angioplasty with stents also used in some patients) achieved similar results to carotid endarterectomy in terms of ipsilateral stroke recurrence three years after the intervention (hazard ratio: 1.04; 95% CI: 0.63–1.70).[232] However, the confidence intervals are wide, and one year after treatment severe (70–99%) ipsilateral stenosis was more common in the endovascular group (14% vs. 4%). Endovascular techniques have evolved since this study was initiated, with greater experience of use of stents. The ongoing CREST (Carotid Revascularisation Endarterectomy vs. Stenting Trial) and the International Carotid Stenting Study (ICSS) will provide further data to clarify whether or not endovascular procedures are as effective as carotid endarterectomy.[233,234]

A post hoc subgroup analysis of the North American Symptomatic Carotid Endarterectomy (NASCET) trial found that the absolute benefits of surgery were significantly greater in elderly people. The absolute risk reduction of ipsilateral ischaemic stroke for people with 70–99% stenosis was 28.9% (number needed to treat [NNT] = 3) in people aged 75 or over, as compared to 15.1% (NNT = 7) in people aged 65–74 and 9.7% (NNT = 10) in people aged under 65.[235] Furthermore, the absolute risk reduction was significant in older patients (aged 75 or over) with lesser degrees of stenosis (50–69%). This finding is supported by pooling of data from the Carotid Endarterectomy Trialists' Collaboration (CETC).[236]

There are some observational data to suggest that surgeons who perform very few carotid endarterectomies per year (less than 5) achieve worse outcomes, and that hospitals with greater throughput (over 100 operations per year) achieve better results[237] (quality of evidence: B2).

Antiplatelet agents

Aspirin is effective in secondary prevention of stroke, despite causing a small increase in risk of haemorrhagic stroke.[215] The size of the risk reduction is similar to that achieved by primary prevention (Table 26). Thienopyridines (clopidogrel, ticlopidine) are effective alternatives.[218] Whether or not adding dipyridamole to aspirin increases the effectiveness, as has been suggested by one trial, the European Stroke Prevention Study (ESPS-2),[238] is currently being reviewed by the Antithrombotic Trialists Collaboration.[239] The combination of clopidogrel and aspirin has been shown to be more effective than aspirin alone in preventing vascular events in patients with acute coronary syndrome and in patients undergoing percutaneous coronary interventions.[240,241]

Statin therapy

The unpublished MRC/BHF Heart Protection Study provides evidence of the effectiveness of statin use in people who have had a stroke (see 'Prevention in people at high risk of stroke' above).

Ineffective therapies

Long-term anticoagulation in people with non-embolic stroke (in the absence of atrial fibrillation or valvular heart disease) confers no benefit, but does increase risk of bleeding.[242] In a recently reported trial which compared warfarin to aspirin for prevention of recurrent ischaemic stroke in patients who had a prior non-cardioembolic stroke, non-significant advantages in terms of lower stroke rates and major haemorrhage were found for aspirin over warfarin (stroke rates: 16% vs. 18%; major haemorrhage rates: 1.5% vs. 2.2%).[243]

Acute treatment of stroke

Diagnosis

The accuracy of clinical diagnosis depends upon the setting and the time after onset of symptoms when the diagnosis is made. A study in Ohio found that 62 out of 86 (72%) patients diagnosed as having had a stroke or TIA by ambulance personnel had this diagnosis confirmed in hospital.[244] A study in Los Angeles found higher levels of accuracy were achieved by ambulance personnel in association with the use of a screening instrument (the Los Angeles Prehospital Stroke Screen [LAPSS]). Eighty-six per cent of patients diagnosed as having had a stroke on the LAPSS had this diagnosis confirmed in hospital.[245] Estimates of the accuracy of diagnosis in Accident and Emergency vary between a predictive value of 81 and 95%.[246,247] The main source of error is distinguishing stroke from other causes of acute neurological deficit, such as post-ictal deficits, systemic infection, tumours and toxic metabolic disturbances. In the OCSP, out of 325 patients diagnosed as having a 'clinically definite first stroke' by an experienced physician after admission, only 5 turned out to have different final diagnoses (2 subdural, 2 glioma, 1 metastasis).[248] Only 3 out of 411 patients diagnosed as not having had a stroke were subsequently found (on the basis of CT scan or autopsy) to have had one. Infarcts on a CT scan are most apparent after a few days, though up to half of patients with a clinically definite stroke will not have a diagnostic lesion on a CT scan.[249]

In their review of the evidence, the Intercollegiate Working Party for Stroke concluded that little directed research has been carried out to assess the process of diagnosis for stroke, and that 'No research has evaluated critically the role of brain imaging.'[11] There are three reasons for performing brain imaging (CT or MRI scan) in acute stroke: to identify other causes for the symptoms (as discussed in the preceding paragraph), to exclude cerebral haemorrhage and to assess eligibility for thrombolysis in centres where this is given.

CT scanning (or other brain imaging) has a role to differentiate cerebral infarction from haemorrhage, since this will help determine both acute treatment and secondary prevention strategy. In this regard, case series show that it becomes more difficult to distinguish cerebral haemorrhage from cerebral infarction as time elapses after the stroke, and that after two weeks the scan may be classified incorrectly.[250] While early CT can accurately identify intracerebral haemorrhage, it can be difficult to differentiate between a primary intracerebral haemorrhage (PICH) and haemorrhagic transformation of an infarct (HTI). The possibility of mistaking an HTI for a PICH decreases the earlier the CT scan is performed.[248]

As acute treatments which require early intervention become available (*see* below), early clinical diagnosis may be less adequate. For example, in a series of 70 patients who were examined within 6 hours of onset of symptoms, and diagnosed at that time as having had an anterior circulation stroke, 6 were found to have different final diagnoses (3 metabolic upset, 1 migraine, 1 alcohol withdrawal, 1 hysteria).[251] Furthermore, of the 64 patients who did have a stroke, in 15 it was not an anterior circulation stroke, but something else (e.g. intracerebral haemorrhage, small vessel occlusion).

Echocardiography can identify cardiac sources of embolus in patients with stroke and clinical evidence of cardiac disease. There is evidence from observational studies that patients with intracardiac thrombus benefit from anticoagulation.[252]

Acute interventions

A large number of interventions in acute stroke have been reviewed by the Cochrane Stroke Group. Interventions that show some promise, but for which there is insufficient evidence of effectiveness to recommend them currently outside clinical trials, include cooling therapy (on the basis of patho-physiology)[253] and fibrinogen-depleting agents (ancrod).[254] Treatments that are in common use in several parts of the world for which no evidence of effectiveness was found include anticoagulants for acute stroke,[255] including low-molecular-weight heparins,[256] deliberate lowering of blood pressure in acute stroke,[257] and surgery for primary supratentorial intracerebral haemorrhage.[258]

Two interventions for which there is some evidence of beneficial effect are antiplatelet therapy and thrombolysis. Aspirin, at a dose of 160–300 mg daily, started within 48 hours of onset of symptoms, leads to a small but significant reduction in risk of death or dependency (6% risk reduction) (quality of evidence: C1).[259] Thrombolysis increases risk of death, but reduces dependency in survivors so that, overall, risk of death or dependency is reduced.[260] By the end of follow-up, thrombolysis administered within 6 hours of onset of stroke resulted in a 17% reduction in the odds of death or dependency. Indirect comparison of the different thrombolytic agents that have been used in trials suggests that recombinant tissue plasminogen activator is associated with fewer deaths and greater chance of a good outcome (alive and independent) (quality of evidence: B1).[260] Interpretation of the data on thrombolysis remains controversial. In the USA, thrombolysis is more widely accepted as a 'proven' treatment on the basis of the National Institute of Neurological Disorders and Stroke (NINDS) trial, which found a better chance of a good outcome in patients treated with tissue plasminogen activator (tPA) at both 3[261] and 12 months after the stroke.[262,263] However, other trials, such as the European Co-operative Acute Stroke trials (ECASS I and II), did not find that tPA was effective.[264,265] The conclusion of the Cochrane review of this evidence was that:

> The data are promising and may justify the use of thrombolytic therapy with intravenous recombinant tissue plasminogen activator in experienced centres in selected patients. However, the widespread use of thrombolytic therapy in routine clinical practice at this time cannot be supported. Further trials will be needed to identify which patients are most likely to benefit from treatment and the environment in which it may best be given, before thrombolytic therapy should be adopted on a wider scale.[260]

Organisation of stroke care

Organised inpatient care in stroke units leads to better survival, less dependency, and greater likelihood of patients living at home after one year as compared to conventional inpatient care. The odds of death or institutionalised care at final follow-up (median one year) were reduced by 24% (greater than the effect of any individual drug), and the odds of death or dependency by 25% in patients who received stroke-unit care.[169] Stroke-unit care is not associated with any increase in length of hospital stay. There is no evidence that services which aim to avoid hospital admission for stroke patients can achieve the same benefits as inpatient stroke units.[165] A trial comparing stroke-unit care with general ward care with stroke team support, or domiciliary stroke care with specialist team support, found significantly better outcomes for the group that received inpatient stroke-unit care as compared to the other models of care (which loosely fit under the broad definition of 'organised' stroke care).[266]

There is no evidence from randomised trials as to how soon after their stroke patients should be admitted to stroke units. The poorer survival in UK hospitals, as compared to some European centres which are associated with more intensive management of the early phases of acute stroke, has been cited as circumstantial evidence for the importance of more intensive acute stroke care (quality of evidence: B3).[267]

Models of care that support early discharge from hospital reduce length of stay, but the effects on patient and carer outcomes and on overall costs of this approach are unclear.[268,269] For example, a London study showed that community-based rehabilitation (after, on average, 34 days in hospital) can achieve similar outcomes in terms of activities of daily living at one year to slightly longer periods in hospital (average 40 days), though patients in the early discharge group were found to have higher levels of anxiety.[270] There are similar uncertainties over the effects of day-hospital rehabilitation.[271]

Stroke rehabilitation

The overall package of 'stroke-unit care', as outlined in 'Acute management and rehabilitation of stroke' in Section 5, is effective, which is evidence for the role of rehabilitation in stroke as a whole. This rehabilitation is multi-disciplinary. The evidence for the individual components of the rehabilitation process is reviewed below. In general, the evidence for the individual components is a lot weaker than the evidence for the rehabilitation process as a whole. However, demonstrating that one part of the system looked at in isolation does not work is not evidence that that part is not necessary for the effective provision of rehabilitation.[272]

Treatment of swallowing difficulties

Observational studies using historical controls suggest that recognising and treating swallowing difficulties in stroke patients will reduce risk of pneumonia.[273] However, there is a lack of evidence available to guide care and feeding of these patients.[274] Percutaneous endoscopic gastrostomy (PEG) feeding may improve outcome and nutrition as compared with nasogastric tube feeding, but this is based on two small trials only.[274,275]

Physiotherapy

A systematic review of randomised trials of physiotherapy after stroke identified seven trials involving 597 patients.[276] Patients who received more intensive physiotherapy did better in terms of a composite outcome of death or deterioration at the end of follow-up (OR: 0.54; 95% CI: 0.34–0.85). A separate meta-analysis reached similar conclusions.[277] Since these reviews, a randomised trial of physiotherapy with three groups (arm training, leg training and a control group) in 101 patients with severe disability following a middle cerebral artery stroke demonstrated that greater intensity of rehabilitation improved functional recovery and health-related functional status.[278] There is a growing evidence base looking at specific interventions such as electrical stimulation for the prevention and treatment of post-stroke shoulder pain,[279] and electromyographic feedback to improve limb function,[280] but clear conclusions about the effectiveness or otherwise of these interventions cannot be drawn.

Speech and language therapy

There is too little evidence from randomised controlled trials about the effects of speech and language therapy after stroke to draw any conclusions as to whether it is effective or ineffective.[281] A systematic review of observational studies concluded that intensive targeted therapy is effective for some specific dysphasic syndromes (quality of evidence: B2).[282]

Occupational therapy

Recent randomised controlled trials have demonstrated the effectiveness of domiciliary occupational therapy for stroke, in both patients who stay at home[283] and patients after discharge from hospital.[284] A meta-analysis of controlled studies (including some randomised trials) of occupational therapy for older people (i.e. not just stroke patients) found some evidence in support of occupational therapy in other settings, such as nursing homes and psychogeriatric wards.[285]

Treatment of post-stroke depression

Trials have been performed of both pharmacological and psychological treatments of post-stroke depression. A recent systematic review concluded that patients with depressive symptoms after stroke do respond to short-term treatment with antidepressants, but that there is a lack of trials of sufficient size to draw conclusions as to the role of psychological treatments in post-stroke depression.[135]

Integrated care pathways

One approach to achieving co-ordinated care that has been tried is the integrated care pathway, in which a co-ordinator or case manager is responsible for ensuring that patient care follows a pre-defined template. In one trial, this approach was compared to a conventional multi-disciplinary approach in which individualised care objectives were set depending upon patient progress. However, the integrated care pathway approach was found to be associated with slower recovery and poorer quality-of-life scores.[286]

Late rehabilitation

Most research on rehabilitation has been directed at therapy in the first few months following stroke. One trial of physiotherapy for patients who had a stroke at least a year earlier found that minimal late intervention could lead to small improvements in mobility, but the improvements were not maintained[287] (quality of evidence: C1–2). A small trial of more intensive therapy found that this led to reduced dependence and increased social function – an effect that appeared to be sustained.[288]

Family support services

There is no evidence that family care workers can reduce the emotional impact of stroke for patients,[289] but there is consistent evidence from two randomised controlled trials that provision of such services can lead to significant psychosocial benefits for carers.[186,187]

Other services

Many other aspects of stroke care have been evaluated. For example, trials of information provision[290] and of educational programmes[291] for patients and carers have been performed, but have not demonstrated any clear benefits.[292] Two small trials provide some evidence that cognitive rehabilitation may improve alertness and sustained attention for patients with attention deficits, but there is insufficient data to conclude whether or not this leads to any improved functional independence.[293] It is unclear whether cognitive rehabilitation has any effects on memory deficits following stroke.[294]

There is little research to support the provision of most equipment, such as walking sticks, frames or even wheelchairs. However, in many cases the benefits are so obvious that research is not likely to be sensible (e.g. provision of a wheelchair to someone unable to walk). Ankle/foot orthoses have been researched a little, and there is some evidence from non-randomised studies that they facilitate walking.[295] However, this was not confirmed in a more recent randomised study.[296]

Sub-arachnoid haemorrhage

Investigations in sub-arachnoid haemorrhage

These have recently been reviewed by van Gijn and Rinkel.[297] CT scans detect the characteristic appearance of blood in the basal cisterns. However, false-positive diagnoses are possible on CT if there is generalised brain oedema leading to venous congestion in the sub-arachnoid space. CT scanning within 12 hours is 98% sensitive (i.e. will miss 2% of patients with sub-arachnoid haemorrhage).[298] MRI scanning is as accurate as CT scanning in the early stages, but is better than CT at detecting extravasated blood later on.[297] Lumbar puncture can exclude sub-arachnoid haemorrhage in patients with a negative scan, but a traumatic tap (i.e. the lumbar puncture needle entering a vein) can be mistaken for blood in the sub-arachnoid space. The risks of this are reduced the later after the onset of symptoms that the lumbar puncture is performed, since this allows xanthochromia (caused by lysis of red cells in the cerebrospinal fluid) to develop, which gives a characteristic appearance to the fluid.[297]

Angiography is the gold standard for detecting aneurysms, but has a 1.8% rate of neurological complications.[299] Techniques such as MR angiography and CT angiography are nearly as accurate as angiography and are safer.[297]

Treatment of sub-arachnoid haemorrhage

Case series and a small randomised controlled trial suggest that surgical evacuation of large haematomas in the acute phase may improve survival and outcome (quality of evidence: B2).[297]

There are medical, surgical and endovascular approaches aimed at preventing re-bleeding. A review of antifibrinolytic therapy (e.g. tranexamic acid) found no evidence of benefit, with an odds ratio of poor outcome of 1.05 (95% CI: 0.72–1.26).[300] However, the reviewers noted that the trials were performed more than 10 years ago, and that new strategies might overcome the ischaemia-inducing potential of the treatment. Operative clipping of the aneurysm is standard practice (quality of evidence: B3). A Cochrane review identified one randomised controlled trial addressing the timing of surgery after aneurysmal sub-arachnoid haemorrhage.[301,302] Patients operated on late had more re-bleeding and delayed ischaemia, but this was not apparent if the patient was on nimodipine. The Cochrane reviewers concluded that timing of surgery was not a critical factor in determining outcome following sub-arachnoid haemorrhage, based on the limited evidence available. An alternative to surgery is the use of coil embolisation to pack the aneurysm.[303] To date, there is insufficient evidence to judge the value of coil embolisation as compared to surgical intervention.[297] One randomised trial ($n = 109$) has been published which compared coil embolisation to surgical ligation of ruptured intracranial aneurysm, and found no difference in clinical outcome at three months between the groups.[304] The ongoing MRC-funded International Sub-arachnoid Aneurysm Trial (ISAT) is a randomised trial comparing neurosurgical clipping with endovascular coil treatment for ruptured cerebral aneurysm causing acute sub-arachnoid haemorrhage. It is anticipated that this trial will report in 2002.

With regard to prevention of secondary cerebral ischaemia, a systematic review of calcium antagonists in sub-arachnoid haemorrhage found that nimodipine is effective in reducing risk of poor outcome (death or severe disability), achieving a risk reduction of 18% (95% CI: 7–28%).[305] Other neuroprotective agents have been evaluated, but no clear-cut evidence of benefit has been found for any of these.[304] Other aspects of the medical management of sub-arachnoid haemorrhage, such as avoidance of treatment of hypertension in the acute phase and prevention of hypovolaemia through use of intravenous saline are currently justified on the basis of the underlying pathophysiology (quality of evidence: B3).[297]

Cost-effectiveness studies

Two systematic reviews have recently summarised the economic evaluations of stroke care that have been performed.[306,307] Both reviews commented that the overall quality of the evaluations tended to be poor. Two areas for which a number of cost-effectiveness studies were found were carotid endarterectomy and anticoagulation in atrial fibrillation.

Cost-effectiveness of carotid endarterectomy

Two studies were identified that examined the cost-effectiveness of carotid endarterectomy for symptomatic carotid artery stenosis. In one study, carotid endarterectomy was found to be the dominant strategy (i.e. to lead to cost savings and better outcome),[308] while in the other the cost per QALY was $4715, at 1998 prices.[309] However, neither of these studies took into account the cost of identifying which patients with symptoms are suitable for surgery. If this is taken into account, the cost per QALY rises to $46 746, at 1998 prices.[310]

Two studies looked at the cost-effectiveness of the procedure for asymptomatic carotid artery stenosis, but came up with very divergent estimates: $8484 and $60 605 per QALY, at 1998 prices.[309,311] Neither of these considered the additional costs of screening to identify carotid stenosis in asymptomatic patients. Four studies which have included these costs give very variable estimates of the cost-effectiveness, ranging from a simple injunction not to do it (on the basis that screening programmes are more costly and lead to worse outcomes than not screening) to a cost of $41 864 per QALY, at 1998 prices.[307]

Cost-effectiveness of anticoagulation in atrial fibrillation

Two cost-effectiveness analyses of anticoagulation in atrial fibrillation both concluded that warfarin was highly cost-effective, except in people at low risk of stroke, with a cost per QALY of $9200, at 1998 prices, in patients at medium risk of stroke, and was cost saving (i.e. better outcome at lower cost) in patients at high risk of stroke.[312,313] Lightowlers and McGuire, whose study was based in the UK, estimated that the cost per life-year gained free from stroke over 10 years ranged from −£400 (i.e. resource saving) to £13 000. The frequency of anticoagulation monitoring was the factor that most influenced the results.[313]

An economic evaluation of primary care-based anticoagulation management as compared to traditional hospital-based care found that it was more expensive (£170 per annum per patient compared to £69),[314] but the higher cost needs to be set against the potential for improved control.[148]

7 Models of care and recommendations

In a rational health care system, need for stroke services is dictated by how common stroke is, and what can be done to either prevent it, or treat, rehabilitate and care for people who suffer a stroke. In this section, the interpretation of the evidence base for stroke services is considered by reviewing the various guidelines that have recently been published in the UK for stroke. The National Service Framework for Older People recommendations conform to these guidelines, and are summarised at the end of each relevant subsection. Secondly, the implications of full implementation of these guidelines are considered by outlining the number of patients that might be expected in a given population. Next, priorities for stroke service development are considered, taking into account current uptake of services, how effective they are, and the population to which they are applicable.

Guidelines for stroke care

Evidence-based guidelines have been produced by a number of different organisations in the UK. These include the North of England Evidence-Based Guideline Development Project,[315] the Scottish Intercollegiate Guidelines Network (SIGN),[316] the Royal College of Physicians of Edinburgh Consensus Conferences (ECC) on stroke,[317] and the Intercollegiate Working Party (IWP) for stroke which produced the National Clinical Guidelines.[11] There have been no UK-based guidelines on primary prevention of stroke, but there has been a recent statement from the Stroke Council of the American Heart Association, so this has been included in this analysis.[43] While there are some differences in detail, these guidelines are broadly in agreement with each other. They are summarised below, and differences are discussed.

Primary prevention of stroke

For the primary prevention of stroke, the guidelines of the American Heart Association, which are summarised in Table 27, are mostly uncontroversial. The recommendations in the top half of the table are

Table 27: Summary of guidance for primary prevention of stroke.

Hypertension	'Regular screening for hypertension (at least every two years in adults) and appropriate management.' (AHA)
Smoking	'Smoking cessation for all current smokers is recommended.' (AHA)
Diabetes	'Careful control of hypertension in both type 1 and type 2 diabetics is recommended. Glycaemic control is recommended to reduce microvascular complications.'
Asymptomatic carotid stenosis	'Endarterectomy may be considered in patients with high-grade asymptomatic carotid stenosis performed by a surgeon with < 3% morbidity/mortality rate.' (AHA)
Atrial fibrillation	'Antithrombotic therapy (warfarin or aspirin) should be considered for patients with non-valvular atrial fibrillation based on an assessment of their risk of embolism and risk of bleeding complications.' (AHA) 'Higher-risk patients should be considered for warfarin at a target INR of 2.5. Aspirin may be a safer alternative to warfarin in some of these patients.' (SIGN)
Hyperlipidaemia	'Patients with known coronary heart disease and elevated LDL-cholesterol levels should be considered for treatment with a statin.' (AHA)
Obesity	'Weight reduction in overweight persons is recommended.' (AHA)
Physical inactivity	'Regular exercise (30 minutes of moderate-intensity activity daily).' (AHA)
Poor diet/nutrition	'At least five daily servings of fruit and vegetables.' (AHA)
Alcohol abuse	'No more than 2 drinks per day for men and 1 drink per day for non-pregnant women.' (AHA)
Hyperhomocysteinaemia	'Use of folic acid and B vitamins may be considered.' (AHA)
Oral contraceptive use	'Oral contraceptives should be avoided in women with additional risk factors (e.g. cigarette smoking or prior thromboembolic events).' (AHA)

AHA, American Heart Association;[43] SIGN, Scottish Intercollegiate Guidelines Network.[324]

derived from randomised controlled trial evidence; in the lower half of the table reasonable extrapolations from observational studies are made.

One area where the guideline differs from UK practice is carotid surgery for asymptomatic carotid artery stenosis. Cost-effectiveness studies have demonstrated that it is not cost-effective to screen for asymptomatic lesions,[307] so the issue is really whether patients who incidentally are found to have carotid artery stenosis should be operated on. The operation, while effective, only confers a small reduction in absolute risk. Therefore the skill of the surgeon is critically important, since a high complication rate would outweigh the potential benefits of surgery. UK guidelines such as SIGN and the Edinburgh Consensus Conferences have avoided making specific recommendations about carotid artery surgery in this circumstance.[318,319]

Another area of controversy is the optimal treatment of atrial fibrillation. A recent review has challenged the accepted orthodoxy that warfarin is the preferred treatment to aspirin.[212] Warfarin is more effective than aspirin, but the latter is safer. Therefore the treatment decision depends upon assessment of both stroke risk and haemorrhage risk in individual patients. Decision analysis can be a useful tool to guide therapeutic decisions in individual patients.[320] However, there are important gaps in the evidence, most notably with regard to treatment in the elderly, who are both at higher risk of stroke and at higher risk of haemorrhage.[321] The Birmingham Atrial Fibrillation Treatment of the Aged (BAFTA) randomised controlled trial has been set up to address this issue.[322] The wording of both the AHA and SIGN statements reflects this uncertainty, though other guidelines have been more forceful in advocating warfarin therapy.[323]

Guidelines will need to be updated once the results of the MRC/BHF heart protection study have been published, to reflect the wider indications for statins.[207]

NSF implementation

The NSF for Older People requires that general practices should build on registers developed for the coronary heart disease NSF, and develop a systematic approach for:

- identifying those at high risk of stroke
- identifying and recording modifiable risk factors of people at high risk of stroke
- providing and documenting the delivery of appropriate advice, support and treatment
- offering a regular review to those at risk of stroke.

Prevention in people who have had a TIA or stroke

The guidance issued by SIGN, the Intercollegiate Working Party (IWP) and the Edinburgh Consensus Conferences (ECC) for secondary prevention are mostly in agreement with each other (see Table 28).

These guidelines were produced prior to both the publication of the PROGRESS trial[222] and the completion of the MRC/BHF heart protection study.[207] One implication of PROGRESS is that it is worth lowering blood pressure in people who have had a stroke, whether or not they are defined as being hypertensive. While the PROGRESS trial used two specific agents (the diuretic indapamide and the ACE inhibitor perindopril), the reductions in stroke risk observed are of the order of magnitude that would be anticipated given the blood pressure reductions that were achieved, so the result is probably generalisable to blood pressure-lowering regimes in general (including non-pharmacological approaches). A second implication is that it may be worth lowering blood pressure as much as can be tolerated. Once the MRC/BHF heart protection study has been published, statin use in stroke patients will need to be incorporated into guidelines.

All patients should have their blood pressure checked and be started on an antiplatelet agent. There is some controversy over what dose of aspirin should be used. There is no evidence that higher doses (e.g. 300 mg/day) are any more effective than lower doses (e.g. 75 mg/day).[326] There is also some disagreement

Table 28: Summary of guidance for secondary prevention of stroke.

Hypertension	'All patients should have their blood pressure checked, and hypertension persisting for over one month should be treated.' (IWP) 'Control of hypertension . . . should be advocated once the initial event has stabilised.' (SIGN)[325]
Antiplatelet therapy	'All patients not on anticoagulation should be taking aspirin (50–300 mg) daily, or a combination of low-dose aspirin and dipyridamole modified release. Where patients are aspirin intolerant an alternative antiplatelet agent (clopidogrel 75 mg daily or dipyridamole MR 200 mg twice daily) should be used.' (IWP) 'Antiplatelet therapy, normally aspirin (75–300 mg/day), should be prescribed as early as possible.' 'Dipyridamole or clopidogrel should be considered as an alternative to aspirin in patients with contraindications to aspirin, or who are intolerant of aspirin.' 'Dipyridamole should be considered in addition to aspirin, especially in patients with recurrent stroke or TIA despite aspirin.' (SIGN) 'Treatment should be with 75–150 mg aspirin, continued long term.' 'Clopidogrel and the combination of aspirin and modified-release dipyridamole are . . . alternatives.' 'Insufficient evidence in view of cost to justify clopidogrel or dipyridamole as first-line treatment.' (ECC)
Anticoagulation	'In the presence of atrial fibrillation, mitral valve disease, prosthetic heart valves or within 3 months of myocardial infarction, anticoagulation should be considered for all patients who have ischaemic stroke.' (IWP) 'Warfarin should be considered for use in patients with non-valvular atrial fibrillation . . . after cardio-embolic stroke from valvular heart disease and recent myocardial infarction.' (SIGN) 'Patients who have had a TIA or ischaemic stroke and are in atrial fibrillation should be considered for long-term treatment with warfarin (Target INR 2.5).' (ECC)
Carotid endarterectomy	'Any patient with a carotid artery area stroke, and minor or absent residual disability, should be considered for carotid endarterectomy.' (IWP) 'Carotid endarterectomy has a role in preventing stroke in patients with recent (within 6 months) carotid territory symptoms in association with severe stenosis of the ipsilateral carotid artery, and who are fit for surgery. Surgery should be targeted at patients at highest risk of further stroke, and performed as soon as possible after the initial event.' (ECC)
Other risk factors	'All patients should be assessed and treated for other vascular risk factors and advised about lifestyle factors.' (IWP)

IWP, Intercollegiate Working Party for Stroke National Clinical Guidelines;[11] SIGN, Scottish Intercollegiate Guidelines Network; ECC, Edinburgh Consensus Conferences on Stroke.

as to the role of alternative antiplatelet agents. While the guidelines agree that the high cost of clopidogrel excludes it from being an appropriate first-line agent, recommendations on the use of aspirin in combination with dipyridamole differ. It would seem sensible to await the conclusions of the Antithrombotic Trialists Collaboration[239] before recommending combination therapy on the basis of one trial which has been subject to some criticism.[327] It is plausible that combination therapy of clopidogrel and aspirin will have a role, given the success of this combination in ischaemic heart disease, for example in 'aspirin failures' (i.e. people who suffer recurrent strokes/TIAs while on aspirin). The different guidelines are in agreement as to the role of warfarin post-stroke (indicated in atrial fibrillation, recent myocardial infarction and in the presence of valvular heart disease), and on the role of carotid endarterectomy. With regard to this latter procedure, the guidelines appropriately emphasise the importance of early investigation after a TIA or minor stroke because of the high risk of early recurrence in a patient with a significant carotid artery stenosis.

Acute treatment of stroke

Recommendations on acute management of patients with stroke are summarised in Table 29. Despite the absence of direct research evaluating the role of brain imaging, the guidelines all recommend that CT (or MRI) scans should be performed on all patients, ideally within 48 hours (or 24 according to the Edinburgh Consensus statement). The rationale for early CT scanning is to identify non-stroke pathology, differentiate haemorrhage from infarct, and identify possible indications for neurosurgical intervention. CT scanning cannot make a reliable positive diagnosis of stroke.[248] Early CT scanning is essential to exclude haemorrhage where acute medical interventions such as thrombolysis are being considered. The necessity to perform a CT scan before administering aspirin is uncertain and opinion varies, though aspirin is likely to do some harm if given to someone who has had an intracerebral haemorrhage.

Use of aspirin in acute stroke is uncontroversial. Trials have demonstrated efficacy using both 160 mg and 300 mg doses.[259] The UK recommendations on thrombolysis are conservative compared to North American practice, but are an appropriate reflection of the available evidence (*Note*: thrombolysis only has a restricted licence for use in the UK).[260] The SIGN and IWP guidelines differ on the role of neurosurgery for cerebral haemorrhage. There are insufficient data from trials to recommend whether neurosurgery should or should not be used.[258] The recommendation of compression stockings by the IWP is an extrapolation from evidence on the role of compression stockings to prevent deep vein thrombosis (DVT) in patients undergoing various kinds of surgery, and not based on trials in stroke patients.[328]

There is a general consensus that in order to treat people with acute stroke in a way that is consistent with the guidelines, patients should be urgently referred to specialist secondary care services, and that patients with moderate or severe symptoms should be admitted to hospital (to a stroke unit). Within hospital, there is consensus on the basis of physiological principles that stroke patients should be monitored and treated for fever, hyperglycaemia, dehydration and hypoxia, and that their airways should be maintained and risks of aspiration minimised.[267]

NSF implementation

The NSF for Older People makes specific recommendations for the management of acute stroke:

- a brain scan within 48 hours
- aspirin, if a diagnosis of haemorrhage is unlikely.

It also makes more general observations about the importance of appropriate management of the general condition of a stroke patient (such as hydration, hyperglycaemia, blood pressure, etc.).

Organisation of stroke care

A key component of recommendations on organisation of stroke care is the importance of stroke units. This recommendation has a strong evidence base.[169] However, the stroke-unit trials included a heterogeneous set of patterns of care, and so it is difficult to be prescriptive about what constitutes 'stroke-unit care', and a range of models are available that probably meet the relevant criteria (*see* 'Stroke-unit care' in Section 5). There is a difference in emphasis between the IWP and the ECC regarding the appropriate setting for acute care and rehabilitation. This will in part have been influenced by the publication of a trial of alternative

Table 29: Summary of guidance on acute treatment of stroke.

Diagnosis	'Stroke is primarily a clinical diagnosis. Confirmation, using imaging, will be needed if there are unusual clinical features.' 'The diagnosis should always be reviewed by a neurologist or physician with special interest in stroke.' (IWP)
Setting for acute care	'Patients should only be managed at home if acute care guidelines can be followed, care services are able to provide adequate and flexible support within 24 hours, and the services delivered at home are part of a specialist stroke service. Otherwise, patients should be admitted to hospital for initial care and assessment.' (IWP)
CT scanning/brain imaging	'Brain imaging is required as a matter of urgency if there is a clinical deterioration in the patient's condition, sub-arachnoid haemorrhage is suspected, hydrocephalus secondary to intracerebral haemorrhage is suspected, trauma is suspected, or the patient is on anticoagulant treatment, or has a known bleeding tendency.' 'Brain imaging should be undertaken in all patients within 48 hours unless there are good clinical reasons for not doing so.' (IWP) 'All patients with acute stroke should undergo CT brain scanning as soon as possible – preferably within 48 hours – and no later than seven days.' (SIGN) 'All patients with symptoms suggestive of a stroke should be referred to the stroke service for assessment, including CT brain scan, ideally within 24 hours.' (ECC)
Aspirin	'300 mg should be given as soon as possible after the onset of stroke symptoms (if a diagnosis of haemorrhage is considered unlikely).' (IWP) 'Early treatment with aspirin (150–300 mg daily) is recommended, starting as soon as intracranial haemorrhage is excluded by CT brain scanning.' (SIGN) 'Should be commenced within 48 hrs, or as soon as the diagnosis of cerebral infarction has been made (dose 150–300 mg).' (ECC)
Thrombolytic therapy	'Thrombolytic treatment with tissue plasminogen activator (tPA) should be given only in a specialist centre, within 3 hours of stroke onset (when haemorrhage has been definitely excluded).' (IWP) 'It is reasonable to use thrombolytic therapy (for example rtPA) in highly selected patients in a carefully monitored environment.' (ECC)
Other drug therapies	'No other drug treatment aimed at treatment of the stroke should be given unless a part of a randomised controlled trial.' (IWP)
Neurosurgery	'Neurosurgical opinion should be sought for cases of hydrocephalus.' (IWP) 'Urgent neurosurgical assessment should be available for selected patients, such as those with large cerebellar infarcts or hydrocephalus, and for selected cases of cerebral haemorrhage.' (SIGN)
Compression stockings	'Where stroke has caused weak or paralysed legs, full-length compression stockings should be applied (unless contraindicated) to prevent venous thrombosis.' (IWP) 'Physical methods of preventing DVT in stroke patients should be evaluated.' (ECC)
Other	'There should be local policies for the early management of hypertension, hyperglycaemia, hydration and pyrexia.' (IWP)

IWP, Intercollegiate Working Party for Stroke; SIGN, Scottish Intercollegiate Guidelines Network; ECC, Edinburgh Consensus Conferences on Stroke.

strategies for stroke care,[266] which preceded the November 2000 Edinburgh Consensus meeting, but came after the IWP had published its report. The general consensus now, echoed in the NSF for Older People, is that patients with acute stroke should be admitted to hospital.

With regard to setting for subsequent specialist rehabilitation, the trials of early discharge provide some evidence that community-based rehabilitation can achieve similar results to hospital-based care. Community-based rehabilitation services are an important part of a comprehensive service for stroke patients, but need to be linked to the specialist stroke services.

Both SIGN and ECC make recommendations on the importance of early assessment of patients with suspected TIAs in order to identify those who might benefit from carotid endarterectomy (*see* Table 30).

Table 30: Summary of guidance on organisation of stroke care.

Services for patients with suspected TIAs	'Patients with suspected TIA or minor stroke who are not admitted to hospital should have rapid access for urgent assessment and investigation (CT brain scanning, carotid Doppler examination and echocardiography).' (SIGN) 'For patients with symptoms suggestive of TIA, all clinicians should have rapid access to specialist advice and investigation. If assessment in a neurovascular clinic is agreed to be appropriate by the referring clinician and the specialist, this should be carried out within a week.' (ECC)
Stroke services	'Every organisation involved in the care of stroke patients over the first six months should ensure that stroke patients are the responsibility of and are seen by services specialising in stroke and rehabilitation.' 'The stroke service should comprise a geographically identified unit, a co-ordinated, multi-disciplinary team, staff with specialist expertise in stroke and rehabilitation, education programmes for staff, patients and carers, and agreed protocols for common problems.' (IWP) 'We emphasise the importance, and urge the further development, of well-organised and co-ordinated stroke services.' (ECC)
Hospital services	'Acute inpatient care for patients with major stroke should be organised as a multi-disciplinary stroke service based in designated units.' (SIGN) 'Any patient with moderate or severe symptoms should be referred with the expectation of admission to a stroke unit.' 'Strong evidence exists in favour of care being provided in dedicated stroke units.' (ECC)
Community services	'Specialist day hospital rehabilitation or specialist domiciliary rehabilitation can be offered to outpatients with equal effect.' 'Patients not admitted to hospital should be seen by a specialist rehabilitation team.' (IWP) 'Community-based rehabilitation services should develop partnerships with stroke services.' (ECC)
Setting for rehabilitation	'Specialist stroke services can be delivered to patients, after the acute phase, equally effectively in hospital or in the community, provided that the patient can transfer from bed to chair before going home.' (IWP) 'Management in a stroke unit which combines both acute assessment and the full range of rehabilitation should be the pathway of choice.' 'For those patients able to be rehabilitated at home . . . this is preferred by some patients.' (ECC)

IWP, Intercollegiate Working Party for Stroke; SIGN, Scottish Intercollegiate Guidelines Network; ECC, Edinburgh Consensus Conferences on Stroke.

This model of care has not been formally evaluated, but has logic given that surgery is of greatest benefit the earlier that it is performed.

NSF implementation

The NSF for Older People recommends:

- urgent referral of patients with suspected TIA to a rapid-response neurovascular clinic managed by a clinician with expertise in stroke for investigation and treatment
- that all patients who may have had a stroke will usually require urgent hospital admission, and that they should be treated by specialist stroke teams within designated stroke units.

Stroke rehabilitation

Of the guideline groups, the IWP is the only one so far to have focused on the specifics of rehabilitation (*see* Table 31). While the evidence base for some of the recommendations is lacking (*see* Section 6), they reflect a broad-based consensus of opinion.

Table 31: Summary of guidance on rehabilitation.

Multi-disciplinary assessment	'A multi-disciplinary assessment using a formal procedure or protocol should be undertaken and documented in the notes within 24–48 hours of admission. The protocol should include assessment of consciousness level, swallowing, pressure sores risk, nutritional status, cognitive impairment, communication, and the patient's needs in relation to moving and handling.' (IWP) 'Rehabilitation following stroke is an inter-disciplinary process.' (ECC)
Management	'Protocols should be adhered to for management of urinary and faecal incontinence and constipation, nutritional support and enteral feeding, prevention and management of shoulder pain, and discharge planning.' 'Goal-setting should involve the patient, and family if appropriate.' (IWP)
Therapists	'Patients with specific communication difficulties should be assessed by a speech and language therapist for their suitability for intensive therapy.' (IWP) 'A physiotherapist with expertise in neurodisability should co-ordinate therapy to improve movement performance of patients with stroke.' (IWP) 'All patients with difficulties in activities of daily living should be assessed by an occupational therapist with specialist knowledge in neurological disability.' (IWP)
Mood	'Patients would be screened for emotionalism, depression and anxiety within the first month of stroke, and their mood kept under review. When diagnosed, an antidepressant should be considered.' (IWP) 'There is evidence to support an individual intervention which could be drawn from the following: antidepressants for depression or emotionalism; psychological therapies; support approaches (including patient and carer support groups).' (ECC)

IWP, Intercollegiate Working Party for Stroke; ECC, Edinburgh Consensus Conferences on Stroke.

NSF implementation

The NSF for Older People recommends:

- early, expert and intensive rehabilitation in a hospital stroke unit
- that a stroke care co-ordinator should:
  - co-ordinate assessment and individual care plans
  - ensure arrangements for support and secondary prevention are in place prior to discharge
  - ensure efficient flow of relevant information to community-based professionals
  - ensure smooth transfer between care settings
  - ensure needs for home adaptations are identified and met prior to discharge.

While the actions and tasks specified by the NSF are important, there is no evidence that making use of a specialist stroke care co-ordinator is the best way of achieving them. Indeed, the limited evidence available suggests that some models that use a stroke co-ordinator may be harmful.[286] Stroke care co-ordinators have not been evaluated in this role, and alternative approaches adopted by district stroke services may be as effective at lower cost.

Carers and families

Guidance on services for carers and families is summarised in Table 32.

NSF recommendations

The NSF for Older People recommends:

- patients and carers should be involved in planning their care and safe discharge from hospital
- patients and carers should be provided with a named stroke care co-ordinator they can contact.

Again, there is no evidence to support the NSF's recommendation of using a stroke care co-ordinator to support patients and carers after transfer out of hospital. What is needed is an organisation, service or contact point to enable patients and carers to access support services after leaving hospital.

Continuing care

The NSF recommends: 'Recovery from stroke can continue over a long time, and rehabilitation should continue until it is clear that maximum recovery has been achieved. Some patients will need ongoing

Table 32: Summary of guidance on services for carers and families.

Management	'Carers should receive all necessary equipment and training in moving and handling, in order to position and transfer the patient safely in the home environment.' (IWP)
Information	'Families should be given information on the nature of stroke and its manifestations and on relevant local and national services, and patients and carers should be involved in decisions.' (IWP)
Carer stress	'Stroke services must be alert to the likely stress on carers.' (IWP)
Family support	'Family support workers should be involved to help reduce carer distress.' (IWP) 'Carers may experience considerable stress and there is evidence that this can be reduced by interventions such as family support services.' (ECC)

IWP, Intercollegiate Working Party for Stroke; ECC, Edinburgh Consensus Conferences on Stroke.

support, possibly for many years. These people and their carers should have access to a stroke care co-ordinator who can provide advice, arrange reassessment when needs or circumstances change, co-ordinate long-term support, or arrange for specialist care. Following a stroke, any patient reporting a significant disability at six months should be reassessed and offered further targeted rehabilitation if this can help them to recover further function.'[9]

Towards a quantified model for stroke care

Synthesising the epidemiology of stroke with the recommendations of the various expert committees that have reviewed the evidence on stroke care, it is possible to define what the ideal level of service provision might be for stroke care for a given population. This is summarised in Figures 5 and 6 for a 'typical' population of 100 000 based on UK data. Figure 5 focuses on services to prevent stroke (both primary and secondary prevention), and Figure 6 (*see* overleaf) focuses on the treatment and rehabilitation needs of people with stroke.

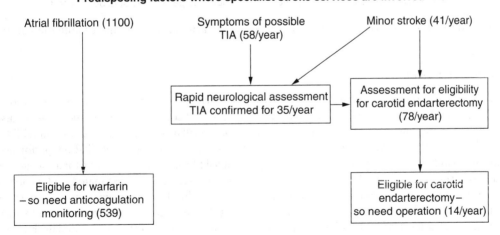

Numbers in parentheses indicate likely number of prevalent or incident (per year) patients.
See 'Summary of epidemiology of stroke at level of primary care trust' above for numbers.
See text for further explanation.

Figure 5: Estimate of ideal level of service provision for a population of 100 000: prevention of stroke.

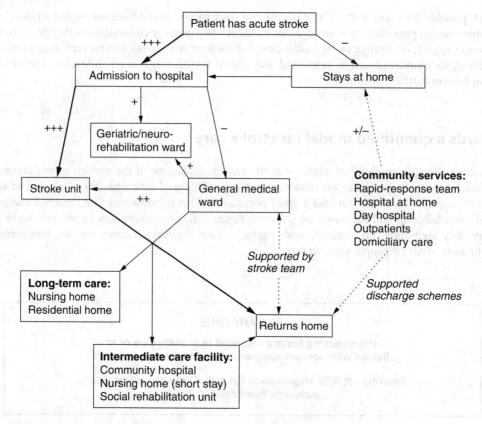

Bold arrows reflect desired pathway.
+ indicates that the proportion of patients who follow this pathway should be increased.
– indicates that the proportion of patients who follow this pathway should be reduced.

Figure 6: Ideal service provision for a population of 100 000: acute treatment and rehabilitation of stroke.

Prevention services

Much of the disease prevention activity that is carried out in primary care is not specific to stroke, though it has an important impact on stroke incidence as discussed in Section 4. The specific areas of disease prevention that impinge upon specialist services are atrial fibrillation and assessment of suitability for carotid endarterectomy (*see* Figure 5). From a prevalence survey of atrial fibrillation performed in Northumberland, it was estimated that 49% of people in atrial fibrillation were eligible for anticoagulation based upon criteria from a pooled analysis of trial results.[50] Therefore, of the estimated 1100 people with atrial fibrillation in a population of 100 000, approximately 561 should be on aspirin and 539 on warfarin. Thus provision should be available to monitor the anticoagulation (whether in primary care or in hospital anticoagulation clinics) of 540 patients per 100 000 population. It is difficult to estimate how many patients in primary care present with a possible TIA, given that the epidemiological data are based on confirmed TIAs. However, if a 40% misdiagnosis rate of GPs is assumed,[97] then a rapid-access neurological assessment clinic would need to see 58 patients per year with suspected TIA (and possibly more with minor stroke if these were not admitted to hospital). Using the methodology of Ferris *et al.*[160] applied to the population estimates summarised in 'Summary of epidemiology of stroke at level of primary care trust' in

Section 4, it can be estimated that 14 carotid endarterectomies per 100 000 population would represent optimum provision.

Treatment and rehabilitation services

It is more difficult to present a single model of treatment and rehabilitation services. While there is strong consensus on the importance of stroke units and the value of a co-ordinated, multi-disciplinary approach, the optimum mix of hospital- as opposed to community-based services will depend upon the locality (urban or rural), and on what services are already present. While the current evidence favours inpatient rehabilitation, there have been few trials that have directly compared inpatient to outpatient rehabilitation.[268] The emphases of the guidelines are shown in Figure 6. In essence, they recommend that a greater proportion of patients should be admitted to hospital, and of those, more should receive their rehabilitation on a stroke unit. With regard to the numbers involved, 221 people per 100 000 might be expected to have a stroke per annum (including recurrent strokes) (*see* 'Summary of epidemiology of stroke at level of primary care trust' in Section 4). If 20% of these are assumed to die early, and if 70% of the remainder are assumed to have a moderate or severe stroke (i.e. will require admission to a stroke unit for rehabilitation), and if the average length of stay is assumed to be 30 days,[172] then this equates to a need for a 12-bedded stroke unit per 100 000 population, assuming 85% bed occupancy (which will allow for some fluctuation in numbers). Most of the stroke units included in the systematic review of their effectiveness were of similar size (6–15 beds),[170] but are likely to have served far larger catchment populations ($\geq 300\,000$). Therefore, a model of care whereby the majority of stroke patients are admitted to a stroke unit is not sustainable without radical organisational change within the hospital sector. This raises the question of whether locality-based rehabilitation in intermediate care facilities might not be an appropriate model of care. Such intermediate care facilities would need to specialise in stroke, and would need to treat sufficient numbers of patients to develop and maintain that expertise, which in turn means that the locality service would need to have a sufficiently large catchment area. Such models have not been evaluated, and trials of this pattern of care vs. stroke units in district general hospitals need to be performed.

A stroke service also requires access to neurosurgical expertise for the management of patients with sub-arachnoid haemorrhage, and those with stroke who develop complications such as hydrocephalus that require neurosurgical intervention.

Continuing care

Most of the research on models of care is directed at treating 'incident' cases of stroke, i.e. the acute treatment and rehabilitation needs of people in the early phases after stroke (perhaps up to one year). However, from a primary care perspective, the needs of incident cases are dwarfed by those of prevalent cases. How best to meet the long-term needs of patients with stroke is an under-researched area, and models of care that address these needs should be developed and evaluated. As noted above, the NSF recommends use of stroke co-ordinators. The National Clinical Guidelines for Stroke make the following recommendations.[11]

- Any patient with disability at 6 months or later after stroke should be assessed for a period of further targeted rehabilitation to be given where appropriate.
- Patients and their carers should have their individual psychosocial and support needs reviewed on a regular basis.
- Health and social services professionals should ensure that patients and their families have information about the statutory and voluntary organisations offering services specific to these needs.

Standard three of the National Service Framework for Older People relates to intermediate care.[9] The standard is that 'Older people will have access to a new range of intermediate care services at home or in designated care settings, to promote their independence by providing enhanced services from the NHS and councils to prevent unnecessary hospital admission and effective rehabilitation services to enable early discharge from hospital and to prevent premature or unnecessary admission to long-term residential care.'

It is difficult to quantify the longer-term needs of stroke survivors, but on the basis of data from the OCSP (*see* 'Survival following stroke' and 'Incidence of disability following stroke' in Section 4) that 70% of stroke patients survive to one year, and that 35% of these patients remain functionally dependent, it can be estimated that about 54 new stroke patients per 100 000 population will require continuing care (either institutional or domiciliary) one year after their stroke. The actual level of service needed will be greater than this, since it relates to prevalent rather than incident cases. Prevalence surveys of disability suggest that in a population of 100 000 one might anticipate 1000 stroke survivors with residual disability. In the absence of an evidence base, it is difficult to be prescriptive about what services should be available. Such services need to be considered within the broader context of disability management and services for elderly people.

Priorities for stroke care

The quantified model described in 'Towards a quantified model for stroke care' above is of an 'ideal' service, which ignores financial constraints and cost-effectiveness. These aspects cannot be ignored when considering what should be the highest priorities in developing local services. What is most relevant in this context is the marginal benefit (i.e. the impact of moving from the current service provision to the optimum) of each service development. This can be approximated by estimating the gap between current service provision and the optimal service, what it would cost to fill that gap, and what would be the outcome in terms of health benefits.

Stroke prevention

In Table 33, the effects of each intervention, in terms of number of strokes that would be prevented, is estimated by using the typical rate of stroke that occurred in the control groups of the trials on which evidence of effectiveness is based. The table does not directly try to evaluate the relative cost-effectiveness of different interventions, but rather the impact of full implementation of current recommendations.

Table 33 can only offer a crude estimate of the relative value of prioritising each of the intervention strategies, since it would be possible to increase the relative cost-effectiveness of each of the interventions by targeting them at individuals who had the most to gain. For example, while the average number needed to operate on to prevent a stroke with carotid endarterectomy in the European Carotid Surgery Trial was 14, this could be reduced to 3 if operations were only performed on particular high-risk individuals.[331] Secondly, only some of the direct costs are included. Thus, for hypertension, only the cost of the drugs are considered, and not the costs of assessment and monitoring. Similarly, for carotid endarterectomy, only the costs of the operation itself are taken into account. The costs of anticoagulation, on the other hand, are derived from studies that will have given a more accurate assessment of total costs. Thirdly, the table does not take account of the costs of treating strokes. Thus it is not possible to draw any conclusions as to the overall cost-effectiveness of each of the interventions as compared with not implementing them. Nevertheless, it is possible to draw some tentative conclusions from the table as to the relative priority that should be accorded to increasing uptake of each of the stroke prevention strategies.

In terms of cost per stroke averted, optimising uptake of aspirin is much the most cost-effective strategy. Next comes use of anticoagulation in atrial fibrillation, followed by treating hypertensive patients with

Table 33: Estimate of marginal costs and benefits of optimising service provision to prevent stroke.

Intervention	Current uptake* /100,000	Estimated optimal uptake* /100,000	Shortfall /100,000	Cost of treatment per person/year	Risk of stroke off treatment (pa)	Number of strokes prevented pa if switch from current to optimal care†	Cost per stroke prevented
Achieve tight control of BP of people already on treatment	2,718[47]	9,591	6,873	‡Low £19 High £116[329] (drug costs only)	0.3%[84]	7.2	£18,095 £110,476
Treat hypertension in people not on treatment	9,591	36,545	26,954	Low £19 High £116 (drug costs only)	0.3%	38.4	£18,095 £110,476
Anticoagulate eligible patients in AF	253	539	286	£70–80[314,320]	3.3%[330]	5.6	£3,850
Aspirin for patients with CHD or AF not on warfarin	4,410	7,000	2,590	£1	2.9%[215]	15.8	£164
Aspirin post-stroke	945	1,500	555	£1	6%[55]	9.0	£62
Carotid endarterectomy	9	14	5	£1,940 (costs of operation only)	17% over 5 years[331]	0.35 over 5 years	£27,700

*Derived from data in Sections 4 and 5.
†Derived from risk reductions quoted in Section 6.
‡Low estimate: derived from cost of generic 'old' antihypertensive agents: thiazides and β-blockers; high estimate: derived from newer antihypertensive agents.

low-cost generic agents (β-blocker or thiazide), as per the British Hypertension Society guidelines (low-cost option in Table 32).[332] The costs of identifying and following up such people are not taken into account. The former could be minimised if best use is made of the potential for opportunistic screening. The next priority would be improving access to carotid endarterectomy. Optimising treatment of hypertensives using newer agents (high-cost option in Table 32) would appear to be a much lower priority. The most important strategy in terms of reducing the number of strokes is the initiation of treatment in hypertensive people not currently on medication.

Maximal implementation of all these strategies might be estimated to reduce the incidence of stroke by about 0.74/1000, which would reduce the total age-adjusted incidence of stroke by about a third. This is less than the 40% target that has been set by Government.[8] To achieve these targets, lifestyle factors such as smoking, physical activity and diet (*see* Tables 9 and 12) must also be tackled. Population-based approaches that aim to reduce the level of a risk factor in the whole population rather than simply in high-risk individuals also need to be considered. For example, Rose estimated that a 5% lowering of blood pressure in the UK population would result in a 30% reduction in stroke incidence, whereas treating everyone with a diastolic blood pressure above 100 mmHg would only reduce the incidence by 15%.[147]

An analysis of secondary prevention of stroke strategies performed by Hankey and Warlow suggested that in terms of cost per stroke prevented, simple advice to stop smoking was the most cost-effective strategy, and carotid endarterectomy the least cost-effective.[333] Table 34 summarises their results. In the table, the relative cost-effectiveness of clopidogrel and carotid endarterectomy has been reversed compared with how they appeared in the original publication. This is to compensate for the fact that endarterectomy is a one-off procedure with long-term benefit, whereas medical therapies need to be long term to sustain benefit.

Stroke treatment and rehabilitation

Hankey and Warlow looked at acute treatment strategies (also shown in Table 34). They concluded that the highest priority should be to establish a stroke unit that delivers organised stroke care through a

Table 34: Summary of Hankey and Warlow's analysis of cost (in Aus$) per stroke prevented (secondary prevention) or per death/dependency avoided (acute stroke treatment) (adapted from Hankey and Warlow).[333]

		Cost
Acute stroke treatment	Stroke unit	?0
	Aspirin	83
	Thrombolysis with tPA	36,000
Secondary stroke prevention	Smoking cessation: advice	0
	Diuretics for hypertension	1,350
	Aspirin for sinus rhythm	2,000
	Anticoagulation for AF	>1,200
	ACE inhibitor for hypertension	18,000
	Aspirin and dipyridamole for sinus rhythm	18,500
	Smoking cessation: nicotine patches	19,600
	Statins for hypercholesterolaemia	41,000
	Carotid endarterectomy for severe symptomatic stenosis to prevent one stroke per year for three years	182,000
	Clopidogrel for all in sinus rhythm	74,000

multi-disciplinary team. Since they postulate (rather optimistically) that a stroke unit could be set up by redistributing existing secondary care resources, this strategy comes out as highly cost-effective, since it has no additional costs attached to it.

With regard to treatment and rehabilitation, it is more difficult to identify relative priorities, since a more sophisticated outcome measure than strokes avoided needs to be used, and the data that are available tend to focus on discrete medical treatments rather than patterns of care. Nevertheless, the establishment of stroke units, as emphasised in the guidelines considered earlier in this section and recommended by Hankey and Warlow, can be considered a first priority.

Conclusions

The key components of a strategy for primary stroke prevention include identification and treatment of hypertension, identification and treatment of atrial fibrillation, careful control of hypertension in diabetes, lifestyle advice with regard to smoking, diet, weight, and exercise, and treatment with a statin of patients with known coronary heart disease and elevated cholesterol.

The same issues apply to secondary prevention, but because the risks of subsequent strokes are high, each is of relatively greater importance and effectiveness. In addition, patients should be on aspirin, or another antiplatelet agent if aspirin-intolerant. Patients with a TIA or minor stroke should be assessed rapidly for carotid endarterectomy, which should be performed in a centre with a low complication rate. This might necessitate use of regional or sub-regional units.

There is consensus that the vast majority of patients with acute stroke should initially be assessed in hospital. Aspirin is an effective acute treatment for ischaemic stroke, and is preferably administered after brain imaging has been performed to rule out intracerebral haemorrhage. Thrombolytic therapy is a reasonable treatment to give in selected patients, but only in specialist centres in a carefully monitored environment. Further research is required before such a model of care can be 'rolled out' to a wider population.

There is strong evidence that acute care and rehabilitation of stroke patients is best carried out in stroke units that offer an organised, multi-disciplinary approach to care. All stroke patients should have access to such care. The extent to which rehabilitation should be performed in central stroke units and the extent to which it can be performed as effectively in community settings has to be resolved. Community-based rehabilitation has not been demonstrated to be as effective as stroke-unit care, but it is impractical to expect existing models of stroke-unit care (with an average unit size of 6–15 beds) to cater for the needs of a typical DGH catchment area. Therefore, locality-based models of intermediate care need to be developed and evaluated.

8 Approaches to audit and outcome measures

Several publications have given advice on the appropriate mechanisms of audit of stroke care, and what measures to use for this. The purpose of this section is to summarise these recommendations and targets.

Saving Lives: Our Healthier Nation

The target of this Government White Paper is to reduce the death rate from coronary heart disease and stroke and related diseases in people under 75 years by at least two-fifths by 2010 – saving 200 000 lives in total.[8]

This is a useful target for monitoring the overall impact on health of a wide variety of factors. The value of this indicator is that it broadens the perspective beyond the health services to other factors that influence health, such as lifestyle and socio-economic circumstances.

The National Service Framework for Older People

This includes milestones that the NHS is required to meet in developing stroke services.

- April 2002: Every general hospital which cares for people with stroke will have plans to introduce a specialised stroke service model from 2004.
- April 2003: Every hospital which cares for people with stroke will have established clinical audit systems to ensure delivery of the National Clinical Guidelines for stroke care.
- April 2004: Primary care trusts will have ensured that:
    - every general practice, using protocols agreed with local specialist services, can identify and treat patients identified as being at risk of a stroke because of high blood pressure, atrial fibrillation or other risk factors
    - every general practice is using a protocol agreed with local specialist services for the rapid referral and management of those with transient ischaemic attack (TIA)
    - every general practice can identify people who have had a stroke and is treating them according to protocols agreed with local specialist services
    - every general practice has established clinical audit systems for stroke.
- April 2004: 100% of all general hospitals which care for people with stroke will have a specialised stroke service as described in the stroke service model.

Outcome indicators for stroke

A working group for the Department of Health reviewed the possible value of a series of 24 health outcome indicators for stroke.[334] Their recommendations are summarised in Table 35. They categorised the indicators into five types:

- A: to be implemented generally on a routine basis
- B: to be implemented generally by periodic survey
- C: to be implemented where local circumstances allow on a routine basis
- D: to be implemented where local circumstances allow by periodic survey
- E: to be developed further either because the link with effectiveness is not clear or because the indicator specification is incomplete.

When interpreting variations in health outcome indicators, four major categories of explanation need to be considered: differences in measurement technique; chance; differences in case-mix; and differences in quality of care. Process measures (such as use of aspirin) are more sensitive to genuine differences in the quality of care than outcome measures (such as hospital-specific mortality), and are easier to interpret, provided that there is a proven link between process and outcome.[335]

Table 35: Summary of recommendations of working group on health outcome indicators for stroke.

Topic area	Indicator	Category
Reduction/avoidance of risk of first/subsequent stroke	Incidence of hospitalised stroke	A
	Population-based incidence of stroke	C
	Percentage of GP patients with BP recorded in previous 5 years	A
	Median and inter-quartile range of systolic BP within a GP population	B
	Percentage of GP patients identified as hypertensive whose most recent systolic BP is less than 160 mmHg	C
	Percentage of GP patients who have a prescription for aspirin therapy at six months after non-haemorrhagic stroke	B
	Percentage of GP patients with atrial fibrillation who have a prescription for anticoagulant therapy	D
Reduction of death from stroke	Case fatality rate within 30 days of a hospital admission for stroke	A
	Case fatality rate within 30 days of stroke (inpatient or community-based treatment)	C
	Population-based mortality rates	A
Reduction/avoidance of complications from stroke	Percentage of patients for whom a formal swallowing assessment is undertaken within 24 hours of stroke	E
	Incidence of pressure sores during inpatient stay within a hospital population with stroke	A
	Percentage of patients within a community provider population who, six months following stroke, have one or more pressure sores	B
	Rate of emergency re-admissions within 30 days of discharge with a diagnosis of stroke	D
Improving function and well-being after stroke	Multi-professional involvement in the week following admission with stroke	B
	Distribution of Barthel ADL score at discharge from hospital with stroke	A
	Distribution of Barthel ADL score six months after stroke	B
	Assessment of aphasia six months after stroke	E
	Assessment of outdoor mobility six months after stroke	E
	Assessment of social functioning six months after stroke	E
	Assessment of depression six months after stroke	E
	Change in Barthel ADL score between discharge and six months after stroke	D
	Percentage of people admitted with stroke who return to pre-admission category of residence	A
	Percentage of people who live in pre-admission category of residence six months after stroke	B
	Percentage of people not hospitalised living in pre-stroke category of residence six months after stroke	D
	Patients' or carers' knowledge of available health and social services six months after stroke	E
	Patient satisfaction six months after stroke	E
	Carer burden six months after stroke	E

The National Sentinel Audit for stroke

The Royal College of Physicians developed an audit tool for stroke under the guidance of the Intercollegiate Working Party.[10] This audit covered the organisation and facilities for treating stroke, the case-mix of admitted patients, and the process of care with regard to initial assessment, rehabilitation, secondary prevention, discharge planning, communication with carers, and follow-up and review. This model of audit provides a useful tool for monitoring the hospital care of stroke patients, offering the opportunity for comparative data between trusts (as in the national audit that the Royal College of Physicians carried out), or comparisons within the same trust over time.

9 Research priorities

Prevention of stroke

The NSF for Older People is promoting the introduction of care pathways which enable rapid investigation of patients with possible TIA and minor stroke. Such models have an underlying rationale, but have not been evaluated. Formal testing would enhance plans to implement this initiative.

Acute stroke treatments

As noted in the Edinburgh Consensus statement, 'While trials of the efficacy of novel drugs in acute stroke and secondary prevention are vital, there is an urgent need for greater funding for non-drug treatment and, in particular, into aspects of stroke service delivery and organisation.'[317] While acute drug treatments for stroke are emerging, such as aspirin and thrombolysis in specific circumstances, there are major non-pharmacological questions to address. These include issues around the general management of acute stroke patients, such as how intensively they should be monitored, and how early rehabilitation should start. Cost-effectiveness of different intensities of acute care needs to be evaluated.

Rehabilitation

There is a growing evidence base for stroke rehabilitation. Some of the most important evidence comes from evaluations of complex packages of care, such as stroke units. It has been argued that studies that are focused on the specific components of rehabilitation, which include precise definitions of what is involved, are needed to complement this research.[336] Thus, rather than simply asking general research questions such as 'Does physiotherapy improve outcome following stroke?', more specific questions that detail the amount and type of physiotherapy, and the specific nature of the problem that the physiotherapy is to address (e.g. shoulder pain), need to be answered.

However, there is just as significant a role for research that focuses on the overarching activities and processes that are central to the nature of rehabilitation.[337] Thus the research agenda should aim to:

- investigate ways to improve goal-setting and assessment
- understand the interrelationships between disease, impairment and contextual factors, and the interrelationship between disability and participation
- investigate ways of modifying behaviour (i.e. optimising activity) in the context of disabling illness.

Organisation and models of stroke care

While it is clear that stroke units are an effective model for the delivery of hospital-based care for patients with stroke, stroke units as currently constituted (5–15 bedded units) will not be able to cope with the stroke workload of a typical DGH (25–35 stroke inpatients at any one time).[10] Therefore, new models need to be developed and evaluated that can offer alternatives to stroke-unit care of equal efficacy. These might include intermediate care facilities, such as community hospitals, locality-based stroke rehabilitation units, or other community-based facilities such as domiciliary teams and day hospital services. The one trial that compared hospital stroke-unit care to alternative models of multi-disciplinary care found that outcome was significantly worse in those patients not randomised to stroke-unit care, but this trial cannot be generalised to all settings, or indeed all non-stroke-unit models of care. Further trials are needed comparing different models against what is now the recognised standard of care in an inpatient stroke unit.

Research has tended to focus on treatment of incident rather than prevalent stroke patients, i.e. care in the first year following stroke, rather than long-term support. Models need to be developed and tested that provide long-term support to stroke patients. These should include models that are not stroke-specific, but focus on the more general issues of disability management. The stroke co-ordinator promoted by the NSF for Older People is one such model, but it needs formal evaluation. Another model that has been promoted is regular patient reassessment.[338] However, the frequency and nature of these contacts need to be defined.[339] Other models might include general practice-based packages of care for patients identified as having had past strokes. Development of such models would be timely, given the requirement of the NSF for general practices to develop stroke registers.

Level of funding of stroke research

Rothwell points out that there are major disparities in the level of research funding, comparing the three major causes of death and disability in the world: heart disease, cancer and stroke.[340] Most research funding comes from disease-specific charity organisations, non-disease-specific funding bodies (government or charity) and from industry (pharmaceutical). Between them, these funding bodies spend significantly more on research into heart disease and cancer than into stroke. He recommends that non-disease-specific research-funding bodies, such as the Medical Research Council, the Wellcome Trust and the National Co-ordinating Centre for Health Technology Assessment, should take these disparities into account when deciding upon their own priorities.

Appendix 1: The WHO ICIDH-2 model of illness, now the ICF model

The WHO ICIDH model

In 1980 the World Health Organization (WHO) published an International Classification of Impairments, Disabilities and Handicaps (ICIDH) which was based upon earlier work.[1-3] It was conceived of as being complementary to the International Classification of Diseases (ICD), which is essentially a classification of disease (pathology). The ICIDH classification has not been as widely used as the ICD, but there certainly have been publications both researching into it and using it. Badley[4] stated that over 1000 articles had been published relating to its use at that time.

In 2000 a new revision was finalised, and the new classification is known as the International Classification of Functioning, Disability and Health (ICF) but is still also referred to as the ICIDH-2. It does not differ greatly in most respects, but it does add one further dimension and it has changed some of the terminology. The new dimension is one of *context*; it emphasises that all ill people must be seen within a context – as described below. The new terminology is to use the words 'activities' and 'participation' in place of disability and handicap, respectively.

The model is still an incomplete model of illness, especially in missing out the whole domain of 'quality of life'. It is also not easy to draw distinctions between the levels using the definitions, and the classification itself is probably not usable in any routine sense. The model currently on the website (www3.who.int/icf/icftemplate.cfm; accessed 29/11/01) has an overview table shown below (Table A1.1).

Table A1.1: The ICF overview table.

	Functioning and disability		Contextual factors	
Components	Body structures and functions	Activities and participation	Environmental factors	Personal factors
Domains	Body structures Body functions	Life areas Tasks, actions	External influences on functioning and disability	Internal influences on functioning and disability
Constructs	Change in body functions (physiological) Change in body structures (anatomical)	Capacity: executing tasks in a standard environment Performance: executing tasks in current environment	Facilitating or hindering impact of features of the physical, social and attitudinal world	Impact of the attributes of the person
Positive aspects	Functional and structural integrity Impairment	Activities Participation Activity limitation Participation limitation	Facilitators Barriers/hindrances	Not applicable Not applicable

This appendix elaborates on the model, hopefully clarifying it so that it is easily understood. The ideas put forward here were used as the basis for the National Clinical Guidelines for Stroke, and have been discussed in other articles.[5] Tables A1.2 and A1.3 give the overview.

Although not explicitly published as a framework for rehabilitation, the WHO ICIDH has been developed as such (see Table A1.2 below and Table A1.3 overleaf). The WHO ICIDH model considers that any disease (i.e. pathology) may cause or be associated with abnormalities at three higher levels: abnormalities of the person; alterations in behaviour; and changes in social position. These are referred to respectively as impairments, disabilities and handicaps. (**In the ICF they are referred to as impairments, activity limitations and participation limitations.**) To make the model more complete one must incorporate disease or pathology, which refers to abnormalities at the level of the organ. A brief description and discussion of the four descriptive levels follows. Next the model should incorporate the environment or context, and the ICF does this. Finally quality of life is included in the amended model, drawing on ideas discussed by Post et al.[6]

Table A1.2: Rehabilitation model – the WHO ICIDH-2 framework.

Level of illness

Term	Synonym	Comment
Pathology	Disease/diagnosis	Refers to abnormalities or changes in the structure and/or function of an *organ or organ system*
Impairment	Symptoms/signs	Refers to abnormalities or changes in the structure and/or function of the *whole body* set in *personal context*
Activity (was disability)	Function/observed behaviour	Refers to abnormalities, changes or restrictions in the interaction between a person and his or her environment or *physical context* (i.e. changes in the *quality or quantity of behaviour*)
Participation (was handicap)	Social positions/roles	Refers to changes, limitations, or 'abnormalities' in the *position* of the person in their *social context*

Contextual factors

Domain	Examples	Comment
Personal	Previous illness	Primarily refers to *attitudes, beliefs and expectations* often arising from previous experience of illness in self or others, but also to personal characteristics
Physical	House, local shops, carers	Primarily refers to local physical *structures*, but also includes people as *carers* (not as social partners)
Social	Laws, friends, family	Primarily refers to *legal* and local *cultural* setting, including expectations of important others

Note: This model is usually prefaced with the words, 'In the context of illness, . . . '.

Table A1.3: Expanded model of illness.

System	Experience/location:	
	Subjective/internal	Objective/external
Level of illness		
Person's organ *Pathology*	**Disease** Label attached by person, usually on basis of belief	**Diagnosis** Label attached by others, usually on basis of investigation
Person's body *Impairment*	**Symptoms** Somatic sensation, experienced moods, thoughts, etc.	**Signs** Observable abnormalities (absence or change), explicit or implicit
Person in environment *Behaviour*	**Perceived ability** What person feels they can do, and feeling about quality of performance	**Disability/activities** What others note person does do, quantification of that performance
Person in society *Roles*	**Role satisfaction** Person's judgement (valuation) of their own role performance (what and how well)	**Handicap/participation** Judgement (valuation) of important others (local culture) on role performance (what and how well)
Context of illness		
Internal, personal context	**Personality** Person's beliefs, attitudes, expectations, goals, etc.	**Past history** Observed/recorded behaviour prior to and early on in this illness
External, physical context	**Salience** Person's attitudes towards specific people, locations, etc.	**Resources** Description of physical (buildings, equipment, etc.) and personal (carers, etc.) resources available
External, social context	**Local culture** The people and organisations important to person, and their culture, especially family and people in same accommodation	**Society** The society lived in and the laws, duties and responsibilities expected from and the rights of members of that society
Totality of illness		
Quality of life *Summation of effects*	**Happiness** Person's assessment of and reaction to achievement or failure of important goals and sense of being a worthwhile person	**Status** Society's judgement on success in life; material possessions

Pathology

Much illness can be traced to abnormalities within organs in the body. Organs may function abnormally for several reasons. Trauma may cause destruction of part or all of the organ. Disruption of the blood supply may cause reduced function or complete death of some of the organ. Micro-organisms may damage or destroy part or all of the organ. The cells of the organ may change their function due to alterations in their genetic control, causing (for example) tumour formation or the production of more or less of their normal product. In nerve cells especially, the properties of the cell membrane might be altered subtly so that the cell changes its behaviour. In all these ways, and in many other ways, the function of the organ can be disturbed.

Within this level there are of course many subdivisions and categorisations. Some of the categories relate to presumed aetiology (congenital or acquired, due to infectious agents or physical agents, etc.). Some classifications give biochemical detail, others give structural detail, and yet others give macroscopic details. However, the common feature is that all these sub-categories are within the organ, and often within the cell.

Impairment

Just as cells and tissues come together to form unitary structures known as organs, so organs and organ systems (such as the cardiovascular system or endocrine system) come together to form a single structure, the organism or body. Abnormalities that arise at the level of the organism are referred to as impairments. Individual impairments may arise from more than one pathology. More importantly, some patients may only experience an impairment when they have two or more pathologies; this appearance of abnormalities independent of specific components is the essence of a higher-order system. For example, osteoarthritis of a hip may be asymptomatic until there is extra stress upon the hip, as might occur if the patient has a stroke (a second pathology) or moves to live somewhere where she can only have a bath, not a shower (an environmental or contextual change).

Disability, or functional limitations

The third level to be affected is the interaction that occurs between a person and his or her environment. This interaction is best described as behaviour. The WHO ICIDH refers to change in the third level as disability (or now refers to it more accurately as *activity limitations*). The other phrase used by many people to refer to changes in behaviour is the functional consequences of a disease. In practice the changes are almost always measured or conceived of in terms of dependence, either upon other people or upon special equipment.

Disability is therefore considered to refer to alterations in the quality or quantity of an individual's goal-directed behaviour, or their activities. In other words, a person may need to change the way they achieve their goals, or may achieve them more slowly, or may depend upon special equipment, or may not be able to achieve them at all. All these changes are 'disabilities', although they are more accurately and appropriately referred to as changes in behaviour or activity *at the level of* disability.

Handicap

Handicap is the most difficult concept to define and measure. It is best considered as referring to changes in or restrictions on the person's social position and social role functioning in some way. Handicap is ultimately a personal matter. How someone feels changed or restricted by their illness in terms of their social position and social role functioning can only be judged by that individual in conjunction with the people who are directly involved with that person.

The revised ICIDH refers to this level as the level of *participation*, and this also emphasises the fact that this level refers to or describes the person's participation in or involvement in social (culturally determined, personally important) activities.

A simplified analysis

This model can easily be simplified, and perhaps clarified in the following way. The fundamental unit of behaviour is the individual (human) person. Abnormalities in that person's organs or an abnormality of the organism itself therefore directly affect the 'behavioural unit', restricting or altering its abilities. Therefore pathology and impairment form one level concerning the individual person who then interacts with his or her environment.

The observed behaviour (i.e. the interaction between the person and his or her environment) can then be analysed in two ways. The first is *descriptively*, usually focusing on independence and normality, where change is referred to as disability. The second is in terms of the *meaning attached* to that behaviour by the person and by others, where any change in the meaning attributed to behaviour (which may itself have changed) may be referred to as handicap. The ICF implicitly recognises this distinction, putting body structures and functions together and activities and participation together (*see* Table A1.1).

Context

The revised ICIDH has added a vital further dimension, that of context. As soon as one considers behaviour and participation in society, it is necessary to consider not only the individual but their environment. Furthermore, one cannot only consider the physical environment but one must also consider the personal environment (other people), the legal environment and the cultural environment (expectations of relevant other people). The WHO ICIDH also considers, correctly, that the person's own personal history is an important part of the context.

Thus, for simplicity, the context of an illness can be divided into three:

- *personal*: the individual's own previous experiences and current expectations
- *physical*: the structures around the person, both near and far
- *social*: the influence of other people, including the influence of society as manifest in its laws and customs.

This may be too simple, but it does cover the main areas and it does emphasise that one must look well beyond the disease itself when considering its management.

Summary and conclusion

In summary, illness can be analysed thus. A person is a behavioural unit, and changes within the person (i.e. pathology) may affect the person's range of intrinsic functions and skills (i.e. give impairments), thereby influencing and constraining his or her behaviour and behavioural repertoire. However, while the person lives, he or she will interact with the environment. The behaviour can be observed and described, which constitutes the description at the level of 'disability'; furthermore, that behaviour will have meaning attributed to it by the person and by relevant others, which then constitutes the person's state at the level of handicap.

It must be emphasised that the WHO ICF is a descriptive model. Its whole intention is to allow a description and classification of an individual's state or circumstances. This is necessary for rehabilitation, but not sufficient. Several other factors need to be considered when analysing a patient's situation. These include the context of the illness (i.e. the past history of the illness, the patient's stage in life, the family's involvement), the patient's desires or life philosophy, and the patient's reactions to the illness.

Furthermore, the clinicians must take into account the context of the person (the physical environment, the personal environment, the local social facilities, financial considerations, the legal situation, etc.). A comprehensive awareness of illness needs to recognise these 'hidden variables'.

General insights from the model

This model is not simply of academic interest; it leads to many useful insights. Although hopefully many of these will be apparent, a brief résumé of the more important lessons will be given here.

Time, and the focus of attention

Initially, in managing any illness, it is both necessary and correct to devote most resources to establishing the underlying pathology (if any), because there may be specific treatments available. Furthermore, the pathology has a major influence on determining prognosis. However, even in the initial stages changes in behaviour are important. For example, the patient may need care (usually nursing care) because of dependence (i.e. disability).

Once the pathology is established and treated, attention should rapidly switch to the level of disability. At first this attention may relate to the patient, but soon attention must broaden to include the patient's normal (home) environment (family, house, etc.). Later still, the focus of attention should move on to consider social roles (i.e. handicap) and to investigate the social environment.

An important corollary of this change in focus over time is an exponential increase in timescales. Pathologically centred processes occur in short timescales – minutes, hours or, at most, days. Processes relating to behaviour take weeks, months or years to be complete. Processes relating to handicap may take years, decades or even centuries to finish, because they often involve changing society as much as changing the person.

Patient and environment

This model forcibly reminds us that patients are people, coming from their own physical and social environment. Therefore, as attention moves from pathology to handicap, so attention must move from the ill individual to the physical, personal and social environment of that individual. Disability and handicap can only be considered in the context of the individual person's own environment – their family, friends, workmates, home, etc. Rehabilitation must take this into account.

Hospital systems

Hospitals have increasingly had to cope with a mixture of processes, some relating to pathology and some relating to disability. This mixing of pathologically centred processes with behaviour centred processes leads to an obvious conflict between two different systems, because the former takes place in a short timescale, and the latter in a long timescale. In other words, there are two systems (pathological diagnosis/treatment, and disability diagnosis/treatment) trying to run at greatly different speeds within a single system (the hospital). The conflicts are obvious; patients are usually labelled 'bed-blockers' or 'patients with social problems'.

Furthermore, hospitals provide an environment quite alien to most people, and certainly divorced from a patient's reality. Therefore it is difficult to judge or treat disability accurately in a hospital setting, especially when considering any behaviour beyond the most basic, such as feeding.

One solution may be for hospitals to disentangle the two major processes occurring here, having relatively few beds devoted to high-speed, high-tech medicine and surgery and a much greater number of beds in a separate location devoted to recuperation and (where needed) active rehabilitation. These might be termed 'complex care wards'.

Interventions

It seems logical, and it is probably true, that interventions will be more effective the closer they are to the root cause of an illness. In other words, where an illness can be traced to a specific pathology, it is considered more efficient to 'cure' that pathology than to give symptomatic treatment (i.e. to treat impairments). However, it is important to remember that the price of achieving a cure of the pathology may sometimes be a much higher level of impairment, disability or handicap.

The model also reminds us that interventions should not only be directed at the patient. It is often more important and more effective to alter the environment. This might include rehousing, providing a wheelchair, teaching relatives how to transfer the patient, and teaching work colleagues how to communicate with the individual. It may also include changing the environment to reduce or remove factors causing the illness itself (for example, increasing the tax on cigarettes or alcohol).

Loose relationships

It must be emphasised that, though the various systems interact with each other, the relationships are only general and are not tight. In other words, in most instances a fixed pathological lesion does not equate with a defined impairment, a defined impairment does not equate with a definite level of dependence, nor does a specific level of disability equate to a fixed handicap. There are major opportunities for clinically silent pathology, impairment or disability.

Equally importantly, the effects of abnormalities can jump levels. For example, a right hemianopia (an impairment) may cause no disability, but if the person is a car driver then the person may lose their driving licence and hence their job. The fact that the effects of any specific pathology, impairment or disability can vary so much means that there is ample opportunity for intervention to ameliorate the consequences.

The nature and strength of the interrelationships between the different levels of illness has only recently been investigated to a significant degree.[7–10] There is an urgent need to investigate these relationships systematically, especially to study the importance and effects of any interaction between different impairments, so that rehabilitation interventions can be more rationally targeted.[11,12] The effects of intervening variables also need to be researched.[13]

Measures

Many measures used in health care consist of two or more items which are amalgamated to form a single scale or score. Much has been written about the process of constructing health measures.[14–16] This model emphasises two specific considerations.

The component items of a measure should all relate to (come from) the same level. Some measures fail to observe this rule, and their validity and utility must be questionable. One widely used measure illustrates this. The Oxford Handicap Scale[17] contains one question on impairment ('Does the patient have any residual symptoms?') and most of the other questions concentrate upon reduced mobility (a disability). The scale does not touch on handicap despite its name. Any measure which mixes items from different levels, for example, pathology items with impairment items, or impairment items with disability items, must be considered intrinsically invalid.[14]

Secondly, when evaluating a service, one must choose measures that assess outcome at the appropriate level. The levels of interest to most patients are those of handicap and disability. Another area of interest is that of well-being, which is probably close to quality of life.

Observation vs. implication

Another way to consider the model is in terms of those characteristics of an illness that can be observed, and are externally verifiable, and those characteristics which are simply deduced or implied.

All behaviour is externally observable and thus objective and verifiable. We can state whether someone does actually dress independently, walk fast, talk, undertake work, etc. Opinions may vary on the quality of the behaviour (e.g. its standard), but there is external evidence which can (for example) be recorded on a videotape.

Opinions may differ significantly about the reasons for the observed abnormalities and also about whether someone 'should' be more or less competent. Nonetheless, measures of disability are usually objective, provided those measures record actual behaviour observed in the relevant setting and do not attempt to qualify the observations or to interpret them.

Handicap, in contrast, is almost all implied; most of the ideas are externally imposed constructs. We may say externally that we believe that an individual is acting the roles of mother, wife and housekeeper. The person concerned, however, may see herself as a servant and slave, or as a boss, or in other ways (e.g. as a daughter). There is no externally verifiable truth.

A few impairments may be externally observable. For example, a reduced range of passive movement or a facial disfigurement are both easily verified externally. However, most are implied constructs, particularly in the field of neurology. Weakness (reduced voluntary motor power) is perhaps objective, but the label applied (e.g. upper motor neuron weakness) is often a construct deduced from other evidence. Often there is little disagreement with such an obvious label as weakness (though pain in the limb may contribute to the weakness), but other frequently used labels such as spastic weakness, apraxia, spasticity, or neglect are all much less certain.

Furthermore, in neurological practice, many of the impairments are deduced from behavioural observations, even if the behaviour is controlled and constrained so as to highlight postulated impairments. For example, neglect may be diagnosed as a result of performance (behaviour) on a series of tests (a test battery), or aphasia after performance on another series of tests. However, it is well recognised that other impairments can cause failure on the tests. Blindness is an obvious example, neglect can cause a reduced score on some tests of aphasia,[18] and aphasia makes it difficult to test visual fields and many other areas.

Thus, this model suggests that, contrary to popular belief, measures of disability are generally objective, whereas statements about pathological diagnosis and symptoms and signs are often much more subjective, depending upon deductions made by an observer who may be biased. Studies on the reliability of objective neurological examination of patients after stroke emphasise the unreliable (subjective) nature of many of these observations.[19,20]

Normality

Most measures assume a normal state, usually as a standard against which the patient is judged. However, it is often difficult to know what is normal in many situations. At the level of disability, the concept of normal becomes almost redundant. In Western culture at least, most people take personal responsibility for dressing, feeding, toileting and walking, but the individual chooses almost all other behaviour, and may choose not to undertake many behaviours (e.g. cooking, driving a car). At the level of handicap, it must be accepted that role performance is unique and can only be compared with the individual's past roles and with the expectations of the person and their social circle (family, friends, colleagues, etc.).

Therefore, the term normal is difficult to use. It may be better to talk instead of change, and sometimes the actual state will fall outside generally accepted normal limits for that individual. For some items no normal limits will exist, for some they will depend upon personal, cultural or other characteristics, and for some the limits will be quite closely defined and will be common to more or less everyone.

Prognosis

Prognosis is usually related to the pathology because the pathology determines the prognostic field for that illness. If two people have foot drop, the prognosis will be different if one has motor neuron disease and the other a recent stroke. Within a disease group there will be differences between patients, but knowing the pathology will enable one to determine the correct prognostic items.

Therefore, it is essential to know pathology when giving a prognosis, both because it determines the prognostic field and because it often determines which observations can be used as specific prognostic factors. Thus, in terms of the model, a change in one system (at one level) may not determine specific changes at other levels but may nonetheless have a pervasive influence upon future performance in other levels.

The rehabilitation team

The successful management of an illness requires involvement and intervention at all levels affected by that illness. Once a stroke has stabilised, all other factors up to and including housing and employment need to be considered and acted upon. If not, the management of the illness will not be considered successful by the patient.

Therefore this model shows that the team of people needed to help anyone with an illness is likely to include a wide range of professions so that all aspects of the illness can be covered. Furthermore, in chronic illness it is likely that any effective team will normally span a variety of agencies and departments, such as health, social services, employment, education and housing (depending upon the country).

Patient goals

This model reminds us that, when considering rehabilitation, it is vital to take into account the goals of the patient. Indeed, it is often also important to take into account the goals of the family and sometimes the goals of other carers, funding agencies, etc.

The vocabulary

It is noticeable that the terms used (pathology, impairment, disability and handicap) are all negative. They all relate to the abnormal state. They do not have positive counterparts. None of the terms used now started with their current meaning.

References for Appendix 1

1 Nagi S. *An Epidemiology of Disability Among Adults in the USA.* MMFQ/Health and Society, 1976, pp. 439–67.

2 Duckworth D. The need for a standard terminology and classification of disablement. In: Granger CV, Gresham GE (eds). *Functional Assessment in Rehabilitation Medicine.* Baltimore, MD: Williams and Wilkins, 1984, pp. 1–13.

3 Granger CV. A conceptual model for functional assessment. In: Granger CV, Gresham GE (eds). *Functional Assessment in Rehabilitation Medicine.* Baltimore, MD: Williams and Wilkins, pp. 14–25.

4 Badley EM. An introduction to the concepts and classifications of the international classification of impairments, disabilities and handicaps. *Disabil Rehabil* 1993; **15**: 161–78.

5 Wade DT, de Jong BA. Recent advances in rehabilitation. *BMJ* 2000; **320**: 1385–8.

6 Post MWM, de Witte LP, Schrijvers AJP. Quality of life and the ICIDH: towards an integrated conceptual model for rehabilitation outcomes research. *Clin Rehabil* 1999; **13**: 5–15.

7 Farmer JE, Eakman AM. The relationship between neuropsychological functioning and instrumental activities of daily living following acquired brain injury. *Appl Neuropsychol* 1995; **2**: 107–15.

8 Heinemann AW, Linacre JM, Wright BD, Hamilton BB, Granger C. Relationships between impairment and physical disability as measured by the Functional Independence Measure. *Arch Phys Med Rehabil* 1993; **74**: 566–73.

9 McSweeny AJ, Grant I, Heaton RK, Prigitano GP, Adams KM. Relationship of neuropsychological status to everyday functioning in healthy and chronically ill persons. *J Clin Exp Neuropsychol* 1985; **7**: 281–91.

10 Wade DT, Legh-Smith J, Langton Hewer R. Depressed mood after stroke: a community study of its frequency. *Br J Psychiatry* 1987; **151**: 200–5.

11 Wade DT. Epidemiology of disabling neurological disease: how and why does disability occur? *J Neurol Neurosurg Psychiatry* 1996; **61**: 242–9.

12 Whyte J. Toward a methodology for rehabilitation research. *Am J Phys Med Rehabil* 1994; **73**: 428–35.

13 Peters DJ. Disablement observed, addressed, and experienced: integrating subjective experience into disablement models. *Disabil Rehabil* 1996; **18**: 593–603.

14 Wade DT. *Measurement in Neurological Rehabilitation.* Oxford: Oxford University Press, 1992.

15 Bowling A. *Measuring Disease.* Buckingham: Open University Press, 1995.

16 McDowell I, Newell C. *Measuring Health. A guide to rating scales and questionnaires.* Oxford: Oxford University Press, 1987.

17 van Swieten JC, Koudstall PJ, Visser MC, Schouten HJA, van Gijn J. Interobserver agreement for the assessment of handicap in stroke patients. *Stroke* 1988; **19**: 604–77.

18 Al-Khawaja I, Wade DT, Collin CF. Bedside screening for aphasia: a comparison of two methods. *J Neurol* 1996; **243**: 201–4.

19 Tomasello F, Mariana F, Fieschi C *et al.* Assessment of interobserver differences in the Italian multicentre study on reversible cerebral ischaemia. *Stroke* 1982; **13**: 32–4.

20 Goldstein LB, Bertels C, Davis JN. Interrater reliability of the NIH stroke scale. *Arch Neurol* 1989; **46**: 660–2.

Appendix 2: Summary of reviews of the Cochrane Stroke Group

This includes reviews on the Cochrane Library up to and including *Issue 4*, 2001. The date after each statement represents the last time a substantial update of this review was performed.

Review	Reviewers' conclusion
Prevention of first stroke	
Effective/promising treatments	
Antiplatelet therapy for preventing stroke in patients with non-valvular atrial fibrillation and no previous history of stroke or transient ischaemic attacks	'Considering all randomised data, aspirin modestly (by about 20%) reduces stroke and major vascular events in non-valvular AF. For primary prevention among AF patients with an average stroke rate of 4.5%/year, about 10 strokes would be prevented yearly for every 1000 given aspirin.'[1] (8/99)
Carotid endarterectomy for asymptomatic carotid stenosis	'There is some evidence favouring CEA for asymptomatic carotid stenosis, but the effect is at best barely significant, and extremely small in terms of absolute risk reduction.'[2] (8/99)
Oral anticoagulants for preventing stroke in patients with non-valvular atrial fibrillation and no previous history of stroke or transient ischaemic attacks	'Adjusted-dose OAC (achieved INRs of 2–3) reduces stroke as well as disabling/fatal stroke for patients with non-valvular AF, and these benefits were not substantially offset by increased bleeding among participants in randomised clinical trials. Limitations include relatively short follow-up and imprecise estimates of bleeding risks from these selected participants. For primary prevention in AF patients who have an average stroke rate of 4%/year, about 25 strokes and about 12 disabling fatal strokes would be prevented yearly for every 1000 given OAC.'[3] (8/99)
Thienopyridine derivatives (ticlopidine, clopidogrel) vs. aspirin for preventing stroke and other serious vascular events in high-vascular-risk patients	'The available randomised evidence shows that the thienopyridine derivatives are modestly but significantly more effective than aspirin in preventing serious vascular events in patients at high risk (and specifically in TIA/ischaemic stroke patients), but there is uncertainty about the size of the additional benefit. The thienopyridines are also associated with less gastrointestinal haemorrhage and other upper gastrointestinal upset than aspirin, but an excess of skin rash and diarrhoea. The risk of skin rash and diarrhoea is greater with ticlopidine than with clopidogrel. Ticlopidine, but not clopidogrel, is associated with an excess of neutropenia and of thrombotic thrombocytopenic purpura.'[4] (8/99)
Ineffective/unproven treatments	
Antithrombotic drugs for carotid artery dissection	'There were no randomised trials comparing either anticoagulants or antiplatelet drugs with control. There is, therefore, no evidence to support their routine use for the treatment of extracranial internal carotid artery dissection. There were also no randomised trials that directly compared anticoagulants with antiplatelet drugs, and the reported non-randomised studies did not show any evidence of a significant difference between the two. We suggest that a randomised trial including at least 1000 patients in each treatment arm with this condition is clearly needed.'[5] (7/00)

Review	Reviewers' conclusion

Treatment of acute stroke

Effective/promising treatments

Antiplatelet therapy for acute ischaemic stroke	'Antiplatelet therapy with aspirin, 160 to 300 mg daily, given orally (or per rectum in patients who cannot swallow), and started within 48 hours of onset of presumed ischaemic stroke reduces the risk of early recurrent ischaemic stroke without a major risk of early haemorrhagic complications and improves long-term outcome.'[6] (5/99)
Thrombolysis for acute ischaemic stroke	'Thrombolytic therapy increases deaths within the first 7 to 10 days, and deaths at final follow-up. Thrombolytic therapy also significantly increases symptomatic and fatal intracranial haemorrhage. These risks are offset by a reduction in disability in survivors, so that there is, overall, a significant net reduction in the proportion of patients dead or dependent in activities of daily living. The data from trials using intravenous recombinant tissue plasminogen activator (tPA), from which there is the most evidence on thrombolytic therapy so far, suggest that it may be associated with less hazard and more benefit. There was heterogeneity between the trials and the optimum criteria to identify the patients most likely to benefit and least likely to be harmed, the agent, dose, and route of administration, are not clear. The data are promising and may justify the use of thrombolytic therapy with intravenous recombinant tPA in experienced centres in selected patients. However, the widespread use of thrombolytic therapy in routine clinical practice at this time cannot be supported. Further trials will be needed to identify which patients are most likely to benefit from treatment and the environment in which it may best be given, before thrombolytic therapy should be adopted on a wider scale.'[7] (7/99)

Ineffective/unproven treatments

Anticoagulants for acute ischaemic stroke	'Immediate anticoagulant therapy in patients with acute ischaemic stroke is not associated with net short- or long-term benefit. The data from this review do not support the routine use of any type of anticoagulant in acute ischaemic stroke.'[8] (2/99)
Calcium antagonists for acute ischaemic stroke	'No evidence is available to justify the use of calcium antagonists in patients with acute ischaemic stroke.'[9] (10/99)
Cooling therapy for acute stroke	'There is currently no evidence from randomised trials to support the routine use of physical or chemical cooling therapy in acute stroke. Since experimental studies showed a neuroprotective effect of hypothermia in cerebral ischaemia, and hypothermia appears to improve the outcome in patients with severe closed head injury, trials with cooling therapy in acute stroke are warranted.'[10] (5/99)
Corticosteroids for acute ischaemic stroke	'There is not enough evidence to evaluate corticosteroid treatment for people with acute presumed ischaemic stroke.'[11] (10/98)
Fibrinogen-depleting agents for acute ischaemic stroke	'Although ancrod appears to be promising, it is not possible to draw reliable conclusions from the available data.'[12] (11/96)
Gangliosides for acute ischaemic stroke	'There is not enough evidence to conclude that gangliosides are beneficial in acute stroke. Caution is warranted because of reports of sporadic cases of Guillain-Barré syndrome after ganglioside therapy.'[13] (8/00)

Review	Reviewers' conclusion

Treatment of acute stroke

Ineffective/unproven treatments Continued.

Glycerol for acute stroke	'This systematic review suggests a favourable effect of glycerol treatment on short-term survival in patients with probable or definite ischaemic stroke, but the magnitude of the treatment effect may be minimal (as low as a 3% reduction in odds). Due to the relatively small number of patients and that the trials have been performed in the pre-CT era, the results must be interpreted cautiously. The lack of evidence of benefit in long-term survival does not support the routine or selective use of glycerol treatment in patients with acute stroke.'[14] (5/00)
Haemodilution for acute ischaemic stroke	'The overall results of this review are compatible with both a modest benefit and a moderate harm of haemodilution therapy for acute ischaemic stroke. As used in the randomised trials, this therapy has not been proven to improve survival or functional outcome.'[15] (8/99)
Interventions for deliberately altering blood pressure in acute stroke	'There is not enough evidence to evaluate the effect of altering blood pressure on outcome during the acute phase of stroke. Oral CCBs, ACE inhibitors and glyceryl trinitrate all appear to lower blood pressure in patients with acute stroke.'[16] (2/01)
Interventions for dysphagia in acute stroke	'Too few studies have been performed, and these have involved too few patients. PEG feeding may improve outcome and nutrition as compared with NGT feeding. Further research is required to assess how and when patients are fed, and the effect of swallowing or drug therapy on dysphagia.'[17] (3/99)
Low-molecular-weight heparins or heparinoids vs. standard unfractionated heparin for acute ischaemic stroke	'Low-molecular-weight heparin or heparinoid appear to decrease the occurrence of deep vein thrombosis compared to standard unfractionated heparin, but there are too few data to provide reliable information on their effect on other important outcomes, including death and intracranial haemorrhage.'[18] (8/01)
Mannitol for acute stroke	'There is currently not enough evidence to decide whether the routine use of mannitol in acute stroke would result in any beneficial or harmful effect. The routine use of mannitol in all patients with acute stroke is not supported by any evidence from randomised controlled clinical trials. Further trials are needed to confirm or refute the routine use of mannitol in acute stroke.'[19] (10/00)
Nitric oxide donors (nitrates), L-arginine, or nitric oxide synthase inhibitors for acute ischaemic stroke	'There is currently no evidence from randomised trials on the effects of nitric oxide donors, L-arginine, or nitric oxide synthase inhibitors in patients with acute ischaemic stroke.'[20] (8/97)
Pentoxifylline, propentofylline and pentifylline for acute ischaemic stroke	'There is not enough evidence to assess the effectiveness and safety of methylxanthines after acute ischaemic stroke.'[21] (6/96)
Piracetam for acute ischaemic stroke	'There is some suggestion of an unfavourable effect of piracetam on early death, but this may have been caused by baseline differences in stroke severity in the trials. Piracetam does not appear to reduce dependency for stroke patients.'[22] (1/99)
Prostacyclin and analogues for acute ischaemic stroke	'Too few patients have been studied in randomised trials to allow conclusions to be drawn about the effect of prostacyclin treatment on survival of people with acute stroke.'[23] (1/98)

Review	Reviewers' conclusion
Treatment of acute stroke	

Ineffective/unproven treatments Continued.

Surgery for primary supratentorial intracerebral haemorrhage	'There is not enough evidence to evaluate the effect of craniotomy or stereotactic surgery, or endoscopic evacuation in patients with supratentorial intracerebral haematoma.'[24] (12/98)
Theophylline, aminophylline, caffeine and analogues for acute ischaemic stroke	'There is not enough evidence to assess whether theophylline or its analogues reduce mortality or morbidity, or are safe, in people with acute ischaemic stroke.'[25] (3/99)
Thrombolysis (different doses, routes of administration and agents) for acute ischaemic stroke	'There is not enough evidence to conclude whether lower doses of thrombolytic agents might be safer or more effective than higher doses in acute ischaemic stroke. It is not possible to conclude whether one agent might be better than another, or which route of administration might be best. No comparative data for streptokinase have been found.'[26] (4/98)
Tirilazad for acute ischaemic stroke	'Tirilazad mesylate increased the combined end-point of 'death or disability' by about one-fifth, but did not alter case fatality, when given to patients with acute ischaemic stroke. Although further trials of tirilazad are now not warranted, analysis of individual patient data from the trials may help elucidate why tirilazad appears to worsen outcome in acute ischaemic stroke.'[27] (7/01)
Vasoactive drugs for acute stroke	'There is not enough evidence to reliably evaluate the effect of altering blood pressure on outcome after acute stroke. CCBs, β-blockers, and probably ACE inhibitors, prostacyclin and nitric oxide, each lowered BP during the acute phase of stroke. In contrast, magnesium, naftidrofuryl and piracetam had little or no effect on BP.'[28] (4/00)
Vinpocetine for acute ischaemic stroke	'There is not enough evidence to evaluate the effect of vinpocetine on survival or dependency of patients with acute stroke.'[29] (7/97)

Treatment of sub-arachnoid haemorrhage	

Effective/promising treatments

Calcium antagonists for aneurysmal sub-arachnoid haemorrhage	'Calcium antagonists reduce the proportion of patients with poor outcome and ischaemic neurological deficits after aneurysmal SAH; the risk reduction for case fatality alone is not statistically significant. The results for 'poor outcome' are statistically robust, but depend mainly on trials with oral nimodipine; the evidence for nicardipine and AT877 is inconclusive. The intermediate factors through which nimodipine exerts its beneficial effect after aneurysmal SAH remain uncertain.'[30] (7/99)

Ineffective/unproven treatments

Antifibrinolytic therapy for aneurysmal sub-arachnoid haemorrhage	'Antifibrinolytic treatment does not appear to benefit people with aneurysmal sub-arachnoid haemorrhage. However, the trials were all done more than 10 years ago. New strategies may counteract the ischaemia-inducing potential of antifibrinolytic treatment and lead to improved outcome. A trial of combined antifibrinolytic and anti-ischaemia treatment is under way.' (7/98)
Circulatory volume expansion for aneurysmal sub-arachnoid haemorrhage	'The effects of volume expansion therapy have not been studied properly in patients with aneurysmal sub-arachnoid haemorrhage. At present, there is no sound evidence for or against the use of volume expansion therapy in patients with aneurysmal sub-arachnoid haemorrhage.'[31] (7/99)

Review	Reviewers' conclusion

Treatment of sub-arachnoid haemorrhage

Ineffective/unproven treatments Continued.

Timing of surgery for aneurysmal sub-arachnoid haemorrhage	'Based upon the limited randomised controlled evidence available, the timing of surgery was not a critical factor in determining outcome following a sub-arachnoid haemorrhage. Since the publication of the only randomised controlled study in 1989, techniques for the treatment of sub-arachnoid haemorrhage have progressed, questioning the validity of the conclusions in the modern era. Currently, most neurovascular surgeons elect to operate within 3 or 4 days of the bleed in good-grade patients to minimise the chances of a devastating re-bleed. However, the treatment of patients in poorer grades warrants further scrutiny in a randomised controlled trial.'[32] (11/00)

Secondary prevention of stroke

Effective/promising treatments

Anticoagulants for preventing stroke in patients with non-rheumatic atrial fibrillation and a history of stroke or transient ischaemic attacks	'The evidence suggests that anticoagulants are beneficial, without serious adverse effects, for people with non-rheumatic atrial fibrillation and recent cerebral ischaemia.'[33] (2/95)
Anticoagulants vs. antiplatelet therapy for preventing stroke in patients with non-rheumatic atrial fibrillation and a history of stroke or transient ischaemic attacks	'The evidence from one trial suggests that anticoagulant therapy can benefit people with non-rheumatic atrial fibrillation and recent cerebral ischaemia. Aspirin may be a useful alternative if there is a contraindication to anticoagulant therapy. The risk of adverse events appears to be higher with anticoagulant therapy than aspirin.'[34] (2/95)
Antiplatelet therapy for preventing stroke in patients with non-rheumatic atrial fibrillation and a history of stroke or transient ischaemic attacks	'Aspirin may reduce the risk of vascular events in people with non-rheumatic atrial fibrillation, but the effect shown in the single trial was not statistically significant.'[35] (2/95)
Carotid endarterectomy for symptomatic carotid stenosis	Carotid endarterectomy reduced the risk of disabling stroke or death for patients with stenosis exceeding ECST-measured 70% or NASCET-measured 50%. This result is generalisable only to surgically fit patients operated on by surgeons with low complication rates (less than 6%).[36] (3/99)

Ineffective/unproven treatments

Anticoagulants for preventing recurrence following ischaemic stroke or transient ischaemic attack	'There appears to be no clear benefit from long-term anticoagulant therapy in people with non-embolic presumed ischaemic stroke or transient ischaemic attack. There appears to be a significant bleeding risk associated with anticoagulant therapy.'[37] (9/97)
Anticoagulants (oral) vs. antiplatelet therapy for preventing further vascular events after transient ischaemic attack or minor stroke of presumed arterial origin	'For the secondary prevention of further vascular events after transient ischaemic attack or minor stroke of presumed arterial origin, there is insufficient evidence to justify the routine use of low-intensity oral anticoagulants (INR 2.0–3.6). More intense anticoagulation (INR 3.0–4.5) is not safe and should not be used in this setting.'[38] (12/99)

Review	Reviewers' conclusion

Secondary prevention of stroke

Ineffective/unproven treatments Continued.

Eversion vs. conventional carotid endarterectomy for preventing stroke	'Eversion CEA may be associated with low risk of arterial occlusion and re-stenosis. However, numbers are too small to definitively assess benefits or harms. Reduced re-stenosis rates did not appear to be associated with clinical benefit in terms of reduced stroke risk, either peri-operatively or later. Until further evidence is available, the choice of the CEA technique should depend on the experience and familiarity of the individual surgeon.'[39] (8/00)
Local vs. general anaesthesia for carotid endarterectomy	'There is not enough evidence from randomised trials comparing carotid endarterectomy performed under local as opposed to general anaesthetic. Non-randomised studies suggest potential benefits with local anaesthetic. However, these studies are likely to be significantly biased.'[40] (8/96)
Patch angioplasty vs. primary closure for carotid endarterectomy	'Limited evidence suggests that carotid patch angioplasty may lower the risk of peri-operative arterial occlusion and re-stenosis. It is unclear whether this reduces the risk of death or stroke.'[41] (5/96)
Patches of different types for carotid patch angioplasty	'There is not enough evidence to differentiate between venous and synthetic patches in carotid endarterectomy.'[42] (5/96)
Percutaneous transluminal angioplasty and stenting for vertebral artery stenosis	'There is no evidence as yet to assess the effects of percutaneous transluminal angioplasty for vertebral artery stenosis.'[43] (5/97)
Percutaneous transluminal angioplasty and stenting for carotid artery stenosis	'There is no evidence as yet to assess the relative effects of carotid percutaneous transluminal angioplasty in people with carotid stenosis.'[44] (7/97)
Routine or selective carotid artery shunting for carotid endarterectomy (and different methods of monitoring in selective shunting)	'The data presently available are too limited to either support or refute the use of routine or selective shunting in carotid endarterectomy. Large-scale randomised trials using no shunting as the control group are required. No one method of monitoring in selective shunting has been shown to produce better outcomes.'[45] (12/94)

Organisation of stroke care

Effective/promising treatments

Organised inpatient (stroke unit) care for stroke	'Stroke patients who receive organised inpatient care in a stroke unit are more likely to be alive, independent, and living at home one year after the stroke. The apparent benefits are not restricted to any particular subgroup of patients or model of stroke unit care. No systematic increase was observed in the length of inpatient stay.'[46] (10/98)

Ineffective/unproven treatments

Services for helping acute stroke patients avoid hospital admission	'There is currently no evidence from clinical trials to support a radical shift in the care of acute stroke patients from hospital-based care.'[47] (5/99)
Services for reducing duration of hospital care for acute stroke patients	'ESD services provided for a selected group of stroke patients can reduce the length of hospital stay. However, the relative risks and benefits and overall costs of such services remain unclear.'[48] (5/99)

Review	Reviewers' conclusion
Rehabilitation following stroke	

Effective/promising treatments

Cognitive rehabilitation for attention deficits following stroke	'There is some indication that training improves alertness and sustained attention, but no evidence to support or refute the use of cognitive rehabilitation for attention deficits to improve functional independence following stroke.'[49] (5/00)

Ineffective/unproven treatments

Cognitive rehabilitation for memory deficits following stroke	'There is insufficient evidence to support or refute the effectiveness of cognitive rehabilitation for memory problems after stroke.'[50] (2/00)
Electrical stimulation for preventing and treating post-stroke shoulder pain	'The evidence from randomised controlled trials so far does not confirm or refute that electrical stimulation around the shoulder after stroke influences reports of pain, but there do appear to be benefits for passive humeral lateral rotation. A possible mechanism is through the reduction of glenohumeral subluxation. Further studies are required.'[51] (4/99)
Information provision for stroke patients and their care givers	'The results of the review are limited by the variable quality of the trials and the wide range of outcome measures used. The general effectiveness of information has not been conclusively demonstrated. Future work should address the expressed needs of patients and carers and seek to identify appropriate teaching strategies which can be successfully implemented within clinical practice'[52] (1/01)
Pharmacological treatment for aphasia following stroke	'The main conclusion of this review is that drug treatment with piracetam may be effective in the treatment of aphasia after stroke. Further research is needed to explore the effects of drugs for aphasia, in particular piracetam. If a trial is done, this must be large enough to have adequate statistical power. The safety of the drug should be of primary interest. Researchers should examine the long-term effects of this treatment, and whether it is more effective than speech and language therapy.'[53] (7/01)
Speech and language therapy for aphasia following stroke	'The main conclusion of this review is that speech and language therapy treatment for people with aphasia after a stroke has not been shown to be either clearly effective or clearly ineffective within a RCT. Decisions about the management of patients must therefore be based on other forms of evidence. Further research is required to find out if speech and language therapy for aphasic patients is effective. If researchers choose to do a trial, this must be large enough to have adequate statistical power, and be clearly reported.'[54] (7/99)
Speech and language therapy for dysarthria due to non-progressive brain damage	'There is no evidence of the quality required by this review to support or refute the effectiveness of speech and language therapy interventions for dysarthria following non-progressive brain damage. There is an urgent need for good-quality research in this area.'[55] (9/00)

Citations of Cochrane Reviews

1 Benavente O, Hart R, Koudstaal P, Laupacis A, McBride R. Antiplatelet therapy for preventing stroke in patients with non-valvular atrial fibrillation and no previous history of stroke or transient ischemic attacks (Cochrane Review). In: *The Cochrane Library. Issue 4*. Oxford: Update Software, 2000.

2 Chambers BR, You RX, Donnan GA. Carotid endarterectomy for asymptomatic carotid stenosis (Cochrane Review). In: *The Cochrane Library. Issue 4*. Oxford: Update Software, 2000.

3 Benavente O, Hart R, Koudstaal P, Laupacis A, McBride R. Oral anticoagulants for preventing stroke in patients with non-valvular atrial fibrillation and no previous history of stroke or transient ischemic attacks (Cochrane Review). In: *The Cochrane Library. Issue 4*. Oxford: Update Software, 2000.

4 Hankey GJ, Sudlow CLM, Dunbabin DW. Thienopyridine derivatives (ticlopidine, clopidogrel) versus aspirin for preventing stroke and other serious vascular events in high vascular risk patients (Cochrane Review). In: *The Cochrane Library. Issue 4*. Oxford: Update Software, 2000.

5 Lyrer P, Engelter S. Antithrombotic drugs for carotid artery dissection (Cochrane Review). In: *The Cochrane Library. Issue 4*. Oxford: Update Software, 2000.

6 Gubitz G, Sandercock P, Counsell C. Antiplatelet therapy for acute ischaemic stroke (Cochrane Review). In: *The Cochrane Library. Issue 4*. Oxford: Update Software, 2000.

7 Wardlaw JM, del Zoppo G, Yamaguchi T. Thrombolysis for acute ischaemic stroke (Cochrane Review). In: *The Cochrane Library. Issue 4*. Oxford: Update Software, 2000.

8 Gubitz G, Counsell C, Sandercock P, Signorini D. Anticoagulants for acute ischaemic stroke (Cochrane Review). In: *The Cochrane Library. Issue 4*. Oxford: Update Software, 2000.

9 Horn J, Limburg M. Calcium antagonists for acute ischemic stroke (Cochrane Review). In: *The Cochrane Library. Issue 4*. Oxford: Update Software, 2000.

10 Correia M, Silva M, Veloso M. Cooling therapy for acute stroke (Cochrane Review). In: *The Cochrane Library. Issue 4*. Oxford: Update Software, 2000.

11 Qizilbash N, Lewington SL, Lopez-Arrieta JM. Corticosteroids for acute ischaemic stroke (Cochrane Review). In: *The Cochrane Library. Issue 4*. Oxford: Update Software, 2000.

12 Liu M, Counsell C, Wardlaw J. Fibrinogen-depleting agents for acute ischaemic stroke (Cochrane Review). In: *The Cochrane Library. Issue 4*. Oxford: Update Software, 2000.

13 Candelise L, Ciccone A. Gangliosides for acute ischaemic stroke (Cochrane Review). In: *The Cochrane Library. Issue 4*. Oxford: Update Software, 2000.

14 Righetti E, Celani MG, Cantisani T, Sterzi R, Boysen G, Ricci S. Glycerol for acute stroke (Cochrane Review). In: *The Cochrane Library. Issue 4*. Oxford: Update Software, 2000.

15 Asplund K, Israelsson K, Schampi I. Haemodilution for acute ischaemic stroke (Cochrane Review). In: *The Cochrane Library. Issue 4*. Oxford: Update Software, 2000.

16 Blood Pressure in Acute Stroke Collaboration (BASC). Interventions for deliberately altering blood pressure in acute stroke (Cochrane Review). In: *The Cochrane Library. Issue 4*. Oxford: Update Software, 2000.

17 Bath PMW, Bath FJ, Smithard DG. Interventions for dysphagia in acute stroke (Cochrane Review). In: *The Cochrane Library. Issue 4*. Oxford: Update Software, 2000.

18 Counsell C, Sandercock P. Low-molecular-weight heparins or heparinoids versus standard unfractionated heparin for acute ischaemic stroke (Cochrane Review). In: *The Cochrane Library. Issue 4*. Oxford: Update Software, 2000.

19 Bereczki D, Liu M, do Prado GF, Fekete I. Mannitol for acute stroke (Cochrane Review). In: *The Cochrane Library. Issue 4*. Oxford: Update Software, 2000.

20 Bath FJ, Butterworth RJ, Bath PMW. Nitric oxide donors (nitrates), L-arginine, or nitric oxide synthase inhibitors for acute ischaemic stroke (Cochrane Review). In: *The Cochrane Library. Issue 4*. Oxford: Update Software, 2000.

21 Bath PMW, Bath FJ, Asplund K. Pentoxifylline, propentofylline and pentifylline for acute ischaemic stroke (Cochrane Review). In: *The Cochrane Library. Issue 4.* Oxford: Update Software, 2000.

22 Ricci S, Celani MG, Cantisani AT, Righetti E. Piracetam for acute ischaemic stroke (Cochrane Review). In: *The Cochrane Library. Issue 4.* Oxford: Update Software, 2000.

23 Bath PMW, Bath FJ. Prostacyclin and analogues for acute ischaemic stroke (Cochrane Review). In: *The Cochrane Library. Issue 4.* Oxford: Update Software, 2000.

24 Prasad K, Shrivastava A. Surgery for primary supratentorial intracerebral haemorrhage (Cochrane Review). In: *The Cochrane Library. Issue 4.* Oxford: Update Software, 2000.

25 Mohiuddin AA, Bath FJ, Bath PMW. Theophylline, aminophylline, caffeine and analogues for acute ischaemic stroke (Cochrane Review). In: *The Cochrane Library. Issue 4.* Oxford: Update Software, 2000.

26 Liu M, Wardlaw J. Thrombolysis (different doses, routes of administration and agents) for acute ischaemic stroke (Cochrane Review). In: *The Cochrane Library. Issue 4.* Oxford: Update Software, 2000.

27 The Tirilazad International Steering Committee. Tirilazad for acute ischaemic stroke (Cochrane Review). In: *The Cochrane Library. Issue 4.* Oxford: Update Software, 2000.

28 The Blood Pressure in Acute Stroke Collaboration (BASC). Vasoactive drugs for acute stroke (Cochrane Review). In: *The Cochrane Library. Issue 4.* Oxford: Update Software, 2000.

29 Bereczki D, Fekete I. Vinpocetine for acute ischaemic stroke (Cochrane Review). In: *The Cochrane Library. Issue 4.* Oxford: Update Software, 2000.

30 Feigin VL, Rinkel GJE, Algra A, Vermeulen M, van Gijn J. Calcium antagonists for aneurysmal subarachnoid haemorrhage (Cochrane Review). In: *The Cochrane Library. Issue 4.* Oxford: Update Software, 2000.

31 Feigin VL, Rinkel GJE, Algra A, van Gijn J. Circulatory volume expansion for aneurysmal subarachnoid hemorrhage (Cochrane Review). In: *The Cochrane Library. Issue 4.* Oxford: Update Software, 2000.

32 Whitfield PC, Kirkpatrick PJ. Timing of surgery for aneurysmal sub-arachnoid haemorrhage (Cochrane Review). In: *The Cochrane Library. Issue 4.* Oxford: Update Software, 2000.

33 Koudstaal PJ. Anticoagulants for preventing stroke in patients with non-rheumatic atrial fibrillation and a history of stroke or transient ischemic attacks (Cochrane Review). In: *The Cochrane Library. Issue 4.* Oxford: Update Software, 2000.

34 Koudstaal PJ. Anticoagulants versus antiplatelet therapy for preventing stroke in patients with non-rheumatic atrial fibrillation and a history of stroke or transient ischemic attacks (Cochrane Review). In: *The Cochrane Library. Issue 4.* Oxford: Update Software, 2000.

35 Koudstaal PJ. Antiplatelet therapy for preventing stroke in patients with non-rheumatic atrial fibrillation and a history of stroke or transient ischemic attacks (Cochrane Review). In: *The Cochrane Library. Issue 4.* Oxford: Update Software, 2000.

36 Cina CS, Clase CM, Haynes RB. Carotid endarterectomy for symptomatic carotid stenosis (Cochrane Review). In: *The Cochrane Library. Issue 4.* Oxford: Update Software, 2000.

37 Liu M, Counsell C, Sandercock P. Anticoagulants for preventing recurrence following ischaemic stroke or transient ischaemic attack (Cochrane Review). In: *The Cochrane Library. Issue 4.* Oxford: Update Software, 2000.

38 Algra A, De Schryver ELLM, van Gijn J, Kappelle LJ, Koudstaal PJ. Oral anticoagulants versus antiplatelet therapy for preventing further vascular events after transient ischaemic attack or minor stroke of presumed arterial origin (Cochrane Review). In: *The Cochrane Library. Issue 4.* Oxford: Update Software, 2000.

39 Cao PG, De Rango P, Zannetti S, Giordano G, Ricci S, Celani MG. Eversion versus conventional carotid endarterectomy for preventing stroke (Cochrane Review). In: *The Cochrane Library. Issue 4.* Oxford: Update Software, 2000.

40 Tangkanakul C, Counsell C, Warlow C. Local versus general anaesthesia for carotid endarterectomy (Cochrane Review). In: *The Cochrane Library. Issue 4*. Oxford: Update Software, 2000.

41 Counsell C, Salinas R, Warlow C, Naylor R. Patch angioplasty versus primary closure for carotid endarterectomy (Cochrane Review). In: *The Cochrane Library. Issue 4*. Oxford: Update Software, 2000.

42 Counsell C, Warlow C, Naylor R. Patches of different types for carotid patch angioplasty (Cochrane Review). In: *The Cochrane Library. Issue 4*. Oxford: Update Software, 2000.

43 Crawley F, Brown MM. Percutaneous transluminal angioplasty and stenting for vertebral artery stenosis (Cochrane Review). In: *The Cochrane Library. Issue 4*. Oxford: Update Software, 2000.

44 Crawley F, Brown MM. Percutaneous transluminal angioplasty and stenting for carotid artery stenosis (Cochrane Review). In: *The Cochrane Library. Issue 4*. Oxford: Update Software, 2000.

45 Counsell C, Salinas R, Naylor R, Warlow C. Routine or selective carotid artery shunting for carotid endarterectomy (and different methods of monitoring in selective shunting) (Cochrane Review). In: *The Cochrane Library. Issue 4*. Oxford: Update Software, 2000.

46 Stroke Unit Trialists' Collaboration. Organised inpatient (stroke unit) care for stroke (Cochrane Review). In: *The Cochrane Library. Issue 4*. Oxford: Update Software, 2000.

47 Langhorne P, Dennis MS, Kalra L, Shepperd S, Wade DT, Wolfe CDA. Services for helping acute stroke patients avoid hospital admission (Cochrane Review). In: *The Cochrane Library. Issue 4*. Oxford: Update Software, 2000.

48 Early Supported Discharge Trialists. Services for reducing duration of hospital care for acute stroke patients (Cochrane Review). In: *The Cochrane Library. Issue 4*. Oxford: Update Software, 2000.

49 Lincoln NB, Majid MJ, Weyman N. Cognitive rehabilitation for attention deficits following stroke (Cochrane Review). In: *The Cochrane Library. Issue 4*. Oxford: Update Software, 2000.

50 Majid MJ, Lincoln NB, Weyman N. Cognitive rehabilitation for memory deficits following stroke (Cochrane Review). In: *The Cochrane Library. Issue 4*. Oxford: Update Software, 2000.

51 Price CIM, Pandyan AD. Electrical stimulation for preventing and treating post-stroke shoulder pain (Cochrane Review). In: *The Cochrane Library. Issue 4*. Oxford: Update Software, 2000.

52 Forster A, Smith J, Young J, Knapp P, House A, Wright A. Information provision for stroke patients and their caregivers (Cochrane Review). In: *The Cochrane Library. Issue 4*. Oxford: Update Software, 2000.

53 Greener J, Enderby P, Whurr R. Pharmacological treatment for aphasia following stroke (Cochrane Review). In: *The Cochrane Library. Issue 4*. Oxford: Update Software, 2000.

54 Greener J, Enderby P, Whurr R. Speech and language therapy for aphasia following stroke (Cochrane Review). In: *The Cochrane Library. Issue 4*. Oxford: Update Software, 2000.

55 Sellars C, Hughes T, Langhorne P. Speech and language therapy for dysarthria due to non-progressive brain damage (Cochrane Review). In: *The Cochrane Library. Issue 4*. Oxford: Update Software, 2000.

References

1 Office for National Statistics. *Mortality Statistics: cause. Review of the Registrar General on deaths by cause, sex and age, in England and Wales, 1999.* London: The Stationery Office, 2000.

2 Office for Health Economics. *Stroke.* London: Office for Health Economics, 1988.

3 Secretary of State for Health. *The Health of the Nation: a strategy for health in England.* Cm 1986. London: HMSO, 1992.

4 Sarti C, Rastenyte D, Cepaitis Z, Tuomilehto J. International trends in mortality from stroke, 1968 to 1994. *Stroke* 2000; **31**: 1588–601.

5 Wolfe CDA, Tilling K, Beech R, Rudd AG for the European BIOMED Group. Variations in case fatality and dependency from stroke in Western and Central Europe. *Stroke* 1999; **30**: 350–6.

6 Wolfe CDA, Giroud M, Kolominsky-Rabas P *et al.* for the European Registries of Stroke (EROS) Collaboration. *Stroke* 2000; **31**: 2074–9.

7 Sudlow CLM, Warlow CP. Comparable studies of the incidence of stroke and its pathological types. Results from an international collaboration. *Stroke* 1997; **28**: 491–9.

8 Secretary of State for Health. *Saving Lives: Our Healthier Nation.* London: The Stationery Office, 1999.

9 National Health Service Executive. *National Service Framework for Older People.* London: Department of Health, 2001.

10 Rudd AG, Irwin P, Rutledge Z *et al.* The national sentinel audit for stroke: a tool for raising standards of care. *J R Coll Lond* 1999; **33**: 460–4.

11 Intercollegiate Working Party for Stroke. *National Clinical Guidelines for Stroke.* London: Clinical Effectiveness and Evaluation Unit, Royal College of Physicians, 2000.

12 Hatano S. Experience from a multicentre stroke register: a preliminary report. *Bull World Health Organ* 1976; **54**: 541–53.

13 Bamford J, Sandercock P, Dennis M, Burn J, Warlow C. A prospective study of acute cerebrovascular disease in the community: the Oxfordshire Community Stroke Project – 1981–86. 2. Incidence, case fatality rates and overall outcome at one year of cerebral infarction, primary intracerebral and sub-arachnoid haemorrhage. *J Neurol Neurosurg Psychiatry* 1990; **53**: 16–22.

14 Office for National Statistics. *Mortality statistics: cause. Review of the Registrar General on deaths by cause, sex and age, in England and Wales, 1998.* London: The Stationery Office, 1999.

15 Adams HJ, Bendixen BH, Kappelle LJ *et al.* Classification of sub-type of acute ischaemic stroke. Definitions for use in a multi-centre clinical trial. *Stroke* 1993; **24**: 35–41.

16 Madden KP, Karanjia PN, Adams HP, Clarke WR and the TOAST investigators. Accuracy of initial stroke subtype diagnosis in the TOAST study. *Neurology* 1995; **45**: 1975–9.

17 Lee LJ, Kidwell CS, Alger J *et al.* Impact on stroke subtype diagnosis of early diffusion-weighted magnetic resonance imaging and magnetic resonance angiography. *Stroke* 2000; **31**: 1081–9.

18 Kistler JP, Furie KL. Carotid endarterectomy revisited. *NEJM* 2000; **342**: 1743–5.

19 Petty GW, Brown RD, Whisnant JP *et al.* Ischaemic stroke subtypes: a population-based study of functional outcome, survival and recurrence. *Stroke* 2000; **31**: 1062–8.

20 Bonita R, Thomson S. Sub-arachnoid hemorrhage: epidemiology, diagnosis, management, and outcome. *Stroke* 1985; **16**: 591–4.

21 Locksley HB. Report on the co-operative study of intracranial aneurysms and sub-arachnoid haemorrhage. VI. Natural history of sub-arachnoid haemorrhage, intracranial aneurysms and arteriovenous malformations. *J Neurosurg* 1966; **25**: 219–39.

22 Taub NA, Wolfe CDA, Richardson E, Burney PGJ. Predicting the disability of first-time stroke sufferers at 1 year. *Stroke* 1994; **25**: 352–7.

23 Henon H, Godefroy O, Leys D *et al*. Early predictors of death and disability after acute cerebral ischemic event. *Stroke* 1995; **26**: 392–8.

24 Hier DB, Edelstein G. Deriving clinical prediction rules from stroke outcome research. *Stroke* 1991; **22**: 1431–6.

25 Gladman JRF, Harwood DMJ, Barer DH. Predicting the outcome of acute stroke: prospective evaluation of five multivariate models and comparison with simple methods. *J Neurol Neurosurg Psychiatry* 1992; **55**: 347–51.

26 Davenport RJ, Dennis MS, Warlow CP. Effect of correcting outcome data for case-mix: an example from stroke medicine. *BMJ* 1996; **312**: 1503–5.

27 Rothwell P. Interpretation of variations in outcome in audit of clinical interventions. *Lancet* 2000; **355**: 4–5.

28 Bamford J, Sandercock P, Dennis M, Burn J, Warlow C. Classification and natural history of clinically identifiable subtypes of cerebral infarction. *Lancet* 1991; **337**: 1521–6.

29 Toni D, Duca RD, Fiorelli M *et al*. Pure motor hemiparesis and sensorimotor stroke. Accuracy of very early clinical diagnosis of lacunar strokes. *Stroke* 1994; **25**: 92–6.

30 Wade DT. *Measurement in Neurological Rehabilitation*. Oxford: Oxford University Press, 1992.

31 Stojcevic N, Wilkinson P, Wolfe C. Outcome measurement in stroke patients. In: Wolfe C, Rudd A, Beech R (eds). *Stroke Services and Research: an overview with recommendations for future research*. London: The Stroke Association, 1996, pp. 261–80.

32 Wade DT, Collin C. The Barthel ADL Index: a standard measure of physical disability? *Int Disabil Stud* 1988; **10**: 64–7.

33 Holbrook M, Skilbeck CE. An activities index for use with stroke patients. *Age Ageing* 1983; **12**: 166–70.

34 Harwood RH, Ebrahim S. *Manual of the London Handicap Scale*. Nottingham: University of Nottingham, 1995.

35 World Health Organization (WHO). *International Classification of Impairments, Disabilities and Handicaps*. Geneva: WHO, 1980.

36 Dennis MS, Bamford JM, Sandercock PAG, Warlow CP. Incidence of transient ischemic attacks in Oxfordshire, England. *Stroke* 1989; **20**: 333–9.

37 Laloux P, Jamart J, Meurisse H *et al*. Persisting perfusion defect in transient ischaemic attacks: a new clinically useful sub-group? *Stroke* 1996; **27**: 425–30.

38 Kelly-Hayes M, Robertson JT, Broderick JP *et al*. The American Heart Association stroke outcome classification. *Stroke* 1998; **29**: 1274–80.

39 World Health Organization. *International Classification of Disease*, 9th revision. London: HMSO, 1977.

40 World Health Organization (WHO). *International Classification of Disease*, 10th revision. Geneva: WHO, 1992.

41 Mant J, Mant F, Winner S. How good is routine information? Validation of coding for acute stroke in Oxford hospitals. *Health Trends* 1998; **29**: 96–9.

42 World Health Organization (WHO). *International Classification of Functioning, Disability and Health. ICF*. Geneva: WHO, May 2001.

43 Goldstein LB, Adams R, Becker K *et al*. Primary prevention of ischaemic stroke. A statement for health care professionals from the Stroke Council of the American Heart Association. *Stroke* 2001; **32**: 280–99.

44 Ebrahim S, Harwood R. *Stroke Epidemiology, Evidence, and Clinical Practice* (2e). Oxford: Oxford University Press, 1999.

45 Warlow CP. Epidemiology of stroke. *Lancet* 1998; **352** (Suppl. 3): 1–4.

46 MacMahon S, Peto R, Cutler J *et al.* Blood pressure, stroke, and coronary heart disease. Part 1. Prolonged differences in blood pressure: prospective observational studies corrected for the regression dilution bias. *Lancet* 1990; **335**: 765–74.

47 Erens B, Primatesta P (eds). *Health Survey for England: cardiovascular disease 1998.* London: The Stationery Office, 1999.

48 Brand FN, Abbott RD, Kannel WB, Wolf PA. Characteristics and prognosis of lone atrial fibrillation: 30-year follow-up in the Framingham Study. *JAMA* 1985; **254**: 3449–53.

49 Kopecky SL, Gersh BJ, McGoon MD *et al.* Lone atrial fibrillation in elderly persons: a marker for cardiovascular risk. *Arch Intern Med* 1999; **159**: 1118–22.

50 Sudlow S, Thomson R, Thwaites B *et al.* Prevalence of atrial fibrillation and eligibility for anticoagulants in the community. *Lancet* 1998; **352**: 1167–71.

51 Wheeldon NM, Tayler DI, Anagnostou E *et al.* Screening for atrial fibrillation in primary care. *Heart* 1998; **79**: 50–5.

52 Shinton R, Beevers G. Meta-analysis of relation between cigarette smoking and stroke. *BMJ* 1989; **298**: 789–94.

53 Gatling W, Budd S, Walters D, Mullee MA, Goddard JR, Hill RD. Evidence of an increasing prevalence of diagnosed diabetes mellitus in the Poole area from 1983 to 1996. *Diabet Med* 1998; **15**: 1015–21.

54 Bennett N, Dodd T, Flatley J, Freeth S, Boiling K. *Health Survey for England 1993.* London: HMSO, 1994.

55 Burn J, Dennis M, Bamford J *et al.* Long-term risk of recurrent stroke after a first ever stroke: the Oxfordshire Community Stroke Project. *Stroke* 1994; **25**: 333–7.

56 Geddes J, Fear J, Tennant A *et al.* Prevalence of self-reported stroke in a population in northern England. *J Epidemiol Community Health* 1996; **50**: 140–3.

57 O'Mahony P, Thomson RG, Dobson R *et al.* The prevalence of stroke and associated disability. *J Public Health Med* 1999; **21**: 166–71.

58 Dennis M, Bamford J, Sandercock P, Warlow C. Prognosis of transient ischaemic attacks in the Oxfordshire Community Stroke Project. *Stroke* 1990; **21**: 848–53.

59 Bots ML, van der Wilk EC, Koudstaal PJ *et al.* Transient neurological attacks in the general population: prevalence, risk factors, and clinical relevance. *Stroke* 1997; **28**: 768–73.

60 Wolfe C, Stojcevice N, Stewart J. The effectiveness of measures aimed at reducing the incidence of stroke. In: Wolfe C, Rudd A, Beech R (eds). *Stroke Services and Research: an overview with recommendations for future research.* London: The Stroke Association, 1996, pp. 39–86.

61 Hart CL, Smith GD, Hole DJ, Hawthorne VM. Alcohol consumption and mortality from all causes, coronary heart disease, and stroke: results from a prospective cohort study of Scottish men with 21 years of follow-up. *BMJ* 1999; **318**: 1725–9.

62 Sacco RL, Elkind M, Boden-Albala B *et al.* The protective effect of moderate alcohol consumption on ischaemic stroke. *JAMA* 1999; **281**: 53–60.

63 Gillum LA, Mamidipudi SK, Johnston SC. Ischaemic stroke risk with oral contraceptives: a meta-analysis. *JAMA* 2000; **284**: 72–8.

64 O'Connell J, Gray CS. Atrial fibrillation and stroke prevention in the community. *Age Ageing* 1996; **25**: 307–9.

65 Lip GYH, Golding DJ, Nazir M *et al.* A survey of atrial fibrillation in general practice: the West Birmingham Atrial Fibrillation Project. *Br J Gen Pract* 1997; **47**: 285–9.

66 Levy S, Maarek M, Cournel P *et al.* Characterisation of different subsets of atrial fibrillation in general practice in France. The ALFA study. *Circulation* 1999; **99**: 3028–35.

67 Kannel WB, Wolf PA, Benjamin EJ, Levy D. Prevalence, incidence, prognosis, and predisposing conditions for atrial fibrillation: population-based estimates. *Am J Cardiol* 1998; **82**: 2–9N.

68 Psaty BM, Manolia TA, Kuller LH *et al*. Incidence of and risk factors for atrial fibrillation in older adults. *Circulation* 1997; **96**: 2455–61.

69 Furberg CD, Psaty BM, Manolio TA *et al*. Prevalence of atrial fibrillation in elderly subjects (the Cardiovascular Health Study). *Am J Cardiol* 1994; **74**: 236–41.

70 Feinberg WM, Blackshear JL, Laupacis A *et al*. Prevalence, age distribution and gender of patients with atrial fibrillation. *Arch Intern Med* 1995; **155**: 469–73.

71 Go AS, Hylek EM, Phillips KA *et al*. Prevalence of diagnosed atrial fibrillation in adults. National implications for rhythm management and stroke prevention: the anticoagulation and risk factors in atrial fibrillation (ATRIA) study. *JAMA* 2001; **285**: 2370–5.

72 Sudlow M, Rodgers H, Kenny RA, Thomson R. Population-based study of use of anticoagulants among patients with atrial fibrillation in the community. *BMJ* 1997; **314**: 1529–30.

73 Wolf PA, Abbott RD, Kannel WB. Atrial fibrillation: a major contributor to stroke in the elderly. The Framingham Study. *Arch Intern Med* 1987; **147**: 1561–4.

74 Benjamin EJ, Wolf PA, D'Agostino RB *et al*. Impact of atrial fibrillation on the risk of death: the Framingham Heart Study. *Circulation* 1998; **98**: 946–52.

75 Lake FR, Cullen KJ, de Klerk NH *et al*. Atrial fibrillation and mortality in an elderly population. *Aust N Z J Med* 1989; **19**: 321–6.

76 Lin H-J, Wolf PA, Kelly-Hayes *et al*. Stroke severity in atrial fibrillation. *Stroke* 1996; **27**: 1760–4.

77 Sandercock P, Bamford J, Dennis M *et al*. Atrial fibrillation and stroke: prevalence in different types of stroke and influence on early and long-term prognosis (Oxfordshire Community Stroke Project). *BMJ* 1992; **305**: 1460–5.

78 Atrial Fibrillation Investigators. Risk factors for stroke and efficacy of antithrombotic therapy in atrial fibrillation. Analysis of pooled data from five randomised controlled trials. *Arch Intern Med* 1994; **154**: 1449–57.

79 SPAF Investigators. Predictors of thrombo-embolism in atrial fibrillation: clinical features of patients at risk. *Ann Intern Med* 1992; **116**: 1–5.

80 Hart RG, Pearce LA, McBride R *et al*. Factors associated with ischaemic stroke during aspirin therapy in atrial fibrillation: analysis of 2012 participants in the SPAF I-III clinical trials. *Stroke* 1999; **30**: 1223–9.

81 SPAF III Writing Committee. Patients with nonvalvular atrial fibrillation at low risk of stroke during treatment with aspirin. *JAMA* 1998; **279**: 1273–7.

82 SPAF Investigators. Predictors of thromboembolism in atrial fibrillation. II. Echocardiographic features of patients at risk. *Ann Intern Med* 1992; **116**: 6–12.

83 Wolf PA. Prevention of stroke. *Lancet* 1998; **352** (Suppl. 3): 15–18.

84 Prospective Studies Collaboration. Cholesterol, diastolic blood pressure, and stroke: 13,000 strokes in 450,000 people in 45 prospective cohorts. *Lancet* 1995; **346**: 1647–53.

85 Hebert PR, Gaziano JM, Chan KS, Hennekens CH. Cholesterol lowering with statin drugs, risk of stroke, and total mortality. *JAMA* 1997; **278**: 313–21.

86 Iso H, Jacobs DR Jr, Wentworth D *et al*. for the MRFIT Research Group. Serum cholesterol levels and six-year mortality from stroke in 350,977 men screened for the Multiple Risk Factor Intervention Trial. *NEJM* 1989; **320**: 904–10.

87 European Carotid Surgery Trialists' Collaborative Group. MRC European Carotid Surgery Trial: interim results for symptomatic patients with severe (70–99%) or with mild (0–29%) carotid stenosis. *Lancet* 1991; **337**: 1235–43.

88 North American Symptomatic Carotid Endarterectomy Trial Collaborators. Beneficial effect of carotid endarterectomy in symptomatic patients with high-grade carotid stenosis. *NEJM* 1991; **325**: 445–53.

89 Executive Committee for the Asymptomatic Carotid Atherosclerosis Study. *JAMA* 1995; **273**: 1421–8.

90 Inzitari D, Eliasziw M, Gates P *et al.* The causes and risk of stroke in patients with asymptomatic internal-carotid artery stenosis. *NEJM* 2000; **342**: 1693–700.

91 Barnett HJM, Gunton RW, Eliasziw *et al.* Causes and severity of ischaemic stroke in patients with internal carotid artery stenosis. *JAMA* 2000; **283**: 1429–36.

92 Ogren M, Hedblad B, Isacsson S-O *et al.* Ten-year cerebrovascular morbidity and mortality in 68-year-old men with asymptomatic carotid stenosis. *BMJ* 1995; **310**: 1294–8.

93 Dennis MS, Bamford JM, Sandercock PAG, Warlow CP. Incidence of transient ischaemic attack in Oxfordshire, England. *Stroke* 1989; **20**: 333–9.

94 Sempere AP, Duarte J, Cabezas C, Claveria LE. Incidence of transient ischaemic attacks and minor ischaemic strokes in Segovia, Spain. *Stroke* 1996; **27**: 667–71.

95 Brown RD Jr, Petty GW, O'Fallon WM *et al.* Incidence of transient ischaemic attack in Rochester, Minnesota, 1985–9. *Stroke* 1998; **29**: 2109–13.

96 Gibbs RGJ, Newson R, Lawrenson R *et al.* Diagnosis and initial management of stroke and transient ischemic attack across UK Health Regions from 1992 to 1996. Experience of a national primary care database. *Stroke* 2001; **32**: 1085–90.

97 Martin PJ, Young G, Enevoldson TP, Humphrey PR. Overdiagnosis of TIA and minor stroke: experience at a regional neurovascular clinic. *Q J Med* 1997; **90**: 759–63.

98 Toole JF, Lefkowitz DS, Chambless LE *et al.* Self-reported transient ischaemic attack and stroke symptoms: methods and baseline prevalence. The ARIC Study 1987–89. *Am J Epidemiol* 1996; **144**: 849–56.

99 Bamford J, Sandercock P, Dennis M *et al.* A prospective study of acute cerebrovascular disease in the community: the Oxfordshire Community Stroke Project 1981–86. 1. Methodology, demography and incident cases of first ever stroke. *J Neurol Neurosurg Psychiatry* 1988; **51**: 1373–80.

100 Stewart JA, Dundas R, Howard RS *et al.* Ethnic differences in incidence of stroke: prospective study with stroke register. *BMJ* 1999; **318**: 967–71.

101 Du X, Sourbutts J, Cruickshank K *et al.* A community-based stroke register in a high-risk area for stroke in north-west England. *J Epidemiol Community Health* 1997; **51**: 472–8.

102 National Institute of Epidemiology. *Public Health Common Data Set 1996*. Guildford: University of Surrey, 1997.

103 Wolfe CDA, Rudd AG, Howard R *et al.* The incidence and case fatality rates of stroke in a multi-ethnic population. The South London Stroke Register. *J Neurol Neurosurg Psychiatry* 2002; **72**: 211–16.

104 Bamford J, Sandercock P, Warlow C, Gray M. Why are patients with acute stroke admitted to hospital? *BMJ* 1986; **292**: 1369–72.

105 Tilling K, Sterne JAC, Wolfe CDA. Estimation of the incidence of stroke using a capture-recapture model including co-variates. *Int J Epidemiol* 2001; **30**: 1351–9.

106 Williams GR, Jiang JG, Matchar DB, Samsa GP. Incidence and occurrence of total (first ever and recurrent) stroke. *Stroke* 1999; **30**: 2523–8.

107 Broderick J, Brott T, Kothari R *et al.* The Greater Cincinnati/Northern Kentucky Stroke Study. Preliminary first ever and total incidence rates of stroke among blacks. *Stroke* 1998; **29**: 415–21.

108 Thorvaldsen P, Asplund K, Kuulasmaa K *et al.* for the WHO MONICA project. Stroke incidence, case fatality, and mortality in the WHO MONICA project. *Stroke* 1995; **26**: 361–7.

109 Office for National Statistics. *Key Health Statistics From General Practice 1998*. Series MB6 no. 2. London: Office for National Statistics, 2000.

110 Dennis MS, Burn JPS, Sandercock PAG *et al.* Long-term survival after first ever stroke: the Oxfordshire Community Stroke Project. *Stroke* 1993; **24**: 796–800.

111 Samsa GP, Bian J, Lipscombe J, Matchar DB. Epidemiology of recurrent cerebral infarction. A Medicare claims-based comparison of first and recurrent strokes on 2-year survival and cost. *Stroke* 1999; **30**: 338–49.

112 Wild S, McKeigue P. Cross-sectional analysis of mortality by country of birth in England and Wales, 1970–92. *BMJ* 1997; **314**: 705–10.

113 Maheswaran R, Elliott P, Strachan DP. Socioeconomic deprivation, ethnicity, and stroke mortality in Greater London and south-east England. *J Epidemiol Community Health* 1997; **51**: 127–31.

114 Ebrahim S. Stroke mortality – secular and geographic trends: comment on papers by Maheswaran and colleagues. *J Epidemiol Community Health* 1997; **51**: 132–3.

115 Smith GD, Hart C, Blane D, Hole D. Adverse socioeconomic conditions in childhood and cause-specific adult mortality: prospective observational study. *BMJ* 1998; **316**: 1631–5.

116 Charlton J, Murphy M, Khaw K *et al.* Cardiovascular diseases. In: Charlton J, Murphy M (eds). *The Health of Adult Britain. Vol. 2.* London: The Stationery Office, 1997, pp. 76–81.

117 Office for National Statistics. Mortality statistics: cause. Review of the Registrar General on deaths by cause, sex and age, in England and Wales, 1986. Series DH2 no. 13. London: The Stationery Office, 1988.

118 Corwine LI, Wolf PA, Kannel WB *et al.* Accuracy of death certification of stroke: the Framingham study. *Stroke* 1982; **13**: 818–21.

119 Thorvaldsen P, Davidesen M, Bronnum-Hansen H and Schroll M for the Danish MONICA Study Group. Stable stroke occurrence despite incidence reduction in an aging population. *Stroke* 1999; **30**: 2529–34.

120 Thorvaldsen P, Kuulasmaa K, Rajakangas AM *et al.* for the WHO MONICA project. Stroke trends in the WHO MONICA project. *Stroke* 1997; **28**: 500–6.

121 Stegmayr B, Asplund K, Wester PO. Trends in incidence, case-fatality rate, and severity of stroke in Northern Sweden, 1985–91. *Stroke* 1994; **25**: 1738–45.

122 Bonita R, Broad JB, Beaglehole R. Changes in stroke incidence and case-fatality in Auckland, New Zealand, 1981–91. *Lancet* 1993; **342**: 1470–3.

123 May DS, Kittner SJ. Use of Medicare claims data to estimate national trends in stroke incidence, 1985–1991. *Stroke* 1994; **25**: 2343–7.

124 Brown RD, Whisnant JP, Sicks JD *et al.* Stroke incidence, prevalence and survival: secular trends in Rochester Minnesota through 1989. *Stroke* 1996; **27**: 373–80.

125 Shahar E, McGovern PG, Sprafka M *et al.* Improved survival of stroke patients during the 1980s. The Minnesota Stroke Survey. *Stroke* 1995; **26**: 1–6.

126 Barker WH, Mullooly JP. Stroke in a defined elderly population, 1967–85. A less lethal and disabling but no less common disease. *Stroke* 1997; **28**: 284–90.

127 May DS, Casper ML, Croft JB, Giles WH. Trends in survival after stroke among Medicare beneficiaries. *Stroke* 1994; **25**: 1617–22.

128 Wade DT. Stroke (acute cerebrovascular disease). In: Stevens A, Raftery J (eds). *Health Care Needs Assessment. Vol. 1.* Oxford: Radcliffe Medical Press, 1994, pp. 111–255.

129 Lawrence ES, Coshall C, Dundas R *et al.* Estimates of the prevalence of acute stroke impairments and disability in a multiethnic population. *Stroke* 2001; **32**: 1279–84.

130 Jorgensen HS, Nakayama H, Raaschou HO *et al.* Outcome and time course of recovery in stroke. Part II. Time course of recovery. The Copenhagen Stroke Study. *Arch Phys Med Rehabil* 1995; **76**: 406–12.

131 Wade DT, Skilbeck CE, Langton-Hewer R. Selective cognitive losses after stroke. Frequency, recovery and prognostic importance. *Int Disabil Stud* 1989; **11**: 34–9.

132 Wade DT, Langton-Hewer R. Outcome after an acute stroke: urinary incontinence and loss of consciousness compared in 532 patients. *Q J Med* 1985; **221**: 347–52.

133 Wade DT, Langton-Hewer R. Functional abilities after stroke: measurement, natural history and prognosis. *J Neurol Neurosurg Psychiatry* 1987; **50**: 177–82.

134 Wade DT, Langton-Hewer R, David RM, Enderby P. Aphasia after stroke: natural history and associated deficits. *J Neurol Neurosurg Psychiatry* 1986; **49**: 11–16.

135 House AO, Hackett ML, Anderson CS. Effects of antidepressants and psychological therapies for reducing the emotional impact of stroke. *Proc R Coll Physicians Edinb* 2001; **31**(58): 50–60.

136 Dennis M, O'Rourke S, Lewis S *et al.* Emotional outcomes after stroke: factors associated with poor outcome. *J Neurol Neurosurg Psychiatry* 2000; **68**: 47–52.

137 Kotila M, Numminen H, Waltimo O, Kaste M. Depression after stroke: results of the FINNSTROKE study. *Stroke* 1998; **29**: 368–72.

138 Greveson G, James O. Improving long-term outcome after stroke – the views of patients and carers. *Health Trends* 1991; **23**: 161–2.

139 Blake H, Lincoln N. Factors associated with strain in co-resident spouses of patients following stroke. *Clin Rehabil* 2000; **14**: 307–14.

140 Wade DT, Leigh-Smith J, Hewer RA. Effects of living with and looking after survivors of a stroke. *BMJ* 1986; **293**: 418–20.

141 Scholte op Reimer WJM, de Haan RJ, Rijnders PT, Limburg M, van den Bos GAM. The burden of caregiving in partners of long-term stroke survivors. *Stroke* 1998; **29**: 1605–11.

142 Han B, Haley WE. Family caregiving for patients with stroke: review and analysis. *Stroke* 1999; **30**: 1478–85.

143 Dennis M, O'Rourke S, Lewis S, Sharpe M, Warlow C. A quantitative study of the emotional outcome of people caring for stroke survivors. *Stroke* 1998; **29**: 1867–72.

144 Anderson CS, Linto J, Stewart-Wynne EG. A population-based assessment of the impact and burden of caregiving for long-term stroke survivors. *Stroke* 1995; **26**: 843–9.

145 Carnwath TCM, Johnson DAW. Psychiatric morbidity among spouses of patients with stroke. *BMJ* 1987; **294**: 409–11.

146 Ingall T, Asplund K, Mahonen M, Bonita R for the WHO MONICA Project. A multinational comparison of sub-arachnoid hemorrhage epidemiology in the WHO MONICA Stroke Study. *Stroke* 2000; **31**: 1054–61.

147 Rose GR. *The Strategy for Preventive Medicine.* Oxford: Oxford University Press, 1992.

148 Fitzmaurice DA, Hobbs FDR, Murray ET *et al.* Oral anticoagulation management in primary care with the use of computerised decision support and near patient testing. A randomised controlled trial. *Arch Intern Med* 2000; **160**: 2343–8.

149 Fitzmaurice DA, Hobbs FD, Delaney BC, Wilson S, McManus R. Review of computerized decision support systems for oral anticoagulation management. *Br J Haematol* 1998; **102**: 907–9.

150 Ansell JE, Patel N, Ostrovsky D, Nozzolillo E, Peterson AM. Long-term patient self-management of oral anticoagulation. *Arch Intern Med* 1995; **155**: 2185–9.

151 Whittle J, Wickenheiser L, Venditti LN. Is warfarin underused in the treatment of elderly persons with atrial fibrillation? *Arch Intern Med* 1997; **157**: 441–5.

152 Munschauer FE, Priore RL, Hens M *et al.* Thromboembolism prophylaxis in chronic atrial fibrillation: practice patterns in community and tertiary care hospitals. *Stroke* 1997; **28**: 72–6.

153 Bratzler D *et al.* Warfarin use in Medicare patients with atrial fibrillation. *Arch Intern Med* 1997; **157**: 1613–17.

154 Stafford RS, Singer DE. Recent national patterns of warfarin use in atrial fibrillation. *Circulation* 1998; **97**: 1231–3.

155 Whincup P. *Preventing Recurrent Strokes: are opportunities being missed?* London: Stroke Association, 1997.

156 McCallum AK, Whincup PH, Morris RW *et al.* Aspirin use in middle-aged men with cardiovascular disease: are opportunities being missed? *Br J Gen Pract* 1997; **47**: 417–21.

157 Campbell NC, Thain J, Deans HG, Ritchie LD, Rawles JM. Secondary prevention in coronary heart disease: baseline survey of provision in general practice. *BMJ* 1998; **316**: 1430–4.

158 Bhatti TS, Harradine K, Davies B *et al.* First year of a fast track carotid duplex service. *J R Coll Surg Edinb* 1999; **44**: 307–9.

159 McCollum PT, da Silva A, Ridler BD, de Cossart L. Carotid endarterectomy in the UK and Ireland: audit of 30-day outcome. The Audit Committee for the Vascular Surgical Society. *Eur J Vasc Endovasc Surg* 1997; **14**: 386–91.

160 Ferris G, Roderick P, Smithies A *et al.* An epidemiological needs assessment of carotid endarterectomy in an English health region. Is the need being met? *BMJ* 1998; **317**: 447–51.

161 Gibbs RGJ, Todd J-C, Irvine C *et al.* Relationship between the regional and national incidence of transient ischaemic attack and stroke and performance of carotid endarterectomy. *Eur J Vasc Endovasc Surg* 1998; **16**: 47–52.

162 Bamford J, Sandercock P, Warlow C, Gray M. Why are patients with acute stroke admitted to hospital? *BMJ* 1986; **292**: 1369–72.

163 Wolfe CD, Taub NA, Bryan S *et al.* Variations in the incidence, management and outcome of stroke in residents under the age of 75 in two health districts of southern England. *J Public Health Med* 1995; **17**: 411–18.

164 Wolfe CDA, Taub NA, Woodrow J *et al.* Patterns of acute stroke care in three districts of southern England. *J Epidemiol Community Health* 1993; **47**: 144–8.

165 Langhorne P, Dennis MS, Kalra L, Shepperd S, Wade DT, Wolfe CDA. Services for helping acute stroke patients avoid hospital admission (Cochrane Review). In: *The Cochrane Library. Issue 4.* Oxford: Update Software, 2000.

166 Bamford J. Clinical examination in diagnosis and subclassification of stroke. *Lancet* 1992; **339**: 400–2.

167 Ebrahim S, Redfern J. *Stroke Care: a matter of chance. A national survey of stroke services.* London: Stroke Association, 1999.

168 Clinical Standards Advisory Group. *Report on Clinical Effectiveness Using Stroke Care as an Example.* London: The Stationery Office, 1998.

169 Stroke Unit Trialists' Collaboration. Organised inpatient (stroke unit) care for stroke (Cochrane Review). In: *The Cochrane Library. Issue 4.* Oxford: Update Software, 2000.

170 Langhorne P, Dennis M (eds). *Stroke Units: an evidence-based approach.* London: BMJ Books, 1998.

171 Evans A, Perez I, Harraf F *et al.* Can differences in management processes explain different outcomes between stroke unit and stroke team care? *Lancet* 2001; **358**: 1586–92.

172 Fan CW, McDonnell R, Johnson Z *et al.* Hospital-based stroke care in Ireland: results from one regional register. *Ir J Med Sci* 2000; **169**: 30–3.

173 Audit Commission. *The Way to Go Home: rehabilitation and remedial services for older people.* London: The Audit Commission for Local Authorities and the National Health Service in England and Wales, 2000.

174 Enderby P. *A Survey of Community Rehabilitation in the United Kingdom.* Sheffield: University of Sheffield, 1999.

175 Newman P. *Aspects of Intermediate Care: a literature review.* Anglia and Oxford Regional Office, 1997.

176 McCormack B. The developing role of community hospitals: an essential part of a quality service. *Qual Health Care* 1993; **2**: 253–8.

177 Ritchie LD, Robinson K. Community hospitals: new wine in old bottles. *Br J Gen Pract* 1998; **38**: 1039–40.

178 Treasure RAR, Davies JAJ. Contribution of a general practitioner hospital: a further study. *BMJ* 1990; **300**: 644–6.

179 Tomlinson J, Raymond NT, Field D, Botha JL. Use of general practitioner beds in Leicestershire community hospitals. *Br J Gen Pract* 1995; **45**: 399–403.

180 Rudd AG, Irwin P, Rutledge Z *et al.* Regional variations in stroke care in England, Wales and Northern Ireland: results from the National Sentinel Audit of Stroke. *Clin Rehabil* 2001; **15**: 562–72.

181 Office of Population Censuses and Surveys. *Survey of Disability in Great Britain.* Report no 1. London: HMSO, 1985.

182 Barer DH. Stroke in Nottingham: the burden of nursing care. *Clin Rehabil* 1991; **5**: 103–10.

183 Knapp P, Young J, House A, Forster A. Non-drug strategies to resolve psycho-social difficulties after stroke. *Age Ageing* 2000; **29**: 23–30.

184 Christie D, Weigall D. Social work effectiveness in two-year stroke survivors: a randomised controlled trial. *Community Health Studies* 1984; **8**: 26–32.

185 Forster A, Young J. Specialist nurse support for patients with stroke in the community: a randomised controlled trial. *BMJ* 1996; **312**: 1642–6.

186 Mant J, Carter J, Wade DT, Winner S. Family support for stroke: a randomised controlled trial. *Lancet* 2000; **356**: 808–13.

187 Dennis M, O'Rourke S, Slattery J, Staniforth T, Warlow C. Evaluation of a stroke family care worker: results of a randomised controlled trial. *BMJ* 1997; **314**: 1071–7.

188 Bosanquet N, Franks P. *Stroke Care: reducing the burden of disease.* London: Stroke Association, 1998.

189 NHS Executive. *NHS Reference Costs 1999.* NHS Executive, 2000.

190 Caro JJ, Huybrechts KF and Duchesne I for the Stroke Economic Analysis Group. Management patterns and costs of acute ischemic stroke: an international study. *Stroke* 2000; **31**: 582–90.

191 Barton S (ed.). *Clinical Evidence: a compendium of the best available evidence for effective health care.* Issue 4. London: BMJ Publishing Group, 2000.

192 Contributors to the Cochrane Collaboration and the NHS Centre for Reviews and Dissemination. *Evidence from Systematic Reviews of Research Relevant to Implementing the 'Wider Public Health' Agenda.* York: NHS Centre for Reviews and Dissemination, 2000.

193 Rees K, Lawlor DA, Ebrahim S, Mant J. A national contract on heart disease and stroke. In: Contributors to the Cochrane Collaboration and the NHS Centre for Reviews and Dissemination. *Evidence from Systematic Reviews of Research Relevant to Implementing the 'Wider Public Health' Agenda.* York: NHS Centre for Reviews and Dissemination, 2000.

194 Chaloupka FJ, Wechsler H. Price, tobacco control policies and smoking among adults. *J Health Econ* 1997; **16**: 359–73.

195 Choi BCK, Ferrence RG, Pack AWP. *Evaluating the Effects of Price on the Demand for Tobacco Products: review of methodologies and studies.* Ontario Tobacco Research Unit, 1997.

196 Chapman S, Borland R, Scollo M, Brownson RC, Dominello A, Woodward S. The impact of smoke-free workplaces on declining cigarette consumption in Australia and the United States. *Am J Public Health* 1999; **89**: 1018–23.

197 Smee C. *Effect of Tobacco Advertising on Tobacco Consumption: a discussion document reviewing the evidence.* London: Department of Health, 1992.

198 NHS Centre for Reviews and Dissemination. Preventing the uptake of smoking in young people. *Effect Health Care* 1999; **5**: 12.

199 Sowden AJ, Arblaster L. Mass media interventions for preventing smoking in young people (Cochrane Review). In: *The Cochrane Library. Issue 1.* Oxford: Update Software, 2000.

200 Gepkens A, Gunning SL. Interventions to reduce socioeconomic health differences: a review of the international literature. *Eur J Public Health* 1996; **6**: 218–26.

201 Connor J. Randomised studies of income supplementation: a lost opportunity to assess health outcomes. *J Epidemiol Community Health* 1999; **53**: 725–30.

202 Hillsdon M, Thorogood M. A systematic review of exercise promotion strategies. *Br J Sports Med* 1996; **30**: 84–9.

203 Ness A, Powles J. Fruit and vegetables, and cardiovascular disease: a review. *Int J Epidemiol* 1997; **26**: 1–13.

204 Marshall T. Exploring a fiscal food policy: the case of diet and ischaemic heart disease. *BMJ* 2000; **320**: 301–5.

205 Plehn JF, Davis BR, Sacks FM *et al.* Reduction of stroke incidence after myocardial infarction with pravastatin. The Cholesterol and Recurrent Events Study (CARE). *Circulation* 1999; **99**: 216–23.

206 Scandinavian Simvastatin Survival Study Group. Randomised trial of cholesterol lowering in 4444 patients with coronary heart disease: the Scandinavian Simvastatin Survival Study. *Lancet* 1994; **344**: 1383–9.

207 Kmietowicz Z. Statins are the new aspirin, Oxford researchers say. *BMJ* 2001; **323**: 1145.

208 Doll R, Peto R, Hall E, Wheatley K, Gray R. Mortality in relation to consumption of alcohol: 13 years' observations on male British Doctors. *BMJ* 1994; **309**: 911–18.

209 Collins R, Peto R. Antihypertensive drug therapy: effects on stroke and coronary heart disease. In: Swales JD (ed.). *Textbook of Hypertension.* Oxford: Blackwell Scientific Publications, 1994, pp. 1156–64.

210 Hart RG, Benavente O, McBride R, Pearce LA. Antithrombotic therapy to prevent stroke in patients with atrial fibrillation: a meta-analysis. *Ann Intern Med* 1999; **131**: 492–501.

211 Benavente O, Hart R, Koudstaal P, Laupacis A, McBride R. Antiplatelet therapy for preventing stroke in patients with non-valvular atrial fibrillation and no previous history of stroke or transient ischemic attacks (Cochrane Review). In: *The Cochrane Library. Issue 4.* Oxford: Update Software, 2000.

212 Taylor FC, Cohen H, Ebrahim S. Systematic review of long-term anticoagulation or antiplatelet treatment in patients with non-rheumatic atrial fibrillation. *BMJ* 2001; **322**: 321–6.

213 Chambers BR, You RX, Donnan GA. Carotid endarterectomy for asymptomatic carotid stenosis (Cochrane Review). In: *The Cochrane Library. Issue 4.* Oxford: Update Software, 2000.

214 Benavente O, Moher D, Pham B. Carotid endarterectomy for asymptomatic carotid stenosis: a meta-analysis. *BMJ* 1998; **317**: 1477–80.

215 Antiplatelet Trialists' Collaboration. Collaborative overview of randomised trials of antiplatelet therapy. 1. Prevention of death, myocardial infarction, and stroke by prolonged antiplatelet therapy in various categories of patients. *BMJ* 1994; **308**: 81–106.

216 Johnson ES. A meta-regression analysis of the dose–response effect of aspirin on stroke. *Arch Intern Med* 1999; **159**: 1248–53.

217 Hankey GJ, Sudlow CLM, Dunbabin DW. Thienopyridines or aspirin to prevent stroke and other serious vascular events in patients at high risk of vascular disease. A systematic review of the evidence from randomised trials. *Stroke* 2000; **31**: 1779–84.

218 Hankey GJ, Sudlow CLM, Dunbabin DW. Thienopyridine derivatives (ticlopidine, clopidogrel) versus aspirin for preventing stroke and other serious vascular events in high vascular risk patients (Cochrane Review). In: *The Cochrane Library. Issue 4.* Oxford: Update Software, 2000.

219 Hebert PR, Gaziano JM, Sau Chan K, Hennekens CH. Cholesterol lowering with statin drugs, risk of stroke, and total mortality. An overview of randomised trials. *JAMA* 1997; **278**: 313–21.

220 Gueyffier F, Boissel J-P, Boutitie F *et al.* for the INDANA Project collaborators. Effect of antihypertensive treatment in patients having already suffered from stroke: gathering the evidence. *Stroke* 1997; **28**: 2557–62.

221 PROGRESS Management Committee. Blood pressure lowering for the secondary prevention of stroke: rationale and design of PROGRESS. *J Hypertens* 1996; **14** (Suppl. 2): S41–6.

222 PROGRESS Collaborative Group. Randomised trial of a perindopril-based blood-pressure-lowering regimen among 6105 individuals with previous stroke or transient ischaemic attack. *Lancet* 2001; **358**: 1033–41.

223 Rodgers A, MacMahon S, Gamble G *et al.* for the UK TIA Collaborative Group. Blood pressure and risk of stroke in patients with cerebrovascular disease. *BMJ* 1996; **313**: 147.

224 Cina CS, Clase CM, Haynes RB. Carotid endarterectomy for symptomatic carotid stenosis (Cochrane Review). In: *The Cochrane Library. Issue 4.* Oxford: Update Software, 2000.

225 Cao PG, De Rango P, Zannetti S, Giordano G, Ricci S, Celani MG. Eversion versus conventional carotid endarterectomy for preventing stroke (Cochrane Review). In: *The Cochrane Library. Issue 1.* Oxford: Update Software, 2001.

226 Tangkanakul C, Counsell C, Warlow C. Local versus general anaesthesia for carotid endarterectomy (Cochrane Review). In: *The Cochrane Library. Issue 4.* Oxford: Update Software, 2000.

227 Counsell C, Salinas R, Warlow C, Naylor R. Patch angioplasty versus primary closure for carotid endarterectomy (Cochrane Review). In: *The Cochrane Library. Issue 4.* Oxford: Update Software, 2000.

228 Counsell C, Warlow C, Naylor R. Patches of different types for carotid patch angioplasty (Cochrane Review). In: *The Cochrane Library. Issue 4.* Oxford: Update Software, 2000.

229 Crawley F, Brown MM. Percutaneous transluminal angioplasty and stenting for vertebral artery stenosis (Cochrane Review). In: *The Cochrane Library. Issue 4.* Oxford: Update Software, 2000.

230 Crawley F, Brown MM. Percutaneous transluminal angioplasty and stenting for carotid artery stenosis (Cochrane Review). In: *The Cochrane Library. Issue 4.* Oxford: Update Software, 2000.

231 Counsell C, Salinas R, Naylor R, Warlow C. Routine or selective carotid artery shunting for carotid endarterectomy (and different methods of monitoring in selective shunting) (Cochrane Review). In: *The Cochrane Library. Issue 4.* Oxford: Update Software, 2000.

232 CAVATAS investigators. Endovascular versus surgical treatment in patients with carotid stenosis in the Carotid and Vertebral Artery Transluminal Angioplasty Study (CAVATAS): a randomised trial. *Lancet* 2001; **357**: 1729–37.

233 Spence D, Eliasziw M. Endarterectomy or angioplasty for treatment of carotid stenosis? *Lancet* 2001; **357**: 1722–3.

234 Stroke Editorial Office. Major ongoing stroke trials. *Stroke* 2001; **32**: 1449–57.

235 Alamowitch S, Eliasziw M, Algra A *et al.* for the NASCET Group. Risk, causes, and prevention of ischaemic stroke in elderly patients with symptomatic internal carotid artery stenosis. *Lancet* 2001; **357**: 1154–60.

236 Rothwell PM. Carotid endarterectomy and prevention of stroke in the very elderly. *Lancet* 2001; **357**: 1142–3.

237 Hannan EL, Popp J, Tranmer B *et al.* Relationship between provider volume and mortality for carotid endarterectomies in New York State. *Stroke* 1998; **29**: 2292–7.

238 Diener HC, Cunha L, Forbes C *et al.* ESPS 2: dipyridamole and acetylsalicylic acid in the secondary prevention of stroke. *J Neurol Sci* 1996; **143**: 1–13.

239 Sudlow C and Baigent C on behalf of the Antithrombotic Trialists Collaboration. Different antiplatelet regimens in the prevention of vascular events among patients at high risk of stroke: new evidence from the antithrombotic trialists' collaboration. *Cerebrovasc Dis* 1998; **8** (Suppl. 4): 68.

240 Yusuf S, Zhao F, Mehta SR *et al.* for the Clopidogrel in Unstable Angina to Prevent Recurrent Events Trial Investigators (CURE). Effects of clopidogrel in addition to aspirin in patients with acute coronary syndromes without ST-elevation. *NEJM* 2001; **345**: 494–502.

241 Mehta SR, Yusuf S, Peters RJG *et al.* for the CURE Investigators. Effects of pretreatment with clopidogrel and aspirin followed by long-term therapy in patients undergoing percutaneous coronary intervention: the PCI-CURE study. *Lancet* 2001; **358**: 527–33.

242 Liu M, Counsell C, Sandercock P. Anticoagulants for preventing recurrence following ischaemic stroke or transient ischaemic attack (Cochrane Review). In: *The Cochrane Library. Issue 4*. Oxford: Update Software, 2000.

243 Mohr JP, Thompson JLP, Lazar RM *et al.* for the Warfarin-Aspirin Recurrent Stroke Study Group. A comparison of warfarin and aspirin for the prevention of recurrent ischaemic stroke. *NEJM* 2001; **345**: 1444–51.

244 Kothari R, Barsan W, Brott T *et al.* Frequency and accuracy of prehospital diagnosis of acute stroke. *Stroke* 1995; **26**: 937–41.

245 Kidwell C, Starkman S, Eckstein M *et al.* Identifying stroke in the field: prospective validation of the Los Angeles Prehospital Stroke Screen (LAPSS). *Stroke* 2000; **31**: 71–6.

246 Libman RB, Wirkowski E, Alvir J, Rao TH. Conditions that mimic stroke in the emergency department. *Arch Neurol* 1995; **52**: 1119–22.

247 Kothari RU, Brott T, Broderick JP, Hamilton CA. Emergency physicians: accuracy in the diagnosis of stroke. *Stroke* 1995; **26**: 2238–41.

248 Sandercock P, Molyneux A, Warlow C. Value of computed tomography in patients with stroke: Oxfordshire Community Stroke Project. *BMJ* 1985; **290**: 193–7.

249 Davenport R, Dennis M. Neurological emergencies: stroke. *J Neurol Neurosurg Psychiatry* 2000; **68**: 277–88.

250 Dennis MS, Bamford JM, Molyneux AJ, Warlow CP. Rapid resolution of signs of primary intracerebral haemorrhage in computed tomograms of the brain. *BMJ* 1987; **295**: 379–81.

251 Allder S, Moody AR, Martel AL *et al.* Limitations of clinical diagnosis in acute stroke. *Lancet* 1999; **354**: 1523.

252 Kapral MK. Preventive health care: update 2. Echocardiography for the detection of a cardiac source of embolus in patients with stroke. *Can Med Assoc J* 1999; **161**: 989–96.

253 Correia M, Silva M, Veloso M. Cooling therapy for acute stroke (Cochrane Review). In: *The Cochrane Library. Issue 4*. Oxford: Update Software, 2000.

254 Liu M, Counsell C, Wardlaw J. Fibrinogen-depleting agents for acute ischaemic stroke (Cochrane Review). In: *The Cochrane Library. Issue 4*. Oxford: Update Software, 2000.

255 Gubitz G, Counsell C, Sandercock P, Signorini D. Anticoagulants for acute ischaemic stroke (Cochrane Review). In: *The Cochrane Library. Issue 4*. Oxford: Update Software, 2000.

256 Counsell C, Sandercock P. Low-molecular-weight heparins or heparinoids versus standard un-fractionated heparin for acute ischaemic stroke (Cochrane Review). In: *The Cochrane Library. Issue 4*. Oxford: Update Software, 2000.

257 Blood Pressure in Acute Stroke Collaboration (BASC). Interventions for deliberately altering blood pressure in acute stroke (Cochrane Review). In: *The Cochrane Library. Issue 4*. Oxford: Update Software, 2000.

258 Prasad K, Shrivastava A. Surgery for primary supratentorial intracerebral haemorrhage (Cochrane Review). In: *The Cochrane Library. Issue 4*. Oxford: Update Software, 2000.

259 Gubitz G, Sandercock P, Counsell C. Antiplatelet therapy for acute ischaemic stroke (Cochrane Review). In: *The Cochrane Library. Issue 4*. Oxford: Update Software, 2000.

260 Wardlaw JM, del Zoppo G, Yamaguchi T. Thrombolysis for acute ischaemic stroke (Cochrane Review). In: *The Cochrane Library. Issue 4*. Oxford: Update Software, 2000.

261 National Institute of Neurological Disorders and Stroke rt-PA Study Group. Tissue plasminogen activator for acute ischemic stroke. *NEJM*. 1995; **333**: 1581–7.

262 Kwiatkowski TG, Libman RB, Frankel M *et al.* for the NINDS study group. Effects of tissue plasminogen activator for acute ischemic stroke at one year. *NEJM* 1999; **340**: 1781–7.

263 Wood AJJ. Treatment of acute ischemic stroke. *NEJM* 2000; **343**: 710–22.

264 Hacke W, Kaste M, Fieschi C *et al.* Intravenous thrombolysis with recombinant tissue plasminogen activator for acute hemispheric stroke. *JAMA* 1995; **274**: 1017–25.

265 Hacke W, Kaste M, Fieschi C *et al.* Randomized double blind placebo controlled trial of thrombolytic therapy with intravenous alteplase in acute ischaemic stroke (ECASS II). *Lancet* 1998; **352**: 1245–51.

266 Kalra L, Evans A, Perez I *et al.* Alternative strategies for stroke care: a prospective randomized controlled trial. *Lancet* 2000; **356**: 894–9.

267 Wolfe C, Rudd A, Dennis M, Warlow C, Langhorne P. Taking acute stroke care seriously. *BMJ* 2001; **323**: 5–6.

268 Early Supported Discharge Trialists. Services for reducing duration of hospital care for acute stroke patients (Cochrane Review). In: *The Cochrane Library. Issue 4.* Oxford: Update Software, 2000.

269 Weir RP. *Rehabilitation of Cerebrovascular Disorder (Stroke). Early discharge and support: a critical review of the literature.* Christchurch: New Zealand Health Technology Assessment, 1999.

270 Rudd AG, Wolfe CDA, Tilling K, Beech R. Randomised controlled trial to evaluate early discharge scheme for patients with stroke. *BMJ* 1997; **315**: 1039–44.

271 Dekker R, Drost EA, Groothoff JW, Arendzen JH, van Gijn JC, Eisma WH. Effects of day-hospital rehabilitation in stroke patients: a review of randomized clinical trials. *Scand J Rehabil Med* 1998; **30**: 87–94.

272 Wade DT. Research into the black box of rehabilitation: the risks of a type III error. *Clin Rehabil* 2001; **15**: 1–4.

273 Agency for Health Care Policy and Research (AHCPR). *Diagnosis and Treatment of Swallowing Disorders (Dysphagia) in Acute-Care Stroke Patients.* Rockville, MD: Agency for Health Care Policy and Research, 1999.

274 Bath PMW, Bath FJ, Smithard DG. Interventions for dysphagia in acute stroke (Cochrane Review). In: *The Cochrane Library. Issue 4.* Oxford: Update Software, 2000.

275 Norton B, Homer-Ward M, Donnelly MT, Long RG, Homes GKT. A randomised prospective comparison of percutaneous endoscopic gastrostomy and nasogastric tube feeding after acute dysphagic stroke. *BMJ* 1996; **312**: 13–16.

276 Langhorne P, Wagenaar R, Partridge C. Physiotherapy after stroke: more is better? *Physiother Res Int* 1996; **1**(2): 75–88.

277 Kwakkel G, Wagenaar RC, Koelman TW, Lankhorst GJ, Koetsier JC. Effects of intensity of rehabilitation after stroke: a research synthesis. *Stroke* 1997; **28**(8): 1550–6.

278 Kwakkel G, Wagenaar RC, Twisk KWR *et al.* Intensity of leg and arm training after primary middle-cerebral artery stroke: a randomised controlled trial. *Lancet* 1999; **354**: 191–6.

279 Price CIM, Pandyan AD. Electrical stimulation for preventing and treating post-stroke shoulder pain (Cochrane Review). In: *The Cochrane Library. Issue 4.* Oxford: Update Software, 2000.

280 Moreland JD, Thomson MA, Fuoco AR. Electromyographic biofeedback to improve lower extremity function after stroke: a meta-analysis. *Arch Phys Med Rehabil* 1998; **79**: 134–40.

281 Greener J, Enderby P, Whurr R. Speech and language therapy for aphasia following stroke (Cochrane Review). In: *The Cochrane Library. Issue 4.* Oxford: Update Software, 2000.

282 Enderby P, Emerson J. Speech and language therapy: does it work? *BMJ* 1996; **312**: 1655–8.

283 Walker MF, Gladman JRF, Lincoln NB, Siemonsa P, Whiteley T. Occupational therapy for stroke patients not admitted to hospital: a randomised controlled trial. *Lancet* 1999; **354**: 278–80.

284 Gilbertson L, Langhorne P, Walker A, Allen A, Murray GD. Domiciliary occupational therapy for patients with stroke discharged from hospital: randomised controlled trial. *BMJ* 2000; **320**: 603–6.

285 Carlson M, Fanchiang S-P, Zemke R, Clark F. A meta-analysis of the effectiveness of occupational therapy for older persons. *Am J Occup Ther* 1996; **50**: 89–98.

286 Sulch D, Perez I, Melbourn A, Kalra L. Randomised controlled trial of integrated (managed) care pathway for stroke rehabilitation. *Stroke* 2000; **31**: 1929–34.

287 Wade DT, Collen FM, Robb GF, Warlow CP. Physiotherapy intervention late after stroke and mobility. *BMJ* 1992; **304**: 609–13.

288 Werner RA, Kessler S. Effectiveness of an intensive outpatient rehabilitation program for postacute stroke patients. *Am J Phys Med Rehabil* 1996; **75**: 114–20.

289 Mant J. Overview of the evidence for Stroke Family Care Workers. *Proc R Coll Physicians Edinb* 2001; **31** (Suppl. 8): 44–9.

290 Mant J, Carter J, Wade DT, Winner S. The impact of an information pack on patients with stroke and their carers: a randomised controlled trial. *Clin Rehabil* 1998; **12**: 465–76.

291 Rodgers H, Atkinson C, Bond S *et al.* Randomised controlled trial of a comprehensive stroke education program for patients and caregivers. *Stroke* 1999; **30**: 2585–91.

292 Knapp P, Young J, House A, Forster A. Non-drug strategies to resolve psycho-social difficulties after stroke. *Age Ageing* 2000; **29**: 23–30.

293 Lincoln NB, Majid MJ, Weyman N. Cognitive rehabilitation for attention deficits following stroke (Cochrane Review). In: *The Cochrane Library. Issue 4.* Oxford: Update Software, 2000.

294 Majid MJ, Lincoln NB, Weyman N. Cognitive rehabilitation for memory deficits following stroke (Cochrane Review). In: *The Cochrane Library. Issue 4.* Oxford: Update Software, 2000.

295 Lehmann JF, Condon SM, Price R, DeLateur BJ. Gait abnormalities in hemiplegia: their correction by ankle-foot orthoses. *Arch Phys Med Rehabil* 1987; **68**: 763–71.

296 Beckerman H, Becher J, Lankhorst GJ, Verbeek ALM. Walking ability of stroke patients: efficacy of thermocoagulation of tibial nerve blocking and a polypropylene ankle foot orthosis. *Arch Phys Med Rehabil* 1996; **77**: 1144–51.

297 Van Gijn J, Rinkel GJE. Sub-arachnoid haemorrhage: diagnosis, causes and management. *Brain* 2001; **124**: 249–78.

298 Van der Wee N, Rinkel GJ, Hasan D, van Gijn J. Detection of sub-arachnoid haemorrhage on early CT: is lumbar puncture still needed after a negative scan? *J Neurol Neurosurg Psychiatry* 1995; **58**: 357–9.

299 Cloft HJ, Joseph GJ, Dion JE. Risk of cerebral angiography in patients with sub-arachnoid haemorrhage, cerebral aneurysm and arteriovenous malformation: a meta-analysis. *Stroke* 1999; **30**: 317–20.

300 Roos YBWEM, Rinkel GJE, Vermeulen M, Algra A, van Gijn J. Antifibrinolytic therapy for aneurysmal sub-arachnoid haemorrhage (Cochrane Review). In: *The Cochrane Library. Issue 4.* Oxford: Update Software, 2000.

301 Ohman J, Heiskanen O. Timing of operation for ruptured supratentorial aneurysms: a prospective randomised study. *J Neurosurg* 1989; **70**: 55–60.

302 Whitfield PC, Kirkpatrick PJ. Timing of surgery for sub-arachnoid haemorrhage (Cochrane Review). In: *The Cochrane Library. Issue 2.* Oxford: Update Software, 2001.

303 Byrne JV, Sohn MJ, Molyneux AJ. Five-year experience in using coil embolization for ruptured intracranial aneurysms: outcomes and incidence of late rebleeding. *J Neurosurg* 1999; **90**: 656–63.

304 Vanninen R, Koivisto T, Saari T *et al.* Ruptured intracranial aneurysms: acute endovascular treatment with electrolytically detachable coils: a prospective randomised study. *Radiology* 1999; **211**: 325–36.

305 Feigin VL, Rinkel GJE, Algra A, Vermeulen M, van Gijn J. Calcium antagonists for aneurysmal sub-arachnoid haemorrhage (Cochrane Review). In: *The Cochrane Library. Issue 4.* Oxford: Update Software, 2000.

306 Evers A, Ament A, Blaauw G. Economic evaluation in stroke research: a systematic review. *Stroke* 2000; **31**: 1046–53.

307 Holloway RG, Benesch CG, Rahilly CR, Courtright CE. A systematic review of cost-effectiveness research of stroke evaluation and treatment. *Stroke* 1999; **30**: 1340–9.

308 Nussbaum ES, Heros RC, Erickson DL. Cost-effectiveness of carotid endarterectomy. *Neurosurgery* 1996; **38**: 237–44.

309 Kuntz KM, Kent KC. Is carotid endarterectomy cost-effective? *Circulation* 1996; **94** (Suppl. 2): 194–8.

310 Matchar DB, Pauk JS, Lipscomb J, Moore WS (eds). *A Health Policy Perspective on Carotid Endarterectomy: cost, effectiveness and cost-effectiveness.* Philadelphia, PA: WB Saunders, 1996, pp. 680–9.

311 Cronenwett JL, Birkmeyer JD, Nackman GB *et al.* Cost-effectiveness of carotid endarterectomy in asymptomatic patients. *J Vasc Surg* 1997; **25**: 298–311.

312 Gage BF, Cardinalli AB, Albers GW, Owens DK. Cost-effectiveness of warfarin and aspirin for prophylaxis of stroke in patients with nonvalvular atrial fibrillation. *JAMA* 1995; **274**: 1839–45.

313 Lightowlers S, McGuire A. Cost-effectiveness of anticoagulation in non-rheumatic atrial fibrillation in the primary prevention of ischemic stroke. *Stroke* 1998; **29**: 1827–32.

314 Parry D, Fitzmaurice D, Raftery J. Anticoagulation management in primary care: a trial-based economic evaluation. *Br J Haematol* 2000; **111**: 530–3.

315 Eccles M, Freemantle N, Mason J and the North of England Aspirin Guideline Development Group. North of England evidence-based guideline development project: guideline on the use of aspirin as secondary prophylaxis for vascular disease in primary care. *BMJ* 1998; **316**: 1303–9.

316 Scottish Intercollegiate Guidelines Network (SIGN). *SIGN Guidelines: an introduction to SIGN methodology for the development of evidence-based clinical guidelines.* SIGN Publication No 38. Edinburgh: SIGN, 1999.

317 Royal College of Physicians of Edinburgh (RCPE). *Consensus Statement: stroke treatment and service delivery.* Edinburgh: RCPE, 2000.

318 Scottish Intercollegiate Guidelines Network (SIGN). *Management of Carotid Stenosis and Carotid Endarterectomy.* Pilot edition. SIGN Publication No 14. Edinburgh: SIGN, 1997.

319 Royal College of Physicians of Edinburgh. *Consensus Conference on Medical Management of Stroke 26 and 27th May 1998 – consensus statement (updated November 2000).* Edinburgh: Royal College of Physicians of Edinburgh, 2000.

320 Thomson R, Parkin D, Eccles M *et al.* Decision analysis and guidelines for anticoagulant therapy to prevent stroke in patients with atrial fibrillation. *Lancet* 2000; **355**: 956–62.

321 Palaretti G, Hirsh J, Legnani C *et al.* Oral anticoagulation treatment in the elderly: a nested prospective case control study. *Arch Intern Med* 2000; **160**: 470–8.

322 Fitzmaurice DA, Mant J, Murray ET, Hobbs FDR. Anticoagulation to prevent stroke in atrial fibrillation. *BMJ* 2000; **321**: 1156.

323 Goreclick PB, Sacco RL, Smith DB *et al.* Prevention of a first stroke: a review of guidelines and a multidisciplinary consensus statement from the National Stroke Association. *JAMA* 1999; **281**: 1112–20.

324 Scottish Intercollegiate Guidelines Network (SIGN). *Antithrombotic Therapy.* SIGN Publication No 36. Edinburgh: SIGN, 1999.

325 Scottish Intercollegiate Guidelines Network (SIGN). *Management of Patients with Stroke 1. Assessment, investigation, immediate management and secondary prevention.* Pilot edition. SIGN Publication No 13. Edinburgh: SIGN, 1997.

326 Johnson ES. A meta-regression analysis of the dose–response effect of aspirin on stroke. *Arch Intern Med* 1999; **159**: 1248–53.

327 Barnett HJM, Eliasziw M, Meldrum HE. Prevention of ischaemic stroke. *BMJ* 1999; **318**: 1539–43.

328 Wells PS, Lensing AW, Hirsh J. Graduated compression stockings in the prevention of post-operative venous thrombo-embolism: a meta-analysis. *Arch Intern Med* 1994; **154**: 67–72.

329 BNF Editorial staff. *British National Formulary 40*. London: BMA and Royal Pharmaceutical Society of Great Britain, 2000.

330 Hart RG, Pearce LA, McBride R *et al*. Factors associated with ischaemic stroke during aspirin therapy in atrial fibrillation. Analysis of 2012 participants in the SPAF I-III clinical trials. *Stroke* 1999; **30**: 1223–9.

331 Rothwell PM, Warlow CP. Prediction of benefit from carotid endarterectomy in individual patients: a risk modelling study. *Lancet* 1999; **353**: 2105–10.

332 Ramsay LE, Williams B, Johnston GD *et al*. British Hypertension Society guidelines for hypertension management 1999: summary. *BMJ* 1999; **319**: 630–5.

333 Hankey GJ, Warlow CP. Treatment and secondary prevention of stroke: evidence, costs, and effects on individuals and populations. *Lancet* 1999; **354**: 1457–63.

334 Rudd A, Goldacre M, Amess M *et al*. (eds). *Health Outcome Indicators: stroke. Report of a working group to the Department of Health*. Oxford: National Centre for Health Outcomes Development, 1999.

335 Mant J, Hicks N. Detecting differences in quality of care: the sensitivity of measures of process and outcome in treating acute myocardial infarction. *BMJ* 1995; **311**: 793–6.

336 Pomeroy VM, Tallis RC. Need to focus research in stroke rehabilitation. *Lancet* 2000; **355**: 836–7.

337 Wade DT. Research into rehabilitation: what is the priority? *Clin Rehabil* 2001; **15**: 229–32.

338 The King's Fund. Consensus conference: treatment of stroke. *BMJ* 1988; **297**: 126–8.

339 Young JB. The primary care stroke gap. *Br J Gen Pract* 2001; **51**: 788–801.

340 Rothwell PM. The high cost of not funding stroke research: a comparison with heart disease and cancer. *Lancet* 2001; **357**: 1612–16.

4   Lower Respiratory Disease*

Sarah Walters and Derek J Ward

1 Summary

Statement of the problem

Respiratory disease has a substantial impact on the health of populations at all ages and every level of morbidity. Acute upper respiratory infections are the commonest illnesses experienced by individuals throughout life, accounting for over 27% of all GP consultations. Asthma and chronic obstructive pulmonary disease are the cause of almost 5% of all admissions and bed-days, and lower respiratory infections are responsible for almost 11% of deaths. While still uncommon, TB rates appear to be rising and it remains an important problem in some communities. Cystic fibrosis is the commonest inherited disorder in the UK and is an important cause of death in young adults. Improvements in survival mean increasing use of expensive medications and medical technologies.

Sub-categories

The principal sub-categories of lower respiratory disease considered in this review were chosen on the basis of their public health or health service impact, and are:

1 lower respiratory infections in children
2 lower respiratory infections in adults, including pneumonia
3 asthma
4 chronic obstructive pulmonary disease (COPD)
5 tuberculosis
6 cystic fibrosis.

Upper respiratory conditions (including allergic rhinitis), influenza, lung cancer, neonatal respiratory problems, occupational diseases, sleep-disordered breathing, diffuse parenchymal lung disease (a wide range of conditions that include fibrosing alveolitis and sarcoidosis) and other respiratory disorders are not specifically reviewed in detail in this revision. Together, these conditions account for 7% of deaths and 2.5% of hospital admissions, and form a substantial part of the workload of respiratory physicians.

---

* This is an update of a chapter written for the first edition by HR Anderson, A Esmail, J Holowell, P Littlejohns and D Strachan.

Prevalence and incidence

In 1999, lower respiratory disorders (excluding lung cancer) accounted for 17.6% of all deaths, 7.1% of finished consultant episodes (FCEs) and 10.2% of inpatient bed-days, and during 1991–92, these conditions were the reason for 12.1% of general practitioner consultations.

Acute respiratory infections in children

Acute lower respiratory infections comprise a wide range of poorly defined clinical syndromes causing considerable distress and possible long-term lung damage. Population surveys suggest that about 20% of children are affected by bronchitis or bronchiolitis, and 1–5% suffer pneumonia at some time. Risk factors for bronchitis include male sex, the North or West regions of the UK, poor socio-economic status, large families, white ethnic group, tobacco smoke exposure and bottle feeding. Of children aged 0–4 years, 157.8 per 1000 consult GPs annually with bronchitis or bronchiolitis, and admissions account for 24.3 per 10 000 FCEs in this age group. Including pneumonia, lower respiratory infections account for 3% of childhood deaths. Infection rates are seasonal, varying 2–3-fold during the year, and overall rates of hospital admissions appear to be falling. Whooping cough is now rare, with almost all eligible children immunised (up from a low point of just over 30% in 1979).

Lower respiratory infections in adults

Respiratory tract infections in adults are major causes of morbidity and mortality in the community. They are the stated reason for 16% of all adult GP consultations and resulted in over 50 million antibiotic prescriptions during 1995. Community-acquired pneumonia affects approximately 500 adults per 100 000 annually (230–360 per 100 000 all ages), 32% of whom are hospitalised. There is a marked seasonal distribution in infections, with a peak between January and March. Pneumonia has a case fatality rate of approximately 3% and is identified as the cause of 11% of adult deaths (3.3% in adults under 65 years). Pathogens are identified in only 45–70% of pneumonia, and classification by infective aetiology may not be helpful. However, *Streptococcus pneumoniae*, *Haemophilus influenzae* and influenza A are the commonest pathogens (> 50%), along with *Mycoplasma* in epidemic years. Nosocomial pneumonia is a significant burden on the health service and has a case fatality rate of 36%. There are currently no readily available UK figures on its occurrence, but in the USA its incidence is estimated at 5–10 per 1000 of all admissions (120–220 per 1000 admissions to ITU).

Asthma

Asthma is a clinical diagnosis characterised by episodic wheezy dyspnoea resulting from chronic inflammation of the airways and increased responsiveness to a variety of stimuli. Wheezing within the last 12 months is reported by up to 38% of children and a third of adults, and is more frequently reported for children living in Southern England or Wales, from poor socio-economic backgrounds and those exposed to tobacco smoke. Doctor-diagnosed asthma is reported for 21% of children and by 12% of adults, and about 4–6% of children and 4–13% of adults are thought to require regular medical supervision. The incidence of asthma is highest in the first 7 years of life (2–3% per annum) and then levels off at 0.7% per annum, so that the cumulative incidence by age 23 is 30% and age 33 is 43%. About 50% of regular childhood wheezing persists to early adulthood. Data is lacking on patterns of asthma attacks and utilisation of services over an individual's lifetime. Trends in asthma are difficult to interpret, suggesting little change in lifetime prevalence. However, there may be a shift towards more severe asthma among individuals, and self-reported asthma, GP consultations, prescriptions of anti-asthma drugs and hospital admissions increased during the 1990s, especially in children, though asthma incidence may now be falling. Even so, there may still be under-diagnosis in the community and up to 3.4% of undiagnosed 12–14 year olds may display severe symptoms. Mortality rates appear to have been stable since 1979 (small increase in 15–25 year age group) and age-standardised mortality rates have fallen since the 1980s. Fatal asthma is rare, occurring in 6.7 per million aged 0–14 years and 6.7 per million aged 15–44 (diagnostic confusion and transfer may influence rates in older adults). In 1999, there were 1521 deaths due to asthma, compared with 1969 in 1992.

Chronic obstructive pulmonary disease

The term 'COPD' is used to describe a syndrome of chronic progressive airflow obstruction which is not completely reversible. It is due to a number of pathological and clinical entities that frequently overlap (e.g. emphysema, a pathological diagnosis, or chronic bronchitis, defined clinically by the presence of a productive cough for at least 3 months of two successive years). The condition is rare in people who have never smoked, and the prevalence of COPD reflects the patterns of smoking in the population, with a strong social class gradient. Chronic bronchitis (i.e. chronic productive cough) affects 17% of men and 6% of women of middle age, whereas COPD affects 5% and 3% of middle-aged men and women, respectively. Prevalence of COPD is rising among women, reflecting secular trends in smoking. Mortality rates for COPD have declined in the last 30 years and the condition now accounts for 5.7% male and 4.0% female adult deaths, a significant number of which were premature (168 per million before age 65).

Tuberculosis

The majority of cases of TB affect the lungs, and can vary in severity from a fulminant infection to sub-clinical disease, which may be reactivated at times of stress or immunocompromise. TB is a notifiable disease, and while this underestimates the total prevalence, notifications provide useful data on patterns and trends. Rates have risen since 1988 at approximately 1% per year, with the highest rates in London (34 per 100 000) and lowest in the Eastern Region (5 per 100 000). Deaths remain relatively rare (300 per year) and case fatality rates continue to fall in all age groups. Ethnicity is a major risk factor in the UK (169–178 per 100 000 in South Asian communities and 7 per 100 000 in whites), although prevalence decreases with time of residence in the UK, and while rates are falling in Indian and Caribbean groups, they are rising in Black African, Pakistani, Bangladeshi and other groups. In the UK, there is currently little overlap between the population with HIV and those previously exposed to TB. About 2% (4.3% in London) of notifications are in those who are also HIV positive. UK data also indicate a rise in the problem of drug resistance for TB; isoniazid resistance is present in 6.3% of isolates from those with no previous history of TB, and 17.0% of others. Equivalent figures for multi-drug-resistant TB are 1% and 11%.

Cystic fibrosis

Cystic fibrosis is the product of a variety of genetic defects inherited in an autosomal recessive fashion and results in secretions (especially those from the lung, pancreas, sweat glands and reproductive tract) becoming more viscous. Thick lung mucus readily becomes infected, and respiratory disease is the cause of most deaths. One in 25 carries a defective gene and approximately 1 in 2500 live births are affected by cystic fibrosis annually. Case registry data indicate that there are 7500 individuals in the UK with cystic fibrosis, of whom 43% (and rising) are adults. Prevalence depends upon age (440 per million aged 0–14 years, 300 aged 15 to 24, and 35 aged 25+) and while current median survival is 28 years, the current birth cohort may expect this to be more than 40 years. While the condition is a rare cause of death overall (< 0.1%), it accounts for 23% of all deaths due to respiratory disease in those aged 5–25 years (1.4% overall).

Services available and their effectiveness

Respiratory diseases are managed at all levels of the health service. Patients with chronic conditions use primary care services and outpatients to manage their ongoing care, a major feature of which is self-care and patient decision making. There is insufficient evidence of effectiveness to claim that a substantial unmet need for inpatient services exists in the community.

Acute respiratory infections in children

Over 80% of lower respiratory infections in childhood are treated by GPs, accounting for 16% of consultations in those aged 0–4 and 9% in those aged 5–15. Most inpatient referrals are managed by general paediatric services, resulting in 2.1% of all FCEs and 1.8% of bed-days for those aged 0–14.

Primary preventive activities include reducing passive exposure to tobacco smoke, promoting breast-feeding and vaccinating against whooping cough and measles. The use of antibiotics to treat viral upper respiratory tract infections is ineffective at preventing bacterial lower respiratory infections and may result in increased antibiotic resistance. No norms for treatment services exist, and management may include antibiotic therapy where bacterial infection is suspected, and supportive care in an environment appropriate to the severity of the illness. The diagnosis is primarily clinical and the choice of antimicrobial drug is usually made without microbiological findings.

Lower respiratory infection in adults

Most (67–95%) adults with community-acquired pneumonia are treated outside hospital, and pneumonia accounts for 0.3% of all adult consultations. Up to a third of pneumonia cases are admitted and they comprise 0.43% of FCEs in those aged 15–64, and 2.2% of FCEs in over-65s. Nosocomial pneumonia results in 7–9 extra days in hospital for each patient affected.

The use of antibiotics to treat viral upper respiratory tract infections is ineffective at preventing lower respiratory infections and may result in increased antibiotic resistance. Pneumococcal vaccination is recommended in those for whom infection would be more common or serious, and may prevent re-admission with pneumonia in those over 60 years admitted for any reason. Diagnosis in the community is primarily clinical – X-ray and other investigations being reserved for slow responders to treatment and to exclude cancer. No norms exist for treatment services, although UK guidelines for management exist and have recently been updated. Treatment includes antibiotics and supportive care in an environment appropriate to the severity of the illness. The diagnosis is primarily clinical and the choice of antimicrobial drug is usually made without microbiological findings. Neuraminidase inhibitors may reduce the duration of influenza and are recommended for those at risk of secondary complications, but their place in influenza prevention is not yet established, nor is the nature of the at-risk groups who might benefit from treatment.

Asthma

GP consultations for asthma represent 7% of the total for children, and 1–2% for adults. In addition, self-referral to A&E departments is common, resulting in 40–50% of all asthma admissions (at least as many again are also seen in A&E and discharged). Asthma admissions have risen since the 1970s and now account for 6% of FCEs in childhood and 2% of those in adults.

There is currently limited scope for primary prevention outside of the occupational setting, other than efforts to limit *in-utero* and postnatal exposure of babies and young children to environmental tobacco smoke. However, secondary prevention does have an important role and includes the avoidance of precipitating factors (passive tobacco smoke, moulds, infections and allergen exposure, especially house dust mite and pet allergens, although the evidence that allergen avoidance is effective is relatively weak) and the control of the outdoor environment (especially ozone). There is currently no place for screening.

There are no norms for asthma treatment services, and in general the facilities for diagnosis, investigation and ongoing management are available to GPs and hospital doctors alike. Management of chronic asthma occurs at all levels of the health service, while the management of acute severe asthma may require investigations and therapies unavailable in the community; the British Thoracic Society recommends that such inpatients are managed by respiratory specialists. However, the criteria for admission vary widely. The treatment of chronic and acute severe asthma is subject to UK evidence-based and consensus guidelines. The mainstay of chronic treatment is by (usually inhaled) drugs, and guidelines emphasise the inflammatory basis of asthma and the need to use regular anti-inflammatory drugs in preference to anti-spasmodic medications 'as needed'. Spacer devices for inhalers are probably as effective as nebulisers for drug delivery, and the place of nebulisers for chronic therapy is unclear. The principles of care are becoming more proactive, and engage the patient in monitoring their condition and self-management according to predefined protocols. Education alone does not improve outcomes, although intensive behavioural interventions may do so. The role of allergen desensitisation and physiotherapy is unclear, while acupuncture and hypnotherapy are ineffective. The provision of specialist asthma nurses has increased recently, but there is evidence that specialist nurse-led interventions in hospital have no effect on patient-related outcomes. There is a move towards increasing specialisation of asthma treatment in primary care through general practitioners with a special interest, and specialist asthma nurses.

Chronic obstructive pulmonary disease

Overall, 1.4% of the population consults their GP for COPD each year, and this condition accounts for 2% of FCEs and over 3% of bed-days in adults. As for asthma, the pyramid of disease severity has a broad base in the community, with only 10% being referred to secondary care.

COPD is a chronic, progressive, irreversible disease, and stopping smoking both prevents its development and slows its progress. Other (secondary) preventive activities include vaccination against influenza and pneumococcal disease. The clinical diagnosis requires confirmation by pulmonary function tests (spirometry), which also help to stratify severity, and other radiological and invasive tests may be helpful to exclude other diseases. Spirometry is not universally available in primary care. There are no norms for the provision of treatment services. Management is subject to UK-based guidelines and concentrates upon smoking advice, the treatment of acute (often infective) exacerbations with antibiotics, corticosteroids and oxygen, symptomatic treatment with bronchodilators and inhaled anti-inflammatory drugs to maximise any reversible airflow limitation, and domiciliary oxygen in selected severe cases. The balance between primary and secondary care for ongoing care is unclear. Physiotherapy alone is probably of no benefit, although formal multi-disciplinary rehabilitation programmes are beneficial. Screening of patients with chronic cough, wheeze or breathlessness and/or smokers for COPD has been recommended to allow early smoking cessation interventions, but there is a lack of objective evidence of effects on mortality or of the most appropriate methods of delivering screening.

Tuberculosis

The historical decline in TB owes much to improvements in the population's social and nutritional status and later introduction of effective drug therapy. Mass screening is no longer practised in the UK, although the school immunisation programme is still recommended. Vaccination is also recommended for immigrants from countries where TB is common, and children born to high-risk families. The prevention and control of TB in the UK is the subject of published guidelines, and there remains the provision of designated TB services with facilities for contact tracing and administering chemoprophylaxis or vaccination. Drug treatment requires 6–9 months of therapy, and while reminder cards, monetary incentives, lay worker involvement and clinic supervision have all been shown to improve compliance, evidence from the UK suggests that directly observed therapy does not.

Cystic fibrosis

Evidence of improved outcomes exists for care undertaken in specialist centres for cystic fibrosis, and this is the subject of recommendations by special interest groups. However, care may be shared with local respiratory services and GPs using a variety of models. The majority of care occurs on an outpatient basis and requires a multi-disciplinary approach including paediatricians and physicians specialising in cystic fibrosis, specialist nurses, dietitians, physiotherapists and social workers. On average, patients attend outpatients 4.6 times annually and admission rates vary between 0.3 and 2.0 times per person per year. Handover of adolescent patients from paediatric to adult services is recommended and most patients continue to attend school and work full-time.

Screening may be carried out on an antenatal or postnatal basis and may detect up to 70% of cases. A population-based screening programme is not yet available in the UK, but a national neonatal screening programme has been recommended. The availability and content of treatment services are the subject of guidelines by special interest groups. The mainstay of drug therapy is early aggressive treatment with high doses and prolonged courses (often parenteral or nebulised) of antibiotics to prevent colonisation of the lung by some organisms and to treat recurrent infective exacerbations. Patients should be segregated according to colonisation by the organism *Burkholderia cepacia*. There is increasing evidence that segregation should be extended to include patients with transmissible strains of other organisms, including *Pseudomonas aeruginosa*. Many patients self-administer intravenous treatments. Those with pancreatic insufficiency should use enzyme supplements and additional fat-soluble vitamins, and oral or parenteral feeding may also be required. A proportion of patients gain benefit from Domase alpha to reduce sputum viscosity, and all require physiotherapy (usually self-conducted) to clear secretions (some gain benefit from nebulised bronchodilators prior to physiotherapy). Those with end-stage lung disease may gain benefit from single lung or lung–heart transplantation, and approximately 5% develop liver failure and may require liver transplantation.

Quantified models of care

The prevention, treatment and rehabilitation of lower respiratory disease is complex, but of the various models available, the two considered most relevant for purchasers for these conditions are the natural history model and the service model. Decision points within these models focus upon the balance between preventive and therapeutic services, between primary and secondary care, and between specialist and generalist care within each of these settings.

It is argued that the direction of marginal shifts in provision of health services for most lower respiratory conditions should probably be:

- treatment → prevention
- secondary/tertiary care → primary care and patient enablement.

However, *within* each of these settings there is a general view that treatment should be provided by specialists in respiratory conditions, rather than generalists. These specialists are usually in the hospital setting specialist respiratory physicians, and in the primary care setting, general practitioners with a specialist interest, or nurses with specialist training.

Thus within each care setting, the general marginal shift should be:

- generalist care → specialist care.

For some conditions, such as cystic fibrosis, increasing specialisation of care can produce significantly better clinical outcomes, and there is a clear need for increased specialisation and more tertiary care provision.

This conclusion does not deny the value of hospital care in the diagnosis and management of difficult or unusual cases. Neither does it deny the value of intensive respiratory care for clinically severe patients, or the therapeutic effectiveness of antibiotics and anti-asthmatic therapy currently available in both hospital and community settings.

Outcome measures and audit methods

In general, it is easier to specify the desired direction of changes than to set quantified targets. Improvements in the scope and linkage of health information and greater use of clinical audit are suggested as means of facilitating needs assessment and monitoring outcomes.

Information and research requirements

There is a need for further research into the incidence of acute respiratory illness in the community, variations in referral, diagnosis and management, and the overlap of disease severity at service interfaces. Consensus guidelines for clinical management are incompletely evaluated in terms of efficacy, and the extent to which population mortality and morbidity can be reduced by treatment is uncertain. Future prospects for prevention depend upon further aetiological research and the continued development of vaccines.

2 Statement of the problem

General approach to the task

The original brief required a concise review of the whole of lower respiratory disease, following the framework for research reviews. However, the range of disease entities is broad and therefore this chapter focuses on a specific group of disorders *and does not attempt to cover the full range of conditions that fall within the remit of the respiratory specialist.* The areas for detailed review (acute infections in childhood, acute infections in adults, COPD, asthma, tuberculosis and cystic fibrosis) were chosen on the basis of their public health impact, the demands they place upon specialist (respiratory and other) services, and the costs incurred in their management.

Tables and figures displaying data relevant to the full range of lower respiratory disease are collected in **Appendix B** and referenced in **bold** type. Tables and figures displaying data of relevance to the detailed reviews of specific groups of conditions are included in the text and indicated using Roman numerals.

We are aware that the main purpose of the review is to help purchasers of health care. However, in considering interventions and their effectiveness we have included some aspects of prevention, which are not the direct responsibilities of the purchasers. It is our belief that purchasers need such information to set their own efforts in context and to influence other agencies to help in reducing health problems.

The first version of this chapter was prepared collaboratively by five authors (HRA, AE, JH, PL and DS). The conditions subject to detailed review were included as appendices and were the work of single authors. Two authors prepared this revision (SW and DW), one of whom (SW) also provided the detailed review of cystic fibrosis, not included in the first series.

Changes from the first edition

While following the protocol common to all in the Needs Assessment series, the structure of this chapter has been considerably altered since the first edition. In its original form, specific conditions subject to detailed review were included in referenced appendices. The information in these appendices has now been integrated into the main text. In addition, cystic fibrosis has been added to the list of conditions reviewed in detail.

Routine data summarised in the tables and figures collected in **Appendix B** and accompanying text have all been updated to 1998–99 for mortality and hospital episode statistics (finished consultant episodes and occupied bed-days), and 1991–92 for GP consultations. Detailed discussions on the sub-categories under review have been amended to reflect changes in the understanding and coding of certain conditions, especially asthma and chronic obstructive pulmonary disease. Similarly, new data on incidence and prevalence have been included for asthma and TB, where recent trends are more fully explored, and cystic fibrosis. New developments in the organisation and delivery of services related to specialisation (and sub-specialisation for cystic fibrosis), treatment pathways (for asthma and chronic obstructive pulmonary disease in particular) and the role of multi-disciplinary team members (asthma, chronic obstructive pulmonary disease and cystic fibrosis) are more fully considered. Finally, recent developments in prevention and treatment are also considered, and highlight the growth of evidence-based and consensus guidelines (pneumonia, asthma, chronic obstructive pulmonary disease, TB and cystic fibrosis). In particular, new evidence is considered on the use of existing and novel therapies for influenza, chronic obstructive pulmonary disease, asthma (for which an extensive review is provided) and cystic fibrosis.

The nature of the public health problem

Scale

Respiratory disease has a substantial impact on the health of populations at all ages and every level of morbidity. Acute upper respiratory infections are the commonest illnesses experienced at all ages, leading to school absence, loss of productivity, widespread consumption of non-prescribed medicines and a substantial burden of consultations in general practice. Lower respiratory infections impinge upon inpatient and mortality statistics. Asthma is one of the commonest chronic diseases of childhood, and COPD in adults is a major contributor to sickness absence, premature retirement, disability and mortality in old age. Tuberculosis, although now rare in the UK, remains a problem among certain immigrant groups, and is likely to re-emerge elsewhere as the AIDS epidemic progresses. Cystic fibrosis is an increasingly important cause of death among young adults, and improvements in survival mean increasing use of expensive medication and medical technology.

Table B.1 shows the percentage of all deaths, hospital discharges, inpatient bed-days and general practitioner consultations attributable to various respiratory diseases nationwide. **Table B.2** translates these proportions into the number of deaths and respiratory workload for a given population size. The relative importance of all respiratory conditions and of particular diagnostic categories varies considerably according to age (*see* **Figures B.1 to B.8**).

Major issues

The major issues in the field of lower respiratory disease relate to the balance of care between primary, secondary and tertiary care, and the cost, availability and cost-effectiveness of expensive new drugs and technologies.

Balance of care

There is widespread debate about the balance of care between primary, secondary and tertiary care for both common and rare respiratory conditions and, within each level of care, about the appropriate balance of care between generalists and those with specialist interests and training. In general there is scanty evidence on which to base decisions about balance of care.

New drugs and technologies

Because respiratory disease is so common, new drugs in this field represent important potential costs to the NHS. New drugs on the horizon in this field include new anti-inflammatory therapies for asthma and COPD and new drugs in the treatment of cystic fibrosis. Inhaled therapies have been converted to CFC-free inhalers, with cost implications.

Diseases included (ICD-9 and ICD-10 codes)

International Classification of Diseases (ICD) codes relevant to respiratory disease are shown and discussed in **Appendix A**. These are based on diagnoses, but for certain purposes other classifications (by site, chronicity, cause or age) may be more appropriate. These issues are discussed further in **Appendix A.**

We have selected for this review groups of conditions which make an important contribution to at least one of the indicators shown in **Table B.2** and which are broadly 'lower respiratory' in nature. Cystic fibrosis is included because it makes a significant contribution to morbidity and mortality in young adults, and because of the expensive nature of some of the interventions used in its treatment. Although it is no longer the cause of substantial mortality and morbidity, tuberculosis is included because it makes special demands upon chest medicine services and is a particular problem in certain districts with substantial immigrant populations. Conditions included in the review are:

- lower respiratory infections in children
- lower respiratory infections in adults
- asthma (ICD-9 493, ICD-10 J45–46)
- chronic obstructive pulmonary disease (COPD) (ICD-9 490–492 and 494–496, ICD-10 J41–44)
- respiratory tuberculosis (ICD-9 011–012, ICD-10 A15–16)
- cystic fibrosis (ICD-9 277, ICD-10 E84).

Each section of this chapter presents detailed information relating to acute lower respiratory infections in children (acute bronchitis, bronchiolitis, pneumonia and whooping cough), acute lower respiratory infections in adults (pneumonia and influenza), asthma, chronic obstructive airway disease, respiratory tuberculosis and cystic fibrosis.

Diseases excluded (ICD-9 and ICD-10 codes)

- Upper respiratory infections (ICD-9 460–465, ICD-10 J01–06) and other upper respiratory conditions (ICD-9 470–478, ICD-10 J01–06) have been excluded because, although they are extremely common and cause a lot of minor morbidity, their impact upon mortality is small and the related hospital workload is often in ear, nose and throat surgery, which is the subject of a separate review.
- Lung cancer (ICD-9 162, ICD-10 C33–34) is a major cause of death, particularly among middle-aged and elderly men, and places a substantial burden upon inpatient services in general and chest medicine. It is considered as a separate review in the Health Care Needs Assessment series.
- Neonatal respiratory problems (ICD-9 769–770, ICD-10 P28).
- Occupational diseases such as farmers' lung (ICD-9 495, ICD-10 J67), coalworkers' pneumoconiosis (ICD-9 500, ICD-10 J60) and other dust diseases (ICD-9 501–505, ICD-10 J60–67) are not discussed in detail, although such conditions may present special local problems in some areas.
- Other respiratory conditions (ICD 510–519, ICD-10) are also not discussed in detail since the category includes a heterogeneous assortment of conditions. The category is nevertheless important in terms of the burden on inpatient services and demands on respiratory specialists.

During 1999, these conditions together accounted for 7% of all deaths, 2.5% of finished consultant episodes (FCEs) and 3.3% of bed-days.

3 Sub-categories

Lower respiratory infections in children

Acute lower respiratory tract infections (LRTI) in children include a wide variety of diagnoses that frequently represent poorly defined clinical syndromes used as convenient diagnostic labels, without any implication of specific site of involvement in the respiratory tract.

- **Acute bronchitis (ICD-10 J20):** Unspecified bronchitis (ICD8 and ICD-9 490, ICD-10 J40) is more usually acute than chronic in children, and should be included in estimates of disease incidence. It may present with cough and/or wheeze. The presence of stridor (noise on inspiration) is characteristic of laryngotracheobronchitis ('croup'). This relatively benign illness does not appear as a separate entity in published statistics.
- **Acute bronchiolitis (ICD-10 J21):** This is combined with acute bronchitis in ICD8. The distinction is controversial, as there is rarely pathological evidence to implicate the smaller rather than the larger airways. Bronchiolitis is usually applied to the more severe illnesses without evidence of pulmonary consolidation in the first year of life, and is closely related to respiratory syncytial virus (RSV) infection. It is rarely diagnosed in children over 12 months of age, although RSV infection may occur at any age.
- **Pneumonia (ICD-10 J12–J17):** Strictly, this diagnosis is only applicable when there is radiological or pathological evidence of pulmonary consolidation, but is much more widely applied as a label for severe illness, particularly by parents. Subdivisions by cause (viral, ICD-9 480; pneumococcal, ICD-9

481; other bacterial, ICD-9 482) or by presumed site (bronchopneumonia, ICD-9 485; 'other' pneumonia: organism unspecified, ICD-9 486) are of little use for epidemiological work in children.

- **Whooping cough (ICD-10 A37):** This is primarily a clinical diagnosis, as culture of *Bordetella pertussis* is inconsistent, particularly after the early days of the illness. It is included here because its severe effects are mainly confined to the respiratory system.

These are illnesses of concern for three reasons.

- They are an important contribution to childhood mortality, particularly in the postnatal period (although case fatality of the average episode is low).
- They cause considerable distress in the child and arouse anxiety among parents.
- Although episodes are usually self-limiting, there is concern about the long-term consequences for respiratory health in adulthood.[1] There is controversy about whether observed associations between childhood LRTI and later cough, phlegm and poor lung function are a result of 'lung damage' or simply a reflection of a chronic tendency of some children to develop all kinds of chest troubles (asthma being one possible explanation for such continued susceptibility).

Currently, the objective of services is to prevent death and distress, and to minimise long-term health consequences of these conditions.

Cause

There is a poor correspondence between the infecting agent and clinical manifestations. However, the distinction between bacterial and viral illnesses potentially affects management. A more detailed aetiological classification may be required if specific antiviral therapies are developed.

The majority of LRTI in infants and young children in the developed world have a viral aetiology,[2] predominantly parainfluenza types 1–3 (35%), respiratory syncytial virus (22%), influenza types A or B (12%) and adenovirus (7%).[2] *Streptococcus pneumoniae* and *Mycoplasma pneumoniae* account for most of the pneumonias in children above four years of age.[3] *Mycoplasma pneumoniae* accounts for about 15% of other LRTI in children.[2]

Comorbidity

Infants with pre-existing cardiorespiratory disease (congenital heart disease, bronchopulmonary dysplasia, cystic fibrosis) or immunosuppression are at increased risk of death during acute episodes of LRTI.[4] More vigorous therapeutic regimes may be justified in these vulnerable children, but their impact on the total requirement for services is likely to be small.

Children with asthma are much more common and are at increased risk of episodes labelled as bronchitis or pneumonia.

Lower respiratory infections in adults

Respiratory tract infections are a major cause of morbidity and mortality in the community and the most important burden on the health service after mental illness.[5] They represent the commonest condition seen by general practitioners, accounting for 16% of all adult consultations. They are the fifth most important reason for sickness benefit claims.[5]

In the 1970s in England and Wales, 25 million prescriptions were written for antibiotics for respiratory infections per year,[6] rising to a peak of over 50 million prescriptions a year in 1995 (Prescription Pricing

Authority website). In 1994, the annual cost of prescribed antibiotics exceeded £160 million. More recent information on prescribing patterns is not routinely available, but there is no evidence to suggest that the burden of illness due to respiratory tract infections has decreased over the last decade.

Within ICD-9 and ICD-10, pneumonia and influenza are coded as follows:

	ICD-9	ICD-10
Influenza	487	J10–11
Pneumonia	480–486	J12–J18

Pneumonia

Pneumonia is one of the most serious lower respiratory tract infections and accounts for about ten times as many deaths in the UK as all other deaths from infectious diseases combined. In those under 65 years of age, pneumonia deaths equal those from all other infections.[7] There are nearly four times as many deaths from pneumonia in England and Wales in the 5–49 year age group every year as there are from asthma.[8] The case fatality in community-acquired pneumonia ranges from 3% to 15%.[9–11] Although definitions of pneumonia vary, it is estimated that in England and Wales, one person per 1000 in the general adult population is admitted to hospital with pneumonia annually.[12]

ICD-9 and 10 include codes for pneumonia attributable to specific causes (viral causes, ICD-9 480, ICD-10 J12; pneumococci, ICD-9 481, ICD-10 J13; and other bacteria, ICD-9 482, ICD-10 J14–15), but such classification is often unsatisfactory since no pathogen can be demonstrated in 30–55% of cases. Non-specific codes, which include bronchopneumonia (ICD-9 485, ICD-10 J180) and pneumonia, organism unspecified (ICD-9 486, ICD-10 J181–189), are commonly used in routine statistics, particularly as a non-specific certified cause of death in patients with other chronic conditions. Recent changes in the coding of death certificates have been introduced in an attempt to minimise this ambiguity, and the usefulness of the ICD codes in the classification of pneumonia is discussed more fully in **Appendix A**.

Cause-specific pneumonias (i.e. with a named organism) are a potentially preventable cause of premature mortality, accounting for four times as many deaths under 50 years of age as there are from asthma. They may usefully be subdivided into infections acquired in the community and in hospital (nosocomial pneumonia), the latter presenting special problems of prevention and therapy.

Asthma

Asthma is characterised by recurrent episodes of airflow limitation that are usually reversible either spontaneously or with appropriate treatment. It is accompanied by symptoms of breathlessness, wheezing, chest tightness and cough.[14] It is caused by variations in airways resistance which occur because the airways have an increased level of responsiveness to a variety of stimuli. Its pathological basis is thought to be a type of chronic non-infective inflammation.[14–16]

Asthma is of concern for three reasons.

- It is one of the commonest chronic diseases of childhood and a major cause of acute and chronic morbidity at all ages, including school absence in children and loss of time from work in adults. There is evidence that asthma is under-diagnosed and under-treated and thus the 'community effectiveness' of anti-asthma medications is limited, despite their proven efficacy, at least in the short term.

- It incurs major costs in terms of prescribed medications, general practitioner and consultant (paediatric, respiratory medicine, geriatrics and general medicine) time, and hospital admissions. Indicators of service use and prescribing have been increasing in recent years.
- It has been listed as a potentially avoidable cause of premature mortality (0–44 years). Although uncommon in absolute terms, asthma mortality is appreciable relative to other causes, and while admissions are less common in adults relative to childhood, mortality is more frequent.

ICD codes

In ICD-9, it is 493, and in ICD-10 it is J45 and J46.

1 There is diagnostic confusion and overlap with other conditions. In children the main overlapping condition is acute bronchitis (ICD-9 466, ICD-10 J20, J21). In adults the main areas of overlap are diseases characterised by chronic airflow obstruction (ICD-9 490, 491, 497 ICD-10 J40–43); some analyses group all of these together with asthma, but this is unhelpful because asthma has different health care requirements.
2 Coding rules have changed at each revision of the ICD in line with changing concepts of asthma vis-à-vis COPD. Broadly, the rules have shifted with successive revisions away from giving priority to bronchitis towards giving more priority to asthma.
3 The ICD code does not indicate the severity of asthma, which may vary from subclinical to life-threatening. Conceptually, severity reflects two factors, the first being the actual physical disturbance and the second the risk of sudden life-threatening deteriorations. Medical decisions are made with both factors in mind. Various clinical classifications of asthma have been proposed,[17] but these have no ICD counterpart, and tend to be part of a spectrum of clinical and pathophysiological characteristics. In practice it is probably useful to distinguish chronic asthma and acute asthma but there are all shades of severity and combinations of these.
4 Chronic asthma may lead to airway remodelling and eventually to an element of fixed airflow obstruction similar to COPD.[18]
5 Asthma tends to be under-diagnosed and doctors in both the primary and secondary sector vary in their diagnostic practice.[19–22]
6 The diagnosis of asthma indicates not only the current clinical 'state' but also the tendency to asthma, i.e. the asthmatic 'trait'. Thus a patient may have 'asthma' but be currently free of symptoms.
7 In older adults, it may be difficult to distinguish chronic asthma from COPD. Although aetiology differs, symptoms and in some instances medication used may be similar.[23]
8 In both children and adults, the medical care of asthma is influenced by the increased likelihood of comorbidity due to other conditions belonging to the 'atopic' group, namely eczema and hay fever. These add to the total burden of illness and also tend to be associated with increased severity and worse prognosis.[24]

Sub-categories of asthma

For health service purchasing and provision, the most important sub-categories are acute asthma and chronic asthma. Ideally, sub-categorisation by severity would also be useful. Unfortunately, neither of these sub-categories are accessible through the routine information systems. ICD-10 now separates acute severe asthma (J46) from other forms of asthma (J45).

Chronic obstructive pulmonary (airways) disease

The term COPD is used to describe a syndrome of chronic progressive airflow obstruction, which is not fully reversible. The airflow limitation is usually both progressive and associated with an abnormal inflammatory response to inhaled particles or gases.[25]

The term COPD formerly embraced the pathological diagnosis of emphysema and the clinical diagnosis of chronic bronchitis, defined by a productive cough for at least three months of the year for two successive years. However, a productive cough may be present without airflow limitation, and airflow limitation may develop without a chronic cough, and chronic bronchitis may not necessarily lead to progressive impairment of respiratory function and life expectancy. For this reason, these terms are not now used interchangeably with the preferred diagnosis of COPD.

Diagnosis requires lung function to be measured. Life expectancy is related to the reduction in lung function. COPD was responsible for 4.8% of all deaths in 1999, although diagnostic confusion with chronic asthma may occur, particularly in the elderly, and statistics based upon diagnosis alone should be interpreted cautiously.

COPD poses a major public health problem in terms of:

- mortality, particularly in middle and old age. The three diagnoses remain among the principal certified causes of death, although their relative contribution is declining, particularly among men. There is also evidence that impaired ventilatory function (related mainly to COPD) is a risk factor for premature death from cardiovascular disease, independent of smoking
- chronic respiratory disability and recurrent chest infections, leading to premature retirement, loss of productivity, general practitioner contacts and use of hospital resources.

These diseases rarely occur among those who have never smoked, and their progression can be slowed if smoking patients give up smoking. Childhood respiratory infections may also be an important risk factor.[1] Thus, much of the public health burden is potentially preventable.

ICD codes

COPD is a relatively new overarching diagnostic term introduced because of considerable diagnostic confusion between chronic or unspecified bronchitis (ICD-9 490–491, ICD-10 J40–42) and emphysema (ICD-9 492, ICD-10 J43) in adults. A diagnosis of COAD or COPD (coded to chronic airways obstruction, ICD-9 496, ICD-10 J44) is increasingly used for adult patients with cough, phlegm and/or breathlessness with evidence of irreversible reductions in ventilatory function. In an individual patient, all of these components may be present, or one or other may be dominant at any particular time. Asthma is distinguished from these categories on the basis of reversibility of airflow obstruction, although there is substantial overlap in terms of clinical presentation and therapeutic management, particularly in the elderly. The ICD-9 and ICD-10 codes relating to COPD and asthma are shown below.

ICD-9 description	ICD-9 code	ICD-10 code	ICD-10 description
Bronchitis, not specified as acute or chronic	490	J40	
Chronic bronchitis	491	J41	Chronic bronchitis, type specified
		J42	Chronic bronchitis, unspecified
Emphysema	492	J43	
Asthma	493	J45	Asthma, specified or unspecified
		J46	Status asthmaticus
Chronic airways obstruction, not elsewhere classified	496	J44	Chronic obstructive pulmonary disease

Tuberculosis

This infectious disease still affects millions of people worldwide, but until recently has been a diminishing problem in the UK.[26] While the disease can affect any organ, the lungs are involved in 75% of cases.[27] Primary infection with the tubercle bacillus can result in clinical disease, or in a contained form of disease without clinical symptoms that may subsequently be reactivated at times of stress or immune compromise. Thus, there is a spectrum of pulmonary tuberculosis, from a fulminant disease to an asymptomatic carrier state. The latter is particularly important as it may spread the disease.

Historically, tuberculosis (TB) prevention and treatment has been the responsibility of a respiratory physician working from a chest clinic. Appropriate antibiotic therapy is curative and prevents cross-infection. Concern is growing about the increasing prevalence of drug-resistant TB infections in the UK and elsewhere.

It is of concern for two reasons:

- it is a preventable cause of death
- it is communicable.

The public health problem in the UK is greatest among immigrant groups, although certain groups of people are particularly at risk, e.g. immunosuppressed patients and those with HIV infection. In America, the risk of patients with HIV infection acquiring TB is estimated to be 500 times greater than the general population.[28] Although the current impact of HIV on TB in the UK appears small, trends in HIV infection and clinical AIDS could have a major influence on future patterns of tuberculosis and its impact on services.

Tuberculosis is commonly subdivided according to the site of involvement: pulmonary (ICD-9 011, ICD-10 A15–A16), other respiratory (ICD-9 012, ICD-10 A15–A16) and non-respiratory (ICD-9 013–019).

Cystic fibrosis

Cystic fibrosis (ICD-9 277.0, ICD-10 E84) is the commonest inherited disorder in Caucasian populations. Inherited by the autosomal recessive route, one person in 25 carries one of a variety of genetic defects affecting a single gene responsible for production of a protein called CFTR (cystic fibrosis transmembrane conductance regulator). CFTR acts as a chloride channel and genetic defects in this gene affect transport of salt and water across cell membranes. This primarily affects exocrine secretions in the lungs, pancreas and sweat glands. In the lung, this causes thickening of mucus, which can readily become infected with opportunistic bacteria. If untreated, chronic infection leads to bronchiectasis, respiratory failure and death. Although it is a multi-system disorder, respiratory disease is the main cause of death in 95% of cases. Defective production of exocrine enzymes in the pancreas results in steatorrhoea and malabsorption. A high concentration of sodium and chloride in the sweat is used as a diagnostic test. Other organs affected include the male reproductive tract (absence of the vas deferens in a high proportion of patients, causing infertility) and the liver.

It is of concern because:

- the prevalence is rising rapidly, particularly among adults, due to very marked increases in survival and improvements in treatment
- the cost of treating this disease is very high. The average NHS cost has recently been placed at around £8000 per patient per year, but this varies according to age and severity
- it is now an important cause of death and hospital admission among young adults.

There is potential for prevention by use of prenatal genetic screening, and to prevent long-term morbidity by early diagnosis and aggressive treatment in specialist centres. Treatment is centred on aggressive management of respiratory infections, including use of nebulised and intravenous antibiotics, to minimise lung damage, maximise lung function and allow individuals to pursue a normal active lifestyle. Individuals need regular respiratory physiotherapy, an active exercise programme, a high-calorie diet, vitamin supplements and pancreatic enzyme supplements. Where possible, treatment is undertaken at home, work or school to minimise impact on lifestyle. In severely affected individuals, life can be prolonged by heart–lung or double-lung transplantation. Survival and clinical status are significantly increased if a centre specialising in treatment of cystic fibrosis is responsible for care.

The link between genotype and phenotype is not completely clear. The commonest mutation affecting the cystic fibrosis gene is the delta-F-508 mutation, responsible for just over two-thirds of all mutations in the UK population. Pancreatic sufficiency is retained in about 10% of patients with cystic fibrosis, and appears to be associated both with a favourable prognosis and also with absence of the delta-F-508 mutation, but this association is not absolute. Therefore, at present it is not possible to predict phenotype from the genotype.

Use of sub-categories in this chapter

The six sub-categories described above have sufficient clinical, epidemiological and public health differences to be dealt with separately throughout most of this chapter. However, in the sections concerned with models of care, outcomes, targets and research, some categories have been collapsed into lower respiratory infections (adult and children) and obstructive lung diseases (asthma and COPD).

4 Prevalence and incidence

Morbidity

Table B.3 summarises the principal findings from ad hoc surveys of prevalence and incidence of lower respiratory disease. Many respiratory problems are characterised by acute episodes occurring periodically in people with chronic symptoms or increased susceptibility. Measures of prevalence, i.e. numbers of people affected, are the most commonly reported index. Incidence may be estimated from recall of episodes over a defined prior period (often from birth), i.e. cumulative incidence. Few surveys offer information on the incidence of spells of illness (comparable to hospital admission rates), which may be the most relevant measure for planning acute services.

Acute lower respiratory infections in children

Population surveys

A number of large population surveys of respiratory disease in childhood carried out in the 1960s and 1970s included questions relating to bronchitis and pneumonia (*see* Table 1). More recent evidence is not available, reflecting the declining interest in these conditions. There are major problems posed by the definition and by incomplete recall of disease episodes by parents.[29]

Table 1: Estimates of incidence of acute lower respiratory illness in early childhood obtained by parental recall from population surveys of British children.

Place	Date	Number studied	Illness	Cumulative incidence	By age	Notes
Kent[36]	1964	4,700	Bronchitis	23.0%	5	
			Pneumonia	3.0%	5	
National (1958 cohort)[31,37]	1965	10,500	Pneumonia	3.0%	5	
				1.0%	1	
		14,000	Bronchitis with wheezing	17.0%	7	(i)
Selected urban and rural areas in England and Wales[31,32]	1966	11,500	Bronchitis	23.0%	6–10	(ii)
				9.0%	1	
			Pneumonia	5.0%	6–10	(ii)
				1.8%	1	
			Whooping cough	16.0%	6–10	
				1.6%	1	
National (1970 cohort)[30]	1975	13,500	Bronchitis	17.0%	5	
			Pneumonia	1.6%	5	

(i) should probably be considered as a manifestation of asthma.
(i) and (ii) unpublished analyses of data.[31]

These surveys suggest that about 20% of children are affected by bronchitis (probably including bronchiolitis) at some time in early childhood, but estimates of the cumulative incidence of pneumonia are less consistent (ranging from 1% to 5%). Many of the illnesses recalled as bronchitis may have been episodes of wheeze related to asthma.

Epidemiological surveys have found associations of bronchitis, bronchiolitis and pneumonia in children with the following factors.

- **Sex:** The male:female ratio is about 1.3:1.[30]
- **Region:** Marked regional variation exists in reported bronchitis, but not pneumonia.[30,31] High bronchitis incidence is reported in north and west England, and Wales, and low incidence in Scotland and East Anglia.
- **Poor socio-economic status:** There are strong trends for both parental recall of bronchitis and pneumonia.[30,32] Effects are partly related to family size/composition, parental smoking and, possibly, infant feeding.
- **Sibship size:** Lower respiratory illnesses in the first two years of life are more common in large families.[30,31] There is some evidence of an association with day-care attendance.[2]
- **Ethnicity:** A lower incidence of bronchitis among inner-city ethnic minorities than among inner-city whites has been reported, though based on small numbers.[33]
- **Parental smoking:** A strong, consistent and dose-related association has been reported, particularly in children under three years of age.[34,35]
- **Breastfeeding:** Findings are less consistent, though they tend towards an increased risk of LRTI in bottle-fed children. This may be due to confounding by parental smoking.
- **Prematurity and low birth weight:** These are related to bronchiolitis and pneumonia, particularly in early life, but not to bronchitis.[30]

General practice consultations

There are three principal sources. These data principally rely on clinical diagnoses with only limited reference to laboratory and radiological tests, and therefore caution is required when comparing rates of disease with those from other sources (e.g. special studies or hospital data).

- **National Morbidity Studies 1981–2 and 1991–2:** Acute bronchitis is a much more common presentation in general practice than pneumonia. In the Fourth National Morbidity Survey 1991–2, 157.8 per 1000 people aged 0–4 consulted during the year with one or more episodes of acute bronchitis (including bronchiolitis), whereas the figure for pneumonia was only 3.7 per 1000 (**Table B.7**). The male:female ratio was 1.12:1 for acute bronchitis and 1.48:1 for pneumonia, consistent with the cumulative incidence data from surveys. In 1991–92, 1.2 per 1000 children consulted for whooping cough, almost a tenfold fall from 1981–82, but this figure will vary from year to year.
- **Medical Research Council Collaborative Study 1964–66:** A special study of respiratory illnesses in selected practices,[38] this provides more detail on the clinical syndromes encountered in general practice and in hospital than is available in the other two sources, but is based on a relatively small number of cases.
- **RCGP Weekly Returns Service 1967–90:** This continuous monitoring using 'spotter' practices highlights the marked seasonality in acute LRTI, with a two- to threefold variation in incidence of acute bronchitis and three- to fourfold variation in incidence of pneumonia during childhood.[39] This places high demands upon primary and secondary care during the winter months, upon which may be superimposed epidemics of pertussis, measles and influenza.

Hospital admissions

- **Rates of admission:** In England in 1998–99, there were 24.3 FCEs per 10 000 children aged 0–14 for acute bronchitis (including bronchiolitis) and 13.4 per 10 000 for pneumonia (including influenza). The 0–4 year age group accounted for over 99% of FCEs for acute bronchitis and over 75% of FCEs for pneumonia. The male:female ratio for acute bronchitis and bronchiolitis was higher than for incidence or general practice data (1.5:1), but was lower for pneumonia (1.3:1).
- **Regional variations:** Variations by hospital region cannot be adequately described from published statistics because admissions for acute bronchitis are not presented by region. The available data, relating to chronic/unspecified bronchitis and pneumonia, may be influenced by diagnostic transfer from acute bronchitis.
- **Time trends:** National rates of admission for bronchitis, bronchiolitis and pneumonia in childhood have been falling. The rates for 1985 were about 10% lower than the equivalent figures for 1982. More recent data indicate that the rate of FCEs for 1998–99 is higher than the admission rate for 1985 (37.7 vs. 21.8 per 10 000), but the change to recording FCEs confuses the interpretation of these data, and it is not possible to comment on the trend in admissions during this time period. Further reductions may well have occurred since 1985.

Infectious disease notifications

Information on notifications of infectious disease is available from the Health Protection Agency website on www.hpa.org.uk/infections/topics_az/topics.asp.

Figure 1 shows notifications of whooping cough by age group 1980–98. There has been a quite dramatic decline in notifications, particularly in children under 10 years of age. Figure 2 shows immunisation uptake for whooping cough from 1966 to 1998, demonstrating a large rise in the proportion of eligible children immunised by 1998.

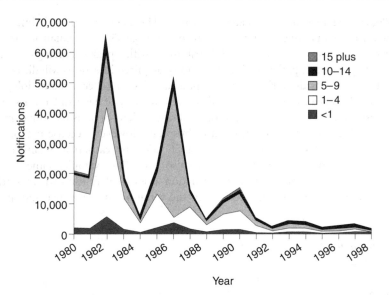

Figure 1: Notifications of whooping cough, England and Wales, by age group, 1980–98. Data from Health Protection Agency website.

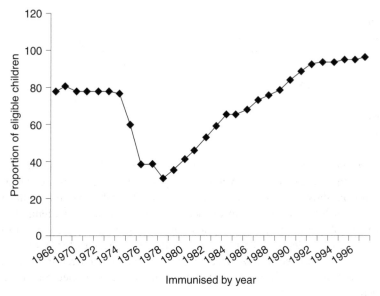

Figure 2: Proportion of eligible children immunised by target date, 1968–97. Data from Health Protection Agency website.

Lower respiratory infections in adults

Community-acquired pneumonia

The incidence of community-acquired pneumonia varies from 230 to 360 per 100 000 population at all ages, and 470 per 100 000 in the adult population.[9–11,40] Recent UK figures put the incidence slightly higher at 500 per 100 000, with 32% of episodes treated in hospital. The incidence is high in infants, falls in young children, and then rises again to over 1000 per 100 000 beyond age 45. The median age at onset is 59 years (mean 48–51 years). There is a marked seasonal distribution, with a peak occurring between January and March. Approximately 3% of all patients with community-acquired infections will die and 5–22% will be admitted to hospital. This wide variation in hospital admission reflects methodological differences between surveys as well as health service factors such as availability of beds and admission policy.

It is possible to estimate the relative contribution of various micro-organisms from community surveys of pneumonia where the case has been admitted to hospital. However, because pathogens can only be demonstrated in 45–70% of pneumonias,[10,11,41] classification by causative organism is not entirely satisfactory. Clinical definitions of pneumonia may also vary. For example, some surveys have used evidence of chest infection with radiological confirmation as a case definition whereas others have used clinical findings only. These factors help account for the variation in prevalence and incidence rates in different studies.

Streptococcus pneumoniae	34–36%
Haemophilus influenzae	10%
Influenza A	6–7%
Staphylococcus aureus	1%
Escherichia coli	1%
Legionella pneumophila	0.5–15%
Proteus mirabilis	0.5%
Actinomyces israelii	0.5%
Mycoplasma pneumoniae	1–18%
Chlamydia psittaci	1%
Influenza B	2%
Respiratory syncytial virus (RSV)	2%
Adenovirus	2%
Parainfluenza virus	2%
Cytomegalovirus	0.5%

Streptococcus pneumoniae, Haemophilus influenzae and influenza A virus are the commonest pathogens causing community-acquired pneumonia. *Mycoplasma pneumoniae* epidemics occur about every four years.[42] Some organisms show seasonal patterns of infection. Microbiology may differ in patients with chronic respiratory disorders, immunocompromised patients or alcoholic patients. In epidemic years, *Mycoplasma* is the most common cause of pneumonias requiring hospital admission.[43] Influenza pneumonia also occurs in epidemics; the most recent in the UK was in the winter of 1989–90 when 25 000 excess deaths were estimated to have occurred, 82% of which occurred in people over 75 years of age.[44] *Legionella* accounts for 2–5% (up to 15% in one survey)[9] of cases of pneumonia,[11] of which about a third will have been acquired abroad.

Risk factors for death from community-acquired pneumonia include age, tachypnoea, hypotension, hypothermia, diabetes mellitus, neoplasm, neurological disease, leukopenia, bacteraemia and more than one lobe affected.[45]

Nosocomial pneumonia

Despite the significant economic burden that it represents, the aetiology and pathogenesis of nosocomial pneumonia is poorly understood and there are no readily available UK figures on its incidence. However, data from the USA suggest that the incidence of nosocomial pneumonia ranges from 5–10 cases per 1000 patient admissions[46] and up to 120–220 per 1000 admissions in intensive-care units.[47] Hospital-acquired pneumonia accounts for 10–19% of all nosocomial infections.

Risk factors for nosocomial pneumonia include age greater than 70 years, admission to an intensive-care unit, chronic lung disease and thoracic and upper abdominal surgery.[47] Several of these risk factors are amenable to modification and it has been estimated that approximately a third of the mortality may be preventable.[48] American studies[47] suggest a 36% fatality rate, with increased risk related to the type of organism, bilateral radiographic changes, the presence of respiratory failure, age and inappropriate antibiotic therapy.

Asthma

Prevalence and incidence as indicators of health needs

Most studies were not done with health needs in mind and lack relevant data on severity and other clinically relevant aspects of the illness. Thus, knowledge of prevalence and incidence is not readily translated into a measure of health need. Also, because asthma is a treatable and suppressible condition, prevalence could, theoretically, reflect treatment in the community. This will have implications for outcome indicators.

Table 2 shows various indicators of asthma morbidity and mortality by broad age group taken from the data in **Appendix B** and from ad hoc studies. The following discussion deals with some of these in more detail and includes a list of references to UK studies of prevalence and incidence.

Table 2: Summary of available information on morbidity and mortality statistics for asthma and symptoms of wheeze (percentages). Figures updated to include Health Survey for England 1996, which includes different age groups.

	Age group (%)			
	0–14	**15–44**	**45–64**	**65+**
Morbidity and mortality				
Incidence per year	1–2			
Lifetime incidence	30	32	34	34
Current wheezing or 12-month period prevalence	12–18	10 (19% 16–44)	15–22	24
Persistent wheezing	4	4	6	
Severe acute attacks	1			
Disabling disease	1–2		3	
Diagnosis of asthma	4–6 (21% 2–15)	4 (15% 16–44)	10	10
Requiring regular treatment or care	4–6	4–9	4–9	4–13
Mortality	0.00020	0.00067	0.00247	0.0108

Prevalence of current asthma

Because of the variable level of diagnosis of asthma in children it is customary to use wheezing as the indicator of asthma in prevalence surveys. This approach is less helpful in middle-aged and elderly groups because wheezing may be a symptom of COPD. Prevalence may be recorded as 'current', but it is preferable to record the reported prevalence over the previous year (12-month period prevalence) to permit comparability between surveys. These rates will include a considerable proportion of subjects with mild disease, and in the elderly it may be difficult to infer the proportion who have asthma rather than wheezing associated with COPD. Very few studies have measured the severity of asthma in such a way as to aid the evaluation and planning of clinical care and services.

Overall, the prevalence of asthma sufficiently severe to require regular medical supervision is very similar across all ages – about 4% – and this figure appears to be rising. In children, 7–10% of all 12–14 year olds in the UK report more than four attacks per year, and 5% of adults report themselves to be on regular anti-asthma medication.

Information on the prevalence of symptoms has recently been incorporated in the Health Survey for England,[49] and a review of respiratory symptoms and lung function in young people was also carried out using this survey.[50] The important findings from these surveys are summarised in Table 3 and Figures 3 to 5. Overall, one third of adults and 28% of children had a history of wheezing. The prevalence of

Table 3: Risk factors for wheeze in the last 12 months for adults and children, by sex, 1995–96 for adults and 1995–97 combined for children.

	OR	95% Confidence interval
Factors associated with prevalence of wheeze in last 12 months in adults		
Males		
Exposure to other people's smoke > 20 hours a week	1.19	1.05, 1.35
Ex regular smoker	1.46	1.28, 1.60
Less than 20 cigarettes a day	2.07	18.4, 2.34
20 cigarettes or more a day	3.44	3.00, 3.93
Social class IIIN	1.15	1.04, 1.56
Social class IIIM	1.43	1.18, 1.72
Social class IV	1.24	1.00, 1.52
Social class V	1.48	1.15, 1.90
Suburban dwelling	1.13	1.01, 1.25
Urban dwelling	1.15	1.01, 1.31
Females		
Exposure to other people's smoke 6 to 19 hours a week	1.32	1.17, 1.49
Exposure to other people's smoke > 20 hours a week	1.4	1.24, 1.58
Ex smoker	1.67	1.51, 1.85
Less than 20 cigarettes a day	2.03	1.83, 2.25
20 cigarettes or more a day	2.76	2.40, 3.19
Suburban dwelling	1.17	1.06, 1.29
Urban dwelling	1.3	1.15, 1.46
Factors associated with prevalence of wheeze in last 12 months in children		
Boys aged 2 to 15		
Five or more in household	0.8	0.66, 0.97
Father has diagnosed asthma	2.11	1.63, 2.74
Mother has diagnosed asthma	2.15	1.69, 2.73
Girls aged 2 to 15		
Suburban dwelling	1.46	1.10, 1.94
Rural dwelling	1.63	1.18, 2.24
Five or more in household	0.8	0.65, 0.98
Father has diagnosed asthma	1.39	1.04, 1.87
Mother has diagnosed asthma	1.74	1.34, 2.26

Source: Health Survey for England.

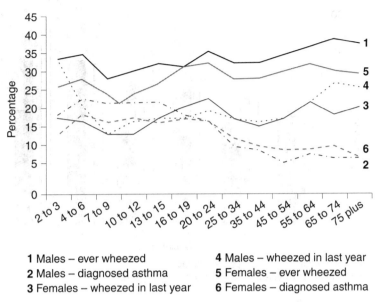

1 Males – ever wheezed
2 Males – diagnosed asthma
3 Females – wheezed in last year

4 Males – wheezed in last year
5 Females – ever wheezed
6 Females – diagnosed asthma

Figure 3: Proportion of children and adults with various respiratory symptoms by age and sex, 1995–96 for adults and 1995–97 combined for children.
Source: Health Survey for England.

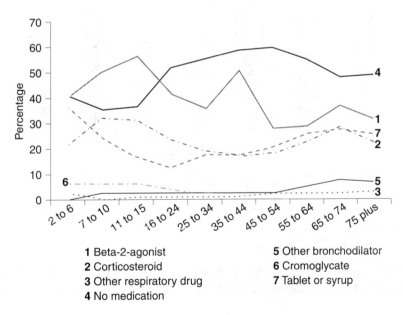

1 Beta-2-agonist
2 Corticosteroid
3 Other respiratory drug
4 No medication

5 Other bronchodilator
6 Cromoglycate
7 Tablet or syrup

Figure 4: Proportion of children and adults who have ever wheezed and who had most recent attack within five years who are currently receiving certain types of drug treatment, 1995–96 for adults and 1995–97 combined for children.
Source: Health Survey for England.

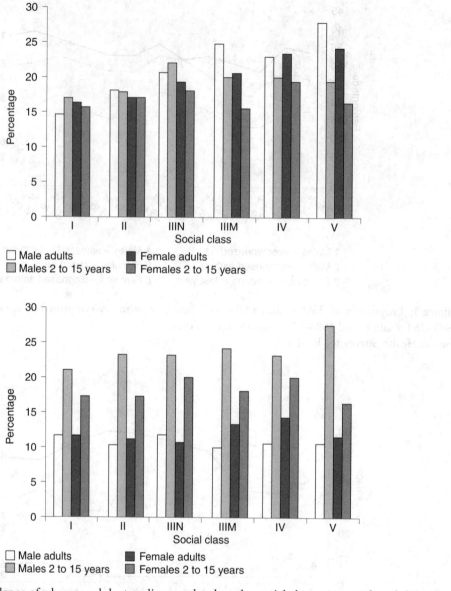

Figure 5: Prevalence of wheeze and doctor-diagnosed asthma by social class, 1995–96 for adults and 1995–97 combined for children.
Source: Health Survey for England.

doctor-diagnosed asthma was 12% in adults and 21% in children. Of those reporting wheezing or asthma, 47% of adults and 62% of children had been prescribed medication for their symptoms in the last 12 months.

Incidence

Incidence is a measure of the rate at which people develop asthma for the first time. In the National Child Development Study 1958 cohort, incidence was highest in the first seven years of life (approximately 2–3%

per annum) and then levelled out at 0.7% per annum from ages 11 to 23.[51] The cumulative incidence to age 23 was about 30%, and to age 33 was 43%, which agrees with studies of general practice records.[52–54] These are higher than previous figures because asthma has a good prognosis in childhood – only about 20% of early wheezers (50% in more severe cases) persist to age 23. The health service implication is that a much higher proportion of the population will require care for asthma at some time during their life than is apparent from the prevalence figures.

Incidence during childhood is strongly associated with pneumonia, hay fever and eczema, and more weakly with male sex, antepartum haemorrhage, whooping cough, migraine and recurrent abdominal pain. From 17–33 years, incidence is strongly related to cigarette smoking and hay fever, and more weakly to female sex, albuminuria in pregnancy, eczema and migraine. Smoking in pregnancy is weakly associated with childhood asthma, but more strongly with incidence after age 16. Relapse at 33 years is associated with atopy and current smoking. These suggest several preventive measures may both reduce incidence and improve prognosis of asthma.[54]

For understanding health needs it is also important to have information about the patterns of acute asthma attacks experienced by individuals, i.e. incidence (spells). High utilisation may be due to a higher number of patients presenting for care or to a similar number of patients presenting more frequently. Because there is a lack of data about the epidemiology of acute episodes of asthma it is difficult to estimate the risk of fatality in an attack or understand the dynamics of care of acute asthma.

Prognosis

About 50% of young children with regular wheezing will still have symptoms in early adult life. The longer-term prognosis is uncertain. Mortality follow-up of patients with asthma reveals a considerable cumulative risk of mortality.[55] There is also evidence that chronic asthma is associated with the development of fixed airflow obstruction or remodelling similar to that seen in COPD.[18]

Sex difference

Incidence and prevalence are higher among boys than girls, but by the late teens the incidence has become higher in girls. Prevalence is fairly similar between the sexes during adult life.

Trends

Temporal changes to reported asthma prevalence may be difficult to interpret due to an increasing acceptance of the label 'asthma'. However, there have been a small number of studies in children that have reported the prevalence of recurrent symptoms, principally wheezing in the absence of respiratory infection, using the same questionnaire instrument. Overall, these suggest an overall rise in symptom prevalence.[56–60] In the UK, one survey suggested that the prevalence of wheezing among 5–11 year olds rose by more than 30% during the period 1982–92, while a separate study from Aberdeen found that wheezing prevalence rose from 10 to 20% between 1964 and 1989 along with a general rise in the symptoms of other atopic diseases (hayfever and eczema).[60] Similar changes have been observed for children in the USA.[60] However, data for adults is lacking and there is little evidence regarding changes to the severity of asthma symptoms. These are areas that need further research. In children, more marked changes have occurred in the prevalence of a diagnosis of asthma,[56,58,61] GP consultations[62] and hospital admissions,[63] all three of which are susceptible to non-epidemiological influences.

Trends in self-reported asthma, GP consultations, inpatient treatment, mortality and prescribing for asthma have been reported in a recent epidemiological overview of asthma.[64] Self-reported asthma has risen in all age groups, most markedly in children between 1984 and 1991. Prescriptions for asthma drugs rose from 12.71 million items in 1980 to 31.25 million items in 1993. However, the extent to which this reflects an increased awareness of asthma and appropriate treatment compared to an increase in either incidence or severity is not clear. There is evidence from a recent survey in children aged 12–14 that substantial asthma morbidity is still going undiagnosed and untreated,[65] with up to 3.4% displaying severe symptoms that were untreated.

When viewed over the long term, there is evidence of an increase in asthma mortality.[66] An epidemic of asthma deaths was experienced in the mid-1960s but this subsided to prior levels, probably due to the correction of its cause (iatrogenic effect of a new anti-asthmatic preparation).[67] Following this there was further evidence of an increase in mortality from 1973 to 1985 among the 5–35 age group.[66] An analysis of mortality from 1979–89 (within ICD 9th revision) up to age 45 indicated that the only significant increase was within the 15–25 age group (averaging +2% per year), with the other groups showing no change.[68] In adults over 65 the trend is upward, but difficult to interpret because of the scope for transfer from the more numerous COPD deaths. Age-standardised mortality rates for asthma have been falling in the UK since the early 1990s.[64]

Geographical, social and ethnic effects on incidence and prevalence

In children, asthma may be more prevalent in the south of the UK than in the north.[69] The prevalence also appears to be relatively high in Wales.[32] Little is known about geographical factors and adult asthma although there is clearly some variation.[70] In the 1996 Health Survey for England, adult asthma prevalence appeared to be slightly higher in the south.[49]

Most studies of infants and young children report a positive influence of social factors on the incidence of wheezing illness, possibly reflecting greater exposure to infections and tobacco smoke in the manual classes.[71–73] After the age of about five the effect of social factors tends to fade.[51] In the past there was probably a class effect on labelling,[74–76] but this has not been observed in recent studies. Among adults, a diagnosis of asthma is still reported more by non-manual classes.[77] Analysis of the ONS disability survey indicates that disability associated with asthma is two to three times more frequent in manual than in non-manual classes. It is relevant here to note evidence that adult asthmatics of manual social class have been found to have potentially greater degrees of reversibility of air flow obstruction.[78] Asthma in childhood has a measurable though small effect on employment prospects and on social status.[79] There is some evidence that mortality is higher in adults from lower social classes.[80]

In the recent Health Survey for England, self-reported wheezing in the last 12 months showed a noticeable positive social class gradient for adult men and women, but the gradient was less clear for children and doctor-diagnosed asthma (*see* Figure 5).

Two epidemiological studies have examined the question of ethnicity and asthma in children. One found no relationship with ethnicity.[81] The other, while finding no relationship with asthma, did find a higher prevalence of wheezing in whites and those from Caribbean communities.[33] It is unlikely that the ethnic composition of a district will have a significant effect on health needs for asthma. There is no epidemiological evidence relating to ethnicity in adults although there are reports which indicate that hospital use may be greater among Asian asthmatics.[82] Studies in the USA indicate that more frequent and severe asthma in adult blacks can be explained by social and environmental factors.[73]

Chronic obstructive pulmonary (airways) disease

The prevalence of chronic bronchitis and COPD is closely related to the smoking habits of the population.[83] There has been a decline in morbidity attributed to chronic bronchitis over the last 40 years. However, the UK continues to have high prevalence rates compared to other developed countries even after controlling for smoking habits.[84] Table 4 summarises population-based surveys of the

Table 4: Prevalence (%) of chronic respiratory symptoms in general populations in the UK (1950s to 1990s)[49,85,87-96]

	Men				Women			
	Cough	Phlegm	Persistent cough and phlegm	Wheeze	Cough	Phlegm	Persistent cough and phlegm	Wheeze
Leigh (urban England) (1956) (55–64 years)	30	33	18	38				
Great Britain selected general practices (1958) (45–64 years)	47	41		38	21	18		32
Glamorgan (rural Wales) (1957) (55–64 years)	31	28	26	48	13	13	8	48
Annandale (rural Scotland) (1958) (55–64 years)	29	23	20	44	15	14	11	38
Rhondda Fach (industrial Wales) (non-miners) (1961) (55–64 years)	42	35	29		16	16	10	
Peterborough (industrial) (1961) (55–64 years)	31							
Holt-cromer (residential seaside town) (1961) (55–64 years)	22							
Halesworth (rural) (1961) (55–64 years)	20							
Scotland general population (1965–75) (45–64 years)	26				14			
England, Scotland and Wales (1970) (55–64 years)			25				9	
England, Scotland and Wales (general population) (1972) (37–67 years)	30			32	20			24
England, Scotland and Wales (national cohort of men) (1978) (40–59 years)			16					
London (urban general practice) (1985) (55–64 years)	27	27	21	34	15	12	9	21
Southern England (general rural population) (1990) (55–64 years)	19	19	15		13	12	8	
England (general population – Health Survey for England) (1995–96) (55 years and over)				38				31

prevalence of chronic cough and phlegm over the last 40 years. Chronic bronchitis as defined by the Medical Research Council (persistent cough with phlegm production) now affects about 17% of men and 6% of women in middle age. The prevalence of COPD is lower (about 5% in men and 3% in women of middle age).[85] Prevalence increases with age, and is found to be higher in men.[86]

Comparing these figures with surveys carried out during the 1950s and 1960s suggests that prevalence is declining, in line with trends in the smoking habits of this age group.

Both productive cough and impaired lung function are much more common in poorer socio-economic groups, in northerly regions and Wales, and among urban rather than rural populations.[86] These variations are only partly explained by smoking habits.

Tuberculosis

Tuberculosis is a notifiable disease, and although they give an underestimate of the true level of disease, notifications provide a useful indicator of trends in the level of disease.

Notifications declined steadily since recording began in 1913, but have levelled off since the mid-1980s (*see* Figure 6). Since 1988, notifications have risen slightly year on year at a rate of approximately 1% per annum for respiratory TB and 4% per annum for non-respiratory TB (*see* Figure 7). This reversal in decline has also been seen in America, where it has been attributed to HIV infection, but this does not appear to be the case in the UK at present.

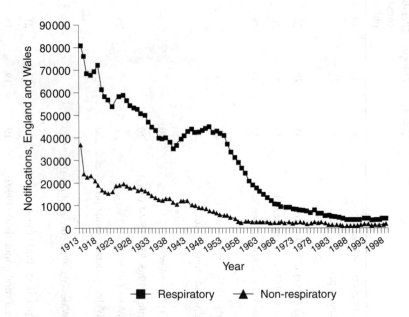

Figure 6: Notifications of tuberculosis in England and Wales, 1913–98.
Source: Health Protection Agency website (www.hpa.org.uk).

Notification rates show wide regional variations, with the highest rates and greatest rise since 1993 being in London (34.0 per 100 000, rising from 28.3 per 100 000 in 1993), and the lowest rate being in the Eastern region (5.0 per 100 000).[97]

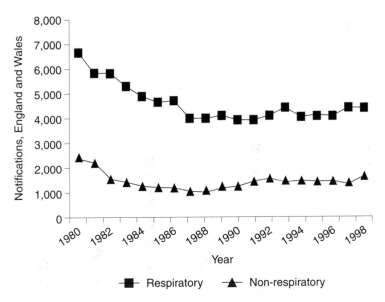

Figure 7: Notifications of tuberculosis in England and Wales, 1980–98.
Source: Health Protection Agency website (www.hpa.org.uk).

TB and HIV infection

TB in those with HIV infection is most commonly the result of reactivation of a dormant infection and therefore occurs in those previously exposed to TB.[98] In the UK, there currently appears to be little overlap between the subpopulation with HIV infection and those with previous tuberculous infection.[99] The proportion of AIDS cases in whom TB occurs is relatively small (5% of AIDS cases by July 1990; between 4 and 6% in 1998),[100] and less than 0.5% of patients notified with TB in 1988 were identified as having AIDS.[101] By the 1993 survey of notifications, this proportion had risen to 2.0% of all eligible adult cases, and this was higher in London (4.3%) than elsewhere (0.8%).[102] However, the likely future impact of HIV on TB is uncertain.

TB and ethnicity

The MRC study in 1983[27] showed considerable differences between ethnic groups in the estimated yearly rates of notifications of respiratory TB in England and Wales, subsequently confirmed by further surveys of notifications in 1988 and 1993[102] (*see* Figure 8). Notification rates have generally decreased in the white, Indian and Black Caribbean groups, but have increased in the Black African, Pakistani, Bangladeshi and other ethnic groups since 1988.

Amongst immigrants from the Indian subcontinent, prevalence rates decrease as period of residence in the UK increases, particularly beyond five years.[103] The majority of the increase in cases in the Black African and other ethnic groups in 1993 was also due to recent immigration.[102]

Non-respiratory TB is more common in patients of Indian subcontinent origin (46% non-respiratory cases, compared with 16% in the white population).

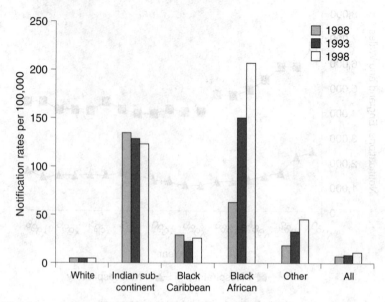

Figure 8: Notification rates per 100 000 population by ethnic group for tuberculosis in England, 1983–93.
Source: Kumar *et al.*[98] and Health Protection Agency website (www.hpa.org.uk).

TB and other risk factors

Age is a major risk factor for tuberculosis, and notification rates increase with age in all ethnic groups. Among white patients, the majority of cases are in older age groups,[104] while the greatest proportion of cases in patients from the Indian subcontinent occur in those aged under 35 (*see* Figure 9).[103]

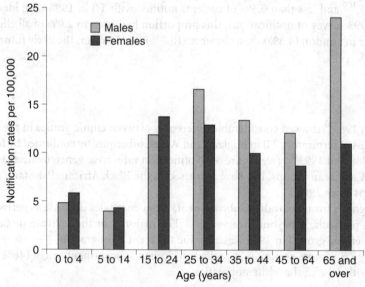

Figure 9: Notification rates of TB by age and sex, England and Wales, 1998.
Source: Health Protection Agency website (www.hpa.org.uk).

The homeless constitute a major risk group, with a confirmed prevalence of 1.5% (1500 per 100 000) in one study.

Drug resistance

Resistance to one or more anti-tuberculous drug is a global problem. A study in 1998 for the World Health Organization identified the total prevalence of resistance to a single drug to be 12.6% globally, and 1.9% in England and Wales.[105] Recent data from the UK Mycobacterial Resistance Network suggest that isoniazid resistance occurs in 6.3% of isolates in individuals with no previous history of TB, and in 17.0% of those with previous history of TB. Multi-drug resistance occurs in 1.0% of those with no previous history, and 11.0% of those with a previous history.

Cystic fibrosis

People who carry the defective gene comprise about one in 25 of the population, and the great majority of these individuals have no clinical abnormality. Approximately 1 in 2500 live births are affected by cystic fibrosis in the UK, i.e. approximately 250 births in England and Wales per year. The United Kingdom Cystic Fibrosis Survey*,[106] which is a case register, estimates that there are 7500 individuals in the UK with cystic fibrosis, of whom 57% are under 15 years of age and 43% are adults (*see* Figures 10 and 11). The proportion of adults was expected to rise to over 50% by the year 2000. This gives a prevalence of approximately 140 affected individuals per million resident population. Prevalence is higher in the 0 to 14 years age group (440 per million) and 15 to 24 age group (300 per million), but is lower in the over 25 age group (35 per million). The prevalence in the UK is rising by approximately 160 individuals per year, of whom the majority are adults.[107] Current median survival is around 28 years of age, but survival of the current birth cohort is predicted to exceed 40–50 years.

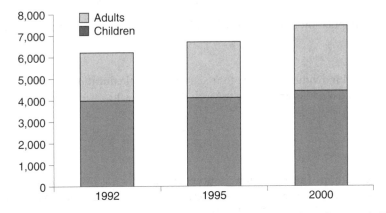

Figure 10: UK cystic fibrosis population, based on estimates or projections from 1992 UK Cystic Fibrosis Survey Data.[165]

Prevalence varies little across the country. The disease is much more common in Caucasian populations than in those from other ethnic backgrounds, but still occurs in these groups, although much more rarely. Cystic fibrosis can in particular be underdiagnosed in people with an ethnic origin in the Indian subcontinent.

---

* The function of the UK Cystic Fibrosis Survey has now been taken over by the enhanced UK Cystic Fibrosis Database at the University of Dundee.

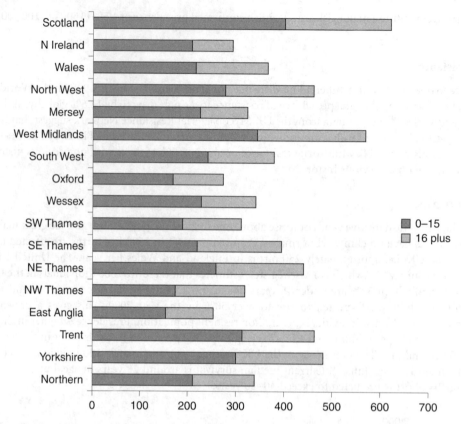

Figure 11: Regional population of cystic fibrosis patients (adults and children): 1992 regional boundaries.[165]

The majority of affected individuals are able to undertake normal education and full-time employment, but one quarter of affected adults are unable to work due to ill health.

Mortality

Lower respiratory conditions (including lung cancer) account for 23% of all deaths. They account for almost 15% of all deaths up to age 65, increasing thereafter due to a rising contribution from COPD and pneumonia to almost 25% (**Figures B.1** and **B.2**).

Lower respiratory infection in childhood

Lower respiratory infection in childhood is rarely fatal (15 per million 0 to 14-year-olds in 1999), yet bronchitis, bronchiolitis and pneumonia account for 3% of all deaths in this age group (**Table B.4**). Deaths due to acute LRTI in childhood are mainly a problem of the first year of life. Deaths up to 28 days should be excluded from consideration, as they will be heavily influenced by cases of respiratory distress syndrome in premature babies. In England and Wales during 1989, bronchitis, bronchiolitis and pneumonia together accounted for 5% of all post-neonatal deaths.[108] In 1999, deaths due to bronchitis, bronchiolitis, pneumonia and whooping cough comprised 2.9% all deaths in the 0–4 age group. The male:female ratio at this age is about 1.4:1, closely reflecting the sex difference in admissions and somewhat greater than that for incidence. For children aged 5–14, the male:female ratio rises to 1.9:1. Children of parents in social class IV or V are three times more likely to die of respiratory conditions at ages one to four than children in social classes I or II.[109] This is somewhat greater than the social class differential in incidence suggested by survey data. Post-neonatal mortality and deaths at ages 5–14 are less strongly related to parental social class. Regional variations in mortality are difficult to interpret in the absence of good data on geographical patterns of incidence.

Pneumonia in adults

Pneumonia is frequently recorded as the cause of death, especially in the very old, where other chronic diseases may have predisposed to death. Changes in the coding of underlying cause of death in England and Wales from 1984 onwards now give precedence to certain other conditions mentioned on the death certificate when pneumonia is recorded as the primary cause, but this does not entirely solve this problem.

Pneumonia (all forms) was certified as the underlying cause in 10.7% of all deaths in 1999 (after implementing the new coding rules as discussed above). In the 15–64 age group, this proportion was 3.3%, representing rates of 22 per million at age 15–44 years and 198 per million at age 45–64 years (**Table B.4**).

Asthma

Mortality is best thought of as an indicator of case fatality rather than of morbidity and it is notable that the ratio of mortality to prevalence increases rapidly with age.[19,22,23,56,57,63,70,85,110–115] Asthma mortality has a high profile, but accounts for less than 0.25% of all deaths (**Table B.1**); an average general practice could expect to experience the death of a child with asthma only once in 1000 practice-years. There is concern that asthma mortality has risen over the past 20 years, but this is mainly a problem in older adults, where transfer of deaths from COPD poses a major problem of interpretation. Among children and young adults, where diagnostic transfer is less problematic, the actual rates of fatal asthma are low: 2.3 per million (0.4% of all deaths) at age 0–14 and 6.3 per million (0.8% of all deaths) at age 15–44 (**Table B.4**). Asthma mortality in children has not increased during the 1990s.

Chronic obstructive pulmonary disease

While mortality attributed to chronic bronchitis has decreased considerably over the last 30 years,[116,117] mortality due to chronic airways obstruction (a new ICD code introduced in 1979), and later COPD (ICD-9 496, ICD-10 J40–47), has been increasing. This is probably due to an increasing shift in diagnostic labelling from chronic bronchitis and emphysema (ICD-9 490–492, ICD-10 J40–43) rather than a change in the epidemiology of COPD.[118] However, overall death rates from these three conditions combined have been declining over the past 30 years. In 1999, these three diseases were certified as the underlying cause of 5.7% of all male deaths and 4.0% of all female deaths. The majority of these deaths occurred in elderly people, but in middle age (45–64 years) 194 people per million died of chronic bronchitis, emphysema or COPD, 3.4% of all such premature deaths.

Tuberculosis

Pulmonary tuberculosis now accounts for less than 0.1% of all deaths (about 300) in the UK per year. Age-specific mortality rates for tuberculosis have been declining in England and Wales since the mid-1900s. Case-fatality rates continue to decrease in all age groups, although the overall annual mortality rate declined by only 0.13% between 1974 and 1987. This is because the incidence of disease in those over 75 years has declined more slowly than in the rest of the population and the size of this age group has increased.[119]

Cystic fibrosis

Overall, cystic fibrosis is a rare cause of death, accounting for less than 0.1% of all deaths. However, in children and young adults aged 5–25 it is the second most important respiratory cause of death (after pneumonia), accounting for 23% of all respiratory deaths, and 1.4% of all deaths, in these age groups. Median survival continues to increase, and is currently around 28 years. Survival is improving for each successive birth cohort, and for the current birth cohort it is expected to exceed 40 years.[120]

5 Services available

Health care sectors concerned

Respiratory conditions are managed at all levels of the health service. Acute conditions or acute exacerbations of chronic conditions involve primary care services, and in some cases result in hospital admission including the use of intensive-care units and the whole range of emergency services. Patients with chronic respiratory conditions use primary care services and outpatients. Self-care and patient decision making is a major feature of the management of chronic conditions and of their acute exacerbations.

Patients with respiratory diseases are managed by the specialties of paediatrics, adult general medicine, respiratory medicine, cardiothoracic surgery and geriatrics. Varying degrees of sub-specialisation are observed within respiratory medicine. The care is essentially medical, i.e. using clinical assessment and treatment with drugs and other non-surgical supportive treatment. Respiratory diseases are also the concern of public health medicine and non-health agencies concerned with air quality, living conditions and smoking control.

Provision of respiratory specialist care

The British Thoracic Society (BTS) now recommends one consultant with a specialist interest in thoracic medicine per 60 000 population (the previous figure proposed in the late 1970s was one per 150 000, and in the 1990s, one per 100 000). This would bring the UK into line with the European average for respiratory consultant provision. Figures from the Royal College of Physicians of London Consultant Census showed that in 1996 there were 426 consultants citing a specialist interest in thoracic medicine in England and Wales, representing 0.8 per 100 000, with considerable regional variation. By 2003 this figure had risen to 502 consultants, or 1 per 100 000. This figure includes consultants working in academic and research posts. Expansion in consultant numbers occurred in thoracic medicine at a similar rate to medical specialties in general (7% per annum) during the 1990s, but has fallen to 5.7% per annum since 2000 (figures from British Thoracic Society). Diagnostic facilities are used by a minority of patients and include lung function laboratories, radiology, blood gas analysis, endoscopy, allergy testing and microbiology.

Supporting services are used by only a minority of patients and include physiotherapy, specialist home care nurses, rehabilitation and domiciliary oxygen.

Service availability and utilisation

Table B.1 shows the proportion of all hospital discharges, hospital bed-days and general practice consultations attributable to various respiratory diseases, for both sexes and all ages combined. These estimates are based on reliable recent data (i.e. hospital admissions data for England 1998–99, cause-specific and overall mortality for England and Wales from the Office for National Statistics 1999, and the Fourth National Morbidity Survey in General Practice 1991–92), with rates calculated using the appropriate mid-year population estimates. These figures represent the workload directly attributable to respiratory illness. Such data are only indirectly related to the measures of incidence and prevalence discussed above. Coexisting respiratory disease is often an important but unquantified factor contributing to case fatality in other diseases (e.g. myocardial infarction), and may substantially prolong length of stay (e.g. after surgical operation).

Table B.2 translates these figures into the experience of a hypothetical 'average' district with a population of 500 000 people of similar age and sex distribution to that of England and Wales in 1999. In any specific district, these figures will be subject to a degree of modification to take account of geographical variations related to environmental, occupational, social and other factors. It must also be remembered that some respiratory conditions are undergoing marked trends in both their epidemiology and medical care.

Tables B.5–B.8 are provided as a resource for readers wishing to derive estimates of case load based on local population estimates and national age-specific rates of utilisation.

Figures B.3, B.5 and **B.7** show the hospital admissions, inpatient bed-days and general practice consultations due to lower respiratory conditions at different ages. **Figures B.4, B.6** and **B.8** show equivalent figures for all respiratory causes. Interpretation of these figures should take account of the different all-cause rates at different ages. The corresponding rates of service use (related to age-specific population denominators) are shown in **Tables B.5–8**.

Excluding lung cancer, lower respiratory conditions account for 7.8% of all FCEs (approximately 6% of hospital admissions) and about 85% of the admissions due to all respiratory diseases. The remaining respiratory admissions are mainly due to upper respiratory conditions (principally to ENT units) in children, and to lung cancer and non-specific symptoms in older adults. Most of the paediatric admissions for lower respiratory conditions are for acute respiratory illnesses and asthma, whereas in middle and old age, COPD and pneumonia assume greater importance.

The age-related pattern of bed occupancy is broadly similar, although the contribution of lower respiratory conditions to inpatient bed-days in the elderly is greater than their share of admissions. This reflects the tendency for old people to be admitted with pneumonia, but then retained in hospital because of multiple disease problems or inadequate social support. This problem is seasonal and contributes to the widespread shortage of acute medical beds in the winter months. Planning of inpatient services needs to allow for this seasonal phenomenon.

Lower respiratory conditions account for about 16% of all consultations in general practice, proportionately more in children and the elderly than in middle age. Much of this workload is attributable to asthma and acute lower respiratory infections. These graphs also emphasise the substantial contribution of upper respiratory conditions (which are excluded from this review) to workload in primary care (overall they account for 22% of consultations, and 50% of consultations in children under 5).

Lower respiratory infections in children

Available routine statistics and ad hoc surveys show that over 80% of lower respiratory tract infections in children are treated by general practitioners. Bronchitis, bronchiolitis and pneumonia (including influenza) account for 19% of all GP consultations in the 0–4 years age group and 9% of all GP consultations in the 5–15 years age group (**Table B.7**). Whooping cough accounted for a further 0.8% in 1981–82, and 0.1% in 1991–92, although this has almost certainly declined in more recent years.

General paediatric hospital services receive most of the inpatient referrals, either from the general practitioner or through casualty. These conditions have few implications for outpatient services. Of all hospital admissions at ages 0–14 years, acute bronchitis, bronchiolitis and pneumonia (including influenza) accounted for 2.3% of admissions in 1985, 3.35% in 1996, and 2.1% of FCEs in 1998–99. However, they also account for a lower proportion of occupied bed-days (1.79% in 1998–99; **Tables B.5** and **B.6**). The burden posed by whooping cough varies from year to year since the disease follows a four-year epidemic cycle. In 1985 whooping cough accounted for 0.3% of all paediatric hospital admissions and a similar proportion of occupied bed-days. By 1996, this had fallen to 0.06% of admissions and 0.03% of bed-days, and in 1998–99, 0.06% of FCEs but 0.07% of bed-days.

There are no norms for the provision of services for treating lower respiratory infections. Wide variations in service use may arise because of the epidemic or seasonal nature of lower respiratory infections.

Primary preventive health care includes reduction of passive exposure to tobacco smoke, promotion of breastfeeding, and vaccination against whooping cough and measles, for which GPs and community services are responsible.

Lower respiratory infection in adults

The health care sectors concerned with the management of influenza and community-acquired or nosocomial pneumonia in adults are based on the natural history of the disease. Ad hoc surveys show that 67–95% of adults with community-acquired pneumonia are treated at home by general practitioners.[10,121] Pneumonia and influenza account for 0.3% of all GP consultations in the 15+ age group (**Table B.7**), but diagnosis in the community is difficult.

In general practice, the diagnosis is mainly on the basis of clinical history and examination. A convalescent chest radiograph may be taken to confirm resolution of the infection, and in smokers to exclude underlying cancer of the lung. Slow responders to treatment may have further investigations, especially during epidemics of *Mycoplasma*, *Legionella* or influenza.

Between 5% and 33% of all patients with community-acquired pneumonia will be admitted to hospital. In 1998–99, pneumonia and influenza accounted for 0.43% of all FCEs in the 15–64 age group and 2.2% of FCEs in the over-65 age group (**Table B.5**). Because of the age-related pattern of bed occupancy discussed above, pneumonia and influenza account for 4.6% of occupied beds in the over-65s.

The main activities for preventing community-acquired pneumonia concern smoking reduction and the vaccination against influenza and *Streptococcus pneumoniae* of special risk groups.

Two-thirds of nosocomial pneumonias occur in patients who have undergone thoracic or upper abdominal surgical procedures or who have had intensive respiratory care such as assisted ventilation. It has been estimated that excess stay in hospital as a direct consequence of nosocomial pneumonia ranges from 7 to 9 days per affected patient. Twenty-five per cent of all extra days spent in hospital are due to nosocomial pneumonia, and 40% of the extra costs attributable to nosocomial infections are due to nosocomial pneumonia.[122] The direct cost of nosocomial pneumonia in the USA has been estimated as approximately $1.1 billion annually.

No norms exist for the provision of services for treating lower respiratory infections in adults. However, there are guidelines for the management of community-acquired pneumonia.[123] The clinical management of certain other conditions, such as stroke, and of post-operative patients is partly directed at preventing nosocomial pneumonia.

Asthma

The main data about the use of services for asthma are summarised in Table 5. Most are taken from routine sources tabulated in **Appendix B**, but Table 2 also includes data from some ad hoc surveys. Interpretation of routine utilisation data needs to take into account the way in which the data were collected, especially the process of diagnosis, which is subject to much variation and confusion in the case of asthma.

Table 5: Summary of data on service use for asthma, all expressed per hundred population per year.

	Percentage by age group			
	0–14	15–44	45–64	65+
Patients consulting GP	2.8	1.5	1.7	1.8
Consultations with GP	7.1	1.1	1.8	1.7
GP home visits	2			
Referral to outpatients	1		1–2	
Prescribed anti-asthmatic drugs	6	4	4	
A&E attendance (without admission)	1			
Hospital admissions (spells)	0.69	0.35	0.39	0.65
Hospital bed-days	1.17	1.16	1.84	4.87

Most data on the activity of GPs are from the Royal College of General Practitioners (RCGP) volunteer practices, which are scattered about the country,[124] but limited data are also available from ad hoc surveys of practice populations.[22,125,126] About 2% of the population consult their general practitioner annually for asthma, accounting for 1.4% of all consultations (**Table B.7**). The four National Morbidity Surveys in General Practice (1955–56, 1970–71, 1981–82 and 1991–92) show that there has been an increase in patients consulting between 1970–71 and 1980–81 and again in 1990–91, accompanied by a fall in consultations per patient consulting.[62] This is consistent with the postulated increase in the prevalence or severity of asthma, although an artefactual explanation associated with changing diagnostic fashions and health behaviour of patients cannot be excluded. Since 1993 there is some evidence that the number of new consultations for asthma episodes in primary care has fallen, making a change in diagnostic preference less likely as an explanation for the previous observed rises.[127]

No routine data about outpatient use by diagnosis are available. Data from the RCGP morbidity survey are unreliable because of the small numbers of referrals in the sample. Ad hoc surveys in children and adults indicate that about 10–15% of those consulting are referred.[115,125] Very little is known about rates of attendance at Accident and Emergency (A&E) departments for acute asthma because here again no data are collected routinely. Ad hoc surveys of children indicate that for every child admitted, one is seen in A&E and sent home.[58,125] Data from over 10 years ago suggested a trend away from GP domiciliary visits and towards A&E attendance,[58] while other evidence indicates that there is a marked increase in self-referral to hospital for acute asthma in children, the current level being about 40–50% of admissions.[63] The impact of NHS Direct on use of other services for asthma is as yet unclear.

Asthma admissions in children have increased dramatically since the early 1970s,[63–64] particularly for the pre-school age group, and asthma represents an important contributor to the workload in paediatrics, accounting for 3.5% of all FCEs at ages 0–14 years. The increase is not explained by diagnostic transfer or an increase in readmission rates. In adults, asthma accounts for about 2.3% of FCEs and 1.8% of bed-days (**Tables B.5** and **B.6**), and there has been only a modest rise in admissions in young adults and no trend in older adults.[64,128] Because of the large pool of asthma in the community, at least some of the increase could be explained by a shift towards hospital as the preferred place to treat acute asthma in children,[58] or alternatively, the increase could be explained by epidemiological factors.[57] Asthma admission rates vary across different regions by a factor of about two. Limited information from Scotland and from the Oxford Record Linkage Study indicates that social class does not have an important effect on admissions. There is no evidence concerning ethnic factors.

There are no norms for the provision of services for asthma. Evidence-based guidelines for hospitalisation in acute asthma are now available,[25,140] but it is not possible to construct a norm from this information. For the management of chronic asthma the evidence is even less clear. The tools of diagnosis, investigation and treatment are to a large extent available to general practitioners and hospital doctors alike. However, it is not clear where the general balance between primary and secondary care, and within each setting the balance between generalist and specialist care, should lie, nor is it clear which is the most suitable method of managing recall for ongoing care in each setting. Therefore it is not possible to construct norms for asthma service provision. Patients with severe acute asthma admitted to hospital should be under the care of a specialist in respiratory medicine or respiratory paediatrics.

Primary prevention

Asthma probably results from an interaction between genetically susceptible individuals and environmental factors, and it is thought that the wide geographical variations which exist are explained by environmental factors. Little is known about the cause of asthma itself.[127] However, interventions to prevent whooping cough and smoking in pregnancy may reduce incidence of childhood and later-onset asthma.[54] Risk factors for earlier onset in childhood include a family history of atopy, increased levels of allergic antibodies, artificial feeding, exposure to tobacco smoke and higher exposure to house dust mites.

A large number of precipitating factors have been identified, including respiratory infections, emotional upset, exercise, allergens and irritant atmospheres. The relative public health importance of these is poorly understood. Factors in the indoor environment have received most attention, particularly allergens of animal origin (house dust mites, pets),[130,131] moulds[113] and passive smoking.[132,133] Standards for indoor levels of house dust mite have been proposed,[134] although there is little evidence that methods currently available have any significant impact on either house dust mite levels or asthma symptoms.[167,168] No standard for tobacco smoke exists, and the approach has been to discourage it altogether. Young adults who have ever had asthma should not smoke, since this increases risk of relapse in later adulthood[54] and increases the risk of COPD. Breastfeeding may delay onset of wheezing in at-risk infants,[72] and is promoted for this and many other reasons. Specific problems arise in the workplace where there may be exposure to allergens and other asthmogenic substances not encountered elsewhere.

Control of precipitating factors in the outdoor environment is even less developed. Rarely a man-made source of aero-allergen exposure can be identified and controlled. There is recent interest in the role of air pollution in aetiology of and exacerbation of existing asthma, especially levels of ozone, although evidence that this is important in the UK is lacking.[135]

Where it is possible to control exposure to allergens or irritants, one approach may be to concentrate on individuals known to be at risk because they are atopic or of atopic parentage.

Overall, there is very little preventive care for asthma and the main activity is probably the control of active and passive smoking and limitation of exposure to known occupational precipitants. Other agencies are responsible for housing and domestic environment, air pollution and occupational hazards.

Secondary prevention

Undiagnosed asthma may be detected by screening for symptoms suggestive of asthma with a simple questionnaire. It has been suggested that this could be done through schools or by surveys of practice populations. Although asthma may be identified at a pre-symptomatic stage by tests of bronchial hyper-reactivity, no screening test of sufficient sensitivity or specificity exists and if it did there would be other factors to consider before considering a screening programme. The American Thoracic Society does not recommend screening.[136]

Diagnosis and treatment

The diagnosis and treatment of asthma have been the subject of recent consensus statements and other reviews. Diagnosis is usually based on clinical history and examination, but may be supplemented by lung function tests, chest X-ray and therapeutic trial where other conditions (primarily COPD) are considered. Overlap with COPD in older subjects has led many clinicians to ensure that any reversible component of airways obstruction is identified and treated using bronchodilating and anti-inflammatory drugs. Most diagnosis and treatment comes within the realm of the general practitioner, although spirometry, which is not universally available in primary care, is required for diagnosis and assessment of COPD and its differentiation from asthma.

Individuals with asthma carry a long-term susceptibility to the disease, and the chronic inflammation now believed to be the basis of this susceptibility may be present even when the patient is symptom-free. The development of the inflammatory concept has led to an increasing emphasis on the use of anti-inflammatory rather than anti-spasmodic drugs, and on regular rather than ad hoc regimes of care.

The aims of treatment are mixed:

- to reduce exposure to precipitating factors (*see* above)
- to reduce or abolish disability
- to reduce or abolish symptoms
- to reduce the incidence of acute severe attacks
- to reduce the risk of death in an attack
- to achieve a target level of lung function
- to improve long-term prognosis.

The clinical care of asthma is a regular topic in medical journals directed at a general medical readership. There have recently appeared consensus statements which provide guidelines on the clinical management of asthma in adults[16,137] and children.[138] The original consensus groups were initially composed mainly of respiratory specialists. These were recently updated for both adults and children, have become more evidence based in approach and have incorporated guidance for treatment in primary care.[25,139,140]

There is a potential conflict between the aims of the doctors and those of their patients. This applies for example to the question of how intensively acute attacks should be treated and the lengths to which regular treatment should go in order to prevent attacks. Confidential enquiries have demonstrated that some deaths occur quickly, in patients who do not appear to be particularly ill.[141–143] It may be that these patients had unrecognised severe asthma (a well-demonstrated entity) or that the attack was indeed very quick and severe. Some patients exhibit what is termed 'brittleness' and may deteriorate suddenly. Although doctors may wish to treat each attack as if it were potentially fatal, this is probably not an attitude that can be sustained by patients on a day-to-day basis. Similarly, patients with chronic symptoms may prefer to live with a certain level of symptoms rather than have the extra burden of treatment. They may prefer to 'normalise' their illness rather than consider themselves to be chronically ill. This may explain why some severely affected patients delay treatment or seeking medical attention.[144] Thus the expectations and objectives of carers may conflict with those of the patient. In contrast, parents may be so concerned about their or their child's asthma as to want treatment or hospitalisation that is not needed on medical grounds.[145]

Assessment will determine the type, level and place of treatment. Clear guidelines are available with recommendations for treatment of childhood asthma, acute asthma attacks and chronic treatment and monitoring of asthma.[16,140,13] These include clear guidelines for specialist referral (to a respiratory physician or respiratory paediatrician) for clarification of diagnosis or for assessment of treatment.[140]

Chronic asthma

Despite its high prevalence, chronic asthma is still under-diagnosed. Diagnosis and investigation of chronic asthma should include a high level of clinical suspicion among any adult or child presenting with wheeze, a full clinical and occupational history, measurements of lung function that should include spirometry and serial measurements of peak expiratory flow rate where required, challenge with methocholine, histamine or exercise, and might also include non-invasive markers of airway inflammation, and measurement of allergic status. Facilities to undertake these investigations are not universally available in primary care, and their correct application requires appropriate training of the health professional responsible. There are guidelines available for the appropriate provision of spirometry services.[146]

Evidence-based guidelines recommend a stepped approach to treatment that is tailored to the severity of asthma symptoms and patient response at each stage.[25,140] Guidelines differ slightly for adults and children, and treatments are set out in Table 10 (see p. 314). The aim is to step up therapy until optimum asthma control is obtained, and attempt to step down once asthma is controlled to keep the patient on the minimum level of effective therapy. A minority of patients with severe asthma under specialist care will require more intensive therapy, including the use of oral steroid-sparing agents.

A wide variety of devices are available for the delivery of inhaled therapies, including metered-dose aerosol inhalers, dry powder inhalers, spacer devices and nebulisers. Current guidelines[140] recommend a pressurised metered-dose inhaler with a spacer, but the choice of device also needs to be based on patient preference and ability to use the device correctly.

Non-drug treatment that has been tried in asthma includes acupuncture, homeopathy, ayurvedic medicine, herbal medicine, ionisers, osteopathy and chiropractic, and Buteyko. There is no good evidence for the effectiveness of these alternatives. Treatment of allergic rhinitis, which coexists in many individuals with asthma, may also improve asthma symptoms.

Effective monitoring of peak expiratory flow combined with self-management plans is a vital element of management of asthma. The principles of care are becoming more proactive, with increased use of treatment plans in which procedures for the patient to make decisions about prescribed treatment and when to obtain medical assistance are agreed. There is increased emphasis on self-management and, to assist this, various schemes for self-monitoring have been devised. These may take the form of a card carried by the patient (e.g. National Asthma Campaign adult asthma card). Evidence-based and consensus guidelines for self-management are available,[16,25,140] and devices for the self-monitoring of lung function are available on prescription.

Acute episodes of asthma

Acute episodes of asthma do not all require hospitalisation, and many can be managed in the community by following self-management plans tailored to the patient. The severity of an asthma attack can be assessed by symptoms (breathlessness, ability to talk, level of consciousness, respiratory rate, use of accessory muscles, wheeze, pulse and pulsus paradoxus), peak expiratory flow rate, blood gases and oxygen saturation. Clear guidelines are available on when patients should contact a clinician or self-refer to hospital, and on investigation, treatment and admission to hospital and intensive care during an acute attack.[25,140] However, it is important to note that because the course of acute asthma is unpredictable, assessment of severity incorporates the doctor's perception of the risk of deterioration and this leads inevitably to a degree of variation in the way that the same patient would be managed by different doctors.[147,148] Individual patients do not always fit into guideline categories, and clinical assessment remains an important variable in treatment.

The mainstay of treatment of acute episodes includes frequent or continuously administered inhaled or nebulised β_2-agonists, oral glucocorticoids and oxygen. To this may be added inhaled anticholinergics, intravenous methylxanthines, intravenous magnesium, parenteral β_2-agonists and assisted ventilation. Peak flow measurement forms the basis of monitoring and clinical treatment decisions.

Education

Self-care is an indispensable aspect of the domiciliary care of asthma. Education aims to improve self-care by educating the patient about their illness and its medical treatment, by training the patient to perform necessary techniques (e.g. using inhaler) properly, and by helping them monitor the illness and make appropriate decisions about adjusting treatment and seeking assistance.

Dynamics and organisation of care

The majority of care for chronic asthma and for non-life-threatening attacks of acute asthma takes place in the community setting and primary care.

Acute asthma

Most treatments for non-life-threatening attacks of acute asthma are available in the domiciliary setting, but more severe acute cases tend to be referred or self-refer to hospital. As mentioned above, the assessment of severity is influenced by the perception of risk of deterioration. Figure 12 (*see* overleaf) shows the possible pathways for a child with an acute asthma attack. One feature of acute asthma is that a sizeable proportion self-refer, including calling an ambulance. Guidelines suggest thresholds at which self-referral should occur, based upon written self-management plans and/or advice on what to do if symptoms of an attack occur.[25,140] In some areas there is a formal self-admission policy.[149] Guidelines also suggest pathways and decision points for referral to clinicians, direct self-referral to hospital, and routes of management once in hospital, including admission to intensive-care units.[25,140]

Chronic asthma

For chronic asthma, the majority of care takes place in the community. In recent years there have been marginal shifts in management of asthma from secondary to primary care, but within each setting there has been a marginal shift towards the management of asthma by respiratory physicians (secondary care) and general practitioners with a special clinical interest (primary care), together with the use of specialist asthma nurses (in both primary and secondary care). Increasing numbers of general practices offer asthma clinics, and the majority of hospitals offer special respiratory clinics for adults, and some offer special paediatric respiratory clinics. Adolescents with asthma may come under the care of their general practitioners, a paediatrician or respiratory physician depending on local policy.

Although the above pattern of marginal shifts from secondary to primary care and, within each setting, from general to specialist care is established, the general balance between primary and secondary care, and general and specialist care within each setting is still variable, and the correct balance is not yet known. In

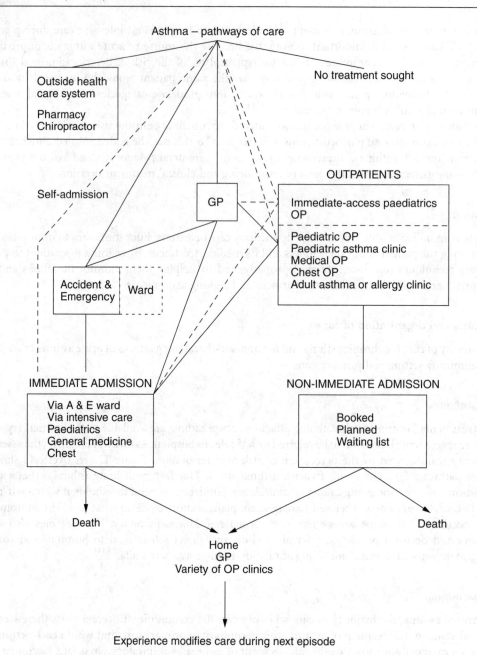

Figure 12: Possible pathways of care for asthma in the UK. Solid lines represent departures from the basic NHS referral system. OP, outpatients.

particular we do not know which patients benefit most from regular specialist review. Shared care between primary and secondary care, led in either the primary or secondary care setting, is also established in some areas, although there are several different models for this.[286] The best method of arranging ongoing review for those with chronic asthma in either primary or secondary care is also unclear, and a high proportion of patients do not want practice-initiated review.[150]

Emergency care

Because this may be needed urgently, other arrangements are required. One is the self-admission or open-access policy based upon written advice on what to do when symptoms occur that has been referred to above. The other is the need for a rapid response by ambulances: recently crews have been trained in the emergency treatment of asthma.

Chronic obstructive pulmonary (airways) disease

Among people of all ages, about 1.4% consult their general practitioner each year for chronic bronchitis, emphysema and obstructive airways disease (**Table B.7**). The proportion is greatest among the elderly (4.5%) and a further 15% of the over-65 age group consult with acute or unspecified bronchitis which probably includes many cases of chronic disease. Recurrent consultations are common, with an average of three per year among elderly patients consulting for bronchitis, emphysema or COPD. Consultation rates (spells) and patient consultation rates (people) are much higher among males than females.

This condition accounts for about 2% of all FCEs and a somewhat greater proportion (3.2%) of all inpatient bed-days (**Table B.5** and **Table B.6**). Most admissions are in those aged 65 or more, where it accounts for 5% of FCEs and bed-days. The increase in hospitalisation for 'chronic airways obstruction' has been balanced by a decline in hospitalisation for 'chronic bronchitis'.

As for asthma, the pyramid of care has a broad base in the community and sharp apex in the hospital. This means that small shifts in referral practice will have relatively greater effects on hospital use.

There are no norms for the provision of services for COPD. British Thoracic Society guidelines provide indications as to when referral for hospital care might be appropriate in the management of ongoing care and acute exacerbations.[330] As for asthma, the tools of diagnosis, investigation and treatment are to a large extent available to general practitioners and hospital doctors alike and referral habits vary greatly.

The main aetiological factor in COPD is smoking, and its control is the most important preventive activity. An effective smoking prevention programme would therefore dramatically reduce the associated morbidity and mortality. In addition, smoking cessation remains the only proven means of preventing the deterioration of lung function in individuals with the disease.[151] Other agencies are responsible for housing and domestic environment, air pollution and occupational exposures.

Vaccination against influenza and/or pneumococcal disease and early treatment with antibiotics are employed in a variable fashion to prevent or reduce the impact of these diseases on patients with COPD.

Diagnosis is made on clinical history and is confirmed by pulmonary function tests (peak expiratory flow rate, forced expiratory flow rate in one second – FEV_1). Access to testing equipment in primary care and training in its use is not universal. A diagnosis of COPD implies that airflow obstruction is present; the significance of symptoms (typically cough and phlegm) with no deterioration in lung function is unclear. Differential diagnosis from asthma can present a problem.[23] A chest X-ray may be helpful in excluding other diseases, but will only be abnormal in severe forms of the disease (associated emphysema). Many clinicians attempt to ensure that any potentially reversible airways obstruction is identified and treated using bronchodilating and anti-inflammatory treatments.

COPD is an incurable disease, although smoking cessation can alter the prognosis for an individual. The natural history involves a gradual deterioration of lung function leading to shortness of breath, increasing exercise intolerance and finally heart failure and death. The speed of deterioration is variable; in some patients it can be rapid. The wide spectrum of disease severity means that general practitioners manage most patients, with a minority (about 10%) being referred to hospital.[124,126] Assessment of the severity of both chronic and acute disease using tests of lung function is an important aspect of management.

Management in most cases involves the following.

- Smoking advice. Smoking cessation can stop the rate of deterioration, but lung function will not improve.[152]
- The treatment of acute exacerbations, usually acute respiratory tract infections, with antibiotics.
- Symptomatic treatment with bronchodilator drugs and/or steroids is often attempted to maximise any airways reversibility. These can be administered in tablet form or inhaled using either simple devices or more sophisticated nebulisers.
- In the most severe forms of the disease, oxygen can be used. This can be provided in various ways and can be given intermittently or on a long-term basis. However, the use of domiciliary oxygen therapy for end-stage chronic respiratory failure is variable.

Historically, treatment has been on a demand basis but recently there has been a move towards regular surveillance and early intervention in acute exacerbations. There are various ways that this can be achieved, e.g. respiratory nurses, general practitioner clinics and outpatient departments. There has been an increase in the use of respiratory health workers for chronic lung disease (mainly COPD, but also chronic asthma). Their purpose is to provide continuity, support and education. In general practice, there has been a growth of clinics for asthma, usually run by a practice nurse with additional training. Active physical training and rehabilitation of patients has been recommended by some as it may improve exercise tolerance.[153]

Tuberculosis

The main causes of the reduction in morbidity and mortality due to tuberculosis were improvements in the social and nutritional status of the general population and the introduction of effective drug therapy.

In the past, prevention and treatment have been carried out through the school BCG immunisation programme, the mass chest X-ray service (to identify infected individuals), and a national network of chest clinics with the responsibility for treating cases and undertaking contact tracing. As the number of cases has diminished the cost–benefit of these programmes has changed and the pattern of management has been modified. Screening of new immigrants is still undertaken by port authorities in conjunction with departments of public health medicine and chest clinics, and is still recommended.[154] Contact tracing continues and individuals are either treated if found to be infected, given prophylactic drugs if at high risk, or monitored.

There is no longer a mass-screening programme and the school immunisation programme has been phased out in some areas.[155,156] However, because of the uncertainty surrounding the impact of HIV infection on TB in this country, and the cessation of fall in incidence of TB, continuation of the schools BCG immunisation programme was recommended until 1995–96,[157] and is still currently recommended in guidelines from the Department of Health.[154] BCG vaccination is also currently recommended for high-risk groups, including immigrants from countries where TB is common, and infants born into high-risk families.[158]

Guidelines for the control and prevention of tuberculosis in the UK have been published.[154,159] The provision of designated TB services has ensured that the decline in morbidity and mortality initiated by public health measures has continued. However, there remain sporadic outbreaks in schools and new cases in ethnic minority groups and susceptible people (including homeless individuals).

Treatment is mainly with drugs for varying periods of time (6–12 months). There have been various recommendations published by the British Thoracic Society,[158–161] the World Health Organization[162] and other agencies.[163] Despite these guidelines there is evidence that prescribing habits still vary.[164]

Unlike other respiratory infections, tuberculosis has predominantly been managed at special outpatient clinics equipped with facilities for contact tracing. However, in many areas the chest clinic as originally set up has disappeared and its function is shared between respiratory physicians and departments of public health. Patterns of services vary depending on the prevalence of disease in the community (ethnic minority groups) and local availability of respiratory physicians and public health doctors.

Cystic fibrosis

Cystic fibrosis is a chronic condition that is managed across health care sectors. There is evidence that outcome is improved if care is undertaken by a hospital specialist who has a major specialist interest in the condition. However, care can be shared with a local hospital physician and general practitioner, using a variety of different models. The majority of care takes place on an outpatient basis, including intravenous antibiotic treatment, nebulised antibiotics and mucolytics, self-administered physiotherapy, nutritional management and pancreatic enzyme supplementation. Outpatient care is usually undertaken by specialist multi-disciplinary teams, including physicians or paediatricians, specialist nurses, physiotherapists, dietitians and social workers. Handover of adolescent patients to adult specialists is recommended. All patients with cystic fibrosis require lifelong specialist medical supervision and treatment. Severely affected patients may require oxygen and non-invasive ventilatory support. Heart–lung or double-lung transplantation is performed on a few selected patients with end-stage lung disease.

Diagnosis may be made on the basis of symptoms or as part of a local neonatal screening programme, using a combination of sweat electrolyte concentrations and genetic typing.

Overall, cystic fibrosis contributes a very small proportion of GP consultations, hospital admissions and hospital bed-days (under 1%). The majority of care takes place in hospital outpatients.

Screening

Two forms of screening are possible for cystic fibrosis. The first detects carriers of the defective gene before birth of an affected child. The second is the screening of newborn babies to detect cystic fibrosis early. This would permit early treatment, which should improve clinical prognosis for the affected child, and may also prevent the birth of a second affected child into a family before the first is diagnosed.

Genetic screening is possible using a simple test, taking cells from a mouthwash and screening these for the six most commonly occurring alleles in the UK population, about 85% of all abnormal alleles. It can be offered in several different ways. In the antenatal clinic it can be offered either sequentially (screen mother first and father if mother is positive) or as a couple (couple is either positive or negative, but individual results are not given). It can also be offered to schoolchildren or through general practice. Finally, it can be offered to relatives of affected patients, known as 'cascade' screening.

The uptake varies according to the model used. In the antenatal model, the test has the potential to detect 70% of cases of cystic fibrosis, and the uptake is around 70%, thus reducing its potential to prevent cystic fibrosis to around 50% of cases, assuming all affected pregnancies are terminated.

Population carrier screening programs are not universally available in the UK, and methods vary according to region.

Neonatal screening is possible using the Guthrie blood spot that is used to detect other inborn errors of metabolism such as phenylketonuria and congenital hypothyroidism. This test is cheap, and there appear to be short-term benefits to babies and young children with cystic fibrosis, but there is still controversy as to whether long-term prognosis is improved.

Treatment

The majority of care for patients with cystic fibrosis takes place as outpatients, with inpatient care reserved for those with complicated disease, severe disease, or lacking social support to undertake treatment at home. The majority of patients with cystic fibrosis are able to attend school and work full-time. Adults have 80% the rate of employment of normal adults, with 50% able to work, and a further 25% being in full-time education.

In a study for the Clinical Standards Advisory Group,[165] patients attended outpatients an average of 4.6 times a year, with a range of 0.5 to 8.1 times per year (*see* Table 6). Admission rates ranged from 0.3 to 2.0 per patient per year. However, in a survey of adults with cystic fibrosis, 40% had no hospital admissions and 45% no courses of home intravenous antibiotics in the previous year.[166] Among adults, the mean number of admissions was 1.7, the mean number of home intravenous antibiotic courses was also 1.7, and the mean number of ward visits was 2.7 per patient per year. There was a marked relationship to severity of disease, with patients in the more severe group requiring a mean of five admissions per year.

Where dedicated beds were available, the provision ranged from 1.7 to 7.7 per 100 patients, with a mean of 3.8, but the majority of clinics admit patients to general medical or paediatric beds. The level recommended by the British Paediatric Association is 6 to 8 beds per 100 patients.

Table 6: Activity rates per 100 patients per year for cystic fibrosis in specialist clinics.[165]

| Activity | Rate per 100 patients per year | | |
	Mean	Range	*n*
New referrals	10	2–19	13
Follow-up appointments	465	50–813	10
Admissions	96	36–204	9

Organisation of care

It has been recommended by the British Paediatric Association, the British Thoracic Society and the Clinical Standards Advisory Group (CSAG) that patients with cystic fibrosis (both paediatric and adult) should have access to specialist centres for their treatment. The Clinical Standards Advisory Group defined various levels of care (*see* Table 7). Level I was the national specialist centre, level II a regional specialist centre, level III a local specialist centre and level IV a local cystic fibrosis clinic or general hospital.

Table 7: Staffing levels of cystic fibrosis centres in relation to BPA recommendations, expressed as number of sessions (half days) per 50 patients attending the clinic. The latter denominator includes those attending for shared care.

Staff type	Mean	Maximum	Minimum	Recommended	Units with adequate staff
Consultant sessions	1.55	5.5	0	3–4	3
Junior medical sessions	1.16	5.9	0	5	1
Other medical sessions	0.42	3.2	0	2	2
Physiotherapist sessions	3.13	11.6	0	20	0
Dietitian sessions	1.20	4.4	0	2–3	1
Social worker sessions	0.81	4.4	0	3	3
Nurse specialist sessions	6.16	20.8	0	10	4
Secretarial sessions	0.87	9.4	0	2	4
Other sessions	0.36	3.2	0	–	–

Source: Walters and Jordan.[165]

Definitions of specialisation depended largely on the number of patients cared for, with a level III centre requiring a minimum of 40 to 50 patients.[167]

The Cystic Fibrosis Trust, British Paediatric Association and British Thoracic Society produced joint clinical guidelines for the care of patients with cystic fibrosis.[168] These have recently been updated by the Cystic Fibrosis Trust into a document on standards of clinical care for patients with cystic fibrosis.[169] These embrace the concept of a specialist centre, staffed by a multi-disciplinary team skilled in dealing with cystic fibrosis patients and their families. They lay down consensus standards for staffing and facilities at such centres, although few existing centres currently meet the required standards.

The Clinical Standards Advisory Group reviewed access and availability of specialist services for patients with cystic fibrosis in 1992[167] and again in 1995.[165] In the latter report, access was measured both by interviews with clinicians and purchasers and also by surveys of patients and parents of children with cystic fibrosis. It was noted that although access to specialist care had improved, it was still not universal and also varied between regions (*see* Figure 13).

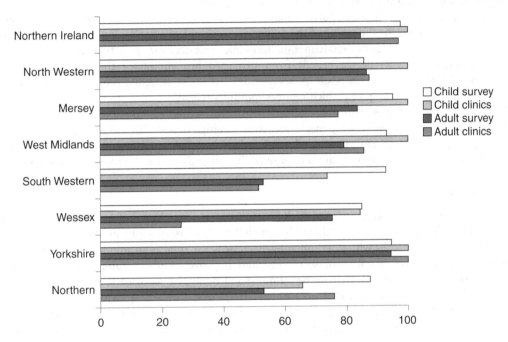

Figure 13: Proportion of patients attending specialist clinics by region comparing estimates made by clinic directors and estimates made by patients themselves through surveys.
Source: Walters and Jordan.[165] (*Note*: not all regions were studied in this survey.)

The concept of shared care was also introduced in the CSAG reports. In this instance, shared care means care shared between a specialist centre and a local hospital, rather than a hospital and general practitioner. This has been widely practised as a method of improving convenience for patients, whilst at the same time permitting specialist input into care, but as yet it has not been very well evaluated. It may take the form of alternating visits between local and specialist clinics, annual appraisals by a specialist clinic, peripatetic or visiting clinics from specialists to local hospitals, or other less formal types of arrangement.

The Cystic Fibrosis Trust is in the process of developing methods to accredit specialist clinical services for patients with cystic fibrosis based upon their standards document.

Drug therapy

The mainstay of treatment for cystic fibrosis is aggressive early therapy with antibiotics to reduce the impact of recurrent infective exacerbations on the respiratory tract. Antibiotics may be given orally for treatment of some organisms. However, respiratory infection frequently progresses from organisms sensitive to oral antibiotics (*Haemophilus influenzae*, *Staphylococcus aureus*, some strains of *Pseudomonas aeruginosa*) to organisms that require intravenous antibiotics (most strains of *Pseudomonas aeruginosa*, *Burkholderia cepacia*). A high proportion of adult patients are colonised by organisms resistant to several antibiotics. This has important implications for infection control in hospital, since outbreaks of infection due to both *Burkholderia cepacia* and *Pseudomonas aerginosa* have been attributed to contact between patients in hospital and social settings. The Cystic Fibrosis Trust has produced guidelines on cross-infection with *Pseudomonas aeruginosa*,[170] and has produced guidelines for *Burkholderia cepacia*,[171] suggesting that patients should be segregated in wards and outpatient clinics.

Antibiotics need to be given in high doses for relatively long periods of time to penetrate the sputum and have effect, and treatment does not often eradicate the organism.

A large proportion of patients or parents may be trained to give their own intravenous antibiotic treatment at home, either for the whole of the course, or to complete a course initiated in hospital. The Cystic Fibrosis Trust has produced guidelines on antibiotic treatment for cystic fibrosis.[172]

A proportion of patients derive benefit from nebulised bronchodilator therapy given prior to physiotherapy to prevent bronchospasm. A proportion also derive benefit from recombinant human deoxyribonuclease (Dornase alpha), which reduces sputum viscosity.

All patients with cystic fibrosis who are pancreatic insufficient require treatment with pancreatic enzyme supplements given prior to and during meals, sometimes in high doses, with the goal of normalising fat absorption and producing normal growth and weight gain. Fat-soluble vitamin supplements are required, notably vitamins A, D and E. Some patients require additional oral or enteral feeding to maintain weight.

Non-drug therapy

Physiotherapy is essential to clear infected sticky secretions from the chest and maintain lung function. This is usually performed by the patient themselves, with the help of parents for younger children. A variety of devices are available to assist with physiotherapy. Exercise is also used as an adjunct to physiotherapy to maintain fitness, increase clearance of secretions, and improve well-being and functional capacity. Nutritional supplementation, which may be administered orally, by nasogastric tube or gastrostomy, may be required for some patients. Patients with end-stage lung disease may require oxygen, and non-invasive ventilation at home or in hospital may be used by patients awaiting lung transplantation. The Cystic Fibrosis Trust has produced guidelines for physiotherapy and nutritional management in cystic fibrosis.[173,174]

Patients who develop severe end-stage lung disease may benefit from lung transplantation (single lung, double lung or heart–lung). Approximately 5% of patients develop liver failure, and this may require liver transplantation. The number of patients who can benefit from transplantation is limited by the supply of donor organs. In 1990–92, 40 cystic fibrosis patients per year had lung or heart–lung transplants.

Health care resource groups

The health care resource groups (HRGs) of relevance to lower respiratory disease are described in **Appendix A**.

The total number of FCEs and bed-days according to HRG, together with the percentage of all grouped episodes in 1995–96, are shown in **Table B.9**. It should be noted that the HRG data were provided from a central resource for this project. When compared to data on FCEs for respiratory diagnoses collected during the same period, only a fraction of respiratory episodes have been coded to HRGs. Data are also missing on some key respiratory HRGs, including cystic fibrosis (D17), some tuberculosis (D19), pulmonary embolus (D9 to 11), respiratory neoplasms (D25) and sleep-disordered breathing (D31). The reason for the incomplete nature of the data provided is not known. Data were not provided according to age group, so further analysis is not possible. No data were available on costs for HRGs.

6 Effectiveness of services

In this section, the nature and quality of evidence relating to the effectiveness of particular interventions is indicated in parentheses and bold type using the agreed criteria (*see* Introductory chapter on strength of the recommendation [A–D] and quality of evidence [I–IV]).

Prevention

Smoking (AII-2)

There is ample observational but sparse experimental evidence indicating that a reduction in active and passive smoking would reduce the incidence, prevalence and severity of a wide range of respiratory diseases, including infections and obstructive airways diseases, across the whole age range. Because about a third of the population smokes, there is scope for major improvement. Benefits would be both short and long term and include reductions in lung cancer and non-respiratory diseases. Smoking control strategies can operate at national and local levels by reducing uptake as well as encouraging cessation (BI). The most effective strategies seem to be the raising of price, increasing no-smoking areas, and provision of advice and nicotine chewing gum by general practitioners.[175] In quality-adjusted life-year (QALY) terms, advice by the general practitioner to a patient to stop smoking is probably one of the most cost-effective interventions available to the NHS.[176]

Passive exposure to tobacco smoke is associated with bronchitis and bronchiolitis in children under 5 (especially where the mother smokes), and evidence from China, where few mothers smoke, suggests a postnatal effect of paternal smoking. Damage from smoking may begin before birth,[177] and antenatal and postnatal services have an opportunity to influence smoking behaviour, although experimental evidence is not available to confirm whether this reduces subsequent LRTI in the offspring.

Passive exposure to tobacco smoke is also associated with asthma symptoms in children aged 2 to 15, and there is good observational evidence to suggest that reduction in environmental tobacco smoke (ETS) would be beneficial, and to pursue this without formal trial[178] (AII-2). Reducing exposure of children to environmental tobacco smoke is likely to produce health gain by reducing both acute and chronic respiratory disease (BII-2).

In patients with existing COPD, stopping smoking is the most effective treatment (AI). A number of evaluative studies have assessed the respective effectiveness of chest physicians, smoking clinics and nurse counsellors in smoking control, but no single method offers a substantial advantage over the others.

Other inhaled hazards (B-III)

In the outdoor environment, it is not known whether a reduction in existing levels of air pollution from fossil fuel combustion would reduce the incidence and burden of respiratory disease, including asthma, to any extent, and there is considerable uncertainty about the cost-effectiveness of this approach. Aero-allergens implicated in asthma reflect patterns of agriculture, local authority planting policies, and fashions in gardening, but it is not known to what extent changes would be beneficial.

The beneficial effect of reduction of hazards in the workplace has been demonstrated (AII).

In the indoor environment, evidence of improvement in asthma after removal from damp, mouldy premises is anecdotal. The targeting of individuals with asthma or those known to be at risk of developing asthma because of the existence of other atopic diseases, or a family history of atopy, with strategies to lower the levels of exposure to known important precipitants over which there is some control has been suggested to reduce the burden of asthma. In the home, the main agents to be reduced are allergens (house dust mites, pets, moulds) and irritants (tobacco smoke).

Trials have shown that house dust mites can be controlled by various procedures, but unless radical changes can be made to the household arrangements and unrelenting control measures instituted, there is recolonisation.[179] Systematic reviews have shown that there is no evidence that currently available methods of house dust mite control have any effect on asthma (DI).[180,181] The effect of removing objects or animals to which an individual is sensitive is likely to be beneficial (BIII), but may be difficult in practice. There is no evidence that maternal antigen avoidance during pregnancy reduces atopic disease in offspring, and it may have important detrimental effects on maternal or fetal nutrition (DI).[182]

Breastfeeding (BII-2)

Observational evidence indicates that this may reduce the incidence of lower respiratory infections and, in atopic families, delay the onset of wheezing illness. Community and other perinatal services may play a role in promoting and supporting breastfeeding.

Immunisation

Whooping cough

The efficacy of whooping cough (pertussis) vaccination has been demonstrated by randomised controlled trials (AI). The MRC field trials found the vaccine to be effective in reducing primary infection and dissemination of infection to secondary cases. A decline in uptake in the mid-1970s was accompanied by a return of epidemic pertussis in the UK (whereas in the USA, where vaccine uptake was maintained, notification rates remained low). Uptake has been rising throughout the 1980s and is now at record levels (over 75% among 2-year-olds nationwide).[183] The proportion immunised rose further during the 1990s (see Figure 2).

Concern has been focused on neurological side-effects, particularly acute encephalopathy, the risk of which is increased threefold after pertussis vaccination.[184] However, the overall numbers of deaths, hospital admissions and severe neurological illnesses in the population would be reduced by increasing pertussis vaccine uptake.[185] Thus, at a public health level, the risk of adverse reactions to whooping cough vaccine is low compared with the benefits – although individual families may not come to the same conclusion.

Measles

The efficacy of measles vaccination has been demonstrated by randomised controlled trials (AI). Lower respiratory illnesses may be due to secondary infection following measles, particularly in the first year of life. Measles vaccine is given in the UK as part of the measles, mumps and rubella vaccine at 13 months and again at 3–5 years. This schedule may have some indirect impact through a reduction in incidence, particularly if high levels of uptake can be achieved. Newer vaccines which promote effective immunity when used at six months of life may further reduce this problem, although they have so far only been evaluated in developing countries.[186]

Pneumococci

The efficacy of pneumococcal vaccines has been established in younger age groups in other, mainly developing countries. Such evidence is not available specifically for the elderly, the main group of concern in the UK. The effectiveness of pneumococcal vaccination has been evaluated by systematic review and found to be high in healthy low-risk individuals, but lower in high-risk individuals (BI).[187] An evaluation of current recommendations by case–control study showed the vaccine to be effective in splenectomised patients and those with chronic disease (BII-2),[188] but a randomised controlled trial has shown it to be ineffective in patients over 50 with previous community-acquired pneumonia (DI).[189] Thus the prevention of pneumonia by the use of pneumococcal vaccine remains controversial. American guidelines from the Communicable Diseases Centre[190] recommend its use for:

- immunocompromised adults at increased risk of pneumococcal disease
- adults with asymptomatic or symptomatic HIV infection
- immunocompetent adults who are at increased risk of pneumococcal disease because of chronic illness (AIII).

In the UK, the vaccine is recommended for use in all people over two years of age in whom pneumococcal infection will be either more common or serious (BI).[191] The main controversy concerns the use of pneumococcal vaccine in immunocompetent adults who are at increased risk of pneumococcal disease.

Randomised clinical trials carried out in 1976–77 established the efficacy of pneumococcal vaccination in South African gold miners.[192,193] Studies in Papua New Guinea[194] and on hyposplenic patients in the USA[195] also showed significant reductions in the occurrence of pneumonia in immunised groups. Based on the results of these earlier trials, a licence was granted in the USA for pneumococcal vaccine for use in patients at risk for serious pneumococcal infections (the elderly, patients with chronic illness and the immunocompromised).

Reports of vaccine failure in some targeted populations in the USA led to uncertainty about the vaccine's efficacy.[196–198] However, these studies have been criticised because they have included too few patients and because of other methodological problems.[199] Two carefully conducted case–control studies have shown polyvalent pneumococcal vaccine to have an aggregate efficacy of between 60% and 70% in preventing pneumococcal bacteraemia in the elderly,[198,200] and a very large case–control study[201] established the efficacy of pneumococcal vaccination in preventing pneumonia in patients admitted to hospital.

It is probably because of doubts concerning the efficacy of pneumococcal vaccine and the conflicting evidence from the different trials that only about 10% of the target population in the USA have been immunised.[202] It is also likely that clinicians underestimate the impact of pneumococcal disease because establishing a definitive diagnosis in non-bacteraemic patients is often not possible. In the UK, where there are no recommendations concerning the use of vaccine, use of this vaccine is negligible.

Because of the low uptake of pneumococcal vaccination in the UK, several authors have argued for a different approach. Evidence from the Oxford Record Linkage Study has shown that many patients hospitalised for, or dying from, pneumonia have been discharged from a hospital within the previous five years.[203,204] This suggests that there may be an epidemiological rationale for immunising all patients over a certain age who are admitted to hospital for any reason.

The methodology of the Oxford study was used in a similar study[205] in the USA and produced similar results. The Shenandoah study showed that approximately 62% of patients discharged with a diagnosis of pneumonia had been discharged from hospital in the previous four years.[205] The authors were able to demonstrate that discharged patients with any diagnosis had a 6–9% probability of readmissions with pneumonia within five years and that immunising a few high-risk patients could prevent many of these readmissions. Cost–benefit analysis showed that costs of vaccination would be approximately one-third the costs of hospital care for unvaccinated discharged patients readmitted with pneumonia.

Cost-effectiveness analysis indicates that the 23 valent pneumococcal vaccine can improve the health of elderly people for a reasonable expenditure and compares well with influenza vaccination in terms of healthy years gained for a given expenditure.[206] There is therefore sufficient evidence to suggest that purchasers should make it a requirement that all patients over the age of 60 who are admitted to hospital for any reason should have pneumococcal vaccination (AII-2).

Influenza

In contrast to pneumococcal vaccination, there are established guidelines for immunisation against influenza[207] and recommendations are circulated to doctors by the Chief Medical Officer on a yearly basis. Vaccination is not recommended for the attempted control of the general spread of influenza but is recommended for people at special risk (evidence for recommendation graded AI). Groups recommended for vaccination include the elderly suffering from certain chronic diseases and those living in residential homes and long-stay hospitals. There is evidence from a systematic review that influenza vaccination may reduce exacerbations in patients with chronic obstructive pulmonary disease (AI).[208] However, a similar review has found no beneficial effect of influenza vaccine in patients with asthma (CI).[209]

There is strong evidence from systematic reviews that influenza vaccination is effective in reducing mortality, hospital admissions and incidence of pneumonia in the elderly (AI).[210] Immunisation programmes are highly cost-effective, resulting in estimated net cost savings of between 1 and 235 US dollars per person (AII-2).[211,212]

Tuberculosis

Immunisation with BCG (bacille Calmette-Guèrin) is used in the prevention of TB. The calculated protective efficacy of BCG varies according to type of tuberculosis and age group. It is around 50% for pulmonary TB, but higher for miliary TB, meningitis and for mortality reductions (AI).[213–215]

Because of the decline in the prevalence and incidence of tuberculosis, the cost-effectiveness of many prevention programmes at district level is being questioned. However, continuation of immunisation of high-risk individuals, health care workers and schoolchildren is currently still recommended (CIII).

Immunisation against other pathogens

Trials of respiratory syncytial virus vaccine have found it to be ineffective and possibly harmful (EI).[4] Vaccines to prevent colonisation with *Pseudomonas aeruginosa* in cystic fibrosis have not been shown to be effective and may be harmful (DI).[216]

Screening

Asthma

Increased bronchial reactivity in subjects without symptoms may be predictive of later asthma, but cannot be advised as a screening procedure because few of the criteria for screening can be satisfied. Screening of schoolchildren for symptoms suggestive of undiagnosed asthma is not strictly screening because the disease is not subclinical. Uncontrolled trials of such 'screening' followed by medical intervention where indicated show a temporary improvement in morbidity.[217] Recent evidence from a controlled trial indicates that the effectiveness of this approach is very limited.[218] This result vindicates the position adopted in a previous review of child health screening in which it was recommended that such programmes should not be introduced without further evaluation (DI).[219]

It is possible to identify, through family history and indicators of atopy, individuals at increased risk of developing asthma in response to environmental allergens. Screening along these lines may be useful in certain occupations (BII-2). It might also be useful in advising families about pets, furnishings, etc. (CIII), but this approach has not been evaluated (DIII).

Chronic obstructive pulmonary disease

At present, there is no case for screening unselected asymptomatic individuals with spirometry to identify individuals at increased risk of developing COPD (DIII).[136] COPD is frequently under-diagnosed and associated with significant health impact.[220,221] The place of spirometric testing (case finding) in symptomatic individuals or smokers who are at risk of developing COPD is not clear (CIII), although it is certainly feasible and does not increase costs of health care.[222,223] A systematic review suggested that in symptomatic patients, addition of spirometric testing does not increase smoking quit rates,[224] but studies since this review suggest increased quit rates.[225]

Tuberculosis

The value of selective screening (immigrants, health workers, etc.) for tuberculosis has recently been reassessed, and guidance recommends its continuation. There is evidence that the incidence in high-risk groups can be reduced by this strategy (BIII).

Cystic fibrosis

A systematic review of screening for cystic fibrosis was carried out by Murray et al.[226] This review considered both antenatal screening to detect carriers, and neonatal screening. It concluded that antenatal screening should be introduced as a routine, and that health authorities (now primary care trusts) should consider introduction of neonatal screening (BI). They estimated costs of screening to be approximately £46–53 000 per pregnancy detected, and £4400 to £6400 per case diagnosed early for neonatal screening.

Other systematic reviews of neonatal screening suggest that such screening may be beneficial (BI),[227] or that further information is needed before recommending that existing programmes for cystic fibrosis be extended (CI).[228,229] Nevertheless, national neonatal screening is to be implemented for cystic fibrosis in the UK[230] on the basis of more recent studies from the USA.[231]

An economic evaluation from the USA differed in its conclusion regarding antenatal carrier screening from that of Murray et al. It concluded that only 41% of births were preventable, and that screening resulted in a net cost per birth averted of over $1 million, with a cost per QALY of over $8000 (CII-2).[232]

Other preventive measures

Antibiotics in acute respiratory infections

The non-selective use of antibiotics to treat upper respiratory tract infections or acute bronchitis in healthy adults or children in general practice has occasionally been considered justified in order to prevent bacterial lower respiratory complications of viral infections. However, this strategy is likely to be ineffective in upper respiratory illness,[233] and may result in unnecessary adverse effects (DI).[234] In addition, a systematic review and randomised controlled trials from Australia[235] and Thailand[236] have shown that overall (in adults and children) the use of antibiotics in acute bronchitis confers little overall benefit (CI).[237] However, acute bronchitis can be difficult to distinguish from community-acquired pneumonia in the primary care setting. The use of antibiotics in this way is also thought to promote the emergence and spread of antibiotic-resistant organisms and this is a significant argument against their unselective use. A reduction in the use of antibiotics in this context forms part of a national strategy to encourage the 'prudent use' of these drugs in order to tackle the growth of such resistance.[234]

Neuraminidase inhibitors in influenza

There is evidence to show that neuraminidase inhibitors shorten the duration of influenza symptoms but not yet serious complications (AI).[238] Their use is recommended by the National Institute for Clinical Excellence for treating 'influenza-like illness' in adults at risk from serious complications of influenza infection at times when influenza is circulating in the community.[239]

Neuraminidase inhibitors may also be effective in preventing influenza (AI). Randomised controlled trials have shown efficacy in preventing experimental infection,[238] cross-infection among household contacts[240,241] and during community administration.[242,243] However, there is no evidence as to their efficacy in preventing serious complications of influenza, and these trials do not specifically consider those in the population at risk of such complications, i.e. those who are currently the target group for immunisation. These groups include the elderly, health care workers, and people with COPD, asthma and cystic fibrosis. The cost-effectiveness of using these drugs for prophylaxis is not known.

Prevention of nosocomial pneumonia

Established surveillance programmes exist in many hospitals to prevent nosocomial infections. These are usually the responsibility of trained infection control nurses. The role of infection control nurses includes conducting surveillance of infections, applying policies for preventive patient care practices (e.g. urinary catheter care) and reducing wasteful environmental culturing. In some cases, rates of surgical wound infections are reported to surgeons to encourage more careful operating techniques.[122]

The efficacy of infection control nurses was highlighted in a large study in the USA[122] which found that an infection control nurse working together with a clinician with a special interest in infection control and practising epidemiological surveillance and control techniques could prevent about one-third of all nosocomial infections. The same may not be true for nosocomial pneumonia but specific action could probably achieve some reduction.

It has been suggested that much of the surveillance work that is at present carried out in hospital relies too much on process measures,[244] e.g. establishing baseline measures of the prevalence of pathogens. A lot of effort is also expended in evaluating established control measures and reinforcing patient care practices. However, trying to reduce nosocomial infections by using outcome measures would require setting as an objective the reduction of the nosocomial pneumonia rate from the present level of 10–19%, with possible additional outcome measures being reductions in the overall extra hospital stay and reductions in the extra costs attributable to this condition.

A potentially effective surveillance system to prevent pneumonias would include post-operative surveillance with results reported back to surgeons,[122] possibly as a part of existing audit activity. Surveillance of pneumonia occurring in medical patients would need to encompass high-risk groups in areas such as stroke units, intensive-care units and neonatal intensive-care units. At present there is little activity of this type in the UK.

There are no cost-effectiveness studies or randomised trials evaluating the role of infection control nurses. However, based on experience in the USA and the theoretical possibilities for prevention, there is some case for this type of service. The strength of the recommendation and the quality of evidence for infection control nurses can be graded as CIII.

Contact tracing and chemoprophylaxis for tuberculosis

In addition to immunisation with BCG (bacille Calmette-Guèrin), key strategies for TB prevention include contact tracing and chemoprophylaxis. The cost-effectiveness of identifying cases through contact tracing remains uncertain (CIII).[245,248] However, the effectiveness and cost-effectiveness of chemoprophylaxis with isoniazid, for which contact tracing is a prerequisite, have been studied. Isoniazid is effective in preventing active TB and death from TB (AI).[249] An economic evaluation showed chemoprophylaxis to result in an absolute cost saving in men aged 20 recently infected. For older men aged 55 with no risk other than lifelong presence of TB bacillus, the cost per QALY was calculated at between £629 (no discount) and £11 000 (discount) (AII-2).[250,251]

Clinical services

Lower respiratory infections in adults and children

Management is by antibiotic therapy against bacterial infections (AI) and supportive treatment, depending on severity (AIII). The choice of antimicrobial drug is usually made without definite information about the infecting organism (which in children is often a virus). Even if a satisfactory sample can be obtained, microbiological results come too late to guide initial therapy, and the role of the chest radiograph in this decision has not been clarified. Cost-effectiveness is rarely addressed but, as inpatient costs predominate, this will be influenced more by the level of the health system where the patient is treated than by details of diagnosis and therapy. Evidence is emerging that oral antibiotics can be used in most hospitalised patients, shortening length of stay (BI).

Lower respiratory infections in children

Evidence-based guidelines on the management of community-acquired pneumonia in childhood are available.[377] Given the predominantly viral nature of acute LRTI in young children, treatment is most often supportive (*see* below) rather than specific (antibiotics). Clinical signs and symptoms do not reliably distinguish between bronchitis and pneumonia, or between viral and bacterial illness. It has been suggested that all children over one year with pneumonia should receive antibiotics,[3] and a chest X-ray may assist such a decision. Microbiological tests rarely influence immediate clinical management, but can be justified in the severely ill child as a guide to subsequent changes of treatment.

The most important management decisions are determined by the clinical severity of the illness, rather than by a specific pathological or microbiological diagnosis. Regardless of cause, children in respiratory failure require transcutaneous monitoring of hypoxia, oxygen therapy, and occasionally may need mechanical ventilation. On the other hand, the vast majority of children with LRTI recover spontaneously without even antibiotic therapy.

A recent systematic review demonstrated that bronchodilators may have significant benefit for children with bronchiolitis[252] (BI). However, randomised controlled trials in infants with bronchiolitis have shown no substantial benefit from bronchodilators, humidified air or physiotherapy,[3] although a recent meta-analysis indicates that steroids may have a role in improving symptoms and reducing length of stay.[251] A specific aerosolised treatment for respiratory syncytial virus (Ribavirin) is under evaluation, but is expensive. It may have a role for vulnerable infants with pre-existing cardiorespiratory disease, but is not currently recommended for use in previously healthy infants.[3] Early data also show benefit from leukotriene-receptor antagonists ('antileukotrienes'),[252] and these medications warrant further evaluation.

Unselective use of antibiotics for upper respiratory illness and acute bronchitis in general practice has been suggested as an approach to preventing bacterial lower respiratory complications of viral respiratory infections. However, this strategy is likely to be ineffective, to result in unnecessary adverse effects and to promote widespread antibiotic resistance (DI; *see* above).

Community-acquired pneumonia in adults

General practitioners can treat 80% of community-acquired pneumonia effectively provided that appropriate antibiotics are employed.[10] Consensus guidelines for management of community-acquired pneumonia in adults have recently been updated by the British Thoracic Society, and made evidence based (AI).[123] The new guidelines offer guidance on the investigation and management of community-acquired pneumonia. A prediction rule is available to determine which patients are at low risk and may be managed at home, but this is derived from the USA and has not been tested in a prospective trial (CIII).[253]

Treatment in the community should reflect the prominence of *Streptococcus pneumoniae* and *Haemophilus influenzae* and these organisms should be covered by the initial antibiotic in any patient with community-acquired pneumonia (AIII).[123,254] In addition, therapy should cover *Mycoplasma pneumoniae* during regular epidemics. Routine treatment for *Staphylococcus aureus* and *Legionella pneumophila* should not be instituted except in the case of influenza epidemics or if there is a local outbreak of *Legionella*. Monitoring of local and national patterns of disease will help guide therapy in these areas.

There is evidence that for hospitalised patients who can take oral antibiotics, there is no difference in clinical outcome when compared to intravenous antibiotics, but length of stay is reduced (BI).[255] In hospitalised patients treated with intravenous antibiotics, there is evidence that these can be safely converted to oral therapy after 2 days, with substantial cost saving (54%) (AI),[256,257] and once converted to oral therapy, complications are rare and patients may be discharged home (AII-2).[258]

About 6% of admitted patients will die. Risk factors for mortality include age, treatment with digoxin and raised blood urea.[11] Treatment with an appropriate antibiotic prior to admission improves outcome. Figures for 1982–83 suggest that the average length of stay in hospitalised patients who survive is 10.8 days; 80% return to work within six weeks.

The impact of adherence to management guidelines has been studied. There was no overall impact on mortality, but unplanned transfer to intensive care was reduced, and bacteriological investigation increased (CIII).[259]

Clinical care of patients with chronic asthma

Patients with chronic symptoms usually present with acute attacks. However, for the purposes of this paper it will be simplest to deal with acute and chronic asthma separately. This follows the approach of the latest guidelines.

Diagnosis

In both adults and children there is a problem of under-diagnosis which, in turn, is associated with worse treatment.[19,21,65,126,260] Since this phenomenon began to be publicised, there has been a doubling in the proportion of wheezy children diagnosed as having asthma.[56,58,61] The situation remains less than satisfactory. Some doctors treat all patients with COPD with bronchodilators initially so that any reversible element can be identified and treated (not evaluated). This carries a risk of over-treating COPD patients with bronchodilator drugs. Guidelines state clearly when patients should be referred to specialists (respiratory paediatricians or physicians) for diagnosis and assessment.[140]

Drug treatment

Drugs used have all been tested for efficacy using randomised clinical trials with outcomes such as improvement of lung function, reduction of symptoms, improved activity and reduced need for other therapy (AI). However, recent evidence indicates that one preparation (fenoterol, which is not much used in the UK) may be associated with increased mortality. There is also concern about the effects of long-term regular administration of short-acting beta agonists generally,[261,262] and current guidance[25,140] suggests that regular use of short-acting beta agonists should be avoided. In addition there is evidence that the mainstay of anti-inflammatory treatment (inhaled steroids) is not as free from systemic side-effects as was first hoped. There is a need for more placebo-controlled long-term trials designed to look for adverse effects. A summary of available recent evidence on effectiveness of drug therapy for both chronic and acute asthma is provided in Table 8 (*see* overleaf). This evidence has been translated into guidelines, and a summary of the current guidance on stepped drug therapy for chronic asthma is provided in Table 10.

The place of nebulisers in the treatment of both acute and chronic asthma is unclear. There is evidence that the use of spacer devices with inhalers is as effective as nebuliser therapy and may confer advantages in children (CI).[263–265]

The impact of current services and therapy on chronic symptoms of asthma at a population level is unsatisfactory, with surveys consistently reporting high proportions of patients with disabling symptoms despite treatment or without treatment at all,[125,266] and underuse of preventive therapy.[22,267] Poor treatment also occurs in Accident and Emergency[243] and on admission.[22,269,270] Possible reasons include:

- variability between doctors in prescribing
- failure to identify and treat all patients
- inadequate efficacy of the drugs
- lack of patient co-operation with care (poor 'compliance' or 'adherence').

One community study has shown a better level of control of asthma among more compliant patients, indicating that such control is beneficial.[242] Recent controlled trial evidence indicates that standard setting in general practice improves both the process and outcome of care for children with wheezing (BI).[271] Another controlled trial failed to show an effect on outcome of GP group education.[272] There is a strong anecdotal impression that since the introduction of inhaled steroids, crippling asthma in children has become extremely rare. The recent flurry of audit activity and consensus statements on treatment guidelines should lead to more consistent approaches to the management of chronic asthma. There is some evidence that guidelines when applied in practice improve prescribing practice (BI) but have no impact on other outcomes, including patient-related outcomes (CI) and hospitalisation rates[273] (BI). In Canada, prescribing habits improved, but there was little evidence that guidelines improved patient outcomes (CIII).[274,275]

Self-care with drugs is a feature of asthma therapy and, for this reason, a variety of systems have been devised to enable the patient to monitor their condition using symptoms (and peak flow measurements) and to act appropriately by changing their medication or seeking help. This is still not adequately evaluated. Uncontrolled trials show evidence of benefit (CII-1),[276,277] but this does not seem to be due to the peak flow monitoring.[277]

Table 8: Summary of recent available evidence on effectiveness of drug therapy for asthma.

Authors	Title	Reference	Study type	Summary
1 Inhaled corticosteroids				
Calpin C, Macarthur C, Stephens D, Feldman W, Parkin PC	Effectiveness of prophylactic inhaled steroids in childhood asthma: a systematic review of the literature	*J Allergy Clin Immunol* 1997; **100**: 452–7	Systematic review	A 1	Clear evidence of beneficial effect on cough, wheeze, beta agonist and oral steroid use. Minor adverse effects noted
Hatoum H, Schumock G, Kendzierski D	Meta-analysis of controlled trials of drug therapy in mild chronic asthma: the role of inhaled corticosteroids	*Ann Pharmacother* 1994; **28**: 1285–9	Systematic review	A 1	Regular corticosteroids should be used if repeated doses of B-2 agonist are needed
Salmeron S, Guerin JC, Godard P *et al.*	High doses of inhaled corticosteroids in unstable chronic asthma: a multicentre, double-blind, placebo-controlled trial	*Am Rev Resp Dis* 1989; **140**: 167–71	RCT	A 1	High-dose inhaled corticosteroids control symptoms and improve lung function in chronic unstable asthma
Adams N, Bestall J, Jones PW	Budesonide for chronic asthma in children and adults	Cochrane Library: Update Software, 2001	Systematic review	A 1	Budesonide is significantly better than placebo in controlling symptoms of mild persistent asthma
Adams N, Bestall J, Jones PW	Inhaled beclomethasone vs. placebo for chronic asthma	Cochrane Library: Update Software, 2001	Systematic review	A 1	Beclomethasone is significantly better than placebo in controlling symptoms of mild persistent asthma
Adams N, Bestall J, Jones PW	Inhaled fluticasone propionate for chronic asthma	Cochrane Library: Update Software, 2001	Systematic review	A 1	Fluticasone is significantly better than placebo in controlling symptoms of mild persistent asthma
Booth P, Wells N, Morrison A	A comparison of the cost-effectiveness of alternative prophylactic therapies in childhood asthma	*Pharmacoeconomics* 1996; **10**: 262–8	Economic evaluation	B 1	Open-label study. Fluticasone is more effective than cromoglycate in symptom control, lung function improvement, fewer adverse effect reports. Total drug cost was higher for cromoglycate. Fluticasone is more effective and cost-effective

Author	Title	Source	Study type	Grade	Level	Comments
Lipworth B	Systemic adverse effects of inhaled corticosteroid therapy: a systematic review and meta-analysis	*Arch Intern Med* 1999; **159**: 941–55	Systematic review	A	1	Adrenal suppression worse above 1.5 mg a day. Fluticasone causes greater adrenal suppression than other inhaled steroids. Bone mineral density, cataract and bruising also affected by similar doses. 400 mcg/day beclomethasone inhibits growth
Price D, Appleby J	Fluticasone propionate: an audit of outcomes and cost-effectiveness in primary care	*Resp Med* 1998; **92**: 351–3	Economic evaluation	D	1	Fluticasone resulted in improved lung function, reduced use of other medication, reduced asthma nurse and GP attendances. However, it was still more expensive than alternative treatment. Study was not randomised. No conclusion can be drawn

2 Oral corticosteroids

Author	Title	Source	Study type	Grade	Level	Comments
Rowe B, Spooner C, Ducharme F, Bretzlaff J, Bota G	Corticosteroids for preventing relapse following acute exacerbations of asthma	Cochrane Library: Update Software, 1999	Systematic review	A	1	A short course of corticosteroids following assessment for acute severe asthma reduces relapses and decreases beta-agonist use without an increase in side-effects
O'Driscoll B, Kaira S, Wilson M *et al.*	Double-blind trial of steroid tapering in acute asthma	*Lancet* 1993; **341**: 324–7	RCT	A	1	A short course of corticosteroids given for acute asthma can safely be stopped abruptly
Levy ML, Stevenson C, Maslen T	Comparison of a short course of oral prednisone and fluticasone propionate in the treatment of adults with acute exacerbations of asthma in primary care	*Thorax* 1996; **51**: 1087–92	RCT	B	1	No difference in treatment failure or relapse rate
Edmonds M, Camargo C Jr, Pollack C *et al.*	Early use of inhaled corticosteroids in the emergency department treatment of acute asthma	Cochrane Library: Update Software, 2001	Systematic review	C	1	Inhaled corticosteroid reduces hospital admission in those not taking oral corticosteroid only when compared with placebo

Table 8: Continued.

Authors	Title	Reference	Study type		Summary
Edmonds M, Camargo C Jr, Saunders L et al.	Inhaled steroids in acute asthma following emergency department discharge	Cochrane Library: Update Software, 2001	Systematic review	C 1	No significant relapse rates when comparing oral and high-dose inhaled corticosteroids, or the combination of both vs. oral corticosteroids alone
Manser R, Reid D, Abramson M	Corticosteroids for acute severe asthma in hospitalised patients	Cochrane Library: Update Software, 1999	Systematic review	D 1	High doses (over 80 mg per day prednisolone or equivalent) show no significant advantage over lower doses in initial management of acute severe asthma in terms of lung function or respiratory failure
3 Short-acting beta-2 agonist					
Walters EH, Walters J	Inhaled short-acting beta-agonist use in asthma: regular vs. as-needed treatment	Cochrane Library: Update Software, 2001	Systematic review	A 1	Regular beta-2 agonists produce no clinically important benefits over as-required use of this medication
Chapman K, Kesten S, Szalai J	Regular vs. as-needed inhaled salbutamol in asthma control	*Lancet* 1994; **343:** 1379–82	RCT	B 1	Regular salbutamol resulted in fewer exacerbations, less medication use and better asthma control. No difference in lung function
Van Schayck C, Dompeling E, van Herwaarden C et al.	Bronchodilator treatment in moderate asthma or chronic bronchitis: continuous or on demand? A randomised controlled study	*BMJ* 1991; **303:** 1426–31	RCT	C 1	The rate of lung function decline was slower in patients taking drugs on demand, with no difference in symptoms
Spitzer W, Suissa S, Ernst P et al.	The use of beta agonists and the risk of death and near death from asthma	*NEJM* 1992; **326:** 501–6	Case–control study	D 2.2	Use of regular high-dose beta agonists by metered-dose inhaler was associated with increased risk of death from asthma. Less for nebuliser use, no risk for oral steroids or cromoglycate. The higher the dose, the greater the risk of death

Authors	Title	Reference	Type	Grade	Level	Comments
Shrestha M, Bidadi K, Gourlay S et al.	Continuous vs. intermittent albuterol at high and low doses in the treatment of severe acute asthma in adults	Chest 1996; **110:** 42–7	RCT	B	1	Continuous administration improves lung function
Rudnitsky G, Eberlien R, Schoffstall J et al.	Comparison of intermittent and continuously nebulised albuterol for treatment of asthma in an urban emergency department	Ann Emerg Med 1993; **22:** 1847–53	RCT	C	1	No difference in lung function or admission rates, except in post hoc group with very severe airflow obstruction
Travers A, Jones A, Kelly K et al.	Intravenous beta-2 agonists for acute asthma in the emergency department	Cochrane Library: Update Software, 2001	Systematic review	D	1	No difference between intravenous and nebulised delivery of beta-2 agonists in any clinical outcomes

4 Long-acting beta-2 agonists

Authors	Title	Reference	Type	Grade	Level	Comments
Shrewsbury S, Pyke S, Britton M	Meta-analysis of increased dose of inhaled steroid or addition of salmeterol in symptomatic asthma (MIASMA)	BMJ 2000; **320:** 1368–73	RCT	A	1	Where asthma is not controlled on low-dose inhaled corticosteroids, addition of long-acting beta-2 agonists produced significant clinical benefits when compared with increasing the dose of inhaled corticosteroids
Fish JE, Israel E, Murray JJ et al.	Salmeterol powder provides significantly better benefit than montelukast in asthma patients receiving concomitant inhaled corticosteroid therapy	Chest 2001; **120:** 423–30	RCT	A	1	Adding salmeterol to inhaled corticosteroids produces greater benefit than adding montelukast to inhaled corticosteroids
Lundback B, Rawlinson D, Palmer J	Twelve-month comparison of salmeterol and salbutamol as dry-powder formulations in asthmatic patients	Thorax 1993; **48:** 148–53	RCT	A	1	Salmeterol more effective than salbutamol in control of symptoms and drug use, especially if overnight relief required
Pearlman D, Chervinsky P, LaForce C et al.	A comparison of salmeterol with albuterol in the treatment of mild to moderate asthma	NEJM 1992; **327:** 1420–5	RCT	A	1	Salmeterol more effective than albuterol in symptom control, drug use and lung function
Britton M, Earnshaw J, Palmer JBD	A twelve-month comparison of salmeterol with salbutamol in asthmatic patients	Eur Resp J 1992; **5:** 1062–7	RCT	A	1	Salmeterol more effective than salbutamol in control of symptoms, lung function and drug use

Table 8: Continued.

Authors	Title	Reference	Study type			Summary
de Benedictis F, Tuteri G, Pazzelli P, Niccoli A, Mezzetti D, Vaccaro R	Salmeterol in exercise-induced bronchoconstriction in asthmatic children: comparison of two doses	*Eur Resp J* 1996; **9:** 2099–103	RCT	A	1	Salmeterol is more effective than salbutamol in exercise-induced asthma
Greening A, Ind P, Northfield M, Shaw G	Added salmeterol vs. higher-dose corticosteroid in asthma patients with symptoms on existing inhaled corticosteroid	*Lancet* 1994; **344:** 219–24	RCT	A	1	Salmeterol is more effective than increasing dose of inhaled steroids
Woolcock A, Lundback B, Ringdal N, Jackes L	Comparison of addition of salmeterol to inhaled steroids with doubling the dose of inhaled steroids	*Am J Resp Crit Care Med* 1996; **153:** 1481–8	RCT	A	1	Salmeterol is more effective than increasing dose of steroids
Wilding P, Clark M, Coon J *et al.*	Effect of long-term treatment with salmeterol on asthma control: a double-blind randomised crossover study	*BMJ* 1997; **314:** 1441–6	RCT	A	1	Salmeterol may permit reduction in dose of inhaled steroids
Rutten van Molken M, van Doorslaer E, Till M	Cost-effectiveness analysis of formoterol vs. salmeterol in patients with asthma	*Pharmacoeconomics* 1998; **14:** 671–84	Economic evaluation	C	1	There was no difference in effectiveness or cost between the two long-acting beta agonists. Choice of drug should therefore be based on cost in each country

5 Anticholinergic agents

Plotnick L, Ducharme F	Should inhaled anticholinergics be added to beta-2 agonists for treating acute childhood and adolescent asthma?	*BMJ* 1998; **317:** 971–7	Systematic review	A	1	A single dose does not reduce hospital admission but does improve lung function. Multiple doses improve lung function and reduce hospital admission, but only in school-age children with severe exacerbations

Author	Title	Reference	Study type	Grade		Comments
Plotnick L, Ducharme F	Combined inhaled anticholinergics and beta-2 agonists for initial treatment of acute asthma in children	Cochrane Library: Update Software, 1999	Systematic review	B	1	Single doses have no effect, but multiple doses reduce hospital admission and improve lung function in children with acute severe asthma when added to beta-2-agonists
Osmond M, Klassen T	Efficacy of ipratropium bromide in acute childhood asthma: a meta-analysis	*Acad Emerg Med* 1995; **2**: 651–6	Systematic review	B	1	Ipratropium, when combined with beta-agonist, produced a significant increase in lung function, but no difference in clinical parameters. In very severe asthma there may be a reduction in lung function
Everard M, Kurian M	Anticholinergic drugs for wheeze in children under the age of two years	Cochrane Library: Update Software, 1999	Systematic review	C	1	Parents preferred ipratropium, and symptom scores were better, but there was no difference in hospitalisation rates, oxygen saturation, treatment response or length of stay
Aaron S	The use of ipratropium bromide for the management of acute asthma exacerbations in adults and children	*J Asthma* 2001; **38**: 521–30	Systematic review	A	1	Significantly improves lung function and reduces hospital admission when combined with salbutamol, compared with salbutamol alone

6 Leukotriene antagonists

Author	Title	Reference	Study type	Grade		Comments
Fish JE, Kemp JP, Lockey RF *et al.*	Zafirlukast for symptomatic mild to moderate asthma: a 13-week multi-centre study	*Clin Ther* 1997; **19**: 675–90	RCT	B	1	Zafirlukast improves symptoms when compared with placebo in patients otherwise not taking regular anti-asthma medication
Suissa S, Dennis R, Ernst P *et al.*	Effectiveness of the leukotriene receptor antagonist zafirlukast for mild to moderate asthma. A randomised, double-blind, placebo-controlled trial	*Ann Intern Med* 1997; **126**: 177–83	RCT	B	1	Zafirlukast improves symptoms when compared with placebo in patients otherwise not taking regular anti-asthma medication
Nathan RA, Bernsteain JA, Bieloray L *et al.*	Zafirlukast improves asthma symptoms and quality of life in patients with moderate reversible airflow obstruction	*J Allergy Clin Immunol* 1998; **102**: 935–42	RCT	B	1	Zafirlukast improves symptoms when compared with placebo in patients otherwise not taking regular anti-asthma medication

Table 8: Continued.

Authors	Title	Reference	Study type		Summary
Ducharme FM, Hicks GC.	Anti-leukotriene agents compared to inhaled corticosteroids in the management of recurrent and/or chronic asthma	Cochrane Library: Update Software, 2001	Systematic review	C 1	No significant difference in exacerbation rate, but symptom control was better with inhaled corticosteroids
Fish IE, Israel E, Murray JJ et al.	Salmeterol powder provides significantly better benefit than monteleukast in asthma patients receiving concomitant inhaled corticosteroid therapy	Chest 2001; **120:** 423–30	RCT	A 1	Adding salmeterol to inhaled corticosteroids produces greater benefit than adding monteleukast to inhaled corticosteroids
7 Delivery of inhaled therapy					
Cates C	Holding chambers vs. nebulisers for beta-agonist treatment of acute asthma	Cochrane Library: Update Software, 2002	Systematic review	A 1	Holding chambers produce outcomes at least equivalent to nebulisers, and may have some advantages over nebulisers in children
Turner M, Patel A, Ginsburg S, FitzGerald JM	Bronchodilator delivery in acute airflow obstruction	Arch Intern Med 1997; **157:** 1736–44	Systematic review	A 1	Bronchodilator delivery using metered-dose inhaler with spacer is equivalent to use of nebuliser in adults with airflow obstruction
Muers M, Corris P (eds)	Nebuliser Project Group of the British Thoracic Society Standards of Care Committee. Current best practice for nebuliser treatment	Thorax 1997; **52** (Suppl. 2): S1–104	Guideline	C 5	Evidence-based guideline suggests large-volume spacers are as effective as nebulisers for many patients. Need for large study to determine in which patients use of nebulisers is beneficial

Other treatments

A summary of available evidence for non-drug therapy, including psychoeducational interventions, is given in Table 9 (*see* overleaf). There have recently been a number of trials and systematic reviews of psychoeducational care, including self-management plans, in the field of asthma management which are summarised in Table 9. The general conclusion is that the benefit is dependent on the type of educational process used, and is generally modest (BI). Interventions may be cost-effective but the net saving is small (BI).[278,279]

Desensitisation using allergen immunotherapy is popular in some other European countries but is not generally recommended because of relative ineffectiveness and dangers.[280] Physiotherapy is prescribed for some patients but its rationale in asthma has been questioned,[281] and there have been no controlled trials. Acupuncture has attracted interest but a meta-analysis of trials indicates that it is not effective.[282] Many years ago an MRC working party concluded that hypnotherapy is not indicated. There is insufficient evidence for the effectiveness of homeopathy.[283] Recent guidelines reviewed evidence for a wide range of complementary and alternative therapies for asthma, including traditional Chinese medicine, acupuncture, air ionisers, homeopathy, hypnosis, spinal manipulation, physical training, breathing exercises, speleotherapy, dietary interventions and weight reduction for obese patients. There is very little evidence for effectiveness of any of these interventions,[140] although some merit further investigation.

Investigations

The use of lung function tests in the assessment of asthma is variable. There is even more variability in the use of lung function monitoring. The same applies to chest X-ray. Both of these procedures seem clinically appropriate but their use has never been tested by means of a trial. Similarly, allergen skin tests have never been shown to improve outcome.

Organisation of care

GPs vary in their use of specialist referral and in their reasons for requesting it.[148,149] They also differ in their preferences and dependence on specialist outpatient clinics for the continuing care of the patient. An increasing proportion of practices are providing special asthma clinics in primary care. The longer-term care of asthmatics in hospital outpatients has never been supported by evidence of benefit. A considerable proportion of long-term outpatients have no clinical reason for continuing to attend (DI).[284]

A systematic review of asthma care concluded that there was no conclusive evidence to favour one type of care (specialist or generalist) over another. However, specialist care tended to be of higher quality, and shared care between hospital and primary care can be as good as hospital-led care, and also cheaper by about £40 per annum (BI).[285] Another trial of integrated care between hospital and primary care showed no benefit to patients, but the patients preferred it, and there were small savings to the patients and health service (BI).[286] There is thus evidence to support shared care for patients with asthma between hospital and primary care, and limited evidence that this care should involve a specialist. However, the optimum balance for ongoing care between primary and secondary care, and between generalists and specialists within each of these settings, has not been clearly established. Trials that have been published to date vary in their design, but overall suggest limited benefit may accrue from specialisation of care within primary care (*see* **Tables B.1 to B.3**).[287–290]

Another organisational variant is the provision of an asthma nurse with responsibility for education and training in the use of medications. There is insufficient evidence to conclude that this type of provision is more effective than standard care,[287] but there is evidence that this type of care is safe.[289] A recent trial

Table 9: Summary of recent evidence of effectiveness of non-drug therapy for asthma, including psychoeducational interventions.

Authors	Title	Reference	Study type		Summary
1 Psychoeducational interventions, including written self-management programmes					
Gibson P, Coughlan J, Wilson A et al.	Self-management education and regular practitioner review for adults with asthma	Cochrane Library: Update Software, 2001	Systematic review	B	Self-management reduces hospital admissions and attendance, visits to the doctor, days off work or school and nocturnal symptoms, but does not affect lung function. A written plan has greater effect on hospitalisation and lung function. Best results occur with written care plans	1
Devine E	Meta-analysis of the effects of psychoeducational care in adults with asthma	Res Nurs Health 1996; **19**: 367–76	Systematic review	B	Education and relaxation-based behavioural therapy improve multiple measures of functioning and well-being in adults with asthma. Effect estimates could not be reliably calculated for other interventions	1
Madge P, McColl J, Paton J	Impact of a nurse-led home management training programme in children admitted to hospital with acute asthma: a randomised controlled study	Thorax 1997; **52**: 223–8	RCT	B	Readmissions reduced from 25% to 8% if asthma education follows acute admission in children	1
Lahdensuo A, Haahtela T, Herrala J et al.	Randomised comparison of guided self-management and traditional treatment of asthma	BMJ 1996; **312**: 748–52	RCT	B	Confers benefit on absence from work, attacks, need for treatment, emergency consultations and hospital admissions	1
Taitel M, Kotses H, Bernstein I, Bernstein D, Creer T	A self-management programme of adult asthma. Part II: cost-benefit analysis	J Allergy Clin Immunol 1995; **95**: 672–6	Economic evaluation	B	Reduced asthma attacks and improved self-management and cognitive measures at six months. Not analysed by intention to treat. Net saving was US$267 per patient	1

Osman L, Abdalla M, Beattie J *et al.*	Reducing hospital admission through computer-supported education for asthma patients	*BMJ* 1994; **308**: 568–71	Randomised trial	B	2.2	Severe cases had lower hospitalisation rates when they received enhanced education with personalised computerised booklets compared to normal education, and also less sleep disturbance. No difference in drug use or GP consultations was found
Trautner C, Richter B, Berger B	Cost-effectiveness of a structured treatment and teaching programme on asthma	*Eur Resp J* 1993; **6**: 1485–91	Economic evaluation	B	5	Case series. Reduction in severe asthma attacks noted; reduced hospital days and days of absence from work. Savings were DM12 850 per year (all) and DM5900 per year direct. Likely to overestimate benefit
Gibson P, Coughlan J, Wilson A *et al.*	Limited (information only) patient education programmes for adults with asthma	Cochrane Library: Update Software, 1999	Systematic review	C	1	Use of limited asthma education appears to be of no benefit, although there may be a minor effect when used in emergency departments
Bernard-Bonnin A, Stachenko S, Bonin D, Charette C, Rousseau E	Self-management teaching programmes and morbidity of paediatric asthma: a meta-analysis	*J Allergy Clin Immunol* 1995; **95**: 34–41	Systematic review	C	1	Effect sizes were very small. Self-management teaching had no effect on emergency visits, hospital admissions, hospital days, asthma attacks or time off school
Kauppinen R, Sintonen H, Tukiainen H	One-year economic evaluation of intensive vs. conventional patient education and supervision for self-management of new asthmatic patients	*Resp Med* 1998; **92**: 300–7	Economic analysis	C	1	Lung function measures were better at one year in the intervention group. No improvement in quality-of-life measures. Intervention cost more and overall was not more cost-effective than conventional education
Drummond N, Abdalla M, Beattie J *et al.*	Effectiveness of routine self-monitoring of peak flow in patients with asthma	*BMJ* 1994; **308**: 564–7	Randomised trial	C	3	Prescribing a peak flow meter slightly increased GP consultations. In severe asthmatics, oral steroid use increased. No other significant difference in wide range of clinical and symptomatic outcomes

Table 9: Continued.

Authors	Title	Reference	Study type			Summary
2 Exercise and physical training						
Scholtz W, Haubrock M, Lob-Corzilius T, Gebert N, Wahn U, Szczepanski R	Cost-effectiveness studies of ambulatory educational programmes for children with asthma and their families	*Pneumologie* 1996; **50**: 538–43	Economic evaluation	B	5	Exercise training was effective overall in reducing a weighted score derived from clinical and quality-of-life criteria. Training saves DM97 per unit of effectiveness per year
Ram F, Robinson S, Black P	Physical training in asthma	Cochrane Library: Update Software, 1999	Systematic review	C	1	Improved cardiopulmonary fitness at the expense of more exacerbations
3 Complementary therapies						
Linde K, Jobst K	Homeopathy for chronic asthma	Cochrane Library: Update Software, 2000	Systematic review	C	1	Minor effects on lung function, symptoms and drug use, but insufficient evidence to assess role of homeopathy in asthma
Abramson M, Puy R, Weiner J	Allergen immunotherapy for asthma	Cochrane Library: Update Software, 1999	Systematic review	C	1	Immunotherapy may reduce symptoms and medication use, but the possibility of severe adverse reactions must be considered
Linde K, Jobst K, Panton J	Acupuncture for chronic asthma	Cochrane Library: Update Software, 1999	Systematic review	C	1	Trials of poor quality. Only one trial showed possible improvement in lung function. The role of acupuncture in treatment of asthma is uncertain
4 Other therapies						
Abramson MJ, Puy RM, Weiner JM	Is allergen immunotherapy effective in asthma? A meta-analysis of randomised controlled trials	*Am J Resp Crit Care Med* 1995; **151**: 969–74	Systematic review	C	1	Meta-analysis suggested benefit on symptoms, medication use and lung function, but many adverse reactions. No anaphylaxis, but risk of 1 in 500. Recommendation to treat balanced by need for care

showed that an asthma nurse providing intervention according to the British Thoracic Society guidelines on the role of such a nurse had no impact on any patient-related outcome measures, although a marginal improvement in prescribing occurred.[288] This study also showed improvements in diagnosis of asthma.

Care of chronic asthma in primary care is based around the use of guided self-management incorporating educational interventions together with self-management plans. Guided self-management reduces morbidity and the need for hospital services (BI)[321] (*see* Table 10 overleaf).

Clinical care of acute asthma

Drug treatment

Acute asthma causes great distress and may lead to death; it is one of the classic medical emergencies. Many attacks are of lesser severity. No controlled trials of treatment vs. non-treatment have been done though some trials comparing different treatments have been reported and there is one instance of an uncontrolled trial of no treatment (AIII).[292] Doctors vary in the way they treat acute asthma in general practice,[147] at A&E and in hospitals.[19,268,270,293] Evidence-based guidelines are now becoming available for the management of acute and chronic asthma.[25,140] These give clear guidance on when referral to hospital is required, and on procedures once at hospital for admission to hospital and to intensive care. It is acceptable to treat a relatively mild episode intensively because of the known unpredictability of attacks. Confidential enquiries always identify a proportion of patients who have been treated inadequately though it is not known whether, if proper care had been instituted, these patients would have survived.

Available recent evidence on effectiveness of drug treatment in acute asthma is summarised in Table 8. It is now clear that oral corticosteroids are as effective as intravenous steroids in patients able to take oral medication (AI).[294–296] A single dose of intravenous magnesium sulphate is now incorporated into guidance on treatment of acute severe asthma (AI).[297]

It has been observed that in spite of advances in medical care of asthma the death rate remains at the level of the late 1950s and may be increasing slightly in young adults. All other things being equal, this might be interpreted evaluatively to indicate that little can be done to alter asthma mortality. If this is the case, the reason for treating asthma should be to relieve distress. It is accepted that it does so and no trial would be ethical. The length of stay for asthma has decreased markedly over recent years, which might indicate either more effective treatment or a lower threshold of admission.

Other treatment

Antibiotics are sometimes given but a randomised trial of hospital patients demonstrated that they are of no value.[298] Physiotherapy is often ordered in hospital but this is variable, its rationale is unclear, and it has never been evaluated.[281] Oxygen administration improves oxygenation and is one reason for admitting patients with acute asthma. Ventilation is required in seriously ill patients to maintain oxygenation, and it can be shown to do so.

Investigations

Lung function tests are accepted as essential for assessment and monitoring of acute attacks but are not regularly done in general practice and only variably in hospitals. Blood gases give important information about the state of the patient although their use is variable and, in children, uncommon. Recently non-invasive measures of oxygenation using pulse oximetry have been introduced. Trial evidence indicates that there is no benefit in taking a chest X-ray of a patient who has been X-rayed on a previous occasion.[299] Microbiology of throat or sputum is often ordered in admitted patients but has not been evaluated. Other

Table 10: Steps in the treatment of chronic asthma in adults and children.

Asthma severity	Treatment (adults)	Alternatives (adults)	Treatment (children)	Alternatives (children)
Step 1: Intermittent. *Symptoms less than once a week, FEV_1 or PEF > 80% predicted with < 20% variability*	Inhaled β_2 agonists as required (also used at all subsequent steps)	Inhaled ipratropium, oral β_2 agonists, theophyllines	Inhaled β_2 agonists as required (also used at all subsequent steps)	Inhaled ipratropium
Step 2: Mild persistent. *Symptoms more than weekly but less than daily. FEV_1 or PEF > 80% predicted, variability 20–30%*	Inhaled glucocorticoid 200 to 800 μg beclomethasone equivalent	Sustained-release theophylline or Cromone or leukotriene modifier	Inhaled glucocorticoid 200–400 μg beclomethasone equivalent	As for adults
Step 3: Moderate persistent. *Symptoms daily, FEV_1 or PEF 60–80% predicted, variability > 30%*	*Add* long-acting inhaled β_2 agonists (LABA). If ineffective increase glucocorticoid up to 800 μg beclomethasone equivalent. If ineffective stop LABA and try other therapies	Sustained-release theophylline or long-acting oral β_2 agonists or leukotriene modifier	*Add* long-acting inhaled β_2 agonists (LABA). If ineffective increase glucocorticoid up to 400 μg beclomethasone equivalent. If ineffective stop LABA and try other therapies. If under 5 consider referral to respiratory paediatrician	Sustained-release theophylline (if over 5) or leukotriene modifier
Step 4: Severe persistent. *Symptoms daily with frequent exacerbations and limitations of physical activities. FEV_1 or PEF < 60% predicted and variability > 30%*	Higher-dose inhaled glucocorticoid (> 1000 μg beclomethasone equivalent) plus one or more of the following: sustained-release theophylline; leukotriene modifier; long-acting β_2 agonists		If under 5 refer to respiratory paediatrician. For children aged 5 and over, consider higher dose inhaled glucocorticoid (800 μg beclomethasone equivalent) plus one or more of the following: sustained-release theophylline; leukotriene modifier; long-acting β_2 agonists	
Step 5: Continuous use of oral corticosteroids	*Add* oral corticosteroids and refer to specialist care		*Add* oral corticosteroids and refer to respiratory paediatrician	

Source: Adapted from British Thoracic Society Guidelines[140] and GINA guidelines.[25]

general medical work-up tests (full blood count, urine microscopy and culture, and electrolytes) may be done but the level varies from hospital to hospital. The rationale for this practice is weak and the effect on outcome has not been evaluated.

Hospitalisation

Criteria for admission to hospital vary considerably. Evidence-based guidelines provide indications as to when hospitalisation in acute asthma is appropriate.[25,140] As a form of treatment, hospitalisation has never been evaluated. Studies into the appropriateness of admission may be useful in answering this question. A randomised controlled trial investigating the use of an asthma liaison nurse in children admitted to hospital found that this intervention increased readmissions.[300] Another study of nurse-led education following admission in children showed improvements in readmission rates. Therefore the evidence for effectiveness is conflicting (CI).[301] A controlled trial among adults had a more successful outcome.[302]

Organisation of care

The different routes of referral to hospital have rarely been evaluated. On the basis of an uncontrolled evaluation, the Edinburgh 'self-admission' arrangements were considered to reduce mortality.[149] The benefits of the marked shift towards self-referral to hospital in recent years have not been demonstrated, though parents appear to be satisfied with such arrangements.[145] The British Thoracic Society Guidelines recommend that all patients with hospitalisation due to acute asthma should be under the care of a respiratory specialist.[140]

Education

The role of education has been reviewed[303] and a meta-analysis of trials is available.[304] Trial evidence suggests that education alone, while it may increase knowledge, does not improve outcome.[305] Interventions which are effective are those which are more intensive (and expensive) and behaviourally rather than educationally based. The effectiveness of psychoeducational interventions is summarised in Table 9. In general the evidence that educational interventions in adults with asthma are effective is limited but it seems they are effective (BI). Educational interventions have been adopted into widespread practice in the care of both acute and chronic asthma.

One trial of education to improve the care of children admitted to hospital did not improve outcome and increased readmissions,[300] and another reduced readmissions.[301] Guided self-management plans for patients with asthma reduce exacerbation rates and overall morbidity.[290]

Chronic obstructive pulmonary disease

COPD is incurable and progressive. Assessment of the effectiveness of different forms of management is difficult because the relationship between lung function and morbidity, as measured by quality-of-life indices, is complex and not particularly close. Indeed the emotional state of the patient suffering with COPD is probably as important as lung function in determining well-being. The degree and rate of deterioration in lung function, however, are a good predictor of mortality.

Management of COPD is centred around initial diagnosis and monitoring, reduction of risk factors for deterioration (cigarette smoking), the management of stable COPD (using bronchodilators, inhaled glucocorticoids, pulmonary rehabilitation and long-term oxygen therapy where indicated), and the management of acute exacerbations.

Investigations

There is a general debate on the costs and benefits of direct general practitioner access to radiology departments.[306] There are now guidelines laid down by radiologists regarding criteria for X-rays which are likely to reduce the frequency of unnecessary X-rays.[307]

Bronchoscopy is often indicated to exclude other diseases, particularly lung cancer.

Spirometry with reversibility is essential for the diagnosis and monitoring of patients with COPD. Sophisticated pulmonary function tests are probably only required in a minority of patients but there has been no formal evaluation of their use.

Drug treatment

Long-term bronchodilator drugs and steroids may give symptomatic relief but have not been shown to affect prognosis.[308] There have been a number of large recent studies on effect of inhaled corticosteroids in COPD, some of which have yet to report in full. In general the evidence suggests that long-term inhaled corticosteroids have either no or marginal effect on lung function decline or exacerbations (DI), but may have a positive effect on quality of life (BI).[309–311] Oral corticosteroids improve lung function and quality of life in the short term in a proportion of patients with COPD, but cannot be used long term because of unacceptable side-effects (CI).[312]

The place of bronchodilator therapy in COPD also remains unclear. A systematic review of long-acting bronchodilators concluded that there was no effect on exacerbations or exercise tolerance, little effect on lung function but greater effects on symptoms and quality of life (BI). Individual trials of regular inhaled bronchodilator therapy have demonstrated both beneficial effects[312–317] (on lung function and quality of life) and detrimental effects.[318] A systematic review suggests that there are overall beneficial effects on symptoms, lung function and quality of life, at least in the short term.[319] There is little if any evidence that ipratropium combined with beta-2 agonists may be more effective than beta-2 agonists alone (CI).[320]

Long-term domiciliary oxygen has been shown to reduce mortality in a number of studies (AI), but patients with hypoxaemic disease, i.e. those who might benefit from the provision of oxygen, represent a minority of cases.[321,322] A systematic review has concluded that long-term oxygen therapy only improves survival in COPD patients with moderate to severe hypoxaemia (AI).[323] At present there is little evidence to support its use in patients with milder hypoxaemia. A study in the UK revealed a geographical mismatch between the issue of oxygen equipment and anticipated need.[324]

Antibiotics and oxygen therapy in acute exacerbations probably reduce risk of death (BII-2). A systematic review of antibiotics for acute exacerbations of COPD concluded that antibiotics improve symptoms, reduce their duration and improve lung function, and that the effect is greater for hospital inpatients than outpatients (AI).[325] A systematic review suggests there is reasonably good evidence to support the use of mucolytic agents in COPD and chronic bronchitis (BI). The place of theophyllines in management of acute exacerbations and stable COPD is also unclear, there being evidence of modest benefit in some patients, but balanced by adverse side-effects (CI).[327–329] Guidelines have been produced for the management of COPD in the UK, which incorporate guidance on investigation and diagnosis, assessment, management of chronic disease and acute exacerbations and organisation and management of care (BIII).[330]

Other treatments and services

The appropriate balance between primary and secondary care remains controversial. There have been no formal trials. Some audits of outpatient clinics suggest that up to 30% of follow-up visits may be inappropriate.[284,331] There has been little research on criteria for hospital admission. In severe hospitalised cases a decision on whether a patient should be ventilated has to be made, but little research has taken place on the necessary criteria. Most hospitalised patients are treated by general physicians rather than respiratory specialists. Evidence in asthmatics suggest that generalists are less likely to monitor and follow up patients, which may also be true in COPD.[21]

There has been little evaluative research on GP hospital vs. district hospital admissions.

There has been some work comparing regular surveillance by a nurse specialist with a demand-led service (BI).[332,333] This approach may prolong the life of severe cases at greater expense to the health service.

Observational studies and controlled trials indicate that stopping smoking slows the progression of disease (AI).

There remains debate over the benefits of chest physiotherapy.[84] A systematic review suggests no evidence of effect (CI).[334]

Nocturnal non-invasive positive pressure ventilation has recently been introduced for the management of hypercapnic patients with COPD. However, at present there is insufficient evidence to determine its benefit – some patients appear to derive great benefit, but these cannot be identified a priori.[335]

There have been a number of recent evaluations of both educational interventions and formal pulmonary rehabilitation programmes in patients with COPD. Education alone reduced hospital admission and GP attendance, and produced cost savings (BI).[336] Several systematic reviews suggest there is some evidence for clinically significant benefit from pulmonary rehabilitation, particularly that which incorporates exercise training (AI),[337–342] but there was no evidence of cost savings in an economic evaluation (DI).[343]

Tuberculosis

Drug therapy for tuberculosis has been shown to be effective in numerous randomised controlled trials (AI), but regimens shorter than six months have not been shown to be as effective as those of six months' duration.[344] Guidelines for both prevention and control, and for chemotherapy of tuberculosis in the UK have been produced (AIII).[154,159,161] Because of the duration of treatment, non-compliance is a problem.[164]

A systematic review of strategies to improve compliance with treatment showed that reminder cards, monetary incentives, lay worker involvement and clinic staff supervision increased completion, but directly observed therapy did not[345] (BI). However, the place of directly observed therapy is not yet clear, with more than one consensus statement considering it to be both effective and cost-effective.[346,347]

Cystic fibrosis

The treatment of cystic fibrosis is complicated, because of the multi-system nature of this condition, although it is usually undertaken by a respiratory specialist (adult or paediatric) because lung disease is responsible for most of the mortality associated with the condition. Care of patients with cystic fibrosis requires a partnership between patient, family, specialist doctor and multi-disciplinary team, and the general practitioner. There have been no formal evaluations of the role that the general practitioner can play in management of cystic fibrosis, and the majority of care is provided by the hospital, usually as an outpatient or supported in the community by hospital staff. There is evidence from observational studies that survival is improved for patients who are treated in specialist centres with specialist multi-disciplinary teams, that there is some clinical benefit, and that patients and families prefer this mode of treatment (AIII). The evidence for benefit where care is shared between a specialist clinic and a local hospital is less clear, although this form of care is frequently recommended as a method of delivering specialist care to patients who live at a distance from a main centre (CIII).

Antibiotics

Three systematic reviews have all concluded that treatment of patients chronically colonised with *Pseudomonas aeruginosa* using nebulised antibiotics is beneficial. This benefit may be demonstrated in terms of improved lung function, reduced hospital admissions, fewer intravenous antibiotic courses and improved survival (AI).[348–350]

There is also evidence from a well-designed trial that early treatment with oral and inhaled antibiotics can prevent chronic colonisation with *Pseudomonas aeruginosa* if given when the organism is first detected (AI). Since chronic colonisation with this organism is an adverse prognostic indicator, this treatment is likely to prove beneficial.[318]

Continuous oral anti-staphylococcal antibiotics, when given from infancy for two years, reduce cough, hospital admissions and length of stay (AI).[352] However, there is little evidence for the effectiveness of this treatment beyond two years of age.

Other drug therapy

Both oral steroids and non-steroidal anti-inflammatory drugs have been evaluated to see if they reduce the progression of lung disease in cystic fibrosis. In a systematic review of oral steroid therapy, high-dose oral corticosteroids at a dose of 1–2 mg/kg on alternate days appear to slow the progression of lung disease in children (CI),[353] but at the expense of serious side-effects including growth retardation, cataracts and abnormalities in glucose metabolism. A systematic review of non-steroidal anti-inflammatory drugs[354] essentially covered a single trial, which demonstrated that lung function decline was reduced in children aged 5–13, the use of antibiotics was reduced and nutritional status improved (CI).[355] Although no serious side-effects were seen, the trial had low power to detect these, and their use was not recommended.

Two systematic reviews have been produced concerning the effects of dornase alpha in cystic fibrosis. Both concluded that the drug produces small but significant gains in lung function when used for a short period (six months) in patients with moderate impairment, and without serious adverse effects (BI).[356,357] The long-term effects are, as yet, unknown. The drug is expensive, and an economic evaluation has not yet been published. Hypertonic saline produces similar gains when given over a period of two weeks, and direct comparison with dornase alpha is needed (CI).[358]

There is evidence that enteric-coated microsphere preparations of pancreatic enzyme supplements improve fat absorption when compared to non-enteric-coated preparations (AI).[359] However, the dose should not exceed 10 000 lipase units per kilogram, and should be adjusted until steatorrhoea is controlled (AI).[360] Higher doses may lead to colonic strictures (EIII).[361]

Physiotherapy

Three systematic reviews were identified that evaluated the effectiveness of physiotherapy in the treatment of cystic fibrosis. Two suggested that physiotherapy was effective when compared to no treatment (AI), reducing the decline in lung function.[362,363] One review suggested that there was no significant difference between the modalities of physiotherapy treatment tested, but the other suggested that the forced expiration technique was probably less effective than the positive expiratory pressure mask, exercise and directed coughing in the acute exacerbation. The reviews did not test the same modalities, however, so it is still unclear which type of treatment is preferable. One review suggested that exercise plus physiotherapy is superior to physiotherapy alone.[362]

The third systematic review evaluated the new mechanical vibrator device that has recently become available in North America. It concluded that the vibrator was not significantly better than other forms of physiotherapy, and its use is not recommended (DI).[364]

Other non-drug therapy

Although the use of enteral tube feeding and oral calorie supplements in cystic fibrosis is widespread, systematic reviews of the evidence show trials to be of poor quality and evidence for the use of these forms of treatment lacking.[365,366]

Observational studies show that for some patients, heart–lung, lung or liver transplantation can increase survival and quality of life (AIII).

Management of care

One study has examined the effectiveness and cost of home intravenous antibiotic therapy in cystic fibrosis, when compared to hospital treatment. The randomised trial found no difference in clinical outcome. Improved family and personal life were offset by increased fatigue in patients. The cost was approximately half that of an inpatient course of intravenous antibiotic therapy (BI).[367] Home intravenous antibiotic therapy is in widespread use for both adults and children with cystic fibrosis.

Cost-effectiveness

Studies of cost-effectiveness are rare. The most useful lines of enquiry are likely to be:

- shifts towards ambulatory and primary care
- the use of formal shared care protocols
- identification and study of high users
- shifting of costs between public sectors and between the public and private sectors.

Except for asthma (*see* below), available evidence of the cost-effectiveness of individual interventions is discussed above in the relevant disease sections on clinical effectiveness.

Asthma

The costs of asthma have been described in a number of reports.[370,371] Some of the issues are covered in a recent review.[372] In the community, the chief costs relate to doctor time and drugs. One controlled trial of the effects of clinical standard setting in general practice found improvements in outcome were associated with increased use of resources.[266] The other focus of interest has been the potential savings in hospital care arising from more adequate primary care. A descriptive study among adult asthmatics admitted to hospital concluded that 73% of admissions could have been avoided by better ambulatory care with proportionate savings.[373] Other techniques of examining cost-effectiveness have been tried but are not convincing methodologically.[374,375] In the USA, cost-effectiveness estimations are being built into some programmes.[374]

7 Models of care

The prevention, treatment and rehabilitation of lower respiratory disease are complex, but of the various models available, the two considered most relevant for purchasers for these conditions are the natural history model and the service model. Decision points within these models focus upon the balance between preventive and therapeutic services, between primary and secondary care, and between specialist and generalist care within each of these settings.

In the natural history model, the central concept is the following chain of events:

aetiology → pathophysiology → manifestations of disease → consequences of disease.

In this model the concern is to achieve an appropriate balance between interventions at different points of the chain.

In the service model the focus of interest is the use of health services, and the main concern is that patients be treated in an appropriate way in an appropriate place by appropriate personnel.

It is argued that the direction of marginal shifts in provision of health services for most lower respiratory conditions should probably be as follows:

treatment → prevention

secondary/tertiary care → primary care and patient enablement.

However, *within* each of these settings there is a general view that treatment should be provided by specialists in respiratory conditions, rather than generalists. These specialists are usually specialist respiratory physicians in the hospital setting, and in the primary care setting, general practitioners with a specialist interest, or nurses with specialist training. That is to say, within each care setting, the general marginal shift should be:

generalist care → specialist care.

For some conditions, such as cystic fibrosis, increasing specialisation of care can produce significantly better clinical outcomes, and there is a clear need for increased specialisation and more tertiary care provision.

The diagnosis and management of difficult or unusual cases, including those not covered by this review, and of cystic fibrosis, should continue to be the responsibility of an accredited respiratory specialist with special expertise in the individual condition. There is some evidence that management of acute exacerbations of chronic lower respiratory conditions (asthma and COPD) requiring hospitalisation should also be undertaken by a respiratory specialist.

A useful feature of these models is that they allow the collapsing of most lower respiratory conditions into only two groups: lower respiratory infections, which tend to be acute and limited in duration, and asthma and COPD, which are chronic diseases with acute exacerbations. Cystic fibrosis forms a third special case due to its different aetiology and need for specialist management.

Lower respiratory infections

Natural history model

Given the lack of specific treatment for most lower respiratory infections in children, and the strong observational evidence implicating environmental tobacco smoke, greater emphasis on prevention by reducing parental smoking can be justified. Among adults, there should be greater emphasis on smoking reduction.

A policy of immunising patients over 60 admitted to hospital with pneumococcal vaccine should be considered. This may mean shifting resources from primary care towards hospital. A policy of immunising all elderly people against influenza is very important.

Service model

The main resource implications of lower respiratory infection arise from inpatient care. Its high incidence in the community, of which only a minority of episodes reach hospital, implies that small shifts in the threshold of referral and admission could have a major impact on hospital resources. In the absence of a comprehensive evaluation of the clinical and economic costs and benefits of different balances between primary and secondary care, there should be caution in recommending any major shifts in activity. However, given that few patients who are admitted receive intensive supportive care, the direction of any marginal shift should be towards primary rather than inpatient care. Guidelines are now available which should improve the marginal shift towards management of lower respiratory infections in the community.

Parental anxiety and expectations are often an important determinant of the threshold of referral (including self-referral) of children to Accident and Emergency departments, and of subsequent admission. This may or may not be deemed appropriate. Key policy decisions to be made relate to the extent to which clinical considerations should prevail over parental choice, and whether general practitioners or Accident and Emergency departments are better placed to assess clinical severity.

There is scope for developing a degree of consensus about the criteria for 'appropriateness' of admission, and of subsequent continuation of inpatient care (marginal bed-days). There is also scope to reduce the reliance on intravenous antibiotic therapy in hospitalised patients, and thus reduce length of stay.

There is evidence to suggest that if pneumonias are treated correctly at an early stage by general practitioners, then fewer patients will be admitted to hospital. This may mean a changing role for respiratory physicians towards providing more advice to general practitioners on the epidemiology of pneumonias and on their treatment in the primary care setting.

Asthma and chronic obstructive pulmonary disease

Natural history model

There are a number of points in the natural history of asthma where it is possible to intervene. At present, the main thrust of activity is to use asthma drugs to reduce morbidity associated with chronic asthma and to prevent or reduce the intensity of acute exacerbations. Although the scope for primary prevention using existing knowledge is not altogether clear, there might be benefits in expanding this aspect, but not at the expense of treatment. It is possible that with more determined efforts to uncover under-diagnosis and inadequate treatment there may be a need to expand primary care further. Within the domain of treatment there is a shift towards a model in which asthma is viewed as a chronic disorder which should be treated in a proactive or anticipatory fashion, rather than as a series of episodes each of which is managed reactively. All of these shifts will require more resources at the primary care level though they might lead to savings through reductions in hospital care.

While a minority of COPD cases are caused by mainly genetic factors, the majority are the result of smoking, which is not only a primary cause, but is detrimental at all points of the chain. The shift must therefore be towards smoking control.

Service model

The care of both asthma and COPD implies a dual relationship between the patient and doctor or even, in more severe cases, a triangular relationship between patient, general practitioner and hospital doctor.

Patients with acute asthma may need to short-circuit the referral system to hospital by self-referral. The latter may be ad hoc or formalised as an agreed 'open-access' policy and backed up by written self-management plans for individual patients. Whatever the arrangement, it is clear that the dominant service model is one of reliance on community care with backup from specialist and inpatient facilities. Because of the severity 'pyramid', a small shift in referral towards hospital will have a disproportionate effect on hospital workload. There is evidence that the balance of care of acute asthma in children is shifting towards the hospital, but since this is not accompanied by evidence of benefit, further increases should be questioned.

The health service 'career' patterns of patients may not be well represented by examination of available utilisation data. All kinds of patterns exist and there is room for some shifting towards those which are more appropriate. Although the marginal shift should probably be away from hospital care for the management of chronic asthma, within both primary and secondary care, at least for some patients, a shift towards specialist care may be of benefit. In particular, the reduction of inappropriate use of hospital services would lead to considerable savings in that sector. Empowerment of patients through education, review and written self-management plans may reduce morbidity and the use of all levels of health services. The optimum methods of organising asthma and COPD services in primary care are still to be determined. There is some evidence that care can be effectively delivered by specially trained asthma and respiratory nurses working in primary care. The consequent increase in resources required by primary care services needs examination. These resources include trained personnel (medical and nursing), and provision of and training in the use of spirometric equipment. Some patients will continue to require assessment and ongoing management under a respiratory specialist.

There is some evidence that for acute exacerbations of asthma and COPD, patients fare better when under the care of a respiratory specialist rather than a general physician.

Tuberculosis

Natural history model

Because most patients with tuberculosis are infected in other countries, the direction is away from prevention through BCG, or early detection through mass X-ray, towards detection through clinical services, screening of immigrants and good contact tracing. However, BCG is still recommended for high-risk groups and for schoolchildren.

Service model

Treatment of tuberculosis needs to be overseen by a respiratory or infectious disease specialist. However, there is scope for developing further community and ambulatory care interventions to improve completion of therapy, which in turn will reduce antibiotic resistance.

Cystic fibrosis

Natural history model

As an inherited condition, there is potential to prevent the disease by population screening for carriers and antenatal detection with termination of affected pregnancy. At present it is not clear whether this will be beneficial or cost-effective. There is also potential to prevent decline in lung function by screening newborn infants and instituting early therapy, and there is some evidence that this is effective. There is therefore scope to move towards prevention and early intervention.

There is also evidence that exacerbations of disease may be prevented and clinical progress improved by the use of a number of drugs. In this instance, treatment is seen as both therapeutic and preventive, in that it reduces the consequences of disease.

Gene therapy is currently undergoing trials, and may in future form a method of intervening in the natural history of the disease. At present, it is still in the early trial phase.

Service model

Cystic fibrosis is the single condition in this review where there is good evidence that care directed by respiratory specialists with special expertise in cystic fibrosis is of benefit. However, much of this care can be successfully delivered in the community, with the patient and family taking responsibility for self-management, including delivery of quite complex forms of treatment such as intravenous antibiotic therapy and enteral feeding. The majority of support for such community-based treatment is provided by specialist hospital-based teams, and community services and primary care are rarely actively involved in care delivery. There is scope for further involvement of primary care and community care teams, but the opportunity cost of educating these professionals to care for a very small number of patients should be considered – it might be more cost-effective to use hospital-based community support unless the patient lives at a great distance from the treatment centre. The clinical nurse specialist plays an important role in delivery of hospital-based community support, although the role has not been subjected to formal trial. In general, there should be a marginal shift towards management of uncomplicated respiratory exacerbations at home, which may require provision of additional hospital-based and primary-care based support.

Care for children may be shared between a large specialist centre and a local hospital, particularly for patients who would otherwise have to travel long distances, but the optimum method of delivery of shared care is not known – there are various models, including alternating visits, annual assessments and peripatetic visiting clinics. At present there is insufficient evidence to recommend the use of shared care for adults with cystic fibrosis.

Infection control is a major issue in cystic fibrosis, and provision of inpatient facilities and outpatient clinic facilities that permit segregation of patients chronically infected with certain types of organism is increasingly being recommended, which may have implications for capital building programmes in hospitals.

8 Outcome measures

General points

We interpret outcome measures loosely to include either indicators that directly measure the effects of health care on the respiratory status and subsequent health of an individual or population ('true outcomes' or 'health gain'), or indirect indicators of progress towards the achievement of those goals through changes in policy, service provision or reduction of risk factors.

To measure outcome requires not only the existence of good measures of respiratory health status but also a means by which the level of these measures can be related to planned interventions. Because of the present lack of outcome measures it is often necessary to rely on measures of the structure and process of care, particularly if targets are contemplated.

The British Thoracic Society Guidelines for treatment of acute asthma have recently identified a number of specific areas for detailed monitoring of routine and emergency care in both a primary care and hospital setting.[140]

Prevention

A   Structure.

1   National and local policies to reduce smoking.
2   Housing fitness standards and building regulations.
3   Air pollution control (including sources of *Legionella*).
4   Availability of effective means of anti-smoking help.
5   Regulation of inhaled hazards in the workplace.
6   Policies for immunisation (pneumococci, influenza, whooping cough).
7   Hospital control of infection policies.
8   Neonatal and possibly antenatal screening programmes for cystic fibrosis.

B   Process.

1   Implementation of anti-smoking policies and other policies related to the quality of inhaled air to include reducing environmental tobacco smoke exposure.
2   Achievement of coverage by immunisation which is adequate for control of the disease in question.

C   Outcome.

1   Reduction in smoking.
2   Reduction in occupational lung disease.
3   Reduction in diseases amenable to control by immunisation – whooping cough, influenza, pneumococcal pneumonia.
4   Reduction in hospital-acquired pneumonia.
5   Reduction in notifications of communicable diseases.
6   Reduction in mortality.

Clinical services

A   Structure.

1   Agreed management guidelines for drug treatment, investigation, outpatient referral and discharge, hospital admission and discharge criteria. Increasingly, these should be based on evidence of efficacy.
2   Access to general practitioners, paediatric and adult medicine specialists and to specialists trained in respiratory medicine.
3   Access to nurse-run structured care for patients with asthma in primary care. Use of structured record in primary care for patients with asthma.
4   Access to specialists in paediatric and adult respiratory medicine who specialise in cystic fibrosis. Adequate facilities to allow segregation of inpatients and outpatients in cystic fibrosis clinics. Access to home intravenous therapy with appropriate support for patients with cystic fibrosis.
5   Access to the full range of respiratory diagnostic facilities, including lung function tests, microbiology, radiology, endoscopy and pathology.
6   Access to appropriate drugs, delivery systems and respiratory function self-monitoring equipment such as peak flow meters.
7   Access to an intensive-care unit.
8   Ambulance services trained in the emergency care of acute asthma.
9   Policies and protocols for reducing spread of communicable respiratory disease from affected patients. Designated individual in primary care trust responsible for the control of TB.

B   Process.

1   Adherence to protocols and guidelines. Audit, including that of selected deaths.
2   Equity. Investigation of variations between areas, social classes and ethnic groups which are not justified by differences in need for care.
3   Levels of unmet need in the community to include access to tertiary specialist centres for patients with cystic fibrosis.
4   Level of education and self-management.
5   Proportion of patients inappropriately using hospitals.
6   Proportion of patients with self-management plans for asthma and COPD in whom these are appropriate (those with moderate to severe symptoms, with frequent exacerbations, requiring emergency interventions, seeing different doctors).
7   Proportion of patients with asthma or COPD and persisting or severe symptoms who are referred for specialist assessment.
8   Proportion of practices using a structured (guideline-based) recording system for clinical care of asthma.

C   Outcome.

1   Reduction in morbidity. For chronic respiratory disease, this could be measured using simple self-completed questionnaires. These could be used in the service context or on a community basis.
2   Improved patient-assessed disease control and quality of life. This can be assessed using a variety of existing methods.
3   Patient satisfaction with care.
4   School absence; work absence.
5   Mortality. Deaths in young and even middle-aged people should, in principle, be amenable to prevention by reducing case fatality.
6   Proportion of patients with active asthma that is well controlled. The British Thoracic Society Guidelines suggest patients should have few symptoms, be able to use inhalers correctly, be taking inhaled steroids, have normal lung function ($> 80\%$ predicted FEV_1), and have an asthma action plan.

9 Targets

Targets are used to quantify the rate of change or to specify a desired level of the target indicator. Some will have been shown to be achievable and some may be achievable only in theory. Often it will be easier to obtain consensus about the desired direction of change (perhaps more appropriately termed 'goals') than to set quantitative targets.

Measures of the outcome of health service intervention usually reflect other influences, such as epidemiological factors or the intervention of other agencies. For example, the prevalence of disabling asthma probably reflects both epidemiological and medical care influences. Similar limitations apply to some risk factors, such as smoking, where the influence of the NHS may be partly at a national policy level and also involve other agencies. Furthermore, at a local or regional level many 'true' outcome indicators may be based on small numbers and therefore be inappropriate for target setting at these levels. This limits the utility of outcome targets and implies that measures of process will be more credible targets. This, however, presupposes that a link between process and outcome has been established by other means (e.g. randomised controlled trial). This is rarely the case for respiratory disease.

The social class gradient found in most respiratory diseases raises the following question. Should this be seen as a mitigating factor or as a failure to meet targets of equity?

Prevention

1 **Smoking:** A significant reduction (of 35% in men, 29% in women and 33% in 11- to 15-year-olds) in smoking was proposed by Government.[375] These targets have been modified in the *Smoking Kills* document. For children, a reduction from 13% to 11% by 2005 and 9% by 2010 is now proposed. For adults, a reduction from 28% to 26% by 2005 and 24% by 2010 is proposed. In pregnancy, a reduction from 23% to 18% by 2005 and 15% by 2010 is proposed.

2 **Immunisation:** The FPHM has proposed a 1995 target of 95% pertussis immunisation by the age of one year, and of 95% measles immunisation by the age of two years. The World Health Organization also recommends this target. This has been achieved in the UK, and efforts to continue this level of coverage should continue with this as the target.

3 **Air quality:** Air quality guidelines for Europe have been published and should be observed. The Expert Panel on Air Quality Standards produces air quality guidelines for the UK and efforts should be made to adhere to these targets, and the targets outlined in the National Air Quality Strategy.

4 **Cooling systems:** There should be monitoring of cooling systems which are potential sources of *Legionella* dissemination. A perhaps ambitious target could be that none are contaminated.

5 **Pneumococcal immunisation:** A target of immunisation of all patients over 60 who have been admitted to hospital with pneumococcal vaccine was suggested in the last edition. The evidence that this is effective is weak. However, all groups for whom immunisation is suggested in the current edition of *Immunisation for Infectious Disease* should receive such immunisation.

6 **Influenza immunisation:** All at-risk groups should be immunised.

Morbidity

1 **Reduction in morbidity in the population:** Reduction in morbidity from asthma is certainly a goal and in theory it is achievable because surveys indicate considerable under-treatment. There is recent evidence which suggests that reductions are possible in practice (in children), but it would be inappropriate to set a quantified target without much better epidemiological information on determinants and time trends. The current uncertainty about adverse effects of treatment on morbidity needs to be kept in mind.

2 **Notifications of whooping cough:** A target of at least 50% reduction by 1995 was suggested (FPHM), and this has been achieved – there was a 93% reduction in three-year moving average notifications between 1982 and 1998. There is no target set by the World Health Organization, but it would seem reasonable to set a target of at least maintaining with progress towards a further 50% reduction in notifications by 2010.

3 **Notifications of measles:** A target of 80% reduction by 1995 was suggested (FPHM) and achieved, with a 95% reduction in three-year moving average notifications between 1982 and 1998. The World Health Organization has set a target of eradication, but no target date has been set. Eradication is theoretically achievable, and a target of a further 50% reduction in notifications by 2010 should be attainable.

4 **Reduction in readmissions for asthma:** This would be measurable and may be achievable. The question is whether it is desirable. Further evaluation is needed before a target can be set.

The following are goals, but quantifiable targets cannot be set:

5   **Reduction in nosocomial infections.**
6   **Improved quality of life and disease control in chronic disease.**
7   **Satisfaction with services.**
8   **Reduction in unscheduled use of primary care for asthma and COPD.**

Mortality

At a district level, mortality from the conditions listed below is too low to monitor.

1   **Tuberculosis:** A target of zero is achievable except for immune-deficient patients.
2   **Pertussis:** Mortality is already low but case fatality is higher in children with other serious diseases. Immunisation is not wholly protective. While a further reduction is desirable, a quantifiable target is difficult to define.
3   **Asthma:** In theory there is scope for a reduction in mortality because acute asthma is treatable and a proportion of deaths have been associated with inadequate care. For this reason asthma mortality in ages 5–44 has been listed as avoidable. It is not known to what extent this may be possible in practice. Neither do we know enough about trends and geographical variations in epidemiological influences to be able to interpret trends. Thus a reduction of mortality in this age group, though desirable, may not be achievable. Deaths are too few for targets to be set locally.
4   **Cystic fibrosis:** In theory a target of no deaths between the ages of 1 year and 16 years may be achievable, but would be difficult to monitor at local level due to small numbers of patients in individual districts. Therefore a target cannot be set. However, mortality in the paediatric age group should be minimised, and survival could be monitored at regional level.

Clinical and service targets

1   **Distribution of respiratory specialists:** The distribution of doctors accredited in respiratory medicine together with necessary laboratory and investigative backup should be arranged so that all patients requiring such services have access to them. Whether specialists should be in groups or single-handed needs discussion.
2   **Setting up and adherence to guidelines for clinical management:** These should be evidence based where evidence exists, the methodology should be adequately described, and ideally they should be drawn up by multi-disciplinary teams and regularly reviewed.
3   **Level of uptake of peak flow meters:** Until more is understood about the benefits of self-monitoring, a target cannot be set.
4   **Implementation of self-management plans:** These appear to be promising in the management of asthma. Further evaluation is required before setting a target that all chronic asthmatics should have them. However, all patients with moderate to severe asthma should have these plans and every patient with asthma should have written advice on when to seek help.
5   **Improved levels of patient education and self-care skills:** It would be reasonable to set a target that all patients with chronic respiratory disease should have a basic understanding of their illness and its treatment, and that they should know what to do in an emergency, and how to reduce exposure to exacerbating factors.
6   **Appropriateness of admissions and other hospital utilisation:** Appropriateness protocols are still in the development stage but have potential. In time it may be possible to set target levels for the proportion of appropriate admissions and distribution of length of stay.

7 **Notifications of tuberculosis:** These should be complete and within a set time, to enable an appropriate response.

8 **Setting up and adherence to protocols for management of outbreaks of TB, and for contact tracing, chemoprophylaxis and completion of courses of treatment**.

9 **Cystic fibrosis services:** All patients with cystic fibrosis should have access to a specialist in cystic fibrosis (tertiary-level service) supported by a specialist multi-disciplinary team.

Changes in information required to facilitate needs assessment at a local level

The information changes suggested below refer not only to improvements or additions to the standing systems but also to methods which might be applied on a sample basis when required. Operationally, there are three categories:

1 routine data as they are at present, or in a modified form
2 new data to be collected at the point of service use
3 data to be collected from community surveys.

Changes in information required to enable targets to be met in future and to enable outcomes to be monitored

1 **Local assessment of needs:** Will often (particularly in the short term) involve extrapolation from national data. It is therefore desirable that, where possible, local developments in information use standard methods so that comparison with national figures can continue.

2 **Maintain and improve communicable disease notification system:** In particular there is a need to improve feedback to primary care trusts to enable rapid response to problems.

3 **Improve and standardise diagnostic recording of deaths and admissions:** This applies not only to the underlying cause but also to comorbidity revealed by other causes recorded.

4 **Support, extend and standardise general practitioner systems for recording clinical activity:** This would provide at the primary care level a basis for assessing demand for care and the response to it.

5 **Develop methods of obtaining diagnostic data from Accident and Emergency departments and outpatient clinics:** These are being developed at present. A national minimum data set would improve ability to make comparisons between primary care trusts.

6 **Linkage of hospital admissions:** Use of the NHS number, which is also being considered, would facilitate linkage. This information would not only give information about demand and patterns of use, but would also be a useful focus for audit.

7 **Modify existing prescription analysis (PACT) to include the recording and coding of age:** The existing system codes only whether the patient is exempt or not (though age of the child is recorded on the prescription) and even these data cannot be linked to specific drug data. Some respiratory drugs are disease-specific and data improved in this way would give better information about the use of medicines for these illnesses.

8 **Improve information obtained from schools:** There are two main possibilities. The first would be to adopt a standard structured school medical examination. The second would be to include in school absence records a suitable comment about the medical cause of absence, e.g. 'chest illness'.

9 **Develop simple, practical and valid methods of measuring morbidity in the community by questionnaires:** Such procedures could also obtain data on treatment, service use and satisfaction.

10   **Develop practical methods of measuring severity of illness at service interfaces:** This would enable variations in process and outcome to be interpreted.

11   **Develop simple, standard and comparable measures of respiratory risk factors at a local level:** These would enable variations in morbidity to be interpreted, and risk factor intervention to be prioritised and monitored. Factors include smoking, industrial exposures, air pollution, indoor hazards, social class and ethnic composition.

12   **Maintain the national cystic fibrosis clinical database:** This would allow local service planning, and provide information for local audit. At present this is maintained by charitable funding.

13   **Develop standardised templates for respiratory disease across GP computer systems and standardise use of coding:** This would allow collection of data on incidence, prevalence and use of services in primary care at the population level and facilitate monitoring, audit and needs assessment.

Health outcomes

1   **Audit of deaths:** Numbers of deaths are routinely available but some simple means of auditing care and prevention prior to the death should be considered. This exercise would concentrate on 'premature' deaths with the aim of learning more about both immediate and more distant factors contributing to death and using such knowledge to improve and monitor care and prevention locally. Confidential enquiries have been undertaken for asthma deaths, and could usefully be undertaken for other causes, including deaths from cystic fibrosis in the paediatric age group, to identify service-related factors contributing to the deaths.

2   **Surveys of morbidity, treatment and patient satisfaction:** The main chronic respiratory diseases are common and easily measured by simple survey techniques.

3   **Admissions and re-admissions:** These are an important outcome of ambulatory care in conditions where it is believed that hospitalisation may be avoided by appropriate care. Similarly, readmissions may also reflect a lack of appropriate arrangements following the earlier admission.

Process

1   **Analysis of variability between districts in process and outcome measures:** This is one level up from measurement of individual clinical process and outcome. If it is possible to assume that underlying morbidity is broadly similar across districts, large variations in outcome indicate different levels of care, whereas large variations in process indicate inefficiency or unmet need.

2   **Measures of the appropriateness of admission:** This concept has been developed in the USA and is based on consensus criteria of appropriateness. It need not be disease-specific.

3   **Audit of adherence to protocols or clinical guidelines.**

4   **Surveys of risk factors for disease, in so far as these are targets for intervention.**

System factors and balance of care

1   **Range and level of severity at service interfaces:** These can be measured and are necessary if district variations or trends are to be interpreted adequately.

2   **Mode of referral for acute illness:** This is easily measured and of great importance in acute severe illness.

3 **Ratio of regular to short-term attenders at outpatients:** This would not be an appropriate outcome measure for patients with cystic fibrosis, or those with rare chronic respiratory diseases, including diffuse parenchymal lung disease (not assessed in this chapter).

4 **Analysis of the service 'careers' of patients to describe, explain and compare patterns of use at the patient level rather than relying on 'spells' as at present.**

Research priorities

1 Development of standard methods suitable for monitoring at a community level morbidity and quality of life, treatment, and patient factors such as satisfaction with care, stigma and self-care skills.

2 Measurement and monitoring of the incidence of acute respiratory illness. For certain conditions with acute exacerbations there are very few epidemiological data on acute illness. Without this, it is difficult to assess need or interpret utilisation data.

3 Identification of the scope for prevention through environmental control of known precipitants in the home and outdoor environment.

4 Aetiological research directed at preventable factors.

5 Continued development and evaluation of vaccines, especially those against pneumococci and respiratory syncytial virus, and *Pseudomonas aeruginosa* in cystic fibrosis.

6 Evaluation of the prevention and treatment of hospital-acquired pneumonia.

7 Investigation of the impact of treatment on the natural history of obstructive lung disease, including iatrogenesis.

8 Case–control studies of adverse outcomes such as deaths, readmissions, etc. The fact that confidential enquiries into circumstances of death are not controlled limits their conclusions.

9 Appraisal of the extent to which population mortality and morbidity can be reduced by treatment.

10 Investigation of the reasons for the variability which exists between doctors and hospitals in the approach to diagnosis and management and the use of investigations and services.

11 Development of simple and standard ways of measuring disease severity at service interfaces and of ensuring uniform diagnostic recording.

12 Evaluation of those elements of consensus guidelines for which evidence of efficacy is lacking.

13 Assessment of the benefits and costs of various models of care, including marginal shifts to and from primary, secondary and tertiary care. This could include assessment of cost-effectiveness of GP asthma clinics, peripatetic clinics in primary care, various models of shared care, and models of care for patients with cystic fibrosis (tertiary, secondary and primary balance).

14 The role of specialist nurses and the most cost-effective use of their time and skills need further defining.

15 Evaluation of factors that lead to appropriate and inappropriate use of hospital admission, discharge, outpatient referral and outpatient discharge.

Appendix A: Classification of respiratory diseases

Mode of presentation of respiratory disease

The respiratory tract has a limited range of responses to infection, irritation, allergy or structural change. The symptoms encountered are therefore rarely disease-specific, posing problems for clinical diagnosis and epidemiological surveys. For example, cough may be a symptom of self-limiting upper respiratory infection, asthma, bronchitis, pneumonia, tuberculosis or lung cancer, whereas chronic breathlessness on exertion may indicate disease of the cardiovascular system rather than airflow limitation, emphysema or fibrosis of the lung.

The detection of rare but serious pathology in patients presenting with common symptoms poses a diagnostic task for respiratory medicine services. Respiratory illnesses may progress rapidly from an apparently innocuous 'common cold' to life-threatening pneumonia or bronchospasm. Although this occurs rather infrequently, it influences both clinical attitudes to the management of acute episodes and lay expectations of the services that should be provided.

Diagnostic labels

A wide range of apparently site-specific diagnostic terms are used in acute respiratory disease (e.g. bronchitis, bronchiolitis, laryngotracheobronchitis). These are rarely supported by any direct evidence of the site of involvement, and the ability to discriminate disease affecting different parts of the lower respiratory tract by clinical examination is poor. Consolidation of the lung seen on X-ray confirms the presence of pneumonia, but this diagnosis may be applied on clinical grounds alone.

The diagnosis of chronic obstructive lung disease is equally problematic. A conceptual distinction between potentially reversible airflow obstruction (due to bronchospasm) and irreversible airflow obstruction (associated with structural lung disease) is widely accepted, although many patients appear to have both. Clinical fashion in the labelling of these conditions has changed substantially in recent years. Historically, 'chronic bronchitis' and 'emphysema' were used interchangeably to describe adult patients with chronic lung disease. Since the 1980s, the less specific (but perhaps more honest) terms 'chronic obstructive airways disease' (COAD) or 'chronic obstructive pulmonary disease' (COPD) became increasingly popular.

The term COPD is now the internationally accepted term embracing all of the clinical labels or acronyms shown below, either alone or in combination:

- emphysema
- chronic bronchitis
- chronic obstructive bronchitis
- chronic airflow limitation (CAL)
- chronic airflow obstruction (CAO)
- chronic airways obstruction (CAO)
- non-reversible obstructive airways disease (NROAD)
- chronic obstructive pulmonary disease (COPD)
- chronic obstructive lung disease (COLD)
- some cases of chronic asthma.

Diagnostic fashions in paediatric practice have led to increasing use of the asthma label as a replacement for the previously more popular 'wheezy bronchitis'.

These issues have major implications for the interpretation of data coded to ICD classifications.

Site of involvement

Respiratory diseases are broadly divided into those affecting the 'upper' respiratory tract (nose, pharynx and larynx) and 'lower' respiratory diseases (affecting the trachea, bronchi or lungs). Diseases of the middle ear, although anatomically part of the respiratory tract, are generally excluded.

Episodes of illness may progress from upper respiratory involvement to lower respiratory symptoms, due to either physiological response (e.g. asthma), invasion of the intrathoracic airways by the primary pathogen (e.g. viral pneumonia) or secondary bacterial infection (e.g. exacerbation of chronic bronchitis by influenza).

Infections and allergies affecting the upper respiratory tract are extremely common and pose a substantial burden of minor morbidity, loss of productivity, school absence, etc. Few episodes progress to lower respiratory involvement, but when they do they generate much of the respiratory inpatient workload.

Chronicity

The distinction between acute episodes and chronic disease (or susceptibility) is important in assessing epidemiological information and planning service provision. Much of the workload posed by respiratory disease, particularly in general practice, comprises relatively brief, often self-limiting episodes of illness. These may be superimposed on chronic morbidity, typically in patients with chronic bronchitis or obstructive pulmonary disease (including asthma), but also as a result of rarer conditions such as cystic fibrosis, bronchiectasis or immune deficiency states (including AIDS).

Cause

Several respiratory syndromes may be described or subdivided in terms of presumed cause. This is not always of relevance to clinical management or service provision. For example, the distinction between 'extrinsic' and 'intrinsic' asthma is poorly defined and does not influence choice of treatment, and subdivision into infectious and non-infectious illness may be difficult because infectious episodes are a common cause of acute exacerbations in patients with allergic asthma or COPD.

An attempt to distinguish between viral and bacterial infection forms part of the clinical investigation and management of acute episodes, particularly of lower respiratory illness in hospital. The need to make this distinction is not always clear (e.g. acute lower respiratory illness in children). Even when specific organisms are sought (e.g. in patients hospitalised with pneumonia), they are identified in only a minority of cases. Most common respiratory pathogens are associated with a variety of syndromes involving both upper and lower respiratory tract.

Classification by specific infectious agent is of public health importance where immunisation is available (e.g. pertussis, measles, tuberculosis) or anticipated (e.g. respiratory syncytial virus). Wards for patients with tuberculosis have historically been located at a distance from other medical units and this separation sometimes persists in current arrangements for chest medicine services.

Prevention of non-infectious respiratory disease may usefully be planned by grouping diseases according to presumed cause (e.g. smoking-related diseases, occupational lung diseases).

Age

The distinction between paediatric and adult respiratory disease, although arbitrary, may be of some relevance for planning purposes. Special respiratory problems arise in the neonatal period, which are not part of this review. General paediatric services handle most of the respiratory disease requiring hospitalisation in childhood, whereas in adults the workload may be split between general medical units and specialist chest medicine services.

Classification for health service planning

The International Classification of Diseases (ICD) is extensively used for classifying mortality, morbidity and service use statistics, but several factors affect the interpretation of data coded to the ICD classifications. First, fashions in diagnostic labelling may result in shifts from one ICD code to another over time, and the possibility of diagnostic transfer needs to be considered carefully when reviewing epidemiological information, particularly relating to diseases of the lower respiratory tract. Second, the ICD classification emphasises the aetiology of diseases and, in line with this, routine mortality statistics are tabulated by underlying cause. This tends to underplay the importance of those respiratory conditions which exacerbate other conditions and/or commonly arise as complications, e.g. pneumonia. Different coding conventions apply to hospital admission and other service use statistics which are commonly coded and tabulated by the main condition treated or investigated, rather than by underlying cause. Finally, the ICD code does not reflect the severity of a condition which for a number of respiratory diseases, e.g. asthma, may range from subclinical to life-threatening.

Other ICD-compatible systems have been developed for use in specific settings, e.g. Read codes for classifying primary care episodes and health care resource groups (HRGs) for classifying hospital resource use, but as yet these are not widely used in the UK.

ICD-9 and ICD-10 codes relating to lower respiratory disease

Codes relating to respiratory disease from both the 9th and 10th revisions of the International Classification of Diseases are presented, since the data covered by this review were collected during the period of changeover between the two revisions of the classification. There is not an exact overlap between the two classifications, but where possible the list overleaf gives equivalent coding for each condition.

Codes presented here refer *only* to those conditions referred to in this review, either in the overall review, in analysis of health service and mortality data, or in the individual appendices.

Disease	ICD-9 codes	ICD-10 codes	ICD-10 description (where different)
Pulmonary tuberculosis	011	A15	Respiratory tuberculosis, bacteriologically and histologically confirmed
		A16	Respiratory tuberculosis, not confirmed bacteriologically or histologically
Whooping cough	032	A37	
Malignant neoplasm of trachea, bronchus and lung	162	C33	Malignant neoplasm of trachea
		C34	Malignant neoplasm of bronchus or lung
Malignant neoplasm of pleura	163	C38.4	
Malignant neoplasm of other or ill-defined sites in the respiratory system and intra-thoracic organs	165	C39	
Cystic fibrosis	277.0	E84	
Acute respiratory infections	460–465	J01–J06	
Other disorders of the upper respiratory tract	470–478	J01–J06	
Acute bronchitis and bronchiolitis	466	J20	Acute bronchitis
		J21	Acute bronchiolitis
Viral pneumonia	480	J12	
Pneumococcal pneumonia	481	J13	Pneumonia due to *Streptococcus pneumoniae*
Other bacterial pneumonia	482	J14	Pneumonia due to *Haemophilus influenzae*
		J15	Pneumonia due to other bacteria and *Mycoplasma*
Pneumonia due to other specified organism	483	J16	Chlamydial pneumonia Pneumonia due to other specified infectious organisms
		J17	Pneumonia in diseases classified elsewhere
Bronchopneumonia, organism unspecified	484	J180	
Pneumonia, organism unspecified	485	J181–189	
Influenza (with and without pneumonia)	487	J10	Influenza, virus identified
		J11	Influenza, virus not identified
Bronchitis, not specified as acute or chronic	490	J40	
Chronic bronchitis	491	J41	Chronic bronchitis, type specified
		J42	Chronic bronchitis, unspecified
Emphysema	492	J43	
Asthma	493	J45	Asthma, specified or unspecified
		J46	Status asthmaticus
Bronchiectasis	494	J47	
Extrinsic allergic alveolitis	495	J66	Airway diseases due to organic dusts
		J67	Hypersensitivity pneumonitis due to organic dusts

Disease	ICD-9 codes	ICD-10 codes	ICD-10 description (where different)
Chronic airways obstruction, not elsewhere classified	496	J44	Chronic obstructive pulmonary disease
Coalworkers, pneumoconiosis	500	J60	
Asbestosis	501	J61	Pneumoconiosis due to asbestos and other mineral fibres
		J92	Pleural plaque with or without presence or asbestos
Pneumoconiosis due to other silica or silicates	502	J62	Pneumoconiosis due to talc dust
			Pneumoconiosis due to other dust containing silica
Pneumoconiosis due to other inorganic dust	503	J63	
Pneumopathy due to inhalation of other dust	504	J67	Hypersensitivity pneumonitis due to organic dusts
Pneumoconiosis, unspecified	505	J64	Pneumoconiosis unspecified
		J65	Pneumoconiosis associated with tuberculosis
Respiratory conditions due to fumes and vapours	506	J68	Respiratory conditions due to chemicals, gases, fumes and vapours
Pneumonitis due to solids and liquids	507	J69	Pneumonitis due to food and vomit, oils and essences and other solids and liquids
Respiratory conditions due to other unspecified external agents	508	J70	(includes radiation, drug-induced interstitial lung disorders, and other or unspecified external agents)
Empyema	510	J86	Pyothorax
Pleurisy	511	J90	Pleural effusion not elsewhere classified
Pneumothorax	512	J93	
Abscess of lung and mediastinum	513	J85	
Pulmonary congestion and hypostasis	514	J80	Adult respiratory distress syndrome
		J81	Pulmonary oedema
Post-inflammatory pulmonary fibrosis	515	J84	
Other alveolar and parieto-alveolar pneumopathy	516	J84	
Other diseases of the lung	518	J95	Post-surgical pulmonary disorders
		J96	Acute and chronic respiratory failure
		J98	Other diseases of the lung, mediastinum, diaphragm and respiratory tract, specified and unspecified respiratory disorders
Other diseases of the respiratory system	519	J98	Other diseases of the lung, mediastinum, diaphragm and respiratory tract, specified and unspecified respiratory disorders
		J99	Respiratory disorders in diseases classified elsewhere
Respiratory distress syndrome	769	P28.0	Primary atelectasis of newborn
Other respiratory conditions of newborn and fetus	770	P28.1–P28.9	

Health care-related groups relating to lower respiratory disease

HRG	Description
D01	Lung transplant
D02	Complex thoracic procedures
D03	Major thoracic procedures
D04	Intermediate thoracic procedures with complicating condition
D05	Intermediate thoracic procedures without complicating condition
D06	Minor thoracic procedures
D07	Fibre-optic bronchoscopy
D08	Rigid bronchoscopy
D09	Pulmonary embolus – died
D10	Pulmonary embolus > 69 or with complicating condition
D11	Pulmonary embolus < 70 or without complicating condition
D12	Lung abscess or empyema
D13	Lobar, atypical or viral pneumonia > 69 or with comorbid condition
D14	Lobar, atypical or viral pneumonia < 70 without comorbid condition
D15	Bronchopneumonia
D16	Bronchiectasis
D17	Cystic fibrosis
D18	Pulmonary or pleural tuberculosis
D19	Other tuberculosis
D20	Chronic obstructive pulmonary disease or bronchitis
D21	Asthma > 49 years or with comorbid condition
D22	Asthma < 50 years without comorbid condition
D23	Pleural effusion or pleurisy > 69 or with comorbid condition
D24	Pleural effusion or pleurisy < 70 without comorbid condition
D25	Respiratory neoplasms
D26	Fibrosis or pneumoconiosis
D27	Extrinsic allergic alveolitis or pulmonary eosinophilia
D28	Granulomatous or other lung disease
D29	Inhalation lung injury or foreign body aspiration
D30	Pneumothorax
D31	Sleep-disordered breathing
D32	Respiratory failure
D33	Other respiratory diagnosis > 69 or with comorbid condition
D34	Other respiratory diagnosis < 70 without comorbid condition
E01	Heart and lung transplant
P01	Asthma/recurrent wheeze
P03	Upper respiratory tract disorder
P04	Lower respiratory tract disorder

Appendix B: Main tables and figures

Tables

Table B.1: Percentage of all deaths, GP consultations, finished consultant episodes and bed-days due to lower respiratory disorders, both sexes, all ages combined.

Category			Mortality by underlying cause (England and Wales 1999)		GP consultations (England 1991–92)		Finished consultant episodes (England 1998–99)		Occupied bed-days (England 1998–99)	
Cause	ICD-9	ICD-10	Deaths	Percentage	Consultations per 10,000 pyar*	Percentage	FCE	Percentage	Bed-days	Percentage
Pulmonary TB	011–012	A15–16	299	0.05	2	0.03	1,942	0.02	43,478	0.07
Whooping cough	033	A37	2	0.00	1	0.01	1,001	0.01	4,375	0.01
Ca trachea, bronchus, lung and pleura	162	C33–34	29,493	5.30	8	0.10	90,831	0.76	518,474	0.83
Cystic fibrosis	277.0	E84	119	0.02	3	0.04	12,037	0.10	73,426	0.12
Upper respiratory	460–465, 470–478	J01–06	37	0.01	2,131	27.31	64,589	0.54	130,331	0.21
Acute bronchitis and bronchiolitis	466	J20–21	487	0.09	719	9.21	25,016	0.21	85,901	0.14
Other upper respiratory tract	470–478	J01–06	47	0.01	430	5.51				
Pneumonia	480–486	J12–18	59,273	10.66	29	0.37	122,312	1.02	1,692,778	2.70
Influenza	487	J10–11	585	0.11	205	2.63	3,449	0.03	22,580	0.04
Chronic and unspecified bronchitis	490–491	J40–42	1,736	0.31	91	1.17	7,672	0.06	69,941	0.11
Emphysema and COPD	492+496	J43–44	24,378	4.38	56	0.72	18,372	0.15	127,115	0.20
Asthma	493	J45–46	1,364	0.25	425	5.45	300,613	2.51	1,085,960	1.73
Other COPD	494–495	J47	768	0.14	5	0.06	7,931	0.07	48,661	0.08

Table B.1: Continued.

Category			Mortality by underlying cause (England and Wales 1999)		GP consultations (England 1991–92)		Finished consultant episodes (England 1998–99)		Occupied bed-days (England 1998–99)	
Cause	ICD-9	ICD-10	Deaths	Percentage	Consultations per 10,000 pyar*	Percentage	FCE	Percentage	Bed-days	Percentage
All COPD excl. asthma	490–496	J40–44, 47	26,882	4.83	538	6.89	241,145	2.01	1,989,908	3.17
Pneumoconioses†	500–508	J60–67	1,023	0.18	1	0.01	3,469	0.03	23,355	0.04
Other respiratory	510–519	J68–99	8,057	1.45	34	0.44	137,142	1.15	1,382,152	2.21
All Chapter VIII	460–519	J01–99	97,755	17.58	3,070	39.34	897,735	7.50	6,412,965	10.23
Total Chapter VIII lower respiratory (i.e. excludes upper respiratory J01–06)			97,671	17.56	939	12.03	833,146	6.96	6,282,634	10.02
Total non-Chapter VIII lower respiratory (A15–16 + 37, C33–34, E84)			29,913	5.38	14	0.18	105,811	0.88	639,753	1.02
Total lower respiratory			127,584	22.94	953	12.21	938,957	7.84	6,922,387	11.04

* pyar, person years at risk.
† Includes diseases due to organic dust in ICD-10.

Table B.2: Mortality and service use for 1998–99 in hypothetical district with population of 500 000 with similar population structure to England and Wales.

Cause	ICD-9	ICD-10	Number of deaths	Number of GP consult-ations	Number of finished consultant episodes	Number of bed-days per year	Average occupied hospital beds per day
Pulmonary TB	011–012	A15–16	3	100	20	437	1
Whooping cough	033	A37	0	50	10	44	0
Ca trachea, bronchus, lung and pleura	162	C33–34	280	400	913	5,211	14
Cystic fibrosis	277.0	E84	1	150	121	5,738	16
Upper respiratory	460–465, 470–478	J01–06	2	106,550	649	1,310	4
Acute bronchitis and bronchiolitis	466	J20–21	5	35,950	251	863	2
Pneumonia	480–486	J12–18	562	1,450	1,229	17,012	47
Influenza	487	J10–11	6	10,250	35	227	1
Chronic and unspecified bronchitis	490–491	J40–42	16	4,550	77	703	2
Emphysema and COPD	492+496	J43–44	231	2,800	185	1,277	3
Asthma	493	J45–46	13	21,250	3,021	10,914	30
Other COPD	494–495	J47	7	250	80	489	1
All COPD	490–496	J40–47	255	26,900	2,423	19,998	55
Pneumoconioses*	500–508	J60–67	10	50	35	235	1
Other respiratory	510–519	J68–99	76	1,700	1,378	13,890	38
All Chapter VIII	460–519	J01–99	928	153,500	9,363	66,918	183

Source: Tables B.1, B.4, B.5 and B.6.

* Includes diseases due to organic dust in ICD-10.

Table B.3: Summary of the principal findings from ad hoc surveys of prevalence and incidence of lower respiratory disease.

Respiratory condition		Prevalence	Incidence	Cumulative incidence	Modifying factors
Acute lower respiratory tract infections in childhood	Acute bronchitis			20%	Males > females and north > south; associated with poor socio-economic status, large families, parental smoking, low birth weight (27–32)
	Pneumonia			1–5%	
	Whooping cough			1.6%	
				see Table 1	
Adult respiratory infections	Community-acquired pneumonia		230–360 per 100,000 (470 per 100,000 adults only) (9–12)(37)(42)		Social class V > I, associated with smoking, alcohol and pre-existing illness (10–12)(42)
	Nosocomial pneumonia		0.5–1% of all hospital admissions, 12–22% of ICU admissions (43)(44)		
Tuberculosis		Notifications (annual rate): Indian, Pakistani and Bangladeshi communities 169–178 per 100,000; whites 6.9 per 100,000			Ethnicity, HIV infection
Asthma	Requiring treatment (46)(47), Tables 2, 3	0–14 years: 6% 15–64: 4% 65+: 4% all ages: 4%			South > north (65)
	Current wheezing (any severity)	0–14 years: 12–15% 15–64: 10% 65+: 15–20%		30%	
COPD (81)(82), Table 4	symptomatic	17% men, 6% women			North > south, urban > rural, social
	Significant impairment of lung function	5% men, 3% women			Class V > I (82)

Table B.4: Death rate per million for selected respiratory causes, England and Wales 1999.

Age range (years)		Number					Rate per million				
		0–14	15–44	45–64	65+	Total	0–14	15–44	45–64	65+	Total
Pulmonary TB 011	Male	0	20	39	145	204	0.0	1.8	6.4	42.1	7.9
	Female	0	8	9	76	93	0.0	0.7	1.5	15.7	3.5
	Total	0	28	48	221	297	0.0	1.3	3.9	26.7	5.6
Other respiratory TB 012	Male	0	0	0	2	2	0.0	0.0	0.0	0.6	0.1
	Female	0	0	0	0	0	0.0	0.0	0.0	0.0	0.0
	Total	0	0	0	2	2	0.0	0.0	0.0	0.2	0.0
Whooping cough 033	Male	1	0	0	0	1	0.2	0.0	0.0	0.0	0.0
	Female	1	0	0	0	1	0.2	0.0	0.0	0.0	0.0
	Total	2	0	0	0	2	0.2	0.0	0.0	0.0	0.0
Lung cancer 162	Male	0	154	3,969	14,219	18,342	0.0	13.6	651.0	4,132.0	705.9
	Female	0	136	2,337	8,678	11,151	0.0	12.6	379.2	1,790.3	417.6
	Total	0	290	6,306	22,897	29,493	0.0	13.1	514.4	2,762.6	559.7
Cystic fibrosis 277.0	Male	5	48	1	0	54	1.0	4.3	0.2	0.0	2.1
	Female	7	55	2	1	65	1.4	5.1	0.3	0.2	2.4
	Total	12	103	3	1	119	1.2	4.7	0.2	0.1	2.3
Acute respiratory infections 460–465	Male	1	4	3	7	15	0.2	0.4	0.5	2.0	0.6
	Female	3	2	1	16	22	0.6	0.2	0.2	3.3	0.8
	Total	4	6	4	23	37	0.4	0.3	0.3	2.8	0.7
Acute bronchitis and bronchiolitis 466	Male	22	9	34	117	182	4.3	0.8	5.6	34.0	7.0
	Female	10	5	34	256	305	2.0	0.5	5.5	52.8	11.4
	Total	32	14	68	373	487	3.2	0.6	5.5	45.0	9.2
Other upper respiratory tract 470–478	Male	0	3	12	9	24	0.0	0.3	2.0	2.6	0.9
	Female	1	2	4	16	23	0.2	0.2	0.6	3.3	0.9
	Total	1	5	16	25	47	0.1	0.2	1.3	3.0	0.9
Pneumonia 480–486	Male	70	299	1,481	21,536	23,386	13.6	26.5	242.9	6,258.3	900.0
	Female	52	198	947	34,690	35,887	10.6	18.3	153.7	7,156.9	1,343.8
	Total	122	497	2,428	56,226	59,273	12.1	22.5	198.1	6,783.8	1,124.9
Influenza 487	Male	6	4	17	181	208	1.2	0.4	2.8	52.6	8.0
	Female	2	3	15	357	377	0.4	0.3	2.4	73.7	14.1
	Total	8	7	32	538	585	0.8	0.3	2.6	64.9	11.1

Table B.4: Continued.

Age range (years)		Number					Rate per million				
		0–14	15–44	45–64	65+	Total	0–14	15–44	45–64	65+	Total
Chronic and unspecified bronchitis	Male	4	3	123	946	1,076	0.8	0.3	20.2	274.9	41.4
490–491	Female	3	9	61	587	660	0.6	0.8	9.9	121.1	24.7
	Total	7	12	184	1,533	1,736	0.7	0.5	15.0	185.0	32.9
Emphysema	Male	0	8	166	985	1,159	0.0	0.7	27.2	286.2	44.6
492	Female	1	2	79	475	557	0.2	0.2	12.8	98.0	20.9
	Total	1	10	245	1,460	1,716	0.1	0.5	20.0	176.2	32.6
Asthma	Male	17	61	127	291	496	3.3	5.4	20.8	84.6	19.1
493	Female	6	78	162	622	868	1.2	7.2	26.3	128.3	32.5
	Total	23	139	289	913	1,364	2.3	6.3	23.6	110.2	25.9
Bronchiectasis and alveolitis	Male	0	3	68	267	338	0.0	0.3	11.2	77.6	13.0
494–495	Female	0	4	77	349	430	0.0	0.4	12.5	72.0	16.1
	Total	0	7	145	616	768	0.0	0.3	11.8	74.3	14.6
Chronic airways obstruction	Male	2	11	1,015	11,595	12,623	0.4	1.0	166.5	3,369.5	485.8
496	Female	1	12	792	9,234	10,039	0.2	1.1	128.5	1,905.1	375.9
	Total	3	23	1,807	20,829	22,662	0.3	1.0	147.4	2,513.1	430.1
Pneumoconioses	Male	3	9	56	639	707	0.6	0.8	9.2	185.7	27.2
500–508	Female	4	9	19	284	316	0.8	0.8	3.1	58.6	11.8
	Total	7	18	75	923	1,023	0.7	0.8	6.1	111.4	19.4
Other respiratory diseases	Male	51	47	296	3,159	3,553	9.9	4.2	48.5	918.0	136.7
510–519	Female	27	40	192	4,245	4,504	5.5	3.7	31.2	875.8	168.7
	Total	78	87	488	7,404	8,057	7.8	3.9	39.8	893.3	152.9
Respiratory symptoms	Male	0	1	2	4	7	0.0	0.1	0.3	1.2	0.3
786	Female	0	0	2	3	5	0.0	0.0	0.3	0.6	0.2
	Total	0	1	4	7	12	0.0	0.0	0.3	0.8	0.2
All Chapter VIII	Male	176	461	3,398	39,732	43,767	34.1	40.8	557.3	11,546.0	1,684.3
460–519	Female	110	364	2,383	51,131	53,988	22.4	33.7	386.7	10,548.8	2,021.6
	Total	286	825	5,781	90,863	97,755	28.4	37.4	471.6	10,962.8	1,855.3
All causes	Male	2,973	11,953	42,309	207,064	264,299	576.6	1,058.7	6,939.4	60,172.0	10,171.4
	Female	2,229	6,309	27,060	256,221	291,819	454.9	5,84.4	4,391.2	52,860.7	10,927.3
	Total	5,202	18,262	69,369	463,285	556,118	517.3	8,26.9	5,658.5	55,896.3	10,554.5

Table B.5: Number and rate per million for finished consultant episodes for selected respiratory diagnoses.

Age range (years)		Number (where sex is known)					Rate per million				
		0–14	15–44	45–64	65+	Total	0–14	15–44	45–64	65+	Total
Pulmonary TB A15	Male	10	223	166	201	600	2.1	20.8	28.9	62.2	24.4
	Female	15	197	68	102	382	3.2	19.3	11.7	22.4	15.2
	Total	25	420	234	303	982	2.6	20.1	20.3	38.9	19.7
Other respiratory TB A16	Male	10	231	136	201	578	2.1	21.6	23.7	62.2	23.6
	Female	15	197	68	102	382	3.2	19.3	11.7	22.4	15.2
	Total	25	428	204	303	960	2.6	20.5	17.7	38.9	19.3
Whooping cough A37	Male	463	2	0	1	466	95.1	0.2	0.0	0.3	19.0
	Female	528	6	1	0	535	114.1	0.6	0.2	0.0	21.2
	Total	991	8	1	1	1,001	104.4	0.4	0.1	0.1	20.1
Lung cancer C33–C34	Male	24	1,017	19,378	37,129	57,553	4.9	95.1	3,373.7	11,493.3	2,345.0
	Female	21	976	11,981	20,298	33,278	4.5	95.4	2,064.4	4,461.0	1,320.0
	Total	45	1,993	31,359	57,427	90,831	4.7	95.2	2,715.7	7,380.5	1,825.6
Cystic fibrosis E84	Male	2,667	3,260	35	15	5,977	547.7	304.7	6.1	4.6	243.5
	Female	2,680	3,310	64	5	6,060	579.2	323.6	11.0	1.1	240.4
	Total	5,347	6,570	99	20	12,037	563.0	313.9	8.6	2.6	241.9
Acute respiratory infections J01–J06	Male	32,174	1,466	790	1,619	36,050	6,607.4	137.0	137.5	501.2	1,468.9
	Female	22,546	2,437	1,114	2,435	28,539	4,872.5	238.2	191.9	535.2	1,132.1
	Total	54,720	3,903	1,904	4,054	64,589	5,762.0	186.5	164.9	521.0	1,298.2
Acute bronchitis and bronchiolitis J20–J21	Male	13,665	128	205	484	14,484	2,806.3	12.0	35.7	149.8	590.2
	Female	9,416	197	207	711	10,532	2,034.9	19.3	35.7	156.3	417.8
	Total	23,081	325	412	1,195	25,016	2,430.4	15.5	35.7	153.6	502.8
Pneumonia J12–J18	Male	7,253	6,027	8,850	38,952	61,117	1,489.5	563.3	1,540.8	12,057.6	2,490.2
	Female	5,515	4,725	6,042	44,897	61,195	1,191.9	461.9	1,041.1	9,867.3	2,427.4
	Total	12,768	10,752	14,892	83,849	122,312	1,344.5	513.8	1,289.6	10,776.3	2,458.4
Influenza J10–J11	Male	337	406	307	440	1,493	69.2	37.9	53.4	136.2	60.8
	Female	284	748	299	622	1,956	61.4	73.1	51.5	136.7	77.6
	Total	621	1,154	606	1,062	3,449	65.4	55.1	52.5	136.5	69.3
Chronic and unspecified bronchitis J40–J42	Male	132	291	846	2,594	3,863	27.1	27.2	147.3	803.0	157.4
	Female	70	377	839	2,522	3,809	15.1	36.9	144.6	554.3	151.1
	Total	202	668	1,685	5,116	7,672	21.3	31.9	145.9	657.5	154.2

Table B.5: Continued.

Age range (years)		Number (where sex is known)					Rate per million				
		0–14	15–44	45–64	65+	Total	0–14	15–44	45–64	65+	Total
Emphysema J43–J44	Male	14	255	2,774	9,231	12,275	2.9	23.8	482.9	2,857.5	500.1
	Female	33	169	1,424	4,471	6,097	7.1	16.5	245.4	982.6	241.8
	Total	47	424	4,198	13,702	18,372	4.9	20.3	363.5	1,761.0	369.3
Asthma J45–J46	Male	38,074	30,781	24,570	29,400	122,869	7,819.0	2,877.6	4,277.6	9,100.8	5,006.3
	Female	21,539	70,322	38,665	46,894	177,744	4,654.9	6,874.8	6,662.2	10,306.1	7,050.6
	Total	59,613	101,103	63,235	76,294	300,613	6,277.2	4,831.0	5,476.1	9,805.3	6,042.1
Bronchiectasis and alveolitis J47	Male	139	403	1,063	1,402	3,008	28.5	37.7	185.1	434.0	122.6
	Female	131	614	2,151	2,027	4,923	28.3	60.0	370.6	445.5	195.3
	Total	270	1,017	3,214	3,429	7,931	28.4	48.6	278.3	440.7	159.4
Chronic obstructive pulmonary disease (COPD) J40–J47	Male	163	965	23,515	109,231	133,891	33.5	90.2	4,093.9	33,812.4	5,455.4
	Female	78	1,307	18,383	87,465	107,254	16.9	127.8	3,167.5	19,222.7	4,254.4
	Total	241	2,272	41,898	196,696	241,145	25.4	108.6	3,628.3	25,279.3	4,846.9
Pneumoconioses J60–J67	Male	0	7	357	3,041	3,406	0.0	0.7	62.2	941.3	138.8
	Female	0	1	10	52	63	0.0	0.1	1.7	11.4	2.5
	Total	0	8	367	3,093	3,469	0.0	0.4	31.8	397.5	69.7
Other respiratory diseases J68–J99	Male	3,684	9,540	18,765	43,885	75,902	756.6	891.7	3,266.9	13,584.6	3,092.6
	Female	2,637	6,618	13,876	38,097	61,240	569.9	647.0	2,390.9	8,372.8	2,429.2
	Total	6,321	16,158	32,641	81,982	137,142	665.6	772.1	2,826.7	10,536.3	2,756.5
All Chapter VIII	Male	95,635	50,269	82,042	240,279	468,358	19,640.0	4,698.5	14,283.3	74,378.3	19,083.3
	Female	62,249	87,515	83,010	230,193	463,352	13,452.8	8,555.6	14,303.2	50,590.8	18,379.8
	Total	157,884	137,784	165,052	470,472	931,710	16,625.1	6,583.8	14,293.3	60,465.0	18,726.7
All causes	Male	943,612	1,124,583	1,266,584	1,833,105	5,172,521	193,784.0	105,111.0	220,509.4	567,436.9	210,755.1
	Female	758,658	2,689,907	1,276,045	2,057,819	6,800,957	163,956.2	262,968.7	219,871.3	452,258.0	269,773.3
	Total	1,702,270	3,814,490	2,542,629	3,890,924	11,973,478	179,248.6	182,269.0	220,188.7	500,060.9	240,658.9

Table B.6: Average bed-days per year per million population, and average number of beds in use per day per million population for selected respiratory diagnoses, England 1998–99.

Age range (years)		Bed-days (where sex is known)					Bed-days per million					Average beds in use per day per million population				
		0–14	15–44	45–64	65+	Total	0–14	15–44	45–64	65+	Total	0–14	15–44	45–64	65+	Total
Pulmonary TB A15	Male	74	2,456	2,630	3,279	8,439	15.2	229.6	457.9	1,015.0	343.8	0.0	0.6	1.3	2.8	0.9
	Female	60	1,497	666	5,285	7,508	13.0	146.3	114.8	1,161.5	297.8	0.0	0.4	0.3	3.2	0.8
	Total	134	3,953	3,296	8,564	15,947	14.1	188.9	285.4	1,100.6	320.5	0.0	0.5	0.8	3.0	0.9
Other respiratory TB A16	Male	208	6,108	4,320	6,677	17,313	42.7	570.9	752.1	2,066.9	705.4	0.1	1.6	2.1	5.7	1.9
	Female	262	3,424	1,757	4,775	10,218	56.6	334.7	302.7	1,049.4	405.3	0.2	0.9	0.8	2.9	1.1
	Total	470	9,532	6,077	11,452	27,531	49.5	455.5	526.3	1,471.8	553.4	0.1	1.2	1.4	4.0	1.5
Whooping cough A37	Male	1,823	2	0	0	1,825	374.4	0.2	0.0	0.0	74.4	1.0	0.0	0.0	0.0	0.2
	Female	2,535	14	1	0	2,550	547.8	1.4	0.2	0.0	101.2	1.5	0.0	0.0	0.0	0.3
	Total	4,358	16	1	0	4,375	458.9	0.8	0.1	0.0	87.9	1.3	0.0	0.0	0.0	0.2
Lung cancer C33–C34	Male	127	3,973	75,434	234,437	314,010	26.1	371.3	13,132.9	72,569.9	12,794.4	0.1	1.0	36.0	198.8	35.1
	Female	96	3,810	47,726	152,815	204,464	20.7	372.5	8,223.5	33,585.0	8,110.5	0.1	1.0	22.5	92.0	22.2
	Total	223	7,783	123,160	387,252	518,474	23.5	371.9	10,665.5	49,769.6	10,421.0	0.1	1.0	29.2	136.4	28.6
Cystic fibrosis E84	Male	13,971	22,028	281	156	36,436	2,869.1	2,058.9	48.9	48.3	1,484.6	7.9	5.6	0.1	0.1	4.1
	Female	16,098	20,533	303	56	36,990	3,479.0	2,007.3	52.2	12.3	1,467.3	9.5	5.5	0.1	0.0	4.0
	Total	30,069	42,561	584	212	73,426	3,166.3	2,033.7	50.6	27.2	1,475.8	8.7	5.6	0.1	0.1	4.0
Acute respiratory infections J01–J06	Male	37,734	5,273	4,317	15,943	63,269	7,749.2	492.8	751.6	4,935.1	2,577.9	21.2	1.4	2.1	13.5	7.1
	Female	26,662	5,547	4,848	30,003	67,062	5,762.0	542.3	835.3	6,593.9	2,660.1	15.8	1.5	2.3	18.1	7.3
	Total	64,396	10,820	9,165	45,946	130,331	6,780.9	517.0	793.7	5,905.0	2,619.6	18.6	1.4	2.2	16.2	7.2
Acute bronchitis and bronchiolitis J20–J21	Male	37,677	283	980	5,918	44,862	7,737.5	26.5	170.6	1,831.9	1,827.9	21.2	0.1	0.5	5.0	5.0
	Female	28,331	4,778	762	7,158	41,039	6,122.7	467.1	131.3	1,573.2	1,627.9	16.8	1.3	0.4	4.3	4.5
	Total	66,008	5,061	1,742	13,076	85,901	6,950.6	241.8	150.9	1,680.5	1,726.6	19.0	0.7	0.4	4.6	4.7
Pneumonia J12–J18	Male	26,955	38,499	84,846	590,380	740,980	5,535.6	3,598.4	14,771.5	182,751.9	30,191.3	15.2	9.9	40.5	500.7	82.7
	Female	21,996	26,165	61,212	842,268	951,798	4,753.6	2,557.9	10,547.2	185,109.8	37,754.9	13.0	7.0	28.9	507.2	103.4
	Total	48,951	64,664	146,058	1,432,648	1,692,778	5,154.5	3,089.9	12,648.5	184,123.7	34,023.7	14.1	8.5	34.7	504.4	93.2
Influenza J10–J11	Male	1,237	656	1,869	5,910	9,696	254.0	61.3	325.4	1,829.4	395.1	0.7	0.2	0.9	5.0	1.1
	Female	966	2,717	942	8,252	12,884	208.8	265.6	162.3	1,813.6	511.1	0.6	0.7	0.4	5.0	1.4
	Total	2,203	3,373	2,811	14,162	22,580	232.0	161.2	243.4	1,820.1	453.8	0.6	0.4	0.7	5.0	1.2
Chronic and unspecified bronchitis J40–J42	Male	177	1,774	3,632	17,326	22,909	36.3	165.8	632.3	5,363.3	933.3	0.1	0.5	1.7	14.7	2.6
	Female	154	23,877	4,011	18,990	47,032	33.3	2,334.2	691.1	4,173.5	1,865.6	0.1	6.4	1.9	11.4	5.1
	Total	331	25,651	7,643	36,316	69,941	34.9	1,225.7	661.9	4,667.3	1,405.8	0.1	3.4	1.8	12.8	3.9
Emphysema J43–J44	Male	52	1,197	14,686	66,729	82,668	10.7	111.9	2,556.8	20,655.9	3,368.3	0.0	0.3	7.0	56.6	9.2
	Female	128	768	8,235	35,316	44,447	27.7	75.1	1,418.9	7,761.6	1,763.1	0.1	0.2	3.9	21.3	4.8
	Total	180	1,965	22,921	102,045	127,115	19.0	93.9	1,984.9	13,114.8	2,554.9	0.1	0.3	5.4	35.9	7.0

Table B.6: Continued.

Age range (years)		Bed-days (where sex is known)					Bed-days per million					Average beds in use per day per million population				
		0–14	15–44	45–64	65+	Total	0–14	15–44	45–64	65+	Total	0–14	15–44	45–64	65+	Total
Asthma J45–J46	Male	67,331	89,395	87,114	156,946	400,901	13,827.4	8,355.5	15,166.4	48,582.6	16,334.8	37.9	22.9	41.6	133.1	44.8
	Female	33,740	178,922	148,659	323,426	685,059	7,291.7	17,491.6	25,615.0	7,1081.1	27,174.2	20.0	47.9	70.2	194.7	74.4
	Total	101,071	268,317	235,773	480,372	1,085,960	10,642.7	12,821.1	20,417.7	61,737.3	21,827.1	29.2	35.1	55.9	169.1	59.8
Bronchiectasis J47	Male	512	1,601	5,486	10,416	18,017	105.1	149.6	955.1	3,224.3	734.1	0.3	0.4	2.6	8.8	2.0
	Female	576	2,648	10,597	16,823	30,644	124.5	258.9	1,825.9	3,697.3	1,215.6	0.3	0.7	5.0	10.1	3.3
	Total	1,088	4,249	16,083	27,239	48,661	114.6	203.0	1,392.8	3,500.8	978.1	0.3	0.6	3.8	9.6	2.7
Chronic obstructive pulmonary disease (COPD) J40–J47	Male	735	3,934	137,599	913,549	1,055,909	150.9	367.7	23,955.7	282,788.7	43,023.2	0.4	1.0	65.6	774.8	117.9
	Female	277	5,662	106,256	821,633	933,999	59.9	553.5	18,308.6	180,574.7	37,048.9	0.2	1.5	50.2	494.7	101.5
	Total	1,012	9,596	243,855	1,735,182	1,989,908	106.6	458.5	21,117.6	223,005.3	39,995.8	0.3	1.3	57.9	611.0	109.6
Pneumoconioses J60–J67	Male	0	13	1,563	21,192	22,768	0.0	1.2	272.1	6,560.0	927.7	0.0	0.0	0.7	18.0	2.5
	Female	0	18	55	514	587	0.0	1.8	9.5	113.0	23.3	0.0	0.0	0.0	0.3	0.1
	Total	0	31	1,618	21,706	23,355	0.0	1.5	140.1	2,789.7	469.4	0.0	0.0	0.4	7.6	1.3
Other respiratory diseases J68–J99	Male	28,494	72,603	171,806	462,123	735,355	5,851.6	6,786.0	29,911.0	143,050.0	29,962.1	16.0	18.6	81.9	391.9	82.1
	Female	22,937	54,702	120,590	448,441	646,797	4,957.0	5,347.7	20,778.5	98,556.3	25,656.5	13.6	14.7	56.9	270.0	70.3
	Total	51,431	127,305	292,396	910,564	1,382,152	5,415.7	6,083.1	25,321.2	117,025.5	27,280.3	14.8	16.7	69.4	320.6	76.1
All Chapter VIII J01–J99	Male	200,904	215,228	513,898	2,266,432	3,197,334	41,258.5	20,116.6	89,468.5	701,573.1	130,275.8	113.0	55.1	245.1	1,922.1	356.9
	Female	135,767	305,804	466,167	2,552,824	3,461,348	29,341.1	29,895.8	80,323.8	561,047.9	137,301.1	80.4	81.9	220.1	1,537.1	376.2
	Total	336,671	521,032	980,065	4,819,256	6,658,682	35,451.4	24,896.6	84,872.5	619,370.0	133,835.1	97.1	68.2	232.5	1,696.9	366.7
All causes	Male	3,976,642	6,756,253	5,450,803	12,325,963	28,549,223	816,659.5	631,484.5	948,972.5	3,815,497.0	1,163,242.3	2,237.4	1,730.1	2,599.9	10,453.4	3,187.0
	Female	2,569,791	7,646,858	5,053,527	18,796,077	34,127,493	555,366.3	747,566.5	870,757.3	4,130,915.1	1,353,733.8	1,521.6	2,048.1	2,385.6	11,317.6	3,708.9
	Total	6,546,433	14,403,111	10,504,330	31,122,040	62,676,716	689,337.7	688,228.6	909,662.7	3,999,799.5	1,259,760.1	1,888.6	1,885.6	2,492.2	10,958.4	3,451.4

Source: HES Statistics, England, 1998–99.

Note: This table refers to bed-days where a respiratory diagnosis is mentioned anywhere.

Table B.7: GP consultation rates per 10 000 person years at risk, England 1991–92.

Age range (years)		Consultation rate per 10,000 person years at risk								
		0–4	5–15	16–24	25–44	45–64	65–74	75–84	85 and over	Total
Pulmonary TB 011	Male	0	0	0	1	3	6	5	0	1
	Female	0	0	0	1	1	2	1	2	1
	Total	0	0	0	1	2	4	2	1	1
Other respiratory TB 012	Male	0	0	0	0	0	0	0	0	0
	Female	0	0	0	0	0	0	0	0	0
	Total	0	0	0	0	0	0	0	0	0
Whooping cough 033	Male	9	3	0	0	0	0	0	0	1
	Female	15	5	0	1	0	0	0	0	2
	Total	12	4	0	0	0	0	0	0	1
Lung cancer 162	Male	0	0	0	0	14	45	61	71	9
	Female	0	0	0	0	9	15	17	16	5
	Total	0	0	0	0	11	29	33	30	7
Cystic fibrosis 277.0 (includes other and unspecified metabolic disorders)	Male	5	4	5	2	2	2	1	0	3
	Female	7	3	3	2	1	2	1	2	3
	Total	6	4	4	2	2	2	1	1	3
Acute respiratory infections 460–465	Male	4,527	2,180	1,426	1,015	781	788	747	803	1,410
	Female	4,478	2,713	2,452	1,896	1,359	1,065	928	892	1,980
	Total	4,504	2,439	1,941	1,454	1,067	940	861	870	1,701
Acute bronchitis and bronchiolitis 466	Male	1,664	440	358	374	632	1,148	1,521	1,913	643
	Female	1,488	402	502	615	894	1,136	1,242	1,588	792
	Total	1,578	422	430	494	762	1,142	1,346	1,669	719
Other upper respiratory tract 470–478	Male	349	697	529	354	265	313	243	190	398
	Female	306	581	684	528	359	330	215	118	460
	Total	328	641	607	441	311	322	225	136	430
Pneumonia 480–486	Male	43	19	7	12	23	69	185	269	30
	Female	29	10	8	11	18	48	143	247	28
	Total	37	15	8	12	21	41	126	313	29
Influenza 487	Male	216	164	193	194	172	148	156	190	181
	Female	188	180	262	255	248	185	491	150	228
	Total	202	172	227	224	209	168	178	160	205

Table B.7: Continued.

Age range (years)		Consultation rate per 10,000 person years at risk								
		0–4	5–15	16–24	25–44	45–64	65–74	75–84	85 and over	Total
Chronic and unspecified bronchitis	Male	106	21	12	25	90	303	367	416	80
490–491	Female	92	18	20	38	101	181	221	250	78
	Total	99	19	21	31	95	236	275	292	79
Emphysema	Male	0	0	0	1	9	28	26	24	5
492	Female	0	0	0	1	4	7	3	2	2
	Total	0	0	0	1	6	16	12	7	4
Asthma	Male	1,017	626	249	157	150	197	158	125	300
493	Female	742	460	301	224	215	244	194	104	295
	Total	883	545	275	190	182	223	180	109	297
Bronchiectasis and alveolitis	Male	1	0	1		4	4	10	6	2
494–495	Female	1	0	0	2	7	12	5	10	3
	Total	1	0	0	1	5	8	7	9	3
Chronic airways obstruction	Male	1	0	0	2	39	158	172	178	29
496	Female	0	0	0	3	32	35	90	61	20
	Total	0	0	0	2	35	107	121	90	24
Pneumoconioses	Male	0	0	0	0	2	6	9	6	1
500–508	Female	0	0	0	0	0	1	1	0	0
	Total	0	0	0	0	1	4	4	1	1
Other respiratory diseases	Male	43	10	19	22	34	62	97	107	31
510–519	Female	33	11	27	35	44	59	66	71	37
	Total	38	10	23	28	39	60	78	80	34
Respiratory symptoms	Male	1,114	327	165	202	309	459	519	630	339
786	Female	1,077	364	241	268	379	484	512	498	392
	Total	1,096	345	203	235	344	473	514	531	366
All Chapter VIII	Male	6,643	3,552	2,524	1,956	1,979	2,743	3,192	3,714	2,722
460–519	Female	6,290	3,814	3,712	3,140	2,838	2,877	2,837	1,498	3,404
	Total	6,471	3,680	3,120	2,546	2,405	2,817	2,970	3,273	3,070
All causes	Male	10,245	7,026	6,192	6,072	6,922	8,127	9,001	9,086	6,999
	Female	10,197	7,452	8,942	8,651	8,310	8,389	9,079	9,228	8,575
	Total	10,221	7,234	7,572	7,357	7,610	8,271	9,050	9,193	7,803

Source: Morbidity statistics from general practice, 1991–92.
Number of patients consulting GP for condition within 12 months × 10,000, divided by number of patients at risk.

Table B.8: Analysis of Respiratory Health Care Resource Groups: rates per million, number of episodes in each group in a hypothetical district with a population of 500 000 and population structure similar to England and Wales, and proportion of total recorded FCEs and bed-days attributable to each group.

HRG	Code	Total FCEs	Rate per million	FCEs in hypothetical district	Total FCE (%)	Total bed-days	Bed-days per million	Bed-days in typical district	Daily occupied beds in typical district	Total bed-days (%)
Lung transplant	D01	90	1.7	1	0.0	2,394	46.0	23	0	0.0
Thoracic procedures (complex to intermediate)	D02–D05	18,811	361.1	181	0.4	170,965.3	3,281.5	1,641	4	1.1
Minor thoracic surgical procedures	D06	5,822	111.7	56	0.1	2,900.3	55.7	28	0	0.0
Fibre-optic bronchoscopy	D07	28,813	553.0	277	0.6	1,174.4	22.5	11	0	0.0
Rigid bronchoscopy	D08	6,937	133.1	67	0.1	1,328.6	25.5	13	0	0.0
Lung abscess or empyema	D12	1,282	24.6	12	0.0	15,011.8	288.1	144	0	0.1
Pneumonia – lobar, atypical or viral	D13–D14	39,166	751.7	376	0.8	334,313.3	6,416.8	3,208	9	2.1
Bronchopneumonia	D15	15,455	296.6	148	0.3	160,300.1	3,076.8	1,538	4	1.0
Bronchiectasis	D16	4,346	83.4	42	0.1	34,437.3	661.0	330	1	0.2
Pulmonary tuberculosis	D18	1,385	26.6	13	0.0	15,789	303.1	152	0	0.1
COPD and bronchitis	D20	86,399	1,658.3	829	1.8	700,820.2	13,451.4	6,726	18	4.4
Asthma	D21–D22	114,210	2,192.1	1,096	2.4	771,593.2	14,809.9	7,405	20	4.8
Pleural effusion	D23–D24	10,981	210.8	105	0.2	82,934.2	1,591.8	796	2	0.5
Pneumoconiosis	D26	4,404	84.5	42	0.1	32,095.4	616.0	308	1	0.2
Other interstitial lung disease	D27–D28	1,545	29.7	15	0.0	14,121.8	271.1	136	0	0.1
Foreign body	D29	1,674	32.1	16	0.0	15,415.6	295.9	148	0	0.1
Pneumothorax	D30	4,033	77.4	39	0.1	20,046.3	384.8	192	1	0.1
Respiratory failure	D32	3,643	69.9	35	0.1	25,254	484.7	242	1	0.2
Other respiratory disorder	D33–D34	33,932	651.3	326	0.7	172,645.2	3,313.7	1,657	5	1.1
Chemotherapy with respiratory diagnosis	D98	11,335	217.6	109	0.2	24,151.3	463.6	232	1	0.2
Complex elderly with respiratory diagnosis	D99	39,633	760.7	380	0.8	503,732.6	9,668.6	4,834	13	3.1
Heart and lung transplant	E01	53	1.0	1	0.0	1,526.4	29.3	15	0	0.0
Asthma/recurrent wheeze	P01	32,631	626.3	313	0.7	56,670.8	1,087.7	544	1	0.4
Upper respiratory tract disorder	P02	69,968	1,343.0	671	1.5	92,218.7	1,770.0	885	2	0.6
Lower respiratory tract disorder	P03	45,667	876.5	438	1.0	147,728.3	2,835.5	1,418	4	0.9
Total respiratory		582,215	11,175.0	5,587	12.3	3,399,568.1	65,250.8	32,625	89	21.3
Total all diagnoses (HRG data)		4,719,186				15,991,997				

Table B.9: Analysis of HRG information: proportion of HRG episodes within each specialty attributable to selected respiratory HRGs, England, 1996.

HRG	Code	Total FCEs	General medicine		Respiratory medicine		Paediatrics		Geriatric medicine		Cardiothoracic surgery		General surgery		All the previous specialties		All other specialties	
			FCEs	% speciality total	FCEs	% speciality total	FCEs	% speciality total	FCEs	% speciality total	FCEs	% speciality total	FCEs	% speciality total	FCEs	% speciality total	FCEs	% speciality total
Lung transplant	D01	90	0	0.0	0	0.0	0	0.0	0	0.0	90	0.2	0	0.0	90	0.0	0	0.0
Thoracic procedures (complex to intermediate)	D02–D05	18,811	4,154	0.7	727	1.9	303	0.1	597	0.4	9,568	17.9	1,704	0.2	17,053	0.9	1,758	0.1
Minor thoracic surgical procedures	D06	5,822	3,110	0.5	864	2.3	45	0.0	169	0.1	408	0.8	160	0.0	4,756	0.3	1,066	0.0
Fibre-optic bronchoscopy	D07	28,813	19,027	3.2	7,974	20.9	33	0.0	495	0.3	675	1.3	21	0.0	28,225	1.6	588	0.0
Rigid bronchoscopy	D08	6,937	4,089	0.7	1,240	3.3	85	0.0	13	0.0	1,325	2.5	7	0.0	6,759	0.4	178	0.0
Lung abscess or empyema	D12	1,282	650	0.1	170	0.4	66	0.0	96	0.1	164	0.3	31	0.0	1,177	0.1	105	0.0
Pneumonia – lobar, atypical or viral	D13–D14	39,166	24,369	4.0	1,261	3.3	463	0.2	9,060	6.2	59	0.1	521	0.1	35,733	2.0	3,433	0.1
Bronchopneumonia	D15	15,455	7,226	1.2	322	0.8	7	0.0	5,842	4.0	14	0.0	277	0.0	13,688	0.8	1,767	0.1
Bronchiectasis	D16	4,346	2,217	0.4	1,580	4.1	2	0.0	306	0.2	42	0.1	10	0.0	4,157	0.2	189	0.0
Pulmonary tuberculosis	D18	1,385	1,385	0.2	0	0.0	0	0.0	0	0.0	0	0.0	0	0.0	1,385	0.1	0	0.0
COPD and bronchitis	D20	86,399	56,035	9.3	6,043	15.9	82	0.0	18,056	12.3	149	0.3	249	0.0	80,614	4.5	5,785	0.2
Asthma	D21–D22	114,210	67,865	11.2	5,291	13.9	9,354	4.4	21,741	14.9	74	0.1	473	0.1	104,798	5.8	9,412	0.3
Pleural effusion	D23–D24	10,981	6,535	1.1	719	1.9	90	0.0	1,609	1.1	335	0.6	370	0.0	9,658	0.5	1,323	0.0
Pneumoconiosis	D26	4,404	1,985	0.3	1,445	3.8	21	0.0	575	0.4	143	0.3	15	0.0	4,184	0.2	220	0.0
Other interstitial lung disease	D27–D28	1,545	1,031	0.2	554	1.5	44	0.0	59	0.0	66	0.1	17	0.0	1,771	0.1	–226	0.0
Foreign body	D29	1,674	881	0.1	44	0.1	44	0.0	399	0.3	30	0.1	51	0.0	1,449	0.1	225	0.0
Pneumothorax	D30	4,033	2,889	0.5	262	0.7	7	0.0	313	0.2	231	0.4	85	0.0	3,787	0.2	246	0.0
Respiratory failure	D32	3,643	1,598	0.3	723	1.9	219	0.1	249	0.2	59	0.1	128	0.0	2,976	0.2	667	0.0
Other respiratory disorder	D33–D34	33,932	14,703	2.4	1,760	4.6	7,567	3.5	5,015	3.4	576	1.1	359	0.0	29,980	1.7	3,952	0.1
Chemotherapy with respiratory diagnosis	D98	11,335	2,174	0.4	858	2.3	35	0.0	32	0.0	0	0.0	34	0.0	3,133	0.2	8,202	0.3
Complex elderly with respiratory diagnosis	D99	39,633	16,420	2.7	1,027	2.7	0	0.0	19,537	13.4	10	0.0	291	0.0	37,285	2.1	2,348	0.1
Heart and lung transplant	E01	53	0	0.0	0	0.0	0	0.0	0	0.0	53	0.1	0	0.0	53	0.0	0	0.0
Asthma/recurrent wheeze	P01	32,631	725	0.1	207	0.5	31,417	14.7	13	0.0	5	0.0	18	0.0	32,385	1.8	246	0.0
Upper respiratory tract disorder	P02	69,968	215	0.0	68	0.2	67,324	31.5	0	0.0	13	0.0	292	0.0	67,912	3.8	2,056	0.1
Lower respiratory tract disorder	P03	45,667	360	0.1	142	0.4	44,236	20.7	16	0.0	44	0.1	122	0.0	44,920	2.5	747	0.0
Total respiratory		582,215	239,643	39.7	33,281	87.3	161,444	75.5	84,192	57.6	14,133	26.4	5,235	0.7	537,928	29.7	44,287	1.5
Total all diagnoses (HRG data)		4,719,186	603,406	100.0	38,121	100.0	213,973	100.0	146,236	100.0	53,578	100.0	753,553	100.0	1,808,867	100.0	2,910,319	100.0

Figures

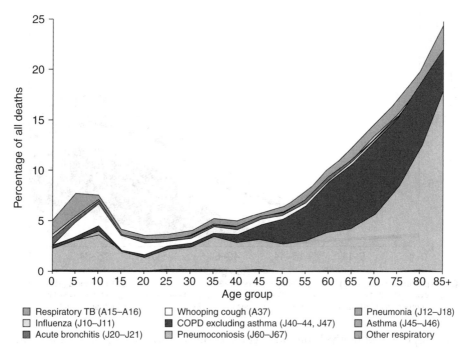

Figure B.1: Proportion of all deaths due to various lower respiratory conditions by age group. *Source*: Mortality Statistics, cause, England and Wales, 1999. Office for National Statistics.

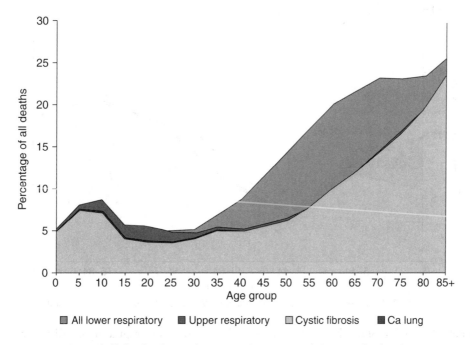

Figure B.2: Proportion of all deaths due to lower respiratory conditions and other important respiratory diseases by age group.
Source: Mortality Statistics, cause, England and Wales, 1999. Office for National Statistics.

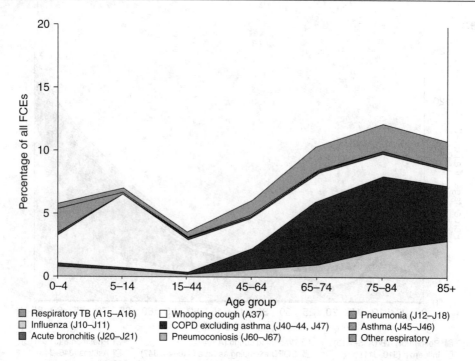

Figure B.3: Proportion of finished consultant episodes due to various lower respiratory conditions by age group.
Source: HES data, England, 1998–99.

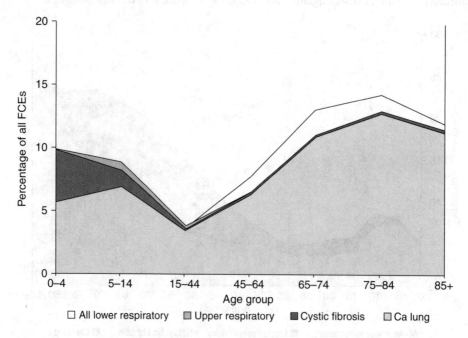

Figure B.4: Proportion of finished consultant episodes due to lower respiratory conditions and other important respiratory diseases.
Source: HES data, England, 1998–99.

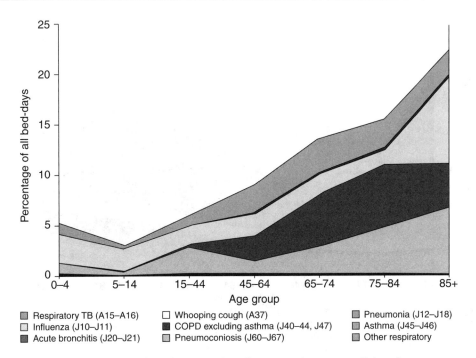

Figure B.5: Proportion of bed-days due to various lower respiratory conditions by age group.
Source: HES data, England, 1998–99.

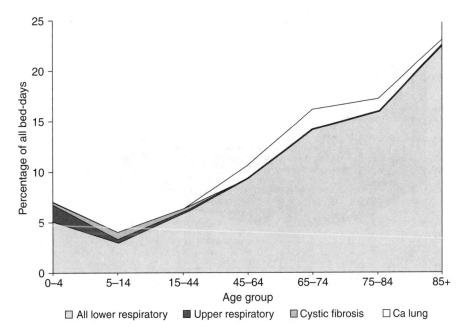

Figure B.6: Proportion of bed-days due to various lower respiratory conditions and other important respiratory diseases by age group.
Source: HES data, England, 1998–99.

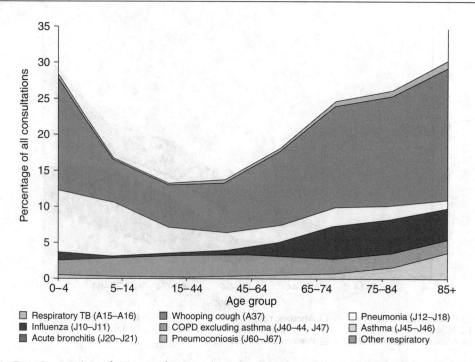

Figure B.7: Proportion of GP consultations due to various lower respiratory conditions by age group. *Source*: Morbidity statistics in general practice, 1991–92.

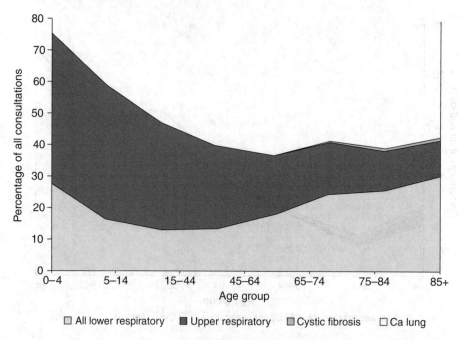

Figure B.8: Proportion of GP consultations due to lower respiratory conditions and other important respiratory diseases by age.

References

1 Barker DJP, Osmond C. Childhood respiratory infection and adult chronic bronchitis in England and Wales. *BMJ* 1986; **293**: 1271–5.

2 Denny FW. Acute respiratory infections in children: etiology and epidemiology. *Pediatr Rev* 1987; **9**: 135–46.

3 Pneumonia in childhood. Editorial. *Lancet* 1988; **1**: 741–3.

4 Milner AD, Murray M. Acute bronchiolitis in infancy: treatment and prognosis. *Thorax* 1989; **44**: 1–5.

5 Black DAK, Pole JD. Priorities in biomedical journal. Indices of burden. *Br J Prev Soc Med* 1975; **29**: 222–7.

6 Antibiotics and respiratory illness. Editorial. *BMJ* 1974; **3**: 1.

7 Office of Population Censuses and Surveys. *Communicable Disease Statistics 1980*. Series MB2 No. 7. London: HMSO, 1980.

8 Charlton JRH, Hartley RM, Silver R, Holland WW. Geographical variation in mortality from conditions amenable to medical intervention in England and Wales. *Lancet* 1983; **1**: 691–6.

9 Macfarlane JT, Finch RG, Ward MJ, Macrae AD. Hospital study of adult community-acquired pneumonia. *Lancet* 1982; **2**: 255–8.

10 Woodhead MA, Macfarlane JT, McCracken JS, Rose DH, Finch RG. Prospective study of the aetiology and outcome of pneumonia in the community. *Lancet* 1987; **1**: 671–4.

11 British Thoracic Society and Public Health Laboratory Service. Community-acquired pneumonia in adults in British hospitals in 1982–1983: a survey of aetiology, mortality, prognostic factors and outcome. *Q J Med* 1987; New Series **62**, No. 239: 195–220.

12 Office of Population Censuses and Surveys. *Hospital Inpatient Enquiry 1980*. Series MB4 1985 No. 27. London: HMSO, 1987.

13 National Institutes of Health and National Heart, Lung and Blood Institute. *Global Initiative for Asthma: global strategy for asthma management and prevention*. Bethesda, MD: NIH, 2002.

14 Holgate ST, Finnerty JP. Recent advances in understanding the pathogenesis of asthma and its clinical implications. *Q J Med* 1988; **66**: 5–19.

15 Barnes PJ. A new approach to the treatment of asthma. *NEJM* 1989; **321**: 1517–27.

16 British Thoracic Society Research Unit of Royal College of Physicians of London, King's Fund Centre. Guidelines for management of asthma in adults. 1. Chronic persistent asthma. *BMJ* 1990; **301**: 651–3.

17 Scadding JG. Definitions and clinical categories of asthma. In: Clark TJH, Godfrey S (eds). *Asthma*. London: Chapman and Hall Medical, 1983, pp. 1–10.

18 Brown PJ, Greville HW, Finucane KE. Asthma and irreversible obstruction. *Thorax* 1984; **39**: 131–6.

19 Speight ANP, Lee DA, Hey EN. Underdiagnosis and undertreatment of asthma in childhood. *BMJ* 1983; **286**: 1253–6.

20 Anderson HR, Bailey PA, Cooper JS, Palmer JC. Influence of morbidity, illness label, and social, family and health service factors on drug treatment of childhood asthma. *Lancet* 1981; **2**: 1030–2.

21 Bucknall CE, Robertson C, Moran F, Stevenson RD. Differences in hospital asthma management. *Lancet* 1988; **1**: 748–50.

22 Gellert AR, Gellert SL, Iliffe SR. Prevalence and management of asthma in a London inner-city general. *Br J Gen Pract* 1990; **40**: 197–201.

23 Littlejohns P, Ebrahim S, Anderson R. Prevalence and diagnosis of chronic respiratory symptoms in adults. *BMJ* 1989; **298**: 1556–60.

24 ARIA in conjunction with the World Health Organization. *Allergic Rhinitis and its Impact on Asthma. Management of allergic rhinitis and its impact on asthma. Pocket guide*. Downloaded from www.whiar.com/.

25 National Institutes of Health and National Heart, Lung and Blood Institute. *Global Initiative for Chronic Obstructive Lung Disease: global strategy for the diagnosis, management and prevention of chronic obstructive lung disease.* NHLBI/WHO Workshop Report. Bethesda, MD: NIH, 2001. Available from www.goldcopd.com/.

26 Joint IUT/WHO Study Group. *Tuberculosis Control.* WHO Technical Report Series no. 671.

27 Medical Research Council Tuberculosis and Chest Diseases Unit. National survey of notifications of tuberculosis in England and Wales. *BMJ* 1985; **291**: 658–61.

28 Barnes PF, Bloch AB, Davidson PT, Snider DE. Tuberculosis in patients with human immunodeficiency virus infection. *NEJM* 1991; **324**: 1644–50.

29 Watkins CJ, Burton P, Leeder S, Sittampalam Y, Wever AMJ, Wiggins R. Doctor diagnosis and maternal recall of lower respiratory illness. *Int J Epidemiol* 1982; **11**: 62–6.

30 Golding J. Bronchitis and pneumonia. In: Butler NR, Golding J (eds). *From Birth to Five. A study of the health and behaviour of Britain's five-year-olds.* Oxford: Pergamon, 1986.

31 Strachan DP (unpublished). Analyses of original data from Colley and Reid (1970) and Strachan *et al.* (1987).

32 Colley JRT, Reid DD. Urban and social origins of childhood bronchitis in England and Wales. *BMJ* 1970; **2**: 213–17.

33 Melia RJW, Chinn S, Rona RJ. Respiratory illness and home environment of ethnic groups. *BMJ* 1988; **296**: 1438–41.

34 Weiss ST, Tager IB, Schenker M, Speizer FE. The health effects of involuntary smoking. *Am Rev Respir Dis* 1983; **128**: 933–42.

35 Fielding JE, Phenow KJ. Health effects of involuntary smoking. *NEJM* 1988; **319**: 1452–60.

36 Holland WW, Bailey P, Bland JM. Long-term consequences of respiratory disease in infancy. *J Epidemiol Community Health* 1978; **32**: 256–9.

37 Strachan DP, Anderson HR, Bland JM, Peckham C. Asthma as a link between chest illness in childhood and chronic cough and phlegm in young adults. *BMJ* 1988; **296**: 890–3.

38 Miller DL. Collaborative studies of acute respiratory disease in patients seen in general practice and in children admitted to hospital. *Postgrad Med J* 1973; **49**: 749–62.

39 Weekly Returns Service of the Royal College of General Practitioners. *Report for 1988.* Birmingham: RCGP Research Unit, 1989.

40 Office of Population Censuses and Surveys. *Communicable Disease Statistics 1988.* Series MB2 No. 15. London: HMSO, 1988.

41 McNabb WR, Shanson DC, Williams TDM, Lant AF. Adult community-acquired pneumonia in central London. *J R Soc Med* 1984; **77**: 550–5.

42 Noah ND. *Mycoplasma pneumoniae* infection in the United Kingdom – 1967–1973. *BMJ* 1974; **1**: 544–6.

43 White RJ, Blainey AD, Harrison KJ, Clarke SKR. Causes of pneumonia presenting to a district general hospital. *Thorax* 1981; **36**: 566–70.

44 Curwen M, Dunnell K, Ashley J. Hidden influenza deaths: 1989–90. In: *Population Trends No. 61.* London: HMSO, 1990, pp. 31–3.

45 Fine M, Smith M, Carson C *et al.* Prognosis and outcomes of patients with community-acquired pneumonia. *JAMA* 1996; **275**: 134–41.

46 Wenzel RP. Hospital-acquired pneumonia: overview of the current state of the art for prevention and control. *Eur J Clin Microbiol Infect Dis* 1989; **8**: 56–60.

47 Celis R, Torres A, Gatell JM, Almela M, Rodriguez-Roisin R, Augusti-Vidal A. Nosocomial pneumonia. A multivariate analysis of risk and prognosis. *Chest* 1988; **93**: 318–24.

48 Gross PA. Epidemiology of hospital acquired pneumonia. *Semin Respir Infect* 1987; **2**: 2–7.

49 Department of Health. *Health Survey for England 1996*. London: The Stationery Office, 1996; www.official-documents.co.uk/document/doh/survey96.

50 Department of Health. *The Health of Young People 1995–1997*. London: The Stationery Office, 1997; www.official-documents.co.uk/document/doh/survey97.

51 Anderson HR, Bland JM, Patel S, Peckham C. The natural history of asthma in childhood. *J Epidemiol Community Health* 1986; **40**: 121–9.

52 Goodall JF. The natural history of common respiratory infection in children and some principles in its management. Wheezy children. *J R Coll Gen Pract* 1958; **1**: 51–9.

53 Strachan DP. The prevalence and natural history of wheezing in early childhood. *J R Coll Gen Pract* 1985; **35**: 182–4.

54 Strachan DP, Butland BK, Anderson HR. Incidence and prognosis of asthma and wheezing illness from early childhood to age 33 in a national British cohort. *BMJ* 1996; **312**: 1195–9.

55 Markowe HLJ, Bulpitt CJ, Shipley MJ, Rose G, Crombie DL, Fleming DM. Prognosis in adult asthma: a national study. *BMJ* 1987; **295**: 949–52.

56 Burr ML, Butland BK, King S, Vaughan-Williams E. Changes in asthma prevalence: two surveys 15 years apart. *Arch Dis Child* 1989; **64**: 1452–6.

57 Burney PG, Chinn S, Rona RJ. Has the prevalence of asthma increased in children? Evidence from the national study of health and growth 1973–86. *BMJ* 1990; **300**: 1306–10.

58 Strachan DP, Anderson HR. Trends in hospital admission rates for asthma in children: change in prevalence or medical care? *BMJ* 1991; **304**: 819–20.

59 Anderson HR. Is the prevalence of asthma changing? *Arch Dis Child* 1989; **64**: 172–5.

60 Sears MR. *Evidence-Based Asthma Management*. Hamilton, Ontario: BC Decker Inc, 2000, pp. 1–12.

61 Hill R, Williams J, Tattersfield A, Britton J. Change in use of asthma as a diagnostic label for wheezing illness in schoolchildren. *BMJ* 1989; **299**: 898.

62 Fleming DM, Crombie DL. Prevalence of asthma and hay fever in England and Wales. *BMJ* 1987: **294**: 279–83.

63 Anderson HR. Increase in hospital admissions for childhood asthma: trends in referral, severity and readmissions from 1970 to 1985 in a health region of the United Kingdom. *Thorax* 1989; **44**: 614–19.

64 Department of Health. *Asthma: an epidemiological overview*. London: HMSO, 1995.

65 Kaur B, Anderson HR, Austin J *et al.* Prevalence of asthma symptoms, diagnosis and treatment in 12–14-year-old children across Great Britain (international study of asthma and allergies in childhood, ISAAC UK). *BMJ* 1998; **516**: 118–24.

66 Burney PG. Asthma mortality in England and Wales: evidence for a further increase, 1974–84. *Lancet* 1986; **2**: 323–6.

67 Inman WHW, Adelstein AM. Rise and fall of asthma mortality in England and Wales in relation to use of pressurised aerosols. *Lancet* 1969; **2**: 279–83.

68 Anderson HR, Strachan DP. Asthma mortality in England and Wales, 1979–89 (letter). *Lancet* 1991; **337**: 1357.

69 Strachan DP, Golding J, Anderson HR. Regional variations in wheezing illness in British children: effect of migration during early childhood. *J Epidemiol Community Health* 1990; **44**: 231–6.

70 Burney PGJ, Papacosta AO, Withey CH, Colley JRT, Holland WW. Hospital admission rates and the prevalence of asthma symptoms in 20 local authority districts. *Thorax* 1991; **46**: 574–9.

71 Leeder SR, Corkhill R, Irwig LM, Holland WW, Colley JRT. Influence of family factors on the incidence of lower respiratory illness during the first year of life. *Br J Prev Soc Med* 1976; **30**: 302–12.

72 Burr ML, Miskelly FG, Butland BK, Merrett TG, Vaughan-Williams E. Environmental factors and symptoms in infants at high risk of allergy. *J Epidemiol Community Health* 1989; **43**: 125–32.

73 Weitzman M, Gortmaker S, Sobol A. Racial, social, and environmental risks for childhood asthma. *Am J Dis Child* 1990; **144**: 1189–94.

74 Graham PJ, Rutter JL, Yule W, Pless IB. Childhood asthma: a psychosomatic disorder? Some epidemiological considerations. *Br J Prev Soc Med* 1967; **21**: 78–85.

75 Hamman RF, Halil T, Holland WW. Asthma in schoolchildren: demographic associations with peak expiratory flow rates compared with children with bronchitis. *Br J Prev Soc Med* 1975; **29**: 228–38.

76 Peckham C, Butler N. A national study of asthma in childhood. *J Epidemiol Community Health* 1978; **32**: 79–85.

77 Blaxter M. Evidence on inequality in health from a national survey. *Lancet* 1987; **2**: 30–2.

78 Connolly CK, Chan NS, Prescott RJ. The influence of social factors on the control of asthma. *Postgrad Med J* 1989; **65**: 282–5.

79 Sibbald B, McGuigan S, Anderson HR. Asthma and employment in young adults. *Thorax* 1992; **47**: 19–24.

80 Office of Population Censuses and Surveys. *Decennial Supplement on Occupational Mortality 1982–83*. London: HMSO, 1986.

81 Johnston ID, Bland JM, Anderson HR. Ethnic variation in respiratory morbidity and lung function in childhood. *Thorax* 1987; **42**: 542–8.

82 Ayres GJ. Acute asthma in Asian patients: hospital admissions and duration of stay in a district with a high immigrant population. *Br J Dis Chest* 1986; **80**: 242–8.

83 Cook DG, Kussick SJ, Shaper AG. The respiratory effects of smoking. *J Smok Relat Dis* 1990; **1**: 45–58.

84 College Committee on Thoracic Medicine. Disabling chest disease: prevention and care. *J R Coll Physicians Lond* 1981; **15**: 69–87.

85 Burr ML, Charles TJ, Roy K, Seaton A. Asthma in the elderly: an epidemiological survey. *BMJ* 1979; **1**: 1041–4.

86 Cullinan P. Respiratory disease in England and Wales. *Thorax* 1988; **43**: 949–54.

87 Higgins ITT, Oldham PD et al. Respiratory symptoms and pulmonary disability in an industrial town. *BMJ* 1956; **ii**: 904–9.

88 Respiratory Diseases Study Group of the Royal College of General Practitioners. Chronic bronchitis in Great Britain. *BMJ* 1961; **11**: 973–9.

89 Higgins ITT. Respiratory symptoms, bronchitis and ventilatory capacity in a random sample of an agricultural population. *BMJ* 1957; **ii**: 1198–203.

90 Higgins ITT, Cochran JB. Respiratory symptoms, bronchitis and disability in a random sample of an agricultural community in Dumfries-shire. *Tubercle* 1958; **39**: 296.

91 Higgins ITT, Cochrane AL. Chronic respiratory symptoms in a random sample of men and women in the Rhondda Fach in 1958. *Br J Ind Med* 1961; **18**: 93.

92 Mcnab GR, Slator EJ, Stewart CJ. Response to a questionnaire on chronic bronchitic symptoms in East Anglia. *Br J Prev Soc Med* 1966; **20**: 181–8.

93 Lambert PM, Reid DD. Smoking, air pollution and bronchitis in Britain. *Lancet* 1970; **i**; 853–7.

94 Hawthorne VM, Fry JS. Smoking and health: the association between smoking behaviour, total mortality and cardiorespiratory disease in West Central Scotland. *J Epidemiol Community Health* 1978; **32**: 260–6.

95 Dean G, Lee PN, Todd GF et al. Factors related to respiratory and cardiovascular symptoms in the United Kingdom. *J Epidemiol Community Health* 1978; **32**: 86–96.

96 Cullinan P. Persistent cough and phlegm: prevalence and clinical characteristics in South East England. *Resp Med* 1992; **86**: 143–9.

97 Public Health Laboratory Service. *Tuberculosis Notification Rates per 100 000 Population, England and Wales, by Region, 1993–1998*; www.phls.co.uk/facts/TBRates/Region.htm.

98 Watson JM. Tuberculosis in perspective. *Commun Dis Rep CDR Rev* 1991; **1**(12): 129.

99 Watson JM, Gill ON. HIV infection and tuberculosis. *BMJ* 1990; **300**: 63–4.

100 Department of Health, Scottish Office, Welsh Office. *Interdepartmental Working Group on Tuberculosis. Prevention and control of tuberculosis in the United Kingdom. UK Guidance on Prevention and Control of Transmission of 1. HIV-related tuberculosis 2. Drug-resistant including multi-drug resistant tuberculosis.* London: The Stationery Office, 1998.

101 Watson JM *et al.* Tuberculosis and HIV infection in England and Wales. *Thorax* 1991; **46**: 311 (Proceedings of the BTS winter meeting 1990).

102 Kumar D, Watson JM, Charlett A *et al.* Tuberculosis in England and Wales in 1993: results of a national survey. *Thorax* 1997; **52**: 1060–7.

103 Springett VH *et al.* Changes in tuberculosis notification rates in the white ethnic group in England and Wales between 1953 and 1983. *J Epidemiol Community Health* 1988; **42**; 370–6.

104 Nunn AJ *et al.* Changes in annual tuberculosis notification rates between 1978/79 and 1983 for the population of Indian subcontinent ethnic origin resident in England. *J Epidemiol Community Health* 1986; **40**: 357–63.

105 Pablos-Mendez A, Raviglione MC, Laszlo A *et al.* Global surveillance for antituberculosis drug resistance, 1994–1997. *NEJM* 1998; **338**: 1641–9.

106 United Kingdom Cystic Fibrosis Survey (1998). Personal communication.

107 Dodge JA, Morison S, Lewis PA *et al.* Incidence, population and survival of cystic fibrosis in the UK, 1968–1995. *Arch Dis Child* 1997; **77**: 493–6.

108 Office of Population Censuses and Surveys. *Mortality Statistics, Cause: England and Wales 1989.* Series DH2 no.16. London: HMSO, 1991.

109 Office of Population Censuses and Surveys. *Occupational Mortality, Childhood Supplement. The Registrar General's decennial supplement for England and Wales, 1979–80, 1982–83.* Series DS no.8. London: HMSO, 1988.

110 Gregg I. Epidemiological aspects. In: Clark TJH, Godfrey S (eds). *Asthma.* London: Chapman and Hall Medical, 1983, pp. 242–78.

111 Anderson HR, Bailey PA, Cooper JS, Palmer JC, West S. Morbidity and school absence caused by asthma and wheezing illness. *Arch Dis Child* 1983; **83**: 777–84.

112 Golding J, Butler N. Wheezing and asthma. In: Butler NJ, Golding J (eds). *From Birth to Five. A study of the health and behaviour of Britain's five-year-olds.* Oxford: Pergamon Press, 1986, pp. 158–70.

113 Strachan DP. Damp housing and childhood asthma: validation of reporting of symptoms. *BMJ* 1988; **297**: 1223–6.

114 Clifford RD, Radford M, Howell JB, Holgate ST. Prevalence of respiratory symptoms among 7 and 11 year old schoolchildren and association with asthma. *Arch Dis Child* 1989; **64**: 1118–25.

115 Hill RA, Standen PJ, Tattersfield AE. Asthma, wheezing, and school absence in primary schools. *Arch Dis Child* 1989; **64**: 246–51.

116 Leck I. Falling death rates from bronchitis. *Lancet* 1988; **ii**: 694.

117 Wiggins J, Lyster W. Will falling death rates from acute and chronic bronchitis continue? *Lancet* 1988; **1**: 286–7.

118 Backhouse A, Holland WW. Trends in mortality from chronic obstructive airways disease in the United Kingdom. *Thorax* 1989; **44**: 529–32.

119 Nisar M, Davies PDO. Current trends in tuberculosis mortality in England and Wales. *Thorax* 1991; **46**: 438–40.

120 Elborn JS *et al. Thorax* 1991; **46**: 881–5.

121 Everett MT. Major chest infection managed at home. *Practitioner* 1983; **227**: 1743–54.

122 Haley RW, Culver DH, White JW *et al.* The efficacy of infection surveillance and control programs in preventing nosocomial infections in US hospitals. *Am J Epidemiol* 1985; **121**: 182–205.

123 British Thoracic Society. Guidelines for the management of community-acquired pneumonia in adults. *Thorax* 2001; **56** (Suppl. 4).

124 Royal College of General Practitioners, Office of Population Censuses and Surveys, and Department of Health and Social Security. *Morbidity Statistics from General Practice: third national study 1981–82.* Series MB5 No.1. London: HMSO, 1986.

125 Anderson HR, Bailey PA, Cooper JS, Palmer JC, West S. Medical care of asthma and wheezing illness in children: a community survey. *J Epidemiol Community Health* 1983; **37**: 180–6.

126 Littlejohns P, Ebrahim S, Anderson HR. Treatment of adult asthma: is the diagnosis relevant? *Thorax* 1989; **44**: 797–802.

127 Fleming DM, Sunderland R, Cross KW, Ross AM. Declining incidence of episodes of asthma: a study of trends in new episodes presenting to general practitioners in the period 1989–98. *Thorax* 2000; **55**: 657–61.

128 Alderson MR. Trends in morbidity and mortality from asthma. *Popul Trends* 1987; **49**: 18–23.

129 Burney P. Why study the epidemiology of asthma? *Thorax* 1988; **43**: 425–8.

130 Platts-Mills TA, Chapman MD. Dust mites: immunology, allergic disease, and environmental control. *J Allergy Clin Immunol* 1987; **80**: 755–75.

131 Platts-Mills TA. Allergens and asthma. *Allergy Proc* 1990; **11**: 269–71.

132 Weitzman M, Gortmaker S, Walker DK, Sobol A. Maternal smoking and childhood asthma. *Pediatrics* 1990; **85**: 505–11.

133 Wood RD, Wu JM, Witorsch RJ, Witorsch P. Environmental tobacco smoke exposure and respiratory health in children: an updated critical review and analysis of the epidemiological literature. *Indoor Environ* 1992; **1**: 19–35.

134 International Workshop Report. Dust mite allergens and asthma: a worldwide problem. *Bull WHO* 1988; **66**: 769–80.

135 Department of Health Advisory Group on the Medical Aspects of Air Pollution Episodes. *Ozone.* London: HMSO, 1991.

136 American Thoracic Society. Screening for adult respiratory disease. *Am Rev Respir Dis* 1983; **128**: 768–74.

137 British Thoracic Society, Research Unit of Royal College of Physicians London, and King's Fund Centre. National guidelines for management of asthma in adults. II. Acute severe asthma. *BMJ* 1990; **301**: 797–800.

138 Warner JO, Gotz M, Landau LI *et al.* Management of asthma: a consensus statement. *Arch Dis Child* 1989; **64**: 1065–79.

139 British Thoracic Society. Revised guidelines on management of asthma 1997. *Thorax* 1997; **52** (Suppl. 1); S2–21.

140 British Thoracic Society and Scottish Intercollegiate Guidelines Network. British guideline on the management of asthma. *Thorax* 2003; **58** (Suppl. 1).

141 British Thoracic Association. Death from asthma in two regions of England. *BMJ* 1982; **285**: 1251–5.

142 Johnson AJ, Nunn AJ, Somner AR, Stableforth DE, Stewart CJ. Circumstances of death from asthma. *BMJ* 1984; **288**: 1870–2.

143 Fletcher HJ, Ibrahim SA, Speight N. Survey of asthma deaths in the Northern region, 1970–85. *Arch Dis Child* 1990; **65**: 163–7.

144 Sibbald B. Patient self-care in acute asthma. *Thorax* 1989; **44**: 97–101.

145 Storr J, Barrell E, Lenney W. Rising asthma admissions and self-referral. *Arch Dis Child* 1988; **63**: 774–9.

146 AARC. Clinical practice guideline. Spirometry, 1996 update. *Respir Care* 1996; **41**(7): 629–36.

147 Anderson HR, Freeling P, Patel SP. Decision-making in acute asthma. *J R Coll Gen Pract* 1983; **33**: 105–8.

148 Henry RL, Milner AD. Specialist approach to childhood asthma: does it exist? *BMJ* 1983; **287**: 260–1.

149 Crompton GK, Grant IWB, Bloomfield P. Edinburgh emergency asthma admission service: report on 10 years' experience. *BMJ* 1979; **2**: 1199–201.

150 Price DB, Wolfe S. Patients' use and views on the service provided. *Asthma J* 2000; **5**: 141–4.

151 Holland WW. Chronic obstructive lung disease prevention. *Br J Dis Chest* 1988; **82**: 32–44.

152 Anthonisen N, Connett J, Kiley J *et al.* Effects of smoking intervention and the use of an inhaled anticholinergic bronchodilator on the rate of decline of FEV_1: the lung health study. *JAMA* 1994: **272**; 1497–505.

153 Sinclair DJM, Ingram CG. Controlled trial of supervised exercise training in chronic bronchitis. *BMJ* 1980; **280**: 519–21.

154 Interdepartmental Working Group on Tuberculosis. *The Prevention and Control of Tuberculosis in the United Kingdom: recommendations for the prevention and control of tuberculosis at the local level.* London: Department of Health, 1996.

155 Joseph CA, Watson JM, Fern KJ. BCG immunization in England and Wales: a survey of policy and practice in schoolchildren and neonates. *BMJ* 1992; **305**: 495–8.

156 Frankenburg RA, Mayon-White RT. The effect of a policy of non-vaccination of schoolchildren on the incidence of tuberculosis in Oxfordshire. *J Public Health Med* 1991; **13**(3): 209–13.

157 Omerod LP. *Childhood Tuberculosis: public health aspects.* Communicable Disease Report 1991. Vol. 1, review number 12.

158 Subcommittee of the Joint Tuberculosis Committee of the British Thoracic Society. Control and prevention of tuberculosis in Britain: an updated code of practice. *BMJ* 1990; **300**: 995–9.

159 Joint Tuberculosis Committee of the British Thoracic Society. Control and prevention of tuberculosis in the United Kingdom: code of practice 1994. *Thorax* 1994; **49**: 1193–200.

160 Omerod LP for a subcommittee of the Joint Tuberculosis Committee. Chemotherapy and management in the United Kingdom: recommendations of the Joint Tuberculosis Committee of the British Thoracic Society. *Thorax* 1990; **45**: 403–8.

161 Joint Tuberculosis Commitee of the British Thoracic Society. Chemotherapy and management of tuberculosis in the United Kingdom: recommendations 1998. *Thorax* 1998; **53**: 536–48.

162 Toman K. *Tuberculosis Case Finding and Chemotherapy.* Geneva: World Health Organization, 1979.

163 Chemotherapy of pulmonary tuberculosis in Britain. *Drug Ther Bull* 1988; **26**(1): 1–4.

164 British Thoracic Society Research Committee and Medical Research Council Cardiothoracic Epidemiology Group. The management of pulmonary tuberculosis in adults notified in England and Wales in 1988. *Respir Med* 1991; **85**: 319–23.

165 Walters S, Jordan D. *Clinical Standards Advisory Group: cystic fibrosis revisited – access and availability of specialist services,* 1996; www.cfstudy.com/sarah/csag2.pdf

166 Walters S. *Association of Cystic Fibrosis Adults Survey (1994).* London: Cystic Fibrosis Trust, 1995.

167 Clinical Standards Advisory Group. *Access and Availability of Specialist Services: cystic fibrosis.* London: HMSO, 1992.

168 Royal College of Physicians. *Clinical Guidelines for Cystic Fibrosis Care: recommendations of a working group.* London: Royal College of Physicians, 1996.

169 Cystic Fibrosis Trust. *Standards of Care: standards for the clinical care of children and adults with cystic fibrosis in the UK 2001.* London: Cystic Fibrosis Trust, 2001.

170 Cystic Fibrosis Trust. Pseudomonas aeruginosa *Infection in Cystic Fibrosis. Suggestions for prevention and infection control.* London: Cystic Fibrosis Trust, 2001.

171 Cystic Fibrosis Infection Control Group. *A Statement on* Burkholderia cepacia. London: Cystic Fibrosis Trust, 1999.

172 Cystic Fibrosis Trust. *Antibiotic Treatment for Cystic Fibrosis. Report of the UK Cystic Fibrosis Trust Antibiotic Group.* London: Cystic Fibrosis Trust, 2002.

173 Association of Chartered Physiotherapists in Cystic Fibrosis. *Clinical Guidelines for the Physiotherapy Management of Cystic Fibrosis.* London: Cystic Fibrosis Trust, 2002.

174 UK Cystic Fibrosis Trust Nutrition Working Group. *Nutritional Management of Cystic Fibrosis.* London: Cystic Fibrosis Trust, 2002.

175 Campbell IA. Stopping patients smoking. *Br J Dis Chest* 1988; **82**: 9–15.

176 Maynard A. Logic in medicine: an economic perspective. In: Philips C (ed.). *Logic in Medicine.* London: BMJ Publications, 1988.

177 Barker DJP, Godrey KM, Fall C, Osmond C, Winter PD, Shaheen SO. Relationship of birth weight and childhood respiratory infection to adult lung function and death from chronic obstructive airways disease. *BMJ* 1991; **303**: 671–5.

178 DiFranza J, Lew R. Morbidity and mortality in children associated with the use of tobacco products by other people. *Pediatrics* 1996; **97**: 560–8.

179 Walshaw MJ. Mite control: is it worthwhile? Editorial. *Respir Med* 1990; **84**: 257–8.

180 Gotzche P, Hammarquist C, Burr M. House dust mite control measures in the management of asthma: a meta-analysis. *BMJ* 1998; **317**: 1105–10.

181 Hammarquist C, Burr M, Gotzche P. House dust mite control measures for asthma (Cochrane Review). In: *The Cochrane Library.* Oxford: Update Software, 1999.

182 Kramer M. Maternal antigen avoidance during pregnancy for preventing atopic disease in infants of women at high risk (Cochrane Review). In: *The Cochrane Library.* Oxford: Update Software, 1999.

183 Faculty of Public Health Medicine. *UK Levels of Health. First report of a working party.* London: Faculty of Public Health Medicine, 1991, pp. 36–44.

184 Miller DL *et al.* Pertussis immunization and serious acute neurological illness in children. *BMJ* 1981; **282**: 1595.

185 Cherry JD. *The epidemiology of pertussis and pertussis immunization in the United Kingdom and the United States: a comparative study.* MSc epidemiology dissertation. London: School of Hygiene and Tropical Medicine, 1983.

186 Rudd PT. Childhood immunization in the new decade. *BMJ* 1991; **302**: 481–2.

187 Fine M, Smith M, Carson C *et al.* Efficacy of pneumococcal vaccine in adults: a meta-analysis of randomised controlled trials. *Arch Intern Med* 1994; **154**: 2666–77.

188 Butler J, Breiman R, Campbell J *et al.* Pneumococcal polysaccharide vaccine efficiency. A evaluation of current recommendations. *JAMA* 1993: **270**(15): 1826–31.

189 Ortqvist A, Hedlund J, Burman L-A *et al.* Randomised controlled trial of 23 valent pneumococcal capsular polysaccharide vaccine in prevention of pneumonia in middle-aged and elderly people. *Lancet* 1998; **351**: 399–403.

190 Leads from the MMWR. Recommendations of the immunization practices and advisory committee. Pneumococcal polysaccharide vaccine. *JAMA* 1989; **261**: 1265–7.

191 Salisbury D, Begg N. *Immunisation against Infectious Disease.* London: Department of Health, 1996.

192 Austrian R, Douglas RM, Schiffman G. Prevention of pneumococcal pneumonia by vaccination. *Trans Assoc Am Physicians* 1976; **89**: 184–94.

193 Smit P, Oberholzer D, Hayden-Smith S, Koornhof HJ, Hilleman MR. Protective efficacy of pneumococcal polysaccharide vaccines. *JAMA* 1977; **238**: 2613–16.

194 Riley ID, Tarr PI, Andrews M. Immunization with a polyvalent pneumococcal vaccine: reduction of adult respiratory mortality in a New Guinea Highlands community. *Lancet* 1977; **1**: 1338–41.

195 Ammann AJ, Addiego J, Wara DW, Lubin B, Smith WB, Mentzer WC. Polyvalent pneumococcal polysaccharide immunization of patients with sickle-cell anaemia and patients with splenectomy. *NEJM* 1977; **297**: 897–900.

196 Simberkoff MS, Cross AP, Al-Ibrahim M *et al.* Efficacy of pneumococcal vaccine in high-risk patients. Results of a Veterans Administration co-operative study. *NEJM* 1986; **215**: 1318–27.

197 Forrestor HL, Jahnigen DW, LaForce FM. Inefficacy of pneumococcal vaccine in a high-risk population. *Am J Med* 1987; **83**: 425–30.

198 Simms RV, Steinmann WC, McConville JH, King LR, Zwick WC, Schwartz JS. The clinical effectiveness of pneumococcal vaccine in the elderly. *Ann Intern Med* 1988; **108**: 653–7.

199 LaForce FM. Adult immunizations: are they worth the trouble? *J Gen Intern Med* 1990; **5** (Suppl.): 557–61.

200 Shapiro ED, Austrian R, Adair RK, Clemens JD. The protective efficacy of pneumococcal vaccine (abstract). *Clin Res* 1988; **36**: 470A.

201 Shapiro ED, Berg AT, Austrian R *et al.* The protective efficacy of polyvalent pneumococcal polysaccharide vaccine. *NEJM* 1991; **325**: 1453–60.

202 Williams WW, Hickson MA, Kane MA, Kendal AP, Spika JS, Hinman AR. Immunization policy and vaccine coverage among adults. *Ann Intern Med* 1988; **108**: 616–25.

203 Fedson DS, Baldwin JA. Previous hospital care as a risk factor for pneumonia. *JAMA* 1982; **248**: 1989–95.

204 Fedson DS. Hospital-based pneumococcal immunization: the epidemiologic rationale and its implementation. *Infect Control* 1982; **3**: 303–9.

205 Fedson DS, Harward MP, Reid RA, Kaiser DL. Hospital-based pneumococcal immunization. Epidemiologic rationales from the Shenandoah study. *JAMA* 1990; **264**: 1117–23.

206 Sisk JE, Riegelman RK. Cost-effectiveness of vaccination against pneumococcal pneumonia: an update. *Ann Intern Med* 1986; **104**: 79–86.

207 Department of Health. *Immunization against Infectious Disease.* London: HMSO, 1990.

208 Poole PJ, Chacko E, Wood-Baker RWB, Cates CJ. Influenza vaccine for patients with chronic obstructive pulmonary disease (Cochrane Review). In: *The Cochrane Library. Issue 4.* Oxford: Update Software, 2002.

209 Cates CJ, Jefferson TO, Bara AI, Rowe BH. Vaccines for preventing influenza in people with asthma (Cochrane Review). In: *The Cochrane Library. Issue 4.* Oxford: Update Software, 2002.

210 Gross P, Hermogenes A, Sacks H, Lau J, Levandowski R. The efficacy of influenza vaccine in elderly persons: a meta-analysis and review of the literature. *Ann Intern Med* 1995; **123**: 518–27.

211 Mullooly J, Bennett M, Hornbrook M *et al.* Influenza vaccination programs for elderly persons: cost-effectiveness in a health maintenance organisation. *Ann Intern Med* 1994; **121**: 947–52.

212 Nichol K, Margolis K, Wuorenma R, Von Sternberg T. The efficacy and cost-effectiveness of vaccination against influenza among elderly persons living in the community. *NEJM* 1994; **331**: 778–84.

213 Colditz G, Brewer R, Berkey C *et al.* Efficacy of BCG vaccine in the prevention of tuberculosis: a meta-analysis of the published literature. *JAMA* 1994; **271**: 698–702.

214 Colditz G, Berkey C, Mosteller F *et al.* Efficacy of bacillus Calmette-Guèrin vaccination of new-borns and infants in the prevention of tuberculosis: a meta-analysis of the published literature. *Pediatrics* 1996; **96**: 29–35.

215 Rodrigues L, Diwan V, Wheeler J. Protective effect of BCG against tuberculous meningitis and miliary tuberculosis: a meta-analysis. *Int J Epidemiol* 1993; **22**: 1154–8.

216 Keogan M, Johansen H. Vaccines for preventing infection with *Pseudomonas aeruginosa* in people with cystic fibrosis (Cochrane Review). In: *The Cochrane Library.* Oxford: Update Software, 1999.

217 Colver AF. Community campaign against asthma. *Arch Dis Child* 1990; **59**: 449–52.

218 Hill R, Williams J, Britton J, Tattersfield A. Can morbidity associated with untreated asthma in primary school children be reduced? A controlled intervention study. *BMJ* 1991; **303**: 1169–74.

219 Hall DMB. *Health for All Children: a programme for child health surveillance.* Oxford: Oxford Medical Publications, 1989.

220 Coultas DB, Mapel D, Gagnon R, Lydick E. The health impact of undiagnosed airflow obstruction in a national sample of United States adults. *Am J Respir Crit Care Med* 2001; **164**: 372–7.

221 McIvor RA, Tashkin DP. Underdiagnosis of chronic obstructive pulmonary disease: a rationale for spirometry as a screening tool. *Can Respir J* 2001; **8**: 153–8.

222 van den Boom G, Rutten-van Molken MP, Folgering H, van Weel C, van Schayck CP. The economic effects of screening for obstructive airway disease: an economic analysis of the DIMCA program. *Prev Med* 2000; **30**: 302–8.

223 Van Schayk CP, Loozen JMC, Wagena A, Akkermans P, Wesseling GJ. Detecting patients at a high risk of developing chronic obstructive pulmonary disease in general practice: cross-sectional case-finding study. *BMJ* 2002; **324**: 1370.

224 Badgett RG, Tanaka DJ. Is screening for chronic obstructive pulmonary disease justified? *Prev Med* 1997; **26**: 466–72.

225 Gorecka D, Bednarek M, Kislo A *et al.* Awareness of airflow obstruction together with antismoking advice increases success in cessation of smoking. *Pneumonol Alergol Pol* 2001; **69**: 617–25.

226 Murray J, Cuckle H, Taylor G *et al.* Screening for cystic fibrosis. *Health Technol Assess* 1999; **3**(8).

227 Pollitt RJ, Leonard JV, Green A *et al.* Neonatal screening for inborn errors of metabolism: cost, yield and outcome. *Health Technol Assess* 1997; **1**(7).

228 Seymour CA, Thomason MJ, Chalmers RA *et al.* Neonatal screening for inborn errors of metabolism: a systematic review. *Health Technol Assess* 1999; **1**(11).

229 www.info.doh.gov.uk/doh/intpress.nsf/page/2001–0208?OpenDocument. Department of Health website, April 2001.

230 Farrell PM, Kosorok MR, Rock MJ *et al.* Early diagnosis of cystic fibrosis through neonatal screening prevents severe malnutrition and improves long-term growth. *Pediatrics* 2001; **107**: 1–13.

231 Merelle M, Nagelkerke A, Lees C, Dezateux C. Newborn screening for cystic fibrosis (Cochrane Review). In: *The Cochrane Library.* Oxford: Update Software, 1999.

232 Rowley P, Loader S, Kaplan R. Prenatal screening for cystic fibrosis carriers: an economic evaluation. *Am J Hum Genet* 1998; **63**: 1160–74.

233 Arroll B, Kenealy T. Antibiotics for the common cold (Cochrane Review). In: *The Cochrane Library.* Oxford: Update Software, 1999.

234 NHS Executive. *UK Antimicrobial Resistance Strategy and Action Plan.* London: NHS Executive, 2000; www.gov.uk/arbstrat.htm.

235 Gordon M, Lovell S, Dugdale AB. The value of antibiotics in minor respiratory illness in children – a controlled trial. *Med J Aust* 1974; **9**: 304–6.

236 Sutrisna B, Frerichs RR, Reingold AL. Randomised controlled trial of effectiveness of ampicillin in mild acute respiratory infections in Indonesian children. *Lancet* 1991; **338**: 471–4.

237 Becker L, Glazier R, McIsaac W, Smuchny J. Antibiotics for acute bronchitis (Cochrane Review). In: *The Cochrane Library.* Oxford: Update Software, 1999.

238 Jefferson T, Demicheli V, Deeks J, Rivetti D. Neuraminidase inhibitors for preventing and treating influenza in healthy adults (Cochrane Review). In: *The Cochrane Library.* Oxford: Update Software, 1999.

239 National Institute for Clinical Excellence (NICE). *Guidance on the Use of Zanamivir (Relenza) in the Treatment of Influenza.* Technology Appraisal Guidance no. 15. London: NICE, 2000.

240 Welliver R, Monto AS, Carewicz O *et al.* Effectiveness of oseltamivir in preventing influenza in household contacts: a randomized controlled trial. *JAMA* 2001; **285**: 748–54.

241 Hayden FG, Gubareva LV, Monto AS *et al.* Inhaled zanamivir for the prevention of influenza in families. *NEJM* 2000; **343**: 1282–9.

242 Monto AS, Robinson DP, Herlocher ML, Hinson JM Jr, Elliott MJ, Crisp A. Zanamivir in the prevention of influenza among healthy adults: a randomized controlled trial. *JAMA* 1999; **282**: 31–5.

243 Hayden FG, Atmar RL, Schilling M *et al.* Use of the selective oral neuraminidase inhibitor oseltamivir to prevent influenza. *NEJM* 1999; **341**: 1336–43.

244 Haley RW. Surveillance by objective: a new priority-directed approach to the control of nosocomial infections. *Am J Infect Control* 1985; **13**: 78–89.

245 Esmonde TFG, Petheram IS. Audit of tuberculosis contact tracing procedures in South Gwent. *Respir Med* 1991; **85**: 421–4.

246 British Thoracic Association. A study of standardised contact procedures in tuberculosis. *Tubercle* 1978; **59**: 245–59.

247 Smieja M, Marchetti C, Cook D, Smaill F. Isoniazid for preventing tuberculosis in non-HIV-infected persons (Cochrane Review). In: *The Cochrane Library*. Oxford: Update Software, 1999.

248 Snider D, Caras G, Koplan J. Preventive therapy with isoniazid: cost-effectiveness of different durations of therapy. *JAMA* 1986; **255**: 1579–83.

249 Rose D, Chechter C, Fahs M, Silver A. Tuberculosis prevention: cost-effectiveness analysis of isoniazid chemoprophylaxis. *Am J Prev Med* 1988; **4**: 102–9.

250 Kellner J, Ohlsson A, Gadomski A, Wang E. Bronchodilators for bronchiolitis (Cochrane Review). In: *The Cochrane Library*. Oxford: Update Software, 1999.

251 Garrison MM, Christakis DA, Harvey E, Cummings P, Davis RL. Systemic corticosteroids in infant bronchiolitis: a meta-analysis. *Pediatrics* 2000; **105**: E44.

252 Bisgaard H, Hermansen M, Vrang C *et al.* Leukotriene receptor antagonist reduces lung symptoms following respiratory syncytial virus bronchiolitis in infants. *Am J Respir Crit Care Med* 2002; **165** (Suppl. 8): 838.

253 Fine M, Auble T, Yearly D *et al.* A prediction rule to identify low-risk patients with community-acquired pneumonia. *NEJM* 1997; **336**: 243–50.

254 Antibiotics for community-acquired pneumonia in adults. *Drug Ther Bull* 1988; **26**: 13–16.

255 Chan R, Hemeryck L, O'Regan M *et al.* Oral versus intravenous antibiotics for community-acquired lower respiratory tract infection in a general hospital: open randomised controlled trial. *BMJ* 1995; **27**: 1360–2.

256 Omidvari K, de Boisblanc B, Karam G, Nelson S, Haponik E, Summer W. Early transition to oral antibiotic therapy for community-acquired pneumonia: duration of therapy, clinical outcomes and cost analysis. *Respir Med* 1998; **92**: 1032–9.

257 Siegel R, Halpern N, Almenoff P, Lee A, Cashin R, Greene J. A prospective randomised study of inpatient IV antibiotics for community-acquired pneumonia: the optimal duration of therapy. *Chest* 1996; **110**: 965–71.

258 Rhew D, Hackner D, Henderson L, Ellrodt A, Weingarten S. The clinical benefit of in-hospital observation in low-risk pneumonia patients after conversion from parenteral to oral antimicrobial therapy. *Chest* 1998; **113**: 142–6.

259 Hirani N, MacFarlane J. Impact of management guidelines on the outcome of severe community-acquired pneumonia. *Thorax* 1997; **52**: 17–21.

260 Jones A, Sykes A. The effect of symptom presentation on delay in asthma diagnosis in children in a general practice. *Respir Med* 1990; **84**: 139–42.

261 Sears MR, Taylor DR, Print DC *et al*. Regular inhaled beta-agonist treatment in bronchial asthma. *Lancet* 1990; **336**: 1391–6.

262 Page CP. One explanation of the asthma paradox: inhibition of natural anti-inflammatory mechanism by beta 2-agonists. *Lancet* 1991; **337**: 717–20.

263 Cates C. Holding chambers versus nebulisers for beta-agonist treatment of acute asthma (Cochrane Review). In: *The Cochrane Library*. Oxford: Update Software, 2002.

264 Turner M, Patel A, Ginsburg S, FitzGerald J. Bronchodilator delivery in acute airflow obstruction. *Arch Intern Med* 1997; **157**: 1736–44.

265 Muers M, Corris P (eds) for the Nebuliser Project Group of the British Thoracic Society Standards of Care Committee. Current best practice for nebuliser treatment. *Thorax* 1997; **52** (Suppl. 2): S1–104.

266 White PT, Pharoah CA, Anderson HR, Freeling P. Improving the outcome of chronic asthma in general practice: a randomised controlled trial of small group education. *J R Coll Gen Pract* 1989; **39**: 182–6.

267 Horn CR, Clark TJH, Cochrane GM. Compliance with inhaled therapy and morbidity from asthma. *Respir Med* 1990; **84**: 67–70.

268 Arnold AG, Lane DJ, Zapata E. Current therapeutic practice in the management of acute severe asthma. *Br J Dis Chest* 1983; **77**: 123–35.

269 Bucknall CE, Robertson C, Moran F, Stevenson RD. Management of asthma in hospital: a prospective audit. *BMJ* 1988; **296**: 1637–9.

270 Osman J, Ormerod P, Stableforth D. Management of acute asthma: a survey of hospital practice and comparison between thoracic and general physicians in Birmingham and Manchester. *Br J Dis Chest* 1987; **81**: 232–41.

271 North of England Study of Standards and Performance in General Practice. *Final Report. Volume III. The effects of setting and implementing clinical standards*. Newcastle upon Tyne: Health Care Research Unit, University of Newcastle upon Tyne, 1990.

272 Johnston IDA, Bland JM, Anderson HR, Lambert HP. Respiratory sequelae of whooping cough (correspondence). *BMJ* 1985; **291**: 482–3.

273 Feder G, Griffiths C, Highton C, Eldridge S, Spence M, Southgate L. Do clinical guidelines introduced with practice-based education improve care of asthmatic and diabetic patients? A randomised controlled trial in general practices in East London. *BMJ* 1995; **311**: 1472–8.

274 Habbick B, Baker M, McNutt M, Cockcroft D. Recent trends in the use of inhaled beta-2 adrenergic agonists and inhaled corticosteroids in Saskatchewan. *Can Med Assoc J* 1995; **153**: 1437–43.

275 Worrall G, Chaulk P, Freake D. The effects of clinical practice guidelines on patient outcomes in primary care: a systematic review. *Can Med Assoc J* 1997; **156**: 1705–12.

276 Beasley R, Cushley M, Holgate ST. A self-management plan in the treatment of adult asthma. *Thorax* 1989; **44**: 200–4.

277 Charlton I, Charlton G, Broomfield J, Mullee MA. Evaluation of peak flow and symptoms-only self-management plans for control of asthma in general practice. *BMJ* 1990; **301**: 1355–9.

278 Taitel M, Kotses H, Bernstein I, Bernstein D, Creer T. A self-management program of adult asthma. Part II. Cost–benefit analysis. *J Allergy Clin Immunol* 1995; **95**: 672–6.

279 Trautner C, Richter B, Berger M. Cost-effectiveness of a structured treatment and teaching programme on asthma. *Eur Respir J* 1993; **6**: 1485–91.

280 Eiser N. Desensitization today. *BMJ* 1990; **300**: 1412–13.

281 Selsby DS. Chest physiotherapy. *BMJ* 1989; **298**: 541–2.

282 Kleijnen J, ter Reit G, Knipschild P. Acupuncture and asthma: a review of controlled trials. *Thorax* 1991; **46**: 799–802.

283 Linde K, Jobst KA. Homeopathy for chronic asthma (Cochrane Review). In: *The Cochrane Library*. Oxford: Update Software, 2002.

284 Leitch AG, Parker S, Currie A, King T, McHardy GJR. Do chest physicians follow up too many patients? *Respir Med* 1989; **83**: 329–32.

285 Eatwood A, Sheldon T. Organisation of asthma care: what difference does it make? A systematic review of the literature. *Qual Health Care* 1996; **5**: 134–43.

286 Drummond N, Abdalla M, Buckingham J *et al*. Integrated care for asthma: a clinical, social and economic evaluation. *BMJ* 1994; **308**: 559–64.

287 Charlton I, Charlton G, Broomfield J, Mullee MA. Audit of the effect of a nurse-run asthma clinic on workload and patient morbidity in a general practice. *Br J Gen Pract* 1991; **41**: 227–31.

288 Premaratne U, Sterne J, Marks G, Webb J, Azima H, Burney P. Clustered randomised trial of an intervention to improve the management of asthma: Greenwich Asthma Study. *BMJ* 1999; **18**: 1251–5.

289 Heard AR, Richards IJ, Alpers JH, Pilotto LS, Smith BJ, Black JA. Randomised controlled trial of general practice-based asthma clinics. *Med J Aust* 1999; **171**: 68–71.

290 Gibson PG, Coughlan J, Wilson AJ *et al*. Self-management education and regular practitioner review for adults with asthma (Cochrane Review). In: *The Cochrane Library*. Oxford: Update Software, 2002.

291 Fay JK, Jones A, Ram FSF. Primary care-based clinics for asthma (Cochrane Review). In: *The Cochrane Library*. Oxford: Update Software, 2002.

292 Roe W. 'Science' in the practice of medicine: its limitations and dangers. *Perspect Biol Med* 1984; **27**: 386–400.

293 Anderson HR. Trends and district variations in the hospital care of childhood asthma: results of a regional study 1970–85. *Thorax* 1990; **45**: 431–7.

294 Stein LM, Cole RP. Early administration of corticosteroid in the emergency-room treatment of acute asthma. *Ann Intern Med* 1990; **112**: 822–7.

295 Pietroni MAC, Milledge JS. IV steroids in acute severe asthma. *Bandolier* 1995; **May**: 15-5.

296 Harrison B, Hart G, Ali N, Stokes T, Vaughan D, Robinson A. Need for intravenous hydrocortisone in addition to oral prednisolone in patients admitted to hospital with severe asthma without ventilatory failure. *Lancet* 1986; **i**: 181–4.

297 Rowe BH, Breatzlaff JA, Boudon C *et al*. Magnesium sulphate for treating exacerbations of acute asthma in the emergency department (Cochrane Review). In: *The Cochrane Library. Issue 1*. Oxford: Update Software, 2003.

298 Graham VAL, Milton AF, Knowles GK, Davies RJ. Routine antibiotics in hospital management of acute asthma. *Lancet* 1982; **1**: 418–20.

299 Gershel JC, Goldman HS, Stein REK, Shelov SP, Ziprkowski M. The usefulness of chest radiographs in first asthma attacks. *NEJM* 1983; **309**: 336–9.

300 Mitchell EA, Ferguson V, Norwood M. Asthma education by community child health nurses. *Arch Dis Child* 1986; **61**: 1184–9.

301 Madge P, McColl J, Paton J. Impact of a nurse-led home management training programme in children admitted to hospital with acute asthma: a randomised controlled study. *Thorax* 1997; **52**: 223–8.

302 Mayo PH, Richman J, Harris HW. Results of a program to reduce admissions for adult asthma. *Ann Intern Med* 1990; **112**: 864–71.

303 Hilton S. Patient education in asthma. *Fam Pract* 1986; **3**: 44–8.

304 Mazzuca SA. Does patient education in chronic disease have therapeutic value? *J Chron Dis* 1982; **35**: 521–9.

305 Hilton S, Sibbald B, Anderson HR, Freeling P. Controlled evaluation of the effects of patient education on asthma morbidity in general practice. *Lancet* 1986; **1**: 26–9.

306 Bury RF. General practice radiology – the poor relation. *Clin Radiol* 1990; **42**: 226–7.

307 Chisholm R. Guidelines for radiological investigations: make the best use of your department of radiology. *BMJ* 1991; **303**: 797–9.

308 Callahan C, Dittus R, Katz B. Oral corticosteroids therapy for patients with stable chronic obstructive pulmonary disease: a meta-analysis. *Ann Intern Med* 1991; **114**: 216–23.

309 van Grunsven P, van Schayck C, Derenne J *et al.* Long-term effects of inhaled corticosteroids in chronic obstructive pulmonary disease: a meta-analysis. *Thorax* 1999; **54**: 7–14.

310 Piaggiaro P, Dahle R, Bakran I *et al.* Multicentre randomised placebo-controlled trial of inhaled fluticasone propionate in patients with chronic obstructive pulmonary disease. *Lancet* 1998; **357**: 773–80.

311 Burge P. EUROSCOP, ISOLDE and the Copenhagen City Lung Study. *Thorax* 1999; **54**: 287–8.

312 Callahan C, Dittus R, Katz B. Oral corticosteroid therapy for patients with stable chronic obstructive pulmonary disease. *Ann Intern Med* 1991; **114**: 216–23.

313 Anthonisen N, Wright E for the IPPB Trial Group. Bronchodilator response in chronic obstructive pulmonary disease. *Am Rev Respir Dis* 1986; **133**: 814–19.

314 Boyd G, Moice A, Pounsford J, Siebert M, Peslis N, Crawford C. An evaluation of salmeterol in the treatment of chronic obstructive pulmonary disease. *Eur Respir J* 1997; **10**: 815–21.

315 Jones P, Bosh T. Quality of life changes in COPD patients treated with salmeterol. *Am J Respir Crit Care Med* 1997; **155**: 1283–9.

316 Levin D, Little K, Laughlin K *et al.* Addition of anticholinergic solution prolongs bronchodilator effect of beta-2 agonists in patients with chronic obstructive pulmonary disease. *Am J Med* 1996; **100**: 40–85.

317 Ulrik C. Efficacy of inhaled salmeterol in the management of smokers with chronic obstructive pulmonary disease: a single-centre randomised double-blind placebo-controlled crossover study. *Thorax* 1995; **50**: 750–4.

318 Van Schayk C, Dompeling E, van Herwaarden C *et al.* Bronchodilator treatment in moderate asthma or chronic bronchitis: continuous or on demand? A randomised controlled study. *BMJ* 1991; **303**: 1426–31.

319 Sestini P, Renzoni E, Rominson S, Poole P, Ram FSF. Short-acting beta-2 agonists for stable chronic obstructive pulmonary disease (Cochrane Review). In: *The Cochrane Library*. Oxford: Update Software, 2002.

320 McCrory DB, Brown CD. Anti-cholinergic bronchodilators versus beta-2 sympathomimetic agents for acute exacerbations of chronic obstructive pulmonary disease (Cochrane Review). In: *The Cochrane Library*. Oxford: Update Software, 2002.

321 Intermittent Positive Pressure Trial Group. Intermittent positive pressure breathing therapy of chronic obstructive pulmonary disease. *Ann Intern Med* 1983; **99**: 612–20.

322 Nocturnal Oxygen Therapy Trial Group. Continuous or nocturnal oxygen therapy in hypoxaemic chronic obstructive lung disease. *Ann Intern Med* 1980; **93**: 391–8.

323 Crockett A, Moss J, Cranston J, Alpers J. Domiciliary oxygen for chronic obstructive pulmonary disease (Cochrane Review). In: *The Cochrane Library*. Oxford: Update Software, 1999.

324 Williams BT, Nicholl JP. Prevalence of hypoxaemic chronic obstructive lung disease with reference to long-term oxygen therapy. *Lancet* 1985; **ii**: 369–72.

325 Saint S, Bent S, Vittinghoff E, Grady D. Antibiotics in chronic obstructive pulmonary disease exacerbations: a meta-analysis. *JAMA* 1995; **273**: 957–60.

326 Poole P, Black P. Mucolytic agents for chronic bronchitis (Cochrane Review). In: *The Cochrane Library*. Oxford: Update Software, 2002.

327 Fink G, Kaye C, Sulkes J, Gabbay U, Spitzer S. Effect of theophylline on exercise performance in patients with severe COPD. *Thorax* 1994; **49**: 332–4.

328 Karpel J, Kotch A, Zinny M, Pesin J, Alleyne W. A comparison of inhaled ipratropium, oral theophylline plus inhaled B-agonist and combination of all three in patients with COPD. *Chest* 1994; **105**: 1089–94.

329 Kirsten D, Wegner R, Jorres R, Magnussen H. Effects of theophylline withdrawal in severe chronic obstructive pulmonary disease. *Chest* 1993; **104**: 1101–7.

330 British Thoracic Society. BTS guidelines for the management of chronic obstructive pulmonary disease. *Thorax* 1997; **52** (Suppl. 5): S1–28.

331 Leitch AG, Parker S, Currie A, King T, McHardy GJR. Evaluation of the need for follow-up in an outpatient clinic. *Respir Med* 1990; **84**: 119–22.

332 Littlejohns P, Baveystock CM, Parnell H, Jones WP. Randomised controlled trial of the effectiveness of a respiratory health worker in reducing impairment, disability, and handicap due to chronic airflow limitation. *Thorax* 1991; **46**: 559–64.

333 Cockcroft A, Bagnell P, Heslop A *et al.* Controlled trial of respiratory health worker visiting patients with chronic respiratory disability. *BMJ* 1987; **294**: 225–8.

334 Jones A, Rowe B. Bronchopulmonary hygiene physical therapy for chronic obstructive pulmonary disease and bronchiectasis (Cochrane Review). In: *The Cochrane Library*. Oxford: Update Software, 1999.

335 Wijkstra PJ, Lacasse Y, Uyatt GH, Goldstein RS. Nocturnal non-invasive positive pressure ventilation for stable COPD (Cochrane Review). In: *The Cochrane Library*. Oxford: Update Software, 2002.

336 Tougaard L, Krone T, Sorknaes A, Ellegaard H for the PASTMA Group. Economic benefits of teaching patients with chronic obstructive pulmonary disease about their illness. *Lancet* 1992; **339**: 1517–20.

337 Lacasse Y, Wong E, Guyatt G, King D, Cook D, Goldstein R. Meta-analysis of respiratory rehabilitation in chronic obstructive pulmonary disease. *Lancet* 1996; **348**: 1115–19.

338 Ries A, Carlin B, Carrieri-Kohlman V *et al.* Pulmonary rehabilitation: joint ACP/AACVPR evidence-based guidelines. *Chest* 1997; **112**: 1363–96.

339 Devine E, Pearcy J. Meta-analysis of the effects of psychoeducational care in adults with chronic obstructive pulmonary disease. *Patient Educ Couns* 1996; **29**: 167–78.

340 Lacasse Y, Guyatt G, Goldstein R. The components of a respiratory rehabilitation program: a systematic review. *Chest* 1997; **1**(11): 1077–88.

341 Ries A, Kaplan R, Limberg T, Prewitt L. Effects of pulmonary rehabilitation on physiologic and psychosocial outcomes in patients with chronic obstructive pulmonary disease. *Ann Intern Med* 1995; **122**: 823–32.

342 Lacasse Y, Brosseau L, Milne S *et al.* Pulmonary rehabilitation for chronic obstructive pulmonary disease (Cochrane Review). In: *The Cochrane Library*. Oxford: Update Software, 2002.

343 Goldstein R, Gort E, Guyatt G, Feeny D. Economic analysis of respiratory rehabilitation. *Chest* 1997; **112**: 370–9.

344 Gelband H. Regimens of less than six months for treating tuberculosis (Cochrane Review). In: *The Cochrane Library*. Oxford: Update Software, 1999.

345 Volmink J, Garner P. Interventions for promoting adherence to tuberculosis treatment (Cochrane Review). In: *The Cochrane Library*. Oxford: Update Software, 1999.

346 Chaulk C, Kazandjian V. Directly observed therapy for treatment completion of pulmonary tuberculosis: consensus statement of the public health tuberculosis guidelines panel. *JAMA* 1998; **279**: 943–8.

347 Moore R, Chaulk C, Griffiths R, Cavalcane S, Chaisson R. Cost-effectiveness of directly observed versus self-administered therapy for tuberculosis. *Am J Respir Crit Care Med* 1996; **154**: 1013–19.

348 Mukhopadhyay S, Singh M, Cater J, Ogston S, Franklin M, Oliver R. Nebulised antipseudomonal antibiotic therapy in cystic fibrosis: a meta-analysis of benefits and risks. *Thorax* 1996; **51**: 364–8.

349 Touw J, Brimicombe R, Hodson M, Heijerman H, Bakker W. Inhalation of antibiotics in cystic fibrosis. *Eur Respir J* 1995; **8**: 1594–604.

350 Ryan G, Mukhopdhyay S, Singh M. Nebulised anti-pseudomonal antibiotics for cystic fibrosis (Cochrane Review). In: *The Cochrane Library*. Oxford: Update Software, 1999.

351 Valerius N, Koch C, Hoiby N. Prevention of chronic *Pseudomonas aeruginosa* colonisation in cystic fibrosis by early treatment. *Lancet* 1991; **338**: 725–6.

352 Weaver LT, Green MR, Nicholson K *et al.* Prognosis in cystic fibrosis treated with continuous flucloxacillin from the neonatal period. *Arch Dis Child* 1994; **70**: 84–9.

353 Cheng K, Ashby D, Smyth R. Oral steroids for cystic fibrosis (Cochrane Review). In: *The Cochrane Library*. Oxford: Update Software, 1999.

354 Dezateux C, Crighton A. Oral non-steroidal anti-inflammatory drug therapy for cystic fibrosis (Cochrane Review). In: *The Cochrane Library*. Oxford: Update Software, 1999.

355 Konstan M, Byard P, Hoppel C, Davis P. Effect of high-dose ibuprofen in patients with cystic fibrosis. *NEJM* 1995; **332**: 848–54.

356 Kearney C, Wallis C. Deoxyribonuclease for cystic fibrosis (Cochrane Review). In: *The Cochrane Library*. Oxford: Update Software, 1999.

357 Cramer G, Bosso J. The role of dornase alfa in the treatment of cystic fibrosis. *Ann Pharmacother* 1996; **30**: 656–61.

358 Wark P, MacDonald V. Nebulised hypertonic saline for cystic fibrosis (Cochrane Review). In: *The Cochrane Library*. Oxford: Update Software, 1999.

359 Dutta S, Hubbard V, Appler M. Critical examination of therapeutic efficacy of a pH-sensitive enteric-coated pancreatic enzyme preparation in treatment of exocrine pancreatic insufficiency secondary to cystic fibrosis. *Dig Dis Sci* 1988; **33**: 1237–44.

360 Beker L, Fink R, Shamsa F *et al.* Comparison of weight-based dosages of enteric-coated microtablet enzyme preparations in patients with cystic fibrosis. *J Pediatr Gastroenterol Nutr* 1994; **19**: 191–7.

361 Smyth RL, van Velzen D, Smyth A, Lloyd D, Heaf D. Strictures of the ascending colon in cystic fibrosis and high-strength pancreatic enzymes. *Lancet* 1994; **343**: 85–6.

362 Thomas J, Cook D, Brooks D. Chest physical therapy management of patients with cystic fibrosis: a meta-analysis. *Am J Respir Crit Care Med* 1995; **151**: 846–50.

363 Boyd S, Brooks D, Agnew-Coughlin J, Ashwell J. Evaluation of the literature on the effectiveness of physical therapy modalities in the management of children with cystic fibrosis. *Pediatr Phys Ther* 1994; **6**: 70–4.

364 Thomas J, DeHueck A, Kleiner M, Newton J, Crowe J, Mahler S. To vibrate or not to vibrate: usefulness of the mechanical vibrator for clearing bronchial secretions. *Physiother Can* 1995; **57**: 120–5.

365 Smyth R, Walters S. Oral calorie supplements for cystic fibrosis (Cochrane Review). In: *The Cochrane Library*. Oxford: Update Software, 1999.

366 Conway S, Morton A, Wolfe S. Enteral tube feeding for cystic fibrosis (Cochrane Review). In: *The Cochrane Library*. Oxford: Update Software, 1999.

367 Wolter J, Bowler S, Nolan P, McCormack J. Home intravenous therapy in cystic fibrosis: a prospective randomised trial examining clinical, quality of life and cost aspects. *Eur Respir J* 1997; **10**: 896–900.

368 Office of Health Economics. *Asthma*. London: Office of Health Economics, 1990.

369 Clark TJH. *The Occurrence and Cost of Asthma*. London: Cambridge Medical Publications, 1990.

370 Buxton MJ. Economic evaluation studies in respiratory medicine. *Respir Med* 1991; **85** (Suppl.): 43–6.

371 Blainey D, Lomas D, Beale A, Partridge M. The cost of acute asthma – how much is preventable? *Health Trends* 1991; **22**: 151–3.

372 Ross RN, Morris M, Sakowitz SR, Berman BA. Cost-effectiveness of including cromolyn sodium in the treatment program for asthma: a retrospective, record-based study. *Clin Ther* 1988; **10**: 188–203.

373 Carswell F, Robinson EJ, Hek G, Shenton T. A Bristol experience: benefits and cost of an 'asthma nurse' visiting the homes of asthmatic children. *Bristol Medico-Chir J* 1989; **104**: 11–12.

374 Wilson-Pessano SR, Scamagas P, Arsham G *et al.* An evaluation of approaches to asthma self-management education for adults: the AIR/Kaiser-Permanente Study. *Health Educ Q* 1987; **14**: 333–43.

375 Secretary of State. *The Health of the Nation*. CM1986. London: HMSO, 1992.

376 Mitchell EA, Anderson HR, Freeling P, White PT. Why are hospital admission and mortality rates for childhood asthma higher in New Zealand than in the United Kingdom? *Thorax* 1990; **45**: 176–82.

377 British Thoracic Society. BTS guidelines for the management of community-acquired pneumonia in childhood. *Thorax* 2002; **57** (Suppl. 1).

5 Coronary Heart Disease

David A Wood, Kornelia P Kotseva, Kevin Fox, Ameet Bakhai and
Tim J Bowker

1 Summary

Statement of the problem

Coronary atherosclerosis manifests as sudden cardiac collapse, acute coronary syndromes, exertional angina, non-fatal arrhythmias, heart failure and death. These manifestations are often collectively referred to as coronary heart disease (CHD). Coronary atherosclerosis is ubiquitous in our population and CHD is the most common cause of death in both men and women in the UK. In some groups it is more common than others, with variations in mortality and morbidity rates being apparent regionally and within socio-economic and ethnic groups throughout the UK.

The principal strategy for reducing the population burden of this disease is primary prevention. The White Paper *Saving Lives: Our Healthier Nation* has made heart disease and stroke a priority. The major lifestyle causes of CHD are known and need to be addressed at a society level.

In patients with CHD, the majority survive their first clinical presentation. In patients with symptomatic disease, morbidity and mortality are reduced through therapeutic and revascularisation procedures and over the longer term by lifestyle changes, risk factor modification and the use of prophylactic drug therapies.

The National Service Framework for CHD has set priorities and targets, and addresses both prevention and treatment in an integrated strategy. In addition to a public health strategy for prevention, a complementary clinical strategy is required for primary prevention of coronary atherosclerosis and its complications, the prompt management of symptomatic disease and then secondary prevention and rehabilitation.

Sub-categories

A clinical strategy for coronary atherosclerosis and its complications encompasses the following sub-categories of patients.

- **Pre-symptomatic:** Individuals at high risk of developing CHD and other atherosclerotic disease and patients with asymptomatic coronary artery disease in the general population.
- **Symptomatic disease:** Individuals with symptomatic manifestations of coronary atherosclerosis (sudden cardiac collapse, acute myocardial infarction (MI), unstable angina, exertional angina and heart failure).
- **Post-symptomatic:** Individuals whose symptoms of CHD have been assessed and managed and who require rehabilitation to reduce the risk of recurrent coronary disease, improve quality of life and increase life expectancy.

Prevalence/incidence

Pre-symptomatic

1 **Individuals at high risk of developing CHD and other atherosclerotic disease:** Overall, 12% of men and 5% of women under 75 years have a CHD risk of $\geq 15\%$ over 10 years and are potentially eligible for treatment.
2 **Individuals with asymptomatic atherosclerosis:** The prevalence of Q-wave abnormalities on resting ECGs in the general population, where no history of CHD is reported, suggest that all clinical estimates of disease frequency underestimate the true burden of disease in the population.

Symptomatic patients

From the Bromley Coronary Heart Disease Register (BCHDR) the incidence of symptomatic disease in 25–75-year-olds per 100 000 per annum is summarised below.

Incidence rates for:	All	Male	Female
Number of cases	620	378	242
Sudden cardiac death	36 (28–44)	57 (43–75)	22 (15–31)
Chest pain, cardiac in origin, no history of CHD	481 (480–482)	583 (582–584)	379 (378–380)
Exertional angina, no history of CHD	122 (108–137)	172 (146–201)	89 (74–106)
Non-fatal acute MI, no history of CHD	75 (64–86)	133 (110–159)	37 (28–49)
Unstable angina, no history of CHD	34 (27–42)	53 (39–70)	22 (15–31)

Other estimates of the incidence and prevalence of symptomatic medical presentations of CHD from regional and national surveys include the following.

- The Health Survey for England found the overall prevalence of exertional angina in the population aged 16 years and over was 2.6% in men and 3.1% in women. In both sexes prevalence increased with age, from negligible in those aged under 35, to almost 1 in 5 in those aged 75 and over. In the same survey 4.2% of men reported having had a 'heart attack', with the prevalence in women being half that in men. Again, in both cases prevalence increased with age.
- The OXMIS study found the overall age-standardised event rate for non-fatal first and recurrent MI in men and women aged 30–69 years per 100 000/annum was 171 and 50, respectively.

Heart failure

In the Hillingdon Heart Failure Study the overall incidence rate for clinical heart failure for all ages was 130 per 100 000/annum. A variety of studies have estimated the prevalence of heart failure to be 3–16/1000 individuals, which rises with age. The prognosis of heart failure is poor. In one study the one-year survival was 62%.

Future epidemiological trends

Mortality rates from CHD are falling. The decline is considered to be primarily a fall in events rather than a decline in case fatality. The decline in smoking is an important contributing factor, as are changes in the national diet. The medical and surgical management of patients presenting with coronary atherosclerosis is also a contributing factor to the decline in CHD mortality by reducing case fatality.

Services available

Pre-symptomatic

There is no national policy for cardiovascular screening of the healthy population in primary care. Such patients are currently detected through new patient checks and opportunistic screening.

Symptomatic

1 **Out-of-hospital cardiac arrest:** Community studies have shown that about 75% of cardiac arrests occur outside hospital. Overall survival from out-of-hospital cardiac arrest remains poor. The NHS plans to continue the single paramedic response system, prioritising emergency calls and reducing response times for life-threatening emergencies from the present 14 minutes for 95% of calls in urban areas to 8 minutes for 90% of all calls in all areas.
2 **Presentation and management of cardiac chest pain in the community:** A patient seeking medical advice for chest pain can do so through their GP or Accident and Emergency (A&E). For the GP the diagnosis can be difficult from the history alone, and the options are to send the patient to A&E (if an acute coronary syndrome is suspected), perform an electrocardiogram (ECG) or refer for an open-access ECG or other non-invasive investigations (e.g. exercise tolerance test), or refer for a cardiology outpatient opinion. The preferred model of care for angina is now hospital-based Rapid Access Chest Pain Clinics. For those presenting directly to casualty, patients can be triaged in a variety of ways, including Chest Pain Assessment Units, and then the doctor can admit, refer to cardiology outpatients or refer back to the GP.
3 **Presentation and management of exertional angina in the community:** Criteria for referring patients with exertional angina from primary care to hospital outpatients are not defined in most districts. There is therefore likely to be a large variation in practice between districts and between GPs within a district. The preferred model of care for patients with exertional angina, which is becoming widely available, is a Rapid Access Chest Pain Clinic (RACPC). A majority of hospitals now provide a chest pain clinic facility, and interest in this approach will continue to grow. However, there is wide variation in the protocols for these 'one-stop clinics', although the overall objective is to have patients assessed within two weeks of presentation.
4 **Presentation and management of acute coronary syndromes:** For patients admitted to hospital with an acute coronary syndrome, the majority first seek advice from their GP, and around a third call an ambulance or present directly to the casualty department. About one in two patients are ultimately managed by a cardiologist. The majority of patients with an admission diagnosis of acute MI are given thrombolytics, with the median time interval between hospital arrival and starting thrombolytic therapy being 76 minutes.
5 **Coronary revascularisation:** Whether by coronary artery surgery or by percutaneous angioplasty, coronary revascularisation can both save lives and improve quality of life. Since 1980 there has been a fourfold increase in the number of coronary artery bypass graft (CABG) operations. Angioplasty and other coronary intervention procedures have increased more rapidly over a shorter time period. There are marked variations in revascularisation rates which are not closely correlated with the coronary disease burden. Revascularisation rates are lower in the UK than in many other Western European countries.

6 **Presentation and management of heart failure in the community:** The majority of patients developing clinical heart failure for the first time present as an acute medical emergency. The rest present to their GP and are either diagnosed and managed in the community or referred for specialist investigation and a consultant opinion. The diagnosis of clinical heart failure can be improved with the addition of echocardiography. More recently, natriuretic peptides are being used as diagnostic markers of heart failure. In practice, patients in the community are commonly diagnosed on clinical criteria alone, often supported by simple investigations such as the ECG and chest X-ray. There is evidence of under-investigation of patients with suspected heart failure. Once the clinical diagnosis of heart failure has been made and the aetiology defined, subsequent management will include diuretics, ACE inhibitors (or AII receptor blockers), β-blockers and spironolactone in some combination. Current evidence suggests underuse of these agents. The way in which these treatments are started, up-titrated and monitored varies considerably. Specialist heart failure nurses are being introduced in some districts to provide liaison care between the hospital and the community.

Post-symptomatic: cardiovascular prevention and rehabilitation

After the acute medical/surgical management of patients presenting with CHD, the clinical strategy is to reduce the risk of recurrent disease, improve quality of life and increase life expectancy. Traditionally, cardiac rehabilitation has focused on supervised exercise sessions, but this is gradually evolving into comprehensive lifestyle programmes based on behavioural models of change. Risk factor management in terms of controlling blood pressure, lipids and diabetes, and the use of prophylactic drug therapies such as aspirin are also becoming an integral part of this approach to reduce cardiovascular disease. And finally, the psychosocial and vocational support required to help patients lead as full a life as possible is also provided.

Service provision still remains inadequate in many parts of the country. There is also wide variation in practice and in the organisation and management of cardiac rehabilitation services.

Effectiveness

Pre-symptomatic patients

1 Individuals at high risk of developing CHD

- **Cardiovascular screening:** The evidence from randomised controlled trials (RCTs) of systematic (unselected) nurse-led multifactorial cardiovascular screening in primary care is disappointing, showing small reductions in total coronary risk, achieved principally through lifestyle change. In contrast, unifactorial intervention trials, usually with drug therapies, show significant benefits in coronary and other vascular morbidity and mortality for both antihypertensive and cholesterol modification therapies in primary prevention.

- **Lifestyle interventions:** Individuals who choose to stop smoking have a lower risk of subsequent CHD. The few RCTs of diet in primary prevention of CHD have principally tested a reduction in saturated fat and have shown no benefit in relation to CHD and total mortality. Trials of diet in relation to surrogate end-points for CHD, namely lipoproteins and blood pressure, have provided evidence that modifying dietary components can favourably influence these risk factors for CHD. RCTs of dietary supplements of vitamins and other food nutrients have provided no convincing evidence to support their use. The adoption of moderate physical activity is associated with a reduced risk of non-fatal coronary disease and both cardiovascular and non-cardiovascular mortality.

- **Blood pressure and blood lipids:** Several large-scale RCTs have demonstrated that blood pressure lowering by drugs reduces cardiovascular morbidity and mortality. Antihypertensive treatment has resulted in a substantial reduction in the risk of stroke and heart failure associated with hypertension. Clinical evidence of the benefit of lowering blood cholesterol in relation to primary prevention of CHD has been obtained from several RCTs. In trials of statins there was a significant reduction in the combined end-point of non-fatal and fatal coronary events and all-cause mortality.
- **Diabetes mellitus:** Although both types of diabetes are associated with a markedly increased risk of CHD, cerebrovascular disease and peripheral vascular disease, there has been no convincing evidence from RCTs that glycaemic control has any benefit in relation to these macrovascular complications, but the control of other risk factors such as blood pressure does reduce coronary and other vascular risk.

Symptomatic patients

1 **Out-of-hospital cardiac arrest:** Direct current cardioversion for ventricular flutter/fibrillation in the context of acute myocardial ischaemia/infarction is life-saving. In specialised areas of care in a hospital where staff are trained in all aspects of advanced cardiopulmonary resuscitation, the chances of surviving a cardiac arrest are optimal. For out-of-hospital cardiac arrests this is not so, and the evidence shows that only a small minority survive to reach hospital and then be discharged alive.
2 **Chest pain in the community:** There is no evidence from RCTs that rapid assessment of chest pain will favourably modify the natural history of exertional angina. Such clinics resolve the diagnosis and initiate appropriate management.
3 **Exertional angina:**
   - **Drug therapy:** There is no evidence from RCTs that any therapeutic drug class used to treat the symptoms of angina has any survival benefit. However, there is trial evidence that prophylactic aspirin, cholesterol-lowering therapy with a statin, and more recently, an ACE inhibitor, reduces the risk of subsequent cardiovascular morbidity and mortality.
   - **Coronary revascularisation:** Revascularisation of selected patients with stable exertional angina, by either coronary artery surgery or coronary angioplasty, can reduce coronary morbidity and mortality.
4 **Acute coronary syndromes:** Q-wave MI, non-Q-wave MI and unstable angina.
   Numerous trials have changed the management of acute coronary syndromes substantially, with further developments still to come. Effective interventions include the following.

   - **Anti-ischaemic therapy:** β-blockers.
   - **Anti-thrombotic therapy:** Antiplatelet therapy with aspirin and clopidogrel, alone or in combination. The National Institute for Clinical Excellence has recommended that all high-risk patients are given a Gp IIb/IIIa receptor blocker as soon as possible on admission with a non-ST elevation acute coronary syndrome.
   - **Acute anticoagulation:** Low-molecular-weight heparin.
   - **Thrombolytic therapy:** For patients with an evolving MI, seen within 12 hours of the onset of symptoms, aged < 75 years. For older patients and those seen after 12 hours, or with other ECG changes, there is no convincing evidence for thrombolytic therapy.
   - **Long-term anticoagulation:** The data for oral anticoagulation in addition to aspirin are contradictory.

- **Interventional therapy:**
  - **Primary angioplasty:** An alternative to thrombolytic therapy in an evolving MI when undertaken by a skilled interventionist.
  - **Early revascularisation:** The benefit of early revascularisation for high-risk patients has been compared with a conservative medical approach in a number of trials, but requires further evaluation.
  - **Late revascularisation:** Patients following an MI are at high risk of reinfarction and coronary death. In the DANAMI trial those patients randomised to an invasive strategy, which included revascularisation of those with abnormal exercise tests, had a better outcome.
- **Other therapies:**
  - **Statins:** Although there is no convincing evidence for statins in the acute phase of the disease, there is compelling evidence for the long-term use of this drug class in reducing the risk of non-fatal and fatal coronary disease, other vascular disease and total mortality.
  - **ACE inhibitors:** In patients with an MI there is evidence of benefit for angiotensin-converting-enzyme (ACE) inhibitors. Patients with symptoms or signs of heart failure at the time of MI, or with echocardiographic evidence of significant LV systolic dysfunction, and more recently those with preserved systolic function, will all benefit from ACE inhibitors.
  - **Anti-arrhythmic drugs:** There is no single trial evidence for the prophylactic use of anti-arrhythmic drugs, other than β-blockers, in the management of acute coronary syndromes. An individual patient meta-analysis of amiodarone following MI found a 13% reduction in the total mortality.
5 **Heart failure:** ACE inhibitors and β-blockers improve survival in all grades of heart failure. Digoxin therapy for patients whose rhythm is sinus in heart failure does not confer any survival benefit but may be useful for symptoms and to reduce hospitalisation. Although there is no clinical trial evidence for diuretic therapy, this treatment was beneficial to patients in heart failure when first used and all therapeutic agents with proven survival benefit are given in combination with diuretics. Few non-pharmacological treatments have been tested in large RCTs. Cardiac transplantation improves survival. LV assist devices may act as a bridge to transplantation. Revascularisation has not been tested in an RCT but case series suggest it is useful in patients with 'viable' myocardium. Complex biventricular pacing improves symptoms in highly selected patients.

Post-symptomatic patients

1 **Lifestyle interventions:** Evidence from observational studies shows that patients who choose to quit smoking have a lower risk of recurrent disease and a longer life expectancy. Three RCTs have shown benefit from dietary modification following an MI, through supplementation with polyunsaturated fatty acids, by reducing the risk of recurrent disease and improving survival. There have been a large number of RCTs of exercise rehabilitation following MI, and two meta-analyses have shown that such rehabilitation reduces overall cardiovascular mortality by 20–25%.
2 **Other interventions:** Although blood pressure elevation in patients with MI is associated with an increased risk of reinfarction, there is no RCT evidence of blood pressure lowering following the development of coronary disease. However, several classes of antihypertensive agents given to selected patients following MI have reduced subsequent coronary morbidity and mortality. There is compelling evidence that use of statins following the development of coronary disease is associated with a survival benefit. In patients with CHD, aspirin and other platelet-modifying drugs, β-blockers, ACE inhibitors and anticoagulation have also been shown in single trials or meta-analyses to reduce total mortality.

Models of care

National Service Framework for CHD

The standards presented in the National Service Framework for CHD should be adhered to and local delivery plans drawn up by relevant partners.

Cardiovascular screening

Screening of individuals in general practice should be multi-factorial and absolute risk of developing CHD calculated using the Joint British Societies Coronary Risk Prediction Chart. All high-risk relevant individuals should receive lifestyle advice in relation to smoking, diet and physical activity. Absolute CHD risk should be the major determinant of whether drugs are used in primary coronary prevention.

Sudden cardiac collapse

Patients with chest pain and no past history of CHD should call 999 or go directly to the nearest A&E department. Patients with known CHD who experience a recurrence of chest pain, or have worsening symptoms, should also seek immediate medical help from the same sources or their GP. When a GP is called to see a patient with chest pain an ambulance should be called at the same time if the pain is considered to be severe. All patients for whom an ambulance is summoned because of chest pain or collapse should be given priority and attended by a paramedical crew trained and equipped for advanced cardiopulmonary resuscitation. Relatives of patients with CHD should be offered the opportunity of training in cardiopulmonary resuscitation (CPR).

Exertional (stable) angina

All patients with exertional (stable) angina should be assessed by a cardiologist through a Rapid Access Chest Pain Clinic to confirm the diagnosis, initiate appropriate management and select those high-risk patients who may benefit from revascularisation. Lifestyle and other risk factors need to be addressed in this patient group. Elective coronary artery surgery in selected high-risk patients relieves symptoms and improves prognosis. The availability of coronary surgery should be proportional to the standardised mortality ratio for coronary disease to ensure an equitable distribution of cardiac services on the basis of clinical need across the country.

Acute coronary syndromes

All patients with acute chest pain need to be assessed in hospital rapidly. Risk stratification of patients with acute coronary syndromes is critical in identifying those individuals at high risk of future events. A clinical history supported by an ECG and newer, more sensitive and specific markers of cardiac damage such as troponin T testing can readily identify patients at high or low risk with acute coronary syndromes. Patients at high risk of adverse events should be admitted to a coronary-care unit and be under the care of a cardiologist. Patients on other wards at high risk after an acute coronary syndrome should also have the input of cardiologists within the first 24 hours. All patients should receive aspirin from a general practitioner or other health worker if chest pain is considered to be cardiac in origin, unless the patient is allergic to aspirin

When faced with ST-elevation MI, there are very few reasons why thrombolysis should not be given promptly, and where contraindicated primary coronary angioplasty should be considered as an emergency. This latter procedure has maximal benefit only if available immediately by an experienced operator in an appropriate centre.

Minimising the time between initiation of thrombolytic or other antiplatelet treatments and both onset of symptoms (call to needle time) and arrival at hospital (door to needle time) will limit the amount of myocardial damage and consequent complications, and reduce mortality and improve quality of life.

Patients at high risk may require elective coronary arteriography during the same admission. Patients not at high risk will require an exercise tolerance test, ideally before discharge, to further differentiate these patients into high or low-risk individuals. Although there is no direct trial evidence for antihypertensive therapy in the acute management of myocardial ischaemia/infarction, the use of intravenous nitrates, β-blockers and ACE inhibitors will all lower blood pressure, and therefore it is reasonable to aim for a target BP of < 140 mmHg systolic and less than 85 mmHg diastolic in all patients in hospital. Nor is there any evidence in the acute situation for cholesterol modification therapy, but the current recommendation is to initiate treatment with a statin if the initial random (non-fasting) cholesterol is > 5.0 mmol/l on admission, but practice is changing and statins are sometimes being prescribed regardless of cholesterol levels. In selecting drug therapies, preference should be given to drugs which have been evaluated in RCTs and have been shown to be both efficacious and safe, and the doses prescribed should be those used in the trials.

Cardiovascular prevention and rehabilitation

All patients who survive their initial symptomatic presentation of coronary atherosclerosis require a programme which addresses all aspects of prevention and rehabilitation, integrated with continuing long-term care in the community. This process of care from hospital to general practice should address lifestyle, other risk factors, prophylactic drug therapies and other aspects of rehabilitation. The latter include knowledge of disease, its causes, treatment and prevention, psychosocial factors and occupational factors. Screening of first-degree blood relatives of patients with premature CHD (men < 55 years, women < 65 years) should be considered.

Heart failure

All patients presenting for the first time with the clinical syndrome of heart failure should undergo specialist assessment to confirm the diagnosis, determine aetiology and initiate appropriate management. Coronary arteriography should be considered in all patients in whom the aetiology is unknown and who may benefit, if they have coronary artery disease, from risk factor modification and revascularisation. The optimal model of care for long-term management of heart failure between the hospital and general practice, in order to reduce the frequency of relapses and hospitalisations and improve survival, needs to be determined.

2 Statement of the problem/introduction

Coronary atherosclerosis is ubiquitous in our population and coronary heart disease (CHD) is the most common single cause of death in both men and women in the UK. Despite a decline in CHD mortality since the 1970s, the UK still has one of the highest death rates from this cause in the world.[153] There are large regional, socio-economic and ethnic differences in CHD mortality in the UK.[2,12,228] Death rates from CHD are higher in Scotland, Northern Ireland and the North of England than in Wales and the South of England. Male manual workers have higher death rates from CHD compared to non-manual workers and the same differences are seen for women. South Asians living in the UK have higher death rates from CHD than average. Although the death rate from CHD has not been falling as fast as in some other countries, it has fallen in both men and women and at all ages under 75 years, but fastest for the youngest (35–44 years) age group. The death rate is also falling across all social groups and for both men and women, but the death rate is falling faster in non-manual workers and therefore the difference in death rates between social groups is increasing. The difference in death rates between South Asians and the rest of the population is also increasing because the death rate from CHD is not falling as fast in South Asians as it is in the rest of the population.

Coronary atherosclerosis manifests as sudden cardiac collapse, acute coronary syndromes (acute myocardial infarction (MI) and unstable angina), exertional angina and death in the community. Coronary atherosclerosis can also present with non-fatal arrhythmias or heart failure. Atherosclerosis also affects the rest of the arterial circulation, principally the aorta and its major branches to the head and limbs. Patients presenting with cerebral ischaemia or infarction, or symptoms of peripheral arterial disease, usually have coronary atherosclerosis as well. For those who survive these other clinical manifestations of atherosclerosis, the commonest cause of death is CHD.

Sudden collapse and death in the community is a first manifestation of many cardiac diseases but most of these deaths are due to coronary atherosclerosis.[21,24] Post-mortem reveals acute thrombosis with acute myocardial infarction or ischaemia, but in only about half the cases. Importantly, the other victims have evidence of myocardial scarring due to one or more previous myocardial ischaemic insults despite the absence of any medical history of CHD. So acute myocardial infarction accounts for only half such deaths and for the other victims there is pathological evidence of one or more premorbid events, some of which may have been symptomatic although not medically assessed. Myocardial scarring alone is therefore a source of lethal ventricular arrhythmias in about half of all sudden cardiac deaths due to coronary atherosclerosis.

When the acute manifestations of coronary artery disease – sudden cardiac death and acute myocardial infarction – are considered together, then one in two patients with new or recurrent disease will have died within 30 days of their acute clinical presentation.[145,146,218,224] About 69% die in the community, 29% die in hospital and the other 2% die within 30 days of discharge.[192] However, when *all* first symptomatic expressions of coronary atherosclerosis are considered together – sudden cardiac death, acute coronary syndromes (acute myocardial infarction and unstable angina) and angina pectoris – the majority of patients survive their *first* clinical presentation, with less than one in five of all such incident events due to sudden cardiac death in the community. Therefore, considerable potential exists amongst those with symptomatic disease to reduce morbidity and mortality through therapeutic and revascularisation procedures and over the longer term by lifestyle changes, risk factor modification, and the use of prophylactic drug therapies such as aspirin, β-blockers, ACE inhibitors, cholesterol modification therapy and anticoagulation.

Coronary artery disease accounts for over half of all new presentations of heart failure, another important clinical expression of coronary atherosclerosis.[42,45] In addition, a history of hypertension is present in about half of all cases of heart failure, although considered to be the primary aetiology in just under a third. When hypertension is added to documented coronary artery disease, then coronary atherosclerosis and its antecedents account for most heart failure presenting in the community.

Given that coronary atherosclerosis presents as sudden death, and non-fatal manifestations of coronary artery disease can cause profound morbidity and a shorter life, the principal strategy for reducing the population burden of this disease is primordial prevention – a societal strategy to prevent the development of atherosclerosis and its clinical sequelae. The Government's White Paper *Saving Lives: Our Healthier Nation* has made heart disease and stroke a priority with the following target by the year 2010: 'to reduce the death rate from heart disease and stroke and related illnesses amongst people under 65 years by at least a further third.'[54] The major lifestyle causes of CHD in the population – diet,[53] smoking[55] and physical inactivity – are known, and need to be addressed at a society level.

The National Service Framework for CHD[139] has set priorities and targets and addresses both prevention and treatment in an integrated strategy. Therefore, in the context of a public health strategy for prevention, a complementary clinical strategy is required for primary prevention of coronary atherosclerosis and its complications, the prompt management of symptomatic disease and then comprehensive prevention and rehabilitation.

3 Sub-categories

A societal strategy addresses the determinants of smoking, unhealthy food choices, obesity, excessive alcohol consumption and physical inactivity in the population. In this context a clinical strategy for coronary atherosclerosis and its complications comprises the following.

1 **Pre-symptomatic:** Screening the healthy population. Identification and treatment of high-risk individuals in the general population through cardiovascular screening followed by lifestyle and proven therapeutic interventions.
2 **Symptomatic disease:** Early assessment and management of symptomatic manifestations of coronary atherosclerosis (sudden cardiac collapse, acute myocardial infarction, unstable angina, exertional angina and heart failure) using proven medical and surgical treatments.
3 **Post-symptomatic:** Cardiac prevention and rehabilitation, to reduce the risk of recurrent coronary heart disease, improve quality of life and increase life expectancy.

Using this three-pronged approach to a clinical strategy for the management of coronary heart disease, it is useful to consider the following patient sub-categories.

Pre-symptomatic

1 **Individuals at high risk of developing CHD and other atherosclerotic disease:** Traditionally, cardiovascular risk factors have been considered individually,[200] such as blood pressure[178] or blood lipid levels,[16] and treatment based on the actual level of a given risk factor regardless of overall multi-factorial (absolute) risk of developing CHD. For example, an individual with a systolic blood pressure of 150 mmHg could have an absolute risk of CHD (taking into account all risk factors) over the next 10 years as high as 35% or as low as just 5%, depending on whether he is a smoker, what his lipoprotein levels are and whether or not he has diabetes mellitus. So assessment and management of coronary risk factors is evolving towards a multi-factorial approach, and whether or not to treat a given level of blood pressure or blood lipids is now being assessed in the context of absolute CHD risk.[107,161,232,233] In the UK, a high-risk individual has been defined as one whose absolute CHD risk over 10 years is ≥ 15%.[90,107,226]
2 **Patients with asymptomatic coronary artery disease and other atherosclerotic disease:** With modern non-invasive techniques, imaging atherosclerosis in the coronary arteries (using MRI or ultra-fast CT scanning for coronary calcification) and other vessels, including the neck (carotids and vertebrals), abdominal aorta and lower limb arteries is now possible. The place of these techniques in assessment and management of asymptomatic disease in the population remains to be established.

Screening for asymptomatic left ventricular dysfunction has been advocated but is as yet unproven.[127]

Symptomatic disease

Patients with coronary atherosclerosis can present clinically in one or more of the following ways:

1 **Sudden cardiac collapse (and death) in the community:** Sudden cardiac collapse in the form of an abrupt loss of consciousness is most commonly due to a ventricular arrhythmia (ventricular tachycardia or fibrillation), and without cardiopulmonary resuscitation and specifically direct current cardioversion, death will quickly follow. Spontaneous reversion of a ventricular arrhythmia to a normal cardiac rhythm in the context of coronary disease does occur and such patients can present with unexplained presyncopal symptoms or loss of consciousness.

2 **Chest pain in the community:** Chest pain is a common symptom in the community and coronary disease is only one of many causes.

3 **Exertional angina:** Chest pain on exertion – a retrosternal tightness or discomfort – which is relieved by rest is the commonest symptomatic manifestation of coronary artery disease. This symptom, called angina, is commonly associated with breathlessness, and breathlessness alone may be an anginal variant.

4 **Acute coronary syndromes:**

- Unstable angina
- Non-ST-elevation myocardial infarction
- ST-elevation myocardial infarction.

The underlying pathology of coronary atherosclerosis, with ruptured plaque and intraluminal thrombosis, is common to all divisions of this syndrome except when triggered iatrogenically during coronary procedures. The distinction between these three diagnostic categories is therefore, to an extent, artificial because it depends on arbitrarily dividing those with myocardial ischaemia, but no myocardial necrosis, from those with ECG and/or laboratory evidence of necrosis, and this is a function of the sensitivity and specificity of enzyme estimation and other tests for myocardial necrosis. Cardiac troponins T and I are very useful for identifying patients with myocardial necrosis. These markers and CK-MB now provide the laboratory basis of diagnosing a myocardial infarction.

5 **Heart failure due to coronary atherosclerosis:** Heart failure is a clinical syndrome which develops as a consequence of cardiac disease, and is recognised clinically by symptoms and signs produced by complex circulatory and neurohormonal responses to cardiac dysfunction. The European Society of Cardiology has defined heart failure as a constellation of symptoms, typically breathlessness and fatigue, signs of fluid retention and evidence of major cardiac dysfunction at rest together with, where appropriate, a clinical response to treatment.[209]

Post-symptomatic: cardiovascular prevention and rehabilitation

After prompt assessment and management of coronary disease – exertional angina, acute coronary syndromes and heart failure – which can include emergency or elective coronary revascularisation, the underlying causes of the disease need to be addressed and patients rehabilitated. The WHO defines the rehabilitation of cardiac patients as:

> . . . the sum of activities required to influence favourably the underlying cause of the disease, as well as the best possible physical, mental and social conditions, so that they may by their own efforts preserve or resume when lost, as normal a place as possible in the community. Rehabilitation cannot be regarded as an isolated form of therapy but must be integrated with the whole treatment of which it forms only one facet.[234]

4 Incidence, prevalence and mortality

Pre-symptomatic

1 **Individuals at high risk of developing CHD and other atherosclerotic disease:** The proportions of men and women (excluding patients with reported CHD or other arterial disease) who are potentially eligible for treatment at different levels of absolute CHD risk in England has been estimated by applying the Framingham risk function[6,7] to the Health Survey for England[157] (*see* Table 1). The Health Survey for England did not measure HDL cholesterol and this has been estimated from the equivalent survey in Scotland.[108] The Scottish survey is based on people aged 13–64, whereas in England the population aged 30–75 years was surveyed. For the 64–75 age group in England the average HDL cholesterol at age 64 years in Scotland was used. Overall, 12% of men and 5% of women under 75 years have a CHD risk of ≥ 15% over 10 years.

Table 1(a): Percentage of men and women aged 30–74 years in England at different levels of CHD risk.

Absolute* CHD risk (%)	Men	Women
≥ 30	3	–
25–29	5	2
20–24	8	2
15–19	12	5

* Framingham function: absolute risk of non-fatal myocardial infarction and coronary death over 10 years.
Source: Health Survey for England 1994.

Table 1(b): Percentage of men and women in England at different levels of CHD risk with a BP of ≥ 140/85 mmHg or cholesterol ≥ 5.0 mmol/l, or both.

CHD absolute risk (%)	Men (%)	Women (%)
Blood pressure > 140/85 mmHg		
≥ 30	3.0	–
25–29	4.3	0.2
20–24	6.5	1.6
15–19	7.8	4.5
Total cholesterol > 5.0 mmol/l		
≥ 30	3.2	–
25–29	4.7	0.2
20–24	7.8	1.7
15–19	10.9	5.1
Blood pressure > 140/85 mmHg and total cholesterol > 5.0 mmol/l		
≥ 30	3.0	–
25–29	4.2	0.2
20–24	6.1	1.6
15–19	7.0	4.5

2 **Individuals with asymptomatic atherosclerosis:** The prevalence of Q-wave abnormalities on resting ECGs in the general population, where no history of CHD is reported, suggest that all clinical estimates of disease frequency underestimate the true burden of disease in the population. The presence of Q-wave abnormalities in apparently healthy individuals is partly explained by so-called silent myocardial infarction, but this could also arise because the patient did not report symptoms to a doctor, or a doctor misdiagnosed the symptoms and attributed them to some other pathology. Finally, Q-waves on an ECG are not always due to coronary artery disease.

Symptomatic patients

The incidence of coronary heart disease – sudden cardiac death, acute coronary syndromes and exertional angina – is only available from specially conducted community surveys. The Bromley Coronary Heart Disease Register (BCHDR) is the first community register in the UK to identify all symptomatic medical presentations of CHD in one population.[194] All incident (first) presentations of sudden cardiac death, acute coronary syndromes (acute myocardial infarction and unstable angina) and exertional angina were registered for Bromley Health District in South-East London (population of 186 053; men and women aged 25–74 years) for the period 1996–98 (Figures 1 and 2).

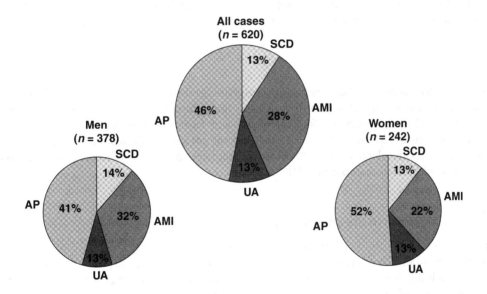

Figure 1: Incidence (first presentation) of fatal and non-fatal cases of coronary heart disease in men and women (< 75 years) in the community. *Source:* Bromley Coronary Heart Disease Register. SCD, sudden cardiac death; AMI, acute myocardial infarction; UA, unstable angina; AP, angina pectoris.

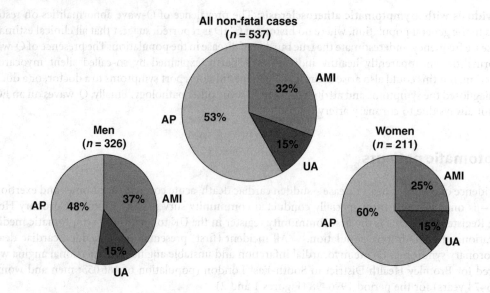

Figure 2: Incidence (first presentation) of non-fatal cases of coronary heart disease in men and women (< 75 years) in the community. *Source*: Bromley Coronary Heart Disease Register. SCD, sudden cardiac death; AMI, acute myocardial infarction; UA, unstable angina; AP, angina pectoris.

Incidence rates for sudden cardiac death, acute coronary syndromes (acute myocardial infarction and unstable angina) and exertional angina derived from this community survey are given in the text and Tables 3, 7 and 8. These incidence rates for a population with an age-standardised CHD mortality under 75 years of 117 for men and 34 for women per 100 000 per annum can be adjusted for districts with different CHD mortality rates in order to estimate the expected number of new cases of disease for other parts of the country. There are no national data on CHD incidence.

Sudden cardiac death in the community

The incidence of sudden cardiac death, as a first manifestation of coronary artery disease, is not available from routine statistics. However, in England the HM Coroner's system requires all unexpected deaths in apparently well individuals with no history of CHD or other disease to have a post-mortem examination. In a national survey of sudden cardiac death undertaken through a random sample of HM Coroners in England in men and women < 65 years with no history of coronary heart disease, 86% of all deaths were attributed to CHD (*see* Table 2).[20] Therefore, it is possible to enumerate the incidence of sudden cardiac death for a district, as a first manifestation of coronary artery disease, from HM Coroner's records, including post-mortem reports and other medical information. Sudden deaths occurring outside the district can still be identified retrospectively as they are all ultimately notified to the health authority according to postal address. The age/sex-specific incidence rates for sudden cardiac death from the Bromley Register are shown in Table 3. The incidence rate for sudden cardiac death (95% CI) due to coronary artery disease for the age group 25–74 years was 36 per 100 000/annum (28–44). The incidence for men was 57 (43–75) and for women it was 22 (15–31).

Table 2: Cardiac causes of sudden unheralded death in England.

HM Coroner's post-mortems in men and women < 65 years		
Coronary heart disease		560 (86%)
Acute ischaemia ± coronary thrombosis	*290 (52%)*	
Myocardial scarring (without acute ischaemia/infarction)	*133 (24%)*	
Coronary atheroma only (without acute ischaemia or scarring)	*137 (24%)*	
Left ventricular hypertrophy		52
Aortic valve stenosis		12
Idiopathic fibrosis syndrome		5
Myocarditis		5
Hypertrophic cardiomyopathy		3
Other rare cardiac causes		14
Total		651

Table 3: Incidence (first presentation) per 100 000 population (25–74 years) per annum (95% CI) of coronary heart disease in men and women in the community.

	Men		Women		All	
	n	Rate (95% CI)	*n*	Rate (95% CI)	*n*	Rate (95% CI)
Angina pectoris	157	172 (146–201)	127	89 (74–106)	284	122 (108–137)
Unstable angina	48	53 (39–70)	31	22 (15–31)	79	34 (27–42)
Acute myocardial infarction	121	133 (110–159)	53	37 (28–49)	174	75 (64–86)
Sudden cardiac death	52	57 (43–75)	31	22 (15–31)	83	36 (28–44)
All	378	414 (374–458)	242	170 (149–193)	620	266 (246–288)

Source: Bromley Coronary Heart Disease Register.

Other contemporary community surveys have recorded sudden and other deaths attributed to CHD in Belfast,[69] Glasgow,[218] Oxford[224] and three other UK health districts[145,146] (*see* Table 9). However, these studies have only focused on acute coronary disease – sudden death, other deaths due to CHD and non-fatal acute myocardial infarction – and included both new (incident cases) and recurrent coronary disease with fatal events recorded up to 28 days after initial medical presentation. In the Oxford Myocardial Infarction Incidence Study,[57] conducted in a district with a similar age-standardised CHD mortality (118 for men and 36 for women per 100 000/annum) to Bromley, the sudden death rate (a fatal infarction in which death occurred before the patient could be seen by a doctor) for men and women (30–69 years) was 27 and 26, respectively.

Chest pain in the community

Chest pain is common in the community and breathlessness can be a variant of angina. The incidence rate for chest pain reported for the first time to medical services (a general practitioner or an Accident and Emergency Department) by patients with no history of CHD, and considered by the doctor to be potentially cardiac in origin, was measured as part of the Bromley CHD register (*see* Table 4). The incidence rate for chest pain for the 25–74 years age group was 481 per 100 000 per annum (480–482); men

583 (582–584) and women 379 (378–380) per 100 000. The age/sex-specific incidence rates are given in Table 5 and Table 6. As the incidence rate for angina in women is about half that in men (*see* below), chest pain is a more common complaint in this group in relation to their true incidence of coronary disease.

Table 4: Number of cases and age-specific incidence rates (95% CI) of chest pain per 100 000 population (25–74 years) per annum (the number and incidence of patients presenting for the first time with chest pain considered to be exertional angina).

Age (years)	All incident chest pain			Non-anginal chest pains		
	n	Incidence	95% CI	*n*	Incidence	95% CI
<25	7	8	5.9, 10	7	8	5.9, 10
25–34	56	120	119, 121	54	116	115, 117
35–44	170	407	406, 408	150	360	359, 361
45–54	307	742	741, 743	229	553	552, 554
55–64	392	1,310	1309, 1311	224	749	748, 750
65–75	384	1,445	1444, 1446	190	710	714, 716
>75	1,316	481	480, 482	854	312	341, 313

Table 5: Number of cases and age-specific incidence rates (95% CI) of chest pain in men per 100 000 population (25–74 years) per annum.

Age (years)	All incident chest pain			Non-anginal chest pains		
	n	Incidence	95% CI	*n*	Incidence	95% CI
<25	3	7	3, 10	3	7	4, 10
25–34	44	187	186, 188	43	183	182, 184
35–44	120	568	567, 569	102	483	482, 484
45–54	182	903	902, 904	124	615	614, 616
55–64	234	1,615	1614, 1616	117	807	806, 808
65–75	213	1,787	1786, 1788	80	671	670, 672
>75	796	583	582, 584	469	343	342, 344

Table 6: Number of cases and age-specific incidence rates (95% CI) of chest pain in women per 100 000 population (25–74 years) per annum.

Age (years)	All incident chest pain			Non-anginal chest pains		
	n	Incidence	95% CI	*n*	Incidence	95% CI
<25	4	9	6.3, 12	4	9	6.3, 12
25–34	12	52	50, 54	11	48	46, 50
35–44	50	243	242, 244	48	233	232, 234
45–54	125	589	588, 590	105	494	493, 495
55–64	158	1,024	1022, 1026	48	311	310, 312
65–75	171	1,167	1166, 1168	43	293	292, 294
>75	520	379	378, 380	385	281	280, 282

Exertional angina

The age/sex-specific incidence rates for exertional angina in patients with no history of CHD from the Bromley CHD register are shown in Tables 7 and 8 (*see* overleaf). The incidence rate (95% CI) for exertional angina for the 25–74 years age group was 122 per 100 000/annum (108–137). The incidence rate for men was 172 (146–201) and for women it was 89 per 100 000/annum (74–106).

Angina is a symptom and therefore there is greater potential for misdiagnosis, particularly in women for whom chest pain is more commonly reported. Therefore angina incidence rates from this register inevitably count some patients who are subsequently shown at coronary arteriography to have normal coronary arteries. Incidence will therefore be inflated by including such healthy people, but refining the diagnosis by electrocardiography, either at rest or on exercise, will underestimate true incidence. This is because the majority of patients with angina due to coronary atherosclerosis have normal resting ECGs, and only two-thirds show changes consistent with myocardial ischaemia (ST-segment and/or T-wave changes) on exercise and some of these will be false positives, particularly among women. So the true incidence of angina lies somewhere between the rate calculated for symptoms alone (regardless of ECG and other findings) and that derived for patients with symptoms, objective evidence of reversible ischaemia and coronary atherosclerosis at angiography.

Prevalence of angina has been estimated in population surveys using a standardised questionnaire. The Health Survey for England[157] used the Rose Angina Questionnaire, and the overall prevalence (angina grade 1 and 2) in the population aged 16 years and over was 2.6% in men and 3.1% in women. It was higher in women than in men in all age groups except for those aged 75 and over, where 7.3% of men and 5.9% of women reported this symptom. In contrast, the overall prevalence of having ever been diagnosed with angina by a doctor was 5.3% in men (3.2% currently) and 3.9% in women (2.5% currently). In both sexes, prevalence increased with age, from negligible in those aged under 35 to almost 1 in 5 in those aged 75 and over (18.3% of men and 17.0% of women). The prevalence of angina as assessed by the Rose Angina Questionnaire showed a different pattern to reported doctor-diagnosed angina: the overall prevalence was lower than for reported doctor-diagnosed angina, and women reported more symptoms than men. Also the Rose Angina Questionnaire gave higher estimates in younger age groups and lower estimates in older age groups than self-reported prevalence. These different measures of prevalent angina can have different applications and from a clinical perspective a doctor diagnosis is more useful because it is not just based on symptoms but also takes account of other clinical information such as risk factors, investigations and a specialist opinion. Angina based on hospital discharges and deaths has no meaning for the community because most patients with exertional angina are never admitted to hospital at the time of their first presentation to medical services.

Acute coronary syndromes

The age/sex-specific incidence rates for non-fatal acute myocardial infarction and unstable angina, in patients with no history of CHD, from the Bromley CHD register are shown in Tables 3, 7 and 8. The incidence rate for acute myocardial infarction for the 25–74 years age group was 75 per 100 000/annum (64–86). The incidence rate for men was 133 (110–159) and for women it was 37 (28–49). The comparable incidence rates for unstable angina are overall 34 (27–42), men 53 (39–70) and women 22 (15–31).

The Belfast and Glasgow MONICA Studies[69,218] and the Oxford Community Study[224] have all recorded non-fatal acute myocardial infarction, surviving up to 28 days after the initial presentation, and these events are based on both new (incident cases) and recurrent coronary disease (*see* Table 9). The MONICA studies in Belfast and Glasgow were both based on patients under 65 years, whereas in Oxford the population studied was up to 79 years old. Unstable angina is not included in these surveys. In OXMIS the overall age-standardised event rate for non-fatal first and recurrent events in men and women aged

Table 7: Number and age-specific incidence rates per 100 000/population (25–74 years) per annum (95% CI) of coronary heart disease in men in the community (12 months' data collection).

Age (years)	Exertional angina			Unstable angina			Acute myocardial infarction			Sudden cardiac death			Total		
	n	Inc.	CI	n	Inc.	CI	n	Inc.	CI	n	Inc.	CI	n	Inc.	CI
25–34	0	0	—	0	0	—	1	4	(0.1–24)	0	0	—	1	4	(0.1–24)
35–44	4	19	(5–48)	1	5	(0.1–26)	11	52	(26–93)	1	5	(0.1–26)	18	80	(47–129)
45–54	26	129	(84–189)	9	45	(20–85)	25	124	(80–183)	6	30	(11–65)	65	327	(253–417)
55–64	65	449	(346–572)	14	97	(53–162)	34	235	(163–328)	17	117	(68–189)	130	897	(749–1065)
65–74	62	520	(399–667)	24	201	(129–300)	50	420	(311–553)	28	235	(156–340)	164	1,376	(1,173–1,603)
25–74	157	172	(146–201)	48	53	(39–70)	121	133	(110–159)	52	57	(43–75)	378	414	(374–458)

Source: Bromley Coronary Heart Disease Register.

Table 8: Number and age-specific incidence rates per 100 000/population (25–74 years) per annum (95% CI) of coronary heart disease in women in the community (21 months' data collection).

Age (years)	Exertional angina			Unstable angina			Acute myocardial infarction			Sudden cardiac death			Total		
	n	Inc.	CI	n	Inc.	CI	n	Inc.	CI	n	Inc.	CI	n	Inc.	CI
25–34	0	0	—	0	0	—	1	3	(0.1–16)	0	0	—	1	3	(0.1–16)
35–44	2	6	(0.8–23)	0	0	—	1	3	(0.1–18)	1	3	(0.1–18)	4	13	(4–33)
45–54	17	53	(31–85)	6	19	(7–41)	4	13	(3–32)	2	6	(0.8–23)	29	91	(61–131)
55–64	53	229	(172–300)	11	48	(24–85)	14	61	(33–102)	6	26	(10–56)	84	363	(290–449)
65–74	55	250	(188–326)	14	64	(35–107)	33	150	(103–211)	22	100	(63–151)	124	564	(469–627)
25–74	127	89	(74–106)	31	22	(15–31)	53	37	(28–49)	31	22	(15–31)	242	170	(149–193)

Source: Bromley Coronary Heart Disease Register.

30–69 years per 100 000/annum was 171 and 50, respectively. The higher event rates in Oxford compared to Bromley are probably explained by the inclusion of recurrent cases of coronary disease in the Oxford study. The event rates for Belfast and Glasgow, where the age-standardised CHD mortality rates are 193 for men and 73 for women and 260 for men and 99 for women, respectively, are much higher than the rates for Oxford and Bromley. The Belfast, Glasgow and Oxford studies describe a community picture for acute coronary events, based on both incident (new) and recurrent cases. However, a complete picture of acute coronary disease must include incident and recurrent cases of unstable angina – namely, the complete spectrum of acute coronary syndromes. Apart from the Bromley CHD Register there are no other contemporary community data on incidence or event rates for unstable angina.

The prevalence of myocardial infarction is reported in the Health Survey for England.[157] Overall in the population aged 16 years and over, 4.2% of men reported having had a 'heart attack' (0.6% in the last 12 months). Among women the prevalence was less than half that of men (1.8% and 0.3%, respectively). In both cases prevalence increased with age; among men aged 65 and over, more than 10% had a 'heart attack', a tenth of them in the last 12 months. From the Rose Angina Questionnaire the prevalence of a 'possible myocardial infarction' was estimated at 8.6% in men and 5.6% in women (more than double the prevalence of a reported doctor-diagnosed heart attack). The term 'heart attack' is not necessarily understood by patients to be an acute myocardial infarction and therefore this term may include patients admitted to hospital with unstable angina or exertional angina as well. As with exertional (stable) angina, it is more useful to use the reported doctor-diagnosed estimates than those from the Rose Angina Questionnaire for reasons already given.

A comparison of case fatalities for Oxford, Glasgow and Belfast for a population less than 65 years is shown in Table 9. About one in two acute coronary events (new and recurrent) are fatal within 28 days.

Table 9: Standardised event rates (new and recurrent) per 100 000 population and case fatalities for acute coronary disease in different populations in the UK.

	Men		Women	
	Event rate	Case fatality (%)	Event rate	Case fatality (%)
Age-standardised[a] event rates for men and women aged 35–64 years				
Belfast[1]	781	40	197	44
Glasgow[1]	823	49	256	49
Oxford[2]	273	39	66	36
Age-standardised[b] event rates for men and women aged 65–79 years				
Oxford[2]	1,350	–	677	–
First event[c] rates for men and women aged 35–64 years				
Oxford[2]	189	–	58	–
Bromley[3]	125	–	35	–

[1] WHO MONICA studies in Belfast and Glasgow.
[2] Oxford Myocardial Infarction Study.
[3] Bromley Coronary Heart Disease Register.
[a] Age standardised.
[b] Age standardisation to a world standard population.
[c] First events in Oxford (non-fatal and fatal definite myocardial infarction (MI), fatal possible MI and unclassifiable coronary death) up to 28 days after medical presentation compared to first events in Bromley (sudden cardiac death in the community and non-fatal acute myocardial infarction admitted alive to hospital).

Case fatality rises with age in both men and women. In the MONICA survey, case fatality was the same for new (incident) and recurrent events in both men and women. As these descriptions of acute coronary events in the community do not include non-fatal cases of unstable angina and exertional angina, the overall case fatality for symptomatic coronary disease appears much worse than it actually is. By including all non-fatal manifestations of coronary atherosclerosis, and in particular exertional angina, the proportion who survive their initial symptomatic presentation to be either assessed as an outpatient or admitted to hospital is substantially higher (about four-fifths of all incident cases) (*see* Figure 2).

The most contemporary national data available on acute coronary syndromes without ST elevation come from the PRAIS-UK registry.[41] This registry conducted throughout 1998 and 1999 involved 1046 patients enrolled from 56 centres throughout the UK. Centres were originally invited by a geographically stratified method based on intervals of catchment populations. About 40% of those hospitals originally invited were unable to participate due to resource limitations and therefore further suitable replacement hospitals were invited, though not fully geographically balanced. The average duration for recruiting 20 consecutive patients in PRAIS-UK was 14 days. The total catchment population of these centres was 24% of the UK. By extrapolation, each centre would admit about 520 patients annually with acute coronary syndromes without ST elevation. In the UK the number of admissions per year would be about 114 000. The range around this figure is between 94 000 and 133 000 with a rate of about 2000 per million population. The baseline characteristics of these patients are shown in Table 10. The average length of stay for patients in PRAIS-UK was 6 days. In-hospital rates of death and death or non-fatal MI were 1.5% and 3.9%. All patients in PRAIS-UK had 6 months follow-up, by which time the rates of death and death or non-fatal MI were 7.3% and 12.5%, respectively. These rates are similar to those seen in the earlier international OASIS study and support the observation that most patients admitted with acute coronary syndromes are at high risk of subsequent major adverse cardiac events.

Table 10(a): Baseline characteristics of 1046 patients admitted with non-ST-elevation acute coronary syndromes in PRAIS-UK.

Baseline characteristics	$n = 1046$
Age (years)	66 ± 12
Gender (% male)	60.8
Diabetes (%)	16.0
Treated hypertension (%)	36.9
Current smoker (%)	22.8
Prior angina (%)	74.6
Prior MI (%)	48.1
Prior PTCA (%)	13.5
Prior CABG (%)	13.4
Prior revascularisation (%)	23.1
Prior coronary disease	81.0

Table 10(b): Outcomes from PRAIS-UK.

Outcomes from PRAIS-UK	In hospital (%)	6 months (%)
Death	1.5	7.6
New MI	4.0	7.7
Refractory/unstable angina	3.4	17.0
Death/MI	4.9	12.2
Death/MI/RFA/UA	7.7	30.0
Stroke	0.5	1.0
Death/MI/stroke	5.4	14.8
Heart failure	7.9	12.6
Major bleed	0.9	1.6

Heart failure due to coronary atherosclerosis

Although coronary artery disease is the principal cause of heart failure, there are other pathologies responsible for this clinical syndrome (*see* Table 11).[45] Incidence of new clinical heart failure can only be estimated from special population surveys. Age/sex-specific incidence rates for incident (new) clinical heart failure were estimated in the first London Heart Failure Study, in Hillingdon (*see* Table 12 overleaf).[42] The overall incidence rate (95% CI) for clinical heart failure for all ages was 130 per 100 000/annum (113–148). The incidence rate for men was 141 (117–169), and for women it was 119 (97–144).

Table 11: Aetiology of incidence (first presentation) of heart failure in men and women in the community.

Aetiology	*n* (%)
Coronary heart disease	79 (36%)
Acute myocardial thrombosis	*42 (19%)*
Not acute myocardial infarction	*37 (17%)*
Hypertension	30 (14%)
Valve disease	16 (7%)
Atrial fibrillation or flutter	10 (5%)
Cor pulmonale	4 (2%)
Alcohol	4 (2%)
Hypertrophic cardiomyopathy	1 (0.5%)
Restrictive cardiomyopathy	1 (0.5%)
Unknown	75 (34%)

Source: London Heart Failure Study I.

There are few data on ethnic variation in heart failure incidence, although it is likely to parallel variations in the incidence of coronary heart disease.

The commonest aetiology of heart failure was CHD, as assessed mainly from non-invasive tests, which accounted for about a third of all cases (*see* Table 11). CHD frequently coexisted with a history of hypertension, which was found in about half of such cases. In the second London Heart Failure Study, in Bromley, using the same methodology, coronary arteriography was undertaken in unselected incident

Table 12: Incidence (first presentation) of heart failure per 100 000 population per annum in men and women (aged 25 years and over) in the community.

Age	Men		Women		All	
	n	Rate (95% CI)	*n*	Rate (95% CI)	*n*	Rate (95% CI)
25–34	0	–	1	4 (0.1–25)	1	2 (0.05–12)
35–44	3	16 (3–47)	3	18 (4–52)	6	17 (6–37)
45–54	4	26 (7–65)	1	7 (0.2–38)	5	16 (5–38)
55–64	21	170 (105–260)	8	67 (29–132)	29	119 (80–172)
65–74	34	388 (269–542)	24	231 (148–343)	58	303 (230–391)
75–84	41	982 (705–1,332)	42	592 (427–801)	83	737 (587–913)
85+	15	1,676 (938–2,764)	23	962 (610–1,443)	38	1,156 (818–1,587)
Total	118	141 (117–169)	102	119 (97–144)	220	130 (113–148)

Source: London Heart Failure Study II.

cases of heart failure under the age of 75 years.[74,76] CHD was the cause of heart failure in at least one in two of these cases (*see* Table 13), and this shows that clinical assessment without angiography underestimates, in absolute terms by about 20%, the real proportion of patients with CHD as the cause of heart failure.

Table 13: Aetiology of incidence (first presentation) of heart failure in men and women < 75 years in the community.

Aetiology	*n* (%)
Coronary artery disease	71 (52%)
Idiopathic dilated cardiomyopathy	17 (13%)
Valve disease	13 (10%)
Hypertension	6 (4%)
Alcohol	5 (4%)
Atrial fibrillation	4 (3%)
Other (determined)	7 (5%)
Undetermined (no angiographic data)	13 (10%)

Source: London Heart Failure Study II.

The Health Survey for England did not estimate the prevalence of heart failure. A variety of studies have however estimated the prevalence of heart failure, suggesting an overall prevalence of 3–16/1000 patients. There is a significant age-related increase in prevalence, with rates of 40–60/1000 in those over 70 years.[130] This prevalence (and the number of admissions) is increasing and this is presumably due to improved survival from myocardial infarction and improved treatments for heart failure.

Heart failure is associated with substantial morbidity resulting in recurrent hospital admissions. Five per cent of hospital admissions may be due to heart failure.[126] Readmission rates are high (up to 50% in the first 3 months). Importantly some studies suggest up to 50% of these admissions may be preventable.[134]

In the second London cohort of 332 cases of incident (new) heart failure followed up for a median of 14 months there were 209 hospitalisations in 127 (38%) of these patients.[44] Seventy-eight patients had one subsequent hospital admission and 49 had two or more (maximum of five) hospital admissions.

Ninety-three (44%) of these 209 admissions were related to worsening of heart failure. The average duration of a hospital admission was 5 days (range 12 to 84 days).

Overall the prognosis of heart failure based on all incident cases is poor. Six thousand deaths per year are thought to be due to heart failure secondary to coronary heart disease. In the first London heart failure study the one-year survival was 62%.[46,130]

The cost to the NHS of heart failure is estimated to be 1–2% of the total NHS budget.[128]

While the majority of heart failure is due to left ventricular systolic dysfunction there are cases of heart failure who have preserved systolic function. A proportion of these have abnormalities of diastolic function. The epidemiology of this poorly defined condition has not been established but may represent up to 50% of new heart failure,[130] although a much lower figure is more likely.

Future epidemiological trends

In England and Wales the decline in CHD mortality did not start until about 1978, and it has been more age related than elsewhere.[153] At ages 35–44 the annual rate of decline is around 5%, reducing to around 2% by ages 55 to 64. At older ages (where most deaths occur) a major fall is still awaited. It is likely that we can now expect a long, continuing decline in CHD mortality of perhaps 3–4% per year, involving both sexes and (before long) all regions and all ages.

The decline in CHD mortality is considered to be primarily due to a fall in events (new and recurrent) but a decline in case fatality is also making a contribution. This fall in event rates is secondary to an abatement of underlying causes, some of which are known and some not. The decline in smoking, particularly amongst men and in higher socio-economic groups, is an important contributing factor, as are changes in the national diet reflecting a reduction in saturated fat consumption. However, there are some worrying trends such as teenage smoking, the rising prevalence of obesity and the lack of physical activity in the general population.

The medical and surgical management of patients presenting with coronary atherosclerosis is also contributing to the decline in CHD mortality by reducing case fatality. There are now a number of different medical and surgical interventions which have been shown, in randomised controlled trials, to reduce coronary and total mortality (*see* Section 6 on 'Effectiveness of services and interventions').

Data from large multi-national registries of patients with acute coronary syndromes demonstrate that about twice as many patients are admitted with unstable angina and myocardial infarctions without ST elevation than with myocardial infarction with ST elevation.[207] The mortality rates for both these groups of patients is similar at 6–12 months. This highlights the fact that, while mortality rates for patients with ST elevation are decreasing, event rates for patients with unstable angina and particularly myocardial infarction without ST elevation are higher than previously realised.

5 Services available

Pre-symptomatic

Screening the healthy population

Screening the healthy population for risk of developing CHD (or other arterial disease) is a prerequisite to identifying and targeting high-risk individuals for lifestyle and, as appropriate, therapeutic interventions.

The overall objective of a cardiovascular screening programme is to detect and treat high-risk individuals in order to reduce the risk of a first non-fatal or fatal ischaemic event.

The following criteria need to be met before a coronary or cardiovascular risk screening programme can be justified.

Criteria for screening for risk of disease	Criteria met
• Disease is common	Yes
• Relationship between risk factors and the subsequent development of disease is quantified	Yes
• Evidence from randomised controlled trials that modifying risk factors reduces the subsequent risk of developing disease	Yes
• Screening tests for risk factors are valid, precise, reproducible, practical and acceptable	Yes
• Screening and management strategy for risk factors which can replicate (or improve on) the results of randomised controlled trials	Some evidence
• Cost-effective use of resources in primary and secondary care, including medical and other health professionals, and the cost of drug treatments	Some evidence

The advantages of screening for high-risk individuals are several. First, it focuses on interventions which are appropriate to the individual. Second, it avoids unnecessary medical action being taken in those who are at low risk as defined within a given population. Third, this approach is consistent with the medical model of care between the patient and the doctor. In this way the risk factor blood pressure, which is continuously distributed in the population, becomes the disease called hypertension (which only some people have) and for which the doctor can then legitimately offer treatment. Finally, the benefit-to-risk ratio improves where benefits of any given intervention in high-risk individuals are larger. By the same token it is a cost-effective use of medical resources. However, it must be remembered that the predictive power of screening tests for an individual is low. Although a person may be classified as high risk, only a minority in that risk category will actually develop the disease within 10 years.

At present there is no national policy for cardiovascular screening of the healthy population in primary care although the principle of identifying and treating those at highest risk of disease is widely accepted following the documented limited impact of unselected screening in primary care.[99,100,230,231] Such patients are being detected through new patient checks and opportunistic screening, e.g. for hypertension or diabetes, but this serendipitous approach, which is likely to vary considerably in its application both between and within (between partners) general practices, means that a proportion of individuals will go undetected. In the Health Survey for England[160] the prevalence of untreated hypertension (defined as a BP > 160/95 mmHg) was 9.9% overall, which is about half of all patients with high blood pressure, and the number of individuals will be considerably higher for the new definition of high blood pressure (> 140/90 mmHg). However, not all such patients will necessarily require antihypertensive therapy as treatment of systolic BP 140–159 mmHg and diastolic BP 90–99 mmHg depends on the clinical context defined by absolute CHD or cardiovascular risk.[107,163,226,233] Opportunistic screening can include some or all of the following.

1 **Lifestyle assessment:** Tobacco exposure (current or former cigarette smoker); obesity (height and weight and calculation of body mass index [weight/height^2] and a measure of central obesity); and physically active or sedentary.

2 **Other risk factors:**

- blood pressure
- lipids
  - random (non-fasting) total cholesterol
  - fasting lipoprotein profile (total cholesterol, HDL-cholesterol, triglycerides and calculated LDL-cholesterol)
- glycosuria, random (non-fasting) glucose, fasting glucose, 2-hour postprandial glucose (but not following a standard glucose load), glucose tolerance test.

3 **Family history:**

- premature CHD: first-degree blood relative (men < 55 years and women < 65 years) with non-fatal or fatal CHD
- premature stroke or other atherosclerotic disease
- diabetes, hypertension, dyslipidaemia.

4 **Screening of blood relatives:** In a patient with a high cholesterol level (say > 8.0 mmol/l) and/or when there is a family history of premature CHD, the systematic screening of first-degree blood relatives for familial dyslipidaemia.

At present, no national general practice data on frequency of cardiovascular screening, what it constitutes, and what action is taken on the results are available.

The potential for risk factor reduction in high-risk individuals is considerable, through both effective lifestyle intervention and the use of efficacious and safe drug therapies for hypertension (low-dose thiazide diuretics or β-blockers as first-line treatment in the absence of contraindications or compelling indications for other antihypertensive agents) and lipids (statins) as demonstrated in clinical trials with disease end-points. However, this potential to reduce risk in primary prevention of CHD and other atherosclerotic diseases is not being realised in practice.

Early detection of asymptomatic coronary artery disease

As sudden cardiac collapse and death is the first and final manifestation of CHD in about 1 in 10 apparently healthy individuals, there is an understandable interest in detecting coronary disease in the asymptomatic phase of its natural history. Sudden death is not the only impetus for a coronary artery disease screening programme. Some patients who survive their first symptomatic presentation may be so disabled by a myocardial infarction that secondary prevention and rehabilitation have little to offer.

For coronary artery disease, magnetic resonance imaging is able to detect and quantify proximal atherosclerotic disease, and ultra-fast CT scanning uses coronary calcification as a surrogate for coronary atheroma.

The objective of a coronary artery disease detection programme is to identify amongst apparently healthy individuals in the general population those who have asymptomatic coronary disease in order to slow disease progression, induce regression, and decrease the risk of acute thrombotic complications. In this way risk of a non-fatal or fatal cardiac ischaemic event can be postponed or even prevented.

However, the following criteria need to be met before a coronary artery disease screening programme can be justified.

Criteria for screening for asymptomatic disease	Criteria met
• Disease is common	Yes
• Relationship between asymptomatic disease and the subsequent development of disease is quantified	Some evidence
• Evidence from randomised controlled trials that modifying risk factors for asymptomatic disease reduces the subsequent risk of developing symptomatic disease	No
• Screening tests for asymptomatic disease are valid, precise, reproducible, practical and acceptable	No
• Screening and management strategy for asymptomatic disease	No
• Cost-effective use of resources	No

For the moment, none of the non-invasive techniques currently available to detect coronary artery disease have met all of the above criteria, and therefore this remains the subject of research.

Symptomatic

Out-of-hospital cardiac arrest

Community studies have shown that about three-quarters of cardiac arrests occur outside hospital, 83% in the victim's home, and that the principal witnesses are members of the victim's family. About half the cases who die have a medical history of coronary disease. In the UK Heart Attack Study only half the arrests were witnessed and in the others the victim was found dead, having last been seen alive several hours previously.[145,146] Importantly, of those that were witnessed, death was truly sudden in only a small minority (13%). Premonitory symptoms were reported by bereaved relatives in at least a third of deaths, and the commonest was chest pain, but symptoms of 'breathlessness', 'indigestion' or 'feeling unwell' were also reported frequently. A call for help before cardiac arrest is made in very few cases and cardiopulmonary resuscitation (CPR) is attempted in less than a third of the deaths that are witnessed. Overall survival after out-of-hospital cardiac arrest remains poor. A total of 111 patients were successfully resuscitated in the UK Heart Attack Study but only half were discharged from hospital alive. Of these, the vast majority had ventricular fibrillation. If the arrest is witnessed the main determinant of survival is the delay from arrhythmia to electrical defibrillation of the heart. There is almost a one-in-two chance of patients who arrest in the presence of a paramedic equipped with a defibrillator surviving to leave hospital alive. Basic life support performed before the arrival of a defibrillator doubles the survival rate, yet cardiopulmonary resuscitation is attempted by lay people in less than a third of the deaths they witness. Attendance by an ambulance crew fully trained in CPR and equipped with a defibrillator is not guaranteed. Nor does a general practitioner necessarily attend a community collapse, preferring instead to summon an ambulance. The NHS plans to continue the single paramedic response system, prioritising emergency calls and reducing response times for life-threatening emergencies from the present 14 minutes for 95% of calls in urban areas to 8 minutes for 90% of all calls in all areas. So there is potential to treat cardiac arrest in the community more effectively.

Presentation and management of cardiac chest pain in the community

A patient seeking medical advice for chest pain can do so through the general practitioner or Accident and Emergency (A&E). The doctor has to decide whether the pain is cardiac in origin and, if so, whether it is due to an acute coronary syndrome or exertional angina. The former requires urgent assessment in hospital whereas the latter can be managed as an outpatient. For the GP, the diagnosis can be difficult from the history alone. Options are to send the patient to casualty, perform an ECG or refer for an open-access 12-lead ECG (and in some hospitals open-access exercise testing is also available) or refer for a cardiology outpatient opinion. Community surveys of angina before the introduction of chest pain clinics found that most patients with 'stable angina' were managed by their GP; only a small minority were referred for specialist opinion and investigations. For those patients presenting directly to casualty, the doctor can admit, or refer to cardiology outpatients or back to the GP. The consequence is up to 25% inappropriate admissions of non-cardiac chest pain to hospital ('chest pain – exclude myocardial infarction') and conversely between 2 and 12% of patients being inappropriately discharged from hospital.[141]

Presentation and management of exertional angina in the community

Criteria for referring patients with exertional angina from primary care to hospital outpatients were not defined in most districts, and therefore a large variation in practice existed between districts and between general practitioners within a district. Some GPs referred patients when they first presented, whereas others managed patients medically and only referred if symptoms could not be adequately controlled with medication alone, or for other reasons.

In one community study of prevalent angina, most patients for whom general practitioners prescribed nitrates had not been investigated in detail.[89,138] Only 64% had had an ECG, 7% an exercise test and 4% a coronary angiogram. One in five of these patients attended a hospital medical clinic during the period of the survey, and half of these were seen by a cardiologist. In a seven-year follow-up of this group of patients, 20% were admitted urgently with chest pain (although only 14% had a confirmed myocardial infarction) and a further 15% were referred for a medical outpatient appointment because of chest pain. Thirty-nine per cent of patients died during this period, of whom two-thirds died from cardiovascular or unknown causes. So if Nottingham was representative of practice elsewhere, then most patients with suspected angina were treated by general practitioners without specialist help.

One model of care for patients with exertional angina, which is now widely available, is a rapid-access chest pain clinic (RACPC).[48,59,103,141,151] For example, a service in Bromley opened in 1996 provided rapid daily assessment of patients with chest pain which, in the opinion of the referring doctor, could be due to angina. All patients had presented with chest pain for the first time, and none had a past medical history of CHD. The RACPC was open from Monday to Friday, 12 midday to 4 pm, and patients could therefore be rapidly assessed without appointment, on either the day they presented or the next working day. Patients considered by the GP to have unstable angina or an evolving myocardial infarction were referred directly to the A&E department in the usual way. Patients with chest pain who went direct to A&E without consulting their GP, and in whom an acute coronary syndrome had been excluded, were also referred to the RACPC for assessment of angina. Patients were reviewed by a cardiologist in training and had a full history, clinical examination, resting 12-lead ECG, chest X-ray and, for those with angina or possible angina, a treadmill exercise test (Bruce protocol) and/or a thallium scan if they were unable to use the treadmill. The results of this service are shown in Table 14(a).[190–193] Twenty-nine per cent of patients were considered to have exertional angina and two-thirds non-cardiac pain. One in 20 patients had an acute coronary syndrome despite the advice to refer such patients directly to casualty. These results are almost identical to those of a RACPC at Newham General Hospital in London where the patient referral criteria were almost identical.[104]

In the Newham clinic the pain had to be of recent onset (within 4 weeks) and younger people (men < 30 years and women < 40 years) were discouraged.

These clinics show that the diagnosis of cardiac chest pain can be resolved, those with coronary disease identified and those with non-cardiac pain appropriately reassured. The difficulty sometimes in distinguishing an acute coronary syndrome from exertional angina in the community is also illustrated by the inappropriate referral of a small proportion of such patients to these clinics. These patients may have been inappropriately managed in the past in general practice and thus not received potential life-saving treatments. Although the majority of patients did not have cardiac pain this should not necessarily be seen as a judgement of the GP's ability to diagnose angina, because the threshold for referral to a RACPC is likely to be lower than that for referral to cardiology outpatients.

In Bromley this service was set up in the context of the Bromley CHD Register and so it was possible to estimate the impact of the RACPC on the number of new diagnoses of CHD in this district. The number of new exertional angina cases increased by 57% as a result of the RACPC. This increase in the number of angina patients assessed in hospital is consistent with previous reports of a low referral rate of angina patients by GPs to a specialist. When a chest pain clinic opens there will inevitably be an increase in the number of new cases of angina identified by the cardiology service, who were not previously referred for a specialist opinion.

Unlike Bromley and Newham, the referral criteria for the chest pain clinics in Edinburgh[48,141] (see Table 14(b)) were more acute ('acute or recent onset' or 'new or increasing or chest pain at rest'). Although

Table 14(a): Rapid-access chest pain clinics.

	Bromley Hospital London (n = 1602)	Newham Hospital London (n = 2160)
Referral criteria	Chest pain considered to be exertional angina and no history of CHD	Recent onset of chest pain (under 4 weeks) and no history of CHD
Acute coronary syndromes	84 (5%)	86 (4%)
Angina	467* (29%)	540 (25%)
Non-cardiac chest pain	1,051 (66%)	1,490 (69%)
Other	–	–

* Definite and possible angina combined.

Table 14(b): Rapid-access chest pain clinics.

	Royal Infirmary Edinburgh (n = 1188)	Western General Edinburgh (n = 278)
Referral criteria	Suspected cardiac chest pain of acute or recent onset and no history of CHD*	New or increasing chest pain, or chest pain at rest, or other chest pain of concern in patients with or without a history of CHD
Acute coronary syndromes	144 (12%)	51 (18%)
Angina	274 (23%)	89 (32%)
Non-cardiac chest pain	768† (65%)	136 (49%)
Other	2 (–)	2 (–)

* Patients with suspected myocardial infarction or unstable angina referred directly for hospital admission.
† Includes 82 patients with chest pain not otherwise specified.

GPs were instructed to send patients with suspected acute coronary syndromes direct to casualty, these referral criteria increased by up to threefold the proportion of patients referred to the chest pain clinic with acute coronary disease, which may actually delay life-saving treatments. The number of hospitals providing a chest pain clinic facility is rapidly increasing but their impact needs to be evaluated.

In the Edinburgh Royal Infirmary service, GPs were asked to provide an initial diagnosis and an indication of their preferred patient management if the chest pain clinic was not available. An unambiguous referral diagnosis was only made in 29% of cases. The GP diagnosis agreed with that of the clinic physician in just a third of the 27% of cases for which the GP proposed hospital admission. Only a fifth of patients required admission from the chest pain clinic. Conversely, of the three-quarters of patients who would have had a GP-requested outpatient review, about 1 in 10 actually required direct admission to hospital. So a positive impact of the chest pain clinic was to reduce intended admissions to hospital by 46%. However, on the negative side, of the 144 patients with an acute coronary syndrome (81% unstable angina), only 26% would have been hospitalised by their GP, thus delaying admission and life-saving treatments for the majority.[141]

Patients with exertional angina assessed in such clinics all have specialist investigations (treadmill exercise testing, radionuclear investigations, etc.) to determine the severity of coronary artery disease and myocardial ischaemia. In the Bromley Rapid-Access Chest Pain Clinic, 85% of patients with exertional angina went on to have an exercise test (87%) or a thallium scan (13%). On exercise testing there was objective evidence of myocardial ischaemia in 72% of patients, and 74% of patients who had thallium scans had a high probability of coronary artery disease. Forty-eight per cent of patients classified as high risk on the basis of these non-invasive investigations proceeded to coronary arteriography; 60% required revascularisation in the form of either angioplasty ± stent implantation (70%) or CABG (30%), 23% were for medical therapy only, and 17% had normal coronary angiograms. Overall, 29% of all patients presenting with exertional angina required revascularisation.

So rapid assessment of chest pain resolves the cardiac diagnosis, provides potential life-saving treatments for those with acute coronary syndromes who might otherwise have been managed in the community, prevents unnecessary hospital admissions and risk-stratifies patients for coronary arteriography and revascularisation.

Presentation and management of acute coronary syndromes

A contemporary description of the presentation and hospital management of acute coronary syndromes comes from a UK Survey of Acute Myocardial Infarction and Ischaemia (SAMII).[21] This prospective clinical survey was undertaken in a random sample of 94 district general hospitals (DGHs) at which 1064 consecutive patients aged < 70 years (approximately equal numbers of men and women) with a working diagnosis of acute myocardial infarction or ischaemia were followed up to discharge.

For patients admitted to hospital with an acute coronary syndrome, the majority first seek advice from their GP and around a third call an ambulance or present directly to the casualty department. There is a difference in the source of medical advice by gender. Men go directly to casualty more frequently than women, who prefer to seek advice from their GP. The time interval from symptom onset to the start of in-hospital treatment is mainly determined by the patient deciding to seek medical advice. Once such advice is sought, the time to admission is longer if this is done through the GP. Once they reach hospital, the majority of patients (57%) are initially assessed in casualty, but 28% are admitted directly to a critical care unit (CCU). For those assessed in casualty, the triaging of patients with chest pain, and a protocol for initiating thrombolytic therapy in the A&E department, are both important determinants of the door to needle time. Sixty-eight per cent of patients who are being managed as an acute coronary syndrome are admitted to a CCU. The others are treated in an acute medical ward. Acute myocardial infarction is more likely to be managed in a CCU. Thirty-two per cent of patients are admitted under the care of a cardiologist, and of those admitted under another specialty about 18% are transferred to a cardiologist prior to discharge. So overall, about one in two patients are ultimately managed by a cardiologist.

Four out of five patients with a working admission diagnosis of acute myocardial infarction were given thrombolytics, and streptokinase was used in a large majority[11,17,70,95,165–167,215] (see Table 15(a)). TPA or another agent was used in 13% of cases. The proportion of patients with a final discharge diagnosis of acute myocardial infarction, who received thrombolytic therapy as part of initial management, falls to about two-thirds. This is explained by a number of factors. The diagnosis of an evolving myocardial infarction depends on characteristic symptoms and dynamic ECG changes with or without laboratory evidence of myocardial necrosis. In the absence of characteristic ECG changes, the physician requires serial blood enzyme estimations to make the diagnosis, but these are neither completely sensitive nor specific, though newer more sensitive measures are now used, such as troponin.[119,122] In those patients with a past history of CHD the initial ECG can be difficult to interpret as there may be residual ST elevation and/or Q-waves. A proportion of patients have contraindications to thrombolytic therapy. The median time interval between hospital arrival and starting thrombolytic therapy in those with an initial diagnosis of acute myocardial infarction was 76 minutes. This interval is almost halved for those initially assessed in a CCU compared to casualty. Importantly, of those patients with a final discharge diagnosis of myocardial ischaemia but no infarction, only 4% received thrombolytic therapy inappropriately. The treatments used in acute myocardial ischaemia are shown in Table 15(b).

Table 15(a): Therapeutic management of acute coronary syndromes in district general hospitals in the UK: acute myocardial infarction.*

Acute myocardial infarction ($n = 447$)		
Initial in-hospital (first 24 hours) management		
Thrombolysis		79%
Streptokinase	85%	
TPA	12%	
Others	3%	
Aspirin		93%
< 150 mg	40%	
≥ 150 mg	60%	
β-blockers		35%
Intravenous	10%	
Oral	97%	
At discharge		
Aspirin		92%
β-blockers		51%
Lipid modification		1.5%
ACE inhibitors		36%
Calcium antagonists		18%
Nitrates		58%
Diuretics		20%
Anticoagulants		2.1%

* Bowker TJ et al. (SAMII principal results paper. Eur Heart J 2000; 21: 1458–63).

Table 15(b): Therapeutic management of acute coronary syndromes in district general hospitals in the UK: acute myocardial ischaemia.

Acute myocardial ischaemia ($n = 614$)		
Initial in-hospital (first 24 hours) management		
Aspirin		83%
< 150 mg	54%	
≥ 150 mg	46%	
Intravenous nitrates		39%
Heparin*		62%
Subcutaneous	28%†	
Other	97%	
At discharge		
Aspirin		83%
β-blockers		46%
ACE inhibitors		25%
Lipid modification		1.2%
Calcium antagonists		54%
Nitrates		78%
Diuretics		24%
Anticoagulants		7.4%*

* Heparin: 'subcutaneous' – unfractionated sc only; 'other' – unfractionated IV; low-molecular-weight sc or IV.
† Some patients receiving sc heparin here subsequently given heparin by another route.

Aspirin is given in almost all patients, although the dose varies from 75 mg to more than 150 mg.[8] Fifty-six per cent of myocardial infarction patients are given a β-blocker but in only 3% is this first given intravenously.[80,235] Thirty-eight per cent are prescribed an ACE inhibitor.[1] Other drug therapy is shown in Table 10.[36]

One in ten patients had exercise electrocardiography prior to discharge and those patients with a final diagnosis of AMI as opposed to myocardial ischaemia were less likely to have this test. Three per cent of patients had coronary angiography at the DGH prior to discharge, and when those booked electively for this procedure are added, the proportion increases to 5%. The median duration of in-hospital stay is about five days, and longer for women than for men. About 13% of patients require bed-to-bed transfer to a specialist cardiac centre because of recurrent myocardial ischaemia, and this is twice as common in those with an initial diagnosis of myocardial ischaemia as opposed to acute infarction. They are also more likely to have a past history of CHD. Altogether, about one in five patients are referred, either as inpatients, or electively as an outpatient, to a specialist cardiac centre. One in three patients are given a place on a cardiac rehabilitation course, and these places are more likely to be offered to incident (new) cases of myocardial infarction.

For patients admitted with acute coronary syndromes without ST elevation, data from PRAIS-UK provide the following information. Of the 1046 patients recruited from 56 selected centres, 71% were admitted through Accident and Emergency, while 28% were admitted directly via general practice or chest pain clinics. Less than 2% of patients were transfers from another hospital, but 9% of patients needed subsequent inter-hospital transfers for coronary investigations and procedures. Chest pain was present on admission in 72% of patients, and about two-thirds of patients had recently had unstable or increasing anginal symptoms. The first admission ward was a CCU for 38% of patients, and an admission or cardiology ward for 45% of patients. Study co-ordinators were asked to recruit patients from all wards with acute coronary syndromes, regardless of age. About half of all patients had input from a cardiologist or physician with an interest in cardiology at any time. Of the 56 PRAIS-UK centres, about half had access to some form of coronary angiography, while 15% of centres had access to coronary interventions and coronary bypass surgery.

Treatment changes between admission and follow-up demonstrate that there is no increase in prescriptions of most agents, including agents such as lipid-lowering therapies, after discharge. Use of agents such as β-blockers is markedly low, even allowing for older patients with comorbidities, and use of agents such as aspirin and statins is lower than other countries in registries performed at the same time, such as ENACT.[72] Work is needed to improve the implementation of an evidence-based prescription policy based on available guidelines for patients with an acute coronary syndrome in the UK.

Coronary revascularisation

Coronary revascularisation by coronary artery surgery or percutaneous angioplasty can both save lives and improve quality of life.[109,111] Patients who are potentially eligible for revascularisation include the following:

1 acute myocardial infarction with evidence following recovery of clinically important reversible myocardial ischaemia

2 acute coronary syndromes (non-Q-wave MI or unstable angina) following appropriate medical management

3 exertional angina with evidence of clinically important reversible myocardial ischaemia, or whose symptoms cannot be controlled by medical therapy.

Primary angioplasty has a potential role in patients with acute myocardial infarction who are ineligible for thrombolytic therapy, including those in cardiogenic shock.

The chosen revascularisation procedure for an individual depends on a number of factors, including coronary anatomy. Coronary artery surgery is preferred on prognostic grounds in patients with left main stem disease (or left main stem equivalent disease) or three-vessel disease, particularly in the presence of impaired LV systolic function.

Coronary artery surgery or percutaneous transluminal coronary angioplasty (with or without stenting) is suitable on symptomatic grounds in patients whose coronary disease does not fall into the above classification.

Since 1980 there has been a fourfold increase in the number of coronary artery bypass graft operations, which totalled 22 160 in 1996–97. Angioplasty and other coronary intervention procedures have increased more rapidly over a shorter time period, and in 1996 there were 20 511 procedures reported. Yet revascularisation rates are lower in the UK than in many other Western European countries. This may partly reflect the relatively lower cardiologist-per-population ratio in the UK compared to other countries.[18] The Department of Health in 2001 was aiming for a 30% increase in the number of consultants in the UK by 2004.

Within the UK there are marked variations in revascularisation rates. The age-standardised rates (per 100 000 population) for CABG and angioplasties by national health authority districts in England show an enormous range, from four in Nottingham to 140 for Brent and Harrow; the average for England is 57. This variation in revascularisation rates is not closely correlated with the coronary disease burden for these districts.

Using CHD mortality as a surrogate for disease burden, there should be a direct correlation between age-standardised CHD mortality rates and interventional rates for coronary disease. The revascularisation rates for a health district should reflect the local burden of clinical disease, and not an arbitrary interventional rate based on clinical practice in other countries.

Presentation and management of heart failure due to coronary artery disease in the community

The majority (67%) of patients developing clinical heart failure for the first time present as an acute medical emergency, most commonly in the context of an acute myocardial infarction.[76] The rest present to their general practitioner and are either diagnosed and managed in the community or referred for specialist investigation (e.g. echocardiography) and a consultant opinion. It is not known what proportion of these patients are managed without a cardiology opinion. The diagnosis of clinical heart failure can sometimes be difficult, in hospital as well as the community, but particularly for the general practitioner without ready access to specialist investigations.[34,75]

A normal ECG and chest X-ray virtually excludes the diagnosis of heart failure but, conversely, abnormalities in either of these investigations are not necessarily diagnostic of clinical heart failure. The accuracy of the diagnosis of heart failure is considerably improved with the addition of echocardiography, which defines cardiac anatomy and assesses left ventricular dysfunction, but the demonstration of impaired systolic function does not necessarily mean the patient has clinical heart failure. More recently, natriuretic peptides are being used as diagnostic markers of heart failure, but their application in clinical practice is still the subject of research.[43] Currently, patients in the community are commonly diagnosed on clinical criteria alone, often supported by simple investigations such as the ECG and chest X-ray. In some districts open-access echocardiography is offered[29] or the patient is referred to a specialist where all cardiac investigations will be undertaken including, as appropriate, cardiac catheterisation.

There is evidence of under-investigation of patients with suspected heart failure. In one study, only 31% of patients with suspected or presumed heart failure had undergone echocardiography.[32] This study also confirmed the figure of approximately 50% for the accuracy of diagnosis of heart failure in primary care.

Once the clinical diagnosis of heart failure has been made and the aetiology defined, subsequent management will include diuretics, ACE inhibitors (or AII receptor blockers), β-blockers and spironolactone in some combination. ACE inhibitors, β-blockers and spironolactone have all been shown to improve the survival of heart failure patients. Current evidence suggests underuse of these agents. While ACE inhibitors are now used in the majority of patients, β-blockers are used in less than 10% of patients with heart failure.[222] The way in which these treatments are started, up-titrated and monitored varies considerably with, in some cases, the general practitioner having sole responsibility and in others, ongoing review organised through specialist heart failure clinics. Specialist heart failure nurses are being introduced in some districts to provide liaison care between the hospital and the community with the intention of reducing the need for recurrent hospital admissions.[129] Not all patients are appropriate for aggressive treatment. For many, palliative care may be the aim.[85]

Post-symptomatic: cardiovascular prevention and rehabilitation

After the acute medical/surgical management of patients presenting with acute coronary syndromes or exertional angina, the clinical strategy is to reduce the risk of recurrent disease and improve quality of life and life expectancy. Traditionally, cardiac rehabilitation has focused on supervised exercise sessions but this is gradually evolving into comprehensive lifestyle programmes – smoking cessation, healthy food choices as well as increased physical activity – based on behavioural models of change. Risk factor management in terms of controlling blood pressure, lipids and diabetes, and the use of prophylactic drug therapies such as aspirin is also becoming an integral part of this approach to reduce cardiovascular disease. And finally, the psychosocial and vocational support required to help patients lead as full a life as possible is also provided. This evolution in the scope of cardiac rehabilitation might now more appropriately be called *cardiovascular prevention* and rehabilitation.

As the scope of cardiovascular prevention and rehabilitation is evolving it is also embracing a broader group of patients with coronary disease. Rehabilitation was initially restricted to patients recovering from a myocardial infarction and those who had had cardiac surgery. With the emphasis now on favourably influencing the underlying causes of the disease, patients presenting with angina, both stable and unstable, are being included after their initial medical or surgical management.

Although the evidence base for cardiovascular prevention and rehabilitation of coronary patients is now amongst the best of any aspect of clinical medicine, service provision still remains inadequate in many parts of the country, despite a rapid increase in the number of cardiac rehabilitation programmes over recent years, many started by the British Heart Foundation. The British Association of Cardiac Rehabilitation[49] puts the total number of programmes at almost 300, but this means that many coronary patients still have no access to such a service. There is also wide variation in practice and in the organisation and management of cardiac rehabilitation services. Thus current service provision fails to meet the national guidelines for cardiac rehabilitation. Most programmes are outpatient, hospital based and concentrate on lower-risk patients who have had myocardial infarction, although many also include patients who have had coronary artery surgery or angioplasty. Women are less likely to receive cardiac rehabilitation than men. The majority of programmes are still exercise centred, although patient education on other aspects of lifestyle and coronary disease is provided in most. A national hospital survey (ASPIRE) of patients with established CHD, undertaken by the British Cardiac Society, still found considerable potential to reduce the risk of recurrent disease through effective lifestyle changes, risk factor management and the appropriate use of proven prophylactic drug therapies.[22] The risk factor management in patients with CHD in Europe is also far from optimal. Surveys of clinical practice such as EUROASPIRE I and II (European Action on Secondary Prevention by Intervention to Reduce Events) have shown that integration of coronary heart disease prevention into daily practice is inadequate and there is considerable potential to further reduce cardiovascular risk in patients with established CHD because many are not achieving these lifestyle and risk factor goals.[65–67]

More recent surveys in general practice have found that nearly two-thirds of patients with CHD have two or more high-risk lifestyle factors that would benefit from change, and there is considerable variation in the prescribing of prophylactic drug therapies between one part of the country and another.

Prescribing of aspirin ranged from 81% to 97%, β-blockers from 32% to 67% and lipid-lowering drugs from 4% to 9%. Several models of care have been evaluated to raise the standards of secondary preventive care, including specialist liaison nurses working between hospital and general practice, postal prompts for patients and general practitioners, health promotion by health visitors and secondary prevention clinics run by nurses in general practice. The liaison nurses had no impact on health outcome, and health visitors and postal prompts were also unsuccessful. A dedicated nurse, however, improved patients' health and reduced hospital admissions.

Hospital remains an appropriate starting point for cardiovascular prevention and rehabilitation because patients with acute coronary disease present through Accident and Emergency departments, or are admitted directly to cardiac care units. Those with exertional angina are being assessed in increasing numbers through hospital, mainly through rapid-access chest pain clinics, but also through cardiology outpatients and Accident and Emergency departments.

Patients with exertional angina are at high risk of progressing to an acute coronary syndrome or coronary death. By addressing lifestyle and other coronary risk factors, and by prescribing aspirin and other prophylactic remedies, the risk of disease progression can be reduced. Yet these patients are not usually included in cardiovascular prevention and rehabilitation programmes, and surveys of risk factor management like ASPIRE have shown that those with angina alone are least well managed compared to patients following myocardial infarction or revascularisation.

6 Effectiveness of services and interventions

Pre-symptomatic patients

Individuals at high risk of developing CHD

Cardiovascular screening

The evidence from randomised controlled trials of systematic (unselected) nurse-led multifactorial cardiovascular screening in primary care is disappointing. The British Family Heart Study[231] and OXCHECK[99,100] both demonstrated small but significant reductions in total coronary risk, achieved principally through lifestyle change. There was no change in smoking habit, but small and significant reductions in weight, blood pressure and cholesterol. Overall, the total coronary risk was reduced by about 12%, the greatest reduction occurring in those at highest risk, and importantly these reductions were sustained in the OXCHECK trial over several years. These results are in contrast to those obtained in unifactorial intervention trials, usually with drug therapies, showing significant benefits in coronary morbidity and mortality for both antihypertensive and cholesterol modification therapies in primary prevention. In addition, antihypertensive therapy reduces the risk of stroke and there is some evidence emerging, at least in the context of coronary patients, that cholesterol modification therapy can also reduce the risk of stroke. So if clear benefit is evident from different unifactorial interventions, then multifactorial intervention should produce at least as great a benefit. And this is so if the multifactorial intervention is accepted. In an analysis of the relationship between compliance with the WHO Factories Study[115,171] intervention programme and CHD incidence, it was shown that the multifactorial prevention programme was effective to the extent that it was accepted. The rationale for multifactorial intervention and its beneficial effect is therefore not in doubt, but such an intervention needs to produce the same changes achieved in each of the single risk factor trials.

Lifestyle interventions

The evidence for lifestyle change – stopping smoking, modifying diet and increasing physical activity – comes from both observational studies and randomised controlled trials. Individuals who chose to stop smoking have a lower risk of subsequent CHD. There has been only one randomised controlled trial of stopping smoking in healthy middle-aged men which showed no evidence of benefit in terms of coronary or total mortality. This result is more a reflection of the limitations of the randomised controlled trial in evaluating lifestyle change rather than an objective assessment of the true impact of stopping smoking on subsequent disease development. The observational data that smokers who quit have lower CHD rates is a much closer approximation to the true impact of stopping smoking, but this relationship is confounded by other lifestyle changes associated with stopping smoking, including favourable dietary changes and an increase in physical activity[156] (level of evidence: II-2).

The principal evidence for diet as a major determinant of CHD comes from epidemiological studies, and no observational studies have reported the effect of dietary change on subsequent disease events. Of the few randomised controlled trials of diet in primary prevention of CHD, most have tested a reduction in fat, principally saturated fat, although some have modified the intake of monounsaturated and polyunsaturated fats as well. These trials have shown no benefit in relation to CHD or total mortality but again, as with the RCTs of stopping smoking, there are a number of important methodological issues in each of these trials, which substantially reduced the chances of obtaining a realistic answer to the dietary hypotheses. There have been many trials of diet in relation to surrogate end-points for CHD, namely lipoproteins and blood pressure.[33] These trials have provided convincing evidence, particularly those conducted under metabolic conditions, that modifying dietary components can favourably influence these risk factors for CHD. Therefore, extrapolating from these dietary risk factor trials, the expectation is that such favourable changes will translate into a lower risk of atherosclerotic disease, but this has not been convincingly demonstrated in disease end-point trials. Finally, there have been a number of RCTs of dietary supplements of vitamins and other food nutrients. Interestingly, β-carotene increased cardiovascular mortality in one trial in the healthy population. So there is currently no convincing evidence to support dietary supplementation with vitamins or other nutrients[30,120,188] (level of evidence: II-2).

There have been no randomised controlled trials of increasing physical activity in the primary prevention of CHD. So the evidence comes from epidemiological studies but, unlike diet, this evidence also includes studies which have related change in physical activity to subsequent disease. The adoption of moderate physical activity is associated with a reduced risk of non-fatal coronary disease and both cardiovascular and non-cardiovascular mortality. There is both observational and trial evidence on the favourable impact of physical activity on other risk factors for CHD, principally lipoproteins. Physical activity raises HDL cholesterol and lowers LDL cholesterol and triglycerides. Physical activity also lowers blood pressure. The same caveats about the confounding effects of other lifestyle changes apply to physical activity as to smoking and diet[86,117,172,177] (level of evidence: II-2).

Blood pressure

Several large-scale randomised controlled trials have convincingly demonstrated that blood pressure lowering by drugs reduces cardiovascular morbidity and mortality. A meta-analysis of these trials comprising a total of more than 40 000 individuals has shown that over an average period of five years a mean diastolic blood pressure difference of 5–6 mmHg between treatment and control groups reduced the risk of stroke by about 40%.[38,39,123] This is only slightly less than the increase in fatal and non-fatal stroke seen in epidemiological studies for a prolonged increase in diastolic blood pressure of 5–6 mmHg. Another meta-analysis comprising a total of about 14 000 individuals showed that blood pressure lowering reduces the development of heart failure by about 50%.[136] However, this meta-analytic approach has also shown that the reduction in risk of coronary heart disease (fatal or non-fatal events) with a five-year reduction of diastolic blood pressure of 5–6 mmHg is about 15%, which is definitely less than the 20–25% increase in coronary heart disease predicted from epidemiology for a prolonged 5–6 mmHg difference in diastolic blood pressure. Thus antihypertensive treatment does result in a substantial reduction in the increased risk of stroke and heart failure associated with hypertension. However, it only incompletely reduces the risk of coronary heart disease.

Hypertension is also a major risk factor in the elderly. A number of randomised controlled trials have shown that antihypertensive drug treatment is clearly beneficial and this benefit extends to the very elderly up to 80 years of age. These trials have also shown that in isolated systolic hypertension, i.e. a form of hypertension common in the elderly population which markedly increases cardiovascular risk, blood pressure lowering by drugs results in a clear-cut reduction in the number of cardiovascular fatal and non-fatal events. Cardiovascular complications reduced by drug treatment are stroke, heart failure and coronary heart disease, with a reduction in all-cause mortality, both in individual trials and in a meta-analysis[186,211] (level of evidence: I).

Blood lipids

Clinical evidence of the benefit of lowering blood cholesterol in relation to primary prevention of CHD has been obtained from several RCTs, and there is now much less concern about the benefits of such treatment overall. There have now been two RCTs of cholesterol modification using statins in primary prevention, namely the West of Scotland Coronary Prevention Study (WOSCOPS)[227] and the Air Force/Texas

Coronary Atherosclerotic Prevention Study (AFCAPS/TexCAPS).[58] In both trials there was a significant reduction in the combined end-point of non-fatal and fatal coronary events. There was no effect on total mortality but neither trial was powered to test the effect of lipid lowering on all causes of deaths. Importantly, there was no evidence of any adverse effects of the statins on non-cardiovascular events and these results are consistent with the three trials of statins in secondary prevention, two of which did show overall benefit in relation to total mortality. Earlier clinical trials of fibrate treatment have not yielded results as clear-cut as those involving other classes of lipid-lowering drugs, principally the statins. Continuing long-term surveillance of all classes of lipid modification therapy of clinical events, both cardiovascular and non-cardiovascular, is necessary (level of evidence: I).

Diabetes mellitus

Although both types of diabetes, type 1 (insulin-dependent) and type 2 (non-insulin-dependent), are associated with a markedly increased risk of CHD, cerebrovascular disease and peripheral vascular disease, there has been no evidence from RCTs that glycaemic control had any benefit in relation to these macrovascular complications. The recent UK Prospective Diabetes Study (UKPDS)[219,220] evaluated different treatment modalities (chlorpropamide, glibenclamide, insulin and metformin) in type 2 diabetes in relation to both microvascular and macrovascular end-points. Glycaemic control reduced the risk of microvascular complications but was not associated with a significant reduction in macrovascular complications. However, lowering blood pressure did significantly reduce coronary events (level of evidence: I for anti-hypertensive therapy).

Individuals with asymptomatic disease

Although non-invasive methods for the detection of asymptomatic coronary artery or other athero-sclerotic disease look promising, more research is needed to evaluate their incremental value above that of conventional risk factor measurements in assessing absolute risk of developing cardiovascular disease in healthy people. Randomised controlled trials are also required to evaluate the impact of a non-invasive screening and intervention programme for coronary artery or other arterial disease on subsequent morbidity and mortality.

Symptomatic patients

Out-of-hospital cardiac arrest

Direct current cardioversion for ventricular flutter/fibrillation in the context of acute myocardial ischaemia/infarction is life-saving, and therefore a randomised controlled trial has never been conducted because observation provided conclusive proof. In a CCU/ITU, Accident and Emergency department and other specialised areas of care in a hospital where staff are trained in all aspects of advanced cardiopulmonary resuscitation, the chances of surviving a cardiac arrest are optimal. For out-of-hospital cardiac arrests this is not so, and the observational evidence shows that only a small minority survive to reach and then be discharged from hospital alive. The central issue is the benefit of different levels of cardiopulmonary resuscitation in the community (paramedical with full resuscitation skills and equipment) through to bystander CPR[210] (level of evidence: II-3).

Despite the present provision of paramedical teams, only 1 in 10 patients are successfully resuscitated, of whom less than half survive to 30 days (about 4% of all cardiac arrests outside hospital). However, only a minority actually has cardiopulmonary resuscitation (about 27%). Paramedical staff have a much higher success rate compared to bystander CPR. There is a fivefold increase in the prospect of surviving out-of-hospital cardiac arrest, from 8% with relative or bystander CPR to 40% for paramedics.[145,146]

Chest pain in the community

There is no evidence from randomised controlled trials that rapid assessment of chest pain will favourably modify the natural history of exertional angina. Such clinics resolve the diagnosis and initiate appropriate management, but their impact on morbidity and mortality is not known.

Exertional angina

Drug therapy

There is no evidence from randomised controlled trials that any therapeutic drug class used to treat the symptom angina has any survival benefit. This includes nitrates, β-blockers, calcium-channel blockers and other agents. However, there is some trial evidence that prophylactic aspirin, cholesterol-lowering therapy with a statin, and more recently an ACE inhibitor, reduces the risk of subsequent cardiovascular morbidity and mortality and can improve survival[47,61,77,93,110,189] (level of evidence I [aspirin] and II-I [statin]).

Coronary revascularisation

Revascularisation of selected patients with stable exertional angina, by either coronary artery surgery or coronary angioplasty, will reduce morbidity and mortality.[13,155,170,201] In an overview of randomised controlled trials comparing coronary artery bypass graft (CABG) surgery with medical therapy in patients with stable angina (not severe enough to necessitate surgery on symptomatic grounds alone, or myocardial infarction), the CABG group had significantly lower mortality than the medically treated group up to 10 years. The odds ratios (95% CI) were 0.61 (0.48–0.77), 0.68 (0.56–0.83) and 0.83 (0.70–0.98) at 5, 7 and 10 years in favour of surgery. The risk reduction was greatest in those with the most prognostically important disease (left main artery and in three vessels). Coronary surgery has also been compared to coronary angioplasty in angina patients. A meta-analysis of randomised trials showed no difference in prognosis between these two initial revascularisation strategies for the combined end-point of cardiac death and non-fatal myocardial infarction; relative risk 1.08 (0.79–1.50). However, 17.8% of patients randomised to percutaneous transluminal coronary angioplasty (PTCA) required additional CABG within a year. The rate of additional non-randomised interventions (PTCA and/or CABG) in the first year of follow-up was 3.37% and 3.3% in patients randomised to PTCA and CABG, respectively. The prevalence of angina after one year was considerably higher in the PTCA group (relative risk 1.56 [1.30, 1.83]), although this difference had attenuated by 3 years. Separate analyses for multi-vessel and single-vessel disease patients were largely compatible, though the rates of mortality, additional intervention and prevalent angina were slightly lower in single-vessel disease.

In the UK, the Randomised Intervention Treatment of Angina (RITA) trial showed similar results (no difference in the combined end-point of death or definite myocardial infarction; relative risk 0.88 [0.59–1.29]).[168] However, 4% of PTCA patients required emergency CABG before discharge and a further 15% had CABG during follow-up. Altogether, 38% and 11% of the PTCA and CABG groups that required revascularisation procedure(s) had a primary event. Repeat coronary arteriography during follow-up was four times more common in PTCA than in CABG patients. The prevalence of angina during follow-up was higher in the PTCA group (32% vs. 11% at 6 months) but this difference became less marked after 2 years and anti-anginal drugs were prescribed more frequently for PTCA patients. The long-term follow-up (median 6.5 years) of RITA-1 continued to show no significant difference in death or non-fatal myocardial infarction.[94] Altogether, a quarter of patients assigned PTCA also had CABG and a further 19% required additional non-randomised PTCA. The prevalence of angina remained consistently higher in the PTCA group. So these revascularisation procedures for patients with angina are equivalent in terms of subsequent death and myocardial infarction. However, those who have PTCA have a much higher need for repeat angiography and further revascularisation (either CABG or repeat PTCA), and are still more symptomatic than those who had surgery.

The role of PTCA has also been evaluated in comparison to medical therapy in the RITA-2 trial.[169] Unlike the comparison with surgery, there was a significantly higher risk of death or definite myocardial infarction in the PTCA group (6.3% vs. 3.3%), with an absolute difference of 3% (95% CI: 0.4–5.7%). This difference was mainly due to one death and seven non-fatal myocardial infarctions related to the revascularisation procedures. Almost one in five patients randomised to PTCA required either emergency ($n = 7$) or elective CABG or further non-randomised PTCA. In the medical group, 23% underwent a revascularisation procedure during follow-up, mostly because of worsening symptoms. Relief of angina and exercise time was significantly better in the PTCA group, and these benefits were greatest in those with more severe angina at baseline. In patients with angina, which is considered suitable for either medical care or PTCA, the greater symptomatic improvement from this form of revascularisation has to be balanced against the short-term excess hazard (principally myocardial infarction and emergency revascularisation).

Acute coronary syndromes: Q-wave MI, non-Q-wave MI and unstable angina

Patients with acute coronary syndromes (acute ST-elevation MI, non-ST-elevation MI and unstable angina) require urgent hospital assessment for three reasons. First, the survival benefit for those patients eligible for reperfusion therapies (thrombolytic agent or combination of thrombolytic with either heparin or Gp IIb/IIIa receptor blocker therapy or primary angioplasty) increases the shorter the interval between onset of symptoms and treatment. Second, in the event of ventricular flutter/fibrillation the chances of successful resuscitation are increased fivefold with a trained paramedic crew in attendance, or if the cardiac arrest occurs in casualty or another specialised hospital area. Third, for those patients not eligible for reperfusion therapies, agents such as clopidogrel and Gp IIb/IIIa receptor blockers have been shown to reduce subsequent combined end-points such as death, stroke or myocardial infarction. There are numerous trials, both recently completed and ongoing, dealing with the management of acute coronary syndromes which have changed the management of acute coronary syndromes substantially, with further developments to come.

Anti-ischaemic therapy

Only β-blockers show clinical evidence of benefit from randomised controlled trials in relation to survival. Intravenous (oral) β-blockade in acute myocardial infarction lowers early mortality by 10–15%. There are no similar trials in unstable angina. There is no comparable evidence for intravenous nitrates. Calcium antagonists – verapamil and diltiazem – can be used for patients with AMI in whom β-blockers are contraindicated, and in the absence of significant LV systolic dysfunction or heart failure. However, a meta-analysis of this class of drugs showed no evidence of benefit in terms of mortality, and may actually increase the risk of dying. Nifedipine, the short-acting calcium-channel blocker, is contraindicated in this context[106,182,185,235] (level of evidence for β-blockers: 1).

Antithrombotic therapy

Antiplatelet therapy

Antiplatelet therapy, principally aspirin, has been shown in randomised controlled trials to reduce the risk of myocardial infarction and death in acute coronary syndromes by up to 70%. Of the second-generation platelet inhibitors, clopidogrel is superior to aspirin in one randomised control trial in terms of achieving a significantly greater reduction in clinical events, and is therefore an appropriate alternative to aspirin when the latter cannot be tolerated. The combination of aspirin and clopidogrel for patients presenting with non-ST-elevation acute coronary syndromes has recently been shown to reduce the combined end-point of cardiovascular death, myocardial infarction and stroke by 20% at a mean follow-up of 9 months. This reduction in the CURE trial was mainly due to a reduction in myocardial infarction. In a prospective subgroup analysis of the patients in the CURE study who underwent coronary angioplasty, the benefit seen was even higher despite the placebo arm switching briefly to open-label clopidogrel for 1 month.[131,132]

Intravenous glycoprotein IIb/IIIa-receptor antagonists are the third generation of platelet inhibitors. Oral agents have been ineffective. There are two distinct types of intravenous agents: monoclonal antibodies (abciximab) and small molecules (tirofiban or eptifibatide). These agents have been evaluated in a number of trials of acute coronary syndromes. Initially these agents were restricted to trials of patients with non-ST-elevation acute coronary syndromes, but more recently they have been tried in combination with thrombolytic agents in the context of ST-elevation acute coronary syndromes. In randomised controlled trials of non-ST-elevation acute coronary syndrome patients, both small-molecule agents have shown a reduction in myocardial infarction and death of up to 25% compared with aspirin and unfractionated heparin alone. The main component of this reduction has been the reduction in myocardial infarction. One notable exception of an intravenous agent not being effective was the GUSTO-IV study of non-ST-elevation in patients with acute coronary syndromes unlikely to go for revascularisation.[181] While a number of theories of inadequate chronic platelet inhibition or rebound platelet activation have been offered for this result, the impact has been that abciximab is not recommended for medical stabilisation of patients with non-ST-elevation acute coronary syndromes. However, in the context of patients going for coronary angioplasty, abciximab was found to be superior to tirofiban in the only head-to-head Gp IIb/IIIa-receptor blocker (TARGET) study to report thus far.[216] It is worth noting that the National Institute for Clinical Excellence has recommended that all high-risk patients are given a Gp IIb/IIIa-receptor blocker as soon as possible on admission with a non-ST-elevation acute coronary syndrome. This guidance has been supported by the recent European and UK guidelines on the management of non-ST-elevation acute coronary syndromes. Despite these strong, clear recommendations there has not been a widespread uptake of Gp IIb/IIIa-receptor blockers except when patients are scheduled to go directly to coronary angiography. However, few patients in the UK are offered urgent angiography due to lack of interventional units[8,15,25–28,64,73,114,132,158–160,181,208,216] (level of evidence for aspirin, clopidogrel: I-1; glycoprotein IIb/IIIa-receptor antagonists as adjuncts to angioplasty and stenting in the context of acute coronary syndrome: I-1; glycoprotein IIb/IIIa-receptor antagonists as medical stabilisation of acute coronary syndrome only: I-1).

Acute anticoagulation

A meta-analysis of the use of unfractionated heparin in acute coronary syndromes has shown only marginal benefit in terms of mortality over the use of aspirin alone. Low-molecular-weight heparin, together with aspirin, is much more effective than aspirin alone and is at least as effective as unfractionated heparin. Low-molecular-weight heparin is being increasingly used in preference to unfractionated heparin because of ease of administration (subcutaneous) and the lack of need for monitoring[9,10,36,40,61,62,79,81,82,88,101,113,208] (level of evidence for unfractionated heparin: 4).

Thrombolytic therapy

In patients with an evolving myocardial infarction (ST elevation >0.1 mm in two or more contiguous leads, or bundle-branch block) seen within 12 hours of the onset of symptoms, aged <75 years, thrombolytic therapy will reduce mortality. For those patients with an anterior MI, there is evidence that rtPA confers additional mortality benefit over streptokinase. For older patients and those seen after 12 hours, or with other ECG changes, there is no convincing evidence for thrombolytic therapy. Nor is there any evidence to support the use of thrombolytic therapy in non-Q-wave MI or unstable angina, and for the latter this treatment may actually have adverse risks. Combinations of thrombolytic agents and Gp IIb/IIIa-receptor blockers are being evaluated. In ASSENT-3, tenecteplase was combined with either unfractionated abciximab or enoxaparin.[202] Both the latter arms did significantly and equally better than the unfractionated heparin arm. The convenience of enoxaparin makes it an attractive addition to thrombolytic agents for reducing the combined end-points of death (by 30 days), reinfarction and refractory ischaemia[11,70,78,102,199,203] (level of evidence for thrombolytic therapies: 1).

Long-term anticoagulation

The data for oral anticoagulation in addition to aspirin are contradictory. While the earlier CHAMP study of 5059 patients with acute myocardial infarction showed no benefit of the combination over 10 years with a mean INR of 1.9, the more recent WARIS-II trial showed a benefit. WARIS-II enrolled 3630 acute myocardial infarction patients and randomised them to either aspirin or warfarin or a combination.[98] The mean INR in the combination group was 2.2 and in the warfarin-alone arm was 2.8. Both these warfarin arms reduced the rate of combined first events of death, thrombo-embolic stroke or reinfarction significantly by 29% and 19%, respectively. The combination arm increased the risk of bleeding fourfold above aspirin but with very low absolute numbers (0.15% to 0.58% major bleeds per year). Patients with both Q- and non-Q-wave infarctions were included in that study. How these results will impact on clinical practice remains to be seen in view of the additional resources needed for this approach. An evaluation of aspirin–warfarin and clopidogrel–aspirin–warfarin combinations would be the next logical step to determine benefits and bleeding rates. Anticoagulation would be appropriate in selective coronary patients at high risk of systemic embolisation (atrial fibrillation, large anterior MI and LV thrombus) (level of evidence: I-2).

Statins in the acute phase

The MIRACL trial evaluated the impact of atorvastatin 80 mg started between 24 and 96 hours after admission and continued for 16 weeks, in 3086 patients with non-ST-elevation acute coronary syndromes. There was a significant reduction in the combined end-points of first event of death, myocardial infarction, stroke or recurrent ischaemia/ischaemic readmission. However, this result was almost completely due to a reduction in recurrent ischaemia/ischaemic readmissions. So the clinical benefit of acute statin therapy remains an open question, but there was little difference in adverse events compared with placebo[175] (level of evidence: I-2).

Hormone replacement therapies in the acute phase of acute coronary syndromes

A variety of hormone replacement therapies are being evaluated in female patients presenting with acute coronary syndromes, and the results of these are awaited.

Interventional therapy

Primary angioplasty

There is evidence of mortality benefit for primary angioplasty as an alternative to thrombolytic therapy in an evolving myocardial infarction when undertaken by a skilled interventionist. However, at present this therapeutic option is not available in the vast majority of hospitals which manage acute coronary syndromes. Primary angioplasty should be considered for patients with evolving MI (same criteria as for thrombolytic therapy) in whom thrombolysis is contraindicated, or for cardiogenic shock (level of evidence: I-1).

Early revascularisation

After medical therapy for acute coronary syndromes the benefit of early revascularisation for high-risk patients, e.g. non-Q-wave MI and unstable angina who settle medically, has been compared with a conservative medical approach. In the FRISC II trial, patients with unstable coronary artery disease (verified by electrocardiography or raised biochemical markers) were randomised to an early invasive or non-invasive treatment strategy. There was a reduction in the combined end-point of death or myocardial infarction (risk ratio: 0.78 [95% CI: 0.62–0.98]). Myocardial infarction decreased significantly, but not mortality. Symptoms of angina and readmission were halved by the invasive strategy. The differences between previous studies and the FRICS II trial[83,225] are probably explained by the large difference in intervention rates and the timing of interventions. Coronary angiography was done within the first 7 days in 96% and 10%, and revascularisation within the first 10 days in 71% and 9% of patients in the invasive and non-invasive groups. This is in contrast to the intervention rates in the TIMI IIb trial (61 vs. 49% at 42 days) and the VANQWISH[19] trial (44 vs. 33% after about 1 year). In the context of non-ST-elevation acute coronary syndromes, the TARGET trial of 2220 patients also demonstrated the benefits of a routine early aggressive approach compared to an initial conservative approach with all patients covered by Gp IIb/IIIa-receptor blockers.[216] The TACTICS trial required all patients randomised to the invasive approach to go for angiography within 4 to 48 hours, with revascularisation if appropriate.[26] Inpatient angiography was provided for patients in the conservative group if they developed refractory ischaemia, cardiac complications or had a positive pre-discharge stress test. The primary outcome was a combination of death, myocardial infarction or a readmission with an acute coronary syndrome within 6 months. Prior to discharge 51% of patients in the conservative group and 97% in the invasive group had angiography, resulting in respective revascularisation rates of 36% and 60%. By 6 months, revascularisation rates were 44% and 61%, and the primary end-point occurred in 19.4% of the conservative group and 15.9% of the invasive group. The relative risk reduction was 22% ($p = 0.025$), mainly due to significant reductions in myocardial infarction and readmission but not mortality.

So the potential of early revascularisation, particularly for high-risk patients, in reducing subsequent morbidity (myocardial infarction) has been shown but requires further evaluation in relation to total mortality. A policy of early revascularisation will require a major increase in resources and manpower. In PRAIS-UK, only 10% of patients had inpatient angiography and another 4% of patients had angiography after inter-hospital transfer. These rates are lower than the conservative arm of the TACTICS trial, demonstrating the marked disparity of resources in the UK compared to other European countries and the USA (level of evidence: 1).

Late revascularisation

Patients following a myocardial infarction (Q-wave and non-Q-wave MI) are at high risk of reinfarction and coronary death. In the DANAMI (Danish Trial in Acute Myocardial Infarction)[124] trial, patients following a myocardial infarction were randomised to an invasive strategy, exercise testing and coronary angiography with revascularisation of those with abnormal exercise tests, or a conservative one. Those randomised to the invasive strategy had a better outcome.

Other therapies

ACE inhibitors

In patients with a myocardial infarction there is evidence of benefit for angiotensin-converting-enzyme inhibitors. Patients with symptoms or signs of heart failure at the time of MI, or with echocardiographic evidence of significant LV systolic dysfunction (ejection fraction < 40%) and more recently, those with preserved systolic function, will all benefit from ACE inhibitors.[1,103,116,237] When an ACE inhibitor is contraindicated the combination of nitrates and hydralazine should be considered (level of evidence: 1).

Anti-arrhythmic drugs

There is no single-trial evidence for the prophylactic use of anti-arrhythmic drugs, other than β-blockers, in the management of acute coronary syndromes. An individual patient meta-analysis of amiodarone following myocardial infarction found a 13% reduction in total mortality. The follow-up period for the studies included varied from 6 months to 4.5 years.[4]

Cardiovascular prevention

The evidence for the long-term use of aspirin (or other platelet-modifying drugs), β-blockade and cholesterol modification therapy is described under 'Cardiovascular prevention and rehabilitation' on p. 425.

Heart failure

Randomised controlled trials of several classes of therapeutic agents have shown survival benefit for patients with clinical heart failure.[180] ACE inhibitors improve survival in all grades of heart failure.[84] This class has largely superseded the use of hydralazine and nitrates (where mortality benefit has been demonstrated in earlier studies) except where renal function precludes ACE inhibitor or AII-receptor antagonist therapy (level of evidence: I-1).

AII-receptor antagonists are appropriate if ACE inhibitors are not tolerated (e.g. because of cough) but their efficacy in addition to ACE inhibitors (particularly in combination with β-blockers) is unclear[37] (level of evidence: I-1).

β-Blockers improve survival in all grades of heart failure but must be initiated and up-titrated cautiously[31,133,152,229] (level of evidence: I-1).

Digoxin therapy for patients whose rhythm is sinus in heart failure does not confer any survival benefit but may be useful for symptoms and to reduce hospitalisation[203] (level of evidence: I-1).

Although there is no clinical trial evidence for diuretic therapy, this treatment was obviously beneficial to patients in heart failure when first used, and all therapeutic agents with proven survival benefit are given in combination with diuretics (level of evidence: III).

Spironolactone in low doses (25–50 mg o.d.) improved survival in one trial of patients with severe heart failure, although worsening hyperkalaemia and renal failure can occur[154] (level of evidence: I-1).

Cardiac transplantation improves survival[97] (level of evidence: II-1).

LV-assist devices may act as a bridge to transplantation. Revascularisation has not been tested in a RCT but case series suggest that it is useful in patients with 'viable' myocardium[74] (level of evidence: II-1).

Complex biventricular pacing improves symptoms in highly selected patients[223] (level of evidence: I-2).

Models of care have in the main not been formally evaluated, although nurse-led interventions have been shown to reduce hospitalisations[129] (level of evidence: I-2).

There is some evidence of increased exercise capacity from physical training in heart failure[68] (level of evidence: I-2).

There are few reliable data on treatment for the specific clinical syndrome of heart failure with preserved systolic function.

Post-symptomatic patients

Lifestyle interventions

Smoking

As there are no randomised controlled trials of stopping smoking after developing symptomatic coronary artery disease, evidence of effectiveness comes from observational studies. Patients who choose to quit, and such evidence comes mainly from those who have had a myocardial infarction, have a lower risk of recurrent disease and a longer life expectancy. This benefit is partly a function of stopping smoking but may also reflect other lifestyle changes made by those who quit, namely healthier food choices, increased physical activity and better compliance with prophylactic drug therapies[164,221] (level of evidence: II-2).

Diet

Three randomised controlled trials have shown benefit from dietary modification following a myocardial infarction by reducing the risk of recurrent disease and improving survival. Dietary supplementation with oily fish (two portions per week) or fish oil capsules in one trial, an α-linolenic acid-based margarine in the second, and a vegetarian diet rich in fruits and nuts in the third all significantly reduced the frequency of subsequent coronary morbidity and mortality. Although there are methodological concerns about some aspects of these trials, the evidence is sufficiently strong to provide support for the current dietary recommendations following the development of coronary disease, and to justify further research[52,19] (level of evidence: I).

Physical activity

There have been a large number of randomised trials of exercise rehabilitation following myocardial infarction, and two meta-analyses have shown that such rehabilitation reduces by 20–25% overall cardiovascular mortality. Whilst this evidence is supportive of a beneficial effect of aerobic exercise, changes in physical activity in these programmes have occurred concurrently with other changes in lifestyle, such as smoking cessation and the adoption of a healthy diet. This was examined in one of the meta-analyses which compared the effects of trials of exercise rehabilitation alone with those including other aspects of lifestyle change. The benefits in reducing coronary morbidity and mortality were only evident in the multifactorial intervention trials. Although there was a favourable trend in the exercise-only trials, this did not achieve statistical significance[24,71,96,118,140,148,149,212] (level of evidence: I).

Obesity

There is no evidence, from either clinical trials or observational studies, of the effect of reducing obesity in coronary patients in relation to subsequent morbidity and mortality. However, because of the adverse effects of obesity on other risk factors, and also because of its adverse haemodynamic consequences, reducing weight is important in obese patients with coronary disease (level of evidence: 0).

Other interventions

Blood pressure

Although blood pressure elevation in patients with myocardial infarction is associated with an increased risk of reinfarction, there is no randomised controlled trial evidence of blood pressure lowering following the development of coronary disease. However, several classes of antihypertensive agents (β-blockers, ACE inhibitors) given to selected patients following myocardial infarction have reduced subsequent coronary morbidity and mortality. So current clinical practice of using antihypertensive therapy in coronary patients with raised blood pressure is supported by this evidence, and that from randomised controlled trials of blood pressure in primary prevention.[162,163]

Blood lipids

In contrast, there is compelling evidence that lipid modification, principally lowering total and LDL cholesterol with statins following the development of coronary disease, is associated with a significant reduction in subsequent morbidity and mortality and an increase in survival. Three randomised controlled trials[173,174,205] have provided consistent evidence of benefit. Whether this benefit is the same across the whole distribution of cholesterol in coronary patients was not clear, particularly for those patients with a total cholesterol of < 4.8 mmol/l. However, the results of the recent Heart Protection Study have now shown in high-risk patients, including those with established CHD, that cholesterol lowering in those with a baseline LDL cholesterol < 2.6 mmol/l gives the same proportionate reduction in cardiovascular events as for those with higher cholesterol levels.[238] So the evidence for lipid modification is strongest for the statins, and this class of lipid modification therapy also has the best safety record so far[16,179,187] (level of evidence: I).

Diabetes mellitus

Hyperglycaemia after myocardial infarction is associated with a poorer prognosis.[121,135] There has been one randomised controlled trial of aggressive blood glucose management with insulin, compared to usual treatment, following myocardial infarction, and one-year mortality was significantly reduced by 25% in the insulin-treated group[125] (level of evidence: I).

Prophylactic drug therapies

In patients with coronary heart disease the following drugs, or classes of drugs, have been shown in single trials or meta-analyses to reduce total mortality. Therefore, in addition to the use of drugs which may be needed to control symptoms and manage blood pressure, lipids and glucose, the following should also be considered.

1 **Aspirin and other platelet-modifying drugs:** Aspirin (at least 75 mg) or other platelet-modifying drugs, in virtually all patients with coronary heart disease or other atherosclerotic disease. The meta-analysis of antiplatelet trials following myocardial infarction provides convincing evidence of a significant reduction in all-cause mortality, vascular mortality, non-fatal reinfarction of the myocardium and non-fatal stroke. In the trials which used aspirin, the most widely tested doses ranged

between 75 and 325 mg per day. There was no evidence of any greater clinical benefit for doses of 160–325 mg compared to 75 mg daily. Nor was any other antiplatelet regimen in this overview more effective than daily aspirin in this dose range. Side-effects from aspirin use, principally gastrointestinal bleeding and peptic ulceration, are lowest in those using 75 mg or less daily. Therefore, for secondary coronary heart disease prevention a maintenance dose of 75 mg of aspirin is recommended for all patients following myocardial infarction and those with other clinical manifestations of coronary artery disease (unstable angina and stable angina). Although there is no clinical trial evidence of treatment beyond a few years it would be prudent to continue aspirin therapy for life. When aspirin cannot be tolerated, alternative antiplatelet therapies such as clopidogrel should be considered. For patients with stroke or transient ischaemic attacks, aspirin at a dose of at least 75 mg daily is recommended and should also be considered for other high-risk patients with peripheral arterial disease[8,14,27,60,112] (level of evidence: I).

2 **β-Blockers:** β-Blockers in patients following acute myocardial infarction. In a meta-analysis of β-blockers following myocardial infarction there was evidence of a significant reduction in all-cause mortality, and in particular sudden cardiac death, as well as non-fatal reinfarction. This clinical benefit was greatest in those patients with left ventricular dysfunction or serious tachyarrhythmias. Therefore, a β-blocker should be considered in patients with no contraindications following myocardial infarction, and particularly for patients at high risk because of mechanical or electrical complications. The evidence for calcium antagonists as a prophylactic therapy following myocardial infarction is not as well established[80,87,91,92,105,137,150,185] (level of evidence: I).

3 **ACE inhibitors:** ACE inhibitors in patients with coronary heart disease. ACE inhibitors in patients with symptoms or signs of heart failure at the time of acute myocardial infarction, those with a large myocardial infarction and those with chronic left ventricular systolic dysfunction will significantly reduce all-cause mortality and the risk of progressing to persistent heart failure. In the absence of clinical heart failure, an assessment of left ventricular function by echocardiography is required. Patients following myocardial infarction with an estimated ejection fraction < 40% would be eligible for treatment with an ACE inhibitor.[1,56,236] The HOPE trial provides further evidence of the benefits of ACE inhibition in patients with coronary disease and preserved left ventricular function,[237] and this has been reinforced by the EUROPA study for patients with stable angina[239] (level of evidence: I).

4 **Anticoagulation:** Anticoagulation following myocardial infarction for selected patients at increased risk of thrombo-embolic events, including patients with large anterior myocardial infarction, left ventricular aneurysm or thrombus, paroxysmal tachyarrhythmias, chronic heart failure and those with a history of thrombo-embolic events[5,183] (level of evidence: II).

7 Quantified models of care and recommendations

National models of care

The National Service Framework (NSF) for Coronary Heart Disease published in 2000 put forward a framework for reducing the burden of CHD in England and modernising CHD services. It set out standards of care (*see* opposite) for the prevention, diagnosis and treatment of CHD and described the interventions and service models for the delivery of these standards. Health authorities (now primary care trusts) and their partners were required to produce local delivery plans and long-term service agreements.

Standards of care

Standards 1 and 2: Reducing heart disease in the population	1	The NHS and partner agencies should develop, implement and monitor policies that reduce the prevalence of coronary risk factors in the population, and reduce inequalities in risks of developing heart disease.
	2	The NHS and partner agencies should contribute to a reduction in the prevalence of smoking in the local population.
Standards 3 and 4: Preventing CHD in high-risk patients	3	General practitioners and primary care teams should identify all people with cardiovascular disease and offer them established comprehensive advice and appropriate treatment to reduce their risks.
	4	General practitioners and primary health care teams should identify all people at significant risk of cardiovascular disease but who have not developed symptoms and offer them appropriate advice and treatment to reduce their risks.
Standards 5, 6 and 7: Heart attack and other acute coronary syndromes	5	People with symptoms of a possible heart attack should receive help from an individual equipped with and appropriately trained in the use of a defibrillator within 8 minutes of calling for help, to maximise the benefits of resuscitation should it be necessary.
	6	People thought to be suffering from a heart attack should be assessed professionally and, if indicated, receive aspirin. Thrombolysis should be given within 60 minutes of calling for professional help.
	7	NHS trusts should put in place agreed protocols/systems of care so that people admitted to hospital with proven heart attack are appropriately assessed and offered treatments of proven clinical and cost-effectiveness to reduce their risk of disability and death.
Standard 8: Stable angina	8	People with symptoms of angina or suspected angina should receive appropriate investigation and treatment to relieve their pain and reduce their risk of coronary events.
Standards 9 and 10: Revascularisation	9	People with angina that is increasing in frequency or severity should be referred to a cardiologist urgently or, for those at greatest risk, as an emergency.
	10	NHS trusts should put in place hospital-wide systems of care so that patients with suspected or confirmed coronary heart disease receive timely and appropriate investigation and treatment to relieve their symptoms and reduce their risk of subsequent coronary events.
Standard 11: Heart failure	11	Doctors should arrange for people with suspected heart failure to be offered appropriate investigations (e.g. electrocardiography, echocardiography) that will confirm or refute the diagnosis. For those in whom heart failure is confirmed, its cause should be identified – treatments most likely to both relieve their symptoms and reduce their risk of death should be offered.
Standard 12: Cardiac rehabilitation	12	NHS trusts should put in place agreed protocols/systems of care so that, prior to leaving hospital, people admitted to hospital suffering from coronary heart disease have been invited to participate in a multi-disciplinary programme of secondary prevention and cardiac rehabilitation. The aim of the programme will be to reduce their risk of subsequent cardiac problems and to promote their return to a full and normal life.

Cardiovascular screening in primary care and relationships to specialist (hypertension, lipids and diabetes) hospital clinics

The model of care developed for cardiovascular screening and intervention in primary care needs to achieve the same risk factor changes achieved in unifactorial trials (blood pressure and lipids) which significantly reduced coronary morbidity and mortality. If such risk factor changes are achieved there will inevitably be a corresponding reduction in clinical disease. Despite the compelling scientific evidence for both lifestyle and therapeutic interventions in primary prevention of CHD and stroke, the evidence that this knowledge can be successfully translated into effective multifactorial risk factor reduction in primary care is disappointing. The conclusion of the multifactorial intervention trials OXCHECK[99,100] and the British Family Heart Study[231] is that lifestyle interventions and appropriate use of drug therapies should be concentrated on individuals at highest risk.

This emphasis on identifying and managing high-risk individuals has been endorsed in the Joint British Societies' recommendations on coronary prevention in clinical practice.[107,233] This new emphasis on multifactorial CHD risk assessment as the principal determinant of how intensively to intervene with lifestyle, and when to consider the use of drug therapies, is an important departure from traditional single risk factor guidance. Beyond lifestyle, the decision to introduce drug therapy for blood pressure or lipids should be strongly determined by the absolute risk of developing CHD or cardiovascular disease. As a general guide, an absolute risk of 15% or greater of developing CHD (equivalent to a cardiovascular risk of $\geq 20\%$) over the next 10 years is considered to be sufficiently high to justify drug treatment, although the physician's final decision about using drug therapy will also be influenced by the patient's age, gender, race, inheritance, coexistent disease and other factors such as life expectancy. In other words, a decision to introduce drug therapy, for example to lower BP, is not simply a function of the BP level alone. It is the whole risk factor context, of which BP is only one contributory factor, which is important. A coronary risk prediction chart is published in the recommendations so that absolute CHD risk (the risk of myocardial infarction and coronary death) over the next 10 years can be estimated. The risk factors used are gender, age, smoking habit, systolic BP, total cholesterol to HDL-cholesterol ratio and diabetes mellitus. There is also a cardiac risk assessor computer program which can be used to calculate both CHD and cardio-vascular (CHD and stroke) risk.

As the identification, investigation and management of everyone at a 15% or higher CHD risk in the population would be hugely demanding on NHS resources, a staged approach to coronary and other arterial disease prevention is recommended. Those at highest risk should be targeted first, and as a minimum, healthy individuals with a 30% or higher CHD risk over 10 years should all be identified and treated appropriately and effectively now. As the scientific evidence clearly justifies risk factor intervention in healthy individuals with a CHD risk lower than 30%, it is entirely appropriate for physicians to progressively expand opportunistic screening and risk factor intervention down to individuals with a 15% CHD risk over 10 years, as long as those at higher levels of risk have already received effective preventive care. Taking a progressive staged approach to coronary prevention in this way ensures that those at highest risk are targeted first and the delivery of care is commensurate with the ability of medical services to identify, investigate and manage patients properly over the long term.

However, not all high-risk people as defined will be eligible for blood-pressure-lowering drug therapy as this also depends on whether the blood pressure, in response to lifestyle advice, remains consistently greater than systolic > 140 mmHg and/or diastolic > 85 mmHg, or there is evidence of target organ damage. The percentages of people with a CHD risk $\geq 15\%$ and a BP > 140 and/or > 85 mmHg are shown in Table 1(b). Similarly, the use of lipid modification therapy also depends on whether the total cholesterol (and LDL cholesterol), in response to lifestyle advice, remains consistently greater than 5 mmol/l (LDL > 3 mmol/l). The percentages of people with a CHD risk $\geq 15\%$ and a total cholesterol ≥ 5 mmol/l are shown in Table 1(b). So, assuming that lifestyle has no effect on the proportion of people requiring BP and/or lipid-lowering therapy, the proportions requiring drug treatment will actually be slightly lower than the 12% and 5% estimated for all risk factors. The therapeutic implication of this multifactorial approach is that lipid-lowering therapies are likely to be used in primary CHD prevention as commonly as antihypertensive therapies. There may actually be a reduction in prescriptions for antihypertensive treatment because elevated blood pressure alone (with the important exception of patients with a systolic BP ≥ 160 mmHg and/or diastolic ≥ 100 mmHg, or evidence of target organ damage at any BP level) will not be sufficient to justify treatment in the absence of other risk factors. In contrast, there will be a considerable expansion in the use of lipid modification therapies, principally statins. Treatment targets in patients whose CHD risk is $\geq 15\%$ over the next 10 years, and for all patients who are started on drug therapies for primary CHD prevention, are defined as follows:

1 BP < 140 mmHg systolic and < 85 mmHg diastolic
2 total cholesterol < 5 mmol/l (LDL-cholesterol < 3 mmol/l)
3 diabetes mellitus should be optimally controlled and blood pressure reduced to < 130 mmHg systolic and < 80 mmHg diastolic
4 aspirin (75 mg) is recommended in individuals who are older than 50 years and are either well-controlled hypertensive patients or men at high risk of CHD.

For some patients a specialist opinion will be required, and there should be agreement on a protocol between general practice and hospital specialist clinics (hypertension, lipid and diabetic) on referral criteria and, conversely, for those assessed in these specialist clinics there should be agreement on the criteria for discharge to continuing care in the community. Audit of the ascertainment of high-risk individuals in general practice and their subsequent management is essential.

In the hospital sector the care of high-risk patients in hypertension, lipid and diabetic clinics should be co-ordinated between specialists based on agreed protocols to ensure a common approach to multi-factorial risk assessment, lifestyle and therapeutic interventions. The care of such high-risk patients treated in specialised hospital clinics should be integrated with general practice to ensure, through the use of agreed common protocols, optimal long-term management. Audit of the impact of common clinical protocols for hospital and general practice on the identification and management of high-risk individuals is strongly recommended.

Organisation of ambulance services for community resuscitation

A fully equipped paramedical ambulance-based team, trained in advanced cardiopulmonary resuscitation (CPR), is only one of several approaches to sudden cardiac collapse in the community.[144,207] About three-quarters of deaths attributed to CHD in people under 75 years occur outside hospital, and 61% are witnessed, usually by a relative or bystander. Importantly, of those that are witnessed, only a minority (about 13%) are instantaneous. Symptoms precede the arrhythmia causing cardiac collapse, principally chest pain, and therefore the potential to manage these patients more effectively exists if the delay between summoning medical help, arrival of a paramedical crew and transport to an Accident and Emergency department can be reduced.

If bystander CPR was performed in all cases, assuming limited success in resuscitation, survival at 30 days would increase from 4% to about 5.5%. Overall case fatality for acute coronary events would be reduced from 45% to 44.7%, an absolute reduction of only 0.3%.

Improving the access of trained staff to community arrests could potentially have a larger impact. Overall case fatality for acute coronary events with all cardiac arrests attended by paramedics could be reduced from 45% to 37%, an absolute reduction of 8%, which represents a 27-fold increase in survival compared to bystander CPR. Based on the most optimistic scenario, in which all community arrests are attended by trained paramedics (or general practitioners), sudden cardiac collapse would still have a high fatality, with 60% or more dying in the community, thus emphasising the priority for primary prevention.

All patients with chest pain who summon an ambulance (or if it is summoned by their GP) should be attended by a paramedical crew trained in advanced cardiopulmonary resuscitation. When the GP has been called, the practitioner should attend the patient as well, even though an ambulance has also been called. In the event of a cardiac arrest, the chances of a successful resuscitation are then maximised. Training the general public in CPR is a considerable task and the impact of bystander CPR is very small indeed. Therefore, it would be better to focus on the close relatives (and friends) of patients with CHD, particularly those who have already survived a cardiac arrest, as these patients are at highest risk of dying suddenly. Other groups would include the police, fire brigade, transport (bus, rail, boat and plane) staff and a small number of selected staff in workplaces.

A policy in general practice of summoning an ambulance at the same time as going to see a patient with chest pain is likely to have the greatest impact on reducing the incidence of sudden death and the interval between symptom onset and thrombolysis for acute myocardial infarction.

Chest pain in the community

All patients presenting for the first time with chest pain which is considered to be cardiac in origin, and where there is no medical history of CHD, should be referred to hospital. Where symptoms are likely to be due to an acute coronary syndrome, urgent transfer to Accident and Emergency, preferably in an ambulance with a trained paramedic crew and facilities for cardiopulmonary resuscitation, is essential. Where the symptoms are those of new exertional angina, the patient should be referred for a cardiological opinion, usually through a rapid-access chest pain clinic, supported by appropriate specialist investigations. For patients with a medical history of CHD whose symptoms become acute or easily provoked or occur at rest, urgent transfer to Accident and Emergency is required. Those patients who experience a recurrence of exertional angina, or have angina which is no longer adequately controlled with medical therapy, require an outpatient cardiology review and further specialist investigation.

Exertional angina

All patients presenting for the first time with the symptom exertional angina should be referred for a cardiological opinion supported by appropriate specialist investigations.[50,142,147,176,197] A rapid-access chest pain clinic is now the preferred way of providing such a clinical service. Referring patients with chest pain for a hospital ECG is a practice which should be abandoned, as it is normal in most patients presenting with new exertional angina. Nor are other open-access tests such as exercise testing or radionuclide investigations advised, because they require specialist interpretation in a clinical context. The traditional practice whereby most patients with angina are managed medically in the community without referral for specialist opinion and appropriate investigations is no longer appropriate. A minority of patients with acute coronary syndromes will be inappropriately managed in the community and thus deprived of life-saving treatments. Of those with exertional angina, some will require revascularisation on prognostic grounds, and they cannot be identified from symptoms alone. In addition, a potentially large number of patients who do not have CHD will be given an unnecessary trial of medical therapy in the community when they could be reassured with no further follow-up required.

Acute coronary syndromes

All patients with cardiac chest pain which may be due to an acute coronary syndrome should be assessed in hospital as quickly as possible.[15,51,196] The ambulance service is usually the best way of achieving this. So when a patient consults general practice with this symptom, if it is considered to be severe, the GP should call 999 at the same time as going to assess the patient. Ambulance crews or general practitioners should always administer at least 150 mg of soluble aspirin to these patients immediately.

Although two-thirds of patients with a diagnosis of AMI receive thrombolytic therapy, this proportion could be increased by using ECG monitoring for dynamic ST/T-wave changes (rather than serial 12-lead ECGs) and more sensitive indices of myocardial necrosis. Triaging the patient quickly through casualty will also increase the proportion of patients eligible for this form of therapy. A written protocol for triage is essential if the door to needle time for thrombolytic therapy is to be the same as that achieved with direct admissions to cardiac care units.

All patients with an acute coronary syndrome should be assessed by a cardiologist within 24 hours of admission, and where this is not possible a written protocol devised by the cardiologist for the management of such patients is essential. This should cover the following.

1 Aspirin (at least 150 mg) for all patients.
2 Thrombolysis criteria and the indications for individual thrombolytic agents.
3 Antiplatelet agents: clopidogrel should be recommended on admission for patients admitted with non-ST-elevation acute coronary syndromes; Gp IIb/IIIa-receptor blockers are recommended for high-risk patients with non-ST-elevation acute coronary syndromes, particularly if scheduled to go for coronary angiography. Guidance should be provided on the use of both clopidogrel and Gp IIb/IIIa-receptor blockers for patients who may need to go to surgery, as they both increase the risk of bleeding, particularly for patients who need to go for coronary artery bypass grafting.
4 β-Blockade: intravenous on admission for ST-elevation MI and oral therapy at the doses prescribed in the clinical trials for all post-MI patients, and for at least three years.
5 ACE inhibitors at the doses prescribed in the clinical trials for patients with symptoms or signs of heart failure at the time of myocardial infarction, or in those with persistent LV systolic dysfunction as assessed by echocardiography (ejection fraction < 40%), or preserved systolic function.
6 Anticoagulants for patients at risk of systemic embolisation with large anterior infarctions, severe heart failure, left ventricular aneurysm or paroxysmal tachyarrhythmias.
7 A written record of cardiac risk factors: tobacco exposure, body mass index (including a measure of central obesity), history of hypertension, hyperlipidaemia and diabetes mellitus. Family history of CHD: relatives, age at which disease developed and/or death and nature of the disease (e.g. MI) and whether there was angioplasty or surgery. For women, exposure to oral contraceptives and HRT, age at menopause and gynaecological history (hysterectomy ± oophorectomy). Action on risk factors should also be recorded: advice to quit tobacco, professional dietary advice given together with a target BMI, advice on how to increase physical activity. BP assessment in hospital with the objective of reducing the systolic pressure consistently below 140 mmHg (< 130 mmHg in patients with diabetes mellitus). Measurement of random total cholesterol on the first blood sample drawn for estimation of blood enzymes, or not later than 24 hours after the onset of symptoms, should also be recorded. If the random total cholesterol is > 5 mmol/l then, in addition to dietary advice, lipid modification therapy should be initiated before discharge. A statin is the drug of first choice at the doses prescribed in the clinical trials. Those with a cholesterol level < 5 mmol/l should have their fasting lipids checked at six weeks to measure total cholesterol, HDL-cholesterol and triglycerides and then calculate LDL-cholesterol. If the total cholesterol is > 5 mmol/l (LDL-cholesterol > 3 mmol/l), then lipid modification therapy should be given as stated above. Blood lipids should be checked again in six weeks. If the target of a total

cholesterol < 5.0 mmol/l (LDL-cholesterol < 3 mmol/l) has not been met, the dose of the statin should be increased. Those with a cholesterol < 5 mmol/l should be monitored, at least annually, because despite diet there may be a requirement for lipid-lowering therapy at a later date. Younger patients (< 55 years for men and < 65 years for women) with CHD and a cholesterol > 5 mmol /l, or any patient whose blood cholesterol is particularly high (> 8 mmol/l) should have their first-degree blood relatives screened for blood cholesterol. This is because of the possibility of familial hypercholesterolaemia, or another inherited form of hyperlipidaemia, which has a sufficiently high risk of arterial disease to justify drug treatment for primary prevention.

8   Fasting blood glucose should be measured. However, because the level may rise acutely during acute myocardial infarction or ischaemia, any elevation of blood glucose in patients who are not clearly diabetic should be confirmed six weeks after the event. The ADA has redefined diabetes mellitus as a fasting blood glucose of ≥ 7 mmol/l or greater. The WHO has proposed new diagnostic criteria and individuals with a fasting plasma glucose of ≥ 7 mmol/l will be designated as having diabetes, those with a fasting glucose of < 7 mmol/l but a two-hour value ≥ 7 and < 11.1 mmol/l as having impaired glucose tolerance (IGT) and those with fasting plasma glucose ≥ 6.1 mmol/l but < 7 mmol/l as having impaired fasting glycaemia (IFG). Patients with CHD whose fasting blood glucose is < 7.8 mmol/l but whose two-hour level is > 7.8 mmol/l and < 11.1 mmol/l, and particularly in those who have hyper-triglyceridaemia (regardless of total cholesterol level), have a higher than expected risk of subsequently developing overt diabetes mellitus and therefore require further fasting blood glucose determinations at annual review.

Rapid-access chest pain clinics are not part of the assessment and management of acute coronary syndromes. This is because they are primarily intended for patients with exertional angina. With such a service fewer patients are admitted unnecessarily to hospital, and a small proportion of patients with acute coronary syndromes are no longer inappropriately managed in the community.

All patients with acute coronary syndromes should be offered a place on a comprehensive cardiovascular prevention and rehabilitation programme.

Heart failure

Patients with heart failure should be investigated and managed according to locally agreed protocols. Examples of these are contained in the NSF for Coronary Heart Disease, Chapter 6, and the SIGN guidelines.[139,180] All patients with heart failure, whether diagnosed in hospital or general practice, should be referred to a cardiologist to confirm (or refute) the diagnosis, determine the aetiology and advise on management. This will include appropriate specialist investigations, principally echocardiography, but also cardiac catheterisation in selected cases. When a cardiology opinion cannot be obtained it is essential to have an ECG, chest X-ray and echocardiogram. These investigations are needed to establish the diagnosis and may also identify the aetiology, including those aetiologies which are potentially remediable with cardiac surgery (e.g. aortic stenosis).

All patients with heart failure due to LV systolic dysfunction in whom an ACE inhibitor is not contra-indicated should receive this class of drug at the doses used in the clinical trials.[180,198,206,209] β-Blockers are indicated in patients with heart failure due to LV systolic dysfunction. For those who are unable to tolerate an ACE inhibitor because of side-effects, e.g. cough, an angiotensin-II-receptor antagonist is an alternative. When renal function is impaired, or deteriorates with the introduction of an ACE inhibitor, a combination of nitrates and hydralazine should be considered. Spironolactone should be added for selected patients with severe heart failure. Diuretics (thiazides and loop) should be used for fluid retention. Arrhythmias (particularly atrial fibrillation [AF]) should be identified and treated and patients who may be appropriate for biventricular pacing or automatic internal cardiac defibrillator (AICD) implantation similarly identified. Digoxin should be a consideration for rate control in AF and for symptomatic benefit in patients in sinus rhythm. Anticoagulation should be considered for those in atrial fibrillation and with dilated ventricles.

Drugs that may be aggravating heart failure should be identified and if possible eliminated (NSAIDs, short-acting calcium-receptor blockers).

The management of heart failure depends on the underlying aetiology, and when this is due to CHD the control of risk factors and revascularisation are both potentially important modalities of treatment.

Patients with heart failure and preserved systolic function should be managed with the aim of symptom control (in the absence of pharmacological trials showing mortality benefits in this particular group). It seems reasonable to treat them with vasodilators and β-blockers.

Patients should be educated to restrict salt and fluid intake, avoid excessive alcohol consumption and maintain (and if possible improve) activity.

Current underutilisation of investigations and therapies suggests that optimal care of heart failure will increase costs through non-invasive and invasive investigations, drugs and human resources (nurses, etc.). However, this may be partially or completely offset by a reduction in costly hospital admissions. Individual trials of drugs and models of care have suggested that optimal treatment results in cost savings.[84,128]

Cardiovascular prevention and rehabilitation from hospital to community

By addressing lifestyle and risk factor management in coronary patients, including the use of prophylactic drug therapies, the risk of progressing to myocardial infarction and coronary death will be reduced.[23,35,107,143,213,214,232–234] In the Joint British Recommendations on Coronary Prevention, patients with established CHD are deemed to be the top priority for prevention, and an integrated cardiovascular prevention and rehabilitation service should be available for such patients.

All hospitals responsible for the acute management of coronary disease should have a comprehensive cardiovascular prevention and rehabilitation service that is fully integrated with all other aspects of cardiac care. This service should be available to all coronary patients (post myocardial infarction, treated unstable angina, exertional angina and those following revascularisation by angioplasty or coronary artery surgery). For those patients who are to be revascularised electively, every effort should be made to achieve ideal lifestyle and risk factor targets, and compliance with appropriate prophylactic drug therapies, before the procedure or operation. Such a service should embrace all aspects of prevention to reduce the patient's risk of subsequent cardiovascular disease, as well as rehabilitation to promote their return to a full and normal life. Integration of care between hospital and general practice through the use of common protocols is essential to ensure optimal long-term lifestyle, risk factor and therapeutic management. Audit of the impact of such protocols is strongly recommended.

Screening of first-degree blood relatives (principally siblings and offspring aged 18 years or older) of patients with premature CHD (men < 55 years and women < 65 years) is encouraged, and in the context of familial dyslipidaemia is essential.

Cardioprotective drug therapy should be considered and prescribed in selected patients: (i) aspirin for all patients; (ii) β-blockers at the doses prescribed in the clinical trials following MI, particularly in high-risk patients, and for at least 3 years; (iii) cholesterol-lowering therapy (statins) at the doses prescribed in the clinical trials; (iv) ACE inhibitors at the doses prescribed in the clinical trials for patients with symptoms or signs of heart failure in the context of MI, or in those with persistent left ventricular systolic dysfunction (ejection fraction < 40%), and those with preserved systolic function; and (v) anticoagulants for patients at risk of systemic embolisation.

8 Outcome measures, audit methods and targets

National audits are required in representative samples of hospitals and general practices to evaluate the process and outcome of care in relation to professional guidelines and nationally agreed targets for CHD. Such audits will give a national picture which can be monitored over time, and they will also facilitate development and evaluation of methodologies (including measurement instruments) which can then be made available for local audits in primary care trusts, hospitals and general practices. An example of such an audit is the National Audit of Myocardial Infarctions (NAOMI) project.

Audits of process and outcome are proposed for the following areas.

Cardiovascular screening

A national sampling frame for general practice is required to audit the identification and management of high-risk individuals.

Process of care

1 All patients joining a practice are given a new patient check, which includes a cardiovascular risk assessment.
2 Absolute risk of CHD or cardiovascular disease is calculated and recorded as well as individual risk factor levels, together with action taken.
3 Risk factor advice in relation to lifestyle (smoking, diet, including obesity, and physical activity) is recorded.
4 For BP, a record of target organ damage (retinopathy, LVH on ECG, renal impairment) and radial femoral delay.
5 For lipids, a record of stigmata (corneal arcus, xanthomata and screening of first-degree blood relatives).
6 For diabetes mellitus, a record of target organ damage (retinopathy, renal impairment including microalbuminuria and proteinuria, neuropathy and skin care).
7 Aspirin prescribed in patients > 50 years who are well-controlled hypertensives on antihypertensive medication.
8 Referral to a specialist (hypertension and/or lipid and/or diabetic clinic).
9 Additional investigations requested for patients with:
   - hypertension: ECG, echocardiography, renal function, catecholamine metabolites, tests for renal artery stenosis, lipids and glucose
   - hyperlipidaemia: renal function, thyroid function, liver function and glucose
   - diabetes mellitus: renal function, lipids.
10 Drugs prescribed: generic names and doses for:
   - hypertension
   - hyperlipidaemia
   - diabetes mellitus.
11 Screening of first-degree blood relatives.

Outcome of care

1 Lifestyle: smoking status, dietary habits (including BMI and central obesity) and physical activity.
2 In high-risk individuals (CHD risk > 15% over 10 years) all patients with severe hypertension (systolic blood pressure > 160 mmHg and/or diastolic blood pressure > 100 mmHg) or associated target organ

damage, familial hypercholesterolaemia or other inherited dyslipidaemia, or diabetes mellitus with associated target organ damage, have the following risk factor targets been achieved?

- BP < 140/85 mmHg
- total cholesterol < 5 mmol/l (LDL-cholesterol < 3 mmol/l)
- diabetes mellitus optimally controlled and BP reduced to < 130/80 mmHg.

3 Compliance with prophylactic aspirin and prescribed therapies for BP, lipids and diabetes mellitus.
4 Quality of life.

Sudden cardiac collapse

A national sampling frame of ambulance services is required, with audit of a random sample of consecutive community collapses.

Exertional angina

A national sampling frame of rapid-access chest pain clinics is required to audit consecutive patients with angina pectoris (but no history of myocardial infarction or revascularisation).

Process of care

1 Referred to a cardiologist or other hospital specialist, or assessment in Accident and Emergency department with or without hospital admission.
2 ECG and exercise tolerance test (or radionuclide scan if unable to exercise) performed.
3 Lifestyle and risk factors recorded (see 'Cardiovascular prevention and rehabilitation' below, items 2 to 5) and action taken.
4 Aspirin prescribed.
5 Psychosocial interventions.
6 Educational interventions.
7 Screening of first-degree blood relatives and action taken.

Outcome of care

1 Lifestyle: smoking status, dietary habits (including BMI and central obesity) and physical activity.
2 BP target of < 140/85 mmHg achieved.
3 Lipid target of total cholesterol < 5 mmol/l and LDL-cholesterol < 3 mmol/l achieved.
4 In diabetes mellitus, good glycaemic control and BP < 130/85 mmHg achieved.
5 Compliance with prescribed prophylactic drug therapy at the doses used in the clinical trials.
6 Quality of life.
7 Blood relatives screened and action that followed.

Acute coronary syndromes

A national sampling frame of district general hospitals is required to audit consecutive cases of acute coronary syndromes.

Process of care

1 Point of contact with the medical services (GP, 999 or direct to casualty) and whether attended by a paramedical crew trained in CPR and/or a GP.
2 Aspirin administered prior to admission to hospital.
3 Thrombolysis: time from onset of symptoms to thrombolytic therapy, door to needle time, place of initial medical assessment (casualty, CCU, other), triaged in Accident and Emergency, type of thrombolytic agents used.
4 β-Blockade: intravenous and/or oral.
5 ACE inhibitor, echocardiography.
6 Cholesterol measured, titration in therapy.
7 Glucose measured and, in diabetes mellitus, insulin therapy used.
8 Anticoagulation.
9 Exercise tolerance test.
10 Referral (emergency or elective) for coronary arteriography with a view to revascularisation (angioplasty ± stenting, CABG).
11 Discharge summary to GP, and follow-up arrangements.

Outcome of care

As for exertional angina.

Heart failure

A national sampling frame of district general hospitals is required to audit consecutive cases of heart failure.

Process of care

1 Number of patients with a diagnosis of heart failure.
2 Specialist who made the diagnosis and whether referred to a cardiologist.
3 Aetiology of heart failure recorded.
4 Percentage echocardiography obtained.
5 Percentage treated with an ACE inhibitor (and dose).
6 Percentage prescribed a β-blocker (and dose).
7 Revascularisation; transplantation.
8 Family screening for familial cardiomyopathy.
9 Use of palliative care services.

Outcome of care

1 Quality of life.
2 Compliance with prescribed drug therapies at the doses used in the clinical trials.
3 Rehospitalisations (including reasons) and mortality.

Cardiovascular prevention and rehabilitation

A national sampling frame of district general hospitals is required to audit consecutive cases of acute coronary syndromes, exertional angina and revascularised patients.

Process of care

1 Patient offered a place on a cardiovascular prevention and rehabilitation programme.
2 Health promotion in relation to lifestyle (smoking, diet and physical activity).
3 BP levels.
4 Lipid levels.
5 Glycaemic and BP control in diabetes mellitus.
6 Prophylactic drug therapy is prescribed, generic names of drugs and doses: aspirin, β-blockers, ACE inhibitors, lipid modification therapy and anticoagulation.
7 Psychosocial intervention.
8 Educational interventions.
9 Exercise tolerance test and supervised exercise sessions.
10 Screening of first-degree blood relatives.
11 Report of patient's lifestyle, risk factors and drug therapies, including risk factor targets, to the GP or practice care team.

Outcome of care

As for exertional angina.

Mortality is not an appropriate outcome of care because a comprehensive cardiovascular prevention and rehabilitation programme, which replicates the process of care in the clinical trials which demonstrated mortality benefit, will inevitably reduce mortality.

9 Information and research requirements

Cardiovascular screening

1 The optimal risk factor model for identifying and targeting high-risk individuals in general practice needs to be defined.
2 Imaginative approaches to lifestyle change also need to be developed.
3 Compliance with drug therapies requires investigation.

Sudden cardiac collapse

1 The optimal response model for sudden cardiac collapse in the community.

Exertional angina

1 The optimal method for diagnosing, investigating and managing exertional angina presenting for the first time in the community requires evaluation. The rapid-assessment chest pain clinic is the preferred model, but this way of diagnosing and managing angina from the community needs to be evaluated.

Acute coronary syndromes

1   The role of the general practitioner in the management of chest pain in the community requires evaluation. If a general practitioner summons an ambulance at the same time as he attends a patient with chest pain, will this shorten the interval between onset of symptoms and appropriate medical therapy, and what impact will this have on the ambulance service and Accident and Emergency departments? Will this approach increase the chances of successful community resuscitation?

2   The role of a chest pain assessment unit also requires evaluation in the context of acute coronary syndromes and whether or not the provision of such a service will increase the identification of such syndromes in the community and thus ensure more appropriate management. Also, does such a service reduce casualty assessments and emergency hospital admissions for chest pain and follow-up appointments for cardiology outpatients? Can such a service delay the appropriate hospital management of patients with acute coronary syndromes?

3   The triaging of patients with chest pain in Accident and Emergency departments requires evaluation in order to develop a model of care which achieves the same standard door to needle time for thrombolytic therapy compared to patients admitted directly to a cardiac care unit.

4   The role of primary angioplasty in the management of acute (anterior) myocardial infarction requires evaluation in a randomised controlled trial in a district general hospital setting.

5   The development of more sensitive and specific assays for myocardial necrosis requires evaluation in the context of Accident and Emergency departments, chest pain assessment units and other outpatient settings to determine whether patients can avoid an unnecessary hospital admission.

6   The contribution of specialists to clinical outcome in acute coronary syndromes requires evaluation because the majority of patients with this acute presentation are managed by specialists other than cardiologists, and one in two patients are never seen by a cardiologist. In the context of protocol-driven management (with the protocol determined by the cardiologist), is clinical outcome any different if the patient is personally attended by a cardiologist compared to any other specialist?

7   Risk stratification of patients with acute coronary syndromes (unstable angina which responds to medical therapy and non-Q-wave myocardial infarction) requires evaluation to determine whether those at highest risk of recurrent coronary disease or death are selected for further investigation.

8   The utility of measuring and acting on a random blood cholesterol measured at the time of admission of patients with acute coronary syndromes, as opposed to delaying such an estimation until a fasting blood sample can be drawn at least six weeks after the acute clinical event, also requires evaluation. In the clinical trials of lipid modification in patients with coronary disease there is no evidence that early treatment will confer any additional benefit. It is important to know whether a delay in measuring and acting on blood lipids, given that care often passes from hospital specialist to the general practitioner, results in less effective care.

Heart failure

1   The role of the cardiologist in relation to the generalist for the diagnosis, aetiological classification and management of heart failure needs to be evaluated as most patients presenting with heart failure to the hospital service are managed by physicians other than cardiologists.

2   As heart failure is associated with a high frequency of recurrent hospital admissions, many of which are due to worsening of the heart failure, the optimal strategy for managing heart failure in the community needs to be defined.

3   Evaluation of new diagnostic tests for heart failure (e.g. the natriuretic peptides) which can be applied in the community is required, and these tests could also be evaluated in patients admitted to hospital.

Cardiovascular prevention and rehabilitation

1   As rehabilitation has traditionally been offered to patients following cardiac surgery or post myocardial infarction, a formal evaluation of models of care for cardiovascular prevention and rehabilitation in patients with angina (both exertional angina and following medical management of unstable angina) is required.

2   The optimal mix and components of a cardiovascular prevention and rehabilitation programme, and the frequency and duration of the programme, require investigation. Several approaches exist for the delivery of cardiovascular prevention and rehabilitation from menu-driven systems, home-based and community-based services and hospital-based programmes. Research is required into the effectiveness of each of these approaches, both separately and together.

3   Lifestyle intervention is the foundation of a cardiovascular prevention programme and research is required to develop more effective ways to help patients stop smoking, make healthy food choices and become physically active over the long term.

4   The integration of care between a hospital-based cardiovascular prevention and rehabilitation programme and the subsequent management of coronary patients in general practice and the community needs to be developed and evaluated. The concept of a cardiac liaison nurse is one approach but there are others and they each need to be evaluated. Other ways of integrating care also need to be considered, such as the common patient-held record.

5   Prescribing drugs at the doses used in the clinical trials which have shown efficacy and safety in relation to prevention of established coronary disease, and ensuring compliance with such treatments over many years, is the only way to replicate the results of the clinical trials. As there are now at least five classes of drugs which can reduce the risk of recurrent disease and improve survival, it is necessary to ensure that appropriate drugs are selected for an individual patient and compliance with such treatments encouraged over the long term. Compliance needs to be monitored and the reasons for non-compliance evaluated.

6   Ethnic minorities pose a particular challenge for cardiovascular prevention and rehabilitation because of cultural and language issues, and these groups require research in their own right to ensure that the lifestyle intervention is appropriate to their culture and the instruments used are offered in the patient's own language and not just English.

7   The involvement of the patient's partner, and other members of the immediate family sharing the same household, could potentially bring about much more effective and sustained lifestyle change in relation to the use of tobacco, food choices and physical activity. The role of the partner in this process requires evaluation to ensure the most conducive environment for lifestyle change.

8   Women are more reluctant to take up a place on a cardiovascular prevention and rehabilitation programme and the reasons for this need to be investigated and measures put in place to ensure that women are able to enjoy the same benefits of such a programme as men.

9   Social class is also a factor in determining whether a patient participates in a cardiovascular prevention and rehabilitation programme, and there is a tendency for response rates to be higher amongst the professional and middle classes, whereas the disease is commonest in working-class men and women. The factors influencing the attitude of different social classes to such programmes require investigation to ensure that all patients take up this service.

10 The elderly are at higher absolute risk of recurrent coronary disease and death and have special requirements in terms of the appropriateness of lifestyle interventions, risk factor management and prophylactic drug therapies. Given competing comorbidity and life expectancy in this group, research is required into the benefits of a cardiovascular prevention and rehabilitation programme and how this can be most sympathetically delivered.

11   There is some evidence to support exercise-based rehabilitation for patients with heart failure and, when this is due to coronary artery disease, other aspects of lifestyle and risk factor management may be important in determining the quality of life and prognosis of these patients. Research is required in patients with chronic LV systolic dysfunction to determine the optimal components of a rehabilitation programme for heart failure.

10 Appendices

A strategy for sudden cardiac collapse in the community

1 A district-wide protocol agreed between the ambulance service, Accident and Emergency and general practice.
2 All 999 calls for 'collapse' to be attended by an ambulance crew trained and equipped for cardio-pulmonary resuscitation.
3 General practitioners to immediately attend all patients reporting chest pain, which could be due to an acute coronary syndrome, and to call an ambulance at the same time.
4 Training of close relatives of patients with established CHD in cardiopulmonary resuscitation.
5 Training of all emergency services, and selected sections of the general public, in cardiopulmonary resuscitation.
6 Auditing the impact of the protocol.

A strategy for diagnosing and managing cardiac chest pain in the community

1 A district-wide protocol agreed between secondary and primary care for patients presenting with chest pain, to general practice or Accident and Emergency.
2 Educating people who develop chest pain to seek medical help early through their general practitioner, or by calling 999. This applies particularly to patients with established CHD who experience a recurrence of symptoms, a worsening of symptoms or symptoms at rest.
3 General practitioners to refer all patients who are thought to have new exertional angina to a rapid-access chest pain clinic, and those who are unstable (acute coronary syndromes) directly to Accident and Emergency.
4 A rapid-access chest pain clinic for new patient assessments to be available in every DGH with an Accident and Emergency department.
5 A triage system for patients attending Accident and Emergency with chest pain in order to prioritise those with acute coronary syndromes for immediate treatment, and referral of those with new exertional angina to the RACPC. Patients with established CHD who are not unstable to be referred to cardiology outpatients.
6 Auditing the impact of the protocol.

A strategy for primary prevention of CHD in high-risk individuals in primary and secondary care

1 A common district-wide protocol agreed between primary and secondary care for the identification and management of high-risk individuals.
2 In primary care, systematic identification of all high-risk (CHD risk $\geq$ 15% over 10 years) individuals through cardiovascular screening:
   - all new patients registering with a general practice – which will ultimately ensure all patients are screened
   - all patients with an existing diagnosis of hypertension, dyslipidaemia or diabetes mellitus

- opportunistic screening of all patients attending for a consultation for whatever reason
- rescreening of all individuals at least once every 5 years and sooner for those whose *projected* 10-year risk to age 60 years is $\geq 15\%$.

3 Nurse-led lifestyle intervention, using a behavioural approach to change, in all high-risk individuals with repeat measurements of BP (if $> 140/90$ mmHg) and cholesterol (if > 5.0 mmol/l), and monitoring of glycaemic control (and other risk factors) in patients with diabetes mellitus.

4 General practitioner-initiated drug treatment at the doses used in the clinical trials in high-risk individuals for risk factors – blood pressure, blood cholesterol and diabetes mellitus – according to an agreed primary/secondary care protocol in order to meet risk factor targets: BP $< 140/85$ mmHg (BP $< 130/80$ mmHg in diabetes mellitus) and optimal glycaemic control in diabetes mellitus ($HbA_{1C} < 7\%$).

5 Referral of selected patients from primary care requiring specialist investigation or management to hypertension, lipid and diabetes clinics according to an agreed primary/secondary care protocol. Discharge of patients from hospital clinics following appropriate specialist investigation and management to primary care.

6 Nurse-led screening of blood relatives in primary care if there is a family history of premature (men < 55 years, women < 65 years) CHD in one or more close relatives or if familial dyslipidaemia is suspected.

7 Auditing the impact of the district protocol in both general practice and specialised hospital (hypertension, lipid and diabetes) clinics.

A strategy for managing acute coronary syndromes

1 A hospital-wide protocol for management of acute coronary syndromes.
2 Triaging of patients in Accident and Emergency to ensure patients eligible for aspirin, thrombolytic therapy and other acute life-saving treatments are managed as quickly as possible. The following treatments at the doses used in the clinical trials to be given in casualty:
- aspirin
- thrombolytic therapy
- intravenous or oral β-blockade
- intravenous nitrates and low-molecular-weight heparin for unstable angina.
3 Primary angioplasty as an alternative to thrombolysis in patients with an AMI but with a major contraindication to thrombolysis, or in cardiogenic shock.
4 Transfer of all patients with acute coronary syndromes to CCU managed by cardiologists.
5 Inpatient angiography for patients with recurrent myocardial ischaemia which does not respond to medical therapy.
6 Initiate prophylactic drug therapies at the doses used in the clinical trials:
- β-blocker
- ACE inhibitor
- cholesterol modification therapy
- anticoagulation.
7 Inpatient pre-discharge exercise test (or an alternative non-invasive assessment of reversible myocardial ischaemia) to determine priority for coronary angiography.
8 Inpatient recruitment to a cardiovascular prevention and rehabilitation programme.
9 Discharge summary to general practitioner specifying diagnosis, lifestyle risk factor and therapeutic targets, and drug therapies.
10 Auditing the impact of the hospital protocol.

A strategy for managing heart failure in secondary and primary care

1 A common district-wide protocol agreed between secondary and primary care for heart failure.
2 All patients presenting for the first time in primary care with heart failure to be referred for a cardiological opinion to confirm the diagnosis and determine aetiology and management.
3 Address the causes of the heart failure, e.g. treating blood pressure and other risk factors for CHD, revascularisation of the myocardium.
4 Initiate drug therapies at the doses used in the clinical trials and other treatments appropriate to the aetiology:
   - loop diuretics
   - ACE inhibitor (or ATII receptor blocker if an ACE inhibitor is not tolerated)
   - hydralazine and nitrate combination where an ACE inhibitor is contraindicated or not tolerated
   - β-blocker
   - spironolactone
   - warfarin.
5 In primary care, general practitioner up-titration of drug treatments and regular assessment for compliance.
6 Auditing the impact of the common clinical protocol for heart failure in secondary and primary care.

A strategy for cardiovascular prevention and rehabilitation of CHD in secondary and primary care

1 A common district-wide protocol agreed between secondary and primary care for cardiovascular prevention and rehabilitation of all patients with CHD.
2 All patients with CHD (acute coronary syndromes, exertional angina and those following coronary revascularisation) to be provided with a hospital-based nurse-led comprehensive cardiovascular prevention and rehabilitation programme which includes the Joint British Societies guidance for lifestyle, risk factor and therapeutic targets, with results summarised in a report to general practice.
3 In primary care, a nurse-led reassessment of patients with CHD following completion of a hospital-based programme which addresses the same targets for lifestyle, risk factors and compliance with drug therapies. Where risk factor and therapeutic targets have not been met, referral to the patient's general practitioner, to initiate drug therapy at the doses used in the clinical trials.
4 In primary care a nurse-led retrospective review of all patients with an existing medical diagnosis of CHD to ensure the lifestyle, risk factor and therapeutic targets are met. Where these targets have not been met, referral to the patient's general practitioner, to initiate drug therapy at the doses used in the clinical trials.
5 General practitioner-initiated drug treatment for risk factors (blood pressure, cholesterol and diabetes mellitus) and as prophylactic therapy (aspirin, β-blocker, ACE inhibitors).
6 Nurse-led screening of first-degree blood relatives if there is a family history of premature (men < 55 years, women < 65 years) CHD in one or more close relatives.
7 Auditing the impact of the common clinical protocol for cardiovascular prevention and rehabilitation in hospital and general practice.

References

1 ACE-inhibitor Myocardial Infarction Collaborative Group. Indications for ACE inhibitors in the early treatment of acute myocardial infarction: systematic overview of individual data from 100 000 patients in randomised trials. *Circulation* 1998; **97**(22): 2202–12.

2 Acheson Report. *Independent Inquiry into Inequalities in Health Report* (Chairman: Sir Donald Acheson). London: The Stationery Office, 1998.

3 US Public Health Service. A clinical practice guideline for treating tobacco use and dependence. *JAMA* 2000; **283**(24): 3244–54.

4 Amiodarone Trials Meta-Analysis Investigators. Effect of prophylactic amiodarone on mortality after acute myocardial infarction and in congestive heart failure: meta-analysis of individual data from 6500 patients in randomised trials. *Lancet* 1997; **350**: 1417–24.

5 Anand SS, Yusuf S. Oral anticoagulant therapy in patients with coronary artery disease: a meta-analysis. *JAMA* 1999; **282**(21): 2058–67.

6 Anderson KM, Odell PM, Wilson PWF, Kannel WB. Cardiovascular disease risk profiles. *Am Heart J* 1990; **121**: 293–8.

7 Anderson KM, Wilson PWF, Odell PM, Kannel WB. An updated coronary risk profile: a statement for health professionals. *Circulation* 1991; **83**: 356–62.

8 Antiplatelet Trialists' Collaboration. Collaborative overview of randomised trials of antiplatelet therapy. I. Prevention of death, myocardial infarction, and stroke by prolonged antiplatelet therapy in various categories of patients. *BMJ* 1994; **308**(6921): 81–106.

9 Antman E, Braunwald E, McCabe CH *et al.* Enoxaparin for the acute and chronic management of unstable angina: results of the TIMI 11B trial. *Circulation* 1998; **98**: I-504.

10 Antman EM, Cohen M, Radley D *et al.* Assessment of the treatment effect of enoxaparin for unstable angina/non-Q-wave myocardial infarction: TIMI 11B-ESSENCE meta-analysis. *Circulation* 1999; **100**: 1602–8.

11 Baigent C, Collins R, Appleby P, Parish S, Sleight P, Peto R. ISIS-2: 10-year survival among patients with suspected acute myocardial infarction in randomised comparison of intravenous streptokinase, oral aspirin, both, or neither. The ISIS-2 (Second International Study of Infarct Survival) Collaborative Group. *BMJ* 1998; **316**(7141): 1337–43.

12 Balarajan R. Ethnicity and variations in mortality from coronary heart disease. *Health Trends* 1996; **28**: 45–51.

13 BARI Investigators. Five-year clinical and functional outcome comparing bypass surgery and angioplasty in patients with multivessel coronary disease. A multicenter randomized trial. Writing Group for the Bypass Angioplasty Revascularization Investigation (BARI) Investigators. *JAMA* 1997; **277**: 715–21.

14 Bertrand ME, Rupprecht HJ, Urban P, Gershlick AH. Double-blind study of the safety of clopidogrel with and without a loading dose in combination with aspirin compared with ticlodipine in combination with aspirin after coronary stenting: the Clopidogrel Aspirin International Co-operative Study (CLASSICS). *Circulation* 2000; **102**(6): 624–9.

15 Bertrand ME, Simmons ML, Fox KAA *et al.* Management of acute coronary syndromes: acute coronary syndromes without persistent ST-segment elevation. Recommendations of the Task Force of the European Society of Cardiology. *Eur Heart J* 2000; **21**: 1406–32.

16 Betteridge DJ, Dodson PM, Durrington PN *et al.* Management of hyperlipidaemia: guidelines of the British Hyperlipidaemia Association. *Postgrad Med J* 1993; **69**: 359–69.

17 Birkhead JS. Time delays in provision of thrombolytic treatment in six district hospitals. *BMJ* 1992; **305**: 445–8.

18 Block P, Petch MC, Letouzey JP. Manpower in cardiology in Europe. The Cardiology Monospeciality Section of the UEMS. *Eur Heart J* 2000; **21**(14): 1135–40.

19 Boden WE, O'Rourke RA, Crawford MH *et al*. Outcomes in patients with acute non-Q-wave myocardial infarction randomly assigned to an invasive as compared with a conservative management strategy. Veterans Affaire Non-Q-Wave Infarction Strategies in Hospital (VANQWISH) Trial Investigators. *NEJM* 1998; **338**: 1785–92.

20 Bowker TJ, Wood DA, Davies MY on behalf of the SADS Steering Group. Sudden unexpected cardiac death: methods and results of a national pilot study. *Int J Cardiol* 1995; **52**: 241–50.

21 Bowker TJ, Turner RM, Wood DA *et al*. A national survey of acute myocardial infarction and ischaemia (SAMII) in the UK: patient characteristics, management and in-hospital outcome in women compared to men. *Eur Heart J* 2000; **21**: 1458–63.

22 Bowker TJ, Clayton TC, Ingham J *et al*. A British Cardiac Society survey of the potential for the secondary prevention of coronary disease: ASPIRE (Action on Secondary Prevention through Intervention to Reduce Events). *Heart* 1996; **75**: 334–42.

23 Bradley F, Morgan S, Smith H, Mant D for the Wessex Research Network. Preventive care for patients following myocardial infarction. *Fam Pract* 1997; **14**: 220–6.

24 Bradley JM, Wallace ES, McCoy PM *et al*. A survey of exercise-based cardiac rehabilitation services in Northern Ireland. *Ulster Med J* 1997; **66**: 100–6.

25 British Cardiac Society Guidelines and Medical Practice Committee and Royal College of Physicians Clinical Effectiveness and Evaluation Unit. Guideline for the management of patients with acute coronary syndromes without persistent ECG ST-segment elevation. *Heart* 2001; **85**(2): 133–42.

26 Cannon CP, Weintraub WS, Demopoulos LA, Robertson DH, Gormley GJ, Braunwald E. Invasive versus conservative strategies in unstable angina and non-Q-wave myocardial infarction following treatment with tirofiban: rationale and study design of the international TACTICS-TIMI 18 Trial (Treat Angina with Aggrastat and determine Cost of Therapy with an Invasive or Conservative Strategy. Thrombolysis In Myocardial Infarction). *Am J Cardiol* 1998; **82**(6): 731–6.

27 CAPRIE Steering Committee. A randomised, blinded trial of clopidogrel versus aspirin in patients at risk of ischaemic events (CAPRIE). *Lancet* 1996; **348**(9038): 1329–39.

28 CAPTURE Investigators. Randomised placebo-controlled trial of abciximab before and during coronary intervention in refractory angina: the CAPTURE study. *Lancet* 1997; **349**: 1429–34.

29 Chambers J, Sprigings D, de Bono D. Open-access echocardiography. *Br J Cardiol* 2001; **8**: 365–74.

30 Chegini S, Katz R. Antioxidant vitamins and coronary artery disease: from CHAOS to HOPE? *Br J Cardiol* 2000; **7**(10): 601–12.

31 CIBIS-II Investigators and Committees. The Cardiac Insufficiency Bisoprolol Study II (CIBIS-II): a randomised trial. *Lancet* 1999; **353**: 9–13.

32 Clarke KW, Gray D, Hampton JR. Evidence of inadequate investigation and treatment of patients with heart failure. *Br Heart J* 1994; **71**: 584–7.

33 Clarke R, Frost C, Collins R *et al*. Dietary lipids and blood cholesterol: quantitative meta-analysis of metabolic ward studies. *BMJ* 1997; **314**: 112–17.

34 Cleland JGF. Diagnosis of heart failure. *Heart* 1998; **79** (Suppl. 2): S10–16.

35 Coats A, McGee H, Stokes H *et al*. (eds). *British Association of Cardiac Rehabilitation. Guidelines for cardiac rehabilitation*. Oxford: Blackwell Science, 1995.

36 Cohen M, Demers C, Gurfinkel EP for the ESSENCE Study Group. A comparison of low-molecular-weight heparin with unfractionated heparin for unstable coronary artery disease. Efficacy and safety of subcutaneous enoxiparin in non-Q-wave coronary events study group. *NEJM* 1997; **337**: 447–52.

37 Cohn JN, Tognoni G. Effect of the angiotensin-receptor blocker valsartan on morbidity and mortality in heart failure: the Valsartan Heart Failure Trial (Val-HeFT). *Circulation* 2000; **102**: 2672.

38 Collins R, Peto R, MacMahon S *et al.* Blood pressure, stroke and coronary heart disease. Part 2. Short-term reductions in blood pressure: overview of randomized drug trials in their epidemiological context. *Lancet* 1990; **335**: 827–38.

39 Collins R, MacMahon S. Blood pressure, antihypertensive drug treatment and the risk of stroke and of coronary heart disease. *Br Med Bull* 1994; **50**: 272–98.

40 Collins R, MacMahon S, Flather M *et al.* Clinical effects of anticoagulant therapy in suspected acute myocardial infarction: systematic overview of randomised trials. *BMJ* 1996; **313**: 652–9.

41 Collinson J, Flather MD, Fox KA *et al.* Clinical outcomes, risk stratification and practice patterns of unstable angina and myocardial infarction without ST elevation: Prospective Registry of Acute Ischaemic Syndromes in the UK (PRAIS-UK). *Eur Heart J* 2000; **21**(17): 1450–7.

42 Cowie MR, Wood DA, Coats AJS *et al.* Incidence and aetiology of heart failure: a population-based study. *Eur Heart J* 1999; **20**(6): 421–8.

43 Cowie MR *et al.* Value of natriuretic peptides in the assessment of patients with possible new heart failure in primary care. *Lancet* 1997; **350**: 1349–53.

44 Cowie MR, Fox KF, Wood DA *et al.* Hospitalisations and deaths in a population-based cohort of incident (new) cases of heart failure. *Heart* 1999; **81** (Suppl. 1): 8.

45 Cowie MR, Mosterd A, Wood DA *et al.* The epidemiology of heart failure. *Eur Heart J* 1997; **18**: 208–25.

46 Cowie MR, Wood DA, Coats AJS *et al.* The survival of patients with a new diagnosis of heart failure: a population-based study. *Heart* 2000: **83**; 505–10.

47 Dargie HJ, Ford I, Fox KM *et al.* Total Ischaemic Burden European Trial (TIBET): effects of ischaemia and treatment with atenolol, nifedipine SR and their combination on outcome in patients with chronic stable angina. *Eur Heart J* 1996; **17**: 104–12.

48 Davie AP, Cesar D, Caruna L *et al.* Outcome from a rapid-assessment chest pain clinic. *Q J Med* 1998; **91**: 339–43.

49 Davidson C, Reval K, Chamberlain DA *et al.* A report of a working group of the British Cardiac Society: cardiac rehabilitation services in the United Kingdom. *Br Heart J* 1995; **73**: 201–2.

50 De Bono D. Investigation and management of stable angina: revised guidelines 1998. Joint Working Party of the British Cardiac Society and Royal College of Physicians of London. *Heart* 1999; **81**(5): 546–55.

51 De Bono DP, Hopkins A. The management of acute myocardial infarction: guidelines and audit standards. Report of a workshop of the Joint Audit Committee of the British Cardiac Society and the Royal College of Physicians. *J R Coll Physicians Lond* 1994; **28**(4): 312–17.

52 De Lorgeril M, Salen P, Martin J-L *et al.* Mediterranean diet, traditional risk factors, and the rate of cardiovascular complications after myocardial infarction. Final report of the Lyon Diet Heart Study. *Circulation* 1999; **99**: 779–85.

53 Department of Health. *Diet and Risk. Report of the Committee of Medical Aspects of Food Policy (COMA)*. London: HMSO, 1994.

54 Department of Health. *Saving Lives: our healthier nation*. London: The Stationery Office, 1999.

55 Department of Health. *Smoking Kills*. London: The Stationery Office, 1998.

56 Domanski MJ, Exner DV, Borkowf CB, Geller NL, Rosenberg Y, Pfeffer MA. Effect of angiotensin-converting enzyme inhibition on sudden cardiac death in patients following acute myocardial infarction. A meta-analysis of randomized clinical trials. *J Am Coll Cardiol* 1999; **33**(3): 598–604.

57 Dovey S, Hicks N, Lancaster T *et al.* on behalf of the Oxfordshire Myocardial Infarction Incidence Study (OXMIS) Group. Secondary prevention after myocardial infarction. *Eur J Gen Pract* 1998; **4**: 6–10.

58 Downs GR, Clearfield M, Weiss S *et al*. Primary prevention of acute coronary events with lovastatin in men and women with average cholesterol levels: results of AFCAPS/TexCAPS (Air Force/Texas Coronary Atherosclerosis Study). *JAMA* 1998; **279**: 1615–22.

59 Duncan B, Fulton M, Morrison S *et al*. Prognosis of new and worsening angina pectoris. *BMJ* 1976; **1**: 981–5.

60 Eccles M, Freemantle N, Mason J and the North of England Aspirin Guideline Development Group. North of England evidence-based guideline development project: guideline on the use of aspirin as secondary prophylaxis for vascular disease in primary care. *BMJ* 1998; **316**: 1303–9.

61 Ad Hoc Subcommittee of the Liaison Committee of the World Health Organization and the International Society of Hypertension. Effects of calcium antagonists on the risks of coronary heart disease, cancer and bleeding. *J Hypertens* 1997; **15**: 105–15.

62 Organisation to Assess Strategies for Ischaemic Syndromes (OASIS-2) Investigators. Effects of recombinant hirudin (lepirudin) compared with heparin on death, myocardial infarction, refractory angina, and revascularisation procedures in patients with acute myocardial ischaemia without ST elevation: a randomised trial. *Lancet* 1999; **353**(9151): 429–38.

63 Eikelboom JW, Anand SS, Malmberg K, Weitz JI, Ginsberg JS, Yusuf S. Ultrafractionated heparin and low-molecular-weight heparin in acute coronary syndrome without ST elevation: a meta-analysis. *Lancet* 2000; **355**(9219): 1936–42.

64 EPILOG Investigators. Platelet glycoprotein IIb/IIIa-receptor blockade and low-dose heparin during percutaneous coronary revascularization. *NEJM* 1997; **336**: 1689–96.

65 EUROASPIRE Study Group. EUROASPIRE. A European Society of Cardiology survey of secondary prevention of coronary heart disease: principal results. *Eur Heart J* 1997; **18**; 1569–82.

66 EUROASPIRE Study Group. Lifestyle and risk factor management and use of drug therapies in coronary patients from 15 countries. Principal results from EUROASPIRE II. Euro Heart Survey Programme. *Eur Heart J* 2001; **22**: 554–72.

67 EUROASPIRE Study Group. Clinical reality of coronary prevention guidelines: a comparison of EUROASPIRE I and II in nine countries. *Lancet* 2001; **357**: 995–1001.

68 European Heart Failure Training Group. Experience from controlled trials of physical training in chronic heart failure. *Eur Heart J* 1998; **19**: 466–75.

69 Evans AE, Patterson CC, Mathewson Z, McCrum EE, McIlmoyle EL. Incidence, delay and survival in the Belfast MONICA Project coronary event register. *Rev Epidemiol Sante Publique* 1990; **38**(5–6): 419–27.

70 Fibrinolytic Therapy Trialists' (FTT) Collaborative Group. Indications for fibrinolytic therapy in suspected acute myocardial infarction: collaborative overview of early mortality and major morbidity results from all randomized trials of more than 1000 patients. *Lancet* 1994; **343**: 311–22.

71 Fletcher G for the Task Force on Risk Reduction. How to implement physical activity in primary and secondary prevention. A statement for health care professionals from the Task Force on Risk Reduction, American Heart Association. *Circulation* 1997; **96**: 355–7.

72 Fox KA, Cokkinos DV, Deckers J, Keil U, Maggioni A, Steg G. The ENACT study: a pan-European survey of acute coronary syndromes. European Network for Acute Coronary Treatment. *Eur Heart J* 2000; **21**(17): 1440–9.

73 Fox KAA. Comparing trials of glycoprotein IIb/IIIa-receptor antagonists. *Eur Heart J* 1999; **1** (Suppl. R): R10–17.

74 Fox KF, Cowie MR, Wood DA, Coats AJ, Poole-Wilson PA, Sutton GC. New perspectives on heart failure due to myocardial ischaemia. *Eur Heart J* 1999; **20**: 256–62.

75 Fox KF, Cowie MR, Wood DA, Coats AJ, Poole-Wilson PA, Sutton GC. A Rapid Access Heart Failure Clinic promptly identifies heart failure and initiates appropriate therapy. *Eur J Heart Failure* 2000; **2**: 423–9.

76 Fox KF, Cowie MR, Wood DA *et al.* Coronary artery disease as the cause of incident heart failure in the population. *Eur Heart J* 2001; **22**(3): 228–36.

77 Fox KM, Mulcahy D, Findlay I, Ford I, Dargie HJ. The Total Ischaemic Burden European Trial (TIBET). Effects of atenolol, nifedipine SR and their combination on the exercise test and the total ischaemic burden in 608 patients with chronic stable angina. *Eur Heart J* 1996; **17**(1): 96–103.

78 Franzosi MG, Santoro E, De Vita C *et al.* Ten-year follow-up of the first mega-trial testing thrombolytic therapy in patients with acute myocardial infarction: results of the Gruppo Italiano per lo studio della sopravvivenza nell'infarto-1 study. *Circulation* 1998; **98**: 2659–65.

79 FRAXIS Study Group. Comparison of two treatment durations (6 days and 14 days) of a low-molecular-weight heparin with a 6-day treatment of unfractionated heparin in the initial management of unstable angina or non-Q-wave myocardial infarction. *Eur Heart J* 1999; **20**: 1553–62.

80 Freemantle N, Cleland J, Young P, Mason J, Harrison J. Beta-blockade after myocardial infarction: systematic review and meta-regression analysis. *BMJ* 1999; **318**: 1730–7.

81 FRISC Study Group. Low-molecular-weight heparin during instability in coronary artery disease. *Lancet* 1996; **347**: 561–8.

82 FRISC II Investigators. Long-term low-molecular-weight heparin in unstable coronary artery disease: FRISC II prospective randomised multicentre study. *Lancet* 1999; **354**: 701–7.

83 FRISC II. Invasive compared with non-invasive treatment in unstable coronary artery disease: FRISC II prospective randomised multicentre study. *Lancet* 1999; **354**: 708–15.

84 Garg R, Yusuf S for the Collaborative Group on ACE Inhibitor Trials. Overview of randomized trials of angiotensin-converting enzyme inhibitors on mortality and morbidity in patients with heart failure. *JAMA* 1995; **273**(18): 1450–6.

85 Gibbs LM, Addington-Hall JM, Gibbs JSR. Dying from heart failure: lessons from palliative care. Many patients would benefit from palliative care at the end of their lives. *BMJ* 1998; **317**: 961–2.

86 Goldbourt U. Physical activity, long-term CHD mortality and longevity: a review of studies over the last 30 years. *World Rev Nutr Diet* 1997; **82**: 229–39.

87 Gottlieb SS, McCarter RJ, Vogel RA. Effects of beta-blockade on mortality among high-risk and low-risk patients after myocardial infarction. *NEJM* 1998; **339**(8): 489–97.

88 Gurfinkel E, Scirica BM. Low-molecular-weight heparin (enoxiparin) in the management of unstable angina: the TIMI studies. *Heart* 1999; **82** (Suppl. I): I15–17.

89 Hampton JR, Barlow AR. Open access. *BMJ* 1995; **310**: 611–12.

90 Haq IU, Ramsay LE, Jackson PR, Wallis EJ. Prediction of coronary risk for primary prevention of coronary heart disease: a comparison of methods. *Q J Med* 1999; **92**: 379–85.

91 Hansen JF. Review of post-infarct treatment with verapamil: combined experience of early and late intervention studies with verapamil in patients with acute myocardial infarction. *Cardiovasc Drugs Ther* 1994; **8** (Suppl. 3): 543–7.

92 Hansen JF, Hagerup L, Sigurd B *et al.* Cardiac event rates after acute myocardial infarction in patients treated with verapamil and trandolapril versus trandolapril alone. *Am J Cardiol* 1997; **79**(6): 738–41.

93 Heidenreich PA, McDonald KM, Hastie T *et al.* Meta-analysis of trials comparing beta-blockers, calcium antagonists and nitrates for stable angina. *JAMA* 1999; **281**(20): 1927–36.

94 Henderson RA, Pocock SJ, Sharp SJ *et al.* Long-term results of RITA-1 trial: clinical and cost comparisons of coronary angioplasty and coronary-artery bypass grafting. *Lancet* 1998; **352**(9138): 1419–25.

95 Hood S, Birnie D, Swan L, Hillis WS. Questionnaire survey of thrombolytic treatment in Accident and Emergency departments in the United Kingdom. *BMJ* 1998; **316**: 274.

96 Horgan J, Bethell H, Carson P *et al.* Working party report on cardiac rehabilitation. *Br Heart J* 1992; **67**: 412–18.

97 Hosenpud JD, Bennet LE, Keck BM *et al.* The registry of the International Society for Heart and Lung Transplantation: fourteenth official report – 1997. *J Heart Lung Transplant* 1998; **16**: 691–712.

98 Hurlen M, Smith P, Arnesen H. Effects of warfarin, aspirin and the two combined on mortality and thrombo-embolic morbidity after myocardial infarction. The WARIS-II (Warfarin-Aspirin Reinfarction Study) design. *Scand Cardiovasc J* 2000; **34**(2): 168–71.

99 Imperial Cancer Research Fund OXCHECK Study Group. Effectiveness of health checks conducted by nurses in primary care: final results of the OXCHECK study. *BMJ* 1995; **310**(6987): 1099–104.

100 Imperial Cancer Research Fund OXCHECK Study Group. Effectiveness of health checks conducted by nurses in primary care: results of the OXCHECK study after one year. *BMJ* 1994; **308**(6924): 308–12.

101 Fragmin and Fast Revascularisation during InStability in Coronary artery disease Investigators. Invasive compared with non-invasive treatment in unstable coronary artery disease: FRISC II prospective randomised multicentre study. *Lancet* 1999; **354**(9180): 708–15.

102 ISIS-3 (Third International Study of Infarct Survival) Collaborative Group. ISIS-3: a randomised comparison of streptokinase vs tissue plaminogen activator vs anistreplase and of aspirin plus heparin vs aspirin alone among 41,299 cases of suspected acute myocardial infarction. *Lancet* 1992; **339**(8796): 753–70.

103 ISIS-4 (Fourth International Study of Infarct Survival) Collaborative Group. ISIS-4: a randomised factorial trial assessing early oral captopril, oral mononitrate, and intravenous magnesium sulphate in 58,050 patients with suspected acute myocardial infarction. *Lancet* 1995; **345**(8951): 669–85.

104 Jain D, Fluck D, Sayer JW *et al.* One-stop chest pain clinic can identify high cardiac risk. *J R Coll Physicians Lond* 1997; **31**: 401–4.

105 Jespersen CM, Hansen JF. Effect of verapamil on reinfarction and cardiovascular events in patients with arterial hypertension included in the Danish Verapamil Infarction Trial II. The Danish Study Group on Verapamil in Myocardial Infarction. *J Hum Hypertens* 1994; **8**(2): 85–8.

106 Jespersen CM. Verapamil in acute myocardial infarction. The rationales of the VAMI and DAVIT III trials. *Cardiovasc Drugs Ther* 2000; **14**(1): 99–105.

107 British Cardiac Society, British Hyperlipidaemia Association, British Hypertension Society and British Diabetic Association. Joint British recommendations on prevention of coronary heart disease in clinical practice: summary. *BMJ* 2000; **320**: 705–8.

108 Joint Health Surveys Unit of Social and Community Planning Research and University College London. *Scottish Health Survey.* Colchester: University of Essex, 1995.

109 Joint Working Group on Coronary Angioplasty of the British Cardiac Society and British Cardiovascular Intervention Society. Coronary angioplasty: guidelines for good practice and training. *Heart* 2000; **83**: 224–35.

110 Juul-Moller S, Edvardsson N, Jahmatz B *et al.* for the Sweden Angina Pectoris Aspirin Trial (SAPAT) Group. Double-blind trial of aspirin in primary prevention of myocardial infarction in patients with stable angina. *Lancet* 1992; **340**: 1421–5.

111 Keogh BE, Kinsman R for the Society of Cardiothoracic Surgeons of Great Britain and Ireland. *National Adult Cardiac Surgical Database Report, 1998.* London: Society of Cardiothoracic Surgeons of Great Britain and Ireland, 1999.

112 Khunti K, Sorrie R, Jennings S, Farooqi A. Improving aspirin prophylaxis after myocardial infarction in primary care: collaboration in multipractice audit between primary care audit group and health authority. *BMJ* 1999; **319**: 297.

113 Klein W, Buchwald A, Hillis SE *et al.* for the FRIC Investigators. Comparison of low-molecular-weight heparin with unfractionated heparin acutely and with placebo for 6 weeks in the management of unstable coronary artery disease. *Circulation* 1997; **96**: 61–8.

114 Kong DF, Califf RM, Miller DP *et al*. Clinical outcomes of therapeutic agents that block the platelet glycoprotein IIb/IIIa integrin in ischemic heart disease. *Circulation* 1998; **98**: 2829–35.

115 Kornitzer M, Rose G. WHO European Collaborative Trial of multifactorial prevention of coronary heart disease. *Prev Med* 1985; **14**(3): 272–8.

116 Latini R, Tognoni G, Maggioni AP *et al*. Clinical effects of early angiotensin-converting enzyme inhibitor treatment for acute myocardial infarction are similar in the presence and absence of aspirin: systematic overview of individual data from 96,712 randomized patients. *J Am Coll Cardiol* 2000; **35**(7): 1801–7.

117 Leon AS, Myers MJ, Connett J. Leisure-time physical activity and the 16-year risks of mortality from coronary heart disease and all-causes in the Multiple Risk Factor Intervention Trial (MRFIT). *Int J Sports Med* 1997; **18** (Suppl. 3): S208–15.

118 Lewin RJ, Ingleton R, Newens AJ *et al*. Adherence to cardiac rehabilitation guidelines: a survey of cardiac rehabilitation programmes in the United Kingdom. *BMJ* 1998; **316**(7141): 1354–5.

119 Lindahl B, Venge P, Wallentin L for the FRISC Study Group. Relation between troponin T and the risk of subsequent cardiac events in unstable coronary artery disease. *Circulation* 1996; **93**: 1651–7.

120 Lonn EM, Yusuf S. Is there a role for antioxidant vitamins in the prevention of cardiovascular diseases? An update on epidemiological and clinical trials data. *Can J Cardiol* 1997; **13**(10): 957–65.

121 Löwel H, Koenig W, Engel S, Hormann A, Keil U. The impact of diabetes mellitus on survival after myocardial infarction: can it be modified by drug treatment? Results of a population-based myocardial infarction register follow-up study. *Diabetologia* 2000; **43**: 218–26.

122 Luscher MS, Thygesen K, Ravkilde J, Heickeendorff L for the TRIM study group. Applicability of cardiac troponin T and I for early risk stratification in unstable coronary disease. *Circulation* 1997; **96**: 2578–85.

123 MacMahon S, Rodgers A. The effects of antihypertensive treatment on vascular disease: reappraisal of evidence of 1994. *Vasc Med Biol* 1994; **4**: 265–71.

124 Madsen JK, Grande P, Saunamaki K *et al*. Danish multicenter randomized study of invasive versus conservative treatment in patients with inductable ischemia after thrombolysis in acute myocardial infarction (DANAMI). *Circulation* 1997; **96**(3): 748–55.

125 Malmberg K for the DIGAMI Study Group. Prospective randomized study of intensive insulin treatment on long-term survival after acute myocardial infarction in patients with diabetes mellitus. *BMJ* 1997; **314**: 1512–15.

126 McMurray J, McDonagh T, Morrison CE, Dargie HJ. Trends in hospitalisation for heart failure in Scotland 1980–1990. *Eur Heart J* 1993; **14**: 1158–62.

127 McMurray JJV, McDonagh TA, Davie AP, Cleland JGF, Francis CM, Morrison C. Should we screen for asymptomatic left ventricular dysfunction to prevent heart failure? *Eur Heart J* 1998; **19**: 842–6.

128 McMurray J, Hart W, Rhodes G. An evaluation of the economic cost of heart failure to the National Health Service in the United Kingdom. *Br J Med Econ* 1993; **6**: 99–110.

129 McMurray JJV, Stewart S. Nurse-led, multidisciplinary intervention in chronic heart failure. *Heart* 1998; **80**: 430–1.

130 McMurray JJV, Stewart S. Epidemiology, aetiology and prognosis of heart failure. *Heart* 2000; **83**: 596–602.

131 Mehta SR, Yusuf S for the CURE Study Investigators. The Clopidogrel in Unstable angina to prevent Recurrent Events (CURE) trial programme; rationale, design and baseline characteristics, including a meta-analysis of the effects of thienopyridines in vascular disease. *Eur Heart J* 2000; **21**(24): 2033–41.

132 Mehta SR, Yusuf S, Peters RJ *et al*. for the CURE Study. Effects of pretreatment with clopidogrel and aspirin followed by long-term therapy in patients undergoing percutaneous coronary intervention: the PCI-CURE study. *Lancet* 2001; **358**(9281): 527–33.

133 MERIT-HF Study Group. Effect of metoprolol CR/XL in chronic heart failure. *Lancet* 1999; **353**: 2001–7.

134 Michaelson A, Konig G, Thimme W. Preventative causative factors leading to hospital admission with decompensated heart failure. *Heart* 1998; **80**: 437–41.

135 Miettinen H, Lehto S, Salomaa V *et al.* Impact of diabetes on mortality after the first myocardial infarction. *Diabetes Care* 1998; **21**: 69–75.

136 Moser M, Hebert PR. Prevention of disease progression, left ventricular hypertrophy and congestive heart failure in hypertension treatment trials. *J Am Coll Cardiol* 1996; **27**: 1214–18.

137 Moss AJ, Oakes D, Rubison M *et al.* Effects of diltiazem on long-term outcome after acute myocardial infarction in patients with and without a history of systematic hypertension. *Am J Cardiol* 1991; **68**(5): 429–33.

138 Murphy J, Connell P, Hampton J. Predictors of risk in patients with unstable angina admitted to a district general hospital. *Br Heart J* 1992; **67**: 395–401.

139 Department of Health. *National Service Framework for Coronary Heart Disease. Modern standards and service models.* London: Department of Health, March 2000; www.doh.gov.uk/nsf/coronary.htm

140 World Health Organization. *Needs and Priorities in Cardiac Rehabilitation and Secondary Prevention in Patients with Coronary Heart Disease.* WHO Technical Report Series 831. Geneva: World Health Organization, 1993.

141 Newby DE, Fox KAA, Flint LL, Boon NA. A 'same-day' direct-access chest pain clinic: improved management and reduced hospitalization. *Q J Med* 1998; **91**: 333–7.

142 NHS Centre for Reviews and Dissemination. Management of stable angina. *Effect Health Care Bull* 1997; **3**: 1–8.

143 NHS Centre for Reviews and Dissemination. Cardiac rehabilitation. *Effect Health Care Bull* 1998; **4**(4): 1–11.

144 NHS Executive. *Review of Ambulance Performance Standards. Final report of the steering group.* London: Department of Health, 1996.

145 Norris RM on behalf of the United Kingdom Heart Attack Study Collaborative Group. Fatality outside hospital from acute coronary events in three British health districts, 1994–95. *BMJ* 1998; **316**: 1065–70.

146 Norris RM. *Sudden Cardiac Death and Acute Myocardial Infarction in Three British Health Districts: the UK heart attack study.* London: British Heart Foundation, 1999, pp. 61–4.

147 North of England Stable Angina Development Group. North of England Evidence-based Guidelines Development Project: summary version of evidence-based guidelines for the primary care management of stable angina. *BMJ* 1996; **312**: 827–32.

148 O'Connor GT, Buring GE, Yusuf S *et al.* An overview of randomized trials of rehabilitation with exercise after myocardial infarction. *Circulation* 1989; **80**: 234–44.

149 Oldridge NB, Guyatt G, Fisher ME, Rimm AA. Cardiac rehabilitation after myocardial infarction: combined experience of randomized clinical trials. *JAMA* 1988; **260**: 945–50.

150 Olsson G, Wikstrand J, Warnold I *et al.* Metoprolol-induced reduction in postinfarction mortality: pooled results from five double-blind randomized trials. *Eur Heart J* 1992; **13**(1): 28–32.

151 O'Toole L, Channer KS. Direct-access exercise electrocardiography: a new service that improves the management of suspected ischaemic heart disease in the community. *Br Heart J* 1995; **73**(2): 200.

152 Packer M, Bristow MR, Cohn JN *et al.* The effect of carvedilol on morbidity and mortality in patients with chronic heart failure. *NEJM* 1996; **334**: 1349–55.

153 Petersen S, Mockford C, Rayner M. *Coronary Heart Disease Statistics. British Heart Foundation Statistics Database.* London: British Heart Foundation, 1999; www.dphpc.ox.ac.uk/bhfhprg

154 Pitt B, Zannad F, Remme WJ *et al.* The effect of spironolactone on morbidity and mortality in patients with severe heart failure. *NEJM* 1999; **341**: 709–17.

155 Pocock SJ, Henderson RA, Rickards AF *et al.* Meta-analysis of randomised trials comparing coronary angioplasty with bypass surgery. *Lancet* 1995; **346**: 1184–9.

156 Prescott E, Hippe M, Schohr P, Hein HO, Vestbo J. Smoking and the risk of myocardial infarction in women and men: longitudinal study. *BMJ* 1998; **316**: 1043–7.

157 Prescott-Clarke P, Primatesta P (eds). *Health Survey for England 1996.* London: The Stationery Office, 1998.

158 Platelet Receptor Inhibition in Ischemic Syndrome Management (PRISM) Investigators. A comparison of aspirin plus tirofiban with aspirin plus hepatin for unstable angina. *NEJM* 1998; **338**: 1498–505.

159 Platelet Receptor Inhibition in Ischemic Syndrome Management in Patients Limited by Unstable Signs and Symptoms (PRISM-PLUS) Study Investigators. Inhibition of the platelet glycoprotein IIb/IIIa receptor with tirofiban in unstable angina and non-Q-wave myocardial infarction. *NEJM* 1998; **338**: 1488–97.

160 PURSUIT Trial Investigators. Inhibition of platelet glycoprotein IIb/IIIa with eptifibatide in patients with acute coronary artery syndromes. *NEJM* 1998; **388**: 436–42.

161 Pyörälä K, De Backer G, Graham I, Poole-Wilson P, Wood D. Prevention of coronary heart disease in clinical practice. Recommendation of the Task Force of the European Society of Cardiology, European Atherosclerosis Society and European Society of Hyptertension. *Eur Heart J* 1994; **15**: 1300–31; *Atherosclerosis* 1994; **110**: 121–61.

162 Ramsay L, Williams B, Johnston G *et al.* Guidelines for management of hypertension: report of the Third Working Party of the British Hypertension Society. *J Hum Hypertens* 1999; **13**(9): 569–92.

163 Ramsay L, Williams B, Johnston G *et al.* British Hypertension Society guidelines for hypertension management: summary. *BMJ* 1999; **319**: 630–5.

164 Raw M, McNeil A, West R. Smoking cessation guidelines for health professionals. A guide to effective smoking cessation inventions for the health care system. *Thorax* 1998; **53** (Suppl. 5): S1–38.

165 Rawles J, Sinclair C, Jennings K, Ritchie L, Waugh N. Call to needle times after acute myocardial infarction in urban and rural areas in northeast Scotland: prospective observational study. *BMJ* 1998; **317**: 576–8.

166 Rawles J. Magnitude of benefit from earlier thrombolytic treatment in acute myocardial infarction: new evidence from Grampian region early anistreplase trial (GREAT). *BMJ* 1996; **312**: 212–16.

167 Rawles J. Quantification of the benefit of earlier thrombolytic therapy: 5-year results of the Grampian early antistreplase trial (GREAT). *J Am Coll Cardiol* 1997; **30**: 1181–6.

168 RITA Investigators. Coronary angioplasty versus coronary artery bypass surgery: the Randomised Intervention Treatment of Angina (RITA) trial. *Lancet* 1993; **341**(8845): 573–80.

169 RITA-2 Trial Participants. Coronary angioplasty versus medical therapy for angina: the second Randomised Intervention Treatment of Angina (RITA-2) trial. *Lancet* 1997; **350**: 461–8.

170 Rogers WJ, Coggin CJ, Gersh BJ *et al.* Ten-year follow-up of quality of life in patients randomised to receive medical therapy or coronary artery bypass graft surgery. The Coronary Artery Surgery Study (CASS). *Circulation* 1990; **82**: 1647–58.

171 Rose G, Tunsdall-Padoe HD, Heller RF. UK heart disease prevention project: incidence and mortality results. *Lancet* 1983; **1**(8333): 1062–6.

172 Rosengren A, Wilhelmsen L. Physical activity protects against coronary death and deaths from all causes in middle-aged men. Evidence from a 20-year follow-up of the primary prevention study in Goteborg. *Ann Epidemiol* 1997; **7**(1): 69–75.

173 Sacks FM, Pfeffer MA, Moye LA *et al.* The effect of pravastatin on coronary events after myocardial infarction in patients with average cholesterol levels. *NEJM* 1996; **335**: 1001–9.

174 Scandinavian Simvastatin Survival Study Group. Randomised trial of cholesterol lowering in 4444 patients with coronary heart disease: the Scandinavian Simvastatin Survival Study. *Lancet* 1994; **344**: 1383–9.

175 Schwartz GG, Olsson AG, Ezekowitz MD *et al*. Effects of atorvastatin on early recurrent ischemic events in acute coronary syndromes. The MIRACL study: a randomized controlled trial. *JAMA* 2001; **285**(13): 1711–18.

176 Scottish Intercollegiate Guidelines Network (SIGN). *Coronary Revascularisation in the Management of Stable Angina Pectoris: a national clinical guideline*. SIGN Publication Number 32. Edinburgh: Royal College of Physicians of Edinburgh, 1998, pp. 19–21.

177 Sesso HD, Paffenbarger RS Jr, Lee IM. Physical activity and coronary heart disease in men: the Harvard Alumni Health Study. *Circulation* 2000; **102**(9): 975–80.

178 Sever P, Beevers G, Bulpitt C *et al*. Management guidelines in essential hypertension: report of the Second Working Party of the British Hypertension Society. *BMJ* 1993; **306**(6883): 983–7.

179 Shepherd J, Betteridge DJ, Durrington PN *et al*. British Hyperlipidaemia Association guidelines on strategies for reduction of coronary heart disease and desirable limits for blood lipid levels. *BMJ* 1987; **295**: 1245–6.

180 SIGN Secretariat. *Diagnosis and Treatment of Heart Failure due to Left Ventricular Systolic Dysfunction*. SIGN Publication Number 35. Edinburgh: Royal College of Physicians of Edinburgh, 1999.

181 Simoons ML for the GUSTO IV-ACS Investigators. Effect of glycoprotein IIb/IIIa receptor blocker abciximab on outcome in patients with acute coronary syndromes without early coronary revascularisation: the GUSTO IV-ACS randomised trial. *Lancet* 2001; **357**(9272): 1915–24.

182 Sleight P. Calcium antagonists during and after myocardial infarction. *Drugs* 1996; **51**(2): 216–25.

183 Smith P. Oral anticoagulants are effective long term after acute myocardial infarction. *J Intern Med* 1999; **245**(4): 383–7.

184 Solomon AJ, Gersh BJ. Management of chronic stable angina: medical therapy, percutaneous transluminal coronary angioplasty, and coronary artery bypass graft surgery. Lessons from the randomized trials. *Ann Intern Med* 1998; **128**(3): 216–23.

185 Soriano JB, Hoes AW, Meems L, Grobbee DE. Increased survival with beta-blockers: importance of ancillary properties. *Prog Cardiovasc Dis* 1997; **39**(5): 445–56.

186 Staessen JA, Fagard R, Thijs L *et al*. for the Systolic Hypertension-Europe (Syst-Eur) Trial Investigators. Morbidity and mortality in the placebo-controlled European Trial on Isolated Systolic Hypertension in the Elderly. *Lancet* 1997; **360**: 757–64.

187 NHS Executive. *Standing Medical Advisory Committee on Use of Statins*. London: Department of Health, 1997.

188 Stephens NG, Parsons A, Schofield PM *et al*. A randomised controlled trial of vitamin E in patients with coronary heart disease: the Cambridge Heart Antioxidant Study (CHAOS). *Lancet* 1996; **347**: 781–6.

189 Stone PH, Gibson RS, Glasser SP *et al*. Comparison of propranolol, diltiazem, and nifedipine in the treatment of ambulatory ischemia in patients with stable angina. Differential effects on ambulatory ischemia, exercise performance, and anginal symptoms. *Circulation* 1990; **82**(6): 1962–72.

190 Sutcliffe SJ, Wood DA. The impact of a rapid access chest pain clinic on the assessment and management of new angina in the community (abstract). *Eur Heart J* 1998; **19** (Suppl. P): P1259.

191 Sutcliffe SJ, Wood DA. Rapid assessment and management of new-onset chest pain in women in the community (abstract). *Eur Heart J* 1998; **19** (Suppl. P): P3776.

192 Sutcliffe SJ, Wood DA. Community presentation and management of new-onset chest pain in women compared to men assessed through a rapid access chest pain clinic (RACPC) (abstract). *JACC* 1999; **33** (Suppl. A): 326A.

193 Sutcliffe SJ, Wood DA. The impact of a rapid access chest pain clinic on the management of new angina in the community. *J Am Coll Cardiol* 1999; **33** (Suppl. A): 392A.

194 Sutcliffe SJ, Sutcliffe AK, Wood DA. The clinical incidence of fatal and non-fatal coronary heart disease in the population (abstract). *Heart* 1999; **81** (Suppl. 1): 91.

195 Tang JL, Armitage JM, Lancaster T *et al.* Systematic review of dietary intervention trials to lower blood total cholesterol in free-living subjects. Commentary. Dietary change, cholesterol reduction, and the public health: what does meta-analysis add? *BMJ* 1998; **316**: 1213–20.

196 Task Force on the Management of Acute Myocardial Infarction of the European Society of Cardiology. Acute myocardial infarction: prehospital and in-hospital management. *Eur Heart J* 1996; **17**: 43–63.

197 Task Force of the European Society of Cardiology. Management of stable angina pectoris. *Eur Heart J* 1997; **18**: 394–413.

198 Task Force of the Working Group on Heart Failure of the European Society of Cardiology. The treatment of heart failure. *Eur Heart J* 1997; **18**(5): 736–53.

199 Assessment of the Safety and Efficacy of a New Thrombolytic Regimen (ASSENT)-3 Investigators. Efficacy and safety of tenecteplase in combination with enoxaparin, abciximab, or unfractionated heparin: the ASSENT-3 randomised trial in acute myocardial infarction. *Lancet* 2001; **358**(9282): 605–13.

200 British Cardiac Society Working Group on Coronary Prevention. Conclusions and recommendations. *Br Heart J* 1987; **57**: 188–9.

201 Bypass Angioplasty Revascularization Investigation (BARI) Investigators. Comparison of coronary bypass surgery with angioplasty in patients with multi-vessel disease. *NEJM* 1996; **335**: 217–25.

202 Digitalis Investigation Group. The effect of digoxin on mortality and morbidity in patients with heart failure. *NEJM* 1997; **336**: 525–33.

203 Global Use of Strategies to Open Occluded Coronary Arteries in Acute Coronary Syndromes (GUSTO IIB) Angioplasty Substudy Investigators. A clinical trial comparing primary coronary angioplasty with tissue plasminogen activator for acute myocardial infarction. *NEJM* 1997; **336**: 1621–8.

204 GRACE Investigators. Rationale and design of the GRACE (Global Registry of Acute Coronary Events) Project: a multinational registry of patients hospitalized with acute coronary syndromes. *Am Heart J* 2001; **141**(2): 190–9.

205 Long-Term Intervention with Pravastatin in Ischaemic Disease (LIPID) Study Group. Prevention of cardiovascular events and death with pravastatin in patients with coronary heart disease and a broad range of initial cholesterol levels. *NEJM* 1998; **339**: 1349–57.

206 Department of Health. *The National Service Framework for Coronary Heart Disease*. London: The Stationery Office, 2000.

207 Task Force of the European Society of Cardiology and the European Resuscitation Council. The pre-hospital management of acute heart attacks. *Eur Hear J* 1998; **19**: 1140–64.

208 Theroux P, Waters D, Qiu S, McCans J, de Guise P, Juneau M. Aspirin versus heparin to prevent myocardial infarction during the acute phase of unstable angina. *Circulation* 1993; **88**: 2045–8.

209 Task Force on Heart Failure of the European Society of Cardiology. Guidelines for the diagnosis of heart failure. *Eur Heart J* 1995; **16**(6): 741–51.

210 United Kingdom Heart Attack Study (UKHAS) Collaborative Group. Effect of time from onset to coming under care on fatality of patients with acute myocardial infarction: effect of resuscitation and thrombolytic treatment. *Heart* 1998; **80**(2): 114–20.

211 Thijs L, Fagard R, Lijnen P, Staessen Y, Van Hoof R, Amery A. A meta-analysis of outcome trials in elderly hypertensives. *J Hypertens* 1992; **10**: 1103–9.

212 Thompson DR, Bowman GS, Kitson AL *et al.* Cardiac rehabilitation services in England and Wales: a national survey. *Int J Cardiol* 1997; **59**: 299–304.

213 Thompson DR, Bowman GS, De Bono DP *et al.* *Cardiac Rehabilitation: guidelines and audit standards.* London: Royal College of Physicians, 1997.

214 Thompson DR, Bowman GS, Kitson AL *et al.* Cardiac rehabilitation in the United Kingdom: guidelines and audit standards. *Heart* 1996; **75**: 89–93.

215 TIMI IIB Investigators. Effects of tissue plasminogen activator and a comparison of early invasive and conservative strategies in unstable angina and non-Q-wave myocardial infarction. *Circulation* 1994; **89**: 1545–56.

216 Topol EJ, Moliterno DJ, Herrmann HC *et al.* Comparison of two platelet glycoprotein IIb/IIIa inhibitors, tirofiban and abciximab, for the prevention of ischemic events with percutaneous coronary revascularization. *NEJM* 2001; **344**(25): 1888–94.

217 Tunstall-Pedoe H, Morrison C, Woodward M, Fitzpatrick B, Watt G. Sex difference in myocardial infarction and coronary deaths in the Scottish MONICA population of Glasgow 1985 to 1991. Presentation, diagnosis, treatment, and 28-day case fatality of 3991 events in men and 1551 events in women. *Circulation* 1996; **93**(11): 1981–92.

218 Tunstall-Pedoe H, Kuulasmaa K, Amouyel P, Arveiler D, Rajakangas AM, Pajak A. Myocardial infarction and coronary deaths in the World Health Organization MONICA Project. Registration procedures, event rates, and case-fatality rates in 38 populations from 21 countries in four continents. *Circulation* 1994; **90**(1): 583–612.

219 UK Prospective Diabetes Study Group. Intensive blood-glucose control with sulphonylureas or insulin compared with conventional treatment and risk of complications in patients with type 2 diabetes (UKPDS 33). *Lancet* 1998; **352**: 837–53.

220 UK Prospective Diabetes Study Group. Tight blood pressure control and risk of macrovascular and microvascular complications in type II diabetes: UKPDS 38. *BMJ* 1998; **317**: 703–13.

221 Van Berkel TFM, Boersma H, Roos-Hesselink JW, Erdman RAM, Simoons ML. Impact of smoking cessation and smoking interventions in patients with coronary heart disease. *Eur Heart J* 1999; **20**: 1773–82.

222 van Veldhuisen DJ, Charlesworth A, Crijns HJ, Lie KI, Hampton JR. Differences in drug treatment of chronic heart failure between European countries. *Eur Heart J* 1999; **20**: 666–72.

223 Varma C, Camm A. Pacing for heart failure. *Lancet* 2001; **357**: 1277–83.

224 Volmink JA, Newton JN, Hicks NR, Sleight P, Fowler GH, Neil HA. Coronary event and case fatality rates in an English population: results of the Oxford Myocardial Infarction Incidence Study. *Heart* 1998; **80**(1): 40–4.

225 Wallentin L, Lagerqvist B, Husted S, Kontny F, Sthle E, Swahn E. Outcome at 1 year after an invasive compared with a non-invasive strategy in unstable coronary artery disease: the FRISC II invasive randomised trial. *Lancet* 2000; **356**(9223): 9–16.

226 Wallis EJ, Ramsay LE, Ul Haq I *et al.* Coronary and cardiovascular risk estimation for primary prevention: validation of a new Sheffield table in the 1995 Scottish health survey population. *BMJ* 2000; **320**(7236): 671–6.

227 West of Scotland Coronary Prevention Study Group. Influence of pravastatin and plasma lipids on clinical events in the West of Scotland Coronary Prevention Study (WOSCOPS). *Circulation* 1998; **97**: 1440–5.

228 Wild S, McKeigue P. Cross-sectional analysis of mortality by country of birth in England and Wales 1970–92. *BMJ* 1997; **314**: 705–10.

229 Witte K, Thackray S, Clark AL, Cooklin M, Cleland JG. Clinical trials update. *Eur J Heart Failure* 2000; **2**: 455–60.

230 Wonderling D, McDermott C, Buxton *et al.* Costs and cost-effectiveness of cardiovascular screening and intervention: the British Family Heart Study. *BMJ* 1996; **312**: 1269–73.

231 Wood DA, Kinmonth A-L, Pyke SDM, Thompson SG on behalf of the Family Heart Study Group. Randomised controlled trial evaluating cardiovascular screening and intervention in general practice: principal results of British Family Heart Study. *BMJ* 1994; **308**: 313–20.

232 Wood D, De Backer G, Faergeman O, Graham I, Mancia G. Pyörälä K. Prevention of coronary heart disease in clinical practice. Recommendations of the Second Joint Task Force of European and Other Societies on Coronary Prevention. *Eur Heart J* 1998; **19**: 1434–503.

233 Wood DA, Durrington P, Poulter N, McInnes G, Rees A, Wray R on behalf of the British Cardiac Society, the British Hyperlipidaemia Association, the British Hypertension Society and the British Diabetic Association. Joint British recommendations on prevention of coronary heart disease in clinical practice. *Heart* 1998; **80**: S1–29.

234 World Health Organization. *Needs and Action Priorities in Cardiac Rehabilitation and Secondary Prevention in Patients with CHD.* WHO Technical Report Series 831. Geneva: WHO Regional Office for Europe, 1993.

235 Yusuf S, Peto R, Lewis J *et al.* Beta-blockade during and after myocardial infarction: an overview of the randomized trials. *Prog Cardiovasc Dis* 1985; **27**: 335–71.

236 Yusuf S, Lonn E. Anti-ischaemic effects of ACE inhibitors: review of current clinical evidence and ongoing clinical trials. *Eur Heart J* 1998; **19** (Suppl. J): J36–44.

237 Yusuf S, Sleight P, Pogue J, Bosch J, Davies R, Dagenais G. Effects of an angiotensin-converting-enzyme inhibitor, ramipril, on cardiovascular events in high-risk patients. *NEJM* 2000; **342**(3): 145–53.

238 Heart Protection Study Collaborative Group. MRC/BHF Heart Protection Study of cholesterol lowering with simvastatin in 20 536 high-risk individuals: a randomized placebo-controlled trial. *Lancet* 2002; **360**: 7–22.

239 Fox KM for the European Trial on Reduction of Cardiac Events with Perindopril in Stable Coronary Artery Disease Investigators. Efficacy of perindopril in reduction of cardiovascular events among patients with stable coronary artery disease: randomised, double-blind, placebo-controlled, multi-centre trial (the EUROPA study). *Lancet* 2003; **362**: 782–8.

6 Colorectal Cancer

Hugh Sanderson, Andrew R Walker and Denise Young

1 Summary

Occurrence

Colorectal cancer is a major cause of mortality and morbidity in the UK and care for this disease uses a significant proportion of health service resources. The key epidemiological characteristics of the disease are given in Table 1.

Table 1: Characteristics of colorectal cancer.

Risk factors	High-fat, low-fibre diet, alcohol, presence of adenomatous polyps, presence of predisposing lower gastrointestinal diseases, previous history of colorectal cancer, family history and genetic syndromes (HNPCC and FAP)
Incidence	618 cases per 1,000,000 population per year (South and West Region, 1995) Rare below the age of 40, the incidence rises steeply and continuously in those over 50 years of age
Mortality	320 deaths per 1,000,000 population per year (South and West Region, 1995)
Survival*	Stage A: 75% Stage B: 57% Stage C: 35% Stage D: 12%

* These are 5-year crude survival rates for patients diagnosed with colorectal cancer in Wessex Region in 1991–95 and include all deaths, not just those due to colorectal cancer.

This chapter considers the options for the provision of care in terms of both cost and outcome to help commissioners gain the best value care for their population. Costs should, however, be interpreted with caution in the light of local variations.

Interventions

Primary prevention

Primary prevention is concerned with reducing the risks of developing colorectal cancer. However, because the causes are not clearly established, prevention is limited to general advice on diet and lifestyle.

Screening and surveillance

This is a disease in which the stage at diagnosis is very significant in relation to prognosis. Consequently, considerable effort has gone into testing ways of achieving early diagnosis, and assessing its impact on mortality. Trials of detection of precancerous changes or early tumours through screening and surveillance have been undertaken. Faecal occult blood testing has been shown to be of similar cost-effectiveness to breast cancer treatment, but compliance is low.

A number of conditions increase the risk of developing colorectal cancer, especially family history, specific syndromes (familial adenomatous polyps; FAP) and a history of polyps or ulcerative colitis. Surveillance of high-risk individuals is widely undertaken although good-quality data on the cost-effectiveness are lacking.

Investigation

This includes basic examination and radiological contrast examination of the bowel. Flexible sigmoid-oscopy (FS) is useful as a quick examination of the rectum and sigmoid colon, but the most important technique is colonoscopy in which the whole of the bowel can be visualised, and biopsies taken of suspicious lesions. Training is required in order to achieve proficiency in the technique, but sigmoid-oscopy services can be provided by nurses,[1] particularly where the examination can be video-recorded for subsequent review.

Treatment

Surgical excision is the main form of initial treatment, but evidence regarding the effect of surgical specialisation on outcomes is contradictory. Similarly, although more extensive dissection resulting in a total mesorectal excision has been shown in non-randomised trials to improve survival, the cost-effectiveness of this technique has not been demonstrated.

Adjuvant radiotherapy has been shown to reduce recurrence rates. There is some inconclusive evidence to suggest that pre-operative therapy is more effective than post-operative therapy in rectal cancer.

Adjuvant chemotherapy is effective for Dukes' stage C cancers and should be used routinely even though there is no consensus on the most effective regime. A multi-centre trial is being undertaken to determine the most effective drugs and mode of administration. Trials to determine the effectiveness of chemotherapy in stage B are also continuing.

There are few UK data on the most cost-effective models for palliative care, but there is evidence that specialist palliative care teams can provide more effective services than conventional care methods. This applies to all malignant disease, and palliative care services are not restricted to colorectal cancer.

2 Statement of the problem

Occurrence

Colorectal cancer is the third most common cancer after lung and non-melanoma skin cancers. It is predominantly a disease of the elderly and an average commissioning agency could expect approximately 543 cases per million people (164 rectal, 379 colon) diagnosed annually and about 296 deaths per million annually.[2,3] Because this is predominantly a disease of the elderly, the age distribution of the population will affect overall incidence. The relevant coding classifications for this disease are given in Appendix I.

Current issues

Because of the strong relationship between stage at diagnosis and prognosis, there is a great deal of interest in finding ways of diagnosing patients earlier. However, although recent trials of faecal occult blood (FOB) testing have shown that reductions in mortality can be achieved, compliance with the screening programme is low, as is compliance with regular FS. As a consequence, there are likely to be difficulties in the design of an effective national screening programme.

There has been some concern in recent years to ensure that colorectal surgery is undertaken by surgeons with a specific interest in the area, and who undertake considerable volumes of colorectal cancer surgery. Despite the attractiveness of the hypothesis that specialists achieve better results, this is not supported by the evidence (but the increasing complexity of management demands care through multi-disciplinary teams). However, the general principles of the Calman–Hine report on the organisation of cancer services will ensure that appropriate services for the care of colorectal cancer patients are available at cancer units and cancer centres.

Relating needs to interventions

Large variations in the availability and use of services exist for many conditions. Consequently one of the key tasks of health service commissioners in planning and monitoring the delivery of service is to identify the need in the population, and estimate the care required for those in need. In order to do this systematically, it is necessary to classify groups of individuals in the population into similar need groups. The appropriate packages of care for each of these need groups can then be determined and from these the total costs of care can be calculated. In addition, measures of the performance of services in meeting targets can be specified in relation to the groups of patients and their packages of care.

3 Sub-categories

This section defines the conditions related to colorectal cancer which require access to health services, and details the various conditions within each group.

Because the stage at diagnosis is so important in determining prognosis and appropriate care, one of the key methods of classification is via pathological staging and grading of colorectal cancers (Appendix II). However, this aspect deals only with classifying patients with diagnosed cancers, and to develop integrated services, a broader classification is required.

Health benefit groups (HBGs) were developed as a way of classifying groups of individuals with similar needs. Health care resource groups (HRGs) provide a way of classifying similar intervention packages. The information can be organised in the form of a matrix in which the vertical axis contains the HBGs defining groups of people with broadly similar needs. The horizontal axis details the number of people falling into each HBG and the health services that they might receive. In order to cover the whole spectrum of conditions and interventions, four matrices have been developed covering the following areas:

- individuals at risk, requiring promotion/prevention interventions
- individuals presenting with symptoms and signs requiring diagnostic/assessment interventions
- individuals with confirmed disease, requiring specific clinical management
- individuals with the continued consequences of disease, requiring support and care.

Appendix III sets out the HBGs and HRGs related to colorectal cancer. Because this provides a structured way of identifying individuals and services, it is used as the basis of this needs assessment chapter. However, because much of the available data is not presented in this format, it can serve only as a map within which to locate other sources of information.

4 Prevalence and incidence

The incidence of colorectal cancer is 618 per 1 000 000 population. The death rate is 320 per 1 000 000. Forty-five per cent of patients are over the age of 75 when a diagnosis of colorectal cancer is made.[4] The age distribution of the population is considered the most important factor determining the overall incidence.

Colorectal cancer is the third most common cancer after lung and non-melanoma skin cancers. The incidence rates for men and women are similar, but colon cancer is about twice as common in women as rectal cancer, whereas in men the incidence of colon and rectal cancers is almost the same.

Colorectal cancer is the second biggest cause of cancer death in this country and the fifth largest cause of death overall. Table 2 gives the age-specific death rates per 1 000 000 population.

Table 2: Colorectal cancer rates per 1 000 000 population (South and West Region, 1995).

	Age (years)				
	0–44	45–64	65–74	75+	Total
Incidence	19	570	1,944	3,415	618
Mortality	6	243	890	2,065	320

Source: South and West Regional Cancer Intelligence Unit.[4]

More than half of all deaths are in the 75+ age group. However, owing to the poor overall survival from this disease it is still a significant cause of premature death, with 163 411 years of life lost each year in England and Wales.[2]

Population at risk

General risk factors

The cause or causes of colorectal cancer are not known. However, several factors are known to increase the chance of development of disease.

High-fat, low-fibre diet

There is considerable evidence to suggest that diet is associated with the development of this disease. Early correlation studies have linked high colorectal cancer rates to countries with a diet high in fat content with a low fibre intake.[5] Observational studies have consistently reported an inverse relationship between a diet that is low in consumption of fruit and vegetables and colorectal cancer.[6–8] One study estimated a relative risk of 1.9 for 'low intake' compared with 'high intake'.[7]

Alcohol consumption

High alcohol intake, particularly beer, has been implicated in the development of rectal cancers.[9] In addition, one study revealed an association between alcohol consumption and colon cancer with a relative risk for drinkers vs. non-drinkers of 4.38 and 1.92 for men and women, respectively.[10]

Tobacco smoking

Recent cohort studies with at least 20 years follow-up have reported a weak positive association between tobacco smoking and colorectal cancer.[11]

Sedentary lifestyle

Observational studies have shown that a sedentary lifestyle increases the risk of colon cancer.[8]

Adenomatous polyps

It has been suggested that most cancers of the colon and rectum evolve from isolated adenomatous polyps (the polyp–cancer theory).[12] The risk of malignant change depends upon the size of the polyp. Small polyps (< 1 cm) represent about 60% of all polyps but only about 1% are malignant. Large polyps (> 2 cm) only represent around 20% of polyps but have a much higher malignancy rate (approximately 50%).

Specific risk factors

Certain groups are at higher than average risk of developing colorectal cancer. These include individuals with:

- ulcerative colitis
- Crohn's disease
- previous history of adenomatous polyp
- previous history of colorectal cancer
- family history
- genetic syndromes.

Ulcerative colitis and Crohn's disease

There is an increased risk of colorectal cancer for patients with long-standing ulcerative colitis and, to a lesser extent, Crohn's disease. The prevalence of ulcerative colitis is around 1600 per 1 000 000 population and that of Crohn's disease about 500 per 1 000 000. In a population of 1 000 000 there will be approximately 2100 patients with inflammatory bowel disease who may require monitoring. The risk of developing colorectal cancer becomes significant between 8 and 10 years following a diagnosis of inflammatory bowel disease.

Family history

Close relatives of people diagnosed with colorectal cancer are at increased risk of this disease. Risk is greater the closer the family relationship, the higher the number of relatives affected and the younger they are at the time of diagnosis.[13–15] A significant family history is defined as close relatives of cases diagnosed before the age of 45 or two or more close relatives with bowel cancer, especially when one or more of the cases is diagnosed at a young age.[16]

Hodgson et al.[17] calculated the lifetime risks of death from colorectal cancer for relatives of index patients with colorectal cancer (see Table 3).

Table 3: Lifetime risks of colorectal cancer in first-degree relatives of patients with colorectal cancer.

Population risk	1 in 50
One first-degree relative affected, diagnosed after age 45	1 in 17
One first- and one second-degree relative affected, diagnosed after age 45	1 in 12
One first-degree relative affected, diagnosed before age 45	1 in 10
Two first-degree relatives affected	1 in 6
Dominant pedigree (50% risk of inheriting genetic predisposition)	1 in 2

Source: Hodgson et al.[17]

Guidelines from the Yorkshire Cancer Organisation suggest that about 10% of the population aged 50 and over have at least one first-degree relative affected by colorectal cancer. This suggests that there are around 31 000 people per 1 000 000 population with a positive family history of colorectal cancer.

Genetic syndromes

Two genetic syndromes which predispose to colorectal cancer are familial adenomatous polyposis (FAP) and hereditary non-polyposis cancer of the colon (HNPCC).

FAP is characterised by the presence of hundreds of polyps lining the large intestine. It is caused by the presence of mutations in the adenomatous polyposis coli (APC) gene; over 80% of families with FAP have an identified APC mutation.[18] Its prevalence has been estimated at around 1 in every 8000–10 000 births[16] and it accounts for approximately 1% of cases of colorectal cancer.[19] Mountney et al.[20] reported a point prevalence of 1 per 35 000, which suggests that there are around 29 affected individuals per 1 000 000 population. If untreated, patients with FAP would usually die of colorectal cancer before the age of 40.[21]

The HNPCC mutation affects approximately 2–5% of colorectal cancer patients and is associated with a lifetime risk of 80%.[18] Data from Glasgow indicate a prevalence of around 190 per 1 000 000 population. HNPCC mutation carriers also have an increased risk of developing other cancers, such as those of the endometrium, ovary, pancreas and larynx.

Previous history of colorectal cancer

Patients who have undergone successful treatment of colorectal cancer are at increased risk of developing a second primary tumour (5% at 25 years).[12] Current survival data suggest that around 210 people per 1 000 000 population of each year's cohort will survive to 5 years and experience the same life expectancy as their peers. Because these are mainly elderly, the pool of 5+ years' survival with a previous history of colorectal cancer is likely to be between 1000 and 1500.

People with symptoms requiring diagnostic interventions

Primary care and referrals

The incidence of new colorectal cancers presenting to the general practitioner is around 3 per 10 000.[22] Patients may present with one or more of the following symptoms which may be associated with colorectal cancer: rectal bleeding, unexplained iron-deficiency anaemia, change in bowel habits, unexplained weight loss, abdominal pain, faecal incontinence, bowel obstruction and production of mucus from the rectum.

Many of these symptoms occur frequently in the general population and may have many medical explanations which causes problems for accurate diagnosis. Researchers have attempted to investigate the predictive value of symptoms for the diagnosis of colorectal cancer, most notably that of visible rectal bleeding. Rectal bleeding is very common, occurring in up to one in six of the general population each year.[23] However, colorectal cancer will be responsible for the bleeding in only a small proportion of these people. In one recent American study, consecutive patients attending clinics were asked if they had noticed rectal blood during the last 3 months and had not sought medical attention. Of 201 individuals who reported rectal bleeding, 6.5% were subsequently found to have cancer of the colon.[24] Goulston and Dent[25] also investigated this issue in a study of 145 patients consulting their general practitioner with rectal bleeding. Colorectal cancer was found responsible for the bleeding in 10% of patients. A similar study was conducted in The Netherlands to examine the predictive value of rectal bleeding in 290 patients aged between 18 and 75.[26] It was found that 20% of patients aged 60–75 and 2% of those aged 50–59 with rectal bleeding had colorectal cancer. Three variables were found to be significantly predictive of colorectal cancer, namely age, change in bowel habit and blood on or mixed with stool.

Approximately 5% of patients with colorectal cancer present asymptomatically or as a result of screening, 63% present symptomatically and 32% present as emergency admissions. Therefore, among a population of 1 000 000 people, 27 present to the health service asymptomatically, 342 symptomatically and 174 as emergencies.

In patients who present with symptoms of colorectal cancer, extra diagnostic investigation is required. British Society of Gastroenterology guidance[27] suggests a rate of at least 2000 per million each for FS and colonoscopy, although not all of these have symptoms suggesting cancer. Patients who present to the health services as emergencies may be suffering from obstruction or perforation. In these cases, a diagnosis of colorectal cancer is usually established after emergency laparotomy.

Confirmed disease requiring specific curative and caring interventions

The rate of progression of disease is variable. Some tumours may be very slow growing while in other cases, local and distant spread may be rapid and uncontrollable. For this reason, it is misleading to use the terms early and late as synonymous with the degree of spread of the disease. Prognosis and treatment are dependent upon the degree to which the cancer has advanced at the time of diagnosis, survival for advanced disease being very poor.

Dukes' staging of colorectal cancer, developed to define the degree of advancement, is a histological grading and does not include metastatic spread.[28] Union Internationale Contre le Cancer (UICC, 1987) modification of this staging is summarised in Table 4 (*see* overleaf) and detailed in Appendix II.

Data from the Wessex Colorectal Audit suggest that approximately 11% of patients are stage A at diagnosis, 33% are stage B, 19% are stage C, 23% are stage D and 13% are unknown (probably mainly C and D; Table 5, *see* overleaf). In a population of 1 000 000 people, one would expect 62 cases of stage A colorectal cancer, 178 cases of stage B, 105 cases of stage C and 127 cases of stage D, with 70 unstaged.

Table 4: Dukes' staging.

Stages

Stage I (A)	Tumour confined to mucosa and submucosa of the bowel wall
Stage II (B)	Tumour penetrating the muscle wall of the bowel
Stage III (C)	Metastasis to regional lymph nodes
Stage IV (D)	Distant metastasis (i.e. distant spread)

Table 5: Distribution of colorectal cancer at diagnosis (1994).

	Colon cases (per million)	Rectum cases (per million)	All cases (per million)
A	6.1 (33)	5.3 (29)	11 (62)
B	24.4 (132)	8.5 (46)	33 (178)
C	13.1 (71)	6.3 (34)	19 (105)
D	17.6 (96)	5.7 (31)	23 (127)
Not known	8.7 (47)	4.2 (23)	13 (70)
Total	69.8 (379)	30.2 (164)	100 (543)

Approximately 40% of patients survive to 5 years, at which point survivors have a life expectancy very similar to the normal population. Survival and treatment effectiveness are dependent on the stage of cancer at diagnosis.[29,30] The stage distribution of colorectal cancer at diagnosis and the associated 5-year survival for each group are shown in Tables 5 and 6.

Table 6: Five-year survival by stage.*

Stage	Colorectal (%)	Rectal (%)	Colon (%)	Rectosigmoid (%)
Overall	41	42	41	40
A	75	71	76	92
B	57	58	57	59
C	35	34	37	27
D	12	8	14	10
Not known	16	20	18	0

* Data from Wessex Colorectal Cancer Audit, 1999.

Consequences of disease

As a consequence of disease, supportive care may be required to relieve symptoms, provide nursing care and alleviate distress. In addition, terminal care may be provided for patients where cure is not achieved.

5 Services available, volumes and costs

This section describes the range of services that may be provided for patients with colorectal cancer at present and identifies the HRGs which cover these interventions, and the costs and volumes of these services. At present, only some of these services can be specified in terms of an HRG code.

There are no specific services for the primary prevention or early detection of colorectal cancer in the general population in the UK. Surveillance is offered in some areas for patients identified as being at increased risk of developing colorectal cancer. Diagnostic methods include colonoscopy, sigmoidoscopy, barium enema, histological assessment of biopsies, ultrasound, computed tomography (CT) scanning, immunoscintology and magnetic resonance imaging (MRI).

Curative treatment includes surgery with or without adjuvant radiotherapy and chemotherapy, and routine follow-up. Palliative care to achieve symptom control may include surgery, radiotherapy and chemotherapy. Terminal care can be based in the hospital, hospice or at home.

Primary prevention

Health promotion

Although direct causal relationships between lifestyle and the development of colorectal cancer are not clearly established, the relevant health promotion advice is provided by many districts (*see* Table 7). Such advice is usually provided in the form of general lifestyle advice and is not specific to colorectal cancer risk (HRGs for primary prevention are not yet defined).

Table 7: Primary prevention advice.

Risk factor	Advice
Diet	Increase intake of fruit and vegetables
Alcohol	Decrease alcohol consumption
Tobacco smoking	Stop smoking
Sedentary lifestyle	Physical activity should be taken at least three times per week for a minimum of 20 minutes on each occasion

Chemoprevention

There is some evidence that the regular use of non-steroidal anti-inflammatory drugs, including aspirin, may reduce the incidence of and mortality from colorectal cancer. However, there is no evidence on which to base an estimate of the frequency of advice to take or prescription for aspirin specifically to avoid colorectal cancer.

Early detection

Early detection of people at average risk

FOB testing and FS are the two most commonly advocated screening methods. General population screening for colorectal cancer is not currently offered within the NHS, but two trials of FOB and colonoscopy have been set up under the auspices of the UK National Screening Committee. At present, fewer than 5% of cases of colorectal cancer are detected by screening.

People at increased risk of colorectal cancer

Patients with a previous history of colorectal cancer, adenomas found symptomatically and ulcerative colitis are usually monitored routinely via colonoscopic surveillance. There are agreed protocols (e.g. Association of Gastroenterology guidelines) and patients who are known to be at substantial risk because of a positive family history or genetic predisposition may be offered a range of services locally or regionally. These may include routine screening surveillance, genetic testing, genetic counselling and, in the case of FAP patients, prophylactic colectomy once multiple adenomas have developed.

Investigations and diagnosis

Misdiagnosis by the GP can lead to delay before the patient is referred for specialist investigation. The most common misdiagnosis is haemorrhoids, often as a result of inadequate investigations. MacArthur and Smith[31] reported delays of over 3 months before hospital referral. There is, however, no strong evidence that longer delay leads to poorer outcomes. Delays can occur at two other stages: first, delays before the patient consults the GP, and second, delays between GP referral and treatment. Macadam[32] reported delays of many weeks in 50% of patients before consulting their GP. Studies have reported that the main reason for patient delay is that they did not consider their symptoms to be serious.[32]

A patient suspected of having colorectal cancer will be referred to a surgeon for diagnostic investigation. A very small number (< 5%) will have been detected through screening. Of the remaining patients, 25–40% may present as an emergency,[33] although this was generally lower in the Wessex Colorectal Cancer Audit (average 20%).

Diagnosis

Symptomatic patients undergo a number of diagnostic investigations including colonoscopy, sigmoidoscopy and double-contrast barium enema. Histological confirmation of the diagnosis is usually required before surgery. Patients with a diagnosis should undergo further investigation to provide information on cancer stage unless the findings are unlikely to influence management.[34] A number of techniques are used including ultrasound, CT scanning, immunoscintology and MRI. Patients who present as an emergency typically require urgent surgery and may have few investigations before proceeding to theatre.

Treatment services

Surgery

Surgery is the mainstay of treatment for the majority of patients. Between 70 and 90% with a diagnosis of colorectal cancer are considered suitable for surgical intervention, although in the Wessex Colorectal Cancer Audit the procedure was considered curative in only 47% of cases; the remainder were palliative or not stated. The proportion of patients presenting as an emergency is about 20%, but may be as low as 10%.[4] The chosen surgical procedure depends on two main factors: whether the patient presents electively or as an emergency, and the position of the tumour in the bowel.

The numbers, rates and costs by HRG for patients with a primary or secondary diagnosis of colorectal cancer are shown in Table 8.

From national hospital data for England (HES, 1994–95) there are 86 237 finished (inpatient and day case) consultant episodes (FCEs) for patients with a diagnosis of colorectal cancer. This is 1759 FCEs per million people, or 3.2 FCEs per new patient with colorectal cancer per year. These consume 514 000 bed-days, which is equivalent to 10 500 bed-days per million or 19 bed-days per new colorectal cancer patient

Table 8: Inpatient episodes for patients with malignancy of the colon/rectum in HRGs F31–F37 (1995–96 Hospital Episode Statistics, England).*

		n (total cases in HRG)	n (diagnosis of malignancy)	n (diagnosis of malignancy/ million)	LOS (malignant)	LOS all cases	Elective cost/FCE (£)	Emergency cost/FCE (£)	Elective cost (£)/ million (80%)	Emergency cost (£)/ million (20%)
F31	Large intestine. Complex procedure	9,512	6,744	138	(16.9)	14.8	3,860	4,306	426,191	118,857
F32	Large intestine. Very major procedure	19,390	11,463	234	(15.2)	13.3	3,331	3,761	623,616	176,013
F33	Large intestine. Major procedure with cc	3,697	862	17.6	(16.4)	13.2	2,835	3,389	39,917	11,929
F34	Large intestine. Major procedure without cc	6,780	938	19	(14.11)	8.8	2,217	2,606	33,698	9,904
F35	Large intestine. Endoscopy	113,632	4,951	101	(0.1)	0.5	464	493	37,483	9,957
F36	Large intestine > 69 with cc	43,748	13,184	270	6.4	904	1,017	1,240	219,573	66,978
F37	Large intestine < 70 without cc	21,940	4,996	102	3.2	657	845	827	68,950	16,863
									1,449,428	410,500
									Total cost	£1,859,928

* Costs derived from National Schedule of Reference Costs, 1998.[35]

per year. Of these, about 30% (509 FCEs per million) are due to surgical procedures on the large bowel HRGs (F31–F35); the remainder are in medical or other procedure HRGs. These surgical HRGs, however, account for 61% of the bed-days (6405 bed-days per million) and, depending upon the number of repeat procedures (i.e. endoscopy, colectomy, colostomy, procedure, etc.), may represent procedures to about 90% of newly diagnosed cancers. These cannot be assigned to stages, but assuming an equal split of 80/20 for elective/emergency HRG costs, the total cost for surgical FCEs (F31–F35) is £1 487 565.

Some patients with metastatic colorectal cancer are suitable for resection of the deposits in the liver. The numbers of liver procedures for patients with a primary diagnosis of colorectal cancer are shown in Table 9. By using the reference costs for these HRGs, the cost of liver procedures can be estimated at £9337 per million people.

Table 9: Liver procedures for patients with a diagnosis of colorectal cancer (1995–96 Hospital Episode Statistics).

	n	*n*/million	Cost/case (£)	Cost/million (£)
GO2 Complex	62	1.3	3,756	4,882.8
GO3 Very major	36	0.7	2,429	1,700.3
GO4 Major > 69 with cc	101	2.1	1,163	2,442.3
GO5 Major < 70 without cc	24	0.5	625	312.5
Total				£9,337.9

Thromboprophylaxis and antibiotic prophylaxis are usually used in patients who undergo colorectal surgery.

Of 4117 operated colorectal cancers in the Wessex Colorectal Cancer Audit, there were 1290 colostomies (31%) and 705 were permanent (17%). This represents 26 and 14% of all colorectal cancers, respectively. These patients require special support from a stoma nurse and the recurring cost of colostomy is estimated to be around £2000 per patient. This suggests a cost of about £150 000 per annum per million.

Some patients may require palliative surgery to reduce symptoms. Local relapse following apparently curative resection of rectal cancer may occur in 20–45% of patients depending on the cancer stage (108–250 per million).[36] Most recurrences occur within 5 years of the initial treatment.

Radiotherapy

Radiotherapy can be used to treat rectal carcinomas. This may be pre-operative, post-operative, primary radical or palliative. There is no established role for adjuvant radiotherapy in the management of cancer of the colon.

Estimated volumes and costs of radiotherapy are shown in Table 10. They are derived in the following way.

- **Pre-operative** radiotherapy is given to some patients with operable but locally advanced rectal cancers to shrink the tumour and enable it to be excised more readily and to prevent local recurrences, hence improving the chance of survival. Studies have also shown a reduction in local recurrence for lower-third rectal cancers of all types. Relevant HRG: W14 complex + imaging 4–12 fractions; estimated as 50% of A + B.
- **Post-operative.** Between 10 and 20% of patients with rectal carcinomas undergoing curative surgery are given post-operative radiotherapy. This group consists mainly of patients with stage C or B

Table 10: Estimated volumes and costs for radiotherapy for rectal cancer for a population of 1 000 000.

	Estimated rate	Number/million	HRG (cost)	Cost/million (£)
Pre-operative	50% A+B	37	W14 (£1,058)	39,146
Post-operative	20% B+C	20	W15 (£1,902)	19,020
			W16 (£2,390)	23,900
Primary radical	20% C+D	13	W15 (£1,902)	12,363
			W16 (£2,390)	15,535
Palliative	20% C+D	13	W04 (£616)	4,004
			W03 (£200)	1,300
Total				115,268

Radiotherapy HRG costs from Northampton Acute Trust, 1997.[37]

tumours, where tumour deposits are outside the wall and 'local' recurrence is a high risk. Radiotherapy is used to contain local spread of the disease, particularly within the pelvis where the disease becomes particularly unpleasant and distressing if recurrent. Relevant HRGs: W15 complex + imaging 13–23 fractions; W16 complex + imaging 24 fractions; estimated as 20% of B + C.

- **Primary radical** radiotherapy may be used in patients with inoperable rectal tumours or those with medical conditions that preclude them from surgery. Relevant HRGs: W15 complex + imaging 13–23 fractions; W16 complex + imaging 24 fractions; estimated as 20% of C + D.
- **Palliative** radiotherapy is used to reduce symptoms in patients with locally advanced rectal cancer who have not previously undergone radiotherapy. Relevant HRGs: W04 simple, no simulator 4–12 fractions; W03 simple, no simulator 0–3 fractions; estimated as 20% of C+D.

Chemotherapy

Chemotherapy is recommended for those with Dukes' stage C colorectal cancer. It is not normally provided for patients with stage A disease, but may be considered for stage B colorectal cancer, where H-nodes are negative but there is extracolonic local spread ('Bad B's'). Therefore, approximately 105 per 1 000 000 people may receive chemotherapy annually for colorectal cancer. However, there are few national data to confirm this. Depending upon the outcome of trials for stage B this may increase.

The usual regime is 5-fluorouracil and folinic acid (5-FUFA). HRGs for chemotherapy are not yet finalised but the draft grouping 'Simple, low cost' covers this regime. Costs for Northampton are estimated at £272 per patient.*

Palliative

Adjuvant chemotherapy may be given to patients with advanced or recurrent colorectal cancer for the palliation of symptoms. The mainstay treatment of palliative chemotherapy is 5-FU.

Because of the difficulties of identifying the diagnosis in statistical returns on chemotherapy courses, and the lack of information on outpatient activity, it is difficult to provide a useful estimate of chemotherapy costs for colorectal cancer.

---

* Since this chapter was written the National Institute for Clinical Excellence has produced guidance on a number of chemotherapeutic agents for colorectal cancer, *see* www.nice.org.uk.

Follow-up

Most patients are followed up as outpatients at intervals ranging from every 3 months to yearly. Investigations performed may include one or a combination of the following: clinical examination, colonoscopy, FS, barium enema, FOB tests, serum carcinoembryonic antigen (CEA) tests, CT scan, chest X-ray, full blood count, liver ultrasound and liver function testing.[38] HRGs for outpatient visits are not yet finalised or costed.

Support services

Palliative care

Palliative care is defined as '. . . active total care offered to a patient with a progressive illness and their family when it is recognised that the illness is no longer curable, in order to concentrate on the quality of life and alleviation of distressing symptoms within the framework of a co-ordinated service.'[39] Palliative care in general has been considered in detail in a separate chapter of the Needs Assessment Reviews.[40] The discussion here focuses mainly on the issues in relation to colorectal cancer, but the design and delivery of palliative care services need to be considered in relation to all patients requiring such care.

A wide range of palliative care services is usually available locally, including specialist palliative care services, such as hospices and mobile palliative care teams, and general services, including primary and hospital care. Voluntary and local authority services also continue to play a large role.

Previous studies of symptom frequency in those with terminal illness suggest that within a population of 1 000 000 people, 270 have pain, 151 have trouble breathing and 164 have symptoms of vomiting or nausea that require treatment. Most colorectal cancer patients with terminal illness usually experience more than one symptom.[40] Cancer patients have been shown to have a higher prevalence of anxiety and depression than the general population.[40] Approximately 106 family members and 80 patients per 1 000 000 may exhibit severe anxiety, fears or worries. These people may need access to more specialist services.

A preliminary estimate of the desirable level of costs of palliative care has been made by the National Council for Hospice and Specialist Palliative Care Services (*see* Table 11). (These are based on policy guidance and represent desired rather than actual levels of provision. It is likely that this overestimates costs in most districts.) These are very preliminary estimates, which will be refined over time, but they provide an initial view of the likely costs. These are based on annual deaths of 2800 per million and are therefore adjusted pro rata to estimate for the 320 deaths per year from colorectal cancer.

Table 11: Target level of resourcing for palliative services.

	Total cost/million (£)	Colorectal cost/million (£)
Community specialist palliative care team	850,000	97,100
Specialist palliative day care	1,000,000	114,300
Hospital palliative care teams	500,000–2,500,000	57,000–285,700
Specialist palliative inpatient care	3,800,000	434,300
Total		554,000–703,000

The Glasgow pilot of HBGs and HRGs for colorectal cancer

This section draws on the experience of Greater Glasgow Health Board (GGHB), which acted as a pilot site for sets of matrices covering three cancer sites including breast, lung and colorectal cancer between October 1996 and June 1997.[41] The summary matrix for colorectal cancer (adjusted for a population of 1 000 000) is shown in Table 12. It illustrates the total costs for a population of 1 000 000 and is based on the detailed matrices in Appendix IV.

Table 12: Colorectal cancer matrices from Glasgow exercise per 1 000 000 population.

Summary matrix	Promotion and primary prevention	Investigation and diagnosis	Initial care	Continuing care	Total
At risk	£106,980				
Presentation		£41,668	£371,200		
Confirmed disease			£3,749,676		
Continuing disease states				£?	
Total					£4,269,523

At present, HRG costs are only available for some services and interventions related to colorectal cancer. Where these are available they have been included in the matrices, and in their absence they have been completed using a variety of sources including price tariffs for GP fundholders, cost data from resource management departments and average specialty costs from routine financial returns. Given local variations, all cost data should be interpreted with caution.

When this pilot was carried out, Matrix 4 was concerned with the care of patients from palliation and supportive services. During the pilot, no information was available on the need for such services by patients with colorectal cancer in the GGHB area and this matrix was not completed. The summary matrix covers only the first three matrices.

6 Effectiveness of services and interventions

This section summarises the available evidence of the effectiveness and cost-effectiveness of services for colorectal cancer.

Primary prevention

Health promotion

There is a paucity of evidence on the effectiveness and cost-effectiveness of most health promotion activities, including lifestyle advice relevant to the prevention of colorectal cancer. Observational and correlation studies provide some support for reductions in colorectal cancer incidence due to lifestyle changes. However, given the complexity of the causal chain linking primary prevention to such reductions, it is difficult to be sure that the observed changes in health status are the result of a particular intervention under study.[42]

Chemoprevention

Evidence of the effectiveness of aspirin as a chemopreventive agent is equivocal with supporting evidence coming from nine observational studies[43–51] and negative evidence from one cohort,[52,53] one case–control[54] and one randomised trial.[55] Supporting observational studies have suggested that regular low-dose aspirin use correlates with a reduction in colorectal cancer risk of between 40 and 50%. Given the relatively low cost of aspirin and the potential health benefit, this issue should be kept under review.

Early detection

Early detection of people at average risk

There is interest in population screening for colorectal cancer. However, the supporting evidence on the effectiveness and cost-effectiveness of the available options is limited. The results of two recent randomised controlled trials of FOB screening have reported reductions in mortality from colorectal cancer of between 15 and 18% (UK and Danish studies, respectively).[56,57] Estimates of the cost per quality-adjusted life year (QALY) from the UK trial show FOB screening to be of similar cost-effectiveness to screening for breast cancer.[58] A multi-centre trial is currently under way in the UK to assess the effectiveness and cost-effectiveness of once-only FS screening for colorectal cancer, and two pilot studies of FOB and colonoscopy were initiated in 2000.[59]

Observational studies suggest that FS may be a more effective screening test then FOB testing. Case–control studies have suggested that it can reduce mortality from colorectal cancers by 60–80%.[60,61] However, it is likely that these figures overestimate the benefits given the biases inherent in observational studies.

Compliance with colorectal cancer screening protocols has been poor in UK trials to date and remains a concern of those interested in population screening. In the FOB testing trial, 57% of participants completed at least one screening but only 38% completed all the FOB tests they were offered.[62] Initial results available from one centre involved in the FS trial indicate a compliance rate of 44%,[62] but more recent studies suggest that compliance rates of around 60% can be achieved.[59]

Early detection of people at increased risk from colorectal cancer

There are inadequate data from well-designed clinical trials to demonstrate the effectiveness and thus cost-effectiveness of surveillance protocols for people known to be at increased risk from colorectal cancer.

In patients in whom polyps have been identified, their removal and histological assessment are common.[63] There are no data on the appropriate management of patients with small polyps not amenable to removal. One trial demonstrated that 3-year colonoscopic surveillance can be as effective as annual follow-up.[64] There is also some evidence that surveillance may only be justified in patients with tubovillous, villous or large adenomas in the rectosigmoid.[65]

There are few effectiveness data supporting reduced morbidity or mortality from routinely screening HNPCC patients. Some studies have suggested that prognosis can be improved in carriers but it is unclear whether this observation is due to surveillance or some other artefact (e.g. earlier diagnosis, longer lead time, improved awareness of signs and symptoms of disease).[66–68]

It is argued that surveillance screening of FAP patients is justified by studies comparing the incidence of malignancies in symptomatic patients with lower rates in asymptomatic cases.[69] However, no evaluations are cited in the literature to date. Once multiple adenomas have developed in these patients the recommended curative treatment is colectomy.[70,71]

Direct evidence of benefit from routine surveillance of patients at increased risk because of a positive family history is also weak. Several studies have demonstrated an increased prevalence of polyps in relatives over controls.[72,73] However, the link to final health outcome is not established.

Routine surveillance of patients with diseases associated with increased risk of developing colorectal cancer (e.g. ulcerative colitis, Crohn's disease) is recommended by the British Society of Gastroenterology. However, as before, there is a lack of documented evidence of health benefit in such patients.

Investigations and diagnosis

Referrals

There is evidence of delays in patient referrals at three stages from the onset of symptoms: first, delays before consulting the GP; second, delays before patients are referred for specialist treatment; and third, in some cases there may be delays from the time of referral until diagnosis and treatment.[32,33,69,74–79] A recent review of the research evidence concluded that there is little to suggest that such delays affect outcomes.[29,32,74,77,80–82]

Diagnosis

The main diagnostic methods (colonoscopy, sigmoidoscopy and double-contrast barium enema) are reported to have similar costs and effectiveness when the latter are used in combination.[83–85] Some studies show that effectiveness improves with operator practice.[86–88]

There is a lack of evidence on the effectiveness and cost-effectiveness of other techniques used (ultrasound, CT scanning, immunoscintology and MRI) in the diagnosis of colorectal cancer.

Treatment

Surgery

Patients undergoing surgery have an estimated average survival of 3 years. However, 5-year survival is dependent upon stage at diagnosis, but after that time the survival curve is no different to that of the rest of the population.

Specialisation

Depending on local provision, surgery may be performed by specialist surgeons or by surgeons with no specialist interest in colorectal surgery. Several observational studies have revealed substantial variations between surgeons in terms of their patient outcomes.[89–100] Such observations are reported to remain after case-mix, skill of the surgeon and chance variations are taken into account.[34] However, a review of the evidence that specialisation and increased patient volume improve outcomes concluded that the available research evidence is contradictory.[15]

Technique

Survival chances are better in patients with rectal cancer when the tumour is removed completely. There is some evidence from non-randomised studies that total mesorectal excision (TME), a surgical technique in which great care is taken to remove all the tissue around the tumour, improves survival and reduces local recurrence rates. It is, however, a longer procedure requiring more theatre time, hospital bed-days and in some cases a temporary stoma.[101,102] The relative cost-effectiveness of this procedure has not been assessed formally. Thus it is not clear that the potential for improved outcomes justifies the required increased resource use. A recent systematic review concluded that 'randomised controlled trials, perhaps comparing total mesorectal excision with conventional surgery plus radiotherapy, are required . . . .'.[16]

Prophylaxis

A review of randomised trials of antimicrobial prophylaxis concluded that it is effective for the prevention of infections in patients who undergo colorectal surgery.[103] Surgical wound infection rates in control patients ranged from 32 to 58%, compared with a pooled figure of 11.1% for patients given antimicrobial prophylaxis. It is not possible to identify the most effective regimen.[16] The Antiplatelet Trialists' Collaboration reported a reduction in the risk of deep vein thrombosis with antiplatelet therapy from 33.6 to 24.8%. The odds of pulmonary embolism were also lower with therapy (1.0% vs. 2.7%).[104]

Patients presenting electively have a higher chance of survival than emergency admissions.[4,90,92–94,97,105] However, a recent review concluded that it is not clear how such emergency admissions can be avoided or outcomes improved.[34]

Radiotherapy

Data from randomised trials demonstrate that adjuvant radiotherapy can reduce local recurrence in patients with operable rectal cancer. However, there is a lack of economic analysis in this area.

Pre-operative

There is strong evidence from meta-analyses (carried out by the Colorectal Cancer Collaborative Group) of pre-operative radiotherapy trials that local recurrence among patients undergoing curative surgery for rectal tumours can be reduced by about 50%.[16] Only a small reduction in overall mortality (4%) was found. However, there were significantly fewer deaths from colorectal cancer in the pre-operative radiotherapy group.[16] The Scottish Intercollegiate Guidelines Network (SIGN) guidelines on colorectal cancer also reviewed the existing randomised trials. They concluded that pre-operative radiotherapy should be given to patients who are considered operable but have tethered rectal cancers.[69,106,107]

Post-operative

A meta-analysis of the results from six randomised trials provides evidence of a 33% reduction in local recurrences with post-operative therapy (stage B and C rectal tumours). As with pre-operative radiotherapy, only a very small overall survival advantage is observed.[16]

Pre-operative vs. post-operative

The Colorectal Cancer Collaborative Group's meta-analysis provides evidence of reduced local recurrences and moderately improved survival in patients receiving pre-operative as opposed to post-operative radiotherapy.[16] This finding is also supported by a study which directly compared pre-operative and post-operative radiotherapy and found that there were fewer recurrences among curatively resected patients with a 1-week pre-operative regime than with a 6-week post-operative regime.[108] However, after a systematic review of the research evidence the SIGN guidelines were unable to reach a conclusion on this issue.

Primary

Primary radical radiotherapy has been shown to be an effective treatment for patients with inoperable rectal tumours or those with medical conditions precluding them from surgery. One study found that small tumours were likely to regress following radiotherapy. Larger tumours were rendered either operable or regressed sufficiently to allow relief from symptoms.[109]

Palliative

Two studies reported subjective improvement of symptoms in 80–90% of patients with presacral recurrences after radical surgery and no prior radiotherapy.[110,111]

Chemotherapy

Adjuvant

The effectiveness of adjuvant chemotherapy in Dukes' stage C colorectal cancers was assessed in a recent systematic overview of randomised trials. The pooled results of 25 studies evaluating prolonged (>3 months) systemic chemotherapy using 5-FUFA suggest an absolute increase in 5-year survival of 6% (range 2–10%).[16] The data reviewed in this area often come from trials including patients with colon cancer only. Thus there is less direct evidence for patients with Dukes' stage C rectal cancers. However, combined chemotherapy and radiotherapy has demonstrated a greater survival benefit in patients with Dukes' stage B and C rectal cancers than radiotherapy alone.[112]

There is a lack of relevant evidence to support the use of adjuvant chemotherapy in patients with Dukes' stage B colon or rectal cancer and these patients should be entered into clinical trials (e.g. the QUASAR study). The use of chemotherapy is not supported by the available evidence in patients with Dukes' stage A colorectal cancer.

There is no consensus as to the most effective chemotherapy regime. Current evidence suggests that the FUFA combination should be recommended but there is no evidence on which of the several FUFA regimens in use is optimal.[16] A 1-week post-operative infusion of 5-FU directly to the liver through the portal vein may reduce mortality by 12%. However, this technique requires further investigation before specific recommendations can be made (e.g. AXIS study).[16]

There is very little evidence on the cost-effectiveness of adjuvant chemotherapy in colorectal cancer patients. Two economic evaluations suggest that it may be relatively cost-effective in patients with Dukes' stage C cancers given intraportally or systemically.[113,114]

Palliative

Chemotherapy in advanced colorectal cancer can have substantial palliative benefit. However, supporting economic evidence is still lacking. Many studies have shown symptomatic benefits and two randomised controlled trials have demonstrated survival advantages of 5–6 months.[115,116] 5-FU remains the mainstay of treatment. However, the optimum regimen is unknown.*

---

* See NICE guidance produced since this chapter was written, www.nice.org.uk.

Palliative care

There is very little research evidence available on the effectiveness and cost-effectiveness of different ways of providing palliative care services for patients with incurable colorectal cancer. Current evidence suggests that a mix of services is necessary and the views of patients and their families should be the main criterion for evaluation of this service. Townsend et al.[117] found that, in ideal circumstances, up to 70% of terminally ill patients would prefer to be cared for at home and for about half of these patients the final choice was home care, allowing for the pressure on carers as the illness progressed. Moreover, of those who finally died in hospital, 63% had stated a preference to die at home. A recent study found that as death approached, patients changed their preference for terminal care from hospital or home to hospice care.[118] Approximately 30% of cancer deaths included in the Regional Study of Care for the Dying died at home.[119]

Overall, there is very little evidence to support the use of conventional care alone (both hospital and community based).[120-125] The main problem of caring for terminally ill patients in a general hospital setting is felt to be the inevitable incompatibility between the demands of acute care and the needs of the terminally ill and their relatives for open-ended conversation and emotional support. Moreover, competing for resources with those who are curable may mean that terminally ill patients have less than adequate provision of care.

North American studies have suggested that the inpatient hospice model is at least as effective as conventional methods of inpatient care and the costs of hospice care are considered to be similar to conventional methods.[123,126-134] One American study found that hospice and specialist palliative care services used a higher number of nursing staff per patient than conventional care, but fewer procedures.[132] There is little evidence on costs or effectiveness from the UK.

There is evidence that specialist palliative care teams can provide more effective services than conventional care methods.[129,135-143] There is some weak evidence to suggest that delayed referrals to specialist palliative care services can increase the time spent in hospital by terminally ill colorectal cancer patients and lead to increased morbidity.[144,145] Home care teams have been shown to reduce the length of stay in hospital of terminally ill patients, some also demonstrating equal or reduced costs.[144,145] Several reports have recommended the use of multi-disciplinary palliative care teams.[146,147]

There is very little comparative evidence for other palliative care services, such as hospital support services, day care, practical support and respite care and hospice at home.

Follow-up

The frequency and nature of follow-up vary widely and there is very little evidence on the benefits of specific and more intensive regimes. Thus, overall the majority of these services cannot be shown to be cost-effective at present.[148-156]

Summary of recommendations

Table 13 (see opposite) provides a summary of the key recommendations for the provision of colorectal cancer services.

Table 13: Summary of recommendations.

	Strength of recommendation	Evidence
Primary prevention		
Health promotion advice	C	III/II
Chemoprevention	C	II
Early detection		
Population screening programme	B	I
Screening high-risk groups	C	III
Surgery		
Access to specialist surgeon	C	III
Radiotherapy		
Adjuvant radiotherapy	B	III
Primary radical	B	III
Palliative	B	III
Chemotherapy		
Adjuvant chemotherapy	A	I
Palliative	A/B	II/I
Follow-up		
Current provision	C	IV
Palliative care		
Specialist palliative care teams	B/A	II/I
Inpatient hospice facilities	B/A	II

See Appendix 5 for definitions.

7 Models of care

Structure of services for colorectal cancer

The recommendations of the Calman–Hine report[157] should form the basis of models of care for patients with colorectal cancer. The recommended structure is 'based on a network of expertise in cancer care reaching from primary care through Cancer Units in district hospitals to Cancer Centres'. Specialisation in cancer care is achieved via three levels of care:

- primary care
- the cancer unit
- the cancer centre.

Primary care must be the focus of care, with effective communication taking place between primary care teams, cancer units and cancer centres. Designated cancer units should be available in most district general hospitals with a full range of supportive services. They should be able to support clinical teams with sufficient expertise and facilities to manage common cancers, including colorectal cancer. The unit should ensure close integration of primary and secondary care and the identification of appropriate rapid referral patterns for patients with symptoms indicating a high risk of malignancy. Designated cancer centres should provide expertise in the management of all cancers, including referrals of more complicated common cancers from cancer units. They should provide specialist diagnostic and therapeutic techniques including radiotherapy.

The application of this model to colorectal cancer services is likely to concentrate the delivery of surgical and chemotherapy services within cancer centres, as well as requiring consideration of the organisation of colonoscopy and surveillance.

Options for colorectal cancer services

This section draws together the evidence on alternative treatments and interventions for colorectal cancer. Given that cancer treatment remains a high priority area for health care commissioners, it is assumed that the decision facing policy makers is *how* to treat colorectal cancer rather than *whether* to treat.

The three main areas in which services for colorectal cancer could be extended are:

- primary prevention – by reducing exposure to factors thought to increase an individual's risk of colorectal cancer
- early detection – by introducing general population screening or screening subgroups known to be at increased risk for colorectal cancer
- treatment – by treating symptomatic disease.

From these categories a list of service options can be drawn up. These include:

- faecal occult blood screening of the general population
- screening first-degree relatives of patients diagnosed with colorectal cancer
- once-only flexible sigmoidoscopy screening of the general population
- systematic follow-up of adenoma patients by endoscopy
- radiotherapy after supposedly curative surgical resection of rectal cancer
- chemotherapy after supposedly curative surgical resection of stage C colon cancer
- surgical resection of hepatic liver metastases for advanced disease.

Primary prevention interventions are not considered further in this section given the lack of direct evidence on the effectiveness of health promotion activities. While some estimates of effect exist, great uncertainty surrounds the costs of such activities and the timing of related health benefits.

The other main area excluded from analysis is the follow-up of patients who have had a supposedly curative resection and aggressive treatment of recurrence. Despite little evidence of effectiveness from randomised trials, this practice is widely established. The problem is in two stages. First, is it worth screening asymptomatic people for recurrence? Second, is it worth treating recurrence once it has been identified? The second issue is more complex because it requires an estimate of the numbers who will benefit and the extent of the benefit, which is rarely reported. Another problem for evaluation in this area is that much of the benefit of follow-up may come from the reassurance provided merely by 'going through the motions' of the monitoring process. Thus, this area is not considered further other than to note the need for further research.

The evidence on the costs and benefits of each option in turn is now considered in order to produce some comparable data and attempt to rank interventions in terms of a common unit of effectiveness.

Faecal occult blood screening of the general population

The MRC trial of faecal occult blood screening for colorectal cancer in the general population reported a reduction in colorectal cancer mortality of 15% in the screened group. This screening trial was also the subject of an economic evaluation lasting more than 10 years. The additional costs of the screening population were £3 058 016 per 100 000 population. When the results of the clinical paper were adjusted for a population of 100 000, the cost per life saved was £37 293.[56,58] The UK National Screening Committee (NSC) sponsored two sites to assess the feasibility, public acceptance and cost-effectiveness of colorectal cancer screening using FOB and colonoscopy for those with strong positive FOB tests. In the mean time, formal advice from the NSC was that no new screening programmes should be introduced pending the outcome of these pilot trials.

Screening first-degree relatives of patients diagnosed with colorectal cancer

There have been no randomised trials to establish the efficacy of screening the relatives of colorectal cancer patients. The following estimates are based on the data of Houlston et al.[72] In England and Wales, 664 cases of colorectal cancer occurred in patients aged less than 45, generating 2445 first-degree relatives (60% parents, 40% siblings). These people would undergo colonoscopic surveillance every 5 years, except for those in whom adenomas were detected, who would be screened every 3 years (11%). Assuming an average life expectancy of 40 years for siblings and 15 years for parents, a total of 13 122 colonoscopies would be required costing a total of £3.5 million. It is estimated that screening would detect 244 cases of colorectal cancer. Of these, only 65% would represent lives saved since a proportion would undergo curative resection even if presenting symptomatically. Thus, 159 lives would be saved at a cost per life saved of £22 090. These estimates do not consider the costs of identifying, contacting and counselling relatives. However, these are likely to be small relative to the costs of investigation. The figures also assume 100% compliance and no net effects on treatment costs.

Once-only flexible sigmoidoscopy screening of the general population

There is no randomised trial evidence on the efficacy of screening for colorectal cancer by once-only FS although a multi-centre trial is now under way in the UK. The following calculations are based on a national screening programme consisting of a single FS at age 58 and colonoscopic surveillance for those found to have high-risk adenomas. A screening interval of 5 years is assumed and three screening rounds are built into the following calculations. There are about 600 000 people aged 58 years in the UK. Assuming 45% compliance, it would cost approximately £60 million to offer the screening to the entire population (FS, £179; colonoscopy, £267; histological assessment of one polyp, £33). Based on the calculations of Atkin et al.,[158] adjusting for a compliance of 45%, it is estimated that 2249 colorectal cancer deaths would be prevented. This equates to a cost per life saved of £26 814.

Systematic follow-up of adenoma patients by endoscopy

One evaluation found that 25% of the total costs of a screening programme were due to adenoma follow-up demonstrating the potential significance of this intervention.[159] However, there is no randomised trial evidence on the health gain of adenoma follow-up by any protocol. Ransohoff et al.[160] calculated that 226 colonoscopic investigations would have to be carried out in order to save one life. This calculation was based on 5-yearly colonoscopy follow-up of a 50-year-old man who had had an adenoma excised. This protocol was estimated to avert around 75% of the colorectal cancer deaths which would have resulted from recurrence. Assuming the cost of colonoscopy is £267, the cost per life saved is £60 342.

Radiotherapy after supposedly curative surgical resection of rectal cancer

A recent meta-analysis concluded that only a small overall survival advantage is observed in patients receiving post-operative radiotherapy.[16] Assuming that 10 000 cases of rectal cancer are diagnosed each year and that 61% are at stages B and C, 6100 patients are eligible for post-operative radiotherapy. It is assumed that a fraction costs £100 on an outpatient basis and that each patient receives 20 fractions. The other costs associated with treatment such as the simulator, planning sessions and clinic visits are assumed to cost £1000 per patient. About 10% of patients suffer an adverse reaction to therapy requiring a 5-day stay in hospital at a cost of £127 per day. The total cost for 6100 patients would be around £18.7 million and an additional 610 lives would be saved. Thus, the cost per life saved is £30 635.

Chemotherapy after supposedly curative surgical resection of stage C colon cancer

Adjuvant chemotherapy in Dukes' stage C colonic cancers was estimated to reduce mortality by around 6%. Approximately 4400 patients are diagnosed with stage C colon cancer each year. The cost of one cycle of chemotherapy on a day-care basis is £319 and an average of eight cycles per patient is assumed. Approximately 30% of patients experience side-effects requiring inpatient admission. The same cost and length of stay assumptions are used as for radiotherapy above. The total cost of treatment is around £15 000 000 and an additional 270 lives would be saved. The cost per life saved is £56 342.

Surgical resection of hepatic liver metastases for advanced disease

Expert opinion suggests that 5% of cases of metastatic colorectal cancer could be cured as a result of resection if guidelines for case selection were carefully adhered to. Each year, 6714 patients present to the health service with advanced colorectal cancer. The mortality rate in these patients following initial admission is 31% and these patients are not considered further.[166] Those who survive will undergo a CT scan to establish the extent of their disease and 5% of these will be eligible for surgical resection. The operation lasts around 4 hours and results in an inpatient stay of 15 days. Theatre time is assumed to cost £5.55 per minute and the same assumptions are made about the costs of an inpatient's stay as for radiotherapy and chemotherapy above. The total cost of treatment is approximately £1.7 million and if 20% of those undergoing surgery are cured, 46 lives are saved. The cost per life saved is £36 385.

Summary

The above results are drawn together in Table 14.

Table 14: Cost per life saved for alternative interventions in colorectal cancer.

Intervention	Cost per life saved (£)
Screening first-degree relatives	22,090
Flexible sigmoidoscopy screening	26,814
Post-operative radiotherapy for rectal cancer	30,635
Resection of liver metastases	36,385
Faecal occult blood screening	37,293
Chemotherapy for colon cancer	56,342
Adenoma follow-up	60,342

Limitations

Given the poor quality of some of the underlying evidence, the results of this exercise must be interpreted with caution by health care commissioners. Potential users of the information must make a judgement about the quality of this data and, in particular, whether it is strong enough for them to base their decisions on. The cost data are particularly difficult to assess, since local cost variations may be substantial and might have an effect on the ranking of these options. Over the next few years costing information should become more reliable and inclusive, and it may then be possible to assess the costs per life saved better.

Some would argue that the measure of effectiveness applied, i.e. lives saved, is unsatisfactory since it does not consider the length of life gained. The application of this unit of outcome implies that saving the life of a 40-year-old has the same value as saving the life of an 80-year-old, a value judgement that many would disagree with. However, the affected age group is relatively homogenous and such comparisons do have some value. To the extent that this is an important issue, it could be argued that it supports the above ranking since the younger age groups are the ones who will tend to benefit most from screening programmes.

Quality-of-life considerations are also omitted from the above calculations. However, an examination of the evidence for colorectal cancer appears to broadly confirm the findings of a study of the breast screening literature which concluded that quality adjustment of life-year gains made little difference to rankings-based life-year gains alone.[162] The main concern regarding quality of life in colorectal cancer treatment relates to adjustment to a colostomy. However, a study of the post-operative life of such patients found them to be 'normal' on a variety of indicators.[163] Only during the terminal stages of disease are the effects likely to be so unpleasant as to be important. This stage of disease is often short for many patients such that lives saved may form a reasonable basis for comparing the costs and benefits of alternative interventions.

8 Outcome measures

The New NHS White Paper provided six principles which underlie the proposed changes. This section outlines the way in which these principles can be used to assess the performance of the NHS in relation to colorectal cancer services by adopting the National Performance Framework. It is designed to support the broader goals highlighted by the White Paper and focus on the results achievable by the health service in a way which is meaningful to all parties concerned.

The six areas of the performance framework are:

1 health improvement
2 fair access
3 effective delivery of appropriate health care
4 efficiency
5 patient/carer experience
6 health outcomes of NHS care.

Table 15 (*see* overleaf) shows how colorectal cancer could be assessed against each of the six areas.

Table 15: Potential performance indicators in colorectal cancer.

Area	Performance indicators
Health improvement	Standardised mortality ratios
Fair access	Waiting times
Effective delivery of appropriate health care:	
Known to be effective	Percentage of patients receiving appropriate treatments
Appropriate to need	Standardised treatment rates by type
	Terminal care
Timeliness	*Stage at diagnosis*
Service organisation	Implementation of Calman–Hine recommendations
Efficiency	Unit costs of care
	Cost per HRG
Patient/carer experience	Waiting times from initial consultation and access to specialist services
	Waiting times from referral to time test results available
	Waiting times from diagnosis to treatment
	Patient anxiety (during diagnosis, treatment, terminal care and follow-up)
	Patient satisfaction with information provision/ involvement in care/dignity in terminal care/symptom control/outcome
	Reassurance (e.g. high-risk patients)
	Complaints
Health outcomes of NHS care:	
NHS success in reducing levels of risk	*Percentage of population adopting low-risk behaviours (e.g. diet)*
	Early detection of risk (?)
	Genetic counselling (?)
NHS success in reducing level of disease, impairment and complications of treatment	Cancer registrations
	Asymptomatic cancers detected at an early stage
	Incidence of avoidable complications (e.g. recurrence, distant metastases, complications of treatment)
	Percentage of patients requiring colostomy
NHS success in restoring function and improving quality of life of patients/carers	*Measurement of physical and mental health status using appropriate measure*
NHS success in reducing premature death	5-year survival
	5-year survival standardised for age and stage

Italics indicate where new data would need to be collected.

9 Information and research requirements

Data requirements

The data requirements of the National Performance Framework (*see* Section 7) are considerable and, if implemented fully, would require the collection of a considerable amount of new data. These data would include:

- stage at diagnosis
- 5-year survival standardised for age and stage
- percentage of asymptomatic cancers detected at an early stage
- incidence of avoidable complications
- percentage of patients requiring colostomy
- percentage of patients adopting low-risk behaviours
- early detection of risk
- provision of genetic counselling
- measurement of physical and health status
- patient anxiety
- patient satisfaction
- provision of reassurance
- number of complaints.

Every region has a cancer registry providing information on the incidence and mortality rates of colorectal cancer. The introduction of the collection of the above data, in particular stage at diagnosis, will increase the potential uses of this disease register.

The experience of the patient and carer(s) is, of course, of paramount importance. In a population of 1 000 000, there are 543 new cases of colorectal cancer per year, of which 309 are terminal. Colorectal cancer is, therefore, a major cause of mortality and morbidity in patients, and the cause of considerable morbidity for family members and carers. Commissioners of cancer services should ensure the collection of appropriate data to ensure the experience of the patient and carer(s) is the best possible.

The role of HBGs in decision making

HBGs have been developed by the National Case-Mix Office as a means of bringing together information on the patient, the services used, costs and (eventual) outcomes. The above sections demonstrate how they might be used in a needs assessment of colorectal cancer; demonstration projects involving other diseases and client groups have also been carried out.

However, further work is required to identify their optimal role in commissioning decisions. For example, the level of detail and amount of effort devoted to the matrices still needs to be determined in order to provide an appropriate balance between the cost of the information and its value in supporting decisions. Another issue is how to achieve consistency and accuracy in data quality so that HBGs can be used in comparisons between the services provided to different populations.

The development of clinical information systems and the electronic patient record should address many of these issues. However, flows of reliable patient-based information that can be used for planning and monitoring will take a number of years to establish.

A model of the natural history of disease

Observational studies and clinical trials have revealed data on the natural history of colorectal cancer that are potentially useful in planning decisions in general and the design of research programmes in particular. However, these data have not been systematically assembled, evaluated, graded and combined into a model for general use.

For example, data collected during the MRC trial of population screening by FOBT could be used to estimate key parameters in the natural history of adenomas and cancer. If these data were assembled into a model then subsequent screening trials, such as the evaluation of FS screening, could have been designed to maximise the efficacy of the intervention. Similar arguments apply to the treatment of symptomatic disease. Variations in medical decision making create 'natural experiments' which can give hints (no more than this) about the way disease progresses. Models of this type would allow the effects of proposed trial protocols to be simulated and revised; the findings of the trial could then be used to validate the model.

The result would be a powerful tool for planning and treatment decision making.

Effectiveness and efficiency

This report has highlighted the lack of information about the clinical and cost-effectiveness of services for patients with colorectal cancer. There is a dearth of information on the relative costs and benefits of preventive activities, screening of average and high-risk individuals, radiotherapy and chemotherapy. The shortage is especially notable in palliative care services, follow-up of treated cases and options for genetics services. More research is needed into the efficacy and cost-effectiveness of the current practice of regular follow-up of patients with a history of colorectal cancer. At present there is a lack of evidence that follow-up is effective in detecting disease recurrence at an earlier stage or reduces disease-specific mortality. Likewise further research is required on the relative costs and benefits of different methods of providing palliative care services. It is essential that the needs and opinions of both patients and carers are taken into account. There are many uncertainties about the clinical and cost-effectiveness of proposals for the organisation of colorectal cancer genetics services. Recommendations have been made in some areas but these are not strongly supported by the existing evidence base. The economic analysis provided in Section 6 of this report is a first attempt to rank selected interventions in terms of a common unit of effectiveness. However, the limitations of this exercise must be noted and commissioners must interpret the results with caution.

Implications of cancer genetics for colorectal cancer services

In recent years, there has been an increase in the number of individuals seeking advice about the risks of developing cancer against the background of their family history. This demand is likely to grow given the ever increasing publicity in the medical literature and popular press. Current services are unco-ordinated and vary from region to region. There are no agreed protocols for determining the level of individual risk or the management of those considered to be at medium or high risk. Health care commissioners need to determine how they are going to respond to the growing demand for colorectal cancer genetic services in their area.

A report by the Genetics Sub-Committee of the Priority Areas Cancer Team in Scotland[164] states that there are three possible options:

- to maintain the current fragmented service
- population screening to identify patients at risk
- to develop a system of screening patients at relatively high risk of developing colorectal cancer.

Current evidence suggests that the third option of a selective approach to screening may be the most cost-effective solution since the incidence of these cancers is very small in the general population. It suggests that the basic aims of genetic services for people concerned about colorectal cancer should be:

- to provide advice and counselling about familial risks
- to identify those who are at medium or high risk on the basis of their family history
- to establish effective screening protocols for the management of these patients.

This report stresses that successful implementation of proposals for colorectal cancer genetic services will require close co-operation between all the parties involved – primary care, genetics clinics and those providing the screening services. The initial point of contact for many individuals concerned about familial cancer risk is primary care. Clinics should provide guidance for primary care staff to assist them in assessing patient risk. Individuals considered to be at medium or high risk should be referred to genetics clinics for a more detailed risk assessment. Agreement is also required on the appropriate screening protocols for individuals at medium and high levels of risk.

The report goes on to define medium-risk individuals as those at three times the population risk and suggests that they should be referred to the relevant cancer unit for surveillance in line with agreed protocols. High-risk individuals are defined as those at over three times the population risk, and it is recommended that they be seen by the cancer genetics co-ordinator for appropriate counselling and DNA testing where a disease-specific mutation has been identified in the family.[164]

Cancer registries

Cancer registers contain valuable information about the incidence and prevalence of malignant disease in the population. However, the failure of registers to be linked into routine health service activity data has greatly limited the application of this information for practical planning and monitoring. Within the new information strategy, effort will need to be put into practical linkage of clinical information to registries, so that an accurate picture of the clinical condition of individuals and their treatments can be collated and used for analysis. To achieve this requires a solution to the issues of confidentiality and the use of named data, and greater consistency and accuracy of clinical record keeping. This is particularly so in the collection of staging information, which is often inadequately recorded in the patient's notes.

While much of this work will be carried out centrally, local organisations (both providers and commissioners) will need to develop better linkages of information systems, provide appropriate incentives to ensure accurate and timely data, and invest in the informatics skills required to turn the raw patient-based data into useful information. This will require investment, but offers a way to improve the efficiency, effectiveness and equity of services. In addition, the proposed collection of a minimum data set by hospices will provide much needed data on the numbers and types of patients receiving hospice-based palliative care.

Cancer trials

As noted in this chapter, there are still unanswered questions about the most effective forms of prevention, early detection, treatment and palliative care for patients with colorectal cancer. Commissioners of health care services should ensure that relevant clinical trials are supported as part of the framework of long-term agreements.

Appendix I: Codings and classifications relevant to colorectal cancer

Diagnosis codes relevant to colorectal cancer (ICD 10)

C180   Mal. neop – Caecum.
C182   Mal. neop – Ascending colon.
C183   Mal. neop – Hepatic flexure.
C184   Mal. neop – Transverse colon.
C185   Mal. neop – Splenic flexure.
C186   Mal. neop – Descending colon.
C187   Mal. neop – Sigmoid colon.
C188   Mal. neop – Overlapping lesion of colon.
C189   Mal. neop – Colon, unspecified.
C19X   Mal. neop – Rectosigmoid junction.
C20X   Mal. neop – Rectum.
C218   Overlapping lesion of rectum, anus and anal canal.

Procedure codes relevant to colorectal cancer (OPCS 4)

H041   Panproctocolectomy and ileostomy.
H042   Panproctocolectomy and anastomosis of ileum to anus and create pouch hfq.
H043   Panproctocolectomy and anastomosis of ileum to anus nec.
H048   Total excision of colon and rectum OS.
H049   Total excision of colon and rectum unspecified.
H051   Total colectomy and anastomosis of ileum to rectum.
H052   Total colectomy and ileostomy and creation of rectal fistula hfq.
H053   Total colectomy and ileostomy nec.
H061   Extended right hemicolectomy and end-to-end anastomosis.
H062   Extended right hemicolectomy and anastomosis of ileum to colon.
H063   Extended right hemicolectomy and anastomosis nec.
H064   Extended right hemicolectomy and ileostomy hfq.
H068   Extended excision of right hemicolon OS.
H069   Extended excision of right hemicolon unspecified.
H071   Right hemicolectomy and end-to-end anastomosis of ileum to colon.
H072   Right hemicolectomy and side-to-side anastomosis of ileum to transverse colon.
H073   Right hemicolectomy and anastomosis nec.
H074   Right hemicolectomy and ileostomy hfq.
H078   Other excision of right hemicolon OS.
H079   Other excision of right hemicolon unspecified.
H081   Transverse colectomy and end-to-end anastomosis.
H082   Transverse colectomy and anastomosis of ileum to colon.
H083   Transverse colectomy and anastomosis nec.
H084   Transverse colectomy and ileostomy hfq.
H085   Transverse colectomy and exteriorisation of bowel nec.
H088   Excision of transverse colon OS.
H089   Excision of transverse colon unspecified.
H091   Left hemicolectomy and end-to-end anastomosis of colon to rectum.
H092   Left hemicolectomy and end-to-end anastomosis of colon to colon.

H093 Left hemicolectomy and anastomosis nec.
H094 Left hemicolectomy and ileostomy hfq.
H095 Left hemicolectomy and exteriorisation of bowel nec.
H098 Excision of left hemicolon OS.
H099 Excision of left hemicolon unspecified.
H101 Sigmoid colectomy and end-to-end anastomosis of ileum to rectum.
H102 Sigmoid colectomy and anastomosis of colon to rectum.
H103 Sigmoid colectomy and anastomosis nec.
H104 Sigmoid colectomy and ileostomy hfq.
H105 Sigmoid colectomy and exteriorisation of bowel nec.
H108 Excision of sigmoid colon OS.
H109 Excision of sigmoid colon unspecified.
H111 Colectomy and end-to-end anastomosis of colon to colon nec.
H112 Colectomy and side-to-side anastomosis of ileum to colon nec.
H113 Colectomy and anastomosis nec.
H114 Colectomy and ileostomy nec.
H115 Colectomy and exteriorisation of bowel nec.
H118 Other excision of colon OS.
H119 Other excision of colon unspecified.
H121 Excision of diverticulum of colon.
H122 Excision of lesion of colon nec.
H123 Destruction of lesion of colon nec.
H128 Extirpation of lesion of colon OS.
H129 Extirpation of lesion of colon unspecified.
H131 Bypass of colon by anastomosis of ileum to colon.
H132 Bypass of colon by anastomosis of caecum to sigmoid colon.
H133 Bypass of colon by anastomosis of transverse colon to sigmoid colon.
H134 Bypass of colon by anastomosis of transverse colon to rectum.
H135 Bypass of colon by anastomosis of colon to rectum nec.
H138 Bypass of colon OS.
H139 Bypass of colon unspecified.
H141 Tube caecostomy.
H142 Refashioning of caecostomy.
H143 Closure of caecostomy.
H148 Exteriorisation of caecum OS.
H149 Exteriorisation of caecum unspecified.
H151 Loop colostomy.
H152 End colostomy.
H153 Refashioning of colostomy.
H154 Closure of colostomy.
H155 Dilation of colostomy.
H156 Reduction of prolapse of colostomy.
H158 Other exteriorisation of colon OS.
H159 Other exteriorisation of colon unspecified.
H161 Drainage of colon.
H162 Caecotomy.
H163 Colotomy.
H168 Incision of colon OS.

H169 Incision of colon unspecified.
H181 Open colonoscopy.
H188 Open endoscopic operations on colon OS.
H189 Open endoscopic operations on colon unspecified.
H198 Other open operations on colon OS.
H201 Fibre-optic endoscopic snare resection of lesion of colon.
H202 Fibre-optic endoscopic cauterisation of lesion of colon.
H203 Fibre-optic endoscopic laser destruction of lesion of colon.
H204 Fibre-optic endoscopic destruction of lesion of colon nec.
H208 Endoscopic extirpation of lesion of colon OS.
H209 Endoscopic extirpation of lesion of colon unspecified.
H218 Other therapeutic endoscopic operations on colon OS.
H219 Other therapeutic endoscopic operations on colon unspecified.
H221 Diagnostic fibre-optic endoscopic examination of colon and biopsy lesion of colon.
H228 Diagnostic endoscopic examination of colon OS.
H229 Diagnostic endoscopic examination of colon unspecified.
H231 Endoscopic snare resect lesion lower bowel using fibre-optic sigmoidoscope.
H232 Endoscopic cauterisation lesion lower bowel using fibre-optic sigmoidoscope.
H233 Endoscopic laser destruct lesion low bowel using fibre-optic sigmoidoscope.
H234 Endoscopic destruct lesion lower bowel using fibre-optic sigmoidoscope nec.
H238 Endoscopic extirp lesion lower bowel using fibre-optic sigmoidoscope OS.
H239 Endoscopic extirp lesion lower bowel using fibre-optic sigmoidoscope US.
H248 Other therap endos ops lower bowel using fibre-optic sigmoidoscope OS.
H249 Other therap endos ops lower bowel using fibre-optic sigmoidoscope US.
H251 Diagnostic endoscopic exam lower bowel and biopsy lesion using fibre-optic sigmoidoscope.
H258 Diagnostic endoscopic exam lower bowel using fibre-optic sigmoidoscope OS.
H259 Diagnostic endoscopic exam lower bowel using fibre-optic sigmoidoscope US.
H261 Endoscopic snare resect lesion sigmoid colon using rigid sigmoidoscope.
H262 Endoscopic cauterisation lesion sigmoid colon using rigid sigmoidoscope.
H263 Endoscopic laser destruct lesion sigmoid colon using rigid sigmoidoscope.
H264 Endoscopic cryotherapy lesion sigmoid colon using rigid sigmoidoscope.
H265 Endoscopic destruct lesion sigmoid colon using rigid sigmoidoscope nec.
H268 Endoscopic extirp lesion sigmoid colon using rigid sigmoidoscope OS.
H269 Endoscopic extirp lesion sigmoid colon using rigid sigmoidoscope US.
H278 Other therap endos ops sigmoid colon using rigid sigmoidoscope OS.
H279 Other therap endos ops sigmoid colon using rigid sigmoidoscope US.
H281 Diagnostic endoscopic exam sigmoid colon and biopsy lesion using rigid sigmoidoscope.
H288 Diagnostic endoscopic exam sigmoid colon using rigid sigmoidoscope OS.
H289 Diagnostic endoscopic exam sigmoid colon using rigid sigmoidoscope US.
H331 Abdominoperineal excision of rectum and end colostomy.
H332 Proctectomy and anastomosis of colon to anus.
H333 Anterior resection rectum and anastomosis of colon to rectum using staples.
H334 Anterior resection of rectum and anastomosis nec.
H335 Rectosigmoidectomy and closure of rectal stump and exteriorisation of bowel.
H336 Anterior resection of rectum and exteriorisation of bowel.
H338 Excision of rectum OS.
H339 Excision of rectum unspecified.
H341 Open excision of lesion of rectum.

H342   Open cauterisation of lesion of rectum.
H343   Open cryotherapy to lesion of rectum.
H344   Open laser destruction of lesion of rectum.
H345   Open destruction of lesion of rectum nec.
H348   Open extirpation of lesion of rectum OS.
H349   Open extirpation of lesion of rectum unspecified.
H404   Trans-sphincteric anastomosis of colon to anus.
H411   Rectosigmoidectomy and peranal anastomosis.

Inpatient HRGs relevant to colorectal cancer. Version 3 (1997)

F31   Large intestine – complex procedures.
F32   Large intestine – very major procedures.
F33   Large intestine – major procedures with cc.
F34   Large intestine – major procedures without cc.
F35   Large intestine – endoscopic or intermediate procedures.
F36   Large intestinal disorders > 69 or with cc.
F37   Large intestinal disorders < 70 without cc.
G02   Liver – complex procedures.
G03   Liver – very major procedures.
G04   Liver – major procedures > 69 or with cc.
G05   Liver – major procedures < 70 without cc.

Radiotherapy HRGs

HRG   Description
w01   Inpatient unsealed source brachytherapy.
w02   Outpatient unsealed source brachytherapy.
w03   Mechanical afterload, high-dose brachytherapy with anaesthetic.
w03   Mechanical afterload, high-dose brachytherapy without anaesthetic.
w05   Mechanical afterload, low-dose brachytherapy with anaesthetic.
w06   Mechanical afterload, low-dose brachytherapy without anaesthetic.
w07   Manual afterload, high-dose brachytherapy with anaesthetic.
w08   Manual afterload, high-dose brachytherapy without anaesthetic.
w09   Manual afterload, low-dose brachytherapy with anaesthetic.
w10   Manual afterload, low-dose brachytherapy without anaesthetic.
w11   Live source, high-dose brachytherapy with anaesthetic.
w12   Live source, high-dose brachytherapy without anaesthetic.
w13   Live source, low-dose brachytherapy with anaesthetic.
w14   Live source, low-dose brachytherapy without anaesthetic.
w15   Teletherapy with technical support, hyperfractionation.
w16   Teletherapy with technical support, > 23 fractions.
w17   Teletherapy with technical support, > 12 and < 24 fractions.
w18   Teletherapy with technical support, > 3 and < 13 fractions.
w19   Teletherapy with technical support, < 4 fractions.
w20   Complex teletherapy with planning, hyperfractionation.
w21   Complex teletherapy with planning, > 23 fractions.

w22   Complex teletherapy with planning, > 12 and < 24 fractions.
w23   Complex teletherapy with planning, > 3 and < 13 fractions.
w24   Complex teletherapy with planning, < 4 fractions.
w25   Complex teletherapy, hyperfractionation.
w26   Complex teletherapy, > 23 fractions.
w27   Complex teletherapy, > 12 and < 24 fractions.
w28   Complex teletherapy, > 3 and < 13 fractions.
w29   Complex teletherapy, < 4 fractions.
w30   Simple teletherapy with simulator, hyperfractionation.
w31   Simple teletherapy with simulator, > 23 fractions.
w32   Simple teletherapy with simulator, > 12 and < 24 fractions.
w33   Simple teletherapy with simulator, > 3 and < 13 fractions.
w34   Simple teletherapy with simulator, < 4 fractions.
w35   Simple teletherapy, hyperfractionation.
w36   Simple teletherapy, > 23 fractions.
w37   Simple teletherapy, > 12 and < 24 fractions.
w38   Simple teletherapy, > 3 and < 13 fractions.
w39   Simple teletherapy, < 4 fractions.
w40   Superficial teletherapy, hyperfractionation.
w41   Superficial teletherapy, > 23 fractions.
w42   Superficial teletherapy, > 12 and < 24 fractions.
w43   Superficial teletherapy, > 3 and < 13 fractions.
w44   Superficial teletherapy, < 4 fractions.

HRG – Condensed Chemotherapy Groups (Draft, 1998)

Group 1

Suitable for administration in a cancer unit or centre.

- Administration fairly straightforward, given staff training.
- Doses fairly standard.
- Low toxicity expected – low risk of myelosuppression.
- Side-effect profile can be managed on an outpatient basis.

e.g. oral regimes, single agent and simple combinations CMF.

Group 2

Suitable for administration in a cancer unit or centre.

- Generally given as an outpatient, but admission may be required during course for complications and side-effects.
- Needs a specialist facility available intermittently.
- Fairly toxic and likelihood of some degree of myelosuppression.

e.g. CHOP, anthracycline regimes.

Group 3

Suitable for administration only in a cancer centre.

- Generally requires admission with trained staff available 24 hours a day.
- Specialist administration – includes protracted infusional regimes.
- Expected toxicity and myelosuppression.

e.g. BEP.

Group 4

Suitable for administration only in a cancer centre.

- Complex regimes.
- Extended admission and extensive specialist support required.
- Expected toxicity and severe myelosuppression.

Extra groups for hormones and biological response modifiers.

Appendix II: UICC staging of colorectal cancer

Dukes' staging of colorectal cancer

Stage A   Tumour confined to the mucosa and submucosa of the bowel wall.
Stage B   Tumour penetrating through the muscle wall of the bowel.
Stage C   Metastasis to regional lymph nodes.
Stage D   Distant metastasis.

Stage grouping

AJCC/UICC				Dukes'
Stage 0	Tis	N0	M0	
Stage I	T1	N0	M0	A
	T2	N0	M0	
Stage II	T3	N0	M0	B
	T4	N0	M0	
Stage III	Any T	N1	M0	C
	Any T	N2	M0	
	Any T	N3	M0	
Stage IV	Any T	Any N	M1	D

Note: Dukes' stage B is a composite of better (T3, N0, M0) prognostic groups, as in Dukes' stage C (Any T, N1, M0 and Any T, N2, N3 M0).

Histopathologic type

This stage classification applies to carcinomas that arise in the colon, rectum or appendix. It does not apply to sarcomas, lymphomas or carcinoid tumours. The histologic types include:

- adenocarcinoma *in situ*
- adenocarcinoma
- mucinous adenocarcinoma (colloid type: > 50% mucinous carcinoma)
- signet-ring-cell carcinoma (> 50% signet-ring cell)
- squamous-cell (epidermoid) carcinoma
- adenosquamous carcinoma
- small-cell (oat-cell) carcinoma
- undifferentiated carcinoma
- carcinoma, NOS.

Histopathologic grade (G)

GX   Grade cannot be assessed.
G1   Well differentiated.
G2   Moderately differentiated.
G3   Poorly differentiated.
G4   Undifferentiated.

Appendix III: HBGs/HRGs for colorectal cancer

The HBG/HRG matrix is a methodology that permits the systematic review of the epidemiology of a condition and the appropriate packages of care for that condition. In order to provide a comprehensive view of health conditions and services, the matrix is split into four components:

- at risk/prevention
- symptomatic presentation/diagnostic investigation
- diagnosed disease/curative service
- continuing consequences of disease/care and palliation.

Matrices have been developed for a number of conditions (including colorectal cancer) and have been piloted in a number of districts as part of the systematic needs assessment process. In these pilots, the methodology was generally found to be useful, although the capture of the necessary data with existing information systems was difficult.

The development of the HBG/HRG matrix will be continued as part of the NHS information strategy, in order to help local users extract useful and comparable information from patient-based information systems and electronic patient records.

Summary

HBGs	Promotion/primary prevention	Investigation and diagnosis	Initial care	Continuing care
At risk Whole population	Health promotion Screening and prophylactic interventions			Community general input
Population at specific risk/screening population Follow-up screening for previously treated disease				
Presentation Asymptomatic, screen detected or incidental finding		Physical examination Chemistry Imaging Cytology Biopsy Special investigation Special support		
Symptomatic presentation				
Confirmed disease Dukes' stage A Dukes' stage B Dukes' stage C Dukes' stage D			Surgery Chemotherapy Radiotherapy Special support	Specialist input Voluntary sector
Continuing disease state *Non-progressive disease* Functional ability Pain Other symptoms *Progressive disease* Functional ability Pain Other symptoms				

Matrix 1: At risk.

HBGs	Numbers/rates	Health promotion*	Screening and prophylactic interventions / Special investigations†	Colon and rectum (f35 cat 2)‡	Special support
Whole population					
Population at specific risk§					
Follow-up screening for previously treated disease					

* Alerting people to change in bowel habits, change in colour of stools, rectal bleeding. Promoting a healthy diet.
† For example, faecal occult blood testing and genetic testing, barium enema.
‡ f35 cat 2: sigmoidoscopy.
§ For example, those with positive family history, ulcerative colitis, previous history of colorectal polyps, hereditary non-polyposis cancer of the colon (HNPCC) and familial adenomatous polyposis.

Matrix 2: Presentation.

HBGs	Numbers/rates	Physical examination	Chemistry	Imaging*	Cytology/ biopsy† (f35 cat 2)	Special investigation	Special support
Asymptomatic, screen detected or incidental finding							
Symptomatic presentation							
Elective‡							
Emergency§							

* Plain X-rays, contrast studies, ultrasound and CT scans.
† This may be through an endoscope (sigmoidoscopy, colonoscopy, etc.).
‡ Presentation might include pain, mass, rectal bleeding and change in bowel habit.
§ Emergency presentation might be with perforation or obstruction.

Matrix 3: Confirmed disease.

HBGs	Numbers/ rates	Surgery Colon and rectum (cat 6 f31, cat 5 f32)	Resection of liver (cat 5 g2, cat 4 g3)	Chemo- therapy	Radiotherapy Teletherapy (W15–W44)	Brachytherapy (W1–W14)	Special support District nursing	Dietetics	Specialist nursing
Dukes' A									
Dukes' B									
Dukes' C									
Dukes' D									

Matrix 4: Continuing disease state.

HBGs	Numbers/ rates	Community general input GP/primary care	Occupational therapy	Physio- therapy	District nursing	Social/ psychological	Other‡	Specialist input*	Voluntary sector†
Non-progressive disease									
Functional ability									
Pain									
Other symptoms									
Progressive disease									
Functional ability									
Pain									
Other symptoms									

* For example, from hospices, etc.

† Services purchased for the voluntary sector wherever appropriate/necessary.

‡ This might include clinical psychology, dietetics, health visiting, midwifery, podiatry/chiropody and speech and language therapy wherever applicable.

Bibliography

Astler VB, Coller FA. The prognostic significance of direct extension of carcinoma of the colon and rectum. *Ann Surg* 1954; **139**: 846–52.

Beart RW Jr, van Heerden JA, Beahrs OH. Evolution in the pathologic staging of carcinoma of the colon. *Surg Gynecol Obstet* 1978; **146**: 257–9.

Castro E *et al.* Carcinoma of the large intestine in patients irradiated for carcinoma of the cervix and uterus. *Surg Gynecol Obstet* 1973; **131**: 45–52.

Eddy DM. Screening for colo-rectal cancer. *Ann Intern Med* 1990; **113**: 373–84.

Gefand D, Ott D. The economic implications of radiologic screening for colonic cancer. *Am J Radiol* 1991; **156**: 939–43.

Goligher J. *Surgery of the Anus, Rectum and Colon* (5e). London: Bailliere Tindall, 1984.

Lennard-Jones JE *et al.* Cancer surveillance in ulcerative colitis. Experience over 15 years. *Lancet* 1983; **ii**: 149–52.

Moss S, Draper GJ, Hardcastle JD, Chamberlain J. Calculation of sample size in trials for early diagnosis of disease. *Int J Epidemiol* 1987; **16**: 104–10.

Mountney L, Sanderson H, Harris J. Colorectal cancer. In: Stevens A, Raferty J (eds). *Health Care Needs Assessment. Volume 1.* Oxford: Radcliffe Medical Press, 1994.

Office of Population Censuses and Surveys. *Incidence, Survival and Mortality in England and Wales. Studies on Medical and Population Subjects 43.* London: HMSO, 1987.

Sandler R, Sandler D. Radiation-induced cancer of the colon and rectum: assessing the risks. *Gastroenterology* 1983; **84**: 51–7.

Souhami R, Tobias J. *Cancer and its Management.* Oxford: Blackwell Science, 1995.

Urdaneta L *et al.* Late development of primary carcinoma of the colon following uretero-sigmoidoscopy. *Ann Surg* 1966; **164**: 503–8.

Willett WC, Stampfer MJ, Colditz GA, Rosuer BA, Speizer FE. Relation of meat, fat and fibre intake to the risk of colon cancer in a prospective study among women. *NEJM* 1990; **323**: 1664–72.

Functional ability

Scoring for the Barthel ADL Index

Bowels

0 incontinent (or needs to be given enemas)
1 occasional accident (once a week)
2 continent

Bladder

0 incontinent, or catheterised and unable to manage alone
1 occasional accident (maximum once per 24 hours)
2 continent

Grooming

0 needs help with personal care
1 independent face/hair/teeth/shaving (implements provided)

Toilet use

0 dependent
1 needs some help, but can do something alone
2 independent (on and off, dressing, wiping)

Feeding

0 unable
1 needs help cutting, spreading butter, etc.
2 independent

Transfer (bed to chair and back)

0 unable, no sitting balance
1 major help (one or two people, physical), can sit
2 minor help (verbal or physical)
3 independent

Mobility

0 dependent
1 wheelchair independent, including corners
2 walks with help of one person (verbal or physical)
3 independent (but may use any aid, e.g. stick)

Dressing

0 dependent
1 needs help, but can do about half unaided
2 independent (includes buttons, zips, laces, etc.)

Stairs

0 unable
1 needs help (verbal, physical, carrying aid)
2 independent

Bathing

0 dependent
1 independent (or in shower)

Total score 0–20

A = independent, B = mild dependence, C = moderate dependence, D = severe dependence, E = very severe dependence.

Severity of pain assessment scoring

Other disabling symptoms

(These may be non-specific for a particular disorder) can include:

- nausea
- vomiting
- lethergy
- malaise
- weight loss
- anorexia
- depression.

The matrix does not take account of severity of symptoms or range of possibilities with current groupings (? to categorise by symptom or severity of symptom).

Basic care

This includes care for basic daily needs.

Specialised care

This includes more specialised care, e.g. nursing, medical, physiotherapy (for contractures), speech therapy for swallowing disorders associated with, for example, Parkinson's disease and motor neuron disease.

Provision of aids and appliances

This includes assessment and instruction for use.

Maintenance of aids and appliances

This may include help with use and continual appraisal.

Family support

This includes counselling for all.

Local and general symptoms of colorectal cancer

	Right colon (%)	Left colon (%)	Rectum (%)
Pain	80	60	5
Mass	70	40	–
Rectal bleeding			60
Change in bowel habit	40	60	80
Weight loss	50	15	25
Vomiting	30	10	–
Obstruction	5	20	5

Appendix IV: Pilot HBG/HRG matrix results from Greater Glasgow Health Board

Matrix 1 outlines the risk factors associated with the development of colorectal cancer, estimating the numbers of people per 1 000 000 population considered to be at increased risk for the disease. It attempts to quantify the costs associated with services aimed at primary and secondary prevention in the different groups.

The different types of diagnostic test available for each type of presentation to the health service and their associated costs are shown in Matrix 2.

Matrix 3 uses Dukes' staging as the relevant HBGs and shows the primary treatments and costs in each group. When this pilot was carried out, Matrix 4 was concerned with the follow-up of patients such as palliation and supportive services. During the pilot, no information was available on the need for such services by patients with colorectal cancer in the Greater Glasgow Health Board area and this matrix was not completed. The summary matrix provided covers only the first three matrices.

Colorectal cancer matrices from Glasgow exercise per 1 000 000 population

Summary matrix	Promotion and primary prevention	Investigation and diagnosis	Initial care	Continuing care	Total
At risk	£106,980				
Presentation		£41,668	£371,200		
Confirmed disease			£3,749,676		
Continuing disease states				£?	
Total					£4,269,523

Matrix 1: Primary and secondary prevention of disease.

	Prevalence	Health promotion	FOB*	Screening endoscopic (F35 = £298)	Genetic	Special support†	Total
Whole population	1,000,000	£50,000					
Low risk	310,000						
Age 50+	448,380	£50,000					
High-fat, low-fibre diet							
High risk							
Positive family history	31,000						
Ulcerative colitis/Crohn's	21,000						
Previous history of CRC	1,500			£5,662			
HNPCC	190			£2,160			
FAP	29						
Total		£100,000	£0	£7,822	£0	£0	£107,822

* 1997–98 cost returns.
† No HRG costs available.

Matrix 2: Diagnosis of disease.

	Prevalence	Examination of bloods, FOB	Endoscopy	Emergency laparotomy	Ultrasound	CT	Total
		£127	£298	£4,000	£32	£78	
Asymptomatic/screen detected	27.15	3,448.05	8,090.7		868.8	2,117.7	
Symptomatic local	407.25	51,720.75	121,360.5		9,774	23,824.13	
Pain	162.9						
Mass	122.175						
Rectal bleeding	134.3925						
Change in bowel habit	285.075						
Obstruction	40.725						
Perforation	24.435						
Generalised							
Weight loss	244.35						
Vomiting	183.2625						
Anaemia	122.175						
Emergency admission	108.6	6,896.1	16,181.4	217,200	868.8	2117.7	
Total	543	62,064.9	145,632.6	217,200	11,511.6	28,059.53	464,468.6

Matrix 3: Treatment of diagnosed disease.

	Preva-lence	Surgery Operations on colon	Operations on rectum	Liver resection	Chemo-therapy Group 1	Group 2	Group 3	Group 4	Radio-therapy Simple palliative	Complex	Special support
Dukes' A	58	£101,243	£67,495	£0	£0	£0	£0	£0	£0	£0	£11,600
Dukes' B	174	£379,661	£253,107	£0	£0	£0	£0	£0	£0	£0	£34,800
Dukes' C	203	£442,938	£295,292	£0	£625,595	£398,591	£185,745	£0	£68,573	£0	£40,600
Dukes' D	145	£237,288	£158,192	£36,250	£0	£113,883	£132,675	£0	£137,147	£0	£29,000
Total	580	£1,161,130	£774,087	£36,250	£625,595	£512,474	£318,420	£0	£205,720	£0	£116,000

Appendix V: Strength of recommendations and quality of evidence

Strength of recommendations

A   Good evidence to support.
B   Fair evidence to support.
C   Poor evidence to support.
D   Fair evidence to reject.
E   Good evidence to reject.

Quality of evidence

I   At least one randomised controlled trial.
II(2)   Well-designed cohort or case-controlled study.
II(3)   Multiple timed series or dramatic results from uncontrolled experiments.
III   Opinions of respected authorities.
IV   Inadequate or conflicting evidence.

References

1 Maule W. Screening for colorectal cancer by nurse endoscopists. *NEJM* 1994; **330**: 183–7.

2 Department of Health. *Public Health Common Data Set 1997: registrations 1991*. Guildford: National Institute of Epidemiology, 1998.

3 Office of National Statistics. *Mortality Statistics, 1994*. London: Office of National Statistics, 1995.

4 Wessex Colorectal Cancer Audit. *Progress Report No 3*. Winchester: Institute of Public Health Medicine, 1996.

5 Burkitt DP. Epidemiology of cancer of the colon and rectum. *Cancer* 1971; **28**: 3–13.

6 Steinmetz KA, Potter JD. Vegetables, fruit and cancer. I. Epidemiology. *Cancer Causes Control* 1991; **2**: 325–7.

7 Block G, Patterson B, Subar A. Fruit, vegetables and cancer prevention: a review of the epidemiological evidence. *Nutr Cancer* 1992; **18**: 1–29.

8 Potter JD, Slattery ML, Bostick RM, Gapstur SM. Colon cancer: a review of the epidemiology. *Epidemiol Rev* 1993; **15**: 499–545.

9 Faivre J. Diet and colorectal cancer. In: Benito E, Giasco A, Hill M (eds). *Public Education on Diet and Cancer*. Amsterdam: Kluwer Academic Publishers, 1992.

10 Hirayama T. Association between alcohol consumption and cancer of the sigmoid colon: observations from a Japanese cohort study. *Lancet* 1989; **2**(8665): 725–7.

11 Heineman EF, Zahm SH, McLaughlin JK, Vaught JB. Increased risk of colorectal cancer among smokers: results of a 26-year follow-up of US veterans and a review. *Int J Cancer* 1995; **59**: 728–38.

12 Morson B. The polyp cancer sequence in the large bowel. *Proc R Soc Med* 1974; **67**: 451–7.

13 Fuchs CS, Giovanucci EL, Colditz GA, Hunter D, Speizer F, Willett WA. A prospective study of family history and the risk of colorectal cancer. *NEJM* 1994; **331**: 1669–74.

14 Hall NR, Finan PJ, Ward B, Bishop D. Genetic susceptibility to colorectal cancer in patients under 45 years of age. *Br J Surg* 1994; **81**: 1485–9.

15 St John DJ, McDermott FT, Hopper JL, Debney E, Johnson W, Hughes E. Cancer risk in relatives of patients with common colorectal cancer. *Ann Intern Med* 1993; **118**: 785–90.

16 Cancer Guidance Sub-Group of the Clinical Outcomes Group. *Improving Outcomes in Colorectal Cancer: the research evidence*. London: NHS Executive, Department of Health, 1997.

17 Hodgson SV, Bishop DT, Dunlop MG, Evans DGR, Northover JMA. Suggested screening guidelines for familial colorectal cancer. *J Med Screen* 1995; **2**: 45–51.

18 Bishop D, Hall N. The genetics of colorectal cancer. *Eur J Cancer* 1994; **30**: 1946–56.

19 Zinzler KW *et al*. Identification of FAP locus genes from chromosome 5q21. *Science* 1991; **253**: 661–5.

20 Mountney L, Sanderson H, Harris J. Colorectal cancer. In: Stevens A, Raftery A (eds). *Health Care Needs Assessment. Volume 1*. Oxford: Radcliffe Medical Press, 1994.

21 Winawer SJ *et al*. Colorectal cancer screening: clinical guidelines and rationale. *Gastroenterology* 1997; **112**: 594–642.

22 Macadam DB. Delay patterns in the diagnosis of gastrointestinal cancer. *J R Coll Gen Pract* 1979; **29**: 723–9.

23 Jones R, Lydeard S. Irritable bowel syndrome in the general population. *BMJ* 1992; **304**: 1542–3.

24 Hefland M, Marton K, Zimmer-Gembeck M, Sox H. History of visible rectal bleeding in a primary care population. *JAMA* 1997; **277**: 44–8.

25 Goulston KJ, Dent O. How important is rectal bleeding in the diagnosis of bowel cancer or polyps? *Lancet* 1986; **2**: 261–5.

26 Fitjen G, Starmans R, Muris J, Schouten H, Blijham G, Knottnerus J. Predictive value of signs and symptoms for colorectal cancer in patients with rectal bleeding in general practice. *Fam Pract* 1995; **12**: 279–86.

27 British Society of Gastroenterology. *Provision of GI Endoscopy and Related Services for a DGH.* London: British Society of Gastroenterology, 1990.

28 Dukes CE. The classification of cancer of the rectum. *J Pathol Bacteriol* 1932; **35**: 323–32.

29 Robinson MHE, Thomas WM, Hardcastle JD, Chamberlain J, Mangham CM. Change towards earlier stage at presentation of colorectal cancer. *Br J Surg* 1993; **80**: 1610–12.

30 Mulcahy HE. *Frequency and Survival Statistics for Colorectal Cancer Based on Data from 777 Patients Derived from St Vincent's Hospital Colorectal Cancer Database.* Dublin: St Vincent's Hospital, 1997.

31 McArthur C, Smith A. Delay in the diagnosis of colorectal cancer. *J R Coll Gen Pract* 1983; **33**: 159–61.

32 Holliday H, Hardcastle J. Delay in diagnosis and treatment of symptomatic colorectal cancer. *Lancet* 1979; **1**: 309–11.

33 Ratcliffe R, Kiff RS, Kingston RD, Walsh SH, Jeacock J. Early diagnosis in colorectal cancer. Still no benefit! *J R Coll Surg Edin* 1989; **34**: 152–5.

34 NHS Centre for Reviews and Dissemination. The management of colorectal cancer. *Effect Health Care Bull* 1997; **3**(6).

35 NHS Executive. *National Schedule of Reference Costs.* London: NHS Executive, 1998.

36 Rich T *et al.* Patterns of recurrence of rectal cancer after potentially curative surgery. *Cancer* 1983; **52**: 1317–29.

37 Lloyd K. Personal communication, 1998.

38 Mella J, Datta S, Biffin A. *Surgeon's Follow-up Practice After Resection of Colorectal Cancer.* London: Royal College of Surgeons of England, 1996.

39 Standing Medical Advisory Committee and Standing Nurse and Midwifery Advisory Committee. *The Principles and Provision of Palliative Care.* London: Joint Report of the Standing Medical Advisory Committee and Standing Nurse and Midwifery Advisory Committee, 1992.

40 Higginson I. Palliative and terminal care. In: Stevens A, Raftery J (eds). *Health Care Needs Assessment. Second series.* Oxford: Radcliffe Medical Press, 1995.

41 Walker A, Jack K, Twaddle S, Burns H. Health Benefit Groups in NHS decision making. In: Sanderson H, Anthony P, Mountney L (eds). *Case-Mix for All.* Oxford: Radcliffe Medical Press, 1998.

42 Scottish Forum for Public Health Medicine. *Health Promotion in Primary Care.* Glasgow: Scottish Needs Assessment Programme, 1996.

43 Kune GA, Kune S, Watson F. Colorectal cancer risk, chronic illnesses, operations and medications: case–control results from the Melbourne colorectal cancer study. *Cancer Res* 1988; **48**: 4399–404.

44 Rosenberg L, Palmer JR, Zauber AG, Warshauer ME, Stolley PD, Shapiro S. A hypothesis: nonsteroidal anti-inflammatory drugs reduce the incidence of large bowel cancer. *J Natl Cancer Inst* 1991; **83**: 355–8.

45 Thun MJ, Namboordiri MM, Heath CW. Aspirin use and reduced risk of fatal colon cancer. *NEJM* 1991; **325**: 1593–6.

46 Greenberg ER, Baron JA, Freeman DH, Mandel JS, Haile R. Reduced risk of large bowel adenomas among aspirin users. *J Natl Cancer Inst* 1993; **85**: 912–16.

47 Logan RFA, Little J, Hawtin PG, Hardcastle JD. Effect of aspirin and non-steroidal anti-inflammatory drugs on colorectal adenomas: case–control study of subjects participating in the Nottingham faecal occult blood screening programme. *BMJ* 1993; **307**: 285–9.

48 Suh O, Mettlin C, Petrelli NJ. Aspirin use, cancer and polyps of the large bowel. *Cancer* 1993; **72**: 1171–7.

49 Giovannucci E, Rimm EB, Stampfer MJ, Colditz GA, Ascherio A, Willet WC. Aspirin use and the risk of colorectal cancer and adenoma in male health professionals. *Ann Intern Med* 1994; **121**: 241–6.

50 Peleg II, Maibach HT, Brown SH, Wilcox CM. Aspirin and nonsteroidal antiinflammatory drug use and the risk of subsequent colorectal cancer. *Arch Intern Med* 1994; **154**: 394–9.

51 Giovannucci E *et al.* Aspirin and the risk of colorectal cancer in women. *NEJM* 1995; **333**: 609–14.

52 Paganini-Hill A, Chao A, Ross RK, Henderson BE. Aspirin use and chronic diseases: a cohort study of the elderly. *BMJ* 1989; **299**: 1247–50.

53 Paganini-Hill A, Hsu G, Ross RK, Henderson BE. Aspirin use and incidence of large bowel cancer in a California retirement community. *J Natl Cancer Inst* 1991; **83**: 1182–3.

54 Evans JMM, McMahon AD, McGilchrist MM, Murray FE, McDevitt DG, MacDonald TM. Non-steroidal anti-inflammatory drugs, aspirin and colorectal cancer: a record linkage study in Tayside, Scotland. *Gastroenterology* 1995; **108**: A464.

55 Gann PH, Manson JE, Glynn RJ, Buring JE, Hennekens CH. Low-dose aspirin and incidence of colorectal tumours in a randomised trial. *J Natl Cancer Inst* 1993; **85**: 1220–4.

56 Hardcastle JD *et al*. Randomised controlled trial of faecal occult blood screening for colorectal cancer. *Lancet* 1996; **348**: 1472–7.

57 Kronborg O, Fenger C, Olsen J, Jorgensen OD, Sondergaard O. Randomised study of screening for colorectal cancer with faecal occult blood test. *Lancet* 1996; **348**: 1467–71.

58 Whynes DK, Neilson AR, Walker AR, Hardcastle JD. Faecal occult blood screening for colorectal cancer: is it cost-effective? *Health Econ* 1998; **7**: 21–9.

59 Atkin W. Implementing screening for colorectal cancer. *BMJ* 1999; **319**: 1212–13.

60 Newcomb PA, Norfleet RG, Storer BE, Surawicz T, Marcus PM. Screening sigmoidoscopy and colorectal cancer mortality. *J Natl Cancer Inst* 1992; **84**: 1572–5.

61 Selby JV, Friedman GD, Quesenberry CP, Weiss N. A case–control study of screening sigmoidoscopy and mortality from colorectal cancer. *NEJM* 1992; **326**: 653–7.

62 Gouldie BM, Pennington CR. Screening for colorectal cancer. *Scot Med J* 1997; **42**: 68.

63 Winawer SJ *et al*. The WHO Collaborating Centre for the Prevention of Colorectal Cancer. Risk and surveillance of individuals with colorectal polyps. *Bull WHO* 1990; **68**: 789–95.

64 Winawer SJ *et al*. Randomised comparison of surveillance intervals after colonoscopic removal of newly diagnosed adenomatous polyps. *NEJM* 1993; **328**: 901–6.

65 Atkin WS, Morson BC, Cuzick J. Long-term risk of colorectal cancer after excision of rectosigmoid adenomas. *NEJM* 1992; **326**(10): 658–62.

66 Kee F, Collins BJ, Paterson CC. Prognosis in familial non-polyposis colorectal cancer. *Gut* 1991; **32**: 513–16.

67 Jarvinen HJ, Mecklin JP, Sistonen P. Screening reduces colorectal cancer rates in families with heriditary non-polyposis colorectal cancer. *Gastroenterology* 1995; **106**: 1405–11.

68 Vasen HF *et al*. Hereditary non-polyposis colorectal cancer: results of long-term surveillance in 50 families. *Eur J Cancer* 1995; **31A**: 1145–8.

69 Scottish Intercollegiate Guidelines Network (SIGN). *Colorectal Cancer*. Edinburgh: SIGN, 1997.

70 Rhodes M, Bradburn DM. Overview of screening and management of familial adenomatous polyposis. *Gut* 1992; **33**: 125–31.

71 Vasen HF *et al*. Molecular genetic tests as a guide to surgical management of familial adenomatous polyposis. *Lancet* 1996; **348**: 433–5.

72 Houlston R, Murday V, Harocopos C, Williams CB, Slack J. Screening and genetic counselling for relatives of patients with colorectal cancer in a family cancer clinic. *BMJ* 1990; **301**: 366–8.

73 Stephenson B, Murday V, Finan P, Quirke P, Dixon M, Bishop D. Feasibility of family-based screening for colorectal neoplasia: experience in one general surgical practice. *Gut* 1993; **34**: 96–100.

74 Rowe-Jones DC, Aylett SO. Delay in treatment in carcinoma of colon and rectum. *Lancet* 1965; **2**: 973–6.

75 Dixon AR, Thornton-Holmes J, Cheetnam NM. General practitioners' awareness of colorectal cancer: a 10-year review. *BMJ* 1990; **301**: 152–3.

76 Goodman D, Irvin TT. Delay in the diagnosis and prognosis of carcinoma of the right colon. *Br J Surg* 1993; **80**: 1327–9.

77 Stubbs RS, Long MG. Symptom duration and pathologic staging of colorectal cancer. *J Surg Oncol* 1986; **12**: 127–30.

78 Crosland A, Jones R. Rectal bleeding; prevalence and consultation behaviour. *BMJ* 1995; **311**: 486–8.

79 Jones RVH, Dudgeon TA. Time between presentation and treatment of six common cancers: a study in Devon. *Br J Gen Pract* 1992; **42**: 419–22.

80 Robinson E, Mohilever J, Zidan J, Sapir D. Colorectal cancer: incidence delay in diagnosis and stage of disease. *Eur J Cancer Clin Oncol* 1986; **22**: 157–61.

81 Clarke PJ, Dehn TCB, Kettlewell MGW. Changing patterns of colorectal cancer in a regional teaching hospital. *Ann R Coll Surg Engl* 1992; **74**: 291–3.

82 Spratt JS. *Neoplasms of the Colon, Rectum and Anus.* Philadelphia: WB Saunders Company, 1984, pp. 247–8.

83 Rex DK *et al.* Flexible sigmoidoscopy plus air-contrast barium enema versus colonoscopy for suspected lower gastrointestinal bleeding. *Gastroenterology* 1990; **98**: 855–61.

84 Kewenter J *et al.* The yield of sigmoidoscopy and double-contrast barium enema in the diagnosis of neoplasms in the large bowel in patients with a positive haemoccult test. *Endoscopy* 1995; **27**: 159–63.

85 Walker AR, Whynes DK, Chamberlain J, Hardcastle J. The hospital costs of diagnostic procedures for colorectal cancer. *J Clin Epidemiol* 1991; **44**: 907–14.

86 Church J. Complete colonoscopy: how often? and if not, why not? *Am J Gastroenterol* 1994; **89**: 556–60.

87 Parry B, Goh H. Quality control in colonoscopy: a Singapore perspective. *Int J Colorectal Dis* 1993; **8**: 139–41.

88 Arblaster M, Collopy B, Elliott P, Mackay J, Ryan P, Woods R. Colonoscopy in a private hospital: continuous quality improvements in practice. *Aust Clin Rev* 1992; **12**: 71–6.

89 Chester J, Britton D. Elective and emergency surgery for colorectal cancer in a district general hospital: impact of surgical training on patient survival. *Ann R Coll Surg Engl* 1989; **71**: 370–4.

90 Runkel NS, Schlag P, Schwarz V, Herfarth C. Outcome after emergency surgery for cancer of the large intestine. *Br J Surg* 1991; **78**: 183–8.

91 Smithers B, Theile D, Cohen J, Evans E, Davis N. Emergency right hemicolectomy in colon carcinoma: a prospective study. *Aust N Z J Surg* 1996; **56**: 749–52.

92 Anderson JH, Hole D, McArdle CS. Elective versus emergency surgery for patients with colorectal cancer. *Br J Surg* 1992; **79**: 706–9.

93 Waldron RP, Donovan IA, Drumm J, Mottram S, Tedman S. Emergency presentation and mortality from colorectal cancer in the elderly. *Br J Surg* 1986; **73**: 214–16.

94 Rice N, Eastwood A, Sheldon T, Steele R, Mella J. *Risk Factors Associated with Survival from Colorectal Cancer.* Unpublished report. York: University of York, 1997 (cited EHCB).

95 McArdle C, Hole D. Impact of variability among surgeons on post-operative morbidity and mortality and ultimate survival. *BMJ* 1991; **302**: 1501–5.

96 Scott P, Jackson T, Al-Jaberi T, Dixon M, Quirke P, Finan P. Total mesorectal excision and local recurrence: a study of tumour spread in the mesorectum distal to rectal cancer. *Br J Surg* 1995; **82**: 1031–3.

97 Riedl ST, Wiebelt H, Bergmann U, Hermanek P. Postoperative morbidity and mortality in colon carcinoma. Results of the German multicenter study of the Study Group Colorectal Carcinoma (SGCRC). *Der Chirurg* 1995; **66**: 597–606.

98 Kingston R, Walsh S, Jeacock J. Colorectal surgeons in district general hospitals produce similar survival outcomes to their teaching hospital colleagues: a review of 5-year survivals in Manchester. *J R Coll Surg* 1992; **37**: 235–7.

99 Hermanek P, Wiebelt H. Staimmer D, Riedl S. Prognostic factors of rectum carcinoma – experience of the German multicenter study SGCRC. *Tumori* 1995; **81**: 60–4.

100 Consultant Surgeons and Pathologists of the Lothian and Borders Health Board. Lothian and Borders large bowel cancer project: immediate outcome after surgery. *Br J Surg* 1995; **82**: 888–90.

101 Karanjia N, Corder A, Bearn P, Heald R. Leakage from stapled low anastomosis after total mesorectal excision or carcinoma of the rectum. *Br J Surg* 1994; **81**: 1224–6.

102 Arbman G, Nilsson E, Hallbook O, Sjodahl R. Local recurrence following total mesorectal excision for rectal cancer. *Br J Surg* 1996; **83**: 375–9.

103 Song F, Glenny AM. Antimicrobial prophylaxis in colorectal surgery: a review of randomised trials. *Health Technol Assess* 1998; **2**(7): 1–110.

104 Antiplatelet Trialists' Collaboration. Collaborative overview of randomised trials of antiplatelet therapy. III. Reduction in venous thrombosis and pulmonary embolism by antiplatelet prophylaxis among surgical and medical patients. *BMJ* 1994; **308**: 235–46.

105 Gordon NLM *et al*. Outcome in colorectal adenocarcinoma: two seven-year studies of a population. *BMJ* 1993; **307**: 707–10.

106 Marsh PJ, James RD, Schofield PF. On behalf of the Northwest Rectal Cancer Group. Adjuvant pre-operative radiotherapy for locally advanced rectal carcinoma: results of a prospective randomised trial. *Dis Colon Rectum* 1994; **37**: 1205–14.

107 Medical Research Council Rectal Working Party. Randomised trial of surgery alone versus radio-therapy followed by surgery for potentially operable locally advanced rectal cancer. *Lancet* 1996; **348**: 1610–14.

108 Frykholm G, Glimelius B, Pahlman L. Pre-operative or post-operative irradiation in adenocarcinoma of the rectum: final treatment results of a randomised trial and an evaluation of late secondary effects. *Dis Colon Rectum* 1993; **36**: 564–72.

109 Taylor R, Kerr G, Arnott SJ. External beam radiotherapy for rectal cancer. *Br J Surg* 1987; **74**: 455–9.

110 Dobrowsky W, Schmid A. Radiotherapy of presacral recurrence following radical surgery for rectal cancer. *Dis Colon Rectum* 1985; **28**: 917–19.

111 Pacini P, Cionini L, Pirtoli L. Symptomatic recurrences of carcinoma of the rectum and sigmoid. *Dis Colon Rectum* 1986; **29**: 865–8.

112 Krook JE *et al*. Effective surgical adjuvant therapy for high-risk rectal cancer. *NEJM* 1991; **324**: 709–15.

113 Messori A *et al*. Cost-effectiveness of adjuvant intraportal chemotherapy in patients with colorectal cancer. *J Clin Gastroenterol* 1996; **23**: 269–74.

114 Brown ML, Nayfield SG, Shibley LM. Adjuvant therapy for Stage III colon cancer: economic returns to research and cost-effectiveness of treatment. *J Natl Cancer Inst* 1994; **86**(6): 424–30.

115 Scheithauer W, Rosen H, Hornek GV, Sebasta C, Depisch D. Randomised comparison of combination chemotherapy plus supportive care with supportive care alone in patients with metastatic colorectal cancer. *BMJ* 1993; **306**: 752–5.

116 Nordic Gastrointestinal Tumour Therapy Group. Expectancy or primary chemotherapy in patients with advanced asymptomatic colorectal cancer: a randomised trial. *J Clin Oncol* 1992; **7**: 425–32.

117 Townsend J *et al*. Terminal cancer care and patients' preference for place of death: a prospective study. *BMJ* 1990; **301**: 415–17.

118 Hinton J. Can home care maintain an acceptable quality of life for patients with terminal cancer and their relatives? *Palliat Med* 1994; **8**: 183–96.

119 Addington-Hall JM, McCarthy M. Dying from cancer: results of a national population-based investigation. *Palliat Med* 1995; **9**: 295–305.

120 Wilkes E. Terminal cancer at home. *Lancet* 1965; **i**: 799–801.

121 Wilkes E. Dying now. *Lancet* 1984; **i**: 950–2.

122 Cartwright A, Hockey L, Anderson JL. *Life Before Death*. London: Routledge & Kegan Paul, 1973.

123 Parkes CM. Terminal care: evaluation of inpatient service at St Christopher's Hospice. Part I. Views of surviving spouse on effects of the service on the patient. *Postgrad Med J* 1979; **55**: 517–22.

124 Mills M, Davis HTO, Macrae W. Care of dying patients in hospital. *BMJ* 1994; **309**: 583–6.

125 Bowling A, Cartwright A. *Life After a Death. A Study of the Elderly Widowed*. London: Tavistock, 1982.

126 Seale CF. What happens in hospices: a review of research evidence. *Soc Sci Med* 1989; **28**(6): 551–9.

127 Kane RL *et al*. Hospice role in alleviating the emotional stress of terminal patients and their families. *Med Care* 1985; **23**(3): 189–97.

128 Kane RL *et al*. A randomised trial of hospice care. *Lancet* 1984; **i**: 890–4.

129 Higginson I, McCarthy M. Evaluation of palliative care: steps to quality assurance? *Palliat Med* 1989; **3**: 267–74.

130 Greer DS *et al*. An alternative in terminal care: results of the National Hospice Study. *J Chron Dis* 1986; **39**: 9–26.

131 Greer DS *et al*. National hospice and study analysis plan. *J Chron Dis* 1983; **36**(11): 737–80.

132 Mor V, Greer DS, Kastenbaum R (eds). *The Hospice Experiment*. Baltimore: Johns Hopkins University Press, 1988.

133 Parkes CM, Parkes J. Hospice versus hospital care – re-evaluation after 10 years as seen by surviving spouses. *Postgrad Med J* 1984; **60**: 120–4.

134 Field D, Ahmedzai S, Biswas B. Care and information received by lay carers of terminally ill patients at the Leicestershire Hospice. *Palliat Med* 1992; **6**(3): 237–45.

135 Zimmer JG, Groth-Junker A, McCusker J. Effects of a physician-led home care team on terminal care. *J Am Geriatr Soc* 1984; **32**: 288–92.

136 Zimmer JG, Groth-Junker A, McCusker J. A randomised controlled study of a home health care team. *Am J Public Health* 1985; **75**: 134–41.

137 Hughes SL *et al*. A randomised trial of the cost-effectiveness of VA hospital-based home care for the terminally ill. *Health Serv Res* 1992; **26**(6): 801–17.

138 Cox K, Bergen A, Norman I. Exploring consumer views of care provided by the Macmillan nurse using the critical incident technique. *J Adv Nurs* 1993; **18**: 408–15.

139 Parkes CM. Terminal care: evaluation of an advisory domiciliary service at St Christopher's Hospice. *Postgrad Med J* 1980; **56**: 685–9.

140 Ventafridda V *et al*. Comparison of home and hospital care of advanced cancer patients. *Tumori* 1989; **75**: 619–25.

141 Creek LV. A homecare hospice profile: description, evaluation and cost-analysis. *J Fam Pract* 1982; **14**: 53–8.

142 Higginson I, McCarthy M. Measuring symptoms in terminal cancer: are pain and dyspnoea controlled? *J R Soc Med* 1989; **82**: 1761–4.

143 Seale C. Death from cancer and death from other causes: the relevance of the hospice approach. *Palliat Med* 1991; **5**: 12–19.

144 McCusker J, Stoddard AM. Effects of an expanding home care programme for the terminally ill. *Med Care* 1987; **25**: 373–84.

145 Higginson I, Wade A, McCarthy M. Effectiveness of two palliative support teams. *J Public Health Med* 1992; **14**: 50–6.

146 Working Group of the Research Unit, Royal College of Physicians. Palliative care: guidelines for good practice and audit measures. *J R Coll Physicians Lond* 1991; **25**(4): 325–8.

147 Cancer Relief Macmillan Fund. *Organisational Standards for Palliative Care*. London: Cancer Relief Macmillan Fund, 1994.

148 Moertel CG *et al*. An evaluation of the carcinoembryonic antigen (CEA) test for monitoring patients with resected colon cancer. *JAMA* 1993; **270**: 174–82.

149 Bruinvels DJ, Stigglebout AM, Kievet J, van Howleingen HC, Habbema D, van de Velde C. Follow-up of patients with colorectal cancer: a meta-analysis. *Ann Surg* 1994; **219**: 174–82.

150 Kievit J, Bruinvels DJ. Detection of recurrence after surgery for colorectal cancer. *Eur J Cancer* 1995; **31A**: 1222–5.

151 Lennon T, Houghton J, Northover J. What is the value of clinical follow-up for colorectal cancer patients? The experience of the CRC/NIH CEA second-look trial. In: *Proceedings of the Nottingham International Colorectal Cancer Symposium*, Nottingham, 1995.

152 Makela JT, Laitinen SO, Kairaluoma MI. Five-year follow-up after radical surgery for colorectal cancer. Results of a prospective randomised trial. *Arch Surg* 1995; **130**: 1062–7.

153 Ohlsson B, Breland U, Ekberg H, Gaffner H, Tranberg KG. Follow-up after curative surgery for colorectal carcinoma. Randomised comparison with no follow-up. *Dis Colon Rectum* 1995; **38**: 619–26.

154 Virgo KS, Vernava AM, Longo WE, McKirgan LW, Johnson FE. Cost of patient follow-up after potentially curative colorectal cancer treatment. *JAMA* 1995; **273**: 1837–41.

155 Audisio RA *et al.* Follow-up in colorectal cancer patients: a cost–benefit analysis. *Ann Surg Oncol* 1996; **3**: 349–57.

156 Edelman MJ, Meyers FJ, Siegal D. The utility of follow-up testing after curative cancer therapy: a critical review and economic analysis. *J Gen Intern Med* 1997; **12**: 18–31.

157 Department of Health. *A Report by the Expert Advisory Group on Cancer to the Chief Medical Officers for England and Wales. A policy framework for commissioning cancer services.* London: Department of Health, 1995.

158 Atkin WS, Cuzick J, Northover JMA, Whynes DK. Prevention of colorectal cancer by once-only flexible sigmoidoscopy. *Lancet* 1993; **341**: 736–40.

159 Wagner J, Herdman R, Wadhwa S. Cost-effectiveness of colorectal screening in the elderly. *Ann Intern Med* 1991; **115**: 807–17.

160 Ransohoff D, Lang C, Kuo S. Colonoscopic surveillance after polypectomy: considerations of cost-effectiveness. *Ann Intern Med* 1991; **114**: 177–82.

161 Umpleby H, Bristol J, Rainey J, Williamson R. Survival of 727 patients with single carcinomas of the large bowel. *Dis Colon Rectum* 1984; **27**: 803–10.

162 de Haes J, de Koning H, van Oortmarssen G, van Agt H, de Bruyn A, van der Maes P. The impact of a breast cancer screening programme on quality-adjusted life-years. *Int J Cancer* 1991; **49**: 538–44.

163 MacDonald L, Anderson R. The health of rectal cancer patients in the community. *Eur J Surg Oncol* 1985; **11**: 235–41.

164 Scottish Office Department of Health. *Commissioning Cancer Services in Scotland: cancer genetic services in Scotland.* Edinburgh: NHS Management Executive, 1998.

Acknowledgements

Thanks are due to the many colleagues who have helped by providing information and advice. Particular thanks are due to Dr Jennifer Smith for data from the Wessex Colorectal Cancer Audit.

7 Cancer of the Lung

Hugh Sanderson and Stephen Spiro

1 Summary

Statement of the problem/introduction

The purpose of this chapter is to provide a concise description of cancer of the lung, its causes and the options for prevention, treatment and care, so that commissioners may develop quantified cost-effective strategies in collaboration with the providers of the various services involved. Detailed recommendations on commissioning have been drawn up by the Cancer Guidance Group of the Clinical Outcomes Group funded by the NHS Executive in England, and this chapter is based largely on that guidance.[1]

The chapter is organised around the concepts of Health Benefit Groups (of conditions), Health care Resource Groups (of interventions) and the Performance Management Framework.[2] The intention is that these can be organised systematically to provide a formal health care framework that identifies the needs, appropriate interventions, standards of care, outcomes and costs for the whole programme of services related to lung cancer. Sections of the chapter deal with the sub-types of lung cancer and related conditions, the relevant interventions, the expected outcomes, costs and monitoring measures. These are then brought together as an example purchasing framework in Appendix VI, which summarises and quantifies the volumes, costs and standards of services related to lung cancer.

The data provided on incidence, costs and outcomes are drawn from various sources and, where possible, adapted to make them as representative of the epidemiological and health care situation per million population as possible. The most useful UK sources are the Public Health Common Data Set,[3] hospital discharge data (either local provider data, or national data from the Department of Health) and the National Schedule of Reference Costs[4] (which provides inpatient HRG costs for medical and surgical care, and since 1999, for radiotherapy as well).

Sub-categories

The sub-categories used in this chapter are those relevant to the purchasing of services. They are:

- the population at risk
- the population presenting with lung cancer
- the population with confirmed lung cancer
- the population with continued consequences of lung cancer.

Prevalence and incidence

It should be noted that cancer of the lung causes significant numbers of deaths and will consume considerable health care resources. Per million people in the UK, there will be about 615 deaths per year (400 men and 215 women) causing about 3720 lost years of life, and the cost of treatment and palliative care will be around £4 million (at 1997 prices).

Services available and effectiveness of services

The key factors involved in purchasing care for cancer of the lung are to do with prevention, treatment and palliative care.

Prevention is concerned almost entirely with reduction in tobacco smoking, both decreasing the numbers of young people starting to smoke, and increasing the numbers of people giving up smoking. This offers the only hope for a reduction in the death rates. The evidence shows that preventive interventions aimed at reducing smoking are highly cost-effective in terms of life-years saved. This is true for both face-to-face interventions and community-based campaigns. However, because of the long-term nature of the carcinogenic exposure, success in achieving reductions in smoking will not result in early reductions in death rates. An investment in prevention now could result in savings in treatment costs in about 10 years.

The cell type and spread of disease determine treatment. Only in cases diagnosed at an early stage, in which the tumour is localised to the lung, is cure possible.

Small-cell tumours are more aggressive, and the main treatment option for limited disease is chemotherapy. This can provide a worthwhile extension of survival, but even for these cases the prognosis is poor. Non-small-cell cancers are less aggressive (although the prognosis is also poor) and, if diagnosed early enough, may be suitable for surgery. For those with limited disease, but not suitable for surgery, radical radiotherapy may be appropriate. The majority of treatment, however, is largely aimed at palliation and controlling symptoms. For this, short-course radiotherapy may be helpful, as may other forms of pain relief and nursing care.

Quantified models of care/recommendations

The service must aim at a reasonable balance of economy of service, with a properly organised assessment process which ensures that those with a reasonable prognosis receive the appropriate diagnostic and treatment services. However, the majority of patients will require good symptom relief and support in hospital, hospice and the community. Although the majority of the resources will be provided for palliative/terminal care, funding should also be available to progress new or innovative treatments and preventive interventions whenever possible. It is particularly important, however, that new forms of treatment are properly evaluated, and wherever possible patients should be enrolled in multi-centre trials if new or unproven treatments are contemplated.

2 Introduction

Definition

Cancer of the lung includes a number of different cell types that affect the lung and associated structures. For the purpose of this specification, the definition includes all malignancies arising in the epithelium of the airways below the larynx and within the lung parenchyma (i.e. bronchogenic carcinoma) and excludes mesothelioma and cancers of other sites with metastatic deposits in the lungs.

The clinical features are described briefly in Appendix I.

Coding and classification

Classifications and codings apply to both the condition and relevant health care interventions and the codes for various systems relevant to lung cancer are shown in Appendix II.

Histological types

Malignancy in the respiratory tract may be subdivided into a number of cell types. The characteristics of the disease, aetiology, prognosis and amenability to treatment differ between types. The major distinction from the point of view of purchasing services is between small-cell (previously known as oat-cell) and non-small-cell tumours because they have different prognoses and require different types of treatment.

Staging

The extent of the disease, together with the physical state of the patient, determines the treatment options and prognosis. Radical treatment to achieve cure is possible in limited disease.

Definitions of limited and extensive disease vary, but those that have been used for limited disease include the following.

- Non-small-cell lung cancer   Staging follows the tumour, node, metastasis (TNM) staging classification. Stage I or II and some Stage IIIa patients are operable.
- Small-cell lung cancer   Cancer is confined to one side of the thorax and ipsilateral mediastinal lymph nodes.

Staging definitions are shown in Appendix IV.

The current position

Cancer of the lung is the most common type of malignancy in England and Wales and has assumed epidemic proportions over the last 40 years as a consequence of social changes and upheavals of the twentieth century, particularly the social consequences of the two world wars, and the widespread adoption of cigarette smoking by all sections of society.

Figures 1 and 2 (*see* overleaf) show the age-specific rates of lung cancer in men and women for birth cohorts from 1900. In men, the highest rates are seen in the cohort born in 1900–05 who started smoking during the 1914–18 war. For women, the highest rates are seen in the cohort born in 1920–25 who started smoking during the 1939–45 war. Subsequent cohorts for both men and women have lower age-specific rates.

In that it is almost entirely due to smoking, the disease could effectively be eliminated over a period of years if all cigarette smoking was to cease. However, not only are there major pressures from commercial

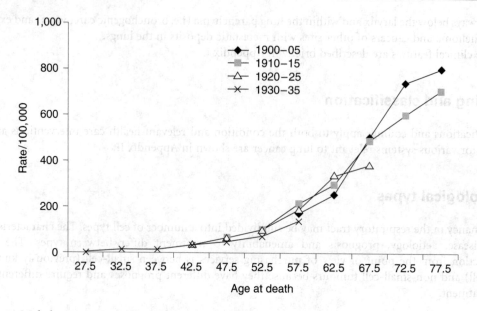

Figure 1: Male lung cancer death rates, England and Wales. Cohorts born in 1900–35.

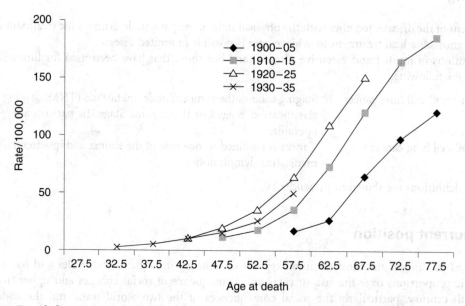

Figure 2: Female lung cancer death rates, England and Wales. Cohorts born in 1900–35.

interests and the media, but also there are important ethical issues about the limits on societies' rights to control individual behaviour. Despite the reductions in smoking rates over recent years, the take-up of smoking in adolescents has not declined. Efforts to address this cannot be divorced from the complex relationship between young people's attitudes to authority, and the confused messages with regard to cigarettes, alcohol and 'soft' drugs.

Apart from prevention/health promotion, the main involvement of health services is in providing curative and caring services. Although most individuals with lung cancer are incurable, much of the focus on research in lung cancer care has been on developing and testing new treatment modalities. However, in order to base purchasing on an adequate evidence base it is also necessary to develop better research on cost-effective ways of delivering pain relief and support in terminal illness.

The Health Benefit Group/Health care Resource Group (HBG/HRG) matrices

Assessment of needs for care can be organised around a matrix that summarises the conditions involved and the relevant interventions. These matrices allow:

- identification of the numbers of cases for each sub-category of conditions related to lung cancer
- specification of the appropriate interventions and the standards for their delivery
- the effectiveness and potential criteria for monitoring the outcome of care
- the cost of providing the interventions to all the cases within the population.

The matrices are split into four categories to encompass the whole range of disease and health care services. Conditions are split as follows.

- **At risk:** Individuals who are at risk of developing the particular condition, and who require health promotion or preventive activities (if any effective ones are available). These may be split into a number of levels of risk, from low to high.
- **Presentation:** Individuals who present with symptoms or signs suggestive of the condition, and who require investigation/assessment in order to confirm the diagnosis. A proportion of these individuals will subsequently be proven not to have the condition. However, this is still a legitimate call on the resources of the health service.
- **Confirmed disease:** Those with a confirmed health condition which requires clinical management.
- **Continued consequences of disease:** Those who require continuing care and/or rehabilitation.

Interventions are divided into:

- promotion/prevention
- diagnostic/assessment
- curative services
- care, palliation and support.

This approach provides the basis of this chapter, and a systematic structure for creating a commissioning document that can be discussed by purchaser and provider. It is very similar to the structure used in a number of programme-budgeting exercises.[5] It also permits the incorporation of performance indicators to measure the efficiency and effectiveness of the care provided within the performance framework. This framework identifies six areas of performance for the assessment and monitoring of delivery of health services:

1 **Health improvement:** To reflect the overall aim of improving the general health of the population.
2 **Fair access:** To ensure fair access in relation to needs irrespective of geography, class, ethnicity, age or sex.
3 **Effective delivery of appropriate health care:** To ensure that care is effective, appropriate and timely, and complies with agreed standards.

4   **Efficiency**: To ensure value for money in use of resources.
5   **Patient/carer experience**: To ensure that the NHS is sensitive to individual needs.
6   **Health outcomes of NHS care**: To ensure the direct contribution of NHS care to improvements in
    overall health.

The use of the condition/intervention matrix with the areas of performance in an integrated health
care framework helps to base the development and monitoring of commissioning plans on local patient
data. In order to achieve this, groupings of types of patient and types of intervention are necessary.
When appropriate individual patient data are available, these can be used to aggregate records, and
identify the numbers of individuals in each sub-category and the numbers of episodes of each type of care
provided. To assess local services, the care provided locally should then be compared with the benchmark
averages, which can be derived from the performance framework, and the best practice recommended
by guideline documents. Because development of these groups and the areas of performance are still
under way, not all of them can be defined completely. However, where possible, definitions are
provided.
   A draft summary HBG/HRG matrix for lung cancer is shown in Appendix III, together with definitions
of each of the relevant HBGs/HRGs. The NHS Information Authority – Case-Mix Programme is defining
and coding the relevant HBGs and HRGs and associating them with the performance indicators in the
Health Care Framework.
   Data do not yet exist in this form in most places, and comprehensive use of HBGs and HRGs is beyond
the information capabilities of most places. However, developments in clinical information systems
should make this possible in the future. In the mean time, the basic structure provides a convenient model
for the presentation of such information as is available and forms the basis of recommendations on how
to develop information systems which will support systematic commissioning of health care. The lack
of good information on rates of incidence/prevalence, intervention and outcomes should not be a reason
for abandoning a systematic approach to thinking about the needs and service requirements. Rather
it identifies what information needs to be developed to undertake the task of commissioning in a
professional manner, and how it should then be used.
   It should be noted that some of the services required are not specific to lung cancer (for instance, the
preventive, diagnostic and palliative care components) although even these services may have some lung
cancer-specific aspects. While these must be included in the lung cancer specification, it is important that
they should not be double counted when developing broader service specifications.

3 Sub-categories of lung cancer

The description of sub-categories is provided in four sections that are relevant to the purchasing of
services.

1 At risk:
   * Whole population
   * Population at specific risk
     – Smokers
   * Previously treated disease.
2 Presentation:
   * Asymptomatic, screen-detected or incidental finding
   * Specific and general symptoms.

3 Confirmed disease:
- Small-cell limited disease
- Small-cell extensive disease
- Non-small-cell operable
- Non-small-cell inoperable, limited
- Non-small-cell extensive disease.
4 Continued consequences of disease:
- Terminal disease/intractable pain.

At risk

Numbers at risk can be identified through factors associated with the development of lung cancer.

Smoking

By far the most important cause of lung cancer is smoking (estimated at 90%).[6] Long-term cigar and pipe smokers who do not inhale do not have such high rates of lung cancer, but cigar and pipe smokers who are ex-cigarette smokers (and hence inhalers) have just as high risks as continuing cigarette smokers.[7]

Passive smoking

Results of individual studies vary, but an excess risk of between 10 and 30% seems to exist for individuals who are passively exposed to tobacco smoke over long periods.[8]

Asbestos

Occupational exposure to asbestos causes both cancer of the lung and mesothelioma (normally of the pleura, but also occasionally of the peritoneum). The latter is almost exclusively due to asbestos. Smokers who are exposed to asbestos have very high risks of lung cancer.[9]

Metal ores

Workers with nickel and chromium ores are at higher risk of developing lung cancer.[10]

Air pollution

Cancer of the lung is more common in residents of urban areas but a substantial part of this difference is due to smoking, social class and occupational exposure. Studies from the USA[11] and Poland[12] have suggested an independent association, and local industrial air pollution in the UK has been associated with high rates of lung cancer.[13] Overall, the attributable risk is likely to be small.

Radon

Exposure to radon in houses increases the risk of lung cancer. Although overall the effect is small, it is potentially significant, particularly in the south-west of England.

4 Incidence and prevalence

For purchasing activity through the HBG/HRG matrix, three 'at-risk' HBGs are identified.

1 The whole population.
2 The population at specific risk, which includes:
   - children and young adults, who are at risk of starting smoking. Per million population there will be about 128 000 children aged 5–14 and 123 000 young people aged 15–24.
   - Smokers who need encouragement and assistance to stop smoking. Twenty-eight per cent of men aged over 16 are smokers and 25% of women aged over 16. This represents about 214 000 people (110 000 men and 104 000 women) per million.
   While there are other risks, there is little that can be done after exposure has occurred, although environmental monitoring and industrial protection are required to minimise exposure to these risk factors.
3 Those treated previously. Individuals with a history of lung cancer who have been treated successfully and are under follow-up. Because of the poor prognosis of this tumour (< 10% survival at 1 year) there will only be about 60 new cases yearly for follow-up.

Those presenting with symptoms

Presentation may be with specific or non-specific symptoms. In addition, some individuals are diagnosed through incidental findings of other investigations. The HBGs are divided into:

- asymptomatic, screen-detected or incidental finding (about 5% of all cases)
- symptomatic presentation. This will include those with suggestive symptoms and a presumptive diagnosis of lung cancer, those with more general symptoms, and those presenting as acutely ill. A definitive diagnosis for these last two groups is made as part of the diagnostic assessment.

Not all of those who present will subsequently be proven to have cancer of the lung, but in these cases the use of resources to exclude the diagnosis is important. There is very little information about the numbers of cases investigated and/or referred with suspected symptoms, so the number of individuals requiring diagnostic services is not easy to identify, either nationally or locally.

As an estimate, in lieu of better information, twice the incidence of lung cancer has been used as an assessment of the numbers of referrals that will require a basic outpatient consultation and simple investigation package. This represents about 1200 referrals of patients with symptoms for assessment per million people. Once the diagnosis has been made, further investigations are required for staging, and these are identified in the treatment matrix.

Diagnosed disease

Incidence and prevalence figures are required to assess the volumes of services that should be purchased for curative services. Because the disease is so lethal, mortality and mean survival figures (*see* Table 1) provide good estimates for incidence and prevalence. However, data to break these down by cell type and extent are difficult to obtain (typically only about two-thirds of cases are confirmed histologically; *see* Table 2). Consequently, the implications for types of services are also difficult to quantify.

Table 1: Age-specific deaths and death rates per 100 000 people (based on rates for England 1994–96, PHCDS).

Age (years)	Males		Females		Total	
	Rate/100,000	*n*	Rate/100,000	*n*	Rate/100,000	*n*
1–4	0.0	0.0	0.0	0.0	0.0	0.0
5–14	0.0	0.0	0.0	0.0	0.0	0.0
15–34	0.2	0.4	0.2	0.1	0.2	0.5
35–64	49.7	94	25.4	48	37.6	142
65–74	385.7	152	172.3	80	269.7	232
75+	608.4	153	182.8	86	329.8	239
All ages	81.0	398	42.3	215	61.3	614

Factors affecting the incidence are described in Appendix V.

Table 2: Estimated percentage of cases by cell type and extent of disease.[14]

	Limited	Extensive	Total
Non-small cell	12 ± 8*	62	80
Small cell	6	14	20
Total	22	78	100

* Up to 15% of non-small-cell lung cancer cases may be suitable for surgery and a further 10% may be suitable for radical radiotherapy.

The numbers for any particular district can be found from the Public Health Common Data Set (PHCDS). Districts which have high concentrations of social class IV/V or a high prevalence of smoking will tend to have higher rates of cancer of the lung than average. Use of the SMR (standardised mortality ratio) by social class or the SRR (standardised registration ratio) for ONS (Office of National Statistics) area types can be used to calculate the expected incidence for a given population (*see* Table 3).

Table 3: New cases per year for a population of 1 million.

	Limited	Extensive	Total
Non-small cell	$74 + 48$	370	492
Small cell	37	85	122
Total	159	455	614

Functional consequences of continuing disease

Advanced lung cancer causes pain, respiratory symptoms (breathlessness) and increasing debility and incapacitation. In addition, the psychological effects of terminal disease affect not just the individual, but also carers and family members. The degree of pain, functional impairment and psychological distress can vary widely and has been described for patients dying of cancer in general,[14] but there is little information on the distribution specifically in relation to lung cancer. Because lung cancer has a very poor prognosis, with only 10% survival at 1 year, and a mean life expectancy of 6 months from diagnosis, the incidence rate provides a reasonable estimate of the numbers of individuals who will experience these functional restrictions to some extent.

It has been estimated that 15–25% of patients dying from cancer receive inpatient hospice care, and between 25 and 65% receive input from a support team or Macmillan nurse. However, these estimates are largely a function of the availability of service, and there is little information on measures of objective need, or easy ways to identify how these estimates should be modified to suit different districts.[15]

This implies that 555 individuals will die during a year, who will experience the symptoms and functional limitations of continuing lung cancer and who are likely to require help of some sort in terms of pain relief, symptom control, nursing care and psychological support.

5 Interventions/services

This section describes the nature, volume and costs of services used to prevent and treat cancer of the lung per million people, and is based upon current guidelines on appropriate care.[1,16]

Services for those at risk of developing lung cancer (whole population/at risk, child smokers, previously treated disease)

Controlling smoking

Smoking prevalence reduction is not only undertaken by the health services. Controls on advertising, availability to young people and taxation policy are also the responsibility of other government agencies.

Health services at the local level deal with two main areas (preventing starting and smoking cessation) and cost estimates for smoking cessation interventions have been taken from guidance issued by the Health Education Authority (HEA)/Centre for Health Economics, York[17] (updated in 2000, *see Thorax.* **55**: 987–99). These estimates are for various options. Smoking cessation guidelines have also been published.[18,19]

Prevention of the uptake of smoking

Education and health services inform about the risks of smoking, and also help to develop young people's self-confidence and self-esteem. The HEA* supplies materials for classroom activities; the major input of staff is teacher time. Training and support for teachers vary from district to district, but are estimated, on average, to be 0.05 WTE health promotion officer/million people (*c.* £1000 per annum; V Speller, personal communication).

Teacher input has been estimated at 3 hours/year in primary school and 6 hours/year in secondary school (not only related to smoking). On the assumption that a population of 1 million has a school-age population of about 153 000 (aged 5–16), of whom about 83 000 will be in 450 primary schools and about

---

* Since this chapter was written the HEA has been superseded by the Health Development Agency (HDA).

70 000 in 70 secondary schools, a cost of about £140 000/year in direct teaching time can be estimated. In addition, materials from the HEA for these schools will cost *c.* £25 000 (non-recurrent). (*Note*: These are not PCT costs.)

Encouraging and supporting quitting

Two types of intervention were assessed by the HEA guidance:

- face-to-face interventions
- community interventions, e.g. 'No Smoking Days'.

Face-to-face interventions range from brief advice (up to 3 minutes) to brief counselling (3–10 minutes) and support with nicotine gum. Brief advice is estimated to cost £492 000 (if undertaken routinely for a population of 1 million and assuming a population reach of 80%). Brief counselling (again if provided routinely and assuming a population reach of 70%) has an additional estimated cost of £2.2 million. Nicotine gum is estimated to incur a further additional cost of £460 000 (assuming a population reach of 50%).

Community interventions assessed were 'Quit and Win' campaigns, which generally involve eligibility for a prize draw for smokers who can demonstrate abstinence for a defined period, and locally organised 'No Smoking Days'. An average cost/average participation 'Quit and Win' campaign is estimated to cost £200 000, and local 'No Smoking Day' activities are estimated at £12 000. The costs to the NHS of encouraging and supporting quitting are shown in Table 4.

Table 4: Summary of costs to the NHS for at-risk population per million (assuming one 'No Smoking Day' and one 'Quit and Win' campaign per year).

HBG	Health education in schools	Health education/ support in primary care	Community interventions	Eligible cases	Total cost
Schoolchildren				153,000	*c.* £1,000
Smokers	£12.80			230,000	£2,952,000
		£0.92		230,000	£212,000
Total					£3,164,000

Note: There are also costs to smokers of time and nicotine gum.

Services for those presenting with symptoms/signs

Screening

No screening services are provided for the early detection of cancer of the lung in the NHS as there is currently no evidence that population screening is effective in reducing mortality. Hypothesis-generating studies assessing the prevalence and incidence of new cancers identified by spiral CT indicate a high level of detection of Stage I cases, but randomised controlled trials will be needed to determine whether this technique identifies cancers early enough to improve mortality. Such a trial has commenced in the USA and is currently being contemplated in various European countries.

Diagnosis

The diagnosis of cancer of the lung is generally made without extensive investigation. However, it may be necessary to undertake further investigation to establish the extent and cell type of the tumour before deciding on the appropriate treatment.

Guidelines recommend that all those with suspicious chest X-ray and history should have bronchoscopy or sputum cytology or computed tomography (CT)-guided fine-needle cytology or core biopsy. However, not all cases are confirmed histologically. Up to 1990 the rate was 50–60%,[20,21] but by 1992–94 this had improved to 70% in the Northern and Yorkshire region.[22]

Referral patterns will vary (and some patients see more than one specialist), but in a recent review of all lung cancer cases in one region (East Anglia; T. Davies, personal communication), 90% of all cases were seen by a physician, 15% by a surgeon and 38% by an oncologist. (Information on the referral patterns of those in whom lung cancer was excluded is not available.) In contrast, data from the Northern and Yorkshire region[22] show that in 1992–94, 61% were seen by a chest physician, 47% by an oncologist and 21% by a surgeon. However, this study also showed substantial variation in the proportion managed by a specialist between both trusts and age groups (86% for those under 70 years, and 63% for those over 70 years).

Lung cancer guidance recommends that all cases are referred to a multi-disciplinary lung cancer team comprising a respiratory physician, radiologist, pathologist, nurse specialist, oncologist, radiotherapist, palliative care specialist and thoracic surgeon.

Average diagnostic costs are small in relation to treatment costs but will include at least one outpatient visit, bronchoscopy in about 50% of cases and chest X-ray. Average diagnostic costs are unknown but unlikely to be more than *c.* £500/patient (*see* Table 5).

Table 5: Summary of diagnosis services.

HBG	Number of individuals	Outpatient visit	Chest X-ray	Rigid broncho-scopy (D08)	Flexible broncho-scopy (D07)	Number of cases	Total cost
Screen detected/ asymptomatic	n/k	n/k	n/k	£418 (day case)	£308 (day case)	n/k	n/k
Symptomatic presentation				£727 (IP)	£488 (IP)		

Services for those with diagnosed disease

The type of service provided depends entirely on the histological type and stage of disease.

Non-small-cell carcinoma, operable

Only patients with potentially curable disease (up to Stage IIB) are considered resectable. Some Stage IIIa tumours are also resectable, particularly if N2 (mediastinal node involvement) disease is only found at resection (usually microscopic nodal involvement).

Selection involves assessment of the general health of the patient, histological diagnosis and staging of the disease. All those considered for surgery will probably have bronchoscopy, a CT scan of the thorax and upper abdomen, and mediastinoscopy if there are enlarged mediastinal nodes on CT (>1 cm in diameter).[1] Current practice varies, and there is little information on the numbers of cases assessed, as distinct from the numbers selected for surgery, but estimates range from 6.7 to 15% of all cases. However, resection rates in the UK are some of the lowest in Europe. Although older patients are less likely to undergo surgery than younger patients, age should not be a barrier to surgery, provided that the patient's performance status is satisfactory.

Mediastinoscopy falls within HRG D04, D05. National average costs (1997–98) are c. £1600–2700. This implies about 74 cases per year per million.

HRG costs for surgical care are now becoming available based on care profiles. A typical profile for surgical care includes:

- 12 days' inpatient stay
- 1.5–2.5 hours' operating-theatre time
- 0.25 days' ITU
- chest X-ray, CAT scan (0.15), mediastinoscopy/mediastinotomy
- group and cross-match/transfuse 2 units
- full blood count and biochemistry
- pre- and post-operative radiotherapy is not recommended.

Current cost estimates for HRG D02 (complex thoracic procedures) are £4183 (elective) and £4151 (emergency). The mean length of stay for HRG D02 (complex thoracic procedures) is 9.4 days (1997–98). Positron emission tomography (PET) scanning can alter clinical stage in up to 30% of patients considered resectable by the above techniques. PET is increasingly recommended as the final staging investigation prior to surgery.[41] Currently there are only five PET scanners available to the NHS in England. Staging algorithms will change with better availability of PET.

Non-small-cell, inoperable, limited disease

For a small number of patients with disease limited to the thorax (approximately 8% of all cases), but unsuitable for operation, radical radiotherapy may be indicated. A recent trial of continuous hyper-fractionated accelerated radiotherapy (CHART) in patients with small-volume but inoperable disease has shown that three daily fractions of radiotherapy (each of 1.5 Gy for 12 days, total 54 Gy) provides a higher response rate than conventional radical radiotherapy. This results in a 24% reduction in the relative risks of death, i.e. 9% absolute improvement in 2-year survival compared with conventional radiotherapy (29 vs. 20%, respectively).[23] Despite this evidence, not all radiotherapy centres have implemented the CHART regime for all suitable patients.

Estimates of the frequency of CHART or conventional radical radiotherapy (the latter probably being given to localised disease considered too bulky for CHART) vary, possibly depending on the availability of resources. An estimate of 8% indicates about 48 cases per year per million people (and may be very much less in other districts, dependent on local practices).[20] In general, cases will have complex planning which should include a CT of the thorax and, for CHART, probable inpatient accommodation. For routine radical radiotherapy, daily visits will be necessary, i.e. 25 visits over a 5-week period. There will also be follow-up visits to outpatients at 2–3-month intervals.

The CHART regime falls into HRG W18 (hyperfractionation, complex with imaging). Other radical radiotherapy regimes will be:

- W15 (complex with imaging, 13–23 fractions) or
- W16 (complex with imaging, 24+ fractions).

See Appendix III for radiotherapy HRG definitions.

The costs per course are £2484, £1902 and £2390, respectively (K Lloyd, personal communication).

There are few data available on chemotherapy costs. However, this regime falls into the 'Toxic, low cost' group for the proposed chemotherapy HRGs, at an estimated cost from one hospital of £336 (£63 per visit, average 5.3 visits).

Non-small-cell, inoperable, extensive disease

The majority of non-small-cell lung carcinoma (NSCLC; 62% of all lung cancer cases) will have progressed beyond the limited stage at diagnosis. In the majority of these patients, palliative radiotherapy will be used at some stage to provide symptom relief. This applies to about 370 cases per year per million population.

On average, cases will receive simple planning and 1–5 fractions of radiotherapy (total dose 20–30 Gy) on an outpatient basis, unless very distant from the radiotherapy centre or very frail (HRG W07 simple and simulator, 4–12 fractions). Some radiotherapy centres have adopted a reduced fraction schedule, which may involve only two or three fractions, which is as effective as longer and more fractionated courses (HRG W06, simple and simulator 0–3 fractions). Estimated costs are £944 and £296, respectively.

Chemotherapy for these patients increases median survival by 3–4 months. There is some evidence of benefit for modern regimes of two or three agents, for patients with ECOG performance status 0 and 1.[42]

Metastatic disease

Depending on the site of metastases, a few fractions of simple radiotherapy may be effective in providing relief of symptoms and pain (HRG W06 simple and simulator 0–3 fractions, cost £296).

Small-cell carcinoma

Small-cell carcinoma is responsible for approximately 20% of all cases, is more aggressive than non-small-cell carcinoma, and is more likely to be widely spread through the lung and to metastasise early. It is radiosensitive, but because of the rapid rate of growth and dissemination, radiotherapy is not effective in achieving cure on its own. The tumour is sensitive to combination chemotherapy.

Limited disease

About 30% of cases of small-cell lung carcinoma (SCLC) are limited (confined to one hemithorax). Surgery may be carried out in a few cases (less than 3% of all SCLC in East Anglia) but the treatment of choice is combination chemotherapy. The recommended duration of treatment is six cycles, one every 3 weeks (chemotherapy, multi-drug high cost £1817, Northampton costs).

Ninety per cent of patients with limited disease will respond, with at least 50% achieving a complete response. However, this is not the same as cure, and many of these patients will subsequently relapse. The administration of mediastinal radiotherapy (W15 complex with imaging 13–23 fractions £1902) is recommended in responding patients and this benefits the median survival, increasing it by 5% at 3 years in patients who have responded to chemotherapy.[24]

Extensive disease

Extensive disease should also be treated with the same chemotherapy regime as for limited disease (chemotherapy group, multi-drug high cost, £1817 per patient course).

Up to 60% of patients respond, with 20% achieving a complete response. Chemotherapy prolongs median survival in limited-disease patients from 3 months untreated to 12–15 months, and in extensive disease from 4 weeks untreated to 6–9 months. The cure rate for patients with limited disease is 7% at 4 years and 0–2% for extensive disease patients. However, fit patients with limited disease and normal biochemical values at diagnosis have a 15–20% chance of cure.

The role of prophylactic cerebral irradiation in prolonging survival is small, but it significantly reduces the incidence of relapse within the brain and the high associated levels of comorbidity and a prolonged stay in hospital (W07 or W08, simple with simulator, 4–12 or 13+ fractions £944, £1417).[25] The effect of chemotherapy on quality of life is beneficial with good control of presenting symptoms. Side-effects should also be tolerable. For those who relapse after a disease-free interval of 1 year, further chemotherapy may by useful, although less so than the initial treatment.

The intensity and duration of chemotherapy may be modified based on stage, performance status and other factors. Costs of chemotherapy are, therefore, variable and a true average figure is not available. HRGs for chemotherapy are not published at the time of writing, but when available will provide estimates of costs for these courses of treatment. Costs quoted in this section are based on costs for draft HRGs from Northampton Acute Trust (*see* Table 6).

Table 6: Summary of treatments and costs (per million population, percentage of all cases).

			Cases	Cost	Total cost
	Local, operable	Surgical resection (12%)	74	HRG D02 £3,750	£277,500
		Mediastinoscopy	37	HRG D04 £1,812	£67,044
Non-small cell (80%) 492	Local disease (inoperable)	CHART (hyperfractionation) Radical radiotherapy 13–24 fractions Radical radiotherapy 24+ fractions (8%) Chemotherapy	48	HRG W18 £2,484 HRG W15 £1,902 HRG W16 £2,390 Toxic low cost £336	£119,232 £16,128
	Widespread disease	Palliative radiotherapy (62%)	370	HRG W07 £944 W06 £296	£174,640 £54,760
	Metastases	Palliative radiotherapy (?25% of all lung cancers)	150	HRG W06 £296	£44,400
Small cell (20%) 122	Limited	Chemotherapy (6%) Plus mediastinal radiotherapy for the 90% who respond	37 33	Multi-drug, high cost £1,817 HRG W15 £1,902	£67,229 £62,766
	Extensive	Chemotherapy Prophylactic cerebral irradiation (14%)	85	Multi-drug high cost £1,817 W07 simple with simulator 4–12 fractions £944	£154,445 £80,240
Total					£1,118,384

Services for those with functional consequences of continuing disease

The majority of patients require palliative care during the terminal phase of their illness, which may last for 3–6 months, and 95% of patients will die of their cancer. Location of care may vary between hospital, hospice, day unit and home. Services provided may include nursing care, pain relief, counselling and support to the patient and family. Models of care have been described in *Palliative and Terminal Care*.[15]

Analysis of service use by 320 terminally ill cancer patients (not only lung) in Wandsworth showed total average costs of £7100. This was made up of an average of 29 inpatient days, six outpatient visits, two day-patient attendances and 13 district nurse visits.[26]

An alternative estimate suggested a rather lower consumption of resources,[27] comprising 14–17 inpatient days, and a requirement for about 50 inpatient hospice beds to provide for the needs of cancer patients in a population of a million. This would imply a cost of *c.* £3.6 million/year at a bed/day cost of £200 per day. From this assessment, if the inpatient hospice requirements are £3.6 million, then the total resource requirements per million people for cancer patients could be £4.5 million (including community and district general hospital services). Since cancer of the lung causes about 25% of the cancer deaths, this would imply a consumption of about £1.1 million for lung cancer patients, or equivalent to *c.* £2000 per patient (for *c.* 550 patients who die of lung cancer each year).

Dedicated funding for terminal/palliative care was provided to districts up to 1994–95 and was *c.* £1 million per million population. However, this did not cover the activity of non-specialist services, such as general practitioners (GPs), district nursing, and use of general beds (both in district general and community hospitals) for nursing and symptom relief.

A survey in 1993 showed that there was considerable use of these services, and a quarter of patients had 20 or more contacts with their GP during the last year of life and 50 or more visits from a district nurse.

Systematic and consistent information about the resources required for the provision of palliative/ terminal care is difficult to obtain. This is partly because the care is distributed across a number of services, including acute hospitals, community services, primary care and contracted private services (hospices).

Recommended patterns of care, requirements for information collection and service standards are detailed in Higginson,[15] but the specific resource implications for patients with cancer of the lung are not known. Palliative care HRGs are under development.

In the light of this uncertainty about the costs of palliative and terminal care, it is difficult to provide more than a very broad range of estimates of the costs of palliative/terminal care for lung cancer patients of £2000–7100 per person, which translates to a total cost per million people of between £1.1 million and £3.9 million.

6 Efficacy/cost-effectiveness of services

Prevention

The evidence on costs and effectiveness of smoking cessation interventions has been summarised by the HEA.[19] (This work has not examined the cost-effectiveness of preventing children from starting smoking.)

Because of the limitations of the studies reported in the literature, the estimates that have been derived are based on a number of assumptions. However, 'the data strongly support the value of smoking cessation programmes compared with almost any other health service intervention'.[17] One problem is the difficulty of ensuring that changes in smoking have been due entirely to the intervention and not another influence. Randomised controlled trials are rare and difficult to arrange when the intervention is to large groups. In addition, the verification of abstinence and the duration of follow-up are other factors which tend to vary and make the literature difficult to compare.

The two types of intervention compared are face-to-face interventions (brief advice, brief counselling, nicotine gum) and community interventions ('No Smoking Day', broader community-wide campaigns and 'Quit and Win' campaigns) (*see* Table 7).

Table 7: Comparison of face-to-face and community interventions.

	Effectiveness	Population reach	Life years gained (lyg)	Cost to NHS (per 1 million people)	Cost/lyg NHS	Cost/ lyg smokers	Cost/ lyg both	Discounted cost/lyg (both)*
Brief advice	2%	80%	6,068	£492,760	£81	£13	£94	£479
Brief counselling	2% (additional gain)	70%	5,310	£2,204,502	£415	£130	£545	£2,787
Nicotine gum	8% (additional gain)	50%	15,202	£561,972	£37	£462	£463	£2,370
'No Smoking Day'	0.15%	90%	568	£11,960	£21	N/A	£21	£107
Broader community-wide campaigns (mid estimate)	0.1%	100%	380	£102,854	£271	N/A	£271	£1,390
'Quit and Win' average cost estimate	8%	1.26%	384	£200,542	£522	N/A	£522	£2,710

* Discounted at 6% p.a.

Screening

Prevention of death through early diagnosis by mass screening (X-ray and sputum cytology) has been evaluated in a number of studies in the USA and Germany.[28,29] These have not shown any benefit in terms of reduced mortality even when high-risk individuals are selected.

Treatment

Surgery for NSCLC

The results of surgery depend upon the selection criteria used, but audit data suggest a 32% relative survival at 5 years. Survival for Stage I NSCLC patients undergoing surgery is quoted as 70% compared with 10% for those who were not operated on. However, selection bias will account for some of this difference, and there are no randomised controlled clinical trials of surgery.

Taking this difference as the most optimistic estimate, the effect of surgery could be estimated as delivering 3 life years per patient, up to 5 years (quality of life is below baseline for up to 6 months post-operatively), at a cost of (£3750 + 1812/2) = £4656. This implies a cost of £1522 per life year gained. This is an underestimate because of the potential gains beyond 5 years, but this may balance the overoptimistic estimate of the difference between surgery and no surgery. (There may be a greater gain due to the avoidance of palliative/terminal care costs.)

Radical radiotherapy for NSCLC

Again, the results will depend upon the patient selection criteria used, but 30% of patients with cancer limited to the thorax treated with the CHART regime survived for 2 years, compared with 20% randomised to conventional radiotherapy. This is equivalent to a gain of 0.2 life years per patient for an extra cost of £698 (£3490 per life year gained).

Meta-analyses of clinical trials in which patients have been randomised to receive radical radiotherapy or radical radiotherapy preceded by chemotherapy highlight a potential benefit of the combined treatment showing a 2-month advantage for the addition of chemotherapy to radiotherapy alone. There is a 4% improvement in survival at 2 years with the addition of cisplatin-containing combination chemotherapy to radiotherapy.[30] Further studies are required to validate these data prospectively.

Palliative radiotherapy for NSCLC

Palliative radiotherapy is effective in relieving specific symptoms, but does not prolong survival. Results from the MRC trial of palliative radiotherapy suggest that two fractions are just as effective in controlling symptoms[31,32] as longer regimes of higher doses. This regime has been adopted in some centres. It should, however, be noted that the longer-term survivors (18 months) of this regime have a risk of radiation myelitis. Although the risk is small (< 5%), the consequence (paraplegia) is severe.

Preliminary trials suggest that a single fraction of intraluminal radiotherapy may be effective in providing palliation, without the risk of myelitis. There are, however, higher costs associated with the equipment, sources and technical skills required in introducing the source via a bronchoscope.

The role of chemotherapy in addition to palliative radiotherapy and best supportive care is uncertain. The meta-analysis assessed every study of chemotherapy vs. best supportive care published before 1995 and showed a small but significant advantage over best supportive care for cisplatin-containing combination chemotherapy. Quality-of-life data remain scarce, but there was a 10% improvement in survival with the addition of chemotherapy in patients with advanced NSCLC at 1 year. Further prospective studies, including quality-of-life assessment and health economic assessment, have verified this claim. Chemotherapy outside clinical trials is discouraged, but is now given increasingly to some PS patients. Four treatment cycles appear to be the optimum.

The cost-effectiveness of conventional radical radiotherapy is difficult to determine, as there are no recent randomised controlled trials of its effectiveness. Laser and selectron therapy have not yet been demonstrated to provide useful results.

Chemotherapy for SCLC

Overall outcome for chemotherapy is 10% survival at 2 years and 5% at 5 years. The results for limited disease are somewhat better at 15–20% at 2 years.

Mean survival without treatment is 3 months for limited disease and 6 weeks for extensive disease. With treatment, this becomes 12–15 months for limited disease and 6–9 months for extensive disease.

The mean survival gain may be estimated as 9–12 months per patient. However, the significant side-effects of chemotherapy may reduce the quality of life. At a cost of £1800 per course of chemotherapy and £1900 for radiotherapy for the 90% of patients who respond (i.e. £3510), the cost per life year is £4680.

A Canadian trial of various regimes indicated that for the most effective regime, an increase in survival of 1.6 months was obtained at a marginal cost of $450, i.e. $3370 per extra life year gained.[33]

Although most estimates of life years gained should be discounted, in the instance of lung cancer treatment, since the duration of life gained is relatively short, this has not been undertaken.

Terminal care

Up to 70% of patients would opt for home care in preference to hospital or hospice if possible, and for half of these patients the final choice was home care. The provision of care in the home has been found to substantially reduce the number of inpatient days, and the extra support at home is no more costly than traditional care,[34] or may be less.[35] Caring for terminally ill patients in a general hospital setting is often felt to be incompatible with the needs of the terminally ill and their relatives for open-ended conversation and emotional support. Hospice or dedicated hospital care may, therefore, be seen as more appropriate.

Summary of efficacy/cost-effectiveness of services

A summary of the efficacy/cost-effectiveness of services is given in Table 8.

Table 8: Service efficacy and cost-effectiveness.

	Intervention	Size of effect*	Quality of evidence†
Prevention	Face-to-face interventions	A	II-1
	Community interventions	A	II-1
Treatment	NSCLC surgery	A	II-2
	NSCLC radical radiotherapy	B	I-2
	NSCLC radical radiotherapy plus chemotherapy	C	II-1
	NSCLC palliative radiotherapy	B	I-2
	SCLC chemotherapy	B	I-2
Support	Palliative care	B	II-1

* A, the procedure has a strong beneficial effect; B, the procedure has a moderate beneficial effect; C, the procedure has a measurable beneficial effect; D, the procedure has no measurable beneficial effect; E, the harms of the procedure outweigh the benefits.
† I-1, evidence from several consistent or one large randomised controlled trial; I-2, evidence from at least one properly designed, randomised controlled trial; II-1, evidence from well-designed controlled trials without randomisation or from well-designed cohort or case–control analytical studies; II-2, evidence from multiple time series with or without intervention (dramatic results from uncontrolled experiments could also be regarded as this type of evidence); III, opinions of respected authorities, based on clinical experience, descriptive studies or reports of expert committees; IV, evidence that is inadequate or conflicting.

7 Models of care and recommendations

Prevention

Prevention of lung cancer through reductions in the numbers of smokers is an effective but long-term strategy. For smokers who give up, the risk of developing lung cancer is a function of the years of exposure to cigarette smoke, and will remain raised but static. Reductions in lung cancer rates are, therefore, only gradual, and the effectiveness of preventing young people from starting to smoke will only become apparent 30–40 years later as they enter their fifties and sixties.

Recommendation for prevention

Investment in prevention is required now if the reductions in smoking are to be achieved. Even then, the reductions in cancer rates will take several years to occur, and cannot be justified in the short term in terms of reductions in treatment costs or life years saved. It is worth bearing in mind, however, that substantial investments in basic research in cell biology and control mechanisms are now being made in order to find new methods of cancer treatment. These are also unlikely to yield significant improvements in patient care for many years (perhaps as many as 20), but are more enthusiastically promoted, although the probability of return on investment is no more certain.

In summary, there is a need to provide a balanced and effective strategy, which will include:

- programmes to prevent children from starting to smoke (support to schools)
- programmes to help people to give up smoking (workplace programmes, National No Smoking Day)
- advice from health professionals (GPs, nurses)
- mass media/fiscal measures/action on advertising (lobbying and local advertising).

It is important to note the time-scale for improvements in lung cancer incidence, and the consequent need to take cost-effective action early.

Screening

As a result of the evaluative studies cited above, screening programmes cannot be recommended, as there is no significant improvement in the prognosis of patients found through screening.

Treatment

Surgery

For suitable tumours, surgical resection offers good outcome at a reasonable cost. Careful selection of cases with thorough pre-operative assessment is likely to ensure good results. Purchasers should discuss the criteria for surgical resection with the providers, and should ensure that the criteria for standards of care in the lung cancer guidance document are followed.

Radical radiotherapy

The CHART regime has been demonstrated to be more effective, though more costly, than conventional radiotherapy. Purchasers should discuss with providers how to ensure that those patients deemed suitable for radical radiotherapy can be treated under the CHART regime.

Palliative radiotherapy

The available evidence suggests that palliative radiotherapy can both be deferred until symptoms are present and be reduced to one or two fractions in many cases. This approach may also be used for the relief of local symptoms and metastases. Adoption of these criteria could potentially reduce the costs of radiotherapy to a district. However, the effect of this on overall costs will be limited because these are dominated by the cost of terminal care, and these are relatively simple and low-cost fractions. In addition, since some radiotherapy departments have already adopted the implications of the MRC trial,[36] the potential gains will not exist in some districts. Purchasers should explore the balance of regimes with providers.

Chemotherapy

The available evidence suggests that survival for SCLC can be extended by 9–12 months on the most cost-effective regime. The evidence for chemotherapy in NSCLC is less clear. Purchasers should discuss with providers how to ensure that patients with SCLC expected to benefit from chemotherapy receive a cost-effective regime. Suitable patients with NSCLC should only receive chemotherapy as part of properly costed multi-centre trials. Purchasers should meet the additional costs of trial entry.

Palliative/terminal care

Palliative care for cancer of the lung is in principle no different to that for other malignant disease. Between 40 and 50 terminal care beds per million people have been recommended, of which 10–12 would be used by patients with cancer of the lung. Home care provision has been recommended at a ratio of four home nurses per million people for patients with severe pain.

In order to provide care for all patients in need it is important for terminal care to be:

- population based
- able to cope with the difficult as well as easy problems
- able to educate health care professionals (both in hospital and in the community) in order to raise the quality of palliative care
- based on an appropriate balance between specialist palliative care and the generalist support of the primary care team.

Continuing education of GPs, hospital doctors and nurses is required together with a well co-ordinated policy on palliative care to ensure that those with the greatest needs get the highest priority for service.

8 Measures of outcomes and targets to monitor services

The measures suggested in this section are based on the six Areas of Performance, and will be better defined as the National Service Frameworks for Cancer are developed.

Prevention

Activity measures should show the interventions undertaken and amount of staff time (including primary care team) devoted to reducing smoking.

The success of preventive activities should be monitored by examining reductions in the rate of starting smoking by children, quit rates achieved by established smokers (these need to be verified by biochemical measures of nicotine and carbon monoxide) and by estimating smoking rates in the community. Methods to ascertain this from sample surveys and extrapolations from other areas (e.g. General Household Survey) need to be explored in order to determine whether the intended reduction in smoking is achieved. It will be important to ensure that such surveys are methodologically sound, and well-designed studies may need to be carried out for 3–5 years in order to determine the actual progress in smoking reduction. Such studies may, however, be costly and should only be undertaken if the information gained is worthwhile.

Over a longer period, reductions in the number of deaths from lung cancer should occur if smoking reductions have been achieved.

Treatment

Efficiency

Costs of treatment regimes should be within an agreed percentage of the national average HRG cost.

Fair access

There should be an agreed rate of access to surgery for operable limited NSCLC disease.

Effective delivery

There should be:

- an agreed rate of entry to CHART for NSCLC inoperable/limited disease
- an agreed rate of use of 1–3 fraction palliative radiotherapy courses for extensive NSCLC
- an agreed rate of early referral to a specialist lung cancer team
- an agreed target rate of histological confirmation and patient/carer experience
- agreed standards of patient explanation for all treatment regimes.

Outcomes of health care

There should be agreed rates of survival/quality-of-life scores for all treatment regimes.

Terminal care

The important elements of terminal care are the relief of symptoms and support of the patient and carers. Fair access should be monitored through the availability of palliative care specialist teams, and the patient/carer experience should be monitored at regular intervals.

9 Information

The data to provide the systematic needs assessment outlined in this chapter are not generally available at the district level. The development of the NHS Information Strategy will focus effort on creating clinical information systems that support patient care, and can also be used to extract epidemiological and management information. An early element of the Information Strategy is the development of a Cancer

Information Strategy which will support the early implementation of electronic patient records for cancer patients. A key component of this strategy will be the specification of agreed minimum data sets (clinical and statistical). These are likely to be based on data sets published by the Royal College of Pathologists and the Royal College of Physicians. This cancer strategy was published in early 2000 and it is likely that in the longer term, the role of cancer registration will become more closely integrated into these clinical information systems.

The essential components of this will include the following.

1   GP computer systems which can provide details of HBGs through the organisation of groups of GPs who are willing to collaborate and ensure the accurate collection of data through their computer systems. This can then be extracted and pooled to provide an estimate of the epidemiology of lung cancer in the population. (This does not need to be 100% of practices as suitable samples could provide sufficiently accurate information.) In addition, the use of services at the primary care level can be assessed, in particular to provide estimates of preventive, diagnostic and palliative/terminal activities.

- Numbers of individuals at risk (smokers, history of asbestos exposure, etc.).
- Numbers of individuals presenting with suspicious symptoms.
- Numbers of individuals referred to hospital and stage at diagnosis (from hospital discharge summary).
- Numbers of individuals with terminal disease.
- Numbers of packages of palliative/terminal care.
- Outcomes of care (survival and quality-of-life measures).
- Numbers of individuals receiving smoking advice and counselling.

2   District hospital clinical systems (and laboratory/radiology department systems) which can provide details of HRGs delivered and performance measures through linking electronic patient records. These need to be linked to demographic details so that the activity can be ascribed to the right population.

- Numbers of individuals seen and assessed in outpatient departments (including diagnostic services).
- Numbers of admissions for surgery (chemo/radiotherapy), palliation and terminal care.
- Standards of care for clinical governance and performance management.

3   Cancer centre clinical systems, similarly linked, which can provide details of HRGs delivered and performance measures through:

- numbers of courses of chemotherapy and radiotherapy
- care standards for clinical governance and performance management.

4   Voluntary sector (hospices, Marie Curie, etc.), which can provide details of HRGs delivered and performance measures through:

- numbers of patients receiving palliative/terminal care in the voluntary sector
- care standards delivered.

5   Community/primary care trust clinical systems.

- Numbers of patients receiving palliative care in community settings.
- Numbers of health education interventions for schoolchildren.

6   Cancer registries ensure completeness of epidemiological data capture and long-term outcome measures.

- Population-based capture of new cases.
- Information on long-term death rates.

10 Research priorities

Case-mix language

Considerable amounts of guidance are available on the evidence for effective processes of care; outcomes and guidelines have been published in the last few years. The interpretation and use of these documents are made more difficult by the use of different groupings and terminology. A set of standard groups, based on clinical terms, and which can be used consistently to extract data from clinical systems, would make the interpretation, application and monitoring of guidance considerably more simple and less expensive.

Curative therapy

The development of better curative treatments needs to be continued because present treatments are effective for only a small proportion of patients. This should come about through well co-ordinated multi-centre trials. Small increases in effectiveness might provide reasonably large increases in the number of life years gained, and districts should ensure that the cost of entry to clinical trials is included in the funding of services.

Palliative care

There is a need for more widely generalisable studies of the relative cost-effectiveness of different models of care for patients with terminal disease, so that evidence-based choices about the development of services can be made.

Appendix I: Clinical features of cancer of the lung

Symptoms

Local symptoms include chest pain, breathlessness, hoarseness and coughing up blood (haemoptysis). However, the presentation may vary widely, and perhaps only half of the total present with a typical picture. This makes it less easy to identify the ideal patterns of referral than for some other tumours. Symptoms of metastatic spread include bone pain, headaches, pain over liver, fever, weight loss and malaise.

Endocrine secretion

Small-cell lung cancers commonly produce ectopic peptide hormones, antidiuretic hormone (ADH) and adrenocorticotrophic hormone (ACTH) being the most common. Their production is a poor prognostic sign. Squamous-cell carcinomas sometimes produce parathormone-like substances that cause hypercalcaemia.

Local invasion

Local growth of the tumour and spread into mediastinal lymph nodes can cause pressure on the other important structures in the chest. These include the great vessels (superior vena cava), pericardium, oesophagus and various nerves. Extensive local tumour may create problems, as well as making it impossible to remove the tumour surgically. Local growth may also invade the chest wall and the ribs.

Metastatic spread

Cancers of the lung tend to spread rapidly to other sites in the body, both through lymphatic channels (to lymph nodes) and through the blood. Initially, lymphatic spread is normally to the hilar, mediastinal, paratracheal and supraclavicular lymph nodes. Common sites of distant metastases are the brain, liver and bones (especially the spinal column), adrenal glands and subcutaneous tissues.

Appendix II: Coding and classification of cancer of the lung

Diagnoses are classified in the *International Classification of Diseases* (*ICD 9* and *ICD 10*). Conditions relevant to lung cancer are also grouped into HBGs, which cover risk, presentation, confirmed disease and irreversible disease.

Interventions are classified in a number of ways. OPCS 4 codes are used for surgical activities, and these are grouped into HRGs for inpatient surgical admissions. Radiotherapy courses are also classified by HRGs, and a draft set of chemotherapy HRGs has been defined. No classification of palliative/terminal care interventions is available yet, although a draft palliative care minimum data set has been published by the National Council for Hospice and Specialist Palliative Care.[37] Palliative care HRGs are under development by the NHS Information Authority.

Conditions

ICD 9

162	Malignant neoplasm of trachea, bronchus and lung.
162.0	Trachea.
162.2	Main bronchus.
162.3	Upper lobe bronchus or lung.
162.4	Middle lobe bronchus or lung.
162.5	Lower lobe bronchus or lung.
162.8	Other.
162.9	Bronchus and lung, unspecified.

ICD 10

C34	Malignant neoplasm of trachea, bronchus and lung.
C340	Malignant neoplasm of main bronchus.
C341	Malignant neoplasm of upper lobe, bronchus or lung.
C342	Malignant neoplasm of middle lobe, bronchus or lung.
C343	Malignant neoplasm of lower lobe, bronchus or lung.
C348	Malignant neoplasm of overlapping lesion of bronchus and lung.
C349	Malignant neoplasm of bronchus or lung, unspecified.

Interventions

OPCS 4 procedures

E46–E63	With a diagnosis from the above list.
E461	Sleeve resect bronch anast HFQ.
E462	Excision of cyst of bronchus.
E463	Excise lesion of bronchus NEC.
E464	Open destr lesion of bronchus.
E468	Partial extirp bronchus OS.
E469	Partial extirp bronchus NOS.

E471	Open-biopsy lesion bronchus NEC.
E472	Closure fistula bronchus.
E473	Repair of bronchus NEC.
E478	Other open operation on bronchus OS.
E479	Other open operation on bronchus NOS.
E481	Fib snare resection lesion lower RT.
E482	Fib laser destruction lesion lower RT.
E483	Fibre-optic destruction lesion lower RT.
E484	Fibre-optic aspiration lower RT.
E485	Fibre-optic removal FB lower RT.
E486	Fibre-optic irrigation lower RT.
E488	Ther fib endoscopy lower RT OS.
E489	Ther fib endoscopy low RT NOS.
E491	Fib endo exam + biopsy lower RT.
E498	Diag fib endoscopy lower RT OS.
E499	Diag fib endoscopy low RT NOS.
E501	Rigid endo snare resec low RT.
E502	Rigid endo laser lesion lower RT.
E503	Rig endos dest lesion low RT NEC.
E504	Rigid endos aspiration low RT.
E505	Rigid endos removal FB low RT.
E506	Rig endos irrigation lower RT.
E508	Rigid ther bronchoscopy OS.
E509	Rigid ther bronchoscopy NOS.
E511	Rigid bronchoscopy and biopsy.
E518	Rigid diag bronchoscopy OS.
E519	Rigid diag bronchoscopy NOS.
E521	Irrigation of bronchus NEC.
E522	Aspiration of bronchus NEC.
E528	Other op bronchus/trachea OS.
E529	Other op bronchus/trachea NOS.
E538	Transplantation of lung OS.
E539	Transplantation of lung NOS.
E541	Total pneumonectomy.
E542	Bilobectomy of lung.
E543	Lobectomy of lung.
E544	Excision of segment of lung.
E545	Partial lobectomy of lung NEC.
E548	Excision of lung OS.
E549	Excision of lung NOS.
E551	Open decortic lesion of lung.
E552	Open excision lesion of lung.
E553	Open cautery lesion of lung.
E554	Open destruction lesion of lung NEC.
E558	Open extirp lesion of lung OS.
E559	Open extirp lesion of lung NOS.
E571	Repair of lung.
E572	Ligation of bulla of lung.

E573	Deflation of bulla of lung.
E574	Incision of lung NEC.
E578	Other open lung operation OS.
E579	Other open lung operation NOS.
E591	Needle-biopsy lesion of lung.
E592	Aspiration-biopsy lesion of lung.
E593	Biopsy lesion of lung NEC.
E594	Drainage of lung.
E598	Other operation on lung OS.
E599	Other operation on lung NOS.
E611	Open excis lesion of mediastinum.
E612	Open-biopsy lesion of mediastinum.
E613	Open drainage of mediastinum.
E614	Mediastinotomy NEC.
E615	Exploration of mediastinum NEC.
E618	Mediastinum open operation OS.
E619	Mediastinum open operation NOS.
E621	Endoscop extirp lesion mediast.
E628	Ther endoscopy mediastinum OS.
E629	Ther endoscopy mediastinum NOS.
E631	Endoscopy + biopsy mediastinum.
E638	Diag endoscopy mediastinum OS.
E639	Diag endoscopy mediastinum NOS.

Appendix III: HBG/HRG matrix

HBG/HRG for lung cancer: summary

HBG	Primary prevention	Investigation and diagnosis	Initial care	Continuing care
At risk				
Whole population	Health education			
Population at specific risk	Screening and prophylactic			
Previously treated disease	Interventions			
	Follow-up care			
Presentation				
Asymptomatic, screen detected or incidental finding		Physical examination		
		Chemistry		
Symptomatic presentation		Imaging		
		Cytology		
		Biopsy		
		Special investigation		
		Special support		
Confirmed disease				
Stage 0, I, II			Surgery	
Stage IIIa, IIIb (limited locally)			Chemotherapy	
Stage IIIa, IIIb (widespread locally)			Radiotherapy	
Stage IV			Special support	
Continuing disease state				
Non-progressive disease				
Functional ability				
Pain				
Other symptoms				
Progressive disease				
Functional ability				Community general input
Pain				Specialist input
Other symptoms				Voluntary sector

HRGs for radiotherapy

HRG	Description
w01	Superficial teletherapy, < 4 fractions
w02	Superficial teletherapy, > 3 fractions
w03	Simple teletherapy, < 4 fractions
w04	Simple teletherapy, > 3 and < 13 fractions
w05	Simple teletherapy, > 12 fractions
w06	Simple teletherapy with simulator, < 4 fractions
w07	Simple teletherapy with simulator, > 3 and < 13 fractions
w08	Simple teletherapy with simulator, > 12 fractions
w09	Complex teletherapy, < 4 fractions
w10	Complex teletherapy, > 3 and < 13 fractions
w11	Complex teletherapy, > 12 and < 24 fractions
w12	Complex teletherapy, > 23 fractions
w13	Complex teletherapy with imaging, < 4 fractions
w14	Complex teletherapy with imaging, > 3 and < 13 fractions
w15	Complex teletherapy with imaging, > 12 and < 24 fractions
w16	Complex teletherapy with imaging, > 23 fractions
w17	Complex teletherapy with imaging and multiple planning, >23 fractions
w18	Complex teletherapy with imaging, hyperfractionation
w19	Complex teletherapy with imaging and multiple planning, hyperfractionation
w20	Teletherapy with technical support, < 4 fractions
w21	Teletherapy with technical support, > 3 and < 13 fractions
w22	Teletherapy with technical support, > 12 and < 24 fractions
w23	Teletherapy with technical support, >23 fractions
w24	Teletherapy with technical support and multiple planning, > 23 fractions
w25	Teletherapy with technical support, hyperfractionation
w26	Teletherapy with technical support and multiple planning, hyperfractionation
w40	Live-source brachytherapy without anaesthetic
w41	Live-source brachytherapy with anaesthetic
w42	Manual-afterload brachytherapy without anaesthetic
w43	Manual-afterload brachytherapy with anaesthetic
w44	Mechanical afterload, low-dose brachytherapy without anaesthetic
w45	Mechanical afterload, low-dose brachytherapy with anaesthetic
w46	Mechanical afterload, high-dose brachytherapy without anaesthetic
w47	Mechanical afterload, high-dose brachytherapy with anaesthetic
w60	Outpatient unsealed-source brachytherapy
w61	Inpatient unsealed-source brachytherapy

Appendix IV: Staging of cancer of the lung

Source: UICC International Union Against Cancer: Hermanek P, Sobin LN (eds). *TNM Classification of Malignant Tumours* (4e). Berlin: Springer-Verlag, 1987.

TNM clinical classification

T: Primary tumour

TX Primary tumour cannot be assessed, or tumour proven by the presence of malignant cells in sputum or bronchial washings but not visualised by imaging or bronchoscopy.

TO No evidence of primary tumour.

Tis Carcinoma *in situ.*

T1 Tumour 3 cm or less in greatest dimension, surrounded by lung or visceral pleura, without bronchoscopic evidence of invasion more proximal than the lobar bronchus (i.e. not in the main bronchus).*

T2 Tumour with any of the following features of size or extent:
  - more than 3 cm in greatest dimension
  - involves main bronchus, 2 cm or more distal to the carina
  - invades visceral pleura
  - associated with atelectasis or obstructive pneumonitis which extends to the hilar region but does not involve the entire lung.

T3 Tumour of any size which directly invades any of the following: chest wall (including superior sulcus tumours), diaphragm, mediastinal pleura, parietal pericardium; or tumour in the main bronchus less than 2 cm distal to the carina*) but without involvement of the carina; or associated atelectasis or obstructive pneumonitis of the entire lung.

T4 Tumour of any size which invades any of the following: mediastinum, heart, great vessels, trachea, oesophagus, vertebral body, carina; or tumour with malignant pleural effusion.†

Notes

* The uncommon superficial spreading tumour of any size with its invasive component limited to the bronchial wall which may extend proximal to the main bronchus is also classified T1.

† Most pleural effusions associated with lung cancer are due to tumour. However, there are a few patients in whom multiple cytopathological examinations of pleural fluid are negative for tumour, the fluid is non-bloody and is not an exudate. Where these elements and clinical judgement dictate that the effusion is not related to the tumour, the effusion should be excluded as a staging element and the patient should be classified as T1, T2 or T3.

N: Regional lymph nodes

NX Regional lymph nodes cannot be assessed.

NO No regional lymph node metastasis.

N1 Metastasis in ipsilateral peribronchial and/or ipsilateral hilar lymph nodes, including direct extension.

N2 Metastasis in ipsilateral mediastinal and/or subcarinal lymph node(s).

N3 Metastasis in contralateral mediastinal, contralateral hilar, ipsilateral or contralateral scalene or supraclavicular lymph node(s).

Staging grouping[38]

	TNM classification		
Stage	**TX**	**NO**	**MO**
Stage 0	Tis	NO	MO
Stage IA	T1	NO	MO
Stage IB	T2	NO	MO
Stage IIA	T1	N1	MO
Stage IIB	T2/T3	N0/N1	MO
Stage IIIA	T1	N2	MO
	T2	N2	MO
	T3	N1, N2	MO
Stage IIIB	Any T	N3	MO
	T4	Any N	MO
Stage IV	Any T	Any N	M1

Summary

Lung

TX   Positive cytology.
T1   < 3 cm.
T2   > 3 cm/extends to hilar region/invades visceral pleura/partial atelectasis.
T3   Chest wall, diaphragm, pericardium, mediastinal pleura, etc. Total atelectasis.
T4   Mediastinum, heart, great vessels, trachea, oesophagus, etc. Malignant effusion.
N1   Peribronchial, ipsilateral hilar.
N2   Ipsilateral mediastinal.
N3   Contralateral mediastinal, scalene or supraclavicular.

Appendix V: Factors affecting incidence of lung cancer

Social class

A consistent gradient in social class and rate of cancer of the lung exists for both males and females (*see* Figures A1 and A2). A substantial part of this effect is due to differences in smoking habit. Districts with high concentrations of residents in social classes IV and V will have higher than average rates for cancer of the lung.

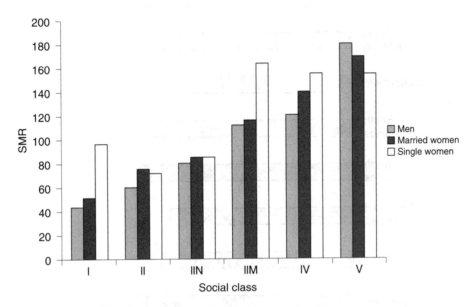

Figure A1: Lung cancer SMR by social class, England and Wales, 1981.

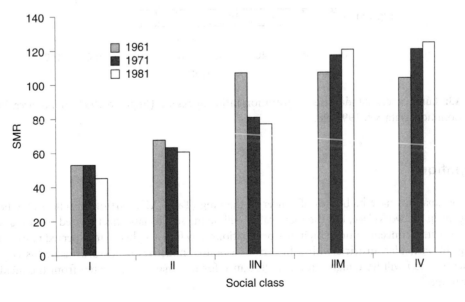

Figure A2: Lung cancer male SMR by social class, England and Wales, 1961, 1971 and 1981.

Geographical location

In general, rates of cancer of the lung are higher in the north than in the south (*see* Figure A3). This variation is likely to be largely due to differences in the social class structure, smoking and occupational exposure.

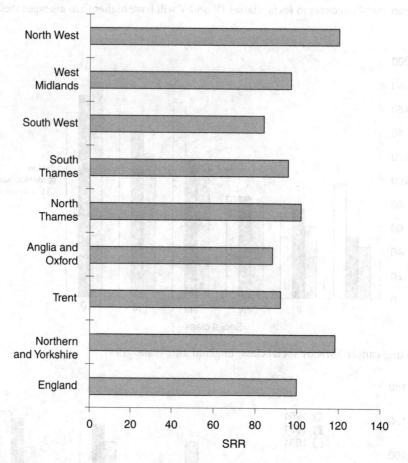

Figure A3: Lung cancer standardised registration ratios by region (England 1984–91). *Source:* Public Health Common Data Set, 1997–98.

Occupation

Certain occupations have high rates of cancer of the lung (Table A1). Part of this effect may be due to carcinogens in the workplace, but the main cause will be the social class effect related to smoking habit.

Districts with a concentration of high-risk occupations may find a higher than expected rate of cancer of the lung. In particular, districts with a history of asbestos industries (dockyards, asbestos component manufacture, etc.) will have high rates. An allowance for this may be calculated from the incidence of mesothelioma.[9]

Table A1: Standardised mortality ratios for selected occupations.

	Men	Married women
High SMRs		
Deck, engine-room hands, lightermen, boatmen	306	365
Steel erectors, scaffolders, steel benders, fixers	247	299
Labourers	246	270
Butchers	187	176
Chemical gas and petroleum process-plant operators	179	211
Low SMRs		
Engineers and technologists	50	49
Farmers, horticulturalists, farm managers	47	57
Professional and related in science and engineering	44	80
Mechanical and aeronautical engineers	34	62
Teachers	29	41

Ethnic origin

Little variation in rates between different ethnic groups has been described in the UK.

Type of district

Several of the above factors can be summarised by the type of district. The Office for National Statistics (ONS) classification of areas is a useful clustering which shows differences in the rates of incidence and mortality (Figure A4).

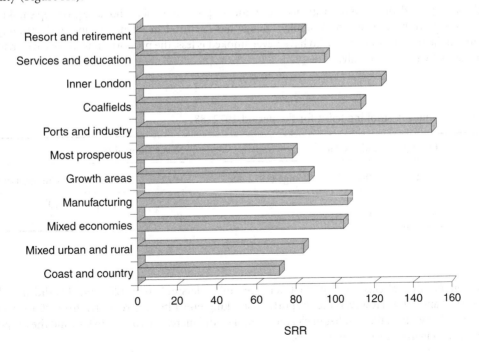

Figure A4: Lung cancer standardised registration ratios by ONS area. *Source*: Public Health Common Data Set.

Trends in incidence

It is important to understand the likely trends in incidence when constructing a long-term strategy for commissioning services for the treatment of individuals with lung cancer. Because of changes in the patterns of smoking, there is likely to be a steady reduction in incidence.

Smoking

The incidence of cancer of the lung is a reflection of past patterns of smoking. The prevalence of smoking in men has been falling for the last 20 years, though for the last 10 years more slowly (c. 1% per year).[39] The rate has also been falling for women, but slightly more slowly than the rate for men (Table A2).

Table A2: Changes in smoking habit.

	Percentage of smokers			Percentage change
	1972	1988	1994–95	1972–94
Men	52	33	28	−24
Women	41	30	25	−16
All	46	32	26	−20

Over the same period, there has been an increase in the proportion of men who have given up smoking and in those who have never smoked. A similar change has occurred in women (Table A3). Although the reduction in the number of people who have never smoked is less, the proportion who have never smoked was substantially greater initially.

Table A3: Changes in smoking habit for the period 1972–88.

Sex	Ex-regular smokers (%)			Never smoked (%)		
	1972	1988	Change (1972–88)	1972	1988	Change (1972–88)
Male	23	32	9	25	35	10
Female	10	19	9	49	51	2

The average number of cigarettes smoked per week by male smokers is 120, and this did not change between 1972 and 1988. However, the proportion smoking non-filter cigarettes fell from 20 to 3% in the same period. For women the number of cigarettes smoked did increase (from 87 to 99), and the proportion smoking plain cigarettes fell from 9 to 1%.

These changes in smoking habit have not been equal between social classes, as shown by the changes in incidence of lung cancer in which the difference between social classes is increasing (Figure A2).

Birth cohorts

Although the smoking habit is changing, the incidence of cancer of the lung is a function of many years of exposure to tobacco smoke. Since smoking habit is largely determined in early adulthood, the smoking experience and hence incidence of disease vary according to the development of smoking patterns in successive cohorts of individuals.[40] Examination of the age-specific rates of lung cancer for the cohorts of men born between 1890 and 1940 show that the 1905 cohort has had the highest rates. For subsequent cohorts the rates have been falling (Figure 1). For women, the 1930 cohort had the highest rate. Subsequent cohorts have had lower rates (Figure 2), but the effects of this on overall mortality have not yet become evident.

In practice, this means that although reduction in smoking is an important objective, especially in the young, the effect on lung cancer incidence will not be apparent for many years. Rapid reductions in lung cancer incidence could not be expected even if all smoking stopped tomorrow.

Appendix VI: An example long-term agreement based on case-mix groups

This example agreement is constructed around the condition of lung cancer and seeks to provide a comprehensive plan for lung cancer, from the stage of potential disease through to terminal disease.

In this agreement, the condition groups (HBGs) have been identified, as have the interventions (HRGs). These are based on the literature and clinical working group advice. These groupings may be used to identify the expected costs and volumes as well as the levels of performance expected within the agreement, and the exercise can be integrated into a higher level of analysis in order to set the detail of this programme in the context of the whole spectrum of conditions and interventions from the NHS.

In working out an agreement, the epidemiology of the population would need to be compared with a national or other benchmark, and the rates of activity and performance measures of the existing service similarly compared. From this base, and consideration of National Service Frameworks and clinical guidelines, the ideal service can be specified, and this forms the basis of a negotiation between purchaser and provider as to what service should be provided for which patients, and the costs and levels of performance expected. Since rapid changes in the delivery of health care are unrealistic, these targets would be set and achieved over a period of years.

The figures supplied in this example are based partly on estimates. The performance standards in particular are provided for illustrative purposes only, and are not intended to be taken as actual recommended standards.

Information to support this level of systematic planning will be available as a product of clinical information systems being developed and implemented as part of the information strategy. This depends upon the extraction of data for primary/community care, secondary care (district general hospital and cancer centre) systems and also population-based registers. These data will be captured as part of the electronic patient record, encoded in clinical terms. Extraction into standard patient groupings minimises the amount of data manipulation required at local level, and ensures comparability of the resulting information. The sources of the data, and the types of data which would need to be extracted, were identified in Section 8.

Example long-term service agreement

Cancer of the lung

1   Parties to the agreement:
   • Midshire Primary Care Trust and its constituent providers:

   – Midshire Acute Trust
   – Midland Cancer Centre
   – Uptown Community Trust
   – Downtown Community Trust
   – Midtown Hospice.

2   Duration of the agreement
   The agreement will be for a period of 5 years, with an option for renegotiation and rolling forwards after 3 years.

3   Objectives

The objective of this agreement is to secure access to efficient, effective and acceptable services for the population of Midshire in respect of the prevention of lung cancer, and the treatment and care of patients with lung cancer, in order to improve the health of the population through prevention of illness and amelioration of disease.

Specifically, the agreement focuses on:

- investing in adequate preventive services
- ensuring increased access to curative surgery, radiotherapy and chemotherapy
- ensuring access to integrated palliative care.

4   Schedule of agreement

This agreement contains a specification of the following:

- Part A: types of patient within the scope of the agreement
- Part B: numbers of patients
- Part C: treatment packages to be provided for them
- Part D: volumes of service and costs (total and by provider)
- Part E: performance measures for delivery of these services.

This schedule is based on a systematic needs assessment process which has compared the incidence/prevalence of patients in the lung cancer HBGs in Midshire with the national average, and also assessed the actual experience of Midshire patients against national averages and the recommendations in the National Service Framework and clinical guidelines.

Costs and performance measures within the six areas of performance have been compared with national benchmarks and levels of performance expected for the service providers for each year within the scope of this agreement, identified and recorded in the schedule of agreement.

Part A: Condition groups (HBGs) within lung cancer

At risk:

- whole population
- population at specific risk
- children
- smokers
- previously treated disease.

Presentation:

- asymptotic, screen detected or incidental finding
- specific and general symptoms.

Confirmed disease:

- small cell, limited disease
- small cell, extensive disease
- non-small cell, operable
- non-small cell, inoperable, limited
- non-small cell, extensive disease
- non-small cell, metastases.

Functional consequences of disease:

- terminal illness.

Part B: Numbers of cases in each Health Benefit Group/year

		1999–2000	2000–01	2001–02	2002–03	2003–04
At risk	Whole population	1,000,000	1,000,000	1,000,000	1,000,000	1,000,000
Population at specific risk	Children	152,000	152,000	152,000	152,000	152,000
	Smokers	230,000	230,000	230,000	230,000	230,000
	Previously treated disease	60	60	60	60	60
Presentation	Asymptomatic, screen detected or incidental finding	61	61	61	61	61
	Specific and general symptoms	1,200	1,200	1,200	1,200	1,200
Confirmed disease	Small cell, limited disease	37	37	37	37	37
	Small cell, extensive disease	85	85	85	85	85
	Non-small cell, operable	74	74	74	74	74
	Non-small cell, inoperable, limited	48	48	48	48	48
	Non-small cell, extensive disease	370	370	370	370	370
	Non-small cell, metastases	185	185	185	185	185
Consequences of disease	Terminal illness/pain	555	555	555	555	555

Part C: Appropriate intervention(s) (HRGs) for each condition group

At risk	Whole population	Promotion	Package of care (HRG)
Population at specific risk	Children	Prevention	Health education
	Smokers		Health education and advice on stopping
	Previously treated disease		Follow-up (HRG XXX)
Presentation	Asymptomatic, screen detected or incidental finding	Assessment	Bronchoscopy (D10, D22)/CAT scan/ mediastinoscopy (D04, D05)
	Specific and general symptoms		Bronchoscopy (D10, D22)/CAT scan
Confirmed disease	Small cell, limited disease	Treatment of disease	Radical chemotherapy (multi-drug, high cost) and radiotherapy (W15)
	Small cell, extensive disease		Radical chemotherapy (multi-drug, high cost) and radiotherapy (W07, W08)
	Non-small cell, operable		Lobectomy (D02), mediastinoscopy (D04, D05)
	Non-small cell, inoperable, limited		Radical radiotherapy (W18)
	Non-small cell, extensive disease		Palliative radiotherapy (W07, W06)
	Non-small cell, metastases		Palliative radiotherapy (W06)
Functional consequences of disease	Terminal illness	Care/support	Inpatient palliative care (HRG XXX)
			Community-based palliative care

Part D: Volumes of service and costs

	Expected numbers/million	Health education	Brief advice	Counsel-ling	OP consult-ation	Rigid bronchos-copy (D10)	Flexible bronchos-copy (D22)	Mediastin-oscopy (D04, D05)	CAT scan	Multi-drug high-cost chemo	Radical RTx (W18)	Proph Rtx (W15)	Palliat. RTx (W07)	Palliat. Rtx (W06)
		£1/head	£2/smoker	£10/smoker	£60	£1,356	£220, £511	£1,812, £194	£150	£1,817	£2,484	£1,902	£944	£296
Based on numbers of episodes, cost per episode and total cost (numbers cost)	1 million													
Specific risk Children	152,000	£152,000												
Smokers	230,000		£460,000											
Previously treated disease	60				£3,600									
Presentation Asymptomatic, screen detected or incidental finding	61				£3,660									
Specific and general symptoms	1,200				£72,000	£81,360	£132,000	£277,500	£22,500					
Confirmed disease Small cell, limited disease	37									67,229		70,374		
Small cell, extensive disease	85									154,445			80,240	
Non-small cell, operable	74													
Non-small cell, inoperable, limited	48										119,232			
Non-small cell, extensive disease	370												174,640	54,760
Non-small cell, metastases	185													27,380
Functional consequences of disease Terminal illness/pain	555													
Total costs		£152,000	£460,000		£79,260	£81,360	£160,620	£277,500	£22,500	£300,000	£119,232	£70,374	£189,606	£82,140

Part E: Service standards schedule (1999–2000) (continued overleaf)

		Promotion	Fair access	Effective delivery	Efficiency	Patient/carer experience	Health outcomes	Health improvement
At risk	Whole population	Prevention Health education						(5% reduction in death rates in 5 years)
Population at specific risk	Children	Health education					Smoking rate in children reduced by 10%	
	Smokers	Brief intervention		50% of consultations with smokers			5% quit rate at 6 months	
	Smokers	Longer counselling		5% of consultations with smokers			15% quit rate at 6 months	
	Previously treated disease	Follow-up (HRG XXX)						
Presentation	Asymptomatic, screen detected or incidental finding	Assessment Bronchoscopy (D10, D22)/ CAT scan/ mediastinoscopy (D04, D05)			<105% of national mean cost			
	Specific and general symptoms	Bronchoscopy (D10, D22)/ CAT scan/ mediastinoscopy (D04, D05)		<105% of national mean cost				

Part E: Continued.

		Promotion	Fair access	Effective delivery	Efficiency	Patient/ carer experience	Health outcomes	Health improvement
Confirmed disease	Small cell, limited disease	Treatment of disease	Radical chemo-therapy (multi-drug, high cost) and radiotherapy (W15)			<105% of national mean cost		25% survival at 1 year	
	Small cell, extensive disease		Radical chemotherapy (multi-drug, high cost) and radiotherapy (W07, W08)			<105% of national mean cost		>6 months above QUAL score of 5	
	Non-small cell, operable		Lobectomy (D02)	Surgery rates >15 % of NSCLC		<105% of national mean cost	Adequate explanation	45% survival at 1 year	
	Non-small cell, inoperable, limited		Radical radiotherapy (W18)		75% receive CHART regime	<105% of national mean cost		25% survival at 1 year	
	Non-small cell, extensive disease		Palliative radiotherapy (W07, W06)		80% receive 1-3 fraction course	<105% of national mean cost		>6 months above QUAL score of 5	
	Non-small cell, metastases		Palliative radiotherapy (W06)			<105% of national mean cost		>6 months above QUAL score of 5	
Conse-quences of disease	Terminal illness/pain	Care/ Support	Palliative care (HRG XXX)	85% of eligible patients managed by integrated team			Patient/ relative satisfaction rating not less than 95% of national		

References

1 NHS Executive. *Guidance on Commissioning Cancer Services: improving outcomes in lung cancer.* London: NHS Executive, 1998.

2 NHS Executive. *The NHS Performance Assessment Framework.* London: NHS Executive, 1999.

3 Department of Health. *Public Health Common Data Set 1997.* London: Department of Health, 1997.

4 NHS Executive. *National Schedule of Reference Costs HSC 1998/100.* London: NHS Executive, 1998.

5 Madden L, Hussey R, Mooney G, Church E. Public health and economics in tandem: programme budgeting, marginal analysis and priority setting in practice. *Health Policy* 1995; **33**: 161–8.

6 Doll R, Peto R. *The Causes of Cancer.* Oxford: Oxford University Press, 1981.

7 Lubin JH, Richter BS, Blot WJ. Lung cancer risk with pipe and cigar use. *J Natl Cancer Inst* 1984; **73**: 377–81.

8 Eriksen MP, LeMaistre CA, Newell GR. Health hazards of passive smoking. *Annu Rev Public Health* 1988; **9**: 47–70.

9 Hammond EC, Selikoff IJ, Seidman H. Asbestos exposure, cigarette smoking and death rates. *Ann NY Acad Sci* 1979; **300**: 473–90.

10 Doll R, Peto R. Occupational lung cancer. A review. *Br J Indust Med* 1959; **16**: 181.

11 Goldsmith JR. The urban factor in cancer: smoking, industrial exposures and air pollution as possible explanations. *J Environ Pathol Toxicol Oncol* 1980; **3**: 205–17.

12 Jedrychowski W, Becher H, Wahrendorf J, Basa-Cierpialek Z. A case–control study of lung cancer with special reference to the effect of air pollution in Poland. *J Epidemiol Community Health* 1990; **44**: 114–20.

13 Lloyd OL. Respiratory cancer clustering associated with localised industrial air pollution. *Lancet* 1978; **1**: 318–20.

14 Cartwright A. Changes in life and care in the year before death 1969–1987. *J Public Health Med* 1991; **13**: 81–7.

15 Higginson I. Palliative and terminal care. In: Stevens A, Raftery J (eds). *Health Care Needs Assessment.* Oxford: Radcliffe Medical Press, 1997.

16 Scottish Intercollegiate Guidelines Network (SIGN). *Management of Lung Cancer.* Edinburgh: SIGN, 1998.

17 HEA/Centre for Health Economics, University of York. *Cost-Effectiveness of Smoking Cessation Interventions.* London: HEA, 1997.

18 Raw M, McNeill A, West R. Smoking cessation; evidence-based recommendations for the health care system. *BMJ* 1999; **318**: 182–5.

19 Parrott S, Godfrey C, Raw M *et al.* Guidance for commissioners on the cost-effectiveness of smoking cessation interventions. *Thorax* 1998; **53**(Suppl. 5): S1–37.

20 Connolly CK, Jones WG, Thorogood J *et al.* Investigation, treatment and prognosis of bronchial cancer in the Yorkshire region of England. *Br J Cancer* 1990; **61**: 579.

21 Watkin WW, Hayhurst GK, Green JA. Time trends in the outcome of lung cancer management: a population study of 9090 cases. *Br J Cancer* 1990; **61**: 590.

22 Northern and Yorkshire Cancer Registry and Information Service (NYCRIS). *Cancer Treatment Policies and their Effects on Survival. Key Sites Study 2 Lung.* Leeds: NYCRIS, 1999.

23 Saunders M, Dische S, Barrett A *et al.* Continuous hyperfractionated accelerated radiotherapy (CHART) versus conventional radiotherapy non-small-cell lung cancer: a randomised multi-centre study. *Lancet* 1997; **30**: 161–5.

24 Pignon J-P, Arriagada R, Itide DC *et al.* A meta-analysis of thoracic radiotherapy for small-cell lung cancer. *NEJM* 1992; **327**: 1618–24.

25 Felletti R, Souhami RL, Spiro SG *et al.* Social consequences of brain or liver relapse in small-cell carcinoma of the bronchus. *Radiother Oncol* 1985; **4**: 335–9.

26 Raftery J, Addington-Hall JM, MacDonald LD *et al.* A randomised controlled trial of the cost-effectiveness of a district co-ordinating service for terminally ill cancer patients. *Palliat Med* 1996; **10**: 151–61.

27 Frankel S, Kamerling B. Assessing the need for hospice beds. *Health Trends* 1990; **2**: 83–6.

28 Berndt R, Nischan P, Ebeling K. Screening for lung cancer in the middle aged. *Int J Cancer* 1990; **45**: 229–30.

29 Fontana RS, Sanderson DR, Woolmer LB *et al.* Lung cancer screening: the Mayo programme. *J Occup Med* 1986; **28**: 746–50.

30 Non-Small-Cell Lung Cancer Collaborative Group. Chemotherapy in non-small-cell lung cancer: a meta-analysis using updated data on individual patients from 52 randomised trials. *BMJ* 1995; **311**: 899–909.

31 Bleehan NM *et al.* Controlled trial of palliative radiotherapy given in two fractions or conventionally fractionated for inoperable NSCLC. *Proceedings of the Fifth World Conference on Lung Cancer* 1988; **4**: A144–8.

32 MRC Lung Cancer Working Party. Inoperable non-small-cell lung cancer. An MRC randomised trial of palliative radiotherapy with two fractions or ten fractions. *Br J Oncol* 1991; **63**: 265–70.

33 Goodwin PJ, Feld R, Evans WK, Pater J. Cost-effectiveness of cancer chemotherapy: an economic evaluation of a randomized trial in small-cell lung cancer. *J Clin Oncol* 1988; **6**: 1537–47.

34 Gray D, MacAdam D, Boldy D. A comparative cost analysis of terminal cancer care in home and hospice. *J Chron Dis* 1987; **40**: 801–10.

35 McCusker J, Stoddard AM. Effects of an expanding home care program for the terminally ill. *Med Care* 1987; **25**: 373–85.

36 Maher EJ *et al.* Who gets radiotherapy? *Health Trends* 1990; **22**: 78–83.

37 Steering Group on Minimum Data Sets. *The Data Manual.* London: National Council for Hospice and Specialist Palliative Care Services, 1995.

38 Mountain CF. Revision in the international staging system for lung cancer. *Chest* 1997; **111**: 1710–17.

39 Office of Population Censuses and Surveys (OPCS). *General Household Survey.* London: OPCS, 1988.

40 Osmond C. Using age period and cohort models to estimate future mortality rates. *Int J Epidemiol* 1985; **14**: 124–9.

41 Van Tinteren H, Hoekstra OS, Smit EF *et al.* Effectiveness of positron emission tomography in the preoperative assessment of patients with suspected non-small-cell lung cancer. The PLUS multicentre randomised trial. *Lancet* 2002; **359**: 1388–93.

42 Spiro SG, Porter JC. Lung cancer – where are we today? Current advances in staging and non-surgical treatment. *Am J Resp Crit Care Med* 2002; **166**: 1166–96.

Acknowledgements

This revision is based on the chapter by Sanderson, Mountney and Harris in the previous edition of *Health Care Needs Assessment*. Additional material has been provided from the English and Scottish guidelines documents, and from the National Schedule of Reference Costs. Costs for radiotherapy and chemotherapy have been provided by Dr K Lloyd based on costing studies in Northampton.

Health Benefit Groups (HBGs) and Health care Resource Groups (HRGs) are being developed by Clinical Working Groups to the specification of the Case-Mix Programme of the NHS Information Authority. The Clinical Working Group for cancers has been chaired by Dr K Lloyd.

8   Osteoarthritis Affecting the Hip and Knee

Jill Dawson, Ray Fitzpatrick, John Fletcher and Richard Wilson

1 Summary

Introduction

Osteoarthritis (OA) is extremely common, particularly among elderly people. It represents a major cause of morbidity, disability and social isolation, especially where the hip and knee are involved. The classification and nomenclature of OA are problematic and the multi-factorial nature of OA is well recognised. Classification might arguably be based on radiological, clinical or symptomatic features. However, each system overlaps with another and no one scheme is ideal. Nevertheless, for the purpose of defining health care need, it is the symptomatic features that truly matter.

Sub-categories

Enormous difficulties are encountered in defining the presence of OA using any single set of criteria, and different criteria are in any case generally needed for different joints. Similarly, no one method of categorising OA is ideal, yet once again a number of constitutional and external risk factors for OA appear to depend crucially on the site affected. We have therefore adopted the simplest sub-categories based on the site – hip or knee – throughout this chapter. Further distinctions are also made according to the severity of symptoms, where the available data permit such distinctions to be made.

Prevalence and incidence

Precise estimates of the prevalence and incidence of OA remain elusive. Reasons for this include problems associated with definition and diagnosis, as well as coding practices. Based on radiographic evidence, it is estimated that between 10% and 25% of people over the age of 55 have OA of the hip and between 14% and 34% of people over the age of 45 have OA of the knee. There is, however, little correspondence between radiographic, clinical or symptomatic evidence of OA. In addition, the presence and extent of radiographic OA does not predict its likely progression to a symptomatic state.

A recent study estimated that symptomatic hip OA affects between 0.7% and 4.4% of adults, while the prevalence of hip disease severe enough to require surgery (which includes causes other than OA) has been put at 15.2 per 1000 people aged 35–85 years. Corresponding prevalence rates for symptomatic OA of the knee are 6.1% for people over 30 and around 7.5% for those in the 55+ age group. A study of people aged

55+ in North Yorkshire further ascertained that between 2% and 3% of individuals reported pain and disability at severity levels consistent with the need to consider knee arthroplasty.

There are a number of factors which modify the risk of OA and which are often joint specific. Thus OA of the hip has little association with obesity, some association with race but limited association with gender, and a strong association with particular occupations, e.g. farming, whereas OA of the knee is strongly associated with obesity, has little or no association with race, chiefly affects women and is related to types of work that involve frequent squatting. It does not appear to be associated with farming.

Services and their costs

Pain is usually the main presenting problem for which patients seek relief and, in general, the first port of call is the general practitioner (GP). Musculoskeletal problems account for around one in ten of all new GP consultations, 18% of which are estimated to be for arthritis. Many services are available to GPs – although there is much local variation – and these include assessment centres, day centres and physiotherapists. However, GPs do not appear to have access to comprehensive sources of information regarding the local services which they may use. The variable extent of direct access to such services and a shortage of specialist physiotherapists are two areas of unmet need of particular relevance to OA. Many inappropriate hospital referrals could be avoided if such services were expanded.

Patients with mild or even moderate symptoms can generally avoid the use of drug therapy altogether – at least for some considerable time. Education, regular telephone contact and improved patient self-efficacy can all help enormously and there is considerable scope for the use of specialist nurse practitioners in this regard.

Where treatment is needed, the majority of patients will require simple analgesia, while in cases where inflammation is active, non-steroidal anti-inflammatory drugs (NSAIDs) may achieve better results but should be used with great care. NSAID usage may increasingly take the form of highly selective cyclo-oxygenase isoform-2 (COX-2) inhibitors which have fewer side-effects, although long-term evaluation is still lacking.

Specialist referral is considered where there are doubts about the diagnosis or when a patient's symptoms have become difficult to control with physical therapy and analgesia and/or their mobility and independence are threatened (although at present referral may be necessary to gain access to various therapists and orthotic services). Where the main consideration is surgery, referral to a surgeon is appropriate, whereas problems concerning diagnosis may be best referred to a rheumatologist. Rheumatology referral is also recommended for assistance with the control of symptoms in those felt to be inappropriate for surgery (which includes the unwilling), where availability permits. Waiting times for hospital outpatient appointments are very variable. Influences on waiting times include the local availability of clinical specialists and the frequency with which consultants follow up patients.

Potential targets for primary prevention include occupational activities, such as repeated lifting and squatting, and there is an enormous need for education and reorganisation of working practices. In practice these are often hard to influence. The avoidance of obesity (in particular) and the encouragement of regular moderate low-impact exercise represent other recurrent themes. In OA of the knee, exercise also encourages the maintenance of muscle strength which is particularly important in this condition. Weight loss (in the overweight) and exercise can also play a role in reducing symptoms once painful symptoms have developed.

Congenital dysplasia of the hip is a known precursor for hip OA in a minority of people and screening can improve the likelihood of obtaining early corrective treatment. The screening method needs to be highly sensitive, however, unlike current methods. It is suggested that such efforts should be concentrated on babies who are known to be at an increased risk based on family history and a number of birth and prenatal factors. Secondary and tertiary prevention is otherwise generally hampered due to ignorance about the causes of symptoms in OA. However, limited evidence suggests that there may be a role for some nutritional factors.

Waiting periods for surgery within the NHS vary across the country, although these statistics are not entirely reliable. Joint replacement (arthroplasty) is only one of a number of forms of surgical intervention that may alleviate OA symptoms of the hip and knee.

Hospital Episode Statistics (HES) reveal that 33 320 primary total hip replacements (THR) and 23 846 primary total knee replacements (TKR) were carried out (chiefly for OA) in English NHS hospitals during 1995–96. It is likely that the demand for TKR surgery will continue to increase relative to THR during the next decade, and there is currently a considerable unmet need for TKR surgery. This will increase the overall demand for resources within orthopaedics. Revision operations represented just over 12% of all THR surgery and almost 6% of all TKRs carried out in the same period. The likely continuing increase in demand for revision operations may lead to longer waiting times for all orthopaedic surgery because such operations are lengthy and require considerable specialist expertise. They also frequently require bone grafting and, in the absence of alternative techniques, a limited supply of allografts may increasingly affect waiting times for these operations.

Effectiveness of services and interventions

There is some evidence to suggest that many GPs are inadequately trained in the management of OA and would welcome further training. While evidence-based guidelines on the management of OA do not exist, practical guidelines (based on professional consensus) do. These could help to encourage better management, although their existence does not appear to be well publicised.

Education, counselling and self-management programmes can all play a very important role in the management of people with OA. In addition, it is recommended that emphasis is placed on increasing the strength of often underused joint-supporting muscles. This alone may alleviate joint pain, particularly in patients with OA of the knee. Patients may also need re-educating in how best to go about their everyday tasks to avoid aggravating the condition. Both methods are best tailor-made to the individual's needs and the involvement of physiotherapists, occupational therapists and other professionals allied to medicine (PAMs) is recommended. Another benefit of involving PAMs includes the assessment and training that they can provide in the use of many orthotic devices (e.g. shoe implants, appropriate use of walking sticks, patella taping) which can assist in significantly relieving symptoms, even in patients whose disease is severe.

For some individuals, available treatments may subject them to considerably greater risks than the underlying condition. The use of NSAIDs, for example, resulted in 147 per 100 000 of the adult UK population being admitted with emergency gastrointestinal problems during 1990–91, and there is now good evidence to show that in almost all cases, simple analgesics, e.g. paracetamol, and topical applications, e.g. NSAIDs, capsaicin, are indicated in preference to orally administered NSAIDs, and their effectiveness is generally the same if taken at adequate levels. Many clinicians appear unaware of this evidence. Highly selective COX-2 inhibitors may alter this view of NSAIDs, but their thorough evaluation is as yet limited.

The success of surgery depends crucially on the appropriate selection of patients and this is relevant to GP referral practices. Currently, there are no evidence-based referral guidelines for GPs. Nevertheless, a number of professional consensus guidelines are available. There is little evidence that these guidelines are used. The availability of orthopaedic specialist services may also affect referral practices and timing, and currently such provision is inadequate in some areas.

Regarding surgery itself, in younger individuals osteotomies may buy time, since arthroplasty is generally more successful and cost-effective for the less active, older age groups. Indeed advanced age, on its own, is rarely a contraindication to surgery. An appropriate standard case definition is once again required for this and all other forms of surgery for OA of the hip and knee which takes account of the best evidence concerning effectiveness, acceptability and cost to patients of treatments. Without such a formulation it is impossible to gauge the extent of any unmet need for treatment in the community. Currently a number of consensus guidelines exist, but further research based on best evidence is required in this area.

THR and TKR are each now considered similarly effective and most people can expect to enjoy more than 15 years' symptomatic relief. The volume of surgery currently differs between the two, however, and while symptomatic OA of the knee is more prevalent than OA of the hip, considerably more hips are replaced. Hip and knee replacement surgery are both considered to be cost-effective. Nevertheless, there is much evidence for considerable variation in outcomes and further evidence to suggest that surgeons' routine practice is not always based on best evidence. There are currently more than 65 hip and 40 knee prostheses on the market, most of which are inadequately evaluated. Indeed, some joint prostheses continue to be used which have been discredited in research studies. Purchasers may in due course wish to specify the use of preferred implants in contracts and limit the use of new relatively untested ones.

Models of care/recommendations

Areas identified as deserving particular attention for future public health interventions are (i) raising general awareness of the benefits of moderate, regular exercise for OA and other conditions, (ii) targeting the avoidance of obesity in both men and women, (iii) increasing education and awareness in the workplace among workers and employers regarding work that involves regular lifting and (iv) the evaluation of alternative or additional means of screening for congenitally abnormal hip joints among infants identified as being at increased risk.

Owing to the large and increasing prevalence of OA, it is recommended that all doctors require training in the management of musculoskeletal problems. Primary care physicians also need continuing training to include this emphasis. Improvements are needed regarding dissemination of information and advice to GPs. This includes the need for evidence-based guidelines on the management and referral of people with OA. There is also an urgent need for comprehensive and regularly updated information regarding the local services that are available to GPs. It is recommended that such information is provided via the Internet and that the responsibility for providing this service needs to be decided, perhaps centrally.

There is currently a shortage of orthopaedic and rheumatology specialist services and there is an acute need for considerable expansion in orthopaedic and rheumatology provision. This need will increase over the next 30 years. An expansion in services provided by professionals allied to medicine, e.g. physiotherapists, is also recommended.

Outcome measures

There has been a lack of standard acceptable outcome measures in the past. Clinical assessments may over-represent the concerns of the clinician rather than those of the patient, and their reproducibility is often questionable. A number of patient-based, condition-specific measures (questionnaires) now exist which make the long-term follow-up of patients more feasible. This is particularly relevant for patients following surgical treatment, because their use reduces the need for additional hospital-based clinical assessments. Such measures are nevertheless designed to compare different treatment groups and study populations and are not generally considered appropriate for the individual assessment of patients. Because outcomes in OA are frequently of a long-term nature and most of these measures are relatively new, a thorough evaluation of their usefulness over the long term is not yet available.

Information and research requirements

GPs require up-to-date information on all services that are available to them in one local source book. Such information needs to be updated regularly and might best be provided on computer websites.

Evidence-based guidelines are needed on the everyday management of hip and knee OA, on indications for specialist referral and for appropriateness and prioritising for surgery. In the mean time, a number of expert consensus guidelines are available. These guidelines need advertising. Much work is currently in progress concerning outcomes assessment, particularly those outcomes which emphasise the patient's perspective. This may help in the future development of guidelines that are evidence based. Research in this area would also benefit from improvements in the quality of hospital-based information, which includes the better application of standard coding practices, many of which are out of date. This in turn relies on the adequate recording of information by clinical personnel.

With some considerable planning and adequate resources, the establishment of national THR and TKR registers could theoretically help to bring about a number of these requirements within one efficient framework.

2 Statement of the problem/introduction

Osteoarthritis (OA), also often called osteoarthrosis or degenerative joint disease, is the most common form of arthritis.[1] It is extremely common in people over 40 years of age and is one of the most prevalent diseases of elderly people.[2] OA may affect one or many joints in the same individual and represents a major cause of morbidity, disability and social isolation. This is particularly so when the main weight-bearing joints, such as the hip and knee, are involved as this may lead directly to reduced mobility.[3–7] This chapter therefore focuses on these particular joints.

In the UK, the proportion of those in the population aged 65 years or older is expected to rise by a quarter from 15% in 1985 to 21% by 2030.[8] This change in population structure, together with the acknowledged association between OA and increasing age, means that OA is assuming recognition as a major public health problem and strain on health care resources.[6,9–14] At the same time, research is leading to rapid changes in our understanding of the disease. It is likely that ultimately this may lead to changes in treatments and policy.[15]

With regard to planning services for OA of the hip and knee, a fundamental requirement is to define the distribution in the population of those people for whom treatment is indicated and desired.[16] While radiographic evidence of OA is common and has been demonstrated to exist in the majority of people by the age of 65 years, and in about 80% of those aged 75 years and above,[2] such evidence does not correspond to clinical criteria, patient-centred criteria or uptake of treatment, and many people with radiographic evidence of OA have few or only mild symptoms. The extent to which a person will be incapacitated by the presence of hip or knee OA, and the likelihood that they will seek a medical opinion or treatment is hard to predict, and the precise role of underlying OA in determining this behaviour is problematic.[17] Nevertheless, from the point of view of health care need, it is *symptomatic* disease that is important.

The clinical characteristics of OA

In most people, OA signs and symptoms are limited to one or only a few joints, and symptoms related to primary OA are generally uncommon in people under the age of 40 years, even when evidence exists of pathological changes having taken place. The involvement of many joints may, therefore, suggest a systemic form of OA,[18] and the presence of severe symptoms in younger people will most usually be associated with underlying factors such as pre-existing joint disorders (e.g. congenital dysplasia of the hip), repetitive occupational-related trauma, old fractures, avascular necrosis or metabolic disorders.[19,20]

The onset of OA is frequently insidious. Symptoms may be continuous or intermittent and their characteristics will depend on the joint involved, although these almost always include pain, which tends to be poorly localised.[18] At first the pain may only be noticed after the joint is used and be relieved by rest. However, when OA becomes severe and advanced, pain is experienced at rest and often awakens the person at night. Joint stiffness is also a feature of OA. It is generally localised and of short duration (less than 30 minutes). Stiffness tends to follow periods of inactivity and is characteristically present first thing in the morning after waking.[18] By the time OA is producing sufficient symptoms to provoke a clinical consultation a cluster of these complaints is quite likely to have emerged.[21]

Severely affected weight-bearing joints bring particular problems with ambulation. A limp is common with hip or knee OA – and is in itself often disturbing to people – but an additional distressing feature, common in OA of the knee, is that the joint may feel unstable, as if it might give way. This sensation can reduce an individual's self-confidence and ultimately their functional independence.[2,18] Advanced disease brings limitation in the range of joint movement, although total loss of movement is rare. Deformity, instability and muscle wasting are all features of advanced, long-standing disease.[18]

Pathogenesis

The known main features of OA aetiopathogenesis are summarised in Figure 1 (*see* opposite).

While a dominant pathological feature of the osteoarthritic joint is focal loss of damaged articular (hyaline) cartilage, it is now understood that OA is a disorder of the whole joint organ and not just the cartilage.[22] The main functions of this particular type of connective tissue are to absorb and accommodate stress in response to mechanical load and to provide a smooth load-bearing surface to facilitate low-friction movement of the joint. Nevertheless, this in turn depends upon loads being properly distributed across its surface and also upon the maintenance of joint stability during movement. A stable joint also requires the integrity of ligaments, muscles and tendons supporting the joint, as well as a well-coordinated nervous system which controls these structures.[23]

At the macroscopic level, the key characteristics of an OA joint are swelling, fibrillation, erosion and eventual loss of articular cartilage, together with the remodelling of underlying bone resulting in subchondral sclerosis, bone cysts, an increase in metaphyseal bone and the development of osteophytes (spurs). The end point of OA is eburnation, in which the focal loss of cartilage at the articulating surface of a bone reaches the stage where the underlying bone becomes exposed and subjected to increasingly localised overloading.[23,24]

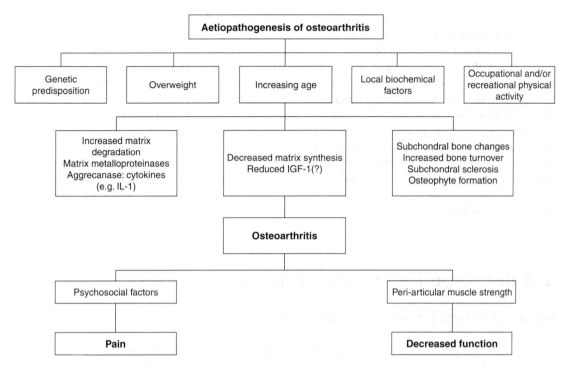

Figure 1: Aetiopathogenesis of osteoarthritis. *Source*: Reproduced with permission from Creamer P, Hochberg MC. Osteoarthritis. *Lancet* 1997; **350**: 503–8.

Prognosis of OA

While the incidence of OA increases with age, there is evidence to suggest that it does not occur as a necessary consequence of ageing, nor is it necessarily a progressive condition.[25,26] Pathological changes in OA tend either to remain stable or to worsen. Nevertheless, both rapid progression and spontaneous regeneration have been described, and patients often experience improvement in their symptoms irrespective of any underlying pathological change.[18] In general, most mild OA does not progress to severe joint damage.[22] There is some evidence to suggest that the risk factors for progression are different from those for the initiation of OA[27] and more limited evidence suggesting that worsening of symptoms may be related to the presence of risk factors, e.g. previous injury, obesity.[28] However, most longitudinal studies have not succeeded in finding any possible explanations for progression.

Examples which illustrate these points include an 11-year follow-up study of people with OA of the hip which found that of 84 subjects who had osteophytes alone on their baseline radiograph, only one developed joint space narrowing. In addition, while two-thirds of patients with symptomatic hip OA progressed radiographically, 5% exhibited radiographic regression.[29] This study also reported that two-thirds of those who entered the study with symptomatic hips experienced a decrease in their pain symptoms over time, despite exhibiting a reduction in the range of movement and difficulties with activities of daily living. Nevertheless, a quarter of patients experienced severe pain.

Another study looked at patients who had been referred to hospital for their hip symptoms.[30] A minority of patients progressed radiographically, albeit over a shorter period of follow-up (median 28 months). It was noted that certain patient characteristics made rapid progression more likely. These characteristics included being female and being of older age at the onset of symptoms. Hip replacement surgery was also used as an indicator of deterioration in this study, with reported symptoms of rest or night pain or poor functional capacity at baseline making hip replacement more likely.[30]

While the natural progression of OA affecting the knee has received considerably more attention than that affecting the hip, the majority of literature is based upon radiographic rather than symptomatic assessment of progression. The prognosis for untreated OA of the knee is noted to be worse than that for the hip (few cases, if any, improve spontaneously), yet progression may be slower[31,32] and disability may increase without an accompanying increase in pain severity.[33] One particular study followed 71 patients for 10–18 years.[32] Radiographic progression was reported in the majority of cases, although changes remained confined to the compartment in which they had first developed. Progression was also more common in women than in men and correlated with worsening symptoms, varus deformity and instability. Overall, evidence would indicate that, in the majority of cases, knee OA will progress radiographically in line with increasing pain and disability, but that this process may be slow.[31] Nevertheless, radiographic change remains a poor surrogate for clinical outcome.[33]

3 Sub-categories of osteoarthritis

Issues of definition and measurement

OA can theoretically be classified in a number of different ways, based on radiological, clinical or symptomatic features, and historically this has been the case. Thus, from an aetiological point of view, OA might be considered primary (idiopathic) or secondary to other disorders (e.g. congenital dislocation of the hip). It may also be monoarticular (affecting one joint) or polyarticular (affecting many joints) and genetic influences can apply here. However, none of these methods of classification is ideal and some may appear rather artificial, particularly since the multi-factorial nature of OA is well recognised.

In a minority of people with OA, the condition is of a generalised nature and involves three or more groups of joints (e.g. hands, feet, knees, hips, spine). It follows that for a proportion of people, OA of the hip or knee will constitute just one of a number of joints affected, often contemporaneously and in accordance with a diagnosis of 'generalised OA'. Although genetic factors are known to be involved in this condition, the genes related to its development remain largely undetermined.[34]

Overall, in recent years OA has increasingly been thought of as a disease process with common risk factors and a variable outcome where subsets could be differentiated according to the site of involvement, associated conditions or patterns of outcome.[35–37] With regard to the hip and knee, a number of constitutional and external risk factors appear to predispose to the development of OA which depend crucially on which of the two sites is affected.

Because of some of the difficulties encountered in defining the presence of OA by any single set of criteria and also because different criteria are needed for different joints, we adopt the simplest sub-categories of hip and knee throughout this chapter. Further distinctions follow according to the severity of symptoms, where the available data permit such distinctions to be made.

Diagnostic criteria and differential diagnosis

It is currently considered neither appropriate, desirable nor realistic that one set of clinical diagnostic criteria be developed for OA. This is because many of the key features come and go and are strongly influenced by other factors, such as general health. In addition, many of the signs and symptoms are non-specific or highly subjective and lack reproducibility. In addition, current clinical and radiographic techniques commonly used to diagnose and assess OA are relatively insensitive to changes in the disease.[35]

Pain and functional impairment are the most usual presenting problems and it is important to determine whether these reported concerns are due to OA or some other condition. This requires careful questioning and physical examination. Many elderly people show radiographic changes of osteoarthritis which are not associated with symptoms, and X-ray confirmation of the diagnosis is frequently not needed, particularly in the general practice setting. An exception to this is when there is doubt about the diagnosis and some other kind of arthropathy is possible.[38] In addition, symptom severity in people with hip or knee OA is frequently associated with anxiety, depression and feelings of social isolation, and it is now known that pain, disability and handicap may to some extent be determined or mediated by such psychological factors.[39,40]

Bony swelling and joint crepitus are features that are found more commonly in OA than in other forms of arthritis. Other main features include use-related joint pain and tenderness, bony and soft tissue swelling, morning stiffness, stiffness related to inactivity, restricted range of movement and problems such as bursitis or tendinitis. Rest or night pain, instability and joint deformities may also be present.[35] The distribution of joint involvement is important in distinguishing between OA and other diagnoses. The differential diagnosis of OA is shown in Table 1.

Table 1: Differential diagnosis of osteoarthritis.

Rheumatoid arthritis
Crystal arthritis (gout and pyrophosphate crystal deposition disease)
Seronegative arthritis, e.g. psoriatic arthritis
Peri-articular syndromes, e.g. bursitis and tendinitis

Source: Reproduced with permission from Scott D. *J R Coll Physicians* 1993; **27**: 391–6.

4 Prevalence and incidence

General points

An assessment of the overall prevalence of OA is made difficult due to differences in the criteria and definitions that have been used in different studies.[41,42] Indeed, there is no clinical, radiological or pathological 'gold standard' against which the epidemiology of OA can be tested.[43] Historically, OA prevalence has therefore been assessed in a number of different ways resulting in a range of rates. The majority of estimates have, however, been based on radiographic assessment. This method commonly uses a system developed by Kellgren and Lawrence in 1957[44] (*see* Table 2), in which cases are defined and graded

Table 2: Kellgren and Lawrence grading system for osteoarthritis.[44]

Grade	Criteria
0	Normal
1	Doubtful narrowing of joint space, possible osteophytes
2	Definite osteophytes, absent or questionable narrowing of joint space
3	Moderate osteophytes, definite narrowing, some sclerosis, possible deformity
4	Large osteophytes, marked narrowing, severe sclerosis, definite deformity

according to the presence of certain radiographic features, such as osteophytes and joint space narrowing. Grading is performed by comparing the index radiograph with reproductions in a radiographic atlas.

The Kellgren and Lawrence system has received much criticism, as it is vulnerable to inconsistent interpretation.[25] Application of the system also revealed the difficulty associated with developing a single formula that is equally suitable for the grading of different joints. For example, the measurement of joint space narrowing is relatively straightforward for the hip and is more often associated with pain than is the presence of osteophytes, whereas osteophyte grade has been demonstrated to have greater validity in defining OA at the knee joint.[45,46] Other problems concern the quality and interpretation of radiographs. Regardless of the difficulties associated with the measurement and classification of OA, radiographically based prevalence estimates are of limited value in defining population requirements for treatment. The main reasons for this are as follows.

- Past joint replacement surgery increasingly affects the figures, because people who have had their painful joint replaced are thereafter excluded from the 'numbers at risk' for primary joint replacement surgery. They also generally have minimal symptoms and so will not appear in symptom-based study samples.
- In the absence of presymptomatic disease-modifying agents, treatment is currently targeted only at reducing symptoms.
- There is a lack of agreement between radiographic evidence of the presence of OA (on which so many prevalence estimates are based) and (i) that of symptoms and (ii) its likely progression (and the timing of that progression) to a symptomatic state.

These general points should be borne in mind for the remainder of this section.

The hip

A number of study prevalence estimates for OA of the hip based on radiographic evidence (with or without symptoms) are summarised in Table 3.

Table 3: Prevalence (%) of radiographic hip OA (Kellgren and Lawrence grades 2–4 and 3 and 4).

Study population (race)	Age (years)	Males			Females		
		n	% with grade† 2–4	3 and 4	n	% with grade† 2–4	3 and 4
Wensleydale, England (white)	55+	102	22	9	149	16	11
Leigh, England (white)	55+	236	25*	7	265	15	5
Watford, England (white)	55+	39	12	4	38	7	0
Oberholen, W Germany (white)	55+	50	16	6	69	10	5
Piestany, Czechoslovakia (white)	55+	180	17	3	196	10	3
Azmoos, Switzerland (white)	55+	93	17	7	130	7	4
Jamaica (black)	55–64	87	1*	0	91	4	4
Nigeria and Liberia (black)	55+	66	3*	2	60	2	1
Phokeng, South Africa (black)	55+	61	3*	1	138	3*	0
All surveys	55+	914	17	6	1,136	10	4
All surveys	55–64	576	14	4	664	8	2

Source: Reproduced with permission from Felson DT. *Epidemiol Rev* 1988; **10**: 1–28.

*$p < 0.01$ compared with unweighted mean rate for sex in all surveys (either 55+ or 55–64 years).

† All figures reported are unweighted means.

Rates range from 3.1% (age 55–74 years)[47] to between 10 and 25% of European Caucasian individuals (over the age of 55 years).[21] In older age groups (> 85 years) the prevalence of hip OA has been put at around 10%.[48] In marked contrast to other OA-affected sites, OA of the hip is more frequent in males than females in the 45–64 years age group, although this becomes less obvious with more severe disease.[49]

While radiographic methods of assessing the presence of OA of the hip or knee show poor agreement with rates obtained by other forms of assessment, e.g. clinical examination,[50,51] evidence currently suggests that radiography is less subject to bias than is clinical assessment.[31] However, a poor relationship has also been demonstrated between radiographic signs of OA affecting the hip and the presence of symptoms or disability. Thus the proportion of patients with (moderate) radiographic hip OA who also report hip pain on most days in the last month has been put at around 28%.[52–54]

Prevalence of symptomatic OA of the hip

Estimates of the prevalence of symptomatic OA of the hip vary. One study reported that symptomatic hip OA affects between 0.7 and 4.4% of adults.[55] Further evidence comes from a recent cross-sectional study of 28 080 people aged 35 and over, resident in the west of England, using questionnaires and clinical examinations (performed on a proportion of the respondents) to assess the prevalence of hip disease. This was assumed to be due to OA in the majority of cases (and hence may be an overestimate). Based on a screening question, having 'hip pain occurring on most days for 1 month or longer during the 12 months before completion of the questionnaire', the prevalence of self-reported hip pain was estimated to be 107 per 1000 for men and 173 per 1000 for women.[16] The prevalence of hip disease severe enough to require surgery was 15.2 per 1000 aged 35–85 years. The prevalence rates of symptomatic disease per 1000 for different sexes and age bands are shown in Table 4.

Table 4: Self-reported pain in either hip.

Age (years)	Men			Women			All usable responses		
	n	Number screen positive	Rate per 1000 (95% CI)	n	Number screen positive	Rate per 1000 (95% CI)	n	Number screen positive	Rate per 1000 (95% CI)
35–44	2,692	150	56 (47–65)	3,052	283	93 (83–104)	5,744	433	75 (69–83)
45–54	2,417	235	97 (86–110)	2,646	442	167 (153–182)	5,063	677	134 (124–143)
55–64	2,194	313	143 (128–158)	2,385	499	209 (193–226)	4,579	812	177 (166–189)
65–74	1,840	244	132 (117–149)	2,212	477	214 (199–233)	4,052	721	178 (166–190)
75–84	887	123	138 (117–163)	1,387	308	220 (200–245)	2,274	431	190 (174–206)
≥85	141	20	140 (89–211)	351	75	211 (172–260)	492	95	193 (159–231)
Total	10,171	1,085	107 (101–113)	12,033	2,084	173 (166–180)	22,204	3,169	143 (138–147)

Source: Reproduced with permission from Frankel S, Eachus J, Pearson N *et al. Lancet* 1999; **353**: 1304–9.

Population incidence studies for OA are all but non-existent, although crucial to an understanding of population requirements for surgery. However, while not specific to OA, and therefore representing a likely overestimate, Frankel *et al.*[16] derived a figure for the incidence of hip disease ('severe enough to require surgery') based on New Zealand clinical hip scores.[56] The incidence rate was calculated from the increase in age-specific prevalence between consecutive age bands. This produced an annual rate of 2.23 (95% CI: 1.56–2.90) per 1000 population in people aged 35 years or over.

The knee

OA of the knee is more prevalent than OA of the hip. Once again, a poor relationship has been demonstrated between radiographic signs of OA of the knee and the presence of symptoms or demonstrable disability.[52–54,57,58] Study estimates based on radiographic evidence are summarised in Table 5.

Table 5: Age-specific prevalence rates (%) of radiological knee OA (Kellgren and Lawrence grades 2–4) in different population groups.

Study location and population		Age group (years)					
		23–34	35–44	45–54	55–64	65–74	75+
NHANES, USA	M	0.0	1.7	2.3	4.1	8.3	
(n = 6,913)	F	0.1	1.5	3.6	7.3	18.0	
Goteberg, Sweden	M						33.3
(n = 81)	F						45.0
Sofia, Bulgaria	M	3.1	3.6	7.0	10.0	9.6	
(n = 4,318)	F	1.6	4.7	9.6	11.3	9.6	
Northern England*	M		7.0	12.1	28.7	42.3	
(n = 1,448)	F		6.0	17.4	48.6	56.3	
Zoetermeer, The Netherlands	M			9.3	16.8	20.9	22.1
(n = 2,957)	F			13.9	18.5	35.2	44.1
Framingham, USA	M					30.8	30.5
(n = 1,420)	F					30.8	41.8
Malmo, Sweden	M		0.0	3.0	4.5	4.5	4.5
(n = 1,179)	F		7.0	4.0	11.0	26.5	36.0

* A combined sample from Leigh, Wensleydale and Watford.

Rates range from 3.8% (ages 25–74 years)[59] to between 14 and 34% (over the age of 45 years).[60] In older age groups (75–79 years) the prevalence of OA of the knee is high, at around 40%.[21] Rates tend to differ between men and women, however. For example, Kellgren and Lawrence reported a prevalence of 40.7% in females and 29.8% in males aged 55–64 years.[61] By the age of 65 years the female:male ratio varies between 1.5:1 and 2:1.[62] The proportion of patients with (moderate) radiographic knee OA who also report knee pain on most days in the last month has been put at 63% of patients (compared with 28% with equivalent definition for the hip) by one American study.[53]

Prevalence of symptomatic OA of the knee

Estimates of the prevalence of symptomatic OA of the knee also vary. A community-based study of Nottingham residents aged 40–79 years reported an overall prevalence of knee pain of 28.7%, increasing with age.[63] However, this was not confirmed as OA related, and other studies have produced much lower figures where confirmatory radiographic evidence was also obtained; these are 6.1% for people aged over 30 and 7–8% for those in the 55+ age group.[21,41,64,65] A study of people aged 55+ in North Yorkshire[66] further ascertained that between 2 and 3% of individuals reported pain and disability at severity levels consistent with the need to consider arthroplasty.

Population incidence studies of knee OA are once again extremely rare and data tend to come from studies of those seeking treatment. These include a primary TKR incidence rate calculated by Williams et al.[67] applying age-specific surgical rates taken from a study of Olmsted County residents, Minnesota[68] to the 1990 English population. These rates were 1.3, 162.1, 208.3 and 391.8 for 45–54, 55–64, 65–74 and 75+ years age groups, respectively, for males, and 44.3, 169.9, 268.4, 642.5 and 235.2 for age groups 45–54, 55–64, 65–74, 75–84 and 85+ years, respectively, for females. The overall calculation produced an annual TKR requirement figure of 28 657. The authors nevertheless stressed that differences in case definition, population characteristics and demographic features between the two countries were all acknowledged as undermining the usefulness of such generalisations.[67,68]

Relationship between population prevalence of hip and knee OA and health care need

Prevalence and incidence of OA based on 'demand'

'Demand' data refer to those people who seek medical advice for their problem, in OA usually pain. However, the onset of pain may be very gradual and the presence of pain may not automatically result in a medical consultation. For example, some individuals may believe that OA is simply an inevitable condition of old age for which little can be done. In this case, sufferers might delay seeking medical assessment and treatment until symptoms become moderately severe. There is thus a dearth of figures representing meaningful incidence rates of OA that are based on 'demand' data.

Demand data may also reflect differences in GPs' referral patterns, and their awareness of the facilities to which they have access.[69] They may also reflect regional variations in the availability of particular health care resources, such as hospital screening services (X-ray or MRI facilities) as well as specialist outpatient departments.[70] The quality of data concerning consultation rates for particular conditions, as well as those for hospital clinic attendance, is often questionable in terms of completeness and consistency of coding over time (see Appendix I). Such data are also unreliable for determining the population requirements for treatments such as surgery. Nevertheless people currently on 'the waiting list' for surgery – or indeed for outpatient appointments – have been considered by some to represent a degree of unmet need,[71] particularly since waiting times may vary from one region to another.

One method has used hospital utilisation rates from the USA (in locations where utilisation approximates roughly to population need) to calculate population needs for primary joint replacement surgery in England. For example, Williams et al.[67] applied, to the 1990 English population, 1987–90 age-specific rates of primary THR per 100 000 person-years based on residents of Olmsted County, Minnesota.[72] These were then used as a very rough proxy for English incident surgical requirements. The rates were 6.8, 56.8, 96.2, 305.7, 173.0 and 147.9, respectively, in males, and 4.6, 23.1, 166.3, 350.2, 421.3 and 162.0 for females, for the age groups < 45, 45–54, 55–64, 65–74, 75–84 and 85+ years, respectively. Application of these rates produced an annual THR requirement of 32 600.

An equivalent calculation for TKR requirement was reported earlier.

Factors that modify risk

While it is agreed that population prevalence figures for hip and knee OA tend to increase steadily with increasing age, there are several additional factors which influence the risk – or timing – of OA development in individuals. OA of different joints involves a different balance of risk factors. In particular, except where OA of the hip and/or knee is involved as part of a generalised, polyarthritic syndrome, each is associated with broadly different risk factors.[21] The most notable examples of risk factors that differ between hip and knee OA are summarised at the end of this section.

Genetic factors

Sex

The relationship between gender and the prevalence of OA is most noticeable in the latter half of adult life. Female gender has been identified as a significant risk factor for OA. Greater life expectancy among women, together with the increasing prevalence of OA with age, results in OA being twice as prevalent in women as in men beyond 55 years of age.[73,74]

OA not only occurs more frequently in females, but also tends to be more severe (particularly beyond age 50) and to involve a greater number of joints. Gender is also associated with the pattern of distribution of OA, with involvement of the interphalangeal joints, the first carpometacarpal joint and knee joints constituting the most usual pattern for women. In contrast, men are more likely to have OA affecting the metacarpophalangeal joints and hips.[75]

The association of OA with gender, along with other specific risk factors (e.g. increased weight and bone mass) and the increasing prevalence of OA in women following the menopause, has signalled the role of oestrogen as an influence.[76] There are theoretical reasons to suspect that female hormones may play a role in OA.

Race/ethnicity

Racial differences have been shown to exist in both the prevalence of OA and the pattern of joint involvement. For example, OA affecting the hips is relatively common in white populations, much less common among black and Native American populations and extremely rare in Asian populations.[75,77] Fewer racial differences are observed for OA of the knee and those differences that have been observed may have been affected by occupational factors.[78] Overall, the question of whether racial differences rest primarily with genetic rather than 'environmental' explanations remains unresolved.

Non-genetic host factors

Age

Age is the most powerful risk factor for OA.[25,79] Lawrence et al.[80] showed that not only was there a marked increase in the occurrence of severe OA (equivalent to the Kellgren and Lawrence system[44] grades 3 and 4) with advancing age, but that this age-related increase appeared to be exponential after 50 years of age. However, the interrelationship between ageing and OA is not yet clear. For example, OA may begin at a relatively young age but only progress to become clinically apparent or symptomatic, and therefore 'more prevalent', as people grow older. There is certainly some evidence to suggest that OA does not occur as a direct consequence of normal ageing, and studies have shown that articular cartilage from patients with OA differs in a number of ways from cartilage of normal elderly individuals.[81,82]

Body weight

Obesity has been strongly linked to OA of the knee and, to a lesser and less consistent[49] extent, of the hip, in cross-sectional and prospective studies.[83,84] For those in the highest quintile for body mass index (BMI) at baseline examination, the relative risk for developing knee OA over the subsequent 36 years has been estimated as 1.5 for men and 2.1 for women in one study.[85] For severe knee OA, the relative risk increased to 1.9 for men and 3.2 for women. In addition, one particular study conducted over a 40-year period was able to show that for women whose baseline BMI values were at least 25 (above the median), weight loss significantly lowered the rate of knee OA.[86] The same study also showed that for women whose baseline weight was under the median, neither weight gain nor weight loss significantly affected their future risk of OA of the knee.

Environmental factors

Occupations and repetitive usage

There is a considerable amount of convincing literature regarding certain occupations which require repetitive use of particular joints over long periods and the subsequent development of site-specific OA. Several studies have found substantially higher rates of hip OA (in men) associated with jobs which require prolonged and frequent heavy lifting – particularly farming – such that hip OA is increasingly regarded as an occupational disease in such cases. By comparison, work which involves kneeling, squatting and climbing stairs, e.g. shipyard work and carpet fitting, is associated with higher rates of OA affecting the knee (in both men and women).[21,83,87–92]

Nutritional factors

There is evidence that antioxidants from the diet and other sources may prevent or delay the development of OA. In particular, vitamin C has been shown to delay the onset of OA in animals in experimental studies, and in the Framingham osteoarthritis study, people in the lowest tertile of vitamin C intake had a threefold increased risk of knee OA progression compared with those who had a higher intake.[94] Inadequate levels of vitamin D also appear to be an important factor in OA progression.[94–96]

Leisure and sports activities

Participation in sport has been associated with an increased risk of lower limb OA.[75,83] This finding is reported for a number of different types of sporting activity. For example, weight-bearing sports activity in women is associated with a two- to threefold increase in radiographic OA affecting the hip and knee.[97] Both hip and, to a greater extent, knee OA have also been shown to be more prevalent among former soccer players, particularly elite players.[98]

As with most other sporting activities, findings regarding risk of hip and knee OA and running are mixed.[99–101] However, there appears to be broad agreement that recreational jogging, rather than high-intensity, competitive running, does not appear to increase the risk of hip or knee OA provided that the joints involved are biomechanically normal.

In summary, OA of the hip has little association with obesity, some association with race but limited association with gender, and a strong association with particular occupations, e.g. farming, whereas OA of the knee is strongly associated with obesity, has little or no association with race, chiefly affects women, and is related to types of work which involve frequent squatting. It does not appear to be associated with farming.

5 Available services and their costs

In general, the services that are available for people who have either hip or knee OA are similar, although each condition requires a different approach. On the occasions when information or treatment differs for either of these joints, this information is highlighted.

Primary care and the primary/secondary care interface

GPs manage the day-to-day care of patients with arthritis and related conditions.[102] In addition to performing the primary assessment of patients with OA, GPs are also responsible for evaluating their need for referral to specialist services and hospital care, and act as gatekeepers in this regard.

Musculoskeletal problems account for around one in ten of all new consultations, 18% of which are estimated to be for arthritis (affecting any site).[103] The annual GP consultation rate for OA is known to have been increasing steadily throughout the last 50 years,[104] although the precise number of GP consultations for OA is unknown and figures relating to those specifically for hip or knee OA are more elusive still. (This is in large part explained by inadequacies and idiosyncrasies inherent in diagnostic coding of primary care databases. Illnesses that are not treated with a drug or occur in people who are not referred may not be recorded on computer.[105] In addition, GPs are only required to record the reason [diagnosis] for a prescription on the first occasion that the drug is prescribed.[106])

There is some evidence to suggest that GPs may only be aware of the more severely affected patients in their practice, as many people with symptoms do not consult their GP about the problem.[107] In some cases patients' perceptions regarding the likely benefit to be gained from a medical consultation (at least before symptoms become moderately severe or disabling) may be low. In general, however, the reasons why some people consult and some do not are known to be complex.[108–111]

The 1990 NHS and Community Care Act led to an expansion in the practice of GPs employing professionals allied to medicine (PAMs) on site. General practice-based specialist outreach clinics and day centres in community hospitals represent other services available to only a proportion of GPs. Arrangements and facilities in these centres differ across the country, although most provide nursing, physiotherapy and/or occupational therapy personnel together with X-ray facilities.

Specialist referral

Indications for referral are discussed later in the chapter (*see* Section 6). When specialist referral is deemed necessary, waiting times to see a specialist vary by region and hospital (and have in some cases resulted from manpower shortages[112]), and despite hospital consultants' views on the inappropriateness of many of the referrals that they deal with, GPs have nevertheless expressed concern at the inadequate provision of orthopaedic surgical services leading to lengthy waiting periods for their patients.[113,114] In some cases this may encourage discussion of private referral, where people have private medical insurance or feel able to afford it.

There are no wholly reliable routine data available regarding GP referral practices for OA of the hip and knee specifically. However, a study of referrals to specialist outpatient clinics throughout the Oxford region revealed joint pain (a category which is likely to have included a high proportion of people with OA) to be the most common reason for referral to hospital-based specialists, at a rate of 43 per 10 000 population per annum.[70] This figure breaks down to 31 in 10 000 referred to an orthopaedic surgeon and 10 in 10 000 referred to a rheumatologist.[115] However, in addition, referral figures coded specifically for people already diagnosed as having OA were given separately. Eight in 10 000 were referred to an orthopaedic surgeon annually; 2 in 10 000 were referred to a rheumatologist.[115] The basis on which GPs choose between surgical vs. rheumatological referral is unknown.

Prevention

While the risk of developing OA increases with age, it does not occur as a direct consequence of normal ageing and this insight, together with evidence about risk factors, suggests that certain primary preventive strategies could be usefully employed where OA of the hip and knee are concerned.

In general, understanding of the role of exercise in relation to OA has changed considerably in recent years, although information may not have filtered through to all health care practitioners,[116] and it is now believed that regular moderate levels of low-intensity exercise within all age groups may help to at least delay the development of symptoms in OA.[117,118] Some of this effect may well be indirect and related to the attenuation of age-related weight gain or the overall beneficial effects on general (including psychological) health.[119] However, an additional benefit of exercise is the maintenance of muscle strength and accompanying improvements in balance,[118,120] as these combine to reduce the risk of falls in elderly people, a factor which contributes to high morbidity.[121–124] Oestrogen replacement is one other potential area of promise in that a number of studies have now reported a reduction in the risk of hip and knee OA associated with its use.[125,126]

Primary prevention most relevant to hip OA

The higher rate of hip OA in men that is associated with occupations in which frequent and heavy lifting is involved suggests a need for increased education and raised awareness among workers at risk and their employers. A concomitant increase is required in the provision and use of lifting aids and machinery, where appropriate, and overall modification of working conditions.

Primary prevention most relevant to knee OA

The major known risk factor for symptomatic OA of the knee, particularly in women, is obesity.[85,127] It follows that every effort should be made to encourage both men and women to eat sensibly and exercise regularly in order to avoid gaining weight during the course of their lifetime.[119] Exercise should aim to strengthen the leg muscles, particularly the quadriceps, since weak quadriceps are known to be associated with symptomatic knee OA.[118]

The high rate of symptom development in people with radiographic evidence of OA suggests that secondary prevention might be practicable. Nevertheless, it is currently unclear precisely what causes the onset of symptoms in people with radiographic changes, and certainly no method is known to prevent their development.[64] Tertiary prevention is hampered by similar problems as there are no modifiable risk factors that are known unequivocally to affect the risk of progression of pain or disability. Nevertheless, recent evidence from the Framingham study suggests that some nutritional risk factors, including vitamin D, have a different effect on late OA than appears to be the case in its early stages, and this effect may be to limit progression.[96]

Treatment and rehabilitation

The appropriate management of individuals with symptomatic OA is necessarily influenced by the age and occupation of the patient, the degree of pain and other symptoms experienced, and their medical history and specific circumstances. Nevertheless, management is likely to include elements of patient education, 'training', alleviation of symptoms (particularly pain) and eventually, where acceptable, surgical intervention.[128–130] There will, however, always be a proportion of people for whom surgery is not an option, due to either reluctance on their part, the primacy of treatment for other coexisting conditions or their extremely poor operative risk. For these patients, and indeed for those waiting (sometimes for lengthy periods) for surgery, other forms of management are required.

The impact of OA means that a multi-disciplinary approach is often needed to treat both the disease and the person. This involves the skills of various health care professionals with a major responsibility falling on the primary care team.[131] The overall aim is to assist patients in attaining their maximum potential in everyday life through the use of education, rehabilitation, medication, surgery and other interventions, including health visitors, social workers, counsellors, dietitians and complementary therapists. The appropriate application of these different elements of treatment rests, in the first instance, on appropriate assessment.

The initial assessment

Most patients present with pain and/or functional impairment as well as anxiety about the underlying cause and prognosis. The GP will need to determine, in the first instance, whether these concerns are due to OA or some other condition. Good management requires a patient-centred rather than a disease-focused approach, and careful questioning is required as well as a physical examination. Indeed an examination of the joint should be carried out even if the history clearly points to OA, as this in itself provides reassurance to patients.[132]

It is necessary to assess and acknowledge the severity of symptoms in a way that is empathetic. While a number of methods exist for measuring the severity of OA symptoms and functional impairment, e.g. arthritis impact measurement scales, WOMAC, Lequesne and others,[133–135] they are not often used within a routine clinical context and it is not clear how useful they would be. Certainly none of these measures make any detailed reference to the coexistence – and impact – of other medical conditions, nor do they take account of people's individual home circumstances, all of which make a crucial difference to the impact of symptomatic hip and knee OA on people's lives. Through careful questioning, the GP will be made aware of the patient's unique clinical and social context and their assessment of the appropriate management will aim to take account of all of these aspects as well as the person's fears and expectations regarding their diagnosis. For example, some people may harbour the fear that a diagnosis of OA means a rapid and inexorable descent into a state of constant pain, extreme disability and dependency.

Details of all remedies that the patient is currently using need to be obtained. This is important and should include any prescribed, 'over-the-counter' or complementary/alternative remedies, as the possibility of drug interactions needs to be borne in mind before initiating any new systemic form of therapy.[136,137] In fact, drug therapy can often be avoided in patients with only localised damage.[138]

The initial assessment by the GP will generally include many elements of education that are outlined below. This includes an explanation about the condition and its likely prognosis, and discussion of the various treatment options together with reassurance that these can help. An emphasis should be placed on the importance of practical elements of self-help, such as ways of protecting the joint (e.g. using a walking-stick, wearing shock-absorbing soles), and obese patients should be counselled and offered assistance regarding the importance of losing weight and the positive effect that this can have on symptoms (especially OA of the knee). The role of exercise should also be discussed, particularly as some people will need 'permission' to use a painful joint.

An important adjunct to the GP's initial assessment is the provision of written information for the patient to take away. This can take the form of key points that were discussed during the consultation, together with information about access to individuals within the primary care team who can provide continuing support and advice. Treatment and progress should be reviewed on a regular basis.[132,139,140]

Education and social–psychological interventions

It is vital that patients are told about the nature and likely outcome of their condition as this will aid their treatment and serve to allay anxiety. It is important that they are made aware of the differences between OA and other forms of arthritis and they should also be informed that the condition frequently stabilises and that surgery is not usually necessary.[133] Patients also need to feel involved with their own management – an increased sense of self-efficacy and empowerment helps to militate against depression and lethargy and may encourage increased social contact.[141–143] Self-management programmes, training in coping strategies, regular telephone contact and counselling are all low-cost interventions of proven benefit which can be offered to patients with OA of the hip or knee.[144–146] There are also a number of organisations that can provide patients with further written information and advice, such as the Arthritis and Rheumatism Council[147] and Arthritis Care.[148]

Exercise, physiotherapy, occupational therapy and orthosis

While specific components of non-pharmacological therapy for patients with symptomatic OA of the hip and knee are often highly joint-specific, a number of general considerations apply to both, and in each case the role of physiotherapists and occupational therapists is of central importance in providing individualised assessment, education and training for patients and their carers.[135,136]

At first, therapists will commonly encounter negative beliefs from patients about the role of exercise.[149] This may be influenced by the widely accepted association between high-level activity, injury and OA, together with the very understandable assumption that painful conditions should be rested. Rest is certainly important, and it is crucial that patients rest when a joint becomes painful during exercise. They are also usually told to keep stair climbing to a minimum.[136,137] Nevertheless, patients, relatives and carers will often need careful explanations and counselling about the detrimental effect of underusing a joint and are therefore taught to balance rest with activity, joint protection with joint loading, weight-bearing with non-weight-bearing, and aerobic with non-aerobic exercise. Hydrotherapy may be offered as a part of physiotherapy, although this may not be widely available.

As with most interventions in OA, the goals of exercise therapy are to reduce pain and improve function. Improving the efficiency and safety of a person's gait is also important, and this can be achieved in part through exercises and training. The importance of walking every day should be emphasised and the judicious use of various orthotic devices may prove invaluable in this regard.

A reduction in the loading forces on the joint is often associated with decreased pain and improved function. A number of safe, simple and cheap orthotic devices are available that can assist in this aim and significantly relieve symptoms, even in patients whose disease is severe. One of the simplest devices, relevant to both hip and knee OA, is the walking-stick (cane). To be most effective, it needs to be held in the hand on the opposite side to the affected joint. This may, however, feel counter-intuitive and often requires some training.[150–153]

The use of shock-absorbing insoles can lessen the impact of heel strike, and shoes with very hard soles should be avoided, as should those which threaten gait stability.[136,137,154,155] The use of a heel lift may confer substantial and dramatic pain relief for many people with OA of the hip.[156]

Medial taping of the patella may relieve painful symptoms in those with OA of the knee which involves the patellofemoral compartment.[157] A light-weight knee brace may also reduce pain in patients with severe medial compartment OA or with lateral instability.[158,159] In addition, lateral heel and sole wedges may relieve symptoms in selected patients.[162]

Diet

People with OA should aim to eat a balanced diet that is rich in vitamins C and D.[93,95,96]

Some individuals may benefit from dietary advice given by a dietitian, particularly those with special dietary needs, e.g. weight reduction. Nutraceuticals, such as avocado/soybean saponifiables, may help to reduce symptoms.

Complementary/alternative therapies

It has been estimated that around 90% of 'rheumatic patients' have each tried on average 13 unproven or 'controversial' remedies,[161,162] and many people feel that they derive benefit from a variety of alternative/complementary therapies, e.g. acupuncture, massage, reflexology. Acupuncture is now available on site in some GP medical centres. Part of the benefit of such therapies undoubtedly relates to the individualised manner of delivery.

Other non-pharmacological treatments for symptomatic OA

A variety of non-invasive, non-pharmacological treatments are available for the relief of pain in OA. These include narrow-band light therapy, cryotherapy (cold air or ice chips), transcutaneous electrical nerve stimulation (TENS),[163,164] pulsed electrical stimulation (Bionicare electrical stimulator) (particularly used for OA of the knee), and heat treatments (including diathermy and ultrasound).

Orthodox drug treatment

Medications for OA are generally directed at the relief of pain rather than disease modification. A study reported in the 1970s that one-sixth of the population believed that medicine could do little or nothing to relieve the symptoms of the various forms of arthritis.[165] Although this figure may well have changed, non-compliance with treatment certainly remains a problem in the management of arthritis generally, with a number of studies suggesting that only between 40 and 60% of patients followed prescribed regimes correctly.[166]

Local/topical application

Topical analgesics, such as methylsalicylate or capsaicin creams, are commonly used as an adjunctive therapy or on their own for patients with knee OA who do not respond to oral analgesics or do not wish to take systemic treatment. Some of these preparations may cause a burning sensation, however, which a proportion of people find unacceptable.[167] Many NSAIDs, such as ibuprofen, are also available over the counter as a topical preparation and these are commonly used for the relief of mild to moderate OA pain.

Intra-articular injections

Local steroid injection into the joint space may temporarily reduce pain quite considerably and increase mobility. This technique may theoretically be used for any joint but is almost never used for the hip. However, it is commonly used for knee OA. The possible reasons for such short-term relief are unclear.[168–170] There is little convincing evidence that repeated use of this treatment may cause harm, and for elderly people with moderate to severe symptoms for whom surgery is not an option this treatment may prove very beneficial.

Intra-articular injections of hyaluronan and other forms of viscosupplementation may also improve symptoms for some individuals.[171,172]

Systemic pharmacological treatments

Systemic pharmacological treatments are usually required when topical pain relief is insufficient. Analgesics, including low doses of NSAIDs, are commonly used in the treatment of mild to moderate OA pain. Simple non-opiate analgesics, such as paracetamol, often work well and although they have no anti-inflammatory effect, side-effects are uncommon and those which might occur, particularly in overdosage (e.g. hepatotoxicity), are equally likely to occur with NSAIDs. In contrast, side-effects from NSAIDs are common – particularly in elderly people – and can be life-threatening. For the present, therefore, NSAIDs should be used as a last resort for pain relief.[138] Highly selective COX-2 inhibitory NSAIDs are increasingly available and may promise fewer side-effects.[173–175]

Where stronger pain relief is required, combination analgesic therapy consisting of paracetamol together with a mild opioid form of analgesic, e.g. dextropropoxyphene (i.e. coproxamol), codeine (cocodamol) or dihydrocodeine (codydramol), are also considered less risky than NSAIDs.[138]

Surgery

While there is hope that new therapies and preventative measures might one day significantly reduce the extremes of OA disability, it is likely that surgical techniques will always play a role for a minority of people with OA. In recent years, total joint replacement (arthroplasty) has displaced many other forms of surgical treatment for OA. Nevertheless, indications remain for these other surgical techniques, which are often used as a means of prolonging the life of the natural joint. This is because arthroplasty generally has a limited life and involves an enormous loss of bone stock which cannot (as yet) be replaced.

In OA of the knee, disease can affect (and be limited to) different compartments of the joint and this has a bearing on which surgical procedures are deemed most appropriate.

Arthroscopy and joint lavage

Arthroscopy is a surgical technique that permits internal examination of a joint in a way that is minimally invasive. It can be carried out under local anaesthesia as an outpatient procedure. Joint lavage, particularly for the knee, will frequently confer symptomatic relief for pain in the earlier stages of OA, although results may be longer lasting in those cases uncomplicated by inflammation.[176]

Osteotomy

Osteotomy involves realigning the articulating surfaces of a joint to allow healing and reduce overloading. It is a preventative procedure used to delay the need for future joint replacement and has a place in the treatment of both the hip and the knee. One particular indication regarding the hip concerns conditions present early in life (e.g. acetabular dysplasia) which can give rise to premature OA, later on.[177]

Arthrodesis

Arthrodesis involves the surgical fusion of bones across a joint space which eliminates all movement at that joint. This procedure is rarely carried out but may be performed on the hip or the knee as a treatment for severe OA when joint replacement would be inadvisable or impossible. This situation may arise if the patient is very young,[178,179] when a joint is grossly deformed or when previous arthroplasty has failed, particularly if failure was due to sepsis.[180–183] Arthrodesis is generally considered a salvage operation and is a relative contraindication for later arthroplasty since the range of movement likely to be achieved is very limited.[184]

Hemiarthroplasty

Arthroplasty involves replacing the patient's diseased joint tissue with metal, plastic or ceramic components. Hemiarthroplasty entails the replacement of only one of the two opposing surfaces of a joint. With regard to the hip, this operation is chiefly carried out for the treatment of fractured femur, which most usually results from trauma (attended in addition by osteoporosis rather than OA). Unicompartmental arthroplasty (UCA) of the knee is indicated when disease is limited to one compartment of the knee only (e.g. lateral or medial condyle), when osteotomy is contraindicated (or has failed), or when the patient is too young, active or heavy to consider total knee replacement (TKR).

Total joint replacement (arthroplasty)

Total joint replacement (arthroplasty) involves fully replacing all the articulating surfaces of a joint. The demand for both primary hip and knee replacement surgery continues to rise and although more THR than TKR operations are carried out in the UK at present, rates of TKR have been increasing much more rapidly in recent years and demand for TKR should equal that for THR in the not too distant future.

As the number of primary operations rises, so too does the demand for revision surgery. While 'revision' increasingly takes many different forms (some more invasive than others), this surgery is on average more costly[185] and less successful than a primary arthroplasty, particularly when it is performed on younger individuals.[73,186] Factors that contribute to both the cost and the success of revision surgery include the higher cost of the prosthesis, the complexity and therefore the length of the operation, and the frequent need for bone grafting, since bone loss (resorption) tends to accompany aseptic loosening, the most common form of arthroplasty failure. While autograft is obviously the preferred option, lack of bone stock frequently leads to the need for allografting. Currently, 1700 femoral heads are collected annually and stored by the Scottish National Blood Transfusion Service for revised THR operations. It has been estimated that this quantity will be insufficient to meet the growing demand if supplies remain at this level.[187] Elsewhere bone banks are gradually being set up. One or two studies have highlighted the small but serious risk of transmitting infection that is associated with using allografts, and the need for stringent screening.[188,189]

Total hip replacement: specifics

The artificial hip joint normally comprises three elements: (i) a ball (usually metal) which replaces the original femoral head that rests on (ii) a metal stem which is inserted into the femur and (iii) a plastic cup which is inserted into the acetabulum. These three elements are collectively referred to as a prosthesis (or implant) and are manufactured by a large number of private companies. Each company makes its own brand which differs from those of competitors in details of design, material and cost.[190]

Early hip prostheses were fixed directly to bone without the use of cement. These were relatively prone to loosening, and during the 1960s acrylic bone cement came into use for the fixation of both acetabular and femoral components, with considerably improved results. These early advances were pioneered by Charnley, who also gave his name to a type of prosthesis which was widely used and still is – except that the prosthesis design has now changed more than once while the name remains largely unchanged.

From the 1970s onwards the number of prosthetic designs has proliferated together with various fixation techniques. For example, further attempts have been made to eliminate the need for bone cement, in particular threaded acetabular cups have been devised which are intended to screw directly into bone. Implants with porous and/or beaded surfaces have also been developed that encourage adjacent bone to grow into the superficial crevices to produce firm fixation. A more recent development has been the introduction of products such as hydroxyapatite as a coating on prostheses. This substance stimulates bone growth with the aim of producing a tighter fit around the prosthesis.

Methods are now increasingly used by which cement may be introduced into the medullary canal of the femur under pressure, although according to a 1996 survey a cement gun is used by only a minority of surgeons (9% of respondents).[191] It is suggested that such techniques have been responsible for a significant reduction in the rate of aseptic loosening of femoral components in recent years,[192] although they are also claimed to have an increased risk of provoking fat embolism, hypotension and death,[193] and await thorough evaluation. Other developments have included the use of ceramic rather than metal femoral heads to reduce wear. Many prostheses are now a hybrid in which the femoral component is cemented and the cup is cementless. Most recently, acetabular and femoral components are being made modular. Most of the different types of prosthesis remain relatively unevaluated.

Data regarding length of hospital stay (LOS) are shown in Figures 2 and 3. The median LOS has decreased gradually for primary THR and to a lesser extent for revision THR. In fact, the LOS varies considerably for people undergoing primary THR and while the majority of patients require between 8 and 14 days,[194,195] this requirement will be strongly influenced by the patient's age and the availability of separate convalescent or rehabilitation facilities.[196,197]

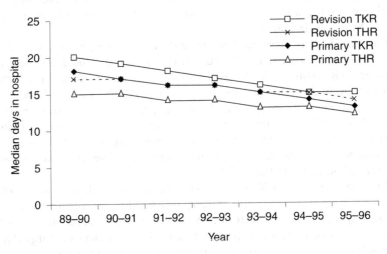

Figure 2: Median length of hospital stay for joint replacement surgery in England, 1989–96.

Following surgery, most patients require at least 3–5 months to gain full strength and energy, and some will take longer. Depending on the type of prosthesis and technique used, rehabilitation may include a period of 6–12 weeks requiring protected weight-bearing on two crutches, followed by gradual transition to walking with a stick.[198] Patients can normally continue with exercises at home after initial instruction, although outcome evaluation every 2–3 years by outpatient visit, questionnaire and/or X-ray is increasingly thought to be of value.[198]

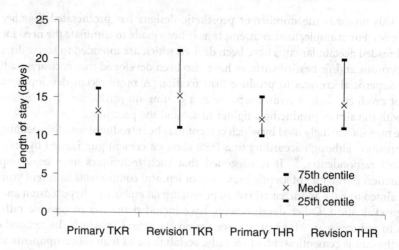

Figure 3: Length of stay plus interquartile ranges for total hip and knee replacement surgery in England, 1995–96.

Total knee replacement: specifics

The knee comprises a number of anatomical elements and is in many ways a more complex organ than the hip. While it is essentially a hinge joint, it also allows a small amount of rotation when in flexion. Sixty-five degrees of flexion are required to walk at a normal pace, 95 degrees to go up and down stairs and 110 degrees to rise from a chair with relative ease.[199]

While OA of the knee is more prevalent than OA of the hip, for reasons that are unclear rates of knee joint replacement are currently lower in this country. One reason may be due to the poorer perceived outcomes following TKR relative to THR based on their past performance. In fact, there has been a significant improvement in the techniques and design of TKRs during the past 20 years,[200,201] such that long-term observational studies now suggest that > 90% of particular designs survive for between 13 and 15 years,[202] and TKR for OA is increasingly being viewed as more reliable and durable than is THR.[203] The early higher failure rates were associated with the use of simple hinged designs, while subsequent designs have attempted to duplicate the anatomy, motion and stability of the knee and have employed the patient's normal soft tissues and ligaments to that end.[204]

The basic design of the modern TKR or 'total condylar arthroplasty' consists of two principal components: a high-density polyethylene tibial bearing which articulates with a polished (usually stainless steel) femoral component. The two parts are not linked mechanically and the stability of the new joint is achieved by a combination of reciprocal shaping of the articulating surfaces and surgical technique, which aims to ensure sufficient tension in the surrounding ligaments and muscles to maintain the two components under compressive loading.

In all TKR prosthetic designs both medial and lateral collateral ligaments are preserved, and in most the anterior cruciate ligament is resected, if it is still intact. Beyond this, two variants of the basic TKR prosthetic design have evolved. One form involves the retention of the posterior cruciate ligament (PCL) and the other substitutes the PCL. To date, survival has not been shown to differ between these two variants.[202,205]

Length of hospital stay (*see* Figures 2 and 3) is on average slightly longer for people undergoing TKR, but is also influenced by patient age, the availability of separate convalescent or rehabilitation facilities[196,197] and the timing of rehabilitation.[195]

The future: therapies for OA disease modification

New therapies which modify the disease itself, rather than simply alleviating symptoms, include agents that aim to restore the equilibrium between cartilage synthesis and degradation. Of particular potential are agents such as doxycycline which selectively block either the release or the action of cytokines, thereby reducing the severity of OA lesions.[206,207]

Another area of increasing interest is that of nutraceuticals. Avocado/soybean unsaponifiables may increasingly be used for the treatment of symptomatic hip and knee OA.[208–210] Glucosamine, chondroitin sulphate and collagen hydrolysate are other examples.[210]

Hospital activity

Waiting times for surgery

Official data on waiting times for THR and TKR surgery are shown in Figures 4 and 5. Median waiting periods (days) for primary THR (163), primary TKR (210), revision THR (131) and revision TKR (105) all increased gradually during the period 1989–96. Of the four operations, waiting times are consistently longest for primary TKR and shortest for revision TKR. During the 7-year period, the largest increase in waiting time (about 2 months) was for primary TKR. While revision surgery would appear to be treated more urgently than primary surgery, there is much variation, as demonstrated by the interquartile ranges for 1995–96.

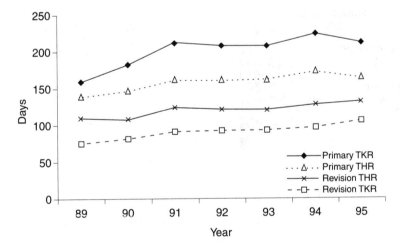

Figure 4: Median waiting times for total hip and knee replacement surgery in England, 1989–96.

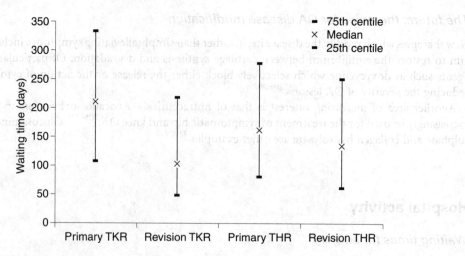

Figure 5: Waiting times plus interquartile ranges for total hip and knee replacement surgery in England, 1995–96.

Surgical rates (based on HES data)

In 1995–96 the principal diagnosis (reason) reported for the majority of people undergoing primary hip and knee replacement was OA (82 and 83%, respectively; *see* Figures 6 and 7). The principal reason given for revision surgery is poorly described (or to be precise, poorly coded).

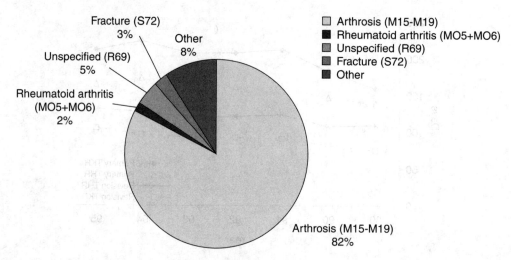

Figure 6: Principal diagnosis for patients undergoing primary total hip replacement surgery in NHS hospitals in England, 1995–96.

Overall, only a tiny proportion (< 5%) of total joint replacement operations are carried out as emergencies. These tend to be THRs (rather than TKRs) for fractured head or neck of femur, although primary implantation of a femoral component alone (hemiarthroplasty) would be a more frequent operation in this case.

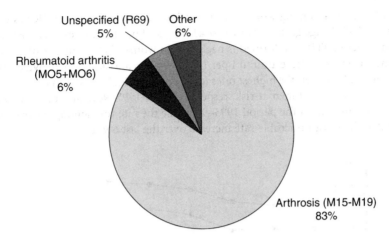

Figure 7: Principal diagnosis for patients undergoing primary total knee replacement surgery in NHS hospitals in England, 1995–96.

The total numbers of operations for total hip and knee replacements that were carried out (for all diagnoses) in NHS hospitals in England during the period 1989–96 are shown in Figure 8. The rate rose steadily for both operations during this period. These figures include a very small proportion of private patients occupying NHS pay-beds (*see* below).

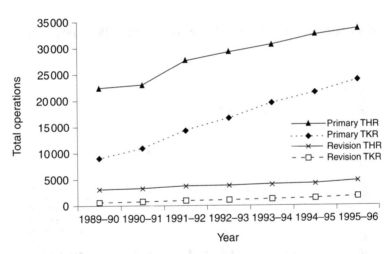

Figure 8: Number of hip and knee replacements in NHS hospitals in England, 1989–96.

In 1989–90, 22 230 primary THR operations were performed, compared with 9068 primary TKRs. By 1995–96 the number of primary THRs had risen to 33 320, while the number of primary TKRs had now reached a similar level (23 846) to that of primary THRs 6 years earlier. The increase in the number of TKRs was faster throughout the period than that of THRs. It is believed that demand for TKR will either equal or overtake that for THR during the next decade, as has already happened in the USA. Currently, evidence would suggest that the population demand for TKR surgery is inadequately provided for and represents a large unmet need.[66,108,198,199,211]

Figures 9 to 12 show that among women an increasing uptake of primary THR has occurred mainly within the 75–84 and 65–74 age groups (rates were 41.5 vs. 35.4 per 10 000 women at risk, respectively, for 1995–96). The number of THRs performed is negligible in women below the age of 45 and is small and constant in women aged 45–54 (rate around 1 per 10 000 women at risk). In men, overall rates of THR are lower than for women. However, the highest rates for primary THR also occur in the 75–84 and 65–74 age groups (27.9 vs. 18.3 per 10 000 men at risk, respectively, for 1995–96), although the rate for the latter age group decreased throughout the period 1993–96, while the rate rose among the over-85s. This oldest age group exhibited the most noticeable rate increase over the last 6 years.

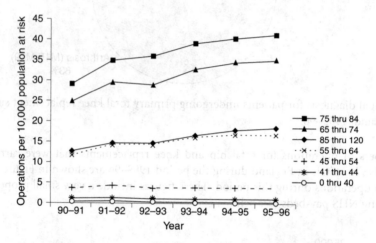

Figure 9: Age-specific rates for primary total hip replacement in NHS hospitals in England, females, 1990–96.

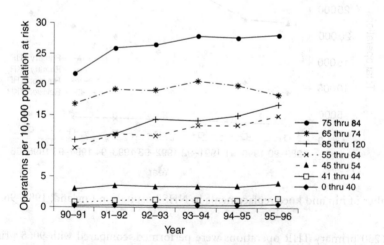

Figure 10: Age-specific rates for primary total hip replacement in NHS hospitals in England, males, 1990–96.

For TKR, once again an increase in surgical uptake has chiefly occurred within the 75–84 and 65–74 years age groups in women (rates were 33.6 vs. 27.7 per 10 000 women at risk, respectively, for 1995–96). Similarly, the number of TKRs performed is negligible in women below the age of 45.

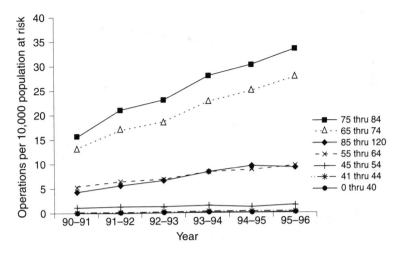

Figure 11: Age-specific rates for primary total knee replacement in NHS hospitals in England, females, 1990–96.

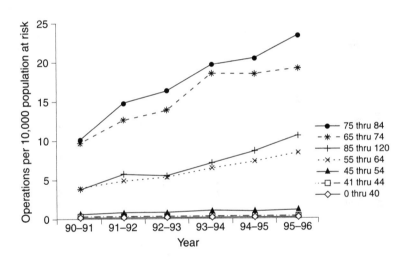

Figure 12: Age-specific rates for primary total knee replacement in NHS hospitals in England, males, 1990–96.

The overall volume of TKR surgery has remained much lower for men than for women, although age-specific rates of surgery are similarly low for men under the age of 45 (around 1 per 10 000 men at risk) and are also similar in the 55–64 and 85+ age groups (8.4 and 10.5 per 10 000 men at risk in 1995–96). However, the rates of surgery for men aged 65–74 and 75–84 are much lower than for women (19.1 and 23.4 per 10 000 men at risk, respectively, 1995–96).

Age- and sex-standardised rates for THR and TKR operations (*see* Figure 13, overleaf) suggest that the rate of THR surgery is levelling off while TKR surgical rates continue to increase, albeit slowly. Standardised rates for revision surgery appear relatively static.

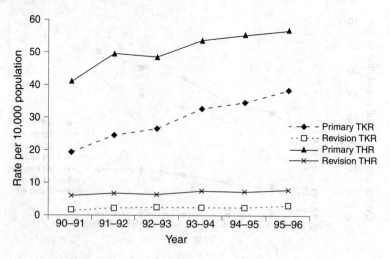

Figure 13: Age- and sex-standardised operation rates for NHS hospitals in England, 1990–96.

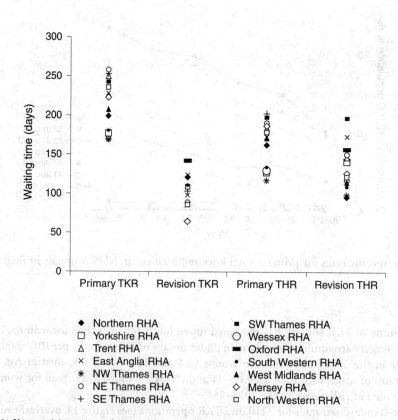

Figure 14: Median waiting times for total hip and knee joint replacement surgery in England during 1995–96 by region of residence.

Regional rates

In an ideal world, once joint replacement has been deemed necessary, any period of waiting might represent an unmet need. Nevertheless, given that a period of delay or preparation is fairly inevitable, regional variation in waiting times may prove more revealing than aggregated figures.

Regional variation in median waiting times for primary and revision THR and TKR for 1995–96 is shown in Figure 14. The range was between 117 days (NW Thames RHA) and 203 days (SE Thames RHA) for primary THR, and between 95 days (Northern RHA) and 196 days (SW Thames RHA) for revision THR.

For TKR median waiting times the range was between 168 days (NW Thames RHA) and 257 days (NE Thames RHA) for primary operations, and between 63 days (Mersey RHA) and 123 days (East Anglia RHA) for revision surgery.

The extent to which these figures can be considered reliable is unknown. Nevertheless, such variation suggests that there may be an unmet need in areas with the longest waiting times. The disparity between waiting times for revision THR, which are similar to those for primary operations, and those for revision TKR, which are considerably shorter than for primary surgery, is worthy of note.

Figures 15 and 16 show that there is enormous variation in surgical rates for both THR and TKR between districts within each region. The two most compelling explanations for this are either that different districts apply different criteria in the decision to proceed to joint replacement surgery or that orthopaedic provision differs between districts (or both). Unfortunately, in the absence of nationally agreed standard objective indications for THR/TKR surgery in the UK, it is not possible to examine this issue.[212]

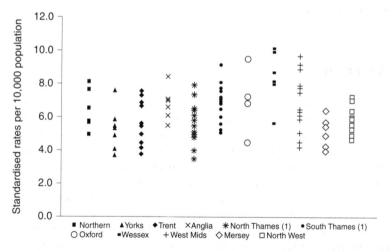

Figure 15: Age- and sex-standardised primary total hip replacement rates for district health authorities in England categorised by region, 1995–96.

Private treatment

Pay-beds in NHS hospitals represent a small fraction of overall private joint replacement activity and represented a fairly steady 900–1200 THRs per year and 400–500 TKRs per year in England throughout the period 1990–91 to 1995–96 (HES data).

Recent data from a Nottingham study (B Williams, personal communication) reveal estimates for the numbers of THR and TKR operations carried out in the independent health care sector (England and

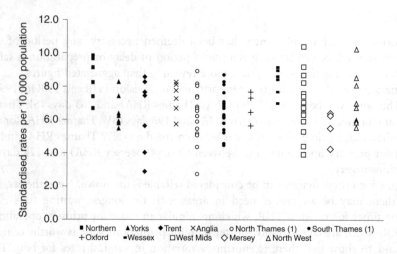

Figure 16: Age- and sex-standardised primary total knee replacement rates for district health authorities in England categorised by region, 1995–96.

Wales only) for the period 1997–98 (*see* Tables A4–A7 in Appendix I). In total, 11 332 THRs and 5965 TKRs (primary and revision operations) were performed in this period. The numbers of primary operations were 10 493 and 5786, respectively. Additional considerations regarding private treatment can also be found in Appendix I.

Costs of OA treatment

A number of studies have attempted to measure the total costs that may be attributed to arthritis (although not specifically for hip and knee OA). OA accounts for the vast majority of these calculations and 56% of people with arthritis are reported as having locomotor disabilities.[213] A full assessment of the costs should include consideration of time lost to work and production, the personal costs to individuals and their families, as well as the costs of all medical and pharmaceutical services used. One such estimate put the total cost of arthritis at around £1200 million for the UK at 1990 prices.[214]

A number of medical costs for arthritis have also been calculated. For example, in the UK it has been estimated that arthritis accounted for £231.3 million of hospital costs during 1989, amounting to around 1.6% of total expenditure. These figures included the cost of all inpatient and outpatient services, although the figure is acknowledged to be a likely underestimate. Arthritis-related general practice costs for the same year were estimated at £44.8 million (2.2% of total expenditure), while pharmaceutical services added a further £219.0 million to the bill. This last figure amounted to almost 10% of the total costs of pharmaceutical services, but did not include the costs of 'over-the-counter' products and therefore represents a considerable underestimate of the true costs of medication provision for arthritis. The overall cost of arthritis to the NHS for 1989 was nevertheless estimated to be £495.08 million.[214]

Costs relating to other aspects of arthritis are even more difficult to estimate. However, the number of days lost from work due to arthritis has been estimated at over 41 million for 1989, leading to approximately £308 million being spent on annual benefit payments. Other costs are less readily quantifiable but include earnings lost due to reduced employment and promotion opportunities as well as early retirement.[215] In addition, people with arthritis may have special requirements and equipment, e.g. handrails, raised toilet seats, to reduce the impact of disability and maintain mobility and independence.[213] Other costs are even harder to quantify but include the impact of pain, loss of self-esteem and depression which all commonly accompany the condition of arthritis.[214–216]

Recent NHS reference costs for specific services and procedures are given in Table 6.

Table 6: Costs of various services and procedures relevant to the treatment of OA of the hip and knee.

	(£)
Consultation with a GP, in GP surgery	10.00[a]
Consultation with a GP, home visit	30.00[a]
Outpatient consultation with an NHS rheumatologist	68.57[b]
Outpatient consultation with an NHS orthopaedic surgeon	53.87[b]
Private hospital consultation	80.00[c]
Session with an NHS physiotherapist (hourly rate)	30.00[a]
Session with an NHS occupational therapist in an orthopaedic hospital	26.00[a]
NHS hospital transport to and from outpatient appointment (ambulance)	33.59[b]
Home visit by district nurse	12.00[a]
Home visit by health visitor	19.00[a]
Home visit by geriatric social worker (hourly rate)	78.00[a]
Knee arthroscopy, NHS as day case	511.00[d]
Private arthroscopy	1,650.00[c]
Primary total hip replacement operation (NHS patient in NHS hospital)	3,737.00[d]
Private primary total hip replacement operation (private wing in NHS hospital)	7,500.00[c]
Primary total knee replacement operation (NHS patient in NHS hospital)	4,207.00[d]
Private primary total knee replacement operation (private wing in NHS hospital)	8,250.00[c]
Revision total hip replacement operation (NHS patient in NHS hospital)	4,613.00[d]
Private revision total hip replacement operation (private wing in NHS hospital)	9,500.00[c]
Revision total knee replacement (NHS patient in NHS hospital)	4,613.00[d]
Private revision total knee replacement operation (private wing in NHS hospital)	9,500.00[c]

Sources: [a] Unit Costs of Health and Social Care 1998;[438] [b] Trust Financial Return 1998;[439] [c] Nuffield Orthopaedic Centre, NHS Trust, Oxford (*Note*: costs subject to variation); [d] National Health Service Reference Costs 1999.[437] These cost figures were obtained by Dr A Gray, Health Economics Research Centre, IHS, Oxford.

6 Effectiveness of services and interventions

Evidence in support (or otherwise) of the various services and interventions available

Figure 17 (*see* overleaf) illustrates points of decision making relevant to the treatment of both hip and knee OA, while Table 7 (*see* pp. 583–4) summarises the overall management of hip and knee OA addressed in this section (this table has adopted the format of a previously published table which summarised data from an earlier date).[139] The quality of scientific evidence regarding different available treatments is shown according to the key given beneath Table 7, together with the strength of any recommendation in support (or otherwise) of their use.

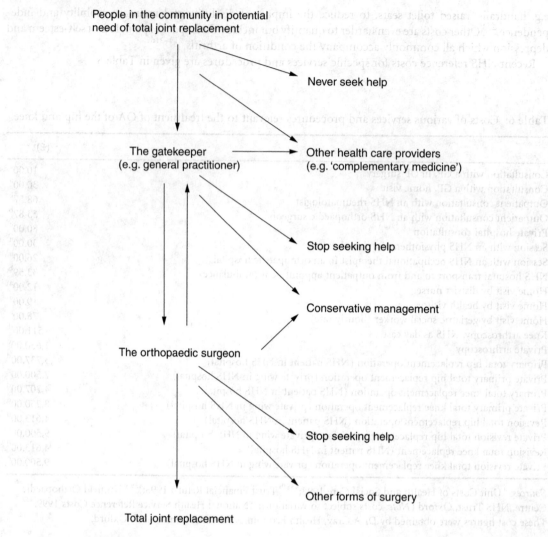

Figure 17: The hypothetical pathway to joint replacement (adapted with permission from Dieppe P *et al. The Hypothetical Pathway to TKR*).

There is in fact a paucity of detailed, clear and relevant evidence from which clinicians, patients and purchasers may make reliable choices about treatment for OA, and outcomes research in OA and orthopaedics has received considerable criticism in the past.[217–221] Many of the criticisms have centred on the lack of relevant available standard validated outcome measures – in particular, measures that take account of the patient's perspective – but there has also been a dearth of well-designed, large-scale (let alone randomised, controlled) studies in this area.

Part of the reason for the poor quality of research-based information on the assessment of outcomes in OA has to do with the long-term nature of these outcomes. For example, with surgical treatment, measurable differences in outcomes between different treatment groups may not arise for 5–10 years. Following up large numbers of people for this length of time is both problematic and costly, and may

Table 7: Management of hip and knee osteoarthritis: the evidence base.

Topic	Quality of evidence*	Strength of recommendation†	Patient selection important	Applies to hip (H) or knee (K)	Reference
Non-pharmacological therapy					
Physiotherapy/muscle exercise programmes	I	A		H or K	Kovar et al.,[254] Panush and Brown,[440] Callaghan et al.,[441] Minor et al.,[269] Ettinger et al.,[271] Fisher et al.[264]
Hydrotherapy/balneotherapy	II-2	B		H or K	Verhagen et al.,[275] Ahern et al.[276]
Shock-absorbing shoe implants	II-2	B	✓	K (or H)	Voloshin and Wosk,[154] Tohyama et al.[442]
Walking-stick (opposite side to symptoms)	III	B		H (or K)	Bount,[151] Brady[152]
Patella taping	I	A	✓	K	Cushnaghan et al.,[157] Balint[128]
Knee bracing	II-2/III	C		H or K	Matsuno et al.[159]
Heat treatments	IV	B		H or K	Brandt[145]
Transcutaneous electrical nerve stimulation (TENS)	I	B		K	Fargas-Babjak et al. Taylor
Cryotherapy (for inflammation)	II-2	B	✓	K	Olson and Stravino,[278] Brandt[145]
Weight loss/dietitian	II-2	B	✓	K (or H)	Felson,[282] Martin et al.,[283] Williams and Foulsham[284]
Other diets: food allergies	IV	C (but rare)	✓	H or K	Panush et al.[443]
Other diets: Vitamin D	II-3	B	✓	H or K	McAlindon et al.[96]
Other diets: Vitamin C	II-3	B		H or K	McAlindon et al.[93]
Other diets	II-3	B and D		H or K	Bourne et al.,[444] McAlindon et al.[93]
Acupuncture	I	D		H or K	Ernst
Arthritis self-help programmes	I	A		H or K	Lorig et al.,[244] Keefe et al.[141]
Telephone contact	II-2	B		H or K	Lorig et al.[244]
Social support	I	A	✓	H or K	Weinberger et al.[445] Weinberger et al.[445]
Pharmacological therapy					
Nutraceuticals (avocado/soybean unsaponifiables)	I	A		H or K	Maheu et al.[208]
Glucosamine, chondroitin sulphate, collagen hydrolysate	II-1/II-2	B		H or K	Leffler et al.,[446] Deal and Moskowitz[210]
Topical analgesics – capsaicin	I	A	✓	H or K	Deal et al.[289]
– NSAIDs	IV	C	✓	H or K	McCarthy et al.,[167] Altman et al.[290]
Non-opioid analgesics	I	A		H or K	Bradley et al.,[293] Williams et al.[447]

Continued overleaf

Table 7: Continued.

Topic	Quality of evidence*	Strength of recommendation†	Patient selection important	Applies to hip (H) or knee (K)	Reference
Opioid analgesics	II-1	B	✓	H or K	Quiding et al.,[448] Rousi et al.,[449]
NSAIDs	I	B and D	✓	H or K	Kjaersgaard Andersen et al.[414] Williams et al.[447]
	II-1				Dieppe et al.,[450] Schnitzer et al.,[451] Tamblyn et al.,[452] Tannenbaum et al.[453]
Adjuvant cytoprotection, e.g. Misoprostol	II-2	B	✓	H or K	Tannenbaum et al.,[453] Shield[303]
Arthrotec (diclofenac and Misoprostol)	II-1	B	✓	H or K	Shield[303]
Intra-articular corticosteroids	I	C	✓	K	Towheed and Hochberg,[454] Creamer[168]
Surgical interventions					
Joint lavage/arthroscopy	I	B and D	✓	K	Ike et al.,[455] Chang et al.,[311] Livesley et al.[176]
Viscosupplementation/hyaluronan injections	I	A	✓	K	Adams et al.,[456] Lohmander et al.[457]
Osteotomy	II-2	B	✓	H or K	Weidenhielm et al.,[458] Werners et al.,[459] Santore and Dabezies[316]
Joint replacement – THR	I/II-2‡	A	✓	H	Bourne et al.,[460] Herberts and Malchau,[381] Laupacis et al.,[461] Rorabeck et al.[462]
– TKR	II-2‡	A	✓	K	Knutson et al.,[463] Kirwan et al.[464]

Table format adapted from Lane NE, Thompson JM. *Am J Med* 1997; **103**: 25–30S.

* Quality of evidence:

I Evidence obtained from at least one properly designed randomised controlled trial

II-1 Evidence obtained from well-designed controlled trials (includes underpowered randomised controlled trials)

II-2 Evidence obtained from well-designed cohort or case–control analytic studies, preferably from more than one centre or research group

II-3 Evidence obtained from multiple time series with or without intervention.

Dramatic results in uncontrolled experiments (e.g. the results of the introduction of penicillin treatment in the 1940s) could also be regarded as this type of evidence

III Opinions of respected authorities, based on clinical experience, descriptive studies, or reports of expert committees

IV Evidence inadequate and conflicting.

† Strength of recommendation:

A There is good evidence to support the use of the procedure

B There is fair evidence to support the use of the procedure

C There is poor evidence for the use of the procedure

D There is fair evidence to reject use of the procedure

E There is good evidence to support the rejection of the use of the procedure.

‡ RCTs have compared various technical factors in arthroplasty, e.g. cemented vs. uncemented, but none have been carried out to compare arthroplasty with an alternative form of treatment.

explain why few studies are carried out. Another problem has concerned appropriate and acceptable outcome measures. Improvements have occurred in this area in recent years and this is discussed further in Section 8.

Effectiveness in the primary care setting: diagnosis, management and referral practice

There is scant information on the effectiveness of OA management in the primary care setting in the UK, and studies based in other countries have different health care systems so their findings may not be generalisable to the UK. This limits any conclusions that may be drawn from reviewing such studies, but their results may nevertheless suggest promising subjects for future study or audit in this country.

One such area of enquiry concerns the comparison of treatment provided by primary care physicians with that by rheumatologists and other hospital-based doctors. Study findings suggest that while primary care physicians are largely responsible for diagnosing and treating joint problems, they may be inadequately trained in this area.[222-230] A UK study also found some aspects of the management of common musculoskeletal problems by primary care physicians to be sub-optimal.[69,231-233] In particular, there is an acknowledged lack of rheumatological expertise in the primary care setting.[139] One way in which this situation might be improved involves the use of rheumatology specialist outreach clinics. A pilot study to evaluate English rheumatology specialist outreach clinics found increased satisfaction expressed by patients and GPs compared with situations in which reliance was solely on hospital outpatient departments. GPs also reported an increase in their own skills and expertise in rheumatology occurring as an indirect effect of these clinics being held in their practice.[234]

In the absence of such facilities, many primary care physicians state that they would welcome management guidelines, either in written format or simply via improved telephone access to consultants for advice.[225,233] In the absence of evidence-based guidelines, consensus guidelines have in fact been produced which usefully cover many key aspects of the management of OA of the hip and knee which are published in the UK.[38,140]

One UK study found that many hospital referrals were in some sense inappropriate.[69] The same study identified GPs' frequent lack of direct access to facilities such as physiotherapy, occupational therapy and orthotics as a major reason for such referrals. General practice-based specialist outreach clinics and day centres in community hospitals are extremely useful to GPs in assisting with the initial assessment of new cases of suspected OA and in providing direct access to therapists. In the absence of such direct access, GPs are obliged to refer patients via a hospital consultant. Interestingly, the same 1991 study also discovered that many GPs *did* in fact have open access to physiotherapy (and other) services of which they were unaware. Nevertheless, many GPs do indeed have no such access at present.

Appointments to see hospital specialists frequently involve a waiting period. One possibility for reducing the waiting time for such appointments is supported by early results from a UK randomised study which recently compared outcomes for specialist physiotherapists vs. sub-consultant surgeons in the initial assessment and management of new GP referrals to outpatient orthopaedic departments. The results showed orthopaedic physiotherapy specialists to be equally effective on the basis of a number of patient-centred outcomes and superior on measures of patient satisfaction.[235] The provision of such services might considerably reduce inappropriate consultant referral (with the associated likely delay in initiation of treatment).[69] At present such services are very rarely provided.

Because there is a considerable overlap between guidelines for specialist referral and issues regarding indications and appropriateness for joint surgery, further consideration of this whole area will be reported in a later section.

Effectiveness of screening

A proportion of hip OA occurs secondary to a congenital or childhood hip disorder (acetabular dysplasia, congenital dislocation, slipped epiphysis or Perthe's disease).[236] The exact proportion that can be accounted for in this way is unclear, but is likely to be small.[236–239] Hip screening has the potential to identify such problems and, in theory, prevent or delay future cases of OA by encouraging their early correction (although data to support this are lacking). However, the neonatal hip screening programme (first introduced in 1969) has been reported as inherently unreliable,[240] with cases no more likely to be detected now than in the past.[241] Whether other methods, e.g. ultrasound, may in due course prove to be more reliable and more cost-effective is currently unknown. Overall, there is wide variation in screening practices and management of this condition throughout the UK, which largely reflects the lack of research.[243] While methods of screening for the presence of pre-symptomatic OA (e.g. genetic screening and biological markers) continue to be developed, there seems little reason currently to recommend such practice on a large scale.

Effectiveness of education, counselling, training and psychological support

Education, counselling, self-management programmes, training in coping strategies and regular telephone contact have each been shown to independently reduce pain, decrease the number of visits to physicians and generally improve the quality of life of people with OA. They may also enhance individuals' continued motivation with any prescribed therapy.[141,144,243–250] Nevertheless, a recently published *Health Technology Assessment*[251] stands as a notable exception to the generally positive findings reported by other studies regarding education, self-efficacy and OA.

This particular study involved an economic evaluation of a primary care-based education programme for patients with OA of the knee and, overall, although the study authors acknowledged that the study suffered from a number of limitations, it failed to demonstrate that any improvements in knowledge, self-efficacy in arthritis management, or health outcomes had occurred after 1 year.

Effectiveness of rehabilitation, exercise and orthosis

While 'joint overload' and vigorous exercise involving damaged or non-normal joints is known to predispose to OA, in general there is compelling evidence to suggest that a moderate level of regular exercise can often reduce pain and disability. It therefore has a palliative role in the management of OA of the hip and knee.[252–256] This may in part be related to the association between lower limb muscle weakness and OA, particularly OA of the knee, since muscle weakness has a mediating role with regard to pain and loss of mobility in people with OA.[257,258] In addition, an interesting relationship was suggested between regular joint motion and osteophyte development by a study reporting increased osteophyte formation in the knees of people who stopped running (for reasons other than knee pain or stiffness) compared with those who continued,[259] and a recent study has demonstrated that muscle strengthening is the intervention that is most likely to have a significant impact on reducing levels of severe mobility limitation in older women with knee pain.[260]

Many studies have now demonstrated the beneficial effects of simple walking exercises for OA of the main weight-bearing joints, and the majority of people with symptomatic OA will benefit from appropriate exercises.[3,145,256,261,262] A moderate level of low-impact aerobic exercise increases cardiovascular endurance and stamina. This is important, because patients with OA usually have decreased endurance. Easy-to-perform, low-rate aerobic exercises, such as walking, swimming, golf and tennis, have now been shown to offer a safe and effective means of improving general fitness, reducing OA-related pain and disability, and increasing performance, despite a lack of change in radiological evidence. The overall benefit of patients' perceptions of improvement and improved confidence in their physical ability should not be underestimated.[254,261–273] Even among elderly people with OA, those with no disability but whose physical performance is low have been identified as more likely to develop joint disability within a 4-year period than similarly affected individuals who were more active.[276] However, compliance with exercise regimens is not assured.

Relevant to symptomatic OA of both hip and knee is the walking-stick. When used properly, this is one of the simplest and most effective orthotic devices for modifying symptoms and increasing confidence.[150–153]

Orthotic devices for OA of the hip

The use of shock-absorbing insoles can lessen the impact of heel strike, and broad-based shoes increase gait stability.[136,137,154,155] In addition, the use of a heel lift has been shown to confer substantial and dramatic pain relief for many people with OA of the hip.[156]

Orthotic devices for OA of the knee

Medial taping of the patella has been shown to relieve painful symptoms in those whose OA involves the patellofemoral compartment.[157] A light-weight knee brace has also been used with some considerable success in reducing pain in patients with severe medial compartment OA and also for those patients experiencing lateral instability.[158,159] In addition, lateral heel and sole wedges may produce excellent results in selected patients, including those with advanced disease.[160]

The benefits of hydrotherapy have been the subject of a Cochrane systematic review.[275] This concluded that despite an overall lack of good randomised controlled trial design, hydrotherapy (spa or otherwise) appeared to confer positive effects on patients with OA and such therapy may be of particular benefit to people with severe symptoms. One of the better designed studies[276] confirmed significant improvements in self-assessed pain and self-efficacy after only 4 days' individual hydrotherapy treatment with a physiotherapist. Improved self-efficacy scores remained for some time after the 4 days' hydrotherapy had ceased, while pain score improvement was only maintained for the duration of the treatment. As with other forms of exercise, this treatment is likely to improve general fitness and overall sense of well-being.

In general, evidence suggests that the majority of people with OA of the major weight-bearing joints will benefit from initial physiotherapy assessment and intervention at all stages and that a relatively short and inexpensive course of therapy may confer long-lasting benefits.[272]

Effectiveness of other miscellaneous forms of therapy

Evidence for the efficacy of other forms of therapy is mixed. Narrow-band light therapy has resulted in highly significant and long-lasting (4–6 months) improvement in pain and decreased disability in patients studied in a small double-blinded randomised controlled trial which compared infra-red with placebo therapies.[277] Cryotherapy (cold air or ice chips) may in some cases relieve pain by reducing inflammation, e.g. for synovitis.[145,278] Transcutaneous electrical nerve stimulation (TENS) has also been shown to relieve pain despite the presence of a strong placebo effect.[261] Similarly, pulsed electrical stimulation has produced significant improvement in knee OA compared with placebo, although the effect may only be short term.[279,280] A review of randomised trials[261] recently concluded that therapeutic heat treatment, including diathermy and ultrasound, did not improve pain or function above the placebo effect in OA joints.

Effectiveness of dietary advice and weight reduction

Dietary advice to encourage weight reduction is recommended, ideally from a dietitian, in patients who are overweight. Evidence for the effects of weight reduction once OA has developed is sparse, although a few studies have shown weight reduction to be associated with a slowing of the rate of progression of OA and/or a favourable effect on symptoms.[281–284] However, patients who are being considered for hip or knee replacement surgery are frequently told to lose weight before surgery when there is no convincing evidence that obesity results in a poorer outcome.[285]

An adequate intake of vitamins C and D should be encouraged, as inadequate levels appear to encourage disease progression in OA.[93–96]

Nutraceuticals, in particular avocado/soybean unsaponifiables, have shown very promising results in recent trials as a treatment for symptomatic hip and knee OA, providing a reduction in symptoms which was equivalent to NSAIDs and better than placebo. This effect persisted beyond treatment cessation.[208–210] Glucosamine, chondroitin sulphate and collagen hydrolysate have also been used with some measurable success.[210]

Beyond this, no evidence exists in support of other specific dietary therapy in the treatment of OA.[136,137,287]

Effectiveness of complementary and alternative therapies

A review of published trials cited three acupuncture studies for treatment of severe symptomatic OA of the knee,[128,287] only one of which found a significant difference in outcome between those who received treatment and controls. All three showed an extremely strong placebo effect. On balance, there is little evidence to support the use of acupuncture in the treatment of OA, although equally there is no reason to discourage people from trying it, given that some people find it helpful.

The placebo effect is clearly present in many alternative/complementary medicine methods (and this is also true of orthodox treatments, of course) but is hard to quantify. Therefore, it is sometimes argued that scientists cannot easily refute the benefits claimed by therapists. The individualised manner of delivery is certainly welcomed by patients,[161,162] and to this extent patients' search for alternative and complementary therapies may represent a need unmet by orthodox practitioners and the health care system as a whole. One important problem with some complementary therapies lies in the risk that patients will discontinue conventional agents without first seeking advice. Use of alternative therapies may also delay the process leading to a medical diagnosis – which may be particularly important if the condition is something other than OA. Other risks stem from the use of 'natural substances,' such as Chinese medicine, which have occasionally been found to contain harmful elements, including undeclared prescription drugs.[162,288]

Overall, orthodox practitioners would be wise to keep an open mind about the value of some complementary therapies if questioned by patients, while at the same time warning them of the possible risks in particular instances.

Effectiveness of analgesia

One study compared topical 10% triethanolamine salicylate with placebo for patients with knee OA and found no difference between the two.[162] There are no published data assessing the effectiveness of topical NSAID preparations. Capsaicin cream has been demonstrated to give a significant improvement in pain scores compared with placebo,[167,289,290] although some people may find the initial local burning sensation that it produces unacceptable.

Regarding systemic treatment, the effect of simple analgesics is quick but tends to last for only a few hours, whereas the effects of anti-inflammatory preparations build up over a few days.[291] A moderate level of pain requires effective pain management and this usually calls for a continuous level of analgesia to be maintained, i.e. given in anticipation of rather than in response to pain.[292] The use of paracetamol has been compared with an NSAID (ibuprofen) in a double-blind study of patients with knee OA, in which both treatments were found to be equally effective.[293] The use of opioid analgesics – while preferable to NSAIDs from the point of view of some side-effects – may increase the risk of falls and accidents, and the use of any analgesic may permit overload and further damage to occur in an affected joint.[294]

Effectiveness of NSAIDs

The use of NSAIDs – which include aspirin – should only be considered when simple analgesics are found to be inadequate for pain control or during inflammatory stages of the disease. The chief consideration at present is the high cost of the side-effects.[138,294]

The mode of action of NSAIDs is complex and not fully understood in OA. Grouping NSAIDs together in any discussion of their action can prove misleading because different NSAIDs have been shown to have differing actions on inflammation mediators. In addition, NSAIDs are now known to have other modes of action in relation to OA cartilage.

There have been many studies of large populations confirming the potency and efficacy of NSAIDs in the treatment of both hip and knee OA. However, Cochrane systematic reviews of the more recent studies of NSAID use for OA in the knee[295] and hip[296] concluded that there was insufficient evidence to distinguish any one NSAID as superior in action. This was published prior to results being available on more recently developed highly selective COX-2 inhibitors, although how these newer NSAIDs might affect elderly people with multiple morbidities is as yet unknown. Nevertheless, the avoidance of side-effects remains a primary consideration. Examples to illustrate the importance of side-effects include findings from one study which has shown that emergency admissions in 1 year (1990–91) for upper gastrointestinal disease which resulted from NSAID use amounted to an overall incidence of 147 per 100 000 (or nearly 15 per 10 000) of the adult population in the UK, with around 3700 deaths resulting directly from complications of peptic ulcer in NSAID users.[297]

Paradoxically, as NSAIDs with more selective effects become available on prescription, the more harmful, non-selective NSAIDs are likely to become increasingly available to patients 'over the counter' thus increasing the risks associated with self-medication.[174]

From a practical standpoint, with unselective NSAIDs the wide diversity of action and side-effects of these drugs result in considerable variation in patient tolerance and response to different preparations,[298] and the prescribing of NSAIDs may therefore involve an element of 'trial and error'.[138] For the moment, it is recommended that well-established formulations are chosen. These include ibuprofen, which can also be obtained over the counter, with diclofenac and piroxicam as other possible structural variants. The reasoning behind this choice is that those which have been in use the longest are least likely to produce idiosyncratic side-effects. They are also likely to be available in generic form and are therefore much cheaper.[138] Ibuprofen has been shown to be the best tolerated of all the NSAIDs, while indomethacin rates as one of the more toxic and should be avoided.[299–302]

Concomitant therapy with H_2-receptor antagonists or antacids is often administered to prevent gastrointestinal side-effects in NSAID users. However, this can prove harmful in the longer term and may simply have the effect of suppressing symptoms but not necessarily the effects of NSAIDs on the gastric mucosa.[301] New formulations are being researched, with one combination, Arthrotec, appearing to confer increased ambulatory activity, as well as increased analgesia compared with diclofenac alone.[303] Arthrotec is only available as a fixed-dose combination at present, and the dose of diclofenac might be considered too high for many elderly patients, particularly if they are taking drugs known to interact with NSAIDs, such as diuretics, antihypertensives, anticoagulants or lithium. In addition, misoprostal itself may result in diarrhoea.[138]

Effectiveness of specialist referral and indications for hip and knee joint replacement surgery

While increased attention has been given to indications for orthopaedic surgery for OA, no evidence-based guidelines currently exist that can help doctors and surgeons decide who might best benefit from surgery. However, there are consensus criteria which address indications for both referral and surgery.

A multi-disciplinary National Institutes of Health (NIH) consensus panel was provided with relevant literature and required to reach agreement on a number of questions, including 'What are the current indications for total hip replacement?'.[304] They concluded that patients were appropriate for THR if they had radiographic evidence of joint damage together with moderate to severe persistent pain or disability not substantially relieved by non-surgical treatments such as analgesics, NSAIDs and physical therapy. They also referred to contraindications, such as medical conditions, that significantly increased the risk of peri-operative complications. The document points out that those aged 60–75 years were once considered ideal candidates for THR but that both younger and older age groups were now increasingly receiving THR. A UK-based workshop similarly emphasised the importance of pain not managed by medical means, followed by loss of movement, increased deformity and progressive disability as the main reasons for surgery for hip and knee OA.[132]

The NIH consensus statement and UK workshop report are both expressed in fairly qualitative terms. A New Zealand consensus panel sought to provide more explicit quantitative guidance in the form of criteria to assess the extent of benefit expected from hip and knee replacement surgery.[56] The literature was summarised and put to groups of health professionals who were required to produce numerical weights of factors that should determine priority for surgery, where priority should be judged in turn by extent of expected benefit. Their final weightings for decisions were as follows: pain, 40%; functional activity, 20%; movement and deformity, 20%; other factors such as multiple joint disease, 20%. It was felt that this system would be particularly valuable in making decisions about waiting time for elective surgery more transparent. This would in turn lead to a system where those with the greatest need and capacity to benefit from surgery would be the highest priority.

A similar multi-disciplinary panel was used in Ontario to agree criteria for appropriateness for referral for possible surgery and also priority in waiting lists for both knee and hip replacement surgery.[305] Their method of developing criteria involved the rating of case scenarios. The panel agreed very substantially on how case scenarios should be assigned following decision algorithms for both appropriateness for referral and urgency and priority on the waiting list. There are striking similarities between the NIH, UK and New Zealand guidelines in the dominance of pain and physical function in criteria. To date, there is little evidence regarding the practical feasibility of using such criteria to assist doctors in deciding whether to refer or surgeons in deciding priorities on waiting lists. There is little evidence of the use of guidelines to address the substantial levels of disagreement about indications for orthopaedic surgery observed among both primary care and specialist doctors.[306,307]

Effectiveness of surgical techniques other than total joint replacement

Arthroscopy can be a valuable tool in the assessment of OA of the knee.[308] It is also a means by which conditions within a joint may be improved during the early stages of symptomatic OA. For example, loose fragments of cartilage may be removed, regions of articular cartilage may be shaved and subchondral bone may be drilled or abraded to stimulate the formation of a new articular surface.[309] The long-term benefits of arthroscopy are hard to predict, although it is suggested that certain patient-related variables are associated with a better outcome, including a short duration of symptoms.[310,311] There is a need for long-term randomised prospective studies in this area.

Joint lavage may prove beneficial for some patients who have not responded to other therapies and for whom a general anaesthetic is undesirable. Any surgical technique, including arthroscopy, usually involves the removal of debris and perhaps certain inflammatory mediators.

The concept of viscosupplementation (supplementing the fluid components inside the joint) has been studied extensively, and products such as modified hyaluronan formulations are continually improving to satisfy the need for tissue and blood compatibility, permeability to metabolites, rheological properties greater than the indigenous synovial fluid (to allow for dilution factors) plus a slow export rate and extended half-life. The procedure is known to relieve the pain of OA and increase mobility in the short term, but it is hoped that it may also delay structural progression of the disease.[172,313]

In a case-series, osteotomy has been shown to produce sustained symptomatic improvement in about 80% of patients treated.[177] In younger active individuals with symptomatic OA of the knee, tibial osteotomy can allow a return to strenuous activities and will frequently delay the need for arthroplasty for up to 12 years, by which time the patient may be more suitable for arthroplasty.[313] Generally, the results of osteotomy depend very much on patient selection, pre-operative planning and surgical technique,[314–317] but the outcome, although very much less predictable than replacement, has the advantage that bone stock is maintained.[177] Generally, this type of surgery is more successful in younger and physically active patients with unilateral knee OA. The outcomes following future arthroplasty of the knee do not appear to be compromised by the prior osteotomy.[318] However, the results are generally not so good for patients having THR subsequent to hip osteotomy.[319,320] Nevertheless, in patients with acetabular dysplasia, timely operative treatment (e.g. periacetabular osteotomy, which involves moving and refixing the acetabulum) can relieve any symptoms, and although more complex and time-consuming than hip replacement, will prevent or greatly delay deterioration of the hip which would in any case eventually need replacing.

With regard to hemiarthroplasty, rarely and in selected cases this operation may be performed in preference to total joint replacement for OA of the hip in which the disease is limited to one small area of cartilage only. The main advantage is the preservation of bone stock in young people in whom future total joint replacement is likely to be indicated. Outcomes for this form of operation are unclear.[76,321,322]

Somewhat more evidence is available regarding unicompartmental arthroplasty (UCA) of the knee.[323–327] While it is technically a more difficult operation than TKR, UCA is claimed to be a less invasive procedure, while maintaining better range of movement, gait and function than TKR. UCA is also said to be an easier operation to revise, should that subsequently become necessary.[324,328] While limited evidence exists in relation to these claims, one economic analysis from the Swedish registry lends support to the cost-effectiveness of the procedure compared with TKR, due to a shorter associated length of hospital stay, fewer complications and cheaper implants.[329]

Effectiveness of total arthroplasty: risks, complications and revision surgery

Outcomes following TKR have improved considerably over the last 20 years, such that joint survival estimates are now similar for both hip and knee arthroplasty, and it has been estimated that within 10 years of surgery fewer than 10% of patients should require revision.[198–200,304,330,331] To this extent, both operations are believed to be successful. However, an appraisal of effectiveness that is based solely on revision rates is not entirely satisfactory.

Despite the overall success rate of hip and knee replacement surgery, an increasing proportion of surgical time is now spent on revising past primary joint replacement operations. There is also considerable variation in the average survival time for different types of joint prosthesis. Even so, there is still very little reliable evidence on which surgeons may base their choice, and recent surveys of all NHS hospitals in England and UK orthopaedic surgeons reported that over 65 different types of hip prosthesis and over 40 different types of knee prosthesis were available for surgeons to choose from.[192,193] New designs are also continually being introduced.[332,333]

In general, the success of arthroplasty may be affected by a number of factors besides the type of prosthesis used. These include the level of experience and expertise of the surgeon,[334,335] as well as patient characteristics such as the type of arthritis or underlying condition which provokes the need for arthroplasty, and patient age, level of physical activity, weight, general health and expectations.[336-338] The appropriate selection of patients for surgery is extremely important and relies upon an adequate case definition for those most likely to benefit from surgery. This should consider symptoms, function and comorbidity.

Following arthroplasty, patients are generally at high risk of developing deep venous thrombosis (DVT), less commonly giving rise to a pulmonary embolism (PE) which may rarely prove fatal.[339-342] A significant risk of developing a DVT also persists for some weeks following hospital discharge.[343-345] Many consider that the serious nature of this condition warrants routine prophylaxis with mechanical means (pulsatile stockings or continuous passive motion), anti-inflammatory agents with antiplatelet activity, warfarin, or a combination of these.[346-348] Indeed 75% of hip surgeons have reported using at least one method of thromboprophylaxis routinely for their patients.[349] This was out of 32 different methods mentioned in the same survey, thereby indicating limited consensus.

However, while the development of DVT is relatively common, the precise risk of subsequent symptomatic PE following arthroplasty in patients who receive no prophylaxis has been estimated as around 1% and the risk of death as no more than 0.2%.[339,350,351] These low estimates of PE risk have therefore led others to conclude that the risk of promoting bleeding that is associated with routine prophylactic anticoagulant therapy may not be justified.[345,350]

Peri- and post-arthroplasty cardiovascular events become increasingly common with advancing age.[352] Elderly patients are also at risk of cognitive dysfunction following major surgery and in around 5% of cases this is long-lasting.[353,354] While anaesthetic techniques have generally improved in terms of risk, a recent large-scale randomised controlled trial concluded that the risk of cognitive dysfunction or cardiovascular events was not affected by whether the anaesthetic was general or epidural.[354]

Epidural anaesthesia and analgesia are standard techniques in orthopaedic surgery of the lower limbs. Compared with general anaesthesia, the benefits of the epidural technique include excellent analgesia, minimal respiratory depression and a significant reduction in intra- and post-operative blood loss due to induced hypotension.[355,356] Urinary retention is a common complication following any major surgery, particularly in elderly men. However, the risk of retention requiring catheterisation is much increased with the use of epidural anaesthesia.[357] A randomised controlled trial of patients having joint replacement surgery has concluded that the use of an indwelling catheter, inserted during the operation and removed the next day, reduces the short- and long-term risks of urinary retention without increasing the risk of urinary infection.[358] Such practice might well prove more acceptable to patients and more cost-effective than urgent catheterisation with the patient fully conscious.

Bilateral arthroplasty may be performed at the same operation. This inevitably involves a longer period under anaesthetic for the patient and a fairly punishing period of rehabilitation, although the length of hospital stay per joint is reduced and the procedure is therefore cheaper. In general, only a minority of surgeons would regularly consider carrying out this operation,[359] and even then younger, fitter individuals tend to be selected.[360] While one study reported that patients aged 80 years or above appear to be at increased risk of cardiovascular and neurological post-operative complications during concomitant bilateral TKR, no such findings have been reported for the equivalent THR procedure.[361,362]

Following arthroplasty, one of the most serious possible complications is deep wound infection. The rate of such infections has been reported as between 0.5 and 2%.[363,364] The more recent use of prophylactic gentamycin-impregnated cement has been shown to reduce the risk of deep infection by comparison with systemic antibiotics in a randomised controlled trial, but the effect did not extend beyond the first year following surgery, which may limit justification for routine use on the grounds of cost.[365]

Specific considerations regarding the effectiveness of THR

A recent structured review of outcomes in primary THR[366] concluded that, given the poor quality of evidence overall, it was not possible to distinguish and recommend any particular prosthesis for use by the NHS in preference to any other. However, the report also concluded that it was hard to justify the use of cementless prostheses at present, and that the more expensive the prosthesis was, the more difficult it was to provide any justification for its selection. One consideration that may make good sense, however, and this consideration applies equally to TKR, is that which takes account of possible trouble in the future, so that prostheses which are conservative of bone stock and which can be removed easily give a better and more successful basis for future revision.[201]

Apart from the many systemic complications that may follow any major surgery, a number of more specific complications may follow THR, and the likely positive effects of the operation need to be balanced against the risks concomitant with any major surgical procedure. For example, data for all elective THRs performed in 10 hospitals in the Oxford region during 1976–85 revealed a rate of eight emergency re-admissions per 1000 THRs within 28 days following discharge and 11 deaths per 1000 within the first 90 days following THR. Both rates increased with age.[367] Most of the deaths or readmissions to hospital were associated with thrombo-embolic or cardiovascular events.

Aseptic loosening of one or more of the components is a particularly serious long-term complication which may affect either or both of the components but which results from a different mechanism in each case.[368] Particular brands of prosthesis are from time to time identified with an abnormally early propensity to loosening.[369] Otherwise, the incidence of radiographic loosening of cemented femoral components is between 30 and 50%, and between 10 and 15% for the acetabular component, 10 years following insertion.[336,370]

An earlier and far more common occurrence following THR is peri-articular heterotopic ossification. This may cause severe problems in around 2–3% of patients, but may be treated successfully by surgical excision combined with radiation treatment.[198] Indeed patients at high risk of this condition may be treated prophylactically with radiation therapy[373,374] or indomethacin.[373]

Dislocation or subluxation of the prosthesis is a complication that more commonly occurs following THR than TKR, generally within the first 6 weeks following surgery. It is associated with poor positioning of the prosthesis by the surgeon or with malpositioning of the patient post-operatively, and it affects between 1 and 3% of cases.[335,374,375] Recurrent dislocation is an indication for revision surgery, although where the position of the implant is satisfactory and the problem is caused by weak abductors the condition may be managed conservatively with bracing and training.[375]

Other possible complications of THR include nerve damage (or palsy) from the surgery, which occurs in around 1% of cases,[376,377] and fracture of an implant component or periprosthetic fracture. Component breakage is now much less common than it used to be and peri-prosthetic fracture most commonly results from a fall.[378,379]

Despite all the risks associated with major surgery in elderly people there is nevertheless evidence to suggest that THR is more successful and cost-effective for elderly women than for any other group of patients, and that advanced age should not be considered a barrier to this type of surgery.[380,381] In addition, there is a suggestion that the (often increased) length of stay for high-risk patients may relate to the timing of rehabilitation and is therefore potentially modifiable. For example, a recent randomised controlled trial[195] was carried out of third-day vs. seventh-day commencement of intensive inpatient rehabilitation by physiotherapy and occupational therapy for high-risk patients (over 70 years of age with considerable comorbidity). This study showed that those who were assigned the third-day protocol required significantly fewer days in hospital, at lower cost. Change scores obtained by patient-based outcome measures before and at 4 months following surgery did not differ. This study would seem to support the early initiation of rehabilitation for THR without the risk of adversely affecting outcomes.

Specific considerations regarding the effectiveness of TKR

A recent UK survey of surgical techniques in TKR[191] revealed that there were 41 different knee implants in use of which five constituted 61% of the total, and while the majority of prostheses now used are of the total condylar resurfacing type, a few surgeons nevertheless continue to use hinged varieties associated with poorer outcomes.[191,382,383]

The type of prosthesis used is only one of a number of technical elements which may influence the ultimate outcome following TKR. One important factor, on which there appears to be no consensus, is whether or not the patella undergoes resurfacing.[384,385] A badly arthritic patella will not track well in the femoral groove and this can lead to complications. However, complications may also arise following resurfacing. Management of the patella and balancing the patellofemoral joint space to avoid maltracking and subluxation is considered to be one of the more difficult aspects of primary TKR surgery, which becomes even more difficult in the revision situation.[386] At present, 32% of surgeons report that they always resurface the patella, while 19% say that they never do.[191]

Another issue concerns the timing of an operation in relation to the stage of the disease. For example, most cases of knee OA begin in the medial compartment only,[387] which suggests that UCA, which may be performed at an earlier stage than TKR, before the anterior cruciate ligament becomes destroyed, might be the most appropriate choice of operation. An additional technical consideration concerns whether the prosthesis is fixed in place with cement or left uncemented. In the UK, 95% of TKRs are cemented. This practice appears to be associated with good results[331,398] and is the cheaper option.[191]

Age is just one of a number of relative contraindications which apply to TKR to a greater extent than to THR, and the decision to proceed with TKR in younger individuals should certainly be weighed against all possible alternatives, e.g. tibial osteotomy.[200] Overweight patients are generally considered to be poor candidates for TKR. However, evidence in support of this stance is fairly mixed and, on balance, suggests that while the results achieved in obese vs. non-obese patients are not as good, early to medium-term outcomes are not significantly compromised by the patient's weight.[388–392]

Following TKR, complications involving the patella are the most common.[393,394] The main problems include patellar dislocation,[395] stress fractures,[396] avascular necrosis,[397] progressive erosion of the articular cartilage in the unresurfaced patella[204] and loosening of the patellar prosthesis.[398] The likelihood of patellofemoral complications may be increased with the use of some types of implant, although evidence for this is sparse.[399] Overall, the majority of such problems are in any case very often self-limiting and may simply be managed with medication, exercises and bracing.[393]

As with THR, aseptic prosthetic loosening is the most common serious long-term complication following TKR. This almost never affects the femoral component, but occurs at the junction between the tibial component and the underlying tibial bone.[199] While tibial component loosening has been related to poor surgical technique,[400] the trabecular bone of the proximal tibia is often abnormally weak in people with OA. It has been suggested that metal-backed tibial components offer the best results with regard to this problem.[199,400]

As with THR, other complications include occasional, usually transient nerve damage[401] and, more importantly, deep infection. The latter complication affects between 0.5 and 2% of knee arthroplasties.[363,364]

In a large prospective study carried out in Sweden, the probability of revision due to infection was reported to be 2% within 6 years for patients with OA.[402]

7 Models of care/recommendations

This section considers a number of scenarios for the management of hip and knee OA and explores the possible consequences of these models. The models are intended to complement one another and are not intended to be alternative approaches.

The public health emphasis

Current evidence would suggest that the prevalence of OA is likely to increase over the next 30 years.[9–11,403] The lack of mobility that results from moderately severe OA symptoms of a lower limb joint can propel individuals towards a rapid deterioration in general health and cardiovascular fitness. This is often further potentiated by other comorbidity.[7,404] Such indirect effects and costs of OA represent some of the many important variables that are exceedingly difficult to evaluate and quantify.

It is clearly more desirable to prevent or at least delay symptomatic OA in whatever ways are feasible, rather than concentrating all efforts on expensive treatments and technologies for the minority of patients who are in the end-stage of the disease. By addressing known modifiable risk factors, primary prevention interventions could theoretically delay or in some cases prevent the development of OA in a significant number of people. The high prevalence of hip and knee OA among elderly people, together with evidence of a number of known risk factors, means that this area is an ideal target for future public health interventions. The following areas deserve particular attention.

1 **Exercise:** Increasingly sedentary lifestyles with low levels of fitness contribute substantially to the major chronic diseases prevalent in industrial societies.[405] Regular moderate (but not excessive) levels of low-impact exercise may assist in delaying the onset of symptomatic hip and knee OA and the associated loss of mobility.[257–259] Exercise can certainly alleviate the symptoms of established OA in some people.[257–260] Indirect effects of exercise that are relevant to OA include the favourable influence on body fat distribution and maintenance of weight loss.[406] Public health initiatives should aim to increase general awareness of the benefits of exercise for this and other conditions.

2 **Obesity:** Obesity is an important modifiable risk factor for both hip and knee OA, but has particular relevance for women and OA of the knee.[85,127] The avoidance of obesity should be a primary target for prevention in both men and women.[63]

3 **Occupational factors:** OA of the hip is in many cases an occupational disease. There is a need for increased education and raised awareness among employers and workers, particularly men, whose work involves regular lifting. Where appropriate, lifting aids and machinery should increasingly be provided and working conditions modified.

4 **Screening:** This is particularly relevant to the hip. Congenitally abnormal joints have an increased likelihood of developing OA of early onset.[240,241,407] Screening programmes require high sensitivity to be cost-effective, and neonatal screening does not meet this requirement currently. The evaluation of alternative or additional methods of screening such as ultrasound or routine examination once children begin to walk is strongly recommended, but overall it is suggested that such efforts should be concentrated on babies who are at increased risk. Risk factors for congenital dysplasia appear to include family history, breech presentation, female sex, oligohydramnios and primiparity.[408–412]

There is little evidence to support the use of other large-scale screening programmes at present. In particular, the use of biological markers of OA (currently being developed) to identify people with asymptomatic disease could not be recommended before effective disease-modifying technologies are available.

The service emphasis

Here changes in existing services are considered. Evidence that relates to the availability of effective treatments and their associated risks as well as the appropriateness of health care setting and personnel will be addressed.

Medical training

In view of the large and increasing prevalence of OA, all doctors require training in the management of musculoskeletal problems. Primary care physicians also need continuing training to include this emphasis because many will have received inadequate training at medical school, but also because guidelines on the prevention and management of OA will continue to change with improving therapies. Current recommendations on the use of medications to manage OA of the hip or knee are summarised below.

Summary of recommendations on the use of medications in the management of hip and knee OA

It is vital that practitioners obtain complete information on any over-the-counter preparations that patients already use before systemic preparations are prescribed. This may also facilitate discussion and guidance about the potential for serious side-effects from NSAIDs, which are becoming increasingly available to people without prescription.

A moderate level of pain requires effective pain management, and this usually requires analgesia to be given in anticipation of rather than in response to pain. The initial choice should be paracetamol 0.5–1 g given 4–6 hourly, up to a maximum of 4 g/day.[132] Paracetamol is available in soluble form for patients who do not like taking tablets. Alternatively, or for those who find paracetamol inadequate, topical NSAIDs may help, e.g. ibuprofen, and capsaicin cream may prove even more effective. However, the latter preparation can produce a localised burning sensation which some people will not tolerate. Topical forms of treatment may nevertheless appeal to those who already take a number of regular oral forms of medication. They also encourage massaging of the affected joint, which many find additionally helpful.

Codeine phosphate, nefopam hydrochloride or combined preparations such as co-proximol are often preferred by patients, although there is little evidence that they work better than paracetamol, and they can be associated with side-effects.[414,415] The use of stronger opioid analgesics should be avoided as they are likely to increase the risk of falls and accidents.

NSAIDs, including aspirin, should only be considered when simple analgesics are found to be inadequate for pain control or during inflammatory stages of the disease. The chief consideration at present is the high cost of the side-effects, particularly in those with any prior history of indigestion or gastrointestinal ulceration or those with renal insufficiency. In addition, other drugs are known to interact with NSAIDs, such as diuretics, antihypertensives, anticoagulants and lithium.

While the newer highly selective COX-2 inhibitors, such as celecoxib, are associated with fewer gastrointestinal events,[175] the renal side-effects may remain even when used at a relatively low therapeutic dose,[415] and their long-term evaluation has not yet occurred. They are also relatively expensive. With older varieties of unselective NSAIDs, the wide diversity of action and side-effects results in considerable variation in patient tolerance and response to different preparations, and the prescribing of NSAIDs may therefore involve an element of 'trial and error'. For the moment, it is recommended that well-established formulations are chosen. These include ibuprofen, which can also be obtained over the counter. Those that have been in use the longest are the least likely to produce idiosyncratic side-effects. They are available in generic form and are therefore much cheaper. Ibuprofen is one of the best tolerated of all NSAIDs, while indomethacin should be avoided.

Concomitant therapy with H_2-receptor antagonists is not recommended as it can prove harmful in the longer term – suppressing symptoms, but not necessarily the effects of NSAIDs.

Improvements in dissemination of information and advice to GPs

Many GPs would welcome guidelines based on best current evidence and expert consensus regarding appropriate management and referral practices for patients with OA. There is a need for guidelines that are evidence based, but a number of specialist consensus guidelines do exist. However, such information is frequently published in specialist journals, rather than the more general medical journals that GPs are most likely to read. Consensus guidelines might also be made available to GPs via the Internet, and this would seem to represent a relatively inexpensive initiative.

A *BMJ* editorial concluded that most protocols raise standards of care and most do more good than harm to patients.[416] The ability to telephone hospital consultants for advice is also considered to be extremely helpful by the proportion of GPs who already have this arrangement. The Internet may in time also make possible consultations that avoid the need for some patients to attend outpatient appointments. An increase in such communication channels is to be encouraged. The expansion of rheumatology and orthopaedic specialist outreach clinics might also increase GPs' skills and expertise,[235] although this would obviously need to be weighed in terms of resource allocation and would require a thorough evaluation.

Comprehensive information needs to be provided for GPs concerning the local availability (and costs) of services (physiotherapy, day centres, occupational therapists, health visitors, social workers, etc.) in one source book (or Internet site) that is updated regularly. This seems an obvious requirement and there is certainly much room for improvement in this area, particularly as GPs are very keen to refer their patients directly to physiotherapy and other services without the need to involve hospital outpatient clinics. The responsibility for providing this service also needs to be decided, perhaps centrally. At present, no one carries this responsibility. Inadequate information results in inappropriate referrals to specialists in some circumstances and, on other occasions, presumably results in no referral being made where one might have been appropriate. This is most certainly an area of unmet need.

Improvements in access to PAMs by GPs, and expansion of these services and roles

Assessment by a physiotherapist with orthopaedic experience (either community or hospital based) is recommended for many patients when they first present with signs of OA of the hip or knee. Practical treatment can then be initiated promptly with the potential to reduce symptoms and the associated need for medications. Physiotherapy can also halt the progression or reduce the speed of decline into disability and dependency. This strategy has the potential to reduce the pressure on outpatient departments, as it would encourage more appropriate referral practices, particularly if referral and triage were to be influenced by physiotherapists. Waiting times could also be reduced in this way. An increased role for physiotherapists and an expansion of this and other services provided by PAMs nevertheless carries major resource implications.[226]

In addition, the regular monitoring of patients with established OA, perhaps with the assistance of nurse practitioners, could improve patients' sense of social support, check their understanding of exercise and drug regimens and enhance their compliance with medication. This could reduce GPs' workload. Regular appointments would mean that any adverse effects of drugs might also be detected sooner. An extension of the roles of specialist PAMs and nurses would need to find acceptance with medical personnel and be assessed on the basis of cost-effectiveness.

Improving the availability of specialist services

The likely increase in the prevalence of hip and knee OA suggests that demand for specialist services will increase over the next 30 years. This has serious implications given that rheumatology has always been undermanned in England and Wales, with many districts having grossly inadequate rheumatology cover during 1983–90. During this period it was also shown that 25% of rheumatology doctors at senior registrar level had had little prior experience in rheumatology.[112]

A report published in 1995 by the British Orthopaedic Association (BOA)[417] was no more reassuring. The report stated that, in 1992, the delay experienced by patients in the UK between referral and being seen by a specialist was 'at the extreme end of the European spectrum'. Furthermore, it stated that there was only one orthopaedic consultant for every 62 000 people in England and Wales and that if the number of consultants was to be doubled, this would still represent a ratio below the average for most other European countries (Figure 18) and would still make no allowance for unmet need and the projected increasing numbers of patients requiring more time-consuming treatment in the future (e.g. patients with complex injuries resulting from sports and high-speed travel, and the higher rate of survival of premature babies).

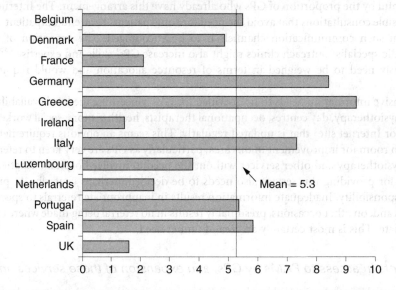

Figure 18: Number of orthopaedic surgeons per 100 000 population in various European countries. *Source*: Reproduced from British Orthopaedic Association. *Consultant Staffing Requirements for an Orthopaedic Service in the National Health Service*. London: British Orthopaedic Association, 1995, pp. 1–27.[417]

The report recommended that no patients should wait longer than 16 weeks for an outpatient appointment, but conceded that at that time the average wait was 24 weeks, with only nine of 161 units able to report waits of 6 weeks or less for a new outpatient appointment.

In response to the BOA report, the Chairman of the BMA's Central Consultants and Specialists Committee stated that an extra 1000 consultants a year were needed for at least 5 years on top of the standard 2% expansion, and that if all else failed, there would have to be a massive expansion of sub-consultant grades instead.[418]

An obvious recommendation is that this situation should be taken extremely seriously by the Government of the day, with more resources targeted towards the expansion of rheumatology and orthopaedic provision. However, even if this were to occur, a medium-term shortfall is inevitable.

Frankel *et al.*'s West of England study[16] generated incidence rates from which a population annual requirement for THR was derived. This requirement was put at 46 600 operations. They calculated that 'actual provision' in England for the same period was 43 500 operations and concluded that current provision of THR surgery is ' . . . of the same order as the incidence of new cases meriting surgery' and that ' . . . demand for the intervention, given agreement on indications, is [therefore] a realistic objective'. These conclusions nevertheless included both NHS and independent-sector operations as representing 'provision', and some might question whether surgery carried out in the independent sector should be considered as equivalent to NHS provision, since it is clearly not equally available to all.[419]

No equivalent data are available for TKR surgery.* However, given that symptomatic knee OA is more prevalent than hip OA, the lower numbers of TKR relative to THR operations would appear to represent a substantial unmet need at present. A national prevalence rate is far less useful than an incidence rate (which cannot be calculated with any confidence), and each is in any case constructed against a background of considerable variation in surgical activity at district level (Figure 16). It is therefore important that purchasers make assessments of the amount of demand that is met for joint replacement surgery based on their resident population. It is important that such analyses are performed taking account of evidence of unexplained variations in the volume of and access to specialist services within the NHS.

It is necessary to use rates standardised for age and sex for determining a district THR or TKR requirement. Reasonable estimates of what constitute 'appropriate levels of surgery' might be forthcoming if the variation in standardised rates for THR and TKR could be explained fully. However, surgical activity at the district level results from the complex interrelationships of need, supply, demand and the influence of clinical decision making. It also encompasses both NHS and private activity.

Quantified need for services

Severe symptomatic hip disease

Frankel *et al.*[16] estimated that, among a large cross-section of people aged 35–85 years, 143 in 1000 reported symptomatic hip disease and 15.2 in 1000 had disease severe enough to require surgery, although the annual incidence of hip disease severe enough to require surgery was estimated at 2.23 in 1000 population. These estimates used population figures taken from the 1991 census. Other findings from the same study were that, within a 12-month period, approximately one-third had consulted a GP about hip pain, around 7% were currently awaiting an outpatient appointment and 2% were awaiting surgery.

A different study[115] reported that of those referred to a specialist for symptomatic OA, specialist referral will probably occur in a 4:1 ratio between orthopaedic surgeons and rheumatologists, respectively. Using this information, together with HES figures on actual hospital activity (which includes people of all ages) and reference costs (Table 6), we calculated cost estimates for a hypothetical population of 100 000 people (Table 8, *see* overleaf). An alternative calculation is then presented which assumes that 25% of those currently treated by surgery will instead be treated conservatively (Table 9, *see* p. 601). This somewhat arbitrary percentage has been adopted purely to illustrate the extent to which costs might be affected by such a change. The second calculation assumes that GP visits would increase by 50% and that the number of physiotherapy referrals would double. It also assumes an 100% shift (increase) towards the use of COX-2 selective NSAIDs (taking one example), as well as a doubling in the length of course for all medications for people with severe hip OA.

---

* Since this chapter was written, the following publication has addressed this issue: Juni P, Dieppe P, Donovan J *et al.* Population requirement for primary knee replacement surgery: a cross-sectional study. *Rheumatology* 2003; **42:** 516–21.

Table 8: Illustrative annual costings for OA of the hip based on a population of 100 000.

Service/procedure		Unit cost	Total cost
Consulted GP about hip pain – 4,767 cases			
Of whom: 9% referred to consultant – 429 cases	1 GP visit, including 2% home visits (h/v)	420 @ £10 in GP surgery 9 @ £30 h/v	
5% referred for physiotherapy, remainder not referred – 4,338 cases	2 GP visits, including 2% home visits (h/v)	4,251 × 2 @ £10 in GP surgery 87 × 2 @ £30 h/v	£94,710.00
Prescribed medicines (40%):		1998 prices:[470]	
Co-codamol 8/500 (48 mg/3 g daily) – 477 cases (10%)		20 × 8/500 mg = 23p = £4	
Ibuprofen (1.2 g daily) – 477 cases (10%)	56-day course:	20 × 400 mg = 32p = £3	
Diclofenac sodium (100 mg daily) – 477 cases (10%)		20 × 50 mg = £1.29 = £7	
Meloxicam (7.5 mg daily) – 477 cases (10%)		30 × 7.5 mg = £10 = £20	£16,218.00
Direct referral to NHS physiotherapist – 238 cases (5%)	1 hour per person	@ £30 per hour	£7,140.00
NHS specialist referral – 334 cases (7%)	Rheumatology Orthopaedics	86 @ £68.57 248 @ £53.87	£19,256.78
No surgery/2 NHS outpatient visits – 253 cases	Rheumatology Orthopaedics	63 × 2 @ £68.57 190 × 2 @ £53.87	£29,110.42
Private specialist referral – 95 cases (2%)		95 @ £80	£7,600.00
No surgery/2 private outpatient visits – 71 cases		71 × 2 @ £80	£11,360.00
NHS surgical rates (all ages/all diagnoses) based on 1995–96 HES data:			
Primary THR NHS – 71 cases	33,320/47,055,204 × 100,000	71 @ £3,737.00	£265,327.00
Three outpatient visits – 71 cases		71 × 3 @ £53.87	£11,474.31
Primary THR private – 22 cases	10,400/47,055,204 × 100,000	22 @ £7,500	£165,000.00
Three outpatient visits – 22 cases		22 × 3 @ £80	£5,280.00
Revision THR NHS – 10 cases	4,637/47,055,204 × 100,000	10 @ £4,613.00	£46,130.00
Three outpatient visits – 10 cases		10 × 3 @ £53.87	£1,616.10
Revision THR private – 2 cases	1,000/47,055,204 × 100,000	2 @ £9,500	£19,000.00
Three outpatient visits – 2 cases		2 × 3 @ £80	£480.00
		TOTAL	£562,377.83

Table 9: Illustrative annual costings for OA of the hip based on a population of 100 000 assuming a 25% decrease in the numbers of NHS patients treated surgically.

Service/procedure	Unit cost	Total cost
Consulted GP about hip pain — 4,767 cases		
Of whom: 9% referred to consultant — 429 cases	1 GP visit, including 2% home visits (h/v)	420 @ £10 in GP surgery 9 @ £30 h/v	
10% referred for physiotherapy, remainder not referred — 4,338 cases	3 GP visits, including 2% home visits (h/v)	4,251 × 3 @ £10 in GP surgery 87 × 3 @ £30 h/v	£136,050.00
Prescribed medicines (40%):		1998 prices[470]	
Co-codamol 8/500 (48 mg/3 g daily) – 238 cases (5%)		20 × 8/500 mg = 23p = £8	
Ibuprofen (1.2 g daily) – 238 cases (5%)	112-day course:	20 × 400 mg = 32p = £6	
Diclofenac sodium (100 mg daily) – 477 cases (10%)		20 × 50 mg = £1.29 = £14	
Meloxicam (7.5 mg daily) – 954 cases (20%)		30 × 7.5 mg = £10 = £40	£48,170.00
Direct referral to NHS physiotherapist — 476 cases (10%)	1 hour per person	@ £30 per hour	£14,280.00
NHS specialist referral — 334 cases (7%)	Rheumatology Orthopaedics	86 @ £68.57 248 @ £53.87	£19,256.78
No surgery/2 NHS outpatient visits — 278 cases	Rheumatology Orthopaedics	69 × 2 @ £68.57 209 × 2 @ £53.87	£31,980.32
Private specialist referral — 95 cases (2%)		95@ £80	£7,600.00
No surgery/2 private outpatient visits — 71 cases		71 × 2 @ £80	£11,360.00
NHS surgical rates (all ages/all diagnoses) based on 1995–96 HES data:			
Primary THR NHS – 53 cases	33,320/47,055,204 × 100,000	53 @ £3,737.00	£19,8061.00
Three outpatient visits – 53 cases		53 × 3 @ £53.87	£8,565.33
Primary THR private – 22 cases	10,400/47,055,204 × 100,000	22 @ £7,500	£165,000.00
Three outpatient visits – 22 cases		22 × 3 @ £80	£5,280.00
Revision THR NHS – 7 cases	4,637/47,055,204 × 100,000	7 @ £4,613.00	£32,291.00
Three outpatient visits – 7 cases		7 × 3 @ £53.87	£1,131.27
Revision THR private – 2 cases	1,000/47,055,204 × 100,000	2 @ £9,500	£19,000.00
Three outpatient visits – 2 cases		2 × 3 @ £80	£480.00
	TOTAL	£480,748.92

In each case, our estimates for services/procedures other than joint surgery do not take account of people aged 85 and above, although costs relating to surgical procedures do. People aged 85+ account for around 2% of THR surgery and, assuming that those unfit for surgery are most likely to be among the very elderly, it may make sense to add around 4% to the cost estimates for services/procedures other than joint surgery to take account of these individuals. The figures presented here are in many cases rough approximations and should only be used or interpreted with extreme caution. There are many hidden costs and large areas of uncertainty. Changes in any of these areas will directly affect any estimates.

Particular points of uncertainty

- The use of over-the-counter medicines as well as GP prescribing practices for OA of the hip and knee.
- The proportion of GP consultations that are home visits. We have assumed 2%, but the proportion is likely to increase in line with the advancing age of patients.
- The proportion of patients whom GPs refer directly for physiotherapy before considering (or while awaiting) specialist referral.
- The proportion of patients with moderate to severe symptoms who do not seek or who refuse treatment.
- The extent to which partners, family and other informal carers provide nursing and other services for people relatively disabled by hip or knee OA.
- Additional treatment/hospitalisation required due to side-effects of medication and whether these will be reduced with next-generation NSAIDs.
- Regional variation in referral practices of GPs and hospital specialist provision.
- The proportion of patients who require hospital transport for outpatient appointments.
- The number of arthroscopies, osteotomies and other operations (apart from total joint replacement) that are carried out for hip or knee OA.
- Variations in length of stay due to post-operative complications and the number/cost of post-operative readmissions.
- Availability, uptake and costs of residential convalescence facilities.

Comparison of the two models implies a reduction in costs of around 15% to the NHS by adopting the second model. It cannot be over-emphasised that this model says nothing about the change in benefit to the patient and that no conclusions may be made regarding cost-effectiveness. Also it is perfectly possible that the patients who were denied surgery would seek private treatment. While this cost would not fall upon the NHS directly it would represent an indirect cost – since some resources are shared – as well as a cost to individuals, insurance companies and, ultimately, society as a whole.

Severe symptomatic knee disease

Cost estimates for OA of the knee are even more problematic than for that of the hip due to the lack of population prevalence and incidence data which reliably take account of symptoms. Based on study figures reported earlier (summarised in the sections on prevalence of OA of the hip and knee), it would be safe to assume that 50% more people are affected by severe symptomatic OA of the knee than the hip, with around 22 in 1000 having disease severe enough to require surgery. Using these assumptions it would be possible to adjust the tables on illustrative costings accordingly. Particular points of uncertainty are identical, although the lower level of surgery relative to the apparent scale of the problem requires explanation.

8 Outcome measures

Until relatively recently, a fundamental reason for the lack of adequate outcome studies in OA and OA-related orthopaedic surgery has been concerned with the lack of standard acceptable outcome measures.[222,368,422,423] For example, the sensitivity and interpretation of methods used to measure and assess outcomes for OA have often been fairly crude, and it has become increasingly clear that clinical assessments of key aspects of outcome (e.g. pain, physical function, range of joint movement) are often inaccurate and not reproducible.[422] Clinical assessments may also overly represent concerns of the clinician, rather than those of the patient.

An alternative method is to use patient-based outcome measures of pain, function, health-related quality of life and satisfaction. Such measures (questionnaires), which are generally used as an adjunct to rather than a replacement for clinical assessments, may provide data that are standardised, reliable, valid, sensitive to change and assess matters of immediate concern to patients.[423–427] An additional merit of these measures is that they render large clinical trials more feasible than is the case where all outcomes are to be assessed by a clinician,[220,428] because following up large numbers of people for a reasonable period is both problematic and costly, particularly if hospital visits and clinical examinations are involved. This partly explains why few high-quality studies have been carried out in the past.

A number of patient-based general health and condition-specific measures have now been developed for application in clinical trials of treatments for OA, e.g. the Western Ontario and McMaster Universities Osteoarthritis Index (WOMAC) and Lequesne Index,[134,220] and more specifically for the evaluation of THR and TKR, e.g. The Oxford hip and knee scores.[426,427] Such measures are designed to compare outcomes between different study populations and treatment groups and are not generally appropriate for the assessment and monitoring of symptoms in individuals.

Outcomes that are considered following treatment for OA, and in particular outcomes following surgical treatment, are usually long term. For example, measurable differences in the relative effectiveness of different joint prostheses may not become evident for 8–10 years, and for this reason many studies of outcomes are retrospective. In the absence of acceptable patient-based measures, a large number of studies to evaluate different joint prostheses tended to focus on rates (and timing) of revision surgery as the main outcome of comparison, frequently using a method called survival analysis.[429] Using the event of revision surgery in this way is problematic because it ignores the fact that there are people who have had an unsatisfactory outcome but who do not have revision surgery. Also the timing of revision surgery may be related to the availability of health services rather than patients' need and will almost certainly involve a lag. The 'survival' and success of joint prostheses are therefore necessarily exaggerated by this method, and it may be that patient-based measures are able to reveal important symptom-based differences in outcomes at an earlier stage following treatment and thereby reduce the period of follow-up that is needed. However, because the more highly condition-specific measures have only been in use for a relatively short time, evidence concerning the full extent of their usefulness (as well as any shortcomings) in detecting such differences is only starting to become available.[108,430,431]

9 Information and research requirements

This section signals priorities important to the accumulation of evidence which would allow informed judgements to be made by purchasers and providers. A number of these priorities relate to primary care and the primary/secondary care interface. For example, GPs have unfortunately only been obliged to provide any numbers or details regarding hospital referrals since April 1990, and such figures as are now available may be difficult to interpret.[115] An example concerns the lack of available statistics on the conditions most commonly referred to outpatient clinics, reasons for referral, and characteristics of those patients who are referred.

In addition, the quality and consistency of coding categories and detail of routinely collected data which relate to primary care and hospital outpatient activity are generally poor. This severely hampers any attempt to provide a clear picture of overall care and provision for people with OA (let alone OA which specifically affects the hip or knee). Thus data gathered from different sources will report on groups with 'arthritis and related conditions', 'joint pain' or 'conditions of the musculoskeletal system' – all somewhat vague terms that are overly inclusive.

Another problem for GPs concerns the dissemination of relevant information about the availability of services that are accessible to them. At present, GPs acquire knowledge of local services in an unsystematic and haphazard fashion. Some information is acquired as a part of continuing medical education (R Walton, personal communication). Otherwise very little information comes directly from health authorities (now primary care trusts), and the dissemination of guidelines and details of available local services is currently the responsibility of individual institutions and service providers and – perhaps surprisingly – such information is not generally available to GPs in one local source book, although some variation is likely across different health care regions in this regard. (GPs used to receive a directory of relevant people and services, all in one booklet, from HAs/FHSAs. However, the last one was produced in 1993 and since then, with changes in health care funding, this was felt to be a 'provider' responsibility; T Jones, personal communication.) It is hoped that Internet websites may go some way towards fulfilling this function, becoming routine over the next few years. (For example, OXWAX, a software package that provides a comprehensive library of medical news updates and available local services, is soon to be used in GP practices throughout the Oxford Region.) This would require someone to take responsibility for regularly updating the information, which would obviously have cost implications. For the moment, information on services is not widely available in any useful format in the NHS (T Lancaster, personal communication; J Bradlow, personal communication).

At the level of secondary care, organisational changes in the NHS have led to the hasty development of 'performance indicators', league-table comparisons between hospital trusts, and so on. Many believe that these kinds of measures are currently too simplistic or ill thought out.[433] Certainly comparisons between different institutions may at times prove misleading. This is because data obtained from different institutions are likely to be of variable quality. However, comparisons between institutions based on such data are also unlikely to involve adequate adjustment for the differences in case-mix that will almost certainly exist between trusts.[434]

Overall we have identified the following information priorities which relate to OA of the hip and knee:

- improvements in recording and accuracy of diagnostic and treatment details in computerised primary care databases and hospital information systems
- the accurate recording and availability of data on private THR and TKR surgery for district residents, to include demographic data
- the establishment of terse, acceptable and standard methods of adjusting outcomes data for differences in case-mix. This represents a formidable challenge to the research community[435,436]
- the availability of inpatient and medium-term morbidity and mortality data for the 90 days following joint replacement surgery, providing absolute figures and figures adjusted for case-mix
- the establishment of clear criteria for specialist referral (to include the consideration of rheumatologist vs. surgeon) and for surgical intervention for clinicians in primary and secondary care, with the aim of better defining and identifying those most likely to benefit
- audit of the outcomes of THR and TKR surgery to include standard measures, providing failure rate (unadjusted and adjusted for case-mix) for the benefit of purchasers and providers alike

- the development of protocols for auditing methods and outcomes measures
- obtaining estimates of the prevalence of local met demand in terms of successful and unsuccessful primary THR and TKR surgery in the district resident population. These estimates should include the use of standard patient-based measures of outcome
- an assessment of the costs and benefits of THR and TKR for varying severity of OA, to assist in setting priorities for health care provision.

With some considerable planning and adequate resources, the establishment of national THR and TKR registers could theoretically help to bring about many of these suggestions within one efficient framework.

Appendix I: The analysis of routine health service data

Diagnostic and operation codes

A tenth edition of the *International Classification of Diseases (ICD-10)* was published in 1993 and was used for all Hospital Episode Statistics (HES) data from 1995–96 onwards.

The NHS Centre for Coding and Classification counsels that, owing to changes in medical knowledge and the requirements of classification itself, there will have been significant changes between the ninth and tenth revisions of the ICD, and states that 'absolute continuity in all or even most areas of data is not possible and should not be sought'. Such changes are likely to affect the HES data presented in this chapter and their interpretation.

The International League against Rheumatism is also currently working on a revision of the *Application of the International Classification of Diseases to Rheumatology and Orthopaedics* (ICD–R&O), including the *International Classification of Musculoskeletal Disorders* (ICMSD), to be compatible with *ICD-10*. This is designed to clarify and standardise the use of terms such as those which apply to the inflammatory polyarthropathies.[465]

The *International Classification of Diseases* diagnostic codes

The most common diagnostic codes relating to OA and used in this chapter are shown in Table A1.

Table A1: Common ICD codes relating to OA.

ICD-9 code (in use prior to 1995)	ICD-10 code* (in use since 1995)	Diagnosis
715	M15.0–M19.9	Osteoarthritis

* These codes are listed in much more detail below.

Details of ICD-10 codes which relate to OA

Codes were kindly supplied by the NHS Centre for Coding and Classification, Leicester.

M15   Polyarthrosis
M15.0   Primary generalised (osteo)arthrosis
M15.1   Heberden's nodes (with arthropathy)
M15.2   Bouchard's nodes (with arthropathy)
M15.3   Secondary multiple arthrosis
M15.4   Erosive (osteo)arthrosis
M15.8   Other polyarthrosis
M15.9   Polyarthrosis, unspecified
M16   Coxarthrosis (arthrosis of hip)
M16.0   Primary coxarthrosis, bilateral
M16.1   Other primary coxarthrosis
M16.2   Coxarthrosis resulting from dysplasia, bilateral
M16.3   Other dysplastic coxarthrosis
M16.4   Post-traumatic coxarthrosis, bilateral

M16.5   Other post-traumatic coxarthrosis
M16.6   Other secondary coxarthrosis, bilateral
M16.7   Other secondary coxarthrosis
M16.9   Coxarthrosis, unspecified
M17   Gonarthrosis (arthrosis of knee)
M17.0   Primary gonarthrosis, bilateral
M17.1   Other primary gonarthrosis
M17.2   Post-traumatic gonarthrosis, bilateral
M17.3   Other post-traumatic gonarthrosis
M17.4   Other secondary gonarthrosis, bilateral
M17.5   Other secondary gonarthrosis
M17.9   Gonarthrosis, unspecified
M18   Arthrosis of first carpometacarpal joint
M18.0   Primary arthrosis of first carpometacarpal joint, bilateral
M18.1   Other primary arthrosis of first carpometacarpal joint
M18.2   Post-traumatic arthrosis of first carpometacarpal joint, bilateral
M18.3   Other post-traumatic arthrosis of first carpometacarpal joint
M18.4   Other secondary arthrosis of first carpometacarpal joint, bilateral
M18.5   Other secondary arthrosis of first carpometacarpal joint
M18.9   Arthrosis of first carpometacarpal joint, unspecified
M19   Other arthrosis
M19.0   Primary arthrosis of other joints
M19.1   Post-traumatic arthrosis of other joints
M19.2   Secondary arthrosis of other joints
M19.8   Other specified arthrosis
M19.9   Arthrosis, unspecified

The hip

Total hip replacement operation: codes and definitions

THRs may be primary or revision/conversion procedures. The strict definition of a primary THR is the replacement of the femoral head and the acetabulum. Should this primary operation fail, a repeat procedure, termed a revision, may be performed. This may necessitate replacement of the acetabular or femoral components, or both. It is occasionally necessary to convert to a THR following previous non-THR surgery of the hip.

For the purpose of estimating primary THR requirements the crucial distinction is between elective procedures and those emergency procedures that are carried out for hip fracture.

Owing to the uncertainties surrounding current coding practices,[466] the operational definition of primary elective THR in the analyses of HES data in this chapter is main procedures coded as THRs only where undertaken for conditions other than fracture (OPCS Operation Codes W37.0–W39).

We have not included operations coded as hemiarthroplasty, which is invariably carried out for fractured femur. In addition, we have counted admissions rather than episodes. The latter can lead to double-counting. These are likely to represent differences in the way that HES data have been analysed by comparison with Williams et al.[67]

OPCS Operation Codes for hip replacement (*see* **Table A2**)

Operations were considered to be primary where the third digit is .1, .8 or .9, and a revision/conversion procedure where the third digit is .2, .3, or .0.

Table A2: OPCS Operation Codes for hip replacement, 4th revision (1988 to present).

Code	Operation
W37–W39	Total hip replacement
W46–W48	Hemiarthroplasty*

* Replacement of the femoral head only, which we have not included.

The knee

TKRs include both femoral and tibial components and are performed almost exclusively as elective procedures. Surgery relating solely to the patellofemoral joint is not considered in our analysis.

OPCS Operation Codes for knee replacement (*see* **Table A3**)

As with the hip and THR, there is diversity in coding practice.[466] Operations were considered to be primary where the third digit is .1, .8 or .9, and a revision/conversion procedure where the third digit is .2, .3, or .0.

Table A3: OPCS Operation Codes for knee replacement, 4th revision (1988 to present).

Code	Operation
W40–W42	Total knee replacement

The coding of TKRs does not suffer from the level of confusion evident with THRs, in which distinction between a true elective THR and a hemiarthroplasty can be particularly problematic. Comparison of the TKR cases recorded for the HES system with information from theatre records revealed 98% accuracy in a 1989–90 survey from six hospitals.[67] This may not be representative of the country as a whole.

Data sources

The following data sources were used to examine aspects of activity levels that may relate to the need for total hip or knee replacement (THR/TKR) surgery:

- Hospital Episode System (HES) data for England
- data on surgical activity in independent hospitals and NHS pay-beds from local and national surveys, and preliminary data from a current Nottingham-based study of independent-sector surgical activity covering all of England and Wales (B Williams, personal communication).

National Health Service data

NHS utilisation data are fundamentally flawed as a measure of population requirements for surgery for the reasons given below.

- Problems of data quality and comparability over time. Trends are difficult to establish accurately when using data collected from any two different sources, e.g. the Hospital Inpatient Enquiry System (HIPE) and the Hospital Episode System (HES). In addition, the incompleteness and inaccuracy of data coding is a problem. Coding systems also change periodically, as was noted above.
- There is an uncertain relationship between supply, demand, professional decision making and requirements.[467] These are clearly interdependent in that patients have no direct access to hospital treatment. It is impossible to distinguish the effects of limits on supply from those of satisfied demand. Public expectations, as well as decisions concerning referral and admission, are influenced by the accuracy of diagnosis by GPs, the perceptions of potential benefit of referral by the GPs and the availability of treatment facilities.
- This data source excludes activity in independent hospitals and NHS pay-beds. The limited current data have been utilised.

The deficiencies of Hospital Activity Analysis (HAA)[466,468] are now compounded by those that have followed the introduction of Körner data since 1987–88. Cross-validation of HAA coding by manual inspection of theatre registers revealed (in 1988) that discrepancies can affect as many as 16% of operations,[469] and KP70 ascertainment data suggest that there were wide variations in the proportion of hospital activity data reported to HES from each district health authority. In addition, ICD-10 has been implemented since 1995 as noted above. The errors inherent in routine data sources must be considered carefully when drawing any conclusions from their analysis. The interpretation of time trends is particularly problematic. It is therefore inappropriate to attempt to derive precise estimates of appropriate operation rates from these data sources.

Private surgery

It is essential to incorporate the level of activity in independent hospitals and NHS pay-beds when attempting to reflect current population levels of THR and TKR surgery. Unfortunately, the record systems of independent hospitals include the underlying diagnosis in only a minority of cases, and not consistently.[470] Until very recently, the only available national data concerning private-sector activity were estimates derived from surveys conducted by the Medical Care Research Unit, University of Sheffield and based on a small sample. These data suggested that a 30% increase in THR surgery in independent hospitals and NHS pay-beds in England and Wales took place between 1981 (6200 operations) and 1986 (8091 operations).[68] The proportion of THR surgery undertaken by the private sector in the respective years was an estimated 26.2% and 27.7%. The Sheffield study estimated that 320 TKRs were undertaken in NHS pay-beds in 1981 and 790 in 1986.[67] Preliminary data from a Nottingham-based study of independent-sector surgical activity have now been made available and are more detailed than the Sheffield study and cover hospitals in the independent sector throughout England and Wales (B Williams, personal communication). These data are presented for hip and knee replacement surgical rates in Tables A4 to A7 (*see* overleaf).

Table A4: Estimated numbers of all total hip joint and knee joint replacement operations in independent hospitals in England and Wales, 1997–98: residents of England and Wales.

Age group (years)	Hip joint	Knee joint	Total
15–44	101	32	133
45–64	2,897	1,204	4,101
65–74	4,625	2,750	7,375
75–98	3,709	1,979	5,688
All ages	11,332	5,965	17,297

Table A5: Estimated numbers of *primary* total hip joint and knee joint replacement operations in independent hospitals in England and Wales, 1997–98: residents of England and Wales.

Age group (years)	Hip joint	Knee joint	Total
15–44	83	32	115
45–64	2,851	1,151	4,002
65–74	4,267	2,718	6,985
75–98	3,292	1,885	5,177
All ages	10,493	5,786	16,279

Table A6: Estimated numbers of all total hip joint and knee joint replacement operations in independent hospitals in England and Wales, 1997–98, by region of residence.

Region of residence	Hip joint	Knee joint	Total
Wales	338	335	673
Northern and Yorkshire	930	369	1,299
Trent	897	400	1,297
Anglia and Oxford	1,462	747	2,209
North Thames	1,538	835	2,373
South Thames	1,906	1,151	3,057
South and West	2,016	1,050	3,066
West Midlands	776	389	1,165
North West	743	490	1,233
London NEC	5		5
England NEC/other	722	200	922
Total	11,333	5,966	17,299

Table A7: Estimated numbers of *primary* total hip joint and knee joint replacement operations in independent hospitals in England and Wales, 1997–98, by region of residence.

Region of residence	Hip joint	Knee joint	Total
Wales	321	335	656
Northern and Yorkshire	862	346	1,208
Trent	897	400	1,297
Anglia and Oxford	1,381	724	2,105
North Thames	1,448	803	2,251
South Thames	1,590	1,134	2,724
South and West	1,876	1,033	2,909
West Midlands	776	349	1,125
North West	713	462	1,175
London NEC	5		5
England NEC/other	625	200	825
Total	10,494	5,786	16,280

References

1 Kelsey JL, Hochberg MC. Epidemiology of chronic musculoskeletal disorders. *Annu Rev Public Health* 1988; **9**: 379–401.

2 Guccione AA. Osteoarthritis, comorbidity, and physical disability. In: Hamerman D (ed.). *Osteoarthritis: public health implications for an aging population*. Baltimore, MD: The Johns Hopkins University Press, 1997, pp. 84–98.

3 Ettinger WH Jr, Afable RF. Physical disability from knee osteoarthritis: the role of exercise as an intervention. *Med Sci Sports Exerc* 1994; **26**: 1435–40.

4 Badley EM. The effect of osteoarthritis on disability and health care use in Canada. *J Rheumatol* 1995; **43** (Suppl.): 19–22.

5 Hochberg MC, Kasper J, Williamson J *et al*. The contribution of osteoarthritis to disability: preliminary data from the Women's Health and Aging Study. *J Rheumatol* 1995; **43** (Suppl.): 16–18.

6 Verbrugge LM, Patrick DL. Seven chronic conditions: their impact on US adults' activity levels and use of medical services. *Am J Public Health* 1995; **85**: 173–82.

7 Philbin EF, Groff GD, Ries MD, Miller TE. Cardiovascular fitness and health in patients with end-stage osteoarthritis. *Arthritis Rheum* 1995; **38**: 799–805.

8 Thompson J. Ageing of the population: contemporary trends and issues. *Popul Trends* 1988; **21**: 18–22.

9 Forbes WF. General concepts of the association of aging and disease. In: Hamerman D (ed.). *Osteoarthritis: public health implications for an aging population*. Baltimore, MD: The Johns Hopkins University Press, 1997, pp. 3–14.

10 Badley EM. Population projections and the effect on rheumatology. *Ann Rheum Dis* 1991; **50**: 3–6.

11 Olshansky SJ, Cassel CK. Implications of the accrual of chronic nonfatal conditions in very elderly persons. In: Hamerman D (ed.). *Osteoarthritis: public health implications for an aging population*. Baltimore, MD: The Johns Hopkins University Press, 1997, pp. 15–29.

12 Finocchiaro C, Abramson MJ, Ryan PF. Arthritis in Australia: an emerging public health problem (letter). *Med J Aust* 1996; **165**: 352.

13 Badley EM. The economic burden of musculoskeletal disorders in Canada is similar to that for cancer, and may be higher (editorial). *J Rheumatol* 1995; **22**: 204–6.

14 Gabriel SE, Crowson CS, O'Fallon WM. Costs of osteoarthritis: estimates from a geographically defined population. *J Rheumatol* 1995; **43**(Suppl.): 23–5.

15 Fenner H. The pharmaceutical industry and therapeutic approaches to osteoarthritis in the next decade. In: Hamerman D (ed.). *Osteoarthritis: public health implications for an aging population*. Baltimore, MD: The Johns Hopkins University Press, 1997, pp. 230–44.

16 Frankel S, Eachus J, Pearson N *et al*. Population requirement for primary hip-replacement surgery: a cross-sectional study. *Lancet* 1999; **353**: 1304–9.

17 Hadler NM. Osteoarthritis as a public health problem. *Clin Rheum Dis* 1985; **11**: 175–85.

18 Moskowitz RW. Osteoarthritis – symptoms and signs. In: Moskowitz RW, Howell DS, Goldberg VM, Mankin HJ (eds). *Osteoarthritis: diagnosis and medical/surgical management*. Philadelphia, PA: WB Saunders, 1992, pp. 255–61.

19 Harris WH. Etiology of osteoarthritis of the hip. *Clin Orthop* 1986; 20–33.

20 Solomon L. Patterns of osteoarthritis of the hip. *J Bone Joint Surg Br* 1976; **58**: 176–83.

21 Felson DT. Epidemiology of hip and knee osteoarthritis. *Epidemiol Rev* 1988; **10**: 1–28.

22 Dieppe P. Osteoarthritis: time to shift the paradigm. This includes distinguishing between severe disease and common minor disability (editorial). *BMJ* 1999; **318**: 1299–300.

23 Bullough PG. The pathology of osteoarthritis. In: Moskowitz RW, Howell DS, Goldberg VM, Mankin HJ (eds). *Osteoarthritis: diagnosis and medical/surgical management*. Philadelphia, PA: WB Saunders, 1992, pp. 39–69.

24 Radin EL, Schaffler M, Gibson G, Tashman S. Osteoarthrosis as the result of repetitive trauma. In: Kuettner KE, Goldberg VM (eds). *Osteoarthritic Disorders.* Rosemont: American Academy of Orthopaedic Surgeons, 1995, pp. 197–203.

25 Cicuttini FM, Spector TD. Evidence for the increasing prevalence of osteoarthritis with aging; does this pertain to the oldest old? In: Hamerman D (ed.). *Osteoarthritis: public health implications for an aging population.* Baltimore, MD: The Johns Hopkins University Press, 1997, pp. 49–62.

26 Kuettner K, Goldberg VM (eds). *Osteoarthritic Disorders.* Rosemont: American Academy of Orthopaedic Surgeons, 1995.

27 Cooper C, Dieppe P, Snow S *et al.* Determinants of the incidence and progression of radiographic knee osteoarthritis. *Arthritis Rheum* 1997; **40**: S331.

28 Felson DT. The course of osteoarthritis and factors that affect it. *Rheum Dis Clin North Am* 1993; **19**: 607–15.

29 Danielsson LG. Incidence and prognosis of coxarthrosis. *Acta Orthop Scand* 1964; **66**: 9–14.

30 Ledingham J, Dawson S, Preston B *et al.* Radiographic progression of hospital-referred osteoarthritis of the hip. *Ann Rheum Dis* 1993; **52**: 263–7.

31 Dieppe P, Cushnaghan J. The natural course and prognosis of osteoarthritis. In: Moskowitz RW, Howell DS, Goldberg VM, Mankin HJ (eds). *Osteoarthritis: diagnosis and medical/surgical management.* Philadelphia, PA: WB Saunders, 1992, pp. 399–412.

32 Hernborg JS, Nilsson BE. The natural course of untreated osteoarthritis of the knee. *Clin Orthop* 1977; **123**: 130–7.

33 Dieppe PA, Cushnaghan J, Shepstone L. The Bristol 'OA500' study: progression of osteoarthritis (OA) over 3 years and the relationship between clinical and radiographic changes at the knee joint. *Osteoarthritis Cartilage* 1997; **5**: 87–97.

34 Ushiyama T, Ueyama H, Inoue K *et al.* Estrogen-receptor gene polymorphism and generalized osteoarthritis. *J Rheumatol* 1998; **25**: 134–7.

35 Dieppe P. The classification and diagnosis of osteoarthritis. In: Kuettner KE, Goldberg VM (eds). *Osteoarthritic Disorders.* Rosemont: American Academy of Orthopaedic Surgeons, 1995, pp. 5–12.

36 Felson DT. Osteoarthritis. *Rheum Dis Clin North Am* 1990; **16**: 499–512.

37 Hutton C. Osteoarthritis revisited and revised. *Ann Rheum Dis* 1994; **53**: 85–6.

38 Scott D. Guidelines for the diagnosis, investigation and management of osteoarthritis of the hip and knee. Report of a joint working group of the British Society for Rheumatology and the Research Unit of the Royal College of Physicians. *J R Coll Physicians* 1993; **27**: 391–6.

39 Salaffi F, Cavalieri F, Nolli M, Ferraccioli G. Analysis of disability in knee osteoarthritis. Relationship with age and psychological variables but not with radiographic score. *J Rheumatol* 1991; **18**: 1581–6.

40 Summers MN, Haley WE, Reveille JD, Alarcon GS. Radiographic assessment and psychologic variables as predictors of pain and functional impairment in osteoarthritis of the knee or hip. *Arthritis Rheum* 1988; **31**: 204–9.

41 Petersson IF. Occurrence of osteoarthritis of the peripheral joints in European populations. *Ann Rheum Dis* 1996; **55**: 659–61.

42 Spector TD, Hochberg MC. Methodological problems in the epidemiological study of osteoarthritis. *Ann Rheum Dis* 1994; **53**: 143–6.

43 Hart DJ, Spector TD. The classification and assessment of osteoarthritis. *Clin Rheumatol* 1995; **9**: 407–32.

44 Kellgren JH, Lawrence JS. *The Epidemiology of Chronic Rheumatism: atlas of standard radiographs.* Oxford: Blackwell Scientific Publications, 1963.

45 Spector TD, Hart DJ, Byrne J *et al.* Definition of osteoarthritis of the knee for epidemiological studies. *Ann Rheum Dis* 1993; **52**: 790–4.

46 Croft P, Cooper C, Wickham C, Coggon D. Defining osteoarthritis of the hip for epidemiologic studies. *Am J Epidemiol* 1990; **132**: 514–22.

47 Tepper S, Hochberg MC. Factors associated with hip osteoarthritis: data from the First National Health and Nutrition Examination Survey (NHANES-I). *Am J Epidemiol* 1993; **137**: 1081–8.

48 Danielsson L, Lindberg H. Prevalence of coxarthrosis in an urban population during four decades. *Clin Orthop* 1997; 106–10.

49 Silman AJ, Hochberg MC. *Epidemiology of the Rheumatic Diseases.* Oxford: Oxford University Press, 1993.

50 Dougados M, Gueguen A, Nguyen M *et al.* Radiological progression of hip osteoarthritis: definition, risk factors and correlations with clinical status. *Ann Rheum Dis* 1996; **55**: 356–62.

51 Bagge E, Bjelle A, Eden S, Svanborg A. Osteoarthritis in the elderly: clinical and radiological findings in 79 and 85 year olds. *Ann Rheum Dis* 1991; **50**: 535–9.

52 Hughes SL, Dunlop D, Edelman P *et al.* Impact of joint impairment on longitudinal disability in elderly persons. *J Gerontol* 1994; **49**: S291–300.

53 Maurer K. *Basic Data on Arthritis: knee, hip, and sacroiliac joints in adults aged 25–74 years, United States, 1971–1975.* Hyattsville, MD: US Department of Health, Education and Welfare, 1979.

54 van Baar ME, Dekker J, Lemmens JA *et al.* Pain and disability in patients with osteoarthritis of hip or knee: the relationship with articular, kinesiological, and psychological characteristics. *J Rheumatol* 1998; **25**: 125–33.

55 Lawrence RC, Helmick CG, Arnett FC *et al.* Estimates of the prevalence of arthritis and selected musculoskeletal disorders in the United States. *Arthritis Rheum* 1998; **41**: 778–99.

56 Hadorn DC, Holmes AC. The New Zealand priority criteria project. Part 1. Overview. *BMJ* 1997; **314**: 131–4.

57 Lethbridge-Cejku M, Scott WWJ, Reichle R *et al.* Association of radiographic features of osteoarthritis of the knee with knee pain: data from the Baltimore Longitudinal Study of Aging. *Arthritis Care Res* 1995; **8**: 182–8.

58 McAlindon TE, Cooper C, Kirwan JR, Dieppe PA. Determinants of disability in osteoarthritis of the knee. *Ann Rheum Dis* 1993; **52**: 258–62.

59 Lawrence RC, Hochberg MC, Kelsey JL *et al.* Estimates of the prevalence of selected arthritic and musculoskeletal diseases in the United States. *J Rheumatol* 1989; **16**: 427–41.

60 Spector TD, Hart DJ. How serious is knee osteoarthritis? *Ann Rheum Dis* 1992; **51**: 1105–6.

61 Kellgren JH, Lawrence JS. Osteoarthrosis and disk degeneration in an urban population. *Ann Rheum Dis* 1958; **17**: 388–97.

62 Hernborg J, Nilsson BE. Age and sex incidence of osteophytes in the knee joint. *Acta Orthop Scand* 1973; **44**: 66–8.

63 O'Reilly SC, Muir KR, Doherty M. Knee pain and disability in the Nottingham community: association with poor health status and psychological distress. *Br J Rheumatol* 1998; **37**: 870–3.

64 Felson DT, Zhang Y. An update on the epidemiology of knee and hip osteoarthritis with a view to prevention. *Arthritis Rheum* 1998; **41**: 1343–55.

65 Odding E, Valkenburg HA, Algra D *et al.* The association of abnormalities on physical examination of the hip and knee with locomotor disability in the Rotterdam Study. *Br J Rheumatol* 1996; **35**: 884–90.

66 Tennant A, Fear J, Pickering A *et al.* Prevalence of knee problems in the population aged 55 years and over: identifying the need for knee arthroplasty. *BMJ* 1995; **310**: 1291–3.

67 Williams M, Frankel S, Nanchanal K *et al.* *Epidemiologically Based Needs Assessment. Total knee replacement. DHA Project: research programme commissioned by the NHS Management Executive.* Crown Publisher, 1992.

68 Quam JP, Michet CJJ, Wilson MG *et al.* Total knee arthroplasty: a population-based study. *Mayo Clin Proc* 1991; **66**: 589–95.

69 Roland MO, Porter RW, Matthews JG *et al.* Improving care: a study of orthopaedic outpatient referrals. *BMJ* 1991; **302**: 1124–8.

70 Coulter A. The interface between primary and secondary care. In: Roland M, Coulter A (eds). *Hospital Referrals*. Oxford: Oxford University Press, 1992, pp. 1–14.

71 Rajaratnam G, Black NA, Dalziel M. Total hip replacements in the National Health Service: is need being met? *J Public Health Med* 1990; **12**: 56–9.

72 Wilson MG, Michet CJ Jr, Ilstrup DM, Melton LJ. Idiopathic symptomatic osteoarthritis of the hip and knee: a population-based incidence study. *Mayo Clin Proc* 1990; **65**: 1214–21.

73 Acheson RM, Collart AB. New Haven survey of joint diseases. XVII. Relationship between some systemic characteristics and osteoarthrosis in a general population. *Ann Rheum Dis* 1975; **34**: 379–87.

74 Felson DT. The epidemiology of osteoarthritis: prevalence and risk factors. In: Kuettner KE, Goldberg VM (eds). *Osteoarthritic Disorders*. Rosemont: American Academy of Orthopaedic Surgeons, 1995, pp. 13–24.

75 Peyron JG, Altman RD. The epidemiology of osteoarthritis. In: Moskowitz RW, Howell DS, Goldberg VM, Mankin HJ (eds). *Osteoarthritis: diagnosis and medical/surgical management*. Philadelphia, PA: WB Saunders, 1992, pp. 15–37.

76 Spector TD, Campion GD. Generalised osteoarthritis: a hormonally mediated disease. *Ann Rheum Dis* 1989; **48**: 523–7.

77 Hoaglund FT, Shiba R, Newberg AH, Leung KY. Diseases of the hip. A comparative study of Japanese Oriental and American white patients. *J Bone Joint Surg Am* 1985; **67**: 1376–83.

78 Andersen S. The epidemiology of primary osteoarthrosis of the knee in Greenland. *Scand J Rheumatol* 1978; **7**: 109–12.

79 Brown KS, Forbes WF. A mathematical model of aging processes. *J Gerontol* 1974; **29**: 46–51.

80 Lawrence JS, Bremner JM, Bier F. Osteoarthrosis. Prevalence in the population and relationship between symptoms and X-ray changes. *Ann Rheum Dis* 1966; **25**: 1–24.

81 Brandt KD, Fife RS. Ageing in relation to the pathogenesis of osteoarthritis. *Clin Rheum Dis* 1986; **12**: 117–30.

82 Sandell LJ. Molecular biology of collagens in normal and osteoarthritic cartilage. In: Kuettner KE, Goldberg VM (eds). *Osteoarthritic Disorders*. Rosemont: American Academy of Orthopaedic Surgeons, 1995, pp. 131–46.

83 Hochberg MC, Lethbridge-Cejku M. Epidemiologic considerations in the primary prevention of osteoarthritis. In: Hamerman D (ed.). *Osteoarthritis: public health implications for an aging population*. Baltimore, MD: The Johns Hopkins University Press, 1997, pp. 169–86.

84 van Saase JL, Vandenbroucke JP, van Romunde LK, Valkenburg HA. Osteoarthritis and obesity in the general population. A relationship calling for an explanation. *J Rheumatol* 1988; **15**: 1152–8.

85 Felson DT, Anderson JJ, Naimark A *et al.* Obesity and knee osteoarthritis. The Framingham Study. *Ann Intern Med* 1988; **109**: 18–24.

86 Felson DT, Zhang Y, Anthony JM *et al.* Weight loss reduces the risk for symptomatic knee osteoarthritis in women. The Framingham Study. *Ann Intern Med* 1992; **116**: 535–9.

87 Coggon D, Kellingray S, Inskip H *et al.* Osteoarthritis of the hip and occupational lifting. *Am J Epidemiol* 1998; **147**: 523–8.

88 Lindberg H, Montgomery F. Heavy labor and the occurrence of gonarthrosis. *Clin Orthop* 1987; 235–6.

89 Vingard E, Alfredsson L, Goldie I, Hogstedt C. Occupation and osteoarthrosis of the hip and knee: a register-based cohort study. *Int J Epidemiol* 1991; **20**: 1025–31.

90 Cooper C, Campbell L, Byng P *et al.* Occupational activity and the risk of hip osteoarthritis. *Ann Rheum Dis* 1996; **55**: 680–2.

91 Cooper C, McAlindon T, Coggon D *et al.* Occupational activity and osteoarthritis of the knee. *Ann Rheum Dis* 1994; **53**: 90–3.

92 Vingard E. Osteoarthrosis of the knee and physical load from occupation. *Ann Rheum Dis* 1996; **55**: 677–9.

93 McAlindon TE, Jacques P, Zhang Y *et al.* Do antioxidant micronutrients protect against the development and progression of knee osteoarthritis? *Arthritis Rheum* 1996; **39**: 648–56.

94 Uitterlinden AG, Burger H, Huang Q *et al.* Vitamin D receptor genotype is associated with radiographic osteoarthritis at the knee. *J Clin Invest* 1997; **100**: 259–63.

95 Keen RW, Hart DJ, Lanchbury JS, Spector TD. Association of early osteoarthritis of the knee with a Taq I polymorphism of the vitamin D receptor gene. *Arthritis Rheum* 1997; **40**: 1444–9.

96 McAlindon TE, Felson DT, Zhang Y *et al.* Relation of dietary intake and serum levels of vitamin D to progression of osteoarthritis of the knee among participants in the Framingham Study. *Ann Intern Med* 1996; **125**: 353–9.

97 Spector TD, Harris PA, Hart DJ *et al.* Risk of osteoarthritis associated with long-term weight-bearing sports: a radiologic survey of the hips and knees in female ex-athletes and population controls. *Arthritis Rheum* 1996; **39**: 988–95.

98 Roos H, Lindberg H, Gardsell P *et al.* The prevalence of gonarthrosis and its relation to meniscectomy in former soccer players. *Am J Sports Med* 1994; **22**: 219–22.

99 Panush RS, Hanson CS, Caldwell JR *et al.* Is running associated with osteoarthritis? An eight-year follow-up study. *J Clin Rheumatol* 1995; **1**: 35–9.

100 Lane NE, Oehlert JW, Bloch DA, Fries JF. The relationship of running to osteoarthritis of the knee and hip and bone mineral density of the lumbar spine: a 9-year longitudinal study. *J Rheumatol* 1998; **25**: 334–41.

101 Lane NE. Physical activity at leisure and risk of osteoarthritis. *Ann Rheum Dis* 1996; **55**: 682–4.

102 Royal College of Physicians. Guidelines for the diagnosis, investigation and management of osteoarthritis of the hip and knee. Report of a Joint Working Group of the British Society for Rheumatology and the Research Unit of the Royal College of Physicians. *J R Coll Physicians Lond* 1993; **27**: 391–6.

103 Office of Population Censuses and Surveys. *Morbidity Statistics from General Practice. Third National Study 1981–2.* London: HMSO, 1986.

104 Croft P. Review of UK data on the rheumatic diseases. 3. Osteoarthritis [published erratum appears in *Br J Rheumatol* 1990; **29**: 488]. *Br J Rheumatol* 1990; **29**: 391–5.

105 Jick H, Jick SS, Derby LE. Validation of information recorded on general practitioner-based computerised data resource in the United Kingdom. *BMJ* 1991; **302**: 766–8.

106 Hollowell J. The General Practice Research Database: quality of morbidity data. *Popul Trends* 1997; 36–40.

107 Vetter NJ, Jones DA, Victor CR. A health visitor affects the problems others do not reach. *Lancet* 1986; **2**: 30–2.

108 Dieppe P, Basler HD, Chard J *et al.* Knee replacement surgery for osteoarthritis: effectiveness, practice variations, indications and possible determinants of utilization. *Rheumatol Oxf* 1999; **38**: 73–83.

109 Prohaska TR, Keller ML, Leventhal EA, Leventhal H. Impact of symptoms and aging attribution on emotions and coping. *Health Psychol* 1987; **6**: 495–514.

110 Wolinsky FD, Johnson RJ. The use of health services by older adults. *J Gerontol* 1991; **46**: S345–57.

111 Miller SM, Brody DS, Summerton J. Styles of coping with threat: implications for health. *J Pers Soc Psychol* 1988; **54**: 142–8.

112 Symmons DP, Jones S, Hothersall TE. Rheumatology manpower in the 1990s. *Br J Rheumatol* 1991; **30**: 119–22.

113 Hicks NR, Baker IA. General practitioners' opinions of health services available to their patients. *BMJ* 1991; **302**: 991–3.

114 Brockway CR, Jones KE. Survey of the opinions of general practitioners about health services in a rural setting. *Public Health* 1993; **107**: 45–52.

115 Bradlow J, Coulter A, Brooks P. *Patterns of Referral. A study of referrals to outpatient clinics from general practices in the Oxford Region.* Oxford: Health Services Research Unit, 1992, pp. 1–42.

116 Clough JD, Lambert T, Miller DR. The new thinking on osteoarthritis. *Patient Care* 1996; **30**: 110–37.

117 Morales TI. The role of signaling factors in articular cartilage homeostasis and osteoarthritis. In: Kuettner KE, Goldberg VM (eds). *Osteoarthritic Disorders.* Rosemont: American Academy of Orthopaedic Surgeons, 1995, pp. 261–70.

118 Slemenda C, Brandt KD, Heilman DK *et al.* Quadriceps weakness and osteoarthritis of the knee. *Ann Intern Med* 1997; **127**: 97–104.

119 DiPietro L, Kohl HW, Barlow CE, Blair SN. Improvements in cardiorespiratory fitness attenuate age-related weight gain in healthy men and women: the Aerobics Center Longitudinal Study. *Int J Obes Relat Metab Disord* 1998; **22**: 55–62.

120 Province MA, Hadley EC, Hornbrook MC *et al.* The effects of exercise on falls in elderly patients. A preplanned meta-analysis of the FICSIT Trials. Frailty and Injuries: Cooperative Studies of Intervention Techniques. *JAMA* 1995; **273**: 1341–7.

121 Guralnik JM, Fried LP, Salive ME. Disability as a public health outcome in the aging population. *Annu Rev Public Health* 1996; **17**: 25–46.

122 Bortz WM. Disuse and aging. *JAMA* 1982; **248**: 1203–8.

123 Wagner EH, LaCroix AZ, Grothaus L *et al.* Preventing disability and falls in older adults: a population-based randomized trial. *Am J Public Health* 1994; **84**: 1800–6.

124 Lord SR, Ward JA, Williams P, Strudwick M. The effect of a 12-month exercise trial on balance, strength, and falls in older women: a randomized controlled trial. *J Am Geriatr Soc* 1995; **43**: 1198–206.

125 Spector TD, Nandra D, Hart DJ, Doyle DV. Is hormone replacement therapy protective for hand and knee osteoarthritis in women? The Chingford Study. *Ann Rheum Dis* 1997; **56**: 432–4.

126 Nevitt MC, Cummings SR, Lane NE *et al.* Association of estrogen replacement therapy with the risk of osteoarthritis of the hip in elderly white women. Study of Osteoporotic Fractures Research Group. *Arch Intern Med* 1996; **156**: 2073–80.

127 Cooper C, McAlindon T, Snow S *et al.* Mechanical and constitutional risk factors for symptomatic knee osteoarthritis: differences between medial tibiofemoral and patellofemoral disease. *J Rheumatol* 1994; **21**: 307–13.

128 Balint G, Szebenyi B. Non-pharmacological therapies in osteoarthritis. *Baillieres Clin Rheumatol* 1997; **11**: 795–815.

129 de Steiger R. Hip. In: Carr AJ, Harnden A (eds). *Orthopaedics in Primary Care.* Oxford: Butterworth-Heinemann, 1997, pp. 83–97.

130 Kelsey JL, O'Brien LA, Grisso JA, Hoffman S. Issues in carrying out epidemiologic research in the elderly. *Am J Epidemiol* 1989; **130**: 857–66.

131 Hynes D. Teamwork needed in arthritis. *Independent Community Pharmacist* 1991; 44–5.

132 Anonymous. Guidelines for the diagnosis, investigation and management of osteoarthritis of the hip and knee. Report of a Joint Working Group of the British Society for Rheumatology and the Research Unit of the Royal College of Physicians. *J R Coll Physicians Lond* 1993; **27**: 391–6.

133 Lequesne MG. The algofunctional indices for hip and knee osteoarthritis. *J Rheumatol* 1997; **24**: 779–81.

134 Liang MH, Fossel AH, Larson MG. Comparisons of five health status instruments for orthopedic evaluation. *Med Care* 1990; **28**: 632–42.

135 Bellamy N, Kean WF, Buchanan WW *et al.* Double-blind randomized controlled trial of sodium meclofenamate (Meclomen) and diclofenac sodium (Voltaren): post-validation reapplication of the WOMAC Osteoarthritis Index. *J Rheumatol* 1992; **19**: 153–9.

136 Hochberg MC, Altman RD, Brandt KD *et al.* Guidelines for the medical management of osteoarthritis. Part II. Osteoarthritis of the knee. American College of Rheumatology. *Arthritis Rheum* 1995; **38**: 1541–6.

137 Hochberg MC, Altman RD, Brandt KD *et al.* Guidelines for the medical management of osteoarthritis. Part I. Osteoarthritis of the hip. American College of Rheumatology. *Arthritis Rheum* 1995; **38**: 1535–40.

138 Bird HA. When are NSAIDs appropriate in osteoarthritis? *Drugs Aging* 1998; **12**: 87–95.

139 Lane NE, Thompson JM. Management of osteoarthritis in the primary-care setting: an evidence-based approach to treatment. *Am J Med* 1997; **103**: 25–30S.

140 The Primary Care Rheumatology Society. *Partnership in Practice: the management of osteoarthritis.* Northallerton: The Primary Care Rheumatology Society, 2000.

141 Keefe FJ, Caldwell DS, Baucom D *et al.* Spouse-assisted coping skills training in the management of osteoarthritic knee pain. *Arthritis Care Res* 1996; **9**: 279–91.

142 Gill TM, Robison JT, Tinetti ME. Predictors of recovery in activities of daily living among disabled older persons living in the community. *J Gen Intern Med* 1997; **12**: 757–62.

143 Creamer P, Hochberg MC. The relationship between psychosocial variables and pain reporting in osteoarthritis of the knee. *Arthritis Care Res* 1998; **11**: 60–5.

144 Rene J, Weinberger M, Mazzuca SA *et al.* Reduction of joint pain in patients with knee osteoarthritis who have received monthly telephone calls from lay personnel and whose medical treatment regimens have remained stable. *Arthritis Rheum* 1992; **35**: 511–15.

145 Brandt KD. Nonsurgical management of osteoarthritis, with an emphasis on nonpharmacologic measures. *Arch Fam Med* 1995; **4**: 1057–64.

146 Mazzuca SA, Brandt KD, Katz BP *et al.* Effects of self-care education on the health status of inner-city patients with osteoarthritis of the knee. *Arthritis Rheum* 1997; **40**: 1466–74.

147 The Arthritis and Rheumatism Council. Various pamphlets. Chesterfield: The Arthritis and Rheumatism Council, 2000.

148 Arthritis Care. Pamphlets/advice. London: Arthritis Care, 2000.

149 Gecht MR, Connell KJ, Sinacore JM, Prohaska TR. A survey of exercise beliefs and exercise habits among people with arthritis. *Arthritis Care Res* 1996; **9**: 82–8.

150 Neumann DA. Biomechanical analysis of selected principles of hip joint protection. *Arthritis Care Res* 1989; **2**: 146–55.

151 Blount WP. Don't throw away the cane. *J Bone Joint Surg Am* 1956; **38**: 695–8.

152 Brady LP. Hip pain. Don't throw away the cane. *Postgrad Med* 1988; **83**: 89–90, 95–7.

153 Brand RA, Crowninshield RD. The effect of cane use on hip contact force. *Clin Orthop* 1980; 181–4.

154 Voloshin A, Wosk J. Influence of artificial shock absorbers on human gait. *Clin Orthop Rel Res* 1981; **160**: 52–6.

155 Bergmann G, Kniggendorf H, Graichen F, Rohlmann A. Influence of shoes and heel strike on the loading of the hip joint. *J Biomech* 1995; **28**: 817–27.

156 Ohsawa S, Ueno R. Heel lifting as a conservative therapy for osteoarthritis of the hip: based on the rationale of Pauwels' intertrochanteric osteotomy. *Prosthet Orthot Int* 1997; **21**: 153–8.

157 Cushnaghan J, McCarthy C, Dieppe P. Taping the patella medially: a new treatment for osteoarthritis of the knee joint? *BMJ* 1994; **308**: 753–5.

158 Rubin G, Dixon M, Danisi M. Prescription procedures for knee orthosis and knee–ankle–foot orthosis. *Orthotics Prosthetics* 1977; **31**: 15.

159 Matsuno H, Kadowaki KM, Tsuji H. Generation II knee bracing for severe medial compartment osteoarthritis of the knee. *Arch Phys Med Rehabil* 1997; **78**: 745–9.

160 Keating EM, Faris PM, Ritter MA, Kane J. Use of lateral heel and sole wedges in the treatment of medial osteoarthritis of the knee. *Orthop Rev* 1993; **22**: 921–4.

161 Houpt JB, McMillan R. Alternative medicine – the challenge of nicht-Schulmedizin (or what is not taught in medical schools) (editorial; comment). *J Rheumatol* 1997; **24**: 2280–2.

162 Panush RS. Controversial arthritis remedies. *Bull Rheum Dis* 1984; **34**: 1–10.

163 Lewis D, Lewis B, Sturrock RD. Transcutaneous electrical nerve stimulation in osteoarthrosis: a therapeutic alternative? *Ann Rheum Dis* 1984; **43**: 47–9.

164 Lewis B, Lewis D, Cumming G. The comparative analgesic efficacy of transcutaneous electrical nerve stimulation and a non-steroidal anti-inflammatory drug for painful osteoarthritis. *Br J Rheumatol* 1994; **33**: 455–60.

165 Dunnell K, Cartwright A. *Medicine Takers, Prescribers and Hoarders.* London: Routledge & Kegan Paul, 1972.

166 Deyo RA, Inui TS, Sullivan B. Noncompliance with arthritis drugs: magnitude, correlates, and clinical implications. *J Rheumatol* 1981; **8**: 931–6.

167 McCarthy GM, McCarty DJ. Effect of topical capsaicin in the therapy of painful osteoarthritis of the hands. *J Rheumatol* 1992; **19**: 604–7.

168 Creamer P. Intra-articular corticosteroid injections in osteoarthritis: do they work and if so, how? *Ann Rheum Dis* 1997; **56**: 634–6.

169 Neustadt DH. Intra-articular steroid therapy. In: Moskowitz RW, Howell DW, Goldberg VM, Mankin HJ (eds). *Osteoarthritis: diagnosis and medical/surgical management.* Philadelphia, PA: WB Saunders, 1992, pp. 493–510.

170 Needleman P, Isakson PC. The discovery and function of COX-2. *J Rheumatol* 1997; **24** (Suppl. 49): 6–8.

171 Henderson EB, Smith EC, Pegley F, Blake DR. Intra-articular injections of 750 kD hyaluronan in the treatment of osteoarthritis: a randomised single-centre double-blind placebo-controlled trial of 91 patients demonstrating lack of efficacy. *Ann Rheum Dis* 1994; **53**: 529–34.

172 Listrat V, Ayral X, Patarnello F *et al.* Arthroscopic evaluation of potential structure-modifying activity of hyaluronan (Hyalgan) in osteoarthritis of the knee. *Osteoarthritis Cartilage* 1997; **5**: 153–60.

173 Ehrlich E, Schnitzer T, Kivitz A. MK-966, a highly selective COX-2 inhibitor, was effective in the treatment of osteoarthritis (OA) of the knee and hip in a six-week placebo-controlled trial. *Arthritis Rheum* 1997; **40**: S85.

174 Hawkey CJ. COX-2 inhibitors. *Lancet* 1999; **353**: 307–14.

175 Emery P, Zeidler H, Kvien TK *et al.* Celecoxib versus diclofenac in long-term management of rheumatoid arthritis: randomised double-blind comparison. *Lancet* 1999; **354**: 2106–11.

176 Livesley PJ, Doherty M, Needoff M, Moulton A. Arthroscopic lavage of osteoarthritic knees. *J Bone Joint Surg Br* 1991; **73**: 922–6.

177 Northmore-Ball MD. Young adults with arthritic hips (editorial). *BMJ* 1997; **315**: 265–6.

178 Roberts CS, Fetto JF. Functional outcome of hip fusion in the young patient. Follow-up study of 10 patients. *J Arthroplasty* 1990; **5**: 89–96.

179 Wedge JH. Hip pain in adolescence. *Clin Orthop* 1987; 93–103.

180 Johnson DP, Bannister GC. The outcome of infected arthroplasty of the knee. *J Bone Joint Surg Br* 1986; **68**: 289–91.

181 Knutson K, Hovelius L, Lindstrand A, Lidgren L. Arthrodesis after failed knee arthroplasty. A nationwide multicenter investigation of 91 cases. *Clin Orthop* 1984; 202–11.

182 Felson DT, Zhang Y, Hannan MT *et al.* The incidence and natural history of knee osteoarthritis in the elderly. The Framingham Osteoarthritis Study. *Arthritis Rheum* 1995; **38**: 1500–5.

183 Frymoyer JW, Hoaglund FT. The role of arthrodesis in reconstruction of the knee. *Clin Orthop* 1974; **101**: 82–92.

184 Mullen JO. Range of motion following total knee arthroplasty in ankylosed joints. *Clin Orthop* 1983; 200–3.

185 Lavernia CJ, Drakeford MK, Tsao AK *et al.* Revision and primary hip and knee arthroplasty. A cost analysis. *Clin Orthop* 1995; 136–41.

186 Stromberg CN, Herberts P, Ahnfelt L. Revision total hip arthroplasty in patients younger than 55 years old. Clinical and radiologic results after 4 years. *J Arthroplasty* 1988; **3**: 47–59.

187 Galea G, Kopman D, Graham BJ. Supply and demand of bone allograft for revision hip surgery in Scotland. *J Bone Joint Surg Br* 1998; **80**: 595–9.

188 Ivory JP, Thomas IH. Audit of a bone bank. *J Bone Joint Surg Br* 1993; **75**: 355–7.

189 Khan MT, Stockley I, Ibbotson C. Allograft bone transplantation: a Sheffield experience. *Ann R Coll Surg Engl* 1998; **80**: 150–3.

190 Newman KJ. Total hip and knee replacements: a survey of 261 hospitals in England. *J R Soc Med* 1993; **86**: 527–9.

191 Phillips AM, Goddard NJ, Tomlinson JE. Current techniques in total knee replacement: results of a national survey. *Ann R Coll Surg Engl* 1996; **78**: 515–20.

192 Mulroy RDJ, Harris WH. The effect of improved cementing techniques on component loosening in total hip replacement. An 11-year radiographic review. *J Bone Joint Surg Br* 1990; **72**: 757–60.

193 McCaskie AW, Barnes MR, Lin E *et al.* Cement pressurisation during hip replacement. *J Bone Joint Surg Br* 1997; **79**: 379–84.

194 Wang A, Hall S, Gilbey H, Ackland T. Patient variability and the design of clinical pathways after primary total hip replacement surgery. *J Qual Clin Pract* 1997; **17**: 123–9.

195 Munin MC, Rudy TE, Glynn NW *et al.* Early inpatient rehabilitation after elective hip and knee arthroplasty. *JAMA* 1998; **279**: 847–52.

196 Weingarten S, Riedinger MS, Sandhu M *et al.* Can practice guidelines safely reduce hospital length of stay? Results from a multicenter interventional study. *Am J Med* 1998; **105**: 33–40.

197 Forrest G, Fuchs M, Gutierrez A, Girardy J. Factors affecting length of stay and need for rehabilitation after hip and knee arthroplasty. *J Arthroplasty* 1998; **13**: 186–90.

198 Harris WH, Sledge CB. Total hip and total knee replacement (1). *NEJM* 1990; **323**: 725–31.

199 Harris WH, Sledge CB. Total hip and total knee replacement (2). *NEJM* 1990; **323**: 801–7.

200 Noble J, Hilton RC. Total knee replacement (editorial). *BMJ* 1991; **303**: 262.

201 Noble J. Total knee replacement – not a bridge too far (editorial). *J Bone Joint Surg Br* 1990; **72**: 173–4.

202 Ranawat CS, Flynn WF Jr, Saddler S *et al.* Long-term results of the total condylar knee arthroplasty. A 15-year survivorship study. *Clin Orthop* 1993; 94–102.

203 Friedman RJ, Poss R. Revision total knee arthroplasty in patients with osteoarthritis. *Rheum Dis Clin North Am* 1988; **14**: 537–44.

204 Insall JN. *Surgery of the Knee.* New York: Churchill Livingstone, 1984.

205 Diduch DR, Insall JN, Scott WN *et al.* Total knee replacement in young, active patients. Long-term follow-up and functional outcome. *J Bone Joint Surg Am* 1997; **79**: 575–82.

206 Ryan ME, Greenwald RA, Golub LM. Potential of tetracyclines to modify cartilage breakdown in osteoarthritis. *Curr Opin Rheumatol* 1996; **8**: 238–47.

207 Pelletier JP, DiBattista JA, Roughley P *et al.* Cytokines and inflammation in cartilage degradation. *Rheum Dis Clin North Am* 1993; **19**: 545–68.

208 Maheu E, Mazieres B, Valat JP *et al.* Symptomatic efficacy of avocado/soybean unsaponifiables in the treatment of osteoarthritis of the knee and hip: a prospective, randomized, double-blind,

placebo-controlled, multicenter clinical trial with a six-month treatment period and a two-month follow-up demonstrating a persistent effect. *Arthritis Rheum* 1998; **41**: 81–91.

209 Boumediene K, Felisaz N, Bogdanowicz P *et al.* Avocado/soya unsaponifiables enhance the expression of transforming growth factor beta₁ and beta₂ in cultured articular chondrocytes. *Arthritis Rheum* 1999; **42**: 148–56.

210 Deal CL, Moskowitz RW. Nutraceuticals as therapeutic agents in osteoarthritis. The role of glucosamine, chondroitin sulfate, and collagen hydrolysate. *Rheum Dis Clin North Am* 1999; **25**: 379–95.

211 Katz BP, Freund DA, Heck DA *et al.* Demographic variation in the rate of knee replacement: a multi-year analysis. *Health Serv Res* 1996; **31**: 125–40.

212 Birrell F, Johnell O, Silman A. Projecting the need for hip replacement over the next three decades: influence of changing demography and threshold for surgery. *Ann Rheum Dis* 1999; **58**: 569–72.

213 Martin J, Meltzer H, Elliot D. *The Prevalence of Disability Among Adults*. London: HMSO, 1989.

214 Wyles M. *Arthritis*. London: Office of Health Economics, 1992.

215 Meenan RF, Yelin EH, Nevitt M, Epstein WV. The impact of chronic disease – a sociomedical profile of rheumatoid arthritis. *Arthritis Rheum* 1981; **24**: 544–9.

216 Ehrlich GE. Social, economic, psychologic and sexual outcomes in rheumatoid arthritis. *Am J Med* 1983; 27–34.

217 Wright JG, Feinstein AR. A comparative contrast of clinimetric and psychometric methods for constructing indexes and rating scales. *J Clin Epidemiol* 1992; **45**: 1201–18.

218 Bulstrode CJK. Outcome measures and their analysis. In: Pynsent P, Fairbank J, Carr A (eds). *Outcome Measures in Orthopaedics*. Oxford: Butterworth-Heinemann, 1993, pp. 1–15.

219 Liang MH, Cullen KE. Evaluation of outcomes in total joint arthroplasty for rheumatoid arthritis. *Clin Orthop* 1984; 41–5.

220 Bellamy N. Outcome measurement in osteoarthritis clinical trials. *J Rheumatol Suppl* 1995; **43**: 49–51.

221 Bellamy N, Kaloni S, Pope J *et al.* Quantitative rheumatology: a survey of outcome measurement procedures in routine rheumatology outpatient practice in Canada. *J Rheumatol* 1998; **25**: 852–8.

222 Goldenberg DL, DeHoratius RJ, Kaplan SR *et al.* Rheumatology training at internal medicine and family practice residency programs. *Arthritis Rheum* 1985; **28**: 471–6.

223 Mazzuca SA, Brandt KD. Clinical rheumatology training in an uncertain future. Opinions of recent and current rheumatology fellows about an extended fellowship in musculoskeletal medicine. *Arthritis Rheum* 1994; **37**: 329–32.

224 Palchik NS, Laing TJ, Connell KJ *et al.* Research priorities for arthritis professional education. *Arthritis Rheum* 1991; **34**: 234–40.

225 Kerr LD. The impact of rheumatology in the primary care setting: one rheumatologist's odyssey. *South Med J* 1995; **88**: 268–70.

226 Madhok R, Green S. Orthopaedic outpatient referral guidelines: experience in an English health district. *Int J Qual Health Care* 1994; **6**: 73–6.

227 Goldenberg DL, Meenan RF, Allaire S, Cohen AS. The educational impact of a rheumatology elective. *Arthritis Rheum* 1983; **26**: 658–63.

228 Crotty M, Ahern MJ, McFarlane AC, Brooks PM. Clinical rheumatology training of Australian medical students. A national survey of 1991 graduates. *Med J Aust* 1993; **158**: 119–20.

229 Renner BR, DeVellis BM, Ennett ST *et al.* Clinical rheumatology training of primary care physicians: the resident perspective. *J Rheumatol* 1990; **17**: 666–72.

230 Kahl LE. Musculoskeletal problems in the family practice setting: guidelines for curriculum design. *J Rheumatol* 1987; **14**: 811–14.

231 Glazier RH, Dalby DM, Badley EM *et al.* Management of common musculoskeletal problems: a survey of Ontario primary care physicians. *Can Med Assoc J* 1998; **158**: 1037–40.

232 Solomon DH, Bates DW, Panush RS, Katz JN. Costs, outcomes, and patient satisfaction by provider type for patients with rheumatic and musculoskeletal conditions: a critical review of the literature and proposed methodologic standards. *Ann Intern Med* 1997; **127**: 52–60.

233 Mazzuca SA, Brandt KD, Katz BP *et al.* Therapeutic strategies distinguish community-based primary care physicians from rheumatologists in the management of osteoarthritis. *J Rheumatol* 1993; **20**: 80–6.

234 Bowling A, Stramer K, Dickinson E *et al.* Evaluation of specialists' outreach clinics in general practice in England: process and acceptability to patients, specialists, and general practitioners. *J Epidemiol Community Health* 1997; **51**: 52–61.

235 Daker-White G, Carr AJ, Harvey I *et al.* A randomised comparison of specially trained physiotherapists versus sub-consultant surgeons in the initial assessment and management of new general practitioner referrals to outpatient orthopaedic departments. *J Epidemiol Community Health* 1998; **25**(abstract).

236 Dieppe P. Management of hip osteoarthritis. *BMJ* 1995; **311**: 853–7.

237 Yoshimura N, Campbell L, Hashimoto T *et al.* Acetabular dysplasia and hip osteoarthritis in Britain and Japan. *Br J Rheumatol* 1998; **37**: 1193–7.

238 Lane NE, Nevitt MC, Cooper C *et al.* Acetabular dysplasia and osteoarthritis of the hip in elderly white women. *Ann Rheum Dis* 1997; **56**: 627–30.

239 Ali GA, Croft PR, Silman AJ. Osteoarthritis of the hip and acetabular dysplasia in Nigerian men. *J Rheumatol* 1996; **23**: 512–15.

240 el Shazly M, Trainor B, Kernohan WG *et al.* Reliability of the Barlow and Ortolani tests for neonatal hip instability. *J Med Screen* 1994; **1**: 165–8.

241 Godward S, Dezateux C. Surgery for congenital dislocation of the hip in the UK as a measure of outcome of screening. MRC Working Party on Congenital Dislocation of the Hip, Medical Research Council. *Lancet* 1998; **351**: 1149–52.

242 Dezateux C, Godward S. A national survey of screening for congenital dislocation of the hip. *Arch Dis Child* 1996; **74**: 445–8.

243 Samuelsson A, Ahlmen M, Sullivan M. The rheumatic patient's early needs and expectations. *Patient Educ Couns* 1993; **20**: 77–91.

244 Lorig KR, Mazonson PD, Holman HR. Evidence suggesting that health education for self-management in patients with chronic arthritis has sustained health benefits while reducing health care costs. *Arthritis Rheum* 1993; **36**: 439–46.

245 Felson DT, Meenan RF, Dayno SJ, Gertman P. Referral of musculoskeletal disease patients by family and general practitioners. *Arthritis Rheum* 1985; **28**: 1156–62.

246 Lorig K, Lubeck D, Kraines RG *et al.* Outcomes of self-help education for patients with arthritis. *Arthritis Rheum* 1985; **28**: 680–5.

247 Keefe FJ, Kashikar Zuck S, Robinson E *et al.* Pain coping strategies that predict patients' and spouses' ratings of patients' self-efficacy. *Pain* 1997; **73**: 191–9.

248 Mazzuca SA, Brandt KD, Katz BP *et al.* Effects of self-care education on the health status of inner-city patients with osteoarthritis of the knee. *Arthritis Rheum* 1997; **40**: 1466–74.

249 Weinberger M, Hiner SL, Tierney WM. Improving functional status in arthritis: the effect of social support. *Soc Sci Med* 1986; **23**: 899–904.

250 Ray R, Koh K, Fong NP, Nair A. Clinical aspects of health screening for senior citizens. *Ann Acad Med Singapore* 1991; **20**: 740–4.

251 Lord J, Victor C, Littlejohns P *et al.* Economic evaluation of a primary care-based education programme for patients with osteoarthritis of the knee. *Health Technol Assess* 1999; **3**.

252 van-Baar ME, Assendelft WJ, Dekker J *et al.* Effectiveness of exercise therapy in patients with osteoarthritis of the hip or knee: a systematic review of randomized clinical trials. *Arthritis Rheum* 1999; **42**: 1361–9.

253 Lane NE, Buckwalter JA. Exercise and osteoarthritis. *Curr Opin Rheumatol* 1999; **11**: 413–16.

254 Kovar PA, Allegrante JP, MacKenzie CR *et al*. Supervised fitness walking in patients with osteoarthritis of the knee. A randomized, controlled trial. *Ann Intern Med* 1992; **116**: 529–34.

255 Minor MA, Sanford MK. Physical interventions in the management of pain in arthritis: an overview for research and practice. *Arthritis Care Res* 1993; **6**: 197–206.

256 Minor MA. Exercise in the management of osteoarthritis of the knee and hip. *Arthritis Care Res* 1994; **7**: 198–204.

257 McAlindon TE, Cooper C, Kirwan JR, Dieppe PA. Determinants of disability in osteoarthritis of the knee. *Ann Rheum Dis* 1993; **52**: 258–62.

258 Dekker J, Tola P, Aufdemkampe G, Winckers M. Negative affect, pain and disability in osteoarthritis patients: the mediating role of muscle weakness. *Behav Res Ther* 1993; **31**: 203–6.

259 Michel BA, Fries JF, Bloch DA *et al*. Osteophytosis of the knee: association with changes in weight-bearing exercise. *Clin Rheumatol* 1992; **11**: 235–8.

260 Lamb SE, Guralnik JM, Buchner DM *et al*. Factors that modify the association between knee pain and limitation of mobility in older women: the women's health and aging study. *Ann Rheum Dis* 2000; **59**: 331–7.

261 Puett DW, Griffin MR. Published trials of nonmedicinal and noninvasive therapies for hip and knee osteoarthritis. *Ann Intern Med* 1994; **121**: 133–40.

262 Chamberlain MA, Care G, Harfield B. Physiotherapy in osteoarthrosis of the knees. A controlled trial of hospital versus home exercises. *Int Rehabil Med* 1982; **4**: 101–6.

263 Borjesson M, Robertson E, Weidenhielm L *et al*. Physiotherapy in knee osteoarthrosis: effect on pain and walking. *Physiother Res Int* 1996; **1**: 89–97.

264 Fisher NM, White SC, Yack HJ *et al*. Muscle function and gait in patients with knee osteoarthritis before and after muscle rehabilitation. *Disabil Rehabil* 1997; **19**: 47–55.

265 Rao A, Evans MF. Does a structured exercise program benefit elderly people with knee osteoarthritis? *Can Fam Physician* 1998; **44**: 283–4.

266 Minor MA. Exercise in the management of osteoarthritis of the knee and hip. *Arthritis Care Res* 1998; **7**: 198–204.

267 La Mantia K, Marks R. The efficacy of aerobic exercises for treating osteoarthritis of the knee. *N Z J Physiother* 1998; **23**: 23–30.

268 Anonymous. Aerobics and weight training relieve knee osteoarthritis. *Dis State Manag* 1997; **3**: 36–7.

269 Minor MA, Hewett JE, Webel RR *et al*. Efficacy of physical conditioning exercise in patients with rheumatoid arthritis and osteoarthritis. *Arthritis Rheum* 1989; **32**: 1396–405.

270 Peterson MG, Kovar Toledano PA, Otis JC *et al*. Effect of a walking program on gait characteristics in patients with osteoarthritis. *Arthritis Care Res* 1993; **6**: 11–16.

271 Ettinger WH Jr, Burns R, Messier SP *et al*. A randomized trial comparing aerobic exercise and resistance exercise with a health education program in older adults with knee osteoarthritis. The Fitness Arthritis and Seniors Trial (FAST). *JAMA* 1997; **277**: 25–31.

272 Marks R, Cantin D. Symptomatic osteo-arthritis of the knee: the efficacy of physiotherapy. *Physiotherapy* 1997; **83**: 306–12.

273 Rejeski WJ, Brawley LR, Ettinger W *et al*. Compliance to exercise therapy in older participants with knee osteoarthritis: implications for treating disability. *Med Sci Sports Exerc* 1997; **29**: 977–85.

274 Guralnik JM, Ferrucci L, Simonsick EM *et al*. Lower-extremity function in persons over the age of 70 years as a predictor of subsequent disability. *NEJM* 1995; **332**: 556–61.

275 Verhagen AP, de Vet HCW, de Bie RA *et al*. Rheumatoid arthritis (RA) and osteoarthritis (OA): balneotherapy for patients with arthritis (Cochrane Review). In: *The Cochrane Library. Issue 3*. Oxford: Update Software, 1998.

276 Ahern M, Nicholls E, Simionato E *et al.* Clinical and psychological effects of hydrotherapy in rheumatic diseases. *Clin Rehabil* 1995; **9**: 204–12.

277 Roos LL, Stranc L, James RC, Li J. Complications, comorbidities, and mortality: improving classification and prediction. *Health Serv Res* 1997; **32**: 229–38.

278 Olson JE, Stravino VD. A review of cryotherapy. *Phys Ther* 1972; **52**: 840–53.

279 Zizic TM, Hoffman KC, Holt PA *et al.* The treatment of osteoarthritis of the knee with pulsed electrical stimulation. *J Rheumatol* 1995; **22**: 1757–61.

280 Trock DH, Bollet AJ, Markoll R. The effect of pulsed electromagnetic fields in the treatment of osteoarthritis of the knee and cervical spine. Report of randomised, double-blind, placebo-controlled trials. *J Rheumatol* 1994; **21**: 1903–11.

281 Felson DT, Chaisson CE. Understanding the relationship between body weight and osteoarthritis. *Baillieres Clin Rheumatol* 1997; **11**: 671–81.

282 Felson DT. Weight and osteoarthritis. *J Rheumatol* 1995; **43** (Suppl.): 7–9.

283 Martin K, Nicklas BJ, Bunyard LB. Weight loss and walking improve symptoms of knee osteoarthritis. *Arthritis Rheum* 1996; **39** (Suppl.): 225.

284 Willims RA, Foulsham BM. Weight reduction in osteoarthritis using phentermine. *Practitioner* 1981; **225**: 231–2.

285 Stern SH, Insall JN. Total knee arthroplasty in obese patients. *J Bone Joint Surg Am* 1990; **72**: 1400–4.

286 Panush RS. Is there a role for diet or other questionable therapies in managing rheumatic diseases? *Bull Rheum Dis* 1993; **42**: 1–4.

287 Black N. Developing high-quality clinical databases (editorial). *BMJ* 1997; **315**: 381–2.

288 Gertner E, Marshall PS, Filandrinos D *et al.* Complications resulting from the use of Chinese herbal medications containing undeclared prescription drugs. *Arthritis Rheum* 1995; **38**: 614–17.

289 Deal CL, Schnitzer TJ, Lipstein E *et al.* Treatment of arthritis with topical capsaicin: a double-blind trial. *Clin Ther* 1991; **13**: 383–95.

290 Altman RD, Aven A, Holmberg CE *et al.* Capsaicin cream 0.025% as monotherapy for osteoarthritis: a double-blind study. *Semin Arthritis Rheum* 1994; **23** (Suppl.): 25–33.

291 Grahame-Smith DG, Aronson JK, Mowat AG. The drug therapy of disorders of bones and joints. In: Grahame-Smith DG, Aronson JK (eds). *Oxford Textbook of Clinical Pharmacology and Drug Therapy.* Oxford: Oxford University Press, 1992, pp. 414–26.

292 Grahame-Smith DG, Aronson JK, McQuay HJ. The relief of pain. In: Grahame-Smith DG, Aronson JK (eds). *Oxford Textbook of Clinical Pharmacology and Drug Therapy.* Oxford: Oxford University Press, 1992, pp. 458–64.

293 Bradley JD, Brandt KD, Katz BP *et al.* Comparison of an anti-inflammatory dose of ibuprofen, an analgesic dose of ibuprofen, and acetaminophen in the treatment of patients with osteoarthritis of the knee. *NEJM* 1991; **325**: 87–91.

294 Brandt KD. Should osteoarthritis be treated with nonsteroidal anti-inflammatory drugs? *Rheum Dis Clin North Am* 1993; **19**: 697–712.

295 Watson MC, Brookes ST, Kirwan JR, Faulkner A. Osteoarthritis: the comparative efficacy of non-aspirin non-steroidal anti-inflammatory drugs for the management of ostoearthritis of the knee (Cochrane Review). In: *The Cochrane Library. Issue 3.* Oxford: Update Software, 1998.

296 Towheed T, Shea B, Wells G, Hochberg M. Osteoarthritis: a systematic review of randomized controlled trials of analgesia and anti-inflammatory therapy in osteoarthritis (OA) of the hip (Cochrane Review). In: *The Cochrane Library. Issue 3.* Oxford: Update Software, 1998.

297 Blower AL, Brooks A, Fenn GC *et al.* Emergency admissions for upper gastrointestinal disease and their relation to NSAID use. *Aliment Pharmacol Ther* 1997; **11**: 283–91.

298 Mazzuca SA, Brandt KD, Anderson SL *et al.* The therapeutic approaches of community-based primary care practitioners to osteoarthritis of the hip in an elderly patient. *J Rheumatol* 1991; **18**: 1593–600.

299 Committee on Safety of Medicines. Relative safety of oral non-aspirin NSAIDs. *Curr Probl Pharmacovig* 1994; **20**: 9–11.

300 Langman MJS, Weil J, Wainwright P *et al.* Risks of bleeding peptic ulcer associated with individual non-steroidal anti-inflammatory drugs. *Lancet* 1994; **343**: 1075–8.

301 Singh G, Ramey DR. NSAID-induced gastrointestinal complications: the ARAMIS perspective – 1997. *J Rheumatol* 1998; **25**: 8–16.

302 Bellamy N, Bensen WG, Beaulieu A *et al.* A multicenter study of nabumetone and diclofenac SR in patients with osteoarthritis. *J Rheumatol* 1995; **22**: 915–20.

303 Shield MJ. Diclofenac/misoprostol: novel findings and their clinical potential. *J Rheumatol* 1998; **51** (Suppl.): 31–41.

304 Anonymous. NIH Consensus Conference: total hip replacement. NIH Consensus Development Panel on Total Hip Replacement. *JAMA* 1995; **273**: 1950–6.

305 Naylor CD, Williams JI, Ontario Panel on Hip and Knee Arthroplasty. Primary hip and knee replacement surgery: Ontario criteria for case selection and surgical priority. *Quality Health Care* 1996; **5**: 20–30.

306 Wright JG, Coyte P, Hawker G *et al.* Variation in orthopedic surgeons' perceptions of the indications for and outcomes of knee replacement. *Can Med Assoc J* 1995; **152**: 687–97.

307 Coyte PC, Hawker G, Croxford R *et al.* Variation in rheumatologists' and family physicians' perceptions of the indications for and outcomes of knee replacement surgery. *J Rheumatol* 1996; **23**: 730–8.

308 Ayral X, Gueguen A, Ike RW *et al.* Inter-observer reliability of the arthroscopic quantification of chondropathy of the knee. *Osteoarthritis Cartilage* 1998; **6**: 160–6.

309 Buckwalter JA, Lohmander LS. Surgical treatment of osteoarthritis. In: Kuettner KE, Goldberg VM (eds). *Osteoarthritic Disorders*. Rosemont: American Academy of Orthopaedic Surgeons, 1995, pp. 379–94.

310 Goldman RT, Scuderi GR, Kelly MA. Arthroscopic treatment of the degenerative knee in older athletes. *Clin Sports Med* 1997; **16**: 51–68.

311 Chang RW, Falconer J, Stulberg SD *et al.* A randomized, controlled trial of arthroscopic surgery versus closed-needle joint lavage for patients with osteoarthritis of the knee. *Arthritis Rheum* 1993; **36**: 289–96.

312 Balazs EA, Denlinger JL. Viscosupplementation: a new concept in the treatment of osteoarthritis. *J Rheumatol* 1993; **20**: 3–9.

313 Coventry MB. Upper tibial osteotomy for osteoarthritis. *J Bone Joint Surg Am* 1985; **67**: 1136–40.

314 Odenbring S, Egund N, Lindstrand A *et al.* Cartilage regeneration after proximal tibial osteotomy for medial gonarthrosis. An arthroscopic, roentgenographic, and histologic study. *Clin Orthop* 1992; 210–16.

315 Migaud H, Duquennoy A, Gougeon F *et al.* Outcome of Chiari pelvic osteotomy in adults: 90 hips with 2–15 years' follow-up. *Acta Orthop Scand* 1995; **66**: 127–31.

316 Santore RF, Dabezies EJ Jr. Femoral osteotomy for secondary arthritis of the hip in young adults. *Can J Surg* 1995; **38** (Suppl. 1): S33–8.

317 Nagel A, Insall JN, Scuderi GR. Proximal tibial osteotomy. A subjective outcome study. *J Bone Joint Surg Am* 1996; **78**: 1353–8.

318 Staeheli JW. Condylar total knee arthroplasty after failed proximal tibial osteotomy. *J Bone Joint Surg Am* 1987; **69**: 28–31.

319 Numair J, Joshi AB, Murphy JC *et al.* Total hip arthroplasty for congenital dysplasia or dislocation of the hip. Survivorship analysis and long-term results. *J Bone Joint Surg Am* 1997; **79**: 1352–60.

320 Ferguson GM, Cabanela ME, Ilstrup DM. Total hip arthroplasty after failed intertrochanteric osteotomy. *J Bone Joint Surg Br* 1994; **76**: 252–7.

321 McConville OR, Bowman AJ Jr, Kilfoyle RM *et al.* Bipolar hemiarthroplasty in degenerative arthritis of the hip: 100 consecutive cases. *Clin Orthop* 1990; 67–74.

322 Prieskorn D, Burton P, Page BJ, Swienckowski J. Bipolar hemiarthroplasty for primary osteoarthritis of the hip. *Orthopedics* 1994; **17**: 1105–11.

323 Emerson RH Jr, Potter T. The use of the McKeever metallic hemiarthroplasty for unicompartmental arthritis. *J Bone Joint Surg Am* 1985; **67**: 208–12.

324 Laurencin CT, Zelicof SB, Scott RD, Ewald FC. Unicompartmental versus total knee arthroplasty in the same patient. A comparative study. *Clin Orthop* 1991; 151–6.

325 Scott RD, Cobb AG, McQueary FG, Thornhill TS. Unicompartmental knee arthroplasty. Eight- to 12-year follow-up evaluation with survivorship analysis. *Clin Orthop* 1991; 96–100.

326 Scott RD, Joyce MJ, Ewald FC, Thomas WH. McKeever metallic hemiarthroplasty of the knee in unicompartmental degenerative arthritis. Long-term clinical follow-up and current indications. *J Bone Joint Surg Am* 1985; **67**: 203–7.

327 Kozinn SC, Scott RD. Surgical treatment of unicompartmental degenerative arthritis of the knee. *Rheum Dis Clin North Am* 1988; **14**: 545–64.

328 Chassin EP, Mikosz RP, Andriacchi TP, Rosenberg AG. Functional analysis of cemented medial unicompartmental knee arthroplasty. *J Arthroplasty* 1996; **11**: 553–9.

329 Robertsson O, Knutson K, Lewold S *et al.* Knee arthroplasty in rheumatoid arthritis. A report from the Swedish Knee Arthroplasty Register on 4,381 primary operations 1985–1995. *Acta Orthop Scand* 1997; **68**: 545–53.

330 Murray DW, Carr AJ, Bulstrode C. Survival analysis of joint replacements. *J Bone Joint Surg Br* 1993; **75**: 697–704.

331 Scuderi GR, Insall JN, Windsor RE, Moran MC. Survivorship of cemented knee replacements. *J Bone Joint Surg Br* 1989; **71**: 798–803.

332 Newman KJ. Total hip and knee replacements: a survey of 261 hospitals in England. *J R Soc Med* 1993; **86**: 527–9.

333 Murray D, Carr A, Bulstrode C. Which primary hip replacement? *J Bone Joint Surg Br* 1995; **77B**: 520–7.

334 Malchau H, Herberts P, Ahnfelt L. Prognosis of total hip replacement in Sweden. Follow-up of 92 675 operations performed 1978-1990. *Acta Orthop Scand* 1993; **64**: 497–506.

335 Hedlundh U, Ahnfelt L, Hybbinette CH *et al.* Surgical experience related to dislocations after total hip arthroplasty. *J Bone Joint Surg Br* 1996; **78**: 206–9.

336 Sutherland CJ, Wilde AH, Borden LS, Marks KE. A ten-year follow-up of one hundred consecutive Muller curved-stem total hip-replacement arthroplasties. *J Bone Joint Surg Am* 1982; **64**: 970–82.

337 Wejkner B, Stenport J, Wiege M. Long-term results of Charnley total hip replacement with special reference to patient's age. *Acta Orthop Belg* 1988; **54**: 59–66.

338 Landon GC, Galante JO, Casini J. Essay on total knee arthroplasty. *Clin Orthop* 1985; 69–74.

339 Lotke PA, Ecker ML, Alavi A, Berkowitz H. Indications for the treatment of deep venous thrombosis following total knee replacement. *J Bone Joint Surg Am* 1984; **66**: 202–8.

340 Flordal PA, Berggvist D, Burmark US *et al.* Risk factors for major thromboembolism and bleeding tendency after elective general surgical operations. The Fragmin Multicentre Study Group. *Eur J Surg* 1996; **162**: 783–9.

341 Fender D, Harper WM, Thompson JR, Gregg PJ. Mortality and fatal pulmonary embolism after primary total hip replacement. Results from a regional hip register. *J Bone Joint Surg Br* 1997; **79**: 896–9.

342 Clarke MT, Green JS, Harper WM, Gregg PJ. Cement as a risk factor for deep-vein thrombosis. Comparison of cemented TKR, uncemented TKR and cemented THR. *J Bone Joint Surg Br* 1998; **80**: 611–13.

343 Planes A, Vochelle N. The post-hospital discharge venous thrombosis risk of the orthopedic patient. *Orthopedics* 1997; **20**(Suppl.): 18–21.

344 Planes A, Vochelle N, Darmon JY *et al.* Risk of deep-venous thrombosis after hospital discharge in patients having undergone total hip replacement: double-blind randomised comparison of enoxaparin versus placebo. *Lancet* 1996; **348**: 224–8.

345 Lotke PA, Steinberg ME, Ecker ML. Significance of deep venous thrombosis in the lower extremity after total joint arthroplasty. *Clin Orthop* 1994; 25–30.

346 Stulberg BN, Insall JN, Williams GW, Ghelman B. Deep-vein thrombosis following total knee replacement. An analysis of six hundred and thirty-eight arthroplasties. *J Bone Joint Surg Am* 1984; **66**: 194–201.

347 Ivory JP, Summerfield J, Thorne S *et al.* Purchasing for quality: the providers' view – total hip replacement. *Quality Health Care* 1994; **3**: 114–19.

348 Paiement GD, Wessinger SJ, Harris WH. Cost-effectiveness of prophylaxis in total hip replacement. *Am J Surg* 1991; **161**: 519–24.

349 Owen TD, Coorsh J. The use of thromboprophylaxis in total hip replacement surgery: are the attitudes of orthopaedic surgeons changing? *J R Soc Med* 1992; **85**: 679–81.

350 Murray DW, Britton AR, Bulstrode CJ. Thromboprophylaxis and death after total hip replacement. *J Bone Joint Surg Br* 1996; **78**: 863–70.

351 Clarke MT, Green JS, Harper WM, Gregg PJ. Screening for deep venous thrombosis after hip and knee replacement without prophylaxis. *J Bone Joint Surg Br* 1997; **79**: 787–91.

352 Kahn RL, Hargett MJ, Urquhart B *et al.* Supraventricular tachyarrhythmias during total joint arthroplasty. Incidence and risk. *Clin Orthop* 1993; 265–9.

353 Moller JT, Cluitmans P, Rasmussen LS *et al.* Long-term postoperative cognitive dysfunction in the elderly ISPOCD1 study. *Lancet* 1998; **351**: 857–61.

354 Williams Russo P, Sharrock NE, Mattis S *et al.* Cognitive effects after epidural vs general anesthesia in older adults. A randomized trial. *JAMA* 1995; **274**: 44–50.

355 Shaw BA, Watson TC, Merzel DI *et al.* The safety of continuous epidural infusion for postoperative analgesia in pediatric spine surgery. *J Pediatr Orthop* 1996; **16**: 374–7.

356 Modig J. Beneficial effects on intraoperative and postoperative blood loss in total hip replacement when performed under lumbar epidural anesthesia. An explanatory study. *Acta Chir Scand* 1989; **550** (Suppl.): 95–100.

357 Williams A, Price N, Willett K. Epidural anaesthesia and urinary dysfunction: the risks in total hip replacement. *J R Soc Med* 1995; **88**: 699–701.

358 Michelson JD, Lotke PA, Steinberg ME. Urinary-bladder management after total joint-replacement surgery. *NEJM* 1988; **319**: 321–6.

359 Ivory JP, Simpson AH, Toogood GJ *et al.* Bilateral knee replacements: simultaneous or staged? *J R Coll Surg Edinb* 1993; **38**: 105–7.

360 Agins HJ, Salvati EA, Ranawat CS *et al.* The nine- to fifteen-year follow-up of one-stage bilateral total hip arthroplasty. *Orthop Clin North Am* 1988; **19**: 517–30.

361 Lynch NM, Trousdale RT, Ilstrup DM. Complications after concomitant bilateral total knee arthroplasty in elderly patients. *Mayo Clin Proc* 1997; **72**: 799–805.

362 Cammisa FPJ, O'Brien SJ, Salvati EA *et al.* One-stage bilateral total hip arthroplasty. A prospective study of perioperative morbidity. *Orthop Clin North Am* 1988; **19**: 657–68.

363 Grogan TJ, Dorey F, Rollins J, Amstutz HC. Deep sepsis following total knee arthroplasty. Ten-year experience at the University of California at Los Angeles Medical Center. *J Bone Joint Surg Am* 1986; **68**: 226–34.

364 Salvati EA, Robinson RP, Zeno SM *et al.* Infection rates after 3175 total hip and total knee replacements performed with and without a horizontal unidirectional filtered air-flow system. *J Bone Joint Surg Am* 1982; **64**: 525–35.

365 Josefsson G, Gudmundsson G, Kolmert L, Wijkstrom S. Prophylaxis with systemic antibiotics versus gentamicin bone cement in total hip arthroplasty. A five-year survey of 1688 hips. *Clin Orthop* 1990; 173–8.

366 Fitzpatrick R, Shortall E, Sculpher M *et al.* Primary total hip replacement surgery: a systematic review of outcomes and modelling of cost-effectiveness associated with different prostheses. *Health Technol Assess* 1998; **2**: 1–64.

367 Seagroatt V, Tan HS, Goldacre M *et al.* Elective total hip replacement: incidence, emergency re-admission rate, and postoperative mortality. *BMJ* 1991; **303**: 1431–5.

368 Schmalzried TP, Kwong LM, Jasty M *et al.* The mechanism of loosening of cemented acetabular components in total hip arthroplasty. Analysis of specimens retrieved at autopsy. *Clin Orthop* 1992; 60–78.

369 Massoud SN, Hunter JB, Holdsworth BJ *et al.* Early femoral loosening in one design of cemented hip replacement. *J Bone Joint Surg Br* 1997; **79**: 603–8.

370 Stauffer RN. Ten-year follow-up study of total hip replacement. *J Bone Joint Surg Am* 1982; **64**: 983–90.

371 Konski A, Pellegrini V, Poulter C *et al.* Randomized trial comparing single-dose versus fractionated irradiation for prevention of heterotopic bone: a preliminary report. *Int J Radiat Oncol Biol Phys* 1990; **18**: 1139–42.

372 Han CD, Choi CH, Suh CO. Prevention of heterotopic bone formation after total hip arthroplasty using 600 rad in single dose in high-risk patient. *Yonsei Med J* 1997; **38**: 96–100.

373 Schmidt SA, Kjaersgaard Andersen P *et al.* The use of indomethacin to prevent the formation of heterotopic bone after total hip replacement: a randomized, double-blind clinical trial. *J Bone Joint Surg Am* 1988; **70**: 834–8.

374 Ritter MA. Dislocation and subluxation of the total hip replacement. *Clin Orthop* 1976; 92–4.

375 Clayton ML, Thirupathi RG. Dislocation following total hip arthroplasty. Management by special brace in selected patients. *Clin Orthop* 1983; 154–9.

376 Navarro RA, Schmalzried TP, Amstutz HC, Dorey FJ. Surgical approach and nerve palsy in total hip arthroplasty. *J Arthroplasty* 1995; **10**: 1–5.

377 van der Linde MJ, Tonino AJ. Nerve injury after hip arthroplasty: 5/600 cases after uncemented hip replacement, anterolateral approach versus direct lateral approach. *Acta Orthop Scand* 1997; **68**: 521–3.

378 Lewallen DG, Berry DJ. Periprosthetic fracture of the femur after total hip arthroplasty: treatment and results to date. *Instr Course Lect* 1998; **47**: 243–9.

379 Morgan B, Mullick S, Harper WM, Finlay DB. An audit of knee radiographs performed for general practitioners. *Br J Radiol* 1997; **70**: 256–60.

380 Garellick G, Malchau H, Herberts P *et al.* Life expectancy and cost utility after total hip replacement. *Clin Orthop* 1998; 141–51.

381 Herberts P, Malchau H. How outcome studies have changed total hip arthroplasty practices in Sweden. *Clin Orthop* 1997; 44–60.

382 Goddard NJ, Coleman NP. Knee replacement – a new epidemic. In: The Institute of Mechanical Engineers and Wallace WA (eds). *Joint Replacement in the 1990s. Clinical studies, financial implications and marketing approaches*. Bury St Edmonds: Mechanical Engineering Publications, 1992, pp. 5–9.

383 Harper WM, Gregg PJ. Trent Regional Arthroplasty Study: interim report and one-year results. In: The Institute of Mechanical Engineers and Wallace WA (eds). *Joint Replacement in the 1990s. Clinical studies, financial implications and marketing approaches*. Bury St Edmonds: Mechanical Engineering Publications, 1992, pp. 49–50.

384 Levai JP, McLeod HC, Freeman MA. Why not resurface the patella? *J Bone Joint Surg Br* 1983; **65**: 448–51.

385 Soudry M, Mestriner LA, Binazzi R, Insall JN. Total knee arthroplasty without patellar resurfacing. *Clin Orthop* 1986; 166–70.

386 Laskin RS. Management of the patella during revision total knee replacement arthroplasty. *Orthop Clin North Am* 1998; **29**: 355–60.

387 White SH, Ludkowski PF, Goodfellow JW. Anteromedial osteoarthritis of the knee. *J Bone Joint Surg Br* 1991; **73**: 582–6.

388 Font Rodriguez DE, Scuderi GR, Insall JN. Survivorship of cemented total knee arthroplasty. *Clin Orthop* 1997; 79–86.

389 Mont MA, Mathur SK, Krackow KA *et al.* Cementless total knee arthroplasty in obese patients. A comparison with a matched control group. *J Arthroplasty* 1996; **11**: 153–6.

390 Sharma L, Sinacore J, Daugherty C *et al.* Prognostic factors for functional outcome of total knee replacement: a prospective study. *J Gerontol A Biol Sci Med Sci* 1996; **51**: M152–7.

391 Hawker G, Wright J, Coyte P *et al.* Health-related quality of life after knee replacement. *J Bone Joint Surg Am* 1998; **80**: 163–73.

392 Smith BE, Askew MJ, Gradisar IA Jr *et al.* The effect of patient weight on the functional outcome of total knee arthroplasty. *Clin Orthop* 1992; 237–44.

393 Goldberg VM, Figgie HE III, Figgie MP. Technical considerations in total knee surgery. Management of patella problems. *Orthop Clin North Am* 1989; **20**: 189–99.

394 Boyd ADJ, Ewald FC, Thomas WH *et al.* Long-term complications after total knee arthroplasty with or without resurfacing of the patella. *J Bone Joint Surg Am* 1993; **75**: 674–81.

395 Merkow RL, Soudry M, Insall JN. Patellar dislocation following total knee replacement. *J Bone Joint Surg Am* 1985; **67**: 1321–7.

396 Scott RD, Turoff N, Ewald FC. Stress fracture of the patella following duopatellar total knee arthroplasty with patellar resurfacing. *Clin Orthop* 1982; 147–51.

397 Wetzner SM, Bezreh JS, Scott RD *et al.* Bone scanning in the assessment of patellar viability following knee replacement. *Clin Orthop* 1985; 215–19.

398 Insall JN, Hood RW, Flawn LB, Sullivan DJ. The total condylar knee prosthesis in gonarthrosis. A five-to nine-year follow-up of the first one hundred consecutive replacements. *J Bone Joint Surg Am* 1983; **65**: 619–28.

399 Healy WL, Wasilewski SA, Takei R, Oberlander M. Patellofemoral complications following total knee arthroplasty. Correlation with implant design and patient risk factors. *J Arthroplasty* 1995; **10**: 197–201.

400 Windsor RE, Scuderi GR, Moran MC, Insall JN. Mechanisms of failure of the femoral and tibial components in total knee arthroplasty. *Clin Orthop* 1989; **248**: 15–20.

401 Rose HA, Hood RW, Otis JC *et al.* Peroneal-nerve palsy following total knee arthroplasty. A review of the Hospital for Special Surgery experience. *J Bone Joint Surg Am* 1982; **64**: 347–51.

402 Knutson K, Lindstrand A, Lidgren L. Survival of knee arthroplasties. A nation-wide multicentre investigation of 8000 cases. *J Bone Joint Surg Br* 1986; **68**: 795–803.

403 Symmons D. Musculoskeletal diseases. In: Charlton J, Murphy M (eds). *The Health of Adult Britain 1841–1994*. London: The Stationery Office, 1997, pp. 140–57.

404 Philbin EF, Ries MD, Groff GD *et al.* Osteoarthritis as a determinant of an adverse coronary heart disease risk profile. *J Cardiovasc Risk* 1996; **3**: 529–33.

405 Blair SN, Booth M, Gyarfas I *et al.* Development of public policy and physical activity initiatives internationally. *Sports Med* 1996; **21**: 157–63.

406 Blair SN. Evidence for success of exercise in weight loss and control. *Ann Intern Med* 1993; **119**: 702–6.

407 O'Brien TM, Moran R, McGoldrick F. The aetiology of degenerative disease of the hip. A review of 400 cases. *Ir J Med Sci* 1989; **158**: 63–6.

408 Gunther A, Smith SJ, Maynard PV *et al.* A case–control study of congenital hip dislocation. *Public Health* 1993; **107**: 9–18.

409 Baronciani D, Atti G, Andiloro F *et al.* Screening for developmental dysplasia of the hip: from theory to practice. Collaborative Group DDH Project. *Pediatrics* 1997; **99**: E5.

410 Yiv BC, Saidin R, Cundy PJ *et al.* Developmental dysplasia of the hip in South Australia in 1991: prevalence and risk factors. *J Paediatr Child Health* 1997; **33**: 151–6.

411 Chan A, McCaul KA, Cundy PJ *et al.* Perinatal risk factors for developmental dysplasia of the hip. *Arch Dis Child Fetal Neonatal Ed* 1997; **76**: F94–100.

412 Geitung JT, Rosendahl K, Sudmann E. Cost-effectiveness of ultrasonographic screening for congenital hip dysplasia in new-borns. *Skeletal Radiol* 1996; **25**: 251–4.

413 Brooks PM, Dougan MA, Mugford S, Meffin E. Comparative effectiveness of 5 analgesics in patients with rheumatoid arthritis and osteoarthritis. *J Rheumatol* 1982; **9** : 723–6.

414 Kjaersgaard Andersen P, Nafei A, Skov O *et al.* Codeine plus paracetamol versus paracetamol in longer-term treatment of chronic pain due to osteoarthritis of the hip. A randomised, double-blind, multi-centre study. *Pain* 1990; **43**: 309–18.

415 Furst DE. Meloxicam: selective COX-2 inhibition in clinical practice. *Semin Arthritis Rheum* 1997; **26**: 21–7.

416 Haines A, Feder G. Guidance on guidelines (editorial). *BMJ* 1992; **305**: 785–6.

417 British Orthopaedic Association. *Consultant Staffing Requirements for an Orthopaedic Service in the National Health Service.* London: British Orthopaedic Association, 1995, pp. 1–27.

418 Court C. Orthopaedic consultants warn of future shortages (letter). *BMJ* 1995; **310**: 419.

419 Dawson J, Fitzpatrick R, Gundle R, Murray D. Provision of primary total hip replacement surgery (letter). *Lancet* 1999; **353**: 2161.

420 Towheed TE, Hochberg MC. A systematic review of randomized controlled trials of pharmacological therapy in osteoarthritis of the hip. *J Rheumatol* 1997; **24**: 349–57.

421 Bellamy N, Kirwan J, Boers M *et al.* Recommendations for a core set of outcome measures for future phase III clinical trials in knee, hip, and hand osteoarthritis. Consensus development at OMERACT III. *J Rheumatol* 1997; **24**: 799–802.

422 Drake BG, Callahan CM, Dittus RS, Wright JG. Global rating systems used in assessing knee arthroplasty outcomes. *J Arthroplasty* 1994; **9**: 409–17.

423 O'Boyle C, McGee H, Hickey A, O'Malley K, Joyce C. Individual quality of life in patients undergoing hip replacement. *Lancet* 1992; **339**: 1088–91.

424 Amadio PC. Outcomes measurements (editorial). *J Bone Joint Surg Am* 1993; **75**: 1583–4.

425 Cleary PD, Reilly DT, Greenfield S *et al.* Using patient reports to assess health-related quality of life after total hip replacement. *Qual Life Res* 1993; **2**: 3–11.

426 Dawson J, Fitzpatrick R, Carr A, Murray D. Questionnaire on the perceptions of patients about total hip replacement. *J Bone Joint Surg Br* 1996; **78**: 185–90.

427 Dawson J, Fitzpatrick R, Murray D, Carr A. Questionnaire on the perceptions of patients about total knee replacement. *J Bone Joint Surg Br* 1998; **80**: 63–69.

428 Dawson J, Fitzpatrick R, Murray D, Carr A. Comparison of measures to assess outcomes in total hip replacement surgery. *Qual Health Care* 1996; **5**: 81–8.

429 Carr AJ, Morris RW, Murray DW, Pynsent PB. Survival analysis in joint replacement surgery. *J Bone Joint Surg Br* 1993; **75**: 178–82.

430 Rissanen P, Aro S, Sintonen H *et al.* Quality of life and functional ability in hip and knee replacements: a prospective study. *Qual Life Res* 1996; **5**: 56–64.

431 Callahan CM, Drake BG, Heck DA, Dittus RS. Patient outcomes following tricompartmental total knee replacement. A meta-analysis. *JAMA* 1994; **271**: 1349–57.

432 Dawson J, Jameson-Shortall E, Emerton M *et al.* Issues relating to long-term follow-up in hip replacement surgery: a review of 598 cases at 7 years comparing two prostheses using revision rates, survival analysis and patient-based measures. *J Arthroplasty* 2000; **15**: 710–17.

433 Appleby J. Promoting efficiency in the NHS: problems with the labour productivity index. *BMJ* 1996; **313**: 1319–21.

434 Radical Statistics Group. NHS 'indicators of success': what do they tell us? *BMJ* 1995; **310**: 1045–50.

435 Guralnik JM. Assessing the impact of comorbidity in the older population. *Ann Epidemiol* 1996; **6**: 376–80.

436 Norton EC, Garfinkel SA, McQuay LJ *et al.* The effect of hospital volume on the in-hospital complication rate in knee replacement patients. *Health Serv Res* 1998; **33**: 1191–210.

437 Department of Health. *National Health Service Reference Costs.* London: Department of Health, 1999.

438 Netten A, Dennett J, Knight J. *Unit Costs of Health and Social Care 1998* [B048]. Canterbury: PSSRU, 1998.

439 Department of Health. *Trust Financial Return 2.* London: Department of Health, 1998.

440 Panush RS, Brown DG. Exercise and arthritis. *Sports Med* 1987; **4**: 54–64.

441 Callaghan MJ, Oldham J, Hunt J. An evaluation of exercise regimes for patients with osteoarthritis of the knee: a single-blind randomized controlled trial. *Clin Rehabil* 1995; **9**: 213–18.

442 Tohyama H, Yasuda K, Kaneda K. Treatment of osteoarthritis of the knee with heel wedges. *Int Orthop* 1991; **15**: 31–3.

443 Panush RS, Stroud RM, Webster EM. Food-induced (allergic) arthritis. Inflammatory arthritis exacerbated by milk. *Arthritis Rheum* 1986; **29**: 220–6.

444 Bourne JT, Kumar P, Huskisson EC *et al.* Arthritis and coeliac disease. *Ann Rheum Dis* 1985; **44**: 592–8.

445 Weinberger M, Tierney WM, Cowper PA *et al.* Cost-effectiveness of increased telephone contact for patients with osteoarthritis. A randomized, controlled trial. *Arthritis Rheum* 1993; **36**: 243–6.

446 Leffler CT, Philippi AF, Leffler SG *et al.* Glucosamine, chondroitin, and manganese ascorbate for degenerative joint disease of the knee or low back: a randomized, double-blind, placebo-controlled pilot study. *Mil Med* 1999; **164**: 85–91.

447 Williams HK, Ward JR, Egger MJ *et al.* Comparison of Naproxen and Acetaminophen in the two-year study of the treatment of osteoarthritis of the knee. *Arthritis Rheum* 1993; **36**: 1196–206.

448 Quiding H, Grimstad J, Rusten K *et al.* Ibuprofen plus codeine, ibuprofen, and placebo in a single- and multi-dose cross-over comparison for coxarthrosis pain. *Pain* 1992; **50**: 303–7.

449 Rousi T, Pohjoli R, Matio J. Tramadol in the treatment of osteoarthritic pain: a double-blind cross-over study versus dextropropoxyphene. *Twelfth European Congress of Rheumatology*, 1991 (abstract).

450 Dieppe P, Cushnaghan J, Jasani MK *et al.* A two-year, placebo-controlled trial of non-steroidal anti-inflammatory therapy in osteoarthritis of the knee joint. *Br J Rheumatol* 1993; **32**: 595–600.

451 Schnitzer TJ, Popovich JM, Andersson GB, Andriacchi TP. Effect of piroxicam on gait in patients with osteoarthritis of the knee. *Arthritis Rheum* 1993; **36**: 1207–13.

452 Tamblyn R, Berkson L, Dauphinee WD *et al.* Unnecessary prescribing of NSAIDs and the management of NSAID-related gastropathy in medical practice. *Ann Intern Med* 1997; **127**: 429–38.

453 Tannenbaum H, Davis P, Russell AS *et al.* An evidence-based approach to prescribing NSAIDs in musculoskeletal disease: a Canadian consensus. Canadian NSAID Consensus Participants. *Can Med Assoc J* 1996; **155**: 77–88.

454 Towheed TE, Hochberg MC. A systematic review of randomized controlled trials of pharmacological therapy in osteoarthritis of the knee, with an emphasis on trial methodology. *Semin Arthritis Rheum* 1997; **26**: 755–70.

455 Ike RW, Arnold WJ, Rothschild EW, Shaw HL. Tidal irrigation versus conservative medical management in patients with osteoarthritis of the knee: a prospective randomized study. Tidal Irrigation Cooperating Group. *J Rheumatol* 1992; **19**: 772–9.

456 Adams ME, Atkinson MH, Lussier AJ *et al.* The role of viscosupplementation with hylan G-F 20 (Synvisc) in the treatment of osteoarthritis of the knee: a Canadian multicenter trial comparing hylan G-F 20 alone, hylan G-F 20 with non-steroidal anti-inflammatory drugs (NSAIDs) and NSAIDs alone. *Osteoarthritis Cartilage* 1995; **3**: 213–25.

457 Lohmander LS, Dalen N, Englund G *et al.* Intra-articular hyaluronan injections in the treatment of osteoarthritis of the knee: a randomised, double-blind, placebo-controlled multicentre trial. Hyaluronan Multicentre Trial Group. *Ann Rheum Dis* 1996; **55**: 424–31.

458 Weidenhielm L, Olsson E, Brostrom LA *et al.* Improvement in gait one year after surgery for knee osteoarthrosis: a comparison between high tibial osteotomy and prosthetic replacement in a prospective randomized study. *Scand J Rehabil Med* 1993; **25**: 25–31.

459 Werners R, Vincent B, Bulstrode C. Osteotomy for osteoarthritis of the hip. A survivorship analysis. *J Bone Joint Surg Br* 1990; **72**: 1010–13.

460 Bourne RB, Rorabeck CH, Laupacis A *et al.* A randomized clinical trial comparing cemented to cementless total hip replacement in 250 osteoarthritic patients: the impact on health-related quality of life and cost-effectiveness. *Iowa Orthop J* 1994; **14**: 108–14.

461 Laupacis A, Bourne R, Rorabeck C *et al.* The effect of elective total hip replacement on health-related quality of life. *J Bone Joint Surg Am* 1993; **75**: 1619–26.

462 Rorabeck CH, Bourne RB, Laupacis A *et al.* A double-blind study of 250 cases comparing cemented with cementless total hip arthroplasty. Cost-effectiveness and its impact on health-related quality of life. *Clin Orthop* 1994; 156–64.

463 Knutson K, Lewold S, Robertsson O, Lidgren L. The Swedish knee arthroplasty register. A nation-wide study of 30,003 knees 1976–1992. *Acta Orthop Scand* 1994; **65**: 375–86.

464 Kirwan JR, Currey HL, Freeman MA *et al.* Overall long-term impact of total hip and knee joint replacement surgery on patients with osteoarthritis and rheumatoid arthritis. *Br J Rheumatol* 1994; **33**: 357–60.

465 World Health Organization. *International Statistical Classification of Diseases and Related Health Problems. Tenth Revision. Instruction manual.* Geneva: World Health Organization, 1993.

466 Rajaratnam G, Black NA, Dalziel M. Total hip replacements in the National Health Service: is need being met? *J Public Health Med* 1990; **12**: 56–9.

467 Morgan M, Mays N, Holland WW. Can hospital use be a measure of need for health care? *J Epidemiol Community Health* 1987; **41**: 269–74.

468 Whates PD, Birzgalis AR, Irving M. Accuracy of hospital activity analysis operation codes. *BMJ Clin Res Ed* 1982; **284**: 1857–8.

469 Skinner PW, Riley D, Thomas EM. Use and abuse of performance indicators. *BMJ* 1988; **297**: 1256–9.

470 BMA and the Royal Pharmaceutical Society. *British National Formulary.* London: BMA and RPS, 1998.

Acknowledgements

We particularly wish to acknowledge the assistance of the following individuals: Dr Alastair Gray, Health Economics Research Centre, IHS, Oxford, for assistance with obtaining NHS service costs; Professor Brian Williams, Department of Public Health Medicine and Epidemiology, UHQMC, Nottingham, for providing numerical data on the independent health care sector; the NHS Centre for Coding and Classification, Leicester, for assistance with diagnostic and operation codes; innumerable individuals in all departments at the Nuffield Orthopaedic Centre, Oxford, for their assistance with clinical details, codings and costings; Marie Montague, Library Manager, IHS, Oxford, for her considerable assistance with reference database searches; Dr Tom Jones, GP Adviser, Oxfordshire Health Authority, Dr Tim Lancaster, Clinical Reader, Department of Primary Health Care, and Dr Robert Walton, GP Tutor and Senior Research Fellow, CRUK GPRG, Department of Pharmacology, Oxford, for information relevant to general practice and GPs; Jean Bradlow, Assistant Director of Public Health, Oxfordshire Health Authority, for information about sources of information on health services in the NHS; Tina Hammond, research assistant, IHS, Oxford, for assisting with reference searches and collating of information.

We also wish to thank the editors and, in particular, the referees for their invaluable contribution and detailed consideration of our work.

9 Cataract Surgery

John R Thompson

1 Summary

Cataract surgery is safe and produces good visual outcomes that measurably improve the quality of life of the people who are treated.[1-4] The number of cataract operations per capita in the UK is lower than in many developed countries, even though epidemiological research shows that the incidence of cataract is just as high. The balance of evidence suggests that UK cataract surgery rates are lower because people are operated on later in the course of the disease.[5-11] The number of cataract operations per year has been increasing for some time in the UK, as it has in other parts of the world, but the UK still lags behind other developed countries.

The existence of a pool of people with moderate degrees of cataract whose surgery is delayed has important implications for the planning of UK health services. Not only does it mean that the number of operations per year will probably continue to grow, but also it suggests that waiting-list initiatives are unlikely to have more than a short-term effect. If waiting lists are reduced then presumably this would simply encourage earlier referral.

The reasons for the comparatively low rates of surgery in the UK are unclear, but may well be associated with the way health care is organised. A recent study in the USA found that cataract surgery is twice as common when paid for on a fee-for-service basis compared with a pre-paid service.[12] It is not certain whether the difference reflects over- or under-utilisation but it is nonetheless important in showing that the organisation of care does influence the level of use.

The main problem in measuring the need for cataract surgery is that there is no objective definition of the point in the progression of the disease at which surgery is justified. Most authorities agree that surgery should be undertaken when the loss of vision due to the cataract interferes with the patient's life.[2,4] This criterion is obviously open to interpretation and gives any health service scope to control the level of surgery. Moderate delay does not appear to worsen the final outcome but does lower the quality of life of the patient while they wait for surgery. For many elderly people who are close to the end of their life, delay means that they never receive treatment.

Cataract is a particular challenge to a state health service in which access to treatment has traditionally been controlled by health professionals. In the consumer-oriented society that is developing in the UK, individuals will want to choose when and from whom they get their health care. It will be the patient who defines need and not the doctor, although of course there will always be a dialogue between the two. The consequence of the shift from medically defined need to patient-defined need will almost certainly be an increase in demand. Indeed, this process is already under way as doctors have become more sensitive to the wishes of their patients. Medical research tends to look at need from the doctor's perspective while in future the patient's perceptions of need may be more relevant.

Given the apparent scope that exists for increasing the number of cataract operations per year, it is vital that the NHS runs as efficiently as possible. The issue of the efficiency of cataract services has recently been addressed by the NHS Executive.[13] In the USA, 80% of cataract surgery is performed as a day-case procedure, while in the UK the rate was until recently closer to 20%,[3] and remains low in many parts of the UK. The saving that would result from a switch from 20% to 80% day-case surgery would free up enough resources to enable the number of cataract operations performed each year to be increased by 25%. As day-case care for routine cataract surgery is just as safe and effective as inpatient care, the transition should be made as soon as possible.

Cataract surgery in the UK is changing so quickly at present that it is difficult for any review to keep up with the pace of that change. There is an inevitable gap of at least two years between the collection of evidence and its publication. Recent trends have brought the level of UK cataract surgery closer to that in other developed countries and it can therefore be assumed that the international differences are less today than they were when the latest published evidence was collected. However, modernisation is not taking place uniformly, and while it is certainly true that there are parts of the UK where a good service is already being provided and, for instance, day-case surgery rates are high, equally there are places that still have some way to go.

2 Introduction and statement of the problem

Cataract is a common condition of later life affecting the lens of the eye and it will, if untreated, eventually lead to severe vision loss. Consequently, cataract has a large impact on the quality of life of many elderly people. Currently the only effective treatment is surgery, but as the operation is relatively straightforward and safe there is no reason why cataract should be a blinding condition in a developed country. Unfortunately, the sheer scale of the problem creates its own difficulties for a health service and the real challenge is how best to provide high-quality eye care to all people affected by cataract.

Elective surgery presents a particular problem for any health service that attempts to cover all members of society. The basic dilemma is whether the service exists to maximise the quality of life of the people it serves, or whether its role is to keep them sufficiently healthy that they do not become an economic drain on society. Any assessment of the need for cataract surgery will depend critically on the answer to that question, for it is perfectly possible for people to cope with most everyday tasks despite a degree of visual impairment. However, although people can cope under such circumstances, their quality of life will be measurably reduced. It is only once the role of the health service has been clarified that questions about the stage of cataract at which to offer treatment and the amount of need can be addressed. In the past, the NHS has offered high-quality surgery but with a comparatively low level of coverage.

This review is an update and extension of the earlier needs assessment of Williams *et al.*[1] Since that original review, cataract surgery in the UK has been transformed by an increased use of local anaesthesia, day-case surgery and phacoemulsification. At the same time, the organisational reforms to the NHS have continued apace. This review concentrates on recent developments in cataract surgery and does not attempt to duplicate all the material in the earlier review.

Definition of cataract

The anatomy of the eye[14] is shown in Figure 1(a) and the structure of the lens is shown diagrammatically in Figure 1(b). The lens sits just behind the iris and its role is to help focus light on to the retina. The lens continues to grow throughout life, adding new layers to its outside. The central portion of the lens is called the nucleus and represents the part of the lens that was present at birth. The outer layers, which are added

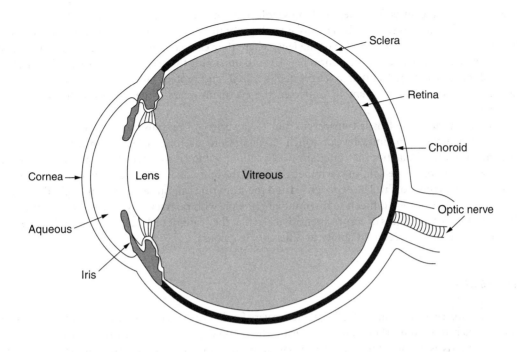

Figure 1(a): Diagrammatic representation of the structure of the eye.

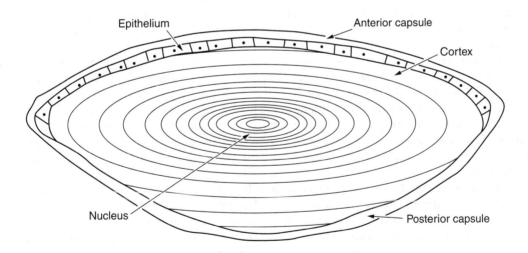

Figure 1(b): Diagrammatic representation of the structure of the lens.

subsequently, are known as the cortex, and this whole body sits within a membrane called the capsule. Cell growth takes place in a layer of epithelial cells at the front of the lens just inside the anterior capsule. As the cells develop they migrate to the edge of the lens, where they elongate, lose their organelles and increase their protein content. These long cells form new layers compacting those laid down earlier in life. The slow growth of the lens and the fact that, once created, lens cells and proteins are very long-lived, mean that a cataract may result from an event that affected the eye many years earlier or from chronic low-level exposures.

In its healthy state, the lens is transparent, but for a variety of reasons, many of which are not fully understood, opacities sometimes develop which stop light from reaching the back of the eye or which cause scattering of light.[15] Opacities that interfere with vision are known as cataracts. In its extreme form, a cataract will allow very little light to reach the retina and the individual will effectively be blind in that eye. In milder forms, vision loss will be experienced and the scattering can cause glare from bright lights which might, for instance, make it difficult to drive at night. People with cataract may also experience changes in refraction, double vision, loss of contrast sensitivity so that they cannot pick out light grey objects against a white background, and a reduced ability to differentiate colours.

Key issues

As cataract surgery is so safe and effective, there are very few issues of quality of care relevant to a developed country. Much more important is how to ensure that people get surgery when they need it. The major problem in needs assessment for cataract is thus to define the point at which a person requires treatment. It is only once this has been done that the size of the problem can be accurately assessed and delays in treatment can be measured. Under a health care system in which the patients buy their health care, people with sufficient resources would be able to define for themselves the point at which they want surgery. The challenge for the NHS is to provide a service for everyone equivalent to that which individuals would purchase for themselves. Without a definition of the time at which surgery can be expected, it is very easy for the provider, or the agency purchasing on behalf of the patient, to save money by delaying treatment.

Economic considerations have led some to question the benefit of operating on the second eye in a patient where both eyes are affected by cataract and vision has been successfully restored to the first eye. Since, in the UK, the individual is not in control of the timing of treatment, the service must ask itself whether its role is to get the individual's vision as close as possible to what it would have been without the cataract, or merely to return them to a state in which they can function independently within society. Although there is considerable research evidence concerning the extent of the benefit to the patient of second-eye surgery, the decision on whether or not the benefit should be delivered is a political and economic one.

There is no doubt that the method of organisation of health care has an effect on the level of provision. The first national cataract audit estimated that in the UK in 1990 there were about 580 cataract operations per 100 000 people aged 50 years or more.[5–7] The corresponding figure for the USA was about 1540 cataract operations, nearly three times as many. Yet there is no evidence of any difference in the incidence rates in the two populations. Some might argue that in the USA, the competitive nature of eye-care provision leads to some unnecessary surgery. However, the size of the discrepancy must lead us to question whether the NHS has been offering a good service to everyone with cataract.

Finally, there is the issue of how best to organise services to provide good-quality care in the most cost-effective way. This issue has recently been addressed in the NHS Executive publication, *Action on Cataracts*.[13] When many senior ophthalmologists started their training, cataract surgery was accompanied by a hospital stay of up to 2 weeks. Now it has been shown that in the large majority of cases, cataract surgery can be performed without any overnight hospital stay. A further potential reorganisation is in the delivery of post-operative care. At present, it is usual for the ophthalmologist to monitor the progress of the patient after surgery in outpatient clinics, but in a few districts ophthalmologists' time has been saved by delegating this post-operative care to community optometrists for routine cases. The argument for day-case surgery is overwhelming but the advantages or otherwise of co-management are yet to be established.

3 Sub-categories

Classification of cataract

The aetiology of most cataracts is not fully understood and so there are no useful schemes of classification based on cause. Congenital and other cataracts of childhood form a special subgroup, as the vast majority of cataracts do not develop until late middle or old age. A few cataracts in adults may be associated with identifiable events such as trauma, but the real difficulty is to classify the remainder, known collectively as age-related cataracts. Some early classification schemes were based on the degree of development of the cataract using vaguely defined terms such as mild and mature. Other schemes use the visual acuity of the subject to describe the degree of cataract. Most scientific studies now differentiate the location of the opacification within the lens, as this may well be related to aetiology. In modern classification schemes, the extent of the different types of cataract is gauged by comparison with standard photographs or diagrams.[16–18] Some researchers have experimented with digitisation of photographs of the lens with a view to obtaining more objective measurements,[19–21] but these methods do not have a role in current medical practice.

None of these classification schemes is particularly well suited to needs assessment. For even the individual's visual acuity will be only loosely related to functional loss and consequent impact on quality of life. Visual acuity is usually measured by asking the individual to read letters of decreasing size on a well-lit letter chart at a distance of six metres. This measurement will not necessarily predict the individual's ability to perform everyday tasks, such as reading a telephone directory in poor light or getting around in the home. Further, it makes no attempt to capture other aspects of vision such as contrast sensitivity, glare or colour vision. Even if all aspects of vision could be measured, they would not adequately describe the impact of the cataract on the individual because each person has their own visual requirements and a cataract that might stop one person from working could be just a minor inconvenience to someone else. The ideal classification for needs assessment would be based on the impact of the cataract on that person's daily life. While researchers have tried to develop questionnaires to measure the impact of cataract, none has gained wide acceptance and quality-of-life measures have had no impact on routine eye care for cataract.

Because there is no classification of cataract that is well suited to needs assessment, this chapter will use a pragmatic division into cataract in children, cataract in adults and posterior capsular opacification.

Cataract in children

Cataracts in children are so rare that although they may result in many years of vision loss, they do not have the same public health importance as age-related cataracts. As well as having different aetiologies,[22] infantile cataracts are special because they are present during the early years of life when the visual pathways linking the eye to the brain are in the process of development. Both bilateral and unilateral cataract can interfere with normal visual development and if treatment is delayed, the damage may be permanent and normal vision may not be achieved, even when the cataract is removed. For this reason it is desirable to operate on infantile cataracts as soon as possible after they are diagnosed which, for congenital cataracts, means within the first few weeks of life.[23,24] In developing countries, childhood blindness due to congenital cataract is still common, often because the children do not get to the health care services soon enough.[25]

Adult cataract

Many different forms of opacification have been described, but the three main types that affect people in later life are nuclear cataracts located in the centre of the lens, cortical cataracts in the periphery, and posterior subcapsular cataracts (PSC) located at the back of the lens just inside the capsule. It is not uncommon to find two or more of these cataract types in the same lens.

The process of formation of the cataract varies with the type. In most people, as they age the lens nucleus becomes harder and yellower.[26] When this process affects vision it is described as nuclear cataract. Breaks in the lens fibres cause spoke-like opacities to develop in the periphery of the lens which, over time, may spread inwards. This is the typical pattern of cortical cataract. PSC starts with the migration and enlargement of epithelial cells, which congregate at the back of the eye and are often centrally located. Cataracts that lie across the visual axis of the lens, such as nuclear cataract and most PSC, will have the most severe impact on visual acuity.

Posterior capsular opacification

When the lens is surgically removed it is impossible to ensure that there are no cells left within the capsule. Sometimes, cells left behind after surgery migrate to the inner surface of the posterior capsule and form an obstruction to light reaching the back of the eye. To the patient, this effect, known as posterior capsular opacification (PCO), will be like the return of their cataract. Fortunately, PCO can be treated by using a laser to make a hole in the posterior capsule. PCO is sufficiently common to make it important that its treatment is allowed for in the assessment of the costs of treating cataract, and the small risk of complications associated with PCO needs to be combined with the risk from the original surgery.

4 The epidemiology of cataract

Cataract in children

A study of a cohort of children born in the UK in 1970 and followed until they were 10 years old showed a rate of bilateral infantile cataract of 2.7 per 10 000 children and a rate of unilateral cataract of 2.0 per 10 000 children.[27] A separate study in Oxfordshire gave an overall rate of about 6 per 10 000.[28] In 1996, the population of England and Wales was just over 50 million and there were about 650 000 live births,[29] which at the reported rates would imply that between 300 and 400 children per year develop infantile cataract. Surgery rates within the NHS are lower, as can be seen from Table 6. Only 130 cataract procedures were performed on children aged under 10 years in England in 1995–96. Presumably the less severe cataracts are not removed until later in life. The UK surveys give broadly similar results to those from other studies in Europe,[30] but two or three times higher than the rates usually quoted for the USA.[31,32] The discrepancy is almost certainly due to the reliance on hospital surveillance data for the American studies, which has led to under-recording.

Children have higher complication rates following cataract surgery than do adults. This is partly due to their much longer survival times, which give greater opportunity for long-term complications to manifest, but it is also related to the stronger inflammatory response seen in children. PCO, which affects about a quarter of adults, is almost universal in children,[33,34] glaucoma affects about 20% of children[35–37] and retinal detachment is also much more common than in adults, but may not occur until the individual is in their twenties or thirties.[38,39] As well as the other complications associated with adult cataract surgery, the disruption to the developing visual system and imbalance between the eyes, especially in unilateral cataract, can create extra problems, chiefly strabismus,[40] amblyopia[41,42] and nystagmus.[43] Lambert and Drack[22] reviewed the visual outcome in children with cataract and found that the outcome depends on age of onset, density of the cataract and promptness of treatment. Up to a quarter of children with bilateral cataract are still blind after treatment.

Adult cataract

Prevalence

Many epidemiological studies have investigated the aetiology of cataract or described the burden of the disease in a community. Aetiological studies tend to be more rigorous and usually measure the extent of any lens opacities on any one of a number of standardised scales, but these scales are hard to relate to the need for surgery. Descriptive studies typically summarise the number of people with a specific vision loss due to cataract, but even this will not tell us how many require surgery. Despite the limitations of the measures used, the studies of cataract surgery rates and of prevalence and incidence give the best currently available indication of need.

Perhaps the finest of the recent epidemiological studies was carried out in Beaver Dam, Wisconsin, USA (Beaver Dam Eye Study, BDES).[44] The population there is mainly of northern European descent and the results might be expected to mirror those that would be found in the UK. Much of the methodology used in that study was adopted by the Blue Mountains Eye Study (BMES) carried out in West Sydney, Australia.[45] Table 1 shows the amount of past surgery found in these two studies. A combination of published and unpublished data from two UK surveys carried out in Melton Mowbray, Leicestershire (Melton Eye Study, MES), is given for comparison. The data for the over-75s come from a survey

Table 1: The prevalence of past surgery in the Beaver Dam Eye Study, the Blue Mountains Eye Study and the Melton Eye Study.

Age (years)	Right eye			Either eye	
	BDES	BMES	MES	BMES	MES
49–54	0.6%	0.8%	NA	1.0%	NA
55–64	1.6%	1.5%	1.1%	1.9%	1.1%
65–74	4.2%	3.0%	1.8%	3.6%	2.9%
75–84	11.6%	12.0%	3.0%	16.1%	4.0%
85+	NA	21.6%	7.5%	31.3%	11.0%

NA, not available; BDES, Beaver Dam Eye Study, USA ($n = 4926$);[44] BMES, Blue Mountains Eye Study, Australia ($n = 3646$);[45] MES, Melton Eye Study, UK, combined results from separate surveys ($n = 1359$).[46]

conducted in 1983[46] and the data for people under 75 come from a survey conducted in 1996. The low surgery rate in the more elderly people may in part be explained by the dates of the surveys. The earlier UK survey was conducted 5 years earlier than the BDES and over a decade before the BMES. However, even the later UK survey of people aged under 75 years found surgery rates for right eyes in people aged 65–74 years that are 43% of the USA rate and 60% of the Australian rate.

A general practice-based survey in inner London[47] found the aphakia (including pseudophakia) rate in people aged 65 years or more was 5.8%, broadly in line with the data from Leicestershire. In the Leicestershire study, it was found that 63% of all visual impairment was due to cataract and that as a result of their examinations, 6% of the subjects were referred to an ophthalmologist for cataract. They compare their rates of aphakia or lens opacities reducing vision to below 6/12 with the rates from the Framingham eye study.[48,49] In people aged 65–74 years, Framingham found 0.7% and London 2%. Over 75 years, Framingham found 3.8% and London 16.4%. These findings suggest that because surgery rates are lower, there is much more treatable visual impairment in the community.

When detailed lens grading was undertaken in a population-based study of people aged 55–74 years in Melton Mowbray, Leicestershire,[50] the results obtained were very similar to those found in studies in the USA. This confirms the impression that the pattern and extent of lens opacities are very similar, even if surgery rates differ.

The BDES also recorded the amount of visually significant cataract – that is, cataract as defined by their grading scheme in eyes that had a logMAR visual acuity, roughly equivalent to 6/9 or worse.[44] The results are shown in Table 2 and are broadly similar to those found in the earlier Framingham study from Massachusetts, USA (see Table 4) and from the BMS from Sydney, Australia.[45]

Table 2: Cataract associated with a visual acuity of 6/9 or worse in the Beaver Dam Eye Study.[44]

Age (years)	Women		Men	
	Worse eye	Better eye	Worse eye	Better eye
43–54	3%	0%	0%	0%
55–64	10%	1%	4%	0%
65–74	30%	8%	14%	3%
75+	46%	25%	39%	13%

Prevalence and ethnicity

Results from the BDES, BMES and MES surveys related mainly to white people of European origin, but 5.5% of the population of the UK are non-white, of whom 30% classify themselves as African-Caribbeans and 49% as South Asian.[51] Differences in the prevalence of cataract in different parts of the world are well established and there is a lot of evidence to suggest differences between ethnic groups living in the same locality. What is unclear is the extent to which these differences reflect genetic or lifestyle factors and to what extent they are due to the generally poorer economic status of immigrant groups.

There is no UK evidence concerning cataract in African-Caribbeans, although in the USA the rate was found to be higher in Baltimore blacks than whites[54] and in Barbados the rate of cortical cataract was found to be higher than in comparable US studies of white populations.[55] The rates for nuclear cataract and PSC were similar. It is well established that glaucoma is more common in African-Caribbeans and so cataract associated with glaucoma might be expected to be more common.[56] Several South Asian communities in the UK have been studied and in every case the prevalence of cataract has been found to be high. For people in their sixties, a study in inner-city Leicester found cataract in 69% of Asians and 30% of Europeans.[52,53] The breakdown by age from the Leicester study is shown in Table 3. In Southall, the corresponding prevalence of cataract in Asians was 86%.[57] Gray surveyed the Bengali population in Tower Hamlets and found an overall cataract rate of 53%. In that study, 5% of their sample needed referral for cataract surgery.[58] A large hospital-based study in Leicester[59] measured the demand incidence for cataract for a 30-month period in the early 1980s. The age-adjusted demand was 5.4% (95% CI: 4.4, 6.5) higher in people of Asian origin compared to whites. There was also some evidence of a difference between subgroups of the Asian community.

Table 3: The prevalence of age-related cataract, aphakia or pseudophakia by age and ethnic origin in the Leicester Eye Study ($n = 369$).[52,53]

Age (years)	Asians	Europeans
40–49	17%	0%
50–59	49%	6%
60–69	69%	30%
70+	93%	64%

Incidence

In a follow-up of the Beaver Dam cohort carried out about 5 years after the original survey,[60] it was found that 6.3% had subsequently had surgery, with the percentages varying with age so that in the 43–54 years age group the incident surgery rate was 0.5%, in the 55–64 age group it was 4%, in the 65–74 age group it was 12% and in those over 75 years it was 20%. Surgery was associated with age and cigarette smoking as well as with characteristics of the lens and of vision measured in the original survey.

Although many of the large population-based eye surveys have returned to their original cohorts to measure incidence and progression of lens opacities, some of the most useful data on incidence come from figures derived from the Framingham prevalence survey.[61] The data are set out in Table 4. The incidence

Table 4: Measured prevalence and estimated 5-year incidence of lens opacities and cataract based on data from the Framingham Eye Study ($n = 2308$).[61]

Age (years)	Any lens opacity		Lens opacity causing a loss of vision*	
	Measured prevalence	Estimated 5-year incidence	Measured prevalence	Estimated 5-year incidence
55–59	16%	10%	2%	1%
60–64	27%	16%	3%	2%
65–69	42%	23%	7%	5%
70–74	59%	31%	10%	9%
75–79	69%	37%	19%	15%
80–84	83%	–	46%	–

* Vision reduced to 6/9 or worse due to the lens opacity.

rates are calculated under a set of assumptions, such as non-differential mortality, that at best will be approximations, and consequently the estimates can only be treated as guides to the true incidence.

A few studies have reported actual measurements of incidence,[62-64] although the definitions of progression are based on specified changes in the grading on standard scales rather than definitions of visually or functionally significant change. Some general features are, however, apparent. First regression is rare and is probably only seen as a result of errors in grading. The rates of progression are higher than the incidence rates for new opacities. PSC has the lowest incidence of the three main types, but once observed, it has the fastest progression rate.

Posterior capsular opacification (PCO)

Posterior capsular opacification is the commonest long-term complication of cataract surgery.[33] The rate of PCO will depend on the surgical technique used, but has also been found to vary with the age of the patient, being common in younger people, and with the type of intra-ocular lens (IOL) implant. IOLs that fill the capsule and present a barrier to cell migration are thought to inhibit the formation of visually disabling PCO.[65] For these reasons, the incidence of PCO has been found to vary widely, with rates ranging up to 50% by 5 years after surgery. The median time to PCO is about 2 years, by which stage 15–20% of patients will be affected. A meta-analysis of published studies of PCO found the average incidence to be 12% at 1 year, 21% at 3 years and 28% at 5 years after surgery.[66] However, the meta-analysis detected significant heterogeneity between studies that they were unable to explain, which suggests that variations in both patient characteristics and local practice are important in determining incidence.

Risk factors

Study of the risk factors for cataract may eventually help us to understand the mechanisms by which cataract is formed, but in the mean time it is more likely to suggest preventive measures. A large number of factors have been associated with cataract, but repeat studies have frequently been contradictory. The inconsistency of much of the evidence stems from the multi-factorial nature of the disease and the difficulty of measuring long-term risk factors. Risk factors have been reviewed regularly.[67-72] Two of the reviews in particular[68,69] illustrate the inconclusiveness of the evidence by reaching quite opposite conclusions about the likely causes of cataract after reviewing the same literature. It is possible that a limited understanding of the genetics of cataract has meant that epidemiological studies have been inconclusive because they have pooled susceptible and non-susceptible subjects. The genetics of cataract is a potentially important area of investigation that is only just beginning to be tackled.

There is some epidemiological evidence that high levels of ultraviolet B (UV-B) radiation in sunlight may be associated with cataract. This relationship was first noticed in ecological studies that found high levels of cataract in places where UV-B exposure is high.[73-75] Attempts to reproduce this finding based on individual measurements have been largely unsuccessful, with only the Waterman Study able to demonstrate a weak association between non-nuclear cataract and UV-B.[76] The lack of a measured effect is probably due to the difficulty of assessing a person's lifetime exposure, which will depend on innumerable factors, such as where they live, the amount of time that they spend outdoors and whether they wear glasses or a hat.[77] Studies based in a single locality may not have a large enough range of lifetime exposures to demonstrate an effect, and multi-centre studies inevitably suffer from confounding. Perhaps the most convincing circumstantial evidence for an association is the fact that so much cortical cataract is found to start in the inferonasal quadrant of the lens[44,45,78,79] which, because of shadowing from the eyebrows and nose, is the segment most exposed to sunlight. Although the evidence is weak, it would seem sensible to advocate that hats and sunglasses which cut out UV-B should be worn in bright sunshine. The design of the sunglasses may be important, for there could be no benefit if the glasses lead to the widening of the pupils yet allow light in through the sides.

The next most important controllable risk factor is probably nutrition. Once again the concern is primarily with lifetime nutritional status, which is exceedingly difficult to measure. There is a lot of weak epidemiological evidence to suggest that antioxidants protect against the development of cataract.[80] This is a sensible hypothesis that might fit in with the UV-B theory. If UV-B releases free radicals in the lens which are responsible for the breakdown of proteins and the breaking of fibres, then antioxidants which help sweep up the free radicals ought to be protective. It is interesting that the human lens contains high concentrations of ascorbate, a very effective antioxidant.[81]

Taylor *et al.*[80] have reviewed the many epidemiological studies which have suggested that vitamins may play a role in preventing or delaying cataract, and subsequently the same team of researchers found a protective effect of vitamin C supplements taken for 10 years or more.[82] Both multi-vitamin supplements and vitamin E supplements were found to be protective against nuclear cataract in a recent longitudinal study.[83] Clinical trial evidence is, however, sparse. Cataract evaluation was added to an existing randomised, double-blind trial of vitamin supplementation and cancer being conducted in Linxian, China, and there was found to be a 43% reduction in the prevalence of nuclear cataract in people aged 65–74 years.[84] A similar study piggy-backed on to a lung cancer trial in Finland found no beneficial effect from more than 5 years of supplementation.[85] Trials of the preventive use of antioxidant supplements are under way in the USA and Australia, but have not yet reported.

Smoking[86–89] and alcohol[90–94] are exposures amenable to intervention that have been linked with cataract. Again the epidemiological evidence is contradictory,[95] and with these exposures the routes by which they might affect the lens are less clear, although cigarette smoking is known to lower antioxidant levels. Both of these exposures may be confounded with nutrition and be indirect measures of social class, which in turn is associated with general health, life expectancy and many factors important for a disease of ageing.

The association between corticosteroid use and the risk of PSC was demonstrated in a series of studies in the 1960s.[71] This finding has raised the question of whether the increased incidence of asthma in children and the resulting use of corticosteroids as a treatment may put more children at risk of cataract in later life. One large Australian study has confirmed an association between inhaled corticosteroids and both PSC and nuclear cataract.[96] Unfortunately, little is known about the importance of dose or duration of use of corticosteroids in cataract risk. Other drugs, such as diuretics and tranquillisers, have been linked with cataract in epidemiological studies but the studies are not consistent and it is difficult to tell whether the risk is associated with the drug, the underlying disease or some other factor associated with the disease. It has been suggested that aspirin is protective against cataract,[91] although not all studies find this,[90,97] and it seems unlikely that prophylactic use would be an effective method of preventing cataract.

People with diabetes have been found to be at increased risk of cataract in many studies,[86,98,99] although this finding has been questioned.[70,100] In a survey in Wisconsin of people with diabetes diagnosed after 30 years of age, the prevalence of past cataract surgery in either eye by age was found to be as follows: 20–54 years, 2.9%; 55–64 years, 5.0%; 65–74 years, 10.7%; 75+ years, 13.5%.[101] Comparison of these figures with those given in Table 1 shows that for people aged under 75 the rate of surgery is two to three times greater. There may be bias in this comparison due to the people with diabetes having increased contact with health services, so increasing the likelihood that they will be offered surgery, but the difference is found in too many studies for it to be dismissed. The likelihood of a causal association is further increased by the laboratory evidence that lenses incubated in high-sugar media will develop cataract. Indeed, the importance of diabetes-related conditions as a cause of cataract may be being underestimated because of the difficulty of defining diabetes and the omission of conditions such as insulin resistance. Various other medical conditions have been associated with cataract in epidemiological studies, including hypertension,[48,49,102] renal failure,[98,103] glaucoma, uveitis and myopia.[104] The evidence is, in each case, rather weak. Severe or prolonged episodes of diarrhoea have been suggested as a possible cause for some cataracts.[98,104,105] The evidence is not conclusive, and even if this is a risk factor it is unlikely to be of major importance in a developed country.

It has been noticed in studies from many countries that cataract extraction is more common in women than in men, but this discrepancy has never been explained. Part of the difference may be explained by the larger proportion of very elderly women, but even the age-adjusted figures show more surgery on women and further research is still needed.

Mortality

A number of studies have identified poorer survival in people with cataract or people undergoing cataract extraction.[106–109] There was some suggestion that this was due to an association between cataract and diabetes,[110] but subsequent studies have found that the poorer survival extends to people without diabetes[111,112] and that it is particularly associated with nuclear cataract. The typical finding of these studies is that the age-adjusted risk of death in people with advanced cataract is about twice that in the general population. This effect is important when assessing the benefits of cataract surgery in terms of years of good vision resulting from the treatment, and survival patterns are also important when assessing the impact of delays in treatment, either through long waiting lists or delays in listing.

According to the First National Cataract Audit,[5–7] the average age at surgery was 76 years. A number of independent studies of private patients in the USA have found the average age at surgery to be about 72 years. So a 4-year delay in surgery might greatly reduce the amount of cataract surgery that is performed because that proportion of patients die in the interim. This would go a long way to explaining why the rate of surgery in the USA is nearly three times that in the UK.[5] It also indicates that earlier surgery and shorter waiting lists could have a dramatic impact on the amount of surgery required.

Based on the age structure for cataract procedures in the UK shown in Table 6 and national statistics on mortality,[113] it is possible to calculate the life expectancy of a person operated on for cataract. Basing the calculations on people aged 50 years or more at surgery, so as to exclude non-age-related cataract, and assuming that the survival pattern of patients with cataract is the same as that of the rest of the population, the life expectancy after surgery is 10.2 years for men and 11 years for women. If the death rates in people with cataract are 1.5 times the national rate, then the life expectancy falls to 8 years and 8.6 years, respectively, and if it is twice the national rate, 6.7 years and 7.2 years, respectively. These differences are clearly important in calculating the benefits of surgery in an economic or cost–benefit analysis.

Analysis of mortality patterns also allows us to estimate how many people die soon after surgery. If the death rate for cataract patients is the same as the national rate, 14% will die within 2 years of surgery. If it is 1.5 times as great, 21% will die, and at twice the national rate, 27% will die. It is easy to see how delayed surgery has acted to reduce the amount of surgery that is performed.

International comparisons

International comparisons are fraught with problems because of the difficulty of standardising for confounding factors and variation in case definition. Nonetheless they are important, not just because of possible relevance to ethnic minorities living in the UK but also because a lot can be learned from studies of cataract surgery rates in places such as Western Europe, North America and Australasia, where the incidence of cataract is similar to that in the UK but health services are differently organised. Such studies allow us to see the impact of changing the definition of need. Although attempts are under way to try to objectify the criteria for cataract surgery, need is still defined subjectively. In countries where there are fewer economic restraints on health care, less conservative definitions of need have resulted in much higher rates of surgery. Information, particularly from places where the patient is more able to define their own need, gives a clue to the UK health services as to just how far the level of surgery may grow.

Some of the most interesting surgery data come from Sweden. In 1991, Sweden introduced a health care guarantee that a cataract patient with a visual acuity of 0.5 (6/12) or less in the better eye could expect surgery within 3 months of listing. In an effort to monitor this guarantee, a national cataract register was set up and run by a small group of enthusiastic ophthalmologists.[114,115]

By 1995, the Swedish cataract register covered 95% of all cataract surgery in that country. A recent analysis[115] has shown that the immediate impact of the guarantee was to reduce waiting times, but after a couple of years the waiting times started to increase again. The guarantee did not have the anticipated effect of removing variations between districts within Sweden, which were still evident in 1995.

The Swedish cataract register collects a minimal set of information on each treated patient, including waiting time, age, sex, employment status, visual acuity, two simple questions of visual function, previous surgery and ocular comorbidity. Based on 1992 data, they estimated that in Sweden there were 4.5 operations per 1000 inhabitants, compared to 5.4 per 1000 in the USA, 2.8 per 1000 in Denmark, 2.7 per 1000 in Norway and 1.8 per 1000 in the UK.[10] The comparatively low rate of surgery in the UK had been noted earlier,[11] and possible explanations have been proposed,[116] but none has satisfactorily explained the discrepancy. Although unexplained, the international comparisons do probably demonstrate the extent to which the NHS needed to expand its service.

An important analysis of time trends in the rates of surgery was made in North Jutland, Denmark,[9] where the rate in 1990 was found to be three times that for the same area in 1980. They found no increase in the proportion of second-eye operations and very little change in the average age at surgery. The increased proportion of very elderly people may have contributed slightly to the rise, but by far the most important factor was the tendency to operate at better levels of visual acuity.

5 Current service provision

Treatments for cataract

There are no medical treatments that have been proved to reverse or even slow down the progress of cataract. If there were, their impact would be dramatic, for it has been estimated that since cataract affects people towards the end of their life, a 10-year delay in the onset would reduce the prevalence in society by 45%.[117] There is some weak evidence to suggest that antioxidant vitamins may be protective against cataract and that avoiding bright sunlight may be beneficial, but these possible preventive measures have not been conclusively demonstrated to work, and in any case they may be of limited use in a well-nourished population from a country with a temperate climate. Consequently, the only currently established treatment is to surgically remove the cataractous lens and replace it with a plastic IOL.[118] Prior to surgery, a person with cataract may be helped by ensuring that their spectacle correction is correct and by sensible adjustments to ambient illumination.

There are three main techniques for cataract surgery. Intracapsular cataract extraction (ICCE) involves the removal of the entire lens, including its capsule. In countries where operating microscopes are available, this technique has been superseded by extracapsular cataract extraction (ECCE) in which the nucleus and cortex are removed through the anterior capsule, leaving the posterior capsule in place. This technique produces faster visual rehabilitation and fewer complications. Over the last decade, a form of ECCE known as phacoemulsification (PE) has become very popular. This technique requires only a very small incision, around 4 mm compared to 10 mm for standard ECCE, and uses a probe that fragments the lens by ultrasound so that it can be removed through a narrow tube. Theoretically, once the surgeon has become skilled in this technique, the smaller incision should lead to even faster visual rehabilitation and even fewer complications. There is, however, little trial evidence of real benefits from PE over ECCE.[4]

There are many types of general anaesthetic (GA) that are suitable for use with day-case surgery, but whichever is used the recovery time from a GA will be longer than that for a local anaesthetic (LA). Because of this, GAs are more suited to use on morning day-case theatre lists,[119] and the running of an efficient day-case unit will require that a large proportion of cataracts be operated on under LA. In one hospital, it was found that consultants who frequently used LAs were the same ones who performed a lot of day-case surgery,[119] so a switch to local anaesthesia is an important accompaniment to increasing the amount of day-case cataract surgery. LAs have other advantages. They have been stated to be safer than GAs,[120–122] although the evidence for this is weak, and to be preferred by patients and medical staff.[120,123] Despite the advantages of LAs, there are some patients for whom they are not recommended, such as those with dementia or communication problems, and those who have a problem lying still.[121]

The standard modern treatment for PCO is neodymium:yttrium–aluminum–garnet (YAG) laser capsulotomy. The laser is focused on the posterior capsule and causes a shockwave that breaks the capsule and hence removes the opacification. The procedure is very effective and safe, although it does have its own rare complications. These include the elevation of intra-ocular pressure, damage to the IOL, retinal detachment and cystoid macular oedema.

Visual acuity at the time of surgery

Some of the best data on cataract surgery in the UK come from the first national cataract audit conducted in 1990.[5–7] A second cataract audit was performed in 1997 and first reports from that work are just becoming available.[8] The first audit attempted to collect data on all cataract surgery conducted in a single week in November 1990 by inviting all NHS consultants to make a return. The second audit relied on volunteering hospitals to collect information on cataract surgery over the period September to December 1997 and to return this information to a central registry. Although both audits may be expected to be broadly representative of current UK practice, the differences in methodology make comparison a little difficult. Among other things, the audits give us a picture of the visual acuity of patients at the time of surgery. The visual acuity of the better eye gives an indication of the visual impairment suffered by the subject, and the visual acuity in the operated eye reflects the stage of the cataract at which surgery takes place. The results for both audits are set out in Table 5.

The first audit[5] showed that even when the best visual acuity in either eye was considered, 16% of patients were blind by the US criterion (best corrected visual acuity less than 3/36) at admission, 6%

Table 5: Visual acuity in the national cataract audits.

Visual acuity	First cataract audit (1990)				Second cataract audit (1997)	
	Better eye		Operated eye		Operated eye	
	At listing	At surgery	At listing	At surgery	At listing	At surgery
6/12 or better	56%	49%	11%	7%	31%	27%
6/18 to 6/24	25%	29%	32%	27%	–	–
6/36 to 6/60	11%	12%	25%	24%	54%	52%
3/60 or worse	8%	10%	32%	42%	15%	21%

despite having no other ocular pathology. A further 37% were visually impaired (better than 6/60 but worse than 6/12), 21% despite having no other ocular pathology. Comparison with the results of the national study of cataract outcomes in the USA is instructive. At surgery in the USA, the percentages with visual acuities of 20/80 (6/24) or less were 8% in the better eye and 34% in the operated eye. If half of the 6/18–6/24 category in the UK audit have a visual acuity of 6/24, the corresponding percentages of patients with 6/24 or less in the UK would be 34% and 79%. These figures suggest much later surgery in the UK.

In the first UK audit, 7% had a visual acuity better than 6/18 in the operated eye at surgery. In one international comparison of four countries, the 1990 UK pattern of pre-operative visual acuity was closest to that of Spain, where 8% had visual acuities in the operated eye better than 0.33 (6/18). The corresponding figure for the USA was 53%, for Canada 36% and for Denmark 36%.[124] An earlier Danish study using 1992 data found only 13% better than 6/18, but even then 44% had a visual acuity of 6/24 or 6/18,[9] compared to 27% found in the first UK audit.

The second audit shows a dramatic shift towards surgery at better visual acuity. From the 7% with visual acuity of 6/12 or better in the operated eye seen in 1990, there had been a rise to 27% by 1997, giving rates much closer to but still lower than the earlier figures for the USA, Canada and Denmark.[124]

Numbers of cataract operations

A steady growth in the number of cataract operations has been noted from many parts of the world.[9,125–127] Some of this increase is undoubtedly due to the ageing of the population, but that effect alone will not explain the dramatic increases that have been noticed. In Denmark, between 1980 and 1991 the number of cataract operations per year increased by 350%, at a time when the size of the elderly population was increasing by 17%.[124] The real explanation for the growth in cataract surgery throughout the developed world has been the tendency to operate earlier. In the Danish study, only 4% of patients in 1981 had a visual acuity of 6/18 or better, while in 1992 this had risen to 42%.

The sharpness of the increase in numbers of operations and the marked shift towards offering surgery at better visual acuities must make us cautious in comparing studies that are even a few years apart. The NHS data for England shows 139 356 cataract procedures for the year 1995–96 (Table 6). One year earlier the

Table 6: Number of cataract procedures performed under the NHS in England for the year 1995–96.

Age (years)	Phacoemulsification	Other cataract extractions	Total
0–9	49	85	130
10–39	848	723	1,571
40–44	475	459	934
45–49	865	912	1,777
50–54	1,334	1,499	2,833
55–59	2,317	2,719	5,036
60–64	3,935	4,697	8,632
65–69	6,318	8,171	14,489
70–74	10,123	13,203	23,326
75–79	11,771	15,929	27,700
80–84	11,912	17,336	29,248
85+	8,804	14,767	23,571
Missing age	33	72	105
Total	58,784	80,572	139,356

figure was 128 334 and before that 112 148, which represents a 24% increase between 1993 and 1995. By 1998–99 the number of NHS cataract procedures had risen to about 170 000 and a target of 250 000 has been set to be achieved by 2003.[128] This would be equivalent to 350 cataract operations per 100 000 people.

Primary care

Ophthalmic conditions are responsible for between 2% and 5% of all general practice consultations but, despite this, GPs lack confidence in diagnosing and treating eye disease. It has been suggested that the chief reason for this is a lack of instruction to medical students in the specialised skills of ophthalmology.[129] Although there is a general lack of confidence in handling ophthalmic conditions, cataract seems to be an exception. In one survey, GPs were asked if they felt confident in diagnosing common eye conditions.[130] The percentages expressing confidence were 30% for senile macular degeneration, 44% for diabetic retinopathy, 36% for chronic glaucoma, but 90% for cataract. In the same survey, only 19% said they would immediately refer on a case of cataract while the remainder felt happy to manage the case themselves until the vision loss became a problem to the patient or when the visual acuity dropped to 6/18 or less.

The fact that GPs are more confident at diagnosing cataract than most other ophthalmic conditions is reflected in their accuracy. A survey of the accuracy of referrals to Burton District General's eye department[131] found 98% accuracy (42/43) in referrals from GPs for cataract, which was even better than the accuracy for optometrist-initiated referrals, which was 88% (52/59). The inaccuracy reflects a disagreement between the ophthalmologist and the referrer as to whether or not the cataract was clinically significant rather than whether or not there was any lens opacity.

Sheldrick et al.[132,133] studied the 2587 consultations with primary care services made by patients from selected general practices in Nottingham. The consultations comprised contacts with both GPs themselves and those with eye casualty. The survey covered a population of just over 36 000 people and lasted for 1 year. In that time 69 patients presented with cataract, defined as a lens opacity reducing the vision to 6/9 or less. This is equivalent to 1.9 new cases per 1000 population per year. Some cases were of bilateral cataract and so the rate can also be expressed as 2.8 eyes per 1000 population per year. If the definition of cataract were restricted to those lens opacities that reduce visual acuity to 6/18 or less, the rate would be 1.8 eyes per 1000 population per year. The rate of cataract surgery locally was, at that time, about 1.4 eyes per 1000 population, so that cataract surgery was being provided for between 50% and 78% of those who could potentially benefit, depending on where the visual acuity threshold was drawn. Age-specific demand incidence for cataract was as follows: 50–59 years, 0.8 cases per 1000 population; 60–69 years, 3.6; 70–79 years, 8.1; 80+ years, 16.4.

General practitioners are obliged to offer an annual health check to all patients aged 75 years or more, which should include an assessment of vision. The Royal College of General Practitioners has advocated the use of a simple question[134] about visual function, but the details of any vision test are not specified in the GP contract.[135] The value of including a vision test has been assessed in a number of trials and these have been reviewed by Smeeth and Iliffe.[136] They looked for evidence of better visual acuity as a result of screening the vision of elderly people and found no indication of any benefit. This disappointing finding conflicts with the evidence from community surveys that show a high level of treatable vision loss due to cataract and refractive errors.[47,137] It may be that the randomised trials merely show that there is no benefit in discovering vision loss if you then do nothing about it.

About half of all cataract referrals are initiated by an optometrist. Even before the introduction of fees for eye tests, a survey found that a quarter of elderly people had not seen an optometrist in the last 3 years.[138] After the introduction of fees, it was suggested that visits to optometrists dropped by a third.[139] It will be interesting to see what effect the removal of these fees will have for, irrespective of sight-test fees, some elderly people are undoubtedly put off visiting an optometrist by fear of the far greater cost involved in replacing their glasses.[135,138,140,141] Optometrists are an important resource that could be used more to supplement the care offered by ophthalmologists, but while optometrists are seen by the public as business people selling expensive glasses there will be a reluctance by some to take advantage of their services.

The UK has fewer consultant ophthalmologists per head of population than most other developed countries, but just as much eye disease. It is not surprising therefore that people in the UK are operated on later in the progress of their disease and that there are long waiting lists. Since it is unlikely that the number of ophthalmologists within the NHS will grow dramatically, it is important to consider whether some of their non-surgical work could be delegated to other health professionals. Within hospitals this might mean giving greater responsibility to nurses or technicians. Outside of hospitals optometrists offer a potential locally based resource of people already trained in eye care. Optometrists could take on some of the routine aftercare of cataract patients, referring back to the ophthalmologist only those cases that need specialist care.

A model of co-managed care has been reported from the USA in which patients were assessed by an ophthalmologist after surgery and if they had no immediate complications or other pre-existing ocular pathology were discharged to the care of an optometrist.[142] Of 2390 cases, 87% were considered appropriate for co-management, and of these 93% had no complications. Using ophthalmologists as the standard, the optometrists had a sensitivity of 59% and a specificity of over 99% for detecting complications. Unfortunately this was not a randomised trial so it is not possible to compare outcomes between co-managed and ophthalmologist-managed patient groups. Lichter gave an American ophthalmologist's view of this study in which he pointed out many of the methodological limitations of the work and questioned whether the patient had anything to gain from such a system.[143] The situation is not quite the same in the UK, where there are proportionately far fewer ophthalmologists and therefore more potential benefit from reducing their workload. Partly in response to the comments made about the original report, the researchers returned to examine in more detail the 41% of cases with complications that they had originally classified as missed by the optometrist.[144] Detailed review by an ophthalmologist and two optometrists raised questions about the quality of care in only four cases. That is, four out of 2458 cases may not have received adequate care.

It is an open question whether the saved ophthalmologists' time resulting from shared management would translate into more patients being treated and whether this would compensate for any poorer outcomes that might result from less highly qualified aftercare. This is an area full of professional rivalry that might make implementation very difficult, as two essentials of co-management are co-operation and communication. There is, however, a lot of experience from the USA of schemes that have developed good protocols.[145]

6 Effectiveness of services

Day-case surgery

Twenty years ago, a cataract patient would have spent up to 2 weeks as an inpatient. Today, patients are unlikely to spend more than a couple of days in hospital, and in some units a large proportion of cataract patients are treated as day cases – that is, the patient is admitted, treated and discharged on the same day. It has been estimated that this saves about 30% of the cost of treatment. In North Yorkshire in the early 1990s the estimated cost of day-case surgery was £222, compared to £366 for inpatient care.[146] A similar saving was found in a case-series in London.[147]

Both randomised trials[146,148–150] and case-series[119,151–154] have shown that in straightforward cases, day-case surgery is just as safe and effective as inpatient care. The key requirement is to identify which patients can safely be treated as day cases. Since 1985, it has been the norm in the USA for cataract surgery under Medicare to be done as an outpatient procedure. Economic pressures combined with patient preference have meant that about 80% of cataract surgery in the USA is carried out as day cases. European rates are not as high as this, but in several countries they remain higher than those achieved in the UK where, in 1993–94, only 20% of cataract surgery was carried out as day cases. In a few UK districts, the day-case rate approaches 80%, but the overwhelming majority of districts range between 0 and 35%.[3]

The major determinants of suitability for day-case surgery relate to the patient's ability to care for himself or herself in the first few days after the operation. Thus patients with psychiatric or social problems may be better off staying in hospital as, in some cases, may patients who live a long way from the unit. To this list, the Royal College of Ophthalmologist Guidelines[2] add patients with pre-existing pathology, such as uveitis, who need close post-operative supervision, and patients who express a preference for inpatient care.

Cooper has reviewed the development of day-case cataract surgery.[123] Some patients like the security of inpatient care, but the majority would either prefer to go home or are indifferent and happy to accept the advice of the consultant.[155] It is important that time is spent explaining to patients how they should care for themselves after surgery so that they feel confident and can avoid harm. If day-case surgery were portrayed to the patient as the norm, there is no reason to suppose that many would express any concern. In a study in Yorkshire, 11% of patients preferred not to have day-case surgery and a further 6.5% were thought by the consultant to be unsuitable, leading to a potential day-case figure very close to the value of 80% seen in the USA.

Rose et al.[156] have reported a randomised trial looking at the use of trained nurses for the pre-operative assessment of day-case cataract surgery cases. They found the nurses to be as good as and more cost-effective than ophthalmologists. However, the trial was very small and although it supports the increased use of co-management within the hospital setting, larger studies are needed before the evidence can be considered conclusive.

The case for switching the vast majority of cataract surgery to day cases is overwhelming and the change will inevitably take place over the coming years alongside the much wider use of local anaesthesia. Overcoming the resistance of consultants who are used to a combination of general anaesthesia and inpatient care and speeding up the change to day-case surgery is a management problem that should be tackled urgently. The Audit Commission's target of 20% day-case surgery has been achieved, but this target was very conservative.[157] In 1992, the Scottish Health Service Advisory Council recommended a target of 30% by the end of 1993 and 80% by 1997.[158] There is no reason why a target of 80% should not be achieved by every district in the UK, yet a third of hospitals still have day-case rates below 50%.[13] The experience of North Yorkshire in attempting to implement a 60% rate for all elective surgery, including cataract, could serve as a useful model for change.

Local vs. general anaesthesia

A joint working party of the Royal College of Ophthalmologists and the Royal College of Anaesthetists produced guidelines on the use of local anaesthetics (LAs).[159] The guidelines specify that all patients should receive a pre-operative assessment that includes full history, examination, blood pressure measurement and urinalysis, and that most should also get blood tests and electrocardiography (ECG). During the operation, verbal contact should be maintained and the patient should be monitored by pulse oximetry, ECG and blood pressure measurement. Intravenous access should be obtained and an anaesthetist should be present in case resuscitation is required.

To monitor the practice of LAs in ophthalmology, in 1996 the Royal College of Ophthalmologists organised an audit which, for 1 week in September that year, collected information on every eye operation that used a LA and then for 3 months collected information on adverse events.[160,161] Theatre records from validation units were used to check the accuracy of the data provided to the audit and to collect some information on the use of GAs.

When initially contacted for the audit, 71% of ophthalmologists said they preferred LAs for cataract surgery and 29% preferred GAs. The proportion who preferred LAs was lower, at 59%, in consultants with 20 or more years' experience. In the audit itself, LAs were used in 87% of PE surgery and 67% of conventional ECCE. PE was the most common type of cataract surgery in this audit and the overall rate of LA use was 80%.

The audit has demonstrated a marked shift in the use of local anaesthesia. In 1984, 63% of ophthalmologists only ever used GAs for cataract surgery. In 1991, 37% said that they used GAs for more than 75% of their cataract surgery. The audit suggests that the rate of GA use has continued to drop.

The audit shows that the joint College guidelines are not being followed completely. For instance, although 96% of patients were monitored during surgery, only 35% had all three forms of monitoring recommended in the guidelines. However, severe systemic adverse events were very rare (0.034% of operations), and occurred with all forms of LA.

PE vs. ECCE

There is no convincing evidence of a difference in visual outcome between PE and ECCE. Because the majority of the studies included in Powe *et al.*'s meta-analysis[162] were American, and by 1991 PE was already popular in the USA, that meta-analysis was able to compare the visual outcome from ECCE and PE. They found no significant difference despite the very large overall sample size. However, the studies included were not randomised trials and it is likely that the PE studies were more recent, so the comparison must be treated with caution. The opportunity for a definitive randomised trial is probably now gone because PE has already become so widely used. A Medical Research Council trial is under way in the UK, but it is relatively small and unlikely to influence practice.

The rationale behind the use of PE is that the smaller incision might lead to fewer complications and faster rehabilitation. The American guidelines[4] reviewed the literature and concluded that although the possible benefits are 'intuitively appealing', there is no definitive evidence to support them.

Complications of surgery

According to the first UK National Cataract Audit, 7% of patients have some complication during surgery, 22% experience some complication in the immediate post-operative period and 20% have some complication at 3 months, including 6% who already have posterior capsular thickening. The rates tended to be higher in patients with some pre-existing ocular pathology.[6]

A literature review of 90 (mostly US) studies covering the period 1979–91 gives pooled complication rates based on data for over 68 000 eyes.[162] However, few if any of these studies are representative of a general population in the way that the UK audit attempts to be and, as such, they may underestimate some of the complication rates. A comparison of the pooled rates with those from the UK audit is given in Table 7.

Table 7: Complication rates associated with cataract surgery, at 3 months for the UK audit and at an average of about 1 year for the meta-analysis.

	First UK National Cataract Audit[6]	Meta-analysis[162]
Peri-operative		
Capsule rupture	3.9%	3.1%
Vitreous loss	1.1%	0.8%
Early post-operative		
Corneal oedema	9.6%	–
Raised intra-ocular pressure	5.3%	–
Endophthalmitis	0.1%	0.13%
Late post-operative		
Cystoid macular oedema	1.2%	1.4%
Retinal detachment	0.1%	0.7%
Dislocation of IOL	0.3%	1.1%
Raised intra-ocular pressure	2.3%	1.4%
Uveitis	1.1%	1.8%
Posterior capsular opacification	6.3%	19.7%

Costs and cost-effectiveness

Studies that purport to compare the benefits of different medical procedures should be treated with extreme caution. In comparing, say, cataract surgery with hip replacement, a measure must be placed on the comparative benefits of good vision and improved mobility, and the result will depend critically on the assumptions that are made. Only clear-cut differences that are robust to changes in the assumptions can be relied on. One attempt to perform such an economic analysis[163] found that, under their assumptions, cataract surgery costs around £500 (at 1983 prices) for every quality-adjusted life year saved. This figure compares favourably with the cost per quality-adjusted life year given for other procedures, such as £750 for hip replacement or £3000 for a kidney transplant. Although this is far from an exact science, cataract surgery comes out well from such economic comparisons.

The impact of economic analyses that seek to compare the treatment of different conditions is limited because health care workers appreciate the strong dependence of the conclusions on subjective prior assumptions.

7 Models of care

Criteria for referral to an ophthalmologist

The referral process is an integral part of health service organisation and, as such, it is difficult to generalise to the UK research that is based on referral processes in other countries where the organisation of health care is different. Such research can at best give pointers to possible approaches, the effectiveness of which would need to be confirmed within the NHS.

Although the process whereby a patient is first seen by an ophthalmologist is vital to the provision of effective care, it has received very little attention from researchers. Cataract referrals are initiated either when a patient notices a deterioration in their vision, or when a problem is detected during a health check. The relative importance of the two routes has not been measured. Improvement in patient-initiated referral is partly a matter of education, so that the public understands the nature of cataract and that it is treatable, and partly a matter of attitude change, so that poorer vision is not accepted as an inevitable consequence of old age. These patient-related factors would also act to improve health service-initiated referral by encouraging attendance for regular eye checks.

Ideally, primary care workers should be able to check a patient's visual acuity and confirm the presence of lens opacities which might be affecting vision. Optometrists, but not all GPs, have the facilities to measure visual acuity accurately at the standard distance of six metres with good lighting. The hospital ophthalmic services are not equipped to cope with a lot of false referrals for cataract and so it is preferable that preliminary checks and first discussions about the advisability of surgery take place in primary care, although final consideration of a patient's suitability for surgery must, of course, remain with the ophthalmologist. Questions of the type used in VF-14 (*see* Table 9) are suitable for use in primary care, as they identify functional vision loss without the need for any special equipment or specialised knowledge. They could, for instance, be incorporated in routine health checks by a practice nurse.

Informal discussion of the need for cataract surgery based on the patient's perception of the importance of their own vision loss would appear to be the best way of deciding whether someone should be referred to an ophthalmologist. However, in a health care system where the patient is not paying directly for the treatment, it is important that they have some idea of when they have a right to surgery. In Sweden, patients were told that they could expect treatment within 3 months if they had a visual acuity of 6/12 or worse due to cataract.[114,115] An alternative approach adopted in New Zealand[164] was to prioritise all patients who want surgery based on reasonably objective criteria. The latter approach may not offer such a good service, but has the advantage of rationing care in a way that can be seen to be fair. In both the informal and more formal systems, control of access to care is concentrated with the ophthalmologist and there has not been any systematic attempt to co-ordinate the criteria used for initial referral with those used for surgery. Similarly there has been no research on the impact that changing the criteria for either referral or surgery would have on the other.

Criteria for first-eye surgery

According to the Guidelines for Cataract Surgery issued by the Royal College of Ophthalmologists in 1995,[2] cataract extraction is justified when the cataract interferes with visual function and the surgeon expects improvement from surgery, or when it will facilitate examination of lesions affecting the posterior segment, or to avoid lens-induced disease. The US guidelines[4] acknowledge similar reasons but try to be a little more objective, differentiating between people with poor visual acuity, defined as 20/50 (6/15) or worse, those with good visual acuity, defined as better than 20/40 (6/12), and those in between with moderate vision. They stress the importance of educating the patient about the likely risks and benefits of surgery. The likely benefits are clearly less for patients with a visual acuity better than 20/40. At 20/40 they consider that surgery is justified if the patient complains of other visual problems, such as glare, or if the vision loss is interfering with the patient's lifestyle.

Neither the UK[2] nor the US[4] guidelines are based on research evidence but rather they reflect the expert opinion of experienced ophthalmologists. Research into objective criteria for cataract surgery is urgently needed, for without them the measurement of need remains highly subjective. Currently, patients do not know when they have a right to expect treatment and commissioners cannot be sure whether the service is meeting the needs of the community. This issue will become more important in the UK when the level of provision approaches that being offered in other industrialised countries. At present it is probably sufficient to know that there is a pool of unmet need, even if it cannot be quantified.

An interesting attempt to study criteria for surgery was made in the Northern Region.[165] Semi-structured interviews were given to consultant ophthalmologists from that region and, as with the US guidelines, led to the conclusion that visual acuity can be usefully categorised as good (defined as 6/9 or better), moderate (6/12 or 6/18), or poor (6/24 or worse). They identified the patient's ability to manage with their current vision, coexisting eye disease, general patient health, patient attitude to surgery and the degree of conservatism of the consultant as important in deciding whether or not to operate. The availability of theatres or beds was not seen as important, but consultant time needed for outpatient follow-up was. Limiting the numbers offered surgery was seen as a way of managing personal workload. Two consultants said that they might list someone early when the waiting list was long, in anticipation of the patient needing surgery by the time they were offered it. The consultants described the moderate visual acuity category as the typical level for advising listing. However, an examination of case notes found that three-quarters of first eyes fell into the poor category at listing.

As part of the health reforms introduced in New Zealand in 1992, a committee was formed to advise the minister on priorities and criteria for elective surgery.[164] The first topic that they considered was cataract extraction. A Delphi process was used to allocate scores to particular patient characteristics that were thought to be related to the need for cataract surgery. Using the results of this investigation they devised a system whereby a patient's priority is judged by summing their score for visual acuity, glare, ocular comorbidity, ability to work, visual function and other disabilities. The weights allocated are shown in Table 8.

The factors chosen, the weights allocated and the very idea of adding together numerical scores can all be criticised,[166] but the basic idea of attempting to define a person's need in an objective way is important, for without such an agreed definition any attempt at needs assessment is futile.

It has been suggested that methods based on a patient's reported visual problems will be open to manipulation by patients who exaggerate their difficulties in order to obtain earlier surgery.[167] This is undoubtedly a real problem, but at its heart is the view that the role of the provider is to police a system of rationing rather than to work with the patient to define the point when surgery would best suit them.

Table 8: New Zealand priority criteria for cataract surgery adjusted from Hadorn et al.[164]

Visual acuity	6/9+	6/12	6/18	6/24	6/36	6/60	CF*
6/9+	0	1	2	3	4	5	6
6/12		7	8	9	10	11	12
6/18			14	15	16	171	18
6/24				21	22	23	24
6/36					28	29	39
6/60						35	36
CF*							40
1 Glare							
None							0
Mild–moderate							5
Severe							10
2 Ocular comorbidity							
None							0
Mild–moderate							5
Severe							10
3 Ability to work or care for dependants							
Not threatened/not applicable							0
Not threatened but more difficult							2
Threatened but not immediately							6
Immediately threatened							15
4 Extent of impairment							
None							0
Mild							5
Moderate							10
Severe							20
5 Other substantial disabilities							
No							0
Yes							5

* CF, count fingers or worse.

Second-eye surgery

People with one eye are at very little disadvantage in their everyday life. Consequently it has been suggested that once the cataractous lens has been removed from the first eye and vision has been successfully restored, there is little advantage in operating on the second eye. Certainly such a policy would offer a great cost saving. The first UK National Cataract Audit[5–7] found that about one-third of all surgery was to the second eye and the second UK audit found a similar result of 35%.[124] In America, two insurers separately proposed imposing severe restrictions on second-eye surgery, although these proposals were subsequently withdrawn.

Both the UK[2] and US[4] guidelines for cataract surgery conclude that the criteria for second-eye surgery should be broadly the same as those for the first eye, even though the evidence for this conclusion was weak. Second-eye surgery should, in theory, improve visual acuity, stereopsis and the field of vision, but it is an open question whether this will translate into marked functional gain. Javitt et al.[168] compared patients undergoing first-eye, second-eye and bilateral surgery using a short questionnaire on visual function. They found a similar improvement in subjective visual function from second-eye surgery as was obtained from first-eye surgery, despite starting from a higher baseline. A subsequent report[169] found greater improvement from bilateral surgery compared to unilateral surgery as measured by VF-14 and subjective reports of trouble with vision and satisfaction with vision. Similar results were found in a UK study[170] and a Spanish study.[171]

In Bristol, a randomised trial was used to measure the short-term effects of second-eye surgery.[172] In the trial, one group was given immediate surgery, while the control group went on to the normal waiting list. At 6 months, when one group had had surgery and the other had not, they found little difference in binocular visual acuity but clear benefits in terms of stereoacuity and self-reported visual problems that impact directly on quality of life.

The balance of evidence is that there is an improvement in the patient's subjective assessment of their vision from second-eye surgery, although the gain may be a little smaller than that obtained from first-eye surgery. Whether this translates into any improved functional ability is less clear. The question of the justification of second-eye surgery depends on the view that is taken about the purpose of the health service. Should it try to maximise individual health or merely seek to maintain a minimum standard? The consensus among UK eye-care workers remains strongly in favour of second-eye surgery.

Developing a local policy

Waiting-list length and waiting times receive a lot of attention in the press and are politically sensitive, but they are susceptible to alteration by short-term measures and they do not give a true indication of the extent of unmet need. A better guide is the fact that, at surgery, UK patients tend to be older and have worse vision than in many other developed countries. This would suggest that in the short term, any increase in resources will merely encourage more and earlier referrals. Unless some attempt is made to control the level of visual disability at which cataract surgery is to be offered, it is likely that demand will grow to soak up the extra resources. Any reasonable attempt to define the level of visual disability which requires cataract surgery would almost certainly result in a sudden increase in demand. Short-term policies aimed at controlling waiting lists must be introduced along with long-term plans which acknowledge that the level of cataract surgery is likely to continue to grow steadily as the population ages and, more importantly, as patients demand earlier surgery.

One way to release resources to meet this anticipated growth in demand is to move towards cheaper but equally effective forms of treatment. Day-case surgery is thought to be about 30% cheaper than inpatient care and suitable for 80% of patients. Transition from an average of 20% day-case care to the realistic target of 80% day-case care would save over 20% of the cataract budget or, alternatively, allow the number of patients treated to increase by over 25% without extra resources. Whether the use of optometrists to manage patients after surgery would offer a saving has not been established, although it would go some small way to freeing up the time of ophthalmologists, enabling them to concentrate on surgery and the care of non-routine cases.

8 Research priorities

The overall quality of surgery and the treatment of complications are probably as good in the UK as they are anywhere in the world. The problems for the NHS are how to ensure that good standards are maintained equally throughout the service, and how to ensure that this high-quality service reaches everyone who needs it within a reasonable length of time. The need for cataract surgery is, in the final reckoning, a matter for the patient, as it depends on their personal visual requirements and the extent to which they feel visually disabled by their cataract. The NHS, however, effectively rations the number of cataract operations that can be performed by controlling the number of ophthalmologists, the amount of theatre time and the budget available. It is not surprising that this leads to delays in listing for surgery and long waiting times. The existence of a small parallel system of private health creates a way of avoiding NHS delays for people who can afford it and is also a source of extra income to many NHS ophthalmologists. As such, private care reduces the pressure on the NHS to improve.

The key research issue for cataract care in the UK is how to structure the service to maximise the number of patients treated. This must mean even more day-case surgery, perhaps with some aftercare provided by optometrists. In all likelihood, a more efficient cataract service would find more work to do, since the freeing of resources would just lead to a broader definition of need. The more logical route of defining need and then planning services to meet that definition is unlikely to be practical, because any reasonable definition would require too great an expansion of services, as can be seen by comparing surgery rates in the UK with those in other developed countries.

Research effort should attack the problem from both directions, by seeking to define need and by looking for greater efficiency. Useful approaches to the definition of need might be to survey ophthalmologists to discover the criteria they would ideally use when deciding whether to offer surgery. Alternatively, it would be interesting to study the stage of disease at which private patients choose to have surgery. It might reasonably be argued that this represents the target at which the NHS should aim.

Day-case surgery has been shown to work effectively in many hospitals and needs to be extended rather than investigated. Co-management is a much less clear issue and although it has operated successfully in other parts of the world, a large multi-centre trial of optometrist aftercare in the UK would seem to be justified.

Major changes in the monitoring and auditing of the care provided by the NHS are already under way and there might well be a role for a cataract register of the type that has been introduced in Sweden. A register is not something that should be introduced lightly for it would involve a considerable amount of work and might just result in increased monitoring without improved care.[173] A requirement is being introduced for trusts to supply information on the quality of care they provide. This will mean that much of the information needed for such a register will be collected by each trust and a cataract register could provide a vehicle for the standardisation of that collection and the pooling of results. A respected body such as the Royal College of Ophthalmologists might be funded to take responsibility for collating the information, especially if the data were sent electronically from trusts. A register would be very valuable in showing trusts how they are performing in relation to others. It would also be helpful for monitoring the effectiveness of future interventions, particularly those that relate to the organisation of care.

Much can be learned from international comparisons, especially when outcome is related to the organisation of services. Although it is sufficient to audit medical outcomes within the UK, aspects of coverage and the timing of surgery would be better studied on a Europe-wide basis so that there would be variation in the organisation of services. Information on the relative performance of health services in other parts of the European Union might help target setting within the NHS.

9 Outcome measures and audit

Powe *et al.* have published a systematic meta-analysis of mostly American studies published between 1979 and 1991, which reported the visual outcome of cataract surgery.[162] They found that 90% of eyes achieved 20/40 (6/12) or better visual acuity and that this figure rose to 95% when eyes with pre-operative comorbidity were excluded.

The first national audit of cataract surgery in the UK detailed the visual outcome of 959 patients treated in a single week in 1990. The usual surgical technique at that time was ECCE. The audit found that overall, 80% of patients achieved 6/12 or better at 3 months after surgery and that this figure rose to 90% in the 537 patients who had no ocular comorbidity. The higher figures from the meta-analysis may just reflect the fact that published case-series are frequently not generalisable to all patients because they tend to be collected by specialists. An international study covering the USA, Canada, Denmark and Spain found no international differences in final visual acuity after adjustment was made for the pre-operative visual acuity and the characteristics of the patient, despite there being considerable differences in methods of surgery between countries.[9]

Fewer studies have reported on measures of outcome from cataract surgery other than visual acuity, although research in this area is increasing. In the USA, Magione et al. used the Activities of Daily Vision Scale (ADVS) and SF-36 measure of health-related quality of life to assess the benefit of cataract extraction in 464 patients.[174] As these scores are compiled from answers to a questionnaire, it is difficult to interpret changes, but one way is to compare the average change with the standard deviation of baseline scores; this is known as the treatment effect size. The results of Magione et al. show a treatment effect of about 0.75 for ADVS at 12 months after surgery, regardless of whether the surgery was to the first eye, the second eye or bilateral.[174] Despite this, health-related quality of life showed a transient improvement at 3 months, but then declined. Unfortunately, there was no control group to show the expected decline in SF-36 over a year in people of this age. The decline was most marked in those patients whose ADVS did not improve after surgery.

Steinberg et al. compared various measures of visual function pre- and post-operatively in 552 first-eye cataract patients.[175] VF-14, a questionnaire measure of visual impairment, improved with a treatment effect of about 1, and 85% of patients reported an improvement in their satisfaction with their own vision. VF-14 is a simple tool for measuring visual function that has been shown to be reliable, valid and sensitive to change. It has been translated from the original US version and used in Canada, Denmark and Spain with comparable results.[176] The questionnaire asks about difficulties due to vision when wearing glasses with each of the 14 activities set out in Table 9. The possible replies are no difficulty (4), a little (3), moderate (2), a great deal (1), or unable (0). The average score over the 14 questions is then multiplied by 25 to get a score out of 100. Any items that are not applicable are excluded from the average. The translated

Table 9: Activities included in the VF-14 scale.

1 Reading small print such as labels on medicine bottles, a telephone book, food labels
2 Reading a newspaper or a book
3 Reading a large-print book or large-print newspaper or numbers on a telephone
4 Recognising people when they are close to you
5 Seeing step, stairs or curbs
6 Reading traffic signs, street signs, store signs
7 Doing fine handwork like sewing, knitting, crocheting or carpentry
8 Writing cheques or filling out forms
9 Playing games such as bingo, dominoes, card games or mah jong
10 Taking part in sports like bowling, handball, tennis, golf
11 Cooking
12 Watching television
13 Driving during the day
14 Driving at night

versions made minor alterations, such as adding crossword puzzles to question 9 and changing the sports in question 10.

Numerous alternatives to VF-14 have been proposed, each using slightly different questions to try to assess functional visual problems. There is no evidence that any of these questionnaires is any better than the others. There is a temptation to design new questionnaires linked to specific study requirements, but the small benefits that might result are likely to be outweighed by the work involved in pre-testing and the lack of comparability with other studies.

The Working Group on Outcome Indicators for Cataract[177] reported to the Department of Health in 1997. They suggested four measures for routine use and a further ten that should be recorded whenever local circumstances allow. These indicators are listed in Table 10. Other indicators were suggested for use in periodic surveys. The majority of the suggested indicators relate to surgery and its outcome, but a few, included under the heading 'to be developed further', extend to include the referral process. In particular, they suggest collection of the rate of referrals to a consultant ophthalmologist per 1000 GPs and the rate of referral to a GP per 1000 NHS eye tests.

Table 10: Cataract outcome indicators for routine use.[177]

Basic set of measures
    Cataract extractions rate per 10,000 population
    Time spent on the waiting list for elective surgery
    Capsulotomy rate per 1,000 cataract extractions at 1 year
    Capsulotomy rate per 1,000 cataract extractions at 5 years

Desirable wherever possible
    Waiting time between GP referral and outpatient appointment
    Visual acuity at referral to a hospital ophthalmologist
    Visual acuity assessed pre-operatively
    Rate of post-operative complications detected before discharge
    Rate of post-operative complications detected between discharge and first outpatient appointment
    Rate of post-operative complications detected between first outpatient appointment and 4 months after surgery
    Readmission rate for care of the operated eye within 30 days of cataract surgery
    Visual acuity at 1 week post operation
    Visual acuity at 4 months post operation
    Difference in visual acuity between the pre-operative and 4-month measurements

Outcome measures play a key role in the development of a good health service, for in general no service should be commissioned without specification of standards that are to be achieved. Although the recommendations of the working group are naturally oriented towards surgery, there is scope for extending these ideas into primary care even if at present the infrastructure for data collection does not exist. If optometrists, for instance, are to be commissioned to contribute to routine post-operative care, then a way must be found for them to supply information on the quality of their performance.

Process measures also have a role in assessing quality of care. Features such as the time spent waiting to be seen in an outpatient clinic, the time spent discussing the need for surgery and the grade of the ophthalmologist are all important indicators of a well-run service.

One obvious danger of an over-reliance on a few indicators is that they may become targets for manipulation. For instance, if limits are placed on the time between listing for surgery and the operation itself, there will be a temptation to delay listing for surgery. For this reason, outcome measures need to cover the whole patient experience and be kept under constant review.

References

1 Williams M, Frankel S, Nanchahal K, Coast J, Donovan J. Cataract surgery. In: Stevens A, Raftery J (eds). *Health Care Needs Assessment.* Oxford: Radcliffe Medical Press, 1994.

2 Royal College of Ophthalmologists. *Guidelines for Cataract Surgery.* London: Royal College of Ophthalmologists, 1995.

3 Nuffield Institute for Health and NHS Centre for Reviews and Dissemination. *Effective Health Care: management of cataract.* Edinburgh: Churchill Livingstone, 1996.

4 US Department of Health and Human Services. *Clinical Practice Guideline Number 4. Cataract in adults: management of functional impairment.* Rockville: AHCPR, 1993.

5 Courtney P. The National Cataract Surgery Survey. I. Method and descriptive features. *Eye* 1992; **6**: 487–92.

6 Desai P. The National Cataract Surgery Survey. II. Clinical outcomes. *Eye* 1993; **7**: 489–94.

7 Desai P. The National Cataract Surgery Survey. III. Process features. *Eye* 1993; **7**: 667–71.

8 Desai P, Reidy A, Minassian D. Profile of patients presenting for cataract surgery in the UK: national data collection. *Br J Ophthalmol* 1999; **83**: 893–6.

9 Norregaard J, Hindsberger C, Alonso J *et al.* Visual outcomes of cataract surgery in the United States, Canada, Denmark and Spain. *Arch Ophthalmol* 1998; **116**: 1095–100.

10 Ninn-Petersen K. Cataract patients in a defined Swedish population 1986–1990. *Acta Ophthalmol Scand* 1997; **75** (Suppl. 221).

11 McPherson K, Strong P, Epstein A, Jones L. Regional variations in the use of common surgical procedures: with and between England and Wales, Canada and the United States of America. *Soc Sci Med* 1981; **15A**: 273–88.

12 Goldzweig C, Mittman B, Carter G *et al.* Variations in cataract extraction rates in Medicare prepaid and fee-for-service settings. *JAMA* 1997; **277**: 1765–8.

13 NHS Executive. *Action on Cataracts. Good practice guidance.* London: Department of Health, 2000.

14 Shun-Shin G. Anatomy of the lens. In: Easty D, Sparrow J (eds). *The Oxford Textbook of Ophthalmology.* Oxford: Oxford University Press, 1999, pp. 453–6.

15 Sparrow J, Frost A. Physical aspects of lens clarity and image degradation. In: Easty D, Sparrow J (eds). *The Oxford Textbook of Ophthalmology.* Oxford: Oxford University Press, 1999, pp. 463–5.

16 Klein B, Klein R, Linton K, Magki Y, Neider M. Assessment of cataract from photographs in the Beaver Dam Eye Study. *Ophthalmology* 1990; **97**: 1428–33.

17 West S, Rosenthal F, Newland H, Taylor H. Use of photographic techniques to grade nuclear cataracts. *Invest Ophthalmol Vis Sci* 1988; **29**: 73–7.

18 Chylack L, Wolfe J, Singer D *et al.* The lens opacities classification system III. *Arch Ophthalmol* 1993; **111**: 831–6.

19 Sparrow J, Brown N, Shun-shin G, Bron A. The Oxford modular cataract image system. *Eye* 1990; **4**: 638–48.

20 Vivino M, Mahurkar A, Trus B, Lopez M, Datiles M. Quantitative analysis of retroillumination images. *Eye* 1995; **9**: 77–84.

21 Vivino M, Chintalagiri S, Trus B, Datiles M. Development of a Scheimpflug slit lamp camera system for quantitative densitometric analysis. *Eye* 1993; **7**: 791–8.

22 Lambert S, Drack A. Infantile cataract. *Surv Ophthalmol* 1996; **40**: 427–58.

23 Lloyd I, Goss-Sampson M, Jeffrey B *et al.* Neonatal cataract: aetiology, pathogenesis and management. *Eye* 1992; **6**: 184–96.

24 Elston J, Timms C. Clinical evidence for the onset of the critical period in infancy. *Br J Ophthalmol* 1992; **76**: 327–8.

25 Jain I, Pillay P, Gangwar D *et al.* Congenital cataract etiology and morphology. *J Pediatr Ophthalmol Strabismus* 1983; **20**: 238–46.

26 Weale R. Ageing changes in the lens. In: Easty D, Sparrow J (eds). *The Oxford Textbook of Ophthalmology.* Oxford: Oxford University Press, 1999, pp. 465–9.

27 Stewart-Brown S, Haslum M. Partial sight and blindness in children of the 1970 birth cohort at 10 years of age. *J Epidemiol Community Health* 1988; **42**: 17–23.

28 Stayte M, Reeves B, Wortham C. Ocular and vision defects in preschool children. *Br J Ophthalmol* 1993; **77**: 228–32.

29 Office of National Statistics. *Birth Statistics 1996.* London: The Stationery Office, 1998.

30 Kohler L, Stigmar G. Vision screening of four-year-old children. *Acta Paediatr Scand* 1973; **62**: 17–27.

31 James L, McClearon A, Walters G. Congenital malformations surveillance data for birth defects prevention. *Teratology* 1993; **48**: 545–709.

32 Edmonds L, Layde P, James L *et al.* Congenital malformation surveillance: two American systems. *Int J Epidemiol* 1981; **10**: 247–52.

33 Apple D, Solomon K, Tetz M *et al.* Posterior capsule opacification. *Surv Ophthalmol* 1992; **37**: 73–116.

34 Markham R, Bloom P, Chandra A, Newcomb E. Results of intraocular lens implantation in pediatric aphakia. *Eye* 1992; **6**: 493–8.

35 Keech R, Tongue A, Scott W. Complications after surgery for congenital and infantile cataracts. *Am J Ophthalmol* 1989; **108**: 136–41.

36 Mills M, Robb R. Glaucoma following childhood cataract surgery. *J Pediatr Ophthalmol Strabismus* 1994; **31**: 355–60.

37 Simon J, Mehta N, Simmons S *et al.* Glaucoma after pediatric lensectomy/vitrectomy. *Ophthalmology* 1991; **98**: 670–4.

38 Kanski J, Elkington A, Daniel R. Retinal detachment after congenital cataract surgery. *Br J Ophthalmol* 1974; **58**: 92–5.

39 Toyofuku H, Hirose T, Scheoens C. Retinal detachment following congenital cataract surgery. *Arch Ophthalmol* 1980; **98**: 669–75.

40 France T, Frank J. The association of strabismus and aphakia in children. *J Pediatr Ophthalmol Strabismus* 1984; **21**: 223–6.

41 Lewis T, Maurer D, Brent H. Development of grating acuity in children treated for unilateral or bilateral congenital cataract. *Invest Ophthalmol Vis Sci* 1995; **36**: 2080–95.

42 Birch E, Stager D. Prevalence of good visual acuity following surgery for congenital unilateral cataract. *Arch Ophthalmol* 1988; **106**: 40–2.

43 Bradford G, Keech R, Scott W. Factors affecting visual outcome after surgery for bilateral congenital cataracts. *Am J Ophthalmol* 1994; **117**: 58–64.

44 Klein B, Klein R, Linton K. Prevalence of age-related lens opacities in a population: the Beaver Dam Eye Study. *Ophthalmology* 1992; **99**: 546–52.

45 Mitchell P, Cumming R, Attebo K, Panchapakesan J. Prevalence of cataract in Australia: the Blue Mountains Eye Study. *Ophthalmology* 1997; **104**: 581–8.

46 Gibson J, Rosenthal A, Lavery J. A study of the prevalence of eye disease in the elderly in an English community. *Trans Ophthalmol Soc UK* 1984; **104**: 196–203.

47 Wormald R, Wright L, Courtney P, Beaumont B, Haines A. Visual problems in the elderly population and implications for services. *BMJ* 1992; **304**: 1226–9.

48 Kahn H, Leibowitz H, Ganley J *et al.* The Framingham Eye Study. I. Outline and major prevalence findings. *Am J Epidemiol* 1977; **106**: 17–32.

49 Kahn H, Leibowitz H, Ganley J *et al.* The Framingham Eye Study. II. Association of ophthalmic pathology with single variables previously measured in the Framingham Heart Study. *Am J Epidemiol* 1977; **106**: 33–41.

50 Deane J, Hall A, Thompson J, Rosenthal A. Prevalence of lenticular abnormalities in a population-based study: Oxford clinical cataract grading in the Melton Eye Study. *Ophthalmic Epidemiol* 1997; **4**: 195–206.

51 Office of Population Censuses and Surveys. *1991 Census General Report: Great Britain.* London: HMSO, 1995.

52 Das B, Thompson J, Patel R, Rosenthal A. The prevalence of age-related cataract in the Asian community in Leicester: a community-based study. *Eye* 1990; **4**: 723–6.

53 Das B, Thompson J, Patel R, Rosenthal A. The prevalence of eye disease in Leicester: a comparison of adults of Asian and European descent. *J R Soc Med* 1994; **87**: 219–22.

54 Tielsch J, Somer A, Witt K, Katz J, Royall R. Blindness and visual impairment in an American Urban population. *Arch Ophthalmol* 1990; **108**: 286–90.

55 Leske M, Connell A, Wu S, Hyman L, Schachat A. Prevalence of lens opacities in the Barbados Eye Study. *Arch Ophthalmol* 1997; **115**: 105–11.

56 Leske M. The epidemiology of open-angle glaucoma: a review. *Am J Epidemiol* 1983; **118**: 166–91.

57 Rauf A, Ong P, Pearson R, Wormald R. A pilot study into the prevalence of ophthalmic disease in the Indian population of Southall. *J R Soc Med* 1994; **87**: 78–9.

58 Gray P. The prevalence of eye disease in elderly Bengalis in Tower Hamlets. *J R Soc Med* 1996; **89**: 23–6.

59 Thompson J. The demand incidence of cataract in Asian immigrants to Britain and their descendants. *Br J Ophthalmol* 1989; **73**: 950–4.

60 Klein B, Klein R, Moss S. Incident cataract surgery: the Beaver Dam Eye Study. *Ophthalmology* 1997; **104**(4): 573–80.

61 Podgor M, Leske C, Ederer F. Incidence estimates for lens changes, macular changes, open-angle glaucoma and diabetic retinopathy. *Am J Epidemiol* 1983; **118**: 206–12.

62 The Italian-American Cataract Study Group. Incidence and prevalence of cortical, nuclear and posterior subcapsular cataracts. *Am J Ophthalmol* 1994; **118**: 623–31.

63 Leske M, Chylack L, He Q *et al.* Incidence and progression of nuclear opacities in the longitudinal study of cataract. *Ophthalmology* 1996; **103**: 705–12.

64 Leske M, Chylack L, He Q *et al.* Incidence and progression of cortical and posterior subcapsular opacities. *Ophthalmology* 1997; **104**: 1987–93.

65 Coombes A, Seward H. Posterior capsular opacification prevention: IOL, lens design and material. *Br J Ophthalmol* 1999; **83**: 640–1.

66 Schaumberg D, Dana M, Christen W, Glynn R. A systematic overview of the incidence of posterior capsular opacification. *Ophthalmology* 1998; **105**: 1213–21.

67 Leske M, Sperduto R. The epidemiology of senile cataracts: a review. *Am J Epidemiol* 1983; **118**: 152–65.

68 Harding J. *Cataract: biochemistry, epidemiology and pharmacology.* London: Chapman and Hall, 1991.

69 Young R. *Age-Related Cataract.* New York: Oxford University Press, 1991.

70 Hodge W, Whitcher J, Satariano W. Risk factors for age-related cataracts. *Epidemiol Rev* 1995; **17**: 336–46.

71 West S, Valmadrid C. Epidemiology of risk factors for age-related cataract. *Surv Ophthalmol* 1995; **39**: 323–34.

72 West S. Age-related cataract – epidemiology and risk factors. In: Easty D, Sparrow J (eds). *The Oxford Textbook of Ophthalmology.* Oxford: Oxford University Press, 1999, pp. 469–74.

73 Hillier R, Giacometti L, Yuen K. Sunlight and cataract: an epidemiologic investigation. *Am J Epidemiol* 1977; **105**: 450–9.

74 Hillier R, Sperduto R, Ederer F. Epidemiologic associations with nuclear, cortical and posterior subcapsular cataracts. *Am J Epidemiol* 1986; **124**: 916–25.

75 Wen-shu M, Tian-sheng H. An epidemiological survey of senile cataract in China. *Chin Med J* 1982; **95**: 813–18.

76 Taylor H, West S, Rosenthal F *et al.* Effect of ultraviolet radiation on cataract formation. *NEJM* 1988; **319**: 1429–33.

77 Rosenthal F, Bakalian A, Taylor H. The effect of prescription eyewear on ocular exposure to ultraviolet radiation. *Am J Public Health* 1986; **76**: 1216–22.

78 Brown N, Harris M, Shun-shin G, Vrensen G, Willekens B, Bron A. Is cortical spoke cataract due to fibre breaks? The relationship between fibre folds, fibre breaks, waterclefts and spoke cataract. *Eye* 1993; **7**: 672–9.

79 Schein O, West S, Munoz B. Cortical lenticular opacification distribution and location in a longitudinal study. *Invest Ophthalmol Vis Sci* 1994; **35**: 363–6.

80 Taylor A, Jacques P, Epstein E. Relations among aging, antioxidant status and cataract. *Am J Nutr* 1995; **62** (Suppl.): 11439–47.

81 Taylor A, Jacques P, Nadler D *et al.* Relationship in humans between ascorbic acid consumption and levels of total ascorbic acid in the lens, aqueous humor and plasma. *Curr Eye Res* 1991; **10**: 751–9.

82 Jacques P, Taylor A. Long-term vitamin C supplementation and prevalence of early age-related lens opacities. *Am J Nutr* 1997; **66**: 911–16.

83 Leske M, Chylack L, He Q *et al.* Antioxidant vitamins and nuclear cataract. The longitudinal study of cataract. *Ophthalmology* 1998; **105**: 831–6.

84 Sperduto R, Hu T-S, Milton R *et al.* The Linxian cataract studies: two nutrition invention trials. *Arch Ophthalmol* 1993; **111**: 1246–353.

85 Teikari J, Virtamo J, Rautalahti M, Palmgren J, Liesto K, Heinonen O. Long-term supplementation with alpha-tocopherol and beta-carotene and age-related cataract. *Acta Ophthalmol Scand* 1997; **75**: 634–40.

86 Leske M, Chylack L, Wu S *et al.* The Lens Opacities Case–Control Study. Risk factors for cataract. *Arch Ophthalmol* 1991; **109**: 244–51.

87 West S, Munoz B, Emmett E, Taylor H. Cigarette smoking and risk of nuclear cataracts. *Arch Ophthalmol* 1989; **107**: 1166–9.

88 Klein B, Klein R, Linton K, Franke T. Cigarette smoking and lens opacities: the Beaver Dam Eye Study. *Am J Prev Med* 1993; **9**: 27–30.

89 Hillier R, Sperduto R, Podgor M *et al.* Cigarette smoking and the risk of development of lens opacities: the Framingham studies. *Arch Ophthalmol* 1997; **115**: 1113–18.

90 West S, Munoz B, Newland E, Emmett E, Taylor H. Lack of evidence for aspirin use and prevention of cataract. *Arch Ophthalmol* 1987; **105**: 1229–31.

91 Harding J, van Heyningen R. Drugs, including alcohol, that act as risk factors for cataract, and possible protection against cataract by aspirin-like analgesics and cyclopenthiazide. *Br J Ophthalmol* 1988; **72**: 809–14.

92 Munoz B, Tajchman U, Bochow T, West S. Alcohol use and risk of posterior subcapsular opacities. *Arch Ophthalmol* 1993; **111**: 110–12.

93 Ritter L, Klein B, Klein R, Mares-Perlman J. Alcohol use and lens opacities in the Beaver Dam Eye Study. *Arch Ophthalmol* 1993; **111**: 113–17.

94 Cumming R, Mitchell P. Alcohol, smoking and cataracts. The Blue Mountain Study. *Arch Ophthalmol* 1997; **115**: 1296–303.

95 Schwab I, Armstrong M, Friedman G, Wong I, Carpenterieri A, Dawson C. Cataract extractions. Risk factors in a health maintenance organization population aged under 60 years of age. *Arch Ophthalmol* 1988; **106**: 1062–5.

96 Cummings R, Mitchell P, Leeder S. Use of inhaled corticosteroids and the risk of cataracts. *NEJM* 1997; **337**: 8–14.

97 Seigel D, Sperduto R, Ferris F. Aspirin and cataracts. *Ophthalmology* 1982; **89**: 47–9.

98 van Heyningen R, Harding J. A case–control study of cataract in Oxfordshire: some risk factors. *Br J Ophthalmol* 1988; **72**: 804–8.

99 Ederer F, Hillier R, Taylor H. Senile lens changes and diabetes in two population studies. *Am J Epidemiol* 1981; **91**: 381–95.

100 Sommer A. Diabetes and senile cataract. *Am J Ophthalmol* 1981; **92**: 134–5.

101 Klein B, Klein R, Moss S. Prevalence of cataract in a population-based study of persons with diabetes mellitus. *Ophthalmology* 1985; **92**: 1191–6.

102 Chen T, Hockwin O, Eckerskorn U *et al*. Cataract and health status. a case–control study. *Ophthalmic Res* 1988; **20**: 1–9.

103 Shun-Shin G, Ratcliffe P, Bron A *et al*. The lens after renal transplantation. *Br J Ophthalmol* 1990; **74**: 267–71.

104 Harding J, Harding R, Egerton M. Risk factors for cataract in Oxfordshire: diabetes, peripheral neuropathy, myopia, glaucoma and diarrhoea. *Acta Ophthalmol Scand* 1989; **67**: 510–17.

105 Minassian D, Mehra V, Jones B. Dehydrational crises from severe diarrhoea or heatstroke and risk of cataract. *Lancet* 1984; **i**: 751–3.

106 Hirsch R, Schwartz B. Increased mortality among elderly patients undergoing cataract extraction. *Arch Ophthalmol* 1983; **101**: 1034–7.

107 Benson W, Farber M, Caplan R. Increased mortality rates after cataract surgery. A statistical analysis. *Ophthalmology* 1988; **95**: 1288–92.

108 Podgor M, Cassel G, Kannel W. Lens changes and survival in a population-based study. *NEJM* 1985; **313**: 1438–44.

109 Cohen D, Neil H, Sparrow J, Thorogood M, Mann J. Lens opacity and mortality in diabetes. *Diabet Med* 1990; **7**: 615–17.

110 Podgor M, Williams B, Cassel G, Sperduto R. Lens changes and incidence of cardiovascular events among persons with diabetes. *Am Heart J* 1989; **117**: 642–8.

111 Thompson J, Sparrow J, Gibson J, Rosenthal A. Cataract and survival in an elderly non-diabetic population. *Arch Ophthalmol* 1993; **111**: 675–9.

112 Klein B, Klein R, Moss S. Age-related eye disease and survival. The Beaver Dam Eye Study. *Ophthalmology* 1995; **113**: 333–9.

113 Office of National Statistics. *Mortality Statistics: general – England and Wales 1993, 1994, 1995*. London: The Stationery Office, 1997.

114 Stenevi U, Lundstrom M, Thorburn W. A national cataract register. 1. Description and epidemiology. *Acta Ophthalmol Scand* 1995; **73**: 41–4.

115 Hanning M, Lundstrom M. Assessment of maximum waiting-time guarantee for cataract surgery. The case of a Swedish policy. *Int J Technol Assess Health Care* 1998; **14**: 180–93.

116 Drummond M, Yates J. Clearing the cataract backlog in a (not so) developing country. *Eye* 1991; **5**: 481–6.

117 Kupfer C. The conquest of cataract: a global challenge. *Trans Ophthalmol Soc UK* 1984; **104**: 1–10.

118 Seward H. Cataract surgery. In: Easty D, Sparrow J (eds). *The Oxford Textbook of Ophthalmology*. Oxford: Oxford University Press, 1999, pp. 1197–204.

119 Strong N, Wigmore W, Smithson S *et al*. Day-case cataract surgery. *Br J Ophthalmol* 1991; **75**: 731–3.

120 Forrest F. Local anaesthesia or general anaesthesia? In: Johnson R, Forrest F (eds). *Local and General Anaesthesia for Ophthalmic Surgery*. Oxford: Butterworth-Heinemann, 1994.

121 Hamilton R, Gimbel H, Strunin L. Regional anaesthesia for 12,000 cataract extraction and intraocular lens implantation procedures. *Can J Anaesth* 1988; **35**: 615–23.

122 Campbell D, Lim M, Kerr M *et al*. A prospective randomised study of local versus general anaesthesia for cataract surgery. *Anaesthesia* 1993; **48**: 422–8.

123 Cooper J. Development of day case cataract surgery: a literature review. *Br J Nurs* 1996; **5**: 1327–33.

124 Norregaard J, Bernth-Petersen P, Andersen T. Changing threshold for cataract surgery in Denmark between 1980 and 1992. *Acta Ophthalmol Scand* 1996; **74**: 604–8.

125 Batterbury M, Khaw P, Hands R, Elkington A. The cataract explosion: the changing pattern of diagnoses of patients attending an ophthalmic outpatient department. *Eye* 1991; **5**: 369–72.

126 Jay J, Devlin M. The increasing frequency of surgery for cataract. *Eye* 1990; **4**: 127–31.

127 Baratz K, Gray D, Hodge D, Butterfield L, Ilstrup D. Cataract extraction rates in Olmstead County, Minnesota, 1980 through 1994. *Arch Ophthalmol* 1997; **115**: 1441–6.

128 Mudd D. A vision of improvement. *Health Manag* 1999; **3**: 14–15.

129 Vernon S. Eye care and the medical student: where should emphasis be placed in undergraduate ophthalmology? *J R Soc Med* 1988; **81**: 335–7.

130 Featherstone P, James C, Hall M, Williams A. General practitioners' confidence in diagnosing and managing eye conditions: a survey in south Devon. *Br J Gen Pract* 1992; **42**: 21–4.

131 Harrison R, Wild J, Hobley A. Referral patterns to an ophthalmic outpatient clinic by general practitioners and ophthalmic opticians and the role of professionals in screening for ocular disease. *BMJ* 1988; **297**: 1162–7.

132 Sheldrick J, Vernon S, Wilson A, Read S. Demand incidence and episode rates of ophthalmic disease in a defined urban population. *BMJ* 1992; **305**: 933–6.

133 Sheldrick J, Wilson A, Vernon S, Sheldrick C. Management of ophthalmic disease in general practice. *Br J Gen Pract* 1993; **43**: 459–62.

134 Williams E, Wallace P. *Health Checks for People Aged 75 Years and Over*. London: Royal College of General Practitioners, 1993.

135 Grindley S, Winyard S. *Losing Sight of Blindness*. London: RNIB, 1997.

136 Smeeth L, Iliffe S. Effectiveness of screening older people for impaired vision in community setting: systematic review of evidence from randomised controlled trials. *BMJ* 1988; **316**: 660–3.

137 Klein B, Klein R, Linton K, De M. The Beaver Dam Eye Study: visual acuity. *Ophthalmology* 1991; **98**: 1310–15.

138 Webster E, Barnes G. Eye tests in the elderly: factors associated with attendance and diagnostic yield in non-attenders. *J R Soc Med* 1992; **85**: 614–16.

139 Rosenthal A. The demand for ophthalmic services. *BMJ* 1992; **305**: 904–5.

140 Landes R, Popay J. 'My sight is poor but I'm getting on now.' The health and social care needs of older people with visual problems. *Health Soc Care* 1993; **1**: 325–35.

141 Reinstein D, Dorward N, Wormald R *et al.* Correctable undetected visual acuity deficit in patients aged 65 and over attending an Accident and Emergency department. *Br J Ophthalmol* 1993; **77**: 293–6.

142 Revicki D, Brown R, Adler M. Patient outcomes with co-managed post-operative care after cataract surgery. *J Clin Epidemiol* 1993; **46**: 5–15.

143 Lichter P. Different providers and different error rates in health care outcomes: cataract co-management at what price? *Ophthalmology* 1993; **100**: 445–6.

144 Revicki D, Poe M. Quality of care in cataract surgery cases experiencing post-operative complications with co-managed care. *J Am Optom Assoc* 1995; **66**: 268–73.

145 Classe J, Alexander L. Protocols for co-management. *Optom Clin* 1994; **4**: 101–22.

146 Percival S, Setty S. Prospective audit comparing ambulatory day surgery with inpatient surgery for treating cataracts. *Qual Health Care* 1992; **1**: 38–42.

147 Aylward G, Larkin D, Cooling R. Audit of costs and clinical outcome of cataract surgery. *Health Trends* 1993; **25**: 126–9.

148 Lowe K, Gregory D, Jeffery R *et al.* Suitability for day-case surgery. *Eye* 1992; **6**: 506–9.

149 Galin M, Boniuk V, Obstbaum S *et al.* Hospitalization and cataract surgery. *Ann Ophthalmol* 1981; **13**: 365–7.

150 Ingram R, Banerjee D, Traynar M *et al.* Day-case cataract surgery. *Trans Ophthalmol Soc UK* 1980; **100**: 205–9.

151 Vernon S, Cheng H. Comparison between the complications of cataract surgery following local anaesthesia with short stay and general anesthesia with a five-day hospitalisation. *Br J Ophthalmol* 1985; **69**: 360–3.

152 Schanzer M, Wilhelmus K. Outpatient cataract surgery by ophthalmology residents in a county hospital. *Ann Ophthalmol* 1985; **7**: 480–2.

153 Elsas T, Guldahl J, Blika A *et al.* Outpatient anterior chamber lens implantation. *Acta Ophthalmol Scand* 1988; **66**: 214–16.

154 Holland G, Earl D, Wheeler N *et al.* Results of inpatient and outpatient cataract surgery. A historical cohort comparison. *Ophthalmology* 1992; **99**: 845–52.

155 Lowe K, Gregory D, Jeffery R, Easty D. Patient perceptions and social impact: preliminary results of the Bristol MRC study. *Eye* 1991; **5**: 373–8.

156 Rose K, Waterman H, Toon L, McLeod D, Tullo A. Management of day-surgery patients with cataract attending a peripheral ophthalmic clinic. *Eye* 1999; **13**: 71–5.

157 Audit Commission. A short cut to better services: day surgery in England and Wales. London: Audit Commission for Local Authorities and the NHS in England and Wales, 1990.

158 Scottish Forum for Public Health Medicine. *Cataract Surgery.* Glasgow: Scottish Forum for Public Health Medicine, 1993.

159 Joint Working Party on Anaesthesia in Ophthalmic Surgery. *Report of the Joint Working Party on Anaesthesia in Ophthalmic Surgery.* London: Royal College of Ophthalmologists, 1993.

160 Eke T, Thompson J. The National Survey of Local Anaesthesia for Ocular Surgery. I. Survey methodology and current practice. *Eye* 1999; **13**: 189–95.

161 Eke T, Thompson J. The National Survey of Local Anaesthesia for Ocular Surgery. II. Safety profiles of local anaesthesia techniques. *Eye* 1999; **13**: 196–204.

162 Powe N, Schein O, Gieser S *et al.* Synthesis of the literature on visual acuity and complications following cataract extraction and intraocular lens implantation. *Arch Ophthalmol* 1994; **112**: 239–52.

163 Drummond M. Economic aspects of cataract. *Ophthalmology* 1987; **95**: 1147–53.

164 Haddorn D, Holmes A. The New Zealand priority criteria project. Part 1. Overview. *BMJ* 1997; **314**: 131–4.

165 Mordue A, Parkin D, Baxter C, Fawcett G, Stewart M. Thresholds for treatment in cataract surgery. *J Public Health Med* 1994; **16**: 393–8.

166 Mordue A, Parkin D. The New Zealand priority criteria project (letter). *BMJ* 1997; **314**: 1765.

167 Smith A. Criteria for cataract surgery: the role of visual acuity and visual function. *Br J Ophthalmol* 1999; **83**: 510–11.

168 Javitt J, Brenner M, Curbow B, Legro M, Street D. Outcomes of cataract surgery. Improvements in visual acuity and visual function after surgery in the first, second and both eyes. *Arch Ophthalmol* 1993; **111**: 686–91.

169 Javitt J, Steinberg E, Sharkey P *et al.* Cataract surgery in one eye or both: a billion dollar per year issue. *Ophthalmology* 1995; **102**: 1583–93.

170 Elliott D, Patla A, Bullimore M. Improvements in clinical and functional vision and perceived visual disability after first and second eye surgery. *Br J Ophthalmol* 1997; **81**: 889–95.

171 Castells X, Alonso J, Ribo C *et al.* Comparison of the results of first and second cataract eye surgery. *Ophthalmology* 1999; **106**: 676–82.

172 Laidlaw D, Harrad R, Hopper C *et al.* Randomised trial of effectiveness of second eye cataract surgery. *Lancet* 1998; **352**: 925–9.

173 Thompson J. The role of registers in epidemiology: a discussion paper. *J R Soc Med* 1989; **82**: 151–2.

174 Magione C, Phillips R, Lawrence M, Seddon J, Orav J, Goldman L. Improved visual function and attenuation of declines in health-related quality of life after cataract extraction. *Arch Ophthalmol* 1994; **112**: 1419–25.

175 Steinberg E, Tielsch J, Schein O *et al.* The VF-14: an index of functional impairment in patients with cataract. *Arch Ophthalmol* 1994; **112**: 630–8.

176 Alonso J, Espallargues M, Andersen T *et al.* International applicability of the VF-14: an index of visual function in patients with cataracts. *Ophthalmology* 1997; **104**: 799–807.

177 Working Group on Outcome Indicators for Cataract. *Outcome Indicators for Cataract.* London: Royal College of Ophthalmologists, 1997.

Acknowledgements

Preliminary work on this review was carried out by Dr Rhian Evans, with help from Mr Nigel Kirkpatrick. My thanks are due to them, to the NHS Executive, to the National Case-mix office in Winchester for supplying the data in Table 5, to Dr T Smith for writing to me on behalf of the Royal College of General Practitioners describing the GP's viewpoint and to Mr I Anderson, who did the same on behalf of the College of Optometrists. However, the views expressed are my own and are not necessarily those of any other individual or organisation.

10 Groin Hernia

Wendy Phillips and Mark Goldman

1 Summary

Statement of the problem

Groin hernia are very common and surgical treatment is recommended for the majority of patients. Groin hernia repair is the commonest general surgical procedure in the UK. Despite the gradual move to day-case procedures, waiting times for surgery have increased.

Sub-categories

Groin hernia are types of abdominal hernia. There are three types of groin hernia, classified according to the anatomical defect: direct and indirect inguinal hernia and femoral hernia. Femoral hernia are more likely to strangulate than are inguinal hernia, and indirect inguinal hernia are more likely to strangulate than are direct ones. It is usually possible to distinguish clinically between inguinal and femoral hernia, but distinguishing between indirect and direct inguinal hernia is less reliable.

Prevalence and incidence

Groin hernia are more common in men than in women, and become increasingly common with advancing age. Up to one in four men will develop a groin hernia at some stage.

Services available

There are three treatment options: make a surgical repair, supply a truss or 'do nothing'. Surgery is recommended for all groin hernia in children and for femoral hernia in adults. Surgery is also the appropriate choice for most adults with indirect hernia, to relieve symptoms and to reduce the risk of serious complications. 'Do nothing' may be the best option in elderly men with a symptom-free direct hernia.

In NHS hospitals in England in 1995–96, there were 87 700 inguinal hernia repairs and 5150 femoral repairs.

There has been a steady rise in the number of inguinal hernia repairs performed since the late 1980s, with a fall in the numbers of procedures classified as an emergency. Waiting times have increased (median wait 85 days) and there is wide variation between health authorities (now PCTs). In 1995–96, just under one-third of such repairs were performed as day cases.

The number of femoral hernia repairs has remained steady, with a slight fall in the numbers classified as an emergency. The percentage of repairs performed as an emergency remains high at 43.7%. Waiting times have also increased (median wait 47 days) and the percentage of procedures performed as day cases is low at 11.9%.

Effectiveness of services and their costs

There are no studies examining the outcomes of conservative treatment, although a randomised trial is being conducted in the USA and results will be available in 2 to 3 years' time. There is no evidence to support the use of trusses for definitive treatment, but they may alleviate symptoms while a patient awaits an operation.

On the whole, studies of effectiveness examine the effect of different surgical techniques for inguinal hernia repair. There are no rigorous trials examining techniques of femoral hernia repair. Other issues that may alter the effectiveness of a procedure include the skill or experience of the surgeon, advice given about mobilisation, the type of anaesthetic used and the volume of hernia that a unit treats.

Randomised controlled trials (RCTs) have mostly examined different surgical techniques. The current debate is between open-mesh repairs and extra-peritoneal laparoscopic mesh repairs. Laparoscopic surgery offers benefits in terms of earlier recovery but requires an experienced surgeon in order to avoid complications and recurrence. The technique incurs more costs for the health service than do open methods, and the procedure takes longer. Laparoscopic repair also requires a general anaesthetic, and so is more difficult to undertake as a day case than is an open-mesh repair.

There is no evidence that the type of admission (day case or inpatient) or the type of anaesthetic affects the outcome.

The recurrence rate may be estimated from the percentage of repairs performed for recurrent hernia. For NHS hospitals in England in 1995–96 this was 7.2%. The true recurrence rate will be much higher, as many patients do not present for further surgery. Large specialist centres quote recurrence rates of approximately 1%. The low rates seen may be due partly to short periods of follow-up and differences in case-mix, but the skill of experienced hernia surgeons is also likely to be a factor.

The estimated total annual NHS cost for the treatment of hernia for a primary care trust (PCT) of 100 000 patients is £160 000.

Quantified models of care and recommendations

The service may be made more cost-effective by increasing day-case surgery and reducing complications and recurrences. The latter requires that surgery is undertaken by experienced surgeons, or at least supervised by them. In part, day-case surgery is limited by the availability of adequate social care for elderly patients.

Societal costs of hernia repair would be reduced by shorter waiting times for surgery and a reduced need for recuperation after it. With modern tension-free repair methods there is no need to limit activity following surgery.

Femoral trusses should no longer be used, as surgery is the treatment of choice for femoral hernia.

Service providers should publish recurrence rates and complication rates following groin hernia surgery.

Extending the use of laparoscopic surgery may increase waiting times for surgery, increase expenditure and result in more complications in the short term (while surgeons are on the learning curve).

2 Introduction and statement of the problem

A hernia (or rupture) is the protrusion of an organ through the part of the body that usually contains it. In the case of groin hernia, this is the protrusion of a part of the intestine through the abdominal wall into the groin.

The majority of patients with a groin hernia will present with a swelling in the groin, with or without discomfort, often described as a 'dragging' sensation. Where the anatomical defect is large, considerable portions of bowel may protrude from the abdominal cavity, causing an unsightly swelling and discomfort. Hernia may sometimes be confused with other causes of groin swellings, but the main problem in diagnosis is differentiating between different types of hernia or being unable to demonstrate a swelling described by a patient. Such a patient will usually present to the general practitioner. In a smaller number of cases, a patient will present as an emergency with an incarceration and/or bowel obstruction. Prompt diagnosis and surgical admission are important in these patients. Six per cent of inguinal hernia repairs and 45% of femoral hernia repairs are performed as emergencies (*see* Section 5).

Groin hernia are important because they are common and may result in discomfort and disfigurement, often interfering with the ability to work in manual jobs. There is also the risk of strangulation (where the blood supply to a section of protruding bowel becomes cut off) and intestinal obstruction (where the bowel contents are prevented from travelling through a trapped portion of intestine). The latter complications are life-threatening. Adjacent structures, such as the testis, may also be affected when the bowel becomes incarcerated or strangulated.

Groin hernia can occur at any age. They are common in babies and small children, become less common in the teens and twenties and then rise in incidence throughout the middle and later years of life.

Conventional treatments for hernia are various forms of surgery and trusses, both of which have been in use for a considerable length of time. An Egyptian papyrus (Ebers 1550 BC) described the use of bandaging (the ancient equivalent of a truss) and the use of cathartics and hot poultices for strangulation. The first description of surgery was by Celsus in AD 25.[1]

Because of the long-standing tradition of surgical repair for groin hernia, there are no randomised controlled trials comparing surgical treatment with no treatment or indeed with a truss. There is little evidence for the effectiveness of trusses and some authors believe they cause complications, especially with prolonged use.[2,3]

The objectives of hernia management are to relieve symptoms, to avoid deformity and to prevent complications. Successful surgery fulfils all these objectives, and provided that complications are minimal, it would appear to be the ideal choice. Traditionally, trusses have been used for patients who are thought to be poor operative risks or where the risk of complications is low. Trusses may control symptoms, but there is little evidence that they can prevent complications. There is some concern that trusses may increase the risk of incarceration or strangulation, especially of the narrow-necked femoral hernia.[2] With improvements in anaesthetic technique and the advent of regional and local anaesthesia, fewer people are unfit for surgery, and so the majority of patients who would benefit from surgery may be offered it.

Hernia do not correct themselves over time and will often deteriorate, with enlargement of the hernia and increasing discomfort. Successful treatment will prevent such complications, and improvements in quality of life have been demonstrated following hernia repair.[4] It is therefore reasonable to conclude that hernia should be treated. The issue then becomes one of access to effective treatment. Inguinal hernia repair rates in England are lower than in the USA, Australia and Norway, so there is some evidence of reduced access to surgery.[2] Much of the mortality from hernia is potentially preventable, because an adequate repair prevents the complications of strangulation or obstruction. There were 311 deaths in England and Wales in 1995 attributed to inguinal or femoral hernia.[5] There is also considerable variation in mortality between countries, with England and Wales having the third highest age-standardised mortality in Europe for abdominal hernia in people aged 5–64 years.[6]

Appendix I lists the diagnostic and procedure codes.

3 Sub-categories

A groin hernia is just one cause of groin swelling, but it should be possible to identify a hernia on clinical examination. Groin hernia are the commonest type of abdominal hernia. There are three distinct types of groin hernia:

- direct inguinal hernia
- indirect inguinal hernia
- femoral hernia.

Where an indirect hernia extends into the scrotum, it may be referred to as an *inguino-scrotal* hernia.

The anatomical deficit is different for each type.[7-10] It is important to distinguish between types because the clinical course and recommended treatment will depend on the category of groin hernia. Complications are far more frequent in femoral hernia than in either type of inguinal hernia. The distinction between direct and indirect may be made reliably only at operation. A study comparing pre-operative diagnosis of inguinal hernia with peri-operative diagnosis found that surgeons correctly diagnosed 76.9% of indirect hernia and 58.9% of direct hernia.[11]

Groin hernia may also be classified as reducible or irreducible depending on whether the abdominal contents may be returned to the abdomen manually. Irreducible hernia (where the contents may not be easily returned to the abdomen) are more likely to result in complications of strangulation and obstruction. When the hernia is small, it may often go undetected.

Data on incidence, prevalence and procedures are all presented using the anatomical categories, as this is the way in which data have been recorded. Patients may also be categorised in terms of the way they present.

- **Patients who do not present for medical care:** This group may or may not have symptoms, and have varying risks of incarceration or strangulation. Many will eventually migrate to one of the other two categories, i.e. they will present acutely or non-acutely with symptoms of their hernia. This category includes patients in whom a hernia is a chance finding when they are examined for other medical purposes. They may or may not have symptoms attributable to the hernia. Approximately half of patients with hernia may be unaware of the problem.[12]
- **Non-acute presentation:** Patients have symptoms, usually of pain in the groin and/or groin swelling. Most present in general practice, where a GP or practice nurse will assess them. Some patients may choose to have an operation to relieve them of their symptoms. Others who are felt to be at high risk of strangulation (particularly those with a femoral hernia) may be advised to have an operation. Some patients with inguinal hernia, especially the elderly, may prefer not to have an operation.
- **Acute presentation:** Patients present acutely with symptoms of complications, usually abdominal pain and/or bowel obstruction. Emergency admission and surgery are required. The cause of the symptoms – the hernia itself – may be missed, especially in a patient who has not had a hernia previously diagnosed. Based on the 1995–96 Health Episode Statistic (HES) data, approximately 8% of all hernia operations are performed as emergencies.

4 Incidence and prevalence

Incidence

There are no population-based studies that measure the incidence of groin hernia. Incidence may be measured only in terms of health care contacts, because many patients may be unaware of their hernia or do not seek medical attention.

Primary care consultations

Demand–incidence data for inguinal hernia have been derived from the fourth national GP morbidity survey,[13] which took place during the financial year 1991–92. Sixty practices volunteered, with a total of 502 493 patients resulting in 468 042 person-years of observation. The data in Table 1 show the numbers of new and first-ever appointments in general practice for inguinal hernia. This incidence rate will underestimate the true incidence, because many people do not seek advice for their hernia and the data set may be incomplete. (Under-reporting by GPs was estimated to be about 5% for consultations but much higher for referrals to secondary care.)

Table 1: Incidence rates (95% CIs) of inguinal hernia per 10 000 person-years at risk.

Age band (years)	Incidence rate in males	Incidence rate in females
0–4	46 (36.5–58.1)	8 (4.3–13.7)
5–15	9 (6.2–13.2)	2 (0.9–4.5)
16–24	11 (7.5–15.4)	1 (0.3–3.1)
25–44	21 (17.8–24.7)	2 (1.2–3.4)
45–64	62 (55.2–69.4)	5 (3.3–7.5)
65–74	118 (103–135)	9 (5.4–14.6)
75–84	182 (159–209)	14 (8.6–23.3)
85 and over	190 (141–259)	37 (18.4–74.2)
All ages	43 (40.4–45.8)	5 (4.2–6.0)

Source: Morbidity Statistics from General Practice. Fourth National Study (MSGP4), 1991–92. First-ever or new consultations per 10 000 patients at risk.

Volunteer practices tended to be larger than average, with younger practice principals. There were also some socio-economic differences between the population studied and the overall population of England and Wales. For instance, ethnic minorities were under-represented in the practice populations.

Data on femoral hernia are not available from MSGP4, because data were analysed at a higher level of diagnostic code. Data have therefore been derived from the third national GP morbidity survey,[14] which took place in the financial year 1981–82. Data were obtained from 48 volunteer practices caring for 332 270 patients and contributing 307 803 person-years to the study. These incidence data are shown in Table 2 (*see* overleaf).

These estimates show femoral hernia incidence in women to be lower than in men. Femoral hernia repairs are more commonly performed in women (*see* Section 5). Women are also more likely to require

Table 2: Incidence rates (95% CIs) for femoral hernia per 10 000 person-years at risk.

Age band (years)	Incidence rate in males	Incidence rate in females
0–4	2 (0.3–7.9)	0 (0.0–5.0)
5–14	0 (0.0–2.0)	0 (0.0–2.2)
15–24	2 (0.8–5.4)	0 (0.0–2.0)
25–44	1 (0.3–2.7)	2 (1.0–3.9)
45–64	1 (0.3–3.1)	2 (0.8–4.3)
65–74	1 (0.0–5.4)	2 (0.5–6.3)
75 and over	9 (3.8–21.2)	7 (3.5–14.1)
All ages	2 (0.5–6.5)	2 (0.5–5.9)

Source: Morbidity Statistics from General Practice. Third National Study (MSGP3),
1981–82. First-ever and new consultations for femoral hernia.

emergency repair for their femoral hernia than are men. It appears that women are less likely to present to their GPs with groin swelling and consequently are at greater risk of strangulation and emergency presentation. Alternatively, GPs may be less likely to diagnose groin hernia in women.

Using the demand–incidence rates from general practice, and the population structure of England (mid-1995 population estimates), the expected numbers of groin hernia patients in an average PCT of 100 000 have been calculated. These are summarised in Table 3.

Table 3: Expected numbers of groin hernia patients in a population of 100 000.

Type of hernia	Inguinal	Femoral
Male	220	7
Female	27	9
Total	247	16

The numbers of surgical procedures performed also form an estimate of incidence, although not all patients are referred for surgical opinion and not all those assessed by a surgeon will be offered surgery. Health service activity data are summarised in Section 5.

Prevalence

Data on prevalence rates come from the GP morbidity survey (MSGP4)[13] and from community studies.

Primary care consultations

Prevalence estimates have been derived from the morbidity survey data (*see* Table 4). These are available only for inguinal hernia.

Table 4: Estimated inguinal hernia prevalence from GP morbidity studies: rates per 10 000 person-years at risk (95% CIs).

Age band (years)	Prevalence rate in males	Prevalence rate in females
0–4	52 (41.5–64.4)	7 (3.9–12.9)
5–15	10 (6.9–14.3)	2 (0.92–4.5)
16–24	14 (10.3–19.2)	2 (0.8–4.4)
25–44	25 (21.6–29.1)	3 (1.9–4.6)
45–64	83 (74.8–91.2)	7 (4.9–9.8)
65–74	156 (139–175)	10 (6.2–15.9)
75–84	262 (234–293)	18 (11.8–28.4)
85 and over	267 (206–343)	35 (15.6–63.5)

Source: MSGP4.[13]

Community surveys

There have been no comprehensive prevalence studies of groin hernia in the wider community. The most comprehensive reference is a paper by Abramson *et al.*[12] They undertook a community survey of men in western Jerusalem using a combination of interview and clinical examination. The prevalence of unrepaired inguinal hernia was recorded as well as any history of hernia repair. The results of their survey are summarised in Table 5.

Table 5: Prevalence of inguinal hernia by age group.

Age group examined (years)	25–34	35–44	45–54	55–64	65–74	75 plus	Total
Number of men examined	620	438	300	322	156	47	1,883
Current prevalence (excluding successful repairs)	11.9%	15.1%	19.7%	26.1%	29.5%	34.1%	18.3%
Lifetime prevalence (including successful repairs)	15.2%	19.4%	28.0%	34.5%	39.7%	46.8%	24.3%

Source: Abramson *et al.*[12]

To ensure consistency of diagnosis, all the examining doctors were trained in the examination and clinical diagnosis of inguinal hernia using the method described by Bailey.[15] While consistency is assured, however, the data will not be entirely accurate, as clinical diagnosis is not always confirmed at surgery.[11] A cough impulse at a scar site was taken as a recurrence. Response rates from those aged under 25 years were low and so the analysis was confined to men aged over 24 years. The poor response rate in the younger group was thought to be a result of service in the armed forces. The response rate for interviews in the 25-plus group was 86%, 91% of whom participated in the follow-up examination.

This study shows an increasing prevalence of inguinal hernia with increasing age in adult males. Hernia were more common on the right in a ratio of 1.3 to 1. One in every five of all hernia showed evidence of recurrence. Only 54% of men with an unoperated swelling reported having a hernia. It is not known how well these results translate to the UK population.

Abramson *et al.* also summarised comparative studies on hernia prevalence from other countries. The results of their study were comparable with those from the other studies and so are likely to be a reasonable estimate. They show that the prevalence estimates from the GP morbidity survey[13] are gross underestimates, even assuming that only half of those with a hernia are aware of it.

Prevalence estimates from other studies are summarised in Table 6, adapted from Abramson *et al.*[12]

Table 6: Prevalence estimates of types of abdominal hernia.

Study	Population	Prevalence rate of hernia
Cohen J, Male E, 1964	Israel. Males aged 17–18 in the cohort born in 1940. Inguinal hernia	0.8%
Zimmerman LM, Anson BJ, 1967[16]	USA. First million drafted in World War I. All hernia	2.0%
Zimmerman LM, Anson BJ, 1967[16]	USA. Selective service registrants; 3 million from World War II. All hernia	8.0%
Nilsson JR, 1937[17]	USA. Routine examination of 7,967 railroad workers. All hernia, including operated	9.5%
Trussell RE, Elinson J, 1959[18]	USA. All abdominal hernia; probability sample of 277 men aged 25 and over	5.3% (25–44 years) 6.0% (45–64 years) 22.9% (65 years plus)
Zimmerman LM, Anson BJ, 1967[16]	UK. Recruits in World War I	0.6–12.5%, depending on age
Edwards H, 1943[19]	UK. Recruits in World War II. Abdominal hernia; 1,300 men aged 35–36 years	11.0%
Yordanov YS, Stoyanov SK, 1969[20]	Pemba (an island close to Zanzibar). Hospital patients or relatives of patients not attending with hernia. Inguinal hernia in 528 men aged over 21 years	25.2%

Several African studies have demonstrated a prevalence in adult males of between 7.7% and 25.2%.[21] It is not possible to comment on possible ethnic differences in hernia prevalence, because studies have used non-comparable samples.

Akin *et al.* studied a series of 27 400 army recruits aged between 20 and 22 years in Turkey in 1995.[22] An inguinal hernia was found in 3.2% of men, with 54.1% being right-sided, 39.7% left-sided and 6.2% bilateral.

Surgery for groin hernia

Using the hospital-episode data for England for the financial year 1995–96, the ratio of primary inguinal hernia repairs to primary femoral repairs was 16.4:1. Although hernia repairs were much more common in men than in women (ratio 7.6:1), femoral hernia repairs were more common in women than in men. The ratio of primary inguinal hernia repair to primary femoral hernia repair is 50:1 in men and 1.9:1 in women. These figures do not reflect the total incidence of groin hernia, as there will be patients who do not present, patients who are not referred from general practice and patients who are not offered or who refuse surgery.

Barwell described a series of over 4000 groin hernia repairs.[21] In these, the ratio of indirect to direct inguinal repairs was 8.3:1 in women and 2.4:1 in men.

Complications of groin hernia

Strangulation and incarceration

Estimates of the risks of strangulation vary enormously, but many of them seem to be based on hearsay rather than on fact. Gallegos[23] studied 476 hernia repairs in a UK hospital population and used Kaplan–Meier survival analysis to estimate the cumulative probability of strangulation over the length of the clinical history. For inguinal hernia, the cumulative probability of strangulation was 2.8% at 3 months, 4.5% after 2 years and 8.6% after 5 years (i.e. an estimated annual strangulation risk of 1.7%). For femoral hernia, the cumulative probability of strangulation was 22% at 3 months and 45% at 21 months. They demonstrated that the cumulative risk of strangulation increased at the greatest rate in the first three months of the history. They also found that patients who were admitted with a strangulated hernia had much shorter clinical histories than those on the waiting list. This suggests that hernia at risk of strangulation may strangulate before patients are referred to hospital.

McEntee et al.[24] undertook a retrospective study of 79 patients who presented with clinical evidence of strangulation between 1979 and 1987. Forty-six patients (58%) had noticed a hernia for at least one month prior to strangulation. Of these, 39% had not reported the hernia to their GP, 41% had reported the hernia to a doctor but had not been referred for surgical opinion and 20% had been assessed surgically with a view to elective repair. Forty per cent of patients had presented within days of developing a hernia. In a smaller study by Allen et al., 18 of 25 patients with strangulated hernia had known of their hernia for over a year before the emergency admission.[25]

Neuhauser made two estimates of the annual risk of strangulation.[26] The first was based on a series of 8633 patients with inguinal hernia described by Berger[27] in 1895 and gave a probability of strangulation or obstruction of 0.4% per annum. Berger questioned patients who came to see him for the fitting of a truss, asking them the length of the history and whether they had had any episodes of obstruction or incarceration. Neuhauser states that Berger's data showed a mortality from incarceration of 8.5%, and therefore increased the rate of strangulation or incarceration by 10% to account for this. It is not at all clear how Berger could have demonstrated a mortality rate from strangulation when he studied live patients.

The second source of data used was an unpublished study in Columbia where almost no routine hernia operations were performed. The numbers of operations on strangulations or incarceration were related to the population at risk. The yearly probability of strangulation was 0.3%. There are several problems with this estimate. It assumes that anyone in the designated population with incarceration or strangulation would have been admitted to hospital and operated on. The data also assume that it was possible to identify accurately a population at risk. The epidemiology of groin hernia appears to vary in different ethnic populations, so the results of studies in Columbia may not be applicable to a European population.[28,29]

Mortality

Mortality from groin hernia may occur from the complications of the hernia (usually strangulation or incarceration) or from the complications of surgery. The mortality rate is much higher following emergency surgery than after elective surgery. Mortality following either emergency or elective surgery has fallen over the years.

Charlton et al.[30] demonstrated huge differences in mortality from abdominal hernia between health authorities for the years 1974–78. These differences were still present even when accounting for differences in population structure and differing levels of deprivation. It seems likely that such inequalities still exist today. These differences may reflect the quality and accessibility of services provided. However, the data refer to all types of abdominal hernia, and it is difficult to be sure that these inequalities would still be present if groin hernia were looked at in isolation.

The largest series of strangulated hernia was described by Frankau in 1931.[31] He studied 1487 strangulated abdominal hernia from a number of hospitals in Britain and Ireland. Mortality rates from strangulation were 12.6% for inguinal hernia and 12.9% for femoral hernia.

Reaveley et al.[6] studied deaths from abdominal hernia in Nottingham over a six-year period. The majority had presented with symptoms of incarceration or strangulation. Of the 20 deaths from inguinal hernia, only half had had a history of the hernia documented in GP records.

Based on 1995–96 HES data, approximately 8% of operations are performed as emergencies. The indication for emergency surgery would be complications, so this figure of 8% gives an estimate of the lifetime risk of strangulation or incarceration. This risk estimate applies to current surgical practice, so complication rates would be much higher if no repairs were done as routine.

Mortality data from death certificates

For the calendar year 1995 in England and Wales, there were 721 deaths where abdominal hernia was given as the underlying cause. Inguinal hernia caused 183 deaths and femoral hernia caused 128; 75.4% of the inguinal hernia deaths and 85.2% of the femoral hernia deaths were in people aged 75 years or over.

Deaths following hernia surgery

In 1995–96, there were 256 deaths in hospital following groin hernia surgery. The numbers of deaths by operation type and admission method are summarised in Table 7. Deaths are more common following emergency surgery than following elective surgery. Death is more common following femoral hernia surgery than following inguinal surgery.

Table 7: Mortality rate from groin hernia repair, using admissions where the discharge method was death.

Mortality rate (number of deaths)	Excision of inguinal sac	Primary inguinal	Recurrent inguinal	Primary femoral	Recurrent femoral
From elective surgery	0% (0)	0.05% (31)	0.09% (5)	0.19% (5)	0% (0)
From emergency surgery	0.29% (3)	2.66% (99)	3.19% (15)	4.33% (96)	4.35% (2)

Source: HES data, 1995–96.

Overall mortality rates following groin hernia repairs are shown in Table 8.

Table 8: Mortality rates from groin hernia surgery.

	Mortality rate, emergency admissions (95% CIs)	Mortality rate, elective admissions (95% CIs)
Inguinal repairs	2.24% (1.9–2.3)	0.04% (0.03–0.06)
Femoral repairs	4.33% (3.5–5.3)	0.18% (0.07–0.47)

Source: HES data, 1995–96.

Trends in groin hernia deaths following surgery are illustrated in Figure 1. These are the numbers of admissions for groin hernia repair where the discharge method was death, i.e. they do not include any deaths that occurred following discharge from hospital.

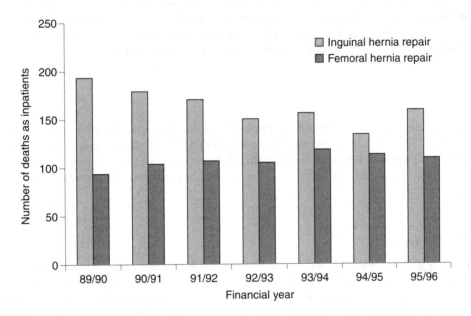

Figure 1: Trends in deaths following groin hernia surgery between 1989–90 and 1995–96 (NHS Hospitals, England).

5 Services available and their costs

Treatment options

The investigation and management of groin hernia are usually straightforward. Patients are not routinely screened for hernia, although one may be detected as part of a physical examination. Small hernia may go unnoticed even by the patient, and not all patients with symptoms or signs present to the GP.

A patient with groin hernia has three choices: no treatment, a truss or surgical repair. PCTs need to develop clear guidelines for referral and management in partnership with surgical colleagues.

No treatment

This has been advocated for small, direct hernia in the elderly and for people regarded as too infirm to withstand surgery. Patient selection on clinical criteria is likely to fail, because the differentiation between direct and indirect inguinal hernia can only be made with certainty at operation.[11] A policy that legitimises patient selection may explain the large numbers of patients whose family doctors do not refer them for a surgical opinion.

Truss

Although there remains a perception amongst patients and some doctors that a truss can be used to manage an inguinal hernia, there is no evidence base to support the truss as a definitive treatment.[2] However, a truss may be used to alleviate symptoms in a patient awaiting surgery. In 1991, an estimated 40 000 trusses were provided annually in the UK.[32] For the 12-month period December 1998 to November 1999, 16 000 trusses were prescribed in England, 32 of them for femoral hernia.*

Surgery

Surgery is of two types: *traditional open surgery* or *laparoscopic repair*. A laparoscopic repair is either *totally extra-peritoneal (TEP)* or *trans-abdominal pre-peritoneal (TAPP)*. The latter repair involves entering the peritoneal cavity, and is being superseded by the TEP approach. The commonest repair uses a mesh prosthesis stapled over the hernial orifice and then covered by peritoneum to prevent local adherence to the bowel.

Inguinal hernia repair

In open surgery an incision is made in the inguinal region, with exposure of the hernia. The sac is excised or reduced. In all but infant hernia procedures, the posterior wall of the inguinal canal is repaired or reinforced, with support and narrowing of the internal inguinal ring. These features are common to all open repairs. The procedure can be carried out under general or local anaesthesia if the hernia is reducible and the patient is not obese.

The precise nature of the surgical repair depends on the operator's preference. Essentially there are two choices.

- The *Shouldice repair*[33] involves overlapping reinforcement of the transversalis fascia.
- The *Lichtenstein technique*[34] involves the insertion of a prosthetic mesh.

It is important to note that most surgeons use a modification of an originally described method, which may have evolved considerably by passage through the hands of several surgeons.

---

* *Source*: Prescription Pricing Authority.

Femoral hernia repair

There are three main methods of femoral hernia repair:

- the *high* approach
- the *transinguinal* approach
- the *low* approach.

Laparoscopic methods and mesh may also be used.

Current service provision

Data on service provision in this report are based on hospital-episode data from NHS hospitals in England (HES data). The data have been analysed on the basis of admissions rather than finished consultant episodes (FCEs). Data have been extracted on the basis of procedure codes (OPCS4; *see* Appendix I). The procedure rates and any trends in service provision in the NHS need to be considered in the light of private health care provision over the same time period.

Volume of surgery

Inguinal hernia repair

In the financial year 1995–96, there were 87 651 inguinal hernia repairs in NHS hospitals in England. Of these, 81 323 (92.8%) were primary repairs and 6328 (7.2%) were recurrent repairs. These represent a crude repair rate (per 100 000) of 180, a crude primary repair rate of 167 and a crude recurrent repair rate of 13.0. Ninety-one per cent of operations were recorded as on men and 7.6% on women, while in 1.6% of admissions the gender was unclassified. There has been a steady increase in the numbers of operations performed annually since the late 1980s. This contrasts with the previous 15 years, when numbers had on average remained static.[21] Between 1989–90 and 1995–96, inguinal hernia repairs rose by 27% in men and 5% in women. It is not clear why there is this gender disparity.

In 1995–96, 89.5% of inguinal hernia repairs were performed as a single procedure (i.e. no additional procedures were performed at the same time). This compares with 83% in 1989–90. This change may have arisen as a result of the increase in day-case surgery, as combined procedures are not suitable for day-case repair. Alternatively, it could be an artefact of the coding or of the data analysis.

Applying incidence rates in general practice to the population in England, there would be an estimated 120 314 new cases of inguinal hernia per annum in England presenting to general practitioners (107 258 men and 13 056 women). For the year 1995–96, there were only 87 651 hernia repairs, which suggests that only 73% of those presenting to GPs have an operation.

Femoral hernia repair

In the financial year 1995–96, there were 5146 femoral hernia repairs in NHS hospitals in England. Of these, 4951 (96.2%) were primary repairs and 195 (3.8%) were recurrent repairs. These represent an overall crude repair rate (per 100 000) of 10.6, a crude primary repair rate of 10.2 and a crude recurrent repair rate of 0.4. The number of femoral hernia repairs performed annually remained steady between 1989–90 and 1995–96, a pattern similar to that seen in the previous 15 years.[21]

Applying incidence rates in general practice to the population in England, there would be an estimated 8012 new cases of femoral hernia per annum in England presenting to general practitioners (3470 men and

4540 women). For the year 1995–96, there were only 5146 hernia repairs, which suggests that only 64% of those presenting to GPs have an operation.

In 1995–96, 83.5% of femoral hernia repairs were performed as a single procedure, compared with 72.5% in 1989–90. Only 31.8% of recurrent femoral repairs were performed as single procedures. The apparent increase in single procedures may have arisen as a result of the increase in day-case surgery. As we remarked earlier, combined procedures are not suitable for day-case repair. Alternatively, it could be an artefact resulting from different methods of analysing the HES data or from the effect of changes in coding practice.

Procedure rates by age and gender

Rates have been calculated using the Office for National Statistics (ONS) mid-1995 population estimates for England. Some of the rates are derived from very small actual numbers, so the confidence intervals for these would be wide.

Inguinal hernia repair

The procedure rates for inguinal hernia are summarised in Table 9.

Table 9: Rates of inguinal hernia repair by age and gender.*

| Age band (years) | Primary repairs | | | | Recurrent repairs | | | |
| | Number of repairs | | Rate per 10,000 population | | Number of repairs | | Rate per 10,000 population | |
	Male	Female	Male	Female	Male	Female	Male	Female
0–4	8,606	856	51.9	5.4	54	5	0.3	0.03
5–14	3,916	732	12.3	2.4	57	5	0.2	0.02
15–24	2,728	155	8.5	0.5	69	5	0.2	0.02
25–44	10,610	854	14.5	1.2	490	27	0.7	0.04
45–64	23,084	1,378	42.5	2.5	2,077	60	3.8	0.11
65–74	14,473	1,041	73.2	4.4	1,866	33	9.4	0.14
75–84	8,608	1,077	93.0	6.9	1,230	37	13.3	0.24
85 plus	1,529	340	70.8	5.2	210	14	9.7	0.22
All ages	73,554	6,433	30.8	2.6	6,053	186	2.5	0.07

* These data exclude 5 admissions where the age was not known and 1420 admissions where the gender was not known.

Age- and sex-specific rates of primary and recurrent hernia repair are shown in Figures 2 and 3 (*see* opposite).

Inguinal hernia repairs are much more common in men than in women at all ages. The age-specific rates are high in infants and in the elderly. Ninety-one per cent of procedures were recorded as performed on men and 7.6% on women, while in 1.6% of procedures the gender was unclassified.

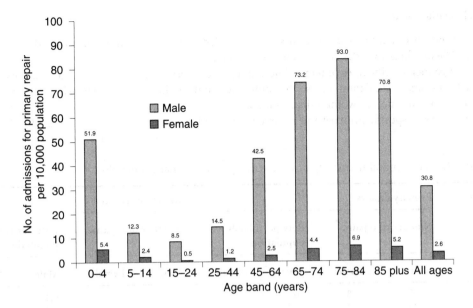

Figure 2: Age- and sex-specific primary inguinal hernia repair rates (NHS Hospitals, England, 1995–96).

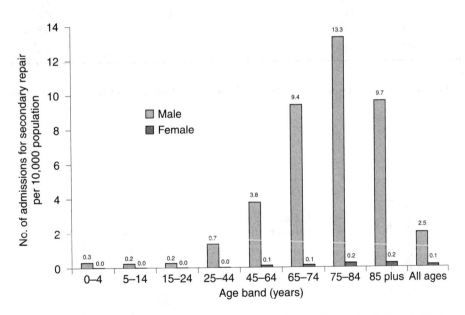

Figure 3: Age- and sex-specific recurrent hernia repair rates (NHS Hospitals, England, 1995–96).

Femoral hernia repair

In 1995–96, 68.1% of femoral hernia repairs were recorded as performed on women and 31.0% on men, while in 0.9% of admissions the gender was not classified.

Age- and gender-specific rates of femoral hernia repair are presented in Table 10. Many of the rates are calculated from small actual numbers, so the confidence limits of the rates would be wide. Femoral hernia repairs are more common in women than in men.

Age- and gender-specific primary and recurrent femoral hernia repair rates are illustrated in Figures 4 and 5.

Table 10: Rates of femoral hernia repair by age and gender, England 1995–96.*

Age band (years)	Primary repairs				Recurrent repairs			
	Number of repairs		Rate per 10,000 population		Number of repairs		Rate per 10,000 population	
	Male	Female	Male	Female	Male	Female	Male	Female
0–4	10	8	0.6	0.5	1	1	0.1	0.1
5–14	28	25	0.9	0.8	3	2	0.1	0.1
15–24	20	32	0.6	1.1	0	1	0.0	0.0
25–44	105	434	1.4	6.1	6	13	0.1	0.2
45–64	426	765	7.9	13.9	22	29	0.4	0.5
65–74	395	756	20.0	31.8	25	29	1.3	1.2
75–84	369	887	39.9	57.0	20	23	2.2	1.5
85 plus	118	501	54.6	77.3	2	17	0.9	2.6
All ages	1,471	3,408	6.2	13.7	79	115	0.3	0.5

Source: HES data, 1995–96.

* These data exclude 1 admission where the age was not known and 72 admissions where the gender was not known.

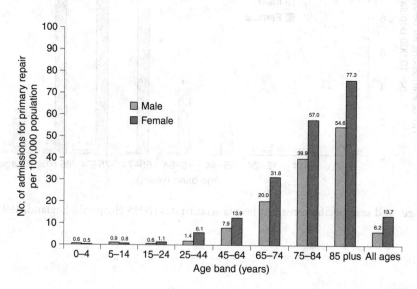

Figure 4: Age- and gender-specific primary femoral hernia repair rates (NHS Hospitals, England, 1995–96).

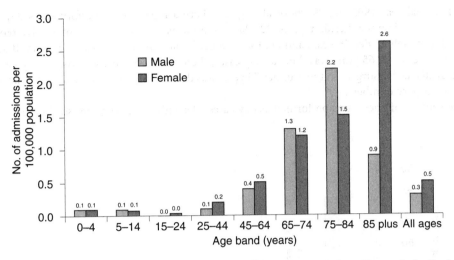

Figure 5: Age- and gender-specific recurrent femoral hernia repair rates (NHS Hospitals, England, 1995–96).

Day-case surgery

Inguinal hernia repair

There has been a steady increase in the percentage of operations performed as day cases over the seven-year period examined. This trend is seen in all three types of procedure, but day-case surgery is much more common in primary repair than in recurrent repair. These trends are illustrated in Figure 6.

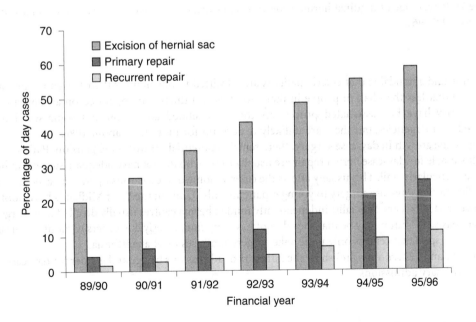

Figure 6: Trends in percentage of inguinal hernia repairs performed as day cases, by procedure type (NHS Hospitals, England, 1989–90 to 1995–96).

For the financial year 1995–96, 29.7% of all inguinal hernia repairs were performed as day cases. Of the 81 126 elective inguinal hernia repairs, 32.1% were done as day cases; 65.5% of elective repairs were performed in people under 65 years and 86.0% were performed in people under 75 years. If all elective surgery in those under 65 years was done as day cases, there would be an 104% rise in day-case surgery numbers. If all elective surgery in those under 75 years was done as day cases, there would be an 168% rise in day-case surgery numbers.

The percentage of operations performed as day cases falls with increasing age (*see* Figure 7).

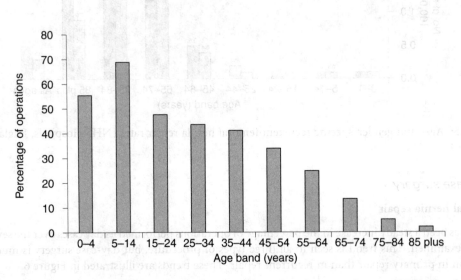

Figure 7: Percentage of inguinal hernia procedures performed as day cases, by age (NHS Hospitals, England, 1995–96).

While it is understandable that elderly patients are admitted to hospital for their hernia repairs, it seems surprising that less than half of people in their twenties and thirties are operated on as day cases. Some patients may have had associated procedures that necessitated admission and some will have been admitted as emergencies, but these are unlikely to account for more than about 10%.

Despite the growth in day-case surgery, there remains potential for further expansion. Patients who are not felt suitable for day-case hernia repair are usually those who do not have adequate support at home or who are particularly frail. This usually affects the elderly. Some day-case units operate an age-based policy, generally offering day-case surgery to younger patients only. Units in the West Midlands have quoted cut-off ages of 65 to 75 years. Specialist independently funded hernia centres usually do all of their surgery on a day-care basis,[35,36] but it may be that they do not have any frail, elderly customers without social support. Some of the specialist centres only undertake surgery that uses local anaesthesia.

Tables 11 and 12 (*see* opposite) show the numbers of admissions by age and gender for day-case surgery and for ordinary admissions.

Table 11: Numbers (%) of day cases for inguinal hernia repair, by age and gender.

Age band (years)	Simple excision of hernia sac			Primary inguinal repair			Recurrent inguinal repair			Total
	Male	Female	Unclassified	Male	Female	Unclassified	Male	Female	Unclassified	
0–4	4,119 (15.8%)	387 (1.5%)	18	733 (2.8%)	119 (0.5%)	0	21 (0.1%)	2	0	5,399 (20.7%)
5–14	2,214 (8.5%)	401 (1.5%)	11	491 (1.9%)	169 (0.6%)	1	37 (0.1%)	3	0	3,327 (12.8%)
15–24	102 (0.4%)	8	0	1,197 (4.6%)	82 (0.3%)	10	22 (0.1%)	2	0	1,423 (5.5%)
25–34	34 (0.1%)	3	0	2,227 (8.6%)	132 (0.5%)	7	57 (0.2%)	3	0	2,463 (9.5%)
35–44	20 (0.1%)	4	0	2,356 (9.1%)	220 (0.8%)	13	64 (0.2%)	2	0	2,679 (10.3%)
45–54	9	4	0	3,552 (13.7%)	256 (1.0%)	24 (0.1%)	127 (0.5%)	1	0	3,973 (15.3%)
55–64	11	0	0	3,467 (13.3%)	145 (0.6%)	12	171 (0.7%)	3	1	3,810 (14.6%)
65–74	7	1	0	2,053 (7.9%)	124 (0.5%)	7	119 (0.5%)	4	0	2,315 (8.9%)
75–84	1	0	0	492 (1.9%)	47 (0.2%)	2	45 (0.2%)	0	0	587 (2.3%)
85 plus	0	0	0	32 (0.1%)	9	0	2	0	0	43 (0.2%)
Unknown	0	0	0	2	0	0	0	0	0	2 (0%)
Total	6,517 (25.0%)	808 (3.1%)	29 (0.1%)	16,602 (63.8%)	1,303 (5.0%)	76 (0.3%)	665 (2.6%)	20 (0.1%)	1 (0%)	26,021 (100%)

Source: HES data, 1995–96.

Table 12: Numbers (%) of ordinary admissions for inguinal hernia repair, by age and gender.

Age band (years)	Simple excision of hernia sac			Primary inguinal repair			Recurrent inguinal repair			Total
	Male	Female	Unclassified	Male	Female	Unclassified	Male	Female	Unclassified	
0–4	3,038 (4.9%)	278 (0.5%)	194 (0.3%)	716 (1.2%)	72 (0.1%)	10	33 (0.1%)	3	3	4,347 (7.1%)
5–14	967 (1.6%)	123 (0.2%)	74 (0.1%)	244 (0.4%)	39 (0.1%)	4	20	2	0	1,473 (2.4%)
15–24	89 (0.1%)	6	5	1,340 (2.2%)	59 (0.1%)	32 (0.1%)	47 (0.1%)	3	0	1,581 (2.6%)
25–34	33 (0.1%)	10	1	2,676 (4.3%)	174 (0.3%)	74 (0.1%)	132 (0.2%)	9	5	3,114 (5.1%)
35–44	24	5	0	3,240 (5.3%)	306 (0.5%)	69 (0.1%)	237 (0.4%)	13	7	3,901 (6.3%)
45–54	49 (0.1%)	6	2	6,339 (10.3%)	483 (0.8%)	154 (0.3%)	642 (1.0%)	28	16	7,719 (12.5%)
55–64	82 (0.1%)	6	7	9,575 (15.5%)	478 (0.8%)	207 (0.3%)	1,137 (1.8%)	28	12	11,532 (18.7%)
65–74	80 (0.1%)	16	3	12,333 (20.0%)	900 (1.5%)	206 (0.3%)	1,747 (2.8%)	29	23	15,337 (24.9%)
75–84	66 (0.1%)	11	8	8,049 (13.1%)	1,019 (1.7%)	156 (0.3%)	1,185 (1.9%)	37	18	10,549 (17.1%)
85 plus	9	3	2	1,488 (2.4%)	328 (0.5%)	18	208 (0.3%)	14	4	2,074 (3.4%)
Unknown	0	0	0	3	0	0	0	0	0	3 (0%)
Total	4,437 (7.2%)	464 (0.8%)	296 (0.5%)	46,003 (74.6%)	3,858 (6.3%)	930 (1.5%)	5,388 (8.7%)	166 (0.3%)	88 (0.1%)	61,630 (100%)

Source: HES data, 1995–96.

Femoral hernia repair

As with inguinal hernia, the percentage of operations performed as day cases has increased (*see* Figure 8), although femoral hernia operations are much less likely to be performed as day cases than are inguinal hernia ones, in part because a much higher percentage of operations are done as emergencies. Recurrent repairs are less likely to be performed as day cases than are primary repairs. Day-case surgery becomes less common with increasing age (*see* Figure 9).

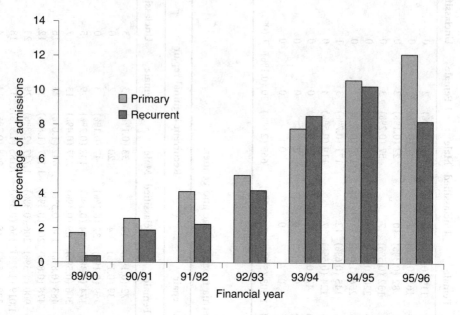

Figure 8: Trends in the percentage of admissions for femoral hernia classified as day cases (NHS Hospitals, England, 1989–90 to 1995–96).

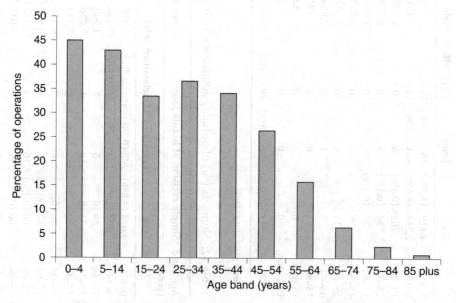

Figure 9: Percentage of femoral hernia operations performed as day cases, by age (NHS Hospitals, England, 1995–96).

In the financial year 1995–96, 12.1% of primary repairs and 8.2% of recurrent repairs were performed as day cases. For primary and recurrent repairs combined, 11.9% of procedures were performed as day cases. In the same year, there were 2807 elective femoral hernia repairs. Of these, only 613 (21.8%) were done as day cases. In total, 52.1% of elective repairs were in people aged under 65 years and 76.2% in people aged under 75 years. If all elective surgery in those under 65 years was done as day cases, there would be an 139% rise in day-case surgery. If all surgery in those under 75 years was done as day cases, there would be a 249% rise in day-case surgery.

The numbers of procedures performed as day cases and as ordinary admissions, by age and gender, are shown in Tables 13 and 14.

Table 13: Numbers of admissions classified as day cases for femoral hernia repair in England.

Age band (years)	Primary repair			Recurrent repair			Total
	Unclassified	Male	Female	Unclassified	Male	Female	
0–4		6	3		1	1	1
15–14	0	13	16	0	2	2	33
15–24	1	8	26	0	0	1	36
25–34	2	35	93	0	1	1	132
35–44	4	43	177	0	4	8	236
45–54	6	126	276	0	5	15	428
55–64	12	228	308	0	14	11	573
65–74	25	366	712	0	24	28	1,155
75–84	14	360	870	0	19	23	1,286
85 plus	5	118	500	0	2	17	642
Not known			1				1
Total	69	1,303	2,982	0	72	107	4,533

Source: HES data, 1995–96.

Table 14: Numbers of ordinary admissions for femoral hernia repair in England.

Age band (years)	Primary repair			Recurrent repair			Total
	Unclassified	Male	Female	Unclassified	Male	Female	
0–4	0	4	5	0	0	0	9
5–14	0	15	9	0	1	0	25
15–24	0	12	6	0	0	0	18
25–34	0	17	58	0	0	1	76
35–44	1	10	106	0	1	3	121
45–54	1	33	116	1	3	3	157
55–64	0	39	65	0	0	0	104
65–74	0	29	44	0	1	1	75
75–84	0	9	17	0	1	0	27
85 plus	0	0	1	0	0	0	1
Total	2	168	427	1	7	8	613

Source: HES data, 1995–96.

Length of stay

Inguinal hernia repair

Length of stay for those admitted has fallen gradually over the last 7 years. These trends are illustrated in Figures 10 and 11. For some procedures the median length of stay was 0 because of the large numbers done as day cases.

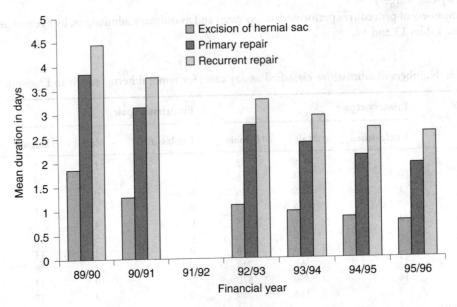

Figure 10: Trend in mean length of stay for inguinal hernia repair (NHS Hospitals, England, 1989–90 to 1995–96).

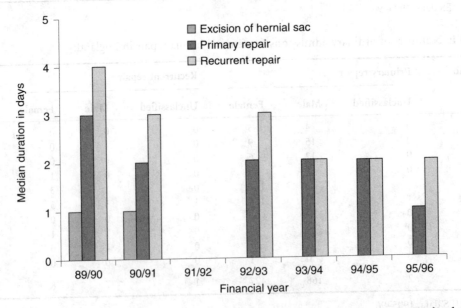

Figure 11: Trend in median length of stay for inguinal hernia repair (NHS Hospitals, England, 1989–90 to 1995–96).

The average length of stay is affected by the increasing numbers of day cases. Table 15 shows the average length of stay for ordinary admissions for 1995–96.

Table 15: Average length of stay for inguinal hernia procedures, excluding day cases.

Procedure type	Excision of hernia sac	Primary inguinal repair	Recurrent inguinal repair	All
Mean duration in days	2.5	2.7	3.0	2.7
Median duration in days	1	2	2	2

Source: HES data, 1995–96.

Femoral hernia repair

Length of stay for femoral hernia repair has fallen steadily (Figures 12 and 13, *see* overleaf). The median length of stay for primary and recurrent repair was 2 days in 1995–96. The mean length of stay was 4.2 days for primary repair and 3.2 days for recurrent repair.

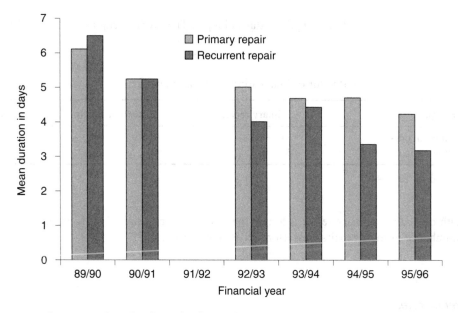

Figure 12: Trends in mean length of stay for femoral hernia repair (NHS Hospitals, England, 1989–90 to 1995–96).

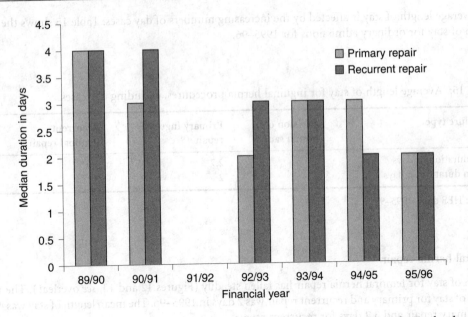

Figure 13: Trends in median length of stay for femoral hernia repair (NHS Hospitals, England, 1989–90 to 1995–96).

When day cases are excluded, the length of stay is longer. The average lengths of stay for 1995–96 are summarised in Table 16.

Table 16: Average length of stay for ordinary admissions in England.

Procedure type	Primary repair	Recurrent repair	All repairs
Mean duration in days	5.0	3.6	4.9
Median duration in days	3	2	3

Source: HES data, 1995–96.

The length of stay for primary repair is longer than for recurrent repair. This is presumably because a higher number of primary repairs are performed as emergencies.

Recurrence rates

Hernia recurrence was included in the high-level performance indicators published by the NHS Executive in June 1999. These are published as a directly age-standardised rate: recurrent repair per 100 000 population per annum, based on HES data for 1997–98. The rate for England was 11, with rates for health authorities ranging from 2 to 17. These figures are difficult to interpret, relating as they do to several types of hernia. Low rates may reflect a reluctance to undertake repair of recurrent hernia, rather than relating to the success of primary repairs.

Inguinal hernia repair

An approximation of the recurrence rate in England under current practices may be obtained from the percentage of procedures for recurrent hernia (in 1995–96, 7.2%).

There has been a steady rise in the percentage of repairs performed for recurrent hernia from the 5.2% seen in 1989–90. It is possible that this represents an increase in the failure rate, but it is perhaps more likely to be a reflection of a greater willingness to operate on recurrent hernia. Whatever the reasons for the rise, it suggests that in routine NHS practice the recurrence rate is nearer to 10% than to the 1% quoted by specialist centres.

Femoral hernia repair

In 1995–96, 3.8% of femoral hernia repairs were for recurrence. There has been a gradual reduction in the proportion of procedures for recurrence from the 5.7% seen in 1989–90.

Emergency repair

Inguinal hernia repair

The percentage of admissions for inguinal hernia that are classified as emergencies has fallen from 9.1% in 1989–90 to 6.0% in 1995–96. This trend is statistically significant ($p < 0.0001$ using the Chi-squared test for trend). In 1995–96, 6.0% of admissions were classified as emergencies. In total, 5.9% of primary repairs and 7.4% of recurrent repairs were classified as emergency admissions. One of the main objectives in undertaking hernia repair is to prevent obstruction and strangulation. This should lead to a fall in emergency admissions. Numbers of admissions categorised by admission method are summarised in Table 17.

Table 17: Numbers (%) of inguinal hernia repairs, by admission method.

Admission method	Gender	Excision of inguinal sac	Primary repair	Recurrent repair	Total	
Elective	Male	9,702 (11.1%)	59,312 (67.7%)	5,608 (6.4%)	74,622	(85.1%)
	Female	1,166 (1.3%)	4,638 (5.3%)	161 (0.2%)	5,965	(6.8%)
	Unclassified	103 (0.1%)	401 (0.5%)	35	539	(0.6%)
Emergency	Male	940 (1.1%)	3,201 (3.7%)	441 (0.5%)	4,582	(5.2%)
	Female	80 (0.1%)	506 (0.6%)	24	610	(0.7%)
	Unclassified	14	20	5	39	
Babies	Male	10	9		19	
	Female	1			1	
	Unclassified	1			1	
Others	Male	302 (0.3%)	83 (0.1%)	4	389	(0.4%)
	Female	25	17	1	43	
	Unclassified	207 (0.2%)	585 (0.7%)	49 (0.1%)	841	(1.0%)
Total		12,551 (14.3%)	68,772 (78.5%)	6,328 (7.2%)	87,651 (100%)	

Source: HES data, 1995–96.

Femoral hernia repair

There has been a small fall in the percentage of admissions classified as emergencies, from 47.4% in 1989–90 to 43.7% in 1995–96. This trend is statistically significant ($p < 0.0001$ using the Chi-squared test for trend). In total, 44.8% of the primary repairs and 23.6% of the recurrent repairs were done as emergencies. In Scottish Health Boards, 47.9% of femoral hernia repairs were done as emergencies.[37] The numbers of admissions categorised by admission method are summarised in Table 18.

Table 18: Numbers (%) of admissions, by admission type.

Admission method	Gender	Primary repair	Recurrent repair	Total
Elective	Male	905 (17.6%)	61 (1.2%)	966 (18.8%)
	Female	1,744 (33.9%)	85 (1.7%)	1,829 (35.5%)
	Unclassified	11 (0.2%)	1	12 (0.2%)
Emergency	Male	563 (10.9%)	17 (0.3%)	580 (11.3%)
	Female	1,642 (31.9%)	29 (0.6%)	1,671 (32.5%)
	Unclassified	11 (0.2%)	0	11 (0.2%)
Babies	Male	0	0	0
	Female	0	0	0
	Unclassified	0	0	0
Other	Male	49 (1.0%)	1	50 (1.0%)
	Female	3	1	4
	Unclassified	23 (0.4%)	0	23 (0.4%)
Total		4,951 (96.2%)	195 (3.8%)	5,146 (100%)

Source: HES data, 1995–96.

A woman is more likely to be admitted as an emergency for a femoral hernia repair than is a man. This may be because women are less likely to present to their GPs with groin swellings, are less likely to be referred for surgery or have to wait longer than men, or because femoral hernia in women is more likely to incarcerate or strangulate. There is some supporting evidence for the first of these explanations from the demand–incidence data in general practice (*see* Section 4).

Waiting times

Inguinal hernia repair

The length of wait has increased steadily over the seven-year period examined (Figure 14, *see* opposite). For inguinal hernia repairs in England in 1995–96, there was a mean wait of 133 days and a median wait of 85 days. For people unable to work as a consequence of their hernia, this length of wait is unacceptable. The median wait in Scotland for inguinal hernia for 1993 was somewhat less, at 56 days.[37]

There are marked variations in waiting times between different health authorities (Figure 15, *see* opposite, and Figures 16 and 17, *see* p. 698), with a twofold difference between the best and the worst.

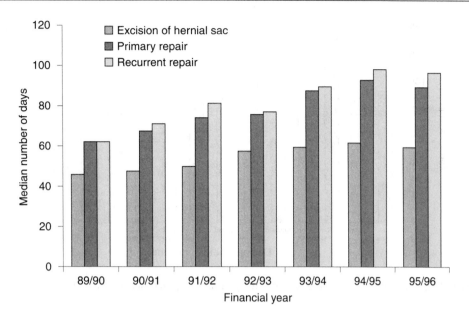

Figure 14: Trends in median length of wait for inguinal hernia repairs (NHS Hospitals, England, 1989–90 to 1995–96).

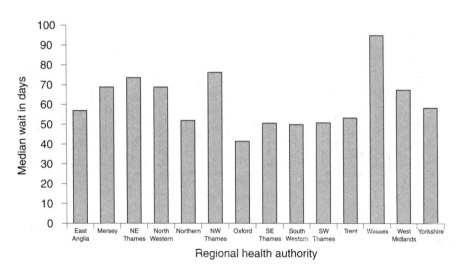

Figure 15: Regional variation in waiting times for excision of the hernial sac (NHS Hospitals, England, 1995–96).

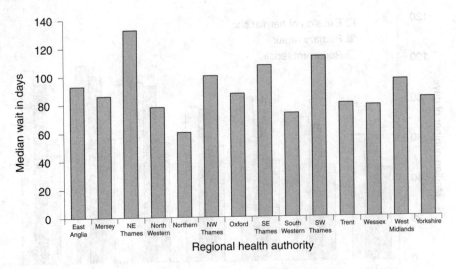

Figure 16: Regional variation in waiting times for primary inguinal hernia repair (NHS Hospitals, England, 1995–96).

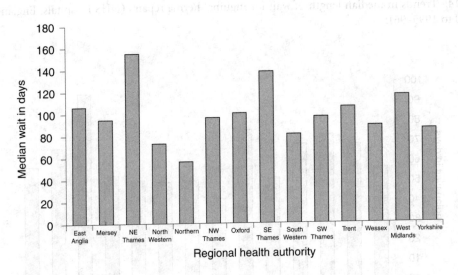

Figure 17: Regional variation in waiting times for recurrent inguinal hernia repair (NHS Hospitals, England, 1995–96).

Femoral hernia repair

Waiting times for femoral hernia have also risen steadily over the 7-year period examined (*see* Figure 18 opposite). This, combined with the static numbers of operations being performed (*see* 'Volume of surgery' on p. 683), suggests that the referral rate for surgery has increased. For the financial year 1995–96, the median wait for femoral hernia repair was 47 days, with a mean wait of 91.5 days. In Scotland in 1993, the median wait was 40 days.[37]

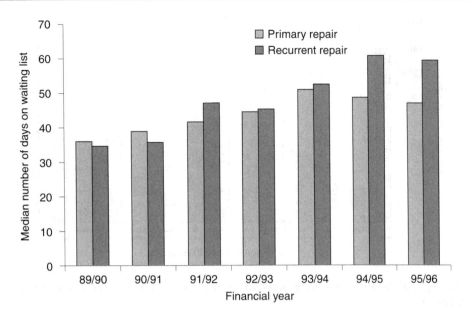

Figure 18: Trends in median length of wait for femoral hernia repair (NHS Hospitals, England, 1989–90 to 1995–96).

Marked variations in waiting times are observed between different regional health authorities (*see* Figure 19, and Figure 20 overleaf), with as much as a sixfold difference between the best and the worst.

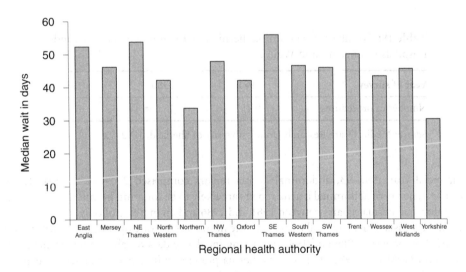

Figure 19: Regional variation in waiting times for primary femoral hernia repair (NHS Hospitals, England, 1995–96).

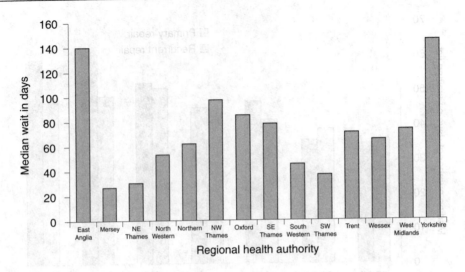

Figure 20: Regional variation in waiting times for recurrent femoral hernia repair (NHS Hospitals, England, 1995–96).

Activity in the private sector

Data on privately funded procedures are not widely available. However, the Medical Care Research Unit at Sheffield University surveyed independent hospitals in England and Wales in three separate years.[38,39] The 1992–93 survey was sent to 217 independent hospitals in England and Wales, 93% of whom replied. The Unit used the results to estimate the numbers of procedures carried out. The results for abdominal hernia are summarised in Table 19.

Table 19: Numbers of abdominal hernia repairs in independently funded hospitals in England and Wales.

Year of survey	1981	1986	1992–93
Number of procedures	9,435	15,664	16,444

Source: Medical Care Research Unit, University of Sheffield, 1992–93.

For the financial year 1992–93, abdominal hernia repairs comprised 2.4% of the private procedure workload. The majority of abdominal hernia repairs are likely to be for groin hernia. There was an increase of 65% in abdominal hernia repairs between 1981 and 1986 and an increase of only 5% between 1986 and 1992–93. This contrasts with an overall increase in the number of private operations of 67% between 1981 and 1986 and 42% between 1986 and 1992–93. Using incidence data on abdominal hernia from the GP morbidity survey GPMS3,[14] 49% of abdominal hernia presenting in general practice were groin hernia. Allowing for this and correcting for the fact that the independent hospital data relate to England and Wales, we would expect 7606 privately funded operations in the UK per year. This is equivalent to 15.5 per PCT of 100 000. In the GP morbidity survey,[14] 5.6% of outpatient referrals for abdominal hernia were to the private sector. Applying this to the number of expected new cases of groin hernia (263; *see* Section 4), we would expect 14.7 referrals per PCT of 100 000. These two estimates, calculated in different ways, are very close, which helps to validate the estimate.

Unfortunately, there are no data more recent than 1992–93 concerning levels of service provision in the private sector. There has been an underlying trend of increasing activity in the private sector, and a recently established specialised hernia repair centre (the British Hernia Centre) appears to be flourishing. They have reported results on thousands of patients.[40] This, along with increasing waiting times in the NHS and anecdotal reports of employers who are willing to pay for procedures for their own staff to avoid long periods of sick pay, suggests that numbers will have continued to rise. From the limited data available, it appears that there has been a greater percentage increase in the number of operations in the private sector than in the NHS, so that private patients may well be referred more frequently than the 5% seen in 1981–82.

Cost of service provision

The costs involved in the treatment of groin hernia are presented in Table 20. Some of these are charges (e.g. ECR charges) and as such will not necessarily be an estimate of the true cost. The actual price paid by a purchaser will often be lower when the service is included in a block contract.

Table 20: Costs and sources for groin hernia services.

Item	Unit cost	Source of cost data
Private day-case surgery. Price includes assessment and follow-up	£895	Informal enquiry to the London Hernia Centre in 1998 for a simple inguinal hernia repair in a fit 45-year-old man
Private GP consultation	£36	Medi Centre charge for consultation lasting up to 15 minutes. September 1998
Inpatient groin hernia repair	£814	HRG H73/H74 (inguinal or femoral hernia repair in a patient aged under 70 years without complications). Average ECR cost for West Midlands trusts, 1998–99
Day-case groin hernia repair	£488	HRG H73/H74 (inguinal or femoral hernia repair in a patient aged under 70 years without complications). Average ECR cost for West Midlands trusts, 1998–99
Outpatient appointment, first visit	£73	Average ECR cost for West Midlands trusts, 1998–99
Outpatient appointment, follow-up	£41	Average ECR cost for West Midlands trusts, 1998–99
General practitioner consultation Practice nurse consultation Practice nurse procedure	£14 £6 £6	Estimates from PSSRU at the University of Kent, based on 1996–97 prices[41]
Truss prescription	£16	Prescription Pricing Authority data for 1997–98. Mean cost of groin truss

Modelling the cost of groin hernia service provision in a PCT

These models are derived from data on existing service provision *and not on a desired model of care*. The model has been kept as simple as possible. It does not include the option of referral and conservative treatment, because there are no data on which to estimate likely numbers for this scenario. In practice, those who are prescribed trusses will require repeat prescriptions and assessments over the years. Data on truss use were based on numbers of prescriptions rather than on numbers of patients, so this will account for the annual expenditure on truss assessments and prescriptions. The majority of expenditure is on surgery.

Assumptions

Only NHS costs have been considered.

- In total, 73% of inguinal hernia and 64% of femoral hernia presenting to general practice are operated on in the NHS.
- In total, 29.7% of inguinal hernia repairs and 11.9% of femoral hernia repairs are performed as day-case procedures.
- In total, 15 groin hernia presenting to a PCT are referred to the private sector (*see* above).
- A patient having inpatient surgery requires two GP appointments, one outpatient (new) appointment and one practice-nurse appointment.
- A patient having private surgery requires one GP appointment and one practice-nurse appointment (assuming a day-case procedure), as prices quoted usually include assessment and one follow-up visit.
- A patient having day-case surgery requires two GP appointments, one outpatient appointment (new) and two practice-nurse appointments.
- A patient having conservative treatment requires two GP appointments, and 55% will be prescribed a truss (based on PPA data).
- In total, 29.7% of inguinal hernia and 11.9% of femoral hernia repairs are performed as day cases.
- Numbers are based on a PCT of 100 000 with the population structure of England.

For a PCT of 100 000 patients, in each year there would be 247 new referrals with inguinal hernia and 16 referrals with femoral hernia. Of the 247 inguinal hernia, 14 would be referred to the private sector, 180 would be operated on in the NHS and 53 would be treated conservatively. Of the NHS operations, 53 would be done as day cases and 127 as inpatient procedures. Of the 16 femoral hernia repairs, five would be treated conservatively, one would be referred to the private sector and ten would be operated on in the NHS. Of the NHS operations, one would be done as a day case and nine would be done as inpatient procedures (*see* Figures 21 and 22 opposite).

NHS costs associated with private surgery

A total of 15 episodes each requiring one GP appointment and one practice-nurse appointment.

Total £300.

NHS costs for inpatient surgery

A total of 136 episodes each requiring two GP appointments, one new outpatient appointment, one surgical inpatient procedure and one practice-nurse appointment.

Total £125 256.

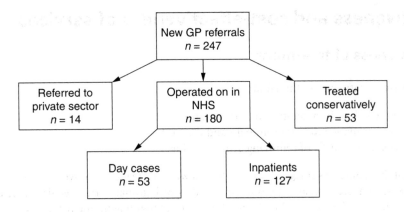

Figure 21: Inguinal hernia: modelling patient flows.

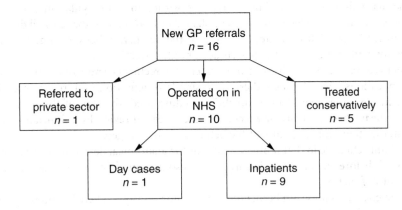

Figure 22: Femoral hernia; modelling patient flows. (Conservative treatment for femorial hernia is not recommended, but in practice some patients may decline surgery and others are not being offered it.)

NHS costs for day-case surgery

A total of 54 episodes each requiring two GP appointments, one new outpatient appointment, one surgical day-case procedure and two practice-nurse appointments.

Total £32 454.

NHS costs for conservative treatment

A total of 58 episodes each requiring two GP appointments. A total of 32 episodes requiring truss prescription.

Total £2136.

Total annual NHS costs

The estimated total annual NHS cost of treatment for hernia for a PCT of 100 000 patients is £160 000.

6 Effectiveness and cost-effectiveness of services

Appropriateness of treatment

The aims of hernia treatment are threefold:

- to eliminate the risk of incarceration or strangulation
- to provide symptomatic relief of groin pain and discomfort
- to give the cosmetic benefit of removing groin swelling.

There is no trial that compares surgery for groin hernia with no treatment or with conservative treatment (i.e. trusses). Research is dominated by outcome studies of inguinal hernia repair, by measurement of recurrence rates and by trials comparing different methods of inguinal hernia repair. Corresponding data for femoral hernia are sparse.

There is a consensus among surgeons that surgery is the treatment of choice in children and in patients with femoral hernia. This is because the lifetime risk of obstruction or strangulation is higher in these two groups of patients. The Royal College guidelines published in 1992 advised that a small direct hernia in an elderly person might be best left untreated.[42] However, the distinction between a direct and an indirect hernia is not easily made clinically, with an accuracy of only 69%.[25]

The effectiveness of surgery is usually measured in terms of recurrence rate, recovery period or return to work, and complications. Unfortunately there is no standard definition of a 'recurrence'. The reported recurrence rate in any series may depend on the procedure used, the skill of the operator, the length of follow-up and the method of identifying recurrences, e.g. regular review by a clinician vs. self-reporting. There are few studies that look at quality of life before and after surgery.

Surgery is certainly effective in that it offers a cure for the anatomical defect in most people. Evaluation of the quality of life before and after hernia surgery has also demonstrated a significant reduction in pain and improvement in function.[4]

Reported recurrence rates for groin hernia repair vary enormously.[43] There has been a general trend for recurrence rates to fall over time, and specialist centres publish very low recurrence rates. The British Hernia Centre claims a recurrence rate of less than 1% over follow-up of one-and-a-half to five years.[40,44] The Shouldice Centre and the Lichtenstein Centre quote similarly low recurrence rates.[33,45] This is probably due in part to the skill and expertise of the dedicated hernia surgeons, but there are also some claims that it is a result of their chosen method.[33] Other series quote recurrence rates for inguinal hernia repair of between 0.7% and 14.3%.[21] Failure of recurrent inguinal hernia repair may be as high as 30%.[46]

In his review of 2105 femoral hernia repairs, Glasgow found recurrence rates of 2% for primary repairs and 7–10% for recurrent repairs.[47] A Spanish series of 93 femoral hernia repairs (using the Lichtenstein technique), with follow-up ranging from 2 to 4 years, reports one recurrence in 93 repairs (recurrence rate 1.1%).[48]

Scottish Health Boards report a recurrence rate of 1% for inguinal hernia and 0.5% for femoral hernia over a 2-year follow-up period,[37] but it is not clear how recurrence has been defined. If the figures have been derived from routine data sources, they are likely to be an underestimate.

In the USA, approximately 10% of all hernia repairs are for recurrent hernia.[49] The equivalent figure for England, using 1995–96 HES data, is 7.2%. These figures will underestimate the true recurrence rate, as they are dependent on the diagnosis and on referral for recurrent repair.

Differences in case-mix are unlikely to account for the large differences in outcome between these overall rates and those quoted by specialist centres. The average age of men operated on at the British Hernia Centre is lower than that for men operated on in the NHS. However, the British Hernia Centre does operate on elderly patients and on patients with a variety of manual and sedentary occupations.[40] They are also happy to operate on patients with large or difficult hernia. Twenty per cent of groin hernia procedures performed at the British Hernia Centre were for large scrotal hernia.[40]

The quality of the available evidence on the effectiveness of interventions (*see* Appendix II) is set out in Table 21.

Table 21: Quality grading of evidence.

Intervention	Size of effect	Quality of evidence
Surgery for femoral hernia	A	III
Truss for femoral hernia	E	IV
Surgery for inguinal hernia	B	III
Truss for inguinal hernia	C	III
Conservative treatment for small direct hernia	B	III
Specialist (hernia unit) care	B	II
Laparoscopic surgery vs. open surgery	C	I

A good-quality systematic review of hernia surgery was published in 1998.[50] It sought to answer six questions in relation to groin hernia repair. The authors' conclusions are summarised in Table 22.

Table 22: Summary of conclusions of systematic review by Cheek *et al.*[50]

Research question	Conclusions
Is local anaesthesia (LA) a safe and effective alternative to general anaesthesia?	LA has fewer adverse effects on respiratory function than does general or regional anaesthesia. Procedures are shorter under LA and outcomes appear to be equivalent.
Is there a difference in outcome between specialist and non-specialist surgeons?	Large series from specialist centres demonstrate low recurrence rates. There are no trials comparing specialist with non-specialist results. Rigorous studies are required.
Are day-case procedures as safe and effective as inpatient surgery?	There is no evidence that outcomes differ between day-case procedures and inpatient surgery. Studies with longer follow-up periods are required to assess the recurrence rate.
Is synchronous bilateral hernia repair as safe and effective as delayed repair?	There was insufficient evidence to allow a conclusion to be reached.
Which method of surgery is the safest and most effective for inguinal hernia repair?	Laparoscopic repair is superior to open surgery in terms of post-operative pain and time to return to work. Recurrence rates and wound infections do not appear to differ.
	The Shouldice repair appears to result in fewer recurrences than do other suture methods. Open-mesh repairs may result in less post-operative pain and lead to faster recovery than does the Shouldice repair.
	It is difficult to draw conclusions on the choice of laparoscopic technique. A totally extra-peritoneal approach may have better outcomes than other laparoscopic methods.
Which method is the safest and most effective for femoral hernia repair?	Unable to draw any conclusions, as the literature was so poor.

The literature search for this review was completed in February 1996. The bulk of new research since this time concerns the use of laparoscopic methods for inguinal hernia repair.

These issues are discussed in more detail in the next section. The discussion relates entirely to inguinal hernia repair because of the paucity of published data on femoral repair.

Anaesthetic alternatives

General, regional (epidural or spinal) and local anaesthesia may all be used for hernia repair. Laparoscopic hernia repair is only possible under general anaesthesia. For open surgery, local anaesthesia is an option, provided that the hernia is reducible and the patient is not obese. Operating under local infiltration anaesthesia does enable the patient to demonstrate the hernia during the operation and to test the repair by straining. These are small advantages to the surgeon, of no real consequence. There is no evidence to support local or general anaesthesia in the early post-operative period or later in terms of return to work. Some patients may have contraindications to general anaesthesia,[51-53] while others will refuse a local anaesthetic.[53] It is also easier to organise day-case surgery when there is no requirement for general anaesthetic administration, because patients may be discharged home almost immediately.

Specialist vs. non-specialist care

Open repair of an inguinal hernia is a procedure learned by surgeons early in training but performed variably. Technical difficulties are minimised by the mesh technique. By contrast the Shouldice repair is demanding and requires a considerable apprenticeship. The Shouldice Clinic in Canada requires staff members to perform 100 procedures as assistants before allowing them to embark alone.[40] Laparoscopic techniques are most demanding of all and at present are carried out only by surgeons with a special interest in minimal-access surgery. During the learning curve, operation times are longer and the surgeon may have to convert to an open technique. This applies to surgeons who have considerable experience of minimal-access surgery in other areas.[54]

There have been no randomised trials comparing treatment at a specialist centre with 'routine' care, although published recurrence rates are lower from specialist centres. A cohort study undertaken in the USA demonstrated better outcomes in patients treated by the specialist hernia team than in those given routine care by general surgeons.[55] Standardisation of care within a general setting may offer benefits.[56]

Day-case vs. inpatient care

Day-case treatment costs less and has the practical advantage that the procedure is less likely to be cancelled because of the lack of a bed. There are no other advantages in terms of outcome to the patient. There has been a long history of day-case surgery; a Scottish surgeon performed nearly 500 outpatient inguinal hernia repairs in 1955,[57] but others have been slow to follow.

The percentage of patients receiving day-case repair is rising year on year as surgeons and patients gain confidence. Inevitably some patients are excluded by the day-case selection criteria. For example, patients undergoing bilateral hernia repair are not appropriate. In general it is the older patient who is likely to be excluded, either through an escalating ASA (American Society of Anaesthetists) grade or through social isolation. In contrast, the British Hernia Centre and the Shouldice Centre undertake the majority of repairs as day cases, even in the very elderly. Presumably patients will not present for surgery if they are unable to make arrangements for their aftercare.

Choice of surgical technique

Comparing the Shouldice repair with the Lichtenstein mesh repair for inguinal hernia, Cheek *et al.*[50] concluded that the two techniques are equivalent, stating that 'neither procedure appears to have a clear advantage over the other'. Their analysis considers operative morbidity and recurrence rate and is heavily dependent on data from randomised, controlled studies.

When the Shouldice technique is compared with open sutured repairs (Maloney darn) based upon the evidence of randomised studies with 2-year follow-up, the Shouldice repair is superior with 'a clear difference' in recurrence rate at 2 years.[50] Cheek *et al.* were unable to make any comparison between mesh repair and sutured repair because 'a paucity of studies meant no conclusions can be drawn'.

Laparoscopic repair of inguinal hernia is the most recently developed surgical technique. It offers a radical new approach, but there are as yet no definitive conclusions regarding its use.* Laparoscopic repair is suitable for reducible hernia, either primary or recurrent. Fewer surgeons are competent to perform laparoscopic repair, whereas an open repair is within the repertoire of all trained general surgeons. The laparoscopic repair has distinct advantages when dealing with a recurrent hernia. It is probably the preferred if more expensive choice when the failure follows original surgery by an open method.[58]

There have been numerous controlled trials since Cheek *et al.* undertook their systematic review. These trials confirm that laparoscopic surgery takes longer than open repair but that the recovery time is shorter.[58–75] Recovery has been measured in terms of time to return to work or to normal activities, global quality of life using the SF36, and severity and extent of post-operative pain.

Two large multi-centre studies have looked at complications and recurrence rate.[45,70] One large such study by the MRC, comparing laparoscopic repair with open hernia repairs (predominantly mesh repairs),[45] found that patients in the laparoscopic group recovered more quickly but that all recurrences and serious surgical complications occurred in this group. However, the major complications occurred in relation to a trans-abdominal technique, which is being superseded by an extra-peritoneal technique. Another large multi-centre trial found laparoscopic surgery to be safer than a conventional open approach, but in this study extra-peritoneal approaches were used.[70] There is an ongoing debate over the costs and benefits of laparoscopic hernia repair, and as yet no consensus has been reached.[76] The EU Hernia Trialists Collaboration has registered a systematic review of laparoscopic vs. open hernia repair with the Cochrane Collaboration.[77]

Prolonged follow-up is desirable when assessing recurrence rates, as over 50% of recurrences occur four or more years after surgery.[21,46] Reported results from randomised controlled trials rarely extend this far.

A recent survey in the West Midlands found that laparoscopic techniques were used in only 35% of the units undertaking groin hernia repair. In each centre, only one or two members of surgical staff would undertake laparoscopic repair, so that only a small proportion of repairs were performed laparoscopically. Mesh repairs were common to all units, and 70% performed some form of open-suture technique.[78] In the USA, more than 80% of repairs involve a mesh prosthesis and are completed as outpatients.[79]

Economic issues

There is one cost-effectiveness study comparing surgery with conservative treatment for groin hernia. Neuhauser modelled elective surgery against the provision of a truss in the elderly (65 years or over). He found no survival benefit from elective surgery in this group of patients.[26] Even assuming a perfect surgeon (i.e. with no recurrences and no mortality from elective surgery), although there was then a survival benefit, the cost per life-year gained was high. There are two main problems with this study. First, the

---

* Since this chapter was written the National Institute for Clinical Excellence has published guidance on laparoscopic surgery for inguinal hernia repair, *see* www.nice.org.uk.

estimates of the annual risk of strangulation may not have been appropriate. Secondly, no account was taken of the quality of life in either group. In addition, it is important to remember that the calculations would be different in a younger group who would stand to lose more of their life expectancy if they died from a complication.

It is impossible from the data available to assess the level of need for hernia repair accurately. There are no good risk estimates for strangulation or incarceration. Neither do we know whether people are offered an operation principally to reduce the risk of complications and premature death, to relieve symptoms or for cosmetic benefit.

People in manual occupations may be on sick leave for prolonged periods of time while waiting for a hernia repair, with considerable cost to the individual, their employers and the Welfare State. If 1% of people waiting for an inguinal hernia repair are unable to work while waiting, with a mean wait of 133 days, this is equivalent to 295 lost years of productivity per annum.

Economic studies of different methods of repair have found that laparoscopic surgery is more expensive because of longer operating times, higher equipment costs and the need for overnight hospital stay.[58,80,81] This may be partly offset by the faster recovery of the patient and earlier return to work.[81] However, the additional costs are borne by the health sector, and the cost benefits would be outside the health sector.

The median time to resume 'normal' activities following surgery varies enormously between studies – any time between 1 and 6 weeks.[40] In the UK, patients are routinely given sick notes for 4 to 6 weeks without assessment of the patient's condition or ability to undertake their usual work. In the USA, median time to return to work and period of post-operative pain have been related to the availability of compensation.[82] Specialist centres undertaking open, tension-free repair recommend early mobilisation, and patients return to work after a median period of 9 days.[40] An American surgeon describes over 20 000 hernia repairs, all undertaken with local anaesthetic, where patients are advised to mobilise immediately (they climb down from the operating table) and resume normal activities on the same day.[83] Patients who do not mobilise are at increased risk of deep venous thrombosis. While sick leave does not affect health care spending, it does have an effect on overall public spending. Current recommendations for time off work need to be reconsidered.

The cost-effectiveness of surgery can best be improved by reducing recurrence and increasing the proportion of procedures performed as day cases.[49]

7 Quantified models of care and recommendations

Inguinal hernia is a common condition and will continue to require considerable surgical resource to relieve symptoms and prevent life-threatening complications. There is a growing understanding of the laparoscopic approach, which is at least equivalent to the open repair, but it is the latter that will remain the mainstay of treatment for some years to come. There is insufficient expertise in the surgical community to support a change to the laparoscopic alternative except for recurrent hernia. However, it is important that the skills are encouraged if there are local pockets of expertise. Present knowledge would advise repair by experienced surgeons, but not necessarily in a specialist centre.

Groin hernia cannot be prevented (although they may be less common in non-smokers), and they tend to increase in size if left. The only effective treatment is surgery. There is a need to identify patients who can probably benefit from surgical intervention and to offer them an efficient service and safe and effective surgery. Many elderly people with an asymptomatic hernia would decline surgery if they felt that their health was not at risk. Unfortunately, it is not possible to give precise estimates of risk to any individual.

The costs of groin hernia may be reduced by increasing day-case surgery, reducing recurrence rates[49] and reducing the time spent off work waiting for or recuperating from surgery. The limiting factor for day-case surgery may be the lack of social support available for many elderly people, rather than strict medical factors.

We offer these recommendations for improvements in the current provision of service.

- Femoral trusses should not be prescribable on an FP10, as there is no clinical justification for their use.[2]
- Day-case surgery should be maximised, as it will free up hospital beds. Acute care throughput per bed is now higher in the UK than in any other Organisation for Economic Co-operation and Development (OECD) country, and some have argued that the pressure on the acute sector could compromise the quality of care.[84] Charges are much less for day-case surgery than for inpatient surgery, so there is potential for saving costs. More patients are suitable for day-case surgery if local rather than general anaesthetic techniques are used.
- Waiting lists have increased steadily over the past few years. This situation needs to be addressed. It may be sensible to introduce a prioritisation scheme so that those who are incapacitated by their hernia would not have to wait long for surgery. It is reassuring to see that, despite an increase in waiting time for operations, the percentage of inguinal hernia operations performed as emergencies has fallen, without a rise in mortality. There has been a very small decrease in the percentage of femoral hernia operations performed as emergencies, and the mortality rate seems fairly stable.
- Laparoscopic surgery is offered routinely in some centres. The surgery takes longer and is more expensive, and longer-term outcomes are probably equivalent to conventional techniques, but recovery time for the patients appears to be reduced.[49,50,58] There is a need for capital investment in equipment and investment in training. A move to laparoscopic surgery would increase costs and would put pressure on inpatient beds, because the surgery cannot be performed under local anaesthetic and fewer patients would be suitable for day-case surgery.
- Specialist hernia centres offer better outcomes in terms of recurrence rates than are achieved routinely in the NHS (1% vs. 5–10%; *see* Section 6). It is difficult to know whether these results are affected by patient selection, with private clinics more likely to operate on young, fit patients who require straightforward repairs. The private centres, however, do claim to be successful with recurrent hernia. As a starting point, all trusts should collect data on the outcomes of hernia repair for publication. Scottish Health Boards all publish 2-year outcomes for hernia repair. English trusts and PCTs should be able to do the same.
- Specialist privately funded hernia centres provide a model of hernia repair provision that could be used in the NHS. At the British Hernia Centre, all operations are performed under local anaesthetic and are done as day-case procedures. Surgeons have extensive experience in hernia surgery. It is feasible for the NHS to operate a similar system, as demonstrated by Kingsnorth and colleagues.[56] As several specialist centres[34,40,51] quote equally low recurrence rates despite using different techniques, it implies that recurrence is related more to the skill of the operator than to the actual technique used.
- The Royal College of Surgeons has collected data on 5500 groin hernia repairs as part of their National Groin Hernia Outcomes Project (NGHOP). The results give valuable information on recurrence rates following NHS surgery. Open-mesh repairs have largely replaced 'darn' methods, and the majority of procedures are being carried out under the supervision of senior surgeons.[85] These changes may have resulted in improved outcomes from hernia surgery.
- With modern 'tension-free' methods, early mobilisation is encouraged and 1–2 weeks of sick leave should be adequate for most people. General practitioners need revised guidance on recommendations for return to work following hernia repair.

Cost-modelling an increase in day-case surgery

An average PCT with lists totalling 100 000 and the population structure of England would expect 247 new inguinal hernia cases and 16 new femoral hernia cases every year (*see* Section 4).

Assumptions are as follows.

- All elective hernia repairs in patients under 65 years of age could be done safely as day cases. Potential numbers of day cases are based on the numbers of elective procedures performed in those aged under 65 years.
- Outcomes from day-case surgery are the same as those for inpatient surgery.[46]
- Only NHS costs have been considered. The costs used are those outlined in Section 5.
- Patients having day-case surgery would require an extra GP consultation and a practice-nurse consultation.
- Numbers are based on a PCT of 100 000 with the population structure of England.

A PCT would expect to commission 8 elective femoral hernia repairs and 166 elective inguinal hernia repairs per year.

For 1995–96, 21.8% of elective femoral hernia repairs were performed as day cases, but 52.1% of patients were aged under 65 years. Assuming a move from 21.8% day-case surgery to 52.1% day-case surgery, 2 patients would be operated on as day cases instead of as inpatients.

For 1995–96, 32.1% of elective inguinal hernia repairs were performed as day cases, but 65.5% of patients were aged under 65 years. Assuming a move from 32.1% day-case surgery to 65.5% day-case surgery, 56 patients would be operated on as day cases instead of as inpatients.

Therefore the total number of patients who would be operated on as day cases instead of as inpatients is 58.

The difference between charges for day-case surgery and for inpatient surgery = £326.

Additional care costs in primary care for day-case surgery = £21.

Therefore the marginal cost saving per hernia repair moved from inpatient care to day-case surgery = £305.

The potential cost saving per PCT per year (for 58 patients) is £17 690.

This calculation assumes that charges are a true estimate of cost and that cost savings can be realised. It does not take into account the cost of developing or expanding a day-case unit, in terms of either building work or staff training. It is also unlikely that staff costs of inpatient care could be reduced. It is perhaps better to consider the opportunity cost of using inpatient beds unnecessarily when the pressures on beds are considerable.

8 Outcomes, audit methods and targets

Recurrence rates

Recurrence rates of less than 1% at 1–2 years are achievable at specialist hernia centres, and this is the standard we should aim to achieve in the NHS. The definition of recurrence would need to take into account the period of observation and a specific definition of recurrent hernia (e.g. whether to include just those presenting for recurrent repair, or whether to invite patients back for clinical assessment). In order to allow comparison, trusts and PCTs should collect and publish recurrence rates for hernia repair in a standardised way, as the Scottish Health Boards do.

Wound infection rates and other complications

Complications of groin hernia surgery include:

- wound haematomas
- wound infection
- sinus formation (unusual with modern suture material)
- scrotal complications, e.g. oedema, testicular atrophy
- urinary retention
- medical problems, e.g. myocardial infarct, pulmonary embolism
- death within 28 days of surgery.

Most centres will be unable to quote their complication rates for surgery, apart from death within 28 days. Published series quote very variable rates, e.g. wound infection rates of 0.13–0.6% and sinus formation rates of 0.1–4.9%.[21] Providers need to develop systems for monitoring complication rates.

9 Information and research priorities

What are the limitations of day-case surgery?

Can hernia at risk of strangulation be predicted?

Some research shows that the risk of strangulation is much higher soon after diagnosis.[23] It also seems to be unusual for femoral hernia to strangulate while a patient is on the waiting list for hernia repair. It may be that those who present for treatment are the ones with long-standing hernia at little risk of strangulation. The percentage of femoral repairs performed as an emergency has changed little over the years, at 45%.

If it is so important to operate on some hernia, should we be raising awareness among patients so that they seek medical advice at an early stage?

Can we ever determine the relative cost-effectiveness of repair vs. conservative management?

Is there a place for the truss in a modern health service?

This would require an RCT measuring quality of life, comparing a truss with surgery for those at low risk of strangulation. Patients using a truss could be offered surgery at the end of the study period. Waiting times for surgery are already five months, so the study could be organised and would not even introduce a delay. At a minimum, there should be a prospective cohort study examining quality-of-life issues in truss users.

Are the additional benefits in terms of quality of life following laparoscopic hernia repair worth the additional cost?

Is there a case for specialisation of hernia services?

This would require an RCT comparing, for example, protocol-driven care by general surgeons with operation by members of a specialist team.

Appendix I: Codes

Diagnostic codes

International Classification of Diseases (ICD). Ninth revision

Code	Description
550	Inguinal hernia
550.0	Inguinal hernia, with gangrene
550.1	Inguinal hernia, with obstruction, without mention of gangrene
550.9	Inguinal hernia, without mention of obstruction or gangrene
551.0	Femoral hernia, with gangrene
552.0	Femoral hernia, with obstruction, without mention of gangrene
553.0	Femoral hernia, without mention of obstruction or gangrene

International Classification of Diseases (ICD). Tenth revision

Code	Description
K40	Inguinal hernia
K40.0	Bilateral inguinal hernia, with obstruction, without gangrene
K40.1	Bilateral inguinal hernia, with gangrene
K40.2	Bilateral inguinal hernia, without obstruction or gangrene
K40.3	Unilateral or unspecified inguinal hernia, with obstruction, without gangrene
K40.4	Unilateral or unspecified inguinal hernia, with gangrene
K40.9	Unilateral or unspecified inguinal hernia, without obstruction or gangrene
K41	Femoral hernia
K41.0	Bilateral femoral hernia, with obstruction, without gangrene
K41.1	Bilateral femoral hernia, with gangrene
K41.2	Bilateral femoral hernia, without obstruction or gangrene
K41.3	Unilateral or unspecified femoral hernia, with obstruction, without gangrene
K41.4	Unilateral or unspecified femoral hernia, with gangrene
K41.9	Unilateral or unspecified femoral hernia, without obstruction or gangrene

READ^{TM} *diagnostic codes and their ICD 10 equivalents* (continued overleaf)

Read diagnostic code	ICD 10
J3012, Bilat.inguinal hernia, with obstruction	K40.0
J3013, Bilat.recur.inguinal hernia, with obstruction	K40.0
J3022, Bilat.inguinal hernia, irreducible	K40.0
J3023, Bilat.recur.inguinal hernia, irreducible	K40.0
J3002, Bilat.inguinal hernia, with gangrene	K40.1
J3003, Bilat.recur.inguinal hernia, with gangrene	K40.1
J3032, Bilat.inguinal hernia, simple	K40.2
J3033, Bilat.recur.inguinal hernia, simple	K40.2
J30y2, Bilat.inguinal hernia, unspecified	K40.2
J30y3, Bilat.recur.inguinal hernia, unspecified	K40.2
J301, Inguinal hernia, with obstruction	K40.3
J3010, Unilat.inguinal hernia, with obstruction	K40.3
J3011, Unilat.recur.inguinal hernia, with obstruction	K40.3
J301z, Inguinal hernia, with obstruction NOS	K40.3
J302, Inguinal hernia, irreducible	K40.3
J3020, Unilat.inguinal hernia, irreducible	K40.3
J3021, Unilat.recur.inguinal hernia, irreducible	K40.3
J302z, Inguinal hernia, irreducible NOS	K40.3
J300, Inguinal hernia, with gangrene	K40.4
J3000, Unilat.inguinal hernia, with gangrene	K40.4
J3001, Unilat.recur.inguinal hernia, with gangrene	K40.4
J300z, Inguinal hernia, with gangrene NOS	K40.4
J303, Simple inguinal hernia	K40.9
J3030, Unilat.inguinal hernia, simple	K40.9
J3031, Unilat.recur.inguinal.hernia, simple	K40.9
J303z, Simple inguinal hernia, NOS	K40.9
J304, Direct inguinal hernia	K40.9
J305, Indirect inguinal hernia	K40.9
J30y, Inguinal hernia, unspecified	K40.9
J30y0, Unilat.inguinal hernia, unspecified	K40.9
J30y1, Unilat.recur.inguinal hernia, unspecified	K40.9
J30yz, Inguinal hernia, unspecified NOS	K40.9
J30z, Inguinal hernia, NOS	K40.9
J3112, Bilat.femoral hernia, with obstruction	K41.0
J3113, Bilat.recur.femoral hernia, with obstruction	K41.0
J3122, Bilat.femoral hernia, irreducible	K41.0
J3123, Bilat.recur.femoral hernia, irreducible	K41.0
J3102, Bilat.femoral hernia, with gangrene	K41.1
J3103, Bilat.recur.femoral hernia, with gangrene	K41.1
J3132, Bilat.femoral hernia, simple	K41.2
J3133, Bilat.recur.femoral hernia, simple	K41.2
J31y2, Bilat.femoral hernia, unspecified	K41.2
J31y3, Bilat.recur.femoral hernia, unspecified	K41.2

READ™ diagnostic codes and their ICD 10 equivalents (continued)

Read diagnostic code	ICD 10
J311, Femoral hernia, with obstruction	K41.3
J3110, Unilat.femoral hernia, with obstruction	K41.3
J3111, Unilat.recur.femoral hernia, with obstruction	K41.3
J311z, Femoral hernia, with obstruction NOS	K41.3
J312, Femoral hernia, irreducible	K41.3
J3120, Unilat.femoral hernia, irreducible	K41.3
J3121, Unilat.recur.femoral hernia, irreducible	K41.3
J312z, Femoral hernia, irreducible NOS	K41.3
J310, Femoral hernia, with gangrene	K41.4
J3100, Unilat.femoral hernia, with gangrene	K41.4
J3101, Unilat.recur.femoral hernia, with gangrene	K41.4
J310z, Femoral hernia, with gangrene NOS	K41.4
J313, Simple femoral hernia	K41.9
J3130, Unilat.femoral hernia, simple	K41.9
J3131, Unilat.recur.femoral hernia, simple	K41.9
J313z, Simple femoral hernia, NOS	K41.9
J31y, Unspecified femoral hernia	K41.9
J31y0, Unilat.femoral hernia, unspecified	K41.9
J31y1, Unilat.recur.femoral hernia, unspecified	K41.9
J31yz, Unspecified femoral hernia, NOS	K41.9
J31z, Femoral hernia, NOS	K41.9

Procedure codes

Office of Population Censuses and Surveys, fourth revision (OPCS4) and READ codes for hernia procedures*

OPCS4	READ	Description
T19	7H10	Simple excision of inguinal hernia sac
T20	7H11	Primary repair of inguinal hernia
T21	7H12	Repair of recurrent inguinal hernia
T22	7H13	Primary repair of femoral hernia
T23	7H14	Repair of recurrent femoral hernia

Four-digit codes are available to give a greater degree of precision.

In the text of this document, primary inguinal hernia repair refers to codes T19 and T20 combined.

---

* Supplementary codes may be required for bowel resection, for example, or for relief of bowel strangulation.

Case-mix groups

Diagnosis-related groups (DRGs)

DRG code	Description
161	Inguinal and femoral hernia procedures in a patient aged > 17 years without complications or comorbidity
162	Inguinal and femoral hernia procedures in a patient aged > 17 years with complications or comorbidity
163	Hernia procedures in a patient aged 0–17 years

Health-related groups (HRGs)*

HRG	OPCS4
F73	T19
F74	T20 to T23

*Where there are complications or comorbidities, HRGs will be lifted to a resource group higher than the two listed. For instance, where the procedure involves a bowel resection, the HRG will be that for bowel resection.

Appendix II: Grading of evidence

Size of effect

A The procedure/service has a strong beneficial effect.
B The procedure/service has a moderate beneficial effect.
C The procedure/service has a measurable beneficial effect.
D The procedure/service has no measurable beneficial effect.
E The harms of the procedure/service outweigh its benefits.

Quality of evidence

I-1 Evidence from several consistent or one large randomised controlled trial.
I-2 Evidence obtained from at least one properly designed randomised controlled trial.
II-1 Evidence obtained from well-designed controlled trials without randomisation, or from well-designed cohort or case–control analytic studies.
II-2 Evidence obtained from multiple time-series with or without the intervention. Dramatic results in uncontrolled experiments (such as the results of the introduction of penicillin treatment in the 1940s) could also be regarded as this type of evidence.
III Opinions of respected authorities, based on clinical experience, descriptive studies or reports of expert committees.
IV Inadequate and conflicting evidence.

References

1 Read R. Historical survey of the treatment of hernia. In: Nyhus L, Condon R (eds). *Hernia* (3e). Philadelphia: Lippincott, 1989, pp. 3–17.

2 Cheek C, Williams M, Farndon J. Trusses in the management of hernia today. *Br J Surg* 1995; **82**: 1611–13.

3 Condon R, Nyhus L. Complications of groin hernia. In: Nyhus L, Condon R (eds). *Hernia* (3e). Philadelphia: Lippincott, 1989, pp. 253–69.

4 Lawrence K, McWhinnie D, Jenkinson C, Coulter A. Quality of life in patients undergoing inguinal hernia repair. *Ann R Coll Surg Eng* 1997; **79**(1): 40–5.

5 Office for National Statistics. *Mortality Statistics Cause*. London: The Stationery Office, 1997.

6 Reaveley A, Nguyen-Van-Tam S, Logan R. Who dies from hernia? *J Epidemiol Community Health* 1998; **52**: 532–3.

7 Condon R. The anatomy of the inguinal region and its relation to groin hernia. In: Nyhus L, Condon R (eds). *Hernia* (3e). Philadelphia: Lippincott, 1989, pp. 18–64.

8 Devlin HB, Kingsnorth A. Groin hernias in babies and children. In: *Management of Abdominal Hernias*. London: Chapman and Hall Medical, 1998, pp. 109–26.

9 Devlin HB, Kingsnorth A. Inguinal hernia in adults. I. The operation. In: *Management of Abdominal Hernias*. London: Chapman and Hall Medical, 1998, pp. 141–66.

10 Devlin HB, Kingsnorth A. Femoral hernia. In: *Management of Abdominal Hernias*. London: Chapman and Hall Medical, 1998, pp. 199–209.

11 Ralphs DN, Brain AJ, Grundy DJ, Hobsley M. How accurately can direct and indirect inguinal hernias be distinguished? *BMJ* 1980; **280**: 1039–40.

12 Abramson JH, Gofin J, Hopp C, Makler A, Epstein LM. The epidemiology of inguinal hernia: a survey in western Jerusalem. *J Epidemiol Community Health* 1978; **32**(1): 59–67.

13 McCormick A, Fleming D, Charlton J. *Morbidity Statistics from General Practice. Fourth national study*. London: HMSO, 1995.

14 Royal College of General Practitioners. *Morbidity Statistics from General Practice. Third national study*. London: HMSO, 1986.

15 Bailey H. *Demonstrations of Physical Signs in Clinical Surgery*. Bristol: Wright, 1942.

16 Zimmerman L, Anson B. *Anatomy and Surgery of Hernia* (2e). Baltimore, MD: Williams and Wilkins, 1967.

17 Nilsson J. Hernia in industry. *Surg Gynaecol Obstet* 1937; **64**: 400–2.

18 Trussell R, Elinson J. *Chronic Illness in a Rural Area: the Hunterdon study*. Cambridge, MA: Harvard University Press, 1959.

19 Edwards H. Discussion on hernia. *Proc R Soc Med* 1943; **36**: 186–9.

20 Yordanov Y, Stoyanov Y. The incidence of hernia on the island of Pemba. *East Afr Med J* 1969; **46**: 687–91.

21 Williams M, Frankel S, Nanchahal K, Coast J, Donavon J. Hernia repair. In: Stevens A, Raftery J (eds). *Health Care Needs Assessment* (1e). Oxford: Radcliffe Medical Press, 1994.

22 Akin ML, Karakaya M, Batkin A, Nogay A. Prevalence of inguinal hernia in otherwise healthy males 20 to 22 years of age. *J R Army Med Corps* 1997; **143**(2): 101–2.

23 Gallegos N, Dawson J, Jarvis M, Hobsley M. Risk of strangulation in groin hernias. *Br J Surg* 1991; **78**: 1171–3.

24 McEntee G, O'Carroll A, Mooney B, Egan T, Delaney P. Timing of strangulation in adult hernias. *Br J Surg* 1989; **76**: 725–6.

25 Allen P, Zager M, Goldman M. Elective repair of groin hernias in the elderly. *Br J Surg* 1987; **74**: 987.

26 Neuhauser D. Elective herniorrhaphy versus truss. In: Bunker J, Barnes B, Mosteller F (eds). *Costs, Risks and Benefits of Surgery*. New York: Oxford University Press, 1977, pp. 223–39.

27 Berger P. Resultats de l'examen de dix mille observations de hernies, Paris. In: *Extrait de Neuvieme Congres Francais de Chirurgie* 1895.

28 Duvie SO. Femoral hernia in Ilesa, Nigeria. *West Afr J Med* 1989; 8(4): 246–50.

29 el Qaderi S, Aligharaibeh KI, Hani IB, Gassaimeh G, Ammari F. Hernia in northern Jordan: some epidemiological considerations. *Trop Geogr Med* 1992; 44(3): 281–3.

30 Charlton J, Silver R, Hartley R, Holland W. Geographical variation in mortality from conditions amenable to medical intervention in England and Wales. *Lancet* 1983; 1: 691–6.

31 Frankau C. Strangulated hernia: a review of 1487 cases. *Br J Surg* 1931; 19: 176–91.

32 Goldman M. Trusses. *BMJ* 1991; 302: 238–9.

33 Glassow F. The Shouldice hospital technique. *Int Surg* 1986; 71: 148–53.

34 Lichtenstein I, Shulman A, Amid P, Monttlor M. The tension-free hernioplasty. *Am J Surg* 1989; 157: 188–93.

35 British Hernia Centre. *The Preferred Method*; www.hernia.org, 1998.

36 Lichtenstein Hernia Institute. *How Long is the Recovery Period After Each Method?*; www.american-hernia.com, 1998.

37 Murray S, Baijal E, O'Driscoll S, Wilkie L, Bashir K, Boyd A. *Scottish Needs Assessment Programme: hernia repair*. Glasgow: Scottish Forum for Public Health Medicine, 1996.

38 Williams B, Nicholl J. Patient characteristics and clinical caseload of short-stay independent hospitals in England and Wales, 1992–93. *BMJ* 1994; 308: 1699–701.

39 Nicholl J, Beeby N, Williams B. Comparison of the activity of short-stay independent hospitals in England and Wales, 1981 and 1986. *BMJ* 1989; 298: 239–42.

40 Kark AE, Kurzer MN, Belsham PA. Three thousand one hundred and seventy-five primary inguinal hernia repairs: advantages of ambulatory open-mesh repair using local anesthesia. *J Am Coll Surg* 1998; 186(4): 447–55.

41 Netten A, Dennett J. *Unit Costs of Health and Social Care*. Personal Social Services Research Unit, University of Kent, 1997.

42 Royal College of Surgeons of England. *Guidelines on the Management of Groin Hernia in Adults*. London: Royal College of Surgeons, 1992.

43 Devlin HB, Kingsnorth A. Inguinal hernia in adults. II. The outcomes. In: *Management of Abdominal Hernias*. London: Chapman and Hall Medical, 1998, pp. 185–97.

44 Kark AE, Kurzer M, Waters KJ. Tension-free mesh hernia repair: review of 1098 cases using local anaesthesia in a day unit. *Ann R Coll Surg Engl* 1995; 77(4): 299–304.

45 MRC Laparoscopic Groin Hernia Trial Group. Laparoscopic versus open repair of groin hernia: a randomised comparison. *Lancet* 1999; 354: 183–8.

46 Anonymous. Activity and recurrent hernia (editorial). *BMJ* 1977; 2: 3–4.

47 Glassow F. Femoral hernia. Review of 2105 repairs in a 17-year period. *Am J Surg* 1985; 150(3): 353–6.

48 Sanchez-Bustos F, Ramia J, Fernandez Ferrero F. Prosthetic repair of femoral hernia: an audit of long-term follow-up. *Eur J Surg* 1998; 164(3): 191–3.

49 Millikan KW, Deziel DJ. The management of hernia. Considerations in cost-effectiveness. *Surg Clin North Am* 1996; 76(1): 105–16.

50 Cheek C, Black N, Devlin H, Kingsnorth A, Taylor R, Watkin D. Groin hernia surgery: a systematic review. *Br J Surg* 1998; 80(Suppl. 1).

51 Glassow F. Inguinal hernia repair using local anaesthesia. *Ann R Coll Surg Engl* 1984; 66: 382–7.

52 Godfrey P, Greenan J, Ranasinghe D, Shabestary S, Pollock A. Ventilatory capacity after three methods of anaesthesia for inguinal hernia repair: a randomised controlled trial. *Br J Surg* 1981; 68: 587–9.

53 Teasdale C, McCrum A, Williams N, Horton R. A randomised controlled trial to compare local with general anaesthesia for short-stay inguinal hernia repair. *Ann R Coll Surg Engl* 1982; **64**: 238–41.

54 Liem M, van Steensel C, Boelhouwer R *et al.* The learning curve for totally extraperitoneal laparoscopic inguinal hernia repair. *Am J Surg* 1996; **171**: 281–5.

55 Deysine M, Grimson R, Soroff H. Inguinal herniorrhaphy. Reduced morbidity by service standardisation. *Arch Surg* 1991; **126**: 628–30.

56 Kingsnorth A, Porter C, Bennett D. The benefits of a hernia service in a public hospital. *Hernia* 2000; **4**: 1–5.

57 Gilbert AI. Day surgery for inguinal hernia. *Int Surg* 1995; **80**(1): 4–8.

58 Wellwood J, Sculpher MJ, Stoker D *et al.* Randomised controlled trial of laparoscopic versus open-mesh repair for inguinal hernia: outcome and cost [published erratum appears in *BMJ* 1998; **317**: 631]. *BMJ* 1998; **317**: 103–10.

59 Aitola P, Airo I, Matikainen M. Laparoscopic versus open preperitoneal inguinal hernia repair: a prospective randomised trial. *Ann Chir Gynaecol* 1998; **87**(1): 22–5.

60 Beets GL, Dirksen CD, Go PM, Geisler FE, Baeten CG, Kootstra G. Open or laparoscopic preperitoneal mesh repair for recurrent inguinal hernia? A randomized controlled trial. *Surg Endosc* 1999; **13**(4): 323–7.

61 Bessell JR, Baxter P, Riddell P, Watkin S, Maddern GJ. A randomized controlled trial of laparoscopic extraperitoneal hernia repair as a day surgical procedure. *Surg Endosc* 1996; **10**(5): 495–500.

62 Champault GG, Rizk N, Catheline JM, Turner R, Boutelier P. Inguinal hernia repair. Totally preperitoneal laparoscopic approach versus Stoppa operation: randomized trial of 100 cases. *Surg Laparosc Endosc Percut Tech* 1997; **7**(6): 445–50.

63 Dirksen CD, Beets GL, Go PM, Geisler FE, Baeten CG, Kootstra G. Bassini repair compared with laparoscopic repair for primary inguinal hernia: a randomised controlled trial. *Eur J Surg* 1998; **164**(6): 439–47.

64 Hauters P, Meunier D, Urgyan S, Jouret JC, Janssen P, Nys JM. Prospective controlled study comparing laparoscopy and the Shouldice technique in the treatment of unilateral inguinal hernia (French). *Ann Chir* 1996; **50**(9): 776–81.

65 Heikkinen TJ, Haukipuro K, Hulkko A. A cost and outcome comparison between laparoscopic and Lichtenstein hernia operations in a day-case unit. A randomized prospective study. *Surg Endosc* 1998; **12**(10): 1199–203.

66 Juul P, Christensen K. Randomized clinical trial of laparoscopic versus open inguinal hernia repair. *Br J Surg* 1999; **86**(3): 316–19.

67 Kald A, Anderberg B, Carlsson P, Park PO, Smedh K. Surgical outcome and cost-minimisation analyses of laparoscopic and open hernia repair: a randomised prospective trial with one-year follow-up. *Eur J Surg* 1997; **163**(7): 505–10.

68 Khoury N. A randomized prospective controlled trial of laparoscopic extraperitoneal hernia repair and mesh-plug hernioplasty: a study of 315 cases. *J Laparoendosc Adv Surg Tech* 1998; **8**(6): 367–72.

69 Kozol R, Lange PM, Kosir M *et al.* A prospective, randomized study of open vs laparoscopic inguinal hernia repair: an assessment of postoperative pain. *Arch Surg* 1997; **132**(3): 292–5.

70 Liem MS, van der Graaf Y, van Steensel CJ *et al.* Comparison of conventional anterior surgery and laparoscopic surgery for inguinal hernia repair. *NEJM* 1997; **336**(22): 1541–7.

71 Liem MS, van der Graaf Y, Zwart RC, Geurts I, van Vroonhoven TJ. A randomized comparison of physical performance following laparoscopic and open inguinal hernia repair. The Coala Trial Group. *Br J Surg* 1997; **84**(1): 64–7.

72 Paganini AM, Lezoche E, Carle F *et al.* A randomized, controlled, clinical study of laparoscopic vs open tension-free inguinal hernia repair. *Surg Endosc* 1998; **12**(7): 979–86.

73 Tanphiphat C, Tanprayoon T, Sangsubhan C, Chatamra K. Laparoscopic vs open inguinal hernia repair. A randomized, controlled trial. *Surg Endosc* 1998; **12**(6): 846–51.

74 Tschudi J, Wagner M, Klaiber C *et al.* Controlled multicenter trial of laparoscopic transabdominal preperitoneal hernioplasty vs Shouldice herniorrhaphy. Early results. *Surg Endosc* 1996; **10**(8): 845–7.

75 Wright DM, Kennedy A, Baxter JN *et al.* Early outcome after open versus extraperitoneal endoscopic tension-free hernioplasty: a randomized clinical trial. *Surgery* 1996; **119**(5): 552–7.

76 Rattner D. Inguinal herniorrhaphy: for surgical specialists only? *Lancet* 1999; **354**: 175.

77 Webb K, Scott NW, Go PM *et al.* on behalf of the EU Hernia Trialists Collaboration. Laparoscopic techniques versus open techniques for inguinal hernia repair (Cochrane Review). In: *The Cochrane Library. Issue 4. Oxford: Update Software, 2000.*

78 Simpson S. Laparoscopic hernia repair in the West Midlands: a survey of current activity, 2000. Personal communication, 1999.

79 Rutkow I. Epidemiologic, economic and sociologic aspects of hernia surgery in the United States in the 1990s. *Surg Clin North Am* 1998; **78**: 941–51.

80 Lawrence K, McWhinnie D, Goodwin A *et al.* An economic evaluation of laparoscopic versus open inguinal hernia repair. *J Public Health Med* 1996; **18**(1): 41–8.

81 Liem MS, Halsema JA, van der Graaf Y, Schrijvers AJ, van Vroonhoven TJ. Cost-effectiveness of extraperitoneal laparoscopic inguinal hernia repair: a randomized comparison with conventional herniorrhaphy. Coala Trial Group. *Ann Surg* 1997; **226**(6): 668–75.

82 Salcedo-Wasicek MC, Thirlby RC. Postoperative course after inguinal herniorrhaphy. A case-controlled comparison of patients receiving workers' compensation vs patients with commercial insurance. *Arch Surg* 1995; **130**: 29–32.

83 Bellis CJ. Immediate return to unrestricted work after inguinal herniorrhaphy. Personal experiences with 27 267 cases, local anesthesia, and mesh. *Int Surg* 1992; **77**(3): 167–9.

84 Appleby J. Hospital beds. *Health Serv J* 1998; 37.

85 Bryan J. Strain of thought. *Health Serv J* 1999; 12–13.

Index

abortion 2.631–75
  audit 2.665–8
  categories 2.640
  effectiveness, services 2.634, 2.660–1
  health promotion, sexual 2.638–9
  incidence 2.632, 2.643–4
  information requirements 2.635,
    2.668–9
  issues 2.631
  models of care 2.635, 2.661–5
  outcome measures 2.635, 2.665–8
  prevalence 2.632, 2.643–4
  problem statement 2.636–40
  recommendations 2.661–5
  research requirements 2.635, 2.668–9
  services available 2.633, 2.652–5
  sex education 2.662
  sub-categories 2.632
  targets 2.635, 2.665–8
aims, HCNA 1.6
alcohol misuse 2.305–65, 2.376–7
  classification 2.312–14, 2.355–61
  context 2.308–9, 2.311
  cost-effectiveness, services 2.307,
    2.340–3
  diagnosis 2.312
  effectiveness, services 2.306–7,
    2.334–43
  identification 2.311–12
  incidence 2.305–6, 2.315–21
  information priorities 2.308, 2.353–4
  integrated response 2.310–11, 2.346–51
  models of care 2.307, 2.343–51
  outcome measures 2.308, 2.351–2
  prevalence 2.305–6, 2.315–21, 2.343–4
  prevention 2.309
  problem statement 2.305, 2.308–12
  research priorities 2.308, 2.353–4
  screening 2.311–12
  services available 2.306, 2.321–34
  strategic options 2.344–6
  sub-categories 2.305, 2.312–14
  targets 2.308, 2.352–3
Alzheimer's disease see dementias
approaches, HCNA 1.9–14
asthma 1.256–7
  clinical care 1.300–15
  cost-effectiveness, services 1.319
  incidence 1.246–7, 1.268–70
  models of care 1.321–2
  mortality 1.277
  prevalence 1.246–7, 1.265–70
  screening 1.296–7
  services available 1.248–9, 1.281–7

  treatment, drug 1.301–8, 1.313
  treatment, non-drug 1.309–15
  treatment steps 1.314–15

benign prostatic hyperplasia (BPH)
    2.91–157
  aetiology 2.96
  assessment (LUTs) 2.106
  audit 2.95, 2.135–6
  autopsy evidence 2.100
  balloon dilatation 2.118–20
  complications 2.92
  cost-effectiveness, services 2.115–33
  costs, services provision 2.113–15
  diagnosis 2.105
  economic evaluation 2.129–33
  effectiveness, services 2.93–4, 2.115–33
  incidence (LUTs) 2.100–4
  models of care 2.94, 2.133–5
  outcome measures 2.95, 2.135–6
  prevalence 2.92, 2.96–8
  prevalence (LUTs) 2.92, 2.100–4
  problem statement 2.91–2, 2.95–9
  prostatectomy 2.116–18
  PSA testing 2.105–6
  recommendations 2.94, 2.133–5
  research needs 2.95, 2.135–6
  services available 2.93, 2.104–15
  sub-categories 2.92, 2.99–100
  sub-categories (LUTs) 2.99–100
  symptoms (LUTs) 2.98–9
  treatments 2.104–29
  treatments, new technologies 2.110–29,
    2.137–47
bowel cancer see colorectal cancer

cancer see colorectal cancer; lung cancer
cataract surgery 1.635–69
  adults 1.641–4
  anaesthesia 1.652–3
  children 1.640–1
  complications 1.653–4
  cost-effectiveness 1.654
  definition 1.636–8
  effectiveness, services 1.651–4
  epidemiology 1.640–7
  international comparisons 1.646–7
  key issues 1.638–9
  models of care 1.655–8
  mortality 1.646
  numbers of operations 1.649–50
  outcome measures 1.659–61
  posterior capsular opacification 1.644
  primary care 1.650–1

  problem statement 1.636–9
  research priorities 1.658–9
  risk factors 1.644–6
  service provision 1.647–51
  sub-categories 1.639–40
  summary 1.635–6
  treatment, cataract 1.647–8
  visual acuity 1.648–9
characteristics, HCNA 1.3–10
CHD see coronary heart disease
child health services, community see
    community child health services
chronic obstructive pulmonary disease
    (COPD) 1.258, 1.270–2
  incidence 1.247
  management 1.315–17
  models of care 1.321–2
  mortality 1.277
  prevalence 1.247
  screening 1.297
  services available 1.249, 1.287–8
  terminology 1.331
colorectal cancer 1.449–502
  characteristics 1.449
  classification 1.478–83
  coding systems 1.478–83
  consequences 1.456
  current issues 1.451
  detection 1.457–8, 1.464–5
  diagnosis 1.458, 1.465
  effectiveness, services 1.463–9
  follow-up 1.468–9
  functional ability 1.489–91
  HBGs/HRGs 1.463, 1.475, 1.485–9,
    1.492–4
  incidence 1.449, 1.452–6
  information requirements 1.475–7
  interventions 1.449–50, 1.451, 1.455–6
  investigation 1.450, 1.458, 1.465
  models of care 1.469–73
  mortality 1.449
  occurrence 1.449, 1.450
  outcome measures 1.473–4
  palliative care 1.462, 1.467–8
  prevalence 1.452–6
  prevention 1.449, 1.457, 1.463–4
  problem statement 1.450–2
  research requirements 1.475–7
  risk factors 1.449, 1.452–4
  screening 1.450
  services available 1.457–63, 1.469–73
  staging 1.484
  sub-categories 1.451–2
  support services 1.462

colorectal cancer (*cont.*):
  surveillance 1.450
  survival 1.449
  treatment 1.450, 1.458–62, 1.465–7
community child health services
  2.543–630
  adoption 2.616
  audiology service 2.620
  charitable sector 2.610
  charter 2.611–12
  Children Act (1989) 2.615
  code of practice 2.614
  costs, services provision 2.544,
    2.559–60
  disabilities, children with 2.547, 2.556,
    2.585–8, 2.599–601, 2.605, 2.608–9,
    2.613, 2.622–3
  disability services 2.570–5
  Education Act 2.614
  effectiveness, services 2.544, 2.576–91
  evidence base 2.548
  fostering 2.616
  health education programmes 2.564–8,
    2.581–2, 2.596–8, 2.604
  health promotion 2.548, 2.568–70,
    2.596–8, 2.617
  immunisation 2.564–8, 2.581–2,
    2.596–8, 2.604, 2.618
  incidence 2.544, 2.554–9
  information 2.545, 2.606–7
  Local Education Authorities 2.554–5,
    2.562–4, 2.577–81, 2.593–6, 2.603–4
  models of care 2.545, 2.591–602,
    2.622–3
  non-government organisations 2.610
  outcome measures 2.603–6
  outcomes 2.545
  prevalence 2.544, 2.554–9
  preventive services 2.568–70, 2.596–8
  problem statement 2.543, 2.546–8
  psychological disorders, children with
    2.553, 2.556–9, 2.576, 2.588–91,
    2.601–2, 2.605–6, 2.609
  psychological pathology 2.547–8
  research requirements 2.545, 2.608–9
  screening 2.564–8, 2.581–2, 2.596–8,
    2.604
  services available 2.544, 2.559–76
  services improvement 2.621
  services, macro-environment 2.570,
    2.585, 2.598–9, 2.604–5
  services, micro-environment 2.568–70,
    2.582–5, 2.596–8, 2.604–5
  services organisation 2.555–6
  services provision, minimum 2.613
  social services departments 2.560–1,
    2.577, 2.592–3
  specialist services 2.619
  sub-categories 2.543, 2.549–53
  targets 2.545, 2.606
  voluntary sector 2.610
contraception 2.631–75
  audit 2.665–8

categories 2.640
cost-effectiveness, services 2.658
costs, services provision 2.646–55
effectiveness, services 2.634, 2.657–9
family planning clinics 2.648
health promotion, sexual 2.638–9
incidence 2.632, 2.641–2
information requirements 2.635,
  2.668–9
interventions 2.657–9
issues 2.631
methods 2.649–52, 2.658–9
models of care 2.635, 2.661–5
outcome measures 2.635, 2.665–8
prevalence 2.632, 2.641–2
problem statement 2.636–40
recommendations 2.661–5
research requirements 2.635, 2.668–9
services available 2.632–3, 2.646–55
sex education 2.662
sub-categories 2.632
targets 2.635, 2.665–8
COPD *see* chronic obstructive pulmonary
  disease
coronary heart disease (CHD) 1.373–435
  acute coronary syndromes 1.423–4,
    1.427–8, 1.430
  ambulance services 1.421–2
  audit 1.426–9
  chest pain 1.422
  detection 1.397–8
  diabetes mellitus 1.409
  effectiveness, services 1.376–8,
    1.407–18
  epidemiological trends 1.395
  exertional angina 1.422, 1.427, 1.429
  heart failure 1.424–5, 1.428, 1.430
  incidence 1.374–5, 1.384–95
  information requirements 1.429–32
  interventions 1.407–18
  models of care 1.379–80, 1.418–25
  mortality 1.384–95
  outcome measures 1.426–9
  post-symptomatic 1.416–18
  pre-symptomatic 1.407–9
  prevalence 1.374–5, 1.384–95
  prevention 1.425, 1.428–9, 1.431–2
  problem statement 1.373, 1.380–2
  recommendations 1.418–25
  rehabilitation 1.425, 1.428–9, 1.431–2
  research requirements 1.429–32
  screening 1.395–7, 1.420–1, 1.426–7,
    1.429
  services available 1.375–6, 1.395–406
  specialist hospitals 1.420–1
  strategies 1.433–5
  sub-categories 1.373, 1.382–3
  symptomatic 1.398–406, 1.409–16
  targets 1.426–9
cystic fibrosis 1.259–60, 1.275–6
  incidence 1.247–8
  models of care 1.322–3
  mortality 1.278

prevalence 1.247–8
screening 1.297
services available 1.250, 1.289–92
treatment 1.317–19

dementias 2.239–303
  assessment 2.265–6, 2.290
  behavioural therapies 2.270–3
  caregivers 2.244
  classification 2.292
  community services 2.255, 2.273–9
  costs, services provision 2.261–3
  course 2.245
  definitions 2.245–7
  delirium 2.247
  diagnosis 2.265–6
  economic evaluation 2.282–3
  effectiveness evaluation 2.282–3
  effectiveness, services 2.241–2,
    2.263–83
  effectiveness, treatments 2.263–83
  future directions 2.291
  hospital specialist care 2.257
  incidence 2.240, 2.248–53
  information systems 2.288–9
  long-stay care 2.257–9
  long-term care settings 2.280–2
  models of care 2.242–3, 2.283–8
  outcome 2.245
  outcome measures 2.290
  pharmacological treatments 2.266–70
  prevalence 2.240, 2.248–53
  primary health care services 2.253–5,
    2.285–6
  primary prevention 2.264–5
  problem statement 2.239, 2.243–5
  psychiatry 2.255–7
  psychosocial therapies 2.270–3
  research 2.289–90
  resources allocation 2.287–8
  resources available 2.253–63
  search strategies 2.293
  service provision levels 2.260–1
  services available 2.240–1, 2.253–63
  sheltered housing 2.257–9
  social support services 2.255
  sub-categories 2.245–8
  subgroups 2.239
  terms 2.293
diabetes mellitus 1.17–74
  abbreviations 1.47
  care, expected 1.56–7
  CHD 1.409
  consensus documents 1.48–9
  cost-effectiveness, services 1.19–20,
    1.31–3, 1.36–7
  costs 1.30–1, 1.60–1
  data for estimates 1.50–4
  definition 1.21–3
  diabetes centres 1.58
  diagnostic criteria 1.21–3
  effectiveness, services 1.19–20, 1.31–7
  end-stage renal failure 1.94–5

glycaemic control 1.33–6
HBGs/HRGs 1.62
health care programme matrix 1.63
incidence 1.18–19, 1.25–7
information requirements 1.20–1,
    1.45–6
models of care 1.20, 1.37–43
outcome measures 1.20, 1.43–5
planning services 1.40–3
prevalence 1.18–19, 1.25–7
problem statement 1.17–18
quality of evidence 1.59
recommendations, Working Group on
    Outcomes 1.64–5
renal disease 1.94–5, 1.107–8
research requirements 1.20–1, 1.45–6
risk factor modification 1.36
Saint Vincent Declaration 1.55
screening 1.29–30, 1.31–3
services available 1.19, 1.27–31
size of effect 1.59
sub-categories 1.18, 1.23–4
diabetic retinopathy, screening 1.32–3
drug misuse 2.367–450
    classification, disorders 2.428–9
    clinical features 2.431–2
    community services 2.399–400
    contact points 2.394–5, 2.414–15
    cost-effectiveness, treatment 2.411–12
    costs, social 2.403–5
    counselling 2.400–1, 2.409–10
    course of problems 2.379
    criminal justice system 2.416–17
    dependence criteria 2.430
    diagnostic definitions 2.380–1
    drug education 2.393–4, 2.405–6
    drugs 2.375–7
    effectiveness, services 2.405–13
    effectiveness, treatments 2.412–13
    GPs 2.397–9
    harm 2.377–9
    hospital inpatient programmes 2.401
    incidence 2.368–9, 2.386–93
    information requirements 2.371–2,
        2.423–7
    intervention models, criminal justice
        system 2.416–17
    minority ethnic groups 2.386
    models of care 2.370–1, 2.413–20
    mortality 2.377
    outcome measures 2.420–3, 2.434
    population sub-groups 2.382–4
    prescribing programmes 2.407–9
    prevalence 2.368–9, 2.386–93
    priority groups 2.384–5, 2.418–20
    problem statement 2.367–8, 2.372–81
    recommendations 2.422–3
    rehabilitation 2.402
    research requirements 2.371–2,
        2.423–7
    residential programmes 2.410–11
    risks 2.377–9
    services available 2.369–70, 2.393–405

services infrastructure 2.433
strategic context 2.374–5
sub-categories 2.381–6
subgroups 2.368
syringe exchange 2.397, 2.406–7
treatment performance indicators
    2.435–7
treatment provision levels 2.402–3
treatment services 2.395–7
treatment tiers 2.414–16

epidemiological approach, HCNA
    1.1–16

femoral hernia *see* groin hernia
fertility services 2.631–75
    audit 2.665–8
    categories 2.640–1
    effectiveness, services 2.634
    health promotion, sexual 2.638–9
    incidence 2.632
    infertility 2.639–40, 2.644–6
    information requirements 2.635,
        2.668–9
    issues 2.631
    models of care 2.635, 2.661–5
    outcome measures 2.635, 2.665–8
    prevalence 2.632
    problem statement 2.636–40
    recommendations 2.661–5
    research requirements 2.635, 2.668–9
    services available 2.634, 2.656–7
    sex education 2.662
    sub-categories 2.632
    targets 2.635, 2.665–8

groin hernia 1.671–720
    anaesthesia 1.706
    audit 1.710–11
    coding systems 1.712–15
    complications 1.679–81, 1.710
    cost-effectiveness, services 1.704–8
    current service provision 1.683–700
    day-case vs. inpatient care 1.706
    economic issues 1.707–8
    effectiveness, services 1.672, 1.704–8
    evidence grading 1.716
    incidence 1.675–81
    information requirements 1.711
    models of care 1.672, 1.708–10
    mortality 1.679–81
    outcomes 1.710–11
    prevalence 1.675–81
    private sector activity 1.700–1
    problem statement 1.671, 1.673–4
    recommendations 1.708–10
    recurrence 1.710
    research priorities 1.711
    services available 1.671–2, 1.681–703
    sub-categories 1.674
    surgery 1.678–9, 1.707
    targets 1.710–11
    treatment options 1.681–3

health care needs assessment (HCNA)
    aims 1.6
    approaches 1.9–14
    characteristics 1.3–10
    epidemiological approach 1.1–16
    objectives 1.6–7
    policy context 1.1–2
    protocol 1.10–14
    scales 1.7–8
    types 1.8–9
heart disease *see* coronary heart disease
hernia, groin *see* groin hernia
hip osteoarthritis *see* osteoarthritis, hip
    and knee

influenza
    immunisation 1.296
    neuraminidase inhibitors 1.298
inguinal hernia *see* groin hernia

kidney disease *see* renal disease
knee osteoarthritis *see* osteoarthritis, hip
    and knee

learning disabilities 2.451–541
    accommodation 2.485–8, 2.505–7,
        2.524
    activities restriction 2.478, 2.493, 2.511
    aetiology 2.466–8
    alternative therapies 2.485–8, 2.505
    autistic spectrum disorders 2.477–8,
        2.492–3, 2.511
    carers' issues 2.480–1, 2.494, 2.512–13
    categories 2.452–3, 2.465–8
    challenging behaviours 2.475–6, 2.492,
        2.508–11
    classification 2.463–5
    client need for services 2.519–21
    commissioning 2.524
    costs, services provision 2.494–5
    day activities 2.488–91, 2.507–8, 2.524
    definitions 2.463–5
    effectiveness, services 2.459, 2.497–513
    families' issues 2.480–1, 2.494,
        2.512–13
    function losses 2.478, 2.493, 2.511
    health care 2.528
    health promotion 2.482, 2.498–500,
        2.523
    impairments syndromes 2.473–4, 2.508
    incidence 2.453–6, 2.468–81
    information requirements 2.461, 2.524,
        2.525–7
    intellectual impairment 2.469–70
    medical conditions 2.478–9
    mental disorders 2.474–5, 2.491–2
    models of care 2.460, 2.513–22
    offending behaviours 2.476
    physical impairments 2.472–3
    policy context 2.462–3
    population need for services 2.514–19
    prevalence 2.453–6, 2.468–81
    primary care 2.482–3, 2.500–1

learning disabilities (*cont.*):
  problem statement 2.451–2, 2.461–5
  research requirements 2.461, 2.525–7
  services available 2.456–9, 2.481–96
  services components 2.513–14
  services provision levels 2.521–2
  social care 2.528
  social consequences 2.479–80, 2.493–4, 2.512
  specialist services 2.483–5, 2.501–5, 2.524
  targets 2.460, 2.523–4
  see also mental illness
lower respiratory disease 1.245–371
  adults 1.255–6, 1.280
  audit 1.251
  bed-day statistics 1.345–6, 1.353
  children 1.254–5, 1.299–300
  classification 1.331–6
  clinical services 1.299–319
  diagnosis statistics 1.343–4
  effectiveness, services 1.248–50, 1.293–319
  GP consultation rates 1.347–8, 1.352, 1.354
  HRGs 1.292–3, 1.349–50
  incidence 1.260–78, 1.340
  information requirements 1.251
  models of care 1.250–1, 1.319–23
  morbidity 1.260–76, 1.326–7
  mortality 1.276–8, 1.327, 1.337–9, 1.341–2, 1.351
  outcome measures 1.251, 1.323–5
  prevalence 1.246–8, 1.260–78, 1.340
  prevention 1.293–9, 1.326
  problem statement 1.245, 1.251–4
  public health problem 1.252–3
  research priorities 1.330
  research requirements 1.251
  services available 1.248–50, 1.278–93
  smoking 1.293
  statistics 1.337–54
  sub-categories 1.245, 1.254–60
  targets 1.325–30
lower urinary tract symptoms (LUTs) *see* benign prostatic hyperplasia
lung cancer 1.503–48
  classification 1.528–30
  clinical features 1.527
  coding systems 1.528–30
  consequences 1.512
  cost-effectiveness, services 1.518–21
  current position 1.505–7
  definition 1.504–5
  effectiveness, services 1.504
  efficacy, services 1.518–21
  HBGs/HRGs 1.507–8, 1.531–2
  histological types 1.505
  incidence 1.504, 1.510–11, 1.535–9
  information requirements 1.524–5
  interventions 1.512–18
  long-term service agreements 1.540–6

models of care 1.504, 1.521–3
  mortality 1.511
  prevalence 1.504, 1.510–11
  problem statement 1.503
  recommendations 1.521–3
  research priorities 1.526
  risk factors 1.509
  services available 1.504, 1.512–18
  smoking 1.512–13, 1.538–9
  staging 1.505, 1.533–4
  sub-categories 1.503, 1.508–12
  terminal care 1.521
  treatment 1.519–21
lung diseases, obstructive *see* chronic obstructive pulmonary disease
LUTs (lower urinary tract symptoms) *see* benign prostatic hyperplasia

measles, immunisation 1.294–5
mental illness *see* learning disabilities; severe mental illness

objectives, HCNA 1.6–7
osteoarthritis, hip and knee 1.549–633
  characteristics 1.554
  classification 1.606–8
  cost-effectiveness, services 1.550–1, 1.564–81
  costs, treatment 1.580–1
  data analysis 1.606–11
  diagnosis 1.556–7, 1.585
  effectiveness, services 1.551–2, 1.581–602
  evidence base 1.583–4
  hospital activity 1.573–80
  incidence 1.549–50, 1.557–63
  information requirements 1.553, 1.603–5
  interventions 1.581–602
  management 1.585
  models of care 1.552, 1.595–9
  NSAIDs 1.589–90
  outcome measures 1.552–3, 1.603
  pathogenesis 1.554–5
  prevalence 1.549–50, 1.557–63
  prevention 1.565
  problem statement 1.553–6
  prognosis 1.555–6
  referrals 1.585
  rehabilitation 1.565–8, 1.586–7
  research requirements 1.553, 1.603–5
  risk factors 1.562–3
  screening 1.586
  services available 1.550–1, 1.564–81
  services need 1.599–602
  sub-categories 1.549, 1.556–7
  surgery 1.569–80, 1.590–5
  treatment 1.565–8
  treatment, drug 1.568–9

pneumococci, immunisation 1.295–6
policy context, HCNA 1.1–2
protocol, HCNA 1.10–14

renal disease 1.75–140
  acute renal failure 1.87, 1.91–2, 1.96, 1.109, 1.126
  categories 1.83
  chronic renal failure 1.87–9, 1.92–5, 1.96–7, 1.109–10
  Cochrane Renal Collaboration (1998) 1.134
  coding systems 1.84–6
  cost-effectiveness, prevention 1.112–16
  cost-effectiveness, services 1.77–9
  diabetes mellitus 1.94–5, 1.107–8
  diagnosing 1.109–12
  effectiveness, services 1.77–9, 1.106–16
  end-stage renal failure 1.89–90, 1.92–5, 1.97, 1.110, 1.126–7
  evaluation 1.81
  evaluation, services 1.126–9
  facilities 1.97–106
  incidence 1.90–5
  modelling future demand 1.79–80
  models of care 1.116–26
  monitoring 1.81
  monitoring services 1.126–9
  planning services 1.119–26
  population need 1.76
  prevalence 1.90–5
  prevention 1.78, 1.107–9, 1.112–16, 1.126–9
  problem statement 1.83–6
  renal replacement therapy 1.78–9, 1.80–1, 1.102–6, 1.113–14, 1.116–26
  research needs 1.81
  research priorities 1.129–31
  services 1.76–7, 1.119–26
  services available 1.95–106
  services estimation 1.116–19
  sub-categories 1.87–90
  transplantation 1.78–9, 1.80–1, 1.102–6, 1.113–14, 1.116–26
  treating 1.109–12
  treatment 1.132–3
  types 1.75
respiratory disease, lower *see* lower respiratory disease

scales, HCNA 1.7–8
severe mental illness (SMI) 2.159–237
  acute psychiatric care 2.187–8
  audit 2.163–4, 2.219–22
  carers' issues 2.190–1
  categories 2.223–4
  classification 2.159
  community services 2.200–1, 2.210–11
  components 2.165–6
  costs, services provision 2.182–99, 2.192–8
  costs, SMIs 2.197–8
  counselling 2.198–9
  CPA 2.186–7
  day activities 2.189–90
  effect size 2.208–10
  effectiveness, services 2.162, 2.199–210

epidemiology 2.176–8
evidence quality 2.208–10
funds allocation 2.217
government documents 2.228
homicide 2.181–2
hospital-based services 2.210–11
incidence 2.160, 2.171–82
information 2.163–4, 2.219–22
liaison psychiatry 2.187
longer-term care 2.188
Mental Illness Needs Index 2.225–7
models of care 2.162–3, 2.210–19
National Service Framework 2.211–12
neurosis 2.171–6
nursing care homes 2.188
official documents 2.228
outcome 2.163–4, 2.219–22
pharmacological treatments 2.202–8
prevalence 2.160, 2.171–82
primary services/secondary services
    2.212–13
problem statement 2.164–7
psychological treatments 2.202–8
psychoses 2.178–80
quantifying needs 2.217–19
rehabilitation 2.189–90, 2.215–17
research 2.219–22
research requirements 2.163–4
residential care 2.213–15
residential care homes 2.188, 2.194–5
secure provision 2.195–7
self-harm 2.181–2
services available 2.160–2, 2.182–99
shelter 2.189–90
sociodemographic factors 2.180
specialist care 2.184–90, 2.195–7
staffing issues 2.191–2
sub-categories 2.167–71
suicide 2.181–2
treatments, cost 2.202–8
users' issues 2.190–1
SMI *see* severe mental illness
stroke 1.141–243
    acute management 1.173–7
    acute treatment 1.183–5, 1.192–3,
        1.206
    audit 1.203–6
    care guidelines 1.189–97, 1.194–5
    care model 1.197–200, 1.207
    care priorities 1.200–3
    Cochrane Reviews 1.225–7

Cochrane Stroke Group 1.218–24
cost-effectiveness, services 1.143–4,
    1.178–88
costs 1.171–8
effectiveness, services 1.143–4,
    1.178–88
HRGs 1.155
ICD codes 1.153–5
incidence 1.142, 1.156–70
key issues 1.146–7
models of care 1.144–5, 1.188–203
mortality 1.145–6
outcome measures 1.203–6
policy, government 1.146
prevalence 1.142, 1.156–70
prevention 1.171–3, 1.179–83,
    1.189–92, 1.197–9, 1.200–3
prognosis 1.149–50
recommendations 1.144–5, 1.188–203
rehabilitation 1.173–7, 1.185–7,
    1.195–6, 1.199, 1.202–3, 1.206
research priorities 1.206–7
risk 1.156–60
sequelae 1.168–70
services available 1.142–3, 1.171–8
sub-arachnoid haemorrhage 1.170,
    1.177–8, 1.187–8
sub-categories 1.141–2, 1.147–56
transient ischaemic attack 1.160–1,
    1.181–3
WHO classifications 1.155–6
WHO ICIDH model 1.208–16

tuberculosis 1.259, 1.272–5
    immunisation 1.296
    incidence 1.247
    models of care 1.322
    mortality 1.277–8
    prevalence 1.247
    screening 1.297
    services available 1.249–50, 1.288–9
    treatment, drug 1.317
types, HCNA 1.8–9

varicose veins 2.1–89
    assessment 2.33–6, 2.53–5
    audit 2.64
    classification 2.13–16, 2.68–9
    coding systems 2.66–7
    cost-effectiveness, treatment 2.62
    costs, services provision 2.31–52

current service provision 2.47–52
decision-making, treatment 2.31–2
effectiveness, services 2.6, 2.53–62
impact 2.12–13
incidence 2.2–3, 2.16–31
information 2.64–5
models of care 2.7, 2.62–3
morbidity 2.30
outcome measures 2.64
population distribution 2.70–7
prevalence 2.2–3, 2.16–31, 2.70–7
problem statement 2.1–2, 2.7–13
research 2.64–5
risk factors 2.22–9
services available 2.3–6, 2.31–52
services configuration 2.45–6
sub-categories 2.2, 2.13–16
surgery 2.42–6
treatment 2.36–45, 2.55–7
venous ulcers 2.1–89
    assessment 2.33–6, 2.53–5
    audit 2.64
    causes 2.10–11
    classification 2.13–16, 2.68–9
    coding systems 2.66–7
    cost-effectiveness, treatment 2.62
    costs, services provision 2.31–52
    current service provision 2.47–52
    decision-making, treatment 2.31–2
    effectiveness, services 2.6, 2.53–62
    impact 2.12–13
    incidence 2.2–3, 2.16–31
    information 2.64–5
    management 2.46
    models of care 2.7, 2.62–3
    morbidity 2.30
    outcome measures 2.64
    prevalence 2.2–3, 2.16–31
    problem statement 2.1–2, 2.7–13
    research 2.64–5
    risk factors 2.22–9
    services available 2.3–6, 2.31–52
    services configuration 2.45–6
    sub-categories 2.2, 2.13–16
    surgery 2.42–6
    treatment 2.36–45, 2.57–61

whooping cough 1.255
    immunisation 1.294
    see also chronic obstructive pulmonary
        disease